INTERNATIONAL BUSINESS

V.K. BHALLA
Professor
Faculty of Management Studies
University of Delhi
DELHI

S Chand And Company Limited
(ISO 9001 Certified Company)

S Chand And Company Limited

(ISO 9001 Certified Company)

Head Office: D-92, Sector–2, Noida – 201301, U.P. (India), Ph. 91-120-4682700

Registered Office: A-27, 2nd Floor, Mohan Co-operative Industrial Estate, New Delhi – 110 044, Phone: 011-49731800

www.**schandpublishing.com;** e-mail: **info@schandpublishing.com**

Marketing Offices:

Chennai	:	Ph: 23632120; chennai@schandpublishing.com
Guwahati	:	Ph: 2738811, 2735640; guwahati@schandpublishing.com
Hyderabad	:	Ph: 40186018; hyderabad@schandpublishing.com
Jalandhar	:	Ph: 4645630; jalandhar@schandpublishing.com
Kolkata	:	Ph: 23357458, 23353914; kolkata@schandpublishing.com
Lucknow	:	Ph: 4003633; lucknow@schandpublishing.com
Mumbai	:	Ph: 25000297; mumbai@schandpublishing.com
Patna	:	Ph: 2260011; patna@schandpublishing.com

First Edition 2013

Reprint 2022

Reprint 2024

ISBN: 978-81-219-4280-5 **Product Code:** H8IBU60BMGT10ENAA13O

PRINTED IN INDIA

By Vikas Publishing House Private Limited, Plot 20/4, Site-IV, Industrial Area Sahibabad, Ghaziabad – 201 010 and Published by S Chand And Company Limited, A-27, 2nd Floor, Mohan Co-operative Industrial Estate, New Delhi – 110 044.

PREFACE

The world economy is going through a historic transformation. We are moving progressively further away from a world in which national economies were relatively isolated from each other by barriers to cross-border trade and investment, distance time zones, language, and national differences in government regulation, culture, and business systems and toward a world in which national economies are merging into a interdependent global economic system. Integrated global economic system, commonly referred as globalization, has been in place for many years. Markets have become truly global for most goods, many services, and especially for financial instruments of all types. This pervasive growth in market interpenetration makes it increasingly difficult for any country to avoid substantial external impacts on its economy. In particular massive capital flows can push exchange rates away from levels that accurately reflect competitive relationships among nations if national economic policies or performances diverse in short run. The rapid dissemination rate of new technologies speeds the pace at which countries must adjust to external events. Smaller, more open countries, long ago gave up illusion of domestic policy autonomy. But even the largest and most apparently self-contained economies are now significantly affected by the global economy. Global integration in trade, investment, factor flows, technology, and communication has been tying economies together.

The most dramatic and significant trends in the world economy has been the rapid sustained growth of international business. The economies are proceeding better than expected but at varying speed—tepidly in many advanced economies and solidly in emerging and developing economies. The acid test of a well-managed company is being able to conceive, develop, and implement effective global strategy. Because of inherent difficulties, global strategy development presents one of the stiffest challenges for managers today. Companies that operate on a global scale today need to integrate their world-wide strategy in contrast to the earlier multinational or multidomestic approach. The earlier strategies would more truly be categorized as multidomestic strategies rather than as global strategies. The implications of a distinction between multidomestic and global strategy are quite profound. In a multidomestic strategy, a firm manages its international activities like a portfolio. Its subsidiaries or other operations around the world each control all the important activities necessary to maximize their returns in their areas of operation independent of activities of other subsidiaries in the firm The subsidiaries enjoy a large degree of autonomy and the firms' activities in each of the national markets in which it operates is determined by the competitive conditions in the national market. In contrast a global strategy integrates the activities of the firm on a world-wide basis to capture the linkages among countries and to treat the entire world as a single borderless market. This requires more than the transferring of intangible assets between countries.

Why then are these changes coming about, and what exactly are they? It is in practice, easier to identify the former than interpret the latter. The reason is that during the past few decades, the emergence of corporate empires in the world economy, based on the contemporary scientific and technological developments, has led to globalization of production. As a result of international production, co-operation among global productive units, the large scale capital exports, "the export of production" or "production abroad" has come into prominence as against commodity export in world economy in recent years. Global corporations consider the whole of the world their production place, as well as their market and move factors of production to wherever they can optimally be combined. They avail fully of the revolution that has brought about instant world-wide communication, and near instant-transformation. Their ownership is transnational; their management is transnational. Their freely mobile management, technology and capital, the modern agent for stepped-up economic growth, transcend individual national boundaries. They are domestic in every place, foreign in none—a true corporate citizen of the world. The greater interdependence among nations has already reduced economic insularity of the peoples of the world, as well as their social and political insularity.

The new global market is not limited to trade in financial instruments. Indeed the world can no longer be as a collection of national economies. The electronic infrastructure that now ties the world together, as well as great advances in the efficiency of conventional transportation, is creating a single global economy. Intellectual capital is most mobile in the world, and it will go where it is wanted, and it will stay where it is well treated. It will flee from manipulation or onerous regulation of its value or use, and no government can restrain it for long. Multinational corporations are rapidly adopting advanced information technologies to increase the efficiency and capabilities of their operations. Valuable information, such as software or financial services, is transmitted digitally. Though, digital technologies are permitting a high degree of integration but has aggravated the gap between countries that are rich and those that are poor and do not have the infrastructural capabilities.

The book reviews the functions and working of the international organizations to indicate much needed reforms, including an appropriate understanding of adjustment programmes. Broader overview of macroeconomic and political factors such as international trade and investment flows, the problems of economic development in emerging economies, the analysis of international and regional institutions such as the World Trade Organization, the International Monetary Fund, the World Bank, and other international development banks, European Monetary System, International Banking, Regional blocks etc. has been provided. It highlights that there has been a creative tension between the regional and multilateral approaches which, although often complicated, has generally advanced trade openness and economic integration. The peculiar conflict in the world economy is the growing trend toward economic integration without a concomitant growth in global political and social institutions to regulate and arbitrate this trend. The economic motives and the key issues that lie behind this deeper integration have been analyzed.

The evolution of trade theory; from old trade doctrines to the new trade theory, has impacted the strategy formulation in international business at two levels. The first *relates* to the continuing support of the free trade doctrine to determine policy for developing areas. As is expected, the push comes from the advanced nations, both at the intergovernmental level and at multilateral institutions like the IMF and the WTO. The *second* impact of trade theory relates to policies pursued by the advanced nations, which relies considerably on the new trade theory doctrines of strategic trade. The uneven power relations between the rich and poor nations of the world permits a continuation of this asymmetrical combination of policies, to which trade theory unfortunately has contributed much. Much of the preoccupation of the policymakers with the micro-theoretic formulations of trade theory, both old and new, are related to a total neglect of the macroeconomic issues relating to the national as well as the world economy. One only expects that the new theories, which are yet to come up, will address some of these limitations. The main objective is to present a comprehensive, up-to-date, and clear exposition of the theory and principles of international business that are essential for understanding, evaluating and suggesting solutions to important international business problems and issues facing the world economy.

The effect of closer global linkages on the economies of countries has been dramatic. Though various choices available to governments among a variety of policy instruments, from a theoretical and empirical perspective, but they have increasingly come to realization that it is very difficult to isolate domestic economic activities from international market events. They find themselves with increasing responsibilities yet with fewer and less effective tools to fulfill these responsibilities. As more part of a domestic economy is exposed to international shifts and changes, these parts are simultaneously becoming less controllable. The same interdependence that has made countries more affluent has also left them more vulnerable. How are national governments to regulate the complexity of multinational production with anything like the firmness with which they once regulated international trade? How does a national government measure capital formation, when much new capital is intellectual? How does it measure the productivity of knowledge workers, where product cannot be counted? If it cannot do that, how can it track productivity growth? How does it track or control the money supply when the financial markets create new financial instruments faster than the regulators can keep track of them? And if it cannot do any of these things with the relative precision of simpler times, what becomes of the great mission of modern governments: controlling and manipulating the national economy? Even if some of these measurement problems are solved, the phenomena they measure will be far more complex and difficult to manipulate them in industrial economies of old. Nevertheless, if the new interventionist gets their way, it could cripple the global economy. Non–tariff measures (NTMs) are often first-best policies to correct market failures. The volume presents an economic perspective on the use of non-tariff measures. Governments use non-tariff measures and services for a growing number of reasons. However as the same NTM used to pursue a public policy objective may also be employed to distort international trade, it can be difficult to distinguish legitimate from protectionist motivations for NTMs. Neither the declared aim of a NTM nor its effect on trade provides conclusive evidence of whether it is innocuous from trade perspective. However, analyzing the nature of these measures——their opaqueness, efficiency, and effect on various groups of society— and their political and economic context can provide important insights.

There was a time when international business was the realm of a few specialists and multinational corporations. Today, the world has changed, and the international business environment profoundly influences firms, governments, and individuals on a daily basis. Corporations, increasingly find their largest growth opportunities stay at home. They recognize the need to obtain the production economies of scale, and are beginning to understand to be in distant markets. They learn about new suppliers abroad, which provide for better and less expensive products. They implement global expansion strategies in which components are produced in one country, assembled in another, and sold in yet other nations around the world. Firms are increasingly linked to each other through global supply arrangements and joint undertakings in research and development. Managers experience that competition is no longer just local, and that they better be ready to face the world, even if their firms stay at home. They recognize the need to obtain the production economies of scale, and are beginning to understand how learning in the international arena contributes to innovation and cost benefits that are crucial to survival. This is one of the most important reasons why a basic understanding of the strategic analysis, formulation and implementation of the various business functions of multinational companies to be so important. The investment policy landscape increasingly includes a combination of voluntary and regulatory initiatives to promote corporate governance, business and ethics, sustainable development, and corporate social responsibility standards.

Corporate social responsibility, though applicable to all types of companies, are increasing significant for international investment, as they typically focus on multinational corporations which, through foreign investments and global value chains, can influence the social and environmental practices of business worldwide.

Individuals are affected by international business more than ever. Its employment effects provide for rapid growth in some areas, and for major dislocations in others. Employees are facing the disturbing reality that workers throughout the world desire their jobs and wondering how to stay competitive. The firms are facing three central issues regarding people: getting them, keeping them, and helping them to improve. Investment in people is time-consuming and costly. But the cost of turnover and the cost of having wrong people are even higher. As management styles have changed among large corporations, so the attitude toward the *people* has evolved from the traditional adversarial relationship between management and labour or between the corporation and the individuals. Indeed employees ceased to be employees and emerge as assets, the sources of strength of an organization. But there is an additional dimension here. Having the right people is not merely a matter of seeking the most gifted or most experienced, but also of investing in a corporate culture that encourages growth, learning, and flexible, creative approach to problem solving. The emphasis is not on the employee's investment of time, talent, and effort in the company for which they work, but on the employer's investment in the employees through training, mentoring, and motivation programmes, and through continuing education. Managing this change and ensuring employees do not become overwhelmed by the speed or extent of these changes is one of the biggest challenges facing the global corporations.

In today's world policies aimed at improving the integration of developing economies into global value chains must look beyond foreign investment and trade. The profound changes in the international business environment has called for a major changes in the marketing functions, an in-depth understanding of the customer in terms of their requirements, needs and wants. Given the country-and customer-specific differences encountered in the international arena, marketing becomes a crucial function of the international business executive. Policymakers need to consider non-equity modes (NEMs) of international production, such as contract manufacturing, service outsourcing, contract farming, franchising, and licensing and management contracts. Today, MNCs explore the possibilities of having strategic alliances through international joint ventures where there are constraints in entering through greenfield investments.

The new millennium is likely to pose new challenges for the international financial managers as the demand for investment capital by the new entrants into the international market economy and the escalating costs of innovations place enormous pressures on the global demand for finance capital and its main supplying agents. In fact, present inadequacy of national capital markets and financial intermediaries, differences in tax regulations, inability of individuals to obtain foreign financial leverage, varying national attitudes toward risk, different rates of inflation, etc. have forced the financial managers of international firms, their bankers, and financial consultants to rethink on domestic oriented concepts which have traditionally influenced the corporate financial decision-making. The determinants of the way in which multinational firms acquire, organise and manage these assets is of critical importance for the success of these firms. The book examines the anatomy and propagation of international financial crises, assesses the adequacy of current regulatory and supervisory practices, and suggests measures that would help to avoid and contain financial crises. Although the near-term macroeconomic effects of the decline appear to have been limited, the longer-term implications might depend on the responses of policymakers and the effectiveness of international co-ordination.

The book is designed in Eight Units: 44 chapters, to cover strategic policy level issues, such as business-government relations, ownership, control of overseas subsidiaries, centralisation of decision-making, and strategic long-range planning. The theoretical developments in the area of international business have been dealt exhaustively since the book aims at providing present and future international managers with the strategic and managerial tools needed for operating globally. However, the communication of the new ideas in international business has been hampered by the fact that the important material is scattered among various journals. The most significant contributions were to be brought together and synthesised to make them readily available to the students. Towards this end, an attempt is made provide a thorough exposition of the developments in international business both at macro and micro level. The book offers a combination of analytical rigor and practical relevance and would be of interest to all those concerned with the international business. Analytical techniques help translate the often vague rules of thumb used by global managers into specific decision criteria. The attempt is to analyse past trends, to identify current issues, and to present the outlook on international business. Accent is on policy approaches, and feasible options for near and medium term action. From this vantage point, the policymakers, business executives, and researchers can then envision the entire panorama of the international business operations and the problems and consideration therein. In placing emphasis on the importance of ideas and theories in structuring expectation and action, an attempt is made to show that conflicts of values are internal to the operations of the international organizations. Broad scope of international business and its effects by presenting leading edge analysis of its various components are covered along with the important functional areas, such as organization development, human resource management, production and logistics, marketing and financial management in the context of globalization. The reader obtains the in-depth exposure to the macro shifts which are redefining the parameters of business, as well insights into the strategic options which firms can choose to respond to these changes. The book also presents the rich array of implementation examples which demonstrate the capability of firms to stay ahead of the game.

One key unique aspect of this book is the fact that it presents concerns and issues in the international business field from global perspective to help and enable readers in developing an understanding of the operations of the multinational firm with the aid of solid theoretical foundation. The detailed knowledge gained by the reader should make him more conversant with the discipline and should provide a strong conceptual foundation on which to build his future business activities and decisions. The text is based on the courses we have taught in the past two decades at the Faculty of Management Studies, Delhi University. Keeping in view the requirements of the students of MBA/Commerce/Business Economics at various Universities/ Institutes, Chartered Accountants, Company Secretaries and other professional courses, the text is designed to fill the gap and also transmit some of the excitement of current thinking and controversy. Since the book is synthesis, I am indebted to all writers who have contributed to the area of finance. I hope that I have interpreted their views correctly. I have made acknowledgement of every idea whose source I have been able to identify, but some writers may have been missed unintentionally. I have benefited greatly from feedback from students and colleagues. Finally, I wish to express thanks and appreciate the diligent support provided by the members of the S. Chand & Company Pvt. Ltd whose high performance standards and in-depth knowledge of publishing have been invaluable in the development of the text.

V.K. BHALLA

CONTENTS

UNIT-III

UNIT-IV

UNIT-VII

Unit I

1

INTERNATIONAL BUSINESS: *AN OVERVIEW*

INTRODUCTION

International business has been growing rapidly in recent decades because of technological expansion, the liberalisation of government policies on cross-border movements (goods, services, and the resources to produce them) the development of institutions need to support and facilitate international transactions, consumer pressures to buy foreign products and services, and increased global competition. This transformation in patterns of international trade, capital and competition in the spatial organisation of social relations and transactions, expressed in transcontinental or interregional flows and networks of activity, interaction and power, has serious consequences for international business strategy. While business leaders have always faced complex challenges, the challenges of today appear more daunting than before. The acid test of a well-managed company is to conceive, develop, and implement an effective global strategy. The combination of better access to resources and a better ability to organise production transnationally increases the pressure on firm to utilise new opportunities lest their competitors do so first and gain a competitive advantage.

By decoupling of space and time, the process (or set of processes) of internationalisation has reduced the modern world to an electronic village, leading to a rapid increase in cross-border economic, political and socio-cultural The Increasing interaction, or integration, of national economic systems through the growth in international trade, investment, and capital flows due to major advances in all technologies, particularly communications, have resulted in an accelerating rate of change in the world. International trade rules have fostered global production net-works, and an associated rise in intrafirm trade, by progressively lowering trade barriers and reducing the likelihood of unpredictable increase. Foreign capital has played a catalytic role in pushing policies in the right direction and contributing a number of resources to the development effort. However, transnational corporations (MNCs) do not substitute for domestic effort: they can only provide access to tangible and intangible assets and catalyse domestic investment and capabilities. Today, more large and small firms, from more countries, in virtually all industries are investing abroad, be it through the expansion of existing facilities, greenfield projects, mergers and acquisitions, the acquisition of assets in the framework of privatisation programmes or through various form of non-equity relationships. Infact, the fragmentation of production processes across international borders is an important new trend, particularly for developing economies. This slicing up the value chain involves separate stages of production being conducted in different countries. Declining communication cost and improved transportation systems permit just-in-time delivery and the coordination of production across borders. Developing economies can expedite their integration into the new production systems by liberalising and improving their tele-communications and transportation sectors.

DEFINITION OF INTERNATIONAL BUSINESS

International business includes any type of business activity that crosses national borders. The *American Heritage Dictionary* defines *international* as "of, relating to, or involving two or more nations" and *business* as "commercial, industrial, or professional dealings." Accordingly, the term *international business,* refers to any commercial, industrial or professional endeavour involving two or more nations.

An alternative way to look at what is meant by *international business* is to distinguish such business from *domestic business.* A domestic business operates in only one country, an international business in more than one. The fundamental characteristic that distinguishes international business from domestic business is that international business involves activities that take place across national borders. The implications of crossing these borders must be considered in all of the decisions and activities that international firms undertake. In addition to this broad, general framework of international business activities, it is also important to recognise specific differences in the way that business is conducted internationally by specifically differentiating between firms described as *multidomestic* and those describe as *global.* The *multidomestic* company does business in more than one country and thereby fits into the international business classification. In other words, a multidomestic firm conducts its foreign business through separate, local entities in foreign countries. The *global* company also operates in more than one country and is an international business. A global firm views all of its foreign entities as interrelated and conduct business on a world wide basis. These are extremes and, in fact, most international companies combine attributes of both, but it is frequently helpful to distinguish between the two. This distinction is helpful in examining international business because the choices that international companies make are influenced by their overall multidomestic or global view.

SCOPE OF INTERNATIONAL BUSINESS ACTIVITIES

The study of international business focus on the particular problems and opportunities that emerge because a firm is operating in more than one country. In a very real sense, international business involves the broadest and most generalised study of the field of business, adapted to a fairly unique across the border environment. Many of the parameters and environmental variables that are very important in international business (such as foreign legal systems, foreign exchange markets, cultural differences, and different rates of inflation) are either largely irrelevant to domestic business or are so reduced in range and complexity as to be of greatly diminished significance. Thus, it might be said that domestic business is a special limited case of international business.

The distinguishing feature of international business is that international firms operate in environments that are highly uncertain and where the rules of the game are often ambiguous, contradictory, and subject to rapid change, as compared to the domestic environment. In fact, conducting international business is really not like playing a whole new ball game, however, it is like playing in a different ball park, where international managers have to learn the factors unique to the playing field. Managers who are astute in identifying new ways of doing business that satisfy the changing priorities of foreign governments have an obvious and major competitive advantage over their competitors who cannot or will not adapt to these changing priorities.

During the past few decades, the emergence of corporate empires in the world economy, based on the contemporary scientific and technological developments, has led to globalization of production. As a result of international production, co-operation among global productive units, the large scale capital exports, "the export of production" or "production abroad" has come into prominence as against commodity export in world economy in recent years. Global corporations consider the whole of the world their production place, as well as their market and move factors of production to wherever they can optimally be combined. They avail fully of the revolution that has brought about instant world-wide communication, and near instant-transformation. Their ownership is transnational; their management is transnational. Their freely mobile management, technology and capital, the modern agent for stepped-up economic growth, transcend individual national boundaries. They are domestic in every place, foreign in none—a true corporate citizen of the world. The greater interdependence among nations has already reduced economic insularity of the peoples of the world, as well as their social and political insularity.

In a world of intensifying competition and accelerating technological change, this complementary and catalytic role can be very valuable. There is more space for firms to pursue their corporate strategies, and enjoying more rights than before. But the economic growth should be accompanied by social and human resource development. The obvious question is: should these increased rights be complemented by firms' assuming greater social responsibility? The notion of social responsibility of MNCs encompasses a broad range of issues of which environmental, human and labour rights have attracted most attention in recent years. In a liberalising and globalising world economy, this question is likely to be asked with increasing frequency and insistence. Today, MNCs, rather being seen as part of the *development problem*, are seen as part of the *solution*. Indeed, if anything, expectation are sometimes far high. MNCs, like other firms respond to government policies. Infact, they are better equipped than national firms to escape the constraints of policies that they find inconvenient. They can move their activities abroad more easily, or use internal channels (e.g. transfer pricing) not open to national firms. In addition, they may contribute, under certain conditions, more than national firms because of their greater access to a whole range of resources. For instance, when an economy open up to trade, MNCs can restructure their affiliates to reach international levels of technology and productivity.

Looking ahead it appears that in the changing economic scenario, international business is a fact of life. The MNCs have become the central actors of the world economy and, in linking foreign direct investment, trade, technology and finance, they are a driving force of a world growth. Contemplating the high-tech world of effective complete markets, in which any contingent claim can be synthesised and any risk can be taken, the importance of internationalisation of production is now well recognised. Managing business in the new millennium will mean some global interactions. The organisations will succeed or fail on the basis of their ability to deal with the dynamic international environment. Their impact on the economic and the social welfare of developed and developing countries is both widespread and critical.

The guiding principles of a firm engaged in (or commencing) international business activities should incorporate a global perspective. A firm's guiding principles can be defined in terms of three broad categories products offered/market served, capabilities, and results (See Exhibit-1). However, this perspective of the international business is critical to understand the full meaning of international business. That is, the firm's

EXHIBIT-1

GUIDING PRINCIPLES IN STRATEGIC PLANNING

Category	*Strategic Area*
Products/Markets	Products offered Market needs
Capabilities	Technology Production capability Method of sale Method of distribution Natural resources
Results	Size/growth Return/profit

senior management should explicitly define the firm's guiding principles in terms of an international mandate rather than allow the firm's international activities to develop as an incidental adjunct to its domestic activities. Incorporating an international outlook into the firm's basic statement of purpose will help focus the attention of managers (at all levels of the organisation) on the opportunities (and hazards) outside the domestic economy.

EXHIBIT-2

STRATEGIC-PLANNING PROCESS

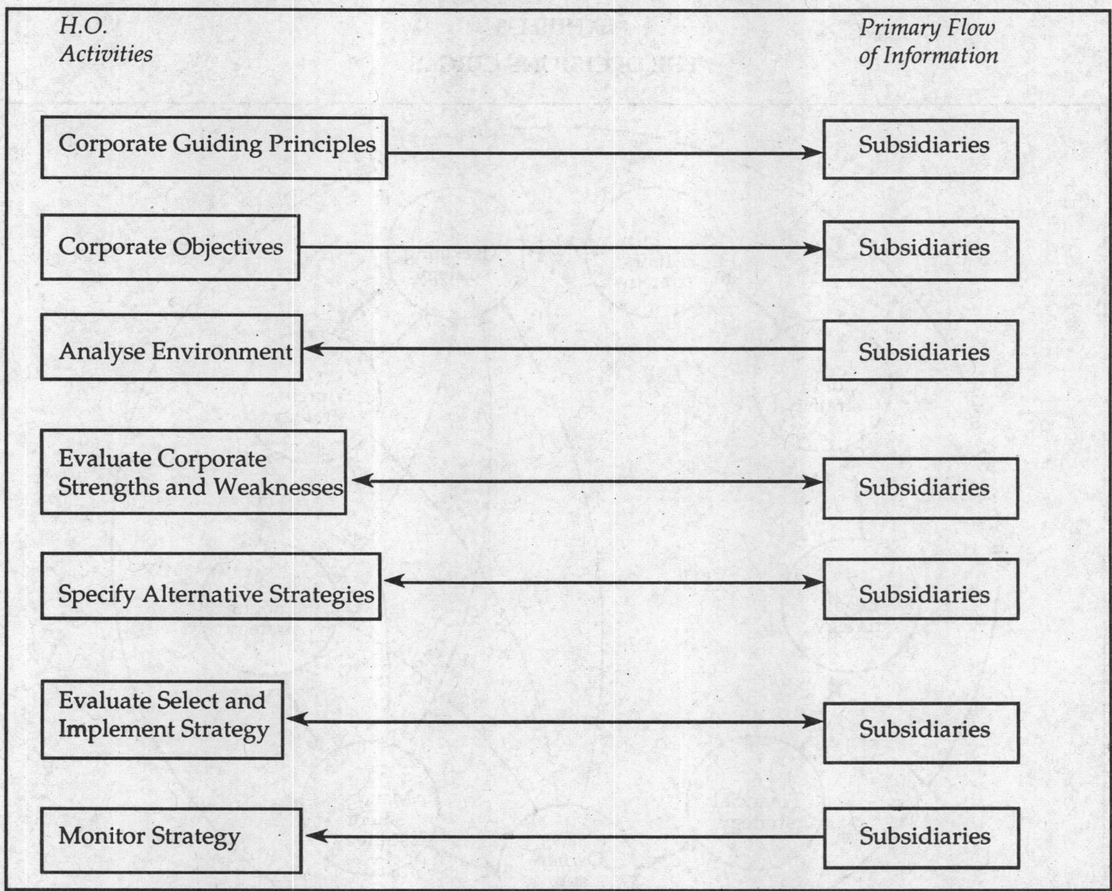

It must be stressed that the impacts of the dynamic factors unique to the playing field for international business are felt in all relevant stages of evolving and implementing business plans. The first broad stage of the process is to formulate a corporate guiding principles. As outlined in Exhibit-2 the first step in formulating and implementing a set of business plans is to define the firm's guiding principles in the marketplace. The guiding principles should, among other things, provide a long-term view of what the firm is striving to become and provide direction to divisional and subsidiary managers vehicle, some firms use "the decision circle" which is simply an interrelated set of strategic choices forced upon any firm faced with the internationalisation of its markets (see Exhibit-3). These choices have to do with marketing, sourcing, labor, management, ownership, finance, law, control, and public affairs. Here the first two—marketing and sourcing—constitute the basic strategies that encompass a firm's initial considerations. Essentially, management is answering two questions: *to whom are we going to sell what, and from where and how will we supply that market?* We then have a series of input

EXHIBIT-3

THE DECISIONS CIRCLE

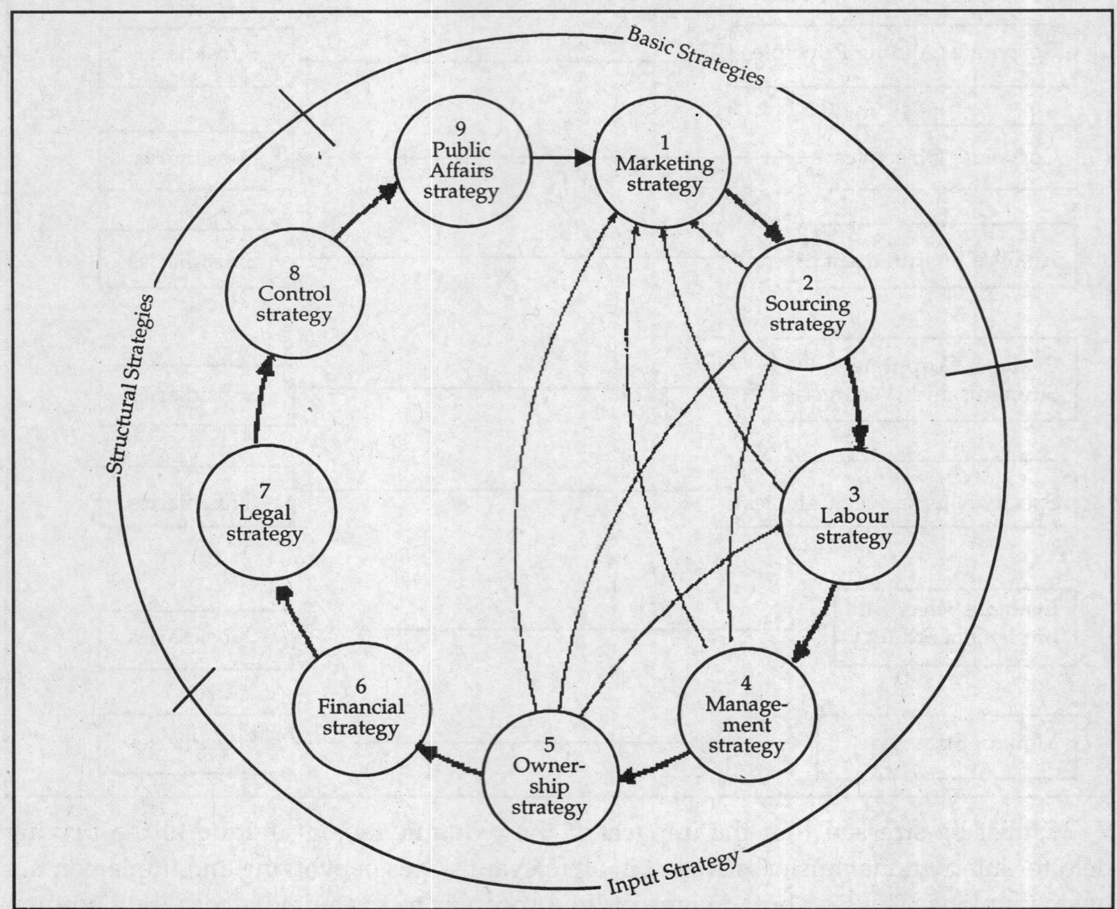

Each strategy area contains a number of subsidiary strategy options. The decision process which normally starts in the marketing strategy area, is an iterative one. As the decision maker proceeds around the decision circle, previously' selected strategies must be readjusted. Only a portion of the possible feedback adjustment loops are shown here.

strategies—labor, management, ownership, and financial. They are in their efforts to develop their own business plans. As an obligation addressed essentially to the query, with what resources are we going to implement the basic strategies? That is, where will we find the right people, willingness to carry the risk, and the necessary funds? A third set of strategies—legal and control—respond to the problem of how the firm is to structure itself to implement the basic strategies, given the resources it can muster. A final strategic area, public affairs, is shown as a basic strategy simply because it places a restraint on all other strategy choices.

Although these strategy areas are shown separately in the decision circle and treated separatel but they obviously do not stand alone. There must be constant reiteration as one moves around the decision circle. The sourcing strategy obviously influences marketing strategy, as well as the reverse. The target market may enjoy certain preferential relationships with other markets. That is, everything influences everything else. Inasmuch as the number of options a firm faces is multiplied as it moves into international markets, decision making becomes increasingly complex the deeper the firm becomes involved internationally. One is dealing with multiple currency, legal, marketing, economic, political, and cultural systems. Geographic and demographic factors differ widely. In fact, as one moves geographically, virtually everything becomes a variable: there are few fixed factors. Exhibit-4 maps some of these complexities.

For our purposes here, a strategy is defined as an element in a consciously devised overall plan of corporate development that, once made and implemented, is difficult (i.e., costly) to change in the short run. By way of contrast, an **operational** or **tactical decision** is one that sets up little or no institutionalised resistance to making a different decision in the near future. Some theorists have differentiated among *strategic, tactical,* and *operational*, with the first being defined as those decisions that imply multi-year commitments; a tactical decision, one that can be shifted in roughly a year's time; an operational decision, one subject to change in less than a year. In the international context, we suggest that the tactical decision, as the phrase is used here, is elevated to the strategic level because of the rigidities in the international environment not present in the purely domestic—for example, work force planning and overall distribution decisions. Changes may be implemented domestically in a few months, but if one is operating internationally, law, contract, and custom may intervene to render change difficult unless implemented over several years.

MAIN DRIVERS OF GLOBALISATION

The second half of the twentieth century saw processes of globalization impacting on people's lives across the world: from cosmopolitan urban centres to rural outposts; from advanced industrial complexes to craft workshops. Increasing interconnectedness and interdependence between people, organizations and governments have been

EXHIBIT-4

VARIABLES IN THE INTERNATIONAL SYSTEM

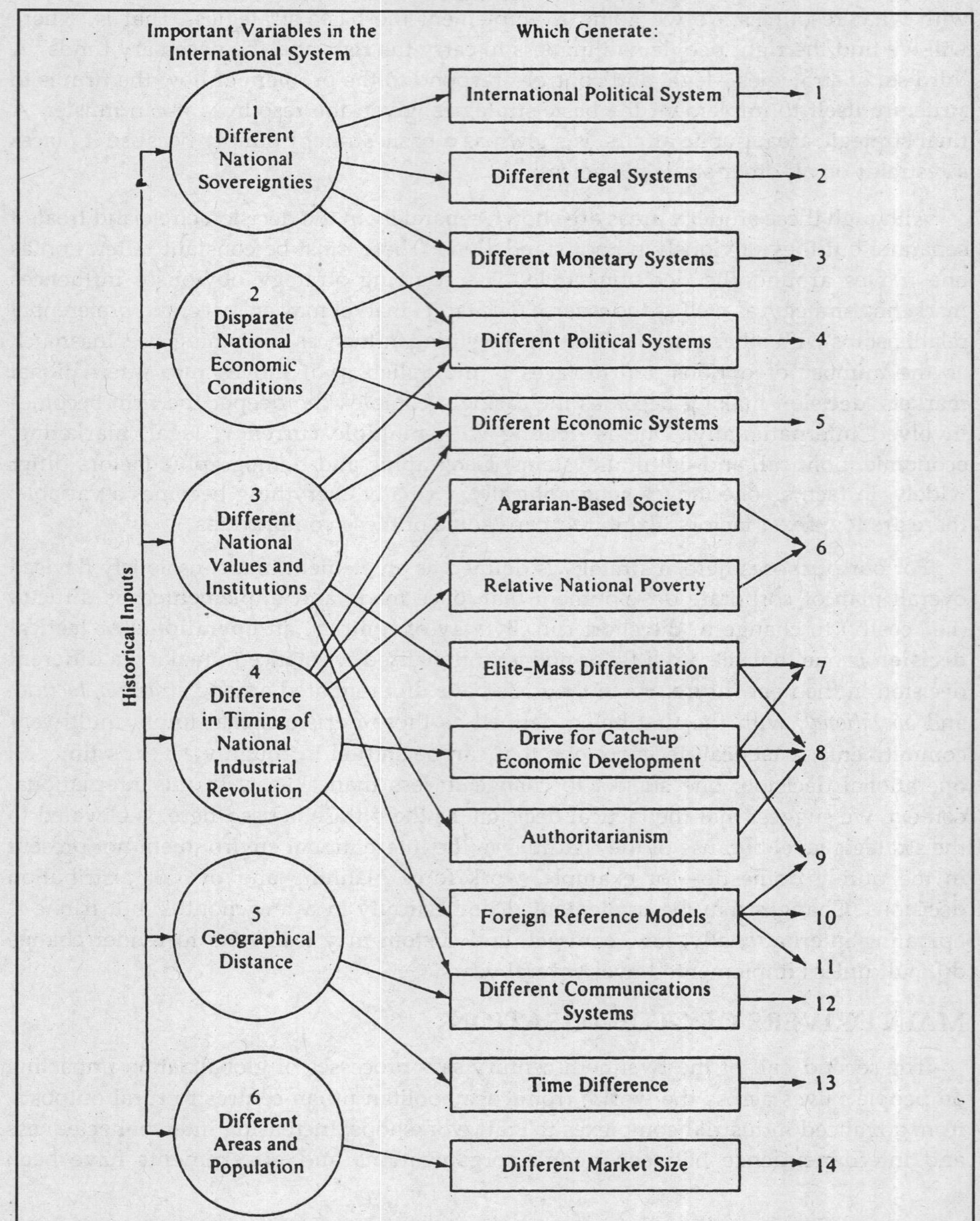

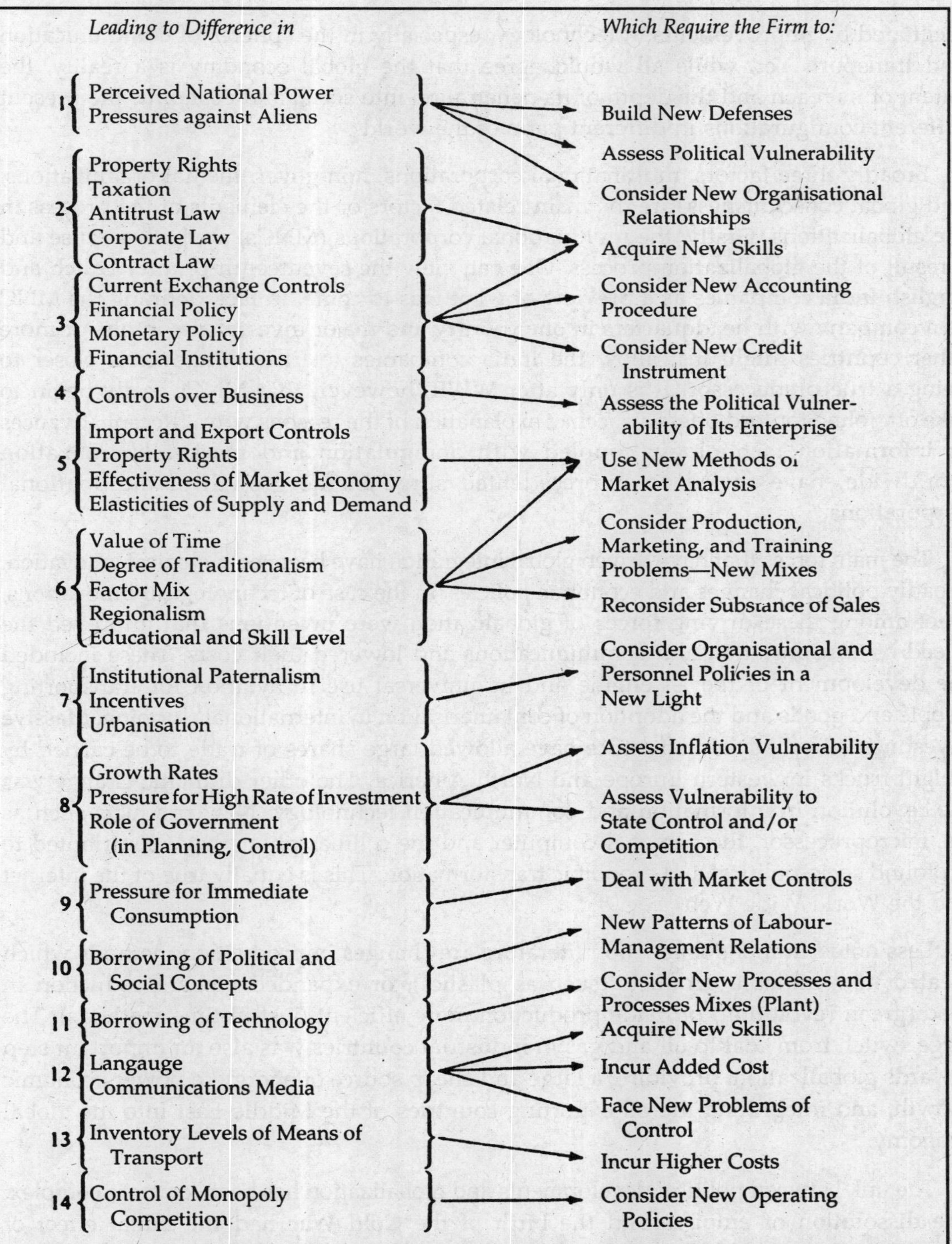

Note: Many important relationships are not charted here. This scheme is presented only as an illustration.

facilitated by improvements in technology, especially in the spheres of communication and transport. Yet, while all would agree that the global economy is a reality, the extent of its reach and the depth of its penetration into social and economic life present different configurations in different parts of the world.

Broadly three factors: multinational corporations, non-governmental organizations, and global consciousness, are the main related factors or the elements of the process in the globalizations. Firstly, the multinational corporations (MNCs) are both a cause and a result of the globalization process. One can view the seventeenth-century Dutch and English India companies as a preview of what was to come. In fact, defining the MNC as a company with headquarters in one country and major investments in one or more other countries might just allow the India companies to fit in. Unilever is closer to being a true predecessor. It is only after WWII, however, that MNCs really begin to take off. John Stopford offers a succinct explanation of the reasons why: "Recent advances in information technology, coupled with deregulation and market liberalization worldwide, have fueled an unprecedented surge in the growth of multinational corporations."

The main forces that have driven global integration have been technological innovation, broadly political changes and economic policies. In the case of technological innovations, chief among these driving forces of globalization were inventions that improved the speed of transportation and communications and lowered their costs. These included the development of the jet engine and its universal use in aviation for transporting people and goods and the adoption of containerisation in international shipping. Massive investments in road infrastructure have allowed large shares of trade to be carried by freight trucks in western Europe and North America. The other dramatic change was the revolution in information and communication technology. New products such as the microprocessor, the personal computer and the cellular phone have contributed to profound socio-political and economic transformation. This is equally true of the internet and the World Wide Web.

Less noted in the globalization literature are changes in production methods which created new tradable products (such as plastics), or expanded global production in food (green revolution) or made production more efficient (just-in-time methods). The large switch from coal to oil and gas in industrial countries was also an important step towards globalization, providing a large and cheap source of energy to power economic growth, and integrating the oil-exporting countries of the Middle East into the global economy.

The link between political developments and globalization has been far more complex. The dissolution of empires and the birth of the Cold War had the initial effect of fragmenting the world and the global economy into a first, second and third world.

The divide between East and West reached its peak in the early 1960s with the construction of the Berlin Wall and the Cuban missile crisis. But well before these dramatic events occurred, the seeds of economic integration had been sown in Europe, with the Marshall Plan providing a huge impetus to economic recovery and integration. Subsequently, with China's economic reform, the fall of the Berlin Wall and the collapse of the Soviet Union, the major political impediments to global economic integration ended.

A key driver of globalization has been economic policy, which resulted in deregulation and the reduction or elimination of restrictions on international trade and financial transactions. Currencies became convertible and balance-of-payments restrictions were relaxed. In effect, for many years after the end of WWII it was currency and payments restrictions rather than tariffs that limited trade the most. The birth of the Eurodollar market was a major step towards increasing the availability of international liquidity and promoting cross-border transactions in western Europe. Beginning in the 1970s, many governments deregulated major service industries such as transport and telecommunications. Deregulation involved a range of actions, from removal, reduction and simplification of government restrictions, to privatization of state-owned enterprises and to liberalization of these industries so as to increase competition.

In the case of trade, liberalization was pursued multilaterally through successive GATT negotiations. Increasingly, bilateral and regional trade agreements became an important aspect of (preferential) trade liberalization as well. But many countries undertook trade reforms unilaterally. In the case of developing countries, their early commercial policies had an inward-looking focus. Industrialization through import substitution was the favoured route to economic development. The subsequent shift away from import substitution may be owed partly to the success of a number of Asian newly-industrializing countries that adopted an export-led growth strategy, but also partly to the debt crisis in the early 1980s, which exposed the limitations of inward-looking policies.

Other points to consider include important actions that contributed to global macroeconomic stability and therefore provided an environment conducive to global integration. These would include the Volcker US Federal Reserve's successful steering of US monetary policy to put an end to US and hence global inflation in the early 1980s and the Louvre Accord, which stabilized major exchange rates. Finally, it would be remiss to exclude the role that international institutions such as the IMF, the World Bank and the GATT played in the process of globalization. They have provided cohesion and greater coherence to international economic policymaking.

The next major factor in globalization is that of the non-governmental organizations (NGOs). The term non-governmental organization or NGO was not in general currency before the UN was formed. When 132 international NGOs decided to cooperate with each other in 1910, they did so under the label, the Union of International Associations. It was only with the United Nations and its reference to organizations not forming part of a government and not working for profit that the term came into widespread usage. It is a messy topic. Whereas the number of MNCs is large, it is identifiable and restricted. NGOs are like the proverbial mushrooms in the rain: they spring up constantly.

The explosive growth of NGOs is a post-WW II phenomenon. It is estimated that there were, as of 2009, about 40,000 international NGOs, as many as 277,000 local ones in Russia, and an astonishing 3.3 million in India.

What exactly is a NGO? There is no generally accepted definition of an NGO and the term carries different connotations in different circumstances. Nevertheless, there are defining traits: an NGO is not a political party, nor is it profit making and it will not engage in violence. In other words, an NGO is an independent voluntary association of people acting together on a continuous basis, for some common purpose, other than achieving government office, making money or illegal activities.

Before the Computer Revolution, communication was mostly slow and one-directional. Thus, the telegraph facilitated authoritarian orders, and was instrumental in calling up troop mobilizations. Steamships allowed for more regular ocean travel than sailing ships, but usually took days to reach their destination. Only with the establishment in the 1960s of direct transnational telephone hook-ups and the provision of relatively inexpensive air travel was it possible for people to either talk or meet conveniently. The lofting of artificial satellites and the advent of cheap computers supported the explosive take-off of NGOs. Originally, their growth seemed to be in the shape of a J curve, similar to that of the MNCs; now it is believed to be much steeper.

Globalization has been defined as increasing interconnection and interdependency. It is only after WW II that one can speak of a rupture. As often said, the awful truth is that "war is the mother of invention." During WW II, research into the launching of missiles took on renewed vigour, especially in the form of German V-2s. The head of the German, and Nazi, programme, Werner von Braun, subsequently was put in charge of the American programme to match the Soviet Union in the period of Cold War. In 1957, the Russians lofted the first artificial satellite into orbit around the earth, Sputnik I. These artificial satellites, now numbering into the thousands, make almost instantaneous communication possible in real time.

Along with the transnational institutional developments, a new consciousness can be said to have arisen: a global consciousness. From space, the astronauts could see the " blue planet" as a single entity, national boundaries simply not showing up. Yet that "space age" seems to have come to an end, at least momentarily. NASA planned its last lunch for July 8, 2011. The economic impact of this ending will be great, in terms of both expenditure and employment.

Telecommunications, weather forecasting, agriculture, forestry and even the search for minerals have all been revolutionized. So has warfare. No power can any longer mobilize its armed forces in secret. The exact location of every building on the planet can be known. And satellite-based global-positioning systems will guide a smart bomb to that location on demand.

Exhibit-5 attempts to provide a chronology of the major events and forces that have contributed to today's globalization.

EXHIBIT-5

Globalisation Chronology

Time	*Economic*	*Political*	*Technological*
1940s	• Establishment of the Bretton Woods System, a new international monetary system (1944-71) • Establishment of GATT (1947) entering into force in January 1948	• Foundation of the United Nations (1945) • Launch of the Marshall Plan (1948–57), a European recovery programme • Founding of the Organization for European Economic Cooperation (1948)	• Expansion of plastics and fibre products, e.g. first nylon stockings for women (1940)
	• Soviet Union establishes the Council for Mutual Economic Assistance (CMEA) for economic cooperation among communist countries (1949-91)	• Decolonization starts (1948-1962). Independence of India, Indonesia, Egypt, for example • China becomes a socialist republic in 1949	• Discovery of large oil fields in the Middle East. especially in Saudi Arabia (1948)
1950s	• Treaty of Rome establishes the European Community (1957). EC and the European Free Trade Association (1959) favour west European integration	• Korean war (1950-53) • Suez crisis (1956)	• Increased use of oil from the Middle East in Europe and Japan • "Just-in-time" production implemented by Toyota
	• Major currencies become convertible (1958-64)	• Decolonization in Africa (15 countries become independent between 1958 and 1962)	• Increasing usage of jet engines in air transport (1957-72)
1960s	• Foundation of the Organization of the Petroleum Exporting Countries (OPEC) (1960)		• First person in space (Yuri Gagarin, 1961) and first man on the moon (Neil Armstrong, 1969)
	• Development of the Eurodollar Market in London which contributed to the expansion of international liquidity		• Integrated circuits become commercially available (1961) • Offshore oil and gas production developed
	• Kennedy Round, 6th session of the GATT (1964-69) • Rapid spread of automobiles and highways in the North accelerates demand and shift in fuels consumption (from coal to oil)	• Erection of Berlin Wall (1961) and Cuban missile crisis (1962) highlight sharp confrontation between East and West	• Green Revolution - transforming agricultural production in developing countries (1960s onwards) • First line of Japan's high-speed train system (shinkansen) opened in 1964 • Mont Blanc Road Tunnel (1965)

	• Trade policies of East Asian countries put more emphasis on exportled development than on import substitution • Elimination of last customs duties within EC (1968)		• Increasing usage of containerization in ocean transport (1968 onwards)
1970s	• Departure from US dollar exchange rate gold standard (1971)	• Yom Kippur war (1973) helps to trigger oil price hike	• First single chip microprocessor (Intel 4004) is introduced (1971)
	• Tokyo Round of the GATT (1973-79)	• EU enlargement to nine members (1973)	
	• Oil price "shocks" (1973-74 and 1979) reverse decades of real oil price declines		
	• Rise of Asian newly industrialized countries • China's economic reform (1978) 1980s		
	• Volcker Fed successfully extinguishes US inflation		• IBM introduces the first personal computer (1981)
	• Developing country debt crisis • Mexico starts market reforms and joins the GATT in 1986	• Enlargement of the EU to 12 members	• Microsoft Windows introduced (1985)
	• Louvre Accord promotes stabilisation of major exchange rates (1987)	• Fall of the Berlin Wall (1989) 1990s	
	• Indian economic reforms launched in 1991 • Establishment of the North American Free Trade Agreement (1994) • Asian financial crisis (1997)	• Dissolution of the Soviet Union (1991) leads to the formation of 13 independent states	• Eurotunnel opens in 1994 linking the United Kingdom to continent • The number of mobile phones increases due to the introduction of second generation (2G) networks using digital technology • Launch of the first 2G-GSM network by Radiolinja in Finland (1991)
	• Establishment of the WTO (1995) following Uruguay Round (1986-94)		• Invention of the World Wide Web by Tim Berners-Lee (1989) - first website put online in 1991. Number of internet users rises to 300 million by 2000
	• Adoption of the euro by 11 European countries (1999)	• Maastricht Treaty (formally, the Treaty on European Union) signed (1992)	
	• Dotcom crisis (2001)		• Container ships transport more than 70 per cent of the seaborne trade in value terms
	• China joins WTO (2001)		• Number of internet users rises to 800 million in 2005
	• End of the Multifibre Arrangement (quantitative restrictions of textiles lifted)	• Enlargement of the EU to 27 members	

GLOBALISATION TRENDS

International trade and investment had been economically important long before industrialization transformed production methods, and before modern technology transformed transport. Wealth generated by companies through international trade and investment could be seen as contributing to the wealth of national economies of sovereign states. The growth of international trade relations, greatly enhanced by industrialization and improvements in transport in the late nineteenth century, has been described as a *process of internationalisation*. Production, companies, and industries were still essentially based in national economies. National economies were to a considerable degree autonomous, and economic policy issues, such as the imposition of tariffs, were matters for national governments to decide. Growth in world trade was a hallmark of internationalization in the period before 1914. The world before the First World War could be accurately described as a global market, reflecting flourishing international flows of goods, services, capital and people. However, the depth of economic integration has been described as 'shallow', characterized by arm's-length transactions between independent companies based in national economies. *Globalization*, by contrast, represents deeper integration, in that international interactions become qualitatively transformed from exchange transactions to long-term, mutidimensional links. Economic globalization, in a sense, has been happening for centuries.

Current trends are towards the increasing globalisation and interdependence of firms, markets and countries. Intense competition among countries, industries, and firms on a global level is a recent development owed to the confluence of several major trends. Among these trends are the decline of tariff and other trade barriers, and attendant rising confidence in foreign investment; the growth of organisation and administrative structures to permit managing resources and risks across sovereign borders and over great distance, the gains in technology and its transfer from one country and firm to another, and perhaps most important, the increasing interdependence of complex technologies economies on one another throughout the value chain.

International trade after WWII entered a long period of record expansion with world merchandise exports rising by more than 8 per cent per annum in real terms over the 1950-73 period. Trade growth slowed thereafter under the impact of two oil price shocks, a burst of inflation caused by monetary expansion and inadequate macroeconomic adjustment policies. In the 1990s, trade expanded again more rapidly, partly driven by innovations in the information technology (IT) sector. Despite the small contraction of trade caused by the dotcom crisis in 2001, the average expansion of world merchandise exports continued to be high – averaging 6 per cent for the 2000-07 period. For the entire 1950-2007 period, trade expanded on average by 6.2 per cent, which is much stronger than in the first wave of globalization from 1850 to 1913. As dollar prices expanded much faster after WWII than before WWI the nominal trade expansion of the former period is more than twice as fast as in the earlier period (9.8 per cent versus 3.8 per cent per annum).

The developments over the last few years in major economies of the world have not been encouraging. There is an apprehension that the process of global economic recovery that began after the financial crisis of the 2008 is beginning to stall and the sovereign debt crisis in the eurozone area may persist for a while. There has been a fall in the rate of world output growth from 2.4 per cent in 2011 to 3.8 per cent in 2010, weighed down by the on-going sovereign debt crisis in Europe, supply chain disruptions from natural disasters in Japan and Thailand, and turmoil in Arab countries.

The abrupt deceleration of trade in 2012 was attributed to slow growth in developed economies and recurring bouts of uncertainty over the future of the euro. Flagging output and high unemployment in developed countries reduced imports and fed through to a lower pace of export growth in both developed and developing economies. Economies in the euro area stalled in 2012 and the sovereign debt crisis flared again in the summer, pushing long-term borrowing costs for Italy and Spain above 6% and stoking uncertainty about the future of the common currency. Growth also slowed worryingly in the US in Q4 (2012), and Japan slipped in and out of recession during the year. As a result, world GDP growth at market exchange rates dropped to 2.1% in 2012 from 2.4% in 2011. This pace of expansion was below the average of 3.2% for the two decades preceding the financial crisis and also below the 2.8% average of the last 20 years including the crisis period (Table 1).

TABLE 1

Real GDP and merchandise trade volume growth by region, 2010-12
Annual % change

	GDP			*Exports*			*Imports*		
	2010	*2011*	*2012*	*2010*	*2011*	*2012*	*2010*	*2011*	*2012*
World	3.8	1.4	2.1	14.1	5.2	2.1	13.6	5.1	1.9
North America	2.6	2.0	2.3	15.0	6.6	4.5	15.7	4.4	3.1
United -States	2.4	1.8	2.2	15.4	7.1	4.1	14.8	3.8	2.8
South and									
Central America[a]	6.2	4.3	2.6	5.2	61	1.4	22.7	12.0	1.8
Europe	2.3	1.7	-0.1	11.0	5.5	0.6	9.4	2.8	-1.9
European Union (27)	2.1	1.5	-0.3	11.7	5.7	0.3	9.1		
Commonwealth of	2.4	-2.0							
Independent States (CIS)	4.7	4.8	3.7	6.1	1.8	1.6	18.8	17.1	6.8
Africa	4.5	0.7	9.3	5.4	-8.5	6.1	8.1	4.5	11.3
Middle East	4.9	5.3	3.3	7.5	5.5	1.2	8.2	51	7.9
Asia	6.7	3.3	3.8	22.7	6.4	2.8	18.2	6.7	3.7

China	10.4	9.2	7.8	28.1	8.8	6.2	22.0	8.8	3.6
Japan	4.5	-0.6	1.9	27.5	-0.6	-1.0	10.1	4.3	3.7
India	10.1	7.9	5.2	25.7	15.0	-0.5	22.7	9.7	7.2
Newly industrialized economics (4)[b]	8.2	4.0	1.8	20.9	7.8	1.6	17.9	2.7	1.5
Memo: Developed economies	2.7	1.5	1.2	13.1	5.1	1.0	10.7	31	-0.1
Memo; Developing and CIS	7.3	5.3	4.7	15.3	5.4	3.3	18.2	8.0	4.6

[a] Includes the Caribbean
[b] Hong Kong, China; Republic of Korea; Singapore and Chinese Taipei.
Source: WTO Secretariat.

Policy responses from the European Central Bank and the Federal Reserve appear to have succeeded in easing the sovereign debt crisis and putting US growth on a firmer footing. Borrowing costs in the euro area have returned to manageable levels since September and joblessness in the US has begun to fall, but progress to date remains fragile. The 2.3% growth in the US was nearly double the 1.2% rate for developed economies as a whole in 2012. Japan's increase for the year was also above average at 1.9%, but the EU's growth was close to zero at –0.3%.

Developing countries and the Commonwealth of Independent States (CIS) collectively raised their output by 4.7% in 2012, with Africa recording the fastest growth of any country or region at 9.3%. China was not far behind at 7.8%, while India recorded a 5.2% increase. However, the newly industrialized Asian economies of Hong Kong (China), the Republic of Korea, Singapore and Chinese Taipei registered a disappointing 1.8% increase as slumping European demand penalized their exports. The next fastest growing region after Africa was Asia (3.8%) followed by the CIS (3.7), the Middle East (3.3%), South and Central America (2.6%), North America (2.3%) and Europe (–0.1%). Aggregate quarterly figures for world GDP growth is likely slowed toward the end of the year as output in the EU contracted in Q4 (2012) and US and Japanese growth slowed.

Improved economic prospects for the United States in 2013 should only partly offset the continued weakness in the European Union, whose economy is expected to remain flat or even contract slightly this year. China's growth should continue to outpace other leading economies, cushioning the slowdown, but exports will still be constrained by weak demand in Europe. As a result, 2013 looks to be a near repeat of 2012, with both trade and output expanding slowly, below their long-term average rates.

The events of 2012 should serve as a reminder that the structural flaws in economies that were revealed by the economic crisis have not been fully addressed, despite important progress in some areas. Repairing these fissures needs to be the priority for 2013.

Attempts by developed economies to strike a balance between short-term growth and increasingly binding fiscal constraints have produced uneven results to date, and finding an appropriate mix of policies has proven to be challenging. Similarly, the amount of progress that developing economies have made in reducing their reliance on external demand is still unclear . As long as global economic weakness persists, protectionist pressure will build and could eventually become overwhelming. The threat of protectionism may be greater now than at any time since the start of the crisis, since other polices to restore growth have been tried and found wanting. To prevent a self-destructive lapse into economic nationalism, countries need to refocus their attention on reinforcing the multilateral trading system. Trade can once again be an engine of growth and a source of strength for the global economy rather than a barometer of instability.

The preliminary estimate of 2.0% growth for world trade in 2012 is 0.5 points below the WTO's most recent forecast of 2.5% from September 2012. The deviation is mostly explained by the worse than expected second-half performance of developed economies, which only managed a 1% increase in exports and a 0.1% decline in imports for the year. The growth of exports from developing economies (including the Commonwealth of Independent States) was in line with earlier predictions, but the rate for imports was less than expected. WTO economists cautioned that their trade forecasts for 2013 and 2014 were difficult to gauge due to divergent outlooks for the US and EU.

These figures refer to merchandise trade in volume terms, i.e., adjusted to account for inflation and exchange rate movements, but nominal (dollar-value) trade flows for both merchandise and commercial services display similar trends. In 2012, the dollar value of world merchandise exports only increased two tenths of one per cent (i.e. 0.2%) to $18.3 trillion, leaving it essentially unchanged. The slower growth in the dollar value of world trade compared to trade in volume terms is explained by falling prices for traded goods. Some of the biggest price declines were recorded for commodities such as coffee (-22 %), cotton (-42%), iron ore (-23%) and coal (-21%), according to IMF commodity price statistics. The value of world commercial services exports rose just 2% in 2012 to $4.3 trillion, with strong differences in growth rates across countries and regions. For example, the US saw its exports of commercial services climb 4% while those of Germany dropped 2% and France's tumbled 7%. On the import side, several European countries recorded sharp declines, including Italy (-8%), France (-10%), Portugal (-6%) and Greece (-18%).

The trade forecast for 2013 assumes 2.1% growth in world output at market exchange rates (unchanged from 2012) based on a consensus of economic forecasters. Risks to the forecast are firmly rooted on the downside and are mostly linked to the sovereign debt crisis in Europe. Accelerated fiscal consolidation in the US could also undermine the forecast if brinksmanship over budget negotiations between the executive and legislative branches leads to miscalculation. As always, unexpected events such as geopolitical tensions and natural disasters could also intrude to disrupt trade. On a more positive note, some factors that held back trade growth in 2012 may subside in 2013, including the recent territorial dispute that soured trade relations between Japan and China.

Indicators of production, business sentiment and employment in the first quarter of 2013 paint a mixed picture of current economic conditions. Purchasing managers' indices suggest that the euro-zone downturn may have accelerated despite continued resilience in Germany. At the same time, the US recorded a strong rise in manufacturing, Japan's production growth was less negative, and China and the Republic of Korea showed modest improvements. Unemployment in the US recently fell to its lowest level since before the economic crisis at 7.6%, whereas the rate for the euro area stands at close to 12%. Together, these indicators point to weak import demand in Europe even as conditions gradually improve elsewhere. In light of the large weight of the EU in world imports (32% in 2012 including trade within the EU, 15% excluding it), this suggests slow growth for trade in the early part of 2013.

Short-term trade developments show the divergent trade performances of major economies over the course of 2012. .Exports from the US and from the EU to the rest of the world (i.e. EU-extra exports) remained relatively strong for most of the year before dipping slightly in final quarter of 2012. Asian exports also held up relatively well, finishing the year on a note after pushing in the third quarter of 2012. Meanwhile , Japan's shipment of goods dropped 11% in second half of 2012 . On the import side, the EU maintained its recent trajectory, with last quarter of 2012 imports from the rest of the world falling to 5% below their level in the middle of 2011, and imports from other EU countries (i.e. intra-EU-trade) slipping by the same amount Japanese imports recorded strong growth or most of the year before dropping 6% in the final quarter of 2012.

Quarterly developments for trade in commercial services show a similar pattern of trade in goods, with year-on –year growth in dollar values flat or declining in Europe and growing in other regions.

The growth of world merchandise trade in 2012 was much lower than one would expect given the rate of world gross domestic product (GDP) growth for the year. Under normal conditions, the growth rate for trade is usually around twice that of GDP, but in 2012 the ratio of trade growth to GDP growth fell to 1:1. No change in world GDP growth is expected for 2013 but there is likely to be a partial return toward the usual ratio of trade growth to GDP growth. In 2013 it should increase to 1.6:1 and then to 1.8:1 in 2014.

Despite the unusually slow rate of trade volume growth in 2012, the ratio of world exports of merchandise and commercial service to world GDP in current dollar terms only dipped slightly, from around 32%, and remained close to its peak value of 33% in 2008 .Finally, it should be noted that slowing economic growth in Europe has a disproportionate impact on world trade due to the fact that by convention trade between EU countries is included in world trade totals. However, if the EU is to be treated as a single entity, which it is for purposes of trade policy, the slowdown in world trade in 2012 would not appear as extreme. In this case world trade growth would be 3.2% in 2012 rather than 2.0%.

The WTO's forecast of 3.3% growth in merchandise trade for 2013 is below the average rate of 5.3% for the last 20 years (1992–2012) and well below the pre-crisis average rate of 6.0% (1990–2008) . The divergence from the 20-year average narrows in the 2-year-ahead forecast for 2014 (5.0%), but it still remains below average. The difference between the pre-crisis trend and current and projected values for world trade appears to be widening, albeit slowly. If WTO's forecast comes to pass, the gap in percentage terms will be 17.0% in 2013 and 17.8% in 2014.

At some point in the future trade growth will again surpass its 20 year average, if only because this average keeps falling with every passing year of sub-par growth. When or if it will manage to bridge the gap with its pre-crisis trend remains to be seen. In addition to a durable level shift in the series, it appears that the fundamental growth rate of world trade volumes has also been reduced. To return to this trend would require a period of very rapid trade expansion at some point in the future, but such a boom in trade does not appear likely any time soon.

Merchandise Trade in Volume (i.e. real) Terms

The volume of world merchandise trade (as measured by the average of exports and imports) registered an increase of just 2% in 2012. If we exclude years in which trade volume declined, this was the smallest annual increase in a data set extending back to 1981. Shipments from developed countries grew more slowly than the world average at 1.0%, while exports of developing economies grew faster at 3.3%. On the import side, developed economies dropped 0.1% last year, while developing economies grew at a 4.6% pace.

After seeing its exports shrink by 8.5% in 2011 following the Libyan civil war, Africa rebounded in 2012 to record the fastest export growth of any region at 6.1%. This was followed by North America, where exports rose 4.5% on the strength of a 4.1% increase the US. Asia only managed to increase its exports by 2.8% in 2012 despite 6.2% growth in China's exports. Contributing to the slow growth in Asia were India and Japan, where exports declined by 0.5% and 1.0%, respectively. Other regions that export large quantities of natural resources saw small increases in export volumes, including the Commonwealth of Independent States (1.6%), South and Central America

(1.4%), and the Middle East (1.2%). This is to be expected since quantities of primary products tend not to change very much from year to year. The region with the slowest export growth was again Europe at 0.6%, but the EU managed to grow even more slowly at 0.3%.

Africa's imports also grew faster than those of any other region at 11.3%, making it the only region with double digit growth in either exports or imports. This was followed by the Middle East (7.9%) and the Commonwealth of Independent States (6.8%), which took advantage of the high average oil prices in 2012 to boost their export earnings to purchase more imports (Table 2). Asia's import growth of 3.7% was driven by a 3.6% increase in China. North America's 3.1% rise was slightly stronger than that of the US (2.8%). South and Central America, with import growth of 1.8%, lagged behind all regions other than Europe, which recorded a 1.9% decline in imports.

TABLE 2

World prices of selected primary products, 2000-12
Annual % change and $/Barrel

	2010	*2011*	*2012*	*2000-12*	*2005-12*
All commodities	26	29	-3	10	10
Metals	48	14	-17	10	10
Food	11	20	-2	7	8
Beverages [a]	14	17	-19	7	8
Agricultural raw materials	32	23	-13	3	4
Energy	26	36	1	12	11
Memo: Crude oil price in $/barrel [b]	79	104	105	60	79

[a] Comprising coffee, cocoa beans and tea.
[b] Average of Brent, Dubai, and West Texas Intermediate.
Source: IMF International Financial Statistics.

Merchandise and Commercial Services Trade in Value (i.e. Dollar) Terms

Commercial services accounted for roughly 19% of total world trade in world goods and commercial services in 2012. The dollar value of world merchandise exports in 2012 was $18.3 trillion, nearly unchanged from 2011. The stagnation in values reduced the average growth rate for the post-2005 period to 8% from 10% last year. This contrasts with the stronger growth rates of 22% in 2010 and 20% in 2011. Meanwhile, world commercial services exports in 2012 were only 2% higher than in 2011 at $4.3 trillion. The 2012 growth rate for transport services was in line with total world commercial services exports at 2%, while travel services grew faster (4%) and other commercial services grew more slowly (1%) (Table 3).

TABLE 3

World exports of merchandise and commercial services, 2005-12
$bn and annual % change

	Value	*Annual % change*			
	2012	*2010*	*2011*	*2012*	*2005-12*
Merchandise	18323	22	20	0	8
Commercial services	4345	10	11	2	8
Transport	885	16	9	2	7
Travel	1105	9	12	4	7
Other commercial services of which:	2350	8	12	1	10
Communications services	100	3	10	-3	8
Construction	110	-4	8	3	10
Insurance services	100	1	0	2	11
Financial services	300	7	12	-4	8
Computer and information services	265	12	14	6	14
Royalties and licence fees	285	8	14	-2	9
Other business services	1145	9	13	2	9
Personal, cultural and recreational services	35	14	13	3	7
Memo: Goods and commercial services (BOP)	22520	19	18	1	8

Source: WTO Secretariat estimates for merchandise and WTO and UNCTAD Secretariat estimates for commercial services.

Some sub-categories of other commercial services grew faster than others. Communications (including postal, courier and telecommunications services) declined by 3%, while construction rose 3% and insurance services increased by 2% in 2012. The biggest decline was observed in financial services (i.e. services provided by banks and other financial intermediaries), which fell 4%. The fastest growing sub-sector of other commercial services was computer and information services, which jumped 6% in 2012. Royalties and licence fees fell 2%, and other business services (including engineering services, legal/accounting services, management consulting, advertising and trade related services, among others) increased by 2%.

In dollar terms, US exports of financial services declined by 4% in 2012, the United Kingdom dropped 13%, Germany slipped 2% and France plunged 20%. Several other EU countries also recorded double digit declines in financial services, including Austria (–11%), Cyprus (–21%), Greece (–29%) and Spain (–11%). Total exports of financial services from Switzerland declined by 8%. Meanwhile, Japan's exports of financial services gained 13% and China's advanced 58%. Finally, the Asian financial centres of

Singapore and Hong Kong, China traded water in 2012 with 0% and 4% growth, respectively. Overall, developed economies' exports of financial services fell 6% while those of developing economies and Commonwealth of Independent States together rose 3%.

The US dollar appreciated against most major currencies between 2012 and 2013, rising nearly 4% on average. Exceptions include the Chinese yuan, which appreciated 2.4% against the dollar, and the Japanese yen, which was more or less unchanged against the dollar (-0.2%). This would tend to understate the value of some trade flows in 2013 and overstate the magnitude of any declines from 2012, particularly for trade not denominated in dollars (e.g. trade within the EU).

The outlook for world trade and output in 2013 and 2014 looks unsettled, as positive economic trends have also been accompanied by more worrisome developments. EU output fell in the fourth quarter of 2012 as the slowdown in Europe finally touched Germany. Monthly indicators of economic activity in January – February, 2013 suggest that the German economy remained relatively resilient in the first quarter of 2013, but the downturn in the rest of the euro area appeared to be intensifying. Most forecasters expect European economies to remain weak in the first half of 2013 before gaining strength later in the year.

Unemployment is falling gradually and private expenditure is picking up in the US, but automatic government spending cuts set to take effect in 2013 could weigh on growth later in the year. Political gridlock may be easing, which could allow more targeted and less sweeping measures to be agreed, with less risk to a promising recovery. The Federal Reserve has signalled that its most recent programme of quantitative easing will not be withdrawn hastily, but as the economy picks up transitioning to a less accommodative policy stance could prove challenging. Japan's new government has prioritized a sizeable fiscal stimulus package and a more accommodative monetary policy as a way to spur economic growth. The former may test the limits of fiscal policy given the size of the country's public debt — estimated by the IMF to exceed 200% of GDP — while the latter may invite charges of currency manipulation. Stimulus-oriented policies will probably provide a boost to Japanese growth and trade in 2013, but how much remains to be seen.

Although China's exports may be hindered by the slowdown in Europe, increased shipments to the US should partly make up for this. Until recently the EU was China's largest trading partner, but the drop in EU imports in 2012 left it in second place behind the US. China's GDP growth is expected to remain strong compared to the rest of the world in 2013, which should provide support for imports from other countries.

In light of these developments, WTO economists are forecasting a small pickup in world trade volume growth to 3.3% in 2013 from 2.0% in 2012. Exports of developed economies should increase by 1.4% while those of developing economies (including the Commonwealth of Independent States) should rise 5.3%. On the import side, the WTO anticipates 1.4% growth in developed economics and 5.9% in developing economies plus CIS (Table 4).

However, these figures for 2014 are provisional estimates based on strong assumptions about the medium-term trajectory of gross domestic product (GDP) and should be interpreted with care. World trade volume growth for that year is expected to improve to 5.0%. Exports of developed and developing economies should increase by 2.6% and 7.5%, respectively. On the import side, developed economies should advance by 3.2% while developing economies should rise 7.4%. The current forecast could be derailed if certain downside risks materialize. These include revived financial market turbulence related to the euro crisis, commodity price spikes, geopolitical tensions, and rising protectionism.

TABLE 4

World merchandise trade and GDP, 2008-2014[a]
Annual % change

	2009	*2010*	*2011*	*2012*	*2013[P]*	*2014[P]*
Volume of world merchandise trade[b]	12.5	13.9	5.2	2.0	3.3	5.0
Exports						
Developed economies	-15.2	13.1	5.1	1.0	1.4	2.6
Developing economies and CIS	-7.4	15.3	5.4	3.3	5.3	7.5
Imports						
Developed economies	-14.3	10.7	3.1	-0.1	1.4	3.2
Developing economies and CIS	-105	18.2	8.0	4.6	5.9	7.4
Real GDP at market exchange rates	-2.5	3.8	2.4	2.1	2.1	2.7
Developed economies	-3.8	2.7	1.5	1.2	1.1	1.9
Developing economies and CIS	2.1	7.3	5.3	4.7	5.0	5.1

[a] Figures for 2012 and 2013 are projections.
[b] Average of exports and imports.
Source: WTO Secretariat for trade, concensus estimates of economic forecasters for GDP.

Trade could still surprise on the upside if Europe returns to growth more quickly than anticipated. However, the most likely result is very similar to last year: a mild recession in the EU restraining exports and imports in both developed and developing economies. The trade forecast assumes a 2.1% increase in world GDP for 2013, with developed economies growing 1.1% and the rest of the world growing 5.0%. The 2014 projection assumes world output growth of 2.7%, with developed economies advancing 1.9% and the rest of the world growing 5.1%. The output figures above refer to real GDP at market exchange rates based on consensus estimates of economic forecasters.

Capital Account Balances and Reserves

In response to a series of financial crises, especially after the East Asian crisis of 1997, many emerging and developing economies adopted new strategies for managing their external economy. These involved greater reliance on exports (resulting in current account surpluses) and the accumulation of foreign exchange reserves, in part to check currency appreciation and also as self-insurance against capital flow reversals.

These strategies led to a shift from being net importers of financial capital to net exporters. As reserves got invested in developed economies, it led to a contradictory phenomenon of capital flowing from emerging countries to capital-rich countries (especially the US). In an accounting sense, this was equated to high saving rates in the emerging market economies (EMEs), especially China. The position of current account balances and reserves in India, in this regard, is somewhat of an outlier as even while holding substantial reserves, it has essentially had a structural current account deficit and is therefore not a contributor to global imbalances in the foregoing sense. Regardless of the merits of holding reserves, it is by now agreed that the relatively stronger external financial position (reserves) of the EMEs made them less vulnerable to the capital reversals following the global financial crisis of 2008 and in that sense a vindication of the strategy of maintaining high reserves.

While holding reserves has been acknowledged to be useful in dealing with the crisis, it has also been argued that excessive reserves involve (quasi-fiscal) costs apart from yielding low returns as countries invest abroad rather than in high-return domestic investments. Furthermore, large fluctuations in the exchange rate could result in significant losses to the value of reserves. For example, if the US dollar weakens, it could result in a loss in value of reserves denominated in dollars. Apart from the holding costs to the economy, high build-up of current account surpluses and reserves has been seen as a major indicator of global imbalances and potential source of instability in the international monetary system. In the global context, it has been argued that reserve accumulation was an outcome of resisting currency appreciation and an attempt to stimulate export-oriented production at the expense of domestic demand. The reserve accumulation by key emerging current account surplus economies, mostly held as dollar assets, supported a strong US dollar in spite of a growing current account deficit in the US. By thwarting exchange rate adjustment, this practice has been contributing to global economic imbalances. On the other hand, it has also been argued that the build-up of reserves is a consequence of loose monetary policies followed by reserve currency-issuing countries. Be that as it may, the fact remains that the issue of exchange rate management, build-up of current account surpluses and of reserves cannot be viewed in isolation and these issues are embedded in a wider ongoing debate on the deficiencies of the international monetary and financial system. For the present, the asymmetry in the balances in terms of current account surplus and reserves is there for the global economy to contend with.

IMPLICATIONS OF THE GLOBAL SHIFT

The changes in composition of the global economy suggest a perceptible shift in the global balance of output of goods (especially manufacturing). While services (in particular financial services) continue to be largely concentrated in advanced economies, a larger share in world population, coupled with higher growth, implies that the EMEs and developing countries will increasingly account for incremental growth in the global market for goods, services, and commodities. A change in the global economic balance driven by supply and demand forces therefore appears to be the 'new normal' and is likely to accentuate in the years to come.

At this juncture, many of the advanced economies are geared to very high levels of private consumption and government expenditure in relation to their GDP. A prolonged slowdown could place further pressure on their budgetary balances and household savings (that are already low) and adversely impact investment and their potential growth. Thus the possibility of low growth setting off a vicious cycle of higher debt and low growth cannot be ruled out.

Therefore, even when the emerging economies (including India) witnessed a slowdown in growth in 2011 due to the renewed bouts of uncertainty in the global economy, there are reasons to suggest that the growth prospects of most of these economies remain robust in the medium to long run. This is due to various factors that drive growth such as demographics and size of the domestic market, apart from more conventional economic drivers such as high rates of investment and savings.

The underlying shift in global economic setting raises the question as to whether future changes in the world economy would unravel in a smooth manner, or be disruptive. Needless to say India, even while carefully responding to the immediate economic challenges emanating from domestic and global sources, will also have to craft and calibrate its policies keeping both outcomes in view.

As for the present, the global situation is marked by volatility in world financial markets, uncertain growth in the advanced economies, and possible disruptions in supplies of energy apart from other geopolitical tensions. There is contradiction between the short-term need for growth and maintaining demand and the need for fiscal consolidation that marks the current policy environment. But even as the world economy, five years after the global financial crisis of 2008, continues to move from one uncertainty to another, there have been continuing efforts in multilateral fora such as the G-20 to bring about greater understanding and coordination in dealing with global imbalances and addressing the weaknesses that might have led to the global crisis, to arrive at measures to revive global growth.

PUBLIC ATTITUDES TO GLOBALISATION

Global integration in product, capital and labour markets has resulted in a more efficient allocation of economic resources over time. The outcome of integration is greater levels of current output and prospects of higher future output. Consumers have a wider choice of products and services at lower prices. Capital can flow to countries which need it the most for economic growth and development. To the extent that technology is embodied in capital goods or is closely linked to FDI flows, openness further improves the growth prospects of developing countries. Allowing workers to move across national borders can alleviate skill shortages in receiving countries or improve dependency ratios in rapidly ageing societies while alleviating unemployment or under-employment in countries providing these workers. Remittances from overseas workers or emigrants can represent a substantial share of national income for these countries.

These benefits are sufficiently tangible and large enough for to suggest broad support for globalization. It has been well recorgnized that trade benefits consumers by offering them a broader range of choice and lower prices and that trade creates market access opportunities for domestic firms. But this is not to deny that there is also a lot of disquiet about the challenges that come with globalization.

Since 2002, the Pew Global Attitudes Project has conducted a series of worldwide public opinion surveys encompassing a broad array of subjects, including attitudes towards trade. Its latest global survey in 2007 (Pew, 2007) was perhaps the most ambitious, covering 47 countries and more than 45,000 interviews. The countries surveyed included: the major industrial countries, such as the United States, Japan and Germany; emerging economies, such as Brazil, China, India and Russia; and least-developed countries, such as Ethiopia and Mali. Pew found that in all 47 nations surveyed, large majorities believed that international trade was benefiting their countries. But accompanying this belief was a fear about the disruptions and downsides of participating in the global economy. People were concerned about inequality, threats to their culture, threats to the environment and threats posed by immigration.

One interesting conclusion from the survey was that there is apparently stronger support for trade in some emerging economies than in industrial countries. Support for globalization appeared to be waning in the industrialized countries even though a majority of the public still supported it. For example, 78 per cent of Americans surveyed in 2002 said that trade was good for their country. In 2007, this was down to 59 per cent. Sharp falls in public support were also seen in Italy, France and even the United Kingdom. In contrast, there was near universal approval of trade in China and India. Ninety-one per cent of those surveyed in China expressed approval of trade. In India, a nearly similar proportion (89 per cent) believed that trade was good for the country.

The results of Pew's Global Attitudes Project are mirrored by other surveys. Since 2004, the German Marshall Fund has undertaken annual surveys of public attitudes in the United States and countries of the European Communities (EC) towards trade and poverty reduction. The 2007 survey showed that US and European support for trade and for the World Trade Organization (WTO) remained high. In the United States, 64 per cent favoured trade while nearly half (48 per cent) also favoured the WTO. In Europe, 75 per cent had favourable views about trade and 58 per cent approved of the WTO. But the German Marshall Fund survey has detected a softening of support since 2004. Interestingly, when it came to job losses, the US and European public both rated outsourcing to another country as its main cause. Furthermore, public attitudes towards emerging economies appeared to be complicated, with China seen more as a threat, while India was perceived more as an opportunity.

For policy-makers who embrace more open markets, there is much to take heart in these results. But rising public concern about some aspects of globalization should also cause them to ponder. For those who believe that the gains from global integration outweigh its costs, it would not be wise to leave these concerns unattended. Perhaps the answer lies in a balance between open markets and complementary policies, along with international initiatives that manage better the risks arising from globalization.

Given our new consciousness, we can no longer act as if it we were not on the edge of global identity, or the problems such as climate change and ecological exhaustion are not occurring on a global scale. Clearly, much of what is going on is economic in nature. This aspect of globalization can most readily be criticized. Powered by neo-liberal ideology, much of economic globalization has the effect of increasing the divide between rich and poor, with the rich getting richer and the poor getting poorer.

If globalization were simply a question of economic, then downside effects outweighs its positive side. However, there is another level, where one can observe much gain. It is in the sense of a growing global consciousness that promotes can be called what the "concept of humanity." This concept has its origin in the Nuremberg trials after WW II (though there are premonitions earlier, especially related to the Armenian question concerning the Turkish "massacre" - or "genocide"? - of millions of their Armenian subjects). At Nuremberg, two extraordinary charges were made: first, that aggressive war was a crime, thus changing thousands of years of its acceptance as a legitimate action; and second, that the Nazis had committed "crimes against humanity."

At this point, the question pushes itself forward: what is this humanity? For centuries, the answer was to be found in philosophers, such as Immanuel Kant, placing its future in some distant time and place, marked by cosmopolitanism. Now the answer is manifesting itself on the ground, in real time. It is this idea that is incorporated in the concept of humanity. It is a concept coming into being. Humanity becoming a sovereign force, asserting itself as such and not, as before, as simply a victim. We are living at the moment of its creation, the beginning of what promises to be a long slow, and uncertain process.

As we can now see, globalization is taking place on many levels. It is helping the growth of MNCs and NGOs, which, in turn, make for increased globalization. It is also fostering the development of global consciousness and, perhaps, global identity. To condemn or approve of globalization as if it were a monolith is to indulge in simplicities.

QUESTIONS

1. Define international business. What are the steps in formulating and implementing a strategic planing process in international business?
2. Critically examine the main drivers of globalisation.
3. Discuss the scope of international business activities in evolving new world economic order.
4. Discuss the public attitudes to globalisation.
5. Explain the concept of decision circle.
6. Does globalisation make it more or less likely that small-to-medium sized businesses will compete worldwide?
7. Discuss the recent globalisation trends and their impact on world economies.
8. Explain the process of internalisation and the important variables in the international system.
9. Almost all opportunities associated with global business are emerging very rapidly. Those who are `selling' and change, or those who discover its advantages, may be inclined to focus on the positive aspects of potential change rather than explore the negative as well. What examples of this are evident to you? Analyse the problems you see with adopting these perspectives without questioning them.

REFERENCES

Acemoglu, D. (2008) *Introduction to modern economic growth, Princeton*: Princeton University Press.

Alcalá, F. and Ciccone, A. (2003) 'Trade, extent of the market, and economic growth 1960-1996', *Department of Economics and Business Working Paper N° 765*, Barcelona: Universitat Pompeu Fabra.—(2004) 'Trade and productivity', *The Quarterly Journal of Economics* 119, 2: 612-645.

Baldwin, R. (2006a) 'Globalisation: the great unbundling(s)', Paper for the Finnish Prime Minister's Of f ice, Economic Council of Finland as part of EU Presidency.

Baldwin, R. and Forslid, R. (2004) 'Trade liberalization with heterogeneous firms', *CEPR Discussion Paper N°* Bernard, A. B., Redding, S.J., and Schott, P.K. (2007b) 'Comparative advantage and heterogeneous firms', *Review of Economic Studies* 74, 1: 31- 66.

Bhagwati, J., Panagariya, A., and Srinivasan, T. N. (1998) *Lectures on International Trade*, Cambridge, M A: MIT Press.

Brander, J. A. and K rugman, P. (1983) 'A 'Reciprocal Dumping' model of international trade', *NBER Working Paper N° 1194*, Cambridge, M A: NBER.

Broda, C. and Weinstein, D.E. (2004) 'Globalization and the gains from variety', Econometric *Society 2004 North American Summer Meeting N° 508*, New York: Econometric Society.

Crafts, N. and Venables, A. J. (2003) 'Globalization in history: Williamson, J.G. (eds) *Globalization in Historical Perspective*, Chicago and London: University of Chicago Press: 323-364.

Davis, D. R. and Weinstein, D. E. (2001) 'An account of global factor trade', The *American Economic Review* 91, 5: 1423-1453.

Deutsches Institut fur Normung (2000) *Economic Benefits of Standardization*, Berlin: Deutsches Institut fur Normung.

Dikhanov, Y. (2005) *Trends in Global Income Distribution, 1970-2000 and Scenarios for 2015*, Human Development Report 2005.

Erdem, E. and Tybout, J. R. (2003) 'Trade policy and industrial sector responses: Using evolutionary models to interpret the evidence', *NBER Working Paper N° 9947*, Cambridge, M A: NBER.

Frankel, J.A. and Romer, D. (1999) 'Does trade cause growth?', *The American Economic Review* 89, 3: 379-399.

Harrison, A. and McMillan, M. (2007) 'On the links between globalization and poverty', *Journal of Economic Literature* 5, 1:123-134.

International Monetary Fund (IMF) (2007a) *World Economic Outlook: Globalization and Inequality*, Washington, DC: IMF.

Irwin, D.A. (2002) *Free Trade Under Fire*, Princeton, NJ: Princeton University Press.

Jones, R. and K. Ierzkowski, H. (2001) 'Globalization and consequences of international fragmentation', in Dornbusch, R., Calvo, G., and Obstfeld, M. (eds) *Money, Factor Mobility and Trade: Festchrift in Honor of Robert A. Mundell*, Cambridge, M A: MIT Press.

Krugman, P.R. and Venables, A. J. (1995) 'Globalization and the inequality of nations', *Quarterly Journal of Economics* 110,4: 857-880.

Maddison, A. (2001) *The World Economy: A Millennial Perspective*, Paris: OECD.

Markusen, J.R., Melvin, J. R., Kaempfer, W.H., and Maskus, K. E. (1995) *International Trade Theory and Evidence*, New York: McGraw-Hill.

Mayer, T. and Zignago, S. (2005) 'Market access in global and regional trade', *CEPII Working Paper N° 2005- 02*, Paris: CEPII Research Center.

McKinsey (2005a) *The Emerging Global Labor Market: The Demand for Offshore Talent in Insurance*, McKinsey Global Institute.

Nunn, N. and Trefler, D. (2008) 'The boundaries of the multinational firm: A n empirical analysis', in Helpman, E., Marin, D., and Verdier, T. (eds) *The Organization of Firms in a Global Economy*, Cambridge, M A: Harvard University Press.

Pew (2007) *World Publics Welcome Global Trade - But Not Immigration*, Pew Global Attitudes Project. Available at http:// w w w.pewresearch.org. Accessed 31/03/08.

Porter, M.E. (1990) *The Competitive Advantage of Nations*, New York, N Y: The Free Press.

Sachs, J. and Warner, A. (1995) 'Economic reform and the process of global integration', *Brookings Papers on Economic Activity* 1, 1-95.

Sapir, A. (2006) 'Globalization and the Reform of European Social Models', *Journal of Common Market Studies* 44, 2:369-390.

Scheve, K. F. and Slaughter, M. J. (2007) 'A new deal for globalization', *Foreign Affairs* July/ August 2007.

Schumpeter, J. (1942) *Capitalism, Socialism and Democracy*, New York: Harper.

Tinbergen, J. (1962) *Shaping the World Economy: Suggestions for an International Economic Policy*, New York: Twentieth Century Fund.

Winters, L . A. and Yusuf, S. (2007) *Dancing with Giants: China, India, and the Global Economy*, Washington D.C.: The World Bank and Institute of Policy Studies.

Yi, K.M. (2003) 'Can vertical specialization explain the growth of world trade?', *Journal of Political Economy* 111, 1: 52-102.

2

INTERNATIONAL BUSINESS THEORIES

INTRODUCTION

Multinational corporations conduct international transactions in many new forms other than traditional exporting and importing. They cut across national boundaries and make a good deal of international trade into intra-firm trade. Financial capital is quite mobile within the corporation, as are senior managerial talent and the technical and managerial know-how which possibly provide the main rationale for the existence of the corporation. A model which assumes factor immobility between nations and which places primary importance upon national boundaries would seem to be utterly irrelevant. One could then argue that trade theory should be abandoned altogether, at least for the analysis of the activities of the multinational corporations. One should treat the world as a single market in which large corporations compete and collude in various ways. The theory of market structure and performance elaborated for the study of the large market would then be appropriate. One would think of all factors of production with the exception of natural resources as mobile. There would still be questions of location to discuss, but these questions would be of interest only to land-owners, property developers, and those concerned with land-use planning. The central economic questions would have to do with productivity in particular industries throughout the vast market and with competitiveness and oligopolistic behaviour.

Yet this approach, in spite of a superficial appeal, is not satisfactory. The main reason is that all factors are not mobile. It is important to know how individual countries (or regions) are affected by the operations of the multinational corporations, whether they locate in one area or another, and whether they raise or lower the welfare of people in particular countries. As long as separate countries (or regions) matter in this sense, the basic concepts of trade theory will continue to be of some relevance.

Advances in trade theory have not kept pace with issues, which concern the majority of nations in guiding policy, particularly in the developing area. Nevertheless, in assessing the usefulness of trade theory, one needs to bear in mind its limited objective. It can hardly be expected to give a precise and detailed description of the real world; and the fact that countries produce more than two products, and industries are not generally perfectly competitive, does not necessarily mean that the theory as usually is useless.

The purpose of theory is to abstract from the complexity of the real world a simplified model of the key relationships between dependent and independent variables, and to explore the positive and normative implications of changes in the "givens" of this hypothetical system. For this purpose, the validity of the empirical foundations of a theory is, obviously within limits, not of such crucial importance, in the sense that the principles of interrelatedness, of systematic response to change, and of optimisation remain valid in the face of wide variations in assumed economic structure.

BASIS FOR TRADE

The main questions on which international trade theory focus are: *Why do countries export and import the sort of products they do and at what relative prices or terms of trade? How are these trade flows related to the characteristics of a country and how do they effect domestic factor prices? What are the gains from trade and how are they divided among trading countries?*

Differences in prices are the basic cause of trade and reflect international differences in costs. *But why should costs differ from country to country ? How can a country produce cameras, sewing machines, and cotton shirts more cheaply than the other country ?* Many people would reply that a country has lower costs because it has lower wages, and wages are important costs. This explanation seems plausible enough; it is firmly based on fact. But it is not adequate. If wage rates were decisive for cost differences and trade, then should undersell the other with higher wages in every product line and every market. Yet a country with lower wages imports labour intensive products from the other country having high wages, and other low-wage countries buy from goods in great variety and enormous quantities. As a matter of fact, the high wage country might be selling more to other countries than it buys abroad, despite its high wages. Differences in wage rates, then, cannot explain trade patterns, and one must look elsewhere for the basis of trade.

An enduring two-way flow of goods must be traced to systematic international differences in the structure of costs and prices : some things must be cheaper to produce at home and will be exported to other countries; some things must be cheaper to produce abroad and will be imported from other countries. This generalisation is basic to the theory of foreign trade, and is known as the principle of comparative advantage. Stated most precisely, it asserts that a country will export the products which it can produce at the lowest relative cost. China, it contends, can export cameras and textiles because it can produce those goods with the least sacrifice of alternative production.

The United States can export machinery and aircrafts because it can produce those goods with the smallest sacrifice. Cameras may be cheaper than machines in both countries, but the cost difference is far from uniform, thus creating opportunities for profitable trade.

SOURCES OF COMPARATIVE ADVANTAGE

A nation's comparative advantage and trade pattern are heavily affected by its resource endowment - both natural and man-made. Nature has decreed important and enduring differences between countries. Some of them are rich in copper, others in petroleum; some have huge waterfalls, others have fertile plains. Some countries have just enough rainfall for rice or cotton cultivation, while some have too much, and others have next to none. Furthermore, some countries have the resource combinations required for the performance of certain vital tasks : one may have the plains and rainfall needed to grow wheat; another may have a rich deposit of iron ore next to a waterway that can carry ore to coal. Finally, some countries have populations large enough to man and support great, complex industries, but others are so very underpopulated that their land cannot even be worked or their ores extracted. In one sense, people are a natural resource; in another, they are a major man-made resource. Mere numbers are the gift of nature. But the skills and attitudes of a population are the work of man and strongly influence a country's comparative advantage. A nation rich in people but poor in skills may be suited to certain tasks, but not to the production and export of manufactured goods. A nation that has very few persons per square mile but has lavished its energies on technical training is likely to enjoy a comparative advantage in the production of precision goods.

Going one step further, we must distinguish between types of skill. Some nations have large numbers of factory workers adept at handling modern machinery. Others have an abundance of engineers and scientists and specialise in new, research-laden products. It has been said, for example, that the United States enjoys a comparative advantage in research and innovation, but that it loses out to its competitors as each of its new products ages, the market for it grows, and the knowledge required to manufacture it is diffused among other countries. The United States, it is argued, has always to race ahead in technology merely to stand still in world markets.

One part of a nation's capital stock is embodied in its labour force as agricultural, and scientific skill. Another part is embodied in physical equipment : roads, airports, harbours, and dams; trucks, aircraft, ships and turbines; factories and office buildings; tractors, lathes, conveyers, and typewriters. These represent the portion of past output that was reserved for investment rather than consumption.

Notice that natural and man-made resources can interact powerfully. Bauxite was not valued as a natural resource until the development of the electrolytic process for extracting aluminum, and of the cheap electric power required to fuel that process. Aluminum itself was not very valuable until the metalworking industries found ways to use it. Pitchblende was a geological curiosity until man's skill and malevolence found a use for uranium, and ways to separate one isotope from others. Population also interacts with technology. Modern mass-production methods need mass markets and are apt to take root first in regions of dense settlement that provide outlets for large lots of standardised products. In consequence, such regions are apt to enjoy a comparative advantage in the export of mass-product articles, and they may well retain their advantage vis-a-vis regions that start later or on a smaller scale. Notice, too, that comparative advantage always has a time dimension. It depends on the state of technology at a given moment and on its subsequent diffusion. It also depends on the history of capital accumulation and, therefore, on the rate of economic growth.

INTERNATIONAL TRADE THEORIES

Mercantilism

The economic doctrine that prevailed during the first two centuries of the development of the modern national state - the seventeenth and eighteenth centuries - was mercantilism. The doctrine of mercantilism has many modern features : it was highly nationalistic, it viewed the well-being of the own nation to be of prime importance, it favoured the regulation and planning of economic activity as an efficient means of fostering the goals of the nation, and it generally viewed foreign trade with suspicion.

The most important way in which a country could grow rich, according to the doctrine of mercantilism, was by acquiring precious metals, especially gold. Single individuals, however, were not to be trusted : they might also like gold, but perhaps they liked other things even more. Left to themselves, they might exchange gold for satin and linen, spices from India, or sugar from Cuba, or indulge in whatever private pleasures they preferred, to the detriment of the stock of precious metals stored in the nation. To prevent such undertakings, the nation had to control foreign trade. Exports were viewed favourably as long as they brought in good, solid gold, but imports were viewed with apprehension as depriving the country of its true source of richness - precious metals. Therefore, trade had to be regulated, controlled and restricted, no specific virtue being in having a large volume of trade.

It was against this background that English classical economics developed, for mercantilism was the credo that Adam Smith and Ricardo rebelled against. English classical economics was an offspring of liberalism and the Enlightenment - of a general philosophy that stressed the importance of the individual and viewed the nation as nothing more than the sum of its inhabitants.

For Smith, as for Ricardo, the supreme object of economics was the consumer : man laboured and produced in order to consume. And anything that could increase consumption, or, to use Ricardo's picturesque phrase, 'the sum of enjoyments', ought to be viewed with favour.

Absolute Advantage

Adam Smith saw clearly that a country could gain by trading. The tailor does not make his own shoes; he exchanges a suit for shoes. Thereby both the shoemaker and the tailor gain. In the same manner, Smith argued, a whole country can gain by trading with other countries.

It takes 10 labour units to manufacture 1 unit of A in country I but 20 labour units in country II, and if it takes 20 units of labour to manufacture 1 unit of good B in country I but only 10 labour units in country II, then both countries can gain by trading.

If the two countries exchanged the 2 goods at a ratio of 1 to 1, so that 1 units of good A is exchanged for 1 unit of good B, country I could get 1 unit of good B by sacrificing only 10 units of labour, whereas it would have to give up 20 units of labour if it produced the good itself. Likewise, country II would have to sacrifice only 10 units of labour to get 1 unit of good A, whereas it would have to give up 20 units of labour if it produced it itself. The implication of this is clearly that both countries could have more of both goods with a given effort, by trading.

This was a simple and powerful illustration of the benefits of trade, and on it Adam Smith rested his plea for non-interference — for free trade as the best policy for trade between nations. Smith's argument seems convincing, but it is not very deep. It was left to Torrens and Ricardo to produce the stronger and more subtle argument for the benefits of trade contained in the theory of comparative advantage.

Comparative Advantage

Ricardo did not object to Smith's analysis. It is obvious that if one country has an absolute advantage over the other country in one line of production in a second line of production, both countries can gain by trading. A great deal of trade, perhaps most trade, is governed by such differences.

But what if one country is more productive than another country in all lines of production ? If country I can produce all goods with less labour cost than country II, does it still benefit the countries to trade ? Ricardo's answer was yes. So long as country II is not equally less productive in all lines of production, it still pays both countries to trade.

We will spend some time elucidating this principle, as it is basic importance to the theory of trade. We may as well start with Ricardo's own model before going on to more modern means of demonstration.

Ricardo used England and Portugal as examples in his demonstration, the two goods they produced being wine and cloth. Being a courteous Englishman, and living in an era when no one had heard about 'under-developed countries', Ricardo assumed that Portugal was more efficient in making both cloth and wine. Table-1 shows how Ricardo summed up the cost conditions in the two countries.

TABLE-1

Cost Comparisons

	Labour cost of production (in hours)	
	1 unit of wine	*1 unit of cloth*
Portugal	80	90
England	120	100

According to this model, Portugal has an absolute advantage in the production of wine as well as in the production of cloth, because the labour cost of production for each unit of the two commodities is less in Portugal than in England. To demonstrate that trade between England and Portugal will, even in this case, lead to gains for both countries, it is useful to introduce the concept of opportunity cost. The opportunity cost for a good X is the amount of other goods which have to be given up in order to produce one (additional) unit of X. Table-2 gives the opportunity costs for producing wine and cloth in Portugal and England. These costs have been constructed on the basis of the information given in Table-1.

TABLE-2

Opportunity Costs

	Opportunity costs for	
	Wine	*Cloth*
Portugal	80/90 = 8/9	90/80 = 9/8
England	120/100 = 12/10	100/120 = 10/12

A country has a comparative advantage in producing a good if the opportunity cost for producing the good is lower at home than in the other country. Table-2 shows that Portugal has the lower opportunity cost of the two countries in producing wine, while England has the lower opportunity cost in producing cloth. Thus Portugal has a comparative advantage in the production of wine and England has a comparative advantage in the production of cloth.

We should now further clarify the meaning of the term 'comparative advantage'. In order to speak about comparative advantage there must be at least two countries and two goods. We compare the opportunity costs of the production of each good in both countries. As long as the two countries' opportunity costs for one good differ, one country has a comparative advantage in the production of one of the two goods, while the other country has a comparative advantage in the production of the other good. As long as this is the case, both countries will gain from trade, regardless of the fact that one of the countries might have an absolute disadvantage in both lines of production.

To illustrate the gains from trade, let us assume that Portugal and England do not trade but produce and consume in isolation. The prices of cloth and wine in the two countries are then determined by their respective costs of production.

In England it takes 120 hours of labour to make 1 unit of wine, while it takes only 100 hours to make 1 unit of cloth, clearly wine must then be more expensive per unit than cloth — 1 unit of wine will cost 120/100, or 1.2 units of cloth. If in Portugal it takes 80 hours of labour to make 1 unit of wine and 90 hours to make 1 unit of cloth, cloth will be more expensive than wine — 1 unit of wine will cost 80/90, or 0.89 units of cloth.

Let us now open the possibility of trade. If England could import 1 unit of wine at a price less than 1.2 units of cloth, she would gain by doing so. If Portugal could import more than 0.89 units of cloth for 1 unit of wine, she, too, would gain. Therefore, if the international price of 1 unit of wine is somewhere between 1.2 and 0.89 units of cloth, both countries will gain by trading.

Let us assume further that in the international market, 1 unit of wine exchanges for 1 unit of cloth. It is then advantageous for England to export cloth and import wine, because in the absence of trade England would have to give up 120 hours of labour for every unit of wine she wants. By trading she can, instead with 100 hours of effort, produce 1 unit of cloth and then exchange this unit of cloth for 1 unit of wine. Under autarky — i.e. a country producing and consuming in isolation — she would have to give up 120 hours of labour for every unit of wine she wanted, whereas with trade she only needs to give up 100 hours. With each 20 hours left over she can produce more cloth and enjoy a higher level of consumption — or the workers can rest, and trade will make possible more leisure with a given amount of consumption. Portugal will also gain from trading. In isolation she would have to give up 90 hours of labour to get 1 unit of cloth. Now she can make 1 unit of wine with the effort of 80 hours of labour and exchange this unit of wine for 1 unit of cloth in the international market. Every 10 hours of labour freed by this process can then be used for either increased production or increased leisure.

Thus trade offers each country the possibility of specialising in the line of its comparative advantage and then exchanging these products for those in which she has a comparative disadvantage. Both countries can reallocate their factors of production to the line where their comparative advantage lies and then export this product and import the other product. In short, with a given amount of resources, each country can consume more by trading than in isolation.

A SIMPLE MODEL

To show how a difference in resource endowments can call forth foreign trade, consider two countries, America and Britain, which are identical in all ways but one. Both of them have 120 man-days of labour available. Both use 2 man-days of labour to grow a ton of potatoes and have enough arable land to employ all their workers in potato-farming. But America's coal deposits are very near to the surface and only 1 man-day of labour is required to dig out a ton, while Britain's deposits are much farther down and 4 man-days of labour are required to dig out a ton. If its whole labour force were employed growing potatoes, America could produce 60 tons per day; 2 man-days of labour can grow a single ton and 120 man-days of labour are available. If, instead, the whole labour force were employed digging coal, America could produce 120 tonnes per day; 1 man-day of labour can dig out a single ton and 120 man-days are available. If, finally, America wished to produce some potatoes and some coal, it could secure any one of several combinations. To produce a single ton of coal, it would have to divert 1 man-day of labour from its potato fields, reducing potato output by half a ton. To produce 2 tons of coal, it would have to divert 2 man-days from the potato fields, reducing potato output by 1 ton.

America's production possibilities are summarised by the line *AB* in Figure-1. The distance *OA* measures the output of coal that would be obtained if the entire labour force worked in the coal mines (120 tons); the distance *OB* measures the output of

FIGURE-1

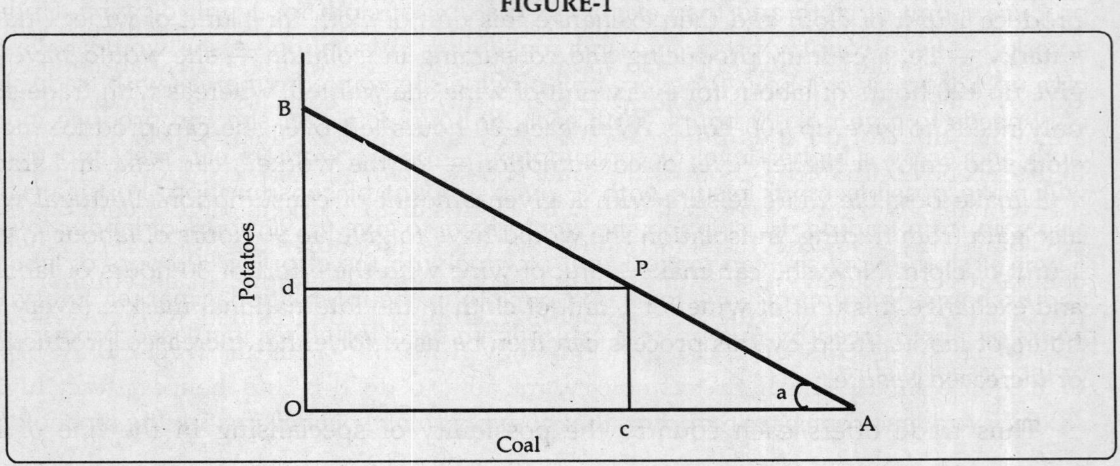

potatoes that would be obtained if the entire labour force worked in in the potato fields (60 tons). Points along the line *AB* describe the combinations of coal and potatoes that could be produced simultaneously. At point *P*, for example, America would be producing *Oc* coal and *Od* potatoes. It would obtain *Oc* coal by foregoing Bd potatoes.

If Americans were not allowed to trade with outsiders, their pattern of consumption would have to coincide with one of the coal and potato combination lying on *AB*. The output mix prevailing at a particular time would, of course, depend on consumer preferences - demand conditions - and on the price of coal in terms of potatoes. That price ratio, in turn, would be given by the comparative labour costs of coal and potato production. Labour is the only variable input (factor of production) used in this very simple economy, and a single man-day of labour can mine a whole ton of coal but can only grow half a ton of potatoes will cost 2 man-days' wages. A ton of coal will be half as expensive as a ton of potatoes, and it will exchange for half a ton of potatoes in America's markets. This same price relationship appears in Figure-1; it is represented by the slope (steepness) of *AB*, the production possibilities frontier. The distance *OB* is half the distance *OA*, indicating that a ton of coal will sell for half a ton of potatoes.

One can arrive at this same result by examining marginal costs. If product markets are perfectly competitive, prices must equal marginal costs. If labour is the only variable input and labour requirements are constant for all output levels, marginal costs must equal labour requirements per unit of extra output multiplied by the wage rate. Hence:

Price of Coal = Marginal Cost of Coal = Wage Rate × Man-days of Labour Needed to Produce a Ton of Coal

Price of Potatoes = Marginal Cost of Potatoes = Wage Rate × Man-days of Labour Needed to Produce a Ton of Potatoes

Therefore :

$$\frac{\text{Price of Coal}}{\text{Price of Potatoes}} = \frac{\text{Man-days Needed to Produce a Ton of Coal}}{\text{Man-days Needed to Produce a Ton of Potatoes}}$$

The wage rate cancels out in this calculation, for it must be the same in both industries.

Britain also needs 2 man-days of labour to produce a ton of potatoes, and consequently could grow 60 tons if it used all its labour in its potato patches. But it needs 4 man-days of labour to dig out a ton of coal, and could mine only 30 tons if it used all its labour in its coal mines. By implication, Britain could produce a single ton of coal by diverting 4 man-days of labour from potato-growing, thereby giving up 2 tons of potatoes. Britain's production possibilities are described by the line *A'B'* in Figure 2. Maximum potato output, *OB'*, is the same as in America, because the two countries are endowed with the same amounts of labour and are equally efficient in potato growing. But maximum coal output, *OA′* is smaller in Britain than in America, for Britain's coal lies somewhat deeper in the ground.

The line *A′B′* in Figure 2 is much steeper than the line *AB* in Figure-1. This difference is explained by the difference in mining costs and implies a difference in relative prices. British coal must be twice as expensive as British potatoes, for labour costs are twice as high. Isolated from the outside world, Britain would produce and consume some combination of coal and potatoes lying on *A′B′* and a ton of coal would be worth 2 tons of potatoes.

But now allow America and Britain to trade and suppose that goods can move between them without transport costs. The opportunity for trade will create a single Anglo-American market and, therefore, a single price for coal in terms of potatoes. This new common price will lie between the national extremesless than the prior British price (2 tons of potatoes per ton of coal) and higher than the prior American price (half a ton of potatoes per ton of coal). Britain can now obtain a ton of coal without surrendering as many potatoes as it had to sacrifice to furnish its own coal. It will tend to specialise in potato-growing and will use its potatoes to buy American coal. America is able to obtain more potatoes for its coal. It will tend to specialise in coal-mining and to use its coal to buy British potatoes.

FIGURE-2

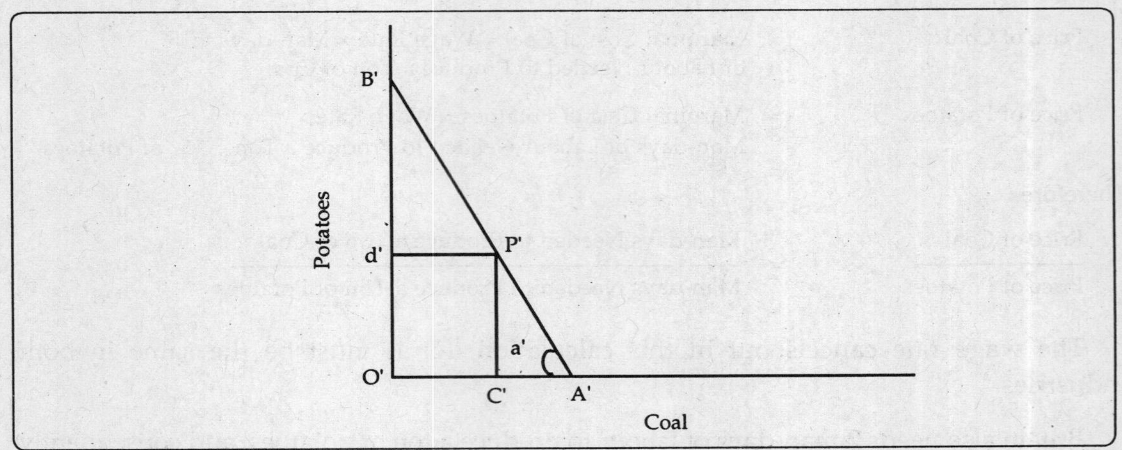

The new common price for coal could also settle at one of the national extremes. In that case, one country would capture all the gains from trade, but the other would be no worse off than it was without trade. If the price came to rest at the old British level, America would garner all the gains from trade; it would get its potatoes cheaper than it could at home. If the price came to rest at the old American level, Britain would garner all the gains from trade; it would get its coal cheaper than it could at home. The determination of the actual price ratio and of the consumption point, *Q* in Figure 3, will depend upon demand conditions in the two countries.

To illustrate this rearrangement of production, suppose that the new Anglo-American coal price is stabilised at 1 ton of potatoes per ton of coal. Britain can now import a ton of coal by growing and exporting a single ton of potatoes. Without trade, by contrast, it had to sacrifice 2 tons of potatoes to produce a ton of coal. In effect, Britain saves 2 man-days of labour on each ton of coal consumed. For its part, America can import a ton of potatoes by mining and exporting a single ton of coal. Without trade, it had to sacrifice 2 tons of coal to produce a ton of potatoes. America saves 1 man-day of labour on each ton of potatoes consumed.

Figure-3 restates these results with greater generality. There, the left hand triangle, OAB, is the American production-possibilities frontier, just as it appeared in Figure-1. The right hand traingle *O'A'B'* is Britain's production-possibilities frontier, taken from Figure-2 but flipped outside-down. If America and Britian could not trade, each would be confined to its own frontier, America at *P* and Britain at *P'*. When they are allowed to trade, they can rearrange production and consumption to mutual advantage. America can specialise in coal-mining, using all its labour to produce *OA* tons. Britain can specialise in potato-farming, using all its labour to produce *O'B'* tons. America can then consume *Oe* tons of coal and export *eA* tons of coal and export *eA* tons to pay for potatoes. Britain can consume O^1F^1 tons of potatoes and exports F^1B^1 tons to pay for coal. America can buy *OF* tons of potatoes (equal to F^1B^1 Britain will export), and Britain can buy O^1e^1 tons of coal (equal to the *P* to *Q*, and British consumption can move from P^1 to *Q*. Which country can consume more of both goods than it did before.

The situation described in Figure-3 is not the only possibility. The point *Q* could

FIGURE-3

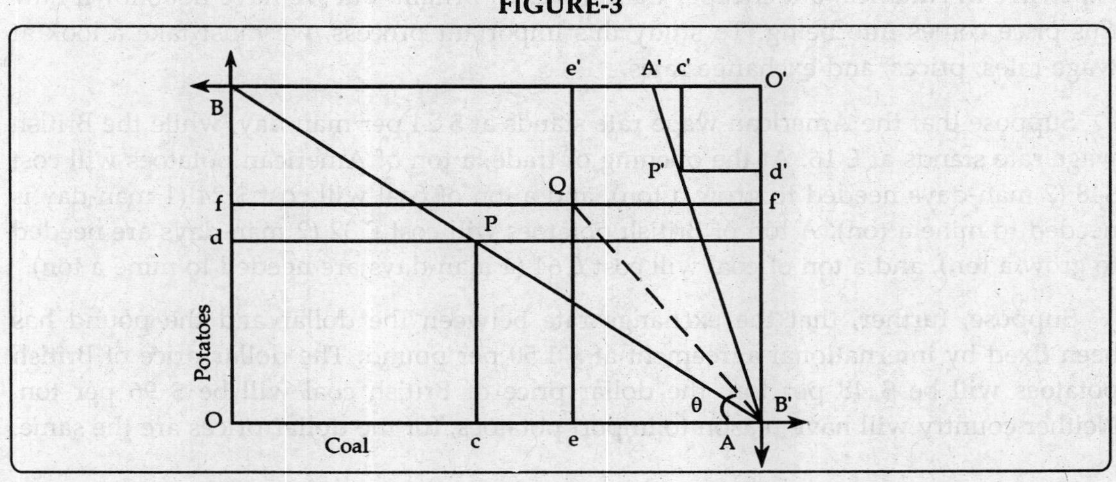

settle down anywhere within the unshaded part of the diagram, depending on demand conditions. Furthermore, *Q* could come to rest on *AB* or *A'B'*, the extreme cases. If *Q* came to rest on *AB*, Britian would specialise completely and take all the gains from trade. America would tend to specialise in coal, but would also grow potatoes. If *Q* came to rest on *A'B'*, America would specialise completely and take all the gains from trade. Britain would tend to specialise in potatoes but would also mine coal.

Figure-3 describes two ways to view the gains from trade. First, it shows that every country can escape the confines of its own resource endowment. Before trade, each country had to consume a combination of coal and potatoes lying on its own production-possibilities frontier. Its choice was restricted by its resource endowment. But trade allows every country to reshuffle output and to consume a combination of commodities it could never produce by itself. In consequence, the individual consumer enjoys a wider range of choice. Figure-3 also shows that trade enlarges global output by allowing every country to specialise in those tasks it does best. Before trade, total coal output was *Oc* plus *c'O'*. With trade it rises to *OA* (an increase of ce plus *e'c'*). Before trade, total potato output was *Od* plus *d'O'*. With trade it rises to *O'B'* (an increase of df plus *f'd'*). This increase in output was required for each country to increase its consumption of both commodities in the fashion described in Figure-3. It also leads to a basic proposition in international economics : Free trade is the best regime for the world as a whole. The increase in coal and potato output shown by Figure-3 is the largest increase possible. Hence, free trade allocates economic tasks to maximise world output and income.

Productivity, Wages and Prices

Figure-3 describes the free-trade price of coal as the slope (steepness) of the dotted line *AQ*. This line is steeper than *AB*, but flatter than *A'B'*. Coal has become more expensive in America, but cheaper than it was in Britain. But we have not shown how this price comes into being. To study this important process, we must take a look at wage rates, prices, and exchange rates.

Suppose that the American wage rate stands at $ 24 per man-day, while the British wage rate stands at £ 16. At the opening of trade, a ton of American potatoes will cost $48 (2 man-days needed to grow a ton), and a ton of coal will cost $ 24 (1 man-day is needed to mine a ton). A ton of British potatoes will cost £ 32 (2 man-days are needed to grow a ton), and a ton of coal will cost £ 64 (4 man-days are needed to mine a ton).

Suppose, further, that the exchange rate between the dollar and the pound has been fixed by international agreement at $ 1.50 per pound. The dollar price of British potatoes will be $ 48 per ton; the dollar price of British coal will be $ 96 per ton. Neither country will have reason to import potatoes, for the dollar prices are the same.

But Britain will import American coal, since British coal costs $ 96 a ton while American coal costs $ 24 a ton.

If both countries' workers were fully employed before trade began, the advent of trade will cause an excess demand for labour in America because of the British demand for American coal. It will also cause unemployment in Britain because of the shift in British demand from domestic to foreign coal. In consequence, wage rates will rise in America and fall in Britain. This change in wages, however, will make British potatoes cheaper than American, whether priced in dollars or pounds, and both countries' consumers will start to buy potatoes in Britain. British farmers will plant larger crops, taking up the labour released from Britain's coal mines; American farmers will cut back their crops, releasing labour to America's mines.

This process will not cease until unemployment disappears in the British coal mines and the labour shortage ends in America's coal mines. And these things will not happen until consumers rearrange their purchases in response to the price changes resulting from the wage-rate change. When, finally, those wage changes have ceased, the price of American coal will be higher than it was to start (because of the increase in American wages), while the price of British potatoes will be lower than it was to start (because of the decrease in British wages). The wage-rate changes will have offset America's higher productivity, allowing Britain's comparative advantage in potato-growing to show through as a lower price.

This same process of adjustment could have been accomplished by changing the exchange rate. Suppose that money wage rates were absolutely rigid in Britain and America but that the exchange rate connecting their currencies was free to fluctuate in response to changes in supply and demand. The British demand for American coal would then be manifest in a demand for American dollars that would drive up the price of the dollar expressed in terms of pounds. This increase in the price of the dollar would lower the cost of British potatoes expressed in dollars and would raise the cost of American coal expressed in pounds. Americans would start to buy British potatoes.

The two-country, two-product, labour-cost model used thus far in this chapter is much like the model developed by Ricardo early in the nineteenth century. Multi-country, multi-commodity versions of that model came into use toward the end of the century and were employed to show that the chief conclusions drawn from Ricardo's work are readily susceptible of generalisation. Infact, these labour-cost models shed much less light on several other aspects of foreign trade : the influence of differences in factor supplies on international specialisation, the impact of economic growth on trade patterns, and the impact of trade on national economies. To study these additional issues, we require more elaborate theoretical models incorporating several factors of production : land, labour and capital.

Factor-Endowments Approach

Ricardo's theory stresses that comperative advantage arises from differences in labour productivity. Swedish economists, Eli Heckscher and Bertil Ohlin argues that the pattern of international trade is determined by differences in factor endowments, rather than differences in productivity.

Like the labour-cost model, it excludes economies of scale, takes no account of transport costs, and assumes that tastes are the same everywhere. But unlike the labour-cost model, it goes on to assume that each country has access to the same technology, and would employ the same methods of production if confronted with identical factor prices. It thereby rules out the differences in relative efficiency that served as the basis for foreign trade in the labour-cost model.

The Heckscher-Ohlin or factor-endowments approach to trade theory proceeds from two suppositions :

1. Products differ in factor requirements - cars require more machine-time (capital) per worker than, say, cotton cloth or furniture, and aircraft require more machine-time than either cars or cotton cloth.
2. Countries differ in factor endowments - some have large amounts of capital per worker (the capital-abundant countries) and some have very little (the labour-abundant countries).

One could, of course, make cars by several methods, differing in capital-intensities. One could use a small machine-shop or an automated plant. One could also weave cloth by many methods, some of them quite highly mechanised. The choice of technique will depend on the prices of the factors of prodcution—the wages paid to workers and the rental prices of machinery (the interest cost of capital and allowances for repair and depreciation). But the factor-endowments model assumes that the product which is most capital-intensive at one set of factor prices is also most capital-intensive at every other set.

The theory then argues that capital-abundant countries will tend to specialise in capital-intensive goods like cars and aircraft, and will export some of their specialities in order to import labour-intensive goods. Similarly, labour-abundant countries will specialise in labour-intensive goods and will lexport their own specialities in order to import capital-intensive goods. To put the proposition in general terms : Trade will be based on differences in factor endowments and will serve to relieve each country's factor shortages.

A numerical example will illustrate this proposition. Suppose that the production of a thousand cars requires the employment of 90 machines and 300 man-years of labour, while the production of a million yards of cloth requires the employment of 30 machines and 600 man-years of labour. If a country's entire stock of machinery and its whole labour force are used in these two industries, one can assert that :

Machines in Use = 90 × Thousand Cars + 30 × Million Yards of cloth

Labour Employed = 300 × Thousand Cars + 600 × Million Yards of cloth

If, next, we know how much machinery and labour is on hand, we can solve these two identities as simultaneous equations, and can thereby obtain a country's full-employment car-and-cloth combination. Consider two countries — a labour-abundant country called Manymen, and a capital-abundant country called Fewmen — with the fixed endowments of machinery and labour shown in Table-3. Replacing "machines in use" and "labour employed" with Manymen's stock of capital (600 machines) and labour supply (6,000 man-years), then solving for cars and cloth, we ascertain that Manymen can produce 4,000 cars and 8,000,000 yards of cloth. Repeating this procedure with Fewmen's endowment, we ascertain that Fewmen can produce 9,000 cars and 3,000,000 yards of cloth. As one would expect, Manymen's output combination is heavily weighted with cloth (the labour-intensive product), and Fewmen's output combination is heavily weighted with cars (the capital-intensive product).

TABLE-3

Factor Endowments and Output Combinations

Factors and Products	*Manymen*	*Fewmen*
Factor supplies :		
Machines (number)	600	900
Labour (man-years)	6,000	4,500
Machines per man-year	0.1	0.2
Full-employment output combination :		
Cars (number)	4,000	9,000
Cloth (yards)	8,000,000	3,000,000
Cars per thousand yards of cloth	0.5	3.0

Clearly, these two countries could gain from trade and would, indeed, be led to trade when brought into contact with each other. Having identical tastes and different output combinations, they would have different price ratios in the absence of trade. Cloth, the labour-intensive good, would be cheap in Manymen, the labour-abundant country, while cars, the capital-intensive good, would be cheap in Fewmen, the capital-abundant country. With the opening of trade and the establishment of common prices, Manymen would specialise in cloth production and would export its speciality in exchange for cars, while Fewemen would specialise in cars and would export its speciality in exchange for cloth. Trade would allow each country to obtain the product it is ill-equipped to manufacture for itself — the one that makes the heaviest demands on its scarce factors of production.

Once again, a free-trade regime is best for the two countries taken together. As in the labour-cost model studied earlier, it works to maximise global output by fostering the most efficient patterns of specialisation.

Factor Substitution and Specialisation

The numerical example we have been examining can be recast geometrically and can then be made somewhat more general. To do so, let us rearrange the "machines-in-use" identity so as to show how much cloth could be produced if the supply of machinery were the only effective constraint on a country's production :

$$\text{Million of Yards of Cloth} = \left(\frac{\text{Machines in Use}}{30}\right) - \left(\frac{90}{30}\right)$$

This capital constraint is represented by the line *MM′* in Figure-4. Next, let us rearrange the "labour-employed" identity to show how much cloth could be produced if the supply of labour were the only effective constraint:

$$\text{Million of Yards of Cloth} = \left(\frac{\text{Labour Employed}}{600}\right) - \left(\frac{300}{600}\right)$$

This labour constraint is represented *LL′* in Figure-4.

FIGURE-4

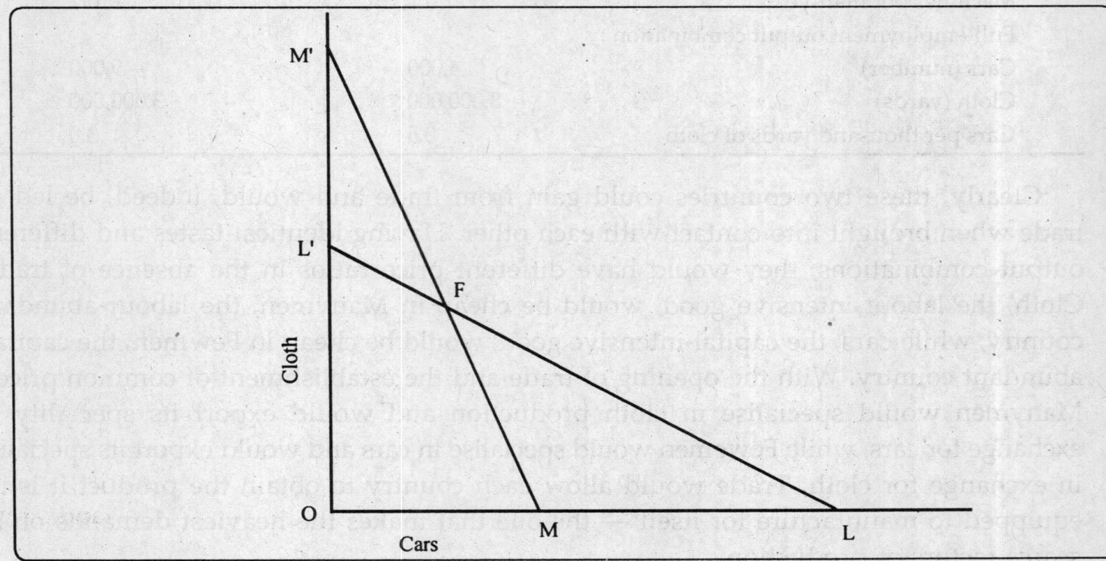

These two constraints, taken together, define a production-possibilities frontier for a two-product, two-factor country. That frontier is *L'FM,* and the full-employment point occurs at the kink, *F*. To the left of the kink, production is constrained by the country's limited supply of labour; to the right of the kink, it is constrained by the limited supply of machines. Were such a country unable to engage in trade, its car and cloth consumption would be confined to a combination on or inside *L'FM*. But were it allowed to trade, it could consume a combination of cars and cloth lying outside *L'FM*. If, for instance, world prices permitted the exchange of a single car for a thousand yards of cloth, that country would consume any combination of cars and cloth lying on *WW'* in Figure-5, and it could escape the limitations imposed by its factor endowment: it could consume *Og* cars and *Oh* cloth by exporting gn cars in exchange mh cloth; it could consume *OL* cars and *OK* cloth by exporting *Km* cloth in exchange for *nL* cars.

Notice, however, that the country portrayed by Figures 4 and 5 has one and only one full-employment point *F*. Were it to respond to consumer demand or to opportunities for trade by producing more than *Om* cloth and less than *On* cars, some of its machines would stand idle and their owners would suffer financial losses. This result derives from an unrealistic assumption regarding technology : that the labour and capital requirements of car and cloth production are entirely rigid. Such a result would not occur at all if manufacturers were able to alter their methods of production. In such circumstances, the owners of idle machines would cut back their rental rates, so as to secure jobs for their machines, and the manufacturers of cars and cloth would respond by choosing more capital-intensive methods of production : they would substitute machinery for labour.

FIGURE-5

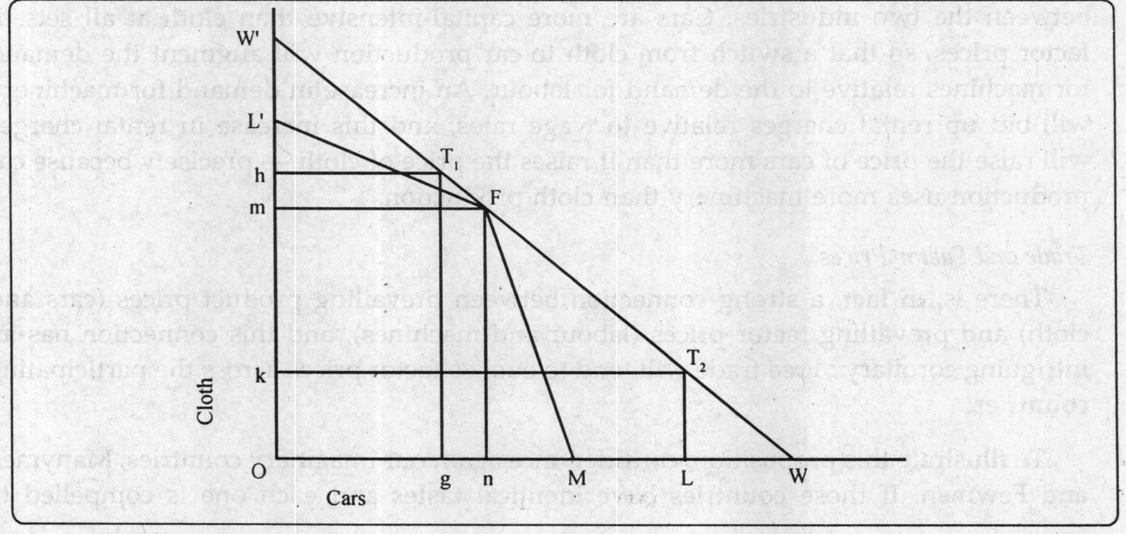

When this sort of factor-substitution is possible, the factor-endowments model changes in two ways. First, the production-possibilities frontier becomes a smooth curve like *XQPY* in Figure 6. Second, the domestic price of cars expressed in terms of cloth comes to depend on the output mix, and will equal the slope of *XQPY* at the point of actual production. If, for example, production were at *P*, involving Ox_1 cars and Oy_1 cloth, the price of cars in terms of cloth would equal the slope of *XQPY* at *P*. If, instead, production were at *Q*, involving Ox_2 cars and Oy_2 cloth, the price of cars would equal the slope of *XQPY* at *Q*

FIGURE-6

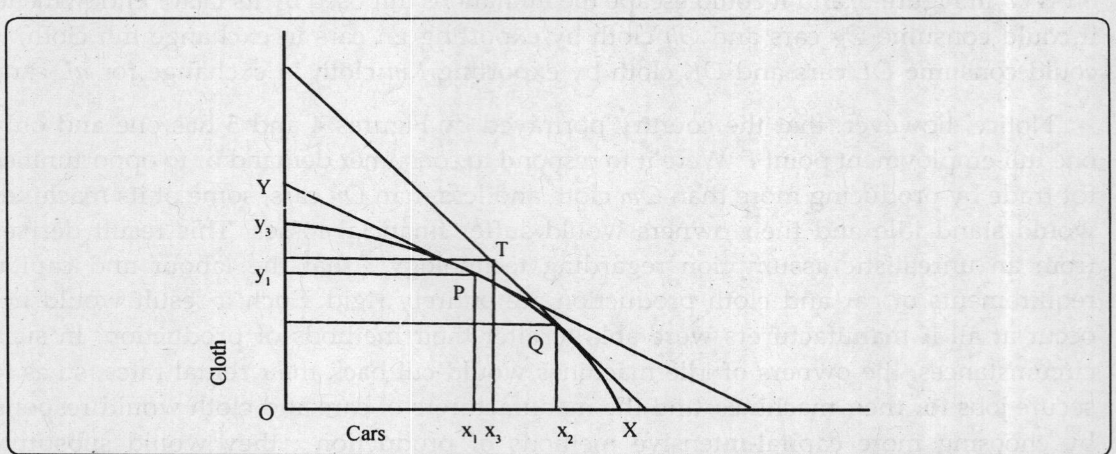

The curve *XQPY* is steeper at *Q* than at *P*, implying a higher price for cars, and more cars are made at *Q*. The price of cars must rise to stimulate production. This link between prices and the product mix arises from the difference in capital-intensities between the two industries. Cars are more capital-intensive than cloth at all sets of factor prices, so that a switch from cloth to car production will augment the demand for machines relative to the demand for labour. An increase in demand for machinery will bid up rental charges relative to wage rates, and this increase in rental charges will raise the price of cars more than it raises the price of cloth — precisely because car production uses more machinery than cloth production.

Trade and Factor Prices

There is, in fact, a strong connection between prevailing product prices (cars and cloth) and prevailing factor prices (labour and machines), and this connection has an intriguing corollary : Free trade will tend to euqlise factor prices across the participating countries

To illustrate this proposition, consider once again our imaginary countries, Manymen and Fewmen. If those countries have identical tastes and each one is compelled to satisfy its own needs, wages will be low in Manymen relative to rental rates on machinery, and wages will be high in Fewmen relative to rental rates. If the two countries can trade with each other, Manymen can relieve its shortage of machinery by importing the capital-intensive product (cars), and its wages will rise relative to rental rates. Fewmen can likewise relieve its shortage of labour by importing the labour-intensive product (cloth) and its wages will fall relative to rental rates.

That is what free trade will do. As wages would be relatively high in Fewmen before trade began, cloth would be expensive compared to cars. With the opening of trade, Fewmen will therefore export cars and import cloth. To do so, it will increase its car production and cut back its cloth production. These shifts in the pattern of production will, in turn, augment Fewmen's demand for machines and will reduce its demand for labour. Manymen, by contrast will increase its cloth production and cut back its car production, and these shifts will augment its demand for labour and will reduce its demand for machines. If there are no transport costs between the two countries, free trade will equalise product prices in Fewmen and Manymen. It will thereby equalise the two countries' factor prices. In actual practice, of course, factor prices are not equal around the world — and the differences are far too great to be explained by transport costs and trade barriers. Hence, the simple model we have been developing cannot be perfectly applicable to the real world; it may ignore important economies of scale, and the fact that modern technology is not available to every country. Yet the tendency described by the Heckscher-Ohlin model — the reduction of factor-price differences through trade — may still be quite important.

Furthermore, available statistics may exaggerate international differences in factor prices. When we compare wage rates around the world, we are comparing rather different things. Some countries' wage statistics are heavily weighted with large returns to skill; others' are dominated by the lower wages of unskilled labour. If one were to compare the wage rates of equally skilled workers, of equally fine land, and so on, being sure to match like with like, factor prices might improve to be more nearly equal than they usually appear.

Suppose, again, that cars and cloth cannot move between the countries. Wages would be higher in Fewmen than Manymen, and if there were no travel costs, workers would migrate from Manymen to Fewmen. If, further, this migration were to continue for as long as wage rates differed, it would render the two countries very much alike. Fewmen would wind up with as many machines and very much more labour than it had to start with, but the ratio of man-years to machines would be exactly equalised in the two countries. This is because the wage-rate difference causing migration would persist for as long as the ratio of man-years were lower in Fewmen than in Manymen. It would only vanish when the ratios were equalised.

This example suggests one more way to look at the gains from trade. It argues that free trade can sometimes substitute for international movements of labour and capital. Factor movements and free trade each serve to reduce differences in factor prices. Factor movements do so by erasing differences in national factor endowments. Free trade does so by offsetting those differences. Trade eliminates the need for a redistribution of productive factors by reallocating economic tasks. It allows every country to make the best use of its own factor endowment.

Leontief Paradox

The Heckscher-Ohlin theory has been one of the most influential in international economics. Most economists prefer the Heckscher-Ohlin theory to Ricardo's theory because it makes fewer simplifying assumptions. It has been subjected to many empirical tests. Beginning with a famous study published in 1953 by Wassily Leontief, many of these tests have raised questions about the validity of the Heckscher-Ohlin theory. Using the Heckscher-Ohlin theory, Leontief postulated that because the United States was relatively abundant in capital compared to other nations, the United States would be an exporter of capital-intensive goods and an importer of labour-intensive goods. To his surprise, however, he found that US exports were less capital intensive than US imports. Since this result was at variance with the predictions of the theory, it has become known as the Leontief paradox.

Table-4 shows the principal findings of Leontief's study in 1953. Since the ratio of imports to exports in terms of capital per worker-year (18,184/14,015) was about 1.30, U.S. exports were less capita-intensive (or more labour-intensive) than U.S. import replacements. Instead of capita-intensive exports and labour-intensive import replacements reqired 30 percent more capital per worker-year to produce than a representative bundle of U.S. exports.

The Leontief paradox stimulated a search for explanations, among them:

i) *Demand bias for capital intensive goods.* The U.S. demand for capital-intensive goods is so strong that it reverses the U.S. compartive cost advantage in such goods.

ii) *Existence of trade barriers*. U.S. labour-intensive imports were reduced by trade barriers (e.g., tariffs and quotas) imposed to protect and save American jobs.

iii) *Importance of natural resources*. Leontief considered only capital and labour inputs, leaving out natural resource inputs. Because natural resources and capital are often used together in production, a country that imports capital-intensive goods may be actually importing natural resource-intensive goods. For example, the United States imports crude oil, which is capital-intensive.

TABLE 4
Capital Position in U.S. Exports and Imports

	Exports	*Import Replacements*
Capital (in 1947 $)	2,550,780	3,091,339
Labour (worker-years)	182	170
Capital per worker-year ($)	14,015	18,184

Source: W. Leontief, 1953. Domestic production and foreign trade: The Americal capital position reexamined, *Proceeding of the American Philosophical Society*, vol. 97 (Nov.), pp. 332-349.

iv) *Prevalence of factor-intensity reversal*. A *factor-intensity reversal* occurs when the relative prices of labour and capital change over time, which changes the relative mix of capital and labour in the production process of a commodity from being capital-intensive to labour-intensive (or vice versa).

Human Skills and Technology-Based Views

The aforementioned explanations were subsequently found to have offered only a partial explanation of the Leontief paradox. Searching for better explanations of the sources of comparative advantage, several scholars challenged the conventional theory of trade which assumed technology and human skills equivalence among different nations. Rather than a seperate theory, the human skills and technology-based view is regarded as a refinement of the conventional theory of trade. It added two new factors of production namely *human skills* and *technology gaps*, to the explanation of comparative advantage sources.

Human skill theorists explained the source of comparative advantage in terms of the comparative abudance of professional skills and other high-level human skills. According to Donald B. Keesing, these include (1) scientists and engineers, (2) technicians and draftsmen, (3) managers, (4) other professionals, and (5) skilled manual workers. Keesing argued that U.S. exports industries employ higher proportions of highly skilled labour than do import-competing industries, Thus, the U.S. exports more skill-intensive manufactures than do other countries. Studies treating professional and skilled human resources as capital reversed the Leontief paradox and found that U.S. exports were actually capital-intensive. The relative abudance of professional and other highly skilled labour in the United States is thus a major source of its comparative advantage in manufacturing products.

Technology theorists argued that certain countries have special advantage as innovators of new products. They also postulated that there was an *imitation lag* that prevent other countries from immediately duplicating the new products of the innovating country. These two conditions gave rise to *technology gaps* in those products that afford the innovating country an export monopoly during the period of imitation lag. In other words, for the duration of imitation gap, the innovator is the only exporter on world markets. Similarly, when a firm discovers a different and more advanced production technique, it will enjoy a cost advantage and dominate the world market for a while (especially if its innovation is legally protected from imitators by the international patent system). For example, it was found that transportation, electrical machinery, instruments, chemicals, and nonelectrical machinery were the five strongest industries in the United States in terms of R&D, which performed 89.4 percent of U.S. total R&D in 1962. These five industries accounted for 72 percent of U.S. exports of manufactures in the same year. As long as technological progress is made, the technology gap would serve as a major source of comparative advantage. As such, technology, like human skills, is a seperate factor of production whose relative abudance of scarcity in a country determines comparative advantage of disadvantage in technology-intensive products. This notion, despite being more than four decades old, still has strong implications for country competitiveness, competitive advantage of MNEs and global R&D management.

Product Life-Cycle Theory

Raymond Vernon proposed the product life-cycle theory in the mid-1960s. Vernon's theory was based on the observation that for most of the 20th century a very large proportion of the world's new products had been developed by US firms and sold first in the United States (e.g., mass-produced automobiles, televisions, instant cameras, photocopiers, personal computers, and semiconductor chips). Vernon argued that the wealth and size of the market gave US firms a strong incentive to develop new consumer products. In addition, the high cost of labour gave US firms an incentive to develop cost-saving process innovations.

Just because a new product is developed by a US firm and first sold in the US market does not mean the product must be produced in the United States. It could be produced abroad at some low-cost location and then exported back into the United States. However, Vernon argued that most new products were initially produced in America. The pioneering firms might have believed it was better to keep production facilities close to the market and to the firm's center of decision making, given the uncertainty and risks inherent in product introductions. Also, the demand for most new products tends not to be based on price. Consequently, firms can charge relatively high prices for new products, which eliminates the need to look for low-cost production sites in other countries.

Vernon went on to say that early in the life cycle of a typical new product, while demand is starting to grow rapidly in the United States, demand in other advanced countries is limited to high-income groups. The limited initial demand in other advanced countries does not make it worthwhile for firms in those countries to produce the new product, but it does necessitate some exports from the United States to those countries.

FIGURE-7

THE PRODUCT LIFE-CYCLE THEORY

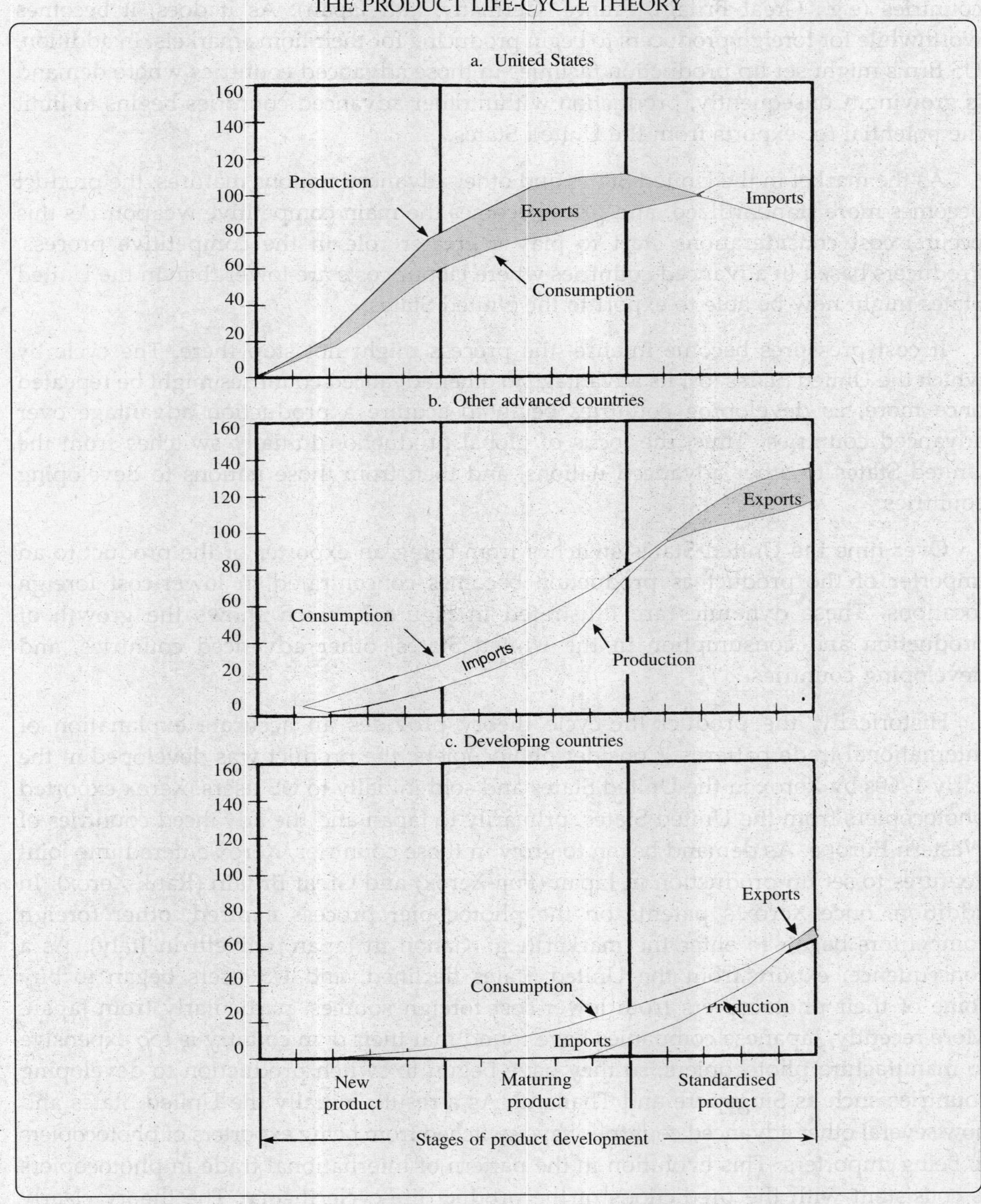

Over time, however, demand for the new product starts to grow in other advanced countries (e.g., Great Britain, France, Germany, and Japan). As it does, it becomes worthwhile for foreign producers to begin producing for their home markets. In addition, US firms might set up production facilities in those advanced countries where demand is growing. Consequently, production within other advanced countries begins to limit the potential for exports from the United States.

As the market in the United States and other advanced nations matures, the product becomes more standardized, and price becomes the main competitive weapon. As this occurs, cost considerations start to play a greater role in the competitive process. Producers based in advanced countries where labour costs are lower than in the United States might now be able to export to the United States.

If cost pressures become intense, the process might not stop there. The cycle by which the United States lost its advantage to other advanced countries might be repeated once more, as developing countries begin to acquire a production advantage over advanced countries. Thus, the locus of global production initially switches from the United States to other advanced nations, and then from those nations to developing countries.

Over time the United States switches from being an exporter of the product to an importer of the product as production becomes concentrated in lower-cost foreign locations. These dynamics are illustrated in Figure-7 which shows the growth of production and consumption in the United States, other advanced countries, and developing countries.

Historically, the product life-cycle theory provides an accurate explanation of international trade patterns. Consider photocopiers; the product was developed in the early 1960s by Xerox in the United States and sold initially to US users. Xerox exported photocopiers from the United States, primarily to Japan and the advanced countries of Western Europe. As demand began to grow in those countries, Xerox entered into joint ventures to set up production in Japan (Fuji-Xerox) and Great Britain (Rank-Xerox). In addition, once Xerox's patents on the photocopier process expired, other foreign competitors began to enter the market (e.g., Canon in Japan, Olivetti in Italy). As a consequence, exports.from the United States declined, and US users began to buy some of their photocopiers from lower-cost foreign sources, particularly from Japan. More recently, Japanese companies have found that their own country is too expensive to manufacture photocopiers, so they have begun to switch production to developing countries such as Singapore and Thailand. As a result, initially the United States and now several other advanced countries have switched from being exporters of photocopiers to being importers. This evolution in the pattern of international trade in photocopiers is consistent with the predictions of the product life-cycle theory. The theory clearly explains the migration of mature industries out of the United States and into low-cost assembly locations.

However, the product life-cycle theory is not without weaknesses. Viewed from an Asian or European perspective, Vernon's argument that most new products are developed and introduced in the United States seems ethnocentric. Although it may be true that from 1945 to 1975 most new products were introduced in the United States, there have always been important exceptions. In recent years these exceptions appear to have become more common. Many new products are now introduced in Japan (e.g., high-definition television or digital audio tapes). More importantly, with the increased globalization and integration of the world economy, growing number of new products are now introduced simultaneously in the United States, Japan, and the advanced European nations (e.g., laptop computers, compact disks, and electronic cameras). This may be accompanied by globally dispersed production, with particular components of a new product being produced in those locations where the mix of factors costs and skills is most favourable (as predicted by the theory of comparative advantage). In short, although Vernon's theory may be useful for explaining the pattern of international trade during the brief period of American global dominance, its relevance in the modern world is limited.

Several facts emerged in connection with product cycles:

1. The export performance of the mature, principal innovating country is better for new products than it is for products approaching maturity;
2. Technology is simplified as the maturing process continues, and products that are initially produced with skilled labour can later be produced by an increased use of automation combined with the use of unskilled labour;
3. The relationship between innovating and imitating countries changes over time. Countries that were once the principal innovators might fall into relative decline. Britain, for example, was the first country to build reailways, at the time with a narrow gauge and small goods wagons. Later, this investment proved to be a drag on progress and subsequent imitators like Germany and the United Sates adapted their railways more successfully to new technological and economic conditions;
4. International trade may increase in the later stages of the product cycle. As a consumer good mature and income rises, products once seen as luxury (e.g., cell phone) become a necessity. General growth of *per capita* incomes broadens the market for mass production.

Linder's Income-Preference Similarity Theory

One of the prominent feature, observed from the pattern of international trade since the 1970s, has been that developed countries trade more with other developed countries. Overall, developed countries among themselves generate about three fourths of total world exports. This fact, by itself, is an indictment of Heckscher-Ohlin's factor-endowment theory. According to the H-O theorem, the incentive to trade is greatest among nations of radically differnt factor endowments. This means that trade would take place in larger part between developed manufacturing countries and developing countries producing primary products (i.e., natural resource commodities such as oil and pertroleum) and labour-intensive goods.

Staffan B. Linder, a swedish economist, divided international trade into two different categores: primary products (natural resource products) and manufacturers. Linder asserts that differences in factor endowments explain trade in natural resource-intensive products but not in manufacturers. He argues that the range of a country's manufactured exports is determined by *internal demands*. International trade in manufacturers takes place largely among developed nations because nations will only export those goods they manufacture at home and will only manufacture at home those goods for which there is a strong domestic demand. Note, however, the MNE may introduce "born national" enterprises whose very first products are destined for foreign markets.

Linder also contends that the more similar the demand preference for manufactured goods in two countries (e.g., the United States and the United Kingdom), the more intensive is the potential trade in manufacturers between them. If two countries have the same or similar demand structures, then their consumers and investors will demand the same goods with similar degress of quality and sophistication, a phenomenon known as *preference similarity*. This similarity boosts trade between the two industrialized countries. To explain the determinants of the demand structure, Linder argues that average *per capital* income is the most important one. Countries with high *per capita* income will demand high-quality, "luxury" consumer goods (e.g., motor vehicle) and sophisticated capital goods (e.g., telecommunications equipment and machinery), while low *per capita* income countries will demand low quality, "necessity" consumer goods (e.g., bicycles) and less sophisticated capital goods (e.g., food processing machinery). Consequently, a rich country that has a comparative advantage in the production of high-quality, advanced manufactuers will find its big export markets in other affluent countries where people demand such products. Similarly, manufactured exports of the poor countries should find their best markets in other poor countries with similar demand structures. Linder also acknowledged that the effect of *per capita* income levels on trade in manufactures may be constrained or distorted by enterpreneurial ignorance, cultural and political differences, transportation costs, and legislative obstacles such as tariffs.

Intra-Industry Trade (IIT)

Intra-industry trade (IIT) occurs when a country is both exporting and importing items in the *same* product classification category. This trade differs from **inter-industry trade**, where a country's exports and imports are in *different* product classification categories. Traditional trade theory dealt only with inter-industry trade, but intra-industry trade clearly constitutes an important segment of international trade. To place the role of this intra-industry trade in context, one merely has to examine the following figures. According to an estimat, 60% of world trade is in manufactured goods and half of this is accounted for by intra-industry trade. Trade in non-manufactures is also subject to this phenomenon. However, for some individual countries, upto 70% of their trade in manufactures is subject to intra-industry trade. It has, furthermore, been increasing over time.

MEASUREMENT OF INTRA-INDUSTRY TRADE

There are a variety of ways to measure intra-industry trade but the simplest is to measure the extent of overlapping trade in a particular commodity or good and express this as a proportion of overall trade, i.e. exports plus imports.

Intra-industry trade can then be expressed as:

$$B_i = \frac{(X_i + M_i) - |X_i - M_i|}{(X_i + M_i)} \times 100$$

where B_i stands for intra-industry trade in commodity *i*, and X_i and M_i the level of exports and imports of the commodity, respectively.

Thus if exports equal ₹ 200 crore and imports ₹ 120 crore then ₹ 240 crore is overlapping trade (i.e. ₹ 120 crore of imports and ₹ 120 crore of exports) while ₹ 80 crore does not overlap. Intra-industry would thus be 75% of the total.

Using our formula this can be deduced from:

$$= \frac{(200 + 120) - (200 - 120)}{(200 + 120)} \times 100$$

$$= \frac{320 - 80}{320} \times 100$$

$$= \frac{240}{320} \times 100$$

$$= 75\%$$

There are several possible explanations for the occurrence of intra-industry trade. Some of these reasons are discussed below.

Product Differentiation

Many varieties of a product may exist because producers attempt to distinguish their products in the minds of consumers in order to achieve brand loyalty, or because consumers themselves want a broad range of characteristics in a product from which to choose. Thus, european firms may produce large automobiles and Indian producers may produce smaller automobiles. The consequence is that some Indian buyers preferring a large car may buy a european product while some european consumers may purchase a smaller, imported car. Because consumer tastes differ in innumerable ways, more so than the varieties of products manufactured by any given country, some intra-industry trade emerges because of product differentiation.

Dynamic Economies of Scale

This reason is related to the product differentiation reason. If IIT has been established in two versions of a product, each producing firm (one in the home country, one in the foreign country) may experience "learning by doing" or what has been called dynamic economies of scale. This means that per-unit cost reductions occurs because of experience in producing a particular good. Due to these cost reduction, sales of each version of the product may increase over time. Since one version was an export and the other an import for each country, intra-industry trade is enhanced over time because of this production experience.

Homogeneous Goods

Intra-industry trade in homogeneous goods can be explained fairly easily by three factors. The *first* is the existence of entrepot or the re-export trade. A considerable proportion of Hong Kong and Singapore's trade is of this type. A country may import goods in bulk which may be shipped out to other neighbouring countries possibly having been broken down into smaller consignments. In this way, one would see the simultaneous importing and exporting of the same goods. The *second* explanation is seasonality, where products are exported during one part of the year and imported during another. This is quite common for agricultural products. The *third* explanation is the cost of transport which may encourage users of a particular good to import it from a bordering country rather than a domestic producer who is located say at the other end of its own country. For similar reasons, the domestic producer may export his good to another country that is located nearby. It is quite common to see this type of cross-border trade take place between land-locked countries such as those found in Europe.

Degree of Product Aggregation

This explanation rests on the observation that IIT can result merely because of the way trade data are recorded and analyzed. If the category is broad there will be greater intra-industry trade than if a narrower category is examined. IIT in the real world may be a statistical artifact because of the degree of aggregation used, even though actual calculations use less broad categories for instance, a product, says chair, can be produced the different materials (e.g. wood and plastic), those countries that are abundant in wood will produce and export wooden chair, and satisfy their demand for plastic chain by importing them. Here, the products being misclassified in that chairs should be recently in sub-categories of the wood and plastic industries and not grouped together.

Differing Income Distributions in Countries

Another explanation of intra-industry trade is that even if two countries have similar per capita incomes, differing distributions of total income in the two countries can lead to intra-industry trade. Consider the hypothetical income distributions plotted in Figure 8. Country I has a heavy concentration of households with lower incomes, while country II has a more "normal" or less skewed distribution. Producers in country I will be concerned primarily with satisfying the bulk of country I's population, so they will produce a variety of the product that caters to consumers with incomes, for example, between y_1 and y_2. Producers in country II will cater to the bulk of country II's households, say those households between y_3 and y_4. Therefore, country II's firms produce a variety of the good with characteristics that satisfy that group. What about a household in

FIGURE 8

INTRA-INDUSTRY TRADE FROM DIFFERING DISTRIBUTIONS OF INCOME

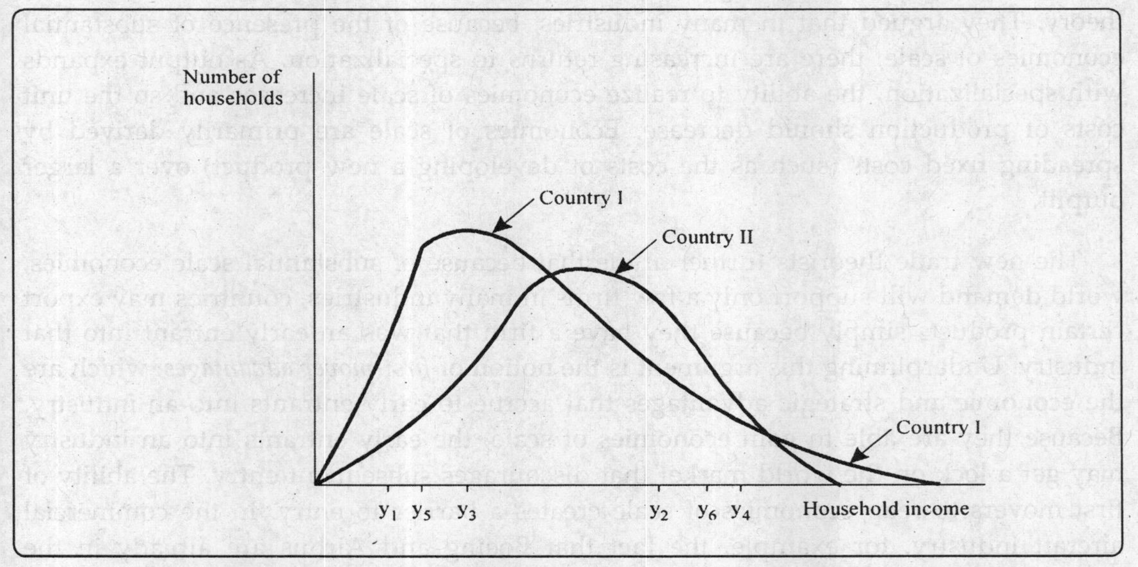

Country I's producers supply varieties of the product catering to households with income between y_1 and y_2, while country II's firms produce varieties to satisfy households with income levels between y_3 and y_4. A household in country I with income y_6 and a household in country II with income y_5 will therefore each consume an imported variety of the good. Intra-industry trade in this general product thus exists.

country I with a high income such as y_6? And what about a household in country II with a low income such as y_5? These consumers will purchase the good from the producers in the other country because their own home firms are not producing a variety of the good that satisfies these consumers. Hence, both countries have intra-industry trade in the product.

How do the theoretical explanations of intra-industry trade measure up in practice? As with all empirical work, methodological problems arise when one tries to test theoretical concepts in practice. The variables that need to be used to model homogeneity, product differentiation, market structure and scale economies are sometimes not available, and the proxies developed are often at best rough approximations. Without minimizing the problem involved in estimating the relationships, the principal empirical works show that variables such as overlapping tastes, product differentiation, market structure, technology, and economies of scale have a positive influence on the level of intra-industry trade between countries. Other factors that were found to have a negative influence were trade barriers and foreign direct investment. Neither of these needs much explanation as one restricts the volume of trade and, hence, the opportunity for intra-industry trade to take place, while the other acts as a replacement for trade.

New Trade Theory

The new trade theory emerged in the 1970s. A number of economists were questioning the assumption of diminishing returns to specialization used in international trade theory. They argued that in many industries, because of the presence of substantial economies of scale, there are increasing returns to specialization. As output expands with specialization, the ability to realize economies of scale increases and so the unit costs of production should decrease. Economies of scale are primarily derived by spreading fixed costs (such as the costs of developing a new product) over a larger output.

The new trade theorists further argue that because of substantial scale economies, world demand will support only a few firms in many industries, countries may export certain products simply because they have a firm that was an early entrant into that industry. Underpinning this argument is the notion of *first-mover advantages,* which are the economic and strategic advantages that accrue to early entrants into an industry. Because they are able to gain economies of scale, the early entrants into an industry may get a lock on the world market that discourages subsequent entry. The ability of first movers to reap economies of scale creates a barrier to entry. In the commercial aircraft industry, for example, the fact that Boeing and Airbus are already in the industry discourages new entry.

This theory suggests that a country may dominate in the export of a good simply because it was lucky enough to have one or more firms among the first to produce that good. This is at variance with the Heckscher-Ohlin theory, which suggests that a country will predominate in the export of a product when it is particularly well endowed with those factors used intensively in its manufacture. Thus, the new trade theorists argue that the United States leads in exports of commercial jet air-craft not because it is better endowed with the factors of production required to man-ufacture aircraft, but because two of the first movers in the industry, Boeing and Mc-Donnell Douglas, were US firms. However, the new trade theory is not at variance with the theory of comparative advantage. Because economies of scale result in an increase in the efficiency of resource utilization, and hence in productivity, the new trade theory identifies an important source of comparative advantage.

How useful is this theory in explaining trade patterns? It is perhaps too early to say, the theory is so new that little supporting empirical work has been done. Consistent with the theory, however, a study by Harvard business historian Alfred Chandler suggests that the existence of first-mover advantages is an important factor in explaining the dominance of firms in certain industries. Also, the number of firms is very limited in many global industries. This is the case with the commercial aircraft industry, the chemical industry, the heavy construction-equipment industry, the heavy truck industry, the tire industry, the consumer electronics industry, and the jet engine industry, to name but a few examples.

Perhaps the most contentious implication of the new trade theory is the argument that it generates for government intervention and strategic trade policy. New trade theorists stress the role of luck, entrepreneurship, and innovation in giving a firm first-mover advantages. According to this argument, the reason Boeing was the first mover in commercial jet aircraft manufacture-rather than firms such as Great Britain's DeHavilland and Hawker Siddely, or Holland's fokker, all of which could have been—was that Boeing was both lucky and innovative. One way Boeing was lucky is that DeHavilland shot itself in the foot when its Comet jet airliner, introduced two years earlier than Boeing's first jet airliner, the 707, was found to be full of serious technological flaws. Had DeHavilland not made some serious technological mistakes, Great Britain might now be the world's leading exporter of commercial jet aircraft!

Boeing's innovativeness was demonstrated by its independent development of the technological know-how required to build a commercial jet airliner. Several new trade theorists have pointed out, however, that Boeing's R&D was largely paid for by the US government; that the 707 was a spin-off from a government-funded military programme. Herein lies a rationale for government intervention. By the sophisticated and judicious use of subsidies, could a government increase the chances of its domestic firms becoming first movers in emerging industries, as the US government apparently did with Boeing? If this is possible, and the new trade theory suggests it might be, then we have an economic rationale for a proactive trade policy that is at variance with the free trade prescriptions of the trade theories.

Krugman's Monopolistic Competition Model

To explain the gains from intra-industry trade and from trade between similar countries, Krugman's monopolistic competition model is perhaps the best known approach, providing a simple but convincing theory of why similar (in terms of technology, endowments) countries gain from trading with each other and why a significant part of that trade may take place within the same industries. It also mentions the reciprocal dumping model, which highlights that, under certain conditions, even trade in identical products may be beneficial. Two basic assumptions, both of which can readily be observed in the real world, are fundamental to Krugman's model: "increasing returns to scale" and "consumers' love of variety."

In the presence of increasing returns to scale (also called "economies of scale"), firms that double their inputs more than double their output. Such situations are quite common. In order to start a business (or maintain operations), firms typically face so-called "fixed" costs, i.e. they have to pay for certain goods or services independently of how much they ultimately produce. Such costs may relate to the time of imployees spent on administrative issues or to investment in machinery and equipment. In addition, a firm incurs variable costs that increase proportionally to the level of output—for instance, a worker can only produce a given number of units per hour and any increase in production requires the hiring of additional workers at the going wage rate. Marginal costs, i.e., the costs of producing an additional unit of output, are therefore constant, but when the overall level of output rises, the fixed costs get distributed over a larger number of units, and, hence, the firm's average costs of production decline. Particularly capital-intensive industries, such as aircraft manufacturing or electronics production, tend to have large fixed costs and economies of scale than often lead to only a few producers worldwide. Increasing returns to scale can also be reaped in the area of services, especially when digital transmission allows for a centralization of certain activities. To illustrate, the retail company Wal-Mart exploits economies of scale in many ways. Wal-Mart has invested continuously in technology to match its stock with customer demand. For example, it introduced a bar code system early on and a software that connects its stores, distribution centres and suppliers, providing detail data on the availability of stock. Such fixed investment in stock management is unlikely to pay off for smallest-sized operations. The use of technology has allowed Wal-Mart to grow and lower its operating costs further through the exploitation of increasing returns to scale. According to an estimate, a 10 per cent increase in total sales volume has decrease Wal-Mart's average cost by 2 per cent. It is also noted that the availability of these technologies, by reducing the costs of tracking stock, has increased Wal-Mart's incentives to add new product lines to its stores, such as pharmacies and auto services. The fact that Wal-Mart is a big retailer gives it a competitive edge in any activity involving a fixed cost, such as contracting with foreign suppliers, which allows Wal-Mart to import at a lower average cost than other retailers.

Since goods can be produced more and more cheaply (i.e., for the same costs, more and more output can be produced), it is certainly economically efficient to produce at a larger scale. The reason why, at the extreme, there is not only one firm producing a single type of product is that consumers prefer to choose from different varieties for each product they buy rather than buy the same one each time, i.e. they have a "love of variety." Taking the example of food, this means that consumers prefer a selection of different restaurants over one pizza restaurant. Consumers' love of variety favours the existence of many small firms, each producing a somewhat differentiated product, while the exploitation of economies of scale makes it worthwhile to organize production in larger firms.

Krugman has built these two opposite tendencies into a simple framework of "monopolistic competition." With larger firms having a cost advantage over smaller ones, the market may cease to be perfectly competitive. In order to abstract away from the complex issue of firm interaction in such a setting, the "monopolistic competition" market structure assumes that each firm produces a product "variety" that is "differentiated" from the varieties produced by other firms. Therefore, each firm has some leeway to set prices without having to fear that consumers immediately switch to a competing supplier for small differences in price. Since a firm has a "monopoly" in its particular variety within the industry, it can set its own price, and since each firm is small compared with the entire market, it does not take into account the impact of its own price on the prices of other firms. At the same time, while these varieties are not exactly the same, they are substitutes for one another, and each firm continues to face competition from other producers in the industry. In fact, the more varieties that exist (i.e. the lower each firm's market share), the lower the price that a firm can charge. By the same token, the more firms there are, the less each firm sells (for a given size of the market) and the higher a firm's average costs. In market equilibrium, price must equal average costs, which, in turn, determines the total number of firms. If price exceeds average costs, new firms would enter the industry as long as profits can be made; conversely, if price is less than average costs, some firms would exit the market.

What happens if two (identical) countries, each with a monopolistically competitive industry, open up to trade? According to traditional models on country differences, there would not be any trade. By contrast, with differentiated goods and increasing returns to scale, trade opening enables firms to serve a larger market (and reduce their average costs) and gives consumers access to an increased range of product varieties. However, as consumers can choose among more varieties, they also become more price-sensitive. Hence, while each firm can produce a larger quantity than before (selling to both the domestic and the foreign market), they can do so only at a lower price. As total sales in the integrated market stay the same, and any individual firm is larger, some firms will go out of business. These effects are best illustrated with a hypothetical example, taken from Krugman and Obstfeld. Assume that two countries, Home and Foreign, each have a monopolistically competitive car sector. Before trade opening, 9,00,000 cars per year are sold in Home and 1.6 million cars in Foreign. Apart from their different market sizes, the two countries are identical in terms of technology, resources and consumer preferences. Assuming certain fixed and variable costs of production as well as a given elasticity of substitution between varieties, Krugman and Obstfeld determine that there are six firms in Home and eight in Foreign. Given the respective market sizes of the two countries, each firm in Home sells 1,50,000 cars, while sales per firm in Foreign are 2,00,000.

Exploiting increasing returns to scale, Foreign firms can produce at a lower average cost and charge a lower price, which the authors determine to be US$ 8,750 as opposed to US$ 10,000 in Home. When Home and Foreign open up to trade, the size of the integrated market is 2.5 million cars (the sum of the two national markets in autarky). Each firm serving this larger market now produces more units (2,50,000 per firm) and the market price for a car has come down to US$ 8,000. However, this also means that the integrated market can only support ten firms in total. In other words, while consumers have a wider range of choice (ten different car varieties instead of six in Home and eight in Foreign before trade opening), the total number of firms (ten) after market integration is less than the sum of firms in autarky.

TABLE 5

Example	*Home market, before trade*	*Foreign market, before trade*	*Integrated market, after trade*
Total sales of cars	9,00,000	16,00,000	25,00,000
Number of firms	6	8	10
Sales per firm	1,50,000	2,00,000	2,50,000
Average cost	$ 10,000	$ 8,750	$ 8,000
Price	$ 10,000	$ 8,750	$ 8,000

The gains form trade in such a scenario are threefold. Firms produce large quantities and better exploit their economies of scale ("scale effect"). Consumers in both countries can choose from a wider variety of products in a given industry ("love-of-variety" effect). At the same time, in an integrated market, they pay a lower price ("procompetitive effect"). Because of these gains, it makes sense that similar countries trade with each other and export/import different varieties of the same good.

While consumers and producers win, those producers that go out of business "lose." It is impossible to know from the above framework who these producers are and in which country the surviving firms will be located. It may be that each country specializes in producing a narrower range of product varieties under free trade than before (while, of course, all varieties are traded and available for consumption in both countries), Yet, firms may also decide to locate predominantly in one market. For instance, if trade is costly, production may concentrate in the larger domestic market, even if there is some demand abroad. By producing near its largest markets, firms can realize economies of scale, while minimizing transport and other trade costs. Thus, the larger country will produce more varieties and be a net exporter in that industry (the so-called "home market effect").

More about the expected trade patterns following liberalization can be gleaned if the basic Krugman model is combined with the traditional approaches concerning country differences. As in the Heckscher-Ohlin model, one country may be relatively abundant in labour and the other country may be capital-abundant, and one of the two goods may be labour-intensive (e.g. food) and the other capital-intensive (e.g. manufacturing). However, unlike in the Heckscher-Ohlin model, one of the industries, manufacturing, has economies of scale, with firms producing differentiated varieties in a monopolistically competitive market.

As in the absence of increasing returns to scale, the capital-rich country would export manufactured goods and import food, and vice-versa for the labour-rich country. If manufacturing is a monopolistically competitive sector, the capital-abundant country will still be an importer of food and a net exporter of manufactured goods. The other country, with a comparative advantage in food production, will export both food and manufactured goods, since it produces different varieties of manufactured goods, which some consumers in the capital-abundant country will appreciate. The trade patterns are depicted in Figure-9, with both countries exporting and importing manufactured goods, but with the capital-rich country running a trade surplus in manufacturing.

FIGURE 9

TRADE PATTERNS WITH COUNTRY DIFFERENCES IN RESOURCES AND A MONOPOLISTICALLY COMPETITIVE SECTOR

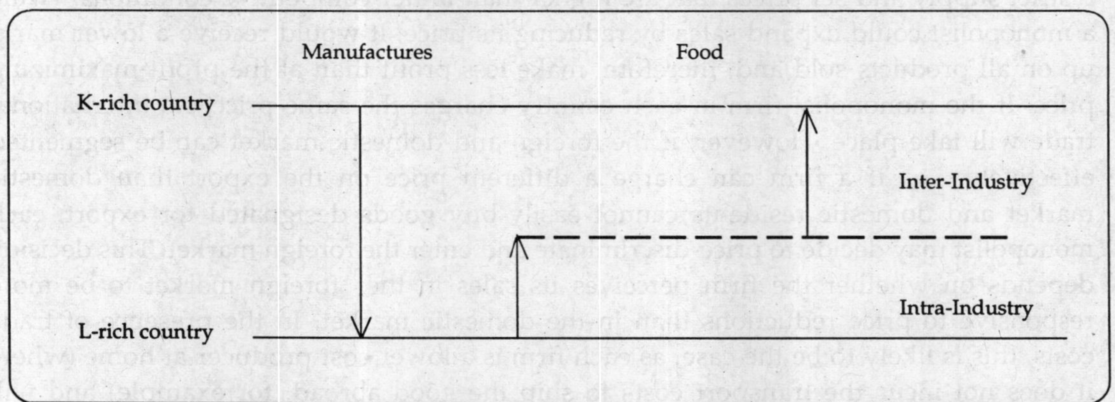

Sources: Krugman and Obsfeld (2006: 127)

Variant of Krugman's Framework

Either provides another approach to explain trade patterns on the basis of Krugman's framework. His variant of the model focuses on trade in intermediate inputs, the production of which is subject to economies of scale that are internal to each firm. The cost of producing the final product is lower the larger the bundle of intermediate varieties used. In turn, the larger the production of the final manufactured good, the larger the number and scale of production of the intermediate. If trade in intermediate inputs is free, it does not matter where in the world the production of manufactureds goods is located in order to realize these economies of scale. However, if trade in intermediate inputs is restricted, producers of final goods would still need to use all the intermediate varieties available in order to manufacture their products at the same cost.

In the presence of trade costs, this will only be possible if all the intermediate and final good production is concentrated in the same country. Hence, this variant of the model can explain the existence of an industrial complex in certain countries. It implies that a reduction of trade costs reduces the need for a concentration of production in any one country.

Reciprocal Dumping

The monopolistic competition model highlights economies of scale as a rationale for trade in similar products and between similar countries. It recognizes that imperfect competition is a necessary consequence of increasing returns to scale at the level of the firm, but disregards most of its consequences. However, imperfect competition, notably the power of firms to price-discriminate between exported and domestically sold products, can itself give rise to international trade between similar countries.

There may be a situation in which the same good is produced by a monopolist in each of two identical countries. In order to maximize profits, monopolists artificially restrict supply and set prices that are higher than under competitive conditions. While a monopolist could expand sales by reducing its price, it would receive a lower mark-up on all products sold and, therefore, make less profit than at the profit-maximizing price. If the monopolist firm in each country charges the same price, no international trade will take place. However, if the foreign and domestic market can be segmented effectively, i.e., if a firm can charge a different price on the export than domestic market and domestic residents cannot easily buy goods designated for export, each monopolist may decide to price-discriminate and enter the foreign market. This decision depends on whether the firm perceives its sales in the foreign market to be more responsive to price reductions than in the domestic market. In the presence of trade costs, this is likely to be the case, as each firm is a lower cost producer at home (where it does not incur the transport costs to ship the good abroad, for example) and will have a lower market share abroad than in the domestic market.

With lower market shares, a firm may double its sales for a given price reduction, but it would need to cut its price much further to double its sales when it has a high market share; hence, a firm is likely to see itself as having less monopoly power abroad and has a higher incentive to keep prices low for exports. If trade costs are not prohibitive, it makes sense for both firms to "dump," i.e. charge a lower price for exports than it charges domestically. By selling in the foreign market, each firm makes additional sales and, hence, profits, even if the price is lower than domestically, while the negative effect on the price of existing sales are imparted on the other firm, not on itself.

In this model, reciprocal dumping leads to two-way trade in the same product, even though trade is costly and, initially, prices have been equal. With the monopoly being replaced by a duopoly situation, consumers in each country benefit from a larger amount of the product in question at a lower average price. While the increased competition represents a benefit, it is, of course, wasteful to spend resources on the shipping of identical products (or close substitutes), and, depending on transport costs, the overall welfare effect may well be negative.

"New New" Trade Theory

"New New" trade theory differs form the "new" trade theory by allowing for differences with respect to firms' marginal costs and fixed market-entry costs that are added to the standard fixed cost of developing a new variety. The basic features of the new theory, introduced in the Melitz model, are in the tradition of monopolistic competition trade models. More precisely, it introduces differences between firms into the Krugman model of "new" trade theory. The economy is endowed with a single factor of production: labour (L). There is a single industry that produces horizontally differentiated products. Each firm produces one single variety using a technology with increasing returns to scale. Competition is imperfect but there are many firms. Firms vary in terms of their total factor productivity. Each firm is assumed to draw its productivity level in a "lottery" after paying a one-time fixed sunk cost of entry (or "invention cost" as Baldwin calls it). This can be thought of as a way to model a situation where the firm invests in research and development (R&D) to develop a new variety and there is uncertainty involved in the R&D process regarding the marginal cost of producing the new variety.

In addition to the sunk "invention cost," if it enters the domestic market, the firm has to pay a fixed entry cost. Similarly, if it wishes to export, market. Depending on the level of its productivity, the firm will thus either produce or exit, and if it produces, it will either produce only for the domestic market or be an exporter. Only firms with sufficiently low marginal costs will be able to sell enough to cover fixed costs. Firms with the lowest marginal costs will find it profitable to pay the entry cost for both the domestic and the export market, while firms with intermediate productivity levels will find it profitable to pay only the entry cost for the domestic market. In other words only the most productive firms become exporters.

Considering a ranking of all firms according to their productivity level, there are three outcomes for firms and two cut-off conditions—that is, two threshold levels of marginal cost. The least productive firms (i.e., those with a marginal cost above the first threshold level) exit the market, those between the first and the second cut-off points enter but only sell on the domestic market and those with the highest levels of productivity (i.e. with a marginal cost lower than the second threshold level) both export and sell domestically. The threshold marginal cost for entering the local market depends on the fixed entry cost of entering the domestic market as well as on prices and demand conditions. Similarly, the cut-off marginal cost for entering the export market is a function of the fixed cost of entering the export market, the trade costs, the price and demand conditions. In this setting, the increases in the exposure to trade through either a transition from self-sufficiency to trade or a reduction of trade costs will force the least productive firms to exit and reallocate market shares from less productive to more productive firms. The increased exposure to trade will always deliver welfare gains.

When entry into new export markets is costly, the exposure to trade offers new profit opportunities only to the more productive firms that can afford to cover the entry cost. This also encourages more market entry as prospective firms respond to the higher potential returns associated with good productivity. At the same time, falling trade costs also reduce the minimum level of productivity that firms need to export successfully and thus, the highest-productivity non-exporters enter the export market and existing exporters see their sales grow as they take advantage of new markets. The increased demand for labour by the more productive firms and new market entrants increases overall wages and forces the least productive firms to exit. In other words, the minimum level of productivity needed to survive increases, prompting the lowest-productivity firms to exit and average industry productivity to increase.

Baldwin and Forslid systematically study the positive and normative aspects of the effects of trade liberalization in the Melitz model. As far as the positive effects of trade liberalization are concerned, they emphasize two main results. First, as mentioned, liberalization has a strong impact on average productivity via a selection effect (the least productive firms drop out of the market) and a reallocation effect (from the less to the more productive firms). Second, trade liberalization leads to an anti-variety effect. Freer trade reduces the number of varieties produced in each country and under reasonable assumptions also reduces the total number of varieties consumed. Using profits to measure the return to capital, the authors also show that the model displays classic Stolper-Samuelson-like behaviour.

Finally, turning to welfare effects, Baldwin and Forslid break down the total welfare impact into *three* partial effects: the negative anti-variety effect, the positive productivity effect, and a positive effect related to a substitution and share-shifting effect in favour of imported varieties. They show that considering all the effects together, the positive productivity and substitution/share-shifting effects outweigh the anti-variety effect, so that the overall impact of freer trade is unambiguously positive.

Bernard et al., examine how firm, industry and country characteristics interact as trade costs fall in a model that embeds differences in firms into a framework of comparative advantage. The model they use has two countries, two factors and two industries. Each industry is populated by a continuum of firms that each produce a single differentiated variety within their industry. Firms vary in their level of productivity, industries vary in factor intensity and countries differ in terms of factor abundance. Using their model, they demonstrate that increased exposure to trade raises the productivity cut-off necessary for survival, which raises average productivity in both industries. In their model, the strength and importance of firm self-selection varies with the interaction between country and industry characteristics. The rise in productivity is more pronounced in the comparative advantage industry, because firms' export opportunities in this industry are greatest. This outcome magnifies the original differences between countries and thereby boosts the welfare gains from trade. By increasing exporters' profits, falling trade costs also reduce the export productivity cut-off level. Here too, responses vary according to country endowments and industry factor intensity. Another interesting effect is related to aggregate productivity growth. Increases in industry productivity reduce the price of the average variety in each industry and thereby elevate the real income of both factors. This effect may even be strong enough to raise the real wages of both factors. The possibility of such an outcome, which also depends on the model's parameters, contrasts sharply with the predictions of the traditional model.

Yeaple proposes an alternative explanation of the economic implications of international trade in the presence of differences among firms. In his model, firms are the same when they start out. Differences arise when they choose to employ different technologies and systematically hire different types of workers. In a two-sector economy, firms in one sector produce a differentiated good. In this sector, firms can choose to employ a medium or high technology. The fixed investment costs for the high technology are higher than for the medium technology are higher than for the medium technology. In the second sector, firms produce the same good, employing a standard low technology. Additionally, workers differ in their skills. High-skilled workers have a comparative advantage in using the high technology whereas medium-skilled workers have a comparative advantage using the medium technology. Therefore, in an equilibrium, firms that choose to use the high technology employ highly skilled workers. As the labour market is competitive, high-technology firms pay a higher wage. Only firms that choose to use the high technology are able to do this and hence attract high-skilled workers. Firms that do not find it profitable to choose the high technology might still find it profitable to use the medium technology and to hire the medium-skilled workers. This might be possible because the medium technology firms pay a lower wage to their workers.

As in Melitz, firms must incur a fixed exporting cost and hence at a sufficiently high level of the latter, only high-productivity firms find it profitable to export. If trading costs are reduced, more firms adopt the better technology, which leads to an improvement in sectoral productivity. It is interesting to note that a reduction in trade barriers even between identical countries raises the relative demand for skilled workers and the skill premium.

National Competitive Advantage

In 1990 Michael Porter of Harvard Business School published the results of intensive research to determine why some nations succeed and others fail in international competition. Porter and his team looked at 100 industries in 10 nations. The book that contains the results of this work, *The Competitive Advantage of Nations*, has made an important contribution to thinking about trade. Like the work of the new trade theorists, Porter's work was driven by a belief that the existing theories of international trade told only part of the story. Porter hoped to explain why a nation achieves international success in a particular industry. Why does Japan do so well in the automobile industry? Why does Switzerland excel in the production and export of precision instruments and pharmaceuticals? Why do Germany and the United States do so well in the chemical industry? These questions cannot be answered easily by the Heckscher-Ohlin theory, and the theory of comparative advantage offers only a partial explanation. The theory

FIGURE 10

DETERMINANTS OF NATIONAL COMPETITIVE ADVANTAGE: PORTER'S DIAMOND

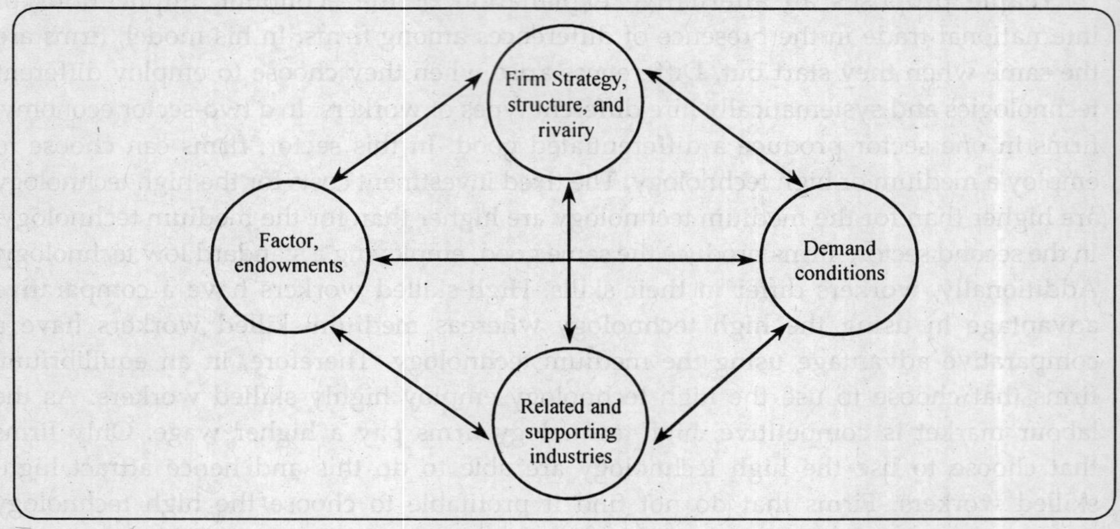

of comparative advantage would say that Switzerland excels in the production and export of precision instruments because it uses its resources very efficiently in these industries. Although this may be correct, this does not explain why Switzerland is more productive in this industry than Great Britain, Germany, or Spain. It is this puzzle that Porter tries to solve.

Porter's thesis is that four broad attributes of a nation shape the environment in which local firms compete, and these attributes promote or impede the creation of competition advantage (Figure-10). These attributes are: i) *factor endowments;* ii) *Demand conditions;* iii) *Relating and supporting industries;* iv) *Firm strategy, structure, and rivalry.*

Porter speaks of these four attributes as constituting the *diamond*. He argues that firms are most likely to succeed in industries or industry segments where the diamond is most favorable. He also argues that the diamond is a mutually reinforcing system. The effect of one attribute is contingent on the state of others. For example, Porter argues, favourable demand conditions will not result in competitive advantage unless the state of rivalry is sufficient to cause firms to respond to them.

Porter maintains that two additional variables can influence the national diamond in important ways: chance and government. Chance events, such as major innovations, create discontinuities that can reshape industry structure and provide the opportunity for one nation's firms to supplant another's. Government, by its choice of policies, can detract from or improve national advantage. For example, regulation can alter home demand conditions, antitrust policies can influence the intensity of rivalry within an industry, and government investments in education can change factor endowments.

Factor Endowments

Factor endowments lie at the center of the Heckscher-Ohlin theory. While Porter does not propose anything radically new, he does analyse the characteristics of factors of production in some detail. He recognises hierarchies among factors, distinguishing between basic factors (e.g., natural resources, climate, location, and demographics) and advanced factors (e.g., communications infrastructure, sophisticated and skilled labour, research facilities, and technological know-how). He argues that advanced factors are the most significant for competitive advantage. Unlike basic factors (which are naturally endowed), advanced factors are a product of investment by individuals, companies, and governments. Thus, government investments in basic and higher education, by improving the general skill and knowledge level of the population and by stimulating advanced research at higher education institutions, can upgrade a nation's advanced factors.

The relationship between advanced and basic factors is complex. Basic factors can provide an initial advantage that is subsequently reinforced and extended by investment in advanced factors. Disadvantages in basic factors can create pressures to invest in advanced factors. The most obvious example of this phenomenon is Japan, a country that lacks arable land and mineral deposits and yet has built a substantial endowment of advanced factors. Porter notes that Japan's large pool of engineers (reflecting a much higher number of engineering graduates per capita than almost any other nation) has been vital to Japan's success in many manufacturing industries.

Demand Conditions

Porter emphasizes the role home demand plays in providing the impetus for upgrading competitive advantage. Firms are typically most sensitive to the needs of their closest customers. Thus, the characteristics of home demand are important in shaping the attributes of domestically made products and in creating pressures for innovation and quality. Porter argues that a nation's firms gain competitive advantage if their domestic consumers are sophisticated and demanding. Such consumers pressure local firms to meet high standards of product quality and to produce innovative products. Porter notes that Japan's sophisticated and knowledgeable buyers of cameras helped stimulate the Japanese camera industry to improve product quality and to introduce innovative models. A similar example can be found in the cellular phone equipment industry, where sophisticated and demanding local customers in Scandinavia helped push Nokia of Finland and Ericsson of Sweden to invest in cellular phone technology long before demand for cellular phones took off in other developed nations. As a result, Nokia and Ericsson, along with Motorola, are today dominant players in the global cellular telephone equipment industry.

Related and Supporting Industries

The Third broad attribute of national advantage in an industry is the presence of suppliers or related industries that are internationally competitive. The benefits of investments in advanced factors of production by related and supporting industries can spill over into an industry, helping it achieve a strong competitive position internationally. Swedish strength in fabricated steel products (e.g., ball bearings and cutting tools) has drawn on strengths in Sweden's specialty steel industry. Technological leadership in the US semiconductor industry until the mid-1980s provided the basis for US success in personal computers and several other technically advanced electronic products. Similarly, Switzerland's success in pharmaceuticals is closely related to its previous international success in the technologically related dye industry.

One consequence of this is that successful industries within a country tend to be grouped into clusters of related industries. This was one of the most pervasive findings of Porter's study. One such cluster is the German textile and apparel sector, which includes high-quality cotton, wool, synthetic fibers, sewing machine needles, and a wide range of textile machinery.

Firm Strategy, Structure, and Rivalry

The fourth broad attribute of national competitive advantage in Porter's model is the strategy, structure, and rivalry of firms within a nation. Porter makes two important points here. His first is that nations are characterised by different "management ideologies," which either help them or do not help them build national competitive advantage. For example, Porter notes the predominance of engineers on the top-management teams of German and Japanese firms. He attributes this to these firms' emphasis on improving manufacturing processes and product design. In contrast, Porter notes a predominance of people with finance backgrounds on the top-management teams of many US firms. He links this to many US firms' lack of attention to improving manufacturing processes and product design, particularly during the 1970s and 1980s. He also argues that the dominance of finance has led to an overemphasis on maximizing short-term financial returns. According to Porter, one consequence of these different management ideologies has been a relative loss of US competitiveness in those engineering-based industries where manufacturing processes and product design issues are important (e.g., the automobile industry).

Porter's second point is that there is a strong association between vigorous domestic rivalry and the creation and persistence of competitive advantage in an industry. Vigorous domestic rivalry induces firms to look for ways to improve efficiency, which makes them better international competitors. Domestic rivalry creates pressures to innovate, to improve quality, to reduce costs, and to invest in upgrading advanced factors. All of this helps to create world-class competitors.

Porter's argument is that the degree to which a nation is likely to achieve international success in a certain industry is a function of the combined impact of factor endowments, domestic demand conditions, related and supporting industries, and domestic rivalry. He argues that for this diamond to boost competitive performance usually requires the presence of all four components (although there are some exceptions). Porter also contends that government can influence each of the four components either positively or negatively. Factor endowments can be affected by subsidies, policies toward capital markets, policies toward education, and the like. Government can shape domestic demand through local product standards or with regulations that mandate or influence buyer needs. Government policy can influence supporting and related industries through regulation and influence firm rivalry through such devices as capital market regulation, tax policy, and antitrust laws.

If Porter is correct, we would expect his model to predict the pattern of international trade that we observe in the real world. Countries should be exporting products from those industries where all four components of the diamond are favorable, while importing in those areas where the components are not favourable. Much about the theory rings true, but the same can be said for the new trade theory, the theory of comparative advantage, and the Heckscher-Ohlin theory. In reality it may be that each of these theories explains something about the pattern of international trade. In many respects these theories complement each other.

IMPLICATIONS FOR BUSINESS

There are three main implications of these theories for international businesses: *location implications, first-mover implications,* and *policy implications.*

Location Implications

One way in which these theories matters to an international business concerns the link between the theories of international trade and a firm's decision about where to locate its productive activities. Underlying most of the theories is the notion that countries have particular advantages different productive activities. Thus, from a profit perspective, it makes sense for a firm to disperse its various productive activities to those countries where they can be performed most efficiently. If design can be performed most efficiently in France, that is where design facilities should be located; if the manufacture of basic components can be performed most efficiently in Singapore, that is where they should be manufactured; and if final assembly can be performed most efficiently in China, that is where final assembly should be performed. The end result is a global web of productive activities, with different activities being performed in varying locations around the globe depending on considerations of comparative advantage, factor endowments, and the like. If the firm does not do this, it may find itself at a competitive disadvantage relative to firms that do.

First-Mover Implications

The new trade theory suggests the importance to firms of building and exploiting first-mover advantages. According to the new trade theory, firms that establish a first-mover advantage with regard to the production of a particular new product may subsequently dominate global trade in that product. This is particularly true in those industries where the global market can profitably support only a limited number of firms, such as the aerospace market, but early commitments also seem to be important in less concentrated industries such as the market for cellular telephone equipment. For the individual firm, it pays to invest substantial financial resources in trying to build a first-mover, or early-mover, advantage, even if that means several years of substantial losses before a new venture becomes profitable. In recent years Japanese firms, rather than their European or North American competitors, have been prepared to undertake the vast investments and bear the years of losses required to build a first-mover advantage. This has been true in the production of liquid crystal display (LCD) screens for laptop computers. While firms such as Toshiba and NEC invested heavily in this technology during the 1980s, many large European and American firms exited the market. As a result, today Japanese firms dominate global trade in LCD screens, even though the technology was invented in the United States.

Policy Implications

The theories of international trade also matter to international businesses because business firms are major players on the international trade scene. Business firms produce exports, and business firms import the products of other countries. Because of their pivotal role in international trade, firms influence government trade policy. By lobbying government, business firms can help promote free trade or trade restrictions. The message for business contained in the theories of international trade is that promoting free trade is generally in the best interests of the home country, although it may not always be in the best interest of an individual firm. Many firms recognise this and lobby for open markets.

Finally, Porter's theory of national competitive advantage also contains policy implications. Porter's theory suggests that it is in a firm's best interest to invest in upgrading advanced factors of production; for example, to invest in better training for its employees and to increase its commitment to research and development It is also in the best interests of business to lobby the government to adopt policies that have a favourable impact on each component of the national "diamond.' Thus, according to Porter, businesses should urge government to increase its investment in education, infrastructure, and basic research (because all these enhance advanced factors) and to adopt policies that promote strong competition within domestic markets (because this makes firms stronger international competitors, according to Porter's findings).

Table-6 below provides a summary of some of the basic characteristics of the trade models (discussed above). Two centuries of economic research on trade have substantially improved our understanding of the gains form trade and thus the causes of trade. It may be noted that early contributions are still relevant but that they are insufficient. New theories have been developed to account for new forms of trade and for new information on trade. No single cause can explain the complex trading relations of today. The old, the new and the "new new" theories should be seen as primarily complementary.

TABLE 6

Trade Theories

	Traditional Trade theory Theory Ricardo, Heckscher-Ohlin	*"New" trade theory Krugman (1980)*	*Heterogeneous firms models Melitz (2003)*
Gains from trade (causes)			
Specialisation	Yes	No	No
Economies of scale	No	Yes	Yes
Pro-competitive	No	Yes	No
Variety	No	Yes	No[1]

Aggregate productivity			
(through selection/reallocation)	No	No[2]	Yes
Trade patterns			
Inter-Industry	Yes	No	No
Intra-industry	No	Yes	Yes
Exporters and non-exporters within industries	No	No	Yes
Distribution			
Trade liberalization affects relative factor rewards	Yes	No	No

1. Variety effects are ambiguous.
2. In the Krugman model, "productivity" in the integrated market also increases in the sense that the same total amount is produced at lower average cost due to exploitation of scale economies. However, the Krugman model is silent about which firms remain in business, since it does not include differences among firms. Once firms are distinguished according to their productivity level, as in the Melitz model, the exit of less productive firms itself leads to improvements in overall industry productivity.

Source: Based on Table 1 of Bernard et al. (2007a).

Concluding, it appears that the evolution of trade theory, from old trade doctrines to the NTT, has impacted policy at two levels. The *first* relates to the continuing support of the free trade doctrine to determine policy for developing areas. As is expected, the push comes from the advanced nations, both at the intergovernmental level and at multilateral institutions like the IMF and the WTO. The *second* impact of trade theory relates to policies pursued by the advanced nations, which relies considerably on the NTT doctrines of strategic trade. The uneven power relations between the rich and poor nations of the world permits a continuation of this asymmetrical combination of policies, to which trade theory unfortunately has contributed much. Much of the preoccupation of the policymakers with the micro-theoretic formulations of trade theory, both old and new, are related to a total neglect of the macroeconomic issues relating to the national as well as the world economy. One only expects that the new theories, which are yet to come up, will address some of these limitations.

QUESTIONS

1. How global efficiency be increased through free trade?
2. With a given level of world resources, international trade may bring about an increase in total world output. Explain.
3. What were the pillars of Mercantilist thought? How were the ideas of Absolute Advantage so devastating to Mercantilist thinking and policy?
4. In the Ricardian analysis, why does each trading partner have an incentive to produce at an endpoint of its production -possibilities frontier.
5. When a country has a comparative advantage in a good ,must it also have an absolute advantage in that good ? Why or why not?
6. If a country has an absolute advantage in a good, must it also have a comparative advantage in that good ? Why or why not?

7. How can a country gain from trade if it is unable to change its production pattern ? How does the factor -endowment theory differ from Ricardian theory in explaining international trade patterns?
8. What factors underlie whether specialisaton in production will be partial or complete on an international basis?
9. What is the "Leontief paradox" and why is it a paradox? What do you think is the major defect in the Leontief test that might have caused the paradox to occur ? Why?
10. What products might be examples of goods that are currently going through or have gone through the various stages outlined in the product cycle theory ?
11. In the Krugman model ,why does the opening of a country to a larger market (world market rather than domestic market alone) lead to lower product prices?
12. Is the existence of product differentiation a necessary condition for the existence of intra-industry trade? Why or why not?
13. Why is an increase in the number of varieties of a good regarded as gain from trade ?Can you think of economic advantages associated with greater product variety ?Explain.
14. How relevant is the theory of comparative advantage to modern trade patterns?
15. How does countertrade work? Is it an efficient economic concept?
16. What is a free trade concept? Is it an efficient economic concept?
17. In what way does the factor endowment theory help to explain why nations trade ?How does the Leo ntief paradox modify this theory?
18. How is theory of absolute advantage similar to that of comparative advantage ? How is it different?
19. What are the main contributions of Porter's theory of competitive advantage?
20. Distinguish between intra-industry trade and inter-industry trade What are some major determinants of intra-industry trade?
21. Of what value is the international product cycle theory in helping to understand why nations trade?
22. What is the basis for trade according to Heckscher-Ohlin ?What products should a country export ? Why ? Using the specific- factors model .explain why you might expect to see certain capital owners and labour groups arguing against expanding trade in a capital - abundant country.
23. "Trade theory assumes that resources are fully employed both before and after trade and that technology remains unchanged. But if the same amounts of resources are actually used ,both before and after trade ,1 don't see how any gain to the world as a whole can occur." Explain the basis for gains from trade to occur even when worker effort and technology remain the same.
24. What role do the factor intensities of production play in the factor proportions theory of trade ? If there were no differences in the factor intensities of the goods produced ,how could that affect the predicted pattern of trade?

REFERENCES

Acemoglu, D. (2008) *Introduction to modern economic growth,* Princeton: Princeton University Press.

Ades, A. F. and Glaescr, E. L. (1999) 'Evidence on growth, increasing returns, and the extent of the market'. *The Quarterly Journal of Economics* 114. 3: 1025-1045.

Aghion. P. and Griffith, R. (2007) *Competition and Growth: Reconciling Theory and Evidence,* Cambridge. MA: MIT Press.

A leala. F. and Ciccone, A. (2003) Trade, extent of the market, and economic growth 1960-1996'. *Department of Economics and Business Working Paper* No *765,* Barcelona: Universitat Pompeu Fabra.

Baldwin, R. (2006a) 'Globalisation: the great unbundling(s)'. Paper for the Finnish Prime Minister's Office. Economic Council of Finland as part of EU Presidency.

Bernard, A. B., Eaton. J.. Jensen. J. B.. and Kortum. S. (2003) 'Plants and productivity in international trade'. *The American Economic Review* 93. 4: 1268-1290.

Bernard, A. B., Redding, S. J., and Schott, P. K. (2007b) 'Comparative advantage and heterogeneous firms', *Review a/Economic Studies* 74, 1: 31-66.

Bernhofen, D. M. and Brovyn, J. C. (2004) 'A direct test of the theory of comparative advantage: The case of Japan', *Journal a/Political Economy* 112. 1: 48-67.

—— (2005) 'An empirical assessment of the comparative advantage gains from trade: Evidence from Japan', *American Economic Review* 95, 1:208-225.

Bowen, H. P., Learner, E. E., and Sveikauskaus, L. (1987)'Multicountry, multifactor tests of the factor abundance theory *'American Economic Review* 77, 5: 791-809.

Branstetter, L.G. (2001) 'A re knowledge spillovers international or intranational in scope?: Microeconometric evidence from the U.S. and Japan', *Journal of International Economics* 53. 1:53-79.

Bustos, P. (2007) 'Multilateral trade liberalization, exports and technology upgrading: Evidence on the impact of MERCOSUR on Argentinian firms', Mimeo, Barcelona: Universitat Pompeu Fabra.

Coe, D. T. and Helpman, E. (1995) 'International R&D spillovers', *European Economic Review* 39, 5: 859-887.

Corden, W. M. (1984) 'The normative theory of international trade', in Jones, R.W. and Kenen.

Davis, D. R. and Weinstein, D. E. (2000) 'International trade as an integrated equilibrium: new perspectives', *The American Economic Review* 90, 2: 150-154.

Deardorff, A. V. (1979) 'Weak links in the chain of comparative advantage', *Journal of International Economics 9,* May: 197-209.

—— (1980) 'The general validity of the law of comparative advantage', *Journal of Political Economy* 88, 1980: 941-957.

—— (2005b) 'How robust is comparative advantage?', *Review of International Economics* 13, 5: 1004-1016.

—— (2005c) 'Ricardian comparative advantage with intermediate inputs', *North American Journal of Economics and Finance* 16, 1: 11-34.

Del Gatto, M.. Mion, G., and Ottaviano, G. 1. P. (2006) Trade integration, firm selection and the costs of non-Europe', Mimeo, University of Bologna.

Dixit, A. K. and Stiglitz, J. E. (1977) 'Monopolistic competition and optimum product diversity', *The American Economic Review* 67, 3: 297-308.

Dollar, D. and Kraay, A. (2002) 'Growth is good for the poor' *Journal of Economic Growth!,* 3: 195-225.

Dornbusch, R., Fischer, S., and Samuelson, P. A. (1977) 'Comparative advantage, trade and payments in a Ricardian model with a continuum of goods', *American Economic Review 61,* 5: 823-839.

Epifani, P. and Gancia, G. (2008) 'Openness, government size and the terms of trade', *IEW Working Paper N° 359,* Zurich: Institute for Empirical Research in Economics.

Ethier, W. J. (1982) 'National and international returns to scale in the modern theory of international trade', *The American Economic Review*, 3: 389-405.

Evenett, S. J. and Keller, W. (2002) 'On theories explaining the success of the gravity equation'. *Journal of Political Economy*

Falvey, R., Greenaway, D., and Yu, Z. (2006b) 'Extending the Melitz Model to asymmetric countries', *University of Nottingham Research Paper No. 2006/07*, Nottingham: Leverhulme Centre for Research on globalization and Economic Policy.

Feenstra, R.(2004) *Advanced International Trade : Theory and Evidence*, Princeton: Princeton University Press.

Fernandez, C., Ley, E., and Steel, M. F. J. (2001) 'Model uncertainty in cross-country growth regressions', *Journal of Applied Econometrics* 16, 5: 563-576.

Frankel, J. A. and Romer, D. (1999) 'Does trade cause growth?' *The American Economic Review* 89, 3: 379-399.

Grubel, H. G. (1967) 'Intra-industry specialization and the pattern of trade', *The Canadian Journal of Economics and Political Science /Revuecanadienne d'Economique et de Science politique* 33, 3: 374-388.

Grubel, H. G. and Lloyd, P. (1975) *Intra-industry Trade : The Theory and Measurement of International Trade in Differentiated Products*, London: Macmillan.

Helpman, E. and Krugman, P. (1985) *Market Structure and Foreign Trade : Increasing Returns, Imperfect Competition and the International Economy*, Brighton: Wheatsheaf Books.

Helpman, E., Melitz, M., and Rubinstein, Y. (2007) 'Estimating trade flows: Trading partners and trading volumes', *NBER Working Paper No. 12927*, Cambridge, MA: NBER.

Helpman, E., Melitz, M. J., and Yeaple. S. R. (2004) 'Exports versus FDI with heterogeneous f inns', *American Economic Review')^*, 1: 300-316.

Hindley, B. and Smith, A. (1984) 'Comparative advantage and trade in services', *The World Economy* 7, 4: 369-389.

Kohli, U. (1993) 'U.S. technology and the specific factors model', *Journal of International Economics* 34, 1-2: 115-136.

Krugman, P. R. (1979) 'Increasing returns, monopolistic competition, and international trade', *Journal of International Economics* 9, 4: 469-479.

—— (1980) 'Scale economies, product differentiation, and the pattern of trade', *American Economic Review* 70, 5: 950-959.

—— (1990) *Rethinking International Trade*, Cambridge, MA: MIT Press.

—— (1991) 'Increasing returns and economic geography '*Journal of Political Economy* 99, 4: 483-499.

Krugman, P. R. and Venables, A. J. (1995) 'Globalization and the inequality of nations'. *Quarterly Journal of Economics* 110, 4: 857-880.

Learner, E. E. (1980) 'The Leontief paradox reconsidered '*Journal of Political Economy* 88, 3: 495-503.

—— (2007) 'A flat world, a level playing field, a small world after all, or none of the above? A review of Thomas L. Friedman's *The World is Flat'*, *Journal of Economic Literature* 45, 1:83-126.

—— Learner, E. E. and Levinsohn, J. (1995) 'International trade theory: The evidence', in Grossman, G. M. and Rogoff, K. (eds) *Handbook of International Economics*, Amsterdam: Elsevier Science: 1339-1396.

Lemieux, T. (2007) 'The changing nature of wage inequality, *NBER Working Paper A'° 13523*, Cambridge, M A: NBER.

Leontief, W. W. (1953) 'Domestic production and foreign trade: The American capital position re-examined', *Proceedings of the American Philosophical Society* 97, 4: 332-349. Reprinted in Richard Caves and Harry G. Johnson (eds) *Readings in International Economics,* Homewood, 111: Irwin (1968)

Levinsohn, J. (1993) 'Testing the imports-as-market-discipline hypothesis', *Journal of International Economics* 35, 1-2: 1-22.

Markusen, J. R. (1983) 'Factor movements and commodity trade as complements', *Journal of International Economics* 14, 3-4: 341-356.

Matsuyama, K. (1991) 'Agricultural productivity, comparative advantage and economic growth', *NBER Working Paper N° 3606,* Cambridge, MA: NBER.

Melitz, M. J. (2003) 'The impact of trade on intra-industry reallocations and aggregate industry productivity', *Econometrica* 71, 6: 1695-1725.

Melitz, M. J. and Ottaviano, G. I. P. (2008) 'Market size, trade, and productivity', *Review of Economic Studies* 75, 1:295-316.

Melvin, J. R. (1989)'Trade in producer services: A Heckscher-Ohlin approach', *The Journal of Political Economy* 97, 5:1180-1196.

Mundell, R. A. (1957) 'International trade and factor mobility', *The American Economic Review* 47, 3: 321-335.

Porter, M. E. (1990) *The Competitive Advantage of Nations,* New York, N Y: The Free Press.

Rivera-Batiz, L.A. and Romer, P.M. (1991) 'Economic integration and endogenous growth', *The Quarterly Journal of Economics* 106, 2: 531-555.

Roberts, M. J. and Tybout, J. R. (1991) 'Size rationalization and trade exposure in developing countries', *Policy Research Working Paper N° 594,* Washington, DC: The World Bank.

Rodriguez, F. and Rodrik, D. (1999) Trade policy and economic growth: A skeptic's guide to the cross-national evidence', *NBER Working Paper N° 7081.* Cambridge, MA: NBER.

Romer, P. M. (1990) 'Endogenous technological change', *The Journal of Political Economy* 98. 5: S71-S102.

Schumpeter, J. (1942) *Capitalism, Socialism and Democracy,* New York: Harper.

Schweinberger, A. G. (1975) 'The Heckscher-Ohlin model and traded intermediate products', *The Review of Economic Studies* 42, 2: 269-278.

Vanek, J. (1968) The factor proportions theory: the N factor case', *Kyklos* 21, October: 749-754. Venture, J. (1997) 'Growth and interdependence', *The Quarterly Journal of Economics* 112, 1: 57-84.

Yeaple. S. R. (2005) 'A simple model of firm heterogeneity, international trade, and wages', *Journal of International Economics* 65, 1: 1-20.

Young, A. (1991) 'Learning by doing and the dynamic effects of international trade', *The Quarterly Journal of Economics* 106,2: 369-405.

Unit II

3

TARIFFS AND OTHER BARRIERS TO TRADE

INTRODUCTION

The contribution of tariffs to total trade costs has decline over time for both developed and developing countries. The formation of the European Union (EU) and the North American Free Trade Agreement (NAFTA) accounted for most of the tariff reductions among developed countries. An important contribution has also been provided by preferential tariff treatment in favour of least-developed countries (LDCs), bringing dutyfree access for most of them to major developed countries. This cnapter does not try to cover all possible policy instruments, but deals with tariffs, quotas, the impact of tariffs, quotas, or tariff-rate quotas, and finally with tariff welfare effects.

THE TARIFF CONCEPT

A tariff is simply a tax (duty) levied on a product when it crosses national boundaries. The most widespread tariff is the *import tariff,* which is a tax levied on an imported product. A less common tariff is an *export tariff,* which is a tax imposed on an exported product. Export tariffs have often been used by developing nations.

Tariffs may be imposed for protection or revenue purposes. A **protective tariff** is designed to reduce the amount of imports entering a country, thus insulating import-competing producers from foreign competition. This allows an increase in the output of import-competing producers that would not have been possible without protection. A **revenue tariff** is imposed for the purpose of generating tax revenues and may be placed on either exports or imports.

TYPES OF TARIFFS

Specific Tariff

A specific tariff is expressed in terms of a fixed amount of money per physical unit of the imported product. A specific tariff is relatively easy to apply and administer, particularly to standardized commodities and staple products where the value of the dutiable goods cannot be easily observed. A main disadvantage of a specific tariff is that the degree of protection it affords domestic producers varies *inversely* with changes in import prices. For example, a specific tariff of ₹ 1,00,000 on autos will discourage imports priced at ₹ 10,00,000 per auto to a greater degree that those priced at ₹ 20,00,000. During times of rising import prices, a given specific tariff loses some of its protective effect. The result is to encourage domstic firms to produce less expensive goods, for which the degree of protection against imports is higher. On the other hand, a specific tariff has the advantage of providing domestic producers more protection during a business recession, when cheaper products are purchased. Specific tariffs thus cushion domestic producers progressively against foreign competitors who cut their prices.

Ad Valorem Tariff

An **ad valorem** (of value) **tariff**, much like a sales tax, is expressed as a fixed percentage of the value of the imported product. Suppose that an ad valorem duty of 15 per cent is levied on imported autos as a percentage applied to a product's value, an ad valorem tariff can distinguish among small differentials in product quality to the extent that they are reflected in product price. Under a system of ad valorem tariffs, a person importing a ₹ 20,00,000 car would have to pay a higher duty than a person importing a ₹ 10,00,000 car. Under a system of specific tarrifs, the duty would be the same.

Another advantage of an ad valorem tariff is that it tends to maintain a constant degree of protection for domestic producers during periods of changing prices. An ad valorem tariff yields revenues proportionate to values, maintaining a constant degree of relative protection at all price levels. An ad valorem tariff is similar to a proportional tax in that the real proportional tax burden or protection does not change as the tax base changes. In recent decades, in response to global inflation and the rising importance of world trade in manufactured products, ad valorem duties have been used more often than specific duties.

Determination of duties under the ad valorem principle at first appears to be simple, but in practice it has suffered from administrative complexities. The main problem has been trying to determine the value of an imported product, a process referred to as **customs valuation.** Import prices are estimated by customs appraisers, who may disagree on product values. Moreover, import prices tend to fluctuate over time, which makes the valuation process rather difficult.

Another customs-valuation problem stems from variations in the methods used to determine a commodity's value. For example, the United States has traditionally used **free-on-board (FOB) valuation,** whereby the tariff is applied to a product's value as it leaves the exporting country. But European countries have traditionally used a **cost-insurance-freight (CIF) valuation,** whereby ad valorem tariffs are levied as a percentage of the imported commodity's total value as it arrives at its final destination. The CIF price thus includes transportation costs, such as insurance and freight.

Compound Tariff

A compount tariff is a combination of specific and ad valorem tariffs. Compound duties are often applied to manufactured products embodying raw materials that are subject to tariffs. In this case, the specific portion of the duty neutralizes the cost disadvantage of domestic manufactures that results from tariff protection granted to domestic suppliers of raw materials, and the ad valorem portion of the duty grants protection to the finished-goods industry.

THE EFFECTIVE RATE OF PROTECTION

In analysing tariffs, economists distinguish between the nominal tariff rate and effective tariff rate. The **nominal tariff rate** is the tariff rate that is published in the country's tariff schedule. It applies to the value of a *finished product* that is imported into a country. A distinction needs to be drawn between the nominal tariff rate, which is) usual *ad valorem* tariff or its equivalent, and the effective rate of protection (ERP). The **effective tariff rate** takes into account not only the nominal tariff rate on a finished product, but also any tariff rate applied to *imported inputs* that are used in producing the finished product. The effective tariff is a measure that applies to a single nation. In a world of floating exchange rates, if all nominal or effective tariff rates rose, the effect would be offset by a change in the exchange rate. It is worth highlighting that nominal tariff may be reflected in more important reductions the effectively applied rates in vertically fragmented processes. For a given tariff cut worldwide, the reduction in total trade costs due to tariff barriers is more important the higher the number of times a product crosses the border during its different production stages. For example, if the value added in each intermediate production stage is assumed to be infinitesimally small, a 1 per cent tariff reduction lowers the cost of producing by N per cent, with N being the number of production stages, since between every production stage the intermediate good crosses a border and incurs a tariff.

An example will help to explain the meaning of this definition. Suppose the world price of shoes is ₹ 2000 and that it takes ₹ 1200 worth of leather at the free-trade world price to make a pair of shoes. In the manufacture of shoes, then, value-added at world prices is ₹ 800. Now suppose Country A levies a nominal tariff of 30 percent on shoe imports but allows leather to be imported duty free. The price of shoes in Country A would rise to ₹ 2600 (i.e. the world price plus the tariff), and consequently the value-added of domestic shoe producers would become ₹ 1400. In other words, they could incur factor costs of ₹ 1400 and still be competitive with a foreign firm whose factor costs were ₹ 800. Value-added in Country A can be 75 percent larger than value-added at the free-trade price [(₹ 1400 - ₹ 800) = 75 percent]. Thus the ERP is 75 percent, while the nominal tariff is only 30 percent. Compare a shoe-producing firm in Country A and its free-trade competitor:

	Firm in Country A	*Free-trade competitor*
Shoe price	₹ 2,600	₹ 2,000
Leather input	₹ 1,200	₹ 1,200
Value-added	₹ 1,400	₹ 800

The high effective rates of protection will attract resources into industries where a country has production costs much higher than abroad, i.e. where it has a comparative disadvantage. As a result, the country's economic efficiency falls.

However, tariff on leather would reduce the effective rate of protection for shoes. The reason is obvious: a tariff on leather increases the price of leather in Country A and raises A firms' costs of production, which means value-added must be smaller for A firms to continue selling shoes at ₹ 2600. In our example, a 20 percent nominal tariff on leather would lead to the following result:

	Firm in Country A	*Free-trade competitor*
Shoe price	₹ 2,600	₹ 2,000
Leather input	₹ 1,440	₹ 1,200
Value-added	₹ 1,160	₹ 800

The effective tariff rate on shoes has fallen from 75 percent to 45 percent [(₹ 1,160 – ₹ 800)/₹ 800 = 45 percent] as a result of the tariff on leather. Shoe producers in Country A will tend to favour tariffs on shoes but oppose tariffs on leather.

A formula for calculating the effective tariff rate follows from the above discussion:

$$e_j = \frac{t_j - \sum_i a_{ij} \cdot t_j}{1 - \sum_i a_{ij}}$$

Where we define the terms above and apply them to the shoe example:

e_j = the effective rate of protection in industry *j*, shoe production

t_j = the nominal tariff rate in industry *j* = 30 percent tariff on shoes

t_i = the nominal tariff rate in industry *i* = 20 percent tariff on leather

a_{ij} = the share of inputs from industry *i* in the value of output of industry *j* at free-trade prices = (₹ 1200/₹ 2000) = 0.60

and the sigma term, Σ, represents summation over all the necessary intermediate inputs i. Therefore the effective rate of protection for shoes is

$$e_j = \frac{30\% - 0.60(20\%)}{1 - 0.60} = \frac{18\%}{0.40} = \frac{0.18}{0.40} = 45\%$$

In this example we had only a single intermediate input, leather. In actual practice, a given product has many intermediate inputs, each with its own nominal tariff rate. The formula uses the share of each such input (a_{ij}) to weight the nominal tariff rates in forming the sum ($\Sigma a_{ij} t_i$).

The tariff structures of many countries show a systematic pattern in which nominal tariff rates increase as the stage of production advances - that is, tariff rates are low (or zero) on raw materials, higher on semi-finished products, and highest on finished manufactures. Such a pattern in nominal tariff rates produces an even greater escalation in effective tariff rates, with very high protection being accorded the higher stages of manufacture. Industrial countries have been accused of using such a tariff structure to preserve their lead in manufacturing and to keep the less-developed countries from developing exports of finished manufactures.

INTERVENTION IN EXPORT MARKETS

In some circumstances export restrictions may be preferred to import restrictions or they may be the only instrument available to address unforeseen difficulties. Therefore, flexibility measures to restrict exports may be needed in a trade agreement to allow governments to be able to address these situations that may not be foreseen at the time that the agreement is signed. Like contingent measures to raise import barriers, in a trade agreement flexibility measures that restrict exports can be useful as they act as a safety valve that allows parties to agree to more extensive commitments.

Governments justify the use of export taxes on several grounds. Governments use export taxes primarily to insulate a country from sudden price rises, to improve government revenue, to develop infant industry to protect the environment etc. It is argued that export taxes are unlikely to be a first-best policy. However, the use of export taxes can be supported on the basis of second-best arguments. Developing more efficient stock markets and financial markets, introducing a flexible exchange-rate regime, extending the tax base and improving the tax administration system could all contribute to solving the problems at a smaller economic cost. Under certain circumstances, a second-best argument for using export taxes, however, can be made.

i) To Control Inflationary Pressures

An increase in the international price of a commodity that is also consumed domestically may create inflationary pressures at home. Import tariffs do not address the problem as their principle effect is to increase domestic prices. Many countries have used export taxes to keep inflation under control.

The rationale for using export taxes to reduce the effects of higher prices from abroad is the following: by making exporting less attractive, export taxes divert part of the production from the foreign to the domestic market. This, in turn, increases domestic supply of the taxed commodity, thus creating a downward pressure on its domestic price that may partially offset the inflationary pressures coming from higher prices abroad. In addition, when export taxes are applied to commodities used in the production processes of other firms, the lower costs for the processing industry may result in lower prices for processed goods.

There are, however, limits to the use of export taxes as an instrument to control inflation. *First,* when export taxes are applied to "intermediate" goods, consumers may not benefit from lower prices. The extent to which lower production costs, due to lower costs of the intermediate commodity, are translated into lower prices for processed goods depends on the market structure. If markets are dominated by a small number of firms that are able to control market prices, consumers might not benefit from lower prices for the processed commodity.

Second, export taxes may have long-term inflationary consequences on the economy. Because of their effect on domestic prices, export taxes may reduce the incentive of firms to invest in the production of the commodity on which they are applied. As a consequence, the long-term supply of the good might fall, thus resulting in higher domestic prices.

Finally, there is a problem of policy coordination. Recent evidence related to the food crisis shows, for example, that while export bans have helped to contain domestic price rises in countries where they have been adopted, they have contributed to a worsened food crisis.

ii) To Increase Government Revenue

Export taxes are a source of tax revenue for the government. To maintain a steady tax revenue during periods of recessions, export taxes can be used as contingent measures. The advantage of using export taxes rather than tariffs to increase government revenue during periods of recession and currency devaluation is that export taxes are a tax on the windfall gains of exporters. Tariffs, in contrast, are a tax on consumers. However, an efficient application of export taxes requires high administrative costs. To reduce domestic instability regarding tax revenue, countries need to use a system of variable tax rates – that is, high rates when export prices are high (e.g. following devaluation) and low rates when they are below a threshold level. The causes that have prompted the implementation of a tax can often peter out quickly. A change in economic conditions requires a quick policy reversal. However, many countries, especially developing countries, lack such political and institutional flexibility.

iii) To Support Industry

Export taxes on intermediate goods act as an indirect subsidy to manufacturing or processing industries as they reduce the domestic price of intermediate products. Therefore, export taxes can be used by governments as an instrument for developing infant industry or for supporting a declining processing industry. The objections raised for the use of import restrictions for these purposes also hold for the use of export taxes: economic intervention can be justified only in the presence of some form of market failure. Other important issues concern their redistributive effects and their distorting effects when international markets are imperfectly competitive. *First,* export taxes on raw commodities redistribute income from primary commodity suppliers to processors. This might increase income inequality within a country and severely affect the poorest sections of the population. *Second,* when markets have imperfect competition, a one-to-one "pass-through" of benefits from farmers to processors cannot be expected. Therefore, export taxes may be ineffective in developing infant industry and introduce further distortions.

iv) To Protect the Environment

Export taxes and bans have frequently been applied to live fishery products, wildlife, and hides and skins of certain endangered species, or to prevent exports of dangerous materials. To understand why and when export taxes are used by governments for the purposes of environmental protection and sustainable development, it is important to understand the causes of environmental problems. These include different sources of market failures and government policy failures. Market failure comes about when property rights are not well defined. If anyone, without restrictions, can fish from the sea, collect wood from the forests or hunt wild animals, the likely result is the over-exploitation of these resources. Government policy failures relate to the failure to introduce adequate environmental taxes to address environmental problems. If appropriately designed, these policies would be the best way for producers and consumers to assume the full cost, inclusive of the environmental damage, of their activity.

When markets and governments fail and no management schemes are in place, the demand from the world market may accelerate the depletion of resources. The use of export taxes may act in these circumstances as a second-best policy. There are, however, some risks associated with this policy. Suppose that a government introduces export taxes on logs to address the problem of deforestation. *First,* low log prices in the home country may encourage inefficient logging practices, thus increasing wastage. *Second,* low prices of inputs may discourage firms from investing in the introduction of sustainable development technologies in the processing industry.

QUOTA

The quota is the most common type of quantitative import or export restriction. A import quota operates by limiting the physical amount of the good or service imported. This reduces the quantity available to common, which in turn causes the domestic price to rise. The domestic price continues to rise until the quantity supplied domestically at the higher price plus the amount of imported allowed under the quota exactly equal the reduced quantity demanded. The quota thus restricts the quantity supplied, causing price to adjust, in contrast to tariff, which increase quantity adjustment by fixing a higher domestic price. A variation of an import quota is the so-called *voluntary export restrict* (VER). A country may establish export quotas to ensure the domestic consumers of a sufficient supply of goods at a low price, to prevent deplection of material resources, or to attempt to raise export price by restricting supply in foreign markets. A specific type of quota that prohibits all forms of trade is an *embargo,* which works like a quota. Countries--or group of countries--may place embergoes on either imports or exports, on whole categories of products regardless of destribution, or specific products to specific countries, or on all products to given countries. Governments impose embargoes in an attempt to use economic means to achieve political gains.

THE IMPACT OF TARIFFS, QUOTAS OR TARIFF-RATE QUOTAS

The restrict trade practices can take different forms, such as tariff surcharges, quotas or tariff-rate quotas (TRQs), since the type of measure to be applied is not prescribed by the relevant WTO rules, other than the obligation to choose the most suitable measure. From an economic point of view, it must be asked what instrument is preferable under what circumstances.

Effects of Tariff, Quota and Tariff-Rate Quota

A common way of analyzing the effects of a tariff and a quota is with the help of a simple demand and supply framework, as shown in Figures 1 and 2. The analysis here assumes the existence of perfect competition and a small economy (i.e. one that is "price-taking" and therefore cannot affect prices by quantitatively varying supply or demand). National economic welfare consists of consumer surplus (the difference between the willingness to pay and the actual price the consumer pays), producer surplus (the sum of profits earned by suppliers) and government tariff revenue. Consumer demand is represented by demand curve D and producers are in a competitive market with supply curve S. Under free trade, consumers purchase at world price PW and demand a quantity equal to D1, domestic suppliers produce S1, and imports fill the excess demand gap. In Figure 1, consumer surplus is given by the sum of a, b, c, d, e and f whereas producer surplus is given by g.

Suppose a country imposes a tariff per unit on foreign imports. The domestic price

FIGURE 1

THE EFFECT OF A TARIFF

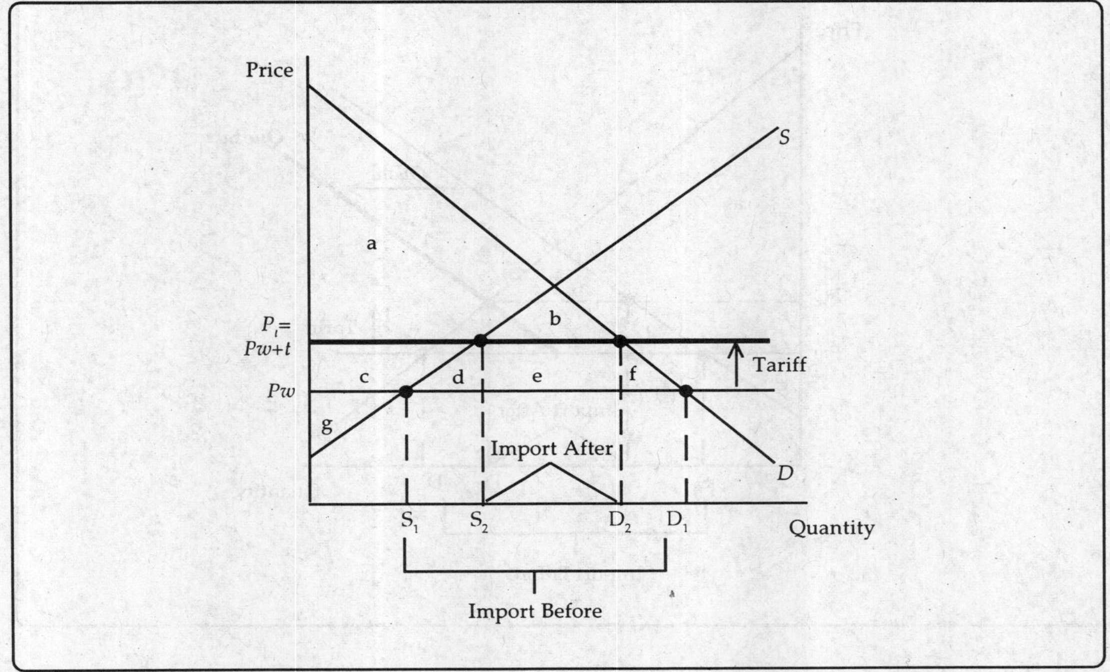

becomes (P_W + t), demand decreases to D_2, and supply increases to S_2. As a consequence, imports fall. Producer surplus increases to $(g + c)$, consumer surplus shrinks to $(a + b)$, but government revenue from the tariff on imports is collected, amounting to e. The sum of national economic welfare in the presence of a tariff is strictly lower than welfare under free trade, with the so-called deadweight loss being equal to $(d + f)$. Owing to the price increase, some consumers are driven out of the market and this loss is captured by triangle f. Moreover, the increase of domestic production entails costs that exceed the costs of the imports they replace. Hence, triangle d captures the loss of surplus associated with domestic production.

Now suppose a government imposes an import quota. This prevents the domestic economy from importing as much as before. Instead, in order to satisfy demand, domestic suppliers have to produce any quantity demanded in excess of the quota. However, since the cost of producing these extra units is strictly higher than the costs of imports, the domestic price rises to P_Q. In Figure 2, the domestic supply curve is now represented in bold. That is, a quota has the effect of shifting the supply curve to the right by the amount of the quota whenever the price is above the world price. The supply curve below the world price does not move, since at these levels of demand it is not profitable

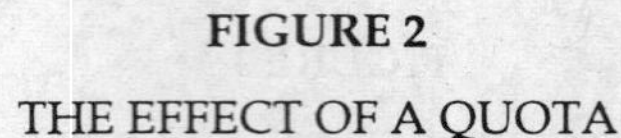

FIGURE 2

THE EFFECT OF A QUOTA

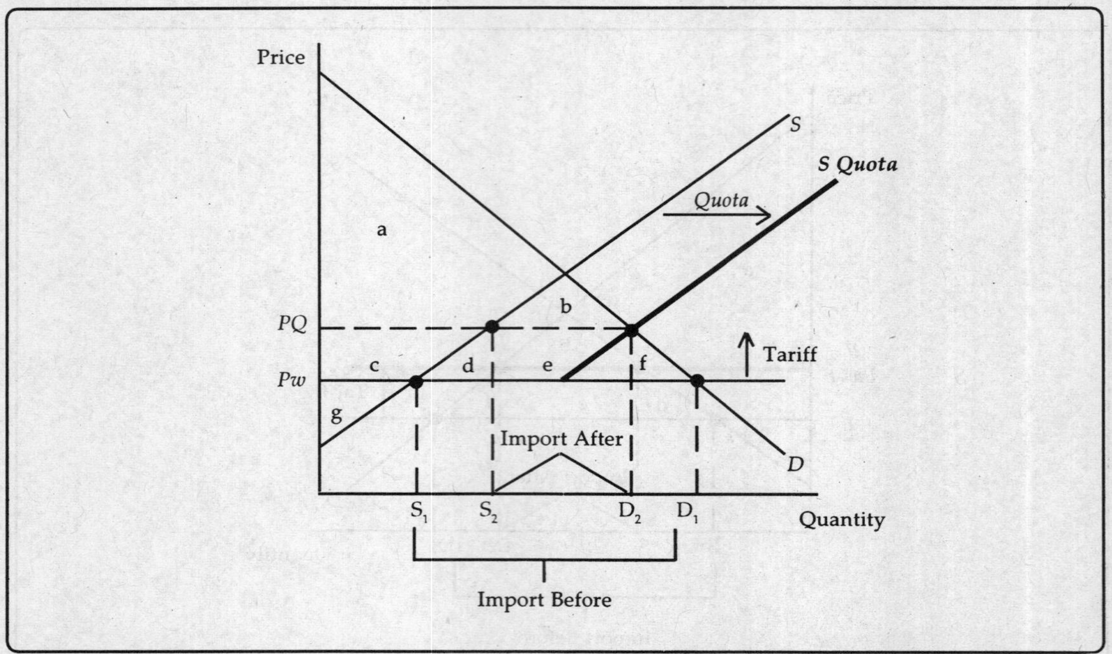

for the licence holders to import. A quota, like a tariff, raises the domestic price and causes deadweight losses equal to *(d + f)*.

While a tariff produces government revenue, an import quota creates a surplus for the licence holders (area $e' + e''$). Theoretically, if the government auctions import rights, the two instruments are equivalent. However, in practice, governments might distribute the quota shares based on historical market shares to importers, who collect the quota rents. Hence, the existence of a quota can provide incentives for importers to engage in inefficient activities aimed at maximising their quota shares. In addition, a quota grants discretion as to how a government allocates import licences. As a result, quotas are considered less transparent and might entail additional inefficiencies, which is why tariffs are commonly seen as a better means of protection.

Further differences exist between tariffs and quotas. A quota interferes directly with the link between prices and quantities, which is essential to the operation of a market-based system. A tariff simply creates a wedge, but allows the price system to function. For instance, if there is an unexpected increase in demand after a tariff or a quota has been imposed, a quota is more protectionist than a tariff. In Figure 3, the demand, represented by D, refers to when the tariff or quota was set. However, the

FIGURE 3

THE DIFFERENCES BETWEEN A TARIFF AND A QUOTA

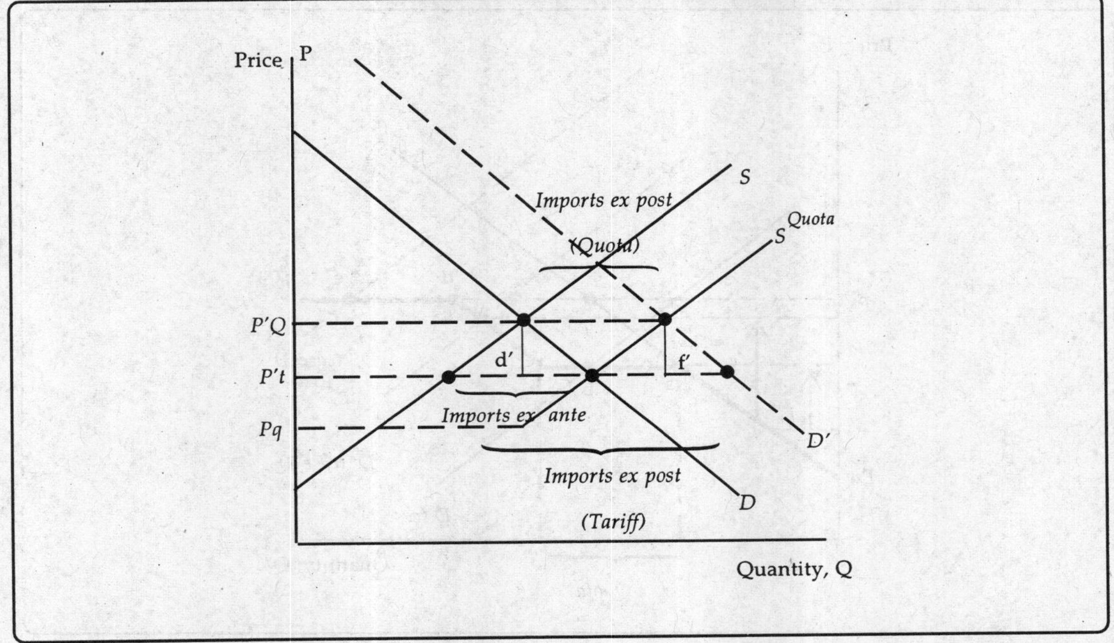

demand unexpectedly expands to D′. With a tariff, the excess demand is satisfied by an increase in imports at price P_t. In the presence of a quota, however, excess demand has to be satisfied by an increase in domestic production, which leads to an increase in the domestic price to P'_Q. Therefore, a quota leads to a further deadweight loss equal to $(d'+f')$ compared with a (previously equivalent) tariff when demand increases.

Safeguard measures, under certain conditions, may also be applied in the form of tariff-rate quotas (TRQs). As its name suggests, a TRQ consists of a quota for a certain volume of imports that may enter the country at a favourable tariff rate known as the in-quota tariff. Any imports exceeding this volume are subject to a higher out-of-quota tariff. Figure 4 illustrates the basic mechanism of a TRQ for three different cases of quota fill and demand. In Case 1, the quota is only partially filled. The applicable tariff on imports is the in-quota tariff, and, hence, the domestic price is equal to $P = P_W + t\ in$ and imports are equal to the amount of the segment that links point *a* to point *b*. Case 2 illustrates a situation in which the quota is filled and additional imports face the out-of-quota tariff. In this case, the out-of-quota tariff rate is high enough to deter imports and foster domestic production at price *P′*. That is, a TRQ has the effect of shifting the supply curve to the right by the amount of the quota. Finally, Case 3 shows a demand curve that is high enough to make even imports subject to the out-of-quota tariff

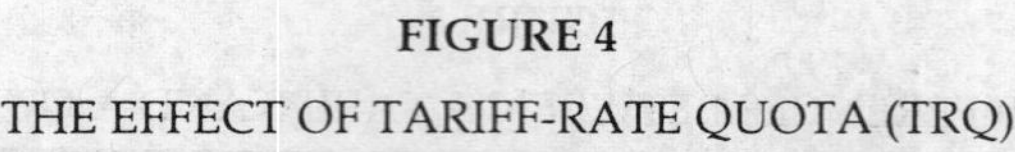

FIGURE 4

THE EFFECT OF TARIFF-RATE QUOTA (TRQ)

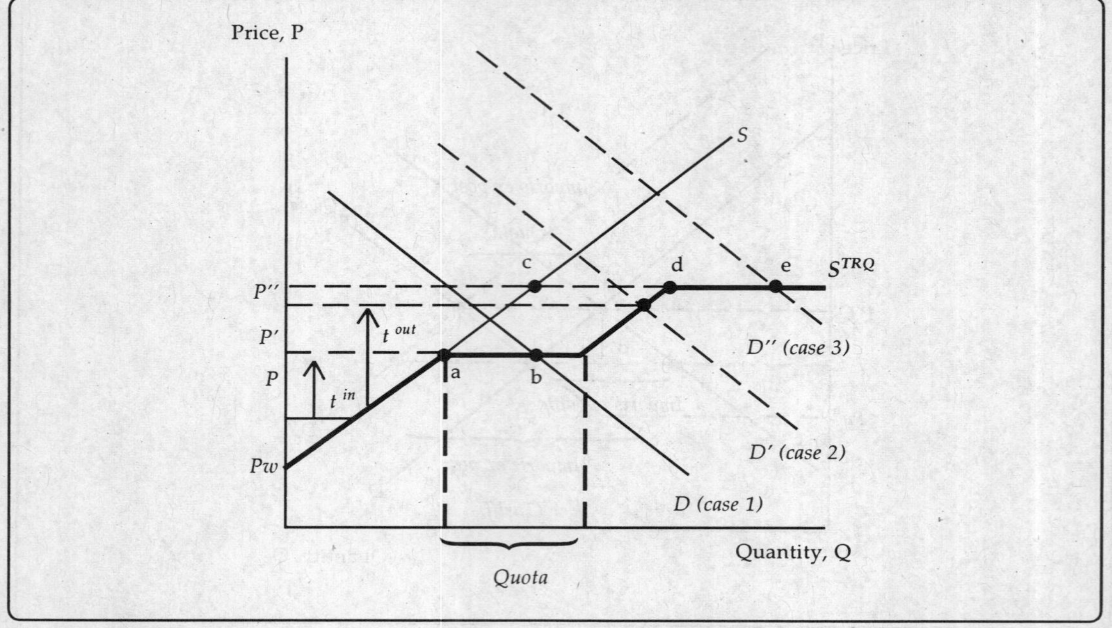

profitable. The price for these additional units of imports is equal to $P'' = P_W + t\ out$ and the volume of additional imports is equal to the amount *de*. Total imports in Case 3 are equal to imports under the in- and out-of-quota tariff, i.e. to the amount *ce*.

Thus, tariffs are more transparent, easy to administer and the revenue created is collected by the government (as opposed to quotas where scarcity premia (quota rents) might be "captured" by exporters or importers depending on the method for allocating quota shares, unless these are auctioned off). However, once political considerations enter the picture, quotas may be the preferred instrument of protection for the very same reasons. For example, fixed quota limits ensure that any demand increases beyond the quota volume are met by the domestic industry and not by imports. Disregarding the added inefficiencies that this creates, governments might see a political advantage in being able to "guarantee" to the affected industry a fixed upper limit on imports.

In general, the existence of quota rents creates specific interests that politicians might wish to acommodate. Since, under the SGA, quota shares are distributed on the basis of historical market shares (and not auctioned off), these may even be transferred to foreign producers, which may help governments appease trading partners and prevent possible retaliatory action emphasizes that policy-makers may on purpose choose quotas as a less transparent instrument in order to conceal political favouritism and reduce the risk of displeasing a large number of voters.

Furthermore, under the assumption that the required adjustment by the domestic industry involves marginal costs that decrease with cumulative production learning, and the first-best policy of production subsidies is unavailable on budgetary or political grounds, the under certain assumptions, quotas are preferable to tariffs in order to increase domestic production at the expense of imports, assuming that trade policy changes are costly and that it makes sense for policy-makers to set a fixed tariff or quota level only once (or a limited number of times). However, the optimal tariff needs to decrease as the adjustment progresses until it reaches zero at the end of the learning period.

A fixed tariff may not offer enough protection early in the adjustment period and be too restrictive towards the end. Conversely, if a quota is set at the long-term consumption level of foreign goods (i.e. the amount of imports once the domestic industry has adjusted), the domestic industry naturally decreases costs until the adjustment is completed. This also implies that quotas require less information about adjustment in the learning period, notably no information on the adjustment process. However, the domestic firms are encouraged to adjust more quickly the higher the effective costs of imports via tariff protection in order to enjoy higher profits as long as possible until the protection phase-out date. By contrast, quotas set at the long-term level of imports (i.e. when marginal costs of the domestic industry have stabilized after the adjustment process) would reduce the incentive to innovate since they do not increase a foreign firm's effective costs as much as tariff protection would do.

TARIFF WELFARE EFFECTS

All the theories on trade illustrate the same basic proposition : *Free trade maximises world output*. Furthermore, these theories show that free trade is beneficial to all of the participating countries. Each country can escape the confines of its own resource endowment to consume a collection of commodities better than the best it can produce. Why, then, do we still hear so much clamor for protective tariffs and other trade barriers ? The answer to this question has two parts. Many fallacious arguments against foreign trade are easily refuted but have a peculiar immunity to logic. Economists can demolish the protectionists' arguments, but speeches about "cheap foreign labour" and the "imperatives of national defense" have enormous popular appeal. Furthermore, several of the arguments for tariffs survive rigorous analysis. Free trade may be best for the world as a whole, but it may not be best from a single country's standpoint : tariffs and other trade barriers may sometimes be employed to redistribute the gains from trade in favour of one country, to redistribute income within a single country, to stimulate domestic employment, or to facilitate economic development. Undoubtedly, a country by restricting imports with a tax can sometimes force down the price at which other countries sell it, and thus improve its terms of trade. However, if it carries the process too far, the loss it suffers by foregoing the consumption of imported products will exceed the gain it takes by reducing foreign prices. The monopolist faces as analogous danger : if he cuts back his output too severely, he will lose more on volume than he gains on price. The fact remains, however : a country that enjoys a strategic position in world trade can rearrange the gains from trade in its own favour by a judicious use of import restrictions.

Figure-5 illustrates the use of tariffs to this end, showing trade in cotton cloth between Fewmen and Manymen. As in an ordinary supply-and-demand diagram, the price of cloth is measured on the vertical axis and the quantity of cloth is measured on the horizontal axis. Look first at Panel A of Figure-5, which shows Fewmen's own supply curve of cotton cloth, S_d, and the supply curve of exports from Manymen, S_f. When the price of cloth is OP_1, Fewmen's own producers will lsupply *Ob* and Manymen's exporters will supply *Oa*. The sum of these two quantities is OQ_1 in Panel *B*, a point on the aggregate supply curve of cotton cloth, S_a, obtained by the addition of S_d and S_f. As Fewmen's demand curve, D_d intersects S_a at R_1, OQ_1 will be consumed at the price OP_1.

Now suppose that Fewmen imposes a 30 per cent tariff, intercepting that fraction of its citizens' expenditure on cotton cloth bought from Manymen's exporters. The

FIGURE-5

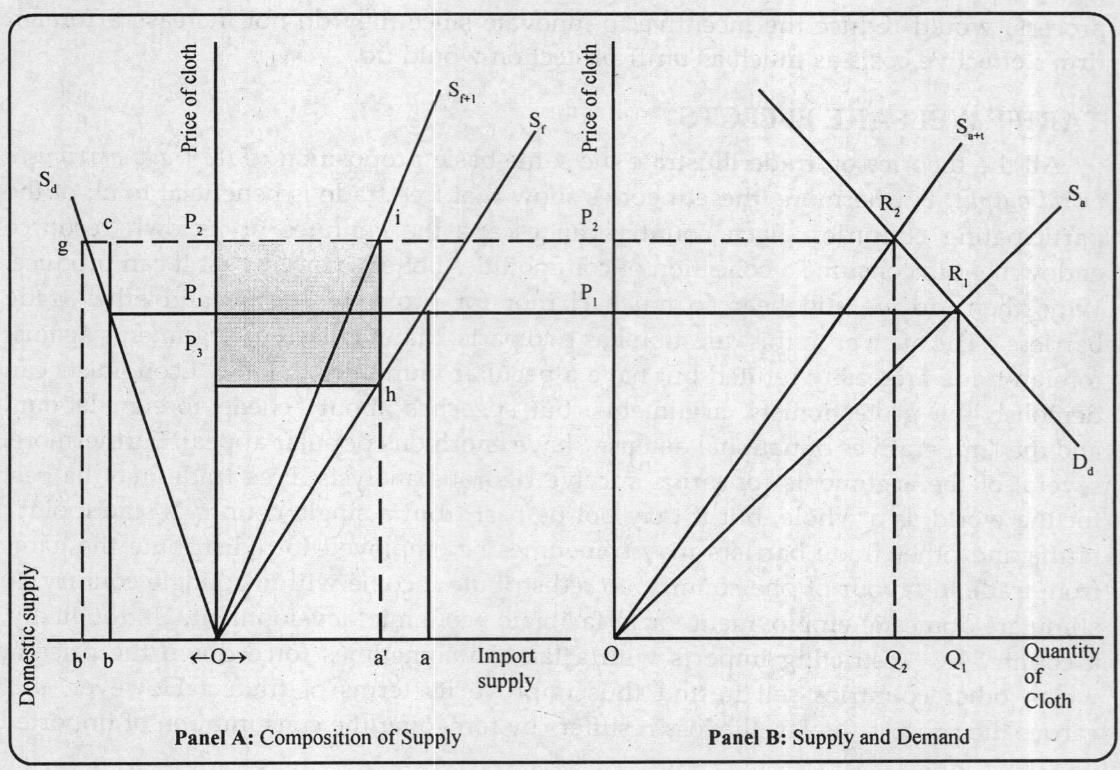

price of cloth in Fewmen has now to exceed the price charged by Manymen; the export supply curve, S_f must be displaced to S_{f+t} so that *ih/ha'* is 30 per cent of *ha'*, and the aggregate supply curve, S_a must shift to $S_{a+t'}$ becoming the sum of domestic supply, S_d and Manymen's export supply with the tariff, S_{f+t}. Supply and demand will be equal at the point R_2 with the quantity consumed at OQ_2 (equal to *Ob'* plus *Oa'*) and the price of cloth at OP_2 in Fewmen's own market.

This tariff on cotton cloth has several effects. Because the price of cloth has risen in Fewmen, there has been a drop in Fewmen's cloth consumption by Q_2Q_1 in Panel B. For that same reason, however, there is a new stimulus to local production, and Fewmen's own output has been enlarged by *bb'* in Panel A. Hence, there is a double squeeze on imports from Manymen—a decrease in consumption and an increase in import-competing production, so that imports from Manymen fall by *a'a* in Panel A. Finally, Fewmen's government collects P_2P_3 of tariff on each yard of imported cloth, for a total of P_2ihP_3, the shaded area in Panel A.

To complete the analysis of Fewmen's tariff, we would have to allow for the impact of this new tax revenue on Fewmen's fiscal policies. It could spend this revenue or remit it to the public by lowering some other tax; the final equilibrium position depends on its decision. Bet let us disregard this last refinement and suppose that the point R_2 locates the exact equilibrium position once the tariff is imposed. Notice the price paid by Fewmen's citizens is higher than it was under free trade (OP_2 is higher than OP_1), but that the price paid to Manymen's exporters is lower than it was free trade (OP_3 is lower than OP_1). Fewmen is able to obtain its imports more cheaply — at a smaller sacrifice of domestic resources. It has secured better terms of trade.

Tariffs and the Distribution of Domestic Income

Tariffs can also be employed to alter the domestic distribution of income. Remember that the product-price differences which give rise to trade have their clear counterparts in factor-price differences. Remember, too, that free trade tends to equalise product prices between the participating countries and, therefore, to equalise those countries' factor prices.

Now let us turn the argument on end. Starting with free trade and equal factor prices in Fewmen and Manymen, let Fewmen impose a tariff on imported cloth. This will raise the price of cloth in Fewmen and lower it in Manymen. It will thereby raise the wage rate in Fewmen and will reduce rental rates on machines. The tariff will encourage Fewmen's cloth production and will discourage its car production, for Fewmen's auto exports will contract with the drop in its cloth imports. In consequence, the tariff will increase Fewmen's demand for labour (the input used intensively in cloth production) and will lower its demand for machines (the input used intensively in car production). It will raise Fewmen's wage rates and reduce Fewmen's rental rates, redistributing income in favour of labour.

This argument has its approximate counterpart in Figure-5. The increase in domestic cloth production caused by the tariff (*Ob* to *Ob′* in Panel *A*) will raise the incomes of the factors of production already employed in the cloth industry, even as it adds to production and employment in that industry. Under free trade, the industry was earning a gross income equal to OP_1eb. With a tariff, it will earn OP_2gb'. The increase can be broken down into two parts : *gcbb′*, which goes to the newly employed factors of production (those that produce the extra cloth *bb′*) and cP_2P_1e, which goes to the factors of production already employed in making cloth (those that produced the original Ob of cloth).

Equity versus Efficiency

Tariffs are an inefficient way to redistribute income. They eat away a part of the pie they are redividing, sacrificing output in the name of equity. Countries with the market power to affect the terms of trade by imposing tariff — and the pressure groups that influence domestic legislative processes — are not necessarily deserving of aid through redistribution.

This conclusion follows directly from free trade. Any deviation from free trade will reduce world production, leaving less to go around. Figure-5 illustrates this point, too. It shows that a tariff replaces low-cost imports with high-cost domestic production. When a tariff is imposed, the last unit of domestic cloth will cost OP_2 dollars to produce (as its price must equal its marginal cost). By contrast, the last unit of imported cloth will cost OP_3 dollars (P_3P_2 dollars less). Hence, the substitution of domestic for foreign cloth fostered by a tariff is wasteful of world resources.

Tariffs and Employment

Tariffs may also be imposed to affect the utilisation of resources — the levels of employment and production. For instance, when two countries start to trade, they may not strike an equilibrium right away. One country's prices may be higher than the other's when those prices are compared at the prevailing exchange rate, and that country will be compelled to reduce its wage rates. If it fails to do so, its least efficient industries will shrink, yet its more efficient industries will not grow to take up the slack. The country will trade from a point on that frontier, and free trade may be worse than no trade at all. If, then, wage rates and other costs are very rigid, a country may gain by restricting its foreign trade. Tariffs will divert demand from foreign to domestic goods, raising domestic output and employment. This result is most likely to occur if the country's unemployed resources are concentrated in its import-competing industries. Tariffs can also combat unemployment caused by a decline in domestic demand during the business cycle, rather than by wage and price disparities revealed at the opening of trade.

Once again, however, tariffs are inefficient policy instruments. They can only stimulate employment by expanding import-competing industries, not the more efficient export industries. Far better, then, to foster wage-rate flexibility or, what may be simpler, to change the exchange rate until a high cost country's prices are aligned with those of its competitors. Such a country should devalue its currency, charging its citizens more for a unit of foreign currency and selling its own currency more cheaply to foreigners. A devaluation raises the domestic price of foreign goods (imports), as foreign currency becomes more expensive. To this extent, it is much like a tariff. But a devaluation also lowers the foreign price of domestic goods (exports), as domestic currency becomes cheaper for foreigners. Unlike a tariff, a devaluation stimulates export industries alongwith import-competing industries, and does not distort resource allocation. To put the same point more strongly; tariffs tend to shift one country's unemployment onto its trading partners. One country's import-competing industries (those that benefit from tariff protection) are other countries' export industries (those that make the best use of their resource endowments). Tariffs are a "beggar-my-neighbour" remedy for unemployment.

Tariffs and Economic Transformation

Most of the standard arguments for tariff protection imply a permanent departure from free trade. One group of arguments, however, advocates a temporary deviation. From time to time, it is said, a country must make major changes in its product mix. It must reallocate resources in a large way, not just at the margin, and may find it easier to make the change behind the protection of a tariff wall.

There are two versions of this argument for transitional protection : one of them promises economies of scale, the other promises economies of age. The first version reminds us that production costs may rise quite steeply for a while, but will begin to fall when output has attained a level which justifies the use of modern machinery and mass-production methods. It consequently recommends that tariffs be imposed to stimulate domestic production and that those tariffs be retained until the growth of the internal market has allowed domestic firms to imitate the most efficient methods used in other countries. Once they are "over the hump", it is argued, domestic producers will become fully competitive and may even be able to export, so that they will not need permanent protection, and tariffs can be cut.

The second version of the argument urges protection for an "infant industry". A young industry may be less efficient than one which has been long established. It may lack seasoned managers, skilled labour, and reliable suppliers of raw materials. Hence, a young industry may warrant protection until it has matured and cut back its unit costs so as to compete with foreign producers. In effect, this version forecasts that temporary tariffs to young industries will actually expand and production-possibilities frontier, and that world output will then be greater because of the transitional departure from free trade.

Both of these versions enjoy widespread respect, for neither has any analytical defect. But enormous problems must be solved in order to apply them correctly. *First,* one must decide which industries can capture sufficient economies of scale or economies of age to survive after tariffs have been removed. If a country protects all its young industries, it will waste precious resources; almost any industry can grow if given sufficient protection, but some will not endure when their tariffs end. Next, one must determine how large a tariff is required to foster the development of a healthy infant. Too much protection will encourage an excessive expansion, and the protected industries will contract when tariffs are removed. Finally, one must decide if the gains are worth the cost. The use of tariffs, even temporarily, will reduce world output during the transition and may even reduce the real income of the country applying them. These direct and certain losses must be weighed against the distant and uncertain gains offered by protection.

Transitional protection can also pose practical problems. Few industries will readily concede that they have grown up and do not need their tariffs. During their adolescence, moreover, they will have acquired influential spokesmen in government, having become important to the national or regional economy. It will then be difficult to strip them of their tariffs and expose them of the competition they grow up to face. Finally, some governments seem to believe that tariffs can create new industries; they restrict imports even when skilled labour, raw materials, and capital are too scarce to allow industrial development.

In brief, the occasions which justify transitional protection may be quite rare, and an indiscriminate application of transitional arguments may do great damage. As with most other tariff arguments, there may be better ways to reach an objective — ways that do not sacrifice income or invite retaliation. Similarly, the trade-creating regional blocks by generating income and efficiency effects may constitute a step toward global free trade.

QUESTIONS

1. Why is a country's demand curve for imports of a good more elastic (or flatter) than the consumer's total demand curve for the good?
2. Why is country's supply curve of exports of a good more elastic (or flatter) than the supply curve of the home producers of the good?
3. Other things being equal, why does greater elasticity in the supply of imports schedule for a good mean that the importing country's consumers of the good are more likely than the foreign suppliers of the goods to bear the burden of an import tariff?
4. How can the tariffs on the import of good lead to decline in consumption of both the import and export good?
5. How does an import quota differ from a tarif? Can a government capture the quota rent? How?
6. What is the difference between an export tax and export subsidy? Which instrument are domestic consumers likely to prefer? Why?

7. If you were an import-competing producer in a growing market, which trade instrument would you prefer—a tariff, an import quota, or subsidy? Why?
8. Is it ever possible for a large country to gain from the imposition of an import quota? Why?
9. Suppose that an export tax rather than an import tariff is used to improve the terms of trade. Will the results be the same? Explain.

REFERENCES

Ball, D.A. and W.A., McCullock, Jr., *International Business— Introduction md Economy,* Plano, Tex.; Business Publications, 1988.

Czinkota, M.R., P. Rivoli, and I.A. Ronkainen, *Introduction Business,* Dryder Press, 1989.

Daniel, J.D., and L.H. Radebaugh, *International Business — Environment and Operations,* Addison - Wasley, 1986.

Garland, J. and R.N. Farmer, *International Dimensions of Busines Policy md Stragegy,* PWS-KENT, 1986.

Gross, R.; and D. Kujawa, *International Business,* Irwin, III. Homewood, 1988.

Heller, H.R., *International Trade,* Englewood Cliffs, N.J.: Prentice-Hall, 1973.

Kefalas, A.G., *Global Business Strategy,* South-Western, 1990.

Rugman, A.D. Lecraw, and L.D. Bosta, *International Business Firm and Environment,* McGraw Hill, 1985.

Crandall, R. (1984) "Import Quotas and the Automobile Industry: The Cost of Protectionism," *Brookings Review,* Summer.

Francois, J. and Hall, K. (1997) "Partial Equilibrium Modeling," in J. Francois and K. Reinert (eds) *Applied Methods for Trade Policy Analysis,* New York: Cambridge University Press.

Hufbauer, G., and Elliott, K. (1994) *Measuring the Costs of Protection in the United States,* Washington, DC: Institute for International Economics.

Messerlin, P. (2001) *Measuring the Cost of Protection in Europe,* Washington, DC: Institute for International

4

'FAIR' TRADE: CONTINGENCY MEASURES

INTRODUCTION

Contingent protection measure are used by governments in importing countries when they feel that firms in exporting countries are conducting their international commerce in a manner which is 'unfair' to their domestic firms. The idea of 'fair' trade defies a workable definition in economics but remains a conceptual notion upon which many countries based their contingent protection. 'Fair' trade is often discussed in the context of the equally indefensible concept of the level playing field. Tariffs are applied to the goods of the exporter at rates which mitigate the perceived economic damage and their removal is contingent upon the 'unfair' practices being halted. Contingent protection measures are applied in two cases--when dumping occurs and when trade-distorting subsidies are used by an exporting country.

Resorting to contingency protection is influenced by external circumstances and *atmospheric.* To ensure that the channels of trade remain open in the global economic downturn, well-balanced contingency measures, designed primarily to deal with a variety of unanticipated market situations, are fundamental to the effectiveness and stability of trading system. The chapter examines the various contigency measures resorted, as well as their implications, for the trading system in terms of how they are designed and deployed.

DUMPING

In theory, dumping is the international equivalent of certain business practices which are considered unacceptable even when firms sell only in their domestic market. The primary unacceptable business practice which anti-dumping measures attempt to address is the international equivalent of predatory pricing. *Predatory pricing is selling below cost to gain a strategic market advantage.*

WHY DO FIRMS DUMP GOODS?

Dumping is generally seen either as an exercise by foreign firms of monopoly power in international trade or as a response to changing demand coupled with an inability to adjust production capacity over the course of the business cycle. Dumping as a reflection of monopoly power, in international trade, can be found essentially in the form of "price discrimination", in which a firm with monopoly or market power charges different prices to consumers in the home and export markets. Charging a lower price to consumers in the export market will be profitable to the monopolist if consumers in the export market are more responsive than consumers at home to price changes, meaning that they will be more inclined to decrease their demand if the price of the product goes up demand is elastic. This difference in demand elasticity between the home and export market can arise if the dumping firm faces competition in the export market but retains a monopoly in its home market.

The assumption that firm has a monopoly in its home market and that the domestic market is oligopolistic is the hallmark of dumping. The presence of competition means any increase in the price charged by the dumping firm will lead consumers to switch to the goods offered by other firms in the domestic market. To sutain price discrimination for the same product, the firm with monopoly power must be able to segment or separate its home and export markets, otherwise arbitrage – the goods selling in the cheaper market will be resold in the high price market – will simply erase the price differential. This segmentation can occur because of trade barriers in the exporting country or high transport costs.

Why should a firm resort to dumping? What are the motives of the firm and the duration of the dumping? The motives include disposing of a surplus, creating goodwill in a new market, predatory dumping (i.e. seeking to establish a monopoly by driving domestic producers out of business), retaliation against dumping by a foreign firm and retaining reduced unit cost through the expansion of output and sales in the export market. The duration of dumping can be sporadic, intermittent or continuous.

In a situation of international oligopoly, the foreign and domestic firms both having market power may competing in both markets, lead to reciprocal dumping. The foreign firm dumps goods in the domestic market and the domestic firm dumps goods in the foreign market. This departs from the usual dumping, where the domestic firm only serves the domestic market while the foreign firm has a monopoly of its own market. Reciprocal dumping creates interesting interactions between the domestic and foreign governments, including tit-for-tat or retaliatory anti-dumping actions.

Reciprocal dumping occurs because of two features: domestic and foreign firms act as competitors and both firms incur transport costs when they export. Competition and the existence of transport cost give the domestic firm a larger share of the domestic market but still leave the foreign firm with a foothold in the domestic market. Furthermore, since a competitor perceives a demand elasticity – that is, the degree of responsiveness to a price change – equal to the industry elasticity divided by its own market share, each firm faces a more elastic – or more price-responsive – demand in its export market. This difference between the demand elasticities faced by the imperfectly competitive firms in the domestic and foreign markets creates the condition for dumping (the f.o.b. – free on board – price for exports is below the price charged in the home market). Since both firms face this difference in demand elasticities in the domestic and foreign markets, there is reciprocal dumping.

If a firm has market power, will it not attempt "predatory" dumping, selling at a sufficiently low price so that domestic producers are eventually driven out of business and the foreign firm is then able to establish a monopoly?

In engaging in predatory dumping, the foreign firm will have to incur losses upfront as it tries to undercut its competitor's price (this presupposes that the foreign and domestic firms have similar cost structures). Assuming that it is successful in eventually driving out its competitor, it will have to subsequently raise its price so as to recoup the initial losses and earn a positive rate of return. But raising its price will invite entrants to the market, which might be new domestic producers or other foreign exporters, thus defeating the purpose of predatory dumping. If it does not raise its price sufficiently, it may not be able to recoup its initial losses. Thus, the set of conditions under which predatory dumping can be successful appears to be quite difficult to realize in practice. However, such instances appear to be rare.

Some of these difficulties of predatory dumping may be overcome by noting that this behaviour could arise if the domestic firm has incomplete information or if credit markets are imperfect. The domestic firm may be unable to secure loans from financial markets which would allow it to survive the initial period of dumping by the foreign firm. The reason for this is that financial markets do not have complete information and project the domestic firm's prospects based on its current profits. Thus, in the face of foreign dumping and losses by the domestic firm, financial markets deny it credit even though in reality the domestic firm may be able to recover if it receives financing to tide it over. Further, the domestic firm may not know for sure whether its foreign rival is a low-cost producer. If the foreign firm is a low-cost producer, the domestic firm will be unable to compete successfully. By dumping, the foreign firm can, irrespective of its actual costs, act like a low-cost competitor and force the domestic firm to close down. Thus, dumping can be a rational strategy even for a high-cost foreign firm so long as its true costs are not known by the domestic firm.

While most explanations of dumping assume that firms who engage in this behaviour must have market power. In certain situation dumping, in the sense of selling in the export market at a price below the average cost of production, can also be the response of firms in perfectly competitive markets during economic downturns. The reason why the price of their goods is that they are unable to reduce their costs as quickly as their price during economic downturns.

In the face of a sudden drop in demand, output price can fall quickly while the firm's lack of flexibility in laying off workers or reducing its capital stock means that it would not be able to adjust its production capacity to the same extent and consequently its costs. Thus, dumping is a natural consequence of a world where perfectly competitive firms face uncertainty in terms of demand for their output and are unable to adjust their production processes quickly. It suggests that dumping may be more frequent in cyclical industries that experience regular fluctuations in demand and in industries where it is difficult to adjust capacity.

Finally, dumping can also be a way for firms to gain valuable experience or increase their technological knowledge, thereby increasing economic efficiency. It is argued that since countries have different levels of technological knowledge, the firms in the technologically backward country can only acquire technical know-how from engaging in production. A firm gains experience from producing goods; the acquired experience enables the firm to produce at lower costs in the future. This provides an incentive for domestic and foreign profit-maximizing firms to continue producing and exporting even if prices are below current costs. This is economically rational for a firm since producing and exporting even when prices are below current costs is a form of investment which pays off in future profitability. And if world demand is high enough, entry into the market by these firms can push down the world price below the opportunity cost of production, with the result that firms in the backward country take part in dumping.

Welfare Effects of Dumping

What are the effects of dumping on the economic welfare of the importing country? With the possible exception of predatory dumping, all other instances of dumping either increase, or at worst, have an ambiguous effect on, the economic welfare of the importing country. Of course, dumping is an example of the exercise of market power. But within this context of imperfectly competitive markets, dumping may increase efficiency in resource allocation. In most circumstances, the welfare of the importing country increases as a result of dumping, as consumers and users of the product benefit from lower import prices, even though the reason for the reduction in price (the dumping) may vary.

Dumping arises from the sensitivity to price of domestic consumers, who would switch to other products if the price is raised. The foreign firm is willing to produce and sell at a price below average cost as a form of investment to increase productivity in the future. So not only are current prices charged by the foreign firm lower but its future price will be lower as well because of the acquisition of technological know-how or of production experience. Business cycle movements and sluggish adjustment in the industry lead the foreign firm to sell at a price advantageous to domestic consumers.

The exception to this general conclusion that dumping is beneficial to the importing country is the case of successful predatory dumping. Domestic consumers and other users of the dumped product may benefit from low prices during the initial stage of dumping but they will face higher prices in the future when the foreign producer acquires monopoly power in the domestic market. If predatory dumping is successful, i.e. the foreign firm's discounted profits from dumping exceed its profits in the no-dumping scenario, consumers will be worse off as initially low prices do not compensate for the higher prices later on.

In the reciprocal dumping the welfare effects of dumping are ambiguous because of two opposing forces. Reciprocal dumping by domestic and foreign firms increases competition and reduces the market power of the incumbent firm in its domestic market. However, economic resources are wasted through the cost of transporting goods between the two countries. Whether welfare rises or not depends on the magnitudes of these two opposing effects.

In all these cases, dumping will be detrimental to domestic industry. The presence of dumped imports increases the competition faced by domestic industry and often leads to a reduction in domestic output. In the predatory dumping case, the domestic industry will cease to exist.

The Benefits and Risks Associated With the Use of Antidumping Actions

To counteract dumping and its economic effects, many countries have turned to anti-dumping law, which allows national authorities to apply antidumping measures on imports as long as dumping has taken place and injury has been caused to domestic industry. Anti-dumping policy can act like a safety valve to let off protectionist steam which might otherwise threaten a government's programme of trade reform. This is an important benefit that should be kept in mind. *How would the greater use of contingent protection affect the behaviour of foreign and domestic firms, trade volumes and the economic welfare of the importing country?*

The effects of anti-dumping measures can be compared with the effects of a tariff on imports. Similar to a tariff, anti-dumping duties will improve the circumstances of domestic producers, raise revenues for government but increase the cost of imports for domestic users or consumers. Thus, the standard economic analysis of tariff protection can be applied to analyze the likely effects of antidumping measures. However, there are important features of anti-dumping policy that this standard analysis will fail to take into account and which need to be considered as well.

(i) Trade Diversion

Anti-dumping duties are not applied to all sources of imports, which raises the possibility of import diversion – i.e. imports from one country are reduced while there is an increase in imports from another country. The application of anti-dumping duties may not significantly reduce the total level of imports, since imports from those sources not subject to antidumping action may just take the place of those subject to the duties.

(ii) Tariff-Jumping Foreign Direct Investment (FDI)

Another complication is that foreign firms who are the subject of anti-dumping action may decide to "jump" the anti-dumping tariff by establishing a presence, through direct investment, in the importing country. There are some who argue that tariff-jumping FDI may be even more of a threat to domestic producers than dumped imports. They argue that a high level of protection in the form of anti-dumping duties may be damaging to an import-competing industry as this would encourage inward FDI, which could be even less desirable to the domestic industry than import competition. A government that is unduly influenced by the domestic import competing industry will consequently set the level of protection low enough to limit direct foreign entry.

(iii) Strategic Behaviour

The presence of anti-dumping legislation may itself affect the strategic behaviour of domestic and foreign firms and in ways that make it difficult to predict the impact on the welfare of the importing country. Strategic behaviour refers to actions taken by firms that are intended to influence the market environment in which they compete, including the behaviour of their competitors. It can include actions to influence rivals to act cooperatively (e.g. form a cartel) or non-cooperatively. The actions have the objective of raising the firm's profits at the expense of rivals. Such behaviour is characteristic of firms which operate in imperfectly competitive markets.

Non-Cooperative Outcomes: In the case of non-cooperative behaviour – i.e. the domestic and foreign firms do not end up colluding with one another in the form of a cartel, for example – the possibility of anti-dumping investigations can lead to a change in the pricing and output behaviour of foreign and domestic firms. Depending on whether firms compete on quantity or on price, the strategic and welfare effects will be different.

The behaviour of both the foreign and domestic firm is altered by anti-dumping policy. Anti-dumping policy creates a credible threat of imposing future duties based on the current margin between the foreign firm's export price and the price it charges in its home market. The domestic firm has an incentive to increase this margin so that there can be a basis for an anti-dumping investigation, while the foreign firm will want to reduce this differential. If firms compete on the basis of quantity, the domestic firm can increase this margin by expanding current production. This drives down price, while the foreign firm will want to lower exports to mitigate the downward pressure on price. So long as the domestic firm has a larger share of the domestic market, it will succeed in decreasing price. Since a reduction in price benefits domestic consumers and users, the presence of anti-dumping policy will tend to increase the domestic country's welfare.

If firms compete on price however, anti-dumping policy will tend to worsen domestic welfare. Competition will force the domestic and foreign firms to charge the same price in the domestic market. This will trigger an anti-dumping duty on the foreign firm because it charges a higher price in its home market, where it has a monopoly and charges the monopoly price. The anti-dumping duty on imports raises the price in the domestic market, penalizing consumers and users.

No matter what definition of dumping is used, if firms compete on the basis of quantity, the domestic firm will increase production in the first period so as to lower price and to create the conditions for an anti-dumping action to be taken against the foreign firm. This will tend to increase welfare in the domestic economy.

One of the reasons for dumping is the firm's desire to maintain production capacity in the face of a reduction in demand. Dumping can result from the combination of a fall in demand and sluggish industry adjustment. For the foreign firm, the ability to "dump" in the domestic market during periods of slack demand reduces the cost of maintaining spare capacity. Under these circumstances, one of the effects of having anti-dumping law in the domestic market may be the reduction of production capacity by the foreign firm. With anti-dumping law, domestic firms can file anti-dumping petitions during downturns, reducing the volume of imports directly during such periods. This antidumping activity raises the cost to the foreign firm of holding excess capacity and leads to a scaling back of its spare capacity. Thus, the volume of imports is reduced indirectly as the foreign firm reduces the scale of its operations. While this helps domestic producers, the overall impact on the domestic economy will be a reduction in economic welfare.

Table-1 shows that anti-dumping investigations initiated by all countries, at a high in 2001 declined almost steadily till 2007. They picked up once again in 2008 but started declining to reach a low in 2011. However, in 2012 they have again increased with 114 investigations (up to June) compared to 68 in 2011 (up to June). In 2011 India topped the list of countries initiating such investigations, but in 2012 (up to June) Brazil is at the top followed by Argentina and Canada. India, the US, and EU with seven investigations each are at fourth spot.

During 2012-13 (1.4.2012 to 31.12.2012), 10 fresh cases have been initiated by the Directorate General of Anti-dumping and Allied Duties (DGAD). The countries involved in these investigations are China PR, the European Union, Korea RP, Malaysia, Mexico, Taiwan, Thailand, Turkey, Saudi Arabia, and the USA.

TABLE-1
Investigations Initiated by Top Ten Users of Anti-Dumping Measures 1995-2012

Country	1995	2001	2002	2003	2005	2007	2008	2009	2010	2011	2011	2012	1995-
											Jan.-June		2012*
India	6	79	81	46	28	47	55	31	41	19	10	7	663
United States	14	77	35	37	12	28	16	20	3	15	9	7	465
European Union	33	28	20	7	24	9	19	15	15	17	8	7	444
Argentina	27	28	14	1	12	8	19	28	14	7	4	10	301
Brazil	5	17	8	4	6	13	23	9	37	16	11	26	258
Australia	5	24	16	8	7	2	6	9	7	18	2	6	241
South Africa	16	6	4	8	23	5	3	3	0	4	1	0	216
China	0	14	30	22	24	4	14	17	8	5	0	4	195
Canada	11	25	5	15	1	1	3	6	2	2	0	10	165
Turkey	0	15	18	11	12	6	23	6	2	2	1	6	154
All countries	157	372	315	234	201	165	213	209	172	155	68	114	4125

Source: WTO *Upto June 2012.

While the OECD (Organization for Economic Cooperation and Development) - WTO - UNCTAD (United Nations Conference on Trade and Development) joint report of October 2012 on G-20[Group of 20] Trade and Investment Measures has pointed towards a slowdown in trade-restrictive measures, the persistence of the global crisis has added to political and economic pressures on governments to resort to contingency trade policies and non-tariff measures (NTMs). Moreover the new measures implemented over the last year can be considered as restricting or potentially restricting trade add to the restrictions adopted since the outbreak of the global crisis. The trade coverage of the restrictive measures put in place since October 2008, excluding those that have been terminated, is estimated to be around 3 per cent of world merchandise trade and 4 per cent of the trade of G-20 economies.

How is the provision of anti-dumping protection to an "upstream" industry likely to also prompt "downstream" industries to seek similar protection. If the increasing input prices associated with upstream anti-dumping protection harm the competitiveness of import-competing downstream firms, then anti-dumping protection provides little benefit to both sectors. They both lose since downstream industries face higher input prices while the upstream industry loses its customers (the downstream sector). However, since protection in the upstream market inflicts injury on downstream industries, this provides them with a basis on which to also seek anti-dumping protection. Hence, there is a tendency for anti-dumping protection to cascade down the production stream, with the protection initially provided to the upstream industry ultimately being extended to the downstream sector as well. Furthermore, the knowledge that the downstream sector will be able to secure similar protection makes it easier for the upstream industry to petition for anti-dumping relief in the first place.

What are the effects of anti-dumping policy in markets where firms compete on the basis of both the price and the quality of their product? One reason why imports may be priced lower than the domestic product is because they have lower quality. If the lower-quality foreign firm is compelled by anti-dumping measures to match the price of the domestic product, it will need to compete more aggressively on the basis of quality. Maintaining a low quality will no longer suffice to compete successfully against domestic firms. This can lead to a quality reversal, in which the foreign firm becomes the quality-producing leader. The quality upgrading of foreign imports as a response to the imposition of trade restrictions, such as a quota, is well-known. Thus, while anti-dumping policy can erase the price differential between imports and domestic output, it can hurt the long-term prospects of the domestic industry by giving the foreign firm the incentive and the opportunity to upgrade the quality of its product.

Finally, an interesting perspective on anti-dumping law is provided by the outcome of strategic interaction not between firms but between governments instead. Hence, the starting point is the reciprocal dumping which is based on the domestic and foreign firms competing in both markets (home and domestic). Both firms also engage in dumping because their free on board (f.o.b.) export prices are less than what they charge at home. The reciprocal dumping outcome resembles a prisoner's dilemma problem, where both parties are worse off as a result of a lack of co-operation. There is economic inefficiency associated with both firms engaging in price discrimination since consumer surplus is lower.

The adoption by the domestic country of antidumping law lowers its economic welfare since the price of imports increases but it improves welfare in the other country. This is because the anti-dumping duty effectively ties the prices charged by the foreign firm in its export and home markets, since the dumping margin reflects the difference between the two prices. Thus, it will be optimal for the foreign firm to reduce the price it charges in its home market to reduce the antidumping duty it faces, increasing welfare in the foreign country. A similar outcome arises when it is only the foreign country which adopts antidumping law: its economic welfare decreases while the domestic country's welfare improves. Only if both countries adopt anti-dumping laws will both their welfare simultaneously increase because the laws eliminate price discrimination globally. The spread of anti-dumping laws worldwide could be seen as a cooperative agreement on the part of governments to avoid the prisoner's dilemma problem.

The strategic interaction between governments is also a motive for anti-dumping actions. It is argued that there is a retaliatory motivation behind countries' use of anti-dumping measures because they appear to take such actions against those that have previously subjected them to anti-dumping investigations. Those who retaliate may believe that previous users of anti-dumping measures are not following a prior commitment to trade openness. Thus, using anti-dumping actions in this strategic fashion is consistent with a strategy of punishing those countries that deviate from this course and deterring such deviation in the future. The recourse to anti-dumping measures which could be targeted at specific countries, than to safeguards.

How Anti-Dumping Measures Can be Used to Facilitate Collusion? Anti-dumping law can lead to tacit collusion between domestic and foreign firms, fixing prices or outputs. The prospect of anti-dumping duties is used by the domestic industry to threaten the foreign industry to agree to collude. If the foreign industry does not agree to collude with domestic industry, the anti-dumping investigation is allowed to proceed with the resulting threat of duties to be imposed on foreign firms. If firms agree to collude, the anti-dumping petition is withdrawn and both domestic and foreign firms will charge higher prices in the domestic market by increasing the artificial scarcity of their output in the importing country. Consumers and other users in the importing country suffer from these higher prices while the domestic government foregoes revenues from anti-dumping duties.

The likelihood that domestic industry will withdraw anti-dumping petitions, and subsequently collude, is affected by the cost of coordinating among the firms and the bargaining strength of domestic industry relative to foreign firms. The greater the number of firms, both domestic and foreign, that need to collude, the greater the coordination costs. This makes the possibility of arriving at an agreement more difficult. The greater the bargaining power of domestic firms, the greater the likelihood of getting foreign firms to agree to collude.

Further there is a possibility of self-enforcing\ agreements between the domestic industry and the foreign firm. The agreements take the form of a promise by the domestic industry not to initiate anti-dumping petitions in exchange for a promise by the foreign firm to export no more than a prespecified amount. For the foreign firm, the main benefit of the agreement is that it can continue to maintain a high price at home. This was not possible when it was faced with anti-dumping action, since under those circumstances it had to channel more of its production to its home market and reduce prices accordingly. For the domestic firms, the agreement means that imports are limited to an amount that is fixed in advance and they are also able to avoid the costs of filing an anti-dumping petition. Even though no anti-dumping suits are initiated, the agreement results in a volume of trade that is not significantly different from the situation when domestic firms were filing such petitions.

Anti-dumping policy influences the incentives for collusion. The domestic market prior to the adoption of anti-dumping legislation may already have cartels to some degree. None of the products sold by the domestic and foreign firms are too different or the cost structure of the firms too dissimilar, the anti-dumping policy can further increase collusion between foreign and domestic firms.

(iv) Other Effects

When the current output level reduces future production costs, domestic and foreign firms may dump products on foreign markets to gain experience. Anti-dumping enforcement, which poses a barrier to below-cost sales by foreign rivals, will reduce the incentive of foreign and domestic firms to undertake this "investment" to gain production experience. This may involve a welfare loss as society foregoes the opportunity of reducing future costs.

A similar concern about the possible impact of anti-dumping actions follows because firms in a technologically backward country can only acquire technological know-how by actually producing that good. The entry of these new firms into the market can result in prices falling below average cost of production. If anti-dumping investigations succeed in penalizing these new entrants, it will put a stop to the process of upgrading by the technologically backward country.

Finally, even in the case of predatory dumping, the welfare consequences of anti-dumping law are ambiguous. Where the domestic firm is hampered by its inability to access credit during the period of predatory dumping, an anti-dumping law may not insulate the domestic firm from this form of dumping. This is because the foreign firm's dumping may take place during a trough in the business cycle, in which case it will be difficult to prove that material injury to the domestic industry arises from dumping and not from other causes.

SUBSIDIES

Although governments usually design trade policies to reduce imports, but sometimes they attempt to encourage exports through subsides. This may occur because of a desire to improve country's trade account, aid a political powerful industry, or help a depressed region in which an export industry is located. Subsidy is broad term that covers any financial contribution by a public body whereby a benefit is conferred. It covers price or income supports (which may not involve a direct transfer or contribution). It also covers private bodies acting on behalf of the government. It is also made clear that such contributions as loans, guarantees, equity infusion and provision of goods are only subsidies if they confer a benefit, that is, are provided at rates that are better than those available on the market.

THE ECONOMICS OF SUBSIDIES

In a perfect market framework, i.e. perfect competition, perfect information, and no externalities (external effects not captured in market prices), subsidizing exports reduces national welfare because it results in the trading partner purchasing its imports more cheaply. However, certain groups in the exporting country are likely to benefit from the subsidy. If the perfect market assumption is relaxed, situations may arise where a government subsidy improves national welfare. An efficient subsidy would correct a market failure, bringing social and private costs and benefits into alignment.

(i) Subsidies in Perfect Markets

When the government of a large country grants an export subsidy to the producers of a particular good or service, these producers will initially earn more on their exports than on their domestic sales and thus they will have an incentive to export more. The price charged to domestic buyers, however, will soon increase to the level of the subsidised export price. Domestic demand will fall. Because the exporting country is assumed to be large, its increased exports will push down the world market price, deteriorating the country's terms-of-trade (i.e. the price of its exports relative to its imports). The importing country's terms-of-trade on the contrary will improve. Overall, despite an increase in traded flows, global welfare will decrease because the subsidy distorts the optimal allocation of resources. The subsidy will affect negatively the welfare of the exporting country, which will suffer both from a deadweight (efficiency) loss and from a terms-of-trade (distributional) loss. While the termsof- trade loss can be seen as a benefit for the importing country in the form of a terms-of-trade gain, the deadweight loss is a net loss for all parties.

The consequences of the subsidy are unevenly distributed in both the exporting and the importing countries. In the importing country, consumers or more generally buyers of the imported product will benefit from a lower price because of the subsidy, but import-competing producers will experience a loss. In the exporting country, subsidized producers will obviously benefit from the subsidy, while domestic consumers will be harmed because they will have to pay a higher price for the subsidized product and taxpayers will lose.

In an export subsidy, the size of the exporting country is crucial. When an export subsidy is implemented by a small exporting country, there is no effect upon the world price. When a large exporting country implements an export subsidy, it increases its exports and at the same time the world supply. This pushes the world price down due to terms of- trade effects. Figure 1 represents the trade flows for one particular good between two large entities, one exporting and one importing country. To simplify, all the exporting country's variables are denoted by an asterisk. The demand of the exporting country for the good is illustrated as D^* and its supply as S^*, generating an export supply curve denoted by *XS*. Similarly, in the importing country, demand for the good is denoted by curve *D* and its supply by curve S, yielding an import demand curve *MD*. In free trade (*FT*), the world price is given by *PFT* which corresponds to the intersection between the import demand and export supply in the world market, shown by point 1 in the middle panel.

The implementation of a specific subsidy (a fixed sum per unit) by the exporting country on its exports, denoted by *s**, shifts the export supply curve out to *XS'*. The export supply curve shifts down by the amount of the subsidy, reflecting the lower marginal cost of exports. Exports increase and the world price falls. In the importing market, the price falls from P_{FT} to P_1 which leads to an increase in demand from D_{FT} to D_1 (a move from point 1 to point 3 on the world market). On the other hand, the export subsidy raises the price in the exporting country and creates a wedge between the prices in the two markets equal to the subsidy. In other words, the price in the exporting country is determined by $P^*_1 = P_1 + s^*$. As a result, consumers in the exporting country reduce their consumption and producers export more at higher prices, as shown by the move from point 1 to point 2 on the export supply curve *XS*. Trade increases from Q_{FT} to Q_1.

The net welfare effect of an export subsidy on the importing country is positive. Indeed, although lower prices lead to lower production levels for import-competing firms, reducing their producer surplus by an amount equal to area *a*, as shown in the right diagram, the loss is more than compensated by an increase in consumer welfare, which equals the sum of *a, b, c* and *d*. In the exporting country, the welfare effect is negative. The consumer welfare loss is equal to areas *A+B*; producers gain *A+B+C* and the government expenditure is the area *B+C+D+E+F+G+H+I*. Therefore, there is a net welfare loss equal to the sum of *B*, the consumer deadweight loss, *D*, a deadweight loss associated with producers, and *E+F+G+H+I*, which is a terms-of-trade loss. The consumer loss is generated because some consumers are driven out of the market, and the producer deadweight loss is explained by the fact that additional and more expensive resources have to be used to increase exports, which would not have taken place without the export subsidy. At the world level, there is a deadweight loss equal to the sum of *b* and *d* plus the portion of the exporting country's terms-of-trade loss that is not compensated by a terms-of-trade gain in the importing country.

A production subsidy would have effects similar to those of an export subsidy. The main difference between the two is that with the production subsidy, the domestic price in the exporting country is pushed down by the fall in the world price prompted by the increase in supply. Consumers in the exporting country gain and so do producers, but the gains are more than offset by the loss to taxpayers.

In addition to subsidies that are provided in relation to some economic activity or another factor, such as production or export levels, governments also frequently provide subsidies to finance wholly or partially the acquisition of fixed assets, such as technology, plant and equipment. Such subsidies may be paid only once or a limited number of times and are often referred to as nonrecurring subsidies. These subsidies can have effects on competition that go beyond the period in which the subsidy is actually provided. They tend to have the effect of increasing investment by some firms in the relevant market. As a consequence, more firms will be active in the industry or existing firms will produce on a greater scale. This may have an impact on the conditions of competition in world markets. The duration of such effects on international competition depends, among other things, on the depreciation rate of the fixed asset and the evolution of demand in the years following the investment.

(ii) Subsidies in the Presence of Market Failures

In the presence of imperfect competition, governments can use subsidies to help national firms earn extra profits. The simplest case is when a government finances predatory pricing by its national producers in export markets. As a result of the predatory prices, domestic producers in the country that is the target of predatory practices are driven out of business and subsidized producers gain a dominant position, which they exploit by setting a monopoly price.

New trade theory models, characterized by imperfect competition in the form of oligopoly or monopolistic competition, were used to identify specific circumstances where intervention in the form of subsidies would be desirable. The intuition is that interventions which alter the strategic relationship between firms can give one firm an advantage over another in imperfectly competitive markets, where each firm's commercial decisions (output and pricing) are dependent on those of its rival. This idea can be illustrated using a simple model.

FIGURE 1

THE EFFECT OF AN EXPORT SUBSIDY IMPLEMENTED BY A LARGE COUNTRY

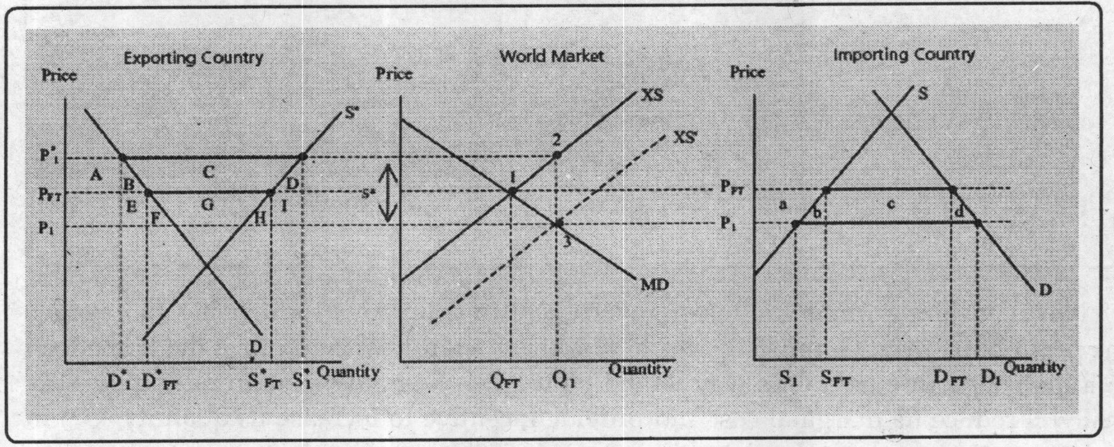

The model has two firms, located in different countries, that only export to a third-country market. The justification for this unrealistic assumption is that it drastically simplifies the welfare analysis: changes in firms' profits correspond to changes in national welfare. Conflicting changes in consumer surplus are assumed away so that in order to maximize national welfare, governments only need to maximize the domestic firm's profits.

Figure 2 is a graphical representation of the model when firms compete. The competition is best understood as firms choosing their production level by taking into consideration how much their rival produces. For instance, without government intervention, the equilibrium is depicted by point *n* in quantity space, which corresponds to the intersection of the two reaction functions $RF_H\ (Q_F\ )$ and $RF_F\ (Q_H\ )$. The home reaction function, $RF_H\ (Q_F\ )$, defines the home firm's quantity that allows the highest profit to be reached, given the quantity of the foreign firm, Q_F. $RF_F\ (Q_H\ )$ can be interpreted in a similar fashion. The home and foreign profits are respectively Π_H and Π_F, and the arrows indicate in which direction profits of the firms increase.

FIGURE 2

OUTPUT SUBSIDY AND REACTION FUNCTIONS IN COURNOT MODEL

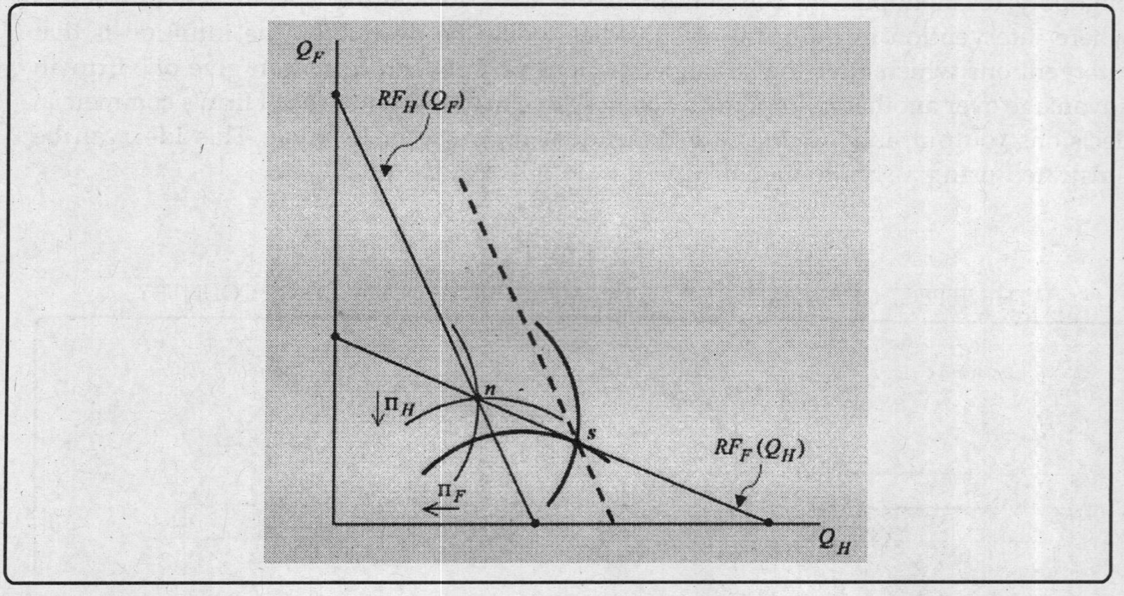

Now consider an interventionist government in country H that wishes to improve the profit of its firm. Graphically, the aim of the government is to move the home firm to a higher profit curve. One way would be to give the home firm an output subsidy that will reduce its marginal cost and provide incentive to increase its quantity (Q_H) in the third country. In Figure 1, an output subsidy shifts the reaction function of the home firm to the right (represented by the dashed line). The new equilibrium is denoted by point *s*. Note that the subsidy's effect is to shift profit from the foreign to the home firm. The home firm is on a higher profit curve and conversely the foreign is on a lower. The main argument illustrated by Figure 2 is that governments can actively use subsidies to shift profits towards the industry receiving the subsidies.

Assuming that firms choose their best output given the output of the other firm, the model shows that a government can increase its national firm's profits by granting it a production subsidy. A production subsidy, which in this case is also an export subsidy, acts as a profit-shifting instrument; profits earned by the competing foreign firm are transferred to the domestic firm, since the subsidy allows the domestic firm to commit to a higher level of output. The intuition behind the proposal for intervention is based on the positive profits earned by both firms and the ability of the government to use subsidies to shift some of the foreign firm's profits to the domestic firm. Since the profits earned by the domestic firm are higher than the subsidy, it pays for the government to implement the subsidy policy. As mentioned, the foreign firm and thus the foreign country are worse off as a result of the subsidy.

This profit-shifting argument in favour of subsidies does not stand up well to changes in assumptions and great care is needed in translating it into policy prescription. If the basic assumptions are relaxed, this *would modify the conclusions*. For example, if each firm is assumed to choose its optimal price given the price of its rival, the results are reversed and the optimal policy for the government is to tax the national firm rather than to subsidize it. However, to identify the industries for which the argument for strategic export promotion is valid would be very difficult in practice.

(iii) Arguments Used by Governments to Justify Subsidies

Governments use subsidies to pursue a variety of objectives, either because they consider that some malfunctioning of the markets impedes them from delivering efficient outcomes or because they consider market outcomes unsatisfactory. Subsidies in the context of environmental policies and research and development (R&D) support tend to be justified on the basis of positive or negative externalities. Subsidies in the context of industrial policies have been related to a variety of market failures, such as learning-by-doing effects, asymmetrical information, and capital market failures. The use of subsidies to redistribute income is not linked to imperfections in the market, but to society's desire to change the market outcome.

Whatever the objective pursued by governments, subsidies tend to be only one of a range of possible instruments to achieve it. The optimal policy instrument is situation-specific and needs to be determined on a case-by-case basis. Subsidies have a number of advantages compared with other instruments. They represent a relatively transparent form of government intervention, to the exten that expenses and recipients are reported in the government's budget. Given their direct impact on prices, subsidies tend to have less undesirable side-effects than other instruments in situations where the government wishes to change market signals (prices), for example in the presence of environmental or knowledge externalities that are not fully reflected in market prices. But subsidies also have disadvantages. Because they have such a direct impact, beneficiaries have a strong incentive to lobby in favour of continued subsidization. In other words, the use of subsidies makes the government prone to undue influence by recipient industry groups or other groups in society. One way of reducing this danger is to link subsidization to objective performance criteria whenever possible.

COUNTERVAILING DUTIES (CVD)

The countervailing duty (CVD) is a *special duty levied for the purpose of offsetting any subsidy bestowed directly or indirectly upon the manufacture, production or export of any merchandise*. From a legal point of view, CVDs are thus similar to anti-dumping duties, in that they are used to raise the domestic prices of imported goods that are considered to be "artificially" low in price. In both cases, the low prices are considered to result from "unfair" practices: dumping of goods by foreign firms in the case of anti-dumping; advantages afforded by foreign governments in the form of production or export subsidies in the case of countervailing duties.

THE ECONOMICS OF COUNTERVAILING DUTIES

In the perfect market, CVDs improve the situation of the producers competing with subsidized imports and provide tariff revenue but they tend to raise the price of goods and harm consumers. Overall, the countervailing country is presumed to be worse off with the duty in place than without it but it could be better off than before the subsidy was imposed. The two main caveats to this proposition are that CVDs can improve the importing country's terms-of-trade, and that they may deter subsidization altogether. This would bring benefits to producers in the importing country who must compete with subsidized goods in their export markets. In the presence of market failures, CVDs can be used for "rent extraction" or capturing profits arising from such failures, which may provide a further argument for using them.

(i) Perfect Markets

When a government imposes a tariff on imports of the subsidized product, its price increases and demand falls. If the country is large enough, this lower demand will depress the world price of the product, mitigating the initial price increase in the protected market and reducing the price in the subsidizing country. Trade falls. If the tariff increase matches the subsidy, trade will return to its pre-subsidy level. The countervailing duty completely eliminates the distortion associated with the subsidy.

In this case, the only effect is a transfer of income from taxpayers in the subsidizing country to the government (taxpayers) in the importing country. Welfare as a result of the CVD is still greater than before the subsidy programme by the amount of the tariff revenue but whether it is greater or smaller than before the imposition of the CVD depends on the relative importance of the distortion introduced by the duty compared to the terms-of-trade gain. If the country is large enough, the terms-of-trade gains could more than compensate the efficiency loss from the duty.

A subsidy granted by a large country will affect importing countries in the same way whether they are large or small. It will increase supply on the world market and will push down the price. The effect of the CVD, however, will differ depending on the size of the country that imposes it. If the country that imposes it is small, the CVD will have no effect on the world price. The tariff increase needed to return to the pre-subsidy price will be less significant than in the large country case and only part of the subsidy will be transferred to the countervailing country. A small countervailing country will no doubt be worse off with the CVD than without it but still with the subsidy. The distortion from the duty will not be offset by a terms-of-trade gain. If only one small importer imposes a CVD, there will be no feedback effect on the subsidizing country. If, however, many small importers countervail, the price will fall and there will be a feedback effect on the subsidizing country.

Why should not the terms-of-trade gains argument be interpreted as a justification for the use of CVDs? First, the subsidizing government is likely to recognize that countervailing duties absorb part of the subsidy and may respond by curtailing or abolishing the programme. Because the importing country gains from the subsidy, it would be worse off in the case where the market returns to the pre-subsidy situation. *Second,* even if the subsidy remains in place, it would be difficult to assess the welfare effect of the CVD. A considerable amount of information on demand and supply would be needed to measure and compare the size of the deadweight loss with the terms-of-trade gain. *Finally,* CVDs may generate positive welfare effects that may exceed the negative distortion effects.There may be a case where the importing country is also exporting the product either to the subsidizing country or to third-country markets, which might be the case because of transport costs. In this case, if the CVD prompts the subsidizing country to eliminate its export subsidy, prices may increase in some of those third markets, which may benefit exporters in the countervailing country. The effects of an export subsidy combined with a CVC are shown in Figure-3. As an export subsidy creates a wedge between the prices in the two markets, the price paid by consumers in the importing country corresponding to P_1 and the price perceived by the producers in the exporting country to $P^*_1 = P_1 + s^*$. The subsidized price causes injury to the domestic producers who then lobby for protection in the form of a countervailing tariff.

FIGURE 3

THE EFFECTS OF AN EXPORT SUBSIDY COMBINED WITH A COUNTERVAILING TARIFF: THE CASE OF LARGE COUNTRIES

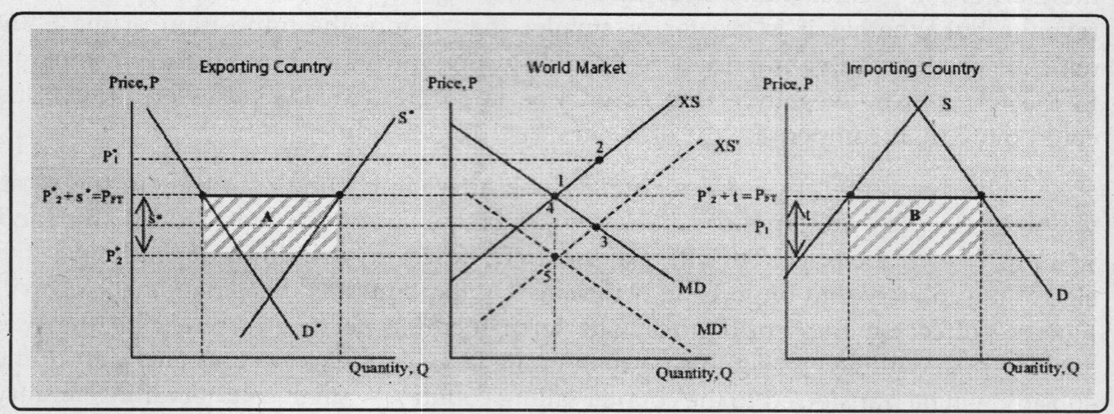

Introducing a countervailing tariff (denoted by *t*) shifts the import demand to the left and drives a second wedge between the prices in the two markets, illustrated by the move from point 3 to points 4 and 5. The tariff has the effect of raising the price in the importing country. However, since the increase is less than the amount of the tariff due to the terms-of-trade effects, part of the tariff is reflected in a decline in the export price. Therefore, the price in the importing country will increase from *P1*, the subsidized price, to the free trade price *PFT* . Similarly, the countervailing tariff will push down the exporters' price to $P^*_2 = P_{FT} - t$. Nonetheless, since the subsidy is still in effect, the true price perceived by the producers is $P^*_2 + s^* = P_{FT}$, which is equal to the price under free trade.

The major implication of a combined policy is that, because output and prices in both markets have returned to their initial free trade levels, the distortionary impact of the subsidy is neutralized. Global welfare returns to its free trade level. The only effect that remains is the transfer of income from the foreign country (*the shaded area A*) to the domestic country in the form of a tariff revenue (*shaded area B*). In other words, what the foreign government spends as an export subsidy is collected by the domestic country in the form of tariff revenue.

If the importing/countervailing country is too small to affect the large exporting country's price, the countervailing tariff raises the price of the good in the importing country by the full amount of the tariff and does not affect the price of the exporting country. In other words, a much smaller countervailing tariff is required to re-establish the subsidized price (*P1*) to the free trade level (*PFT*) in the importing market.

In the production subsidy case, the main difference is that the CVD does not eliminate the distortion. The country that imposes the CVD can completely offset the distortion caused by the subsidy and return to the pre-subsidy situation. Production and consumption in the subsidizing country, however, do not revert to the pre-subsidy situation. Consumers benefit from the tariff-induced reduction of the price (the terms-of-trade effect) while production falls but not all the way to the pre-subsidy level. There is thus both a transfer from taxpayers in the subsidizing country to taxpayers in the importing country and a distortion in the subsidizing country.

(ii) Imperfect Competition in Product Markets

The situation is again more nuanced in markets with imperfect competition. In the presence of imperfect competition, the exporting nation does not necessarily lose and the importing country does not necessarily gain from export subsidies. There is a simple argument where governments subsidize predatory pricing and a more elaborate argument where governments subsidize to improve the strategic position of their producers. The former argument is fairly straightforward. The government of the country targeted by the subsidized predatory pricing should countervail the subsidized imports to prevent damage to domestic producers and the monopolization of its domestic market. While this argument makes some theoretical sense, its validity is limited in practice. *First,* there is very limited empirical evidence suggesting that government-financed predatory pricing occurs to any significant extent. *Second,* assuming that predatory pricing poses a threat, CVDs would only be needed as a remedy if anti-trust law should not or cannot be employed.

(iii) Imperfect Labour Markets

Public support for protection is often based on the perception that competition from imports may lead to costly industry adjustments and cause persistent unemployment. Indeed, there are theoretical arguments in favour of using countervailing duties as a means of facing up to these adjustment costs and the redistribution of resources that results from subsidized imports. This argument assumes that workers' earnings encompass more than the competitive wage. For example, strong labour unions may take advantage of monopoly power to raise wages above the competitive level. Alternatively, employers may raise wages above the competitive level to increase employees' productivity or efficiency.

If workers earn additional income, a foreign subsidy may no longer have an unambiguously beneficial effect. Part of the reduction in domestic producer surplus (the sum of profits earned by suppliers) resulting from the foreign subsidy is not compensated by an increase in consumer surplus (the difference between the willingness to pay and the actual price the consumer pays). If the foreign subsidy has a negative impact on welfare, a CVD that would eliminate it will have a positive effect on welfare but a CVD could enhance welfare even further if the subsidy has a positive effect on welfare.

In theory, trade policy (i.e. the use of CVDs) is only a second-best solution to the type of labour market failure. Economic principles would suggest that the best form of intervention would be to directly address the source of the market distortion. However, it may not be politically acceptable to intervene in the labour market. In this case, there would be a second-best argument for using trade policy, such as CVDs. Moreover, there are a number of other objections to the use of CVDs to address labour market failures. If information problems prevent the use of first-best policies, they may also prevent the use of countervailing duties. More fundamentally, a general safeguard, which is not dependent upon subsidization, may be preferable, even if it is not an ideal response.

However, if subsidies are applied for a limited period and industry adjustment costs are most severe immediately after subsidised imports are introduced, different and possibly greater forms of protection may be needed than for other types of import competition. In particular, it would not require protection measures that facilitate industry adjustment. Long-term adjustment would not be needed because of the temporary nature of subsidies and short-term adjustment would not be advisable because of the high costs associated with this. In other words, if subsidies are applied for a particularly short period, specific contingent measures may be warranted. However, subsidy programmes are generally not temporary. Moreover, other sources of import competition, such as exchange rate fluctuations, may be even more temporary.

Conventional economic wisdom suggests that the hardship of economic upheaval is usually better alleviated with tools other than restrictive trade policies. Retraining programmes, public employment agencies, social security and other measures directly targeted at affected workers introduce less distortions than trade restrictions. However, the taxes levied to finance alternative redistribution policies can also introduce severe distortions. In any case, assuming that there is a case for using trade restrictions to correct the distribution of income, it is again questionable whether CVDs would necessarily be the best protectionist option.

(iv) The Economic Rationale for CVDs

Having examined the welfare effects of subsidies and CVDs, two related questions need to be considered: *why do governments use countervailing duties and what role do CVDs play in trade agreements?* With regard to the first question, the presumption is that governments do not use CVDs solely to improve national or global welfare. Examination of the welfare effects of subsidies and CVDs suggests that in the absence of market failures, CVDs would normally reduce overall national welfare. The question then is why do governments use them. A first answer could be that market imperfections are everywhere. In other words, the cases where CVDs increase welfare would be more frequent than economists tend to believe. Another possible explanation is that governments use CVDs to help producers compete with subsidized imports. The welfare analysis outlined above has shown that the principal beneficiaries of CVDs are indeed those producers. If, governments do not necessarily maximize national welfare but rather pursue policies that benefit certain constituencies, they may indeed use countervailing duties to help producers who have been harmed or are likely to be harmed by foreign subsidies.

In the light of this observation, the related question of the role of CVDs in trade agreements is now considered. If the rationale of a trade agreement is to eliminate beggar-thy-neighbour policies, i.e. policies that have a negative impact on trading partners, countervailing duties can be seen as instruments that allow importing countries to neutralize the negative impact from subsidies.

The government of an importing country can use CVDs to restore the price that existed before the subsidy, thereby leaving domestic consumers and producers unaffected by the subsidy. In the process, it collects tariff revenue which makes it better off than before the subsidy. In this particular case, the negative impact of the subsidy does not necessarily correspond to a reduction in overall economic welfare. If the presumption is that the subsidy does not lead typically to a loss of overall economic welfare but only to a loss of producer surplus (the sum of profits earned by suppliers), the countervailing duty should be seen as an attempt to protect domestic producers from the harmful effects of foreign subsidies rather than to promote global efficiency.

If countervailing duties are intended to neutralize subsidies that inflict a welfare loss on trading partners, they should only be applied when a subsidy can be shown to have this negative effect. CVDs may be part of a larger multilateral system aimed at discouraging trade-distorting subsidies and at facilitating trade concessions. A system of constraining subsidies can only be effective if it is properly enforced. Countervailing duties may be part of the enforcement mechanism. Though in a narrow sense, CVDs are often detrimental to national economic welfare but his view is that there might be systemic gains from the use of countervailing duties by all countries. The threat of CVDs may allow governments to resist political pressures for wasteful subsidization at home. The use of countervailing duties by all countries may also deter subsidies that would injure each nation's exporters in their overseas markets.

OTHER SELECTED MEASURES OF CONTINGENCY PROTECTION

RENEGOTIATION

Contingent measures and renegotiations are two forms of flexibility that serve different purposes. While the goal of contingent measures is to provide temporary protection, renegotiation is intended to be a means through which WTO members seek a permanent rebalancing of concessions within the WTO.

Renegotiations are examples of flexibilty measures defined in terms of procedural disciplines rather than circumstances for their use. Furthermore, they are a permanent form of exception to WTO commitments rather than a temporary suspension of these commitments. Tariff increases within existing bindings – i.e. maximum agreed limits – are examples of flexibilities provided by the nature of the commitments: that is, tariff bound rates are ceilings rather than target levels for tariffs. Export taxes are examples of flexibility measures that apply to exports rather than imports. In the WTO system, they are examples of flexibility measures that are provided by the incompleteness of members' commitments.

Commitments under the WTO can be renegotiated. Article XXVIII of the GATT and Article XXI of the General Agreement on Trade in Services (GATS) define conditions under which WTO members are allowed to withdraw concessions (bound tariff reductions or specific commitments), if compensation is offered to other members affected by the withdrawal. Unlike other contingent measures, which are temporary, renegotiations are permanent measures. In other words, renegotiations alter the commitments of members indefinitely (or, more precisely, until they are renegotiated at a later stage).

SAFEGUARDS

Safeguard provisions are an important element in international trade agreements. They allow policy-makers to make far-ranging commitments taking into account the uncertainty over future events that may require a change in policy. The distinguishing feature of safeguards in trade agreements is their strictly temporary character backed up by the credible threat that other countries will legitimately punish any abuse of the mechanism. This constraint sets the right incentives to make industrial adjustment happen. Furthermore, in a trade agreement, this and other requirements seek to strike a balance between any WTO member's unknown need for flexibility (at the time that the agreement is signed) and the concern of trading partners to minimize the impact of safeguard measures on their interests. The requirement to demonstrate that an increase in imports is the cause of injury to domestic industry and to ensure that injury caused by other factors is not falsely attributed to imports is key in this respect.

In practice, the implementation of this causation/ non-attribution requirement has not been straightforward, as proven by the negative track-record in dispute settlement in this regard. In addition, many observers have criticized the reliance on correlations between imports and injury to demonstrate the impact of imports on domestic industry. Economists have noted the fundamental problem of conceptualizing imports as an exogenous variable and not as one that is determined simultaneously with other injury variables, such as domestic production. Both injury and imports may in fact be the consequence of other events. This view has triggered an academic debate on whether the origin of the shock - foreign or domestic - and a possible identification of responsibilities play a role in pinpointing imports as the cause of injury to domestic industry. Such discussions might eventually also be of practical concern - for instance, in calculating the permissible extent of a safeguard tariff that would not exceed the share of injury due to imports.

TECHNICAL BARRIERS TO TRADE

WTO agreement uses the word *standard* to refer to *voluntary standards*. Mandatory standards imposed by law are referred to as *technical regulations*. The agreement covers the standards that are applied to industrial and agricultural products in order to ensure a level of quality or safety for the consumer. It does not cover subjects falling within the new agreement on sanitary and phytosanitary measures. It does however cover standards drafted as process or production methods if product related, unlike the earlier agreement, which only covered standards drafted as product characteristics.

Standards can create major obstacles to trade. A standard that is designed to deal with a locally made product, and incorporates the design of that product in the standard, can effectively exclude imports from other countries where the design is different. In order to comply a foreign producer may have either to change his production line completely or to create a second production line for export to that particular market. In many cases the producer in question will simply decide not to bother exporting to that market.

Mandatory standards clearly oblige producers seeking to sell in a particular market to conform. If they do not they may face sanctions in the form of seizure, fines or even imprisonment. By definition, voluntary standards do not carry the same consequences and in theory at least producers can ignore them. On the other hand, if they do, they may find it very difficult to sell their products to other industrialists or consumers because they may not match commonly used systems, for example light bulbs with the wrong attachment, or because it may be considered that their products are not the best. Moreover insurance companies usually insist that certain voluntary standards are complied with when insurance is being sought.

With tariffs and other forms of protection being lowered to the point where they have become fairly negligible, standards have become the preferred weapon of protection. Add to this the fact that countries often require that a product not only adhere to a standard, but that it be certified as being in conformity with that standard. This means that the product has to be tested by a recognised laboratory. This procedure is also an attractive way of creating obstacles to trade through administrative delays, refusal of access to a laboratory, the difficulty of carrying out the procedures in a foreign country and so on.

GOVERNMENT PROCUREMENT

Government procurement was not covered by the original GATT agreement. Indeed

Article III, which contained the national treatment principle, explicitly stated that procurement was an exception to that principle. In other words a government could discriminate in favour of domestic suppliers against foreign suppliers.

This type of discrimination has been common. One only has to think of the Buy America provisions in federal and state legislation in the United States. Under EU law there is also a degree of discrimination against non-EU suppliers. However in the EU it is sufficient if a product is in free circulation, that is, if it has been imported into the EU, for it to qualify for treatment.

As well as being deeply embedded in legislation, the use of procurement as a form of industrial policy is even more profound. Nearly all governments use their public money to direct and develop industry. This phenomenon is most obvious in defence and research. Governments are strongly committed to promoting their defence establishments (the so-called military - industrial complex) and nowadays there is even greater pressure to help advance industry's technological base through expenditure on research and development. Add to this the need most governments feel to spend government money to create employment. Domestic employment is not fostered by spending money outside the country on imported goods, however cheap they may be. The instinct to reserve government procurement for domestic purchases, though diminishing in this age of budgetary austerity, is still very deep rooted and strong.

QUESTIONS

1. Define dumping. What do firms dump goods?
2. Discuss the benefits and risks associated with the use of antidumping actions.
3. Explain the economics of renegotiation.
4. Does persistent dumping into the domestic country mean that a foreign government is subsidising the foreign exporting firm? Why or why not?
5. Why do markets have to be kept separate by artificial or natural barriers for dumping to occur?
6. What is the difference between an export tax and export subsidy? Which instrument are domestic consumers likely to prefer? Why?
7. Critically examine the welfare effects of Dumping.
8. Suppose that an export tax rather than an import tariff is used to improve the terms of trade. Will the results be the same? Explain.
9. How do the impacts of an export subsidy in a large country case differ from those in the small country case?
10. "Safeguards provisions are an important element in international trade agreements." Do you agree?
11. Discuss the economics of subsidies. Can government activity use subsidies to shift profits toward the industry receiving the subsidy.
12. Discuss the various contingent measures. How would you choose among different measures?

13. How can an export subsidy by a country actually reduce world welfare?
14. Explain the effect of an export subsidy implemented by a large company.
15. Discuss the concept of Conntervaiting duties (CVD). Why should not the terms-of-trade gains argument be interpreted as a justification for the use of CVD?

REFERENCES

Balassa, B. (1971) The *Structure of Protection in Developing Countries,* Baltimore: Johns Hopkins Press.

Blonigen, B. and Sown, C. (2003) "Antidumping and Retaliation Threats," *Journal of International Economics* 60:249-73.

Corden, M. (1966) "The Structure of a Tariff System and the Effective Rate of Protection," *Journal of Political Economy* 74: 221-37.

Deardorff, A. and Stern, R. (1984) "The Effects of the Tokyo Round on the Structure of Protection," in R. Baldwin and A. Krueger (eds), The *Structure and Evolution of Recent U.S. Trade Policy,* Chicago: University of Chicago Press, pp. 370-5.

Friberg, R, and Ganslandt, M. (2006) "An empirical assessment of the welfare effects of reciprocal dumping," *Journal International Economics 70:* 1-24.

Hufbauer, G. and Erb, J. (1984) *Subsidies in International Trade,* Washington, DC: Institute for International Economics Netherlands Economic Institute (2000) *Evaluation of the Common Organization of the Markets in the Sugar* Sector, September.

Konings, J. and Vandenbussche, H. (2005) "Antidumping protection and markups of domestic firms," *Journal of* International *Economics 65:* 151-65.

Oxfam (2004) "Dumping on the World: How EU Sugar Policies Hurt Poor Countries," Briefing Paper 61, March.

Oxfam (2004) *Dumping on the World, How EU Sugar Policies Hurt Poor Countries,* Oxfam Briefing Paper 61.

Prusa, T. (1992) "Why Are so Many Antidumping Petitions Withdrawn?," *Journal of International Economics* 33: 1-20.

Rutkowski, A. (2007) "Withdrawals of Anti-dumping Complaints in the ED: A Sign of Collusion," *World Economy* 30: '470-503.

Srinivasan, T.N. (1987) "The National Defense Argument for Intervention in Foreign Trade," in R. Stern, (ed.) US. *Trade Policy in a Changing World* Economy , Cambridge, MA: MIT Press, pp. 337-76.

Taylor. C., (2004) "The Economic Effects of Withdrawn Antidumping Investigations: Is There Evidence of Collusive Settlements?" *Journal of International Economics* 62: 295-312.

World Trade Organization (2006) *Overview of Developments in the International Trading Environment,* Annual Report *by* the Director General (WT/TPR/OV/11).

5

TRADE AND PUBLIC POLICIES

INTRODUCTION

International Trade is the exchange of capital, goods, and services across international borders or territories. In most countries, such trade represents a significant share of gross domestic product (GDP). While international trade has been present throughout much of history, its economic, social, and political importance has been on the rise in recent centuries.

Trade agreements are meant to discipline policies that distort trade without constraining governments in their pursuit of other legitimate public policy objectives, such as consumer health and safety protection – even if these happen to affect trade. Thus, while certain non-tariff measures (NTMs) entail trade costs, these costs can be justified for other reasons. The chapter identifies situations in which governments may be prone to employ non-tariff measures for trade competitiveness reasons, even if the stated policy rationale is a different one, or implement an inefficient instrument that may affect trade more than necessary to achieve a given objective. From this analysis, a number of factors relating to the choice of NTMs and the sectors and political context in which they are applied can help distinguish between "legitimate" and "protectionist" (or excessively trade-restrictive) use.

REASONS FOR GOVERNMENT INTERVENTION AND TYPES OF MEASURES

CLASSIFYING NTMs AND GOVERNMENT MOTIVES

There are various ways to categorize both non-tariff measures and the reasons why governments use them namely interventions aimed at increasing national welfare and those motivated by "political economy" goals. The former includes interventions to correct market failures and to exploit a country's or a firm's market power (by manipulating the terms of trade and shifting profits). One key point is that interventions to exploit market power come at the expense of one's trade partners (beggar-thy-neighbour practices), whereas those focused on correcting market failures have trade effects that are unintended consequences of the policy.

Political economy motives reflect the response of political incumbents to special interest groups, usually assumed to be organized producer groups. Political economy motives are likely to lead to policies that shelter favoured producers and reduce trade flows at the expense of national welfare. This suggests a further distinction between non-tariff measures motivated by public policy objectives and those motivated by competitiveness concerns. This does not mean that public policy and competitiveness concerns cannot overlap – for example, when protecting an infant industry whose expansion can increase national welfare. However, there are likely to be many more instances where promoting a domestic producer's interests comes at the expense of the social good. Lastly, motives can be distinguished according to their intended distributional effects – specifically, whether they benefit consumers or producers.

Besides the economic motives of governments for employing non-tariff measures, national welfare and public policy objectives may embrace far more than purely economic issues. Governments are responsible for safeguarding national security. Governments may wish to firmly uphold certain moral and religious tenets. Where a society is made up of different ethnic or religious groups, a high value will be placed upon the preservation of social cohesion. These goals may be compromised if certain goods are freely available in the country, requiring governments to use NTMs so as to restrict their supply via international trade.

NTM can be classified according to whether they are applied at the border, to exports (e.g. export taxes, quotas or bans) and imports (e.g. import quota, import ban), or behind the border. This latter category can be further subdivided according to whether the NTMs are domestic taxes, other charges, and subsidies, or whether they are regulatory. The distinction between border and behind-the-border NTMs appears frequently in the economic literature. In one sense, it is a distinction based on where the measures are applied. However, in another sense, it involves a distinction between measures applied to foreign goods only (at the border) and those applied equally to domestic and foreign goods. This raises a key question about behind-the border measures – i.e. whether, intentionally or *de facto*, they treat domestic and foreign goods differently.

What is common about the interventions collectively called non-tariff measures, irrespective of their motives, is that they have trade effects (either liberal or restrictive). Sometimes the trade effects are simply the by-product of pursuing a particular public policy objective. Other times, the trade effects are the primary goal. Since governments usually claim that their policies have laudable objectives, declared intentions may offer little insight into the motives behind interventions. Instead, motives can best be deduced from the type of NTM chosen, from the sector to which it is applied, from its design and implementation, and from its impact – i.e. whether consumers or producers benefit and whether foreign goods are discriminated against or not.

For the purpose of later analysis of the trade and welfare effects of non-tariff measures, a distinction is made between NTMs that are price, quantity or "quality" focused. A price measure (such as a subsidy) operates by changing relative prices while a quantity measure (such as a quota) works by directly limiting the quantity of some activity. Quality measures (such as a technical barrier to trade measure or a sanitary and phytosanitary measure) change some features of a product or the process by which it is produced. This categorization helps to simplify the analysis of the trade and welfare effects of NTMs by using examples taken from each category rather than by examining exhaustively all NTMs.

Another important theme is the transparency of non-tariff measures. At a conceptual level, transparency can be defined as the absence of information asymmetry, a situation where policy makers and relevant economic agents have the same information. Information asymmetry generates uncertainty for the agents with less information. Those with access to private information may try to manipulate the beliefs of others and thereby indirectly alter economic behaviour. Thus, economic efficiency requires information be made publicly available. In the case of non-tariff measures, it may be important to distinguish between different economic agents – the private sector and other governments – because each is likely to be concerned with different aspects of information. Governments are likely to want information that allows them to better evaluate whether their trade partners are abiding by international commitments. The private sector is likely to be more concerned with information asymmetry that hampers its ability to take advantage of commercially profitable opportunities.

However, motives and impacts of nontariff measures needs to take into account the increasing fragmentation and offshoring of production. The economic theory of fragmentation contends that increased market size makes it profitable to split up the process of production and allow specialization to reduce per unit cost. This division of labour can take place within a country, but if countries differ in their comparative advantages, greater cost savings from specialization can be obtained by offshoring production. This process of fragmentation requires firms to be able to coordinate between production locations and to move parts and components across national borders. This underscores the crucial role of services, particularly telecommunications and transport, in connecting fragmented production blocks. Production fragmentation has an impact on why governments use non-tariff measures and how they influence trade. *First*, where global supply chains are prevalent, it is not possible to disentangle merchandise trade from services trade and foreign direct investment (FDI). This means that NTMs, which affect merchandise trade, are also likely to have an impact on services and FDI flows. Conversely, services and investment regulations are likely to impact merchandise trade as well. *Secondly,* while governments' usual motives for employing NTMs remain – i.e. to address market failures, to exploit market power or to respond to political economy pressures – production fragmentation makes some motives more pressing than others. For instance, governments may see information asymmetry as more critical given that products are now made from parts and components coming from distant and multiple sources. Clearly, the role of NTMs in a world of increasingly fragmented production is a fertile area for future research.

HOW DO NON-TARIFF MEASURES ACHIEVE POLICY OBJECTIVES?

There are a number of methods that governments can follow in choosing non-tariff measures. The economically coherent way to think about government intervention and the choice of NTMs is in the context of a cost-benefit analysis. In broad terms, a cost-benefit analysis involves calculating the net gains to national welfare by implementing one measure relative to an alternative. Here, the presumption is that non-tariff measures will vary in their ability to achieve the policy goal and that they will also differ in their costs. Governments will therefore need to evaluate the benefit from achieving a given policy objective (e.g. the welfare gain from reducing pollution), the contribution that a particular NTM can make to achieving the policy goal, and the cost incurred in applying the NTM. The outcome of the cost benefit analysis determines not only whether government intervention is called for in the first place (the benefit must exceed the cost) but also provides a ranking of the NTMs. In particular, the method should be able to identify the first-best measure – that which produces the largest differential in benefit over cost. It is likely that a cost-benefit analysis would be more information-intensive and technically challenging to apply than some of the simpler methods mentioned above. Benefits and costs need to be quantified and monetary values assigned to them. Informational and resource constraints may explain, at least partly, why some governments do not make more extensive use of cost-benefit analysis in decision-making on NTMs.

More than one NTM can frequently be used to pursue the same policy objective. From the standpoint of economic efficiency, governments should use the NTM that maximizes national welfare – i.e. the first-best NTM. However, NTMs used to pursue legitimate policy objectives can also be used for protectionist purposes, underlining the difficulty of distinguishing "legitimate" from "protectionist" government motives. Several cases of market failures, instances of beggar-thy- neighbour policies, equity motivations, political economy considerations etc. how been discussed below th provide exhaustive coverage on applying NTM to alllied policy objectives.

Correcting Market Failures

Health and Safety of Consumers and Consumer Choice

Information asymmetry refers to a situation where one set of agents involved in an economic transaction or exchange has an informational advantage over other parties. An example is the seller of a used car who has better information about the state of the car than the potential buyer. Another example is the job seeker who has better information about his productivity and aptitude for work than the potential employer. A third example is the case of a producer who sells a sub-standard product which can compromise the health and safety of unwitting consumers.

The existence of information asymmetry can lead to a number of inefficiencies in the market. In the used car example, since buyers know that they are at an information disadvantage they will only be willing to bid a low price – with the result that owners of good quality used cars do not bother to put their cars up for sale, and the used car market ends up being overwhelmed by low-quality cars, i.e. there is adverse selection. In the job-seeking example, information asymmetry may lead the job seeker to expend resources to "signal" his productivity to the potential employer (e.g. attend a more expensive school) even though that decision will not necessarily increase his productivity. In the case of the sub-standard product, sale of the product can cause injuries or even fatalities. As these examples show, markets will not necessarily deliver the most efficient outcomes, and this failure provides a rationale for public action. This explains, for example, why a wide range of consumer goods – food, drugs, vehicles, electrical appliances, safety equipment – face many types of requirements, from design (e.g. toys) to ingredients (e.g. chemicals) to the process of manufacture or production (e.g. pasteurization of milk) and to performance (e.g. helmets). What these measures are designed to do is to weed out those products, whether domestic or foreign, that will compromise the health or safety of consumers.

Information asymmetry is also relevant to international trade. Suppose that countries differ in the safety or quality of the goods that they produce, with the home country specializing in high-quality products and the foreign country specializing in low-quality ones. Imagine that consumers in both countries differ in their preference for quality, with some willing to pay more for high-quality products, and others unwilling to pay more. In this scenario, consumers are also unable to tell the difference between high-quality and lowquality products because these goods are not distinguished by origin. Under these circumstances, the country with high-quality products may lose if it trades with the country producing low-quality products. This arises because trade reduces the average quality of products sold in the market of the high-quality producing country, which spills over to affect the expected welfare of all consumers in the importing country.

The first-best policy is labelling to allow consumers to distinguish between home (high-quality) and foreign (low-quality) products. Consumers with a taste for high-quality goods will purchase home goods and consumers satisfied with low-quality goods will purchase foreign goods, resulting in a two-way trade in equilibrium. Each product will sell for the "right" price – high-quality goods at higher prices and low-quality goods at lower prices. The ability to distinguish between home and foreign products leaves both countries better off as a result of trade because it expands the variety of products available to consumers, and leads to a better match between consumer tastes and products. A similar result if established foreign goods to be labelled according to their country of origin to give the consumer all the necessary information, and unambiguously improves the welfare of the importing country.

Under certain circumstances, export subsidies can also help reduce or eliminate information asymmetry. Consumers in the importing country differ in their taste for quality. Some consumers like high-quality goods and are willing to pay a higher price for them; others would rather pay a lower price for the low-quality good. Unfortunately, the groups are unable to tell the difference between highquality and low-quality products until they make the purchase, i.e. these are "experience goods".

Producers in the exporting country, who make the high-quality product, incur a higher cost of production than producers in the importing country, who make the low-quality good. If both goods circulate in the importing country, consumers will be unable to tell the difference and the price will reflect the average quality of these goods. At such a price, high-quality producers will not be able to export their goods since it will not cover their cost of production. If the high-quality firms are aided by an export subsidy, they can sell their goods at the average price and still earn a profit. Having been introduced to the high-quality product, consumers preferring high-quality goods will be able to make repeat purchases, paying a price that reflects the quality of the good. At this later stage, the highquality producer receives a price that covers his cost of production, and the government can withdraw the export subsidies. Consumers satisfied with low-quality goods benefit as well since they can now identify these goods and pay a lower price for them.

Pollution and the Environment

Another type of market failure that can justify government action is a negative externality such as pollution. Negative externalities arise when an agent's economic activity generates costs to others that the agent does not fully absorb. Hence, the scale of his activity exceeds the socially optimal amount. In recent decades, the public and policy-makers have become increasingly aware of the environmental consequences of certain economic activities. Much of the economic literature focuses on the use of taxes to correct negative externalities — the so-called Pigouvian tax. Nevertheless, many governments have chosen to pursue environmental objectives using non-price measures, such as performance standards, emission quotas, and mandated technologies.

One drawback of trying to reduce pollution through government-mandated technologies is that the incentive to find less costly ways to achieve the same environmental objective is removed. Nevertheless, governments may prefer these measures for distributional or competitive reasons, because of uncertainty about the costs and benefits of abatement, or to avoid the cost of monitoring and enforcement. Regarding distributional or competitiveness concerns, for example, governments may be sensitive to the fact that a pollution tax requires firms to pay for each unit of emission while an emission quota does not. While both instruments might lead the firm to curtail emissions by the same amount, the tax saddles the firm with an additional liability that it does not face with a quota. If policy-makers are uncertain about the true cost of mitigating environmental damage, but are certain that passing beyond a threshold level of environmental damage would be catastrophic, quantity-based measures will be preferred to pricebased measures.

Some of the more complicated and contentious environmental issues involve cross-border externalities. One type of cross-border externality involves countries whose economic activity pollutes or reduces a common resource, damaging all countries. A notable example of this is global warming. Another type of crossborder externality is where the activity occurs in one jurisdiction, but the adverse impacts are partly or fully felt in another jurisdiction.

Cross-border externalities are often compounded by differences in countries' income levels, or institutional and environmental capacities. Since adopting environment-friendly production methods often entails higher costs, this can lead to disagreements between countries about the distribution of the costs and benefits of correcting the externality. A number of GATT/WTO disputes – tuna-dolphin and shrimpturtle – appear to fall within this category. While such differences make it difficult for countries to reach an agreement, markets could play a role in mitigating or eliminating a cross-border externality. Assuming that credible information about the environmental costs of producing a good were available, consumers might be willing to pay more for the product if it was produced without causing environmental harm. Higher prices would provide an incentive for producers to switch to more environment-friendly methods, thereby reducing pressure on the environment.

However, products made by environmentally-friendly processes may not be distinguishable from those made by less environmentally-friendly processes. Tuna caught by fishing methods which leave dolphins unharmed tastes the same as tuna caught by methods lethal to dolphins. This introduces a second market failure – information asymmetry – to the original problem of a cross-border externality.

Given the existence of market failures, open trade is not necessarily optimal. Depending on the strength of consumer preferences for the environment-friendly good, an outright ban of imports from countries that are the source of the environmental externality may be even better than open trade. The rationale is that a ban improves consumer confidence in the products since they know that only environment-friendly goods can be sold. This leads to an increase in demand, i.e. a shift in the demand curve, and to greater consumer surplus. For the importing country, the drawback of an import ban is that some consumers may be indifferent to environment-friendly and environment-unfriendly products, and unwilling to pay a premium for the former. The ban adversely affects them since it limits their choice to the expensive, environment-friendly good.

While there are good reasons to question the advantages of import bans, there are notable examples of products whose trade the international community has banned for environmental reasons, including endangered species (banned under the Convention on International Trade in Endangered Species of Wild Fauna and Flora) and ozone-depleting substances (banned under the Montreal Protocol). Of course, consumer confidence can also be enhanced by a labelling scheme that correctly distinguishes between goods made with little or no harm to the environment and those that impose an environmental cost. Effective labelling would be superior to a ban since it improves consumer confidence without artificially restricting imports. Consumers unwilling to pay a premium for the environment-friendly good are still able to purchase their preferred (low-price) environmentally-unfriendly good.

Infant Industry Protection

In some cases, an agent's economic activity generates benefits for others that the agent does not fully capture. These "positive externalities" represent an important class of market failure that can justify public intervention since the scale of activity is less than the socially optimal amount. One example is infant industry protection. Suppose the conditions for supporting an infant industry exist. The home country has a high-cost industry that finds it difficult to compete with foreign goods, but there are dynamic learning effects that are external to the firm and beneficial to the country. The experience that domestic firms accumulate by producing the good will reduce their costs over time. Furthermore, these learning effects cannot be contained within the firm but are also of benefit to other firms in the industry. This spill-over effect means that a firm does not fully internalize the gains from its learning, and so the prospect of later profit may not be sufficiently attractive to warrant absorbing losses during the initial learning period. This situation provides the necessary justification for extending temporary government support to the industry. Under these conditions, the first-best solution is for governments to use a production subsidy rather than a tariff to assist the infant industry. It directly targets the source of the market failure by supporting learning in the domestic industry without penalizing consumers with a higher price for the product, the principal drawback of using a tariff.

Ideally, the support extended to the infant industry should decline as learning takes place. However, information about the pace of learning may not be known with certainty by the policy-maker. Applying a fixed subsidy rate means that the protection extended to the infant industry will be below the optimum level at the start of the leaning period and too high at the end. Under these circumstances, proposes using a quota instead of a subsidy, noting that it will allow the level of infant-industry protection to adjust automatically as the industry's costs decline. Over time, the quota will become less distortive as the domestic industry's competitiveness improves.

Network Effects/Externalities

Certain products or services are more valuable to a buyer when more consumers use the same product or service. For example, the greater the number of subscribers to a telephone system, the more valuable that network will be to potential subscribers. Likewise, Facebook, Twitter or LinkedIn accounts are more valuable the more "friends", "followers", or professional contacts are drawn into these social networking sites. Such products or services are subject to what have been called "network effects/externalities".

Potentially there is a market failure associated with these networks. An individual decides to join a network because of the benefits he or she will obtain, not because of the benefits existing members will derive from him or her joining. As a result, the size of the network is smaller than the socially desirable size. If there are competing networks, each one of which is owned by a different firm, one way the problem of network size can be resolved is by making them compatible so that clients of one network are connected to the clients of all other networks. Given that each user's utility increases as the size of the network expands, compatibility among networks increases social welfare.

Compatibility can be achieved through adoption of common standards. The key question is whether firms have enough incentives to develop compatibility standards on their own without government intervention. One reason to be sceptical of government intervention is that governments are unlikely to have a significant informational advantage relative to private parties when emerging technologies are concerned, and so cannot be presumed to know which standard is the optimal one. On the other hand, because of the network effects, a product's compatibility increases its value to consumers who will then be willing to pay more for it than for a competing but incompatible product. There may also be a marketmediated effect, as when a complementary good (spare parts, servicing, software) becomes cheaper and more readily available the greater the compatibility of markets..

Monopoly Power

Imperfect competition represents another instance of market failure which occasions various forms of government intervention. Typically though, such measures are directed at the behaviour of firms and not at the products or services they produce. Competition rules will prevent a firm from colluding with others, limit its merger and acquisition activity, and guard against abuse of a dominant position.

A specific example illustrates the role of non-tariff measures in addressing this particular market failure. A small country is only able to source a specific product from a foreign monopolist because it is not produced domestically. The importing government's objective is to expand imports and reduce the artificial scarcity resulting from the foreign monopolist's control of the domestic market. Instead of NTMs being used to restrict trade, in this case NTMs will be used to try to expand trade and/or reduce the price charged by the monopolist. The optimal policy is a price ceiling on the imported product set equal to the monopolist's marginal cost of production. In other words, the foreign monopolist will be allowed to sell to the home country only if it caps its price at the ceiling established by the importing country. (If the monopolist had been a domestic firm, a competition authority would have adopted a similar policy of marginal-cost pricing.)

Beggar-Thy-Neighbour Policies

A country with market power in international trade can increase national welfare by improving its terms of trade (the ratio of export to import prices). If firms competing in international trade have market power – so that one firm's actions have an effect on the profits of its rival(s) – then government actions can shift profits from the foreign firm to the home firm, resulting in a gain in national welfare. In both instances, nontariff measures can be used by the home country to pocket terms-of-trade and profit-shifting gains. These welfare gains will come at the expense of other countries – i.e. these are beggar-thy-neighbour policies.

Manipulating the Terms of Trade with NTMs

The terms of trade can be shifted by trade policy, for instance, an import tariff reduces the demand for imports, so for a large country this will have the effect of reducing the world price of its imports relative to the price for its exports. However, an export tax can have a similar effect on a large country's terms of trade since the reduced availability of a country's export good in world markets should lead to a rise in its price relative to the import product. It turns out that an export subsidy can also shift the terms of trade in favour of the exporting country provided that it has another good that it exports and there are differences in consumption patterns between the importing and exporting countries.

If a country is not constrained in its use of these measures, such as by international agreements, they would be widely used to manipulate the terms of trade. Regulatory instruments, such as technical barriers to trade (TBT) and sanitary and phytosanitary (SPS) measures, would be used to correct market failures and would be set at their socially optimal levels.

However, this result may not necessarily hold in a world where production is increasingly offshored and international trade flows are dominated by intermediate inputs, many of which appear to be highly specialized to their intended use.

Profit-Shifting Non-tariff Measures

Non-tariff measures can also be used to shift profits from the foreign to the home country. This is most relevant in imperfectly competitive markets where firms have market power, and can effectively use NTMs, such as subsidies, export taxes and TBT/SPS measures, to take market share and profits away from foreign rivals.

Suppose that two firms, the home and foreign firm, compete in selling to a third market. Competition between them can take many forms. For instance under Cournot competition, a government can use export subsidies to help the home firm expand output, thereby forcing its foreign rival to contract production and concede market share. The subsidy has the effect of committing the domestic firm to a more aggressive strategy which in turn induces the foreign firm to produce less. From the point of view of the home country, even though the subsidy payment is just a transfer from the government to the home firm, the profit-shifting effect results in the firm's profit rising by more than the amount of the subsidy, creating a net gain to the home country. Note that the export subsidy creates a terms-of-trade loss for the domestic country, but this is more than made up for by the profit-shifting effect of the policy. But if firms compete in prices, the optimal policy will be an export tax rather than an export subsidy under Bertrand competition. Both firms would like to charge a higher price but if only one firm does so it will face lower export demand. However, a price hike would not prove detrimental to the home firm if its rival follows with a price increase of its own. Both firms will earn positive profits as a result. By imposing an export tax on its firm, the home government in effect commits the home firm to charge a higher price for any given price chosen by the rival. This persuades the foreign firm to follow suit – match the home firm's higher price – which benefits it and the home firm as well.

Domestic subsidies in the form of research and development (R&D) subsidies can also be used to shift profits from foreign rivals to domestic firms. This policy turns out to be optimal regardless of whether firms engage in Bertrand or Cournot competition. Basically, the R&D subsidy provides an incentive to the home firm to increase its R&D investments, thereby generating cost-reducing innovation. If the foreign firm is not subsidized in turn by its government, only a small level of R&D spending will be optimal with unfavourable consequences for its ability to generate cost-reducing innovation. The home government's subsidy forces a contraction in the optimal amount of R&D spending by the rival firm, thereby shifting profits from the foreign firm to the home firm.

Although such subsidies dominate discussion in the profit-shifting literature, other non-tariff measures, such as TBT/SPS measures, can play a similar role. Consider a situation in which home and foreign firms are competing in the home market. The home government can impose a new TBT/SPS measure which raises both firms' costs. This measure also burdens consumers, as both firms try to pass on the additional cost in the form of higher prices. Despite this, the home government may find it worthwhile to impose the measure if, as a consequence, the foreign firm is forced to exit the home market, leaving the home firm free to earn monopoly profits, and if the resulting gains outweigh the loss in consumer surplus. The reason that the TBT/SPS measure weighs more heavily on the foreign firm is because it must re-organize production to conform with two different sets of regulations – one for products sold in the home market, and the other for products destined for the foreign market.

Equity

Governments are not only concerned with increasing national income but also with distributing income more equitably. First-best policies for income redistribution are not tariffs or non-tariff measures. In advanced countries, the fiscal system – both on the tax and expenditure side – is used to alter the distribution of income. Particularly in least-developed countries (LDCs), where fiscal systems are less developed and social safety nets often non-existent, governments appear to use trade policy instruments and NTMs in particular to achieve income distribution goals.

Import and export bans and quota restrictions on commodity trade continue to make up a significant part of NTMs in sub- Saharan Africa. The use of export restrictions by a number of emerging economies when commodity prices spiked in 2008 was motivated in part to alleviate the pressure of high food prices on the most disadvantaged.

Political Economy (Protection for Sale)

Political leaders may have other motivations beyond the welfare of citizens. For example, they may depend on financial contributions from special interest groups who want a say in trade policy. In these cases, trade protection is "for sale" to the highest bidder. If policies are being influenced by special interest groups, it should be apparent from the structure of the protection being offered and the nature of the lobbying behind it.

The use of trade taxes – tariffs, import subsidies, export taxes and export subsidies – by "captive" policy-makers under the influence of special interest groups would favour the organized or lobbying sectors. Within organized groups, the import-competing members typically obtain protection while exporting members receive an export subsidy. The Grossman and Helpman also predict that unorganized sectors will be penalized, with import-competing producers facing an import subsidy and exporting sectors penalized with an export tax. Sectors with low elasticities of import demand (export supply) will enjoy higher levels of protection or support. The rationale for this is that the government will prefer to raise contributions from those sectors where increased protection creates the least losses to society. Finally, sectors where import penetration is low will enjoy greater protection. This is because in sectors with large domestic output, producers have much to gain from an increase in the domestic price, while the economy has relatively little to lose from protection when the volume of imports is low.

Politicians captive to special interests might also use TBT/SPS measures or customs procedures as a means of transferring profits to their benefactors. One of the "stylized" findings from the "new new" trade theory is that only the most productive firms in a country are engaged in exports. This stylized fact is explained by firms' widely differing productivity ("firm heterogeneity") and the existence of fixed costs to exporting. These are costs that are incurred by firms only once in order to access a foreign market, such as market information costs, the cost of setting up a distribution system, or the cost of complying with foreign technical regulations. The fixed cost of exporting turns out to be critical in determining which firms will be able to access foreign markets and which firms will fail to do so.

Suppose that the importing country requires all foreign goods to comply with its national TBT/SPS measures. Since this increases the fixed cost of exporting, less productive firms cannot generate enough revenues to cover the higher fixed costs of accessing the foreign market and therefore exit it. This reduces competition in the importing country and increases the market share and profits of domestic firms. A government captive to domestic producers can use compliance with TBT/SPS measures as a way of increasing the profits of these producers.

The lack of transparency of a measure may also be a tell-tale sign of lurking protectionism. Political incumbents have an interest in camouflaging the transfer of income to special interests. The less transparent the measures, the greater leeway incumbents have to serve their principals.

TRADE AND WELFARE EFFECTS OF NTMs

Apart from political economy motives, governments use non-tariff measures to increase national welfare. This means that trade and welfare effects need not move in the same direction. The application of an NTM may reduce trade and yet increase the welfare of the NTM-applying country. The effects largely depend on the nature of the market failure, the type of NTM used, and other market specific circumstances. Nevertheless, the trade effects of the specific measures are highly relevant.

The trade effects of non-tariff measures can be large in a world of deepening economic integration and shaped by complex cross-border production in the form of global supply chains. Using NTMs to pursue beggar-thy-neighbour policies – to manipulate a country's terms of trade or to steal profits from foreign enterprises – is a game that can be played by every country. A government tempted to employ such measures, but concerned about national welfare, will need to worry about the possibility of similar beggarthy- neighbour NTMs being used against it by trade partners. The magnitude of the possible welfare losses from others' opportunistic actions is linked with the size of the trade effects.

Even in the absence of explicit beggar-thy-neighbour policies, and where non-tariff measures are only targeted at genuine market failures, the measures may be opaque, poorly designed, or badly implemented, thus increasing uncertainty and trade costs. Any country – whether the home country or its trading partner – can be guilty of these failings, which will end up reducing trade and the potential welfare gains that the NTMs were intended to achieve in the first place. One area that illustrates the potential problem is conformity assessment.

Conformity assessment procedures are technical procedures — such as testing, verification, inspection and certification — which confirm that products fulfil the requirements laid down in regulations and standards. Generally, exporters bear the cost, if any, of these procedures. Ideally, attestation of conformity should be carried out only once in the most costeffective manner and, subsequently, be recognized everywhere. However, in many instances, authorities in the importing country are not willing to rely on foreign manufacturers' own declarations or reports/certifications by third parties that the required specifications have been met. Whatever the TBT/SPS measure may be, assurance of compliance will be sought from domestic bodies in the importing country. This will unnecessarily raise trade costs if foreign conformity assessment bodies already possess the competence to assure them that products meet the requirements of the importing country.

Since it is impossible to analyse the trade and welfare effect of every non-tariff measure, the following is the focuses on examples regarding quantity, price and quality measures.

(i) Quantity Measures

The classic example of a quantitative restriction is an import quota which fixes trade flows at a given level. If the level of infant industry protection needs to decline over time, and policy-makers lack reliable information about the required policy setting, a quota may serve better than a subsidy. If the safety of foreign products cannot be assured and there is no way for consumers to distinguish between safe and unsafe products, an import ban might be warranted. However, a careful consideration of these latter instances suggests that extenuating circumstances in the form of high information costs were required to justify the use of import quotas. In almost all other circumstances, other non-tariff measures would be preferable to quotas. For example, in the case of infant industry protection, a subsidy is superior to an import quota. Likewise, TBT/SPS measures or labelling schemes work better than a ban in addressing all but the most extreme forms of information asymmetry.

In principle, it is possible to calculate an *ad valorem* tariff rate that, if applied in place of a quota, will have the same trade effect. Even though import levels would be identical, there are critical differences between tariffs and quotas that have an important bearing on welfare. If demand expands because of income or population growth, for example, imports will grow under a tariff but not under a quota. A quota also generates income (quota rent) for importers whereas tariffs generate revenues for government. In addition, the existence of quota rent can lead to an unhealthy struggle among interest groups to acquire these rents, a behaviour known as "rent-seeking", which can either be legal or illegal (e.g. taking the form of bribery or corruption of officials). Since competing groups expend resources to capture the quota rent, rent-seeking adds to the welfare losses or inefficiencies under quantitative restriction that do not exist under tariffs.

If domestic producers have market power, a quota also gives them greater scope to restrict imports than a tariff. While total imports remain the same as under a tariff, domestic producers are able to charge consumers a price greater than the world price plus the tariff equivalent of the quota. This effect is demonstrated most clearly in the case of a monopoly. Under a tariff, the domestic monopolist cannot charge any price above the world price plus the tariff without imports flooding in. However, a quota insulates the domestic market from trade once a given threshold of imports is reached, allowing the monopolist to charge the monopoly price because there is no offsetting inflow of imports.

The case where the import-competing industry is made up of an oligopoly (i.e. a market dominated by a small number of sellers) is more complicated. If the oligopolists compete with one another, it will still be true that a quota gives the domestic firms greater scope to exercise market power. The domestic price ends up being above the world price plus the tariff equivalent of the quota but less than the monopoly price. If the oligopolists collude, it turns out paradoxically that the cartel may charge a lower price under a quota than under a tariff because cartels are subject to defection by members. The higher the price charged by the cartel, the greater the temptation for any single member to cheat by selling more than its allotted share of total output. This opportunistic behaviour is rational for a cartel member even if it risks breaking up the cartel, so long as the additional profit made from cheating is greater than the present value of the reduction in future profits resulting from the cartel's collapse. Given the possibility of a breakdown of the cartel and the lower profits it implies, cartel members may choose to charge a lower price which is just enough to prevent defections.

(ii) Price Measures

Since externalities involve a failure to incorporate the benefit or harm caused by a certain economic activity into market prices, price measures should be the preferred tool to address this type of market failure. Such measures can result in either an expansion or contraction of trade flows. If there is a legitimate case for infant industry protection, for example, a production subsidy reduces imports but also improves economic efficiency by giving domestic firms time to accumulate experience, whose learning in turn benefits the industry as a whole. In effect, there is "too much" trade since the market fails to price in domestic firms' capacity to learn and benefit other firms in the industry. A different pattern will result if a Pigouvian tax is applied to correct pollution at home and the domestic industry is import-competing. Domestic output exceeds the socially optimal amount and "too little" trade is being generated because the market fails to price in the environmental harm created by domestic producers. In this case, the Pigouvian tax results in both the imports and the welfare of the importing country rising.

By its nature, an export subsidy is intended to increase the subsidizing country's trade. If markets are perfectly competitive, an export subsidy moves the terms of trade against the subsidizing country and reduces its welfare. Trade and welfare therefore move in opposite directions. Despite the loss in social welfare, this may well be the chosen trade policy if policy-makers are beholden to producer groups. Organized groups in the export sector will be supported with export subsidies. If markets are oligopolistic, and firms compete in quantity, an export subsidy will move profits to the subsidizing country and increase its welfare. In this case, both trade and welfare move in the same direction. If firms compete in price, an export tax will be required to shift profits from the foreign to the home firm. Since an export tax reduces trade, trade and welfare of the country applying the non-tariff measure move in opposite directions.

An export subsidy could be used to overcome that market failure. Uncertainty in the importing country about the quality of foreign goods acts like a market barrier. The export subsidy allows the foreign producer with the high-quality good to introduce its product to consumers in the importing country by selling at a lower price. If enough consumers there have a taste for the high-quality good, trade expansion will be coupled with a welfare gain for the importing country.

(iii) Quality Measures

A quality measure will require changes to the technical features of imported products which can be either an obstacle to or a catalyst for trade. Requiring exporters to comply with the importing country's TBT/SPS measures can increase trade costs and diminish their export prospects. On the other hand, if compliance with the TBT/SPS measure resolves uncertainty about the quality or safety of the imported product, greater consumer confidence can increase the demand for the item and increase trade. The trade and welfare effects of a quality measure depend on whether it addresses genuine market failures. If the measure is applied only to protect domestic producers, both trade and welfare in the importing country decrease. If, on the other hand, the measure corrects an existing market failure, welfare is likely to increase with ambiguous effects on trade.

Take the extreme case where there are no market failures but where the importing country requires all imported products to comply with a newly introduced TBT/SPS measure. It is possible to distinguish two types of trade costs that would be increased by the requirement to comply with the importing country's regulation. Compliance can increase the variable cost of exporting, with each unit of export incurring an additional cost. Alternatively, compliance can require the exporting firm to revamp its production process or upgrade its technology. In this case, irrespective of the volume of exports, the firm will incur a fixed amount of expenditure if it wants to access the foreign market.

An increase in either fixed or variable costs will have two effects. *First,* it will decrease the volume of exports of those firms who continue to serve the export market. This is sometimes referred to as the intensive margin of trade. *Secondly,* the least efficient exporters will no longer be able to cover their fixed costs of exporting and so would be forced to quit exporting altogether, sometimes referred to as the extensive margin of trade. Where TBT/SPS measures are imposed in the absence of a market failure, social welfare will fall in the importing country. Consumers in the importing country lose out both because the variety of goods is reduced, as some exporters exit the market, and because prices rise as the volume of trade declines. This is not to say that there will be no winners in the importing country. Domestic firms stand to gain because the withdrawal of some exporters and lower sales from remaining exporters reduces competition in the home market.

However, suppose that there is a genuine market failure involving information asymmetry. Consumers in the importing country are uncertain about the safety of the foreign good. Firms in the exporting country may be newcomers to global trade and have little or no reputation to build on. Foreign producers know if their product is safe or not, but consumers in the importing country have no reason to trust their claims. Under these circumstances, there may still be demand for the foreign product, but it is likely to be low. Requiring foreign products to comply with the importing country's TBT/SPS measures can resolve this uncertainty in the mind of consumers. Compliance, however, adds to the exporting firms' cost of production.

Under these conditions, the regulation will have two opposing effects on trade. The need to conform to the new regulation raises the cost of the imported good which will tend to lower the volume of trade. However, enhanced consumer confidence in the safety of the foreign product will increase demand for it. While it is possible that the increased compliance costs will force some exporters to exit the market, others will use their compliance with the regulation as a competitive advantage and increase their market share. In the context of food safety regulations, for instance, more stringent SPS measures in rich importing countries have different impacts on the competitive position of developing countries, exposing the weaknesses of some producers but accentuating the underlying supply-chain strengths of others. Furthermore, some countries use high-quality and safety regulations to successfully position themselves in global markets. Like trade, the effect on welfare is ambiguous and depends on the relative strengths of the forces acting on consumers and domestic producers. The increased cost incurred by foreign exporters to comply with the measure should increase output and revenues for domestic producers. For consumers, there are two opposing effects – a higher price for the product which needs to be weighed against the improvement in the product's safety or quality.

Finally, while Box 1 seems to suggest that an increase (decrease) in trade leads to an increase (decrease) in welfare, this does not necessarily hold under more general conditions. For example, where despite a reduction in trade, welfare improves when the application of a TBT/SPS measure corrects an existing market imperfection. This result is consistent with the argument that sometimes the adverse trade effect of a non-tariff measure is a by-product of pursuing a legitimate public policy goal.

BOX-1

Effect of TBT/SPS Measures on Trade and Welfare

Assume that a country does not produce the good X and meets all its consumption through imports. These imported goods differ widely in quality and consumers are unable to tell them apart. Because of this uncertainty, demand is low (given by the line BD in Figures B.1(a) and (b)) and price is equal to OW. Imports are equal to OA. The government of the importing country requires foreign producers to comply with a quality assurance programme; otherwise their goods will not be allowed to be sold in the country. Compliance raises the costs of foreign producers so that the price they charge rises from OW to OW'. However, consumers are now assured that only high-quality products are being sold in the market which leads to a shift in their demand to BD'. One possible outcome is that total imports rise to OA' in spite of the higher cost of imported goods (see Figure B.1(a)). Some consumer surplus is lost, given by the area labelled WW'EF, as a consequence of the cost of compliance. However, the increased confidence in the higher-quality imports results in a gain equal to the area labelled BEC. Overall, there has been an increase in consumer welfare so in this case both societal welfare and trade increase at the same time. Another possible outcome involves imports declining (see Figure B.1(b)). The increase in consumer confidence is not sufficient to overcome the higher cost of compliance. In this second example, both trade (falling from OA to OA') and societal welfare decline (the loss of WW'EF outweighs the gain of BEC).

THE CHOICE OF NTMs IN LIGHT OF DOMESTIC AND INTERNATIONAL CONSTRAINTS

In many instances, non-tariff measures, even though they affect trade, are first-best policies to address a legitimate public policy objective, such as consumer health and safety protection. However, the same measures can also be employed in a way that distorts international trade. In order to decide in such cases whether an NTM is innocuous, it is useful to determine whether the measure is likely to be pursued for competitiveness reasons rather than the stated public policy rationale or whether it may affect trade more than is necessary to achieve its policy aim.

The question of possible "policy substitution" may arise when international trade agreements limit the use of tariffs and certain types of NTMs but regulate other, less efficient options less effectively.

USE OF NTMs AND DOMESTIC POLICY CONSIDERATIONS

An important reason why governments may choose to pursue trade policy objectives by applying non-tariff measures associated with other public policy goals, or, more generally, may not choose the most efficient measure for this purpose relates to the lack of transparency of certain NTMs regarding their ultimate effect and purpose. This "opaqueness" may make such measures more attractive for politically motivated interventions where beneficiaries and the size of the effects are not easily identified. Other explanations for such policy choices emphasize institutional constraints that entice politicians to choose NTMs with certain characteristics even if these measures are economically wasteful compared with alternative means.

The fact that some NTMs entail a fixed rather than variable cost is another factor that may explain why a government subject to pressure from particular groups may favour NTMs over tariff protection. Finally, the existence of market power in a context of offshoring (and the possibility of extracting profits from exporters) may explain why trade concerns can lead both welfareand politically oriented governments to tamper with domestic policies rather than border policies alone. Each of these explanations is discussed below:

Transparency

Although it has been argued that in competitive political systems, politicians who favour specific interest groups in an inefficient manner would be voted out of office, the political economy literature has increasingly paid attention to the form of government intervention. One branch of the literature presumes that citizens are poorly informed as to the effects of various policies and the extent to which different politicians may be receptive to lobbying. It is not unrealistic to assume that politicians have better information than citizens about whether the conditions for a welfare-improving policy intervention are actually satisfied. In addition, it may be true that citizens remain unsure after a policy is implemented whether the government has acted in the national interest or simply catered to organized interests.

In particular, policies may be chosen that benefit organized interest groups and, at the same time, are justifiable on other widely accepted grounds, such as environmental protection, and, hence, may affect positively the government's reputation with the public at large. This mismatch in information between citizens and the government about both policies and politicians' motivations can lead to the implementation of "inefficient 'sneaky' methods of redistribution over more transparent efficient methods" even when the latter are available.

In the field of trade policy, non-tariff measures may be a means to increase the income of producer lobbies while concealing the associated costs and/or the true benefits of the alleged policy objective (e.g. health, environment) to the public at large. Rather than tariffs that are straightforward in their price impact and cost to consumers, an "opaque" NTM, such as an environmental regulation, may shelter an import-competing sector from foreign competition and, at the same time, be perceived as being in the public interest, even though a proper cost-benefit analysis may not show a net welfare gain. Uncertainty about the justification for, and impact of, different policies cannot explain on its own the use of opaque non-tariff measures, as competition among politicians would allow voters to sanction those politicians that pursue less efficient policies.

However, this changes when the possibility of "government failures" is taken into account. Since in a situation may arise different "types" of politicians are competing for office and voters are unsure as to the true nature of politicians' intentions. In such a case, reputation matters. "Bad" politicians, i.e. those who wish to increase the income received by special interest groups at the expense of the general public, may have an incentive to implement a "public" policy that indirectly benefits the preferred interest group, even though it is not warranted on grounds of national welfare, because open favouritism to certain groups would entail a greater reputational damage.

In other words, by increasing the income of special interest groups through "opaque" rather than direct means, these politicians limit the negative reputational impact. This is because voters cannot be sure that a given public policy is being misused by "bad" politicians, as "good" politicians would pursue the same policy, albeit only if it resulted in an overall net welfare gain. As noted above, this presupposes that citizens are unable to determine the overall costs/benefits of the public policy in question with any degree of confidence both before and after it is implemented. This is a plausible assumption for policy decisions in many areas.

Institutional Constraints

Institutional constraints can make economically less efficient non-tariff measures better for the interests of politicians or social groups that hold political power. First, governments may be limited in their ability to direct benefits to important constituents. They may lack the information necessary to target resources towards their supporters, or the credibility to maintain those policies, without an otherwise inefficient nontariff measure.

Secondly, if the public elects a new government, the interest groups that support the incumbent may lose influence. Inconsistency problems between the government and its supporters lead politicians to try to enact policies that are difficult to reverse. Certain NTMs may be less exposed to the winds of political change. Finally, government policy is not a "monolith", but rather reflects the interests of parochial departments, bureaucrats and legislators. Intragovernmental conflict can create frictions that lead to the implementation of inefficient NTMs favouring one particular interest over another.

Targeting Political Supporters

Some non-tariff measures that are comparatively inefficient, such as a market-distorting regulation, can help the government to target policies towards their favoured constituency. Concretely, a government may prefer a policy that is less efficient if its outcome is more predictable, why such distortionary policies persist,, to illustrate take a case in which removing an inefficient trade measure creates winners and losers in society. For this, presume that the NTM in question is "informationally" efficient, as compensating those that would lose from trade opening requires knowing the extent to which foreign market competition actually causes the harm, while keeping the NTM in place requires no such additional knowledge. It is assumed that information about actual losses is private, i.e. "losers" from trade opening have the incentive to over-report their losses.

If the government worries about excessive spending on compensation policy, it may prefer to sustain the NTM rather than make decisions about how much to compensate. Here, a key assumption is that the effects of an NTM are easier to verify than the effects of trade opening. This argument is less plausible if the costs of over-compensation, are low or the government is equally informed (or equally ignorant) about the effects of an NTM compared with a more efficient redistributive policy.

A similar problem is addressed in the following example. If farmers hold significant political sway, the government may consider providing either a lump-sum transfer (i.e. income support) or price support in order to maintain favour with this group. Price support represents a less efficient instrument because of its effects on product markets, and from a national welfare perspective, the government should prefer a lump-sum transfer. However, despite its negative effects on consumers and trade, governments may prefer price support, which efficiently targets those who are genuinely farmers in the short-run, as farm output is a prerequisite for receiving the subsidy. Conversely, lump-sum payments might go to a larger number of beneficiaries who merely claim or pretend to be farmers. In addition, the price support increases the returns to farming and, in the long run, encourages more entry into farm activities, which further entrenches farmers' political power. Hence, for the government the distortive effects of the price support policy are potentially outweighed by the benefits of solidifying the political power of its favoured constituency.

Policy Reversals

In competitive political systems, governments in power change, which can lead to policy reversals. From the perspective of an interest group, relatively more efficient policy measures such as a one-time subsidy or a tariff may have the disadvantage of being subject to review by new legislatures or other elected officials. By contrast, certain non-tariff measures, such as product regulations, may be defined and implemented by regulatory agencies unaffected by political change and may not be subject to a regular renewal process. Such long-lived but inefficient policies can benefit politicians by increasing interest group support.

Politicians who are unsure about their own re-election prospects receive less from lobbyists for a short-term, reversible policy. However, politicians may nonetheless receive benefits from special interests if they put in place measures, such as product regulations and the related bureaucratic apparatus that last beyond their expected careers. Inefficient NTMs which lack regular oversight also call upon fewer resources to influence the political process and, thus, are less expensive for lobbyists with sufficiently long-term horizons.

Intra-governmental Conflict

Even if legislators do have regular oversight of regulatory policy measures, the bargaining necessary to pass legislation can distort policy decisions. Each legislator must decide how to allocate resources towards policies that benefit the whole country and those that primarily benefit their local constituency. Politicians may be willing to pass a policy of national interest only if, for example, a subsidy is given to an industry located in their home district. As all legislators may need to cater to special interests, inefficient policies can proliferate.

The oversight problem also arises because of a lack of coordination within governments and across agencies that produce and regulate non-tariff measures. Because agency jurisdiction is often allocated according to a function, a given kind of NTM can be the responsibility of a number of overlapping departments or committees within a government. Efficient policy-making requires the contribution and cooperation of a number of agencies with different institutional interests, but these agencies may not value the overall policy goal as much as a parochial interest. As a result, intra-department miscommunication or competition can produce persistently inefficient policies. This implies that reforming NTMs that involve a range of domestic and possibly sub-national regulatory agencies may require broader attention to the potential bureaucratic frictions that prevent cooperation.

FIRM PREFERENCES FOR TRADE MEASURES INDUCING FIXED COSTS

The diverse nature of firms within a particular sector in terms of productivity and size has led to another rationale why trade protection may come in the form of "behind-the border" non-tariff measures rather than border protection. A range of NTMs, such as TBT/SPS measures, have an important fixed cost component, as costly production adjustments have to be made, but per unit costs subsequently decline as more output is sold in the respective market.

Owing to productivity and size differences among firms, fixed cost increases affect firms differently, unlike variable levies that raise costs for every firm by the same percentage. Hence, although a technical product regulation affects both domestic and foreign firms, the fixed costs it entails represent a higher burden for smaller and less productive firms in both countries. As a consequence, the least efficient firms will cease to be competitive and exit the market, while the more productive and larger firms both domestically and abroad will see their profits and market shares increase. Ultimately, behind-the-border non-tariff measures of this sort only benefit the country introducing the measure as a whole if the ratio of very efficient to very inefficient firms is larger at home than in the exporting country. This is in contrast to border measures, which always penalize foreign firms to the benefit of domestic producers.

Under what circumstances, then, would a behind-theborder non-tariff measure rather than border protection be introduced? Of course, like border measures, distortionary behind-the-border measures may also have a negative impact on consumer welfare. However, a politically-oriented government may yield to lobby pressure from domestic producers. Assuming that only the largest and most efficient firms have the means to lobby the government,45 they may gain more from the introduction of a behind-the-border NTM at the expense of small, less productive producers at home (even if some of the gains also go to more productive competitors abroad) than from border protection that shields all domestic firms (including those that do not lobby) from foreign competition.

Lobbying for a more demanding product regulation is more likely the less the government is concerned about social welfare and the fewer foreign firms are active in the domestic market. The reason for the latter is that when trade is already low (e.g. due to largely inefficient foreign firms or existing border protection), an increase in behind-the-border non-tariff measures has a relatively more important effect on domestic competition. To some extent, this is counter-intuitive to the idea of policy substitution, i.e. the increase of behind-the-border NTMs when border measures are liberalized.

At higher levels of regulation, the marginal gain from behind-the-border non-tariff measures declines (and hence the political contributions lobbying firms are willing to make) and at some point becomes smaller than the marginal loss in social welfare (despite the larger weight given to organized producer interest). As a result, behind-the-border NTMs may be set at some "intermediate" level.

Conversely, for border measures targeted exclusively at foreign producers, the domestic producer lobby's marginal gain in profits (and related political contributions) do not decrease with higher levels of protection and lobbies who gain a lot from keeping foreign competition out and governments that care little for social welfare may implement a prohibitive level of border protection, or vice-versa, none at all. In sum, although lobbying for behind-the-border as opposed to border measures simultaneously, it is interesting to note that when behind-the-border NTMs are introduced, the conflict of interest between domestic producers pitting an organized lobby of productive firms against the rest may lead to less restrictive measures than if border protection were pursued.

OFFSHHORING AND BILITERAL BARGAINING

The key feature in international offshoring is the relationship-specific nature of trade between importers and their specialized suppliers abroad. Owing to the specificity of the input, foreign suppliers hold some market power over the importing producer. At the same time, once the input is produced by the exporter according to the importer's specifications and the related investment is sunk, the importer can wield its bargaining power to obtain a share of the foreign supplier's profits. As a result, international prices are determined by bilateral bargaining rather than market clearing. This phenomenon, which has become known as the "hold-up" problem leads to the situation of "under-investment" by foreign suppliers and, hence, an insufficient supply of inputs to domestic producers.

The domestic government now faces a tension in its objective to maximize national welfare: it must provide incentives to foreign input suppliers to produce more and, at the same time, it must help domestic producers importing these inputs to appropriate maximum profits in the bilateral bargaining with the foreign supplier. In order to pursue these different objectives in its foreign trade relationship, the government will not only adjust its tariff policy on inputs, but also employ measures in regard to final products. It will do the former to increase the supply of foreign inputs and the latter in order to affect prices received by producers and, hence, profits all along the supply chain.

Use of NTMs and International Constraints

Governments can use multiple policies to achieve a given objective. In the case of a market failure, the "first-best" policy to address a single distortion is one that offsets the source of the distortion directly. For instance, if the domestic production of a certain good is associated with positive externalities for an economy, a production subsidy is the "first-best" policy – it is welfare-superior to an import tariff. What then happens in a situation where an economy faces a domestic distortion, an externality for example, but also has monopoly power in trade in that it can affect the world price of the given product? In a noncooperative framework, a government would introduce two "first-best" or most efficient policies – a nondistortionary non-tariff measure to tackle the former and a suitable tariff for the latter. However, the "first-best" or most efficient measures may not always be used by governments.

International Constraints

Under the auspices of the GATT/WTO, the last 60 years have seen a dramatic multilateral reduction in tariff barriers owing to agreements that require members to respect the negotiated tariff bindings – ceilings on applied tariffs. If members set tariffs above that binding, they may be subject to a costly dispute initiated by another member. Similar constraints also affect other trade policy measures – for example, non-tariff measures such as import and export quotas as well as export subsidies are generally prohibited, although their use is allowed for "legitimate" reasons in specific cases. Even in preferential trade agreements (PTAs), countries agree to preferential tariffs between themselves and, in customs unions, to set a common external tariff, whereby non-enforcement of these tariffs could generate costly retaliation by other PTA members.

Unlike border measures, disciplining behind-theborder non-tariff measures explicitly under the multilateral trading system, for instance, is more challenging for the following reasons. First, they are typically less transparent. Secondly, NTMs are often highly complex and country-specific. This means that the formulation of general rules to discipline them is likely to involve different authorities who are not used to coordinating with others. Thirdly, while NTMs may have adverse trade effects, some of them are associated with legitimate public policy objectives. Despite these difficulties, NTMs are not left entirely unregulated because members of a trade agreement could otherwise undo any negotiated tariff restrictions by, for instance, imposing different sales taxes for imported and domestic products. Of course, to the extent that countries can use NTMs in import-competing sectors as a means of reducing trade flows, they can undermine commitments previously made with respect to trade policy.

Policy Substitution

It is likely that as countries sign successive rounds of trade agreements that constrain their ability to pursue trade goals through trade policy (tariffs and certain border non-tariff measures), other NTMs, including those behind the border, become attractive tools for terms-of-trade manipulation that shifts costs onto foreign exporters. In other words, there will be incentives for governments to distort their NTMs as a secondary means of protecting import-competing industries. In this context, it is even argued that there is a "Law of Constant Protection".

When tariffs are constrained cooperatively, quotas would be the preferred measure among the set of border NTMs for governments looking for alternative measures. Anti-dumping policies are likely to be used only when the use of quotas is also sufficiently constrained by international agreements. Similarly, if a government cannot respond to competitive pressures abroad by unilaterally restricting market access with an increase in its tariff, it may be drawn into imposing a behind-the-border NTM. For example, it may be tempted to improve the relative cost position of a domestic firm by relaxing technical regulations in its import-competing industry, thereby restricting access to foreign suppliers. Some foreign suppliers who export to these markets may actually lower their prices to remain competitive with domestic producers. However, even such terms-of-trade movement leads to foreign producers absorbing some of the costs of the weakening of domestic technical regulations. Hence, in light of falling trade barriers, this regulatory cost shifting could result in a "race-to-the-bottom" problem where governments might be tempted to relax technical regulations that apply to import-competing industries in the name of international competitiveness – those relating to labour and the environment are prominent examples.

The true source of the "race-to-the-bottom problem" is not that weak foreign technical regulations generate competitive pressures that induce inefficiently low domestic technical regulations. Rather, it is the imperfections in property rights over market access commitments in trade agreements – a government is not free to adjust its policy mix so long as it maintains its market access commitment. For instance, if a government increases technical requirements in its import-competing industry, this industry would be subjected to increased competitive pressure from abroad. However, because trade policy is constrained by an international agreement, the government would not be able to raise its tariff (without a penalty) and maintain its market access commitment.

It is worth noting that instead of a "race-to-the-bottom" problem, it may even be the case that increased constraints on tariff policy imposed by international agreements are accompanied by rising technical regulations. The international cost-shifting incentive described above may instead create a tendency for governments to impose more stringent domestic technical regulations if the domestic firm in an importcompeting industry finds it easier to comply with them, i.e. if the technical regulation improves the relative cost position of the domestic firm. However, even when a technical regulation increases the costs of production more for the foreign firm than the domestic firm, the substitution of technical regulations for tariffs which are constrained by an international agreement is far from straightforward.

Two illustrate, consider two scenarios. First, when tariffs are prohibitive and hence when a small tariff reduction enables minimal participation by the foreign firm, governments are likely to have an incentive to raise technical regulations. This is because the tariff cut increases the marginal benefit of the regulation – because imports become cheaper, the regulation becomes the instrument which can improve the domestic firm's relative cost position and hence its profits. At the same time, by worsening the foreign firm's production costs, and reducing imports, the technical regulation reduces tariff revenues. Hence, if the government cares about tariff revenues, its optimal regulatory response to tariff cuts is less clear. However, prohibitive tariffs are increasingly rare. Secondly, in the case where the foreign firm already has a significant market presence, the relationship between tariff cuts – that deepen foreign penetration even further – and rising technical regulations is more tenuous. Technical regulations reduce consumer surplus. However, a reduction in tariffs diminishes the regulation's marginal impact on consumer surplus because it lowers prices faced by consumers. Similarly, while regulations shift profits to the domestic firm, tariff cuts – by making imports cheaper – diminish the regulation's marginal effect on domestic firm profits.

Given the above, if the government only cares about consumer surplus and the domestic firm's profits, it would respond to tariff cuts by relaxing technical regulations. This suggests that because constraints on the use of tariffs weaken the effectiveness of a technical regulation as an instrument, tariffs and technical regulations are actually complements. It underscores that what matters for policy substitution is not the direct effects of measures, but how the weakening of one measure affects the marginal effectiveness of the other. The government's response is more ambiguous when it also worries about tariff revenues and negative consumption externalities.

A reduction in tariffs, bound by an international agreement, enhances the regulation's marginal effect on the consumption externality because it remains the only instrument to reduce demand in the economy. Similarly, tariff reduction enhances the regulation's marginal effect on raising tariff revenues – constraints on increasing tariffs imply that altering technical regulations is the only way in which the government can influence imports and hence tariff revenue. Hence, if the impact of the regulation on the consumption externality is large and/or if the initial tariff rate is high, the improvement in the regulation's capacity to reduce the externality and raise tariff revenues, on the margin, may offset the reduction of its marginal effects on domestic profits and the consumer surplus. In this situation, governments may respond to tariff reductions by technical requirements, i.e. policy substitution.

In recent years, the proliferation of technical regulations may not be driven by a desire to protect domestic firms' profits when tariffs are constrained by a international agreement, but rather it may reflect a growing awareness of consumption externalities. Governments will have an incentive to increase technical regulations only if the net marginal benefit of the regulation increases with falling tariffs.

QUESTIONS

1. Discuss the reasons for government intervention and types of non-tariff measures (NTMs) application from the perspective of the WTO.
2. Why do you expect a country's trade policy to be different in a country depending upon how wealth is distributed in the country?

3. "Government are more likely to grant protection to industries where the benefits are more concentrated than the costs imposed on others." Do you agree?
4. Identify the situations in which governments may be prone to employ non-tariff measures for trade competitiveness reasons, even if the stated policy rationale is a different one, or implement an inefficient instrument that may affect trade more than necessary to achieve a given objective.
5. Why should democratically elected governments prefer to choose protectionist policies.
6. Critically examine the trade and welfare effects of non-tariff measures (NTMs)?
7. Critically examine the use of non-tariff measures (NTMs) to achieve a range of policy objectives.
8. "Trade barriers raise the real income of scarce factors, which give them a big incentive to lobby for protection." Explain.
9. Define transparency in non-tariff measures. How do non-tariff measures (NTMs) achieve policy objective?
10. Discuss the choice of non-tariff measures (NTMs) in the light of domestic and international constraints.
11. India argues that infant-industry protection of its industry is necessary? What factors support this claim? How would you assess the benefits and costs for targeting an industry?
12. Is it possible to identify disguised protectionism in non-tariff measures (NTMs)?

REFERENCES

Baldwin R.E. (1979), *The Political Economy of US Import Trade Policy*, MIT Press, Cambridge, MA.

Baldwin, R. and Krugman, P. (1988a) "Market Access and Competition: A Simulation Study of 16K Random Access Memories," in R. Feenstra (ed.) *Empirical Research in Industrial Trade*, Cambridge, MA: MIT Press.

—— (1988b) "Industrial Political and International Competition in Wide-bodied Jet Aircraft," in R. Baldwin, (ed.) *Trade Policy Issues and Empirical Analysis*, Chicago: University of Chicago Press, pp. 45-71.

Baldwin, R.E. (1969), The case against infant industry protection. *Journal of Political Economy*, 77, 295-305.

Bardhan, P. (1971) "On Optimum Subsidy to a Learning Industry: An Aspect of the Theory of Infant Industry Protection," *International Economic Review* 12: 54-70.

Beason, R. and Weinstein, D. (1996) "Growth, Economies of Scale, and Targeting in Japan," *Review of Economics and Statistics* 78: 286-95.

Becker, G.S. (1983) A theory of competition among pressure groups for political influence. *Quarterly Journal of Economics*, 98(3), 371-400.

Bhagwati, J. and Ramaswami V.K. (1963) Domestic distortions, tariffs and the theory of optimum subsidy. *Journal of Political Economy*, 71, 44-50.

Corden, W.M. (1957) Tariffs, subsidies and the terms of trade. *Economica*, 24, 235-42.

Cuthbertson, J.M. (1986) The folly of free trade. *Harvard Business Review*, NS 86(5), 122-8.

Dutt, P. and Mitra, D. (2002) "Endogenous Trade Policy through Majority Voting," Journal *of International* Economics 58: 107-34.

Eicher, T. and Osang, T. (2002) "Protection for Sale: An Empirical Investigation: Comment," American Economic Review 92: 1702-1710.

Feenstra, R. (ed.) (1989) *Trade Policies for International Competitiveness*, Chicago: University of Chicago Press.

Finger J.M. (1979), Trade liberalization and public choice perspective, in *Challenges to a Liberal Economic Order*, (eds. R.C. Amacher, G. Harberler and T.D. Willet), American Enterprise Institute, Washington, DC, pp. 421-53.

Flanders, M.J. (1964), Prebisch on protectionism: an evaluation. *The Economic Journal*, 71, 305-26.

Frey, B. (1984), International Political Economics, Blackwells, Oxford.

Gawande, K. and Bandyopadhay, H. (2000) "Is Protection for Sale? Evidence on the Grossman-Helpman Theory of Endogenous Protection," Review *of* Economics and Statistics 82: 139-52.

Goldberg, P. and Maggi, G. (1999) "Protection for Sale: An Empirical Investigation," American Economic Review 89: 1135-1155.

Greenaway, D and Sapsford, D. (1987) Further econometric analysis of the relationship between fiscal dependence on trade taxes and economic development. Public Finance, 42(2), 309-19.

Grossman, G. and Helpman, E. (1994) "Protection for Sole," American Economics Review 84: 833-50.

Heckscher, E. (1935), *Mercantilism*, George Allen and Unwin, London.

Hindley, B. (1983), Trade policy economic performance and Britain's economic problem, in *Policy and Performance in International Trade*, (eds. J. Black and A. Winters), Macmillan, London, pp. 25-42.

IBRD (1987), *World Bank Development Report*, International Bank for Reconstruction and Development, Washington, DC.

Johnson, H.G. (1965) Optimal trade intervention in the presence of domestic distortions, in *Trade Growth and the Balance of Payments*, (eds. R.E. Caves, P. Kenen and H.G. Johnson), North Holland, Amsterdam, pp. 3-34.

Keynes, J.M. (1972), The Collected writings of John Maynard Keynes, Vol. 9, 'Essays in Persuasion.' Mitigation by tariff, in *Essays in Persuasion, Vol. 9, Collected Writings*, Macmillan, pp. 231-44.

Krugman, P. (1984) "Import Protection as Export Promotion: International Competition in the Presence of Oligopoly and Economies of Scale," in H. Kierzkowski (ed.) *Monopolistic Competition in International Trade*, Oxford: Oxford University Press, pp. 180-93.

—— (ed.) (1986) *Strategic Trade Policy and the New International Economics*, Cambridge, MA: MIT Press.

—— (1987) "Is Free Trade Passe?," *Journal of Economic Perspectives* 1: 131-41.

Krugman, P. and Smith, A. (eds) (1994) *Empirical Studies of Strategic Trade Policy*, Chicago: University of Chicago Press.

Leontief, W. (1933), The use of indifference curves in international trade. *Quarterly Journal of Economics*, 47, 493-503.

Lewis, W.A. (1969), *Aspects of Tropical Trade 1883-1965*, Alquist and Wicksell, Stockholm.

Magee, S. (1980) "Three Simple Tests of the Stolper-Samuelson Theorem," in P. Oppenheimer (ed.) *Issues in International Economics*, London: Oriel Press, pp. 138-53.

Markusen, J., Melvin, J., Kaempfer, W., and Maskus, K. (1995) *International Trade Theory and Evidence*, New York: McGraw Hill, pp. 293-300.

Mayer, W. (1984) "Endogenous Tariff Formation," American Economic Review 74: 970-85.

Noland, M. and Pack, H. (2003) *Industrial Policy in an Era of Globalization: Lessons from Asia*, Washington, DC: Institute for International Economics.

Rodrik, D. (1995) "Political Economy of Trade Policy," in G. Grossman and K. Rogoff (eds) Handbook *of International Economics, Vol. Ill*, New York: Elsevier Science B.V., pp. 1457-1494.

6

WORLD TRADE ORGANISATION

INTRODUCTION

The formation of the World Trade Organisation has redefined the structure of the international trade framework. In 1948, after years of negotiations, more than 50 nations signed the Havana Charter to create the ITO, the International Trade Organisation. Several major principles were to govern world trade from then on. One of the principles was the non-discriminatory treatment of parties, and a commitment to reduce tariffs and other trade barriers and eliminate quotas. Services were to be covered just as well as products, owners of patents, and intangible assets were to be protected. Foreign direct investment was to receive fair treatment and domestic-content requirements and public subsidies were to be regulated. But in the 1950s, President Truman decided not to re-submit the ITO charter to Congress for ratification due to perceived threats to national sovereignty and the danger of too much ITO intervention in markets.

The Uruguay Round of Multilateral Trade Negotiations, concluded on 15 December 1993 and the Final Act signed by member countries at a meeting in Marrakesh, Morocco, in April 1994 marked a watershed in the history of multilateral trade in more ways than one. In 1994, the focus was on a totally new organisation which the Uruguay Round negotiations agreed on the World Trade Organisation (WTO). And this WTO, as if by magic, has a lot of components which sound remarkably similar to the provisions of the ITO. Infact, this eighth in the series, was the most ambitious and complex of the trade rounds held since the inception of GATT in 1947. While GATT covered only trade in goods, the scope of multilateral trade negotiations under the Uruguay Round leading to the establishment of the World Trade Organisation (WTO) was extended to cover several new areas such as services, investment and intellectual property rights. Even in the area of goods, agriculture and textiles which were outside the ambit of GATT were brought into the fold of multilateral trade negotiations. The basic principle underlying these Agreements was to have an open trading system based on multilaterally agreed rules.

WORLD TRADE ORGANISATION

The World Trade Organisation (WTO) is the principal international organization governing world trade. It has 150 member countries, representing over 95% of world trade. It was established in 1995 as a successor institution to the General Agreement on Tariffs and Trade (GATT). The GATT was a post-World War II institution intended to promote nondiscrimination in trade among countries, with the view that open trade was crucial for economic stability and peace.

Decisions within the WTO are made by member countries, not WTO staff, and they are made by consensus, not formal vote. High-level policy decisions are made by the Ministerial Conference, which is the body of political representatives (trade ministers) from each member country. The Ministerial Conference must meet atleast every two years. Operational decisions are made by the General Council, which consists of a representative from each member country. The General Council meets monthly, and the chair rotates annually among national representatives.

The United States was an original signatory to the GATT and a leading proponent of the GATT's free-market principles. It continues to be among the countries urging further discussions on opening markets to trade. Although decisions in the WTO are by consensus, the United States has a highly influential role in the WTO because it is the largest trading nation in the world.

Periodically, member countries agree to hold negotiations to revise existing rules or establish new ones. These periodic negotiations are commonly called "rounds." The broader the negotiations, the greater the possible trade-offs, and thus theoretically the greater the potential economic benefits to countries. The multilateral negotiations are especially important to developing countries, which might otherwise be left out of more selective agreements. It must be remembered, however, that trade liberalization also results in job losses and other economic dislocations as well.

DOHA WTO MINISTERIAL CONFERENCE

On November 9-14,2001, trade ministers from member countries met in Doha, Qatar for the fourth WTO Ministerial Conference. At that meeting, they agreed to undertake a new round of multilateral trade negotiations.

Before the Doha Ministerial, negotiations had already been underway on trade in agriculture and trade in services. These on-going negotiations had been required under the last round of multilateral trade negotiations (the Uruguay Round, 1986-1994). However, some countries, including the United States, wanted to expand the agriculture and services talks to allow trade-offs and thus achieve greater trade liberalization.

There were additional reasons for the negotiations. Just months before the Doha Ministerial, the United States had been attacked by terrorists on September 11,2001.

Some government officials called for greater political cohesion and saw the trade negotiations as a means toward that end. Some officials thought that a new round of multilateral trade negotiations could help a world economy weakened by recession and terrorism-related uncertainty. According to the WTO, the year 2001 showed "...the lowest growth in output in more than two decades," and world trade actually contracted that year. Box-1 presents the Doha Declaration.

BOX 1
The Doha Declaration

The Doha Declaration - comprising of a main Declaration, a Declaration on TRIPS Agreement and Public Health and a decision on Implementation related issues and concerns- launches the future work programme of the WTO and includes elaboration and timetables for the current negotiations in agriculture and services and negotiations/possible negotiations in a range of other issues.

Implementation Issues: A number of implementation issues have been addressed in the Decision on implementation related issues and concerns including longer time frame (of six months) for compliance with new SPS and TBT measures, moratorium of two years on non-violation complaints under the TRIPS Agreement, need for special care for initiation of back to back antidumping investigations within a year and co-operation and assistance by members in investigations relating to declared values. The declaration agrees that negotiations on all other outstanding implementation issues shall be an integral part of the work programme. Where specific negotiations are mandated, relevant implementation issues shall be addressed under that mandate and other outstanding implementation issues shall be addressed as a matter of priority by the relevant WTO bodies, which shall report to the Trade Negotiating Committee by the end of 2002 for appropriate action.

Agriculture: The Declaration commits to comprehensive negotiations aimed at: substantial improvements in market access for developing countries; reductions of, with a view to phasing out, all forms of export subsidies; and substantial reductions in trade distorting domestic support being given by the developed countries. It also takes note of non trade concerns of developing countries and their development needs including food security and rural development. Special and differential treatment for developing countries would be an integral part of the negotiations.

Services: The Negotiating Guidelines and Procedures adopted by the Council for Trade in Services would form the basis for continuing negotiations in Services with a view to achieving the objectives of GATS. The declaration recognises the large number of proposals submitted by the members on various sectors including on movement of natural persons.

Industrial tariffs: The negotiations under industrial tariffs would aim at reducing or as appropriate eliminating tariffs, including the reduction of tariff peaks, high tariffs and tariff escalations, as well as non tariff barriers, in particular on products of export interest to developing countries. Product coverage shall be comprehensive and without a priori exclusions with negotiations taking into account the needs and interests of the developing countries including through less than full reciprocity in reduction commitments.

TRIPS: The Work programme mandates negotiations on establishment of a multilateral system of notification and registration of geographical indications for wines and spirits by the 5th session of the Ministerial Conference. The issues related to extension of the higher level of protection of geographical indications to products other than wines and spirits, examination of relationship between the TRIPS Agreement and the Convention on Biological Diversity (CBD), the protection of traditional knowledge and folklore and other relevant new developments would be addressed by the TRIPS Council as part of the Implementation issues. Further, the Declaration on TRIPS and Public Health is one of the most significant outcomes of the Doha Conference. It recognises that the TRIPS Agreement can and should be interpreted and implemented in a manner supportive of WTO members' right to protect public health and to promote access to medicines for all.

WTO Rules: The Declaration mandates negotiations aimed at clarifying and improving disciplines under the Agreement on Implementation and Subsidies and Countervailing Measures while preserving the basic concepts, principles and effectiveness of these Agreements and taking into account the needs of developing countries. It also includes negotiations aimed at clarifying and improving disciplines and procedures under the existing WTO provisions applying to regional trade agreement (keeping into view the developmental aspects of these Agreements). Negotiations are further mandated on improvements and clarifications of the Dispute Settlement Understanding. Addressing outstanding implementation issues on these subjects would be an integral part of these negotiations.

Special and Differential Treatment (S&D): The negotiations shall fully take into account the principle of special and differential treatment for developing countries. It has also been agreed to review all special and differential treatment provisions with a view to strengthening them and making them more precise, effective and operational.

Electronic Commerce: The Work Programme declares that Members will maintain their current practice of not imposing customs duties on electronic transmissions until the Fifth Ministerial Session.

Singapore issues: The issues relating to Trade and Investment, interaction between Trade and Competition, Transparency in Government Procurement and Trade Facilitation will continue to be pursued in the Working Group Study process. Negotiation on these subjects, according to the Work Programme, will take place after the Fifth session of the Ministerial Conference on the basis of a decision to be taken, by explicit consensus, at that session on modalities of negotiations.

Environment: Negotiations on limited aspects of trade and environment (relationship between existing WTO rules and specific trade obligations set out in Multilateral Environmental Agreements, procedures for regular information exchange between MEA and WTO and reduction/elimination of tariff and non tariff barriers to environmental goods and services) has been mandated, along with instructions to the Committee on Trade and Environment to pursue its work on all items on its agenda, giving particular attention to the issues of market access, the relevant provisions of the TRIPS Agreement and labeling.

Labour: The Declaration recognises that ILO is the appropriate forum to address the issue of core labour standards.

Working Groups: The Work Programme has also set up two Working Groups. One to examine the relationship between Trade, Debt and Finance for suggesting solutions, within the WTO mandate, to the problem of external indebtedness of developing countries and to strengthen the coherence of international trade and financial policies, with a view to safeguarding the multilateral trading system from the effects of financial and monetary instability. The other Working group will examine the relationship between Trade and transfer of Technology and to facilitate, within the WTO mandate, increased flow of technology to developing countries.

Negotiations under the Work Programme are to be concluded not later than 1 January 2005 (except negotiation on improving and clarifying the Dispute Settlement Understanding which is to be concluded by end of may 2003). The conduct, conclusion and entry into force of the outcome of negotiations will be treated as parts of a single undertaking (except for DSU). The overall conduct of the negotiations is to be supervised by a Trade Negotiations Committee under the authority of the General Council.

At the Doha meeting, trade ministers agreed that the 5th Ministerial, to be held in 2003, would "take stock of progress, provide any necessary political guidance, and take decisions as necessary," and that negotiations would be concluded not later than January 1, 2005. With the exception of actions on the Dispute Settlement Understanding, trade ministers agreed that the outcome of the negotiations would be a single undertaking, which means that nothing is finally agreed until everything is agreed. Thus, countries agreed they would reach a single, comprehensive agreement containing a balance of concessions at the end of the negotiations.

Negotiations have proceeded at a slow pace and have been characterised by lack of progress on significant issues, and persistent disagreement on nearly every aspect of the agenda. A few issues have been resolved, notably in agriculture. However, the first order of business for the round, the negotiation of modalities, or the methods and formulas by which negotiations are conducted, still remain elusive four years after the beginning of the round.

CANCUN WTO MINISTERIAL CONFERENCE

An important milepost in the Doha Development Agenda round was the 5th Ministerial Conference, which was held in Cancun, Mexico on September 10-14, 2003. The Cancun Ministerial ended without agreement on a framework to guide future negotiations, and this failure to advance the round resulted in a serious loss of momentum and brought into question whether the January 1, 2005 deadline would be met.

The Cancun Ministerial collapsed for several reasons. *First*, differences over the Singapore issues seemed irresolvable. The EU had retreated on some of its demands, but several developing countries refused any consideration of these issues at all. *Second*, it was questioned whether some countries had come to Cancun with a serious intention to negotiate. In the view of some observers, a few countries showed no flexibility in their positions and only repeated their demands rather than talk about trade-offs. *Third*, the wide difference between developing and developed countries across virtually all topics was a major obstacle. The U.S.-EU agricultural proposal and that of the Group of 21, for example, show strikingly different approaches to special and differential treatment Fourth, there was some criticism of procedure.

The aftermath of Cancun was one of standstill and stocktaking. Negouations were suspended for the remainder of 2003. However, in early 2004, then-U.S. Trade Representative (USTR) Robert Zoellick offered proposals on how to move the round forward. The USTR called for a focus on market access, including an elimination of agricultural export subsidies. He also said that the Singapore issues could progress by negotiating on trade facilitation, considering further action on government procurement, and possibly dropping investment and competition. This intervention was credited at the time with reviving interest in the negotiations, and negotiations resumed in March 2004.

On July 31, 2004, WTO members approved a Framework Agreement that includes major developments in the most contentious and crucial issue — agriculture. Because of the importance of agriculture to the Round, the Framework, which provides guidelines but not specific concessions, was regarded as a major achievement. With a broad agreement on agriculture and on other issues, negotiators were given a clearer direction for future discussions. However, the talks settled back into a driftless stalemate, where few but the most technical issues were resolved.

HONG KONG MINISTERIAL DECLARATION

The stalemate in 2005 increased the perceived importance of the 6th Ministerial in Hong Kong as potentially the last opportunity to settle key negotiating issues that could produce an agreement by 2007, the *de facto* deadline resulting from the expiration of U.S. trade promotion authority. Although a flurry of negotiations took place in the fall of 2005, WTO Director-General Pascal Lamy announced in November 2005 that a comprehensive agreement on modalities would not be forthcoming in Hong Kong, and the Doha Round would enter into a decisive phase. The common perception was that quick progress in the negotiations was required to find solutions on key issues, namely agricultural market access, domestic support in agriculture, industrial tariffs and services. Ambitious structural adjustment in agricultural policy and associated trade policy, which have remained "left-over" issues for so many years, is indeed crucial to enabling a balanced and development-focused outcome. In particular, five key objectives (or deliverables) for a meaningful "development package" must be attained to ensure the credibility and sustainability of the multilateral trading system.

First, the Doha Round must result in significantly enhanced and additional real market access and entry for developing countries' exports of manufactured goods, commodities and services in their major markets so as to enable them to grow and prosper. This implies tariff elimination, removal of tariff escalation and peaks, and providing access in services sectors engaged in by developing countries, especially in GATS Modes 4 (movement of natural persons) and 1 (cross-border trade) of services delivery, and addressing non-tariff barriers. The provision of duty-free and quota-free treatment to all LDCs for all their products on a lasting basis, as well as the issue of addressing special concerns of African cotton-producing countries, as contemplated at the Sixth Ministerial Conference of the WTO, are important elements that remain to be implemented fully.

Second, the Doha Round should bring about improvements in multilateral rules that address and remove existing asymmetries and enhance the fairness and equity of the multilateral trading system. Substantially reducing and removing trade-distorting agricultural subsidies is indispensable for levelling the playing field for fair competition in agricultural trade. An appropriate phasing and sequencing of market opening, as well as institutional and regulatory reform, are also important, particularly in the field of services, accompanied by complementary policies in support of building domestic supply capacity.

Third, the development dimension signifies there is enough space for Governments to align the multilateral framework of rights and obligations under WTO with the objectives of national development strategies. This relates to measures such as the more operational special and differential treatment and less-than-full reciprocity rule; preserving tariff revenues; promoting domestic nascent industries and pre-empting de-industrialization; preserving long-standing trade preferences; safeguarding food security, livelihood security and rural development; providing for use of policies and measures to foster commodity-sector production, diversification and competitiveness; universal access to essential and infrastructure services; access to essential drugs; implementation-related issues; and other measures that address the more specific concerns of small island developing States and other vulnerable economies.

Fourth, development solidarity is required from the international community for developing countries in undertaking adjustment and meeting implementation costs, building trade-related infrastructure and supplying capacity-building in trading and marketing. In this context, the Aid for Trade Initiative is an essential complement to the envisaged further trade liberalization under the multilateral trading system. If it provides for additional aid, it can play an important role—along with improved market access, balanced rules and sound domestic policies—in helping developing countries realize sustained gains from trade.

Fifth, it is important to ensure greater coherence and a positive interface between regional trade agreements (RTAs) and the multilateral trading system. In respect of the apparent never-ending tide of regionalism, robust progress in and a successful conclusion to the Doha Round is the best guarantee against the continuing erosion of the multilateral system. Specifically, the WTO rules on RTAs, under negotiation in the Doha negotiations, need clarification and improvement so as to improve compliance and better take into account development aspects of RTAs.

Furthermore, the universality of WTO membership is essential for the legitimacy and governance of the trading system. Accession of about 30 developing countries and countries with economies in transition is thus a systemic priority. However, experience has shown that relatively deep liberalization and stringent reform commitments, including

WTO-plus commitments, have been requested from acceding developing countries, thus affecting their balance of WTO rights and obligations in comparison with the original WTO members. It is thus crucial to ensure fair and equitable terms of accession commensurate with the individual acceding country's trade, financial and development needs, and the provision of increased support in all stages of the accession negotiations, as well as in the post-accession process.

After the suspension of the Round in July 2006, the negotiations were formally resumed in February 2007, followed by active and intense diplomatic activities and consultations at various levels throughout 2007. In July, the centre of negotiations once again returned to Geneva to resume a "bottom-up approach", when chairpersons of the negotiating bodies on agriculture and non-agriculture market access (NAMA) submitted new texts of negotiating modalities in these two priority areas.

Despite these new developments, the positions of major players have remained essentially unchanged since July 2006, when the Round was suspended. Discussions thus continue to centre on trying to find the right balance between agriculture and NAMA and setting numerical targets on various parameters in those two areas. However, unexpectedly, new and difficult issues have been added to the negotiating agenda, such as special flexibilities in NAMA requested for customs unions among developing countries (the Southern Common Market (MERCOSUR) and the Southern African Customs Union (SACU)), while China has recently emphasized that it needs more flexibility as a recently acceded WTO member.

Visible attempts have been made to intensify negotiations in other areas, including services, rules, trade facilitation and trade-related aspects of intellectual property. Most importantly, however, no significant movement was recorded on development issues of special and differential treatment, and implementation issues. Work continued on the operationalization of Aid for Trade, resulting in pledges during the WTO Global Aid for Trade Review on 20 November 2007 to increase funds for this purpose to $30 billion by 2010.

SIGNIFICANCE OF THE NEGOTIATIONS

Trade economists argue that the reduction of trade barriers allows a more efficient exchange of products among countries and encourages economic growth. Multilateral negotiations offer the greatest potential benefits by obliging countries throughout the world to reduce barriers to trade. The gains to the United States and to the world from multilateral trade agreements have been calculated in the billions of dollars.

Multilateral negotiations are especially important to developing countries that might otherwise be left out of a regional or bilateral trade agreement Developing country blocs can improve trade and economic growth among its members, but the larger share of benefits are from the trade agreements that open the markets of the world. Multilateral trade negotiations are also an exercise in international cooperation and encourage economic interdependence, which offers political benefits as well.

When a country opens its markets, however, increased imports might cause economic dislocations at the local or regional level. Communities might lose factories. Workers might lose their jobs. For those who experience such losses, multilateral trade agreements do not improve their economic well-being. Also, if a country takes an action that is not in compliance with an agreement to which it is a party, it might face some form of sanction. Further, some oppose WTO rules that restrict how a country is permitted to respond to imports of an overseas product that employs an undesirable production method, for example a process that might use limited resources or impose unfair working conditions. Thus, while multilateral trade agreements have been found to offer broad economic benefits, they are opposed for a variety of reasons as well.

WTO AND THE TRIPS AGREEMENT

Trade-Related Aspects of Intellectual Property Rights (TRIPS) is expected to have the greatest impact on the pharmaceutical sector and access to medicines. The TRIPS Agreement has been in force since 1995 and is to date the most comprehensive multilateral agreement on intellectual property. The TRIPS Agreement introduced global minimum standards for protecting and enforcing nearly all forms of intellectual property rights (IPR), including those for patents. International conventions prior to TRIPS did not specify minimum standards for patents. At the time that negotiations began, over 40 countries in the world did not grant patent protection for pharmaceutical products. The TRIPS Agreement now requires all WTO members, with few exceptions, to adapt their laws to the minimum standards of IPR protection. In addition, the TRIPS Agreement also introduced detailed obligations for the enforcement of intellectual property rights.

However, TRIPS also contains provisions that allow a degree of flexibility and sufficient room for countries to accommodate their own patent and intellectual property systems and developmental needs. This means countries have a certain amount of freedom in modifying their regulations and, various options exist for them in formulating their national legislation to ensure a proper balance between the goal of providing incentives for future inventions of new drugs and the goal of affordable access to existing medicines.

Patent Protection

The TRIPS Agreement requires WTO Members to provide protection for a minimum term of 20 years from the filing date of a patent application for any invention including for a pharmaceutical product or process. Prior to the TRIPS Agreement, patent duration was significantly shorter in many countries. For example, both developed and developing countries provided for patent terms ranging from 15 to 17 years, whilst in certain developing countries, patents were granted for shorter terms of 5 to 7 years. The TRIPS Agreement also requires countries to provide patent protection for both processes and products, in all fields of technology.

Before TRIPS, many countries provided only process — but not product — patents. *Product patents provide for absolute protection of the product, whereas process patents provide protection in respect of the technology and the process or method of manufacture.* Protection for process patents would not prevent the manufacture of patented products by a process of reverse engineering, where a different process or method from that which has been invented (and patented) is used. For example, national legislation requiring only process patent protection has enabled manufacturers in certain countries to make generic versions of patented medicines. These countries have opted to make use of the transition period that permitted countries to delay, until 2005, patent protection in the areas of technology that authorities require pharmaceutical companies to submit data demonstrating the safety, quality and efficacy of the product. The TRIPS Agreement requires that WTO Members protect undisclosed test data, submitted to drug regulatory authorities for the purposes of obtaining marketing approval, against unfair commercial use. Since countries have considerable discretion to define "unfair commercial use", it is argued that countries can meet their obligations to protect test data by prohibiting "dishonest" use of data. Use by government authorities to assess the efficacy and toxicity of a pharmaceutical would not be affected, in this case.

However, it is now argued that data exclusivity is a requirement of the TRIPS Agreement. The data exclusivity approach grants the originator exclusive rights over their test data and prevents regulatory authorities from relying on the test data to register generic substitutes. Prior to the TRIPS Agreement coming into force, most countries allowed reliance on originator test data to approve generic products. Once test data was submitted by the originator company, the regulatory authorities could rely on the data to approve subsequent applications on similar products, or to rely on proof of prior approval of a similar product in another country. Generic manufacturers need only to prove that their product is chemically identical to the brand-name, original product, and in some countries, that it is bio-equivalent. This approach enabled swift introduction of generics into the market without registration data-related costs. Within the data exclusivity approach, once a company has submitted original test data, no competing manufacturer is allowed to rely on these data for a period of time. Data exclusivity could thus pose an obstacle to effective use of compulsory licences, as the entry of the generic product would be delayed for the duration of the exclusivity period or for the time it takes to undertake a new compilation of test data. The public interest in limiting data protection is to promote competition and ensure that data protection does not become the means to block timely entrance of affordable generic medicines of public health importance.

Transition Periods

The TRIPS Agreement provides for transition periods, permitting developing countries additional time to bring national legislation and practices into conformity with TRIPS provisions. There are three main transition periods. First was the 1995–2000 transition period, at the end of which countries were required to implement the TRIPS Agreement. The 2000–2005 transition period allowed certain countries to delay providing product patent protection in the areas of technology that had not been so protected at the time of the TRIPS Agreement coming into operation in that country. These countries were allowed a further 5 years to put in place a product patent regime for technologies and products, which they had not thus far provided patent protection, such as pharmaceuticals and agro-chemicals. During the transition period, these countries are required to accept patent applications from 1995 onwards and to keep such applications pending, in a patent "mailbox" until the mailbox is opened in 2005 when the applications will be assessed. The third transition period allows least-developed countries (LDCs) until 2006 to implement their obligations under the TRIPS Agreement in view of their economic, financial and administrative constraints. This period may still be extended by the TRIPS Council on request of an LDC Member. LDCs now have a further extension of time, until 2016 with respect to patents on pharmaceutical products and exclusive marketing rights by the Doha Declaration on the TRIPS Agreement and Public Health. Thus, LDCs need not provide for, nor enforce patents and data protection with respect to pharmaceutical products until 1 January 2016. The transition periods have meant that pharmaceuticals or medicines patented before developing countries implemented their TRIPS obligations will not receive patent protection, and thus generic competition is possible. Medicines patented after developing countries have implemented their TRIPS obligations are progressively coming onto the market and will constitute an increasing share of marketed medicines. A substantial change is expected after 2005, when all developing countries will be required to provide patent protection for pharmaceutical products and the mailbox patents are processed.

TRADE RELATED INVESTMENT MEASURES (TRIMS)

The Trade Related Investment Measures Agreement came into effect on 1 January 1995 as part of the Uruguay Round negotiations. It addressed investment measures that were trade related and which violated Article III (National Treatment) or Article XI (general elimination of quantitative restrictions). Basically it prohibited member countries making the approval of investment conditional on compliance with laws, policies or administrative regulations that favoured domestic products.

What is a TRIM?

The Agreement did not define TRIMs, but provided an illustrative list (see Box-1). Examples of TRIMs are: Local content requirements where governments require enterprises to use or purchase domestic products; Trade balancing measures where governments impose restrictions on imports by an enterprise or link the amount of imports to the level of its exports; and finally, the foreign exchange balancing requirements where an enterprise has the level of imports linked to the value of its exports in order to maintain a net foreign exchange earning. However, the lack of a precise definition means that the issue is not always clear cut and there has been considerable disagreement as to whether or not certain measures are covered by the Agreement.

BOX- 2

---

1. TRIMs that are inconsistent with the obligation of national treatment provided for in paragraph 4 of Article III of GATT 1994 include those which are mandatory or enforceable under domestic law or under administrative rulings, or compliance with which is necessary to obtain an advantage, and which require:
   (a) the purchase or use by an enterprise of products of domestic origin or from any domestic source, whether specified in terms of particular products, in terms of volume or value of products, or in terms of a proportion of volume or value of its local production; or
   (b) that an enterprise's purchases or use of imported products be limited to an amount related to the volume or value of local products that it exports.
2. TRIMS that are inconsistent with the obligation of general elimination of quantitative restrictions provided for in paragraph 1 of Article XI of GATT 1994 include those which are mandatory or enforceable under domestic law or under administrative rulings, or compliance with which is necessary to obtain an advantage, and which restrict:
   (a) the importation by an enterprise of products used in or related to its local production, generally or to an amount related to the volume or value of local production that it exports;
   (b) the importation by an enterprise of products used in or related to its local production by restricting its access to foreign exchange to an amount related to the foreign exchange inflows attributable to the enterprise; or
   (c) the exportation or sale for export by an enterprise of products, whether specified in terms of particular products, in terms of volume or value of products, or I terms of a proportion of volume or value of its local production.

TRIMs Elimination and Transition Periods

Under the Agreement member states were given 90 days to notify the WTO of any existing TRIMs. Member states were then given a "transition period" during which their notified TRIMs were to be eliminated. The length of time was based on a state's level of development i.e. developed countries were given 2 years; developing countries were given 5 years; and least-developed countries were given 7 years. Therefore all developing countries should have implemented the TRIMs agreement and eliminated their regulations by 1 January 2000. However, Article 5.3 of the Agreement permits developing and least-developed countries to apply for an extension of the transition period.

Extension Request Negotiations

Discussions about extension requests take place within the WTO Council for Trade in Goods (CTG). The countries submit an extension request to the CTG and then have to justify the request in the face of detailed questioning from other members - the US, EC and Japan have usually been the most active.

WTO DISPUTE SETTLEMENT MECHANISM

As one of the major outcomes of the Uruguay Round, the WTO Dispute Settlement Understanding (DSU) is regarded as one of the central pillars of today's multilateral trading regime. It is expected that this new rule-oriented dispute settlement mechanism (DSM) can replace the GATT's power-based dispute resolution system, thus can bring more equality and protection to developing countries. However, there are also suspicious voices questioning whether the DSM can be really impartial. The fact that developing countries usually find themselves in a weaker position in the WTO compared with industrialized members may indicate that the DSM needs to contribute more efforts to improving the equality status of developing countries. DSU procedure is biased against developing countries. Three primary challenges to equality that developing countries have to face in the new DSM, including lack of legal expertise, constrained financial resources and political and economic pressures. WTO inherits all of the asymmetries that arise when there are substantial differences in bargaining power, since it rests on decentralized enforcement of international obligations.

The WTO Dispute Settlement Mechanism (DSM)

Settling disputes is the responsibility of the Dispute Settlement Body (DSB), which consists of all WTO members. It has the authority to set up panels, adopt or reject panel and Appeal Body (AB) reports, maintain surveillance of the implementation of decided rulings, and authorize limited trade transactions.

The DSM encourages countries to first settle their dispute through bilateral consultation by themselves. If the discussion fails, the parties can bring the dispute to the DSB. Then the DSB establishes a "panel" composed of three experts to investigate the case, after which the panel issues a report with rulings or recommendations. Either side disagreeing with the report can appeal the report at the AB. After reviewing the case based on points of law rather than reexamining the evidence, the AB can uphold, modify or reverse the panel's conclusions by issuing a new report. And the DSB needs to accept or reject the AB's report, but rejection is only possible by consensus. When the case has been decided by the DSB, the losing defendant must bring its actions into line with the decided rulings or recommendations. If it does not comply with the rulings in a certain period of time, and it also fails to reach a mutually-acceptable compensation in negotiation with the complaining side, the latter may ask the DSB for authorization to impose trade sanctions against the other side.

Compared with the GATT mechanism, the DSM of the WTO, "a jewel in the crown of the Uruguay Round," presents profound changes on several aspects: First, the DSM establishes a "single unified dispute settlement system," in contrast to the multiple dispute settlement procedures under GATT. The second change is about the "automaticity". One of the most decisive changes from GATT to the WTO mechanism is the introduction of "negative consensus." Unless there is a consensus establishment of a panel, the panel must be set up. Similarly, decisions of the panel and the AB are also automatically adopted unless there is a DSB consensus to reject them. Third, the establishment of the new appellate procedure and institution - the AB - is another important change. Though the AB only deals with legal issues and does not have the right to reexamine the evidence, it still enhances the possibility that different voices can get heard. In practice, many cases step into the appellate procedure. Fourth, the new DSM procedure has fixed timetable for each step (*Table 1*). This reform not only makes countries able to foresee the time and costs for dispute settlement, it also helps speed up the process thus enhances the WTO efficiency.

TABLE 1

Stages in the WTO Dispute Settlement Process

	How long to settle a dispute?
60 days	Consultations, mediation, etc.
45 days	Panel set up and panelists appointed
6 months	Final panel report to parties
3 weeks	Final panel report to WTO members
60 days	Dispute Settlement Body adopts report (if no appeal)
Total = 1 year	**(without appeal)**
60-90 days	Appeals report
30 days	Dispute Settlement Body adopts appeals report
Total = ly 3m	**(with appeal)**

Source: World Trade Organization, "Understanding the WTO - A Unique Contribution,' http://www.wto.org/english/thewto e/whatis e/tif e/displ e.htm

Fifth, the DSM of the WTO has improved its participation and surveillance mechanism for decision implementation. The AB allows the participation of nongovernmental organizations (NGOs), which shows the increasing accessibility of the DSM. And the DSB decisions can be better implemented with its surveillance mechanism that was virtually non-existent in GATT.

Relative to the power-based GATT system, the DSM of the WTO moves toward a more rule-oriented mechanism. Many scholars expect that this reformed rule-based system can better protect developing countries from the unilateral exercises launched by strong powers, thus enhance the equality in international trade.

The Rule-Based System: Improved Equality for Developing Countries

The Uruguay Round reforms have brought great influence on developing countries' participation and performance in the WTO dispute settlement system. The establishment of a single organizational forum for managing disputes with formalized procedures and greater legal transparency certainly has brought about many positive results that improve the equality status of developing countries.

How the New DSM Enhances Equality

On the one hand, the new DSM in the WTO is a multilateral mechanism for dispute resolution, which provides developing countries with a more favourable environment than that under the bilateral mechanism. Under the rule-based DSM, all the members, no matter they are weak or strong, have the right to resort to the DSM to seek fair and reasonable resolutions for their trade disputes, which is a law-protected equality. The mechanism reduces the instability wising from countries' unilateral actions. And it also increases the transparency of the dispute settlement procedure thus help enhance the fairness.

First, the new DSM improves the bargaining power of developing countries. The system is based on formal legalized rules, thus members are "equal" in front of the law. Even the superpowers need to abide by the regulations. Thus developing countries gain more equality, and hence more power for equal bargaining. Resolving disputes through a judicial route is "particularly beneficial for smaller countries, as without the rules and procedures of the DSU and the extensive obligations in the WTO agreements, they would not have the necessary bargaining power vis-a-vis the larger powers. For instance, Brazil had not pursued a complaint against the EU under the GATT system since it knew the complaint would be blocked. However, under the new WTO mechanism, Brazil notified the EU that it would bring the dispute to the DSB for formal consultation, which is the first step of the WTO dispute settlement procedure. A few days later, the EU made concessions that it had previously held as impossible, and the dispute was resolved. Furthermore, while the GATT system might cripple weaker countries' bargaining power by its "positive consensus" rule, the new WTO DSM improves the situation through the "negative consensus" framework, which greatly reduces the possibility of blockage.

Second, from the angle of independence, under the power-based GATT system, the independence of developing countries was eroded because of their economic and political "dependence" on developed countries. Sometimes they could hardly express their real attitudes. Under the new WTO DSM, as a contrast, a certain level of independence is guaranteed by the fixed legal regulation system. Thus the rule-based arrangements for dispute resolution tend to produce more equal outcomes, mitigating power/wealth disparities.

Third, the general spirit of compliance with the result of the DSM is another optimistic indicator of improved equality. In this rule-based system, the major powers in international trade have indicated that "they will comply with the mandates of the Dispute Settlement reports when they are finalized and formally adopted." And even the most powerful players cannot defy the final rulings without risking harm to the institution. When developing countries file complaints against developed ones to the DSB, even if the result is negative to the developed side, the recommendations or rulings can still be implemented. This situation tends to "reduce asymmetries in post-agreement bargaining power" and enhance developing countries' equality status in the phase of rulings implementation. Besides, countries now get easier access to countermeasures provided through cross-retaliation, which makes developing countries able to impose pressure on developed ones. Thus, as developing members have more assurance as to the implementation situation of the DSM results, their equality status in the system is improved.

On the other hand, considering the concrete DSU provisions, because of the increasing concern on developing countries' particular needs and interests, the DSU provides plenty of provisions offering special favourable conditions to developing countries through the whole dispute settlement procedure. Thus developing countries can enjoy more equality with developed countries.

Article 4.10 of the DSU calls for members to pay special attention to the particular problems and interests of developing countries in consultations. Article 12.10 allows for the extension of the consultation time-period. Article 3.10 states that a developing country involved in a dispute can request that the panel includes at least one panelist from a developing member country if the other side is a developed state. And Article 12.11 provides that the panel report must indicate the form in which the special and differential treatment rules of the DSU have been taken into account, if a developing country member involved in a dispute raises such rules.

At the stage of implementation, according to Article 21.2 of the DSU, particular attention should be paid to matters affecting developing countries interests. As to surveillance, Article 21.8 states that if a case is brought by a developing country, the DSB needs to take into consideration not only the trade coverage of the challenged measures, but also their impact on the economy of the developing country concerned.

Furthermore, Article 27.2 requires the WTO Secretariat to make available legal expertise assistance from the WTO technical cooperation services to any developing member upon its request. And Article 24.1 calls for due restraint in bringing disputes against a least-developed country (LDC) and in asking for compensation or seeking authorization to suspend obligations against a LDC that has lost a dispute.

Inequality in the WTO Dispute Settlement Mechanism

Indeed, the new DSM of the WTO better enables developing countries to use the system for trade dispute resolution. However, many developing members of the WTO are long being among the critics of the new system's inequality since its establishment. The developing countries are still somewhat marginalized under the DSM of the WTO. If this situation continues, in the long run, the WTO legal system may be more and more shaped by developed members' interests and wills, and developing countries may be left less space to stand in. Then what are the real situations and possible explanations of this inequality and marginalization of developing countries in the DSM?

High Costs and Limited Resource Availability

Financial Cost

First, the costs of access of the DSM are very high. And compared with developed states, developing countries actually have fewer resources to invest to defend their WTO rights. It is usually a long process for the WTO to settle a trade dispute through the DSM. As table 1 indicates, approximately, a typical WTO dispute settlement procedure may cost 12 months (without appeal) to 15 month (with appeal), and it will be even longer if including the succeeding implementation phase. Besides the litigation costs, countries initiating disputes in the DSM face income losses from hindered trade during the dispute investigation period. For developing countries, especially those highly relying on their limited exports for national incomes, these potential income and market losses may be more unbearable than the litigation bills.

High costs of WTO dispute settlement erode developing countries' capability, especially those weaker ones', to participate in the DSM. Compared with their developed peers, developing countries usually have fewer financial resources to spend on the WTO litigation. Generally, their economic sizes are smaller, their industries are less profitable, their government budgets are limited, and their limited resources also have to be spent on many other social needs of their own. Thus the high costs actually lower developing countries' status and make them less willing and less able to pursue dispute settlement through the DSM, which can be seen from their less appearance in the system. Furthermore, many developing countries tend to step into a vicious circle. They participate less frequently in the DSM because of high costs, but their less participation makes them not able to benefit from the economies of scale, that is, developed countries can spread the fix costs of developing internal legal expertise over more cases than developing states. As a result, developing countries have to assume higher costs for individual cases.

Financial inequality brings developing countries big obstacles of pursuing WTO dispute settlement. It is theoretically true that they can obtain fund or assistance with lower costs from sources such as private firms and nongovernmental organizations (NGOs). But the problem is: the private sectors in developing countries are relatively weak and less profitable, and they typically view the WTO dispute settlement as the government's job. And other institutions such as NGOs can hardly satisfy the increasing needs given the fact that developing countries are more and more involved in trade disputes and most of them do not have enough resources to invest.

The high financial costs of the WTO dispute settlement trigger inequality in the DSM. With abundant financial resources, developed countries can better afford the WTO dispute settlement thus may use it more frequently than developing states do. Hence it comes out that developing countries do not make full use of the DSM.

Limited Legal Resources

Except for financial investments, legal resources, especially the legal expertise, are also essential for WTO dispute settlement. For instance, in the panel phase, the written request for the panel establishment has to precisely define and limit the scope of the dispute; and the parties involved need to exchange multiple sets of written submissions, present views orally in oral hearings, and answer the questions raised by the panel. All these activities require sufficient legal expertise support. Actually, the shortage of special expertise, personnel and information for legal activities is an important reason why developing countries are suffering inequality and unfavourable outcomes in the DSM.

Industrialized states , also the major players in the WTO, are well equipped with legal experts in the area of the WTO legal system, and they have a worldwide network of commercial and diplomatic representation that feeds their systems with relevant data. In contrast, developing countries have limited legal expertise and it is harder for them to collect data and information because of the lack of networks. Many developing countries have only one or two lawyers to address WTO issues. When small developing countries are involved in disputes with the US or the EU as the other side, the developing ones are obviously in a disadvantageous position concerning legal expertise supply. Though they can buy legal expertise, "scarcity of national administrative resources to identify and prepare cases is a major constraint." Concerning data collection, when the European Commission (EC) realized its lack of such a system after the establishment of WTO mechanism, it hired consultants to identify and report on other countries' trade barriers, which spurred many successful WTO complaints. In contrast, developing countries lack adequate financial as well as human resources to establish such a system in a short time.

Developing countries, to certain extent, can improve their access to WTO litigation services. For example, according to DSU Article 27.2, developing countries can get technical help from the WTO Secretariat. They can also resort to the Advisory Center on WTO Law (ACWL) for legal assistance for dispute cases. And they can go to NGOs and other issue-based organizations or private firms for help.

But the assistance methods' accesses and effects are limited. Taking WTO as an example, its legal assistance services are offered by only two expert attorneys on a limited part-time basis, and the two experts advise developing countries disputants at most one day per week. And the DSU further requires that even the limited assistance can only be provided after a member has decided to bring a dispute into the DSM. Thus developing countries cannot use this assistance to help figure out their "winning probability" thus help decide whether to bring the disputes to the WTO. Moreover, a large number of developing countries are designated as "inactive" for not having paid their assessed contributions to the WTO budget for more than 3 years, and such a designation implies that they are not able to receive technical assistance from the WTO, and a number of other privileges, such as the distribution of documents, are withheld from them. But these "inactive" countries are actually the poor ones that most need the WTO's help. Similarly, the ACWL assistance may also encounter the problem of availability of its resources. On the one hand, the operation fund of the ACWL basically comes from individual countries, and a rich country may be hesitant to provide adequate fund to an organization that often provides litigation assistance directly challenging its own interests. On the other hand, even the limited resources have to be allocated on a fiercely competitive basis. Compared with developed countries, developing countries not only lack legal resources domestically, but also face difficulty in getting assistance from outside.

The financial and legal resource constraints bring about inequality between developing countries and developed states in the DSM, by reducing developing countries' capability to participate in the system. As Besson and Mehdi's finding suggests, developing countries are unlikely to obtain a favourable outcome unless the asymmetry of capacity is corrected.

Inequality Stemming from Power-Based International Relations

The other kind of sources of inequality is about international relations among countries. The WTO is an international organization, the establishment and operation of which are made possible only if member countries are willing to give up a part of their sovereignty to make the institutional contract. This means actions of the WTO may be inevitably influenced by the international political and economic interactions. The DSM is also unexceptional. As what Moon points out, at the law-making stage for establishing the DSM, weaker states have to make concessions to stronger countries for the latter's acceptance of a rule-based system, the result of which is the agreements advantageous to stronger actors. Thus from the beginning, the DSM regulations are more favourable to industrialized countries, and developing countries are more frequently taken to court by developed states under the DSM because of application of its legal provisions.

In the rule-based DSM, power consideration and influence still cannot be denied. As Moon argues, "For reaching a legalized DSM agreement, there should be trade-offs between the stronger-actor-favourable content of law and the fair application of the law." A question here is whether the WTO panels and AB can be really impartial as supposed. Potentially, as the experts are from different countries whose self-interests may also be influenced by powerful states, they cannot totally get rid of the political impacts though this impact may be indirect. Even the AB of the DSM, a basically rule-based institution which should be unbiased in front of the law, is also reluctant to make unequivocal adverse rulings against powerful countries on issues of considerable domestic salience.

Also, the powerful players can use other international political instruments to impose impact on weaker countries, while the latter are actually faced with limited degree of freedom to act. Particularly, since many instruments are outside the WTO's jurisdiction, the WTO can hardly deter such actions. One important kind of political instruments is foreign assistance and economic preferential arrangement provided by developed countries to developing ones. These preferential conditions and financial aid, to some extent, make the poor countries "dependent" on rich economies, thus the latter can ask for favourable political and economic outcomes through imposing pressures on the former. It is not rare that developed countries use foreign aids to press forward their international political and/or economic interests. In the DSM, the developed countries can threaten to reduce or even withdraw the economic benefits they provide to poor countries, and the latter, especially the small ones, can do little to counter such threats thus may retreat and choose not to file the dispute to the WTO. Such actions are basically outside the WTO's authority, thus the institution can hardly do anything about this international political and economic inequality.

Indeed, international politics is intertwined with international economic issues and "power" is greatly influencing the operation of international law. Even the military expenditures gap appears to negatively affect the probability of developing countries to win a dispute. While developed countries can use different political instruments to influence developing countries' actions in and outside the DSM of the WTO, it is hard to say there is a real equality in this system.

Compensation Inadequacy and Lack of Enforcement Capability

Except for the inequalities coming from the imbalances of political power and economic burden, even if developing states launch a complaint and win, it is also difficult for them to get adequate compensation or fully enforce the rulings.

Inadequate Compensation

The time period, from starting a complaint to the end when the complaining side gets the DSB's permission to impose limited trade sanctions ("suspend concessions or obligations"), is a very long procedure. But the WTO retaliation mechanism prescribes that complaints cannot unilaterally take retaliatory actions unless the DSB makes decisions and permits them to, which means that the defendant side is able to violate the WTO laws and hurt the other side's interests during the long time-period, until the WTO recognizes and decides to take action to correct the violations. With economic strength, developed countries can relatively easily affect developing economies even just in a short time. Thus it is possible that before the DSB authorize them to impose trade sanctions, the developing countries' domestic markets and internal economic capabilities have already been badly harmed. For those small developing states, this situation may be even worse.

Even if a developing country as complaint wins in a dispute, the compensation methods under the DSM are limited. Usually it comes out in the forms that the losing defendant withdraws the measures found inconsistent with WTO law, or the winning complaint gets authorization from the DSB to impose limited trade sanctions. Under the current "retaliation-as-compensation" approach, there is no room for retroactive compensation or punishment measures that can help developing countries make up for its previous economic losses that have been already caused before the decision is made. Even if the defendant side corrects its action after the dispute, the complaint still has to assume the economic losses generated before the correction. For developing countries particularly, while their economies are generally weak and vulnerable to outside impact, such burden may be too heavy for them to bear.

Lack of Enforcement Capability

It is also arguable whether developing countries possess adequate enforcement capability to fully implement the WTO rulings or recommendations even if the results are favourable to them. Under the DSM, the final dispute settlement decisions are supposed to be implemented on a decentralized, bilateral basis. The DSM relies entirely on state power for enforcement of its rulings. It may be hard for a developing country to raise tariff rates on certain products imported from a developed country, even if it is authorized to, since this action may hurt itself in turn at the end.

With a relatively weak economy, a developing country may depend on certain imports from developed countries for development; if the products included in the retaliation are actually essential for its own growth, it can hardly be expected that the developing country will really deter or limit the imports. But considering the other side, since most developing countries' markets and economic power are relatively small and weak, whether or not they take retaliatory actions to developed countries' products does not bring much difference to the developed economies, unless they retaliate in alliance, which does not usually happen.. Thus, while the retaliatory actions taken by developing countries to developed states cannot bring much danger or worries to the latter but may incur negative consequences to the users themselves, developing countries actually do not possess real equality with developed countries because of the asymmetry of enforcement capabilities.

THE DSU PROVISIONS - INEQUALITY BEHIND THE ARTICLES

Taking a closer look at the DSU provisions, there is also an interesting story. On the one hand, the Uruguay Round agreement provisions generally demonstrate that strong countries are real beneficiaries. The WTO expanded its coverage to areas such as investment (Agreements on Trade-Related Aspect of Investment Measures, TRIMs), intellectual property rights protection (Agreements on Trade-Related Aspect of Intellectual Property Rights, TRIPs), service trade (General Agreements on Trade in Services, GATS), etc. Because of these agreements, disputes in these areas now can be brought into the DSM. While most of the agreements reflect developed countries' interests, developing countries are actually in an unequal position.

On the other hand, analyzing the special DSU provisions which aim at improving developing countries' status, it is found that they are more declarative than operative. For instance, the Article 4.10 requires that special attention should be problems and interests of developing countries during consultation phase. But this article does not point out concretely on what specific aspects and to what extent the "special attention" should be paid. Since there is no specific implementation measure, in practice it is hard to evaluate whether member countries have really and adequately complied with this provision. And Article 21.2 has the similar problem.

Furthermore, several other provisions regarding special and differential treatment may be difficult to apply, though they seem to be favourable to developing countries. For example, Article 21.7 states that the DSB must consider what further and appropriate action it might take in addition to surveillance and status reports, if a developing country has raised the matter. But it has not been used by any developing country. The reason here is probably that the country has to devote large amounts of resources to analyze and follow the case development, and developing countries hardly possess sufficient resources to do this. Similarly, as discussed earlier, the provisions regarding technical assistance to developing countries are not able to be adequately applied for the sake of the limited resources availability. And till now, the provisions related to LDCs seem to be "useless" since no LDC has been involved in any dispute. Thus, while the DSU provisions, even those favourable to developing countries, cannot be fully applied, further efforts are needed to improve the inequality between developing states and developed ones in the DSM.

THE DOHA AGENDA AND THE ROAD AHEAD FOR WTO: A CRITIQUE

Doha Round talks are overseen by the Trade Negotiations Committee (MNC), whose chair is Director-General Lamy. The negotiations are being held in five working groups and in other, existing bodies in the WTO. Selected topics under negotiation are discussed below in five groups: market access, development issues, WTO rules, trade facilitation, and other issues.

Market Access

Agriculture

The Uruguay Round Agreement on Agriculture called for continued negotiations toward *"...the long-term objective of substantial progressive reductions in support and protection...."* By early 2001, WTO members had achieved some preliminary work in those sectoral negotiations, and later that year, agriculture was wrapped into the broader Doha agenda.

Agriculture has become the linchpin in the Doha Development Agenda. U.S. goals in the new round were elimination of agricultural export subsidies, easing of tariffs and quotas, and reductions in trade-distorting domestic support. The Doha Ministerial Declaration included language on all of these three pillars of agricultural support. It stated that the members committed to *"comprehensive negotiations aimed at substantial improvements in market access; reductions of, with a view to phasing out, all forms of export subsidies; and substantial reductions in trade distorting support."*

The course of the negotiations in the lead up to Cancun were influenced by the reform of the EU's Common Agricultural Policy (CAP). A major issue for the EU was whether or not to approve separation ("decoupling") of payments to farmers based on production. Those types of payments are among the most trade-distorting ("amber box'). On June 26, 2003, EU agriculture ministers approved a reform package that included partial decoupling for certain products. The action was seen by many as a positive step for advancing the trade negotiations.

The EU reform largely addressed one of the three pillars of agricultural reform — domestic support — but did little in a second pillar — market access. In the WTO negotiations on market access, the United States and the Cairns Group support a leveling, or harmonizing, of tariff peaks, or high rates. In comparison, the EU and Japan want flexibility to cut some items less than others to arrive at an average total rate cut.

Another difficulty is "geographical indications," or the protection of product names that reflect the original location of the product. An example is the use of "Bordeaux wine" for wines from the Bordeaux region only. Europeans, joined by India and some other countries, want a mandatory registry of geographical indications that would prevent other countries from using the names. The United States and yet other countries refuse to negotiate a mandatory list, but will accept a voluntary list with no enforcement power. The EU says it will not accept an agriculture agreement without a geographical registry.

Developing countries view reform in agricultural trade as one of their most important goals. They argue that their own producers cannot compete against the surplus agricultural goods that the developed countries, principally the EU and the United States, are selling on the world market at low, subsidized prices. Some African countries also are calling for an end to cotton subsidies, claiming that such subsidies are destroying markets for the smaller African producers.

The July 2004 Framework Agreement provided a basis for which to continue the agriculture talks. On domestic subsidies, subsidies are to be reduced by means of a "tiered" or "banded" approach applied to achieve "harmonization" in the levels of support Subsidizing countries will make a down-payment of a 20% reduction in levels of support in the first year of the agreement. Tariff reduction will utilize a tiered formula with a harmonization component, but with some exceptions for "import sensitive products." The European Union finally agreed to the elimination of export subsidies, considered a major negotiating goal of the United States.

While there was no breakthrough at the December 2005 Hong Kong Ministerial, members agreed to eliminate export subsidies, and "export measures with equivalent effect" by 2013, a date favoured by the European Union (EU). Members agreed to cut domestic support programmes with a *three band methodology*. As the largest user of domestic agricultural subsidies, the EU was placed in the highest band. The United States and Japan were placed in the second band and lesser subsidizing countries were placed in the third band. However, the actual percentage cuts that these bands represent remain subject to negotiation. Members also renewed a commitment to achieve a tariff cutting formula by April 30, 2006. This deadline was not met. In the parallel negotiations on Cotton, members agreed to eliminate export subsidies for cotton and to provide duty-free and quota-free access for LDC cotton producers by year-end 2006. Members also agreed to reduce domestic support for cotton in a more ambitious manner than for other agricultural commodities as an "objective" in the ongoing agricultural negotiations.

Talks to reach modalities proved unsuccessful at a July 23 meeting of the G-6 countries in Geneva and the negotiations were suspended thereafter. Sources of the stalemate in the Geneva talks included U.S. concerns about the magnitude of deviations from market access commitments stemming from the so-called "3-S flexibilities": sensitive products, special products, and the special safeguard mechanism. While each of these flexibilities was incorporated into the July Framework Agreement as negotiating modalities that would allow countries to exempt certain products from the banded tariff formula, the United States contends that the scope envisioned by some countries for these modalities would unacceptably diminish the overall market access gains from the agreement. Conversely, the United States was under pressure at the meeting from the EU and the G-20 group represented by Brazil and India to improve its subsidy reduction offer, but the United States put no new offer on the table. The United States insisted that it will not improve its offer on domestic subsidy reduction unless the EU improves considerably its market access offer and the G-20 countries show a willingness to open their markets not only to agricultural products but to industrial products and services as well.

Services

Along with agriculture, services were apart of the "built-in agenda" of the Uruguay Round. The General Agreement on Trade In Services (GATS), which was concluded in that Round, directs Members to *"...enter into successive rounds of negotiations, beginning not later than five years from the date of entry into force of the WTO Agreement [January 1,1995]... [to achieve] a progressively higher level of liberalization."*

Those negotiations began in early 2000. Negotiating guidelines and procedures were established by March 2001. Under the request-offer approach being used, countries first request changes in other countries' practices, other countries then respond by making offers of changes, and finally the countries negotiate bilaterally on a final agreement The Doha Ministerial Declaration recognized the work already undertaken and reaffirmed the March 2001 guidelines as the basis for continuing the negotiations. It directed participants to submit initial requests for specific commitments by June 30, 2002 and initial offers by March 31, 2003.

The services talks are going slowly. By July 2005 the WTO had received 68 initial commitment offers representing 92 countries (the EU represents 25 members) and 24 offers remained outstanding from non-LDC members (55 if LDCs are included). Only 28 revised offers had been tendered by November 2005, although the July Framework stipulated a March 31, 2005 deadline. All members were to have submitted their initial offers by March 31, 2003. Many have also decried the poor quality of offers, many of which only bind existing practices, rather than offer new concessions and excluded some sectors entirely

At Hong Kong, members committed to submit a second round of revised offers by July 31, 2006, and to submit a final schedule of commitments by October 31, 2006. In order to expedite the negotiating process, members also agreed to employ plurilateral requests to other members covering specific sectors and modes of supply to be completed by February 28, 2006. In response to this deadline, twenty-three plurilateral requests concerning 16 sectors and 3 modes of supply were submitted.

One area of controversy is so-called "Mode IV" services. Mode IV relates to the temporary movement of business persons to another country in order to perform a service on-site. Developing countries want easier movement of their nationals under Mode IV. They claim that the services negotiations have centered on the establishment of businesses in other countries, which has been a focus of developed countries, while there has been no negotiation on Mode IV, which would help them. Developed countries, especially the United States, have opposed discussions on Mode IV services trade. Congress might oppose easier entry for business persons, based on Senate approval of a resolution in the 108th Congress expressing the sense of the Senate that future U.S. trade agreements and implementing legislation should not contain immigration-related provisions. Mode IV services will be a difficult issue to resolve. Fifteen countries have joined a plurilateral request for Mode IV services liberalization to the United States and other developed countries.

Non-Agricultural Market Access (NAMA)

In the Doha Declaration, trade ministers agreed to negotiations to reduce or eliminate tariffs on industrial or primary products, with a focus on "tariff peaks, high tariffs, and tariff escalation." Tariff peaks are considered to be tariff rates of above 15% and often protect sensitive products from competition. Tariff escalation is the practice of increasing tariffs as value is added to a commodity. The talks are also seeking to reduce the incidence of non-tariff barriers, which include import licensing, quotas and other quantitative import restrictions, conformity assessment procedures, and technical barriers to trade. The sectoral elimination of tariffs for specific groups has also be forwarded as an area of negotiation. Negotiators accepted the concept of less than full reciprocity in reductions for developing and least-developed countries.

Doha negotiators agreed to reach modalities for the reduction or elimination of tariffs and non-tariff barriers by the end of May 2003. This deadline was, as were subsequent ones, not met. NAMA issues were not discussed at Cancun, and there was no agreement on the draft texts proposed for consideration at that Ministerial. The July 2004 Framework Agreement adopted the use of a non-linear tariff reduction formula applied on a line-by-line basis, (i.e. one that it can work towards evening out or harmonizing tariff levels), and the Hong Kong Ministerial did agreed to use a Swiss formula. The Ministerial did not agree on the specific equation or coefficients, but negotiators did agreed on an April 30,2006 deadline to resolve these modalities. The Framework Agreement also agreed that tariff reductions would be calculated from bound, rather than the applied, tariff rates.

Negotiators are also grappling with the concept of "flexibility," or the nature and extent of developing country-special and differential treatment, as it relates to formula cuts. In addition to longer implementation times, the July Framework Agreement allows for less than formula cuts for a certain (undetermined) amount tariff lines, keeping a percentage of tariff lines unbound, or not applying formula cuts for an (undetermined) percentage of tariff lines. At Hong Kong, negotiators did agree to provide tariff-free and quota-free access for LCDs by 2008. However, this agreement provides the caveat that 3% of tariff lines can be exempted as sensitive products such as textiles, apparel, and footwear.

Both the United States and the EU have favoured using sectoral tariff elimination as an alterative modality for the NAMA negotiations, but negotiations have stalled on which products to cover and the extent of participation (i.e. whether developing countries or LDCs would be able exempt them selves from commitments). As noted above, the industrial market access talks also encompass negotiations on the reduction of non-tariff barriers (NTBs). No agreements have been reached on what modalities are to be used in negotiating reductions of NTBs.

The April 30 deadline, like so many before, was breached without agreement on the NAMA formula or on other issues. The end of June Geneva summit also failed to reach agreement on NAMA modalities. The United States, Canada, and Switzerland proposed a 5 percentage point differential between the Swiss formula coefficients of developed and developing countries, which is consistent with the EU proposal of a 10 coefficient for developed countries and a 15 coefficient for developing countries. A group of developing countries known as the NAMA-11 proposed that the differential should be at least 25 percentage points. The NAMA talks are being linked more and more to the agricultural talks, with some movement on one becoming increasingly necessary on the other. Developing countries have been unwilling to commit on NAMA without agreement on agriculture, but now some developed countries are tying further agriculture progress to NAMA. The July 23, 2006 G-6 meeting that led to the suspension of the negotiations did not touch on NAMA issues.

Development Issues

Three development issues are most noteworthy. One pertains to compulsory licensing of medicines and patent protection. A second deals with a review of provisions giving special and differential treatment to developing countries. A third addresses problems that developing countries were having in implementing current trade obligations.

Access to Patented Medicines

A major topic at the Doha Ministerial regarded the WTO Agreement on Trade-Related Aspects of Intellectual Property Rights (TRIPS). The issue involves the balance of interests between the pharmaceutical companies in developed countries that held patents on medicines and the public health needs in developing countries. Before the Doha meeting, the United States claimed that the current language in TRIPS was flexible enough to address health emergencies, but other countries insisted on new language.

Section 6 of the Doha document *Declaration on the TRIPS Agreement and Public Health* (TRIPS Declaration), recognized that "*...WTO Members with insufficient or no manufacturing capabilities in the pharmaceutical sector could face difficulties in making effective use of compulsory licensing under the TRIPS Agreement.*" In Section 6, the trade ministers instructed the "*WTO TRIPS Council ".. .to find an expeditious solution to this problem and to report to the [WTO] General Council before the end of 2002.*"

On December 16, 2002, then-TRIPS Council chairman Eduardo Perez Motta produced a draft that would allow countries that lack the manufacturing capacity to produce medicines to issue compulsory licenses for imports of the medicines. All WTO members approved of the chairman's draft except the United States. The U.S. position, representing the interests of the pharmaceutical industry, was that the chairman's draft did not include enough protections against possible misuse of compulsory licenses. The United Slates sought a limit on the diseases that would be covered by the chairman's text, but other countries refused this initiative. The United States decided to oppose the chairman's draft and unilaterally promised not to bring a dispute against any least-developed country that issued compulsory licenses for certain medicines.

One concern of the pharmaceutical industry was that the medicines sent to the developing country might be diverted instead to another country. To address this problem, it was suggested that the medicines be marked so that they can be tracked. Another concern was that more advanced developing countries might use the generic medicines to develop their own industries. For this problem, it was proposed that countries voluntarily "opt-out," or promise not to use compulsory licensing.

On August 30, 2003, WTO members reached agreement on the TRIPS and medicines issue. Voting in the General Council, member governments approved a decision that offered an interim waiver under the TRIPS Agreement allowing a member country to export pharmaceutical products made under compulsory licences to least-developed and certain other members. An accompanying statement represented several "key shared understandings" of Members regarding the Decision, including the recognition that the decision should be used to protect public health and not be an instrument to pursue industrial or commercial policy objectives, and the recognition that products should not be diverted from the intended markets. The statement listed a number of countries that either agreed to opt out of using the system as importers or agreed that they would only use the system in national emergencies or extreme urgency. At the Hong Kong Ministerial, members agreed to a permanent amendment to incorporate the 2003 Decision, which will become effective when it is ratified by two-thirds of the member states.

Special and Differential (S&D) Treatment

In the Doha Ministerial Declaration, the trade ministers reaffirmed special and differential (S&D) treatment for developing countries and agreed that all S&D treatment provisions *"...be reviewed with a view to strengthening them and making them more precise, effective and operational."* In the Declaration, the trade ministers endorsed the work programme on S&D treatment presented in another Doha document, *Decision on Implementation-Related Issues and Concerns* (Implementation Decision). That document called on the WTO Committee on Trade and Development to identify the S&D treatment provisions that are already mandatory and those that are non-binding, and to consider the implications of *"...converting [S&D] treatment measures into mandatory provisions, to identify those that Members consider should be made mandatory, and to report to the General Council with clear recommendations for a decision by July 2002."* It also called for the Committee on Trade and Development 'to examine additional ways in which S&D treatment provisions can be made more effective, to consider ways in which developing countries may be assisted to make best use of [S&D] treatment provisions, and to report to the General Council with clear recommendations for a decision by July 2002.

The negotiations have been split along a developing-country/developed-country divide. Developing countries wanted to negotiate on changes to S&D provisions, keep proposals together in the Committee on Trade and Development, and set shorter deadlines. Developed countries wanted to study S&D provisions, send some proposals to negotiating groups, and leave deadlines open. Developing countries claimed that the developed countries were not negotiating in good faith, while developed countries argued that the developing countries were unreasonable in their proposals.

By the Cancun Ministerial, developing countries had offered about 85 proposals on S&D provisions, but developed countries had agreed to only a handful of these. At Hong Kong, members agreed to five S&D provisions for LDCs, including the tariff-free and quota-free access for LDC goods described under the NAMA.

Implementation Issues

Developing countries claim that they have had problems with the implementation of the agreements reached in the earlier Uruguay Round because of limited capacity or lack of technical assistance. They also claim that they have not realised certain benefits that they expected from the Round, such as increased access for their textiles and apparel in developed-country markets. They seek a clarification of language relating to their interests in existing agreements.

Before the Doha Ministerial, WTO Members resolved a small number of these implementation issues. At the Doha meeting, the Ministerial Declaration directed a two-path approach for the large number of remaining issues: (a) where a specific negotiating mandate is provided, the relevant implementation issues will be addressed under that mandate; and (b) the other outstanding implementation issues will be addressed as a matter of priority by the relevant WTO bodies. Outstanding implementation issues are found in the area of market access, investment measures, safeguards, rules of origin, and subsidies and countervailing measures, among others.

Little progress has been made on implementation issues. The Hong Kong Ministerial Declaration reiterates previous instructions adopted in August 2004, and instructs the negotiating bodies and others to "redouble" their efforts to find solutions to implementation issues. At Hong Kong, a deadline of July 31,2006, was given for the General Council to review progress on implementation issues, and take appropriate action.

Trade Facilitation

The first WTO Ministerial Conference, which was held in Singapore in 1996, established permanent working groups on four issues: *transparency in government procurement, trade facilitation (customs issues), trade and investment,* and *trade and competition.* These became known as the Singapore issues. This issues were pushed at successive Ministerials by the European Union, Japan and Korea, and opposed by most developing countries. The United States was lukewarm about the inclusion of these issues, indicating that it could accept some or all of them at various times, but preferring to focus on market access.

In 2001, the Doha Ministerial Declaration called for further clarification to be undertaken on the four Singapore issues before the 5th Ministerial in 2003 (at Cancun), and for negotiations will take place on the basis of a decision to be taken *by explicit consensus* at the 5th Ministerial. At Cancun, deadlock over the Singapore issues was a contributing factor in the breakup of that summit. After further negotiations during 2004, a compromise was reached in the July 2004 Framework Agreement three of the Singapore issues (government procurement, investment, and competition) were dropped and negotiations would begin on trade facilitation.

Trade facilitation aims to improve the efficiency of international trade by harmonizing and streamlining customs procedures such as duplicative documentation requirements, customs processing delays, and nontransparent or unequally enforced importation rules and requirements. Although negotiations are still in their infancy, the talks have thus far revolved around the scope and obligations of the new disciplines. The scope has thus far revolved around proposals dealing with freedom of transit, fees and formalities, and administrative transparency. Discussions have also occurred concerning the technical assistance and trade capacity building needed by developing countries to implement any subsequent agreement. Developed countries, including the United States and the European Union, favour the negotiation of a concrete rules-based system with appropriate accountability, while some developing countries prefer optional guidelines with "policy flexibility."

Although negotiations have proceeded in a constructive manner, no major breakthroughs in trade facilitation were announced in Hong Kong and the Ministerial declaration did not agree on a date for beginning text-based negotiations. The ministerial served as a review of progress and a discussion of plans for future work.

WTO Rules

Rules Negotiations. The Doha Round negotiations included an objective of "clarifying and improving disciplines" under the WTO Agreements on Antidumping (AD) and on Subsidies and Countervailing Measures (ASCM). The United States sought to keep negotiations on trade remedies outside of the Doha Round, but found many WTO partners insistent on including them for discussion. U.S. negotiators did manage to insert language asserting that *"...basic concepts, principles and effectiveness of these Agreements and their instruments and objectives"* would be preserved. However, Congressional leaders were highly critical of this concession by U.S. trade negotiators.

The Doha Ministerial Declaration also calls for clarifying and improving disciplines on fisheries subsidies, and both the Ministerial Declaration and the Implementation Decision have special provisions on trade remedies and developing countries. In addition to trade remedies, the Declaration calls for clarifying and improving WTO disciplines and procedures on regional trade agreements.

The Declaration identified two phases for the work on trade remedies: *"In the initial phase of the negotiations, participants will indicate the provisions, including disciplines on trade distorting practices, that they seek to clarify and improve in the subsequent phase."* No deadlines were set for these phases. So far, countries are still essentially in the first phase.

The United States has primarily been on the defensive in the rules talks. Many countries have attacked the use of antidumping actions by the United States and other developed nations as disguised protectionism. However, many developing countries are now using antidumping actions themselves, which may goad some countries to re-examine the necessity for discipline. Most of the proposals on trade remedies focus on providing more specificity or restrictions to the AD/ASCM Agreements in terms of definitions and procedures. Yet, no agreements have been reached, even on what is to be negotiated.

The Ministerial Declaration also included several provisions on trade and environment. Among the provisions, the trade ministers agreed to the following: (1) negotiations on the relationship between existing WTO rules and trade obligations in multilateral environmental agreements (MEAs); (2) procedures for the exchange of information between MEA Secretariats and WTO committees, and the criteria for granting observer status; and (3) the reduction or elimination of trade barriers to environmental goods and services. It was agreed at Doha that the WTO's Committee on Trade and Environment would report on these and other issues to the fifth Ministerial (Cancun) and to make recommendations where appropriate. The EU has said that its priorities include observer status for MEAs. The United States is pushing for rules on fisheries subsidies, as mentioned above, and tariff reductions on environmental products.

Despite the setbacks, WTO is essential for easing global poverty. This must be understood. There will be criticism leveraged against the WTO, but it is still the most adequate format for addressing the need to ease global poverty through international trade. It would be counter-productive not to support this indispensable organisation and any other forum that allows for discussion of the sensitive but necessary issues pertaining to trade and poverty. The Doha round was a major test of the commitment towards easing poverty on a global scale. To many who believe in multilateralism, the Cancun meeting has been a disappointment. To restore their confidence, the EU and other relevant powerful countries will now be obliged to prove that even a collectivity of states can find consensus. The enthusiasm, optimism and momentum that came out of the Doha Round, needs to be upheld to ensure essential progress.

It was the WTO's "raison d'etre" to integrate countries into an open trading system, as "an illustration of an open world." This concept not only needs to be upheld but the individual positions also need to be given due consideration. Beyond the 'hard' trade issues at stake in the Doha Round, there is need to deal with moral and development issues. We must understand that measures to enhance economic growth and prosperity have to be anchored in sound moral principles and values. People, increasingly cynical about governments' willingness to fight poverty, have pointed out that combination of trade and development, now on the upsuring, can still produce good results on a rules-based trading system. However, these have to be the right rules. Finally, there also needs to be even-handedness in the architecture of the system. There needs to be increased linkages established between the WTO, the WHO and, a future world environmental organisation to interlink structurally the issues of trade, health, environment, labour and others. Such an inter-linkage would increase global understanding.

With non-tariff measures (N/TMs) coming in new forms and with greater vigour the need was felt to check such tendencies, list they proved counterproductive if retaliatory measures are taken by other countries. Leaders inform like the G-20, World Economic Forum and /he WTO expressed their commitment towards talking the protectionist measures and ensuring an early conclusion of the Doha Round. The WTO/set up a monitoring mechanism for the trade policy measures that members adopted during the financial crisis. However, intentions should translate into actions and protectionist tendencies (Should be nipped in the bud. The developed countries who have been the champions of liberalization and globalization should take the lead in pressing the stop button on rising

WTO NEGOTIATIONS AND INDIA

The Doha Round of trade negotiations at the WTO has been under way since 2001. The negotiations cover several areas such as agriculture, market access for non-agricultural products, trade-related intellectual property rights, rules (covering anti-dumping and subsidies) and trade facilitation. The conduct, conclusion and entry into force of the outcome of the negotiations are parts of a single undertaking, that is "nothing is agreed until everything is agreed".

While the years 2007 and 2008 saw intensive discussions in the WTO and progress achieved on several complex subjects, the negotiations were slow to resume following the December 2008 break at the WTO. Based on discussions during the Mini-Ministerial Meeting held in July 2008, the Chairs of the Negotiating Groups on Agriculture and Non Agricultural Market Access (NAMA) brought out fresh drafts of modalities for Agriculture and NAMA on Decembers, 2008. However, discussions on these texts began only in September 2009 partly due to national elections in the US and India and partly due to a general standstill in Geneva and a reluctance to negotiate seriously with a view to narrowing differences.

Going by the political commitments expressed by WTO members in international fora, India took the initiative and hosted a Ministerial Conference in New Delhi from September 3-4, 2009 which was the first occasion since July 2008 for ministers representing practically all shades of opinion and interests in the WTO to come together. There was unanimous affirmation of the need to expeditiously conclude the Doha Round, particularly in the present economic situation, and for development remaining at the heart of the Doha Round.

The Seventh WTO Ministerial meeting which was the first full Ministerial meeting of the WTO in the aftermath of the global economic meltdown was held in Geneva from November 30-December 3, 2009. While the Conference was not intended as a negotiating forum, it provided a platform for different groups and caucuses to assess the direction of the negotiations. India and her coalition partners reiterated their commitment to upholding the development dimension, the centrality of the multilateral process and the need to safeguard livelihood concerns, particularly of the poor, subsistence farmers in their countries.

The major issues in the current negotiations in the WTO are related to Agriculture and NAMA discussions which resumed on the basis of the draft modalities on Agriculture and NAMA issued by the Chairs of the respective Negotiating Groups on December 6, 2008. As per the draft agriculture modalities, developed countries would have to reduce their bound tariffs in equal annual installments over five years with an overall minimum average cut of 54 percent. Developing countries would have to reduce their bound tariffs with maximum overall average cut of 36 per cent over a larger implementation period of ten years. Both developed and developing members would have the flexibility to designate an appropriate number of tariff lines as sensitive products, on which they would undertake lower tariff cuts. The revised draft modalities propose a special product (SP) entitlement of 12 per cent of agricultural tariff lines. The average tariff cut on SPs is proposed as 11 per cent, including 5 per cent of total tariff lines at zero cuts. This is a special and differential treatment for developing countries. In the case of NAMA negotiations, the tariff reductions are proposed through a non-linear Swiss formula with a three-tiered coefficient of 20, 22 and 25 for formula reductions linked to specific flexibilities for protecting sensitive NAMA tariff lines of developing countries, and a coefficient of 8 for tariff reduction of developed countries.

In services negotiations, the Services Clusters were held in March-April 2009, June 2009, October, 2009 and November, 2009 in which India participated actively. Other than multilateral and plurilateral discussions, bilateral discussions were also held with important trading partners, wherein India conveyed its disappointment over their ambiguous and inadequate signals in the key areas.

A stock taking exercise at the level of senior officials took place in the WTO in March 2010, where members agreed to take the discussions ahead based on the work already done while maintaining the focus on the development dimension of the Round. The positive signals given by world leaders at the G-20 Leaders' Summit held in Seoul in November 2010, imparted a sense of urgency amongst members regarding the Geneva process that was supposed to resume in January 2011. The Director General, WTO, suggested a cocktail approach of discussions combining the Chair-led processes within the negotiating groups and bilateral contacts, both in specific areas and at horizontal level. India was Willing to work with the coalition groups in the WTO towards an early conclusion of the Doha Round. Its stand, however, was unequivocal: the protection of poor, subsistence farmers of developing countries and vulnerable industries was a priority.

In the area of agriculture, discussions were held on the basis of the revised draft agriculture modalities text of 6 December 2008. As per the draft, developed countries would have to reduce their bound tariffs in equal annual installments over five years with an overall minimum average cut of 54 per cent. Developing countries would have to reduce their bound tariffs with a maximum overall average cut of 36 per cent, over a larger implementation period of ten years. Both developed and developing country members would have the flexibility to designate an appropriate number of tariff lines as sensitive products, on which they would undertake lower tariff cuts. Developing countries would have a special products (SP) entitlement of 12 per cent of agricultural tariff lines. An average tariff cut of 11 per cent is proposed on SPs, including 5 per cent of total tariff lines at zero cuts. There are also reductions/disciplines proposed for various categories of domestic and export subsidies.

In the case of Non-Agricultural Market Access (NAMA) negotiations, the tariff reductions were proposed through a non-linear Swiss formula with a three-tiered coefficient of 20, 22 and 25 for formula reductions linked to specific flexibilities for protecting sensitive NAMA tariff lines of developing countries and a coefficient of 8 for tariff reduction of developed countries. With regard to the Sectoral proposal of some countries, by which the tariffs in certain identified sectors were proposed to be brought to zero or near zero levels, India's negotiating position had been that participation in sectoral initiatives must be non-mandatory and on a good faith basis without pre-judging the outcome. Another important aspect of NAMA negotiations pertain to Non-Tariff Barriers (NTBs). With regard to this, India is one of the initial proponents of the Horizontal Mechanism (HM) proposal. It aims to bring in a ministerial decision on "Procedures for the facilitation of NTBs'. This proposal has received the support of more than 100 WTO Member countries. Though the Doha mandate refer to NTBs in the context of 'products of export interest to developing countries', there had been some moves to utilize this increasing market access of remanufactured goods by some countries, led by United States of America. India's negotiating position on this was that since there had been no agreed definition on remanufactured goods, a work programme be required in the first place for defining and distinguishing remanufactured goods in contrast to other second hand goods which might have grave implications on the environment and livelihood aspects of the developing countries. The work programme got support from around 17 countries.

In services, India has been a demander. It has also offered substantial sectoral and modal coverage in its initial offer (January 2004) and the first revised offer (August 2005) of the ongoing services negotiation. At the Signaling Conference (July 2008) which was held on the sidelines of the Mini-Ministerial meeting, some further improvements were also conveyed. However, India's offers/signals are conditional on receiving satisfaction in respect of its Modes 1 / 2 and Mode 4 requests.

The services negotiations at the WTO have been rejuvenated after the G-20 Meeting. Substantive interest has been evinced by all members to intensify the negotiations to make use of the limited window of opportunity to conclude the negotiations. As a part of the plurilateral process (where more than two countries are involved), 22 plurilateral groups have been formed at the WTO in service sectors/ modes. India is the coordinator of the plurilateral requests in Mode 1 (cross-border supply) and Mode 4 (Movement of Natural Persons) - the core areas of its interest in the services negotiations. India is also co-sponsor of plurilateral requests in computer and related services (CRS) and architectural, engineering and integrated engineering services.

India has shown considerable movement from Uruguay Round commitments to revised offers; however its primary requests in Modes 1 and 4 have not been addressed by key developed countries. Some of the major developed country members have shown little or no movement in their Mode 4 offers which is a major cause of concern to India. The US and other developed countries such as Australia are trying to introduce a new approach to services negotiations by way of the clustering initiative. India has opposed this cluster approach on procedural as well as substantive grounds. The lack of progress in services under the Doha Round is not due to problems with the approach of negotiations but because of lack of political will, inadequate response from developed countries in sectors and areas of export interest to developing countries, and little movement in agriculture and NAMA.

Negotiations are taking place in the Negotiating Group on Rules (NCR) aimed at clarifying and improving Disciplines under the Anti Dumping Agreement and the Agreement on Subsidies and Countervailing Measures (ASCM), while preserving the basic concepts, principles, and effectiveness of these agreements and their instruments and objectives. The discussions on Chair's draft text of 18 'December 2008 continued during 2010. Consensus eludes on the bigger issues in anti-dumping such as zeroing, sunset reviews, lesser duty rule, public interest, causation, and anti-circumvention. In Subsidies Agreement, considerable divergence remains in the proposals on specificity, subsidies in the case of inputs provided at regulated prices, and benchmarks for export finance. India has been seeking strengthened anti-dumping rules so as to prohibit the use of zeroing in dumping margin calculation, strengthening of the rules for conduct of sunset reviews, and mandatory application of lesser duty. In the Subsidies Agreement, India is opposed to the enlargement of the scope of prohibited subsidies in the ASCM and /or limiting of the existing flexibilities for the developing countries. In the negotiations on the new disciplines on fisheries subsidies, India is seeking effective special and differential (S&D) treatment for the developing countries, particularly in the light of employment and livelihood concerns for small, artisanal fishing communities and for retaining sufficient 'policy space' so as to enable it to develop its infrastructure.

Another important area of the Doha round is the negotiations on trade facilitation. Simplification of trade procedures by reducing trading costs is in the interest of all WTO members. A Draft Consolidated Negotiating Text on Trade Facilitation was worked out by the WTO members on 14 December 2009. The draft text has since been revised six times in 2010 through discussions in the meetings of the Negotiating Group on Trade Facilitation. India has been actively participating in these meetings and has also tabled a few proposals on 'Customs Cooperation', 'Rapid Alerts System of Customs Union', and 'Appeal Mechanism'. Developed countries do not want to change their trade procedures but expect others to do so. Developing countries have, by and large, adopted an extra defensive approach to negotiations. Least developed countries, in general, do not want to undertake any binding commitment. Capacity constraints and lack of resources are two major factors that prevent developing countries (and least developed countries) from taking on binding commitments in trade facilitation. The current scenario indicates that developed countries and other donors may not invest in building physical infrastructure in these countries, although the July 2004 Framework Agreement clearly links commitments to support and assistance for infrastructure development. It is important that this linkage is respected by the entire WTO membership, particularly the developed countries and that adequate assistance is provided for implementation of commitments so that a high standards agreement on trade facilitation can be reached.

Throughout 2009 and 2010, discussions continued but no headway was made on any sustantive issue in the negotiations. (A summary of India's stand on key negotiating issues is given in Box-3). However, the subject featured on the agenda of almost every

BOX-3
India's Stand on Key Negotiating Issues: A Summary

Agriculture

i) Substantial and effective reductions in overall trade-distorting domestic support (OTDS) of the US and EU;

ii) Self-designation of an appropriate number of special products (SPs);

iii) An operational and effective Special Safeguard Mechanism (SSM);

iv) Simplification and capping of developed country tariffs.

Non-Agricultural Market Access (NAMA)

i) Adequate and appropriate flexibilities for protecting economically vulnerable industries;

ii) Participation in sectoral initiatives only on a non-mandatory and good faith basis without prejudgment of the final outcome, with substantial special and differential treatment provisions for developing countries;

iii) Serious consideration of non-tariff barrier (NTB) textual proposals with wide support such as the horizontal mechanism.

Services

i) Need for qualitative improvement in the revised offers especially on Modes 1 (cross-border supply) and 4 (movement of natural persons);

ii) Appropriate disciplining of domestic regulations by developed countries.

Rules

i) Tightening of disciplines on anti-dumping (deletion of zeroing clause and reiteration of the lesser duty rule)

ii) Effective special and differential treatment for developing countries on fisheries subsidies.

Trade-related Aspects of Intellectual Property Rights (TRIPS)

i) Establishing a clear linkage between the TRIPS Agreement and the Convention on Bio-diversity (CBD) by incorporating specific disclosure norms for patent applications;

ii) Enhanced protection for geographical indications (GIs) other than wines and spirits.

major international meeting and there were strong affirmations of political support for an early conclusion of the Doha Round. Discussions continued in Geneva during March and April 2011, in a variety of formats. Reports on each area of the negotiations were issued on 21 April 2011. These documents provided an overview of the status of negotiations in each area covered in the Doha Development Agenda. While they indicated significant progress in many areas, they also captured the wide gaps remaining on many issues.

The focus then shifted to the possibility of selecting some issues for finalization as an 'early harvest' in time for the Eighth Ministerial Conference of the WTO in December 2011. It began with an attempt to select issues of particular importance to least developed countries (LDCs). However, these attempts did not meet with any success and proved not only unproductive but very divisive as well. Members could not agree on the issues to be included and sought to selectively bring in various issues of commercial interest to them. Gradually, as Members brought in non-LDC issues, the discussion veered away from the LDC issues. The LDC issues include (i) duty free quota free (DFQF) market access; (ii) the rules of origin for DFQF market access; (iii) LDC waiver in services; and (iv) issues relating to cotton (domestic and export subsidies for cotton and tariffs). Some of the issues suggested in addition for an 'LDC plus' package were trade facilitation and the export competition pillar of the agriculture negotiations. There was however little progress in arriving at a consensus on the elements of the early harvest package. The LDCs made it clear that if the LDC package was not delivered at the December 2011 Ministerial Conference, they would be very disappointed. The African Group, the African-Caribbean-Pacific Group, and other groups of developing countries supported an effort to harvest an LDC package for the Conference. India too, supported this stand.

In October-November 2011, concerted efforts were made by some of the developed country members of the WTO to use the G20 Leaders Summit in November 2011 to advance an agenda for the Eighth WTO Ministerial Conference scheduled to be held in Geneva in December 2011. Specifically, they wanted to set the stage for plurilateral agreements on selected issues in the WTO negotiations (rather than multilateral agreements); get WTO members to agree to a commitment abjuring the use of export restrictions; and introduce new issues for negotiation, namely climate change, energy security, and food security. The weeks preceding the Eighth WTO Ministerial Conference saw hectic activity in the WTO as some members attempted to put various issues on the agenda for ministerial decision. These proposals, however, did not receive support amongst WTO members. At the Eighth Ministerial Conference from 15 to 17 December, ministers adopted a number of decisions on intellectual property (IP), electronic commerce, small economies, LDCs' accession, a services waiver for LDCs, and trade policy reviews. A number of members expressed strong reservations about plurilateral approaches. Many members stressed that any different approaches in the work ahead should conform to the Doha mandate, respect the single undertaking, and be truly multilateral, transparent, and inclusive. In looking at future work, a large number of ministers stressed the centrality of development. Many underlined the need to give priority to issues of interest to LDCs, including cotton. Many mentioned the importance of all three pillars in the agriculture negotiations. Many also mentioned trade facilitation, special and differential (S&D) treatment, S&D monitoring mechanism and NTMs. In an unprecedented display of unity, a coalition of more than a hundred developing countries, including India, Brazil, China, and South Africa, met on the sidelines of the Conference and issued a declaration emphasizing the development agenda. They roundly criticized suggestions for plurilateral agreements to replace decision making by multilateral consensus.

In order to promote transparency and provide better understanding of the trade policies and practices of its members, the WTO has a mechanism for regular review of their trade policies. Depending upon its share in world trade, each member's trade policy is reviewed by the WTO at fixed periodic intervals. India's TPR is carried out every four years. The TPR offers an opportunity to other WTO members to ask questions and raise concerns on different aspects of policies and practices of the country under review. The Fifth TPR of India was held on 14 and 16 September 2011 in the WTO. Before the meeting, the WTO Secretariat circulated a compilation of India's written replies to 886 advance questions raised by 26 WTO members. During the review, most of the members commended the resilience of the Indian economy that smoothly withstood the adverse effects of global financial crisis without taking recourse to protectionist measures. Members appreciated India for using its trade policy to promote sustainable development and inclusive growth. Members also noted India's positive engagement in Doha Round negotiations. Some of the members, notably the US, raised concerns in certain areas, namely tariffs and duties, licensing and restrictions, trade defence measures (anti-dumping), SPS & TBT, government procurement, incentive schemes to promote investments and exports and protect agriculture, tariff protection on agriculture, services and investments. Responses to the issues raised were provided in India's Closing Statement on 16 September 2011 (Box-4).

BOX 4

Fifth Trade Policy Review: Issues Raised and India's Responses

---

The Openness of India's Trading Regime: Questions were asked about the openness of India's trading regime. In response India pointed out that year after year, India's imports had outpaced exports. In terms of percentage of GDP, the country's merchandise trade deficit is one of the highest in the world. India has been autonomously reducing its tariffs over the years. The simple average most favoured nation (MFN) tariff rate declined from 15.1 per cent in 2006-7 to 12 per cent in 2010-11. Both the average agricultural and industrial average tariffs have declined over time. The tariffs on 71 per cent of India's tariff lines are between 5 and 10 per cent.

Gap between India's Bound and Applied Rates on Agricultural Products: Some members mentioned the large gap between India's bound and applied rates on agricultural products. India responded that the large gap reflected India's steady and continued autonomous tariff liberalization. During the four years since the last TPR, the tariffs on some agricultural commodities had to be adjusted in the face of high volatility in food prices. In most cases tariffs have been brought down and have stayed down. In a few instances they have been raised again but never above their original levels.

Export Incentives: Questions were asked about export promotion schemes. It was explained that India's export promotion schemes are based on the concept of duty neutralization and providing a level playing field. These schemes are reviewed regularly.

FDI Policy: To a number of questions on FDI policy, India explained that the continuing thrust, during the period since India's last TPR in 2007, has been on making the FDI policy more liberal and investment friendly. The FDI guidelines have been significantly rationalized, simplified, and consolidated, with the aim of providing a single policy platform for reference of foreign investors. Several new sectors, such as petroleum and natural gas and civil aviation were either opened up to foreign investment or significantly liberalized during this period. Efforts were also being made to streamline and simplify the business environment and make regulations conducive to business.

India's IP Policies and Enforcement: On questions related to India's IP policies, India replied that a number of initiatives have been taken to enhance IP protection and enforcement. The changes proposed in the Copyright and Trademark Acts would enhance protection to intellectual property rights (IPRs) in digital technology particularly with regard to the dissemination of protected material over digital networks. These have been supplemented by administrative as well as judicial measures to strengthen the IPR regime. The provisions on IP protection in these laws are further supplemented by border measures to prevent the import of goods involving copyright piracy and counterfeit trademarks. Another initiative taken by Indian customs is the facility for online registration by the right holders through the web-based Automatic Recordation and Targeting for IPR Protection System.

Government Procurement: On this subject, India explained that the procurement of high tech items and high value tenders, above US$ 50,000 is generally open to international bidders. Major reforms are on the anvil for increasing coverage, improving transparency and efficiency, and better enforcement, which are triggered by domestic concerns relating to enhancing the value for money. An omnibus procurement law applicable to the entire country and to all procuring entities, including public-sector enterprises, is being deliberated upon.

Sanitary and Phyto-sanitary (SPS) and Technical Barriers to Trade (TBT) measures: In response to question on India's SPS and TBT measures, India explained that specific trade concerns raised against India have been largely addressed. Regulations adopted in the past have been on the basis of scientific risk analysis.

Export Restrictions: There were some questions on India's use of export restrictions. India responded that export restrictions have been used on some occasions for purposes of domestic supply management but these have been purely on a temporary basis. The ban on the export of rice and wheat had to be extended in 2009 due to a dislocation in production and again in 2010 due to the severest drought in the country in the last forty years. However, the export of wheat and non-basmati rice is now completely free. The export of basmati rice is and has always been free. Restrictions on cotton exports were imposed for only a brief period last year. Cotton yarn exports have been made completely free. Similarly, cotton is also freely exportable.

Other Issues: There were questions related to customs valuation, tariffs, and other charges, internal taxation, import licensing, and the use of trade remedies. In response it was pointed out that India cannot be accused of protectionist intent in its use of trade remedies. If that were the case, then the easy route of increasing the tariffs up to the bound rates could have been used; that has not been done. Anti-dumping measures are legitimate instruments against unfair trade practices. Investigations are carried out in a fair and transparent manner and subjected to strict scrutiny. As a rule India only imposes the lesser duty and not the full dumping margin as is done by some WTO members. This underscores the fact that trade remedies are not used as a protectionist tool. Despite the fact that many members, with very deep pockets, use subsidies as part of their trade policy, India has not imposed a single anti-subsidy measure. As on date, there is only one safeguard duty in force. In the wake of the economic crisis, there was a spurt in application of safeguard investigations in 2009. A total of 14 applications were received but in nine cases, investigations were either terminated or a decision was taken not to impose any safeguard duty. Duties were imposed only in five cases and those too have since been withdrawn. Moreover, India has never taken recourse to quantitative restrictions as safeguard measures. Import licensing affects only a few restricted items primarily on grounds of protection of human, animal, and plant life and the environment. The licensing regime is open and transparent. Licences are granted on a non-discriminatory basis. The relevant regulations are all available in the public domain and the DGFT acts as the nodal agency.

However, the Eighth Ministerial Meeting of the WTO which was held in December 2011 in Geneva provided little political guidance to the members to resolve the issues involved. There was no significant progress in 2012. Efforts are being made for an early harvest on some issues in time for the Ninth Ministerial Conference of the WTO (MC9) to be held in December 2013. India is of the view that any early outcome of the negotiations should invariably address issues of interest to the developing countries, especially the least developed countries (LDCs) and the small vulnerable economies (SVEs). A Draft Consolidated Negotiating Text on Trade Facilitation, revised fourteen times (till December 2012) through discussions in the meetings of the Negotiating Group on Trade Facilitation (NGTF). India is actively engaged in these negotiations and has also tabled a few proposals on 'Customs Cooperation', 'Rapid Alerts System of Customs Union', and 'Appeal Mechanism'. The Draft Text, however, lacks internal balance. The developed countries are holding up the laws and procedures of their own countries as benchmarks and want the developing countries to replicate them. Developing countries have by and large adopted a defensive approach in the negotiations. The developed countries and a few developing countries are making efforts to harvest Trade facilitation' for an early outcome, in time for MC9. India along with most of the developing countries wants issues of market access and trade facilitation to be balanced with developmental issues such as duty free quota, free market access for LDCs, and acceptance of the modalities for reducing cotton subsidies. The G33 group of countries, which is a coalition of 46 developing countries, including India, has tabled a proposal on food security in the WTO on 16 November 201 2. The proposal is for an amendment to certain provisions of the WTO Agreement on Agriculture to allow developing countries greater flexibility in their public stockholding operations for food security purposes. The issue of food security is very important for India and any concession on the trade facilitation front needs to be balanced by acceptance of the G33 proposal in any package deal for MC9.

During the current year, some of the developed country members of the Information Technology Agreement (ITA) of WTO viz. the USA, European Union, and Japan, have proposed expansion of the agreement (called ITA-2) to increase the coverage of IT products on which customs duty would be bound at zero, addressing non-tariff measures, and expanding the number of signatory countries to include new signatories such as Argentina, Brazil, and South Africa. The proponents of ITA expansion have prepared a consolidated list containing around 350 IT products (combining products of interest to all proponents of ITA-2) on which tariff reductions are being sought. This is under active discussion in the WTO and India is carefully examining the proposal.

Negotiations in services have continued primarily in the plurilateral format. Intensive negotiations were held in 2009, 2010, and also till the first half of 2011. These efforts culminated in a report by the Chair of the Committee on Trade in Services - Special Session (CTS-SS) and all subsidiary bodies under the CTS in April 2011. The Chair's report puts forth two views. The developed countries' view is that further progress on market access could include the binding of autonomous liberalization where possible, improved levels of access under commercial presence mode, that is, Mode 3 (including restrictions on foreign equity participation and forms of commercial presence), as well as a robust and satisfactory outcome in Mode 4 (presence of natural persons). The developing countries' view is that there is an imbalance in market access negotiations, as evidenced by the fact that developing country flexibilities have not been taken into account in other members' requests, sectors of export interest to developing countries are not being fully reflected in developed members' offers; developing countries have already made a significant contribution to the Doha Round; and some plurilateral requests and recent proposals have embodied *a* level of ambition going beyond that agreed in Annex C of the Hong Kong Ministerial Declaration. India has already made considerable improvement in its revised offer (from 37 sub-sectors in the Uruguay Round to 95 in the Revised Offer). Some of the major developed country members have shown nil or little movement in their Mode 4 offers, which is an area of interest to India.

QUESTIONS

1. Does the growth of regional trading blocs warrant WTO encouragement? If regional groups had an open membership policy to accept all who applied ,would that be more desirable from a world standpoint?
2. Large countries are likely to have an advantage in any trade war, Why are those countries still willing to join the WTO ,which limits their ability to exploit their market power?
3. Does the chance of countries' to free-ride on concessions of others make the principle of

most-favoured - nation status a weakness of the WTO? Do regional agreements represent an effective way to exclude free riders?

4. When disputes over unfair practices arise ,what standards should be applied to non-market economies, and how different from those applied to firms in market economies must they be to provide comparable treatment?
5. Why does the WTO regard quantitative restrictions as less desirable policy instruments than ad valorem tariffs? How is the current existence of tariff-rate quotas consistent with this preference?
6. Do international negotiations where countries count their gains in terms of greater access to foreign market represent misplaced attention to exports alone ?Regardless of the motive for such negotiations, in what ways do countries gain from cooperating multilaterally?
7. "When a small country reduces its tariffs as part of a WTO agreement ,that is likely to reduce inefficiencies in the country and make it better off, but if the country must increase its payments to others for the right to use their intellectual property ,that is likely to make the country worse off." Evaluate the claim by advocates from developing countries who feel that Uruguay Round agreements were against their interests.
8. If there were no dispute settlement mechanism within the WTO ,how would they weaken the credibility of any multilateral agreements reached? If individual members regard some issues as too important to be addressed by dispute resolution within the WTO, what alternative do they have in responding to WTU panel rulings?

REFERENCES

Czinkota, Michael R. (1994) "Global Neighbors, Poor Relations." *Marketing Management* 2 (4), 46-52. (see chapter 3.)

Davis, Lester A. (1992) *Contribution of Exports* to U.S. Employment Washington, D.C: U.S. Department of Commerce.

Focus: GATT Newsletter. "Uruguay Round results to expand trade by $755 billion." May 1994, 6.

Guide to GAIT Law and Practice (6th edn). Geneva: General Agreement on Tariffs and Trade, 1994, 56

Naisbitt, John (1994) *Global Paradox*. New York: Morrow.

Okamatsu, Sozaburo (1994) "Japan in the World Economy," speech of the Vice Minister of MITI before the Chicago Council of Foreign Relations, 11 May.

Simai, Mihaly (1994) *The Future of Global Governance*. Washington, D.C.: United States Institute of Peace Press. U.S. Senate Committee on Banking. Housing, and Urban Affairs. Subcommittee on International Finance and Monetary Policy (1994) *Renewal of the Export Administration Act*. 103rd Cong. 2nd sess., 3 February, 2 (testimony of Paul Freedenberg).

Wiedersheim-Paul, Finn, H.C. Olson, and L.S. Welch (1978) "Pre-export Activity:

The First Step in the Internationalisation," Journal of International Business Studies, 9 (Spring/ Summer): 47-58.

Yearbook of International Trade Statistics (1956). New York: United Nations.

7

REGIONAL BLOCKS, TRADE LIBERALISATION AND FOREIGN INVESTMENT

INTRODUCTION

Economic integration is proceeding across the world at an unprecedented pace. Globalization has brought enormous benefits for many countries and citizens. But some have been on the losing end of the process, and opposition to further integration is mounting for a multitude of reasons. Trade is just one aspect of globalization, and links with broader economic, political and technological forces are manifold and complex. Certain arguments against open trade are fuelled by a variety of factors - including a general fear of change - that have little to do with further trade opening. Governments responding to anti-trade pressures stemming from anti-globalization arguments risk making poor policy choices. Trade scepticism is clearly a cause of concern, particularly at a time when WTO members are striving to complete the Doha Round. At this crucial juncture, it seems appropriate to revisit the case for regionalism, multilateralism, and globalisation.

REGIONALISM, MULTILATERALISM AND GLOBALISATION

Since the end of World War II under the GATT and WTO, trade policy has *never* been "first-best." One might argue that the multilateral liberalization of international trade under several rounds of GATT has been first-best, and consequently, by construction, has been preferable to the flurry of regional integration agreements over the past 30 years, but the rounds of multilateral liberalizations have been essentially second-best approaches. As Lawrence has noted:

> The postwar experience with both multilateralism and regionalism has been mixed. On the one hand, the multilateral trading system has enjoyed spectacular success in lowering trade barriers on *industrial products.* ... As the focus has shifted away from the relatively easy task of reducing barriers protecting industrial products, achieving agreement has become more difficult. ... In many important

areas, *such as services* and agriculture, liberalization has remained fairly limited, (p. 5; italics added)

Put simply, regionalism has been a second-best policy that has generally sought greater sectoral breadth and depth of integration across goods and services than multilateralism, but has limited itself geographically. By contrast, multilateralism has been a second-best policy that has sought a wider array of countries, but has been more limited in terms of sectoral breadth and depth.

While this appraisal may well be accepted readily by some, to the extent that national consumers' welfare matters to policy makers, the proclivity towards regionalism vs. multilateralism can be readily seen by accounting for three factors. First, services are relatively more expensive to transport than goods. Second, services provided by foreign firms tend to be regulated at a higher level of intensity than domestic firms. Services trade is protected almost exclusively by nontariff barriers. Examples of these barriers are rife. By way of illustration, suppliers are impeded from traveling to receivers by limits on the inflow of temporary workers for construction projects, or by limits on domestic practicing by foreign professionals, such as physicians. Receivers are hindered from going to suppliers by measures that obstruct their traveling abroad for purposes such as tourism or education. Cross-border movement of services themselves is restricted by limitations on foreign content in radio and television broadcasting and in the cinema. As for the provision of services through affiliates, many governments have strictly controlled direct investment by foreigners in sensitive domestic industries such as transportation, telecommunications, banking and advertising. Finally, goods' trade barriers (tariffs) have been relatively less costly to liberalize multilaterally than services' (nontariff) trade barriers.

The relatively greater transportability of goods and the relatively lower trade restrictions on goods - combined with the relatively lower cost of negotiating goods' trade liberalization - has pronounced potential implications for the relative benefits *of regionalism* in goods and services vs. *multilateralism* in goods. At higher relative transport costs for services compared with goods a regional free trade agreement (FTA) in goods and services is welfare superior to a multilateral free trade agreement in goods alone. The combination of these three factors can help explain the relative growth of regionalism vs. multilateralism.

It would be very useful to find from managers' perspectives if these factors have been important in their views of regionalism vs. multilateralism. Many perceptions of regionalism, multilateralism, and globalization will hinge upon "relative trade costs." As these costs are likely even much higher than most have conjectured, even with regard to trading *goods* -much less services. The survey needs to solicit information about these costs. How high do managers think these costs are for "natural" trade costs? For "artificial" (policy-induced) trade costs? There is likely enormous heterogeneity in such costs between goods and services industries, not to mention *across* industries within each group. How have these cost impinged upon managers' views of globalization?

On globalization, to while there is no universally agreed definition economists typically use the term to refer to international integration in commodity, capital and labour markets. Using integration in these markets as the benchmark, it is clear that globalization is not a new phenomenon. Since the mid-19th century, there have been at least two episodes of globalization. The first episode began around the mid-19th century and ended with the commencement of World War I (WWI). The second episode began in the aftermath of World War II (WWII) and continues today. In both these episodes of globalization, rapid trade and output growth went together with major shifts in the relative size of the economies involved. One valuable lesson from history is that globalization has not been a smooth process. It has often been marked by periods of accelerated integration (as observed in the 19th century and in the second half of the 20th century) and by periods of dramatic reversals (as in the inter-war period) sometimes with costly consequences.

Trade, economists have largely focused on "globalization" in the superficial context commanded by where the *customs* - data has most conveniently (or with least cost) led them: *international trade.* However, there is certainly a more appropriate breadth for understanding globalization. Globalization goes beyond the integration of goods, capital and labor markets; it is the full integration of two "societies," in terms of political, social, and cultural norms. Current knowledge *of the simultaneous* determination of trade, capital, and labor flows (especially, by MNCs) is weaker; much of that knowledge could be incorporated more fully and productively +formulating the strategy and policy framework for international business.

REGIONAL INTEGRATION AGREEMENT (RIAs) AND TRADE

Regional integration "which involves arrangements for preferential trade may take a number of forms. The term *trading bloc* is usually reserved by economic theorists for arrangements which take the form either of a free trade area or of a customs union. A *free trade area* involves the elimination of tariffs on trade between the member states, but each member maintains its own national policy towards trade with third countries. Customs inspectors monitor trade at the frontiers between the member states in order to tax trade that might otherwise circumvent high tariff barriers by entering the flea through the member state with the lowest external tariff. In contrast, member states of a *customs union* adopt a common external tariff. Commodities thus flow freely between member states, and there is no need for customs inspection at national borders.

Trading blocs involve the removal of trade barriers, but stop short of further economic integration. A *common market* allows not only for the free improvement of commodities, but also for the free movement of factors of production, *economic union* is used to describe the situation where member states not only participate in a common market, but also promote a high degree of integration in their fiscal, monetary, commercial and welfare policies. Besides these form of economic flows,

Compared to the ideal of free world trade following the WTO convention, the regional trade agreements (RTAs) encompasses both reciprocal bilateral free trade of customs areas and multicountry (plurilateral) agreements. Regional and bilateral trade agreement provide for one type of trade liberalisation and they must be seen in a broader context of alternative method of liberalisation. Members of RTA liberalise trade on *reciprocal* and *preferential* basis. While programmes much as the U.S. African Growth and Opportunity Act (AGOA) and the EU's Everything But Arms (EBA) also liberalise trade preferentially (i.e., different trade partners receive different treatment), the US and EU extend these preferences uniliterally rather than reciprocally. In contrast to both of these type of preferential liberalisation, countries often lower trade barriers in a nondiscriminatory fashion for all trade partners. They might do so multilaterally through GATT/WTO negotiating rounds or *autonomously*, as in the cash of Pakistan in the late 1990s.

Economic Effects of RIAs

The development impacts of RIA membership depend importantly on the countries that are involved, the type of agreement, and its substantive coverage. Recent research suggests that of particular importance to developing countries are whether large industrial countries are members of the agreement, the extent of sectoral exclusions, and the degree to which the RIAs involve "deeper integration"—that is, extend beyond preferential elimination of barriers to trade in goods. In order to understand the economic effects of RIAs, a few definitions are in order.

Trade creation takes place when a member country of the RIA (Country 1) increases its imports from its partner country (Country 2) without a reduction in Country 1's imports from the rest of the world (ROW). This occurs because with the removal of tariffs between member countries, Country 2's products become cheaper than those of Country 1. The increase in (cheaper) imports results in an increase in consumption and a reduction in output in Country 1. Trade creation is beneficial.

Trade diversion takes place when imports from the ROW are replaced in Country 1 by more expensive imports from Country 2. *Why would Country 1 import more expensive goods from Country 2?* Because goods from Country 2 do not pay the import tariff, while ROW goods do. Trade diversion is typically harmful.

Transfers occur between member countries of the trade bloc because removal of tariffs between them means that exports obtain better prices in the partners' markets (a positive transfer), while the costs of imports net of tariffs increase (a negative transfer).

Trade Creation and Diversion and the Type of RIA

Assume that Mexico imports either from the United States or from Japan and applies a 20 percent tariff on all imports. For a given product, the United States sells at a price of $100 and Japan sells at a price of $110. With the 20 percent tariff, the cost to the Mexican consumer is $120 for the good from the United States and $132 for the product from Japan. Consumers import from the cheaper source—from the United States, not Japan. Now assume that Mexico forms an RIA with the United States, along the lines of the North American Free Trade Agreement (NAFTA). Tariffs on imports from the United States fall to zero, and consumers now pay $100. This is a case of trade creation because the United States was already the cheapest source and has become even cheaper, replacing more expensive domestic output and raising consumption as well. Note that the consumer price must fall for trade creation to take place. Since the United States was the only source of Mexican imports to begin with, having an RIA with the United States is identical to unilateral trade liberalization by Mexico and is beneficial.

Assume now that the good is exported by the United States at $110 and by Japan at $100. With the 20 percent tariff, the cost to consumers is $120 for the good from Japan and $132 for that from the United States. The good is imported exclusively from Japan at $ 120. After Mexico forms an RIA with the United States, the cost of imports from the United States is $110, which is lower than the $120 consumer cost for imports from Japan. Consumers switch their source of imports from Japan to the United States. But although the United States is the cheapest source for consumers, it is not the cheapest source for Mexico as a whole. The reason is that although the consumer cost or imports from Japan is $120, the true cost for Mexico is only $100. The $ 100 is the cost in scarce foreign exchange that Mexico pays for imports from Japan, while the additional $20 associated with the 20 percent tariff is simply a transfer from consumers to the government and is not a cost to the nation. To put it differently, before entering the RIA, Mexico paid $100 to the foreign supplier, and after entering the RIA, it pays $110. Thus, Mexico loses $10 per unit of import. This is the cost of trade diversion from a cheaper to a more expensive source. Another way of showing this result is that the consumer price fell by $10 (from $120 to $110), but the government lost $20 in tariff revenue, so the net loss is $10.

Note that trade diversion occurred because the 20 percent tariff is higher than the 10 percent difference in cost between the U.S. and the Japanese good. If the tariff were lower — say, 5 percent — the cost of Japan's imports would be $105, still lower than the U.S. price of $110 free of tariff. Consumers would have continued to import from Japan, the cheapest source, and trade diversion would not have occurred. This example points to an important lesson: RIAs should lower their external trade barriers because that reduces the extent of trade diversion. Another reason for so doing is that reducing external trade barriers makes possible the classical gains from trade. Note also that the welfare impact of an RIA is ambiguous a priori and depends on whether trade creation or trade diversion dominates. Of course, even an RIA that is dominated by trade diversion and has a negative welfare effect can be turned into a beneficial RIA by lowering external trade barriers sufficiently.

In the example above, imports were from either Japan or the United States but not from both. This is relevant for a small country facing imports of a similar good from two large exporters. Countries, however, may import the good from more than one source; this is particularly likely to be the case when a small country imports from another small country and from the ROW. For instance, assume that imports from India and from ROW. Say that the world price for a given product is $100 and Sri Lanka charges an import tariff of 20 percent, or $20. Thus, the import price paid by consumers in (and faced by its producers) is $120. India supply of exports to is not horizontal at $120, as is the case for the ROW. Rather, it is upward sloping: an increase in India supply of exports to Sri Lanka implies a higher (marginal) cost of production because Sri Lanka is a large buyer of India exports (although it is a small buyer of ROW exports). In equilibrium, also sells at $120 because it cannot sell at a price above that of the ROW.*

Assume now that Sri Lanka forms an RIA with India. As long as Sri Lanka continues to import from the ROW, the consumer price remains $120. Since the consumer price remains unchanged, no trade creation takes place. Before the RIA, the Sri Lanka government obtained $20 in tariff revenue for each unit imported from India, and exporters obtained $100. After the RIA, Sri Lanka no longer charges a tariff on India imports for its exports. In other words, Sri Lanka now loses tariff revenue and pays $20 more for its imports from India. This amounts to a transfer of income from Sri Lanka, the importing country, to India the exporting country. Note that this occurs even if the quantity of imports from India remains unchanged (that is, even if supply of exports is vertical or perfectly inelastic), in which case there is no trade diversion.

It is likely, however, that India exports to Sri Lanka's will increase after Sri Lanka import tariff is removed. In that case the loss of tariff revenue for Sri Lanka will be larger. The increase in India exports amounts to trade diversion because total imports

---

* A rare example was a case brought by India against Turkey in 1996. India contested Turkey's imposition of quotas on imports of textile and clothing products, which were required because Turkey had entered into a customs union with the European Union. A WTO panel found that Turkey's measures were inconsistent with GATT Articles XI and XIII and rejected Turkey's assertion that its measures were justified by GATT Article XXIV. On appeal, the Appellate Body upheld the panel's conclusion on the illegality of the quotas but found that the legal interpretation of Article XXIV by the panel was erroneous; the Appellate Body stated that a panel should first ascertain whether an RIA complies with ANjcle XXIV before considering other GATT provisions.

are not affected by the RIA. Since the consumer price is unchanged, the increase in imports from India comes at the expense of reduced imports from the ROW. The (marginal) production cost of the increased imports from India rises from \$100 to \$120, which is higher than the \$100 price paid for ROW imports. Since there is only trade diversion and no trade creation, forming such an RIA lowers the income of the bloc as a whole. India gains by obtaining a better price in Sri Lanka market, and Sri Lanka loses — and it loses more than India gains. The reason is that India additional transfers are obtained by increasing its exports to Sri Lanka, and the increased exports are more expensive to produce than the ROW imports they replace. The difference between India gain and Sri Lanka loss is the net loss) due to trade diversion. It is an inefficiency loss and is not captured by anybody.

To illustrate graphically, assume that a home country and a partner country form an RIA. Both are assumed to be small relative to the rest of the world (ROW), so they take the price of goods from the rest of the world, Pw, as given (Figure-1). D_H represents the home country's demand for imports, S_p represents the partner's supply of exports facing the home country, and S_{ROW} is the supply from the *ROW*. Under free trade, imports equal Q_4, and home country welfare W_H = triangle *ACE*. Assume now that the home country imposes an MFN tariff, *T*. Then the price of imports from the ROW faced by home country producers and consumers rises to $Pw' = Pw + T$, and S_{ROW} shifts

FIGURE 1

A RIA INVOLVING SMALL COUNTRIES

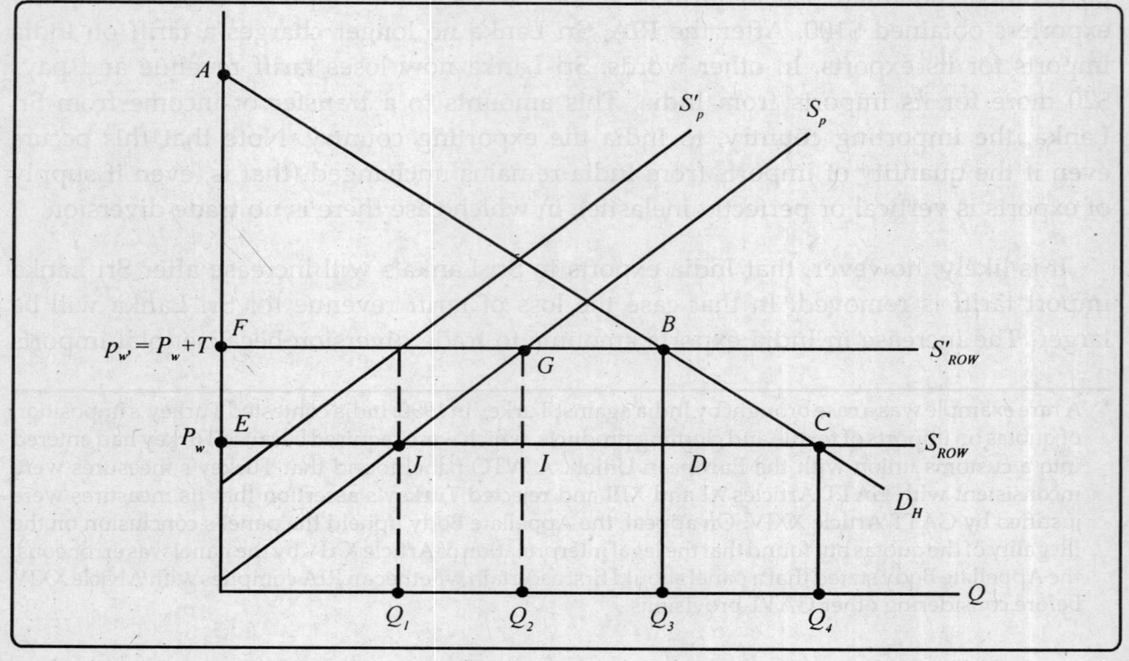

to S'_{ROW}. Similarly, S_p shifts to S_P^1. Imports from the partner country equal Q_1, and imports from the ROW equal $Q_3 - Q_1$, with total imports of Q_3. W_H^{MFN} = surplus *ABF* + tariff revenue *BDEF* and is lower than W_H under free trade by triangle BCD.

Assume that the home country now forms an RIA with the partner country. As the partner country no longer pays the tariff *T*, its export supply curve shifts to S_p. The ROW still pays the tariff *T*, so the home country price remains *Pw'*. Hence, the partner country imports increase from Q_1 to Q_2, while the imports from the ROW fall from $Q_3 - Q_1$ to $Q_3 - Q_2$. This trade diversion results in a worsening in the home country's terms of trade. Welfare is W_H^{RAI} = ABF + *BDIG*. In other words, the RIA has no impact on the consumer surplus because the price is not affected (there is no trade creation), but there is a loss of tariff revenue. W_H^{RAI} is lower than W_H^{MFN} by *EFGI*, the tariff revenue lost on imports from the partner country after forming the RIA. Note that the welfare loss to the home country would occur in the absence of trade diversion as well (for example, the loss would be *EFGI* if S_p were vertical at level Q_2).

The home country welfare loss from the RIA is proportional to the level of partner country imports. Note also that if the MFN tariff were lower than T, the welfare loss from the RIA would be smaller than area *EFGI* both because of lower imports from the partner and because of the lower tariff rate. The partner gains *EFGJ*, which is less than the home country loss of EFGI by the triangle *GIJ*. The reason for the net loss of triangle *GIJ* for the RIA members as a whole is the trade diversion, $Q_2 - Q_1$ This amount was previously imported from the ROW at a cost of Pw but is now produced at a higher marginal cost.

Developing countries are more likely to lose by 'forming a South-South RIA, as opposed to joining a North-South agreement, because the South-South arrangement entails little or no beneficial trade creation. Moreover, there is a high probability that one of the members of a South-South RIA may gain while the other loses. It is the poorest member countries that are likely to lose the most, as the most advanced country will usually have a more developed manufacturing sector. Its manufactures are typically highly protected, and once the RIA is formed, the more advanced country can export them free of tariffs to the poorer member countries. The RIA thus entails an income transfer from the less to the more advanced member countries. Moreover, because the poorer country had more to gain from trading with the North (relative to the more advanced country), it will lose more from creating a South-South RIA. A South-South RIA discriminates against the North and so helps those countries within the bloc that are the closest competitors with the North. Such asymmetric distribution of the gains and losses of integration has led to tensions between members, breakup of RIAs, and even wars. One way to reduce the asymmetry in the distribution of gains and losses, and thus to lessen potential tensions between member countries, is to lower the external trade barriers. The lower the tariff levels with the ROW, the smaller the transfers associated with an RIA.

The foregoing suggests at least three reasons why members of RIAs should lower external trade barriers: (a) to generate classical gains from trade; (b) to lessen the chances that trade diversion will occur;· and (c) to reduce income transfers between member countries resulting from the RIA and the tensions that can arise from such transfers.

THE PROLIFERATION OF REGIONAL PREFERENCE SYSTEMS

More agreements are being signed. Since 1990, the number of RTAs in force rose from 50 to nearly 230. The WTO estimates that another 60 agreements are in various stages of negotiation. The boom in RTAs reflects changes in certain countries' trade policy objectives, the changing perceptions of the multilateral liberalization process, and the reintegration into the global economy of countries in transition from social-ism. This last category accounts for many of the new agreements signed in the early 1990s, when countries in Eastern Europe and the former Soviet Union negotiated RTAs with Western Europe [both the EU and the European Free Trade Association (EFTA)] and with each other. Exhibit-1 presents the frequently cited RTAs and the parties to them.

EXHIBIT-1

TRADING AGREEMENTS AND THE PARTIES TO THEM

Agreement	*Full name*	*Members*
AFTA	ASEAN Free Trade Area	Australlia, Brunei, Canada, Chile, China, Hong Kong (China), Indonasia, Japan, Korea, Malaysia, Mexico, New Zealand, Papua New Guinea, Peru, Philippines, Russia, Singapore, Taiwan (China), Tt land, United States, Vietnam
APEC	Asia Pacific Economic Cooperation	Brunei, Darussalam, Cambodia, Indonesia, Lao People's Democratic Republic, Malaysia, Myanmar, Philippines, Singapore, Thailand, Vietnam
CACM	Central American Common Market	Costa Rica, El Salvador, Guatemala, Honduras, Nicaragua
CAFTA	Central America Free Trade Area	United States, Costa Rica, El Salvador, Guatemala, Honduras, Nicaragua, Dominican Republic
CAN	Andean Community	Bolivia, Colombia, Ecuador, Peru, Republic Bolivariana de Venezuela
CARICOM	Caribbean Community and Common Market	Antigua and Barbuda, Bahamas, Barbados, Belize, Dominica, Gre-nada, Guyana, Haiti, Jamaica, Monserrat, Trinidad and Tobago, St. Kitts and Nevis, St. Lucia, St. Vincent and the Grenadines, Suriname

CEFTA	Central European Free Trade Agreement	Bulgaria, Czech Republic, Hungary, Poland, Romania, Slovak Republic, Slovenia
CEMAC	Economic and Monetary Community of Central Africa	Cameroon, Central African Republic, Chad, Republic of Congo, Equatorial Guinea, Gabon
CER (ANZCERTA)	Closer Economic Relations Trade Agreement	Australia, New Zealand
CIS	Commonwealth of Independent States	Azerbaijan, Armenia, Belarus, Georgia, Moldova, Kazakhstan, Russian Federation, Ukraine, Uzbekistan, Tajikistan, Kyrgyz Republic
COMESA	Common Market for Eastern and Southern Africa	Angola, Burundi, Comoros, Democratic Republic of Congo, Djibouti, Arab Republic of Egypt, Eritrea, Ethiopia, Kenya, Madagascar, Malawi, Mauritius, Namibia, Rwanda, Seychelles,
EAC	East African Community	Kenya, Tanzania, Uganda
ECOWAS	Economic Community of West African States	Sudan, Swaziland, Uganda, *Zambia*, Zimbabwe Benin, Burkina Faso, Cape Verde, Gambia, Ghana, Guinea, Guinea-Bissau, Cote d'Ivoire, Liberia, Mali, Niger, Nigeria, Senegal, Sierra Leone, Togo
EEA	European Economic Area	EU, Iceland, Liechtenstein, Norway Iceland,
EFTA	European Free Trade Association	Liechtenstein, Norway, Switzerland
EMFTA	Euro-Mediterranean Free Trade Area	EU, Algeria, Cyprus, Egypt, Israel, Jordan, Lebanon, Malta, Morocco, Syrian Arab Republic, Tunisia, Turkey, Palestinian Authority
FTAA	Free Trade Area of the Americas	Antigua and Barbuda, Argentina, Bahamas, Barbados, Belice, Bolivia, Brazil, Canada, Chile, Colombia, Costa Rica, Dominica, Dominican Republic, Ecuador, El Salvador, Grenada, Guatemala, Guyana, Haiti, Honduras, Jamaica, Mexico, Nicaragua, Panama, Paraguay, Peru, St. Kitts and Nevis, St. Lucia, St. Vincent and the Grenadines, Suriname, Trinidad and Tobago, United States, Uruguay, Venezuela
GAFTA	Greater Arab Free Trade Area	Bahrain, Egypt, Iraq, Jordan, Kuwait, Lebanon, Libya, Morocco, Oman, Palestine, Qatar, Saudi Arabia, Somalia, Sudan, Syria, Tunisia, United Arab Emirates, Yemen
GCC	Gulf Cooperation Council	Bahrain, Kuwait, Oman, Qatar, Saudi Arabia, United Arab Emirates
MERCOSUR	Southern Common Market	Argentina, Brazil, Paraguay, Uruguay
NAFTA	North American Free Trade Agreement	Canada, Mexico, United States
SACU	Southern African Customs Union	South Africa, Botswana, Lesotho, Swaziland, Namibia
SADC	Southern African Development Community	Angola, Botswana, Democratic Republic of Congo, Lesotho, Malawi,. Mauritius, Mozambique, Namibia, South Africa, Swaziland, Seychelles, Tanzania, Zambia, Zimbabwe
SAFTA	South Asian Free Trade Area	Bangladesh, Bhutan, India, Maldives, Nepal, Pakistan, Sri Lanka
SAPTA	South Asian Preferential Trade Arrangement	Bangladesh, Bhutan, India, Maldives, Nepal, Pakistan, Sri Lanka
WAEMU	West African Economic and Monetary Union	Benin, Burkina Faso, Cote d'lvoire, Guinea Bissau, Mali, Niger, Senegal, Togo

Nearly all countries belong to at least one RTA and some are party to numerous agreements (Box-1). On average, each country belongs to six RTAs, though there is considerable variation across regions and levels of development. East Asian countries sign fewer agreements than countries in other regions. Northern countries have par-ticipated to the greatest extent, each signing, on average, 13 agreements. A substantial number of developing countries (45) have signed bilateral preferential agreements with a Northern partner. However, this activity is not spread evenly across regions. Most activity has been in Eastern Europe, Northern Africa, and Latin America. There are no countries in South Asia that have signed a bilateral agreement with a Northern partner. The enlargement of the EU in May 2004 led to a fall in the number of North-South RTAs in Europe.

Since 2000, several major new trends have emerged in the pattern of regional tratie agreements. One unifying characteristic is that these take RTAs well beyond agreements between adjacent countries. For example,

i) The EU's move toward bilateral market access FTAs and Economic Partnership Agreements (EPAs) with the ACP countries;

BOX-1

Most Countries Belong to More than One RTA

	East Asia and Pacific	*Europe and Central Asia*	*Latin America and the Caribbean*	*Middle and North Africa*	*Sub-Saharan South Asia*	*Africa*	*North*	*Total*
Number of countries	32	36	39	21	8	48	25	209
North-South bilateral								
Countries belonging to at least one RTA	4	12	6	10	0	2	10	44
Average number of RTAs per country	2	1	2	1		1	4	11
Maximum number of RTAs per country	4	4	4	3	0	1	24	40
All others								
Countries belonging to at least one RTA	24	22	33	20	8	47	10	164
Average number of RTAs per country	2	6	8	5	4	4	8	37
Maximum number of RTAs per country	3	12	17	12	9	9	15	77
Total								
Countries belonging to at least one RTA	26	26	35	20	8	48	11	174
Average number of RTAs per country	2	6	8	5	4	4	11	40
Maximum number of RTAs per country	7	12	19	13	9	9	29	98

Note: Bilaterai agreements are defined as an RTA with two members. North is OECD 24 plus Lichtenstein, and South is all other countries.

Source: Published WTO data, World Bank staff.

ii) The shift in the U.S. position toward bilateral preferential agreements; and

iii) The effort of a handful of developing countries to open markets through RTAs.

We turn now to a more in-depth investigation of these trends.

EU Preferential Trade Arrangements

During the 1990s, the EU was an active sponsor of bilateral arrangements with individual countries and groups of countries and was the major player in the RTA game. Prior to the recent accession of 10 new members, the EU had bilateral or regional agreements with 111 countries. Trade agreements became an integral instrument of European foreign policy, particularly in the aftermath of the collapse of the Soviet Union.

Three types of agreements were intended to stabilize the region after 1989. *Europe Agreements* were intended to prepare bordering Eastern European countries for eventual accession into the EU. They involved bilateral agreements between each other and with the EU to reduce tariffs, develop uniform rules of origin, EU-consistent regulatory approaches to services, and common treatment of standards as well as transition rules in sectors such as agriculture. These efforts culminated with the full admission of 10 new countries into the EU in 2004—which is why the number of RTAs registered with the WTO fell for the first time ever. *Euro-Mediterranean Agreements* were intended to build bilateral trade relations between neighbours, with the objective of forming a NAFTA-like free trade area by 2010. Launched in 1995, the EU and 12 countries have been involved in talks on "association agreements" that would subsume some existing bilateral arrangements. To date, bilateral agreements have been signed with Tunisia (1995), Israel (1995), Morocco (1996), Jordan (1997), the Palestinian Authority (1997), Algeria (2001), Egypt (2001), and Lebanon (2002). In general, services liberalization provisions are limited to the restatement of WTO GATS commitments with no new liberalization or with preferential access reserved for suppliers based in member countries. » Dispute settlement is state-to-state based on ad hoc arbitration. *Partnership and Cooperation Agreements* (PCAs) with the Western Balkans, Russia, and the CIS were designed to help promote stability on the border of the EU, and in the case of Russia, expand trade. The EU has been providing technical assistance to these governments to help implement the institutional reforms that are part of the PCAs.

Two new agreements have been added to this list since 2000.

i) *Economic Partnership Agreements (EPAs)* are designed to replace the preferential systems embodied in the Contonou Agreement (the successor to the Lome Convention), which had received a waiver under the enabling clause from GATT Article XXIV, a waiver that expires in 2007. EPAs are designed to promote trade and development in the ACP 77 countries in a WTO-consistent fashion by establishing agreements between large groups of countries forming customs unions

ii) *Free Trade Agreements* with South Africa (which entered into force in 2000), Mexico (2000), and Chile (2003) are designed to open markets and secure trade. Agreements with the Gulf Cooperation Council (GCC) and the Common Market for the South (MERCOSUR) are under active negotiation. These embody free trade provisions for a range of products as well as provisions to liberalize at least some services.

The EU agreements govern services trade in addition to trade in goods. The agreements with Mexico and Chile provide for specific liberalization commitments in the financial sector over and above those included in GATS, with the Chilean agreement adding telecommunications and maritime services. The South African agreement alludes to possible services liberalization, but without commitment. The EU agreements differ in important respects from the U.S. agreements in that they are generally less comprehensive, provide less market access in agriculture, and do not provide for investor-state dispute resolution

The U.S. Embraces Bilateralism

Prior to the present administration, the U.S. had generally eschewed reciprocal preferential trade agreements, whether regional or bilateral. Exceptions included only Canada and Israel in the 1980s and NAFTA in the early 1990s. Indeed, many U.S. trade observers contend that opening NAFTA talks was designed primarily to support multilateral trade negotiations—to spur the Europeans and others into acting on the Uruguay Round. Two years later, the Clinton administration announced its desire to form a Free Trade Area of the Americas (FTAA), and it signed an FTA with Jordan in 2000.

Since the approval of trade promotion authority in 2002, however, the United States has given much greater emphasis to securing bilateral FT As in tandem with its efforts to achieve multilateral liberalization through the WTO. Since 2002 the United States has signed bilateral accords with Australia, Bahrain, Central America plus the Dominican Republic, Chile, Morocco, and Singapore. The United States appears to have intensified its pursuit of RTAs since the Cancun WTO Ministerial (September 2003). Negotiations are officially under way with Colombia, Ecuador, Panama, Peru, SACU, and Thailand. Other economies deemed to be in the queue are Bolivia, Egypt, New Zealand, Pakistan, the Philippines, South Korea, Sri Lanka, and Taiwan (China), and Uruguay This intensified pace may reflect the intention to prod both the multilateral negotiations and the FTAA, as well as to respond to U.S. businesses that fear being shut out of export markets by a growing number of RTAs in which the United States is not a member.

In the broadest of terms, developing countries seek to provide access to their services markets and guarantees in many nontrade areas in exchange for assured access to U.S. goods markets. Key facets of these agreements include.

i) Tariff rates on most nonagricultural products are bound at zero; for example, the U.S.-Chile FTA will bind duties at zero for 85 percent of trade.

ii) Exclusion or delayed liberalization of sensitive products, commonly including agricultural products such as dairy products, cotton, ethyl alcohol, peanuts and peanut butter, sugar, and tobacco for the United States. Some exclusions are due to be phased out according to lengthy timetables; in the Chile-U.S. FTA, for example, all duties will be phased out in 12 years.

iii) Intellectual property rights are conventionally accorded stronger protections than under the WTO's TRIPS agreement, with investor-state suits permitted in the event of disputes.

iv) Investment protections, with provisions for national treatment and nondiscrimination in pre-establishment provisions for companies based in each others markets (though liberal rules of origin indicate foreign subsidiaries located in member countries qualify for eligibility).

v) Services trade are to be open except for those excluded in a negative list; notably excluded are labour service providers, except for the provisional visas held by professionals associated with investing firms.

vi) Labour and environment issues are included in recent agreements, with signatory countries undertaking commitments to enforce their own environmental I and labour laws. Dispute settlement panels are empowered to impose monetary fines rather than using trade sanctions to force compliance.

The United States indicated it would not negotiate changes in its antidumping statutes or on its agricultural subsidies, insisting on addressing both through the WTO's multilateral negotiations.

Developing Countries Actively Pursue Major Markets

The launching of NAFTA spawned a new flurry of interest among developing countries eager to use RTAs to secure market access. Mexico and Chile have been at the forefront of these developments. Mexico, having created a world-class trade negotiating team for NAFTA, turned its attention to Central America and other countries in Latin America. It established arrangements with Costa Rica (1995), Bolivia (1995), Nicaragua (1998), the EU (2000), EFTA (2001), and Japan (2004). After NAFTA was signed, Chile immediately solicited entry into the accord. Rebuffed initially, the country embarked on a wider strategy. Chile established agreements with MERCOSUR (1996),

Canada (1997), Peru (1998), Mexico (1999), Central America (2002), the United States and EU (2003), and EFTA (2004). By 2004, Chile had signed free trade agreements/that provided over 60 percent of its exports with duty-free access to markets around the world.

Many existing regional organizations in Africa also moved aggressively to intensify preferential trade liberalization during the 1990s. For example, the treaty establishing the Common Market for Eastern and Southern Africa (COMESA), which was signed in 1993 to replace the Preferential Trade Area, called for a free trade area by 2000 and a customs union by 2004. The East African Community was formed in the mid-1990s to accelerate economic integration among three COMESA members (Kenya, Tanzania, and Uganda). The SADC Trade Cooperation Protocol was signed in 1996 as part of an effort to reintegrate South Africa into the regional economy after the end of apartheid.

Asian countries have launched similar negotiations since 2001. India has concluded or is negotiating limited arrangements with MERCOSUR and Thailand; MERCOSUR is negotiating with the Andean countries; China has launched bilateral accords with members of the Association of Southeast Asian Nations (ASEAN), to mention a few. In 2004, India, Pakistan, and other South Asian countries announced the South Asian Free Trade Agreement (SAFTA), which is intended to encompass all of the countries of the region.

Many RTAs, Diverse Provisions

RTAs have increasingly been designed to cover much more than liberalization of tariffs and quotas. Box-2 gives a flavor of the range of services and intellectual property rights issues that are addressed in current agreements. Many of these issues have implications for trade, although the precise mechanisms by which trade is affected are not always well defined.

BOX-2

RTAs Cover Many Topics Besides Merchandise Trade

	Standards	*Transport*	*Customs Co-operation*	*Services*	*Intellectual Property*	*Investment*	*Dispute Settlement*	*Labour*	*Competition*
U.S.									
U.S.-Jotxian	No	No	Yes	Yes	Yes	Yes	Yes	Yes	Yes
U.S.-Chile	Yes	No	Yes	Yes	Yes	Yes	Yes	Yes	Yes
U.S.-Singapore	Yes	No	Yes	Yes	Yes	Yes	Yes	Yes	Yes
U.S.-Australia	Yes	No	Yes	Yes	Yes	Yes	Yes	Yes	Yes
U.S.-CAFTA	Yes	No	Yes	Yes	Yes	Yes	Yes	Yes	Yes
U.S. -Morocco	Yes	No	Yes	Yes	Yes	Yes	Yes	Yes	No
NAFTA	Yes	No	Yes	Yes	Yes	Yes	Yes	Yes	Yes
EU*									
EU-South Africa	No	No	No	No	Yes	No	Yes	No	Yes
EU-Mexico	Yes*	Yes	Yes*	Yes	Yes	Yes	Yes	Yes	Yes

EU-Chile	Yes*	Yes	Yes	Yes	Yes	Yes	Yes	Yes	Yes•
Euro-Med. Agreements	No	No	No	No	Yes	No	Yes	No	Yes
South-South									
MERCOSUR	Yes	Yes	Yes	Yes	No	Yes	Yes		Yes
Andean Community									
CARICOM	Yes	No	Yes	Yes	Yes	Yes	Yes	Yes	Yes
AFTA	Yes	Yes	No	Yes	No	Yes	No	Yes	No
SADC		Yes	No	Yes	Yes	No	Yes		
COMESA	Yes	No	Yes	Yes	No	Yes	Yes	Yes	Yes
Other									
Japan-Singapore	Yes	No	Yes	Yes	Yes	Yes	Yes	Yes	Yes
Canada-Chile	No	No	Yes	Yes	Yes	Yes	Yes	Yes	Yes
Chile-Mexico	Yes		Yes	Yes	Yes	Yes	Yes	Yes	Yes

Source: World Bank staff.

* While EU agreements mention cooperation in most of the subject areas, only those in which specific commitments are undertaken receive a "Yes" rating.

• Implementation steps are to be agreed on at a later date.

Many RTAs, Many Rationales

These recent trends highlight different rationales that drive the quest for preferential agreements, but in nearly all cases politics is as important as economics. The classic *North-North* agreement, the European Union, had its origin in politics. The fathers of the European Community, Robert Schumann and Jean Monnet, clearly believed that Franco-German integration through trade and investment would produce a new constellation of common economic interests that would attenuate historic military animosity. As a first step, they felt that placing French and German coal and steel industries under a single authority, the European Coal and Steel Community, would make it impossible for either of these historical enemies to use these resources for military purposes against the other.

Today, for *North-South* agreements, Northern partners often have a complex mix of rationales—rooted in foreign policy, commercial diplomacy, and development policy. In fact, the trade policy has always *been* the principal instrument of foreign policy for the European Union. The United States now appears to be using preferential agreements for reasons that are similarly broad. Both the EU and the United States seek trade agreements that go beyond simple tariff removal to include rules governing services, protection of intellectual property, and adherence to health, labour, and environmental standards.

One goal of developing countries seeking an RTA with a large market, such as the EU or the United States, is simply to secure market access. One should note, however, that most developing countries, especially the least developed countries (LDCs), already enjoy considerable access to these markets for most manufactured products (whether through unilateral preference programmes or because MFN tariffs are already quite low), and RTAs with these countries often exclude agriculture and other politically sensitive products. Nevertheless, RTAs provide some insurance against future protectionist policies, and by reaching an agreement "preemptively," they seek to avoid being left out of a future agreement.

A second objective is to reinforce internal regulatory reforms through external treaty obligations and visible political commitments. Locking in domestic reforms through a foreign trade agreement with the EU clearly motivated countries making the transition from socialism in the 1990s. Mexico under NAFTA was motivated by a similar objective. Guaranteed market access combined with credible domestic reforms can attract foreign direct investment

South-South agreements often reflect a political desire to form or join a broadly based regional initiative, such as ASEAN, COMESA, or MERCOSUR. The drive for economic integration often begins with political objectives. Like France and Germany in the 1950s, the newly established democracies of the Southern Cone formed MERCOSUR in the mid-1980s in the hopes of damping the traditional military hostility between major regional powers — Argentina and Brazil. SADC originated in the 1980s as a coalition opposed to apartheid in South Africa and has more recently turned to creating a free trade area. Some observers note that African customs unions and free trade areas are as active in areas such as conflict resolution as in trade liberalization. Finally, many see relaxed tensions between India and Pakistan as the real payoff from the proposed SAFTA agreement, regardless of what happens to trade barriers in the region. The tentative conclusion of existing studies is that RTAs that expand trade flows appear to have a substantial dampening impact on conflict.

Not all political objectives involve war and peace issues; some *South-South* agreements are designed to pool resources for trade negotiations and trade policy-making. Much as the European Union established a common trade policy with a common commissioner in charge of trade (in part to negotiate more forcefully with the United States in the GATT), so too a driving force for MERCOSUR was to establish a common trade policy relative to the multilateral and hemispheric system.

Entering into a regional agreement may also reflect a desire to deal with region-specific issues—such as transit, water, energy, migration, movement of labour, customs, and standards— that are difficult to broach at the global level. RTAs among CIS countries are arguably an attempt to reconstruct some of the economic linkages that were severed with the disintegration of the Soviet Union and the disorganization caused by the collapse of central planning. Although many of these regional externalities can be handled without a *trade* agreement, RTAs may provide institutions and a framework through which to make progress on these issues.

The wide variation in RTAs flows from the very different motivations countries have for entering into the arrangements. These motivations contribute to greater complexity in rules governing world trade.

Many RTAs Can Complicate Administrative Procedures

An important feature of the rise in the number of RTAs is the growing number of overlapping agreements and the so-called "spaghetti bowl" that has emerged from the proliferation of bilateral agreements The associated myriad of rules strains institutions charged with administering trade agreements. A web of differing trade arrangements can tangle administrative procedures—customs procedures, technical standards, rules of origin, and so on—and thereby raises the costs for both enterprises and governments. This complexity undermines work toward greater trade facilitation in developing countries.

Many agreements between country pairs are duplicated by other agreements to which the same two countries are parties. In Sub-Saharan Africa, for example, about one-half of the pairwise trade relationships covered by an RTA are also covered by another agreement. In other regions, overlapping agreements also comprise a substantial share of the total number of agreements. There would be significant benefits, in terms of lower administrative costs and more effective implementation, from a rationalization of the current structure of overlapping agreements.

Uneven Terms—Hub-and-Spoke Integration

The substantial number of bilateral agreements involving large northern countries, most of which have been signed since 1990, suggests that a hub-and-spoke structure in world trade is emerging. In a hub-and-spoke trading system, the largest markets sign individual agreements with a wide range of peripheral countries among which market access remains restricted. Such agreements can marginalise the spokes, where market access conditions are usually less advantageous than in the hub, which enjoys improved access to all of the spokes. In comparison with a broad .preferential trade agreement, a hub-and-spoke approach in theory generates lower gains, which accrue mainly to the hub. Hubs and spokes are already clearly discernible as the EU and United States extend restrictive rules of origin from one bilateral agreement to another.

Trade Within RTAs is Rising But Preferential Trade is Less Important

Trade between RTA members is growing as the number of agreements increases, and one-third of world trade now takes place between RTA members. Disregarding intra-EU trade, bilateral flows between RTA members have been growing at a rate similar to the growth rate of agreements themselves. This also reveals that the rapid increase in the number of South-South RTAs signed in the past decade has not been matched by much change in trade flows among parties to these agreements. This discrepancy highlights the point made that many new South-South agreements overlap with existing agreements.

Examining total trade flows between RTA partners overstates the amount of trade that takes place on a preferential basis. However, tariff schedules of many RTA members increasingly contain duty-free MFN rates on which no preference can be given. According to an estimate, the amount of preferential trade among RTA members, after accounting for MFN rates of zero, is much lower at 21 percent of world trade. Furthermore, it is often more profitable for enterprises to pay a low MFN tariff when there are high costs to satisfy rules of origin or other administrative procedures that a trader must follow to qualify for preferential treatment under an RTA.

INDIA's REGIONAL TRADING ARRANGEMENTS

India views Regional Trading Arrangements (RTAs) as 'building blocks' towards the overall objective of trade liberalization complementing the multilateral trading system. In the past, India had adopted a very cautious and guarded approach to regionalism. Recognizing that RTAs would continue to feature prominently in world trade, India engaged with its trading partners/blocks with the intention of expanding its export market and began concluding in principle agreements and moving in some cases even towards Comprehensive Economic Cooperation Agreements (CECAs) which covers Free Trade Agreement (FTA) in goods, services, investments and identified areas of economic cooperation. Framework agreements have already been entered into with a number of trading partners with specific road maps to be followed and specified time frames by which the negotiations are to be completed.

So far, India has signed 10 free trade agreements (FTAs) and 5 preferential trade agreements (PTAs) and these FTAs/PTAs are already in force. Further, India is currently negotiating 17 FTAs, including review/expansion of some of the existing ones (Box 3).

BOX 3

India's Regional Trading Arrangements: Recent Developments

- Agreement on South Asia Free Trade Area (SAFTA): The SAFTA Agreement was signed on 6 January 2004 and came into force on 1 January 2006. Under SAFTA, India has granted zero basic custom duty to all LDCs, viz. Afghanistan, Bangladesh, Bhutan, and Maldives, on all items except 25 items relating to alcohol and tobacco. Under the SAFTA Agreement, India has reduced the SAFTA Sensitive List for non-LDCs from 878 to 614 by reduction of 264 tariff lines w.e.f. 6 September 2012. As per the schedule of Tariff Liberalisation Programme (TLP) under SAFTA, India has brought down its peak tariff rates to 5 per cent w.e.f. 1.1.2013
- India-Thailand FTA, Early Harvest Scheme (EHS) under the Framework Agreement for establishing India-Thailand FTA: On 9th October 2003, India and Thailand signed a Framework Agreement for establishing an India-Thailand FTA, which includes trade in goods, trade in services, investment, and other areas of economic cooperation, to be concluded as a single undertaking. Under the EHS, tariff has gradually been eliminated on

a list of 82 common items simultaneously by both sides between 1 September 2004 and 31 August 2006. Under the India-Thailand FTA, it is proposed to provide ASEAN plus tariff concessions. So far 26 rounds of the India-Thailand Trade Negotiation Committee (ITTNC) meetings have been held. The last round was held on 26-27 November 2012 in New Delhi.

- India-ASEAN Comprehensive Economic Cooperation Agreement (CECA): Services and Investment Agreements. The Trade in Goods Agreement, which was signed on 13 August 2009 under the broader framework of the CECA between India and ASEAN has already come into force. Conclusions of negotiations for the Services Agreement and Investment Agreement have been announced during the ASEAN-India Commemorative Summit held on 20 December 2012 in New Delhi. Legal scrubbing for these Agreements will be finalized by February, 2013. The Agreement will be signed during ASEAN Economic Ministers (AEM)-India Consultations in August 2013.
- Regional Comprehensive Economic Partnership (RCEP) Agreement among ASEAN + 6 (Australia, China, India, Japan, Korea, and New Zealand): During the 20th ASEAN Summit held in Cambodia in April 2012, ASEAN States agreed to move towards establishing an RCEP involving ASEAN and its FTA partners. The objective of launching RCEP negotiations is to achieve a modern, comprehensive, high-quality, and mutually beneficial economic partnership agreement among the ASEAN member States and ASEAN's FTA partners. The RCEP will cover trade in goods, trade in services, investment, economic and technical cooperation, intellectual property, competition, dispute settlement, and other issues.
- India - EU Broad Based Trade and Investment Agreement (BTIA): Fifteen rounds of negotiations and a number of intersessional and Chief Negotiator level meetings have been held till date. The 15th round was held during 4-7 December, 2012 in New Delhi. Chief negotiator level meeting was held on 29-30 January, 2013 in New Delhi.
- Global System of Trade Preferences (GSTP): The Agreement establishing the GSTP among developing countries was signed on 13 April 1988 at Belgrade following the conclusion of the First Round of Negotiations. Forty-three countries have ratified the Agreement and become participants. India has offered tariff concessions on 70.08 per cent of dutiable tariff lines with an across-the-board margin of preference (MoP) of 20 per cent on the applied tariffs prevailing on the date of import. India has also unilaterally offered special concessions to LDC participants by granting an MoP of 25 per cent on 77 per cent of all its dutiable tariff lines. The Cabinet Committee on Economic Affairs (CCEA), in its meeting on 23 August 2012, has granted approval for implementing India's schedule of concessions. The tariff concessions are to be implemented thirty days after a minimum of four participants ratify their schedules of concessions. So far India and Malaysia have ratified their schedules.

Source: Department of Commerce, Ministry of Commerce and Industry, Government of India.

In the current situation when WTO negotiations are stalled, world trade has slowed down, and the shadow of protectionist measures looms large, a strategy of diversifying technology intensive exports through the regional process could lead to further trade promotion with trade liberalization (Box 4).

BOX 4

Diversifying Technology-Intensive Export Products Through the Regional Process

---

Two trends in international trade are of great importance in the current global economic environment. One, the growing importance of technology-intensive exports and two, the increasing role of regional trade.

Tradable products can be classified into five different groups based on the technology intensity. (1) Primary products have very little technology basis for retaining comparative advantage, (2) resource-based products having competitive advantages, generally arising from local availability of natural resources and using simple and labour-intensive technology, (3) low technology products having simple technologies mainly embodied in capital equipment, with labour constituting a major element of cost in competitiveness and operating under low-scale economies with low entry barriers, (4) medium technology products comprising skill- and scale-intensive technologies in capital and intermediate products where product development takes place with complex technologies, involving high level of research and development (R&D) expenditure and which require lengthy learning periods and are subject to high entry barriers, and (5) high technology products having advanced and fast changing technologies with emphasis on product design requiring high R&D investment, sophisticated infrastructures, high levels of specialized technical skills, and close interactions between firms and universities/research institutions. Trends in global trade indicate that there has been a proliferation of trade in technology-intensive manufacturing products. Among the globally dynamic products of trade, a significant proportion of items are high and medium technology-intensive items. India has been diversifying into technology intensive products with a fair amount of success with exports of high technology and medium technology products growing faster than the total exports of India during 2004-2011 (Table 1.1). Further, diversifying India's exports to include more technology-intensive product groups is of vital importance.

Table 1.1: India's Trade with Technology Intensive Products

	CAGR		
	2004 to 2007	*2007 to 2011*	*2004 to 2011*
1 Primary products	25.3	17.6	20.8
2 Resources based products	32.4	20.0	25.2
3 Low technology products	13.3	14.5	14.0
4 Medium technology products	27.0	20.0	23.0
5 High technology products	26.6	26.9	26.8
Total exports	24.3	18.8	21.2

In the present global trading environment, export promotion is more strategically pursued through the regional approach. India's export compound annual growth rate (CAGR) is faster with most of the 21 RTAs (covering more than 100 countries) considered here (based on India's level of exports with them, India's membership in some of them, and India's engagement with other continents including Africa), than its overall export CAGR of 19.1 per cent during 1999-2000 to 2010-11 (Table 1.2). Asia is emerging as the most important destination for India's exports through the regional process.

Export potential in medium and high technology-intensive products varies across different RTAs. Decomposition of export potential products into their technology intensities in different regional blocs shows possibility of trade diversification for India in hi-tech product segments. Empirical evidence suggests that India can diversify its exports of technology-intensive products to RTAs. The EU, NAFTA, RCEP, APTA, ASEAN, IOR-ARC, etc. could be some important export destinations with sizeable trade opportunities for technology-intensive exports, though some of these regional arrangements overlap.

Table 1.2: India's Export Performance with Selected RTAs/FTAs

RTA	*Year of Eestabil-shment*	*Value of exports (US$ million)*	*Share in export %*		*Export CAG 2010-11 over 11*	*Trade Rpport-unities (US$ 1999 2000*	*Share in total opportunities available in each RTA(%)*				
			1999-2010-11	*2010-2000*			*Primary Products billion*	*Resource based*	*Low tech-nology*	*Medium tech-nology*	*High tech nology*
1	2	3	4	5	6	7	8	9	10	11	12
With India's membership											
IOR-ARC	1997	77097	17.9	30.7	25.1	51.8	22.5	17.5	11.3	28.0	20.6
RCEP/EAS	2005	51723	14.7	20.6	22.8	155.3	27.3	18.9	8.5	23.3	22.0
BIMST-EC	1997	11673	4.8	4.7	18.6	9.1	38.0	10.8	11.9	24.9	14.4
SAARC	1985	11634	3.9	4.6	21.0	2.5	33.1	25.4	9.7	23.1	8.7
IBSA	2003	7948	1.1	3.2	30.6	11.2	19.8	17.2	7.9	38.8	16.3
With/proposed trade agreement											
EU	1992	45980	26.2	18.3	15.3	205.2	19.9	17.8	16.6	30.4	15.3
GCC	1981	42395	8.7	16.9	26.5	10.0	14.8	17.0	17.1	40.6	10.4
ASEAN	1967	25600	6.1	10.2	24.8	35.1	24.7	17.9	9.8	24.5	23.1
COMESA	1994	7128	2.3	2.8	21.6	3.8	21.1	29.7	10.5	30.5	8.2
MERCOSUR	1991	4730	0.7	1.9	30.4	12.2	14.1	18.6	9.2	41.9	16.2
SACU	1969	4118	0.8	1.6	27.2	3.7	22.9	17.8	9.9	34.5	14.9
Without trade agreement											
NAFTA	1992	27538	24.8	11.0	10.6	93.8	17.8	13.1	14.9	33.6	20.6
APTA	1975	25887	5.9	10.3	25.4	79.5	25.0	19.6	6.2	24.9	24.3
SADC	1992	8158	1.9	3.3	25.3	5.3	19.1	24.1	10.2	34.0	12.6
LAIA	1980	7443	1.5	3.0	26.4	28.4	12.1	17.4	12.9	39.2	18.4
EAC	1967	3994	0.7	1.6	29.0	0.9	12.9	47.1	7.3	25.3	7.3
ECOWAS	1975	3842	1.5	1.5	19.6	3.3	29.8	31.6	12.3	20.6	5.6
CIS	1991	2607	2.9	1.0	8.5	14.8	12.3	15.1	14.2	42.0	16.4
ECCAS	1985	1122	0.1	0.4	33.6	0.3	13.7	30.0	14.9	33.0	8.3
With bilateral trade agreement											
ISLFTA	2000	3503	1.8	3.9	27.7	0.6	20.2	19.1	6.3	20.5	34.0
ISCECA	2003	9816	1.4	1.4	19.4	0.1	25.8	30.7	16.1	22.5	4.9

* Year of establishment / entered into force.

Focused product-market diversification trade and marketing strategies should necessarily entail diversifying India's trade basket, particularly in favour of high and medium technology-intensive products in the targeted RTAs. While this type of focus could also help in avoiding the adverse effects of some RTAs concentrating on primary products involving livelihood concerns of a significant portion of our agricultural and rural communities, care should be taken to avoid inverted duty structures in the 'quid-pro-quo' during RTA negotiations.

Source: Based on study by S.K. Mohanty, (2013), 'Examining Diversification of India's Exports to Developing Countries in a Situation of Partially Affected Global Economy by Recession', Backgrounder for the Economic Survey, MoF, GoI.

Note: The RTAs included in the analysis are: Indian Ocean Rim Association for Regional Cooperation (IOR-ARC), Regional Comprehensive Economic Partnership (RCEP)/ East Asian Summit (EAS), Bay of Bengal Initiative for Multi-sectoral Technical and Economic Cooperation (BIMST-EC), South Asian Association for Regional Cooperation (SAARC), India-Brazil-South Africa Initiative (IBSA), the European Union (EU), Gulf Cooperation Council (GCC), Association of South East Asian Nations (ASEAN), Common Market for Eastern and Southern Africa (COMESA), Southern Common Market (MERCOSUR), South African Customs Union (SACU), North American Free Trade Agreement (NAFTA), Asia-Pacific Trade Agreement (APTA), South African Development Community (SADC), Latin America Integration Association (LAIA), East African Community (EAC), Economic Community of Western African States (ECOWAS), Commonwealth of Independent States (CIS), Economic Community of Central African States (ECCAS), India-Sri Lanka Free Trade Agreement (ISLFTA), India-Singapore Comprehensive Economic Cooperation Agreement (ISCECA).

The challenges for India on the trade front are many. While India has successfully diversified its export basket, more needs to be done on the product diversification front. It also has to reposition itself in its traditional areas of strength like textiles and leather & leather manufactures where it has lost considerable ground, while at the same time making forays into new areas. With multilateral trade negotiations stalled, and RTAs on the rise, India also has to follow a strategic regional trading policy focusing on the potential technology-intensive items in the more important RTAs. Though geopolitical considerations are important, India may have to bargain more in its regional trade negotiations, particularly in cases where livelihood concerns of large pockets of the population are involved, There is also need to address the inverted duty structure in sectors like electronics, textiles, and chemicals and the artificial inverted duty structure caused by some FTAs/RTAs. On the services front, a gold mine of opportunity in sectors like tourism including health tourism is waiting to be tapped.

REGIONAL INTEGRATION AGREEMENTS AND FOREIGN INVESTMENT

Foreign investment has been a driver of integration, increased trade in manufactures, and vertical specialization. As tariff barriers have come down in manufactures, market-seeking, horizontal FDI that once led the way in the import-substitution process has faded importance relative to efficiency-seeking, vertical FDI that looks to locate segments of production in the lowest-cost site. This form of investment is associated with the rise in production chains and trade in components and parts.

To the extant that firms (either domestic or foreign) increase their investment in response to a larger market, or rationalise their production to lower-cost locations

TABLE 1

A Typology of the Entrepreneurial Motivations for Foreign Direct Investment

Motivation for FDI	*Competitive environment host country government*	*Policy response of*	*Likely characteristics of FDI*
1	2	3	4
Access to factors of production	Host country firm(s) have access to certain factors of production (materials, technology etc.) not available/transferable to foreign firms	Passive (unless deemed against national interest) as host country firms are assumed to hold competitive advantage	Acquisition of host country firms
Access to cheaper and factors of production equity (Product cycle hypothesis)	Shift of comparative advantage from emergence of cheaper factor costs in host country	Conditional upon development strategy and requirements to promote technology transfer. Protection of domestic industry by import quotas/tariffs and controls on foreign equity participation	Contractual resource transfers joint ventures with minority participation by foreign firms
Access to products	International competition among similar products. Technical change leaves firms in different countries with competitive advantages in different sub-products	Passive, as mutual benefits perceived for foreign and host country firms	Mutual equity participation

1	*2*	*3*	*4*
Access to customers with local	International trade and competition are limited because of punitive transport costs, or because customers require local production/service	Passive, as foreign firms will be operating in the host country on the same basis as domestic firms	Full manufacturing/service operations, together design facilities
Access to markets Continued (Tariff-jumping FDI)	International competition among similar products. Technical change shifts comparative advantage in favour of foreign firms. Import penetration in host country increases	Protection of domestic industry through import quotas/tariffs etc.	Assembly operations. parts/components from abroad Investment-shunting. Subsidiaries are wholly-owned or involve majority equity participation by foreign firms
Access to future markets Full manufacturing operations. (*Quid pro quo* FDI)		As above industry	Threat of protection for domestic together with local sourcing of parts/components and local R&I) facilities. Joint ventures/technical agreements with host country firms

within the bloc, then there will be benefits in terms of efficiency and welfare. On the other hand, if trade diversion provides the catalyst for FDI, there will be a loss of economic efficiency and welfare. Other provisions of deeper regional integration will also have an effect on FDI. The removal of restrictions on the movement of factors of production (especially the movement of capital should facilitate both intra-bloc FDI and FDI from third countries. And FDI should also be stimulated by the relaxation of ownership and entry requirments, and other liberalising measures to open markets to greater competition.

The liberalisation measures associated with regional integration, however, typically impact in different ways upon intra-bloc FDI and upon FDI from third countries, and also have differential effects according to the underlying entrepreneurial motivation of the investing firm. Firms are motivated to invest overseas for a variety of reasons, and six stylised 'types' of FDI may be identified (Table 1).

i) The first type of FDI is that undertaken to gain access to specific factors of production (for example, resources, technical knowledge, managerial know-how, patents or brand names) owned by a firm, or firms, in the host country. If such factors of production are not available in the home economy of the foreign firm, and are not transferable at arm's length, then the foreign firm must invest locally in order to secure access. This will typically involve an equity stake in an appropriate host-country firm (if the factor is firm-specific), although the factor in question may take the form of a public good available to all firms in the industry. An example of the latter would be an industry consortium to pool research and development (R&D) resources, and whose results were only available to members.

ii) The second type of FDI is that identified by Raymond Vernon in his celebrated product cycle hypothesis and considers investment to gain access to cheaper factors of production (for example, low-cost labour). This type of FDI may be encouraged by the government of the host country if it is pursuing an export-oriented development strategy, in which case it may well provide some form of investment incentive (subsidies, grants, tax concessions and so forth) to the foreign firm. If the government is following an import-substitution policy, on the other hand, foreign firms may only be allowed to participate in the host economy to the extent that they possess technical or managerial know-how that is not available to domestic industry. Such know-how may be transferable on an arm's length basis, in which case the foreign involvement may take the form of a licensing arrangement or other form of contractual resource transfer. Or, if the know-how is not transferable in this way, then a foreign minority stake may be encouraged in a joint venture with a local partner.

iii) The third type of FDI involves international competitors undertaking mutual

TABLE 2

The Effects of Liberalisation Measures on Flows of Foreign Direct Investment into a Trading Bloc/common Market

Motivation for FDI	*Source of FDI*	*Relaxation in ownership and entry requirements*	*Liberalisation of intra-bloc labour movements*	*Liberalisation of intra-bloc capital movements*	*Reduction of intra-bloc barriers to trade*
Access to factors of production	Within bloc	++	0	+	0
	Outside bloc	++	0	0	0
Access to cheaper factors of production	Within bloc	++	0	+	+
	Outside bloc	++	0	0	+
Access to products	Within bloc	++	0	+	+
	Outside bloc	++	0	+	+
Access to customers	Within bloc	++	++	+	0
	Outside bloc	++	0	0	0
Access to markets (Tariff-jumping FDI)	Within bloc	++	0	+	—
	Outside bloc	++	0	0	++
Access to future markets (Quid pro quo FDI)	Within bloc	++	0	+	—
	Outside bloc	++	0	0	++

Notes:

++ indicates a strong positive effect of the liberalisation measure on foreign direct investment

\+ indicates a weaker positive effect of the liberalisation measure on foreign direct investment

0 indicates little or no significant effect of the liberalisation measure on foreign direct investment

— indicates a negative effect of the liberalisation measure on foreign direct investment

investment in one another (either through cross-shareholdings, or through the establishment of joint ventures), in order to gain access to each other's product ranges. The background to this type of FDI is increased competition among similar products as a result of R&D-induced specialisation. Both firms find it difficult to compete in each others' home markets, or in third-country markets for each other's products. If neither product (and hence neither firm) gains the dominant advantage, then the two firms may well invest in each other's area of expertise, and thus promote sub-product specialisation in production.

iv) The fourth type of FDI relates to that undertaken by firms in order to secure access to customers in the host-country market. No underlying shift in comparative advantage either to or from the host country is observed, but exporting from the firm's home base may be impossible (for example, certain services), punitively expensive because of transport costs (for example, bricks), or unfeasible because customers insist on short supply lines (for example, components) or the capability to request immediate design modifications and/or amendments. In particular, the limited tradability of many services (for example, banking, other financial services or retail and wholesale distribution) has been an important factor promoting the growth of FDI in these sectors.

v) The fifth type of FDI relates to the trade diversionary aspect of regional integration. This is commonly known as 'tariff-jumping' FDI and occurs when there are locational advantages for foreign firms in their home country, but the firms are prevented from exporting to the host economy by the existence of tariffs or other barriers to trade. The foreign firms therefore jump the barriers ,by establishing a local presence within the host economy in order to gain access to the local market. The local manufacturing presence need only be sufficient to circumvent the trade barriers, as the foreign firm will want to maintain as much of the value-added in its home economy, hence simple assembly operations will be the norm.

vi) The final type of FDI is that undertaken by foreign firms not with the intention of jumping protective barriers, but with a view to defusing the threat of protection itself. As with tariff-jumping FDI, this follows a systemic shift in comparative advantage in favour of the foreign producers as a result of R&D-induced changes in know-how. The defusion may be achieved either by enhancing directly the benefits (on employment and so on) that FDI confers on the host economy, or by co-opting local firms in joint ventures and thus allocating them a share of the potential benefits. Such *quid pro quo* FDI 1% thus likely to take the form either of full manufacturing operations together with local sourcing of parts and components,

How then are these six types of FDI affected by the various measures which may accompany

regional integration? Table-2 provides a summary of the expected effects of the main provisions, upon both intra-bloc FDI and FDI from third countries.

Clearly the relaxation of ownership and entry requirements to restricted industries will stimulate both intra-bloc FDI and FDI from third countries. This will be the case whether the motivation is to gain access to factors of production, products or markets, or whether liberalisation permits foreign firms access to new customers. The liberalisation of intra-bloc labour movement will have little effect on any type of FDI flow, except for intra-bloc FDI which is undertaken to gain access to customers and where the investing firm's competitive advantage lies in the expertise of its workforce. Various service industries (for example, finance, insurance or consulting) would fit this pattern. The liberalisation of intra-bloc capital movements should have little effect upon FDI from third countries, except perhaps through easing the formation of joint ventures with local partners. But freer capital movement will aid all types of intra-bloc investment for obvious reasons.

Of most interest, however, are the differential effects on FDI of the reductions in intra-bloc barriers to trade that accompany regional integration. The reduction of such barriers should have little effect on FDI undertaken to gain access to specific factors of production, as the acquisition of knowhow, expertise and so on was the primary motivation, not trade. Intra-bloc FDI to gain access to cheaper factors of production will increase as firms within the bloc rationalise their production activities. FDI from third countries may also increase as cheaper locations entice some foreign firms to pursue production within the bloc for export to the higher-cost markets. FDI to gain access to products will also be promoted by reduced barriers to trade as the potential market for the joint venture will be enlarged. In contrast, FDI to gain access to customers should not be significantly affected as, by definition, international trade is either impractical or unfeasible.

The final two types of FDI are both related to the discriminatory aspect of regional integration. Any reduction in intra-bloc barriers to trade will increase the competitive disadvantage (within the bloc) suffered by firms from third countries in relation to firms from within the bloc, and will lead to trade diversion. FDI by the firms from the third countries is therefore a possibility, as they attempt to secure access to the protected market. On the other hand, intra-bloc trade will be stimulated by the reduction in the barriers, and any intra-bloc FDI previously undertaken to secure access to the markets of partner countries may well be reduced.

The various provisions of regional integration agreements thus have quite different effects upon FDI from within the bloc, and from third countries outside the bloc. Furthermore, these effects differ according to the underlying entrepreneurial motivation of the direct investment. Second-round effects may also be identified. For example, much investment in services is linked to investment and/or trade in manufacturing.

THE IMPACT OF REGIONAL INTEGRATION FRAMEWORKS (RIFs) IN FDI DETERMINANTS

(i) The Policy Framework

The majority of RIFs do not explicitly address FDI policy, although there is an increasing tendency for free trade agreements to include investment. Even RIFs postulating a high degree of integration among members, including provisions regarding the movement of capital, may not necessarily contain explicit FDI policy provisions. The overall impact of RIFs on the policy framework for FDI therefore depends on whether a RIF contains provisions liberalising the movement of capital (including FDI capital); on how restrictive the capital movement and investment regimes of the member countries had been prior to the implementation of the RIF; and on other policy- liberalisation provisions contained in the RIFs, notably trade policy. Of these conditions, whether or not a RIF contains explicit FDI provisions — for example, on national treatment, most-favoured-nation treatment, rules of origin, performance requirements, dispute settlement — may be the least important for developed countries and most developing countries as far as inward FDI is concerned, because inward investment regimes are typically open even prior to the implementation of RIFs. The OECD member countries, for example, adopted the Code of Liberalisation of Capital Movements in 1961, though capital-movement liberalisation did not accelerate until after the mid-1970s. Even in many developing countries, at least partially open FDI policies have typically been in place prior to the implementation of a RIF, as the example of Mexico prior to joining NAFTA illustrates. So the direct impact of explicit FDI provisions contained in RIFs on FDI policy determinants is likely to be small in many instances, unless they result in a *considerable* liberalisation of investment regimes.

Other policy provisions contained in RIFs, especially those relevant to trade liberalisation, are likely to be more important in determining FDI. In the overwhelming majority of RIFs, the central elements and the most important factors influencing market-seeking FDI are the liberalisation of trade barriers and the granting of preferential market access to members. Trade liberalisation and trade policy coordination among RIF members contribute to a policy framework conducive to FDI because they create favourable conditions for foreign affiliates within the region to access regional markets for final and intermediate products. They also allow MNCs to establish regionally integrated production networks to enhance their efficiency. In the case of customs unions and free-trade areas, trade discrimination against non-members in the form of tariff barriers makes the size of a regional market more appealing and encourages market-seeking FDI by MNCs not present in the region. The removal of non-tariff barriers, or their harmonisation, also exerts a positive influence on market-seeking FDI.

Apart from trade liberalisation, the harmonisation of related policies among members can also a role as FDI determinant. The "social charter" of the European Union, for example, seeks to ensure that working conditions, wages, social expenditures, etc. would not differ substantially among members and thus give "unfair" location-specific advantages to some member countries. Likewise, European Union environmental regulations seeks to ensure that FDI would not be diverted to members with lax environmental regimes. Such policy harmonisation can act as a brake on a "race to the bottom" in competitive policy liberalisation meant to attract FDI.

Finally, RIFs may also influence the *speed* of FDI (and trade) policy liberalisation. The prospective NAFTA Agreement, for example, prompted Mexico to liberalize its FDI framework even before the Agreement was signed, even though the liberalisation of services and parts of the primary sector accelerated only after Mexico became a signatory. In some cases, however, member countries that are ready to deregulate a particular industry (e.g. financial services in the case of the European Union) may be obliged to wait until the other members of the RIF have reached a similar point. In the European Union not all countries were ready to deregulate their financial services at the same time, and a tier system was introduced to resolve that. But the reverse may also take place: countries that are lagging behind in terms of deregulation of industries and liberalisation of policies may be pressured to move faster by other RIF members. For example, RIF members may be encouraged to privatise, usually with foreign-investor participation, as a means of reducing the share of the public sector in their economies. Even if (as is often the case) pressures to liberalise do not apply to FDI policies per se, they can affect the overall policy framework of a member country in a manner that encourages FDI.

More generally, RIFs can reaffirm their members' commitments to adhere to liberal policies and bring about a momentum to continue the liberalisation process in both FDI and trade. To put it differently: unless RIFs substantially alter national FDI policy frameworks, they will not have a major impact on FDI policy determinants from the point of view of individual countries. Their contribution to FDI policy determinants lies in ensuring member countries' commitment to adhere to a liberal existing policy framework, or to liberalise it if is restrictive, to harmonise policies, to lock in liberalising changes, to increase momentum to liberalise further; to strengthen standards of treatment and protection, and to encourage policies that ensure the proper functioning of markets (e.g. competition policy).

(ii) Economic Determinants

Market size and growth are the FDI economic determinants that are most affected by the implementation of a RIF. Dynamic effects of RIFs in encouraging higher rates of economic growth can help boost inward FDI. Most importantly, the size of the market is redefined under a RIF as the size of the region's market. The possibility of accessing a market wider than that of a single country for tradable goods and services becomes an inducement to invest in the region. This is exemplified by United States FDI in the European Union. A part of United States affiliate sales in the European Union are geared to the regional market: their sales in the European Union in countries other than the host country itself accounted for 31 per cent of their total sales in 1995. All this is made possible by the removal of intra-regional trade barriers within the region, which carries the implication that a single host country's market size is no longer as significant a determinant of market-seeking FDI as it used to be before the implementation of the RIF. The redefinition of market size from national to at least regional is encouraged if a common external tariff is imposed. This can induce at least some import-substituting (tariff-jumping) FDI, as firms previously serving the regional market through exports seek to become "insiders" and switch to FDI. The extent to which this takes place depends on how heavily protected the host (regional) market becomes after the implementation of a RIF, and whether MNCs had already invested in the national markets prior to the RIF. In a liberalising world of falling barriers, the location advantage of a large regional market may not be what it used to be, unless the RIF also dictates some protection, say, through a common external tariff. Of course, even in the absence of a common external tariff, the regional market may still be an attractive location as long as the RIF eliminates obstacles beyond tariff barriers or facilitates business transactions. In addition, there may be advantages associated with becoming an "insider" in a regional area, such as benefiting from rules-of-origin regulations.

All this means that regional integration frameworks increase the geographical scope and size of "effective" markets because they increase the ease of access within member markets through the removal of trade and other barriers. However, even if all trade and investment barriers between countries were removed, cultural, linguistic and other less obvious barriers to doing business would remain, as would the importance of proximity to local consumers. So accessing an individual member country's market, although less significant as an FDI determinant under a RIF, cannot be discounted. In this context, it may be observed that access to European Union markets was an important factor but access to the United Kingdom's market was more significant for all types of FDI.

With the implementation of a RIF, the accessibility of a region's market *from* a given location becomes an important FDI locational determinant. In addition to abolishing customs-clearance procedures that help speed up border crossings, good physical infrastructure, especially in transport and communications, facilitates access to regional markets. The importance of infrastructure as an FDI determinant is therefore enhanced considerably when a RIF comes into effect, for both market-seeking and efficiency-seeking MNCs.

As the importance of market size as an FDI determinant becomes more uniform for all countries that are members of a RIF and as the removal of cross-border barriers within the region increases competitive pressures, determinants related to enhancing efficiency come to play a bigger role for all types of FDI. Increased market size — from national to regional or global — is in itself an efficiency-inducing determinant because it provides the demand dimension that gives rise to the possibility of exploiting economies of scale and scope in production and distribution. Indeed, one of the primary advantages of enlarged markets under RIFs is that they create the demand conditions that allow MNCs to reap economies of scale and scope in all parts of the value chain. On the production side, cost considerations are especially important for efficiency-seeking MNCs. RIFs allow such MNCs to locate each value-added activity of the production process in the most cost-efficient location within the region in order to rationalise operations regionally by taking advantage of productivity-adjusted cost differences in labour, technology, and other resources. In sum, RIFs help to create both the demand conditions and the production conditions needed to improve efficiency in production.

RIFs also influence MNCs' access to resources. In many RIFs, MNCs can access the skills, technologies or other strategic assets available in member countries other than those in which their production operations are located. The European Union, for example, allows all foreign affiliates regardless of their location within the Union to participate in European Union-sponsored R&D projects — subject to certain restrictions on the transfer of technology to non-member countries. When RIFs allow the movement of labour, some labour moves across borders in response to MNC employment opportunities, which may mitigate the importance of the skill-seeking motive for FDI within the region.

Furthermore, RIFs give foreign investors the opportunity to be close to clusters of companies producing similar products or having similar R&D facilities and thus to exploit regional as well as sub-national agglomeration economies and obtain access to created assets. Proximity to a cluster of companies producing similar products or having similar R&D facilities, for example, need not necessarily require that a MNC invests in the same country where these companies or facilities are physically located. It may very well invest in a bordering country in close physical proximity to the cluster of companies or R&D facilities. Thus within regions, a greater concentration of FDI in a few supranational clusters may develop that allows FDI to be more dispersed in terms of *country distribution*, but more concentrated in terms of *geographical space*.

Finally, RIFs promote greater competition to capture expanded markets or increase market shares within the region. Firms may respond to the increased competition for markets by establishing a physical presence, especially if arm's-length competition through trade is hindered by a common external tariff. Increases in intra-regional and extra-regional cross- border acquisitions designed to access resources or defend competitive positions often accompany RIFs.

(iii) Business Facilitation

The primary effect of RIFs on business facilitation FDI determinants is to reduce intra-regional business transaction costs. Such costs arise directly from inadequacies of information, asymmetries in doing business in different countries, the heterogeneity of administrative procedures, and differences in business support measures. Recognising the importance of business facilitation obstacles, some RIFs seek to harmonise efforts to remove them or replace them with comprehensive region-wide programmes for FDI facilitation. APEC has a comprehensive programme to facilitate trade and FDI whose objectives include "smart card" visas for short- term travel; procedures for APEC-wide accreditation of standards; and minimum restrictions on arrival in a member country.

Since RIFs allow a region's market or many of its resources to be more easily accessible by MNCs from any location within the regional bloc, and policy coordination and harmonisation gives rise to a more level playing field, 'business facilitation factors become increasingly important, as they concern matters which individual member countries — and, increasingly, sub-national authorities — can address to distinguish themselves from one another when competing for FDI. Even if some business facilitation measures are harmonised across members, there still remain important differences among members that allow them to compete for FDI. Measures aimed at targeting specific investors, providing social amenities and marketing a country as an investment location usually fall outside the scope of RIFs, and can therefore be used by each RIF member to enhance location-specific advantages. One result is precisely a proliferation of incentives used to attract.

THE POTENTIAL IMPACT OF A POSSIBLE MULTILATERAL FRAMEWORK ON INVESTMENT

The development of an MFI, if such a framework were to be negotiated, would represent a change in the policy-framework cluster of determinants. Although such a framework might also affect some elements of business facilitation (such as investment incentives), it would not involve significant and direct changes in the principal economic determinants. Indeed, by making FDI policies potentially more similar, an MFI would underline the importance of economic (and business facilitation) factors in determining FDI flows.

The precise effect of an MFI on the policy-framework cluster of determinants would depend on its content, including definitions, scope and safeguards. Because an MFI is only a hypothesis, three scenarios, based on differing assumptions, are discussed below for purely analytical purposes. The specific implications of each scenario would vary from country to country in accordance with specific economic and developmental conditions and specific national stances vis-a-vis FDI.

If there were an MFI, how would it affect the volume and pattern of FDI flows? One conceivable outcome of an MFI is that it would help to *increase* FDI flows — and perhaps affect other features of such flows as well. Such an outcome is based in part on the assumption that a multilateral agreement would not only consolidate recent changes towards more liberal policies by many countries but would incorporate "rollback" provisions — requiring countries to commit themselves to reducing or eliminating existing barriers to FDI and strengthening investment protection and the proper functioning of markets. Even in the absence of further liberalisation, a multilateral framework could facilitate investment by providing stronger assurances — as compared with unilateral or even bilateral measures — when it comes to the protection of FDI and the stability of domestic FDI regimes. The presumably greater stability, predictability and transparency resulting from an MFI would create a generally more favourable climate for investors. The impact on inflows might be greatest for those countries that were not already signatories to bilateral, regional, plurilateral or multilateral investment agreements, and countries whose current policies, even if favourable to FDI, are not considered sufficiently predictable by investors. At the same time, whether or not FDI flows would actually increase — and whether there would be a change in the quality and patterns of flows — would depend on the precise content of an agreement, the nature of national commitments and exceptions to the generalised multilateral rules and, of course, the other FDI determinants that would come into play at that point.

A second conceivable outcome of an MFI is that it could actually *reduce* the quantity and quality of FDI flows, because the negotiation of an MFI would take several years, creating uncertainties about the investment climate worldwide and thereby discouraging foreign investors. Further, even if negotiations did produce an agreement, the MFI that would result could conceivably enshrine a less liberal multilateral environment than has already evolved unilaterally or regionally. Such an MFI could also alter the patterns of FDI flows across geographic regions and industries. In particular, an MFI might reduce FDI flows to countries that gain from the currently restrictive policies of their competitors for such investment and increase flows to otherwise desirable locations that are receiving little inward FDI because of uncertainties about policies.

A third conceivable outcome of a possible MFI is that it would have little or no impact on the quantity and quality of FDI flows, as it would not materially alter the policy framework for FDI. One reason why this might be the result is that there has already been significant liberalisation in many countries, in particular in many developing countries and countries in transition, during the 1980s and 1990s; and this liberalisation has contributed to a surge of FDI flows that reached a new record in 1997. Therefore, an MFI that contains, for example, standstill provisions — requiring countries to commit themselves not to introduce new barriers to FDI, lower standards of investment treatment or measures likely to impair the proper functioning of markets — would essentially maintain the status quo, as far as the openness of economies to FDI, their treatment of foreign affiliates and the functioning of their markets are concerned. Finally, on this view, there would be no significant effects on the geographic patterns of FDI flows, as they are largely influenced by other FDI determinants.

On balance, these considerations suggest that an MFI would improve the enabling environment for FDI, to the extent that it would contribute to greater security for investors and greater stability, predictability and transparency in investment policies and rules. This, in turn, could encourage higher FDI flows and potentially some redistribution of those -flows, particularly to countries whose investment climates would newly reflect the multilateral framework. How much difference an MFI would make, however, in terms of the quantity, quality and patterns of *actual* FDI flows is difficult to predict because as in the case of BITs, it is precisely the function of an enabling framework to allow other determinants, and especially economic determinants, to assert their influence.

Expectations about the impact of an MFI on FDI flows (if it were indeed to be negotiated) in comparison to the current regulatory framework and the direction in which it is developing should, therefore, not be exaggerated. There are, of course, other issues that need to be considered in connection with a possible MFI especially the possible role of such an agreement in providing a framework for intergovernmental cooperation in the area of investment.

Although the most profound shifts among FDI determinants result from integrated international strategies, especially complex strategies, the traditional economic determinants related to large markets, trade barriers and non-tradable services are still at work, and account for a large share of worldwide FDI flows. Data on the distribution of sales of foreign affiliates of United States MNCs in host countries are indicative in this regard: two-thirds of MNC activity is still of this type. These figures are higher in the services sector, including trading affiliates, and lower in manufacturing but they do not change the overall outcome.

Some of the largest national markets remain unmatched in size by the largest regional markets or even by entire continents. For example, the market of the European Union during most of its existence has been smaller than the United States market; the market of the African continent (without South Africa) is smaller than that of the Republic of Korea; and the combined markets of the 14 Central and Eastern European countries are smaller than the market of Brazil. As regards trade barriers, even though the general trend has been towards the reduction or even abolition of tariffs and quotas, they continue to remain in force in several (especially developing) countries and in some industries in a much wider group of countries. These continue to generate import-substituting FDI and discourage efficiency-seeking FDI. In non-tradable services, as well as goods that are perishable or need to be adapted to consumer preferences or local standards, the market-seeking motivation, and the corresponding locational attractiveness of host countries, remain as strong as ever. In fact, there has been an explosion of FDI in the services sector as a result of the general trend towards the liberalisation of FDI frameworks for services.

Still, although FDI remains strongly driven by its traditional determinants, the relative importance of different locational determinants for competitiveness-enhancing FDI is shifting. In their quest for competitiveness, MNCs assign a particularly important role to obtaining access to created (or strategic) assets: the principal wealth-creating assets and a key source of competitiveness for firms. Created assets can be tangible like the stock of financial and physical assets such as the communication infrastructure or marketing networks, or intangible. The list of intangible assets is long, but they have a common denominator: knowledge. They include skills, attitudes (e.g. attitudes to wealth creation and business culture), capabilities (technological, innovatory, managerial and leading capabilities), competencies (e.g. to organise income-generating assets productively), relationships (such as interpersonal relationships forged by individuals or contacts with governments), as well as the stock of information, trade marks, goodwill and brainpower. These assets can be embodied in both individuals and firms and they can sometimes be enhanced by clusters of firms and economic activities.

The importance of created intangible assets in production and other economic activities has increased considerably. A large proportion of the costs of many final goods and services, ranging from simple products such as cereals through books and computers to automobiles, consists of the costs of such created assets as R&D, design, advertising, distribution and legal work. Less than 10 per cent of the production cost of automobiles now consists of labour costs; the rest relates to the contributions of various created assets. Moreover, international competition increasingly takes place through new products and processes and these are often knowledge-based. R&D activities leading to new products and processes are costly and risky. At the same time, markets for knowledge-based resources and assets are becoming more open and enterprises-embodying these assets can be bought and sold. The result is that MNCs have taken advantage of these opportunities and used FDI as a major means of acquiring created assets and enhancing corporate competitiveness.

MAKING REGIONALISM COMPLEMENTARY TO MULTILATERALISM

The emergence of a more proactive stance in multilateral negotiations by developing; countries in parallel with an explosion of preferential regional trade agreements (RTAs) around the world raises an important question: *Are these trends complementary, representing different paths to the same desired outcome of faster growth, development, and poverty reduction, or are they competing and incompatible?* In principle, the best outcome for all countries would be a nondiscriminatory trading system; developing countries, in particular, would benefit from a nondiscriminatory trading system because most poor people and many poor countries might find themselves excluded from preferential deals. If the explosion in RTAs implies a higher probability that the majority of developing countries would face greater discrimination than under an MFN (or nondiscriminatory); regime, the world as a whole will be worse off, and individual developing countries may lose substantially

BUILDING BLOCKS *VERSUS* STUMBLING BLOCKS

Whether regional agreements are *building blocks* or *stumbling blocks* to open global markets remains a central question. Proponents of the *stumbling block* theory emphasise that: (1) RTAs may promote costly trade diversion rather than efficient trade creation, especially when sizable MFN tariffs remain — these tariffs create vested interests to maintain preferential margins in "their" markets; (2) proliferating regional agreements absorb scarce negotiating resources (especially in poorer WTO members) and crowd out policy-makers attention; (3) competing RTAs (especially different North-South combinations) may lock in incompatible regulatory structures and standards, and may result in inappropriate norms for developing country partners; and (4) by creating alternative legal frameworks and dispute settlement mechanisms, RTAs may weaken the discipline and efficiency associated with a broadly recognised multilateral framework of rules.

Building block proponents stress that moving forward in smaller steps is often easier to accomplish, and it creates a certain reform momentum: (1) regional/bilateral agreements can help sensitise domestic constituencies to liberalisation and keep the stakes lower to allow for incremental progress on trade; (2) expanding the number and coverage of RTAs can erode vested opposition to multilateral liberalisation because each successive RTA reduces the value of the margin of preference, thereby reducing the discriminatory impact; (3) RTAs are often more about building strategic and/or political alliances or locking in domestic reforms than about actual trade liberalisation and so are not necessarily competitive with multilateral efforts; (4) regional arrange-ments can provide an incubator for developing country firms/producers to learn to trade with RTA partners without facing full global competition; and (5) for some issues, such as regulatory cooperation, RTAs may be a viable and more manageable alternative to, the WTO, where lowest common denominator' outcome trends to prevail.

RTAs can be a complement to multilateral reform, but they are not a substitute. Consider a scenario in which each developing country signed an agreement with the United States, the European Union (EU), Canada, and Japan—the Quad. Each developing country could raise its real incomes by *individually* signing bilateral agreements with the Quad countries; and in some cases they would raise their real incomes more than they would through multilateral accords. But these gains disappear if *all* developing countries were to sign such agreements. In fact, all developing countries would lose relative to a multilateral agreement and even relative to the baseline. This scenario underscores the fact that, while stalled collective action through multilateral channels creates a strong incentive for each developing country to sign a regional agreement, if every country does so, they all lose.

RTAs do alter the incentives for countries to participate in multilateral liberalisation. RTAs can be a stumbling block to multilateral arrangements by creating incentives to resist the preference erosion that can occur through new multilateral liberalisation. However, because the gains are often substantially larger in multilateral agreements, concerns over preference erosion may be limited to a few small countries that could conceivably block a multilateral agreement. Those recalcitrant countries resisting reforms are likely the beneficiaries of preferences associated with distorted agreements encompassing agriculture or the clothing and textile trade, not RTAs. Large developed countries may gain more from signing individual bilateral agreements than they would from a multilateral accord, because they can use the carrot of preferential access to extract concessions in nontrade areas from developing country partners that would be resisted in the -WTO negotiating framework.

From a development perspective, the WTO remains the best-available forum to discipline the use of trade-distorting policies. RTAs can complement the WTO efforts by cooperating on behind-the-border policies, especially on regulation-intensive issues such as services, trade facilitation, and the investment climate. Governments pursuing this agenda through RTAs must adopt rules that are appropriate to their own level of development. To be effective, the rules must target a priority concern, must be enforceable, and must avoid becoming a tax on scarce resources that would be better used elsewhere. Getting the rules "right" so that they promote development has implications for negotiations and enforcement of the resulting disciplines. The potential for inappropriate outcomes is higher in North-South RTAs because the asymmetry in negotiating power can overtake real development priorities.

Reinforcing the complementarity between regionalism and multilateralism and minimising the latent tensions must begin with the completion of the Doha Development Agenda. If the Doha Development Agenda is completed in a way that actually promotes development, it would bring down tariffs, enhance the gains from open regionalism, and discipline any exclusionary effects of regional accords.

All countries could take steps to promote open regionalism—the developing countries, high-income countries, and the international community working together through the WTO. Developing countries are likely to have the greatest success in harnessing trade for growth and poverty reduction if they adopt a three-pronged strategy that involves autonomous liberalisation, active multilateralism, and open regionalism.

High-income countries could promote open regionalism by including agriculture in RTAs. They could adopt more common and nonrestrictive rules of origin across agreements; and, to the extent that these rules set patterns common to most agreements, the burden on customs administration would be reduced. They could work with prospective partners to ensure that new regulations regarding investment and intellectual property are appropriate to the level of development, which would reduce risks of undue enforcement costs. Finally, they could provide trade-related technical assistance not only in the implementation phase but also in the negotiating phase, which could promote greater liberalisation and supply response to new market opportunities in regional or global markets.

The international community, working through the WTO, can reduce discrimination in the system. The procedures associated with RTA disciplines as currently configured are ill-suited to limit either their proliferation or to control their discriminatory provisions. WTO members should establish stronger multilateral surveillance mechanisms to document, analyse, and monitor the effects of RTAs on nonmembers. Expanding the information on the impact of RTAs to stakeholders—firms, consumers, taxpayers—would also help ensure that the potential benefits of liberalisation are both realised and distributed more equitably. Medium-term efforts should focus on implementing WTO disciplines on regional agreements.

QUESTIONS

1. Discuss the alternative forms of preferential trade agreements.
2. Explain the effects of liberalisation measures on flows of foreign direct investment (FDI) into a trading bloc/common market.
3. Critically examine the efficiency gains and losses from preferential trade agreements.
4. Discuss the India's recent regional trading arrangements and export performance with selected RTAs/FTAs.
5. Terms of trade effects are often dominant outcome from custom union formation. What conditions make it more likely that a country will improve its terms of trade at the expense of other member or at the expense of non-members?
6. Discuss the regional integration agreements (RIAs) and trade. What are the economic effects of RIAs.
7. Critically examine the trade liberalising aspects of regional trade agreements and their repercussions for foreign direct investment.
8. Are regional trade agreements building blocks or stumbling blocks.
9. Critically examine the India's strategy of diversifying technology intensive export products to further trade promotion through the regional process.

REFERENCES

Alan Cane, IBM applies to join European Semiconductor Research Project, Financial Times, October 5, 1989, p. 1.

Anne O. Krueger, *Trade and Employment in Developing Countries Synthesis*, University of Chicago press (Chicago), 1983, Chapter 7.

Aronald C. Herberger and Sebastian Edwards, "International Evidence on the sources of Inflation" University of Chicago, Department of Economics, Chicago, 1980, pp. 31-33.

Bergsten, C.F.: America in the World Economy : A strategy for the 1990s, Washington Institute of international economics, 1988.

Bhalla, V.K., International Monetary Corporation, Anmol Publications Pvt. Ltd., New Delhi, 1991

Curzon Price, V.: 1992: European last chance? From common market to single market, occasional paper 81, London, Institute for Economic Affairs, for the Wincott Foundation, 1988.

EC Commission, Europe 1992 - Europe World Partner, European Community news release 28188 (EC Office of Press and Public affairs, October 19, 1988).

Hufbaur, G.C. and J.J. Schott: Prospects for North American Free Trade, Washington, Institute of International Economics, 1991.

John Markoff, IBM, Joins SIEMENS in developing chips, New York Times, January 25, 1990. p. 1.

John R. Harris and Michael P. Todaro, "Migration, Unemployment and Development: A Two Sector Analysis", *American Economic* 'twirl', 50(1), March 1970, pp. 126-42.

Michale Michaely, Demelin Papageorgiou and Armeane M. Chokes, *Liberalizing Foreign Trade : Lessons of Experience in Developing World*, Basic Blackwell (Cambridge, MA), 1991, pp. 196-97.

Praeg, H: "Rationale, objectives and modalities" in Grant Jordan, Praeg and Wanandi, Asia Pacific Economic Cooperation: The Challenge Ahead, Washington, Centre for Strategic and International Studies, 1990.

Ronald I. McKinnon, *'Financial Liberalisation, Monetary Control and Economic Development*, Hohns Hopkins Press, 1991, for an analysis of the in-depth analysis of financial liberalisation episodes.

Schott, J.J. (ed.): More *Free* Trade Areas? Policy Analysis in International Economies 27, Washington, Institute for International Economics, May 1989.

Survey of Europe's Internal Market, *Economist*, July 8, 1989, p. 6.

World Bank, 1991, *Global Economy Prospects and the Developing Countries*, Washington, D.C.

8

THE GLOBAL SERVICES ECONOMY

INTRODUCTION

The services sector covers a wide array of activities ranging from services provided by the most sophisticated sectors like telecommunications, satellite mapping, and computer software to simple services like those performed by the barber, the carpenter, and the plumber; highly capital-intensive activities like civil aviation and shipping to employment-oriented activities like tourism, real estate, and housing; infrastructure-related activities like railways, roadways, and ports to social sector related activities like health and education. Thus, there is no one-size–fits- all definition of services resulting in some overlapping and some borderline inclusions. The National Accounts classification of the services sector incorporates trade, hotels, and restaurants; transport, storage, and communication; financing, insurance, real estate, and business services; and community, social, and personal services. In the World Trade Organization (WTO) list of services and the Reserve Bank of India (RBI) classification, construction is also included.

MODES OF INTERNATIONAL TRADE IN SERVICES

With the founding of the World Trade Organization, the scope of trade liberalisation was extended to new areas, including services, which now account, world-wide, for 70% of value-added and 40% of employment. The modes for international trade in services and the liberalisation thereof are set out in the General Agreement on Trade in Services (GATS). A broad understanding of the notion of trade was adopted, encompassing all modes by which services are delivered internationally. Alongside conventional trade between residents and non-residents, the scope now includes the operations of foreign affiliates in host countries and services supplied by natural persons abroad.

The decision to bring services into the scope of liberalisation highlighted the need for service trade statistics that were more detailed and internationally consistent. Here, the progress over the past decade is beyond dispute, yet the remaining difficulties are still very great, and especially acute in respect of the two modes of service delivery that lie outside the conventional definition of trade.

Goods, Services and Intangibles

The usual criterion of materiality goes back to say, 1850 and has long created a dichotomy between goods and services. This criterion of materiality also enters into statistical definitions to describe physical object goods and intangible service products, as is suggested by the fact that the latter until recently were referred to in the balance of payments as invisibles. In fact, as long as the borderline between goods and services posed no problem, to a large extent as long as information and communication technologies had not yet profoundly altered the modes of production, neither did the immateriality criterion pose a problem as the distinguishing factor between goods and services.

The 1993 revised edition of the United Nations System of National Accounts (SNA) by acknowledging that the product of certain service activities can give rise to the constitution of intangible fixed assets (immaterial investment), strikes a blow to the distinction between goods and services. To acknowledge the existence of intangible assets produced as a result of service activities requires the amendment and clarification of what was a relatively consensual definition of services. Consequently, in the SNA 1993, in addition to the definition stipulating that: i) services are not separate entities over which ownership rights can be established; ii) they are produced to order; iii) they cannot be traded separately from their production; and finally, iv) by the time their production is completed they must have been provided to the consumers.

It was added that there is a group of industries generally classified as service industries that produce outputs that have many of the characteristics of goods, i.e., those industries concerned with the provision, storage, communication and dissemination of information, advice and entertainment in the broadest sense of those terms the production of general or specialized information, news, consultancy reports, computer programs, movies, music, etc. The outputs of these industries, over which ownership rights may be established, are often stored on physical objects: paper, tapes, disks, etc. that can be traded like ordinary goods. Whether characterized as goods or services, these products possess the essential common characteristic that they can be produced by one unit and supplied to another, thus making possible division of labour and the emergence of markets.

The Contribution of the GATS

While the definition of the notion of services has become blurred since the mid-1990s, the definition of international trade in services has in fact been clarified within the institutional framework of multilateral trade negotiations. While the 1948 Havana Charter called for creation of an International Trade Organization which was to lay down principles and rules for trade in goods and services, for nearly half a century trade negotiations dealt with goods alone. Since the Charter was never ratified, the General Agreement on Tariffs and Trade (GATT), which was signed in 1947, continued to be the sole framework for negotiations, limited to trade in merchandise. Following successive rounds of negotiations which led to a substantial decrease in tariff based trade barriers, one of the issues tackled by the Uruguay Round (1986-1994) was non-tariff barriers. At the same time, the United States, backed by the European Union and Japan, pressed for the incorporation of services into the GATT. Ultimately, the World Trade Organization (WTO), established in 1995 at the conclusion of the Uruguay Round, was commissioned to oversee multilateral negotiations in three areas, each of which to be governed by its own agreement: goods (carried forward from the GATT), services (General Agreement on Trade in Services, GATS) and intellectual property (Trade-related Aspects of Intellectual Property Rights, TRIPS).

Extension of the scope of trade liberalisation to the realm of services made it necessary to adopt a common statistical framework at the international level. As required prior to each round of negotiations, Article XIX of the GATS directs the Council, made up of representatives of the Member States, to carry out an assessment of trade in services in overall terms and on a sectoral basis. A broad concept of trade was then adopted, encompassing all of the ways in which services can be provided internationally. As a result, in addition to services recorded in the balance of payments, the GATS added the service activity of foreign affiliates operating in host countries. While trade liberalisation in the realm of goods has been confined to trade in the conventional sense (between residents and non-residents), the opening-up of services led to direct investment being brought into the scope of negotiations.

Under the GATS, a service is deemed to be exported from country A to country B if the service is performed by a provider from A on behalf of a customer from B, regardless of where the service is actually performed. It defined four types of trade in services, depending on who or what (the service, the consumer or the provider) crosses the border (Box-1):

BOX-1

The Four Modes of Trade in Services

Services trade encompasses four modes of delivery:

- *Mode 1 or Cross-border supply* is analogous to trade in goods. An example is software services produced in one country and supplied through mail or electronic means to consumers in another country.
- *Mode 2 or Consumption abroad* occurs when consumers move, e.g. to consume tourism or education services in another country.
- *Mode 3 or Commercial presence* involves foreign direct investment, and includes services supplied through any type of foreign business or professional establishment. An

example is an insurance company owned by citizens of one country establishing a branch in another country.

- *Mode 4 or Presence of natural persons* involves the movement of service-supplying nationals of one country to the territory of another. Examples are a doctor of one country supplying through his physical presence services in another country, or the foreign employees of a foreign bank.

SERVICE TRADE

Trade in some services like transportation of goods is directly dependent on merchandise trade while in some others like financial services it is complementary. However, some other services like tourism and software are near stand-alone services not directly related to merchandise trade. There are many such services and with the spread of telecommunications and computer technology, virtually all commercial services including health care and education have become tradeable across borders without movement of natural persons. The trend towards globalization, reinforced by liberalization policies and the removal of regulatory obstacles, has fuelled steady growth of international investment and trade in services.

GLOBAL TRENDS

In world GDP of US$ 70.2 trillion in 2011, the share of services was 67.5 per cent, more or less the same as in 2001. Interestingly the top 15 countries in terms of services GDP are also the same in overall GDP in 2011. This list includes the major developed countries and Brazil, Russia, India, and China. Among the top 15 countries with highest overall GDP in 2011, India ranked 9th in overall GDP and 10th in services GDP. A comparison of the services performance of the top 15 countries in the eleven-year period from 2001 to 2011 shows that the increase in share of services in GDP is the highest for India (8.1 percentage points) followed by Spain. While China's highest services compound annual growth rate (CAGR) of 11.1 per cent was accompanied by marginal change in its share of services for this period, India's very high CAGR (9.2 per cent) which was second highest was also accompanied by the highest change in its share. This is also a reflection of the domination of the industrial sector along with services in China in its growth, while India's growth has been powered mainly by the services sector.

Despite the higher share of services in India's GDP and dominance of industry over services in China, in terms of absolute value of services GDP as well as growth in services (both decadal and annual in 2001, 2010, and 2011) China is still ahead of India. (Table 1)

Country estimates for 2012 show a deceleration in services growth in some major countries. For example, in 2012 it decelerated to 0.5 per cent from 0.9 per cent (in 2011) in the USA; 8.1 per cent in 2012 from 9.4 per cent (in 2011) in China; and 6.6 per cent in

FY 2012-13 from 8.2 per cent (in FY 2011-12) in India. In Brazil, the services sector grew by a 1.4 per cent in Q3 of 2012 compared to 2.1 per cent in the corresponding period of the previous year.

TABLE 2

Performance in Services : International Comparison

Country	Rank		Overall GDP (US$ billion)		Share of services (percent of GDP)			Change in Share 2011 over 2001	Services growth rate (per cent)			CAGR 2001-11
	GDP	Overall GDP	Services Prices 2011	At current Prices 2011	At constant 2001	2010	2011		2001	2010	2011	
1 US	1	1	14991.3	13225.9	77.0	78.3	78.4	1.4	2.9	2.5	5.1	2.1
2 China	2	3	7203.8	4237.0	40.6	41.9	41.7	1.1	10.4	9.9	8.9	11.1
3 Japan	3	2	5870.4	4604.1	70.6	69.9	70.5	-0.1	1.8	1.1	0.6	0.4
4 Germany	4	4	3604.1	3048.7	70.0	70.8	70.0	0.0	2.5	1.0	1.9	1.3
5 France	5	5	2775.5	2240.5	76.8	79.0	79.2	2.4	1.8	1.9	2.1	1.4
6 Brazil	6	8	2476.7	1126.4	65.4	66.2	66.5	1.1	1.8	5.0	3.1	3.8
7 UK	7	6	2429.2	2381.1	74.0	76.4	76.0	2.0	3.8	1.1	1.2	2.3
8 Italy	8	7	2195.9	1773.1	70.9	73.1	73.1	2.2	2.6	1.4	0.7	0.6
9 India	9	10	1897.6	1322.7	50.1	56.8	58.2	8.1	7.5	9.4	7.4	9.2
10 Russia	10	13	1857.8	947.2	56.3	62.4	62.1	5.8	3.3	3.9	3.6	5.5
11 Canada	11	9	1736.9	1233.5	65.0	69.9	69.7	4.7	3.5	2.6	2.2	2.7
12 Australia	12	11	1515.5	894.5	67.9	69.0	69.2	1.3	3.9	2.3	3.6	3.3
13 Spain	13	12	1478.2	1183.8	63.7	69.8	70.0	6.3	3.6	1.2	1.2	2.8
14 Mexico	14	14	1155.2	956.8	61.4	63.8	64.2	2.8	1.2	5.4	5.0	2.9
15 South Korea	15	15	1116.2	1056.1	60.5	57.0	56.6	-3.9	4.4	3.9	2.7	3.5
World			70201.9	52667.7	68.2	67.6	67.5	-0.7	2.8	2.9	3.6	2.6

Source: Computed from UN National Accounts Statistics accessed on 4 January 2013.

Note: Rank is based on current prices, shares are based on constant prices (US$), growth rates are based on constant prices (US$), CAGR is estimated for 2001-11, construction sector is excluded in services GDP.

While the share of services in employment for many developed countries is very high and in many cases higher than the share of services in incomes, the gap between these shares is relatively less. Except China and India, all the other BRICS countries also have a similar pattern. In the Indian and Chinese cases, there is a wide gap between the two, with gap being wider for India. China's share of services in both income and employment is relatively low due to the domination of the industrial sector, but the gap is also narrower than that of India.

World services export growth (CAGR) reached a high of 12.6 per cent during 2000 to 2008 compared to 6.6 per cent in the 1990s. Growth of world exports of services which declined to - 11.1 per cent due to the global economic crisis of 2008, quickly rebounded in 2010 and grew by 10 per cent. However, the pre-crisis (2008) level of US $ 3.84 trillion was reached and surpassed only after a lag of two years in 2011 when world services exports reached US $ 4.17 trillion with a growth of 11 per cent. The Euro-zone crisis and the global slowdown in 2012 affected services trade as well. Mirroring the trends in world GDP growth and merchandise trade, world exports of commercial services started decelerating from Q4 of 2011 with 5 per cent growth followed by 4 per cent in Q1 of 2012, zero per cent in Q2 of 2012 and - 2 per cent in Q3 2012.

World services-sector FDI rebounded in 2011 after falling sharply in 2009 and 2010, to reach around US $570 billion, registering a growth of 15 per cent over the previous year. FDI in non-financial services, which accounted for 85 per cent of the total, rose modestly, on the back of increases in FDI, targeting electricity, gas, and water as well as transportation and communications. Financial services registered a 13 per cent increase in the value of FDI projects in 2011 reaching US$ 80 billion, though still 50 per cent below the pre-crisis average (2005-2007). FDI projects in banking remained subdued in the wake of the global financial crisis. European banks, which had been at the forefront of international expansion through FDI, were largely absent, with a number of them remaining under government control. In 2012, United Nations Conference on Trade and Development (UNCTAD) estimates indicate a fall in global FDI by 18 per cent to US $ 1.3 trillion, while forecasting a moderate recovery in 2013-14.

GOVERNMENTS INTERVENTION IN SERVICE MARKETS

Services play a key role in supporting production networks. Transport and logistics services are obviously the most important direct services input to international goods trade, but communication, insurance and banking are also key enabling services. A prominent role is additionally played by distribution, business and other after-sales services such as repair and maintenance.

Measures that restrict trade and competition in services markets thus affect not only the economic performance of the sector concerned, but may, particularly with infrastructural services, also have spill-over effects on the economic and export performance of goods and other services industries.

Restrictions on trade in certain goods may impair the efficiency and export competitiveness of services suppliers that rely on those particular products as inputs. Restrictions on the importation of certain medical equipment may raise costs for hospitals when providing related medical services to national and foreign patients, for instance. Measures raising the cost of imported consumer goods would likewise negatively affect retailers, and particularly foreign retailers sourcing many of their products from their home country. Such cross-effects are especially important in light of the growing fragmentation of production processes across countries.

In light of their spill-over effects beyond the industry concerned, restrictions to trade in such "intermediate" services can be argued to be of even greater significance. Similar to the analysis of non-tariff measures for goods trade, there are motivations for governments' intervention in services markets.

(i) Public interest considerations

From a public interest theory standpoint, government intervention in services markets may be justified on efficiency grounds, as well as on equity considerations. Efficiency concerns relate primarily to the existence, in many services industries of instances of market failure, such as asymmetric information (i.e. one party having more information than the other), imperfect competition and externalities. While these failures also appear in goods industries, they seem to be more pervasive in the case of services.

Instances of asymmetric information in services are frequent. This is, essentially, because of the intangible nature of many services. Immateriality implies that consumers cannot easily assess the quality of a service before consuming it. Producers will tend to be better informed. However, they might not have an incentive to supply more information to consumers, as this might be costly to provide, or retaining information may afford a commercial advantage. At the same time, consumers may lack the expertise required to assess much of the technical information they receive. As a result, consumer choice is insufficiently informed for competition to function effectively. This problem is accentuated by the fact that repeat purchases may not always be an avenue to discipline producer behaviour. Services, by their nature, tend to be much more diverse than goods. Consumers may not be willing, or able, to continually purchase identical services.

Though market-based solutions could see producers signalling a commitment to quality, for instance by investing in reputation, customer service, brand name or easily accessible complaint procedures, they are unlikely to be sufficient for high-risk activities. Governments thus often intervene to curb services suppliers from exploiting information asymmetries. As it is generally impossible to impose, verify and ensure compliance with performance requirements by focusing exclusively on the service, governments frequently intervene at the level of the supplier. They may, for instance, require producers to disclose certain information to consumers, or impose qualification or licensing requirements that seek to ensure the competence of the services supplier and thus the quality of the services provided.

Information asymmetries may also be problematic for producers where consumers possess private information, for example about their health status. A lack of generally available information may also engender situations of "moral hazard". For example, where someone other than the consumer bears the full responsibility and consequences of his actions, excessive consumption may result. Insurance markets are a case in point. Imperfect competition is another market failure often encountered in services industries. Many services are supplied through networks: telecommunications, postal services, electricity distribution, environmental and rail transport services are prominent examples. Standardized services provided over such infrastructure or distribution networks often exhibit such large economies of scale that the relevant market can be served most cheaply by a single or small number of firms, i.e. they are often naturally monopolistic/oligopolistic. Unchecked, these markets result in under-supply and prices set above marginal cost. Government intervention is thus warranted, and may imply instituting price controls or enabling competition (e.g. through unbundling services, regulating access to essential facilities, franchising and concessions).

Finally, both negative and positive externalities occur in service markets when the price of a service does not reflect the true cost or benefit to society of producing that service. This results, respectively, in excessive or insufficient consumption. The environmental consequences of heavy road transport or intensive tourism are instances of negative externalities. Network expansion in telecommunications services, increased investment in education or vaccination programmes, on the other hand, are examples of positive externalities.

Government intervention in services industries may also be driven by equity considerations. Many services are inputs into human capital development and, as such, they underpin governments' social objectives. Health and education services are typical examples, but similar considerations may also play a role in sectors such as audio-visual, telecommunications, transport, energy and water services. Unfettered markets would leave certain geographical areas or groups of consumers without affordable prices or adequate supply. The imposition of "universal services obligations" has been one government response to counter these problems.

(ii) Political economy considerations

According to the economic theory of regulation, government intervention is not driven exclusively by the pursuit of the "public interest", but rather, or additionally, by the concerns of special interest groups. Governments may therefore intervene irrespective of the existence of a market failure. Even when intervention is warranted on public policy grounds, governments may still, in deciding which instrument to employ, be "bought" into relying on those measures that benefit more organized groups, generally domestic (or incumbent) producers. In the consist of services industries, political economy consideration are particularly significant in at least four respects

First and foremost, the most transparent form of intervention when it comes to trade policy, i.e. a tariff, is not available in services markets. By definition, governments need to resort to other, often more opaque instruments. This offers greater scope to mask any private interest motivations, and thus potentially reduces the risk of electoral punishment.

Secondly, much less scientific evidence exists on which services intervention might be based and its effectiveness tested. The diverse nature of many services, their intangible nature, and the frequent need to regulate at the producer level all imply that regulation tends to be not only complex, but also much more difficult to assess on the basis of exact criteria applied at the product level. This may, once again, help camouflage governments' true intentions.

Thirdly, the complexity of much services regulation implies that regulators who are less experienced or less resourced might be more easily "captured" by special interest groups even if they intend to act in pursuit of the "public interest". Given such information asymmetries, protection might not even need to be "bought".

Fourthly, given the equity and social concerns attached to many services, consumers might actually side with domestic producers. Consumers may misguidedly fear that, if the interests of domestic producers are no longer upheld, service quality will suffer and/or prices will increase.

BOX 2

Examples of Services-Specific Measures to Pursue Public Policy Objectives

Equitable access

In the transport or telecommunications sectors, governments often want remote regions to be served by such services regardless of profitability. Basic equity objectives also prompt governments to ensure that all citizens have access to education and essential health care at low or zero costs.

Measures include cross-subsidization schemes to ensure that revenues in profitable areas are reinvested in favour of under-developed regions or persons in financial need and licensing conditions which include universal services obligations (for example, commercial hospitals are required to treat a certain percentage of patients free of charge).

Consumer protection

With regard to professional, financial or health services, the complexity of the service that is provided makes it very difficult for consumers to appreciate quality or safety prior to consumption. Services suppliers may exploit such information asymmetries.

Measures include prudential and other technical standards to be complied with by services suppliers; publication requirements on costs, risks, side-effects, etc., so as to enable the consumer to make informed decisions; education and training requirements to ensure competence; and mandatory professional liability insurance.

Reduction of environmental impacts and other negative externalities

Road and air transport cause pollution and noise; tourism could put the environment under stress and disturb natural habitats, etc.

Measures include traffic restrictions over weekends, during night hours or in sensitive areas; zoning laws and building codes; tax/subsidy schemes to mobilize funds for the preservation of cultural heritage.

Macroeconomic stability

Financial institutions may engage in imprudent lending or design complex financial instruments that are insufficiently understood. As a consequence, depositors may lose confidence and withdraw their money, inter-bank lending may suffer, credit supply to the real economy may be hampered, and so forth.

To ensure stability, financial institutions must comply with measures such as minimum capital requirements and higher capital reserves when new financial instruments are provided. They must also diversify assets to limit exposure to individual clients, report on their activities, or put limits on remuneration of management.

Avoidance of market dominance and anti-competitive conduct

Concerns about anti-competitive conduct arise in sectors prone to market concentration (including services with network effects and interconnection needs, such as transport and telecommunications, and liberalized former monopolies).

Measures include limitations on market shares, introduction of price surveillance or mandatory price caps, interconnection guarantees, and government-mandated technical standards to replace company-specific requirements.

(iii) Pervasiveness of Government Intervention

Services industries exhibit hugely different characteristics and market structures. There is a broad range of sectors in which governments play no specific role. Nonetheless, it is widely acknowledged that, given the greater likelihood of market failures and the potentially bigger role played by private interest considerations, government intervention in services markets as a whole is more prominent than in goods markets.

The form of this intervention has changed over time, however. Historically, several infrastructural and social services, especially those provided to the general public (traditionally called "public services"), were directly supplied by government entities, usually in monopoly situations. Recent decades have seen a move away from state ownership towards more reliance on private markets to provide these services. Governments progressively moved back from their role of suppliers and increasingly took on the role of regulators. Once such services were no longer publicly financed and provided, governments were forced to introduce new measures, with the stated objective of promoting economic and social welfare. Indeed, regulation of these services markets has expanded at the same time as the industries concerned have been privatized and opened up to competition.

(c) How do Governments Intervene in Services Markets?

Governments often intervene in services markets in pursuit of a variety of public policy objectives that are unrelated to trade policy considerations. Their interventions might nevertheless raise the cost for services suppliers to enter/establish or operate in a market.

A TYPOLOGY OF SERVICES MEASURES

(i) Types of Services Measures

Classification of services interventions according to whether they affect domestic and foreign services and services suppliers differently, i.e. are discriminatory, and whether they affect the ability of firms to enter/establish in a foreign market or have an impact on their operations, captures virtually all forms of government intervention in services markets. It is also helpful in that it enables a rough distinction between measures that usually reduce the number of suppliers in a market (i.e. those related to market entry/establishment), and thus the quantity supplied at a given price, and measures that raise costs once a market is entered into (i.e. those that impact operations) and result in a given quantity being supplied at a higher price. It also helps to highlight that services interventions comprise measures that affect in the same way foreign and domestic producers seeking access to the domestic market. Measures impacting either entry or establishment in a non-discriminatory fashion may protect national, or incumbent, suppliers, at the expense of foreign or new domestic suppliers. In this regard, some of the measures may actually be restrictive to competition generally, rather than to "foreign competition", i.e. trade.

Thus, what matters for services trade is not just the removal of discriminatory measures but the contestability of the market. Even in a situation where all discriminatory measures were removed, a sector would still remain highly restricted if only a fixed number of suppliers were permitted to operate. Though there would be no discrimination in favour of nationals, the entry of any new supplier to the market, be they foreign or domestic, would still be constrained.

Alternative classifications have also been proposed. They focus more on the type of instrument being used, rather than its effects. For this, four main categories may be distinguished by: (i) quotas and local content requirements; (ii) price-based instruments; (iii) standards, licensing and procurement; and (iv) discriminatory access to distribution networks. These classifications, which are more akin to those employed to classify non-tariff measures applying to goods trade, appear better suited to analyse the economic effects of the various measures, precisely because available literature borrows heavily from traditional (i.e. goods) international trade theory.

BOX-3

Typology of Measures Affecting Services Trade

Measures impacting entry/establishment	Measures impacting operations
Non-discriminatory pharmacies, for example	Restriction on the number of licences for
Reserve requirement for banks, for example	
Discriminatory for example	A limit on the number of foreign architects,
Higher port duties charged on foreign-flagged vessels, for example	

Source: WTO Secretariat, based on Francois and Hoekman (2010).

One instance that is not captured by either classification is when trade is affected by the absence, rather than the presence, of a measure. For example, when there is significant uncertainty about the quality of a service, demand for (and trade of) the service concerned might only increase if certification requirements for suppliers are introduced as these help raise consumer confidence. Instances of natural monopolies or oligopolies provide a further case in point. Unless pro-competitive measures are introduced, dominant incumbent suppliers can, through their control of essential facilities, obstruct access to the market.

(ii) When is a measure a trade restriction?

Much services regulation pursues public policy objectives. Nevertheless, such regulation may unintentionally also have trade-restrictive effects. Or, at the same time as aiming at domestic efficiency or social equity objectives, it might be captured by special interest groups to protect domestic suppliers at the expense of consumers. Economic policy considerations may also lead to services measures being used exclusively for protectionist purposes. They may further affect the choice, among all possible alternatives, of particularly inefficient policy instruments.

Given the pervasiveness of services regulation and its commingling with trade protection a clear identification of which measures are trade restrictions, or a neat separation of the protective component in such measures, is fraught with difficulty. As trade-related implications of services measures depend on the specific characteristics of the service industry in question, and particularly on the market imperfections such measures are designed to correct or equity objectives they are pursuing. Market structures differ widely among services sectors. Services trade includes transactions in highly contestable sectors as well as network industries characterized by large fixed costs of entry, for instance. The trade effects of services measures can thus be expected to be different in these two types of industries.

At the sectoral level, to assess the relative efficiency of different regulatory measures in attaining specific public policy goals, instrument-based classification may be used, first, by addressing discriminatory measures, and then un-discriminatory measures.

First, discriminatory measures that impact either entry/establishment or operations place foreign services and suppliers at a competitive disadvantage relative to domestic services and suppliers. They can be considered trade restrictions almost by definition. They include "traditional" trade measures, such as quantitative restrictions, that impact foreign entry/establishment, and discriminatory taxes or subsidies that affect the cost of foreign suppliers' operations.

International trade theory suggests a ranking of such instruments of protection for goods trade. If the objective of a policy is to expand the output of an import-competing industry, output subsidies can be shown to be a superior instrument to tariffs, and tariffs normally superior to quotas. This ranking should, in principle be as valid for services as it is for goods. Nonetheless, applying a similar analysis to services trade presents a number of challenges. First, tariffs are not necessarily a feasible option for services. Secondly, measures that may have tariff-like effects in terms of raising foreign costs per unit of output are not tariff-like when it comes to generating revenue. Thirdly, and most significantly, the modal definition of services trade implies the possibility that trade restrictions will bring about mode-switching and that factor movements will directly affect market structures.

Tariff-like measures that do not produce any revenue would imply a much greater loss in national welfare than a straight tariff if income from quotas (i.e. quota rents) does not accrue domestically. Generally speaking, quota rents accrue to the owners of the right to import the product in the domestic economy. In the case of services, foreign suppliers generally sell their service directly to domestic consumers, so they are much more likely to collect the quota rents than in the case of goods. Additionally, quotas are often associated with wasteful administration and rentseeking activities, including corrupt practices, that push their social cost above that of tariffs. In imperfectly competitive markets, quotas are shown to be even more wasteful.

If trade is possible through only one mode, a limitation on that mode may render the service concerned nontradable. If modes can be substituted for each other, a prohibitive restriction may not have much effect if the unconstrained mode is the most efficient one. If, however, it is not the first-best option, the switch to the alternative mode may result in deadweight losses induced by trade diversion (though possibly moderated by lower price increases than in the case where this mode-switching option was not available). Thus, any benefits resulting from the multiple modes of services provision at the disposal of suppliers faced with a trade restriction need to be weighed against the additional cost to the importing economy of acquiring the service thorough a relatively inefficient mode.

For those services where cross-border delivery is not feasible, limitations to entry on foreign investment imply that the price and quality of the services concerned are determined exclusively by the domestic market structure. These restrictions on foreign direct investment (FDI) generally take the form of either entry quotas and/or restrictions on foreign equity participation. While the latter restrictions may prevent transfers of technology, skills and know-how, the former have been shown to be more socially wasteful. Foreign FDI might be attracted by returns to investment that have been artificially raised by restrictions on competition and the true social productivity of the investment may thus be lower than the returns to the investor.

As for non-discriminatory measures, some of the general observations are: *First*, non-discriminatory measures affecting entry/establishment, most notably quantitative restrictions, would seem to be difficult to justify on efficiency grounds. By protecting incumbent suppliers from competition, such entry limitations reduce market contestability. They have on occasion been defended for infant-industry type reasons and the fulfillment of universal services obligations through cross-subsidization. However, alternative means have been shown to achieve the same objectives without the need to restrict competition, so that entry limitations are at best second or third-ranking alternatives. *Secondly*, non-discriminatory measures that impact suppliers' operations would seem to be the services measures furthest removed from protectionist purposes. Even when they are pursuing public policy goals, however, they may, intentionally or otherwise, have spill-over effects on trade. For instance, though responding primarily to problems of asymmetric information, certification requirements for professionals have trade and welfare effects that may vary depending on the screening mechanisms chosen. Moreover, such measures might yet again affect supply patterns by inducing suppliers to switch to alternative modes of trading services. As such, a crucial challenge posed by these measures is how to distinguish between when they are used exclusively for public policy objectives and when they are also being used for protectionist purposes.

POLICY ISSUES AND APPROACHES TO SERVICES IN RTAs

While motivations for engagement in services RTAs vary across countries, several factors may be identified. *First* in cases where regional merchandise trade liberalization is considered successful, countries may be encouraged to extend liberalization to services. *Second* services liberalization may be more easily negotiated between a limited set of participants, particularly with economies at similar levels of development with geographical proximity and cultural ties, as they enable a greater degree of reciprocity between regional partners, thus reducing the free-rider problem, than would be possible through multilateral negotiations. *Third*, recognizing the critical importance of services trade for growth and development, many countries accelerated regional initiatives in the search for services export opportunities and greater investment attraction.

There is a greater likelihood of static and dynamic gains from preferential liberalization of services than would be the case with preferential liberalization in the goods area. The potential of RTAs in promoting liberalization of the temporary movement of services suppliers is particularly significant. Regulatory cooperation on mutual recognition or harmonization of professional qualifications and licensing certification and technical standards, competition, and provisions for labour mobility, could further improve welfare. Furthermore, regional services trade offers a supportive environment for national firms by accelerating learning curves, building supply capacities and enhancing international competitiveness. Regional services trade also plays a catalytic role in generating employment and furthering the development of growing regional services industries and firms. By allowing for economies of scale in the production of services, RTAs may support the development of regional infrastructure in key sectors such as transportation, communications and energy.

Gains are expected to be greater from non-preferential than from preferential liberalization, because, among other reasons, the former allows consumers to import from the most competitive sources. Regional liberalization is often sequenced as a transition to multilateral liberalization as it can help strengthen indigenous supply capacities and regulatory effectiveness before they face competition at the global level. Adequate sequencing in the opening of services market could provide long-term dynamic gains. In this sense, RTAs can serve as a "building block" for multilateral liberalization. The sequencing of liberalization particularly matters in those sectors where sunk costs and the incumbent advantages associated with some capital-intensive services are significant, for example infrastructure services, as temporary privileges granted under a preferential RTA may result in preventing the market entry of more efficient suppliers after eventual non-preferential market opening on an MFN basis.

Harnessing the potential of RTAs, particularly South-South RTAs, is of interest to DCs as a means to increase national services exports, and to support the broader objectives of stimulating regional growth dynamics and the development of regional supply capacities and infrastructure development, including through cooperative mechanisms aimed at promoting shared regional infrastructure, policy and regulatory cooperation, and skill-sharing and capacity-building. In some North-South RTAs, developed countries provide support through cooperative mechanisms. There is a need to ensure that supportive mechanisms are made effective, particularly in respect of building supply capacities. Instituting effective cooperative mechanisms, and securing resources for such mechanisms, continues to be at the forefront of regional discussions in developing regions.

Different RTAs have adopted different approaches to services liberalization. For an assessment of the extent to which RTAs have effectively liberalized trade between partners, it is necessary to examine both the services regime and other commitments under agreements, including provisions on investment, integration of labour markets, government procurement, and recognition of licences, certifications and qualifications. Furthermore, various sectoral regulations are also relevant to services trade liberalization. The combined effect of all those disciplines will define the extent of services trade liberalization.

RTAs have adopted distinct approaches in respect of (i) scope; (ii) modalities for liberalization; (iii) depth of commitments; (iv) regulatory cooperation; and (v) other areas of cooperation. On (i) sectoral and modal coverage, existing RTAs tend to provide for universal sectoral coverage, with the exclusion of sensitive sectors such as air and maritime transport and audiovisual services. Liberalization may be based on a progressive approach with an implementation period, especially for DCs (10 years in MERCOSUR). Some agreements provide for separate treatment of investment (NAFTA-type RTAs, MERCOSUR, EU) and movement of persons (NAFTA). Some sector- specific provisions can also contain a liberalization element, including financial services, air, maritime and land transport, telecommunications, professional services and mode-4-type movement.

With regard to (ii) liberalization modalities, RTAs generally follow either a negative or a positive list approach. In the negative list approach, countries list those sectors and modes of supply that they wish to be excluded from the general obligation of not restricting services imports, and remaining restrictions may be subject to negotiated elimination (in some cases with the "ratchet mechanism", which automatically binds unilateral liberalization of new services under the agreement). The positive list approach consists in listing those sectors and modes of supply to whose liberalization countries commit themselves. This approach can, in theory, provide the same level of liberalization as the negative list approach but provides greater flexibility in designing the scope and pace of liberalization commitments. The negative list approach was adopted in NAFTA-type RTAs (CAN, CARICOM), Europe Agreements and EU-Mexico, while the positive list approach was adopted in EU-Chile, ASEAN, MERCOSUR, CACM, Japan-Singapore and United States-Jordan. The definition of rules of origin for services providers is important in determining the level and depth of regional services liberalization vis-a-vis third country services/suppliers.

As regards (iii) the depth of commitments, countries' regional commitment as well as general and sectoral disciplines provided under an RTA would affect the extent to which RTAs can generate effective services liberalization. Liberalization commitment may result either in standstill or rollback of restrictive measures. This is important, since RTAs can go beyond GATS commitment to provide "preferential" market access conditions for regional partners. A series of measures are included to promote effective market access, including improved transparency obligations. Regarding (iv) regulatory cooperation, domestic regulation measures such as qualification requirements also determine the level of liberalization, since such requirements often constitute important market entry barriers to services trade, for example trade in professional services. Harmonization and mutual recognition are pursued under some RTAs (MERCOSUR, NAFTA (accountancy, architecture, engineering), CARICOM), but often on a best-endeavour basis. RTAs can contain market access commitments in government procurement in services and disciplines regarding ESM, monopoly and competition policy.

RTAs AND MOVEMENT OF SERVICES SUPPLIERS

RTAs can provide a promising avenue for service-related temporary movement of persons and workers. They could be relevant for the promotion of movement of workers at all skill levels. This is important, as the existing Mode 4 commitments in the WTO are limited in scope and depth, generally focusing on skilled workers. The existing offers in the ongoing GATS negotiations are largely seen by developing countries as insufficient in respect of contractual services suppliers, independent professionals and semi- and less-skilled service providers. While half of the 70 offers under GATS negotiations have introduced Mode-4-related changes, they often attach professional and educational requirements or sectoral carve-outs.

Some RTAs reflect existing commitments under the GATS while others have moved beyond the GATS in this area, as they have provided for general access for certain categories of personnel and offered additional liberalization. The way in which RTAs treat labour movement varies across regions, ranging from full labour mobility to no effective provision at all. However, many RTAs are yet to achieve their full potential through increased Mode 4 commitments facilitating labour mobility. Even in the most liberal agreement, the transition period and economic assistance to disadvantaged regions are used to mitigate the impact of flow of workers. Most RTAs still focus on facilitating the movement of higher-skilled workers and do not go very much beyond the GATS Mode 4 commitments or unilateral programmes to attract skilled workers. Facilitated movement of people does not always lead to the right to provide services. This will depend on the actual liberalization of particular sectors. Moreover, most RTAs stipulate that the provisions covering labour mobility do not override countries' general migration laws and their right to use residence requirements and related permits and visas.

Regional cooperation in the related field of the labour market, including through visa and migration policy, has also been pursued to promote the provision of services through Mode 4. For instance, the Japan-Philippines Economic Partnership Agreement (2006) has incorporated a commitment regarding visa allocation/quota for the movements of health-care workers.

Some regional groupings have specific initiatives relating to services workers — for example, the *SADC* regional framework aims at developing policy guidelines to attract and retain health professionals in the public sector in order to reverse brain drain in the health sector in the region. Other cooperative processes cover migration-related issues generally, including regular migration and highly skilled migrants. Related mechanisms include COMESA's protocol on the gradual relaxation and eventual elimination of visa requirements and protocol on the free movement of persons, labour, services and the right of establishment and residence, as well as cooperation under the *Thailand-Australia FTA* in facilitating the temporary entry of business people, for example by granting applications offshore. ECOWAS introduced the ECOWAS Passport, thereby eliminating barriers to the cross-border movement of citizens.

NAFTA facilitates the cross-border movement of four categories of persons: business visitors, professionals, infra-corporate transferees, and traders and investors. No party may impose numerical limits or labour market tests as a condition for the entry of intra-corporate transferees, and no limits are imposed on NAFTA visas (TN) issued for one year with an unlimited number of extensions. NAFTA does not alter a member country's general immigration provisions or the requirement for temporary visitors to meet licensing or certification requirements with respect to the exercise of a profession or the delivery of after-sale services.

The *Andean* services regime provides that member countries shall facilitate the free transit and presence of natural persons supplying services, including professional services, and employees of services firms of other member countries in relation to the activities covered by the regime. The Andean Labour Migration Instrument has already introduced significant commitments regarding the free movement of workers, including in the services sector, within the subregion. Any Andean national has the right to enter, reside and work in any Andean country. Therefore, employment in the services sector has been fully opened up to Andean nationals in all member countries. The Andean Community is currently working on a regime for the recognition of licences and certifications in order to make the free movement of natural persons also a reality for accredited occupations and professions.

In *MERCOSUR*, the mechanism for the temporary exercise of professions, which includes the directives for the conclusion of framework agreements for reciprocal recognition between professional bodies adopted in 2003, is expected to promote free trade in professional services. In addition, the elimination of visa requirements for

MERCOSUR nationals, and the MERCOSUR Visa for temporary services suppliers, are important developments. The MERCOSUR Visa allows natural persons to enter, and stay for up to four years, for the purpose of providing services. It applies to managers and directors, administrators, legal representatives, scientists, researchers, professors, artists, sports persons, news persons, highly qualified technicians, and specialists and professionals. The granting of the MERCOSUR Visa is not subject to any economic needs test and is exempt from any requirement for proportionality regarding nationality or wage parity.

COOPERATIVE MECHANISMS UNDER RTAs

Among the arguments for a regional approach to services trade liberalization is the greater viability of cooperative mechanisms. Cooperation can take various forms, including regulatory cooperation, financial, human and institutional capacity- building, trade facilitation and infrastructure-building. Cooperation leading to deeper integration may be more feasible among countries with similar levels of development, social preferences and cultural affinity. The benefits of regulatory cooperation may be particularly great for sectors where trade is impeded by differences in qualification requirements, licences and standards (e.g. professional services) or by visa-related issues. However, there may also be costs, for example those arising from sub-optimal harmonization, which do not properly reflect social preferences and local economic conditions.

Numerous cooperative initiatives focus on *recognition and harmonization of qualifications and standards*, with mutual recognition agreements (MRAs) being a central component. In Europe, mutual recognition of qualifications has been a central pillar for a single services-market.

The recognition of professional qualifications and registration procedures for services suppliers also figures prominently in South-South RTAs. ASEAN is in the process of concluding MRAs for professional services (e.g. engineering, accountancy, architecture, surveying, nursing). MERCOSUR has a mechanism for the temporary exercise of professions, including directives for reciprocal recognition between professional bodies. The Andean Community is working on a regime for the recognition of licences and certifications for accredited occupations. African RTAs have had some success with harmonization programmes: the 1999 SADC Driver's Licence harmonizes the training, examination and licensing of drivers across the region and has facilitated transport services.

Amongst *North-South RTAs*, the *Singapore-Australia FTA* envisages cooperation in the form of academic credits transfer and mutual recognition of academic and vocational qualifications between recognized institutions of higher learning. It also contains a separate chapter on cooperation in education, focusing on quality assurance processes; online and distance education; primary, secondary and higher education systems; technical education and vocational training; industry collaboration for technical and vocational training; and teacher training and development.

Cooperation covers *infrastructure sectors,* including financial services (COMESA Bond Guarantee Scheme, COMESA Yellow Card Scheme, PTA-Reinsurance Company (ZEP-RE)); *energy* (e.g. SADC's Southern African Power Pool, aimed at sound economic, environmental and social practices, coordinating and enforcing regional quality supply standards; measuring systems performance); and *research and development* (including human resource development, e.g. Thailand-Australia FTA). ASEAN, for example, covers the strengthening and integration of infrastructure in transportation, energy and telecommunications (e.g. cooperation for an ASEAN highway, the Singapore-Kunming Rail Link, an ASEAN action plan for open-sky arrangement and a Trans-ASEAN Gas Pipeline Network). COMESA has a number of programmes aimed at facilitating services trade, which focus on transport (i.e. air transport liberalization, the COMESA Carriers' Licence, harmonized axle loading and maximum vehicle dimension, harmonized road transit charges). Other African RTAs also focus on cooperation in transport (e.g. the Yamoussoukro Decision to gradually liberalize air transport, an Africa-wide initiative) and business services, including insurance and logistics services, to facilitate trade within the region.

Many cooperative initiatives also focus on *institution-building*. SADC, through its protocols, aims to enhance more institutionalized sharing of information, and has created a number of new institutions — for example, the Telecommunications Regulators Association of Southern Africa (regulatory cooperation on telecommunications), the Regional Tourism Organization of Southern Africa and the Southern African Power Pool.

Some cooperative mechanisms aim at building *supply capacity.* Amongst North-South agreements, the ACP-EU Cotonou Partnership Agreement (CPA) provides for (and future EPAs will provide for) cooperation regarding labour, business, distribution, finance, tourism, culture, and construction and related engineering services with a view to enhancing their suppliers' competitiveness and increasing trade. The measures envisaged aim at providing ACP residents/citizens with easy access to information and communication technologies. The CPA's "Development Strategies" aim at improving the competitive position, especially of SMEs, including through cooperation in private sector development; product development; sector development (e.g. sustainable tourism development or, in the case of SADC, marketing of the SADC region in close cooperation with the private sector). The Thailand-Australia Agreement aims at investment support and promotion.

The EU implements a *broader cooperative mechanism,* including at a sectoral level (e.g. transport, audiovisual, telecommunications). Programmes have been implemented to support new and potential member States in adopting the *acquis communautaire* in the accession process.

INTERFACE BETWEEN REGIONALISM AND MULTILATERALISM IN TRADE IN SERVICES

There is an intrinsic linkage between RTAs and the multilateral trading system, and DCs face the particular challenge of maximizing benefits from their parallel engagement in multilateral and regional processes. Various dimensions of the interface and coherence need to be taken into account when approaching GATS and RTA negotiations. This is important for DCs, given their limited administrative/institutional capacity to conduct a multitude of negotiations simultaneously and to ensure a coherent framework of rules across agreements; their limited negotiating capacities and bargaining power vis-à-vis economically stronger countries; and their limited capacity to implement international rules. There is a risk that the multiplicity of RTA negotiations may divert human and institutional resources away from multilateral efforts.

WTO rules on RTAs determine conditions under which RTAs in services are allowed to exist and operate. GATS Article V ("Economic integration") establishes an exception to the general MFN principle, with two key requirements to be met: first, services RTAs must have "substantial sectoral coverage" in terms of "number of sectors, volume of trade affected and modes of supply" (no "a priori exclusion of any mode of supply"); and second, RTAs must provide for "the absence or elimination of substantially all discrimination" in terms of national treatment (GATS Article XVII) either through (i) "elimination of existing discriminatory measures" "and/or" (ii) "prohibition of new or more discriminatory measures". This has to be achieved "on the basis of a reasonable time-frame". Moreover, RTAs must be designed to facilitate trade between member States and must not raise the overall level of barriers to services trade against third countries.

Unlike GATT Article XXIV, GATS Article V contains special and differential treatment (SDT). When DCs are party to an RTA, flexibility is to be provided in accordance with the level of development of the countries concerned regarding the two key conditions noted above. In the case of South-South RTAs, "more favourable treatment" may be granted to juridical persons owned or controlled by natural persons of the parties in respect of the requirement to engage in "substantive business operations" in the territory of a party to an agreement. Various interpretations have been put forward as to what constitutes "flexibility" and "more favourable treatment" in Article V:3(b).

MFN market access conditions determine the level of preferences that may be provided in the regional context since preferential treatment is a function of restrictions applied on an MFN basis. Thus, as in the case of goods, MFN liberalization in services could affect the level of such "preferences" or the "GATS plus" element in an RTA. The ongoing GATS negotiations could thus affect the scope of such preferential treatment applied to regional partners in services. Indeed, as noted, several RTAs go beyond GATS commitments. Some RTAs even go further than offers submitted in GATS negotiations (e.g., in financial, express delivery, distribution and audiovisual services). Sometimes, the depth of commitments across sectors is comparable with (or goes beyond) commitments envisaged in plurilateral requests. However, it is also notable that RTAs preserve limitations and sensitivities (for example, in respect of audio-visual services in the EC; maritime and certain professional services in the United States; and cross-border trade in financial services in many countries).

Negotiations are under way regarding *GATS disciplines on domestic regulation,* where DCs face the challenge of striking the right balance between the need to preserve domestic policy flexibility and the need to achieve specific disciplines to underpin their export market access opportunities, including in Mode 4. In this regard, some RTAs incorporate provisions ensuring compliance with future GATS disciplines, for example the Singapore-US FTA services chapter.

Particularly relevant to RTAs are disciplines on recognition under Article VII of GATS. The article governs terms and conditions of recognition agreements and thus affects RTAs' ability in instituting and implementing mutual recognition and harmonization of qualifications and standards In this regard, there arises the question of how this rule will affect RTAs' regulatory cooperation aimed at mutual recognition of qualifications and standards. GATS Article VII requires parties to MRAs "to afford adequate opportunity for interested members to negotiate their accession" and not to "accord recognition in a manner which would constitute a means of discrimination between countries in the application of its standards or criteria for the authorization". Such conditions need to be factored in when designing and implementing MRAs in the regional context.

Regarding subsidies, government procurement and emergency safeguard measures, no GATS disciplines exist in this respect; negotiations are ongoing, but to date have made only limited progress. Thus, RTAs' members have greater leeway in adopting disciplines and commitments which they deem to be appropriate in the regional context, and RTAs appear to have advanced as regards rule-making in some of these areas. Singapore issues dropped in the Doha negotiations are increasingly being pursued in North-South RTAs, entailing disciplines on the right of establishment, investment or government procurement. Thus, some proposals in the GATS negotiations on government procurement, for instance, draw on provisions on government procurement in existing RTAs to open services procurement to international competition. Various RTAs have embarked on regional commitments in those areas, and they may have a bearing on future WTO disciplines.

RTAs, coherent with the MTS, can harness development gains from trade in services by allowing for greater and deeper liberalization while creating viable mechanisms for cooperation for institutional, regulatory and supply capacity-building, competitiveness enhancement and infrastructure development. RTAs can, however, complicate the trading environment through their "spaghetti bowl" effect. South-South RTAs can provide a platform for boosting regional service trade and addressing bottlenecks in trade and production, build up supply capacity and develop trade and transport infrastructure and networks. North-South RTAs can potentially improve market access opportunities for DCs in sectors and modes of supply of export interest to DCs, and incorporate cooperation packages. Effectively implementing such packages can generate substantial development gains. Given the nascent state of the services sector in DCs, the implications of North-South reciprocal market opening in services for DCs' services sectors need to be carefully assessed.

Ensuring development gains from services liberalization and cooperation in the regional context requires DCs to design and implement a judicious domestic regulatory framework and institutions, while carefully approaching international commitments so as to serve their overall development objectives. Adequate impact assessment of trade in services is thus important in identifying strategies and priorities for enhancing developing country competitiveness in services trade and benefiting from the combination of RTAs and the MTS.

QUESTIONS

1. Discuss the four modes of trade in services.
2. Explain the cooperative mechanisms under regional trade agreements (RTAs) to service trade liberalisation.
3. Critically examine the role of services and trade in services for the growth and development prospects of developing countries.
4. Discuss the policy issues and approaches to services in regional trade agreements (RTAs).
5. Critically examine experiences with regional trade agreements' (RTAs) services liberalisation.
6. Explain the interface between regionalism and multilateralism in trade in services.
7. Can RTAs provide a promising avenue for service-related temporary movement of persons and workers?
8. Critically examine the measures that affect the services trade.
9. Discuss the service-specific measures to future public policy objectives.

REFERENCES

Antras, P. and Helpman. E. (2004) 'Global sourcing'. *Journal of Political Economy* 112. 3: 552-580.

—— (2007) 'Contractual frictions and global sourcing', *CEPR Discussion Paper* No *6033*, London: CEPR.

Baldwin. R, and Forslid. R. (2004) 'Trade liberalization with heterogeneous firms,'. *CEPR Discussion Paper* No *4635*, London: CEPR.

Bernard, A.B., Jensen, J. B. Redding, S.J. and Schotl. P.K. (2006) 'firms in international trade'. Mimeo.

Blyde J. and Sinyavskaya, N. (2007) The impact of liberalizing trade in services on trade in goods: An empirical investigation', *Review of Development Economics* 11, 3: 566-583.

Deardorff, A.V. (2001) 'International provision of trade services, trade, and fragmentation'. *Review of International Economics* 9, 2: 233-248.

Feenstra, R.C. and Hanson, G. (1999) 'The impact of outsourcing and high-technology capital on wages: Estimates for the United States, *WIV-WW Quarterly Journal of Economics* 114, 3:907-940.

Feenstra, R.C. and Kee, H.L. (2007) 'Trade liberalisation and export variety: A comparison of Mexico and China', *The World Economy* 30, 1: 5-21.

Gera, S., Gu, W., and Lee, F.C. (1999) Information technology and labour productivity growth.

Grossman, G.M. and Rossi-Hansberg, E. (2006a) 'The rise of offshoring: it's not wine for cloth anymore', Mimeo, Federal Reserve Bank of Kansas City.

—— (2006b) 'Trading tasks: A simple theory of offshoring', *NBER Working Paper No. 12721*, Cambridge, MA: NBER.

Grubel, H.G. (1967) 'Intra-industry specialization and the pattern of trade', *The Canadian Journal of Economics and Political Science /Revuecanadienne d'Economique et de Science politique* 33, 3: 374-388.

Grubel, H.G. and Lloyd, P. (1975) *Intra-industry Trade : The Theory and Measurement of International Trade in Differentiated Products,* London: Macmillan.

Kemp, M.C. (1964) *The Pure Theory of International Trade,* New York: Prentice-Hall.

Krugman, P.R. (1990) *Rethinking International Trade,* Cambridge, MA: MIT Press.

—— and Obstfeld, M. (2006) *International Economics: Theory and Policy,* Boston, San Francisco: Addison Wesley.

Markusen, J.R., Melvin, J.R., Kaempfer, W.H., and Maskus, K.E. (1995) *International Trade Theory and Evidence,* New York: McGraw-Hill.

Maskus, K.E. (2000) *Intellectual Property Rights in the Global Economy,* Washington D.C.: Institute for International Economics.

Porter, M.E. (1990) *The Competitive Advantage of Nations,* New York, N Y: The Free Press.

Rivera-Batiz, L.A. and Romer, P.M. (1991) 'Economic integration and endogenous growth', *The Quarterly Journal of Economics* 106, 2: 531-555.

Romer, P.M. (1990) 'Endogenous technological change', *TheJournal of Political Economy* 98. 5: S71-S102.

Sachs, J. and Warner, A. (1995) 'Economic reform and the process of global integration', *Brookings Papers on Economic Activity* 1, 1-95.

Tang, M.K. and Wei, S.J. (2006) 'Does WTO accession raise income? When external commitments create value', Mimeo.

Young, A. (1991) 'Learning by doing and the dynamic effects of international trade', *The Quarterly Journal of Economics* 106,2: 369-405.

9

GLOBALISATION IN SERVICES: INDIA's OPPORTUNITIES AND CONSTRAINTS

INTRODUCTION

The services sector has been a major and vital force steadily driving growth in the Indian economy for more than a decade. The economy has successfully navigated the turbulent years of the recent global economic crisis because of the vitality of this sector in the domestic economy and its prominent role in India's external economic interactions. At present, the services sector covers a wide range of activities from the most sophisticated information technology (IT) to simple services provided by the unorganized sector, such as the services of the barber and plumber. National Accounts classification of the services sector incorporates trade, hotels, and restaurants; transport, storage, and communication; financing, insurance, real estate, and business services; and community, social, and personal services.

DEFINITIONAL ASPECT OF COMPONENTS OF INVISIBLES

Under the balance of payments (BoP) standard presentation, invisibles form part of the current account and have *three* major heads: *services*, *transfers* and *income*. These three major head are furthre disaggregated into income heads. The details or definitional aspects of components of these head are set out in Box-1.

BOX-1

Definitional Aspect of Components of Invisibles

Item		*Description*
1. Services		
(i)	Travel	'Travel' represents all expenditure by foreign tourists in India on the receipts side and all expenditure by Indian tourists abroad on payments side. Travel receipts largely depend on the arrival of foreign tourists in India during a given time period.
(ii)	Transportation	'Transportation' records receipts and payments on account of the carriage of goods and people as well as other distributive services

	(such as port charges, bunker fuel, stevedoring, cabotage, warehousing) performed on merchandise trade.
(iii) Insurance	'Insurance' consists of insurance on exports/imports, premium on life and non-life policies and reinsurance premium from foreign insurance companies.
(iv) Government Not Included Elsewhere (GNIE)	'Government not included elsewhere (GNIE)' represents remittances towards maintenance of foreign embassies, diplomatic missions and international/regional institutions, while payments record the remittances on account of maintenance of embassies and diplomatic missions abroad.
(v) Miscellaneous Services	'Miscellaneous services' encompass communication services, construction services, financial services, software services, news agency services, royalties, copyright and license fees, personal, cultural and recreational services, management services and business services. Business services comprise merchanting services, trade related services, operational leasing services, legal services, accounting services, business and management consultancy services, advertising services, research and development services, architectural and engineering services, agricultural services, mining and on-site processing services, office maintenance services, environmental services and distribution services.
2. Investment Income	'Investment income' represents the servicing of capital transactions (both debt and non-debt). These transactions are in the form of interest, dividend, profit and others for servicing of capital transactions. Interest payments represent servicing of debt liabilities, while the dividend and profit payments reflect the servicing of non-debt (foreign direct investment and portfolio investment) liabilities. Investment income payments move in tandem with India's external liabilities, while investment income receipts get linked to India's external assets including foreign exchange reserves. In accordance with the BPM5, 'compensation of employees' has been shown under the heading, "income" with effect from 1997-98.
3. Transfers	'Transfers' represent one-sided transactions, i.e., transactions that do not have any quid pro quo, such as grants, gifts, and migrants' transfers by way of remittances for family maintenance, repatriation of savings and transfer of financial and real resources linked to change in resident status of migrants. Official transfer receipts record grants, donations and other assistance received by the Government from bilateral and multilateral institutions. Similar transfers by the Indian Government to other countries are recorded under official transfer payments.

FEATURES OF INVISIBLES IN INDIA's BALANCE OF PAYMENTS

The resurgence of invisibles surplus since the 1990s has helped contain the current account deficit within a narrow corridor with surplus in intermittent years, despite the widening trade deficit. The persistence of current account surplus together with significant capital inflows, in turn, enabled further easing of payment restrictions on current and capital account transactions both for individuals and corporates. A marked feature of India's invisibles is the buoyant services exports particularly software services and business services, and private transfers which are characterised by a shift in the level as well as reduced volatility, providing stability to current receipts. The significant technological transformation of the Indian economy as well as the growth in skilled manpower has enabled this process. The continued leading position of India in software exports as well as transfer receipts during 2007 suggests that they are likely to remain important and stable sources of financial inflows during 2008, although the deepening of the global financial crisis will have some impact.

The deepening of the global financial crisis since mid-September 2008 already pushing many advanced economies – the US, Europe and Japan - officially into recession, many EMEs, including India, started experiencing the adverse impact through various channels. The impact is visible in terms of slowdown in both trade and capital flows with consequences for related services. Furthermore, the contraction in demand, both external and domestic, could lead to a moderation in the demand for other services. Apart from services, the decline in income of the migrant workers due to reduction in wages or job losses following recession could have implications for remittances flows. Furthermore, The fall in global interest rates, capital market crash and poor corporate performance may lead to a contraction in receipts and payments of investment income. Thus, the global financial and economic crisis will have some implications for India's invisibles balance, which have historically helped in the containment of the current account deficit.

MAGNITUDE AND TRENDS IN INVISIBLES

Services GDP

India's services sector has emerged as a prominent sector in terms of its contribution to national and states incomes, trade flows, FDI inflows, and employment. The growth story overall and services of world and India in the 2000s began from almost the same level of around 4-5 per cent in 2000. But over the years, India's overall and services growth rates have outpaced those of the world. Interestingly, unlike world services growth, which has been moving in tandem with its overall growth with mild see-saw movements over the years, India's services growth has been consistently above its overall growth in the last decade except for 2003 (when the former was marginally lower than the latter). The growth of the steadily growing services sector did not fall even during the post 2008 crisis period This was primarily due to higher government spending with the high weighted community, social, and personal services at 19.8 per cent and 17.6 per cent in 2008-09 and 2009-10 respectively, which is more than the rate in 2007-08 and around eight to ten times the rate of 2006-07. This was supported by the good growth in the other two major sectors, 'financial, insurance, real estate, and business services' and 'transport, storage, and communication'. While these two sectors along with 'trade, hotels, and restaurants' were the major contributors to growth before the crisis, during the crisis years of 2008-9 and 2009-10, 'community, social and personal services' assumed a greater role in stabilizing the growth of the services sector. However, the growth of these services decelerated in 2010-11 and was low in 2011-12 due to deceleration in growth of public administration and defence. This, coupled with the lower growth of trade (internal and external) reflected in fall in growth of transport and related activities, led to a relatively lower growth of the services sector and even construction sector. In 2011-12, among the broad services sub-sectors, the highest point contribution to total GDP growth at 34.0 per cent was that of 'financing, insurance, real estate, and business services' followed by 'trade, hotels, and restaurants' (16.9 per cent). Thus, for more than a decade, this sector has been pulling up the growth of the Indian economy with a great amount of stability.

The share of services in India's GDP at factor cost (at current prices) increased from 33.3 per cent in 1950-51 to 56.5 per cent in 2012-13 as per Advance Estimates (AE). Including construction, the share would increase to 64.8 per cent in 2012-13. With an 18.0 per cent share, trade, hotels, and restaurants as a group is the largest contributor to GDP among the various services sub-sectors, followed by financing, insurance, real estate, and business services with a 16.6 per cent share. Both these services showed perceptible improvement in their shares over the years. Community, social, and personal services with a share of 14.0 per cent is in third place. Construction, a borderline services inclusion, is at fourth place with an 8.2 per cent share (Table 1).

TABLE 1

Share and Growth of India's Services Sector (a Factor Cost)

(per cent)

	2000-01	*2005-06*	*2006-07*	*2007-08*	*2008-09*	*2009-10^*	*2010-11@*	*2011-12**	*2012-13***
Trade, hotels, & restaurants	14.6 (5.2)	16.7 (12.2)	17.1 (11.1)	17.1 (10.1)	16.9 (5.7)	16.5 (7.9)	17.2 (11.5)	18.0 (6.2)	25.1# (5.2)
Trade	13.3 (5.0)	15.1 (11.6)	15.4 (10.8)	15.4 (9.8)	15.3 (6.7)	15.1 (8.5)	15.7 (11.5)	16.6 (6.5)	
Hotels & restaurants	1.3 (7.0)	1.6 (17.4)	1.7 (14.4)	1.7 (13.0)	1.5 (-3.3)	1.4 (1.9)	1.5 (10.8)	1.5 (2.8)	
Transport, storage, & communication	7.6 (9.2)	8.2 (11.8)	8.2 (12.6)	8.0 (12.5)	7.8 (10.8)	7.7 (14.8)	7.3 (13.8)	7.1 (8.4)	
Railways	1.1 (4.1)	0.9 (7.5)	0.9 (11.1)	1.0 (9.8)	0.9 (7.7)	0.9 (8.8)	0.8 (5.9)	0.7 (7.5)	
Transport by other means	5.0 (7.7)	5.7 (9.3)	5.7 (9.0)	5.6 (8.7)	5.5 (5.3)	5.3 (7.3)	5.3 (8.2)	5.4 (8.6)	

Storage	0.1	0.1	0.1	0.1	0.1	0.1	0.1	0.1	
	(6.1)	(4.7)	(10.9)	(3.4)	(14.1)	(19.3)	(2.2)	(9.4)	
Communication	1.5	1.6	1.5	1.4	1.4	1.4	1.1	0.9	
	(25.0)	(23.5)	(24.3)	(24.1)	(25.1)	(31.5)	(25.4)	(8.3)	
Financing, insurance, real estate, & business services	13.8	14.5	14.8	15.1	15.9	15.8	16.0	16.6	17.2
	(4.5)	(12.6)	(14.0)	(12.0)	(12.0)	(9.7)	(10.1)	(11.7)	(8.6)
Banking & insurance	5.4	5.4	5.5	5.5	5.6	5.4	5.6	5.7	
	(-2.4)	(15.8)	(20.6)	(16.7)	(14.0)	(11.4)	(14.9)	(13.2)	
Real estate, ownership of dwellings & business services	8.7	9.1	9.3	9.6	10.3	10.4	10.4	10.8	
	(7.5)	(10.6)	(9.5)	(8.4)	(10.4)	(8.3)	(6.0)	(10.3)	
Community, social, & personal services	14.8	13.5	12.8	12.5	13.3	14.5	14.0	14.0	14.3
	(4.6)	(7.1)	(2.8)	(6.9)	(12.5)	(11.7)	(4.3)	(6.0)	(6.8)
Public administration & defence	6.6	5.6	5.2	5.1	5.8	6.6	6.1	6.1	
	(1.9)	(4.3)	(1.9)	(7.6)	(19.8)	(17.6)	(0.0)	(5.4)	
Other services	8.2	7.9	7.6	7.4	7.5	7.8	7.9	7.9	
	(7.0)	(9.1)	(3.5)	(6.3)	(7.4)	(7.2)	(8.0)	(6.5)	
Construction	6.0	7.9	8.2	8.5	8.5	8.2	8.2	8.2	8.2
	(6.1)	(12.8)	(10.3)	(10.8)	(5.3)	(6.7)	(10.2)	(5.6)	(5.9)
Total Services	50.8	53.1	52.9	52.7	53.9	54.5	54.4	55.7	56.5
	(5.4)	(10.9)	(10.1)	(10.3)	(10.0)	(10.5)	(9.8)	(8.2)	(6.6)
Total Services (incl. Construction)	56.8	61.0	61.0	61.2	62.4	62.7	62.6 63.9	64.8	
	(5.5)	(11.1)	(10.1)	(10.3)	(9.4)	(10.0)	(9.8)	(7.9)	(6.5)
Total GDP	100.0	100.0	100.0	100.0	100.0	100.0	100.0	100.0	100.0
	(4.3)	(9.5)	(9.6)	(9.3)	(6.7)	(8.6)	(9.3)	(6.2)	(5.0)

Source: Central Statistics Office (CSO).

Notes:Shares are in current prices and growth in constant prices.

Figures in parenthesis indicate growth rate;

* first revised estimates, @ second revised estimates, ^ third revised estimates,

** Advance Estimate (AE);

includes the shares and growth of both trade, hotels, & restaurants and transport, storage, & communication only for 2012-13.

The CAGR of the services sector GDP at 10 per cent for the period 2004-05 to 2011-12 has been higher than the 8.5 per cent CAGR of overall GDP during the same period. However in 2011-12 and 2012-13, there has also been a deceleration in growth rate of services sector at 8.2 per cent and 6.6 per cent respectively. Among the major broad categorie of services, 'financing, insurance, real estate, and business services', which continued to grow robustly both in 2010-11 and 2011-12 decelerated to 8.6 per cent in 2012-13. While in 2011-12 growth in 'trade, hotels, and restaurants' and 'transport, storage, and communication' slowed down to 6.2 per cent and 8.4 per cent respectively, in 2012-13 ***''trade, hotels, and restaurants' and 'transport, storage, and communication' combined grew by an estimated 5.2 per cent.

Sub-sector wise, among commercial services, in terms of shares, the major services are trade, transport by other means (i.e. excluding railways), banking, and insurance, and real estate ownership of dwellings, and business services, besides construction. In 2011-12, though the growth of 'trade' decelerated to 6.5 per cent, its share improved to 16.6 per cent. The share of 'transport by other means' at 5.4 per cent was almost at earlier levels, while its growth was at 8.6 per cent. Banking and insurance with marginal improvement in its share to 5.7 per cent was the most dynamic sector in 2011-12 with a growth of 13.2 per cent on the top of high growths in the preceding years. 'Real estate, ownership of dwellings, and business services' with a share of 10.8 per cent, which is marginally higher than that of the previous year, also had robust growth of 10.3 per cent. 'Other services' with a share of 7.9 per cent both in 2010-11 and 2011-12 grew at a slower pace of 6.5 per cent in 2011-12. Among 'other services', the two major items are community services, of which education, medical, and health, are the major items; and personal services. Interestingly some items among community services like coaching centres and membership organizations have high growth rates with small shares which are rising. Construction, the borderline services sector, has been the most vulnerable to global events. With a share of 8.2 per cent as in the previous two years, it has been growing unevenly since the global crisis.

State-wise Comparison of Services

A comparison of the share of services in the gross state domestic product (GSDP) of different states and union territories (UTs) in 2011-12 shows that the services sector is the dominant sector in most states of India. States and UTs such as Chandigarh, Delhi, Kerala, Mizoram, West Bengal, Tamil Nadu, Maharashtra, Nagaland, and Karnataka have higher than all-India shares. Chandigarh tops the list with a share of 85 per cent followed by Delhi with 81.8 per cent. Other than Arunachal Pradesh (33.8 per cent), Chhattisgarh (36.7 per cent), and Sikkim (37.0 per cent), the share of services in the GSDP in all other states is more than 40 per cent. In 2011-12, in tune with the general moderation in overall services growth, services growth rates in many states also moderated. But some states continued to register high growth rates with the highest being in Himachal Pradesh at 17.3 per cent followed by Bihar at 16.6 per cent. Among UTs with high services share in GSDP, Delhi with11.5 per cent growth tops the list. While the services revolution in India is becoming more broad-based, with even the hitherto backward states piggy-backing on the good performance of this sector, the initial momentum seems to have slowed down for some north-eastern states like Arunachal Pradesh, Mizoram, and Nagaland after the advantage of base effect is over.

FDI in the Services Sector

The growth of the services sector is closely linked to the FDI inflows into this sector and the role of transnational firms. While the ambiguity in classifying the different activities under the services sector continues, the combined FDI share of financial and non-financial services, construction development, telecommunications, computer hardware and software, and hotel and tourism can be taken as a rough estimate of the FDI share of services, though it could include some non-service elements. This share is 47 per cent of the cumulative FDI equity inflows during the period April 2000- November 2012. The five service sectors are also the sectors attracting the highest cumulative FDI inflows to the economy with financial and nonfinancial services topping the list at US$ 36.04 billion during the period April 2000-November 2012. This is followed by other service sectors—construction development (US$21.77 billion), telecommunication (US $12.62 billion), and computer software and hardware (US $ 11.54 billion). If the shares of some other services or service-related sectors like trading (1.96 per cent), information and broadcasting (1.65 per cent), consultancy services (1.11 per cent), construction (infrastructure) activities (1.06), ports (0.88 per cent), agriculture services (0.80 per cent), hospital and diagnostic centres (0.82 per cent), education (0.36 per cent), air transport including air freight (0.24 per cent), and retail trading (0.02 per cent) are included then the total share of cumulative FDI inflows to the services sector would be 56.08 per cent.

In 2011-12, FDI inflows to the services sector (top five sectors including construction) grew robustly at 57.62 per cent to US $ 12.14 billion compared to the growth of overall FDI inflows at 33.6 per cent. However, in 2012-13 (April-November), overall FDI inflows fell by 43.3 per cent to US$ 15.85 billion from US$ 27.93 billion in the corresponding period of the previous year. Following this trend, FDI inflows in the top five services also fell by 9.7 per cent to US $ 8.19 billion. Among them, while FDI inflows to the top four services ectors fell in the range of 14 to 97 per cent, FDI inflows to the hotel and tourism sector increased by a very high 328 per cent over the corresponding period in the previous year.

The government has taken many policy initiatives to liberalize the FDI policy for the services sector. These include liberalizing the policy on foreign investment for companies operating in the broadcasting sector, like increasing the foreign investment limit from 49 per cent to 74 per cent in teleports (setting up up-linking HUBs/teleports) and direct to home (DTH) and cable networks, and permitting foreign investment (FI) up to 74 per cent in mobile TV; permitting foreign airlines to make foreign investment, up to 49 per cent in scheduled and non-scheduled air transport services; permitting FDI, up to 51 per cent, in multibrand retail trading, (see Box-2); and amendment of the existing policy on FDI in single-brand product retail trading.

BOX-2

FDI in Multibrand Retail Trading

FDI in multibrand retail trading has been permitted subject to specified conditions like the following:

- Fresh agricultural produce, including fruits, vegetables, flowers, grains, pulses, fresh poultry, fishery, and meat products, may be unbranded;

- Minimum amount to be brought in as FDI by the foreign investor, would be US $ 100 million;
- At least 50 per cent of total FDI brought in shall be invested in 'backend infrastructure' within three years of the first tranche of FDI;
- At least 30 per cent of the value of procurement of manufactured/ processed products purchased shall be sourced from Indian 'small industries' which have a total investment in plant and machinery not exceeding US $ 1million;
- Retail sales outlets may be set up only in cities with a population of more than 10 lakh as per Census 2011and may also cover an area of 10 km around the municipal/urban agglomeration limits of such cities;
- Government will have the first right to procurement of agricultural products.

State governments/UTs would be free to take their own decisions in regard to implementation of the policy as retail trade is a state subject. Eleven states/UTs, viz. Andhra Pradesh, Assam, Delhi, Haryana, Jammu and Kashmir, Maharashtra, Manipur, Rajasthan, Uttarakhand, Daman and Diu, and Dadra and Nagar Haveli have agreed to permit establishment of retail outlets under this policy. Constitution of a high-level group under the Minister of Consumer Affairs has also been announced to look into various aspects relating to internal trade and to make recommendations on internal trade reforms to the government, whenever required. FDI in multibrand retail trade would benefit stakeholders across the entire span of the supply chain. Farmers stand to benefit from the significant reduction in post-harvest losses expected to result from the strengthening of the backend infrastructure, which would enable the farmers to obtain a remunerative price for their produce.

Small manufacturers will benefit from the conditionality requiring at least 30 per cent procurement from Indian small industries, as this would enable them to get integrated with global retail chains. This in turn will enhance their capacity to export products from India. As far as small retailers are concerned, organized retail already coexists with small traders and the unorganized retail sector. Studies indicate that there has been a strong competitive response from the traditional retailers to these organized retailers, through improved business practices and technological upgradation. Global experience also indicates that organized and unorganized retail coexist and grow. Consumers stand to gain the most, first, from the lowering of prices that would result from supply-chain efficiencies and secondly, through improvement in product quality due to the combined effect of technological upgradation, efficient grading, sorting and packaging, testing and quality control, and product standardization. Implementation of the policy is also likely to lead to greater FDI inflows, quality employment, and adoption of global best practices.

Source: Based on Inputs from the Department of Industrial Policy and Promotion (DIPP)

India's Services Trade

India's Services Exports

India's services export growth has been faster than that of merchandise exports with the export of services growing at a CAGR of 23.6 per cent during 2001-02 to 2011-12, while merchandise exports grew at a CAGR of 21.4 per cent during the same period. However, growth in services exports became erratic in the post global crisis period. Reflecting the impact of uncertainty in the global economy and weak growth in advanced economies, services exports at US$ 142.3 billion showed a lower growth of 14.2 per cent in 2011-12 as against 29.8 per cent in the preceding year. Growth in services exports decelerated further to 4.3 per cent during H1 of 2012-13 as against 22.7 per cent during H1 of 2011-12 (Table 2).

Growth moderation in services exports was observed in almost all categories. Miscellaneous services, accounting for nearly 75 per cent of total services exports in H1 of 2012-13, grew by 8 per cent during this period as compared to 20.2 per cent in corresponding period of the previous year. Within miscellaneous services, growth in exports of software services, accounting for nearly 46 per cent of total services exports, was in single digit at 9.8 per cent in H1 of 2012-13 compared to the 21.8 per cent in H1 of 2011-12. Some categories like travel, transport, and insurance services showed a negative growth rate leading to lower growth in overall services exports. For 2012-13, NASSCOM has projected a lower export growth in IT and business process management of 8.4 per cent mainly due to reduced spending on technology by US corporations and continued crisis in Europe. While the challenges facing global economic growth persist, the worldwide IT spending is expected to increase by 4.2 per cent in 2013 (from US$ 3.58 trillion in 2012 to US$ 3.73 trillion in 2013). Among nonsoftware services, business services export growth was high at 23.9 per cent in the first half of 2012-13. However, export growth of this category of services has been very erratic in recent years. Communication services export growth was also high at 16.5 per cent.

TABLE 2

India's Export of Services

Commodity Group	*Percentage Share*				*CAGR*	*Growth Rate*[a]			
	2001-02	*2011-12*	*2011-12 (Apr.- Sept.)*	*2012-13 (Apr.- Sept.)*	*2001-02 to 2011-12*	*2010-11*	*2011-12*	*2011-12 (Apr.-Sept.)*	*2012-13 (Apr.-Sept.)*
Travel	18.3	13.0	11.9	10.7	19.4	33.2	16.9	21.3	-5.9
Transportation	12.6	12.8	13.3	12.1	23.8	27.4	28.0	37.1	-4.8
Insurance	1.7	1.8	1.8	1.6	24.8	22.3	35.3	39.8	-9.3
GNIE	3.0	0.3	0.4	0.4	-0.8	21.3	-10.7	30.6	7.7
Miscellaneous	64.4	72.0	72.6	75.2	25.0	29.8	11.3	20.2	8.0
Software Services	44.1	43.7	43.3	45.6	23.5	6.8	17.2	21.8	9.8
Non-Software Services	20.3	28.3	29.3	29.6	27.8	83.4	3.3	18.1	5.4
Of which:									
Business Services	3.0	18.2	17.8	21.2	47.9	112.4	7.7	10.6	23.9
Financial services	1.7	4.2	4.3	3.8	35.2	76.2	-8.3	-6.2	-6.9
Communication Services	4.4	1.1	1.1	1.3	7.8	27.2	2.4	1.1	16.5
Total Services Exports	100.0	100.0	100.0	100.0	23.6	29.8	14.2	22.7	4.3

Source: Computed from RBI data.

Notes: a Growth rate is based on values in US dollar terms. GNIE = Government not included elsewhere.

India's Services Imports

Services imports at US$ 78.2 billion declined by 2.9 per cent in 2011-12, as against an increase of 34.2 per cent in the preceding year. However, imports of services resurged in H1 of 2012-13 and grew sharply by 10.3 per cent as compared to a decline of 0.5 per cent in H1 of 2011-12. This rise in import of services was mainly on account of higher imports of software and business services which increased by 89.7 per cent and 22 per cent respectively during H1 of 2012-13 as against a decline of 47.5 per cent and 4.4 per cent respectively in H1 of 2011-12. However, financial services showed a decline of 34.7 per cent as against an increase of 17.7 per cent in H1 of 2011-12, which is perhaps a reflection of the fragile global financial conditions. Similarly, imports of transportation, travel, insurance also recorded a decline in H1 of 2012-13 as against positive growth in H1 of 2011- 2 (Table 3).

TABLE 3

India's Import of Services

Commodity Group	*Percentage Share*				*CAGR*	*Growth Rate*[a]			
	2001-02	*2011-12*	*2011-12*	*2012-13*	*2001-02 to 2011-12*	*2010-11*	*2011-12*	*2011-12*	*2012-13*
			(Apr.- Sept.)					*(Apr.-Sept.)*	
Travel	21.8	17.6	19.3	15.2	16.4	18.0	24.8	39.4	-12.9
Transportation	25.1	20.9	21.0	18.9	16.8	16.3	18.0	14.5	-1.0
Insurance	2.0	1.9	2.0	1.4	18.3	8.9	7.0	3.6	-23.3
GNIE	2.0	1.0	1.0	0.8	10.7	56.2	-4.9	9.2	-11.3
Miscellaneous	49.0	58.6	56.7	63.7	21.1	44.6	-14.3	-13.4	23.9
Software Services	4.9	1.6	1.7	2.9	6.5	49.5	-42.8	-47.5	89.7
Non-Software Services	44.2	56.9	55.0	60.8	22.0	44.4	-13.0	-11.7	21.9
Of which:									
Business Services	10.9	34.2	33.8	37.4	33.4	53.4	-3.3	-4.4	22.0
Financial services	9.1	10.2	10.7	6.4	20.2	61.2	6.7	17.7	-34.7
Communication Services	2.7	2.0	2.0	0.6	15.5	-15.0	35.2	42.8	-66.2
Total Services Imports	100.0	100.0	100.0	100.0	18.9	34.2	-2.9	-0.5	10.3

Source: Computed from RBI data.

Note: a. Growth rate is based on values in US dollar terms. GNIE = Government not included elsewhere.

India's Balance of Trade in Services

Surplus on account of India's services exports has been a cushioning factor for financing a large part of the merchandise trade deficit in recent years. During 2006-7 to 2011-12, surplus in services exports, on average, financed around 38 per cent of merchandise trade deficit. During 2011-12, net surplus on account of services exports at US$ 64.1 billion stood significantly higher than that in 2010-11 and financed 33.8 per cent of trade deficit. During H1 of 2012-13, with slower growth in services exports and rise in services imports, the surplus at US$ 29.6 billion was 2.8 per cent lower than in H1 of 2011-12, financing 32.6 per cent of trade deficit. Going forward, downward risks to export of services persist as global economic conditions remain less conducive.

Services Employment in India

The pattern of sectoral share of employment has changed over the last two decades with the share of agriculture falling from 64.75 per cent in 1993-94 to 53.2 per cent in 2009-10 and of industries (excluding construction) falling from 12.43 per cent to 11.9 per cent. The shares of the services and construction sectors in employment, on the other hand, increased in the same period from 19.70 per cent to 25.30 per cent and 3.12 per cent to 9.60 per cent respectively. As per the National Sample Survey Office's (NSSO) report on Employment and Unemployment Situation in India 2009-10, on the basis of usually working persons in the principal and subsidiary statuses, for every 1000 people employed in rural India, 679 people are employed in the agriculture sector, 241 in the services sector (including construction), and 80 in the industrial sector. In urban India, 75 people are employed in the agriculture sector, 683 in the services sector (including construction) and 242 in the industrial sector. Construction; trade, hotels, and restaurants; and public administration, education, and community services are the three major employment-providing services sectors.

PERFORMANCE OF SOME MAJOR SERVICES

The performance of the different services based on the different indicators shows that sectors like telecom, tourism, and railways have done well in 2011-12 (Table 4). Shipping and ports show poor performance reflecting the effects of the global slowdown.

Trade

Trade with a share of above 15 per cent in India's GDP in the last seven years (16.6 per cent in 2011-12) and a CAGR of 9.3 per cent during 2004-05 to 2011-12, has grown to ₹ 8,10,585 crore in 2011- 12. As per the A.T. Kearney, Global Retail Development Index 2012 report, India ranked at 5th place remains a high-potential market with accelerated retail market growth of 15 to 20 per cent expected over the next five years. While the overall retail market contributes 14 per cent of India's GDP, organized retail penetration remains low, indicating room for growth. Brazil tops the ranks with retail sales accounting for 70 per cent of Brazil's consumer spending, followed by Chile, China, and Uruguay. In India, the food and beverages segment is seeing increased activity from foreign players, and grocery remains India's largest source of retail sales. Hypermarkets and supermarkets continue to dominate the organised retail market, but cash-andcarry is growing fast, with significant expansion planned from Bharti

Wal-Mart, Metro Group, and Carrefour. Apparel is expected to grow by 9 to 10 per cent annually for the next five years. Players such as Zara, Marks & Spencers, and Mango are actively scouting locations to open more stores across the country. The luxury retail sector saw 20 per cent growth last year, with luxury malls becoming entrenched in Delhi, Mumbai, and Bangalore.

TABLE 4

Performance of India's Services Sector: Some Indicators

Sector	*Indicators*	*Unit*	*Period*				
			2008-09	*2009-10*	*2010-11*	*2011-12*	*2012-13*
Aviation	Airline passengers (domestic and international)	Million	49.5 (a)	54.5 (a)	64.5 (a)	70.2(a)	67.5(a)
Telecom	Telecom connections (wireline and wireless)	Lakh	4297.25	6212.8	8463.2	9513.4	8955.1(b)
Tourism	Foreign tourist arrivals	Million	5.28 (a)	5.17 (a)	5.78 (a)	6.31 (a)	6.65 (a)
	Foreign exchange earnings from tourist arrivals	US $ million	11832 (a)	11136(a)	14193 (a)	16564(a)	17737(a)
Shipping	Gross tonnage of Indian shipping	Million GT	9.28	9.69	10.45	11.06(c)	10.45(d)
	No. of ships	Numbers	925	1003	1071	1122 (c)	1158(d)
Ports	Port traffic	Million tonnes	744.02	850.03	885.45	911.68	455.77(e)
Railways	Freight traffic by railways	Million tonnes	833.31	887.99	832.75	969.78	735.32(c)
	Net tonne kilometers of railways	Million	538226	584760	444515	639768	470956(c)
Storage	Storage capacity	Lakh MT	105.25	105.98	102.47	100.85	101.60
	No. of warehouses	Numbers	499	487	479	468	469

Sources: Directorate General of Civil Aviation, Telecom Regulatory Authority of India, Ministry of Tourism, Ministry of Shipping, Ministry of Railways and Central Warehousing Corporation (Compiled by EXIM Bank of India).

Notes: (a) calendar years, for example 2007-8 for 2007. (b) As on 31st December, 2012, (c) April- December, (d) As on 31 January 2013, (e) April-September. GT is gross tonnage; MT is metric tonnes.

Since 2006, India allowed FDI in single-brand retail to the extent of 51 per cent. In January 2012, the government removed restrictions on FDI in the single-brand retail sector, allowing 100 per cent FDI and from September 2012. FDI in multibrand retail has been allowed up to 51 per cent under the government route and subject to specified conditions (Box 2). While agricultural products could get vastly improved access to markets with the growth of modern retail trade, the revenue to the government could also increase, as at present the retail sector is largely unorganized and has low tax compliance.

Tourism, Including Hotels and Restaurants

Tourism accounts for around 6-7 per cent of global employment (direct and indirect) and 5 per cent of global income as per the United Nations World Tourism Organization (UNWTO). It is one of the largest generators of employment across the world and women account for 70 per cent of the workforce in the travel and tourism industry. Hence it generates more inclusive growth than other sectors. According to the UNWTO, international tourist arrivals surpassed the 1 billion mark for the first time in history in 2012, reaching a figure of 1.04 billion from 996 million in 2011 with 4 per cent growth despite the volatility around the globe, particularly in Europe which accounts for over half of international tourist arrivals worldwide. Emerging economies, with 4.1 per cent growth regained the lead over advanced economies with 3.6 per cent growth, with Asia and Pacific showing the strongest growth at 7 per cent.

In 2013 growth is expected to decelerate slightly and fall in the range of 3-4 per cent with prospects stronger for Asia and Pacific (5-6 per cent). In 2011 international tourism receipts grew by 11 per cent (3.9 per cent in real terms) to an estimated US$ 1030 billion, setting new records in most destinations despite economic challenges in many source markets. International tourism receipts and expenditure for 2012 confirm the positive trend in arrivals. In a significant number of destinations including India (22 per cent) receipts from international tourism increased by 15 per cent or more. According to the UNWTO, the number of international tourist arrivals worldwide is expected to increase by 3.3 per cent a year on an average from 2010 to 2030, resulting in around 43 million more arrivals every year, to reach a total of 1.8 billion arrivals by 2030. As in the past, emerging economy destinations are set to grow faster than advanced economy destinations. As a result, the market share of emerging economies which has increased from 30 per cent in 1980 to 47 per cent in 2011 is expected to reach 57 per cent by 2030, equivalent to over one billion international tourist arrivals.

The contribution of tourism to India's GDP was 6.8 per cent (3.7 per cent direct and 3.1 per cent indirect) and its contribution to total employment generation was 10.2 per cent (direct 4.4 per cent and indirect 5.8 per cent). As per the Twelfth Five Year Plan approach paper, India's travel and tourism sector is estimated to create 78 jobs per million rupees of investment compared to 45 jobs per million rupees in the manufacturing sector. Foreign tourist arrivals (FTAs) in India grew by 9.2 per cent in 2011. However, due to the Euro-zone crisis and global slowdown, FTA growth moderated to 5.4 per cent to reach 66.48 lakh arrivals in 2012. As a result, foreign exchange earnings (FEEs) growth in dollar terms that was 16.7 per cent in 2011 moderated to 7.1 per cent to reach US $ 17.74 billion in 2012. The share of India in international tourist arrivals was just 0.64 per cent (rank 38) in 2011. India's share in the international tourism receipts was relatively higher at 1.61 per cent in 2011 (rank 17), though it is very low compared to countries like the US (11.3 per cent) and even China (4.7 per cent).

Domestic tourism is also an important contributor to the growth of this sector with a 14.34 per cent CAGR of domestic tourist visits from 1991 to 2011. During 2011, there were 851 million domestic tourists, with the top five states, Uttar Pradesh, Andhra Pradesh, Tamil Nadu, Karnataka, and Maharashtra, cumulatively accounting for around 69 per cent of the total domestic tourist visits in the country. The hotels and restaurants sector with a 1.5 per cent share in India's GDP in 2011-12 is also an important sub-component of the tourism sector. There are also many new tourism products that hold significant potential for India like wellness tourism, golf tourism and adventure tourism.

To promote tourism, the government has taken many policy initiatives including a five-year tax holiday for 2, 3, and 4 star category hotels located around all United Nations Educational, Scientific, and Cultural Organization (UNESCO) World Heritage sites (except Delhi and Mumbai) for hotels which start operating w.e.f. 1 April 2008 to 31March 2013; an investment-linked deduction under Section 35 AD of the Income Tax Act extended to new hotels of 2 star category and above anywhere in India, allowing 100 per cent deduction in respect of the whole or any expenditure of capital nature excluding land, goodwill, and financial instruments incurred during the year; and inclusion of 3 star or higher category classified hotels located outside cities with population of more than 10 lakh in the harmonized list of the infrastructure subsector. The Government of India has also taken the initiative of identifying, diversifying, developing, and promoting the nascent/ upcoming niche products of the tourism industry to overcome the 'seasonality' aspect and promote India as a 365 days destination, attract tourists with specific interests, and ensure repeat visits for products in which India has comparative advantage. A committee has been constituted for promotion of golf tourism and wellness tourism and specific guidelines have been formulated to support golf, polo, and wellness tourism. The government has also formulated a set of guidelines on safety and quality norms for adventure tourism. A scheme of Approval of Adventure Tour Operators which is a voluntary scheme open to all bonafide adventure-tour operators has been announced. To attract foreign tourists coming to India for medical treatment, a new 'medical visa' category has been introduced. The government has also formulated guidelines to address various issues governing wellness centres, covering the entire spectrum of the Indian systems of medicine.

At present, there are various challenges that need to be addressed to develop this sector. One of them is the multiple taxes on hospitality- and tourism-related activities which make the tourism product expensive in the form of high hotel rates and high fares; another is the luxury tax which is imposed by state governments leading to high tariffs and low occupancy in hotels. Luxury tax on hotels in some states is very high and varies from 5 per cent to 12.5 per cent and in some cases it is applicable on printed room rates whereas the actual hotel rates offered to guests are much lower. Tourism infrastructure is another area which needs immediate attention where there is plenty of scope for public private partnerships (PPP). User fees could be levied if monuments or tourist sites are developed by the private sector or through PPP. Thus significant opportunities still remain relatively untapped and for faster, sustainable, and more inclusive growth, as envisaged in the Twelfth Five Year Plan, the tourism sector holds a lot of promise.

Some Transport-Related Services

Shipping

Shipping plays an important role in merchandise trade. About 95 per cent of India's trade by volume and 68 per cent in terms of value is transported by sea. As on 31 January 2013, India had a fleet strength of 1158 ships with GT of 10.45 million, with the public-sector Shipping Corporation of India having the largest share of 32.60 per cent. Of this, 356 ships with 9.37 million GT cater to India's overseas trade and the rest to coastal trade. The gross foreign exchange earnings/savings of Indian ships in 2011-12 were ₹ 10,666.45 crore. Despite one the largest merchant shipping fleets among developing countries, India ranks 18th among the 35 flags of registration with the largest registered dead weight tonnage (DWT) with a share of only 1.05 per cent in total world DWT as on 1 January 2012. Leaving aside flags of convenience, Hong Kong has the highest DWT, with a share of 7.6 per cent, while China's share is 3.79 per cent. In 2011 as per UNCTAD, India was ranked 8th among developing countries in terms of container ship operations with 9.95 million twenty foot equivalent units of container (TEUs), with a world share of 1.74 per cent. India is one of the major ship-breaking destinations. In 2011, with a world share of 28.7 per cent (in terms of DWT), it topped the list of shipscrapping nations, scrapping 203 ships of 13.87 million DWT as per ISL Shipping Statistics and Market Review September/October 2012. India is also one of the major countries supplying seafarers.

As a result of the global slowdown, the turbulence experienced by the global shipping industry continued in 2012. The Baltic Dry Index, the barometer of merchandise trade as well as shipping services, has been in the red since the global crisis of 2008, though there were small upswings at the lower end of the index. Like shipping companies worldwide, Indian shipping companies also faced problems of restricted cash inflows due to very low charter hire and freight rates in all segments of shipping. Going by the rough assimilation of various Very Large Crude Carrier (VLCC) fixtures, the average rate tumbled from US$ 13,605 a day in the first quarter of FY 2012-13 to US$ 835, US$ 776, and US$ 1296 in the next three months.

There has been a sharp decline in the share of Indian ships in the carriage of India's overseas trade from about 40 per cent in the late 1980s to 10.4 per cent in 2011-12 with 17.05 per cent share in India's oil imports. Given the relatively low participation of Indian ships in India's trade and given the fact that Indian ships are ageing, with the average age of the Indian fleet increasing from 15 years in 1999 to 16.83 years as on 31 December 2012 (with 41.59 per cent of the fleet over 20 years and 11 per cent in the age group 16-20 years), there is urgent need to increase the shipping fleet so that it is adequate atleast to meet India's trade volumes. This is also an opportune time to increase our depleting shipping fleet to reasonable size as ship prices which had peaked in the middle of 2007-8 have dropped to historical lows in the subsequent years and the trend is continuing even now as on December 2012. A large and modernized shipping fleet will not only lead to higher growth, employment and higher earning/ saving of foreign exchange, but also increase our bargaining power with foreign liners who carry Indian cargo as per their schedule and also discriminate in the rates.

Port Services

Port services are closely connected to shipping services and merchandise trade. The performance of the latter two is also dependent on the efficiency of ports. The total capacity of Indian ports has reached approximately 1245.3 million tonnes as on 31st March 2012. During 2011-12, total traffic handled at all ports at 911.7 million tonnes, grew by 3 per cent over the previous year. Though there was a decline in traffic at major ports, which accounted for more than 60 per cent of total traffic, the 11.5 per cent growth achieved by non-major ports contributed to the overall traffic growth handled by all ports. In the first half of 2012-13 (April-September), traffic handled by Indian ports grew by 1.8 per cent over the corresponding period of the previous year, with the growth of non-major ports (10.3 per cent) compensating for the decline in growth of major ports.

As per the World Shipping Council, Shanghai port ranked at the top in terms of total cargo volume handled with 31.74 million TEUs in 2011. Singapore with 29.94 million TEUs was in second position. The Jawaharlal Nehru Port Trust (JNPT) is ranked 30th in terms of total cargo volume handled with 4.53 million TEUs in 2011. The three port-related performance indicators show improvement in both 2011-12 and April-September 2012 over corresponding previous period. The average output per ship-berth-day improved to 13,374 tonnes for all major ports during 2012-13 (April-September) compared to 12,825 tonnes in corresponding period of 2011-12.The average turnaround time at major Indian ports improved to 4.15 days in 2012-13 (April-September) compared to 5.29 and 5.05 in 2010-11 and 2011-12 respectively and ranged between 1.54 days at Cochin Port to 6.27 days at Kandla Port. The average preberthing detention time (PBDT) for all major ports declined from 2.32 days in 2010-11 to 2.04 in 2011-12. While at first sight this indicates greater efficiency of ports, it could also be due to the lower volumes handled by ports with the global downturn. Even the average turnaround time has been higher in 2011-12 compared to 2008-09. Thus except for average output per ship berth day, the other two indicators have not shown much improvement over the years. Thus efficiency of our ports needs to be improved further (Table 5).

The government has been following the strategy of increasing investment in infrastructure through a combination of public investment and PPP. The Twelfth Five Year Plan with an outlay of ₹ 3,057.47crore (gross budgetary support) for the port sector envisages an increase in capacity of major ports to 1229.29 million tonnes by the end of 2016-17 from the pre-Plan base level of 696.5 million tonnes with 12 per cent average annual growth in capacity addition. While efforts are being made to improve port infrastructure, there is need to upgrade the facilities at existing ports with regard to cargo handling, stevedoring, pilotage services, bunker services, and warehousing facilities; increase the drafts to facilitate trans-shipment of Indian cargo which otherwise takes place outside the country; and rationalize the different port charges to make them comparable with best practice levels. The Maritime Agenda 2010-20 covers some of these issues like full mechanization of cargo handling and movements, having draft of not less than 14 m in major ports and 17 m in hub ports, and shifting of trans-shipment of Indian containers from foreign ports to Indian ports.

TABLE 5

Some Performance Indicators of Ports in India

Indicators							April to September 2011-12		Change in 2011-12 over 2008-09	Change in 2012-13 (Apr.-Sept.) over previous Year
	1990-91	2000-01	2008-09	2009-10	2010-11	2011-12P	2011-12	2012-13		
Average turnaround Time (days)	8.10	4.24	4.20	4.63	5.29	5.05	4.80	4.15	0.85	-0.65
Average pre- berthing detention time (days)	2.16	1.19	1.63	2.16	2.32	2.04	-	-	0.41	-
Average output per ship-berth-day (in tonnes)	3372	6961	9669	9215	9140	13073	12825	13374	3404	549

Source: Transport Research Wing, Ministry of Shipping based on data of Major Ports/Indian Port Association (IPA).

P stands for provisional

Real Estate Services and Housing

Real estate and dwellings has a share of 5.9 per cent in India's GDP and a growth of 7.2 per cent in 2011-12. The growth of the real estate services in particular has been impressive consistently at over 25 per cent since 2005-6 with 26.3 per cent growth in 2011-12. Housing is a basic necessity for human life and is the second largest generator of employment, next only to agriculture. Housing activities have both forward and backward linkages in nearly 300 sub-sectors such as manufacturing (steel, cement, and builders' hardware), transport, electricity, gas and water supply, trade, financial services, and construction which contribute to capital formation, income opportunities, and generation of employment.

In 2012-13 property prices have moderated. As per the National Housing Bank (NHB) RESIDEX index for the quarter July-September 2012 compared to April-June 2012 (covering 20 cities, with 2007 as base year), there is a general decline in prices of residential properties in some smaller towns, while the increase in other cities is mostly marginal. In view of increased urbanization, the housing requirements in urban areas have been witnessing increases over the years. The Eleventh Five Year Plan (2007-12) estimated housing requirement of 24.7 million units in urban areas of which 99 per cent was in the economically weaker sections/lower income groups (EWS/LIG) segment. As per the estimation of the Task Force on Housing Requirements in Urban Areas during the Twelfth Five Year Plan Period (2012-17), the housing requirement in urban areas is 18.7 million units of which 18.5 million are for the EWS/LIG segment. As per a McKinsey Report, the demand for affordable housing will be 38 million by 2030.

To support the growth of the housing and real estate sector, many institutions have been set up especially for financing. While these institutions largely cater to the formal sector, access to finance by the informal market segment largely remains untapped. As this untapped market segment is significant and growing, the Government of India has announced various measures like the Interest Subsidy Scheme for Housing for the Urban Poor and setting up of the Credit Risk Guarantee Fund Trust for Low Income Housing. With support from lending institutions, housing credit has grown substantially over the years, resulting in increased market penetration. The housing loan portfolio of scheduled commercial banks and housing finance companies – the major institutional players – stood at ₹ 6.10 lakh crore as in end-March 2012. However, due to limited housing finance solutions, the gap between housing demand and supply is widening. Besides the mortgage market in India is also underdeveloped. Though mortgages as a percentage of GDP have risen from 3.4 per cent in 2001 to 9 per cent in 2011- 12, the share is relatively lower than in many other countries – such as China (12 per cent), Thailand (17 per cent), Malaysia (29 per cent), Hong Kong (40 per cent), and the USA (65 per cent).

While advanced countries like the US were rattled by the sub-prime crisis, Indian banks have demonstrated a great amount of maturity in their lending for the housing sector. The government has also taken many policy measures for this sector. A number of incentives were given for promoting affordable housing like allowing external commercial borrowings (ECB) for low cost affordable housing projects, increase in investmentlinked deduction of capital expenditure incurred in the affordable housing projects, exemption from service tax payments for construction services related to residential dwellings, and low cost mass housing up to an area of 60 sq. m under the Scheme of Affordable Housing in Partnership. A Credit Risk Guarantee Fund Trust has been established since 1 May 2012, which will be managed by the NHB, and provide default guarantee for housing loans up to ₹ 5 lakh sanctioned and disbursed by the lending institutions without any collateral security or thirdparty guarantees and for new borrowers in the EWS/ LIG category in urban areas. The NHB has also floated a joint-venture mortgage guarantee company – the India Mortgage Guarantee Corporation Pvt. Ltd—which will offer mortgage guarantees against borrower defaults on housing loans from mortgage lenders which will help expand access to housing in India. Renting of residential units has been included in the negative list of services that are exempt from payment of service tax. In order to develop strategic policy intervention to promote rental housing as a viable alternative for addressing the housing shortage, the Government of India has also set up a task force for rental housing. The Rajiv Awas Yojana (RAY), also provides support to states for creation of affordable housing stock and assigning property rights to slum dwellers.

India's housing and real estate sector faces many challenges. While India is among the top countries in terms of housing and workspace needs, it ranks 182nd in construction permission processes according to the World Bank's Doing Business 2013 report. There are 34 procedures and the average time taken is 196 days, which increases the sale value by 40 per cent. Rapid increase in land prices, absence of a long-term funding and lending market at fixed rates, limited developer finance, the Urban Land Ceiling Regulations Act (ULCRA) continuing in some states, existing lower floor area ratio in cities, high stamp duties and difficulties in land acquisition are some other issues which need to be addressed. 'Affordable Housing for All' is another challenge as the demand for housing by the EWS/LIG segment has increased.

Some Business Services

Business services include services like computer-related services, R&D, accounting services and legal services, and renting of machinery in order of importance (shares) as per India's National Accounts. The share of business services in India's GDP, has risen over the years, and these are also the dynamic services with a combined growth rate of 13.5 per cent in 2011-12. They grew at around 20 per cent during 2005-6, 2006-7 and 2008-9 but growth decelerated in the next two years due to the global economic situation.

IT and ITeS

India's IT and ITeS services with exponential growth are a unique export-led success story which has put India on the global map. While India has achieved a brand identity in this sector, other developing countries are trying to emulate India's example. Besides its impact on growth (both direct and indirect), it is also a provider of skilled employment both in India and abroad, generating direct employment for nearly 2.8 million persons and indirect employment of around 8.9 million in 2011-12. The IT-ITeS industry has four major subcomponents: IT services, business process outsourcing (BPO), engineering services and R&D, and software products.

The global slowdown has impacted the revenues of the IT-Business Process Management (BPM) sector, the growth of which decelerated from 15 percent in 2011-12 to an estimated 8.4 percent reaching US$95.2 billion in 2012-13 as per NASSCOM. The deceleration in growth of the dominant export sector (80 percent share) was from 16.5 percent in 2011-12 to 10.2 percent in 2012-13, while domestic revenue growth decelerated from 9.7 percent to a 1.9 per cent (due to currency effect) during these years. In Indian rupee terms domestic revenues have grown at 14.1 per cent in 2012-13 compared to 16.6 per cent in 2011-12. NASSCOM estimate of growth for 2013-14 are 13-15 percent for total IT-BPM revenue, 12-14 percent for exports and 13-15 percent for domestic sector. As a proportion of national GDP, IT and Business Process Management (BPM) sector revenues have grown from 1.2 per cent in 1997-98 to an estimated nearly 8 per cent in 2012-13 (Table 6).

TABLE 6

Overall Growth Performance of the IT-BPM Sector

Year	*Value (US $ Billion)*							*Growth rate (per cent)*		
	2007-08	*2008-09*	*2009-10*	*2010-11*	*2011-12*	*2012-13E*	*2013-14P*	*2011-12*	*2012-13E*	*2013-14P*
Total IT-BPM Services Revenue	52.1	59.9	64.0	76.3	87.7	95.2	106-111	15.0	8.4	13-15
Exports	40.4	47.1	49.7	59.0	68.8	75.8	84-87	16.5	10.2	12-14
Domestic	11.7	12.8	14.3	17.3	19.0	19.3	22-24	9.7	1.9	13-15

Source: NASSCOM

Note: Data excludes Hardware; E: Estimates; P: Projections

While the global slowdown, increasing competition from new countries, and rising protectionist measures in the wake of job losses in developed countries have slightly dimmed the prospects for exports of IT and ITeS services, a great opportunity is waiting in India's domestic market with increasing technology adoption within the government sector and the small and medium business (SMB) sector. The Twelfth Five Year Plan aims to harness the potential of the software and services sector to contribute to the country's development and growth, particularly in terms of investment, exports, employment generation, and contribution to GDP and to retain India's leadership position as a global IT-BPO destination, consolidate and grow in both mature and emerging markets. The government has also announced the National Policy on Information Technology 2012 which aims to maximally leverage the power of ICT to help address the economic and developmental challenges the country faces. Under the National e-Governance Plan (NeGP), the government focuses on making critical public services available electronically and promoting rural entrepreneurship. Of the 31 Mission Mode Projects (MMP), 24 have been approved by the Government of India (with 22 MMPs having gone live).

At central level these are: MCA 21,a complete egovernance project of Ministry of Corporate Affairs, pensions, income tax, central excise and customs, banking, insurance, passport, e-Office, National Population Register (NPR) and UID, India Post, immigration visa, and foreigners' registration and tracking. Some of the issues and challenges related to this sector are the growing competition from developing countries with lower costs, rising protectionist sentiments in developed countries, and transfer pricing issues (See Box 3).

BOX 3

Growing Competition to India's IT and ITeS Services

The IT and ITeS sector has started facing competition from many developing countries. While the EU has the highest share in computer and information services exports, followed by India and the USA, many new competitors like China, Israel and the Philippines have emerged in recent years. Between 2005 and 2011, the annual average growth of computer services was 69 per cent in the Philippines, 28 per cent in Sri Lanka, 59 per cent in Ukraine, 27 per cent in the Russian Federation, 37 per cent in Argentina and 35 per cent in Costa Rica. Even if in some cases the export values are relatively low, the average annual growth of computer services in these economies is well above the average of the top exporters. In the BPO sector, countries such as the Philippines, Malaysia and China in the Asian continent; Egypt and Morocco in North Africa; Brazil, Mexico, Chile and Columbia in Latin America; and Poland and Ireland in Europe are emerging as attractive destinations for voice contracts, posing a significant threat to Indian firms. According to NASSCOM, in the last five years, India has lost about 10 per cent market share to the rest of the world in the world BPO space, most of which is in the voice contract segment.

Though China faces challenges, such as language proficiency, the country is spending large amounts in mission mode to increase English proficiency, and thus may eventually emerge as a threat to India. Though the Philippines, the second largest destination for outsourcing, is currently facing the challenge of appreciating currency, it is a serious competitor having developed both the hardware and software segments of IT. Outsourcing has also become a national issue in several developed countries, like the USA and the UK, who are supporting the local BPO industry through various means. According to industry sources, the BPO industry in the UK employs 800,000 British workers and is emerging as a vital part of the economy.

In such a situation, the Indian BPO industry needs to gear up to address the challenges. Information campaigns to dispel the myths and fears about outsourcing needs to be undertaken by the industry in the developed economies. India should also move up the value chain in software services. Equally important is the need to focus on the large domestic sector where there is a huge opportunity which, if tapped could also lead to lower costs due to scale economies. To address the rising wages in the urban BPO space, there is a need to move more towards rural areas, for which skill development, and English language training with American and different European accents is necessary.

Source : Based on WTO Report and inputs of NASSCOM and EXIM Bank of India.

R&D Services

Among business services, R & D occupies the second position in India's GDP with growth being consistently high at near 20 per cent in the last few years with growth in 2011-12 at 20.5 per cent. Until recently, the competitive advantage in R&D was almost exclusively with the developed economies. Of late, emerging countries are increasingly involved in R&D and innovation, with active involvement of both public and private sectors. Factors such as low cost, access to new markets, availability of knowledge-oriented manpower, favourable regulatory environment, and fiscal benefits play a major role in driving R&D investments towards emerging economies. These countries are also encouraging innovation through legal, regulatory, and policy support.

The US $ 1.5 trillion global gross expenditure on R&D (GERD) for 2013 projected by Battelle and R&D magazine is expected to grow by more than US$ 50 billion over the previous year. In this enormous activity, India's share is 3 per cent with GERD in PPP (purchasing power parity) terms projected at US $ 45.2 billion which is around five times lower than that of China. As a percentage of GDP also it is low at 0.9 per cent. This is partly because the size of the R&D base and absorption capacity is not commensurate with requirements. The share of basic research in India's R&D is estimated to be 26 per cent, applied research 36 per cent, development research 32 per cent, and other research 6 per cent. Government funding of R&D accounts for two-thirds of the total funding. Industry contribution to R&D has been steadily increasing over the years but is still less than a third of the total. Government support for R&D in India tends to focus on classical objectives for public R&D funding such as nuclear energy, defence, space, health, and agriculture.

India is ranked 64th in the global innovation index (GII) in 2012 according to a joint report published by the Institut Européen d'Administration des Affaires i(INSEAD) and World Intellectual Property Organization (WIPO). Though India is ranked better in terms of market sophistication, knowledge and technology outputs, and creative outputs, the country has scored relatively poorly in terms of institutional support, human capital and research, infrastructure and business sophistication for innovation. According to the Global Competitiveness Report 2012-13, India's capacity for innovation has been lower than that of other BRICS countries except Russia. Though India scores better than China, Brazil, and Russia on the quality of scientific research institutions, the research undertaken in such institutions is not percolating down for commercial usage. This is exhibited through its poor score on university–industry collaboration on R&D as compared to other BRICS nations except Russia. Though India scores better than all BRICS nations on availability of scientists and engineers, as compared to the population, the country has one of the lowest ratios of scientists and engineers per million people. Part of this shortage is attributed to the lack of quality higher education institutions. However, even with large population base, India is estimated to have 25 per cent shortage of engineers in the country by 2025 (Table 7).

TABLE 7

Global Competitiveness Index : Innovation Capacity

Country	*Capacity for innovation*		*Quality of scientific research institutions*		*Company spending on R&D*		*University – Industry collaboration on R&D*		*Availability of scientists and engineers*		*PCT patents granted/ million population*	
	Score	*Rank*	*Score*	*Rank*	*Score*	*Rank*	*Score*	*Rank*	*Score*	*Rank*	*Score*	*Rank*
India	3.5	42	4.4	39	3.5	37	3.8	51	5.0	16	1.2	63
China	4.1	23	4.2	44	4.1	24	4.4	35	4.4	46	6.5	38

South Africa	3.5	41	4.6	34	3.5	39	4.5	30	3.4	122	6.8	37
Brazil	3.7	34	4.1	46	3.6	33	4.1	44	3.5	113	2.8	48
Russia	3.3	56	3.6	70	3.0	79	3.4	85	3.8	90	5.4	44
South Korea	4.5	19	4.9	24	4.9	11	4.7	25	4.9	23	16	1.1 9
UK	5.0	12	6.2	3	4.8	12	5.8	2	5.1	12	93.0	18
USA	5.2	7	5.8	6	5.3	7	5.6	3	5.4	5	137.9	12

Source: Global Competitiveness Report 2012-13, World Economic Forum.
Note: PCT—Patent Cooperation Treaty.

The government has stressed the need to enunciate a policy for synergizing science, technology, and innovation and has also established the National Innovation Council. A Science, Technology, and Innovation Policy 2013 has been announced in furtherance of these pronouncements. Increasing GERD to 2 per cent of GDP, from the present level of less than 1 per cent has been set as a national goal. India has declared 2010-20 as the 'decade of innovation'.

Legal Services

Legal services have been growing at a steady rate of 8.2 per cent in each of the years from 2005-6 to 2011-12. The Indian legal profession today consists of approximately 1.2 million registered advocates, around 950 law schools, and approximately 4 to 5 lakh law students across the country. Every year, approximately 60,000–70,000 law graduates join the legal profession in India. India is ranked 45, with a score of 4.5, in terms of judicial independence by the Global Competitiveness Report 2012-13, an improvement from 51st rank in 2011-12. As regards efficiency of the legal framework in settling disputes, India is ranked 59, with a score of 3.8, an improvement from 64th rank a year before. India is ranked at 52nd position when it comes to the efficiency of the legal framework in challenging regulations, with a score of 3.9, a marginal declined from 51st position in the previous year. Though India's rankings are better than most of the South Asian and some South East Asian countries in all the three parameters, there is a need for further improvement particularly in speeding up disposal of cases. The economic growth in India has inevitably led to complex laws and regulations and it is important that lawyers across India have access to the necessary tools to keep pace with the change.

The global financial crisis has not only increased recession-related litigations in developed countries but also encouraged legal outsourcing to cut down costs. India is regarded as one of the best legal process outsourcing (LPO) destinations in view of the low cost of legal professionals (50 per cent to 80 per cent more cost competitive than that of the USA and UK), geographical advantage (Indian time zone is distinct from that of the USA and Britain, allowing it to offer legal services round the clock), language proficiency (emphasis on English education), and the legal system (which is inspired by the legal systems of the USA and UK). Technologically too, the Indian LPO industry has made rapid strides as Indian service providers can make use of advanced means of communication technology. Indian legal service providers offer legal support in the form of research document reviews, drafting of documents, making applications for patents, and various paralegal and administrative tasks.

The National Legal Services Authority (NALSA) has been constituted under the Legal Services Authorities Act 1987 to monitor and evaluate implementation of legal aid programmes and to lay down policies and principles for making legal services available under the Act. Free legal services include payment of court fee, process fees and other charges incurred in legal proceedings, services of lawyers, obtaining and supply of certified copies of orders and other documents in legal proceedings and preparation of appeal, paper book, etc. During the period from 1 April 2012 to 31 October 2012, more than 7.82 lakh persons have benefited through legal aid services in the country. Of them, there were more than 23,000 persons belonging to the scheduled castes and about 20,000 persons from the scheduled tribes. More than 37,000 women and about 5900 children also benefited. During this period more than 54 thousand Lok Adalats have been organized and these Lok Adalats settled more than 17.30 lakh cases. A Para-Legal Volunteers (PLVs) project has been developed by NALSA for the purpose of imparting legal awareness to various target groups. As on 31 December 2012, 73,555 PLVs have been trained in the country and have started functioning, bridging the gap between common people and legal services institutions.

Accounting and Audit Services

Accounting, auditing, and book-keeping services are a part of 'business services'. Accounting services have been growing at around 6-7 per cent since 2005-6 with 7.1 per cent growth in 2011-12. The accounting profession in India is highly developed with the potential to play a greater role internationally. In the US $ 44.5 billion 'other business services' exports of India in 2010, the legal, accounting, management, and public relations services with a value US$ 8.6 billion had a share of 19.3 per cent. This is around five times less than the US exports of US $ 39.1 billion and three times less than China's exports of US$22.8 billion.

There are 53,197 active CA firms as of 27 December 2012. Indian accounting firms are increasingly getting integrated and are providing associated services such as management consultancy, corporate finance, and advisory services in addition to their core business of accounting, auditing, and tax services. Given the high potential for accounting and audit services both domestically and in exports through the outsourcing mode, there is need to revamp the professional development framework to expand the talent pool, deepen the expertise, and enhance the flow of high quality accountancy professionals. Tapping the outsourcing market of the US and other developing countries in niche areas like actuarial and accountancy services would depend on the availability of high-quality experts in tax, insurance, and pension laws of the US and other countries and encouraging setting up of back offices of foreign firms in India. Tie-ups of domestic firms with foreign firms can help gain expertise and markets which would otherwise not be individually available for small domestic accountancy firms. This would also need relaxation in some domestic regulations and obtaining due recognition to Indian qualifications through mutual recognition agreements (MRAs). As with legal services, FDI in accounting services will help improve the competitiveness of the Indian market, and link it better to global markets.

Communication Services

Telecom and Related Services

Telecom services is another sunrise sector in which India has made a mark with the second largest telephone network in the world, after only China. Teledensity, which is an important indicator of telecom penetration, increased from 18.22 per cent in March 2007 to 73.34 per cent as on 31 December 2012, with urban teledensity at 149.55 per cent and rural at 39.90 per cent.

Postal Services

Postal services, a traditional mode of communications all over the world, have also been a popular mode in India, especially rural India. Department of Posts has the largest postal network in the world with 1,54,822 post offices in the country as on 31March 2012. Of these, 1,39,086 are in rural areas and 15,736 in urban. In order to expand the network and further improve people's access to postal services, India Post is also adopting the franchisee model. It has so far opened 1,670 franchisee outlets in areas where it was not possible to open post offices. The Department of Posts has launched 'Project Arrow' as a quality improvement initiative to transform India Post into a vibrant and responsive organization.

With tough competition from courier services offered by the private sector, and emergence of alternate modes of communications such as telecom and information technology, the postal service is diversifying into new areas like e-commerce, B to C address/addresse verification, M to M money transfer, web-based money transfer, social security disbursement and some other social sector-related activities. Besides the already existing instant money order, the Department of Posts launched mobile money remittance services on 15 November 2012 in 18 selected post offices in each of four circles, viz. Kerala, Bihar, Delhi, and Punjab. The Department of Posts has also been given the responsibility of disbursing wages to Mahatma Gandhi National Rural Employment Guarantee Scheme (MGNREGS) beneficiaries through post office savings bank accounts. At present, MGNREGS wages are disbursed through 5.55 crore NREGS accounts in 96,895 post offices. During the current financial year (April-November 2012) wages to the tune of ₹ 9,812 crore have been disbursed. Post offices also have a significant role in disbursement of benefits under various schemes such as pensions and conditional cash transfers to women. The wide reach of post offices is also being utilized for collection of data to compute the rural consumer price index every month in rural areas. While the postal sector is entering into new areas of activity, it has not only to shed its role in some of the traditional activities and areas, but also trim its size and release the resources both physical and human for use in other areas.

BOX 4

An Indicative List of Domestic Restrictions and Regulations in Some Services in India

One major issue in services is the domestic barriers and regulations. Domestic regulations in strict WTO terms include licensing requirements, licensing procedures, qualification requirements, qualification procedures, and technical standards but here other restrictions and barriers are also considered. While there are many domestic regulations in major markets which deny market access to us and therefore need to be negotiated at multilateral and bilateral levels, there are also many domestic regulations in India which hinder the growth of this sector. Since domestic regulations perform the role of tariffs in regulating services, there is need to list the domestic regulations in India which need to be curbed to help growth of the sector and its exports, while retaining those which are necessary for regulating the sector at this stage. An indicative list of some important domestic regulations in India which need to be examined for suitable policy reforms in the services sector is as follows:

Trade and Transport services: Some constraints in these sectors include restrictions on inter-state movement of goods which could ease with the adoption of the model Agriculture Produce and Marketing Committee (APMC) Act by many states; the Multimodal Transportation of Goods Act 1993 which needs revision to ease the existing restrictions on transportation and documentation through different modes of transport, particularly restrictions in the Customs Act which do not allow seamless movement of goods; and restrictions on free movement of cargo between Inland Container Depots (ICDs), Container Freight Stations (CFSs) and Ports.

Construction: In construction, bottlenecks result from continuation of restrictions under the Urban Land Ceiling and Regulation Act (ULCRA) in some states namely Andhra Pradesh, Assam, Bihar, and West Bengal which have not yet repealed it and the confusion in the process required for clearance of buildings even after the repeal of ULCRA by passing of the Urban Land(Ceiling and Regulations) Repeal Act 1999 by the other states. There is also lack of clarity on the role of states as facilitators in the land acquisition policy resulting in increasing number of court litigations adding to risk profile of builders/projects thereby restricting lenders from extending finance to such builders/ projects. There are also restrictions on floor area ratio (FAR) in many states; and other restrictions like the application of bye laws/regulations and its exemptions e.g. increase in FAR which varies from project to project and is sometimes discriminatory. Obtaining environment clearance is another major hindrance.

Accountancy services: While the accountancy professionals were hitherto allowed to operate either as a partnership firm or as a sole proprietorship firm or in their own name since the Indian regulations do not permit exceeding 20 professionals under one firm, the emergence of Limited Liability Partnership (LLP) structure is likely to address this impediment. However, the number of statutory audits of companies per partner is restricted to 20. FDI is also not allowed in this sector and foreign service providers are not allowed to undertake statutory audit of companies as per the provisions of the laws in India. There are also domestic regulations like prohibition on the use of individual logos for partnership and single proprietorship accounting firms. These regulations need to be relaxed and streamlined to facilitate tie-ups and penetrate foreign markets given the potential for exporting these services by the outsourcing mode.

Legal services: In legal services FDI is not permitted and international law firms are not authorized to advertise and open offices in India. Foreign service providers can neither be appointed as partners nor sign legal documents and represent clients. The Bar Council is opposed to entry of foreign lawyers/law firms in any manner. Indian advocates are not permitted to enter into profit-sharing arrangements with persons other than Indian advocates.

Education Services: These come under the concurrent list with multiple controls and regulations by central and state governments and statutory bodies. Regulations of minimum of 25 acres of land to establish a medical college restricts the setting up of medical colleges in cities like Delhi. Patient load factor regulations related to establishment of new medical colleges also need to be in tune with present day equipment-intensive patient care and modern practices and procedures of medical education.

Source: Based on Dr H.A.C. Prasad and R. Sathish (2010), working paper No. 1/2010-DEA on 'Policy for India's Services Sector' with updates from concerned Departments and Institutions.

Moving forward in the coming years, the immediate challenge for the services sector covering myriad activities and areas is growth revival. India's growth has been basically a services led growth pulling up overall growth of the economy. While this could be through a business-as-usual approach, a more targeted approach with focus on big-ticket services could lead to exponential gains for the economy. While software and telecom services have led by example, there are some other important services like tourism including medical tourism and shipping and logistics. Tourism is a bigticket item which can not only lead to higher growth but also more inclusive growth. With world tourist arrivals expected to increase by 43 million every year on an average from 2010 to 2030 and FTAs in emerging countries expected to grow faster than in advanced economies, a goldmine of opportunity in tourism is waiting for India which at present has a paltry share of 0.64 per cent in world tourist arrivals. India has an assorted list of destinations having different types of weather and catering to different types of tourists. However, an image change for Indian tourism is needed with higher investment in tourism infrastructure including through PPP mode. Even user charges could be levied if monuments or tourist sites are developed by the private sector or through PPP. There is urgent need to address issues like high luxury taxes on hotels by states and ensure greater cleanliness and safety for tourists which can help in giving a big boost to this sector. Refunding VAT as done in countries like Thailand and Singapore can also help the tourism sector with ripple effects on sectors like textiles and leather manufacturing, as it can lead to high purchase of these items in which India is price competitive. Shipping services is another major area where the growth impact can be high. With the share of shipping services in India's overseas cargo falling from 40 per cent in the 1980s to just 10.4 per cent in 2011-12, measures to augment the ageing shipping fleet of India are necessary. With global prices at an all-time low, the time is opportune for such purchases which can help in greater foreign exchange earnings/ savings in the future through shipping services which have forward linkage effect even in the export sector and also increase our bargaining power with the foreign liners. Super specialty healthcare is another potential sector with India being one of the cheapest destinations offering quality services.

The other major challenge is to retain and expand our competitive advantage in those services where we have already made a mark. The present advantage in services may not continue forever, with new competitors from other developing countries making rapid strides even in areas where we had the initial advantage as in the case of software services. Further expansion of established services like software and telecom into new markets and greater usage of these services domestically can not only increase services growth but also propel growth in other sectors with greater efficiency in these sectors using knowledge- and technology-based services.

Removing or easing domestic regulations is the third challenge. While removal of market barriers in the form of domestic regulations in other countries depends on multilateral and bilateral negotiations, the myriad restrictions and regulations in the different services domestically need immediate attention. Removing or easing them can lead to dynamic gains for the Indian economy.

The services sector is an uncharted sea throwing up many daunting challenges as well as opening up many exciting opportunities. While many hitherto non-tradable services including those in the government and social sectors are becoming domestically tradable, many services hitherto confined within national borders (like telemedicine) have become internationally tradable. Addressing the challenges of the diverse services sectors and seizing the new opportunities can lead to multiple gains for the services sector and the economy.

QUESTIONS

1. Discuss the salient features of invisibles in India's balance of payments.
2. Critically examine the recent changes in the magnitude and trends in invisibles in India's balance of payments.
3. Discuss the various definitional aspects of components of invisibles under the balance of payments standard presentation.
4. Discuss the increase in the share and growth of India's services in exports and imports in recent times.
5. Explain the performance of some major services in different sectors.

REFERENCES

Apostolos Gkoutzinis (2005), "International Trade in Banking Services and the Role of the WTO: Discussing the Legal Framework and Policy Objectives of the General Agreement on Trade in Services and the Current State of Play in the Doha Round of Trade Negotiations" International Lawyer, Volume 39, No. 4.

International Monetary Fund (1993), 'Manual on Balance of Payments Statistics', 5th edition.

Chami, R., A. Barajas, T. Cosimano, C. Fullenkamp, M. Gapen and P. Montiel (2008), 'Macroeconomic Consequences of Remittances', IMF Occasional Paper No. 259.

Reserve Bank of India (2007), 'Report of the Technical Group on Statistics for International Trade in Banking Services'.

United Nations (2002), 'Manual on Statistics of International Trade in Services'.

World Bank (2007), 'Global Development Finance – The Globalisation of Corporate Finance in Developing Countries'.

Unit III

10

STRATEGIC ISSUES IN INTERNATIONAL MANAGEMENT

INTRODUCTION

The world is changing so fast that many companies find it difficult to keep up. Global competition is the name of the game. Firms must formulate, successfully implement, and control global strategies in order to survive and prosper in the future. The global company is becoming the most viable force in world trade and international relations. The strategic aspects of managing multinational corporations is the focus of this chapter. Hence, our approaches in this chapter is to view the strategic analysis process and international strategy issues as orthogonal to each other. We first review the strategic analysis process, then identify issues of international strategy, and examine these issues in developing a strategy and a structure to operate in the global market. The chapter also covers an integrated strategy of MNCs and the approach of such companies in dealing with the restriction and guidelines put forth by host nations.

INTERNATIONAL STRATEGIC MANAGEMENT: ANALYTICAL FRAMEWORK

Strategic management can be defined as the process of assessing a corporation and its environment in terms of meeting the long-term objectives of the firm, so that it can conform to its environment and take advantage of the opportunities in the market to be best of its ability. Next, the term *international* must be defined in order to fully understand the phenomenon of international strategic management. International may be defined as activities that involve two or more countries. Thus, the concept *international strategic management* can be defined as the effect and interaction of strategic management between two or more nations.

The major aspects of strategy analysis include: setting goals and objectives, performing competitive and industry analysis, analysing resources and capabilities, developing strategic options, choosing a strategy, and implementing that strategy, with feedback loops among all the processes. Figure-1 shows this in simplified model.

International business involves a specific set of issues whose strategic resolution ties into the generic strategic analysis framework in Figure-1. These international

FIGURE-1

THE STRATEGIC ANALYSIS PROCESS

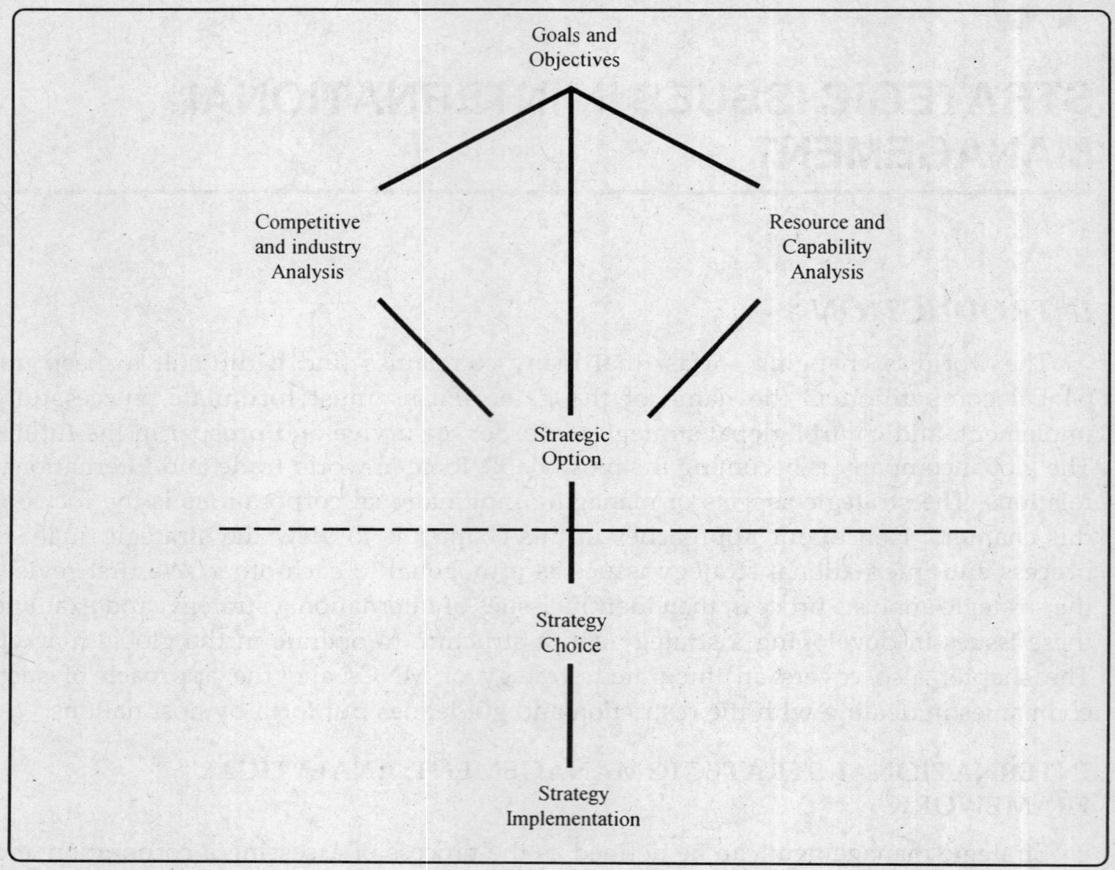

strategy issues are presented in Figure-2 and involve (1) increasing geographic spread (often referred to as 'internationalisation'), (2) achieving local adaptation (often referred to as 'responsiveness'), (3) building global integration (sometimes referred to as) 'globalisation' or 'global strategy'), and (4) multi-business, multi-country and often multi-firm issues such as international strategic alliances and global merger and acquisitions.

In general, the more basic issues in international strategy requires more use of the more basic issues in strategy analysis, as illustrated in Figure-3, although that last international issues of multi-business/multi-firm/multinational moves tends to require heavy emphasis on all five strategic analysis processes. We see heavy reliance on goal

FIGURE-2

INTERNATIONAL STRATEGY ISSUES

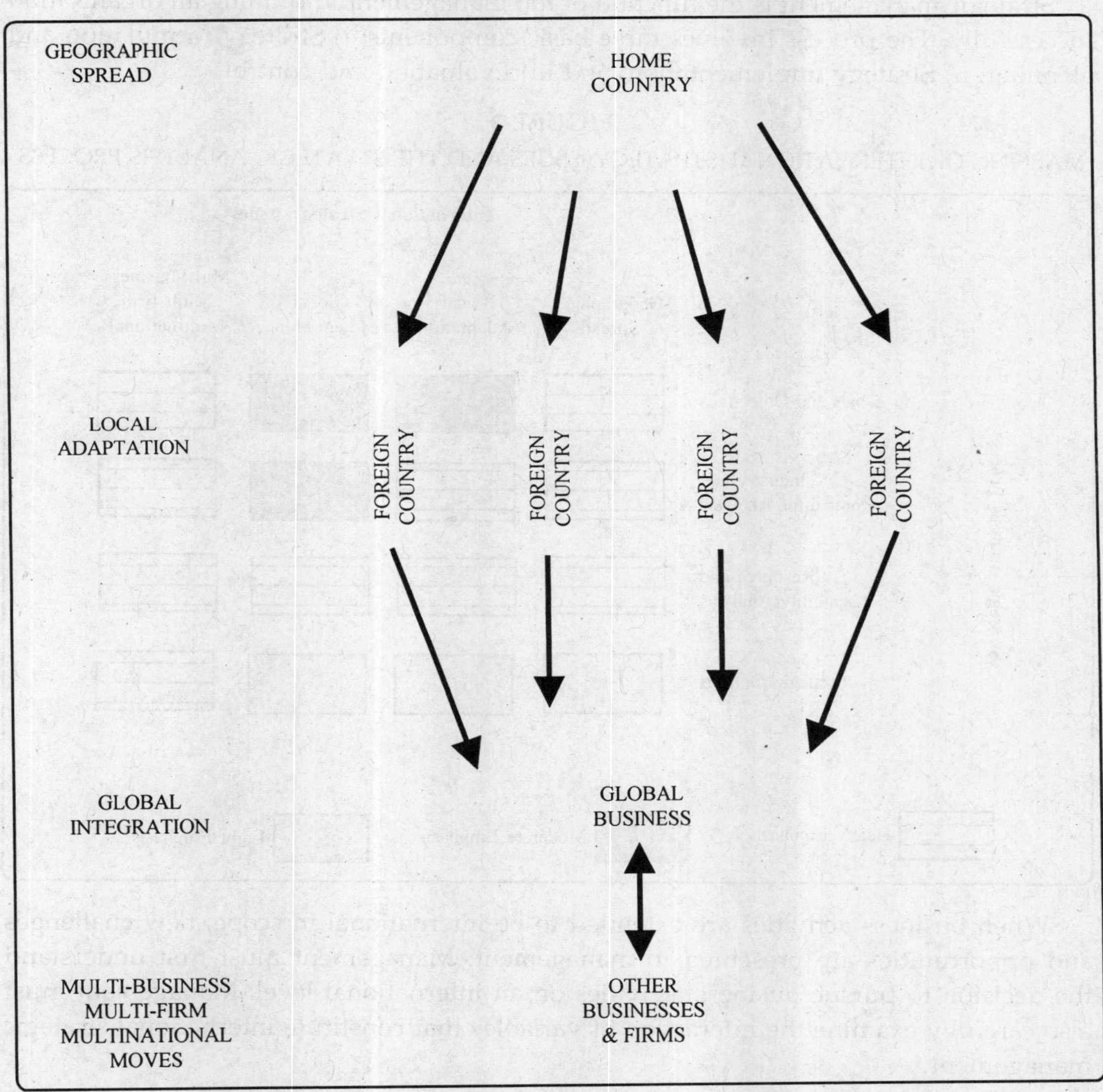

setting, industry analysis, and resource assessment as firm expand internationally. Adaptation and integration are driven largely by issues developed through competitive analysis and resource assessment, while integration must also consider issues revealed by different means of assessing strategic conditions and opportunities.

THE STRATEGIC MANAGEMENT PROCESS

Strategic management is the function of top management in running an organisation successfully. The process involves three basic components: i) Strategy formulation and planning; ii) Strategy implementation; and iii) Evaluation and control.

FIGURE-3

MAPPING OF INTERNATIONAL STRATEGY ISSUES AND THE STRATEGIC ANALYSIS PROCESS

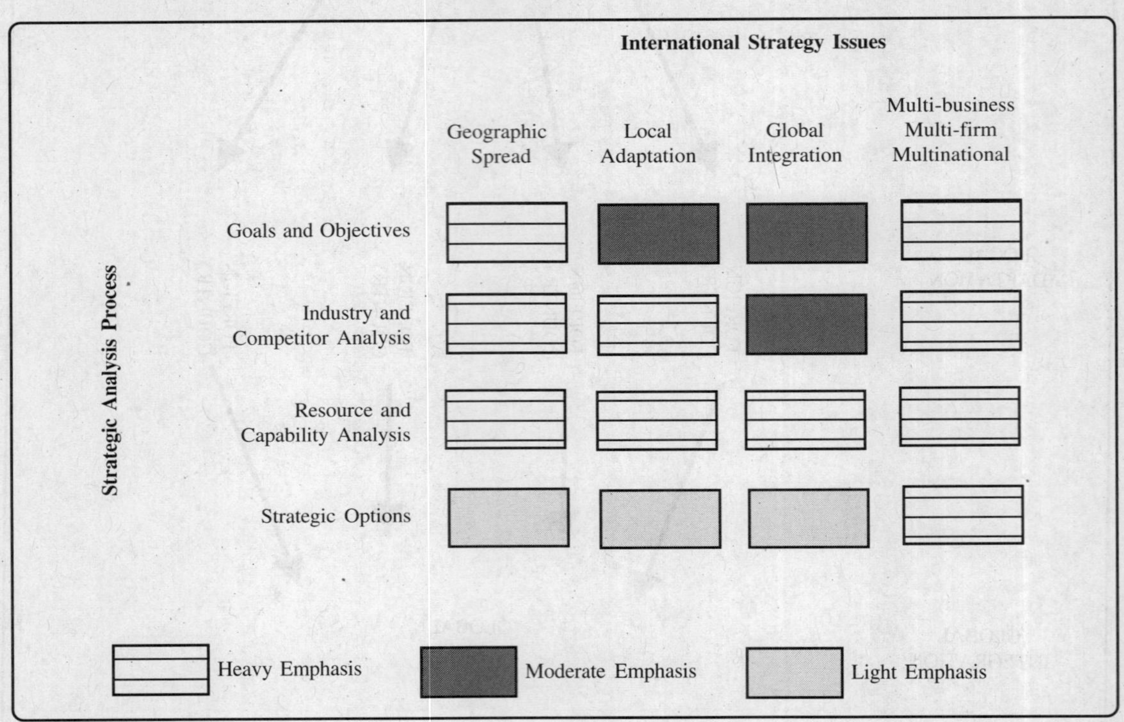

When business activities are extended to be international in scope, new challenges and opportunities are presented to management. Management must first understand the decision to pursue business activities on an international level. Management must also carefully examine the interaction of variables that constitute international strategic management.

Two objectives motivate an organisation to extend its operations to other countries:

1. **Profit:** To take advantage of increasing demand for goods and services in foreign countries.
2. **Stability:** New sources of demand which become evident in other countries may have a positive effect on an organisation's production process.

The following variables are attributed to international strategic management and the various interactions that it encompasses: culture, environment, and government. Each of these variables interacts with the others to create complex situations that must be considered if an organisation's activities are to be managed effectively. Some of the issues that must be addressed before executing strategic management in an international sense are as follow:

Tariffs

Tariffs are government-imposed taxes that are charged on either imported or exported goods. They are imposed as a means of raising revenue or protecting a country's producers from the competition of imported goods.

Payment for International Transactions

International business activity requires the exchange of currencies between countries. Problems may arise relative to foreign exchange rates, as they tend to fluctuate in value.

Government Control Over Profits

Businesses that own facilities in foreign countries would naturally expect to receive profits from their operations. Problems may arise when host country governments regulate foreign access to local currencies, thus, in effect, controlling the amount of profit that parent companies actually receive.

Taxation

Businesses conducting operations in foreign countries are subject to the laws and regulations of those countries. Local taxes may be very high due to the lack of other sources of revenue, thus shifting the tax burden to multinational corporations.

Culture

Different cultures are brought together through international business activity. Complex problems may arise as the result of language barriers and differences in cultural values, tastes, and attitudes.

Each of these issues and their associated variables must be carefully considered in order to ensure effective international strategic management.

STRATEGIC PLANNING *VERSUS* LONG-RANGE PLANNING

In a sense, all strategic planning involves long-range planning, but not all long-range planning involves strategic thinking. In defining strategic planning, it is important to recognise that there is a difference between strategic planning and long-range planning. Long-range planning fails to recognise the changing environment and simply extends present trends into the future. Strategic planning, on the other hand, addresses the wants and needs of an organisation; in other words, it considers a firm's mission. (A mission statement defines a firm's reason for being.) This approach enables a firm to identify its strengths and weaknesses and helps determine what to do in order to get the job done.

Strategic planning provides direction and clarity and identifies where a firm should be three to five years down the road. Strategic planning is not about mechanical data analysis, predictions, and economic forecasts; it is a way of thinking and structuring business ideas—like a game of chess.

The problem with long-range planning is that it is not a way of thinking, but rather a way of formulating a plan to organise, realise, or achieve something, without considering the changing environment. The typical socialist five-year plan is a good example of long-range planning, and it proves the dangers of ignoring economic and political changes.

Strategic planning is often viewed as a team effort in which management responds to complex environmental changes and makes preeminent decisions in times of swift change. In strategic planning, management should answer three strategic questions: *(1) What business to we want to be in? (2) What future direction will we take for development and growth? (3) What is the overall relationship between the external environment in terms of geographic boundaries, target markets, competition, and product offerings and the financial results we seek to achieve?*

MULTINATIONAL FIRMS AND THE ENVIRONMENT

The importance of strategic management in a multinational firm cannot be over-emphasised. The fall of the Berlin Wall (which was followed by reduced tariffs for developing, nonindustrial nations) and improvements in transportation technology are two examples of recent developments that have caused decision makers in multinational corporations to review their procedures for identifying opt mal investment sites abroad. Companies looking to expand into these economic areas face several issues.

One consideration is which market to penetrate. For example, a company needs to understand the restrictions to trade in various regions (i.e., tariffs, quotas, etc.). A community is larger than just one country; it may consist of a group of countries that have aligned themselves for efficiency. These communities are constantly changing, and companies must stay well informed to ensure the competitive advantage of international expansion. Multinational prospects must also consider the long-range implications of international business, one of which is the relationship between the member states of the regional blocs.

The foreign exchange rate can present problems in international markets. Fluctuations in the exchange rate affect the foreign cost structure of products within three to six months. Although this may present gains as well as losses, a company must ask itself if its competencies lie in manipulating different currency positions or are based on certain skills and transferable assets. The foreign exchange rate can have a significant impact on where an organisation will expand.

Multinational expansion provides companies entry to certain regions of the world which have a distinct advantage in terms of tax and wage differentials. Management must exercise careful judgment in evaluating the different types and amounts of incentives. Incentives to companies locating in specific areas take a variety of forms, such as programmes for training and housing.

Companies that seek new markets in foreign countries must do an environmental analysis, both internal and external. The most common environments that organisations evaluate are the economic, technological, societal, political, and ecological. The economic environment is the most critical and also the most difficult to analyse because it deals with the national economic scene. A number of economic trends are of particular interest to businesses, including the stability of the currency the projected growth in the gross national product, the expected growth in the consumer price index, and changes in the tax structure.

In many cases, the technological environment may be the deciding factor in expansion. The success of a business can depend on its ability to stay on the cutting edge of technology. Several technological trends that may interest a firm are microcircuits, solar heating and other alternative energy sources, and metal alloys.

The political environment, which includes regulations, is an extremely critical variable in the long-term efficiency and success of a firm. Firms in regulated industries need to pay special attention to environmental trends in order to be able to predict future courses of action. Significant issues in the political environment include corporate taxes, retirement age, public interest groups, and government permits.

Finally, the ecological environment must be recognised. This area has come under severe scrutiny as people seek to make the earth a safer place. Today, firms must carefully plan projects so as not to have an adverse impact on the environment. Issues in the ecological environment that are of broad interest include clean water requirements, emission standards, bans on certain types of businesses, and noise and air pollution requirements.

STRATEGIC PLANNING

Management sets the course for an organisation through the formulation of organisational plans. Organisations are attempting to respond to the growing need to anticipate changes in the environment—both internal and external—through organisational planning. Although this type of effective planning has dominated outstanding organisational performance, the complexity of change has increased so dramatically that additional planning has become fundamentally important.

A strategy is the "big picture" in terms of what a firm is capable of doing. A strategic plan is made up of a strategy and the time-related details for carrying out that strategy. It should include: i) Marketing mix (the target market); ii) Drain on company resources; iii) Anticipated sales and profits; and iv) Control procedures to ensure that the plan is following its intended course

Strategic planning does not take place in a vacuum. The plan is used by marketing, accounting, production, human resources, and all the other specialists. A strategic plan lets everybody in the firm know what they are trying to accomplish and it gives direction to the whole business effort. Effective strategic planning requires that all aspects of the plan are carried out efficiently at all levels of operation. Every departmental decision is capable of casting a shadow on the final outcome of the strategic plan; therefore, all levels of operation must carry out their assignments completely.

Planning has been defined as drawing from the past to decide in the present what to do in the future. When a company implements strategic planning, it must first analyse its present situation and then formulate and implement those strategies that will be most beneficial in the long run. Extreme care and precision are required to match resources with market opportunities over the long term. Strategic planning differs from day-to-day operational planning in that it is very long term in purpose and direction. Because a company's very existence may rest on the outcome of the strategic plan, it is considered to be an extremely intense and important aspect of company development.

Solid commitment to the strategic plan and its anticipated outcome must be built from the top level of management all the way down through the operational levels. Unlike operational day-to-day planning, where one change after another may be implemented to facilitate an outcome, the final outcome of a strategic plan may take years to realise. Without proper guidelines (policies), a strategic plan may not have the flexibility to achieve its final outcome, which is why it is critical to select a plan that has been well thought out and focuses on the very best interest of the company. Everyone in a company will feel the consequences of a poorly constructed strategic plan. *An operational plan ensures the smooth flow of work on a day-do-day basis; in contrast, a strategic plan indicates a company's present position as well as what its position is destined to be in the future.*

The Basic Stages of Strategic Planning

Step 1: Assess Corporate Strategy

This process requires a firm to assess its own position relative to its environment. In doing so, an organisation must include a SWOT (strengths, weaknesses, opportunities, or threats) analysis to determine its strengths and weaknesses. After analysing its strengths and weaknesses, an organisation must evaluate its potential and identify where the opportunities and threats lie in the external environment. Strategic analysis allows an organisation to define its range of strategic alternatives and choose the one most appropriate for its present external environment.

Step 2: Strategy Formulation

In the process of strategy formulation, an organisation first creates and set of realistic and comprehensive goals and objectives. An appropriate strategy is then selected based on the result that the organisation wants to accomplish. Strategy formulation allows an organisation to identify the strategy that can best meet its realistic goals.

Step 3: Strategy Implementation

This is the most important step in strategic planning. A plan that is formulated perfectly but implemented incorrectly will not produce the desired result. The implementation strategy must have an operational plan that can organise and move resources when they are needed. To do this effectively, such variables as culture, personnel, and the structure and design of the organisation must be assessed.

Many companies find the consequences of not planning adequately and then not implementing correctly extremely hazardous. With the arrival of the computer age, the external and internal environments at most companies are constantly changing. Technology is constantly improving, government regulations are constantly changing, and management policies and personnel are constantly being replaced. This view is even more apparent in the world market. Those who cannot plan in a multicultural mode will lose market share in the global economy. Those who cannot adapt to new technology, changes in foreign policy, and cultural differences will be dropped from the world market as others who plan and implement better strategies take their place. Lack of planning in the global market can mean loss of profits or even failure to survive.

Types of Strategies Used in Strategic Planning

In order to be successful in the international market, a firm must be astute, because the environment changes rather quickly. The real key to being astute in this global situation is to have good strategic planning tools and the ability to use them. In order for a firm to be successful in an international market, it must know when to use certain strategies and when to make adjustments to them to gain an advantage over the competition. There are two basic strategy typologies used by organisations. The first is tied to the scope of an organisation (either global or national) and its market share objectives (high or low). The second typology is seen as a continuum and is made up of the home market mode, the multidomestic mode, and the global mode. In order to be successful, a firm must choose the appropriate strategy in terms of its objectives and implement it effectively.

The first typology of strategy includes four basic strategic orientations. The first is the *global high share strategy*. In this strategy, firms that operate in world markets and want high market shares use pricing, promotions, and products that are popular in world markets. Very large corporations that compete in international markets usually use this type of strategy. IBM is a good example; it expands into new areas, keeps prices competitive, and advertises aggressively. The second type of strategy is the *global niche strategy*, which is used by organisations that operate in world markets but wants to achieve only a low market share. Small firms competing in global markets use this strategy to gain a small market share by trying to pursue a speciality. The third strategy is the *national high share strategy*, which is used by companies that want high volume and low cost in a competitive national market. Firms that use this strategy do not have to pay the tariffs and quotas that global firms do. Therefore, they can also take advantage of government subsidies and tax breaks. The fourth strategy is the *national niche strategy*. Firms that use this type of strategy specialise in national markets where there are few competitors. They survive on the hope that large international corporations will find these markets unattractive and choose not to pursue them.

The second typology is made up of three modes: the home market oriented mode, the multidomestic mode, and the global mode. Firms, that are just entering the global marketplace use the *home market oriented mode*. Basically, they produce goods overseas for export to their original environment. They do so in order to lower production costs and still produce goods geared toward the home market. Firms in the *multidomestic mode* choose to compete in several different foreign markets. They develop specific strategies to fit markets in specific countries. They do not try to take products or services that fit the market in one country to another country. Firms that use this type of strategy usually compete globally. Firms in the *global market mode* pursue an integrated strategy in major world markets. There are no national boundaries to determine where their products can be sold. They compete in the world market.

A UNIFIED MODEL FOR INTERNATIONAL PURPOSES

Countries differ socially, economically, technically, and politically. In order to be successful in the international business environment, it is essential that these differences be recognised and taken into consideration in managing international activities. Several basic questions should be asked when considering opportunities in foreign markets: *Should we go international? In what parts of the world should we look for such opportunities? How soon should we begin our venture in the international market? What are the best means to exploit these opportunities?* In deciding whether to enter foreign markets, management should:

1. Evaluate the opportunities for the firm's products and services in foreign markets, as well as the potential threats, problems, and risks associated with such opportunities.
2. Evaluate the strengths and weaknesses of the firm's managerial, material, technical,

and operational (finance, marketing, etc.) capabilities to determine whether the necessary resources are available to successfully exploit potential opportunities in foreign markets.

Two basic steps are used in developing a model for international strategy: an environmental analysis and an internal resources audit. The general focus of the **environmental analysis** is on the discovery and evaluation of business opportunities and threats and the associated problems and risks. In an international sense, three different levels of environmental analysis should be considered: (1) multinational, (2) regional, and (3) country. Multinational environmental analysis consists of broadly identifying, forecasting, and monitoring critical factors in the world environment. It involves the study of global technological developments, various trends in government intervention, and changes in overall values and lifestyles. These items are evaluated in terms of their degree of impact, both now and in the future. Regional environmental analysis focuses on a more detailed study of the critical factors within a definite geographic area (e.g., Western Europe, the Middle East). This level is directed toward identifying marketing opportunities for a company's products, services, and/or technology in a specific region. The third level, country environmental analysis, involves an even more refined examination of the critical environmental factors. This level continues to focus on the economic, legal, political, and cultural factors in an even smaller number or refined group of countries. This analysis, however, must be oriented toward the specific strategy to enter each individual market in order ensure successful planning.

The second step which aids in the development of an international strategy is the *internal resources audit*. The primary purpose of this audit is to appropriately match a company's managerial, technical, material, and financial resources with those required for successful operation. This audit is related to the business rather than the environment. It focuses on key business success factors, which are simply defined as the key factors essential for success in a particular business. This audit is also considered to be country related in that the amount of resources required will vary relative to the country involved.

Hence, formulating a unified model for international purposes must include:

i) Evaluating international opportunities, threats, problems, and risks;
ii) Evaluating a firm's strengths and weaknesses in order to exploit opportunities in foreign markets;
iii) Defining a firm's scope relative to international business involvement;
iv) Formulating a firm's international corporate objectives; and,
v) Developing specific corporate strategies for a firm as a whole—an international corporate strategy.

STRATEGIES AT STRATEGIC BUSINESS UNITS

The factors that affect strategy at the strategic business unit (SBU) level are significantly modified in multinational operations. All of the factors involved in the marketing mix are affected in some way by the international environment, competition, institutions, and the legal systems. The product itself is very important. Design, packaging, and special needs to accommodate certain sizes and dimensions for consumers in different countries are very important. Promotion is also governed by local practices. Price is frequently determined by cultural customs that influence the amount of money that should be spent on a product. Distribution is affected by, among other things, availability of roads and other transportation channels. A firm must consider all of these factors in order to be successful.

Financial strategies should address currency exchange rates. Fluctuations in exchange rates can cause many problems in terms of profits. Production strategies must cope with the logistical problems that accompany inadequate transportation systems, a dearth of suppliers, and a largely unskilled work force. Personnel strategies should consider laws and customs in regulating work and authority.

The specifics of management functions vary among countries. Managers have different expectations in terms of motivation and leadership style. Different countries have different management hierarchies, motivational techniques, and long-range planning priorities. Control strategies are very important to multinational firms, as are functional strategies, such as communication habits and decision-making skills. If a multinational organisation is to survive and prosper, it must be able to adapt.

One of the most important factors that affects MNCs is the host country's culture. People in different parts of the world have different beliefs. Language is also an important consideration. The same word can take on a different meaning in a different culture. Before a company plans to integrate into another country, extensive research must be done on the area's culture. An important cultural factor that affects management is how competition is viewed. This can influence motivation, leadership style, the compensation system, and the type of people hired.

An additional factor in the success of MNCs is the use of comparative management, which is defined as the analysis of cross-cultural management practices and techniques. Many international managers fail because they are unfamiliar with patterns in the local culture. The American way of doing things is not always the proper way in other cultures. Combining cultures in managerial decisions promotes understanding. To work effectively in a foreign country, a manager must understand the culture of the host country. For example, AT&T representatives at the company's first privately held exhibit in Tokyo were well prepared. In addition to language skills, they had also acquired information about the shared knowledge, beliefs, and values of potential Japanese customers, as well as their ways of interacting and conducting business.

A corporation should also consider local attitudes and beliefs in terms of time value, punctuality or promptness, achievement, work, and change. These factors have a major influence on the business functions of a MNC and may require adaptation.

Sociocultural components include religion, folklore, music, and art. Advertising a product in a commercial with music in the background may not be appropriate in certain cultures. Americans may enjoy the music, but other cultures may find it distasteful or even sacrilegious.

Material culture involves technology and how a product will interact in a specific culture. For example, what if all Ford automobiles sold in India had the steering wheel on the left side? They would be unsuccessful because most Indians drive on the right side of the vehicle. This would be both a cultural and a technological error.

Education plays a major role in the success of a MNC. A company can both improve product quality and achieve its goals by sharing technology and information. Implementing this idea in a multicultural research and development programme can improve a company's product line. When a product that is successful in the United States needs to be adjusted to suit a new region, both cultures can work together to create a suitable product. Participants in a multinational venture need to sit down and communicate their differences. For example, exchanging gifts is customary in some countries, whereas in the United States it is seen as bribery. Differences in language must also be addressed. These differences should be discussed before a programme begins.

There are so many differences between cultures that it is impossible to cover them all at once. The point is that in order *to* be successful, a manager of a MNC should be sensitive to and aware of these differences. A manager will gain the respect of his or her employees by trying to understand what they stand for and what their beliefs are, and the same is true for the employees. By understanding the differences in other cultures, a MNC fosters better employee relations, which in turn affects output and the operation in general in a foreign region. Many companies have failed in the past due to a lack of knowledge about other cultures. It is important for a MNC to gain an advantage over its competitors, and one way to do so is by understanding the culture of its host country.

While learning about a host country's culture, it is also important to build excellent communication channels. In the international market, a complex pattern of communication is often created by the combination of diversity of activities, spread of operations, pressures of environment and competition, and individual characteristics of the panics involved.

All top-level managers in an integrated multinational business need channels for communication and information. These channels are important in keeping subsidiary managers from developing self-serving arguments against integration. All the branches of a MNC should be focused on the same goals. Communication channels have a strong influence on the overall integrated strategy. A functional channel provides feedback on market performance of existing products, requests for new products and review of development projects. Functional channels are limited when communication on a key competitive issue is misinterpreted, which is usually due to a lack of knowledge about the host country.

Global strategic decisions affect the entire company. Managers value input from subsidiaries and work back and forth with top executives in decision making. This type of dialogue requires open lines of communication, even at lower levels. It also means that a company must learn to trust and respect the decisions of lower level managers.

Two-way communication can sometimes result in heated debates. As people split into factions, they begin to distrust one another. Moreover, when subsidiary managers participate in global strategic decision making, they come to view the decisions as their own. This leads to debate over who is right, as people defend their decisions. When information and ideas are exchanged freely, global strategic decision making can be both informative and productive. It allows managers at all levels to express their opinions and hear the opinions of others. When managers feel that their views are taken into consideration, they are likely to be satisfied with the strategic decisions made.

The communication channel that involves interface with senior management can be formal or informal. It includes programme plans and possible environmental strategies. These plans involve a specific purpose and are aimed at a specific area in need of improvement. The programme discussed well in advance and involves a specific purpose. An environmental strategy is a response to important conditions or issues in the natural environment, such as worker code-termination. Here, a subsidiary manager brings the problem to the attention of corporate management at headquarters, although sometimes it is better for a subsidiary to act autonomously and depart from corporate patterns.

When top management cannot resolve or deal directly with an issue that affects an operation in the integrated network, the corporate managing committee has the final decision in the issue resolution process. For example, a subsidiary that feels that its budget is insufficient can approach the corporate managing committee with a request to have it increased. Some integrated companies assign key senior executives as local advocates. They represent key subsidiary or regional interests at corporate headquarters in order to facilitate communication. *A strong global market requires strong localism.* The integrated strategies for communication must be brought to the attention of the performance of the strategic business units. Thus, a balance must be struck between decision making and communication.

LAWS AND REGULATIONS

One of the most difficult and complicated areas that affects a MNC is the different laws and regulations involved in international trade. Special attention should he given to researching the legal systems of the countries in which a MNC operates. In the world of business, the legal environment is based on the following laws: i) **Islamic law:** Derived from interpretation of the *Qur'an* and the teachings of the Prophet Mohammed; ii) **Socialist law:** Derived from the Marxist socialist system; iii) **Common law;** Derived from English law; and iv) **Civil or code law:** Derived from Roman law.

Procedural justice is defined as the extent to which the dynamics of a multinational's strategic decision-making process for its subsidiary units is judged to be fair by subsidiary top management. This term can be broken down into five parts: (i) There is a need for two-way communication in every interaction. (ii) Lower level managers and workers have the right and responsibility to challenge their managers. (iii) The head office must acknowledge and he aware of the local situation at subsidiaries. (iv) When a final strategic decision is made by top management, it is relayed down through the chain of command; and (v) The head office is consistent in its decision making as it affects subsidiaries. This allows management to judge strategic decision making across subsidiary units to be just.

The more subsidiaries a corporation has in different countries, the more regulated that company will become. Domestic laws, host country laws, and international laws all must be considered. A MNC based in the United States can suffer extreme levels of taxation. The higher the income, the higher the income tax. Double taxation takes place by taxing the stockholders and investors. In addition, a subsidiary can be taxed by its host country, which puts it in the position of triple taxation. There is also capital gains tax, which is paid on the sale of an asset at a greater amount of cost. Many countries that host MNCs have a tax treaty. The countries involved sign a treaty in which each country outlines its tax laws and programmes.

Tariffs and quotas ate another national legal force. Tariffs raise funds and at the same time protect the wen-being of a country's free enterprise system. Quotas are enacted to protect domestic producers.

Another important factor that a company should consider before going multinational is the right to keep property in the event of a crisis. A legal option that is open to certain countries is the right to seize foreign-owned property within national borders. This is known as expropriation or confiscation, and it is legal as long as a country has defined it by law.

There are three classifications of international legal forces: (1) contract enforcement; (2) solutions to jurisdiction, interpretation, and enforcement problems; and (3) patents, trademarks, and trade secrets. It is usually difficult to solve a multinational problem that involves a contract, because contracts are usually handled through goodwill. Sometimes, however, arbitration can be effective. Trademarks protect against counterfeiting. They are usually good for 10 to 15 years, but the specifics vary from county to country and can affect a company's profits. Copyrights protect the rights of authors, while trade secrets protect information that companies want to keep confidential. Patents protect the rights of inventors of new products and are usually good for 10 to 15 years, although, again, they vary from country to country. MNCs should look into the laws and regulations that govern contracts in order to prevent espionage.

QUESTIONS

1. What is international strategic management? What are the sources of competitive advantage available to international business that are not available to purely domestic firms?
2. What are steps in international strategy formulation? How do international strategy formulation and international strategy implementation differ?
3. What are the basic types of functional strategies most firms use? Is it likely that some firms have different functional strategies?
4. Describe the role and importance of distinctive competence in international strategy formulation?
5. How can a poor SWOT analysis affect strategic planning?
6. Should the same managers be involved both for formulating and implementing international strategy, or should each part of the process be handled by different managers? Why?
7. Some of the primary ways that MNCs use strategic planning to benefit from economic integration efforts is through strategic alliances and acquisitions. How do MNCs do this?
8. Multinational companies do not formulate worldwide strategies, but rather regional strategies. What does this statement mean and how does it help us better understand international business?

REFERENCES

Ball, George W.: *Global Companies*, Prentice-Hall, Englewood cliffs, N.J., 1982.

Barnett, R.J. and R.E. Muller, *Global Reach*, Simon & Schuster, New York, 1974.

Copeland, L. and Lewis Griggs: *Going International: How to make Friends and Deal Effectively in the Global Market Place*, Random House, New York, 1985.

Davis S., *Managing and Organising Multinational Corporations*, Pergamon Press, N.Y., 1977.

Desatnick, R.L. and M.L. Bennett, *Human Resource Management in the Multinational Company*, Nicholas Press, N.Y., 1978.

Drucker, Peter: *Post-Capitalist Society*, Harper Business, New York, 1993.

Hampton, David R., C.E. Summer, and R.A. Weber: *Organisation Behaviour and the Practice of Management*, Scott, Foresman, Glennieu, Ill, 1987.

Higgins, James M. and Julian W. Vineze: *Strategic Management and Organisational Policy*, CBS College Publishing, N.Y., 1993.

Godiwalla, Y.H.: *Multinational Planning—A Global Approach*, Long Range Planning, April, 1986.

Kefalas, A.G.: *Global Business Strategy*, South-Western, Cincinnati, Ohio, 1990.

Korth, Christopher, *International Business*, Prentice-Hall, Eaglewood Cliffs, N.Y., 1985.

Majaro, Simon: Marketing: *A Strategic Approach to World Market*, George Allen and Unnin, London, 1977.

Peters, T., and R.H. Waterman: *In Search of Excellence,* Harper & Row, N.Y., 1982.

Peter, Michael: *The Competitive Advantage of Nations,* Free Press, New York, 1990.

Reich, Robert: *The Work of Nations,* Alfred A. Knopf, New York, 1991.

Ricks, D.A., *Big Business Blunders,* Dow Jonesfrewin, Homewood, Ill., 1983.

Robock, Stefan and Kenneth Simmonds, *International Business and Multinational Enterprises,* Howin, Homewood, Ill., 1983.

Rue, Lestic W., and Phyllis G. Holland, *Strategic Management: Concept and Expereinces,* McGraw Hill, New York, 1986.

Said, A.A. and Luiz R. Sommons, *The Soveriegns: Multinational* Corporation as World Powers (ed.), Prentice-Hall, Gonglewood Cliffs, N.J., 1975.

Walter, Ingo and Tracy Murray: *Handbook of International Management: International Corporate Planning,* John WIley, New York, 1988.

11

INTERNATIONALISATION OF SERVICE FIRMS

INTRODUCTION

In recent times, the service sector's share of the economy of the largest nations has grown quite drastically. Increasing international investments by service firms and the importance the sector has led to the formulation of new specific business strategies. The chapter begins with a discussion of theoretical findings about the internationalisation of service and manufacturing firms, as well as how the two generic types of firms, that is manufacturing and service, are related. The internationalisation of service firms, and the effects that the most commonly cited characteristics of such firms have on the internationalisation process is then focused on; concentrating on the most crucial and obvious issues that a service-providing firm must deal with during its internationalisation. This is followed by an outline of strategic considerations for service firms.

THEORETICAL MODELS ON INTERNATIONALISATION OF SERVICES AND MANUFACTURING FIRMS

One of the most well-known models on foreign direct investment has been provided by Dunning. This model, often called the *eclectic paradigm* or the *OLI-framework*, explains foreign direct investments by a framework that incorporates trade theory and transaction cost theory. Foreign direct investment is believed to be caused by ownership-specific advantages, location-specific advantages and internationalisation ability. The main idea behind the model is that firms willing to operate in a foreign market are facing a disadvantage since they do not know the market or its local competitors. This disadvantage must be compensated with an owner-specific advantage. In other words, location-specific advantages, such as inexpensive labour or a large market, provide incentives for foreign direct investments. The ownership-advantages, e.g. process or product advantages, compensate for foreign market disadvantages. Furthermore, it is beneficial to internalise the function, which may be caused by high transaction costs in the market for this specific function, instead of selling it to a local firm via a market.

Another widely quoted model on internationalisation is the Uppsala-model which is reduced through organisational learning rests on the assumption that firms are facing high uncertainty when starting operations outside the domestic market. They are consequently reluctant to make large capital investments. One way to overcome this uncertainty is to build the internationalisation of the firm gradually. Initial, small capital investments will increase the knowledge of the foreign market, and of overseas operations *per se*, through incremental investments in the foreign market. The internationalisation is seen as a process where firms gain knowledge about the foreign business environment gradually, which results in gradually increased investments.

The idea of incremental investments has been exemplified by an establishment chain. This chain of sequentially increased investments abroad starts when a firm initiates foreign operations through exports from the domestic factories. The firm then gradually increases efforts to internationalise its activities and contact a local sales agent. As long as the experience is successful, this evolution will continue, which may result in opening a local sales subsidiary and eventually a manufacturing subsidiary.

In other words, this model describes the internationalisation process as having several distinct stages. The stages are linked in a continuously evolving process without clear distinctions between them, and that it is only the manifestations of these phases that develop stage-wise. In other words, attitudes and cognition are assumed to develop continuously, while behaviour, which in this case would be investment patterns, is assumed to develop stage-wise.

Thus, a general description of the characteristics of the internationalisation process may be as follows. At first, the firm or its managers are not interested in, or are unaware of, any internationalisation possibilities, which in the initial stage usually is exports. Exports may then be initiated after intentional or unintentional action by external or internal actors. In a third phase, managers are more actively evaluating and considering the possibilities to export its products, but they are still acting on an experimental basis. Later, exports become more common and the efforts are likely to expand. However, unsuccessful initial attempts may limit expansion. In a fifth phase, the firm is seen as an experienced exporter and will often continue its internationalisation through agents, sales subsidiaries and, finally, manufacturing subsidiaries. In other words, the process involves continuously increased degrees of foreign direct investments.

One can distinguish three stages in the internationalisation process: *initiation, expansion* and *consolidation*. These three stages of resource commitment constitute the basis parts in the internationalisation life-cycle dimension. The initiation phase is characterised by high uncertainty and indecisiveness, since the idea of becoming an international competitor is likely to be unfamiliar and new to most firms. The expansion phase occurs when the firm has attained some experience of foreign markets, with satisfactorily successful results. The uncertainty is gradually reduced as familiarity and knowledge are gathered and the foreign activities grow. Consolidation occurs when the firm is experienced internationally, and usually involves slowed growth. The consolidation phase is also likely to result in attempts to coordinate international activities on a cross-national basis. In other words, operations are coordinated globally in an attempt to reap economies of scale and/or scope.

THEORETICAL MODELS AND SERVICE FIRMS

Foreign direct investments by service firms are positively affected by factors such as large host markets, small cultural distance between home and host country, the openness of the host market, the foreign direct investment by a global oligopolistic competitor, high growth of the firm itself and the desire to service clients globally. There are four commonly cited factors that are assumed to stimulate service firms toward internationalisation:

1. Clients that have internationalised their activities may demand that the service supplier provide a global network and/or global experience.
2. Economies of scale may lower the costs per unit of sales for the service firm and consequently provide an incentive for globalisation.
3. Economies of scope may provide incentives for the service firm to use the experience gained from one specific activity worldwide. This will lower the costs for each new performance of the activity.
4. If a major competitor globalises its activities, the service firm may have to become global itself if it wants to keep its position in the competitive race.

How does service firms relate to that on manufacturing firms? These two categories of firms are often treated as having widely different characteristics of their production and sales processes, which is assumed to cause different types of internationalisation process. Each internationalisation process is treated as being a separate and unrelated phenomenon. This seems to be a too simplistic approach to separate manufacturing of physical goods from production of services in general terms. And it is consequently extremely important to go beyond this superficial treatment; that is, beyond a dichotomous view of the world. The production and sales processes contain both elements that are similar in nature as well as those that are highly different. Furthermore, each category of firms contains a great variety of firms and products. It is not sensible to categorise all firms as being either a physical good producer having specified characteristics, or a service producer having other specified characteristics.

A service is to be seen as *a product, the main purpose of which is to provide a service.* A physical good is *a product, the main purpose of which is to supply tangible goods.* Consequently, products are hereafter defined as being either services, physical goods or combinations of the two.

If one is to separate the two types of firms, based on these general terms, three characteristics of services must be sided as the reasons to differentiate the production of services from that of physical goods. These three characteristics are *simultaneity, perishability* and *intangibility*. *Simultaneity* means that the buyer consumes the service at the same moment it is produced by interacting with the producer; that is, simultaneous production and consumption. *Perishability* means that the service cannot be prefabricated, stored and delivered to the consumer at a later moment. The perishability factor is consequently closely related to the simultaneity factor. *Intangibility* means that he consumer may have difficulties of knowing what the producer really is offering, which is caused by asymmetrical information between the buyer and the seller.

Thus, it is too simplistic to separate the production of services and physical goods on a general basis. Still, the characteristics of services may nevertheless be helpful when one wants to characterise different types of manufacturing and service providing firms. The characteristics called simultaneity, perishability and intangibility are regarded to constitute the main causal variables to the outcome of the operations of a firm.

A MODIFIED VIEW

Most, if not all, products contain some elements of service features and some elements of physical goods. Accordingly, the degrees of service content, or physical good content, can be an insightful component when one tried to understand the effects on the internationalisation process based on the specific characteristics of the product. But the main issue to concentrate on is where is it in the total process of delivering a product to a final consumer that the physical good and/or service-contents are performed. Traditionally, it is whether the consumer experiences the service or physical good content most intensely that has been the determinant of whether a product is considered to be a physical good or a service.

Consequently, one can characterise products, including both goods and services, as well as their production and sales processes by the service intensity. Products contain different degrees of mechanical or man-made service offering as well as different degrees of reliance on physical goods. Products can be said to be good-embodied, that is, the final product is supplied in the form of a physical good, or service-embodied, that is, the final product is supplied in the form of a service.

Goods-embodied services are services that required physical goods to be at hand. This type of product can be exemplified by an automated teller machine—a machine that provides the service of cash withdrawal—a service that bank personnel used to provide. On the other hand, physical goods may also be provided through services, that is, service-embodied goods. This may be exemplified by a restaurant dinner. In general, services always contain elements sourced from either people or a product, and/or contain a technology-embodied feature.

A physical good can consequently be seen as a manifestation of performed services. For instance, an auto-manufacturer can be seen as selling the services of sourcing inputs, modifying these inputs, assembling and styling the parts, and distributing the manifestation of these services—the car—to the consumer. The manufacturing firms provide services, and the physical good is a result of performed service and manufacturing processes.

A comparison can be made between the lease of a car, which traditionally has been defined as supply of a service, and the purchase of a car, which traditionally has been defined as supply of a physical good. From the customer's user-perspective these two different types of transactions are very similar. The customer gets to use a car when and how much he or she wants. The difference appears when the question of risk is approached. Who stands the risk of a stolen or crashed car? Who has to account for the car in the balance sheet? Without making the comparison too detailed, one can state that the differences between the two alternatives are basically of a financial and risk-related nature. Further, some types of service firms may have more characteristics in common with some types of manufacturing firms than with other types of service firms, and the other way around.

To exemplify, the degree of interaction or the degree of simultaneity between the producer and the customer is determined by the need for a customised product. It does not matter whether the product is a service or a physical good. If the customer wants a customised physical good, the degree of interaction is likely to be higher than if the customer wants a standardised service. The reasoning is contrary to the idea that the degree of simultaneity is always higher in service firms than in manufacturing firms.

INTERNATIONALISATION OF SERVICE FIRMS

Internationalisation of service firms may be defined as a firm providing products supplied through production and sales processes that are characterised by high degrees of simultaneity, perishability and/or intangibility.

The Establishment Chain and Entry Strategies for Service Firms

The general argument in this context is that firms characterised by high degrees of simultaneity, intangibility and perishability in the production process do not face the same investment alternatives in their internationalisation process as a firm characterised by low degrees of simultaneity, intangibility and perishability. A modified hypothetical establishment chain for a service firm may be that the firm starts its internationalisation by performing project-type customer-ordered studies or work abroad by temporarily placing employees with the client. These types of projects may be done on an *ad hoc* or long-term basis, and can perhaps be performed at the home country office. A second step may be to open an office abroad, which can be operated by travelling domestic employees or by locally recruited personnel. A third step may be to open several offices abroad and to recruit a larger share of local personnel. This step is comparable to a foreign manufacturing subsidiary for a manufacturing firm.

Thus, there are generally three modes of international involvement that are connected with service firms. One mode is the export of final services, which can be said to involve a situation where, for instance, a bank sells a financial solution to customer based in a foreign country. A second mode is contractual agreements on intermediate services, which can be exemplified by a management consultant firm that analyses the operations of a firm in a foreign country. A third mode is service provision directly by a foreign establishment. A classification of the three most obvious foreign country entry strategies for service firms is: internal development; acquisitions of local firms; and licensing a service concept to a local firm. Other strategies are to develop internal ventures, which is a situation where an individual department within the firm operates internationally. Or the firm may seek internationalisation via joint ventures or alliances.

To explain the main features of the internationalisation process of service firms, the eclectic paradigm may be used. The ownership-specific advantage for service firms is usually almost entirely resting within the employees and within firm-specific concepts, or service delivery systems, that can be kept proprietary at least to some extent. These two parts' historical performance constitutes the firm's reputation on the market.

The long-term possibilities to maintain an ownership-specific advantage can be argued to be higher if the firm's conceptual service system is the major factor behind the firm's success. If an advantage is based only on the abilities of the employees themselves, the firm is in a more risky situation since these people are able to leave the firm overnight. Furthermore, it is likely to be easier to signal a quality signal to customers if the system is the important part of a firm's offering. On the other hand, a system, in the sense of standardised work routines and models for analysis and product design, can be easier to imitate by competitors.

Manufacturing firms that establish operations abroad are often seeking advantages from inexpensive factors of production, large markets or reduced transportation costs. The service firm is usually also seeking customer closeness and is thus highly influenced by cultural differences. The location-specific advantages that the service firms seek can perhaps be argued to be more of an intangible nature than those that manufacturing firms seek or are influenced by. For instance, local customers originating from the same country as the service firm may be likely to select this firm as the supplier to their local operations. On the other hand, cultural differences between the international service firm and local customers may make it difficult to provide excellent service.

The internationalisation aspect of the eclectic-paradigm is highly applicable when discussing service firms and internationalisation. Internationalisation is almost by definition done in service firms that start up activities abroad. But there are factors both working in favour of and against internalising the foreign operations. Native employees can be a crucial asset when the service firm wants to approach local customers, since these employees know the culture. They may also have an already developed experience record that the firm can use as the bridge to a new market. Cooperation with local firms may, on the other hand, provide opportunities to develop crucial relations with customers or other actors rapidly, and may also provide legitimacy and a good reputation.

Accordingly, a truly fundamental issue that faces an internationalising firm is the meeting with new values. This issue about internationalisation is addressed under the term *psychic distance.* Psychic distance has been defined as *'the sum of factors preventing the flow of information from and to the market'*. Thus this concept includes such disparate factors as language barriers, differences in taste among consumers, and differences in values, behaviour and attitudes.

When discussing psychic distance in relation to service providing firms, there is one important factor that must be addressed. One of the most crucial assets for a service firm is its reputation. In fact, the reputation, or the experience record, of a service firm may be the main, or perhaps the only, source for a customer to control the quality of the service offered before the actual transaction. The experience record has been described as a curriculum vitae for the service firm.

Consequently, a large psychic distance between the service firm and its customer is likely to increase the probability that the experience record is not assessed to its full value by the client. There may be several reasons for this. First, the experience record does not appear as valuable for the customer as the firm would like, since the customer may have alternative views on manners in which business should be done. Secondly, a large psychic distance is likely to increase the possibility that the service firm does a less than satisfactory job due to communication problems.

Internationalisation via Network Growth

The very nature of the characteristics simultaneity and intangibility point to the value and need for a service firm to have relevant personal contacts with other firms that are important to the industry. The evolution of service firms is usually highly influenced by networks, which is consistent with on the internationalisation processes within manufacturing firms. Networks, cooperative arrangements and personal relationships are often very important factors for possibilities to perform, and results of, foreign operations.

There is reason to believe that networks are relatively more important for service firms than for manufacturing firms in buyer-seller relationships, Since the service often is produced through personal interaction between seller and buyer. This implies that the surrounding network to a service firm, and its resulting opportunities, are main factors influencing the internationalisation of service firms.

The network's role in the internationalisation process depends on, for instance, the degree of a firm's internationalisation in comparison with its business environment. This reasoning is summarised in Figure 1. The early starter operates in a business environment with few and relatively insignificant international relationships. The firm consequent has little knowledge and experience of foreign markets, and does not hold international contacts that can be used to attain such knowledge. As a result, the firm is likely to be influenced by initiatives from familiar or unfamiliar external actors in the internationalisation process. The internationalisation is often initiated by spontaneously emerging opportunities. Relying on external actors, such as agents or middle men, is a common way to overcome the lack of experience. However filled with risk, acquisitions of local firms and their personnel are other ways to overcome the lack of knowledge. The early starter also faces the problem of reaching a position built on trust from its international counterparts, since the local firms often have not dealt with foreign firms previously.

FIGURE-1

THE INTERNATIONALISATION OF A FIRM IN RELATION TO THE INTERNATIONALISATION OF ITS BUSINESS ENVIRONMENT

		Degree of internationalisation of the business environment	
		Low	*High*
Degree of internationalisation of the firm	*Low*	The early starter	The late starter
	High	The lonely international	The international among others

The lonely international is characterised by a firm that has become a successful international actor in a business that is domestic in its nature; that is, a successful early starter. In this new situation, the early starter has succeeded in becoming international and holds a major advantage over competitors that have not internationalised that operations. The advantage will come from the experience and knowledge of relationships in international business, and from possibilities to attain new types of resources. The firm has, for instance, access to networks in several countries and may initiate new types of business ventures. The firm is more likely to affect the internationalisation of others rather than being affected by others. One of the most important tasks of the lonely international is to pursue international integration of its activities.

The late starter is a firm that is domestic in its operations, but is active in a highly international industry. This means that the firm is likely to face difficulties when it wants to internationalise its activities. Distribution channels may be occupied, its lack of international experience will create difficulties, or international competitors may have become large and unwilling to let new firms enter the global scene. A large late starter can often make rapid steps in its internationalisation through acquisitions, even though this may cause risks due to lack of international experience as compared to other large internationalised firms. The smaller firms are more dependent on other firms and their relations, but are on the other hand usually quite flexible to find a niche position in the international market.

The international among others is an international firm that operates in an international industry. Here, further internationalisation will be marginal, and dependent on how the firm's entire global operations perform and act in a complementary manner. These types of firms are likely to be able to rely on external sourcing to a greater extent than other firms, since they are likely to be located in large, international networks. In this situation, the firm is likely to gain heavily from effective global coordination of its activities, and is consequently often focused on his matter. The international among others is often operating in a global and oligopolistic market.

The service firm can attempt to enter global networks with foreign counterparts in order to reap gains from efficiency in scale and scope. The internationalisation can be attained through multi-firm collaboration or networking.

An important issue during the internationalisation process of a firm is the selection of distribution channels. The exporter of physical goods is dependent on finding economically efficient and effective distribution channels. However, the most effective and efficient channels are often occupied. The exporter of products characterised by high simultaneity and perishability do not face this problem. These firms are not dependent on existing distribution channels. They are able to create their own distribution channel(s) through interacting with the customer during production and consumption of the product. The network contacts are not needed for intermediation between the seller and the buyer, but the need for network contacts to develop customer relationships are still crucial.

Consequently, the internationalisation process of firms is highly affected by the personal experience and characteristic of leading managers. These persons' international outlooks, personal and business experience and their relations with important actors in the industry will have significant influence over the internationalisation process.

Thus, the process will, for instance, depend on visionary management, spontaneous decision-making and a desire to meet challenges.

INTERNATIONALISATION STRATEGIES IN SERVICE FIRMS

Strategic Thinking in Service Firms

Service firms to a large extent have done their strategic decisions in a *ad hoc* manner based on emerging tendencies and spontaneous opportunities. They often neglect their strategic thinking. Questions as in which competitive domain the firm was operating, which clients they served and did not serve, which core services they offered and did not offer, and how the firms could expand their business operation had not been analysed properly, or at all.

Obviously, one effect of high degrees of simultaneity between the buyer and the seller during the production process is that the internationalisation becomes closely tied to each customer relation, and is not altogether under the control of the service firm itself. The service firm must tailor-make its operations to the demands of each customer. For instance, if an accountant firm wishes to serve a U.K.-based multinational firm in U.K. as well as in France, it must know and provide service related to tax laws in each country in addition to industry-specific knowledge. This forces the service provider to be flexible towards each customer during the internationalisation process.

Furthermore, the simultaneity factor relates closely to the issue of customer selection for service firms in their internationalisation process. It may be tempting to merely supply services to foreign operations of domestic customers, since the close interaction between seller and buyer in combination with a large psychic distance will make it more difficult to sell to foreign firms.

This can be described as a passive internationalisation process, since the firm follows its existing customers. This strategy can be a good way to internationalise one's operations while holding down the risk level. Once the firm has become successful in providing services to familiar customers in an unfamiliar country, it may try to take another step.

The most obvious disadvantage with the passive internationalisation strategy is the potential dependency on old customers, which may result in a lack of control over customer focus and product offerings. To a very large extent, it is likely to be the customers that decide the goals and focus of the specific activities. Furthermore, due to the passive strategy the service firm may not be able to learn about and understand the specific environment—that is, the local country in which business is done—which is dangerous for a long-term competitive position.

A high degree of perishability for service-based products implies that there may be benefits from internationalisation *per se*. Due to perishability, the service firm is always pressed to schedule tasks as efficiently as possible, avoiding periods with lack of work in-between projects. In other words, economies of scope are likely to be quite substantial due to the perishability factor, since the activities characterised by perishability can become infrequently used if there are not complementary operations that can employ these resources.

Being present on a larger number of geographical markets should consequently decrease the risk of being out of projects, and can result in better capacity utilisation. As long as employees hold the relevant competence, it is possible to move people to projects in other countries if business is slow in the domestic country. Since the largest cost for these types of firms most often consists of wages and salaries, the potential benefit from high capacity utilisation is substantial. This reasoning rests on the assumption that employee costs, that is wages and salaries, are treated as fixed costs.

The intangible of products is likely to result in increased necessity of being physically located in the local market if the firm is to receive orders. If the firm is not located in the market, it may be difficult for the customers to understand the firm's abilities. In fact, being located on the specific market may be the only way to overcome the intangibility problem, unless the firm's experience record speaks for itself. That is, the firm is so well reputed that customers believe in its quality even before it starts to sell its products on the market in question.

The Intermingling Internationalisation Strategy

A service firm has a good opportunity to connect its offer to the specific needs and interests of each customer. This behaviour, if successful, also increases the possibilities that the service firm is able to hold a long-term relationship with the customer, since the offering is highly customised and thus valuable for the customer. Firms can increase the customer's value of their offering through knowledge about customer behaviour and innovative ability to redesign the roles of the sellers and buyers. Firms' key strategic tasks today are said to the reconfiguration of roles and relationships among this constellation of actors (that is, suppliers, business partners, allies and customers) in order to mobilise the creation of value in new forms and the new players.

The goal of firms ought not be to create value for customers, but to mobilise customers to create their own value from the company's offerings.

The idea of redesigning value for customers is closely connected to simultaneity; that is, the simultaneous production and consumption of products. The supplier of products with high degrees of simultaneity will receive unique understanding of and plentiful information about the customer's operations and sources of competitive advantage. This understanding can be used to develop an offering that results in high value for the customer and that, due to its intangibility, may he difficult to match for competitors.

This results in the proposition that competitive advantages can be gained through value-sharing with customers due to redesigned product offerings. In other words, the firm will strive to intermingle its own value-chain with one or several value-chains of customers. This strategy is apparent for service firms since they often are forced to become internationalised by their customers.

MANAGERIAL IMPLICATIONS

There are significant opportunities for service firms to grow internationally with limited financial risk-taking. The possibilities to provide services from domestic offices or through temporary offices abroad staffed with domestic personnel require low financial investments, which increases the flexibility of the entire internationalisation process. At the same time, there is a crucial risk to consider. The internationalising service-providing firm risks a deteriorated reputation due to its inability to maintain a quality standard in a new and culturally different market. The internationalisation process can be seen as an interplay between the high risk of a reduced experience record, and the relatively low financial risks that a service firm must take.

Main Considerations during Initiation

Another critical conclusion on the internationalisation of service firms concerns the initial steps towards a foreign market. The initiation of internationalisation is described as a phase highly influenced by network contacts and one's own abilities to become international. Thus, one important issue to deal with is the development of a potentially valuable and rich system of network contacts at an early stage in the internationalisation.

Even though it may at the time be less obvious which role and value that each contact ultimately may have, it is still important to nurture relations carefully. Furthermore, as the first steps towards internationalisation often are taken by an external actor, usually a customer, it is important to select customers, if at all possible, in order to facilitate and improve the internationalisation process. By following a customer to a new and unfamiliar market, the firm may achieve its internationalisation through a low-risk mode. This strategy yields a possibility to develop an understanding of the specific market and of internationalisation *per se*, gradually, without having to face a high risk of a deteriorated reputation.

If managers of service firms want to he successful in their investments outside the domestic market, they should map their initial network, analyse how the present relations have been developed, and analyse how the present network can be utilised to provide bridges into new markets.

The key to success lies in network contacts. Another important step towards internationalisation may be to recruit personnel with earlier experience of international operations and a rich international network of contacts.

Main Considerations during Expansion

The second phase of internationalisation, the expansion, is to a high extent influenced by new experience, knowledge and confidence gained through the international operations. Consequently, new relationships will yield additional opportunities, and virtuous or vicious circles are likely to occur during this phase. Initial success may lead to increased desire and ability to expand, and the other way around. However, even if the firm is successful at first, it should develop a system of elements that control growth! Rapid international growth' may result in problems to maintain a high quality standard of provided services.

One way to overcome the quality problem is to systemise the entire service-providing concept. A well-developed system for service production is more likely to result in an even production of high quality service, than if the service production operations are based entirely on the individual's performance. Newly recruited personnel are also likely to need substantial time to develop the skills necessary to provide the quality standard that the firm currently sells, and customers are likely to notice the difference immediately. Moreover, the sales of intangible products will benefit if the firm is able to develop system concepts that can be sold or perhaps licensed to the customer. This will be especially valuable when there is a significant psychic distance between the seller and the buyer, or between the firm and its newly recruited personnel in the foreign country.

Main Considerations during Consolidation

The implication for firms offering products with high perishability is to start operating in several activities with substantial economies of scope. In this way, the activities can complement each other in times of slow demand. This will result in a higher capacity utilisation, and consequently a better economy of production.

The simultaneous production and consumption of products imply an opportunity to customise one's own activity closely to the activities of the customer. This will consequently increase the value of one's offer for the customer. In this sense, the switching cost for the customer to select a new supplier can he increased if the customisation is successful. Learning from customers will be facilitated, which in turn will enhance opportunities to pursue continuous change. Both these factors are crucial for long-term survival and growth.

In other words, by redesigning the products that are offered to the market, a firm may he able to interrelate the customers' value-creating activities to one's own. This strategy has as its potential results a redefinition of responsibilities and roles, and increased total value for both seller and buyer. The goal is then to share this newly created value with the customer to the benefit of birth. Consequently, the service firm should aim at integrating knowledge and relationships, or competence and customers, during its internationalisation.

Thus the success of different strategic choices for internationalising firms offering products characterised by high degrees of simultaneity, perishability and intangibility will be influenced by two main categories of abilities: *First,* the potential to build relationship-driven product offerings to the customers. These will be based on the connection between the firm's value- creating activities and those of the customers. In other words, the opportunity to customise, or integrate, one's own value-chain with that of customers is obvious due to the simultaneity factor. *Secondly,* the ability to select effectively from numerous investment alternatives where the selection is based on the risk of a reduced experience record and the ability to handle this risk. One of the most important trade-offs for these types of firms is that between the risk of a deteriorated experience record and the benefits of increased economies of scale and scope. In order to minimise the risk of a deteriorated experience record, the firm should strive to develop service systems or concepts.

QUESTIONS

1. Discuss the main characteristics of internationalisation of service firms. What basic factors must be addressed when managing international service operations?
2. Define internationalisation of service firms. Explain the various modes of internationalisation of service firms.
3. Explain the internationalisatin of a firm in relation to the internationalisation of its business environment.
4. Discuss the theoretical and conceptual issue of internationalisation in manufacturing and service firms.
5. Critically examine the internationalisation strategies in service firms.

REFERENCES

African Development Bank: *African Development Report 1998,* Oxford University, 1998.

Asian Development Bank (ADB): *Asian Development Outlook 1998,* Oxford University, 1998

Bhalla, V.K.: *International Financial Management*, Anmol Publishers Pvt. Ltd., Delhi, 1999.

Brewer, Thomas L. and Stephen Young: *The Multilateral Investment System and Multinational Enterprises,* Oxford University, 1998.

Chudnovsky, D. and A. Lopez: "Market or policy driven? The foreign direct investment boom in Argentina", *Oxford Development Studies,* 25, 1997.

Cohen, M.A., M. Fisher, and R. Jaikumar, International Manafacturing and Distribution Network: A Normative Model Framework; In K. Ferdowd (ed.), *Managing International Manufacturing,* North-Holland, 1989.

Dunning, J., *International Production and Multinational Enterprise,* George Allen and Irwon, 1981.

Edwards, Sebastian: *Crisis and Reform in Latin America: From Despair to Hope,* Oxford University, 1995.

Estrin, Saul, Kirsty Hughes and Sara Todd: *Foreign Direct Investment in Central and Eastern Europe: Multinationals in the Transition,* Pinter and The Royal Institute of International Affairs, 1997.

Institute of International Finance, Inc.: *Capital Flows to Emerging Market Economies,* The Institute of International Finance, Inc., 1998.

John H.Dunning: Explaining International Production, Unwin Hyman, Boston, 1988.

John H.Dunning: The Globalisation of Business; Routledge, London, 1993

Meyer, Klaus, E.: *Direct Investment in Economies in Transition,* Edward Elgar, 1998.

Motta, Massimo and George Norman: "Does economic integration cause foreign direct investment?, *International Economic Review,* 37, 4 (November), 1996.

Richard D.Robinson: International Business Management (Second Edition), The Dryden Press, Hinsdale, Illinois,1978

Robert Z.Aliber: The Multinational Paradigm; The MIT Press, Cambridge, 1993

Ruigrok, W. and R. Van Tulder: *The Logic of International Restructuring,* Routledge, 1995.

UNCTC: Transnational Corporations in World Development - Trends and Prospects; New York,1988.

United Nations: World Investment Report 1994 - Transnational Corporations, Employment and the Workplace, New York, 1994.

Wells, Louis T.: "Promoting foreign investment opportunities and pitfalls for host countries, in Organisation for Economic Co-operation and Development, *Promoting Foreign Direct Investment in Developing Countries* (Paris: OECD), 1993.

12

INTERNATIONAL PRODUCTION

INTRODUCTION

International production — activity under the aegis of transnational corporations (MNCs) — continues to grow strongly. The main agent of international production, foreign direct investment (FDI), does not flow evenly across countries. This unevenness persists, and in some cases increases, over time. While this has long been a feature of the international economy, there are significant elements of change The growth of FDI in the past two decades or so has been accompanied by changes in its geographical pattern, indicating shifts in the investment climate in host countries and in the economic factors driving the location of international production. New locations are becoming attractive relative to old ones. The activities relocated across countries by direct investment are changing. Within MNCs, the specific corporate functions undertaken by parent firms and foreign affiliates (ranging from marketing to research and development (R&D)) are changing in scope and depth. Sources of FDI are also increasing and shifting. In this chapter, we shall examine the extent to which it is possible to offer a unifying interdisciplinary paradigm which might be used as a framework by which all the relevant variables affecting international production may be better identified, interpreted and evaluated. Further, the mapping of FDI patterns —in the aggregate, by industry and by functional activity—in the chapter throws light on the location of FDI and its industrial and functional distribution across countries.

AN INTERDISCIPLINARY APPROACH

It is not long before, in his attempts to explain international production, the economist needs to draw upon the help of other disciplines. This is for a number of reasons all to do with characteristics of the subject matter to be explained. In discussing these we will distinguish those which are primarily (i) external (or exogenous) to firms; and (ii) those which are internal (or endogenous) to firms.

The External Environment

Of the non-economic variables which are most likely to affect international production, the political and legal aspects are among the most important. Domestic firms, seeking to invest in their own country, take as given the legal, ideological and political environment; that is to say the role played by those non-economic forces, including the affect which they have on efficiency of international intermediate products markets is assumed to be the same for all firms. Once firms enter a different geography and national jurisdiction, these variables become relevant in affecting both their competitive advantage and the modality of their foreign involvement. In some cases, these non-economic differences may be of little significance; in other cases they may be crucially important. To identify non-economic variables affecting international production and to hypothesise about their impact on FDI, needs the help of various disciplines. In this context, it may be pointed that social, cultural and ideological issues are both difficult to evaluate and to pinpoint to a particular discipline. Yet they are importance in decision-making on international production. For example, it is widely accepted that attitudes to wealth creation and income distribution, economic incentives, work and authority, are crucial in any explanation of the economic prowess of particular nations, and of the level and pattern of consumption. Variations in cultural heritage, religious perspectives, political ideologies and moral values fashion such attitudes. Work systems, social norms and patterns of leisure differ not only between developed and developing countries, but within these countries; while the character of societal relationship and the extent to which these have been subject to foreign domination or influence in the past, may strongly influence a country's attitude towards inward direct investment, and particularly the extent to which it prefers to conclude equity partnership with foreign firms rather than accept 100 per cent owned foreign affiliates.

Each of the issues so far identified interact with each other. Attitudes to entrepreneurship, authority and work may affect the industrial policies of a country; those towards foreigners may influence the nature of its external economic relationships; those towards thrift, economic security and leisure may help fashion a government's fiscal and social programme and income distribution policy; those towards authority and leadership may constrain or encourage the growth of private or public hierarchies; those towards women in a society, the level and pattern of its educational budget and employment legislation.

There are other disciplines which relate to the environment in a less central way. The regional and urban geographer, for example, is a specialist whose interest is in the spatial distribution of economic activity. His special skills relate more to the logistics of transversing space and the location of value-adding activity within particular countries. He is much more interested in the determinants and efficiency of inter-spatial linkages, both between producers along a value-added chain and across value-added chains. Primarily the regional scientist is interested in explaining the 'where' of production; but insofar as spatial costs are regarded as a form of market failure, they may impinge on the competitive advantages and organisational modalities of firms. The extent to which the internationalisation of production requires special treatment essentially depends on the extent to which the transversing the national boundaries introduces a new spatial dimension.

Factors Internal to the Firm

As in decisions relating to domestic production, the interaction between economic, organisational, financial, marketing and management variables affecting international production is a complex one and is sometimes difficult to disentangle. However, when an enterprise engages or contemplates engaging in value-adding activity in different countries, a new order of complexity enters into the three main areas of decision taking (as traditionally identified by business schools): *organisation, management* and *marketing*. Management is, at the same time, the easiest and most difficult to deal with: easiest because in its approach to an understanding of business conduct, performance and strategy, it embraces many of the concepts of the industrial economist; the most difficult because of the generality and lack of theoretical underpinning of many of the issues (the discipline of strategic management is especially prone to this). Recent work on management has strongly oriented itself to identifying and evaluating the competitive advantages of MNCs and the management related variables which make for a foreign location. Only to a limited extent have intra-firm organisational issues been of interest to scholars of management; except in so far as the strategy of ownership is itself regarded as a management tool.

By contrast — and as one might expect — the way in which firms organise themselves to supply goods for sale to foreign markets or engage in value-added activities outside national boundaries has been central to the interest of organisational theorists. Here, four organisational issues which directly bear on the international production decision may be identified. The **first** is the form of organisation (both formal or informal) which might influence the way in which investment decisions are taken. These break down into components such as : 'What modifications are required to the form of hierarchical organisation as a consequence of being international ?' *Which of the various variants of M structure are suitable for which types of overseas operations ? How might these vary over time and according to the type of value-added activity being undertaken ? To what extent are adaptations required to the organisational culture or an enterprise when it produces abroad ? and 'How far do the costs of these adaptations affect the way it penetrates foreign markets ?* The **second** organisational issue concerns the locus of decision-taking within hierarchies, and the rationale of alternative governance structures. *To what extent, and in which functional areas are decisions most likely to decentralise ?* Bridging the first and second issues, is the way in which particular functional activities are organised across national boundaries. The **third** organisational question relates to the vertical or horizontal interaction between the participating stakeholders in organisations; and especially on the manner by which work is organised, performance is monitored and conflicts of interest resolved; and the **fourth** the way in which internal and external contractual relationships are handled. Once again country-specific differences would suggest the cross-border organisational relationships may differ in substance, if not in kind, from those facing the purely domestic firm.

Today, MNCs forge and sustain a network of relationships with foreign firms, and is affected by the internationalisation process *per se*, including the transition from exporting or licensing to FDI. This approach contrasts with the internalisation theory in that it argues that a firm's ownership advantages will depend no less on the success of its external relationships with other firms in the network. The multinational firm may use its network position to effectively "externalise" some of its activities without losing control of its crucil intangible assets. The internalisation of markets is often best regarded as a process by which network positions are established and changed, the result of which may substantially influence the MNCs product, marketing and purchasing strategies. A second, and rather different approach to network analysis, is more on networks as a form of organisational relationship between firms, and as a means of overcoming the differences of the allocation of resources by pure markets or pure hierarchies, considering firms as mutually related units, usually located in linked positions, rather than standing as completely independent units.

No less important are the forms of relationships which exist in the network. For instance, the relationship between US firms, which tend to be based on a formal, hierarchical or contractual relationship, while between Japanese firms are based more on mutual trust, respect and integrity. Moreover, since, in Japan, the primary sub-contractor usually bears most of the economic risk of the relationship (and has most to lose by severing the relationship), an important governance cost commonly faced by US and European contracting firms is removed, and hence the Japanese networking system brings with it an organisational advantage to the firms at the hub of the network. Again, the appropriate channels of entry with location-specific variables are being considered as an independent rather than a dependent variable. There is need to formulate the international marketing strategy of firms, both in respect of the type of products which different markets may require, and of the scope of markets (e.g. general or niche) which companies should aim to cultivate the objective to identify and evaluate the competitive strategies most likely to be successful.

As firms become more multinational their options for financing their capital expenditures become wider; and there is little evidence to suggest that, in the absence of government intervention, firms have been constrained in their foreign production and decisions by the lack or cost of finance in their home countries; they will simply seek funding from the least expensive or least risky source. The way in which firms organise their trans-border transactions, the relative advantages of different degrees of equity investment and between equity investment and non-equity capital rests on the balance between financial risk and control. The lower the former relative to the importance of the latter, the more internal hierarchies will be preferred to external relations with independent firms. To formulate a general paradigm about the reasons why firms extend their territorial boundaries from particular countries, the transaction cost minimising and strategic type explanations have emerged as the dominant analytical tools. While increasing attention is now being paid to entrepreneurship as an engine of growth, most discussions on competitive advantages by business historians have tended to centre on the ability of enterprises to coordinate their value added activities across national boundaries and over time. The issue of the 'where' of international business activity does not seem to have captured the interest of business historians.

The question now arises: *'What, if any, is the analytical interface between these different disciplinary strands'? Is there a unifying paradigm which links the explanations? To what extent can one widen the paradigm to embrace non-economic variables? Is it simply a matter of identifying political, legal, organisational, marketing and other variables and adding these to those encompassed in economic models; or does one need to look for a new, or newer paradigms?* The eclectic paradigm offers a cohesive and systematic framework in integrating the kind of analysis with that of other disciplines to answer the kind of questions raised. The basic reason for this is that the ownwership, location and internationalisation (OLI) configuration described by the eclectic paradigm both has applications outside the economics, and draws upon the ideas and concepts of other disciplines. Table-1 sets out the kind of interdisciplinary approach, suggesting that each of the unidisciplinary explanations for international production can be interpreted in terms of the OLI configuration of relationships. It is possible to evaluate the role of managerial, marketing, financial, organisational, political and legal factors on the competitive advantages of firms, the locational advantage of countries and the way in which firms organise the resources within their control and/or those they seek to obtain from other firms. Here, it may be pointed that technological advances and particularly the emergence of a number of generic technologies, e.g. information and communications technology, robotics, biotechnology, etc., together with the rapid growth of strategic alliances among firms are having a marked impact on the nature and growth of firms and the form of their cross-border organisational relationships.

'Why' Sub-Paradigm - O-Advantages

The competitive advantage of firms are not only economic; and they are certainly not determined by the firms themselves. Country-specific political, legal, ideological and cultural differences may fundamentally affect the ability of firms to generate and sustain competitive advantages. For instance, competition and anti-trust legislation (a legal instrument) in one country might prevent firms from merging or forming collaborative alliances, but in another it may allow it. Assuming such mergers and alliances to be beneficial to the firms' attempt to capture international markets, firms may have their competitive advantages increased or lowered as a result. Similarly, a firm's competitive prowess may be directly related to its ability to minimise the cost of transactions associated with different organisational relationships both within or across national boundaries. A full appreciation of cross-border differences in the way in which subcontracting is organised, and in consumer perceptions, preferences and reactions to different marketing techniques may be the crucial ingredient to success in some sectors; in others competitive advantage might rest more on the way in which firms handle their incentive systems and employee relations. And to gain access to knowledge and understanding of the local legal, political and cultural environment, has always been a potent reason for concluding joint ventures when penetraging foreign markets.

TABLE-1

An interdisciplinary approach to the eclectic paradigm

	Ownership advantages	*Location advantages*	*Internationalisation advantages*
1. Management	* Management, culture, experience, strategy	* Comparative resource endowments	* Form of involvement as part of firms competitive posture/strategy
	* Quality of Management * Product quality * Economies of scope * Co-ordinating options	* Configuration options * Oligopolistic strategy	* Strategic partnering
2. Organisation	* Organisational culture/ resources/structure * Complementary assets to core advantages	* Environmental compexity * Ease of transfering organisational structures and external relationships	* Transaction costs : both inter- and intra-firm. * Strategic parterning.
	* Synergistic economies		* Markets/hierarchies clan options
	* Nature of external relationships (e.g. networking) forms	affecting organisational	* Cultural differences
3. Marketing	* Product characteristics	* Inter-country social and cultural differences * Physical distances	* Transaction costs with respect to * Segmented markets a) entry modes
	* Goodwill/brand names * Network advantages	* Need for product customisation	b) agency costs c) supplier relationships * Control of distribution
4. Finance	* Access to finance capital on favourable terms	* Exchange rates	* Market failure in capital/ exchange markets
	* Portfolio diversification across national boundaries	* Controls on sourcing, capital and dividend, remissions, etc.	* Agency costs * Network analysis
5. Political Science as international	* Cultures, ideologies as affecting 'O' advantages * Economic systems	* Role of power groups (e.g. trade unions) * Politically induced incentives and barriers FDI	* Transaction costs arising from political risk relations * Negotiating/bargaining
	* Structure of government * Lobbying ability/bargaining power	* Inter-country political relations	* Government intervention

6. Regional Science	* Multiplant economics * Ability to improve or reduce cost of transport, Information/communications	* Spatial distance * Transport costs	* Spatial costs of organising hierarchies
7. Law	* Legal infrastructure * Patent/contract/company law * Code of conduct	* Extraterritoriality * Restrictive practices legislation	* Litigation procedures * Efficiency of contract law (in protecting property rights)
8. Economic & Business History	* Entrepreneurship	* Tariffs and other import controls	* To capture economies of common governance
	* Economics of vertical integration	* Size of markets	* Quality control
	* Organisational forms. Access to resources/markets	* Government regulations	* Agency costs
	* Interpersonal relationships	* State's role in enforcing contracts * Behavioural norms	* Cost of enforcing contracts

'Where' Sub-Paradigm

There is much in common between the various interdisciplinary attempts to explain the 'where' of international production. The variables considered by the modern economic geographer and regional scientist are virtually the same as those as the earlier researchers on FDI but the techniques of analysis are now considerably more sophisticated. The business analyst is inclined to pay more attention to industry — and firm specific characteristics and the behaviour of competitors affecting the targeting of foreign markets, the location of different kinds of production and the timing of the FDI.

Political scientists and legal scholars generally seek to identify, but not to measure, the politically and legally oriented variables likely to favour the choice of production sites. Indeed, as a general observation, with the possible exception of seeking of quantify economic risk and the general political climate of a country, there have been few attempts to subject political or legal variables to statistical testing. Perhaps the most comprehensive acknowledgement of the whole range of non-economic factors affecting the location of MNCs activity are the efforts of the international banks and specialist institutions which seek, on behalf of their clients, to rank countries by their perceived suitability to foreign direct investment. However, the weights applied to the variables identified as making up the attractiveness are completely subjective.

Most of the efforts to assess the significance of locational variables by non-economists, have been cross-sectional; the major exception is by marketing scholars who have looked into the timing of the different stages of the internationalisation process; and how an appropriate marketing strategy might vary according to changes in the size and character of a country's market and the policies pursued by the host governments. The role of cultural specific variables in affecting the location of subsidiaries, the locational variables influencing subcontracting has particularly interested some organisational theorists. Some geographers have also concerned themselves with the location of

MNC activity within particular region or countries. The factor endowments and market failure paradigm can be used to explain the interface between non-economic factors and the location of value adding activities; and also of the way in which firms are likely to respond to change in the value of these variables.

'How' Sub-Paradigm

It is, however, in the examination of the organisation of international economic activity by firms that the most exciting analytical advances have been made outside economics. Here, without question, the dominant mode of thought has been the transaction-cost paradigm, which is at the heart of explaining and identifying the characteristics of market failure. Indeed some commentators feel that the main tenets of the paradigm, as developed mainly by economists, have been inappropriately applied in other disciplines to explain situations it was not intended to explain.

The transaction-cost paradigm is useful in identifying situations in which the structure of the principal/agent relationship is appropriate. Viewed in this way, a purchase of a component from a supplier is no different than purchasing an hour's work from a mechanic. In both cases, a firm measures the intra-hierarchical transaction (or agency) costs in terms of the incentives and policing costs necessary to ensure quality control, optimum delivery schedules etc. In as much as organisation theory can help us identify and measure costs between production units in different countries, it can add much to our understanding of the 'how' of international production. Marketing theory is also using a transaction cost approach to identifying modes of penetrating new markets. To an extent, disciplinary labels are meaningless, for the concepts and techniques used to evaluate the modes of entry into a particular market, which vary along a continuum from non-equity to 100 per cent subsidiaries are exactly those which economists and business analysts might have been expected to deploy.

Economic and business historians have focused especially on the growth of international production as a form of cross-border vertical or horizontal integration. In recent years, they too have increasingly used a transaction cost paradigm on their studies. The history of organised exchanges has been traced in terms of the interplay between the costs of transacting and the institutional framework of society. In the pre-modern world, the cost of enforcing contracts was often prohibitive; most transactions were highly personalised, and the role of the state as a contract-enforcement agency was limited. By contrast, over the past two centuries, all costs of transacting have been substantially reduced as a result of the development of uniform weights and measures, contract law, new behavioural norms, and improvements in both market co-ordinating and hierarchial exchange mechanisms. The transaction cost paradigm is used to explain the replacement of foreign distribution and marketing agents by sales subsidiaries of the exporting firms. We now return to the political scientists, who are concerned with forms of governance; and the whole issue of public bureaucracy has overtones of the transaction costs and principal/agents paradigm. In the context of explaining the modes of international production, their main interest is the extent to which the external political environment (in the way identified) may affect the transaction costs and/or forms of internal governance by MNCs; and of how this might vary between countries. *'Would the establishment and operational costs of dealing with bureaucracy be lower in a joint venture compared with a 100 per cent subsidiary?' 'What are the costs of obtaining the necessary approval to set up a production facility in a foreign country rather than licensing a local firm to produce the same product?' 'To what extent do governments discriminate against MNC subsidiaries that do not engage in local subcontracting?'* These are all issues which involve an analysis of the political costs of engaging in alternative exchange relationships. Finally, the legal dimension. The extent to which firms prefer full control over their affiliates or are willing to relinquish *de jure* control to external agents may rest on the legal provisions for protecting the firm against an abuse of the agent's position. Indeed, the failure of markets to operate efficiently may be directly related to the uncertainty of the participants as to any legal obligations each may bear to the other about the nature of the good, service or right transacted, and to the capability and fairness of the legal system to redress breaches and/or abuse of contract as and when they occur. Similarly, the extent to which firms may wish to conclude strategic alliances may be affected by the provisions of the anti-trust legislation. Translated into the international dimension, the issue of extra territoriality and the insurance against political risk — in so far as each affects the transaction costs of both hierarchies and markets — are of direct relevance to the way in which firms may organise their trans-border activities.

GLOBAL TRENDS IN INTERNATIONAL PRODUCTION

The growth of international production is an important part of the process of globalisation. *International production* refers to that part of the production of goods and services of countries that is controlled and managed by firms headquartered in other countries. Firms can exercise control of production in countries ("host countries") other than their own ("home country") either through the ownership of a minimum share of equity—that is, a minimum share in the capital stock or assets — of the enterprises in which the production takes place, or through contractual (non-equity) arrangements that confer control upon them. Exercising control and having a voice in the management of an enterprise located abroad ("foreign affiliate")—whether through capital investment or through contractual arrangement—leads to international production.

Firms that engage in international production—transnational corporations (MNCs)—establish, under the common governance of their headquarters, international production systems in which factors of production move, to a greater or lesser extent, among units located in different countries. These systems increasingly cover a variety of activities, ranging from research and development (R&D) to manufacturing to service functions such as accounting, advertising, marketing and training, dispersed over host-country locations and integrated to produce final goods or services. They are also increasingly being established, especially in developed countries, through mergers between existing firms from different countries or the acquisition of existing enterprises in countries by firms from others. Once internationally dispersed production units under common governance are established, mobile and location- bound factors of production to which a MNC has access in home and host countries (and sometimes even third countries) are combined in each unit in ways and for production that contribute the most to the firm's economic and strategic objectives. From the perspective of factor use—as distinct from that of location as host or home country for enterprises engaged in international production — *all* of the production that takes place in these MNC production systems (in parent firms or home-country units as well as foreign affiliates or host-country units) constitutes international production. Viewed from the perspective of home and host countries, however, it is, respectively, the production in foreign locations by a country's own firms, and the production by foreign firms in a country's own locations, that constitute international production.

International production gathered strength across all major indicators (sales, value added, assets, exports and employment), in 2011 (Table-1). The underlying factors for this increase were two-fold. *First,* the relatively favourable economic conditions during the year, especially in emerging markets but also in some developed countries like the United States, increased demand for the goods and services produced by foreign affiliates representing the breadth of FDI stock. *Second,* that stock continued to be augmented by new FDI flows during the year, as MNCs increased their internationalization.

Employment in foreign affiliates rose noticeably during the year, as MNCs continued to expand their production abroad in response to the rise in market opportunities in emerging markets. Globally, foreign affiliates accounted for 69 million jobs in 2011, an 8 per cent increase over the previous year. This stands in stark contrast to the 2 per cent increase in employment projected globally for 2011. Developing and transition economies increasingly account for the majority of employment in foreign affiliates. China alone, for example, accounted for 18.2 million, or 28 per cent, of the total in 2010. This trend continued to be driven by increased FDI generated by both efficiency- and market-seeking motivations, with much of the recent momentum being driven by the latter. A rapidly expanding middle class has attracted FDI in both the manufacturing and the services sectors as MNC executives seek to go "local" and improve their positions in emerging markets.

Foreign affiliates' sales and value added also rose in 2011, continuing their recovery from the lows during the crisis. After dipping in 2009, sales generated by foreign affiliates rebounded in 2010 This trend continued into 2011, with sales rising 9 per cent over the previous year, hitting a record $28 trillion. Likewise, value added increased, reaching $7 trillion, or roughly 10 per cent of global GDP. Although M&As, especially in developed economies, have driven sales and value added figures in the past, the strong recent growth in international production originating in emerging markets has come largely from MNCs pursuing the organic growth of their own facilities and joint ventures with local companies. In developing and transition economies rising international production is often generated from new production capacity, through greenfield investment, rather than through a change in ownership of existing assets.

The financial performance of foreign affiliates also improved in 2011. The rate of return on outward FDI rose 0.9 percentage points to 7.3 per cent. Although this increase brings it near its 2005 high of 7.6 per cent, it remains below the more than 10 per cent returns of the early 1980s. This long-term structural decline in performance is likely to be the result of the changing industry composition of FDI stock over time, with a shift from capital-intensive, high-return activities in the primary sector to services-related activities with relatively lower returns.

The world's largest MNCs reflect these global trends in international production, though they also suggest that the top 100 MNCs, mostly from developed economies, continue to struggle in their activities at home. Foreign sales of the largest 100 MNCs in the world increased almost 20 per cent in 2011, while their domestic sales - largely in developed economies - rose 13 per cent (Table-2). Foreign employment likewise expanded, rising 4 per cent for the year, while domestic employment slumped, falling 3 per cent. Although some of this differential represents the easier expansion of sales and employment in emerging markets than in mature markets, it also highlights the sluggish recovery of developed economies in the aftermath of the crisis. These trends in sales and employment are likely to be reinforced by the increasing impact of austerity policies, particularly in Europe, and a possible return to recession in many developed economies in 2012.

TABIE-1

Selected indicators of FDI and international production, 1990-2011

(Billions of dollars, value at current prices)

Item	*1990*	*2005-2007 pre-crisis average*	*2009*	*2010*	*2011*
FDI inflows	207	1 473	1 198	1 309	1 524
FDI outflows	241	1 501	1 175	1451	1 694
FDI inward stock	2 081	14 588	18 041	19 907	20 438
FDI outward stock	2 093	15 812	19 326	20 865	21168
Income on inward FDI [a]	75	1 020	960	1 178	1 359
Rate of return on inward FDI [b]	4.2	7.3	5.6	6.3	7.1
Income on outward FDI [a]	122	1 100	1 049	1 278	1 470
Rate of return on outward FDI [b]	6.1	7.2	5.6	6.4	7.3

Cross-border M&As	99	703	250	344	526
Sales of foreign affiliates	5 102	20 656	23 866	25 622[c]	27 877[c]
Value added (product) of foreign affiliates	1 018	4 949	6 392	6 560 [C]	7 183[c]
Total assets of foreign affiliates	4 599	4 3623.	7 4910	75 609[c]	82 131[c]
Exports of foreign affiliates	1 498	5 003	5 060	6 267[d]	7 358[d]
Employment by foreign affiliates (thousands)	21 458	51 593	59 877	63 903[c]	69 065[c]
Memorandum:					
GDP	22 206	50 411	57 920	63 075[e]	69 660[e]
Gross fixed capital formation	5 109	11 208	12 735	13 940	15 770
Royalties and licence fee receipts	29	156	200	218	242
Exports of goods and non-factor services	4 382	15 008	15 196	18 821[e]	22 095[e]

Source: UNCTAD.

a Based on data from 168 countries for income on inward FDI and 136 countries for income on outward FDI in 2011, in both cases representing more than 90 per cent of global inward and outward stocks.

b Calculated only for countries with both FDI income and stock data.

c Data for 2010 and 2011 are estimated based on a fixed effects panel regression of each variable against outward stock and *a* lagged dependent variable for the period 1980-2009.

d Data for 1995-1997 are based on a linear regression of exports of foreign affiliates against inward FDI stock for the period 1982-1994. For 1998-2011, the share of exports of foreign affiliates in world export in 1998 (33.3 per cent) was applied to obtain values.

e Data from IMF, *World Economic Outlook*, April 2012.

Note: Not included in this table are the value of worldwide sales by foreign affiliates associated with their parent firms through non-equity relationships and of the sales of the parent firms themselves. Worldwide sales, gross product, total assets, exports and employment of foreign affiliates are estimated by extrapolating the worldwide data of foreign affiliates of MNCs from Australia, Austria, Belgium, Canada, the Czech Republic, Finland, France, Germany, Greece, Israel, Italy, Japan, Latvia, Lithuania, Luxembourg, Portugal, Slovenia, Sweden, and the United States for sales; those from the Czech Republic, France, Israel, Japan, Portugal, Slovenia, Sweden, and the United States for value added (product); those from Austria, Germany, Japan and the United States for assets; those from the Czech Republic, Japan, Portugal, Slovenia, Sweden, and the United States for exports; and those from Australia, Austria, Belgium, Canada, the Czech Republic, Finland, France, Germany, Italy, Japan, Latvia, Lithuania, Luxembourg, Macao (China), Portugal, Slovenia, Sweden, Switzerland and the United States for employment, on the basis of the shares of those countries in worldwide outward FDI stock.

In contrast, Internationalisation indicators for the largest 100 MNCs domiciled in developing and transition economies, reveal the relative strength of their home economies. While foreign assets of those economies rose 7 per cent in 2010, a rate faster than that of the largest 100 MNCs, the rise could not keep up with the remarkable 23 per cent increase in domestic assets. Sales at home also outpaced foreign sales in terms of growth, though both easily surpassed growth rates seen among developed-economy MNCs.

The only area where this trend did not hold was in employment, where the growth of foreign jobs outpaced that of domestic jobs in 2010.

TABLE-2

Internationalisation statistics of the 100 largest non-financial MNCs worldwide and from developing and transition economies
(Billions of dollars, thousands of employees and per cent)

Variable	*100 largest MNCs worldwide*					*100 largest MNCs from developing and transition economies*		
	2009	*2010*[a]	*2009-2010 % Change*	*2011*[b]	*2010-2011 % Change*	*2009*	*2010*	*% Change*
Assets								
Foreign	7147	7495	4.9	7 776	3.7	997	1 068	7.1
Domestic	4396	4417	0.5	4 584	3.8	2 154	2 642	22.6
Total	11 543	11 912	3.2	12 360	3.8	3 152	3710	17.7
Foreign as % of total	62	63	1.0[c]	63	0.0[c]	32	29	-2.9[c]
Sales								
Foreign	4602	4870	5.8	5 696	17.0	911	1 113	22.1
Domestic	2377	2721	14.5	3 077	13.1	1 003	1 311	30.7
Total	6979	7590	8.8	8 774	15.6	1 914	2424	26.6
Foreign as % of total	66	64	-1.8[c]	65	0.8 c	48	46	-1.7[c]
Employment								
Foreign	8568	8684	1.4	9 059	4.3	3 399	3726	9.6
Domestic	6576	6502	-1.1	6 321	-2.8	4 860	5112	5.2
Total	15144	15 186	0.3	15 380	1.3	8 259	8837	7.0
Foreign as % of total	57	57	0.6[c]	59	1.7[c]	41	42	1.0[c]

Source: UNCTAD.
a Revised results.
b Preliminary results.
c In percentage points.

For both groups of MNCs, however, their investment behaviour is indicative of their intention to follow through with their proactive internationalization plans. The top 100 MNCs undertook FDI projects worth $374 billion in 2011, largely driven by a minority of the group's members. During the year, the group concluded $194 billion in gross cross-border deals, representing 20 per cent of M&A purchases in the world by value. The share of cross-border deals in their total deals, both domestic and foreign, reached 72 per cent in 2011, a level significantly higher than that of the preceding two years (roughly 50 per cent). Greenfield investments fell slightly to $180 billion in 2011, though this amount still represented 20 per cent of all greenfield investment projects.

FDI activity by the largest 100 MNCs from developing and transition economies slowed in 2011, after nearly doubling in 2010. As a group, these MNCs completed $119 billion of FDI projects in 2011 ($109 billion, excluding MNCs that are also members of the top 100 MNCs worldwide). Greenfield investments reached $66 billion, or 55 per cent of their total FDI projects, accounting for roughly 7 per cent of total projects around the world. The value of gross cross-border M&As completed by the group in 2011 jumped 42 per cent to $53 billion, or roughly 5.5 per cent of all deals. VimpelCom Ltd (Russian Federation) was the primary driver of this increase, completing $23 billion in deals during the year.

QUESTIONS

1. Discuss the interdisciplinary approach to the eclectic paradigm
2. To what extent can one widen the eclectic paradigm to enhance non-economic variables in international production?
3. Discuss the recent global trends in international production.
4. "International production can be interpreted in terms of the ownership, location and internationalisation (OLI) configuration described by the eclectic paradigm." Explain.
5. Discuss the changes in the key indicators of foreign direct investment and international production during last two decades.
6. Describe the sourcing and vertical integration decisions facing international production management.
7. Identify and discuss the basic locations decisions in international production management.

REFERENCES

Aghion, P. and Griffith, R. (2007) *Competition and Growth: Reconciling Theory and Evidence,* Cambridge, M A: MIT Press.

Bacchetta, M. and Jansen, M. (2003) 'Adjusting to trade liberalization: The role of policy institutions and WTO disciplines', *W TO Special Studies N° 7,* Geneva: World Trade Organization.

Baldwin, R. (2006) 'Offshoring and globalisation: What is new about the new paradigm?', Mimeo, Geneva: Graduate Institute of International Studies.

Blyde, J. and Sinyavskaya, N. (2007) 'The impact of liberalizing trade in services on trade in goods: An empirical investigation', *Review of Development Economics* 11, 3: 566-583.

Boulhol, H. and Fontagne, L. (2006) 'Deindustrialisation and the fear of relocations in the industry', *Working Paper N°2006 - 07,* Paris: CEPII research center.

Brander, J. A. and Krugman, P. (1983) 'A 'Reciprocal Dumping' model of international trade', *NBER Working Paper N° 1194,* Cambridge, M A: NBER.

Brou, D. and Ruta, M. (2007) 'Economic Integration, Political Integration or Both?', Mimeo.

Bustos, P. (2007) 'multilateral trade liberalization, exports and technology upgrading: Evidence on the impact of MERCOSUR on Argentinian firms', Mimeo, Barcelona: Universitat Pompeu Fabra.

Carruthers, R., Bajpai, J., and Hummels, D. (2003) 'Trade and logistics: A n East Asian perspective', in Kharas, H. and Krumm, K. (eds) *East Asia Integrates,* Washington, DC: The World Bank: 77-94.

Caselli, F. and Wilbur, J.C. (2001) 'Cross-country technology diffusion: The case of computers', *The American Economic Review* 91, 2: 328-335.

Dew-Becker, I. and Gordon, R.J. (2005) 'Where did the productivity growth go? Inflation dynamics and the distribution of income', *NBER Working Paper N° 11842,* Cambridge, M A: NBER.

Dikhanov, Y. (2005) *Trends in Global Income Distribution, 1970-2000 and Scenarios for 2015*, Human Development Report 2005.

Djankov, S., Freund, C., and Pham, C. S. (2006) 'Trading on time', *Policy Research Working Paper N° 3909*, Washington, DC: The World Bank.

Feenstra, R.C. and Kee, H.L. (2007) 'Trade liberalisation and export variety: A comparison of Mexico and China', *The World Economy* 30, 1: 5-21.

Feenstra, R.C. and Lewis, T.R. (1994) 'Trade adjustment assistance and Pareto gains from trade', *Journal of International Economics* 36, 3-4: 201-222.

Frankel, J.A. and Romer, D. (1999) 'Does trade cause growth?', *The American Economic Review* 89, 3: 379-399.

Fujita, M., Krugman, P.R., and Venables, A.J. (1999) *The Spatial Economy*, Cambridge, M A: The MIT Press.

Galor, O. and Mountford, A. (2006) 'Trade and the great divergence: The family connection', *American Economic Review* 96, 2: 299-303.

Griffith, R., Redding, S.J., and van Reenen, J. (2000) 'Mapping the two faces of R&D: Productivity growth in a panel of OECD industries', *CEP Discussion Paper N° 0458*, London: Centre for Economic Performance, LSE.

Hanson, G.H., Mataloni, R.J., and Slaughter, M.J. (2005) 'Vertical production net works in multinational firms', *The Review of Economics and Statistics* 87, 4: 664- 678.

Hausman, W.H., Lee, H., and Subramanian, U. (2005) 'Global logistics indicators, supply chain metrics and bilateral trade patterns', *Policy Research Working Paper N° 3773*, Washington, DC: The World Bank.

Helpman, E., Melitz, M., and Rubinstein, Y. (2007) 'Estimating trade f lows: Trading partners and trading volumes', *NBER Working Paper No. 12927*, Cambridge, M A: NBER.

Hummels, D. (2007) 'Transportation costs and international trade in the second era of globalization', *The Journal of Economic Perspectives* 21, 3: 131-154.

Kiyota, K. (2007) 'On testing the law of comparative advantage', *RSIE Discussion Paper N° 556*, Ann Arbor: University of Michigan.

Krugman, P. R. and Obstfeld, M. (2006) *International Economics: Theory and Policy*, Boston, San Francisco: Addison Wesley.

Krugman, P. R. and Venables, A. J. (1995) 'Globalization and the inequality of nations', *Quarterly Journal of Economics* 110,4: 857-880.

Lai, E. L. (1998) 'International intellectual property rights protection and the rate of product innovation', *Journal of Development Economics* 55, 1: 133-153.

Lawrence, R.Z. (2008) *Blue-Collar Blues: Is Trade to Blame for Rising US Income Inequality ?*, Washington DC: Peterson Institute for International Economics.

Lemieux, T. (2007) 'The changing nature of wage inequality', *NBER Working Paper N° 13523*, Cambridge, M A: NBER.

Levinsohn, J. and Petropoulos, W. (2001) 'Creative destruction or just plain destruction?: The U.S. textile and apparel industries since 1972', *NBER Working Paper n° 8348*, Cambridge, M A: NBER.

Lileeva, A. and Trefler, D. (2007) 'Improved access to foreign markets raises plant-level productivity... for some plants', *NBER Working Paper No. 13297*, Cambridge, M A: NBER.

Maskus, K. E., Otsuki, T., and Wilson, J. S. (2005) 'The cost of compliance with product standards for firms in developing countries: an econometric study', *Policy Research Working Paper N° 3590*, Washington, DC: The World Bank.

Mayer, T. and Ottaviano, G. I. P. (2007) 'The Happy Few: The internationalisation of European 34) firms', *Bruegel-CEPR EFIM2007 Report*, Brussels: Bruegel Blueprint.

Mayer, T. and Zignago, S. (2005) 'Market access in global and regional trade', *CEPII Working Paper N° 2005- 02*, Paris: CEPII Research Center.

Syverson, C. (2008) 'Prices, spatial competition, and heterogeneous producers: An empirical test', *Journal of Industrial Economics*, Forthcoming.

13

OPERATION MANAGEMENT IN INTERNATIONAL COMPANIES

INTRODUCTION

In the past, MNCs primarily built their international production networks through FDI (equity holdings), creating an internalized system of affiliates in host countries owned and managed by the parent firm. Over time, MNCs have also externalized activities throughout their global networks, known to be as global value chains (GVCs). They have built interdependent networks of operations involving both their affiliates and partner firms in home and host countries. Depending on their overall objectives and strategy, the industry in which they operate, and the specific circumstances of individual markets, MNCs increasingly control and coordinate the operations of independent or, rather, loosely dependent partner firms, through various mechanisms. These mechanisms or levers of control range from partial ownership or joint ventures, through various contractual forms, to control based on bargaining power arising from MNCs' strategic assets such as technology, market access and standards. Such mechanisms are not mutually exclusive and they can be as much complements as substitutes to FDI. From a policy perspective, to pursue the integration of developing economies into global value chains it is no longer enough to focus on attracting FDI and MNC affiliates on the one hand, or to promote arm's-length trade on the other. Policymakers need to consider a myriad of alternative networked forms of MNC operations, each of which comes with its own set of development impacts and policy implications. The focus of the chapter is on the operational choices and trade-offs.

INTERNATIONAL PROCUREMENT

Once a firm decides to purchase rather than manufacture, then the question is whether it should buy locally or internationally. The decision depends on many factors such as: i) Local shortages (persistent, seasonal, cyclical); ii) Foreign exchange controls; iii) Differential costs due to tariffs, nontariff barriers, insurance, freight etc.; iv) Nature of the firms internationalisation; v) Skills available for importing; vi) The sensitivity of customers or labour; and vii) The appeal of foreign goods. In addition, there are other factors like restraints imposed by intercompany or intracompany agreements. Sometimes, the licensing or technical assistance contract may involve tied buying. Local shortages may lead to high or unstable prices. International purchases involves both foreign export controls and local import restrictions.

There are different types of import restrictions being adopted by different countries. Some forms are: i) Absolute quotas; ii) Tariff rate quotas - tariff rate increases with quantity imported; iii) Quotas by source - quotas are assigned to certain supplying countries; iv) Absolute prohibitions - US against Cuba; v) Special tariffs like countervailing duties for dumping; vi) Voluntary import quotas - US imposition on Japan for several products; and, vii) Voluntary export quotas - Japan imposed on its exports to the US.

Sourcing strategy includes a number of basic choices companies make in deciding how to serve foreign markets. One choice relates to the use of imports, assembly, or production within the country to serve a foreign market. Another decision involves the use of internal or external supplies of components or finished goods. There is no commonly accepted definition of "offshoring" in the public debate nor in the economic literature. However, the term "offshoring" is widely used as a particular subcategory of "outsourcing". The latter has been defined as *"the act of transferring some of a company's recurring interval activities and decision rights to outside providers, as set in a contract"*. The typical consequence of such a decision is a decline of employment in the plant/firm which is doing the "outsourcing" and a rise in employment in the plant/firm from which the supplies are sourced thereafter. The vagueness of the term is often related to the fact that it is not made clear if the change in sourcing of supplies refers to the plant level, the firm level or to the national level. The term "recurring interval activities" might include a given level of in-house supplies in a stagnant business environment, but the meaning is less clear in an expanding environment in which additional supplies from the outside do not necessarily result in an absolute reduction of employment but tend to limit its expansion. It is also useful to distinguish between a replacement of the supplies which takes place between plants of the same firm or from a non-affiliated firm (control-ownership), and whether the new sourcing is from plants in the home country or abroad (location). In certain cases, the sourcing decision goes hand-in-hand with new investment abroad, which leads some observers to focus the outsourcing debate on outright plant closures, with output being replaced by new greenfield investment abroad. But this latter definition seems to be too narrow to capture the scope of outsourcing discussed here.

Type of Outsourcing

Four types of "outsourcing", using location and control/ownership as distinguishing criteria, are:

1. *Captive onshore outsourcing* implies a shift in intra-firm supplies to an affiliated firm in the home economy.
2. If the shift in sourcing of supplies benefits a non-affiliated firm in the home economy, one can describe it as *non-captive onshore outsourcing*. The term "onshore" could be replaced in both cases by "local" or "domestic".
3. *Captive offshoring* describes a situation in which future supplies are sourced from an affiliated firm abroad.
4. The fourth variant of outsourcing may be labeled *non-captive offshoring* and refers to the case when the new supplier is a non-affiliated firm and located abroad.

From an international perspective, the latter two categories of outsourcing, namely captive and non-captive offshoring, are of particular interest.

FIGURE 1

TYPES OF OUTSOURCING

		Located in home economy	Located abroad
Shifting intra-firm inputs/supplies to	Non-affiliated firm	local/domestic/ onshore outsourcing	offshore outsourcing = offshoring
	Affiliated firm	captive onshore outsourcing	captive offshore outsourcing = captive offshoring

A major problem with the definitions above is that they do not concord easily with officially collected economic data. Outsourcing decisions are made at the micro level of plants or firms, while the official data are generally collected at the sectoral and national level. In the case of "offshoring", current statistical concepts do not allow a link to be made between import statistics and a management decision to substitute a product/ service produced in-house by an imported product. Moreover, in contrast to merchandise trade, services trade flows recorded in balance of payments (BOP) statistics are generally not broken down by region and country, which hampers analysis of the geographic aspects of services offshoring. A further difficulty in services trade statistics is due to the importance of the large internal services transactions of multinational firms. Many of these internal across-border transactions might not be reported.

Another obstacle arises if one attempts to look at the sectoral breakdown of offshoring. The sectoral affiliation of a firm might not match the product or service which is offshored. An automobile company might offshore its accounting services and a bank might offshore its IT services. Employment and the net value-added produced in the home country in the automobile (banking) sector might fall as a consequence of offshoring without a corresponding increase in the imports of automobiles (financial services). These difficulties in the sectoral allocation of offshored activities also affect the estimate on the offshore potential of an economy. Obviously, services activities can also be offshored by non-services sectors.

THE ECONOMICS OF OUTSOURCING

MNCs manage global value chains through internalization (ownership) and externalization (including non-equity modes (NEMs)). NEMs and FDI can be substitutes or complements, with the choice based on relative costs, benefits and associated risks. MNCs, like all firms, can decide to conduct such activities in-house (internalization) or they can entrust them to other firms (externalization) – a choice analogous to a "make or buy" decision. Internalization, where there is a cross-border dimension, results in FDI, whereby the international flows of goods, services, information and other assets are intra-firm and under the full control of the MNC. Externalization results either in trade, where the MNC exercises no control over other firms, or in non-equity inter-firm arrangements in which contractual agreements condition the operations and behaviour of host country partner firms.

The choice between internalization and externalization is typically based on the relative costs and benefits, the associated risks, and the feasibility of each option. Internalization of cross-border activities brings with it the costs of running complex, multi-plant, multicurrency operations, which tend to increase the greater the social, cultural and political differences between locations. It also implies internalizing the full extent of risk associated with the activity, including capital exposure and business uncertainty. Finally, it assumes that the technical capability, skills and know-how required to perform the activity are either present in the firm, or not prohibitively expensive or time-consuming to acquire.

Balanced against the costs of internalization are the obvious advantages of retaining full control of value-chain activities. To start with, MNCs will want to maximize "value capture" – externalization clearly implies giving up part of the profits generated along the chain. Secondly, internalization avoids the transaction costs associated with finding suitable third parties and then stipulating contractual arrangements that tend to become more complex the greater the perceived risks associated with loss of control over parts of the value chain and over assets and valuable intellectual property (IP). Finally, internalization also eliminates the costs of managing relationships with NEM partners on a continuous basis, including flows of knowledge, goods and services; communication and information flows; and monitoring and control of compliance with contractual obligations.

Externalization has a number of intrinsic advantages. These include shifting of certain costs and risks to third parties, as well as gaining rapid access to the assets and resources third parties may bring to the partnership. These can be "hard" assets, such as plants and equipment, access to low-cost resources, technological capability and knowhow, or often equally important "soft" assets, such as networks and relationships in host countries. Externalization allows the MNC to establish a more effective internal division of labour, freeing scarce resources to be used in other segments of its value chain – in other words, it allows a focus on "core business". Externalization is clearly more feasible if the knowledge and intellectual property required to conduct the activity are transferable, i.e. not tacit and to some extent standardized or codified.

From the MNC's perspective, the terms of contracts underpinning non-equity relationships are aimed at minimizing the cost of externalization and at protecting the assets, technology and IP exchanged. Non-contractual levers of control can also play a role in minimizing costs and risks to the MNC – the superior bargaining power of the MNC will alleviate concerns related to giving up a measure of control over part of its value chain. The degree of control given up by the MNC, the costs and associated risks of externalization, and the type of contractual and non-contractual levers which come into play, vary by mode, context and relative bargaining power of MNCs and non-equity trades (NEM) partners.

In building their international production networks, MNCs therefore have to decide not only on a location, but also on the mode of control and coordination of international operations. In the classic economic model describing this decision-making process, the ownership-location-internalization (OLI) model, the choice of mode in host countries is between ownership (FDI) and arm's length trade or licensing. Non-equity modes of international production represent an evolution of this model; they allow MNCs to enter a "middle ground" in their global value chains (GVC) governance by externalizing activities while still maintaining a level of control, i.e. improving the trade-off between the advantages and the costs of externalization. (Figure-2).

FIGURE 2

NON-EQUITY MODALITIES: A MIDDLE GROUND BETWEEN FDI AND

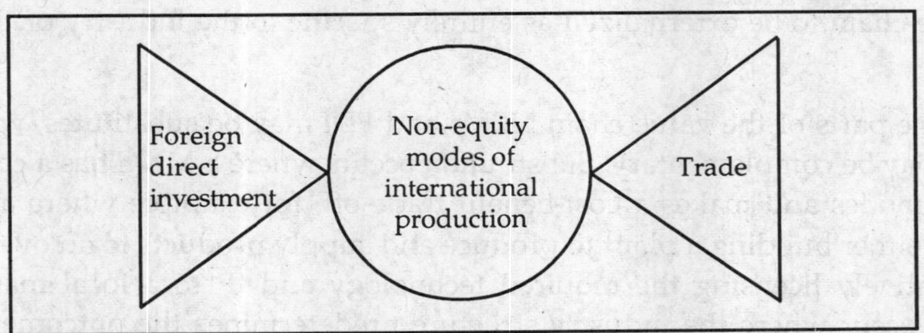

The choice is thus no longer between control through ownership (FDI) or no control (trade), but between a range of modes in which control is exercised in various configurations and to various degrees. Thus, in the case of wholly owned host country affiliates, control is defined purely by ownership; in the case of NEMs, control is exercised through contracts and bargaining power (Table-1). Equity joint ventures are a special case in which MNCs' control flows from a mix of equity and non-equity governance.

TABLE 1

Different Modes of MNC Governance in Global Value Chains

Types of governance	*Translation to modes of international operation*	*OLI-model*		
		Ownership advantages	*Locational advantages*	*Internalization advantages*
Control through ownership	FDI, direct participation in host-country firms	✓	✓	✓
Contractual levers of control	Contractual agreement conditions the behaviour of a host country firm	✓	✓	—
Control based on bargaining power	Host-country firm dependence on access to MNC strategic assets and the MNC network conditions its behaviour	✓	✓	—
No control	Arm's-length market transactions, trade	✓	—	—

Source: UNCTAD, adapted from Dunning (1980).

The ultimate ownership and control configuration of a GVC is thus the outcome of a set of strategic choices by the MNC. The type of non-equity modes that are available or appropriate along GVCs varies by value chain segment. Figure 3 shows that NEMs are not specific to any particular part of the value chain or type of activity – MNCs are generally prepared to externalize any activity that is not fundamental to competitive advantage in their market or industry and that can be carried out at lower cost or more effectively by third parties (including overseas), when the risks associated with externalization are limited or can be contained. Activities that are knowledge-intensive or high value added are not precluded. While certain patterns of NEM activity have emerged in different industries, it is useful to view the propensity of any given segment of a value chain to be externalized as entirely specific to the industry or the individual MNC.

In some parts of the value chain NEMs and FDI may be substitutes, while in others the two may be complementary. Substitution occurs where a MNC has a choice between different modes and makes a cost-benefit trade-off, for example where a firm has the option of either building a plant to produce and supply products to an overseas market, or alternatively licensing the required technology and IP to a local manufacturer. It may also occur where the industry structure predetermines the outcome of the trade-

FIGURE 3

SELECTED NEM-TYPES ALONG THE VALUE CHAIN

Corporate service and support processes				
• Business process outsourcing				
Technology/Intelectual property development				
• Contact R&D, Contract design, in-licensing				
Procurement/in-bound logistics	**Operations/ manufacturing**	**Out-bound logistics/ distrubution**	**Sales, service provisions, marketing**	**Aftersales and services**
• Contract farming • Procurement hubs • Contract manufacturing (intermediates)	• Contract manufacturing (assembly/final product) • Out-licensing	• Contract logistics	• Franchising • Management contracts • Concessions • Brand-licensing	• After-sales services outsourcing • Call centres

off. For example in the electronics industry, in most cases construction of a fully owned new components or assembly plant by a design- or brand-owner no longer makes economic sense in the presence of large and sophisticated global contract manufacturing firms.

Complementarity is a characteristic of MNC coordinated international production systems, which encompass a web of owned affiliates and third-party NEM relationships; both modes of operation are an integral part of the chain of global value creation. Moreover, complementarity may exist at the same stage in the value chain, where for example directly owned retail outlets coexist with franchise outlets, or where foreign affiliates are established to manage and facilitate NEM relationships (e.g. a commercial, procurement or logistics entity to support multiple contract manufacturing relationships in the same overseas market).

The composition of a MNC-governed GVC, and its ownership and control configuration, are dynamic. The partners in NEM relationships evolve over time. In some industries, NEM partner firms have grown into MNCs in their own right, not unusually expanding their NEM operations to new production bases or markets through FDI. Examples include Foxconn (Taiwan Province of China) (contract manufacturing) and Arcos Dorados (Argentina) (franchising). The mix of FDI and NEMs within GVCs can also shift as technologies and standards change. The evolution of MNC strategies in transition economies, broadly from FDI to franchising after the region opened up to international investors, is a case in point.

Make-or-Buy: Onshore or Offshore?

The major determinants of the make-or-buy decisions are the following: (i) technical and institutional separability; (ii) to what extent the task is standardized; (iii) transaction and managerial costs within the firm relative to outside suppliers; (iv) production costs; and (v) the size of the market.

Separability is obviously a precondition for outsourcing. Recent innovations, particularly in IT, have made an increasing number of service tasks separable in time and space. Services that basically collect, manipulate or organize information can be codified, digitized and separated from other tasks within the firm, and then become candidates for outsourcing. A number of entirely new information-based services and occupations have also emerged with the diffusion of IT. Examples are software developers and IT consultants and help-desk services, but also search services, and new types of media and content have opened opportunities for new independent service suppliers.

Standardization and automation were important driving forces in the development of extensive networks of more or less independent suppliers in the car industry. Once information-based services have been codified, digitized and separated, they can also be standardized and in some cases automated. Some can even be reduced to a set of instructions or tasks that workers can follow routinely. Examples of information-based services that can be codified, standardized and outsourced are accounting, billing, payroll, booking and many more. These are typically non-core tasks, both in manufacturing and services companies, and are increasingly outsourced to specialized external suppliers. In addition, as computer software has become standardized, many IT services have also become non-core and can be outsourced.

Managerial costs can be considerable within large companies and probably increase more than proportionally with the complexity of the task and the number of tasks being conducted. Furthermore, many of these costs are independent of the production volume (they are fixed) and constitute a higher share of total cost the smaller the scale of production. With outsourcing, such fixed managerial costs are limited to searching for a supplier and negotiating a contract, and these costs can be considerably lower than setting up in-house production. This is the most important reason why outsourcing is attractive. There are also variable managerial costs such as monitoring and coordinating production. These costs are usually lower with in-house production than with outsourcing, and make outsourcing less attractive. The make-or-buy decision is thus based on finding the balance between fixed and variable costs that results in the lowest total costs. The more standardized an activity, the lower the managerial cost of outsourcing. This is illustrated in figure-2, which shows the relationship between unit cost (including fixed and variable managerial costs and production costs) and standardization. A task is more standardized as we move to the right on the horizontal axis. At low levels of standardization, when the task in question is specific to the firm, it is likely to be produced in-house. The least standardized tasks are typically the strategic or core tasks and these are likely to remain in-house. The same goes for new tasks that are not (yet) standardized and high-skilled tasks that cannot easily be codified, while the standardized tasks are the first to be outsourced.

The relevance of market size for the make-or-buy decision was recognized at least as early as the 1950s. If firms must reach a minimum scale in order to break even, the number of firms that can operate profitably is limited by the size of the market. Likewise, within a firm a minimum scale is needed in order to employ specialists in all tasks and keep them fully occupied. But as firms grow, a larger administration is needed in order to coordinate activities and govern relations between divisions and individuals. At one point the cost of additional administration exceeds the benefits of additional tasks or components being produced in-house. Outsourcing is thus a way of avoiding expanding unit costs, but the existence of a network of outside suppliers requires a sufficiently large market.

Market size is important for one more reason that has to do with the risks related to outsourcing. The outsourcing firm must be sure that the supplier delivers the agreed quantity and quality of inputs at the agreed time, whether it is a service or a component. If not, the production process can be brought to a halt and in an environment with just-in-time production systems this can be extremely costly. Furthermore, if quality is not as agreed, the value of the outsourcing firm's brand name can deteriorate. If the market is large and there are a large number of alternative firms to search among, the chance of finding a good match is better and the chance of finding an alternative should a supplier fail is also better.

Turning to the other side of the outsourcing agreement, there are also uncertainties facing the outside supplier. Producing the agreed quality and quantity may require investment in new skills, new equipment and product development. Workers in call centres in India, for example, have to learn how to speak English the American way in order to enter into outsourcing contracts with American customers and they may have to install software that is compatible with the customers' and so on. If these investments are of little value outside the outsourcing contract, the sub-contractor may be left with costly but useless assets should the outsourcing firm breach or terminate the contract. Also, for this reason the types of tasks and components that are first outsourced are those that are standardized. This is the least risky for both parties. Standardization facilitates international trade, it also facilitates outsourcing.

If the outside supplier is located in the same country as the outsourcing firm, one should expect that production costs are the same, since the factors of production are purchased in the same market. If the activity in question can be offshored to a low-cost location, there are additional gains in terms of lower production costs, but there are also additional managerial costs. The latter depend on whether offshoring is through foreign direct investment (captive offshoring) or through entering a contract with an independent foreign supplier. In the case of captive offshoring, the costs of acquiring local knowledge about laws and regulations, the availability of non-tradable local inputs and so on have to be incurred in addition to the cost of setting up or acquiring the foreign firm. The additional managerial costs of non-captive offshoring consist only of searching for a partner and negotiating a contract. Captive offshoring thus involves a stronger commitment of the firms' resources than offshoring to independent suppliers.

There are also additional variable managerial costs related to offshoring. These are due to differences between the two countries involved in terms of language, laws, government regulations, currency, and usually also due to distance, since even digitized service provision requires some face-to-face communication between the contracting parties. The emphasis of many service-exporting countries on liberalization of service delivery through the movement of natural persons (mode 4 in the GATS) clearly indicates that face-to-face communication is still important. The additional costs related to differences between countries should be about the same for both types of offshoring, while it still holds that monitoring and coordination costs are lower within the firm (captive offshoring) than with outside suppliers (non-captive offshoring).

Fixed managerial costs differ between the four types of outsourcing as follows:

Captive offshoring > local in-house production > non-captive offshoring > local outsourcing.

Unit production costs are lowest with offshoring, and in figure-4 this compensates for higher fixed managerial costs and makes captive offshoring cheaper than domestic in-house production at high levels of standardization. Finally it is recalled that monitoring and coordination costs are lower with in-house production (at home or abroad) and lower with domestic outsourcing than non-captive offshoring. Unit cost as a function of the degree of standardization for all four types of outsourcing are depicted in Figure-4.

Figure-4 shows that an activity needs to reach a certain level of standardization before it is profitable to outsource it. When that threshold is reached it is still the best option to keep production within the firm, but locate production to a low-cost country. With further standardization it becomes profitable to outsource the activity to an independent supplier, but to a local one. Only at relatively high levels of standardization will it pay off to offshore to an independent producer, given the cost function depicted in the figure-4. Moving from left to right on the standardization axis can be interpreted as moving from the strategic core of the firm towards non-core, standard activities. It is important to bear in mind that while developing software is the core business of a

FIGURE 4

COSTS, STANDARDIZATION AND TYPES OF OUTSOURCING

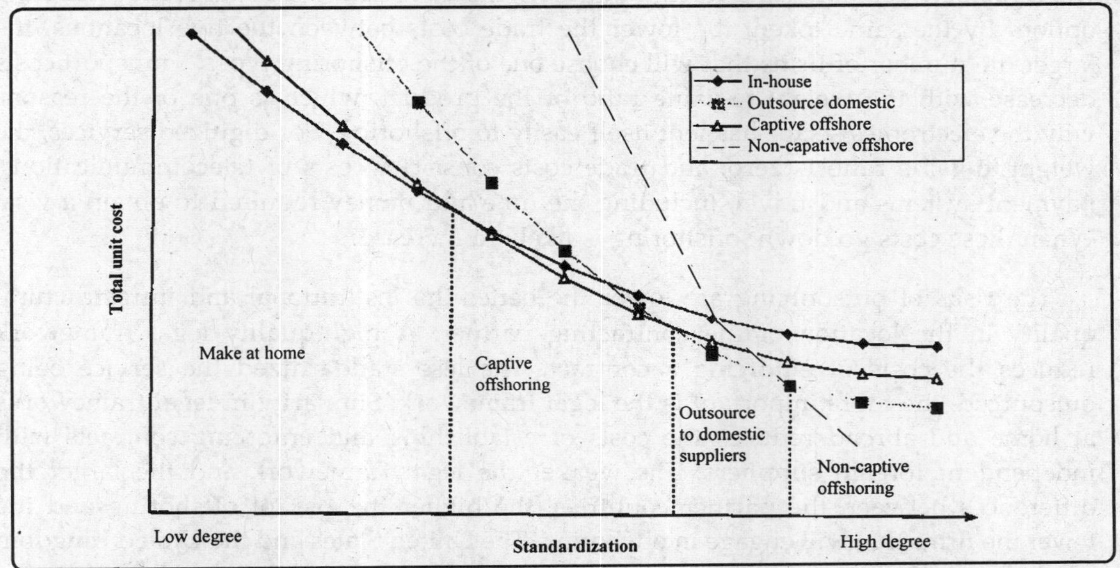

software firm, it is not a core business of, say a bank, and the latter will outsource maintenance and adaptation of software to outside suppliers while a software firm will not. A high degree of standardization is closely related to mature technology. Figure-4 can thus be interpreted to mean that high-technology firms undertaking mainly high-technology activities are likely to retain most activities in-house, although they do engage in captive offshoring to some extent. Low-technology firms undertaking mainly low-technology activities, in contrast, are likely to outsource.

The shape and position of the curves in Figure-4 depend on the characteristics of the firm in question. It is well known that even firms in the same country and the same industry differ widely in terms of productivity and costs. A high-productivity firm is able to produce more from a given amount of inputs than a low-productivity firm. A highly productive firm can afford to pay higher fixed costs than a less productive firm, and is therefore more likely to both outsource and offshore. Its reward for doing so is to further improve its cost competitiveness. The firms with the lowest productivity, in contrast, are unable to offshore and may not even be able to compete with those who do, and could be driven out of business. This is a creative destruction process where the least productive firms will be driven out of business while larger and more productive firms prevail and expand, improving average productivity in the offshoring industry as a whole.

The shape and position of the curves in Figure-4 also depend on relative wages in the two countries involved, communication and travel costs between the two locations, and differences in the general business climate in the two locations. The larger the wage gap between home and foreign locations, the more firms will choose the offshoring option. By the same token, the lower the trade costs between the two locations, the larger the number of firms that will choose one of the offshoring types. Transport costs decrease with the weight-to-value ratio of the product, which is one of the reasons why the electronics sector has lent itself easily to offshoring. For digitized services, the weight-to-value ratio is zero, and trade costs consist of costs of telecommunications, payment systems and travel, including the time and money required to obtain a visa. When these costs go down, offshoring is likely to increase.

The risks of outsourcing are lower the better the institutional and infrastructural quality in the location of the contracting partner. A high-quality legal framework reduces the costs of enforcing a contract. The less standardized the service being outsourced, the more important is the legal framework. Similarity in legal frameworks at home and abroad reduces the costs of establishing and enforcing contracts with independent foreign suppliers. The weaker the legal framework and the larger the differences between the partner countries, the higher the risk of offshoring and the fewer the firms that will engage in offshoring. The United States and the United Kingdom are the leading outsourcing countries. India's and Ireland's success in attracting offshoring business has been partly attributed to their English-speaking workforce. Outsourcing from the other leading industrial countries is much less extensive. Furthermore, their sourcing of services tends to be from countries which are closer to home geographically and/or culturally. A large share of German outsourcing contracts goes to Central Europe, while a large share of Spain's outsourcing contracts go to Latin America.

Low wages and poor quality of institutions and infrastructure typically go together. Therefore, offshoring businesses are more likely to go to middle-income countries than to least-developed countries. Among the low-income and least-developed countries, large countries are more likely to attract outsourcing businesses. Finally, it should be noted that institutional and infrastructural quality at the national level are not always the most relevant variable to look at. In some cases, notably in India, software parks and other special zones have excellent infrastructure and effective one-stop-shops for sorting out the legal formalities of establishing and running a business, even if the average quality in the country as a whole leaves much to be desired.

Thus, the driving forces for outsourcing and offshoring services are first and foremost technology development, notably ICT, and economic growth. Growth leads to and feeds on a higher degree of specialization. Developments in IT have made it possible to standardize, digitize and outsource a number of services, of which some are offshored. The location of offshored services depends on: labour costs; trade costs; the quality of institutions particularly the legal framework; the tax and investment regime, the quality of infrastructure particularly telecommunications; and the skills - particularly language and computer skills.

Improvement in the regulatory environment, such as trade liberalization for imported inputs, lifting of foreign investment restrictions, favourable taxation and low-interest export credits have complemented the dynamic export performance of the two largest IT traders, namely Ireland and India. Thus, offshoring is likely to be concentrated on non-core standardized services. Large and highly productive firms are the most likely to engage in offshoring. Host countries of offshoring activities are likely to be relatively low-cost, with good telecommunications infrastructure, and a reasonably good record on the rule of law. Being close to the offshoring partner in terms of physical distance and/or language and culture also helps.

IMPLICATIONS OF OUTSOURCING AND OFFSHORING

(a) Implications for the Outsourcing/Offshoring Country

Since services account for between two-thirds and three-quarters of total employment in developed economies, productivity gains in this sector are essential to economic growth and improvements in welfare. Furthermore, since services constitute a large and growing share of GDP in developed as well as emerging economies, world trade growth would probably slow down relative to world income growth in the long run if services were not traded. World trade has been an important engine of world growth and development during the post-World War II period and trade in services, including offshoring, will sustain this process. In short, offshoring contributes to a continuation of the post-World War II trend of increased international integration, where trade as a share of GDP has increased and led to growth through specialization, technology diffusion and shifting comparative advantage. It is not new, but represents a deepening of existing trends.

Innovation can take the form of development of new goods, services or processes. New goods and services are typically specific to the innovating firm and are produced in-house. However, as the product, service or process matures, it becomes standardized and a possible candidate for outsourcing. The process at the firm level is one of adding new innovations at the technology frontier, spinning off mature goods and services while maintaining a focused and productive organization. The finance sector springs to mind as the most prominent service sector subject to this dynamic. However, services such as entertainment, media, software development, engineering, architecture, design and even education and health, have started to standardize and outsource routine tasks. In the health sector, this could enable highly skilled health personnel to focus on providing and improving treatment rather than spending a lot of time on routine tasks. Both in manufacturing and services, what is typically retained within the organization are those tasks that are of strategic importance and hence the tasks that contribute directly to distinguishing the final product from that of competitors.

At the national level the process is one of changing comparative advantage with the accumulation of physical and human capital, and shifting the areas of specialization to higher-technology activities. IT has opened the services sector to this dynamic, and vertical disintegration in service sectors is increasingly common. An indication of the extent to which a sector is vertically integrated is the ratio of value added to gross output, i.e. the share of the sales value that has been produced in-house. The most important in-house production factor is labour. Typically, vertically integrated industries have a high share of compensation to employees in their total cost structure. Compensation of employees, taxes and operating surplus represent the value that is created within companies, while material inputs and the different categories of services inputs are purchased from other companies.

The total impact on the economy of reduced costs in the service sectors depends on how the savings are spent. The cost savings could be passed on to customers through lower prices, or they could be captured by the firms through higher profits or by workers through higher wages. The more competitive the market, the larger the share of cost savings will be passed on to customers through lower prices. If the tax rate and profit margin are kept constant, the price of business services and administrative support services would decline by the same percentage as the cost. If firms avoid passing cost savings on to customers, and maintain their output prices, the profit margin would increase in business services and in administrative support services. This could lead to a higher investment rate in the sector and better services in the longer run, which could in turn have a similar effect as a lower price, There is, however, no one-to-one relationship between profit margin and investment, and all or part of the additional profits could simply add to shareholders' consumption expenditure. If the cost savings from outsourcing was captured by the remaining workers in the outsourcing companies, some of the gains would be spent, and some would be saved, contributing to higher investment. It would probably also lead to pressure for higher wages in other sectors which draw on the same pool of skills - and subsequent pressure to outsource to save costs.

In reality, the gains from outsourcing are a mix of elements, but lower costs contribute to higher income and more investment, whichever way the gains from outsourcing and offshoring are spent. The difference is the relative importance of these effects and probably the time it takes for the gains to work their way through the economy, is known that the total employment level and the aggregate trade balance of an economy are determined by domestic macro-economic policy, while trade policy and technical changes at home and abroad affect the composition of trade and employment. Offshoring services to non-affiliated firms abroad has the same effect as trade in intermediate inputs in general: it improves productivity in the offshoring firm through lower costs of each individual offshored input and through a broader variety of inputs. Further, it has the usual effect of reducing the relative income of the production factor that is used intensively in the import-competing activity. In most conceivable cases this improves welfare for the world as a whole.

Captive offshoring introduces an additional dimension into the analysis since it affects the relative endowments of capital and labour both in the outsourcing and recipient country. In general an outflow of capital results in a shift in employment from capital-intensive to labour-intensive sectors in the capital-exporting country. The opposite is true in the capital-importing country. This is to some extent counterbalanced by the repatriation of profits. In any case, the capital flows will probably have to be larger than observed for captive offshoring of services to have a discernible effect on the total composition of employment.

It is also important to ask what is the alternative to offshoring. It may well be a defensive strategy by the offshoring company in order to maintain market share in the face of increased import competition in the market for its final output. In that case, the alternative to offshoring is not domestic production but a loss of market share and downsizing. This is particularly relevant in industries that perform a mix of high-skilled and low-skilled activities, where the low-skilled activities constitute a relatively large share of total costs.

(b) Impact of Outsourcing on the Service-Exporting Country

The impact for service-exporting countries draws on insights from the theory of multinational enterprises, FDI and trade. The possible gains from FDI in host countries are: employment creation (in cases of unemployment and underemployment); increase in total investment (in capital-constrained host countries); technology spillovers; linkages to the local economy etc. A possible negative effect can be crowding out of local industries. The IT-enabled services sector in many of the major exporters (India, Ireland and the Philippines) is mainly producing for exports and thus falls under the export-platform FDI category. This type of FDI is unlikely to crowd out local industries, particularly if unemployment and capital constraints exist in the host country.

Many of the IT-enabled services enterprises that export from India and other poor countries would probably not have established there at all if not for the purpose of exporting, since local demand for such services is unlikely to have initiated or sustained them. This is because the existence of specialized services suppliers requires that both the supplier and the customer have IT hardware (computers and telecommunication lines), and computer and telecommunication penetration in India is low. The telephone penetration rate (fixed and mobile lines) was only 5.2 per 100 inhabitants in 2002, while in the Philippines it was about 22. This compares for example to 33 lines per 100 inhabitants in China and 40 in Mexico. Indian domestic sales in the software and services industry accounted for $3.4 billion out a total of $15.9 billion sales in 2003/04.

India and the Philippines have substantial unemployment and underemployment problems and they are also capital-constrained. Therefore, jobs created and investments made in the IT services exporting sector are likely to be net additions to total employment and investment. The number of software-related jobs created in India in order to service the US market was about 135,000 in 2004, while there were 195,000 "active export focused IT professionals" in 2003, while the corresponding figure for the Philippines was 20,000.

Ireland is not capital-constrained and does not have an unemployment problem today, but some 15-20 years ago it was among the European countries with the highest unemployment rate, at almost 17 per cent in 1985 and 1986. The unemployment rate went down to 3.9 per cent in 2001, but picked up slightly after 2001 following the burst of IT bubble. ICT (both software and hardware) has been an important part of Ireland's amazing catch-up with the leading EU economies since it became a member in 1973. ICT services accounted for 7 per cent of total employment in services in 2002. Foreign-owned enterprises play a more important role in ICT manufacturing, where 97 out of 136 enterprises were foreign-owned and accounted for 84 per cent of employment and 97 per cent of turnover. Ireland has been highly successful in attracting export platform FDI and foreign-owned firms accounted for 89 per cent of Ireland's services exports in 2002. Furthermore, over time the foreign firms have established linkages to the local economy and their demand for skilled labour has motivated investment in human capital.

The extent to which captive offshoring creates linkages and/or spillovers to the local economy is crucial for its development effect. Linkages are found to be small for export-platform FDI in general. Spillovers are more difficult to measure and entail technology transfers, for example via a skills pool on which domestic and foreign companies can draw. Another impact stems from investments in infrastructure that are made in order to attract or accommodate foreign firms, but also benefit local firms and the community at large. Finally, there could be a demonstration effect, inspiring local entrepreneurs as well as other foreign companies to invest in the same country. In particular, if one or more of the major multinationals offshore to a country, others are more likely to follow suit.

Export-led growth in the newly industrialized Asian countries (NICs) in the 1960s was founded on investments in industries that were at the frontier of the countries' technological capacity and for which domestic demand had not yet reached levels that could sustain a scale-effective industry. These exporting industries became recipients of technology transfers from abroad and channels for technology diffusion to local suppliers, creating linkages and thereby serving as engines of growth. Rapid export growth from export processing zones, in contrast, has not generated sustained development unless the exporting industries have over time become integrated into the local economy. Drawing on this experience, it can be concluded that the development effect of hosting offshored services depends on the extent to which these services become integrated with the local economy over time.

Turning to the impact on income distribution in exporting countries, it has been noted that in Mexico, outsourcing of manufacturing activities from the United States has actually led to an increase in demand for skills and an increase in wage inequality - the opposite of what one would expect in trade between a rich and a poorer country. The reason is that while the activities being outsourced are relatively unskilled and labour-intensive in the United States, they are relatively skills-intensive in Mexico due to the differences in industrial structure between the two countries. A similar effect is observed in outsourcing of services to e.g. India, although the evidence is more of an anecdotal nature. Routine information processing is low-skilled labour intensive in the United States and other developed countries, but the skills requirement is well above what the average Indian worker possesses. Besides, multinational companies tend to pay higher wages than local companies, further contributing to wider wage gaps. Therefore, offshoring is likely to increase employment and exports in India, but may not have a similarly favourable effect on income distribution, at least in the first instance.

OFFSHORING AND THE GATS

Offshoring is related to the GATS Agreement, and what opportunities might exist for extending opportunities for trade involving offshoring under transparent and predictable multilateral arrangements. Since 1995, the GATS has provided a framework for the liberalization of virtually all services sectors. Based on a so-called "positive list approach", it allows governments to undertake specific commitments sector by sector and according to four modes of supply. *Cross-border supply* (mode 1) is defined to cover services flows from the territory of one Member (A) into the territory of another Member (B); *consumption abroad* (mode 2) refers to situations where a service is supplied in the territory of Member A to a service consumer of another Member B; *commercial presence* (mode 3) implies that a service supplier of one Member (A) establishes a commercial presence in the territory of another Member (B) to provide a service; and the *presence of natural persons* (mode 4) consists of persons of one Member (A) entering the territory of another Member (B) to supply a service.

The most relevant mode of supply for offshoring activities is the so-called "cross-border supply" of services (or "mode 1"), which is defined as "the supply of a service from the territory of one Member into the territory of another Member" (Art. 1:2(a)). Examples of cross-border delivery include international transport, the supply of services through telecommunications or mail, as well as services embodied in exported goods. Electronic transactions also fall inter alia under mode 1.

In the discussions on electronic commerce, there was a generally shared view among WTO Members that the GATS was technologically neutral, in the sense that it does not contain any provisions that distinguish between the different technological means through which a service may be supplied. This principle, referred to as "technological neutrality" means, in particular, that mode 1 specific commitments undertaken during the Uruguay Round, when Internet was not widely used by the business community, do cover Internet transactions. The principle of technological neutrality has been endorsed by a recent WTO dispute settlement panel. In the United States - Gambling dispute, the Panel considered that the definition of mode 1 in Article 1:2(a) does not contain any indication as to the means that can be used to supply services cross-border. This indicates that the GATS does not limit the various technologically neutral possible means of delivery under mode l. A market access commitment for mode 1 implies the right for other Members' suppliers to supply a service through all means of delivery, whether by mail, telephone, Internet, etc., unless otherwise specified in a Member's Schedule. One should note, however, that this panel report has been appealed. It is thus too early to consider this statement as formally endorsed by WTO Members.

Should an Internet transaction also be considered as mode 2, defined as the supply of a service "in the territory of one Member to the service consumer of any other Member" (so-called "consumption abroad", Art. 1:2(b)). For mode 1, the supplier is situated outside the territory of the Member having undertaken the commitment. In theory, the main distinction between mode 1 and mode 2 is that the service is delivered within the territory of the Member for the former mode and outside the territory in the case of mode 2. However, electronic delivery blurs this distinction, and the physical presence of the consumer is not necessarily a relevant criterion for determining the place of delivery of a service. So far, WTO Members have discussed this issue mainly in relation to financial services and have not reached a clear understanding on how to address it. As the same problem arises in all sectors where services can be supplied electronically, and as these have increased with the development of the Internet, this means that the scope for potential controversial situations has expanded as well. However, in practice, a problem may only arise when, for a given sector; the level of commitment is different for mode 1 and mode 2 (for instance, there is an "Unbound" for mode 1 and a "None" for mode 2). An understanding among Members on whether mode 1 and /or mode 2 are/is relevant for electronic supply might facilitate negotiations. Pending an agreed solution, the best approach may be to ensure a similar level of commitments for both modes 1 and 2.

The degree of market opening consolidated under the GATS is determined by specific commitments undertaken by each Member in its national schedule. GATS specific commitments can be defined as legal guarantees enjoyed by foreign services suppliers, governing conditions of access to a market and conditions of competition vis-a-vis domestic suppliers. In GATS terms, the concept of market access entails six quota-type and other specified restrictions. National treatment refers to the obligation to accord to services and service suppliers of other Members treatment no less favourable than the treatment accorded to national services and service suppliers. Members have the possibility to select the sectors and modes of supply for which they are ready to undertake specific commitments. Moreover, these specific commitments can be qualified with various types of limitations, thus allowing a Member to tailor them to its specific national policy objectives. Therefore, specific commitments undertaken under mode 1 - and mode 2 - in relevant sectors (professional services, computer services, financial services, but also health and education, for instance) do guarantee a certain level of transparency and predictability to countries supplying services under these modes, including offshoring-related services. Full market access and national treatment commitments mean that the "importing" Member cannot maintain or implement any of the six market access measures listed in Article XVI and cannot discriminate, de jure or de facto, against foreign services and service suppliers. Moreover, the undertaking of specific commitments triggers the application of other GATS disciplines, related in particular to transparency requirements, good regulatory practice, behaviour of monopolies, and also the Annex on Telecommunication Services.

Services trade in most sectors is heavily regulated and the need to regulate is likely to increase as competition develops. The GATS explicitly recognizes the right of Members to regulate, and introduce new regulations, on the supply of services within their territories in order to meet national policy objective. Members reaffirmed this principle in the Negotiating Guidelines which provide the framework for the current negotiations; Policy objectives include, inter alia, the protection of the consumer or the need to ensure the quality of the service and/or the qualifications of the supplier. The GATS does not seek to influence policy objectives, but establishes a framework of rules to ensure that services regulations are administered in a reasonable, objective and impartial manner, and are not more burdensome than necessary. Furthermore, Members are currently developing disciplines to ensure that certain types of non-discriminatory measures (qualification requirements and procedures, technical standards and licensing requirements) are based on objective and transparent criteria, and do not constitute unnecessary barriers to trade in services. Applying these measures to cross-border trade raises a number of questions which should be given closer consideration. For instance, does a measure impact differently on services supplied electronically as opposed to those supplied by suppliers who are present within the territory of the Member (modes 3 and 4)? Does the electronic supply of services call for different types of regulatory approaches? For instance, how are qualification and licensing requirements enforced with respect to suppliers situated outside the territory of the "importing" Member?

Another relevant aspect of the GATS framework is its exception provisions. Article XIV, for instance, contains general exceptions which are obviously pertinent for electronic transactions. This provision allows in certain conditions Members to depart from their GATS obligations, including their specific commitments, to take measures necessary to achieve certain public policy objectives, such as the protection of public morals and the maintenance of public order. In this context, it is also worth noting that Article XIV(c) permits, inter alia, Members to take measures necessary to protect the privacy of the personal data of individuals and the confidentiality of individual records and accounts, and to prevent deceptive and fraudulent practices.

The current services negotiations offer an opportunity to improve existing commitments, and undertake new commitments. But how far have modes 1 and 2 been consolidated in Members' schedules in previous negotiations? A WTO Secretariat study reveals that mode 1 has attracted overall far fewer commitments than mode 3, for instance. One explanation may be that Members have considered this mode of supply not to be technically feasible for given sectors (which they sometimes explicitly indicated with an "Unbound*"). Indeed, cross-border supply is irrelevant - and will remain so - for a number of activities which, by their very nature, require physical proximity between the consumer and the supplier (hotel and restaurant services, hairdressing services, for instance). However, one should note that the assumptions concerning the "technical feasibility" of trading services cross-border may have changed since the end of the Uruguay Round as a result of technological developments. Uncertainties about how to enforce regulatory measures with respect to suppliers situated abroad may be another explanation which prompted governments to retain the right to prohibit all suppliers for reasons of "regulatory prudence". But the main characteristic of mode 1 commitments is that they are mostly consolidated as "None" (i.e. no limitation) or "Unbound"; limitations are less common than for mode 3, for instance; fewer types are used (they include mainly nationality, residency and commercial presence requirements) and they are found mainly in financial, telecoms and professional services. Another interesting characteristic is that the level of bindings for individual modes, including mode 1, does not differ significantly between developed and developing countries. However, such general patterns would need to be interpreted with care since, for a given mode, there may be big variations from one sector to another. Specific commitments undertaken with respect to mode 2 are significantly more liberal than those for the other three modes of supply. Most of the time, limitations scheduled for

* Much of this case focuses on one particular electronics product – a laptop computer. Its production process exhibits many interesting features that illustrate the changing nature of offshoring within the electronics industry more broadly. While describing how this particular product is intertwined with the fragmentation phenomenon, some of the characteristics that differentiate the electronics sector from other manufacturing sectors are also examined. Such an analysis sheds light not only on the more fundamental forces driving the fragmentation process, but also ultimately its limitations.

mode 1 have not been repeated under mode 2. This may be a potential source of difficulty given the discussions surrounding the status of electronic transactions.

It is important to recall that the absence of specific commitments in a given sector does not mean the absence of trading opportunities. In fact, actual access conditions for services supplied electronically, in particular information technology services and business process outsourcing, tend to be rather liberal. Of course, scheduling commitments in relevant sub-sectors would add transparency and predictability for business operators.

It is also useful to recall that some general GATS disciplines do apply to services trade even in the absence of specific commitments. The most important of such disciplines is no doubt the obligation not to discriminate among services or services suppliers based on their nationality (MFN obligation). Other generally applicable disciplines include transparency requirements (obligation to publish all measures of general application and to establish enquiry points mandated to respond to other Members' information requests), establishment of administrative reviews and appeals procedures and disciplines on the operations of monopolies and exclusive suppliers.

While modes 1 and 2 are no doubt most relevant for the development of offshoring activities, the fact that two-thirds of all offshoring is "captive" offshoring suggests that lifting foreign investment restrictions may contribute to developing offshoring activities in "exporting" countries. Mode 3 commitments by the countries "exporting" offshoring activities may further contribute to the development of offshoring centers, in particular in developing countries.

Is the GATS equipped to promote further liberalization of offshoring-related services? Some commentators consider that the current framework is "far from ideal". In addition to the uncertain status of electronic delivery as in relation to mode 1 and mode 2, the main criticism concerns the current classification system, which would inadequately reflect "new" services, as well as the "positive list approach" which, coupled with the request-offer process used in the negotiations, would slow down liberalization efforts. Proposals to correct these perceived deficiencies range from the use of model schedules for cross-border trade of IT and BPO services (such schedules were used in the negotiations on telecommunications and maritime transport, for instance), to undertaking a horizontal commitment to liberalize cross-border trade in a wide range of services (such horizontal commitments would mean, in fact, adopting a negative list approach for modes 1 and 2).

Overall, the past experience has shown that opportunities provided by technological change contribute markedly to economy-wide productivity gains, which are the source of all lasting income gains. All major technological changes require adjustment of production capacities and the employment structure. In the (net) offshoring economies, flexibility in periods of adjustment reduces the losses which some firms and employees inevitably will experience at the beginning. The adoption of new technologies and management methods is usually stretched over a significant trial and error period and the normal turnover rates (or churn rates) in the labour markets accommodate structural changes to a large extent. In ten years' time, "the new wave of globalization" brought by the offshoring of services will be compared with previous revolutions such as e-commerce. The projections of the expansion of e-commerce in the mid-90s was not as significant as predicted, but this new technology has found its niche in the retail distribution. Likewise, offshoring of IT and IT-enabled services will increase significantly in size in the coming years without upsetting national employment levels in the countries which offshore, given the normal turnover rates in labour markets. Neither will it dramatically change the overall employment situation in the countries providing the offshored services, given their large labour force growth in the years ahead. Finally, as far as the GATS is concerned, offshoring is one of many services sectors that could be subject to multilateral market access commitments under GATS auspices, aimed at increasing predictable and transparent trading opportunities.

LAPTOP COMPUTER: A CASE STUDY

What makes the production of a laptop computer an interesting case study to examine? By many accounts, the production of a laptop is the epitome of the fragmentation process. First, creation of the final good requires various components, such as semi-conductors, a hard drive, motherboard, memory and display panels, that are frequently designed, produced and assembled in different locations, potentially in different countries, by firms with differing types of contractual arrangements with the end-good producer. Second, such a product is interesting to study because, in many instances, firms have established a sales process in which they permit and even encourage (through price incentives) the customer to create a highly specialized "made to order" product. This feature will highlight the sensitivity of this product to the increasing importance of "timeliness", i.e. the difficulty that firms have to hold a large inventory. This is increasingly being recognised by economists as a new factor driving fragmentation.

Many computer firms that make laptops (e.g. Dell, IBM/Lenovo, etc.) have developed internet sales techniques which allow customers to tailor the design of their computers to their specific tastes or needs. The firm, therefore, has an important role at the beginning and end of the production process – e.g. designing the overall product as well as marketing (advertising, sales) it to end-users. One implication of accommodating customized demand, however, is that the producer becomes constrained in its ability to hold available inventory. Nevertheless, this level of customer demand would not be possible but for advances in telecommunications and information technology.

Many of the steps in the production of the laptop take place via a fragmented production process – e.g. the motherboard may be produced in Japan, the hard drive in Singapore, the memory in the Republic of Korea, the display panel in Chinese Taipei, the microprocessor in Malaysia, etc. – and everything is assembled into a recognizable computer in China. Economic research has documented a number of patterns in the production process and can help to explain the rationale for the fragmented approach and its implications.

First, consider the basic relevance of the decline since 1957 in air transport costs. This is likely to have substantial implications for an industry such as electronics for a number of different reasons. *First,* while the cost of air transport has fallen, for any given weight of the product being transported air shipment is still much more expensive than ocean shipping. One implication of this is that the first products that would be costeffective to ship by air once air transport prices start to decline would be lightweight products with high unit values. Many electronics products fall into this category, including laptop computers. *Second,* the reduction in air transport costs may affect the production process for goods for which "timeliness" is important. The reduction in air transport costs not only helps explain why products such as laptop computers might be traded (imported and exported) internationally, but it can also help to explain why the production process has become so fragmented.

Consider again the full process by which laptops are produced and consumed. Time is an important factor influencing global specialization and trade. Time is valuable because it allows retailers to respond to fluctuations in demand without holding large quantities of inventory. Products where timely delivery is important will be produced near the source of final demand. While this would appear to run counter to the example of the laptop computer, for which consumers are located primarily in the United States or Europe while production takes place largely in South East Asia, a closer inspection suggests that this is not necessarily the case.

With the availability of air transport reducing the timeliness factor for trade between the consumer markets and South East Asia, the source of almost final demand (assembly of components) need not be in close proximity to consumer demand. Nevertheless, even with air shipping, the need for timeliness between the assembly needs and the production of component inputs may drive the localization of production of those components to be within an accessible distance. Indeed the need for timeliness leads to a geographical clustering of economic activity. If final assembly takes place in two locations and component production has increasing returns to scale, component production will tend to cluster around just one of the assembly plants.

In addition to the reduced cost of air shipping, there may also be "quality improvements", although these are more difficult to measure accurately. Nevertheless, in addition to a reduction in average shipping time, improvements in reliability might be measured via a reduction in the variance of shipping times. Technological innovations, such as improvements in methods for handling cargo, may also allow more sensitive products to be shipped internationally in addition to improvements in insurance coverage. Furthermore, there have also been substantial innovations in the telecommunications sector which allow greater fragmentation in the production process. For example, widespread adoption of bar codes and digital scanning results in less costly tracking of components and permits greater distance between different stages of the production process. So the production and assembly of the motherboard, hard drive, display panel, memory and microprocessor for a laptop need not all take place on a single factory floor – in fact, their production can take place at different factories in different countries at different times. Again, such innovations allow producers of intermediate goods and assemblers to hold smaller amounts of inventory. This is particularly important for products that rapidly depreciate in value.

Given the substantial differences in transport costs across countries, there is likely to be a role for the public sector in influencing how transport costs affect the fragmentation of the electronics industry. For example, some of the improvements in the quality and cost of air shipping as an alternative to ocean shipping involve not only technological innovations in the manufacture of aircraft, but also improvements in logistics, public infrastructure and regulatory conditions. In the context of air shipping, important factors include customs clearance delays (trade documentation), the quality of adjoining transport links (such as road haulage and rail) as well as airport efficiency and openness to trade (for example, the number of airports with paved runways capable of accommodating cargo airplanes). Finally, for a fragmented process such as the production of laptops, it may also be important for the country to have reliable access to e-business networks as well as "electronic data interchange" between producers and freight-forwarding companies..

When it comes to understanding the fragmentation of the production process for a product such as a laptop computer, separate from the question of transport costs is the issue of contractual relationships between firms involved the production process. Specifically, are they subsidiaries of a multinational firm, or are these arm's-length transactions occurring between suppliers and buyers? Are these long-term and/or repeat contracts, or are these components purchased from a spot market?

While a laptop computer can be relatively customized by the consumer, he/she is typically asked to choose from an available menu of parts and components when designing the computer's specifications. It is frequently the case, however, that these components tend to be standardized inputs. Thus, more arm's-length trade is expected than intra-firm trade in this sort of sector. As a result of contractual difficulties, goods are initially manufactured in the North, where product development takes place. As the goods become more standardized, the manufacturing stage of production is shifted to the South to take advantage of lower wages. The organization of the production process is also affected by incomplete contracts. This type of model gives rise to a new version of the product cycle in which manufacturing is first shifted to the South to subsidiary firms, and only at a later stage to independent firms in the South.

The share of arm's-length trade has increased at the expense of intra-firm trade within Japanese multinationals in East Asian countries over time. While this trend is observed for all machinery sectors, it is much stronger for the electronics sector. Clearly, as electronic goods become standardized, contractual difficulties arise less often, and arms length trade with specialized producers becomes more efficient.

QUESTIONS

1. Critically examine the elements of global supply chain management. How quality affects the global supply chain?
2. Explain how inventory management is a key dimension of the global supply chain. Illustrate the functioning of a global supplier networks.
3. Critically examine the various steps in global sourcing process.
4. Describe the different dimensions of global manufacturing strategy.
5. Discuss the different alternatives for transporting products along the supply chain from suppliers to customers.
6. Critically examine the basic issues in international logistics and materials management.
7. Why is effective operation management important for an international firms?
8. What is an international operation management? How does a firm's corporate strategy affect its operation management?
9. How do materials management and physical distribution differ?

REFERENCES

Amiti, M. and Wei, S.J. (2005) 'Fear of service outsourcing: is it justified?', *Economic Policy* 20, 42: 308-347.

Anderson, J.E. (1979) 'A theoretical foundation for the gravity equation', *American Economic Review* 69, 1: 106 -116.

Antras, P., Garicano, L., and Rossi-Hansberg, E. (2006) 'Offshoring in a knowledge economy', *Quarterly Journal of Economics* 121, 1: 31-77.

Antras, P. and Helpman, E. (2004) 'Global sourcing', *Journal of Political Economy* 112, 3: 552-580.

Baldwin, R. (2006) 'Offshoring and globalisation: What is new about the new paradigm?', Mimeo, Geneva: Graduate Institute of International Studies.

Baldwin, R. and Robert-Nicoud, F. (2007) 'Offshoring: General equilibrium effects on wages, production and trade', *NBER Working Paper No. 12991*, Cambridge, M A: NBER.

Basel Committee on Banking Supervision (2005) 'Outsourcing in financial services', Basel: BIS.

Basker, E. (2007) 'The causes and consequences of Wal-Mart's growth ', *The Journal of Economic Perspectives* 21, 3: 177-198.

Basker, E. and Van, P.H. (2007) 'Wal-Mart as catalyst to U.S.-China trade', *Department of Economics Working Paper N° 0710*, Columbia, MO: University of Missouri.

Bernard, A.B., Jensen, J. B., and Schott, P. K. (2006b) 'Falling trade costs, heterogeneous firms, and industry dynamics', *Journal of Monetary Economics* 53, 5: 917-937.

Blinder, A.S. (2006) 'Offshoring: The next industrial revolution?', *Foreign Affairs* 85, 2: 113-128.

Davis, D.R. and Harrigan, J. (2007) 'Good jobs, bad jobs, and trade liberalization', *NBER Working Paper N° 13139*, Cambridge, M A: NBER.

Deloitte Touche Tomatsu (2006) Global Financial Services Offshoring: Scaling the Heights.

—— (2007) *Global financial services offshoring Report 2007: Optimizing offshore operations.*

Ekholm, K. and Hakkala, K. (2006) 'The effect of offshoring on labor demand: Evidence from Sweden', CEPR *Discussion Paper N° 5648*, London: CEPR.

Feenstra, R.C. and Hanson, G. (1999) 'The impact of outsourcing and high-technology capital on wages: Estimates for the United States, 1979-1990', *Quarterly Journal of Economics* 114, 3: 907-940.

—— (1996) 'Globalization, outsourcing, and wage inequality', *The American Economic Review* 86, 2: 240-245.

Gancia, G. and Zilibotti, F. (2005) 'Horizontal innovation in the theory of growth and development', in Aghion, P. and Durlauf Steven (eds) *Handbook of Economic Growth, Edition 1*, A msterdam, North Holland: Elsevier: 111-170.

Gorg, H., Henley, A., and Strobl, E. (2004) 'Outsourcing, foreign ownership, exporting and productivity: An empirical investigation with plant level data', *Globalisation, Productivity and Technology Research Paper N° 20 04/08* , Nottingham: Leverhulme Centre.

Grossman, G. M. and Helpman, E. (2003) 'Outsourcing versus FDI in industry equilibrium', *Journal of the European Economic Association* 1, 2-3:317-327.

—— (2005) 'Outsourcing in a global economy', *Review of Economic Studies* 72, 1: 135-159.

Grossman, G. M. and Rossi-Hansberg, E. (2006a) 'The rise of offshoring: it's not wine for cloth anymore', Mimeo, Federal Reserve Bank of Kansas City.

Hijzen, A., Gorg, H., and Hine, R. (2005) 'International outsourcing and the skill structure of labour demand in the United Kingdom', *The Economic Journal* 115, 506: 860-878.

Hobday, M. (2001) 'The electronics industries of the Asia- Pacific: Exploiting international production networks for economic development', *Asian-Pacific Economic Literature* 15,1: 13-29.

Price Waterhouse Coopers (2005) *Offshoring in the financial services industry: Risk and rewards.*

Spencer, B. (2005) 'International outsourcing and incomplete contracts', *Canadian Journal of Economics* 38, 4: 1107-1135.

UNCTAD (2004) *Service offshoring takes off in Europe - In search of improved competitiveness*, Geneva: UNCTAD, Roland Berger Strategy Consultants.

van Welsum, D. and Reif, X. (2006) 'Potential offshoring: Evidence from selected OECD countries', in Collins, S. M. and Brainard, L . (eds) *Brookings Trade Forum 2005, Offshoring White-Collar Work*, Washington, DC: Brookings Institution. Paris, OECD

van Welsum, D. and Vickery, G. (2005) 'Potential Offshoring of ICT-intensive using occupations', DSTI Information Economy Working Paper, DST I/ICCP/IE(20 04)19/FINAL , OECD, Paris.

World Trade Organization (W TO) (2005) 'Offshoring Services: Recent Developments and Policy Issues', *World Trade Report 2005 - Exploring the linkages between trade, standards and the W TO*, Geneva: WTO.

14

ENHANCING GLOBAL COMPETITIVENESS

INTRODUCTION

Competitive economies are those that have in place factors driving the productivity enhancements on which their present and future prosperity is built. A competitiveness supporting economic environment can help national economies to weather business cycle downturns and ensure that the mechanisms enabling solid economic performance going into the future are in place. The competitive environment that international business face is, to a certain extent, a function of the technological environment and the degree of technological innovations attributed to the competitive environment. Technological change and worldwide flow of information are fundamentally reshaping how companies and nations do business. Firms and nations are trying to understand the implications for their competitive strategies. But there is a conflict. The pressures of technological competition increasingly drive corporations towards global strategies while stimulating nationalistic impulses to protect and secure the national technology base from international competition. Misperceived notions, about how governments can promote domestic economic growth are, as a result, complicating the development of an international mind-set needed by both firms and nations to prosper in the emerging techno-global environment. In this context, policymakers are being confronted with new economic management challenges. Today's dynamic economic environment underscores the importance of not losing sight of long-term competitiveness fundamentals amid short-term urgencies. The challenge before policy makers is to formulate constructive policy in such areas as capital formation, human resources, technology and trade; to develop the political consensus necessary for action and to make sure that economic policy is structured so that it enhances the ability of the firms to compete in world markets.

WHAT IS COMPETITIVENESS?

Competitiveness is the contribution of a country's assets, either inherited (e.g. natural resources) or created (e.g. infrastructure) and the processes (e.g. manufacturing) which transform them into economic results, and which meet the test of the international market. A nation's competitiveness is the degree to which it can, under free and fair market conditions, produce goods and services that meet the test of international markets while simultaneously expanding the real income of its citizens. Competitiveness at the national level is based on superior productivity performance and the economy's ability to shift output to high productivity levels which in turn can generate high level of real wages.

The level of productivity, in turn, sets the sustainable level of prosperity that can be earned by an economy. In other words, more-competitive economies tend to be able to produce higher levels of income for senior citizens. The productivity level also determines the rates of return obtained by investments in an economy. Because the rates of return are the fundamental drivers of the growth rates of the economy, a more-competitive economy is one that is likely to grow faster in the medium to long run.

For most people, national productivity is an obscure economic term. Simply saying that productivity is key to economic performance does not shed light on how to achieve it. But when the productivity of Indian firms is contrasted to that of foreign firms, and the productivity of the Indian economy to that of their nations, productivity appears in a different light. These comparisons show in stark terms why productivity is so crucial to the standard of living, and more important, what contributes to it. Large trade deficits, high rate of inflation, poor foreign exchange resources, unemployment, poverty etc. are not the sum total of the competitiveness problem, but they signal a need to reconsider such issues as quality, education, innovation, and investment that together point the way towards productivity.

The concept of competitiveness thus involves static and dynamic components: although the productivity of a country clearly determines its ability to sustain its *level* of income, it is also one of the central determinants of the returns to investment, which is one of the key factors explaining an economy's *growth potential*.

DETERMINANTS OF COMPETITIVENESS

The determinants of competitiveness are many and complex. Economists have long tried to understand what determines the wealth of nations. This attempt has ranged from Adam Smith's focus on specialization and the division of labor to neoclassical economists emphasis on investment in physical capital and infrastructure and, more recently, to interest in other mechanisms such as education and training, technological progress (whether created within the country or adopted from abroad), macroeconomic stability, good governance, the rule of law, transparent and well-functioning institutions, firm sophistication, demand conditions, market size, and many others. Each of these conjectures rests on solid theoretical foundations. The central point, however, is that they are not mutually exclusive—two or more of them could be true at the same time.

However, many of these conjectures are, in fact, simultaneously true. The main drivers of an economy's growth potential can be grouped into 12 pillars of competitiveness:

THE 12 PILLARS OF COMPETITIVENESS

FIRST PILLAR: INSTITUTIONS

The institutional environment is determined by the legal and administrative framework within which individuals, firms, and governments interact to generate income and wealth in the economy. The importance of a solid institutional environment has become even more apparent during the current crisis, given the increasingly direct role played by the state in the economy of many countries.

The quality of institutions has a strong bearing on competitiveness and growth. It influences investment decisions and the organization of production and plays a central role in the ways in which societies distribute the benefits and bear the costs of development strategies and policies. For example, owners of land, corporate shares, or intellectual property are unwilling to invest in the improvement and upkeep of their property if their rights as owners are insecure.

The role of institutions goes beyond the legal framework. Government attitudes toward markets and freedoms, and the efficiency of its operations, are also very important: excessive bureaucracy and red tape, overregulation, corruption, dishonesty in dealing with public contracts, lack of transparency and trustworthiness, and the political dependence of the judicial system impose significant economic costs to businesses and slow the process of economic development. Proper management of the public finances is also critical to ensuring trust in the national business environment.

Although the economic literature has mainly focused on public institutions, private institutions are also an important element in the process of wealth creation. The recent global financial crisis, along with numerous corporate scandals, has highlighted the relevance of accounting and reporting standards and transparency for preventing fraud and mismanagement, ensuring good governance, and maintaining investor and consumer confidence. An economy is well served by businesses that are run honestly, where managers abide by strong ethical practices in their dealings with the government, other firms, and the public. Private-sector transparency is indispensable to business, and can be brought about through the use of standards as well as auditing and accounting practices that ensure access to information in a timely manner.

SECOND PILLAR: INFRASTRUCTURE

Extensive and efficient infrastructure is an essential driver of competitiveness. It is critical for ensuring the effective functioning of the economy, as it is an important factor determining the location of economic activity and the kinds of activities or sectors that can develop in a particular economy. Well-developed infrastructure reduces the effect of distance between regions, with the result of truly integrating the national market and connecting it at low cost to markets in other countries and regions. In addition, the quality and extensiveness of infrastructure networks significantly impact economic growth and reduce income inequalities and poverty in a variety of ways. In this regard, a well-developed transport and communications infrastructure network is a prerequisite for the ability of less-developed communities to connect to core economic activities and basic services.

Effective modes of transport for goods, people, and services—such as quality roads, railroads, ports, and air transport—enable entrepreneurs to get their goods and services to market in a secure and timely manner, and facilitate the movement of workers to the most suitable jobs. Economies also depend on electricity supplies that are free of interruptions and shortages so that businesses and factories can work unimpeded. Finally, a solid and extensive telecommunications network allows for a rapid and free flow of information, which increases overall economic efficiency by helping to ensure that businesses can communicate, and that decisions made by economic actors take into account all available relevant information.

THIRD PILLAR: MACROECONOMIC STABILITY

The stability of the macroeconomic environment is important for business and, therefore, is import the overall competitiveness of a country. Although it is certainly true that macroeconomic stability alone cannot increase the productivity of a nation, it is also recognized that macroeconomic disarray harms the economy. The government cannot provide services efficiently if it has to make high-interest payments on its past debts. Running fiscal deficits limits the government's future ability to react to business cycles. Firms cannot operate efficiently when inflation rates are out of hand. In sum, the economy cannot grow in a sustainable manner unless the macro environment is stable. It is important to note that this pillar focuses only on macroeconomic stability, so it does not directly take into account the way in which public accounts are managed by the government.

FOURTH PILLAR: HEALTH AND PRIMARY EDUCATION

A healthy workforce is vital to a country's competitiveness and productivity. Workers who are ill cannot function to their potential and will be less productive. Poor health leads to significant costs to business, as sick workers are often absent or operate at lower levels of efficiency. Investment in the provision of health services is thus critical for clear economic, as well as moral, considerations.

In addition to health, this pillar takes into account the quantity and quality of basic education received by the population, which is increasingly important in today's economy. Basic education increases the efficiency of each individual worker. Moreover, workers who have received little formal education can carry out only simple manual work and find it much more difficult to adapt to more advanced production processes and techniques. Lack of basic education can therefore become a constraint on business development, with firms finding it difficult to move up the value chain by producing more-sophisticated or value-intensive products.

For the longer term, it will be essential to avoid significant reductions in resource allocation to these critical areas, given that government budgets in many countries will need to be cut to reduce public debt brought about by the present stimulus spending.

FIFTH PILLAR: HIGHER EDUCATION AND TRAINING

Quality higher education and training is crucial for economies that want to move up the value chain beyond simple production processes and products. In particular, today's globalizing economy requires economies to nurture pools of well-educated workers who are able to adapt rapidly to their changing environment. This pillar measures secondary and tertiary enrollment rates as well as the quality of education as assessed by the business community. The extent of staff training is also to be taken into consideration because of the importance of vocational and continuous on-the-job training—which is neglected in many economies—for ensuring a constant upgrading of workers' skills to the changing needs of the evolving economy.

SIXTH PILLAR: GOODS MARKET EFFICIENCY

Countries with efficient goods markets are well positioned to produce the right mix of products and services given supply-and-demand conditions, as well as to ensure that these goods can be most effectively traded in the economy. Healthy market competition, both domestic and foreign, is important in driving market efficiency and thus business productivity, by ensuring that the most efficient firms, producing goods demanded by the market, are those that thrive. The best possible environment for the exchange of goods requires a minimum of impediments to business activity through government intervention. For example, competitiveness is hindered by distortionary or burdensome taxes and by restrictive and discriminatory rules on foreign direct investment (FDI)— limiting foreign ownership—as well as on international trade. The economic slowdown, with the consequent drop in trade and rise in unemployment, has increased the pressure on governments to adopt measures to protect domestic firms and jobs. Yet limiting global trade would not only amplify the current downturn, but in the longer term it would also reduce growth—in particular in developing countries.

Market efficiency also depends on demand conditions such as customer orientation and buyer sophistication. For cultural reasons, customers in some countries may be more demanding than in others. This can create an important competitive advantage, as it forces companies to be more innovative and customer oriented and thus imposes the discipline necessary for efficiency to be achieved in the market.

SEVENTH PILLAR: LABOR MARKET EFFICIENCY

The efficiency and flexibility of the labor market are critical for ensuring that workers are allocated to their most efficient use in the economy and provided with incentives to give their best effort in their jobs. Labor markets must therefore have the flexibility to shift workers from one economic activity to another rapidly and at low cost, and to allow for wage fluctuations without much social disruption. Efficient labor markets must also ensure a clear relationship between worker incentives and their efforts, as well as the best use of available talent—which includes equity in the business environment between women and men.

EIGHTH PILLAR: FINANCIAL MARKET SOPHISTICATION

The present economic crisis has highlighted the role of a sound and well-functioning financial sector fur economic activity. An efficient financial sector allocates the resources saved by a nation's citizens as well as those entering the economy from abroad to their most productive uses. It channels resources to those entrepreneurial or investment projects with the highest expected rates of return, rather than to the politically connected. A thorough and proper assessment of risk is therefore a key ingredient. Business investment is critical to productivity. Therefore economies require sophisticated financial markets that can make capital available for private-sector investment from such sources as loans from a sound banking sector, well-regulated securities exchanges, venture capital, and other financial products. This has been once again underscored by the liquidity crunch experienced by businesses and the public sector in developing and developed countries in recent times. In order to fulfill all those functions, the banking sector needs to be trustworthy and transparent, and—as has been made so clear recently—financial markets need appropriate regulation to protect investors and other actors in the economy at large.

NINTH PILLAR: TECHNOLOGICAL READINESS

This pillar measures the agility with which an economy adopts existing technologies to enhance the productivity of its industries. In today's globalized world, technology has increasingly become an important element for firms to compete and prosper. In particular, information and communication technologies (ICT) have evolved into the "general purpose technology" "of our time, given the critical spillovers to the other economic sectors and their role as efficient infrastructure for commercial transactions.

Therefore ICT access (including the presence of an ICT-friendly regulatory framework) and usage are included in the pillar as essential components of economies' overall level of technological readiness.

In this context, whether the technology used has or has not been developed within national borders is irrelevant for its effect on competitiveness. The central point is that the firms operating in the country have access to advanced products and blueprints and the ability to use them. Among the main sources of foreign technology, FDI often plays a key role. In this respect, it is particularly worrisome that, after four years of solid growth resulting in a record global FDI stock of US$ 1.9 trillion in 2007, FDI has declined by an estimated 15 percent in 2008 with further deterioration expected for 2009, especially for developing countries. This development is due to shortages in finance and a more risk averse attitude of businesses.

It is important to note that, in this context, the level of technology available to firms in a country needs to be distinguished from the country's ability to innovate and expand the frontiers of knowledge. That is why technological readiness need to be looked seperate from innovation, which is captured in the 12th pillar below.

TENTH PILLAR: MARKET SIZE

The size of the market affects productivity because large markets allow firms to exploit economies of scale. Traditionally, the markets available to firms have been constrained by national borders. In the era of globalization, international markets have become a substitute for domestic markets, especially for small countries. There is vast empirical evidence showing that trade openness is positively associated with growth. Even if some recent research casts doubts on the robustness of this relationship, the general sense is that trade has a positive effect on growth, especially for countries with small domestic markets.

Thus, exports can be thought of as a substitute for domestic demand in deterrnining the size of the market for the firms of a country. In today's highly interdependent world, recovery from the present downturn will require that countries increase the amount of goods that they purchase from each other, thus spurring demand. Further lowering barriers to trade would support this process.

ELEVENTH PILLAR: BUSINESS SOPHISTICATION

Business sophistication is conducive to higher efficiency in the production of goods and services. This leads, in turn, to increased productivity, thus enhancing a nation's competitiveness. Business sophistication concerns the quality of a country's overall business networks as well as the quality of individual firm's operations and strategies. It is particularly important for countries at an advanced stage of development, when the more basic sources of-productivity improvements have been exhausted to a large extent. The quality of a country's business networks and supporting industries, the quantity and quality of local suppliers and the extent of their interaction, is important for a variety of reasons. When companies and suppliers from a particular sector are interconnected in geographically proximate groups ("clusters"), efficiency is heightened, greater opportunities for innovation are created, and barriers to entry for new firms are reduced. Individual firms' operations and strategies (branding, marketing, the presence of a value chain, and the production of unique and sophisticated products) all lead to sophisticated and modern business processes.

TWELFTH PILLAR: INNOVATION

The final pillar of competitiveness is innovation. Although substantial gains can be obtained by improving institutions, building infrastructure, reducing macroeconomic instability, or improving human capital, all these factors eventually seem to run into diminishing returns. The same is true for the efficiency of the labor, financial, and goods markets. In the long run, standards of living can be expanded only with innovation. Innovation is particularly important for economies as they approach the frontiers of knowledge and the possibility of integrating and adapting exogenous technologies tends to disappear.

Although less-advanced countries can still improve their productivity by adopting existing technologies or making incremental improvements in other areas, for those that have reached the innovation-driven stage of development, this is no longer sufficient to increase productivity. Firms in these countries must design and develop cutting-edge products and processes to maintain a competitive edge. This requires an environment that is conducive to innovative activity, supported by both the public and the private sectors. In particular, this means sufficient investment in research and development (R&D) especially by the private sector, the presence of high-quality scientific research institutions, extensive collaboration in research between universities and industry, and the protection of intellectual property. In times of crisis, it will be important to resist pressures to cut back on the R&D spending both at the private and public levels that will be so critical for sustainable growth going into the future.

THE INTERRELATION OF THE 12 PILLARS

Although the 12 pillars of competitiveness are described separately, this should not obscure the fact that they are not independent: not only are they related to each other, but they tend to reinforce each other. For example, innovation (12th pillar) is not possible in a world without institutions (1st pillar) that guarantee intellectual property rights, cannot be performed in countries with a poorly educated and poorly trained labor force (5th pillar), and is more difficult in economies with inefficient markets (6th,

7th, and 8th pillars) or without extensive and efficient infrastructure (2nd pillar).

Stages of Development and the Weighted Index

Different pillars affect different countries differently. In the first stage, the economy is *factor-driven* and countries compete based on their factor endowments: primarily unskilled labor and natural resources. Companies compete on the basis of price and sell basic products or commodities, with their low productivity reflected in low wages. Maintaining competitiveness at this stage of development hinges primarily on well-functioning public and private institutions (pillar 1), well-developed infrastructure (pillar 2), a stable macroeconomic framework (pillar 3), and a healthy and literate workforce (pillar 4).

As wages rise with advancing development, countries move into the *efficiency-driven* stage of development, when they must begin to develop more efficient production processes and increase product quality. At this point, competitiveness is increasingly driven by higher education and training (pillar 5), efficient goods markets (pillar 6), well-functioning labor markets (pillar 7), sophisticated financial markets (pillar 8), a large domestic and/or foreign market (pillar 10), and the ability to harness the benefits of existing technologies (pillar 9). Finally as countries move into the *innovation-driven* "stage, they are able to sustain higher wages and the associated standard of living only if their businesses are able to compete with new and unique products. At this stage, companies must compete through innovation (pillar 12), producing new and different goods using the most sophisticated production processes (pillar 11). The concept of stages of development is integrated into the Index by attributing higher relative weights to those pillars that are relatively more relevant for a country given its particular stage of development. That is, although all 12 pillars matter to a certain extent for all countries, the relative importance of each one depends on a country's particular stage of development, to take this into account, the pillars are organized into three subindexes, each critical to a particular stage of development.

The *basic requirements subindex* groups those pillars most critical for countries in the factor-driven stage. The *efficiency enhancer subindex* includes those pillars critical for countries in the efficiency-driven stage. And the *innovation and sophistication factors subindex* includes the pillars critical to countries in the innovation-driven stage. The three subindexes are shown in Figure 1.

The specific weights, to each subindex in every stage of development are shown in Table-1. The Global Competitiveness Report 2009-2010 attributes the specific weights to each subindex at each stage of development as follows:

TABLE-1

Weights of the Three Main Subindexes at Each Stage of Development

Subindex	*Factor driven stage (%)*	*Efficiency driven stage (%)*	*Innovation driven stage (%)*
Basic requirements	60	40	20
Efficiency enhancers	35	50	50
Innovation and sophistication factors	5	10	30

The United States tops the overall ranking in *The Global Competitiveness Report 2008-2009*. Switzerland is in second position followed by Denmark, Sweden and Singapore. Finland (6), Germany (7), Netherlands (8), Japan (9) and Canada (10) are the other countries in the top 10 list. The United Kingdom, while remaining very competitive, has dropped by three places and out of the top 10, mainly attributable to a weakening of its financial markets. Among the BRIC (Brazil, Russia India and China) economies, India ranks 50th, a drop of two places from the last year's 48 spot, while China has improved its ranking to the 30th spot. Only, India has dropped in the ranking, while Russia (51) and Brazil (64) have jumped from last year's 58th and 72nd positions, respectively.

FIGURE 1

THE 12 PILLARS OF COMPETITIVENESS

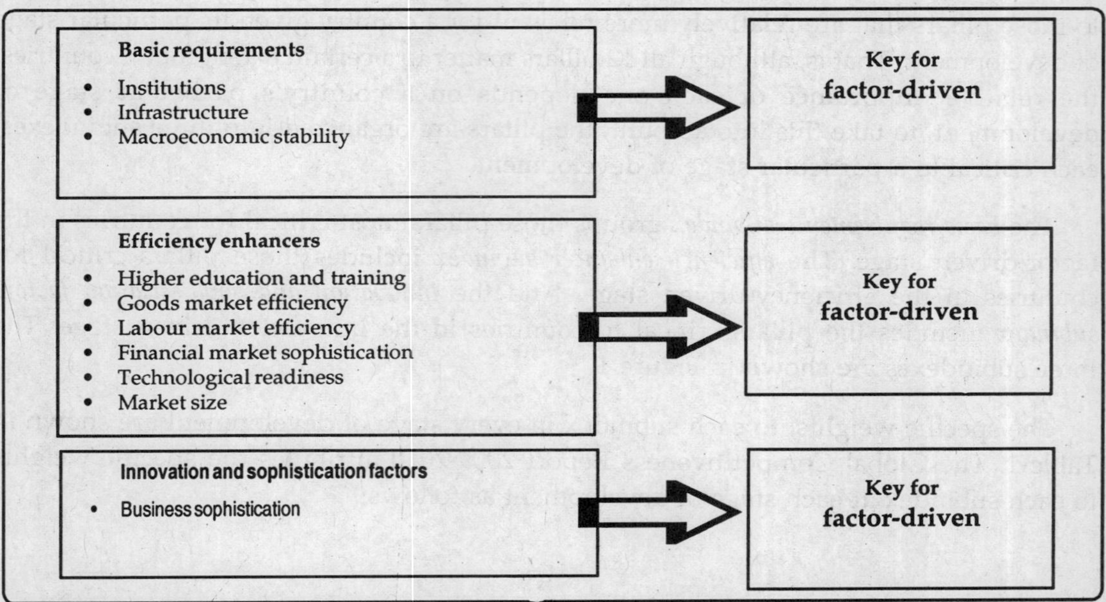

COMPETITIVENESS AND CHANGING CORPORATE STRUCTURES

Global aspirations of companies everywhere constitute a major force that is reshaping the world economy. No firm can ignore the international dimensions. Even the most domestically oriented business is likely to find that it is operating in somebody else's international market. This inter-linked economy have been so rapid that they have outrun the capacity of many companies and managers to make adjustments both to their organisational structures and to their underlying nationalistic assumptions and outlook.

What kind of changes at the organisational level are required to cope with an increasingly complex and faster moving international environment? Many companies grappling with this question recognise the need to speed up decision-making by reducing bureaucracy and streamlining and flattening the organisation. Some are seeking more flexible structures, experimenting with task forces and project teams. Some are decentralising to focus resources on particular markets, to push "ownership" further down the line and to become generally more responsive to local markets. The nub of the problem is the balance that has to be struck between central authority and local authority. If the pendulum swings too close to the centre, the corporate outposts are left floundering between an inappropriate strategy and local realities; too far in the other direction and the centre may be dragged towards the strongest outposts with no capacity for radical moves when these become necessary. It is the classical dilemma that all global companies experience.

At the same time, however, some firms identify almost the opposite of these trends as necessary to obtain the maximum benefit from global opportunities. Some are seeking to coordinate and structure their activities so that their business work together as appropriate on all major issues such as strategy, products, services and resourcing. Others are focussing on the integration of their worldwide business and acquisition.

A strategic approach to management development requires an organisation to take a worldwide view of its management resources. The main issue here is whether to pursue a centralised or decentralised approach. In decentralised multinational firms, responsibility for the early development of managers has been traditionally desolved to the subsidiaries. The corporate centre usually only becomes involved in the development of individuals when they start to assume more senior jobs or significant international responsibilities. Some firms believe strongly in the merits of decentralisation and aim to respond to local conditions within an overall strategic framework set by head office. Their structure is likely to consist of a corporate centre based in the parent country and loose connections of scattered subsidiaries in countries abroad. Communication flows up and down the hierarchy through chains of command and the subsidiaries operate very much as separate companies.

Such firms face a particular dilemma. They may wish to respond to local sensibilities by recrimiling local managers and giving the job in subsidiaries to locals. This prevents synergy between the various subsidiaries and leads to the 'power hug' when overall strategy is formulated at the centre of the organisation, much of the information that is needed to monitor and adopt the strategy is situated in the organisation's outposts. Because information is a source of power, the people there naturally try to retain hold of it. This is an increasingly serious handicap as the need to ensure free passage of information and to distribute ownership of strategy across the organisation becomes ever more pressing in an era of fast moving world markets. Breaking down "power hug" is one of the most important tasks facing international firms in the future. The search for right international strategies and structures continues. In this search, models like the *transnational corporation* and the *heterarchy* can help to clarify and stimulate thinking about the future of international organisations.

Most of the transnational corporations have traditionally built their international operations around one of three strategies. These strategies are: (i) to establish a strong local presence felt through responding to different international market requirements; (ii) to operate as global companies, making themselves fiercely competitive by achieving substantial cost advantages from centralised global scale of operations; and, finally, to develop as international companies whose key strategic capability lies in exploiting parent company knowledge through worldwide diffusion and adaptation. Today, however, no firm can any longer afford to base its strategy one focus. If companies are to cope with the complex international environment, they must have an equally complex and multi-faceted business strategy. Firms operating worldwide must pursue global, multinational and international strategies simultaneously. They must become truly transnational and have an integrated networking structure.

Traditionally, companies have subsidiaries which are either clearly dependent on the corporate centre (as in global companies) or strongly independent (as in multinational firms). Increasingly, however, these relationships are overly simple. International business now demands that every part of an organisation collaborators, shares information, solve problems and collectively implements strategy. An integrated network is needed to share decision-making and enable components, products, resources, information and people to flow freely between the transnational's interdependent units.

A major problem in any worldwide business is that managers in key positions are often limited by narrow perspectives and parochial interests, leading to substandard decision-making. In particularly complex, multi-tiered organisations, this problem is often exacerbated by conflicting interests and overlapping responsibilities. The commitment of every individual employee has to be won to the overall corporate agenda. To develop such a consensus, each individual must understand, share and "internalise" the company's purpose, value and key strategies.

The degree of success that companies achieve in their globalisation policies will depend greatly on their approach to international human resource management (HRM). Major HRM concerns include : identifying and retaining highly qualified people; ensuring sufficient quality and quantity of management at the appropriate time; ensuring management succession; sustaining and improving performance at all levels in all areas of business; increasing the depth of talent in the organisation; making sure that people have the technical and managerial skills to compete; making the management competence and culture that are required sufficiently clear to people; total quality management and changing people's attitudes to quality; establishing training as part of the management culture; gaining top management and line management interest in human resource development; and, finally, linking HRM to strategic objectives. Addressing all these issues is a major challenge in a purely domestic setting. The challenge lies in ensuring that human resource management adequately responds to new international market orientation. International recruitments — attracting people with international experience and visions — is accordingly a growing concern.

The transnational organisation makes difficult demands, however. Much more effort has to be put into welding the organisation together. Travel increases exponentially and a high price has to be paid in terms of exhaustion. The transnational is also an 'untidy', multi-dimensional affair; often it is not clear where decisions are made. Nor does it necessarily solve the problem of "power hug". Traditionally companies have controlled their operations through one of the three methods : (i) highly formalised and institutionalised control mechanisms; (ii) centralised decision-making; and (iii) relied on socialisation to instil a common corporate culture and a shared perspective among its managers. Since the very nature of the multi-dimensional transnational results in a dramatic expansion in the number of issues that need to be integrated, a single method of controls is insufficient. All three processes are needed.

For firms entering new markets, a special challenge is to find new business partnerships and build new relationships. Developing joint ventures and close cooperation with companies in other countries means accepting that such cooperation much change the way that a firm looks at its own tasks and activities. Corporate leaders are beginning to learn what the leaders of nations have always known : in a complex, uncertain world filled with dangerous opponents, it is best not to go it alone. Many firms are now forming strategic alliances with companies in other countries to gain access to new markets and technology, to achieve global spread or to share the costs of research and development. These alliances go beyond the limited scope of the traditional joint venture in that they are central to the fundamental, long-term interests of the partners. Companies may even establish such alliances with firms with whom they are competing in other markets and products. For instance, General Electric deals with companies that are 'competitors in the morning, customers at lunch, and joint venture partners in the afternoon'.

One of the most significant factors driving the ever faster rate of changer is the desire of companies to outpace their rivals in developing new products and delivering them to the market place. Under the impact of time-based competition, product life cycles are accelerating and becoming ever shorter. As world economy is becoming more integrated, so too are the internal operations of firms becoming more interdependent. The challenge is to get different functions such as research and development, engineering, production, marketing and distribution working much more closely together than in the past, replacing rivalry with collaboration.

Consumers will increasingly demand products that can be delivered in their own time and space. Firms are to consider how they might create "instantaneous" products and services that can be delivered within the blink of an eye of their conception. Few firms may be capable but thinking about how this might be done could speed up even the slowest firms.

Perhaps the most dannting impact of this much increased rate of change is that many firms now "going international" for the first time do not have the option of a slow, cautious "let's test the water gradually" approach. The luxury of a low-risk, slow learning process simply no longer exists. Firms relatively new to the international scene face such problems as lack of detailed market knowledge, unfamiliarity with different distribution channels and having to cope with different product standards.

Many firms are aware of the need to keep pace with faster-moving, often contradictory trends (such a simultaneous globalisation in some market sectors and fragmentation in others), and to identify changing life values, new consumer habits and emerging customer attitude. Some are highly aware of the need to respond positively to growing popular concern about both the global and local environments.

More and more companies realise that service and know-how constitute an increasingly important part of their competitive edge. With products becoming increasingly similar and technological advances offering only fleeting advantage in many industries, service will become ever more important. Maintaining constantly high-quality service is difficult enough in the domestic market, but managers will have to understand how to deliver it in international markets too.

The other major factor that is driving firms to give more attention to international business is the speed of market changes. A number of inter-related forces are propelling this acceleration. Perhaps the most fundamental trend is the globalisation of communications. The allied forces of computers and telecommunications are bringing about the *annibilation of space*. In telecommunications, companies are moving to a single worldwide information network, just as economicallly the world is becoming one global market place. They are moving toward the capability to communicate anything to anyone anywhere, by any form - voice, data, text or image - at the speed of light. The international currency market has become a largely speculative one whose roller-coaster movements can overnight undermine the best laid plans of any company. The problem of currency management mean a fundamental change of mind-set. They must regard themselves as financial institutions as well as makers of products and services. In other words, the management of currency must move to the centre of strategy-making and not be left as an afterthought to decision-making.

Like the transnational, the heterarchy uses a wide range of approaches to control and coordinate its operations; it may use arm's-length arrangements such as joint venture for some tasks or it may insist on "managing" by decree in others. Whatever method it uses, the heterarchy always aims to find the best means to achieve the task rather than adhering to a standardised format. Integration occurs through "normative means" such as corporate culture, shared values and managerial style.

The heterarchy describes an organisation that is composed of reciprocally, interdependent and geographically dispersed centres, which are held together by hard strategies, norms and information. The heterarchy has many kinds of centres, allocating head quarters' functions to wherever is most appropriate in the world, and allowing overseas "subsidiaries" to undertake strategic and global roles for the whole company. No dimension, whether product, function or country, reigns permanently supreme. The heterarchy is flexible and takes into account shifts in the business environment; at a certain moment, global product management is important; at another perhaps integration of total R&D is paramound.

It is argued that global and multinational companies can stifle the flow of innovation throughout the organisation. On the one hand, independent subsidiaries within multinationals can sometimes block new ideas and innovations developed at the corporate centres. On the other, a centralised global company may be unable to introduce local innovations because of unmotivated or incapable local managers. Instead of encouraging local innovations or imposing ideas from the centre, the transnational allocates worldwide product responsibilities to different national subsidiaries according to their relative skills and strengths. This not only taps the particular expertise of the business unit but also confirms its identity in the company's global operations. This approach constitutes the transnational's most vital strength; its ability to facilitate organisational learning by fostering a flow of intelligence, ideas and knowledge around the organisation. Search for a new business mind-set is one of today's most important challenges. Triumph of process over structure is a key indication of this change. What is important is not how responsibilities are divided but how people can pull together to pursue new opportunities. In the international arena of the future, it is the ability of people from different countries and cultures to pull together that will be crucial for the success of the international firm.

Internationalisation of business is not merely a challenge waiting around the corner. It is already here, and any company with ambitions of global expansion can ill afford to ignore its implications. Internationally advanced companies have recognised for some time that the distances between domestic and export markets are fast crumbling in virtually every part of the world. Almost any kind of domestic business is seeing, or soon will see, its markets invaded by foreign players. These companies may still think of themselves as national operations, yet are nonetheless directly experiencing the impact of internationalisation. They are being forced to learn the lesson that if they will not go to the international market, it will come to them. Those companies that have read the writing on the wall and are making concerted efforts to become truly international do not underestimate the size of the challenge. They are stepping into the unknown.

RESTRUCTURING BUSINESSES: A WAY TO BUILD WORLD-CLASS COMPANIES IN DEVELOPING COUNTRIES

Over the past two-plus decades, waves of liberalization have all but washed away protectionist barriers in developing countries. As nations integrated themselves into the world economy, multinational corporations externalises its part of its operation to a host-country-based partner firm in which it has no ownership stake, while maintaining a level of control over the operation by contractually specifying the way it is to be conducted, a cross-border non-equity mode NEM of MNC operation arises. When a MNC externalizes part of its operations to a specifications may relate to, for example, the design and quality of the product or service to be delivered, the process and standards of production, or the business model that the partner firm must adhere to. In distinction to purely arm's-length transactions, they have a material impact on the conduct of the business, requiring the host-country partner firm to, for example, make capital expenditure, change processes, adopt new procedures, improve working conditions, use specified suppliers, and so forth.

Thus the defining feature of cross-border NEMs, as a form of governance of a MNC's global value chain, is control over a host-country business entity by means other than equity holdings, although each type of NEM has its own particularities. A parallel can be drawn with FDI. The defining feature of FDI, to distinguish it from other forms of investment, is a significant level of control (a minimum equity stake of 10 per cent in host-country business entities) and a long-term interest in the host-country operation. This issue of a long-term interest also arises in the case of NEMs, as partner firms become an integral part of the MNC's global value chain (GVC) and their performance is an integral part of the MNC's overall competitiveness.

The various forms of NEM, summarized in Table 2, can also be compared to FDI in terms of their motivation. Some, such as contract farming, are resource-seeking; some are efficiency seeking (contract manufacturing, outsourcing); and some are market-seeking (brand licensing, franchising). Furthermore, some types of NEM are similar to FDI in that they entail a "package" of assets, resources, technology and know-how to be put in the care of host-country firms, as in the case of contract manufacturing, outsourcing, franchising and concessions. Other NEM types are more "narrow asset transfers", as in the case of licensing, management contracts, or some sub-types of franchising such as distributorships or agencies.

TABLE 2

Definitions of Selected Types of Cross-Border NEMs

NEM type	*Definition*
Contract manufacturing Services outsourcing	Contractual relationships whereby an international firm contracts out to a host country firm production, service or processing elements of its GVC (extending even to aspects of product development). All go under the general rubric of "outsourcing". Services outsourcing commonly entails the externalization of support processes including IT, business and knowledge functions.
Contract farming	Contractual relationship between an international buyer and (associations of) host-country farmers (including through intermediaries), which establishes conditions for the farming and marketing of agricultural products.
Licensing	Contractual relationship in which an international firm (licensor) grants to a host country firm (licensee) the right to use an intellectual property (e.g. copyrights, trade marks, patents, industrial design rights, trade secrets) in exchange for payment (a royalty). Licensing can take various forms, including brand licensing, product licensing and process licensing. In-licensing refers to a company acquiring a licence from another firm; out-licensing entails sale of intellectual property to other firms.
Franchising	Contractual relationship in which an international firm (franchisor) permits a host country firm (franchisee) to run a business modelled on the system developed by the franchisor in exchange for a fee or a mark-up on goods or services supplied by the franchisor. Franchising includes international master franchising, with a single equity owner of all outlets in a market, and unit franchising, with individual entrepreneurs owning one or more outlets.
Management contracts	Contractual relationship under which operational control of an asset in a host country is vested to an international firm, the contractor, which manages the asset in return for a fee.
Concessions	Contractual relationship under which operational control of an asset in a host country is vested to an international firm, the concessionaire. The firm manages the asset in return for an entitlement to (part of) the proceeds generated by the asset. Concessions are normally complex agreements, such as build-own-transfer (BOT) arrangements, which might include elements of investment by the MNC or ownership of the asset for a period. Legally they can be structured in many ways, including as public–private partnerships (PPPs).
Strategic alliances Contractual joint ventures	Contractual relationship between two or more firms to pursue a joint business objective. Partners may provide the alliance with products, distribution channels,

manufacturing capability, capital equipment, knowledge, expertise, or intellectual property. Strategic alliances involve intellectual property transfer, specialization, shared expenses and risk. Contracts set forth terms, obligations, and liabilities of the parties but do not entail the creation of a new legal entity.

Source: UNCTAD.

The defining features of NEMs – coordination and control of independent firms through contractual and non-contractual means, with a material impact on the conduct of their business – in some instances blur the rigid distinction between FDI, NEMs and trade. In some industries such as electronics, contract manufacturers are very large operators The defining features of NEMs – coordination and control of independent firms through contractual and non-contractual means, with a material impact on the conduct of their business – in some instances blur the rigid distinction between FDI, NEMs and trade. In some industries such as electronics, contract manufacturers are very large operators

NEMs are therefore inextricably linked with international trade and FDI, shaping global patterns of trade in many sectors. In industry segments such as automotive components, consumer electronics, garments, hotels and IT and business process services, contract manufacturing and services outsourcing represent a very large share of total trade. NEMs are thus a major "route-to-market" for countries aiming at export-led growth, and a major point of access to MNC global value chains.

MNC governance, control and coordination of hostcountry operations through NEMs can be indirect. In contract farming, the numbers of individual suppliers are so great that arrangements with MNCs are made by intermediaries. For example, in 2008 Olam (Singapore) sourced 17 agricultural commodities from approximately 200,000 suppliers in 60 countries (most of them developing countries). Similarly, in 2008 food manufacturer Nestlé (Switzerland) had more than 600,000 contract farmers in over 80 developing and transition economies as direct suppliers of various agricultural commodities. Contractual relationships between a MNC and host-country farmers can be channelled through associations of farmers, cooperatives or other intermediaries, which then establish conditions for the production of farm products. In the garments industry, large intermediaries such as Li & Fung (Hong Kong, China) arrange production in dozens of countries for branded clothing companies such as Gap (United States) via its long-standing relationship with independent contractors. Similarly, in franchising, extended networks of business outlets are often governed through a master franchisee that contracts rights for an entire market (a country or region) in which it manages relationships with individual unit franchisees.

The means of control and the sources of bargaining power in NEM relationships vary by type. Partnerships are seldom equal, with power relationships depending on a range of factors which vary by NEM-type and industry, and include the capabilities and other assets possessed by MNCs and partner firms. In each NEM-type contractual levers of control are complemented with elements of soft bargaining power that strengthen MNCs' governance of GVCs (Table 3).

TABLE 3
MNCs' Contractual Levers and Sources of Bargaining Power

Modes	*Contractual levers of MNC control over host-country firms*[a]	*Sources of MNC bargaining power*
Contract manufacturing Services outsourcing Contract farming	• Specifications for design, process, product or service, and quality • Commercial terms and capital expenditure obligations/assurances • Supply guarantees and restrictions on side-selling • Obligations to purchase specific inputs (e.g. seeds, fertilizer) • Obligations regarding the MNC's CSR practices	• Access to the MNC internal market, guaranteed sales • Access to MNC know-how, supplies of inputs, logistics network • Existence of many potential contract suppliers
Licensing	• Obligations placed on the licensee restricting or conditioning the use of the intellectual property	• Access to know-how, intellectual property • Access to the MNC internal market where part of a subcontracting arrangement • Existence of many competing licensees
Franchising	• Obligations placed on the franchisee conditioning the use of the intellectual property and the running of the business (e.g. use of the supply network, choice of suppliers, service levels, capital expenditure, CSR)	• Access to the MNC supply and business support network • Market strength of established brand names • Existence of alternative choices of franchisees
Management contracts	• Obligations regarding the state and maintenance of the asset and future investments (capital expenditure obligations/assurances)	• Access to MNC managerial competencies and know-how, supply network, and intellectual property

Source: UNCTAD.

a. Contractual arrangements also include obligations on the part of MNCs.

At the same time, partner companies in host countries possess or can develop "countervailing power", often with the support of their government. Sources of such countervailing power on the part of NEM partners include specialized knowledge (including patents and other intellectual property), advanced productive capabilities (e.g. the ability to scale operations quickly), access to key assets or resources (including human resources) or knowhow related to the local market of the NEM partner. This countervailing power can also be exercised in a number of ways, including in negotiations defining the terms of a contract.

Ultimately, it is the MNC which orchestrates the value chain. Thus, the most important source of MNC bargaining power, outweighing any countervailing forces that a host-country NEM may put forward, is its role as the coordinator of the GVC itself. This has implications for both partner firms and developing countries. The MNC's governance of its integrated international production network and of the web of loosely dependent entities that make it up allows it to regulate access to the network and to set the conditions. Thus the segmentation or "fine-slicing" of value chains into ever more numerous and discrete activities that can be carried out by partner firms in any location plays into the hands of MNCs. It also makes them important interlocutors for policymakers aiming to stimulate the development of specific economic activities in specific locations, independent of whether such development is driven by FDI or domestic partners' investment.

THE SCALE AND SCOPE OF CROSS-BORDER NEMS

NEMs are an important part of MNC-governed GVCs, and are growing rapidly. NEM activity is becoming ever more widespread geographically, though there are significant variations by mode and industry. To assess the extent to which MNCs govern global value chains it is no longer sufficient to consider equity ownership (FDI) alone as a control mechanism. However, analysing non-equity modes is complex, because the web of directly owned, partially owned, contract-based and arm's-length forms of international operation of MNCs is tangled, and some of the distinctions between the different modes are blurred. Moreover, the relationship between FDI, NEMs and trade is also intertwined in many GVCs.

Cross-border NEM activity worldwide is estimated to have generated about $2 trillion of sales in 2010 in selected modes. Of this amount, contract manufacturing and services outsourcing accounted for about $1 trillion, franchising for $330–350 billion, licensing for $340–360 billion, and management contracts for some $100 billion.

Contract manufacturing and services outsourcing as a whole clearly top the list on all major indicators, including total sales generated, value added, exports, worldwide employment and employment in developing countries as indicated by selected industries (Table 4). Nevertheless, other NEM types are often significant on individual quantitative indicators (e.g. franchising, for employment generation in developing countries) or in terms of qualitative impacts. Looking at major indicators by NEM type also hides significant differences by industry. Sales, value added and employment in more technology-intensive industries such as electronics, automotive components and pharmaceuticals, where contract manufacturing is concentrated in a number of major international operators, are different from those in traditional labour-intensive industries such as garments, footwear and toys, which are characterized by large numbers of smaller producers, at best aggregated under international operators specializing in GVC coordination. Equally, grouping businesses as diverse as retail, quick-service restaurants and business services under the single banner of franchising undoubtedly hides wide variations in value added and employment.

TABLE 4

Key Figures of Cross-Border NEMs, Selected Industries, 2010

(Billions of dollars and millions of employees)

	Estimated NEM-related worldwide			
	Sales	*Value added*	*Employ-ment*	*Employment in developing economies*
Contract manufacturing - selected technology/capital intensive industries				
Electronics	230–240	20–25	1.4–1.7	1.3–1.5
Automotive components	200–220	60–70	1.1–1.4	0.3–0.4
Pharmaceuticals	20–30	5–10	0.1–0.20	.05–0.1
Contract manufacturing - selected labour intensive industries				
Garments	200–205	40–45	6.5–7.0	6.0–6.5
Footwear	50–55	10–15	1.7–2.0	1.6–1.8
Toys	10–15	2–3	0.4–0.5	0.4–0.5
Services outsourcing				
IT services and business process outsourcing	90–100	50–60	3.0–3.5	2.0–2.5
Franchising				
Retail, hotel, restaurant, and catering, business and other services	330–350	130–150	3.8–4.2	2.3–2.5
Management contracts - selected industry				
Hotels	15–20	5–10	0.3–0.4	0.1–0.15

	Estimated NEM-related worldwide		
	Fees	*Associated sales*	*Associated value added*
Licensing			
Cross-industry	17–18	340–360	90–110

Source: UNCTAD estimates.

There are large variations in relative size. In the automotive industry, contract manufacturing accounts for 30 per cent of global exports of automotive components and a quarter of employment. In contrast, in electronics, contract manufacturing represents a much larger share of trade and employment. In labour-intensive industries such as garments, footwear and toys, contract manufacturing is even more important.

Putting different modes of international production in perspective, cross-border activity related to selected NEMs of $2 trillion compares with exports of foreign affiliates of MNCs of some $6 trillion in 2010. However, NEMs are particularly important in developing countries, which in many industries account for almost all NEM-related employment and exports, compared with the developing country share in global FDI stocks of 30 per cent and in world trade of less than 40 per cent. NEMs are also growing rapidly. In most cases, the growth of NEMs outpaces that of the industries in which they operate.

A WAY TO BUILD WORLD CLASS COMPANIES IN DEVELOPING COUNTRIES

Due to onslaught of MNCs, many local companies in developing countries lost market share or sold of business, but some fought back. They held their own against this onslaught, restructured their businesses, exploited new opportunities, and built world-class companies that are giving the MNCs from developed countries a run for their money. What strategies did these globally competitive businesses deploy to overcome the myriad obstacles that their home environments pose? Why and how did some of them move from their dominant positions at home to establish an international presence? Must every emerging-market company follow suit? What sequence of steps should winnable giants take to build stronger businesses at home or to enter markets overseas?

BLUNTING THE MULTINATIONALS' EDGE

At first glance, MNCs from developed countries appear to hold near-insurmountable advantages over businesses in newly industrializing countries. They not only possess well-known brand names, efficient innovation processes and management systems, and sophisticated technologies but also have access to vast reservoirs of finance and talent. Western European and American companies, for instance, can raise large sums of money at a low cost because of their well-established financial markets. They can hire talent easily because the labor markets on both continents work well. Most developing countries lack the soft infrastructure that makes markets work efficiently. Because of institutional voids - the absence of specialized intermediaries, regulatory systems, and contract-enforcing mechanisms - corporations in emerging markets cannot access capital or talent as easily or as inexpensively as European and American corporations can. That often makes it tough for businesses in developing countries to invest in R&D or to build global brands.

Nevertheless, these companies in developing countries can overcome such disadvantages, for three reasons. *First*, when multinational companies from the developed world explore business opportunities in emerging markets, they must confront the same institutional voids that local companies face. However, executives from multinational companies are used to operating in economies with well-developed institutional infrastructures and are therefore ill equipped to deal with such voids. Western organizations, for instance, rely on data from market research firms to tailor their products and marketing strategies to compete in different markets. They also count on supply chain partners to make and deliver products to customers inexpensively. When these companies attempt to move into countries that don't have sophisticated market researchers or reliable supply chain partners, they find it difficult to deploy their business models. By contrast, the managers at local companies know how to work around institutional voids because they've had years of experience doing so. Their familiarity with the local context allows them to identify and meet customers' needs effectively. Moreover, business groups such as India's Tata Group, the Philippines' Ayala Group, and Turkey's Koc Group have created mechanisms for raising capital and developing talent They can, for instance, raise money from the local stock market by trading on their reputations. These groups can also spread the cost of training executives in-house by deploying their managers across businesses. Such mechanisms allow many local companies to compete effectively with foreign giants.

Second, once companies from emerging markets have demonstrated a degree of success, they, too, can tap capital and talent markets in developed countries. Like American and European companies, they can raise money by, say, listing themselves on the New York Stock Exchange or on Nasdaq. Emerging giants often become investors' darlings, making it easy for them to sell equity shares or bonds. In the talent market, intermediaries from developed countries that are trying to fill the gaps in the soft infrastructure in emerging markets help local businesses become more competitive. In recent years, American and European business schools have launched education programmes in developing countries. This has allowed emerging-market companies to retrain their existing managers and to hire people with the same skills that executives in multinational companies possess.

Third - and this is often downplayed by executives -multinational companies are reluctant, sometimes rightly so, to tailor their strategies to every developing market in which they operate. They find it costly and cumbersome to modify their products, services, and communications to suit local tastes, especially since the opportunities in developing countries tend to be relatively small and risky. Further, their organizational processes and cost structures make it difficult for them to sell products and services at optimal price points in emerging markets; they often end up occupying small, superpremium niches. Local companies don't suffer from those constraints, particularly since they operate in just a few geographic markets. In fact, once emerging-market companies improve the quality of their products and services, they are able to cater to customers at home as well as, if not better than, multinational companies.

MARKET STRUCTURES IN DEVELOPING COUNTRIES

The structure of markets in developing countries helps local companies counter their multinational rivals. The markets for finished goods (products) and raw materials (factors of production) can be broken up into four distinct components in developing countries.

At the apex of the market pyramid is the *global tier*. In the product market, this section consists of consumers who want offerings to have the same attributes and quality that products in developed countries have and are willing to pay global prices for them. In the talent market, this tier consists of top-notch managers, such as newly minted graduates from the Indian Institutes of Management, who demand global-level salaries. Immediately below that is the *glocal tier*. In the product market, this tier consists of consumers who demand customized products of near-global standard and are willing to pay a shade less than global consumers do. An example would be Chinese and Indian executives who prefer to stay in a Shangri-La or Taj hotel rather than at a Four Seasons. In the talent market, this section consists of high-quality managers who will work only for local companies even if the pay is a little less than it would be at multinational corporations. Consumers in the *local tier* are happy with products of local quality and at local prices. In the talent market, managers in this section will put up with less-than-world-class working conditions as long as they are paid higher-than-average salaries. The *bottom segment* of the market consists of people who can afford only the least expensive products. Multinational corporations typically compete for consumers and talent only in the global tier. Meanwhile, smart local companies, which dominate the local tier, move into the glocal tier and also create breakthrough products for the bottom segment as economies liberalize. These businesses often become emerging giants.

Because of the institutional voids in developing countries, multinational companies find it difficult to serve anything but the market's global tier. In product markets, the lack of market research makes it tough for multinational companies to understand customers' tastes, and the paucity of distribution networks makes it impossible for them to deliver products to customers in the hinterland. In talent markets, they don't have enough knowledge about the local talent pool to design policies that will attract and motivate employees at the glocal, local, and bottom-of-pyramid tiers. Therefore, when a developing country opens up, multinational companies rush into the global tier, and local companies dominate the local tier. There are immense opportunities in the bottom tier, but companies have to use radically different strategies to crack it open. Over time, the glocal tier becomes the battleground between local and foreign corporations. Since glocal customers demand global products with local features, several emerging-market companies have used their knowledge of local markets to serve customers better than multinational firms have been able to. Companies' successes depend on their ability to exploit their competitive advantages. Since emerging giants both circumvent institutional voids and tailor their strategies to local markets better than multinational companies do, they initially take on foreign competitors by capitalizing on their ability to navigate their home turf. They do that by using one of three strategies.

EXPLOIT UNDERSTANDING OF PRODUCT MARKETS

Many emerging-market companies have become world-class businesses by capitalizing on their knowledge of local product markets. They've kept multinational rivals at bay by judiciously adapting to the special characteristics of customers and business ecosystems at home. These emerging giants have also exploited similarities between geographically proximate developing markets to grow across borders.

Product markets often turn out to be unique because customers' needs and tastes are idiosyncratic. Local companies are the first to realize that and to build businesses around distinctive national characteristics. For instance, Jollibee Foods thrives because it realizes that Filipinos like their burgers to have a particular soy and garlic taste; Nandos is growing in South Africa by providing cooked chicken that suits local palates; and Polio Campero is doing the same in Guatemala. Over the past ten years, these companies have profitably battled American giants like McDonald's and KFC. They have also used their understanding of local preferences to cater to the tastes of the diaspora from their home markets. Jollibee serves Fil-ipino communities in Hong Kong, the Middle East, and California; Nandos has expanded into the United Kingdom and Malaysia; and Polio Campero sells to Latino communities in Ecuador, El Salvador, Honduras, Mexico, Nicaragua, and Peru, as well as parts of the United States. Haier became a leader in China's white goods market, in the teeth of competition from GE, Electrolux, and Whirlpool, mainly because it was able to develop products tailored to the needs of Chinese consumers. For example, when Haier discovered that customers in rural China were using the company's washing machines to clean vegetables like sweet potatoes, the company modified its product designs to accommodate that need. The humid weather in Chinese cities such as Shanghai and Shenzhen requires people to change clothes frequently, so Haier created a tiny washing machine that cleans a single set of clothes. Because the model uses less electricity and water than a regular washing machine does, it has become an instant hit in China's coastal cities. Haier's strategy compels the company to manufacture a large variety of products, but the company exploits its expert knowledge of the Chinese market - knowledge that is hard for multinational companies to obtain — by developing a product for every need.

Haier has also painstakingly created a distribution and service network that covers not only urban markets on the east coast of China but also markets in semi-urban and rural China. In a country where reliable after-sales service and national distribution aren't common, Haier's investments in those two areas have yielded formidable sources of competitive advantage. Product markets often turn out to be hard to penetrate because companies need specialized infrastructures, distribution channels, or delivery systems to meet customers' needs. Most multinational companies are ill equipped to pioneer the development of such systems.

Interestingly, Haier took care to cement its leadership at home before venturing abroad. By 1991, the company had become China's biggest manufacturer of refrigerators, but it wasn't until 1995 that Haier set up its first joint venture, in Indonesia. It then quickly moved into the Philippines, Malaysia, and Yugoslavia over the next two years. Germany became the first Western market for Haier-branded refrigerators in 1997, and two years later, Haier entered the United States, setting up a design center in Boston, a marketing operation in New York, and a manufacturing facility in South Carolina. In the U.S. market, the Chinese giant has focused on entering price-sensitive segments and on learning how to establish partnerships with American retailers such as Best Buy, Home Depot, and Wal-Mart. In 2005, research firm Euromonitor International reported that Haier had a 26% share of the U.S. market for compact refrigerators (the kind found in college dormitories and hotel rooms) and a 50% share of the market for low-end wine cellars. Haier's ability to develop products for small segments has stood it in good stead overseas: In July 2006, Wal-Mart's Web site listed 59 Haier products, many aimed at college students.

Haier's travels epitomize the globalization journey that emerging giants make when they embrace opportunities in product markets. They instinctively turn to other emerging markets when they initially venture abroad because they have the capabilities to respond to opportunities in such countries. Because of their knowledge of products and cost bases, however, they aren't content with operating only in developing countries. When they enter advanced markets, they tend to avoid head-to-head competition with foreign companies; they focus on niche opportunities that allow them to capitalize on their existing strengths. This approach helps emerging giants gradually stretch their capabilities even as they learn how to operate in developed markets. The experience helps them enlarge their footprints in advanced countries and compete more effectively with multinational giants when their home markets mature. For instance, Haier's experience in Europe and the United States will benefit the company as Western retailers such as Carrefour and Wal-Mart become important distribution channels in China.

BUILD ON FAMILIARITY WITH RESOURCE MARKETS

Some emerging-market companies have gained competitive advantage by exploiting their knowledge about local factors of production - the markets for talent and capital - thereby serving customers both at home and abroad in a cost-effective manner. For instance, consider Indian information technology majors such as Tata Consultancy Services, Infosys Technologies, Wipro, and Satyam Computer Services, all of which have excelled in recent years at catering to the global demand for software and services. This is partly because India's education system produces many engineers and technical graduates; local companies hire these people at salaries much lower than those that engineers in developed markets earn. Since institutional voids pervade the talent market in India, however, it is very difficult for foreign companies to capitalize on the same human resources. Multinational software service providers, such as Ac-centure and EDS, have a hard time sorting talent in a market where the level of people's skills and the quality of educational institutions vary wildly. In fact, as talent becomes scarcer in urban centers like Bangalore and Delhi, Indian companies will maintain their advantage, because they know how to lure people from India's second-tier cities better than multinational companies do.

Transnational giants also find it tough to operate in an economy with a poor physical infrastructure and to cope with the Indian regulatory apparatus. India's software companies recognized the possibility of providing services to overseas customers at least a decade before Western companies acknowledged the feasibility of hiring Indian software professionals. Consequently, the Indian firms gained experience early, which has kept them ahead of their foreign rivals. Recently, some Indian companies have also been able to tap the global capital and talent markets, nullifying more of their overseas rivals' inherent advantages.

Some companies have exploited their knowledge of local factors of production and supply chains to build world-class businesses. Taiwan-based Inventec, for instance, is among the world's largest manufacturers of notebook computers, PCs, and servers, many of which it makes in China and supplies to Hewlett-Packard and Toshiba. It also makes cellular telephones and portable music players for other multinational companies. Inventec's customers benefit from the low costs of manufacturing products in China without having to invest in factories there. They are also able to use China's talented software and hardware professionals, who can design products quickly in an industry where product life cycles are notoriously short. Inventec has mastered the challenges associated with sourcing electronic components from around the world, assembling them into quality products at a low cost, and shipping them to multinational companies in a reliable fashion. Recently, Inventec started selling computers in Taiwan and China under its own brand name. The computers have a Chinese operating system and software, so Inventec doesn't compete directly with its customers-yet.

Likewise, Bunge, the world's largest processor of oilseeds, has created a supply chain that links Brazil's farmers to consumers all over the world. Bunge's savvy trading organization tracks the supply of and demand for oilseeds, which lets executives decide when to buy oilseeds; when and where to crush them; and when and where to transport oil and oil meal for consumer, agricultural, and industrial use. Bunge charters approximately 100 ships; it leases warehouses and crushing plants all over the world;

and it even takes equity positions in ports. That infrastructure allows the company to respond quickly to changes in customer requirements and helps it cope with logistics problems, such as those caused by Hurricane Katrina in 2005. Finally, the $24 billion company feeds supply and demand data to Brazil's farmers, along with advice about everything from fertilizers to harvesting techniques, so they can plant the most profitable kinds of oilseeds. Bunge's sales grew by 235% between 1997 and 2004, from $7.4 billion to $25.1 billion. Its net income has risen by about 425% over the same period, from $83 million to $469 million.

Businesses that are built around raw materials are usually global from their inception, either because they serve customers in advanced markets or because they are part of a global value chain. As they grow, these emerging giants expand their footprints in three ways. *First*, they look for customers in advanced markets that they can serve from their home bases. *Second*, as factor markets at home become saturated and thus more expensive, these businesses look for other developing countries that offer similar resources. *Finally*, these companies move up the value chain, selling branded products or offering solutions to niche segments. That's exactly what India's information technology leaders are doing. After establishing themselves as reliable providers of IT services in North America, they moved into Latin America and Asia. By setting up operations in developing countries such as China and Russia, they have started exploiting the large pools of talent in those countries. They have also acquired small consulting firms in the United States and Europe, thereby enhancing their ability to develop high-end solutions for customers.

TREAT INSTITUTIONAL VOIDS AS BUSINESS OPPORTUNITIES

The third way to build emerging giants is for private sector businesses to fill institutional voids. Only governments can set up certain institutions, but companies can own and profitably operate many kinds of intermediaries in product and factor markets.

Many institutional intermediaries facilitate the flow of information in markets; these include newspaper publishers and database vendors. Some intermediaries enhance the credibility of the claims sellers make - for instance, accounting firms, quality-certification firms, and accreditation agencies. Others analyze information and advise buyers and sellers; these include rating agencies, product-rating companies and publications that rank universities and professional schools. Private sector institutions can also facilitate transactions, either by aggregating and distributing goods and services or by creating forums where buyers and sellers can conduct their own transactions. The aggregators - venture capitalists, private-equity firms, and banks in the financial market; retailers in the product market; and, to some extent, universities in the talent market-help buyers and sellers find each other. Stock exchanges, online auction sites, and job sites on the

Internet serve as forums where transactions can take place in the financial, product, and talent markets, respectively.

Multinational companies enjoy an edge in the intermediaries business because they bring expertise, credibility, and experience to the table. However, emerging-market companies can take them on for three reasons. First; many intermediaries are people intensive, so running them requires familiarity with the local language and culture. Second, intermediaries are information intensive, and it takes local expertise to access scattered information and analyze data of variable quality. Third governments consider some institutions, such as media, banking, and financial services, to be of national importance. They often prohibit multinational companies from setting up those institutions or force them to collaborate with local companies.

Resource markets can be separated into the four tiers one global and three local. Multinational companies are suited to serve as intermediaries in the global tier, but local firms are better able to cater to the other tiers. For example, multinational banks serve large blue-chip customers in emerging markets because evaluating those companies' credit worthiness is relatively straightforward. Those businesses produce high-quality financial statements, get them audited by globally reputable accountants, and, if their shares are listed overseas, follow international accounting norms. However, evaluating the credit of small and medium enterprises is tough. Domestic banks, with their local knowledge and informal connections, cater to this segment better than foreign banks do. In Turkey, for example, the likes of Citibank skim the top of the corporate market whereas local banks, like Garanti Bank Turkey and Akbank, cater to Turkish businesses better than the multinational banks do.

Several emerging giants have learned to play the role of market institutions. Consider Old Mutual, an insurance company that realized that South Africa lacked mutual funds and other long-term investment products. Old Mutual responded by creating insurance policies for poor people that had the features of savings accounts. By marketing the policies to millions of South Africans, the company became a large financial services firm. When the South African economy integrated itself with the world market in the early 19905, Old Mutual moved into other African countries, such as Botswana, Kenya, Malawi, Namibia, and Zimbabwe, and listed itself on the Johannesburg and London stock exchanges.

To take another example, Agora is one of Poland's most successful media companies. It publishes Poland's biggest newspaper, *Gazeta Wyborcza* (GW), which commands 43% of the national readership and has a 62% share of national newspaper advertising revenues. The paper started in April 1989 as an organ for the Solidarity political movement, but after Solidarity's victory in Poland's elections in June 1989, Agora's founders made the newspaper an independent organization. Agora filled the information void in Poland by providing not only news coverage but also a vehicle for advertising. Since GW's readers are educated, live in urban areas, and have plenty of disposable income, the newspaper's advertisers include travel agencies, automakers, cellular phone companies, pension funds, and so on. The company trades on the Warsaw and London stock exchanges, which has enabled it to raise capital to fund its growth. In 1993, the company sold approximately 20% of its shares to Cox Enterprises, an American media company. The alliance enabled Agora to get expertise and capital from Cox.

China's Emerge Logistics is another company that has exploited an institutional void in an emerging market to create a profitable business. Although China has plenty of eight-lane highways, delivering goods isn't easy because the transportation system is underdeveloped. No trucking firm operates nationally; in fact, the average Chinese trucking company owns only one or two vehicles. In addition, separate government bodies regulate air, rail, road, and river transport, and several levels of government impose tolls on vehicles. These factors add to companies' costs and hinder them from distributing products. Emerge Logistics, one of China's few third-party logistics services providers, helps multinational companies sell products all over the country by capitalizing on its understanding of the disjointed transportation system and the baffling bureaucracy. Operating from a warehouse an hour away from Shanghai, Emerge Logistics takes foreign companies all the way through the delivery process-from filing import applications before goods enter the country to collecting payments from customers. The company coordinates the transfer of goods among different modes of transportation and takes orders from Chinese customers for its clients' products. By doing the billing itself, Emerge Logistics also facilitates direct sales by Western multinational companies to Chinese customers.

Exploiting institutional opportunities often doesn't create a launchpad for globalization. That doesn't mean these businesses stay small, however. In markets such as Brazil, China, India, and Russia, institutional businesses can become quite large even if they focus only on the domestic market. In smaller emerging markets, companies that try to fill institutional voids can grow by exploiting adjacent opportunities. A print media company, for instance, can expand into electronic media; a bank can diversify into asset management and investment banking; and a privately owned business school can set up a medical, law, or technology school. Doing so often paves the way for these businesses to go global at a later stage.

THE IMPORTANCE OF EXECUTION AND GOVERNANCE

Identifying the right growth strategy is critical for building a world-class business, but execution and governance determine whether companies in emerging markets can realize their potential. While that may be true about building great companies anywhere, excellent execution and good governance are particularly valuable in newly industrializing countries. Financial and talent resources in emerging markets are scarce, but companies that can execute well end up getting more out of them. And since resource providers cannot rely on the enforcement of contracts in emerging markets, good governance - organizational mechanisms that ensure that a company lives up to its commitments to investors, customers, employees, and business partners-allows an organization to acquire a reputation that is invaluable in its dealings with constituents. It can, for instance, access the best resources at the lowest cost.

The manner in which emerging-market companies achieve good governance varies greatly. Countries put different weights on the extent to which a governance system should protect shareholders, employees, and other constituents. The laws regarding corporate governance differ across nations, with greater similarities among those that share economic links such as trading connections. Governance practices vary even more. However, only companies that zealously protect the interests of shareholders and employees, and ensure that both receive competitive returns on investment, become emerging giants.

Is it better to be more global? The answer may appear to be yes. Well-managed companies do spread their wings over time and enter many geographic markets. There is a correlation between global scope and performance. But executives shouldn't confuse that with a causal relationship. What is important is whether global scope results in competitive advantage rather than being the result of advantage derived in some other fashion.

There's more than one way to skin the proverbial cat: Some emerging giants operate in several countries, but others sell only at home. In fact, the United Nations Conference on Trade and Development's list of top 50 emerging-market companies that the correlation between size and degree of globalization in these businesses (as measured by market value) is, at 0.4, low. Moreover, the financial performance of world-class companies that have diversified across countries isn't superior to the performance of those that haven't. Emerging giants can thus be successful even if they don't have global footprints.

QUESTIONS

1. What is competitiveness ?Critically examine the behavioral factors influencing countries' business practices.
2. Discuss the types of competition found in the global environment. Outline the forces that encourage or limit competition.
3. What strategies did the global competitive businesses deploy to overcome the myriad obstacles that their home environment pose? Why and how did some of them move from their dominant positions at home to establish an international presence?
4. Discuss the main drivers of an economy's growth potential.

5. What kind of changes at the organizational level are required to cope with an increasingly complex and faster moving international economic environment?
6. Critically examine the role of FDI in building export competitiveness . How can institutional voids be treated as business opportunities?
7. Discuss the relationship between competition and technology in international business. Explain how companies can succeed internationally in terms of competition and technology.
8. How does international competition differ from domestic competition? Why has the competitive environment in international business intensified?
9. What sequence of steps should winnable giants take to build stronger businesses at home or to enter markets overseas?

REFERENCES

Alesina, A., E. Spolaore, and R. Enrico. 2005. "Trade, Growth and the Size of Countries." In P. Aghion and S. Duriauf. eds., *Handbook of Economic Growth*, 1st Edition, Volume 1. Amsterdam: Elsevier. 1499-1542.

——. 1998. *Endogenous Growth*. Cambridge, MA: MIT Press.

Barro, R. J. and X. Sala-i-Martin. 1992. "Convergence." *Journal of Political Economy* 100 (April): 223-51.

Becker, G. S. 1993, *Human Capital: A Theoretical and Empirical Analysis, with Special Reference to Education*, 3rd Edition. Chicago: University of Chicago Press.

Canning, D., M. Fay, and R. Perotti. 1994. "Infrastructure and Economic Growth." in M. Baldarassi, L. Paganetto, and E. Phelps, eds. *International Differences in Growth Rates.* New York: Palgrave Macmillan.

Drzeniek Hanouz, M., T. Geiger, and A. Panov. 2008. "Ukraine's Performance across the Twelve Pillars of Competitiveness." *The Ukraine Competitiveness* Report 2008. Geneva: World Economic Forum. 47-100.

Easterly, W. 2002. *The Elusive Quest for Growth.* Cambridge, MA: MIT Press.

Fischer, S. 1993. "The Role of Macroeconomic Factors in Growth." *Journal of Monetary Economics* 32 (3): 485-512.

Frenkel, J. and D. Romer. 1999. "Does Trade Cause Growth?" *American Economic Review* 89 (3): 379-99.

Gramlich. E. M. 1994. "Infrastructure Investment: A Review Essay." *Journal of Economic Literature* 32 (3): 1176-96.

Grossman, G. and E. Helpman. 1991. *Innovation and Growth in the World Economy.* Cambridge, MA: MIT Press, Chapters 3 and 4.

Hawksworth J. and G. Cookson. 2008. *The World in 2050: Beyond the BRICs: A Broader Look at Emerging Market Growth Prospects.* London: Pricewaterhouse Coopers.

Kaufmann D. and T. Vishwanalh. 2001. "Toward Transparency: New Approaches and their Application to Financial Markets." *World Bank ObserverlS* 111: 41-57.

OECD (Organisation for Economic Co-operation and Development). 2009. *Assessing Policy Responses to the Economic Crisis: Investing in Innovation for Long-Term Growth.* May. Paris: OECD.

Porter, M. 1990. The *Competitive Advantage of Nations.* New York: The Free Press.

Rodrik, D. and F. Rodriguez. 1999. "Trade Policy and Growth: A Skeptics' Guide to Cross National Evidence." *NBER Working Paper* No. 7081, April. Cambridge. MA: National Bureau of Economic Research.

Romer, P. 1990. "Endogenous Technological Change." *Journal of Political Economy W* (October): X71-S102.

Sachs, J. 2001. *Macroeconomics and Health: Investing in Health lot Economic Development: Report of the Commission on Macroeconomics and Health,* Geneva World Health Organisation.

Sala-i-Martin, X, and E. V. Artadi, 2004. "The Global Competitiveness Index." *The Global Competitiveness Report 2004-2005.* ' Hampshire: Palgrave Macmillan. 51-80.

Sala-i-Martin X., J. Blanke, M. Drneziek Hariouz, T. Geiger, I. Mia and F. Paua. 2008. "The Global Competitiveness Index: Prioritizing the Economic Policy Agenda," *The Global Competitiveness Report 2008-2009.* Geneva: World Economic Forum. 3-41.

Schultj. T. W. 1961. "Investment in Human Capital." *American Economic Review* 1 (2): 1-17.

Shleifer, A. and R. Vishny. 1997, "A Survey of Corporate Governance." Nobel Symposium on Law and Finance, August, 1995. *Journal of Finance 52* (June): 737-83.

Swan, T. W. 1956. "Economic Growth and Capital Accumulation." *Economic Record* 32 (2): 334-61.

Overview." Paper prepared for LAEBA, Second Annual Meeting. November 28-29, 2005. Tel Aviv University.

UNCTAD (United Nations Conference on Trade and Development). 2008. *World Investment Report 2008.* New York and Geneva: United Nations.

———. 2009. *Assessing the Impact of the Current Financial and Economic Crisis on Global FDI Flows.* New York and Geneva: United Nations.

Zingales, L. 1998. "Corporate Governance." In P. Newman, ed. *The New Palgrave Dictionary of Economics and the Law.* New York: Macmillan.

15

INTERNATIONALISATION OF TECHNOLOGICAL INNOVATION

INTRODUCTION

Economic growth in recent years has been achieved largely through technology innovations in various fields of science and industry. Technological innovation refers to innovation that draws on the available science-technology base. As such it acts to link existing technological resources to economic output. Although R&D is often an important element in the process, it is insufficient by itself because the successful realisation of an innovation depends on a host of other factors, such as the market environment and management disposition towards continuing to pursue the innovation. Application of technology and R&D can occur at any point during the series of activities that make up the innovation process. The development of new capabilities applies to both technical functions and managerial ones: organizational and marketing innovation is as important as technical innovation to growth and competitiveness. This is true for the industrialized countries that are at the technology frontiers, as well as for developing countries that need to catch up in terms of technology. Given the large gap between the developed and developing countries in terms of technological advancement, the latter continue to rely heavily on technology transfer from the former in their development process. However, sustainable economic development requires that countries do more than simply "open up" and passively wait for new technologies to flow in. It demands active, continuous technological effort by enterprises, along with government policies that help firms attract technologies, use them effectively and innovate. Technology requires efforts to absorb and adapt; it has strong "tacit" elements that cannot be embodied in equipment or codified in instructions or blueprints. Tacit knowledge can only be transferred effectively if the recipient develops capabilities to learn and incorporate the knowledge. It must seek new information, experiment with the technology, find new ways of organizing production and train its employees in new skills. It involves not just the enterprise itself but also interaction with other firm and institutions.

INNOVATION MATTERS FOR ALL COUNTRIES

Technological innovation means the introduction of new products, processes or services into the market. Innovation does not necessarily mean pushing the frontiers of knowledge, particularly in a developing-country context. Rather, innovations can be *new to the user* but not necessarily *new to the world*. The nature of innovation - and of required capabilities - varies greatly between activities according to their technological complexity, the creation of new technology being at one extreme and the use of existing technologies at the other. Figure 1 shows an illustrative pyramid, with the least complex technological functions (in terms of innovative efforts) at the base, and the most demanding ones at the top. While these categories are generic activities in all three sectors—primary, manufacturing and services—they can be adapted to different technologies to take account of particular machinery, process, product and organizational characteristics.

- The starting point is the acquisition of basic production capabilities to absorb and use existing technology. This sounds easy but it is not, at least in order for capabilities to match relevant global best practice and for activity that goes beyond simple assembly. Reaching internationally acceptable levels of production efficiency and quality in complex activities is very demanding. Many enterprises fail to do this, even after years of operation, unless they invest sufficiently in collecting information, creating new skills and developing appropriate management structures.
- Absorption and adaptation of technology are particularly challenging if conditions are significantly different from those at the origin of the technology, and if local support and supply structures are weak.
- Adaptation, in turn, can grow into significant technological improvement and technological learning, with systematic efforts made to improve product and process performance. At this stage, many firms start monitoring international technological trends and selecting those technologies that can feed into their own efforts.
- Finally there is the frontier innovation stage, when firms design, develop and test entirely new products and processes.

RESEARCH & DEVELOPMENT

R&D comprises creative work undertaken on a systematic basis in order to increase the stock of knowledge, including knowledge of man, culture and society, and the use of this stock of knowledge to devise new applications. R&D involves novelty and the resolution of scientific and technological uncertainty. It includes basic and applied research along with development.

FIGURE 1

STAGES OF TECHNOLOGY DEVELOPMENT BY INNOVATION EFFORT

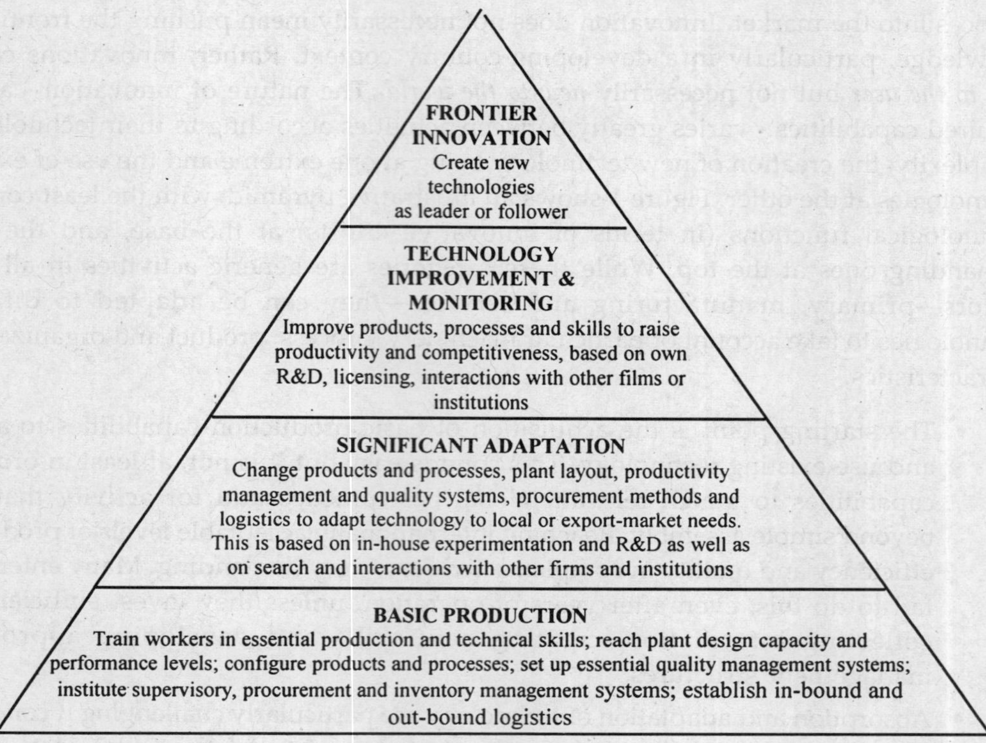

- *Basic research.* The objective of basic research is to gain a more comprehensive knowledge or understanding of the subject under study without specific applications in mind. In industry, basic research is defined as research that advances scientific knowledge but does not have specific immediate commercial objectives.
- *Applied research.* The objective of applied research is to gain the knowledge or understanding to meet a specific, recognized need. In industry, applied research includes investigations to discover new scientific knowledge that has specific commercial objectives with respect to products, processes, or services.
- *Development.* Development is the systematic use of the knowledge or understanding gained from research directed towards the production of useful materials, devices, systems or methods, including the design and development of prototypes and processes.

There is a direct relationship between R&D and growth. The long-term impacts on economic growth of public R&D and business R&D have been found to be strong and significant. Business R&D undertaken in other countries also plays an important role.

Moreover, increased domestic business R&D accentuates the positive impact of both public and foreign business R&D. In other words, business R&D (either domestic or foreign-funded) has both a direct impact on a country's economic growth and an indirect one through improved absorption of the results of public R&D and R&D performed in other countries.

Enterprises are the principal agents of innovation today, but they do not innovate and learn in isolation. They rely on intricate (formal and informal) links with other firms and with public research institutions, universities and other knowledge creating bodies like standards and metrology institutes. In undertaking innovation, they react to government policies on trade, competition, investment and innovation. They seek human resources for innovation from the education and training system, and they draw upon the financial system for funding innovative efforts. The complex web within which innovation occurs is commonly referred to as the "national innovation system" (NIS).

As the internationalization of production deepens and communication costs decline, each NIS increasingly draws on knowledge created in other systems. Rapid technical progress and the rising costs and risks of innovation force innovators to seek centres of scientific excellence internationally. Global production networks - in which MNCs play the leading role - link together the productive activities that underly innovation. Parent companies are instrumental in such networks, providing the initial technology to their affiliates and helping them absorb, adapt and subsequently upgrade it. As a result, the innovation systems of more and more countries are becoming interlinked in a global network in which technological activity is international and information networks span the world.

From an economic development perspective it is becoming increasingly important to take part in this international exchange. Those countries that are in a position to do so stand a better chance of accessing new technologies at an early stage, as well as commercializing innovations developed in their own NIS. However, the capabilities needed for participating are unequally distributed among countries which increases the risk of a further widening of already large development gaps.

Different ways of Internationalising innovation

There are three main categories of innovation internationalization. In the first category, national enterprises and MNCs as well as individuals are engaged in the international commercialization of technology developed at home. The second category relates to domestic and international technical and scientific collaborations among private and public institutions, including domestic firms and MNCs, universities and research centres. International innovation by MNCs is the third category. The MNC is the only institution that, by definition, can control and carry out within its boundaries the process of innovation across the globe. Table-1 shows the taxomony of internationalisation of innovation.

TABLE 1
Taxonomy of Internationalisation of Innovation

Category	*Actors*	*Forms*
International exploitation of nationally produced innovations	Profit-seeking (national and transnational) firms and individuals	• Exports of innovative products • Cession of licenses and patents • Foreign production of innovative goods internally designed and developed
International techno-scientific collaborations	Univerities and public research centres National and international firms	• Joint scientific projects • Scientific exchanges, sabbaticals • International flows of students • Joint ventures for specific projects • Production agreements with exchange of technical information and/or equipment
International generation of innovations	MNCs	• R&D and other innovative activities both in home and host countries • Acquisitions of existing R&D units or greenfield R&D investment in host countries

ENHANCING TECHNOLOGICAL INNOVATION CAPABILITIES

The impact of technological progress is not uniform. *Product* innovation may be used to encourage consumption; and, with rising incomes, consumer demand becomes more differentiated—which further stimulates product innovation. *Process* innovation can dramatically cut the costs of production. Some new technologies are opening entirely new areas of activity. The application of information technology is a good example. In most developed and newly industrialising countries, activities with greater innovation potential (and hence the output of high-technology industries, including in the services sector) have grown faster than that of others. Exports have risen faster than total production — a manifestation of globalisation—and, within exports, high-technology products have grown more rapidly. Sustained economic growth hence increasingly calls not only for the application of new technologies, but also for a shift in the productive structure from low- to high-technology activities.

An analysis of FDI and technology has to take account of this changing context. The world is facing not just rapid technical change, but also shrinking economic space and dramatically intensifying competition. And this emerging new competition places stringent demands on governments. These demands vary by level of development, of course. Industrial countries, generally speaking, focus on achieving — or even pushing beyond — frontier innovation. They seek to improve their "national innovation systems".

Developing countries, in general, are more likely to focus on adapting existing technologies more effectively. Nevertheless, firms in a number of developing countries are among the innovators, especially in emerging areas that offer niches of opportunity. Examples include biotechnology, information technology or new areas of services industries. In every case, countries have to cope with the new competition and changing flows of knowledge and productive factors — all in a far more open economic environment in which there is a "renaissance of capitalism". This new competition is the *first reason* why the analysis of FDI and technology in host developing economies today must differ from that, say, of three or four decades ago. The *second reason* is the way the technology has evolved. Much of early development thinking assumed technology transfer and diffusion in developing countries to be relatively easy, and framed the analysis of MNCs in that context. The main need was thought to be for physical investment. Technologies were transferred "embodied" in new equipment or in patents or blueprints; their efficient use was, if considered at all, taken as given. The structuralist approach supported industrial development behind protective barriers; the neoclassical approach favoured market-driven resource allocation with free trade and international investment flows. Both assumed that countries passively received and deployed technologies from abroad, and did not differ in their ability to use technology. Thus, there was a tendency towards uniform development strategies for all developing countries. In the area of technology, policy and research attention focused on modes of technology transfer and its defects. It largely ignored how well countries coped with the technologies they imported. Moreover, the "soft" side of technology transfer and absorption—organisation and managerial practices, tacit knowledge and the like—was neglected.

The consequences of neglecting technology absorption are evident under both strategies. Import substitution, by removing the competitive spur to learning, led to technological inefficiency and lags. Liberalisation helped technology development in the countries that had built up a strong base of absorptive capabilities, but by ignoring the needs of costly learning and by — incorrectly — assuming efficient markets, delayed or hindered it in others. There is growing divergence rather than convergence in national capabilities: "getting prices right" is thus not a sufficient condition for sustained development. There is now ample evidence that the technological leaders in the developing world adopted specific strategies on technology, different from both classic import substitution and free markets.

TECHNOLOGICAL LEARNING AND DEVELOPMENT

Technology is not sold like physical products, in fully embodied forms; nor does it flow by osmosis when agents are exposed to more advanced systems of knowledge. It has important *tacit elements* that need effort to master. The process is incremental and path dependent. It often faces an uncertain environment where the skills, information, networks and credit needed are not readily available. The main features of technoligcal learning are:

i) Technological learning is a real and significant process. It is conscious and purposive rather than automatic or passive. Firms using a given technology for similar periods need not be equally proficient: each would travel on a different learning curve according to the intensity and efficacy of its capability-building efforts.

ii) Firms do not have full information on technical alternatives. They function with imperfect, variable and rather hazy knowledge of technologies they are using.

iii) Firms may not know how to build up the necessary capabilities — learning itself often has to be learned. The learning process faces risk, uncertainty and cost. For a technological latecomer, the fact that others have already undergone the learning process is both a benefit and a cost. It is a benefit in that they can borrow from the others' experience (to the extent this is accessible). It is a cost in that they are relatively inefficient during the process (and so have to bear a loss if they compete on open markets).

iv) Firms cope with uncertainty not by maximising a well-defined function but by developing organisational and managerial satisfying routines. These are adapted as firms collect new information, learn from experience and imitate other firms. Learning is path- dependent and cumulative.

v) The learning process is highly technology-specific, since technologies differ in their learning requirements. Some technologies are more embodied in equipment while others have greater tacit elements. Process technologies (like chemicals) are more embodied than assembly technologies (machinery or automobiles), and demand different (often less) effort. Capabilities built up in one activity are not easily transferable to another.

vi) Different technologies have different spillover effects and potential for further technological advance. Specialisation in technologies with more technological potential and spillovers has greater dynamic benefits than specialisation in technologies with limited potential.

vii) Capability-building occurs at all levels — shop-floor, process or product engineering, quality management, maintenance, procurement, inventory control, outbound logistics and relations with other firms and institutions. Innovation in the sense of formal R&D is at one end of the spectrum of technological activity; it does not exhaust it. However, R&D becomes important as more complex technologies are used; some R&D is needed just for efficient absorption.

viii) Technological development can take place to different depths. The attainment of a minimum level of operational capability (know-how) is essential to all activity. This may not lead to deeper capabilities, an understanding of the principles of the technology (know-why): this requires a discrete strategy to invest in deepening. The deeper the levels of technological capabilities aimed at, the higher the cost, risk and duration involved. The development of know-why allows firms to select better the technologies they need, lower the costs of buying those technologies, realise more value by adding their own knowledge, and to develop autonomous innovative capabilities.

ix) Technological learning is rife with externalities and interlinkages. It is driven by links with suppliers of inputs or capital goods, competitors, customers, consultants, and technology suppliers. There are also important interactions with firms in unrelated industries, technology institutes, extension services, universities, associations and training institutions. Where information flows are particularly dense, clusters emerge with collective learning for the group as a whole.

x) Technological interactions occur within a country and with other countries. Imported technology is generally the most important initial input into learning in developing countries. Since technologies change constantly, moreover, access to foreign sources of innovation is vital to continued technological progress. Technology import is not, however, a substitute for indigenous capability development — the efficacy with which imported technologies are used depends on local efforts to deepen the absorptive base. Similarly, not all modes of technology import are equally conducive to indigenous learning. Some come highly packaged with complementary factors, and so stimulate less learning.

All these features mean that technology development faces extensive coordination on problem, externalities, missing markets and cumulative effects. More importantly, firms face learning problems: learning to use new technologies, even those existing elsewhere, requires new skills, effort and institutional change. The diffusion of technologies even in industrial countries poses challenges; in developing countries, it is generally far more difficult. This is why simply exposing firms to unregulated markets may not lead to sufficient technological learning. Firms may not be able to bear the costs involved or link their own learning processes with those of other firms that provide them with inputs or buy their outputs and so affect their own competitiveness. (Such technological interdependence can lead to under-investment by all linked firms.) And mastering new technology is not just a once-for-all task. It is a process that requires continuous *upgrading* and *deepening* of all kinds of intellectual capital, as well as of supporting networks and institutions. Without this, countries can remain at the bottom of the technology ladder where their competitive edge lies in simple assembly or processing based on cheap labour — once wages rise they lose this edge. Thus, as they master the simpler elements of technology, they have to move into more advanced technological capabilities. As technologies change, they have to upgrade their own capabilities to remain competitive. As they gain competence in simple activities, they have to move into more advanced ones, although this process may not necessarily be linear. At each stage, learning needs new knowledge, skills and organisation. At every stage, it becomes more challenging. In the new technological context, the challenges themselves become greater. The confluence of the two new analytical factors noted is that the building of new capabilities is critical to technology development in the emerging global competitive scene, even for developing countries that are not "innovators".

The enterprise is at the core of technology development, but it operates within a system. The main elements of this system are market and competitive signals (the incentive regime), factor markets and institutions. This interacting "triad" comprises the structure within which firms learn and create technology. Random firm-level factors aside, systems differ in their ability to stimulate, support and coordinate technological effort. Systemic differences arise from how efficient the various markets and institutions are, and the extent to which governments can improve them when they are deficient. The risks of market and institutional failure always exist and they are particularly high where learning, information, coordination and externalities are involved. To deal with these risks is all the more difficult in many developing countries. The ability of governments to overcome them, create new markets and strengthen institutions is then the crucial factor in technology development.

TRANSFER OF TECHNOLOGY

The transfer and dissemination of technology and the promotion of innovation are among the most important benefits that host countries seek from FDI. MNCs are the dominant source of innovation. Direct investment by them is an important mode of international technology transfer, possibly contributing to local innovative activities in host countries. But attracting technology and innovative capacities and mastering, upgrading and diffusing them throughout the domestic economy require government support—through national policies and international treaty making.

The policies on technology transfer have changed. Most governments have moved from direct controls and restrictions to market-friendly approaches—improving the business and FDI environment, strengthening legal and other institutions and enhancing the skills and raising the capabilities of local enterprises. Market-friendly approaches are themselves shifting—from providing an enabling environment to stronger pro-innovation (technology seller) regimes, while continuing to encourage technology transfer. In the international arena, national market-friendly approaches are complemented by TRIPS, restrictions on performance requirements and a number of other agreements. Important choices remain on the right balance between regulation and markets in the transfer of technology. The realization that developing countries, particularly the LDCs, need special support has led to some mandatory requirements on technology transfer. But implementation remains an issue.

The Need for Policies to Promote Technology Transfer

In a world of rapid technological change and intense competition, creating acquiring and efficiently using new technologies is a vital ingredient of growth. In the generation and dissemination of new technologies, MNCs can provide them in many forms: internalized in FDI, through non-equity forms (such as strategic alliances) and at arm's length (licensing and other contracts and arrangements). The rising cost of innovation, the perceived need to protect and control intangible assets and the liberalization of policies are leading MNCs to use FDI as the main mode for allowing access to valuable technologies. As a result, the role of FDI in international technology transfer is growing. Indeed, many new technologies, particularly those used in integrated production systems, are available only through FDI

Making the best use of FDI-mediated technology transfer requires policy support in the host economy. To start with, MNCs with the most suitable technologies have to be attracted. Then they have to be induced to transfer the technologies that offer the best potential for local development. If MNCs start with simple technologies suited to the low wage and low skill setting of many developing countries, they have to be persuaded to upgrade them as wages and skills rise. In more advanced economies, they have to be induced to transfer the technology development process itself, undertaking more design and R&D locally. The development impact of technology transfer through FDI goes well beyond what happens within foreign affiliates—it extends to diffusing technology and technological capabilities to local suppliers and buyers and contributing to local innovation capacity.

In all these areas, there is a risk that markets will not by themselves optimize technology transfer and development. International technology markets are imperfect and fragmented, dominated by a few large enterprises, mostly MNCs. Once transferred, the efficient use of technology faces problems that may call for policy intervention. Some imperfections are inherent to transactions in information; others arise from weak institutions and markets in host countries, from a legacy of inefficient policies (say, on trade and competition) or from the strategies of technology suppliers. For these reasons, most countries have used policies to influence technology transfer by MNCs.

Shifting Towards a More Market-Friendly Approach in National Policies

Developed and developing countries have differed in their technology transfer policies. Most developed countries are significant innovators and both sell and buy new technology. Their concerns have been mainly to strengthen the technological position of their firms—through more stringent IPRs, though several countries, such as Japan and Switzerland, did not fully protect and enforce IPRs at critical stages of development—and encourage local innovative activity by foreign affiliates. Developing countries, as importers of technology, have tried to improve the terms and conditions of technology transfer, strengthen the bargaining position of local firms and promote technology diffusion and generation, sometimes by a relaxed application of IPRs They have also used incentives and performance requirements to induce greater technology transfer and diffusion by MNCs and to encourage technology generation by local firms.

This pattern is changing: countries are converging in their policies on technology transfer. Developed countries are strengthening IPR protection, while reducing remaining barriers to MNC activities. (But competition policies still counter the abuse of market power by large firms.) Developing countries have moved from the direct regulation of technology transfer towards a more market-friendly approach. Most policy changes have been national, but international investment agreements (IIAs) mirror this pattern. There are now few developing countries with comprehensive systems for vetting technology contracts, either between independent firms or between MNCs and their affiliates.

Many countries—developed and developing —had slack IPR systems until recently, in part to encourage technological capability development in local firms. Most now offer stronger IPR protection, with the TRIPS Agreement providing the international setting. But the case for strengthening IPRs in countries with a weak technological base remains in dispute. The case is more valid for developing countries whose enterprises are launching into innovation or that host (or would like to host) high-technology MNC activities (sensitive to weak IPRs). But non-innovative poor countries may not receive greater technology inflows and yet have to pay more for patented products and technologies.

Another set of measures on FDI-related technology transfer is less obvious. In the past, many economies restricted FDI as the mode of technology transfer while encouraging imports in other forms to promote local R&D capabilities. Of the ones that succeeded, Japan, the Republic of Korea and Taiwan Province of China are the best-known examples But such strategies did not work well in other countries, largely because the context and the way strategies were applied differed.

Controls on inward FDI (used, among other things, to regulate technology transfer) have declined in recent years. But governments use other policy tools more actively to promote technology transfer and development by MNCs. These include targeting technology-intensive activities and functions by promotion agencies seeking to attract new FDI incentives for existing foreign affiliates to upgrade technologies and undertake more R&D and the encouragement of greater local content and stronger local linkages by MNCs

The development and refinement of investment promotion tools — this can cover both the attraction of new investments and the upgrading of existing ones — is perhaps the cutting edge of FDI policies for technology transfer. Mature industrial countries use them as actively as developing countries, Ireland and Singapore are cases in point, showing how this is done and how it needs to be combined with improvement in local capabilities. Policies directed only at foreign investors are unlikely to work if the environment is not conducive to more advanced technological activity.

THE RIGHT MIX OF POLICY INSTRUMENTS AND CONDITIONS

Direct Controls

Direct controls on technology transfer and FDI did not fully succeed largely because they did not address two issues: the information and administrative requirements of technology regulation, and the absorption and upgrading of imported technology. Take the first. It is difficult for any government to dictate effectively to private enterprises the best technology to buy, the most economical terms for procuring it and the optimal structure of transfers over time. On the FDI front, it is similarly difficult for governments to dictate which technologies to transfer or how much to restrict entry to encourage infant local enterprises. The difficulties are far greater in developing countries, where information and skills are more scarce, institutional structures more rigid and local enterprises and institutions less developed.

Controls thus tended to impose uniform, inflexible rules across industries, stipulating the duration of contracts, payment terms, foreign shares and the like without taking the specific circumstances into account. This led in some cases to the transfer of older, less valuable technologies, sometimes barring access to new technologies. The transfer process itself tended to be shallow and incomplete, because the seller had little incentive to transfer more complex segments of the technology or to help the buyer continuously to upgrade technologies over time. The outright prohibition of restrictive clauses in technology transfer contracts by a number of countries often raised the price of the technology and reinforced the propensity to provide less valuable technologies.

The second issue was that regulations focused on the cost of the transfer, not on the conditions needed for the effective absorption and upgrading of imported technology. It was simply assumed that the technology would be used efficiently and would keep abreast of new developments. This often turned out to be optimistic. It imposed costs on host countries, saddling them with technological lags and inefficiencies. Moreover, the settings for implementing restrictive technology transfer policies—protected regimes that gave few incentives to firms to master and upgrade imported technologies—concealed these inefficiencies and added to the ineffectiveness of such policies.

Stipulating greater local ownership—or requiring transfers

Many countries sought to encourage technology absorption by stipulating foreign equity shareholding or insisting on minority joint ventures. The presumption was that greater local ownership would lead to better absorption and diffusion of technology. Where imposed on reluctant technology sellers, however, the results were often not in accordance with expectations. The strategy worked best in countries that had strong local firms, a large skills base and an export-oriented environment. It also worked in some large developing countries. For instance, in India, joint ventures—stipulated by domestic equity ownership requirements—were found to have generated substantial local learning and transfers of technology

The scant evidence on technology transfer requirements suggests that, for the reasons mentioned above, they too did not work well. The requirements tended to raise the cost of transfer to MNCs, inducing them to provide less valuable knowledge or invest less in rooting the technology locally. They thus appeared to be less effective than joint venture requirements.

Providing behavioural incentives

The effectiveness of incentives for technology transfer to host countries depends on the competitive environment and the capabilities of local suppliers Where the host economy is open to competition and local suppliers are capable, incentives enhance technology transfer. Some countries used incentives not only to attract MNCs into high-technology activities but also to encourage foreign affiliates to move into more complex technologies and R&D. But they were successful not because they gave exceptionally generous incentives—but because they created other preconditions for MNCs to deepen technological activity (such as more advanced skills, better local suppliers, more active and innovative research institutions).

Strengthening IPRs

The strengthening of IPRs can be beneficial for some types of technology transfer, but implementing the IPR regime can be costly and challenging. And its effects on development and on FDI flows are controversial. Stronger IPRs can increase the scope for the abuse of market power by technology owners, and developing countries with weak competition policies may not be able to cope with this effectively. Stronger IPRs may also raise the cost of technologies without the compensation, at least in LDCs, of stimulating local innovation or international technology transfer. However, strong IPRs are likely to benefit developing countries with an advanced industrial sector, stimulating local innovation and increasing MNC transfer of technology-intensive activities or R&D functions.

In sum, policies to regulate and stimulate technology transfer through FDI can work, but under special conditions (table 2). Where these conditions do not exist, attempts to control contracts and transfer arrangements may not produce the desired results.

TABLE 2
Technology import strategies, policies and conditions

Strategy objective	*Policy*	*Policy instrument*	*Condition*
Promote domestic technological capabilities by minimizing reliance on FDI	- Conditions on FDI - Incentives to partnership agreements - Government support to domestic firms - Foster national flagship firms	- Foreign ownership restrictions - Financial and tax incentives to local firms - Technical support, R&D promotion programmes - Effective export promotion - Encourage hiring of foreign experts, licensing and capital goods imports	- Exposure to international competition (as by strong export orientation) - Availability of skilled labour - Financial resources - Entrepreneur's willingness and ability to undertake risky technology investment - Institution able to support skill, technology and export activity
Promote FDI with minimal government intervention in the expectation that it will involve technology transfer	- Encourage large FDI inflows - Relax FDI restrictions - Ensure macroeconomic stability	- Remove FDI restrictions or provide incentives - Liberalize trade - Foster competition and well-structured IPR regimes - Provide good infrastructure - General FDI promotion	- Efficient and credible institutions to administer market-friendly policies - High local absorptive capacity
Promote technology transfer by FDI with proactive government intervention	- Target specific MNCs - Provide incentives for MNCs to upgrade their technologies	- Industrial parks and advanced infrastructure - Well structured IPR regimes - High level skills and strong training system geared to activities promoted - Rigorous quality standards - Targeted incentives for activities and/or firms	- Institutions able to handle incentives - Institutions able to select technologies - Institutions for technology support and skill formation
Mixed strategy	- Promote linkages with domestic economy - Build local technological capabilities - Encourage deepening of MNC activity	- Business incubators - Information clearing-houses - Industrial parks - Supporting R&D - Supporting joint ventures, licensing and collaboration - Supporting training of domestic labour force	- Institutions able to bargain with MNCs - Institutions able to plan strategically - Ability to integrate skills financial markets, infrastructure and technological capability development

ROLE FOR INTERNATIONAL ORGANIZATIONS IN PROMOTING THE SPREAD OF TECHNOLOGY

There is often a mismatch between technologies developed at the world frontier (i.e., in the advanced economies that produce most innovations) and the needs of the adopting country. The lack of effective enforcement of intellectual property rights and the inability to pay for innovation in less developed economies lead firms in the advanced economies to target the needs of their own domestic markets. As a result, technologies that travel through trade may not be appropriate for importing countries.

Inappropriate technologies limit the extent of technical development. Importantly, these problems cannot easily be solved by individual countries' policies. For instance, the enforcement of intellectual property rights may imply a *prisoner's dilemma* whereby each developing country prefers other countries to enforce property rights in order to encourage producers in advanced economies to manufacture technologies more appropriate to their needs. This suggests an important role for international organizations in coordinating the enforcement of property rights and in encouraging the production of technologies more appropriate to the needs of less-developed countries. As free-riding problems in patent policy are more severe the larger the number of independent countries involved in the global economy, the significance of an international patent agreement increases with the number of sovereign decision-makers.

Several issues on the role of the multilateral trading system (and of international organizations in general) in promoting the international spread of technology are still open to discussion. These issues include the meticulous design of intellectual property rights agreements (e.g. differential rules for least developed countries, harmonization of criteria for patentability of novelty), the role of other policies (e.g. subsidies, temporary movement of people, monitoring), and the extent to which such policies should be embedded in a multilateral trade agreement.

An area receiving special attention concerns environmentally sound technologies, with provisions for their transfer to developing countries are more common in international environmental agreements. These instruments, while market-friendly, accept the need for the commercial transfer of technology but seek to ensure that transfers are not harmful in environmental terms. They encourage MNCs to transfer environmentally sound technologies to developing countries that may otherwise not be able to use them.

Overall, most provisions consist of "best endeavour" commitments rather than mandatory rules. These have on the whole proven to be somewhat ineffective. International instruments with built-in implementation mechanisms, including finance and monitoring, have a better implementation record—but these are scarce, used mainly for such "public goods" as environmental protection rather than technology transfer.

The concerns promoting earlier interventions in technology transfer have not disappeared, since market and institutional failures remain to be addressed. What has changed is the perception of how best to tackle them. The current thinking is that measures to strengthen local capabilities, markets and institutions are more likely to promote technology transfer and development than interventions in the contractual process. There is, however, a need to retain preferential treatment for developing countries. Indeed, the requirement that TRIPS places on developed countries to promote transfers to LDCs suggests that this is generally accepted.

Some questions to be tackled in the future: *how to operationalize transfer-of-technology provisions for developing countries in international agreements? How to further encourage technology transfer? How to handle the anti-competitive effects of technology transactions? And how to strengthen national innovative capacity?* There is thus a need to consider stronger international cooperation in technology generation, transfer and diffusion.

QUESTIONS

1. Discuss the stages of technology development by innovation effort.
2. Explain the different ways of internationalising innovation.
3. Critically examine the various issues involved in the transfer of technology.
4. Discuss the role of technology and technology transfer in the international business environment.
5. Discuss the impact of technological innovation capabilities.
6. Explain the ways to operationalise transfer of technology provisions for developing countries in international agreements. How can the anti-competitive effects of technology transactions be handled.
7. Using information technology as the example, weigh the positive and negative effects of this technology at four levels: global, national, business, personal.

REFERENCES

Anne O. Krueger, *Trade and Employment in Developing Countries Synthesis,* University of Chicago Press (Chicago), 1983, Chapter 7.

Bergsten, C.F.: America in the World Economy : A strategy for the 1990s, Washington: Institute of International Economics, 1988.

Bhagwati, Jagdish N.: The Theory of Political Economy,, Economic Policy and Foreign Investment, in Public Policy and Economic Development: Essays in Honour of Ian Little, (ed) by Maurice Fg Scott and Deepak Lal (ed), Oxford University Press, Oxford 1990.

Drucker, P.F. : The New realities, Harper and Row, New York, 1989.

Freeman, C.: Technology Policy and Economic Performance, Pinter, London, 1987.

Ghemawat, P. and Spence, A.M.: Modeling Global Competition, in Competition in Global Industries, ed. M. Porter, Boston, Harvard Business School.

———, 1989, "The Competitive Advantage of Nations", New York, The Free Press.

Kogut, B.: Designing Global Strategies: Comparative and competitive value-added chains. Sloan Management Review, Summer, 1985, pp.15-28.

———, 1989, "The Competitive Advantage of Nations", New York, The Free Press. Reich, R. and E. Mankin: Joint Ventures With Japan Give Away Our Future, Harvard Business Review, March-April, 1986, pp. 78-86.

Lall, Sanjaya, "India" in John H. Dunning (ed.): Multinational enterprises, economic structure and international competitiveness, Chichester, John Wiley and Sons, 1986, pp. 309-335.

Martinussen, John.,"Transnational corporations in a developing country: The Indian Experience", New Delhi, Sage Publications, 1988, 228 p.

Michale Michaely, Demelin Papageorgiou and Armeane M. Chokes, *Liberalising Foreign Trade : Lessons of Experience in Developing World,* Basic Blackwell (Cambridge, MA), 1991, pp. 19607.

Ohmae, K.: Triad power: The coming shape of global competition, Free Press, New York, 1985.

Porter, M.E., 1985, "Competitive Advantage", New York :McMillan Press.

Reich, R. and E. Mankin: Joint Ventures With Japan Give Away Our Future, Harvard Business Review, March-April, 1986, pp. 78-86.

Siddharthan, N.S., "In-house R and D, imported technology, and firm size : lessons from Indian experience", The Developing Economies, 26 : 212-221, September 1988.

Yamamura, K.: Caveat Emptor: The industrial policy of Japan, in Krugman, P. (ed.), Strategic Trade Policy and the New International Economies, MIT press, Cambridge, Mass., 1986.

Yamamura, K.: Caveat Emptor: The industrial policy of Japan, in Krugman, P. (ed.), Strategic Trade.

16

GLOBAL e-BUSINESS

INTRODUCTION

Communication and transportation networks have improved dramatically over the last few decades , far-flung nations around the globe are now within the reach. As a result, companies have jumped into international markets, outsourced operations to overseas manufacturers and suppliers, and established subsidiaries around the world. E-business promises to further shrink the global economy as people everywhere reach products on the Web, buy and sell products on e-commerce sites, and manage international supply chains with collaborative software and e-market places. The combination of broadband capabilities, connectivity, standard languages (.html, .xml), wireless communication and portability have given birth to the digital age and its most pervasive manifestation: the Internet. The Internet is a global network connecting millions of computers across the world, exchanging data, opinions, information and news using a common architecture, the Internet Protocol (IP). In essence, the Internet is a global tool since it has abolished physical distance for the transmission of data, images and sounds and it has standardised the transmission protocol as well as the machine software, making it possible for any computer in the world to be part of network and to 'talk' to other computers. In fact, the Internet and its attendant power have made it possible for many companies to conduct global business at a much more discernible and attainable level. As a result of the Internet and new information technology, many of the myths about globalization can be unmasked. New economies and efficiencies of scale have been created. Not too long ago, only a few companies had the resources to compete on a global scale. According to one theory, globalization is a conspiracy by big companies against smaller markets. Some companies, of course, are bigger, financially, man others. That's a testimony to the market-based economy that more and more markets are choosing to adopt. But no company or group of companies is calling all the shots. Small and midsize companies are getting in on the act and thriving globally. Now, more than at any time in history, almost any size firm with the vision and ambition to do so can extend its reach globally.

WHAT IS GLOBAL E-BUSINESS?

Global e-business is not a simple undertaking. It involves a variety of complex issues. Moreover, failure to adequately address the IT element can alienate entire markets and erode the relationship between a company and the marketplace. A comprehensive global e-business strategy can greatly help to ensure a place in the global economy, thus enabling a business to take advantage of a world of possibilities.

Global e-business strategically uses IT to take apart physical supply chains and reassemble them in better ways, create highly focused communications for specific cultures, and select the parameters needed to support multiple markets.

Global e-business adapts specific IT to a company's products and message to best meet the varied expectations of markets around the world. In addition, global e-business is, in many ways, a complete revolution of how a company perceives distance, time, and location.

Global e-business is the most powerful communications medium the business world has ever known, in large part because of its reach into factories, offices, and homes around the world. The substantially lower cost of communication via the Internet has dramatically lessened the importance of distance. For many products that can be digitized—such as pictures, video, sound, and words—distance will become a nonfactor. The same is true for services. And even for most products, because of the Internet, distance will have much less an effect on overall business costs.

In the physical world, time and season predominate the flow of goods and services around the world. We see this in the hours of operation—activities that occur by time of day and in social and climactic seasons. The virtual marketplace, on the other hand, is always open. The seller need not be awake, or even physically present, for the buyer to be served by the seller. The Internet is independent of season. Time can thus be homogenized—made uniformly consistent for all buyers and for all sellers.

Because any screen-based activity can be operated anywhere on earth, location does not play an important part in most business decisions. Is it even relevant? Does location mean where the firm is officially registered? Is it where most of the people employed by the company work? Or is it where the server is physically located? In most cases, it simply doesn't matter.

Following the recent decade's IT explosion, a world marketplace awaits, with its entire attendant of consumers and competition. An initial presence on the Internet can be relatively easy and inexpensive to establish. And any company that has a presence on the World Wide Web is international by definition, whether it chooses to become a global company or not.

Global e-business exploits the Internet's ability to level the playing field for all participants, regardless of size, especially as it relates to a company's ability to communicate with customers, employers, suppliers, investors, and other targeted groups. No other media can claim this ability. No individual or company has a better right to establish a place on the Web than any other. Mere purchasing of limited physical space in newspapers or magazines, or buying time on radio or TV, cannot achieve such presence. No other medium can even come close to achieving the level of scalability that the Internet can achieve, i.e., the ability to leverage its own power and impact to much higher levels and with a much broader global reach.

Global e-business eliminates the historic rigid hierarchy of business processes. According to leading corporate strategists, Individual workers must be given maximum autonomy, and the patterns of communications within a worldwide organization should resemble a knowledge-based ecology more than a flowchart. All of this is irrespective of a company's size and physical location.

The internet would increase the globalisation of markets, reinforce global cost reduction, foster global competition and weaken governments' barriers open trade (See Table-1). The challenge for businesses of all sizes—especially smaller ones—that

TABLE-1

Effects of the Internet on Globalisation

Market globalisation	• Increase global commonality in customer needs and tastes (facilities customised standardisation and strengthen appeal of global brands: Barbie online)
	• Enables global customers and global channels (facilitates global sourcing)
	• Supports global marketing (enhances global brands and standardises search)
	• Makes global products more rapidly visible
Cost reduction	• Exploits differences in country costs and facilitates competition from low-cost small-scale companies from emerging markets
	• Enhances global sourcing
	• Speeds up global logistics
	• Reduces product development costs
Foster global competition	• Makes competitive comparisons easier
	• Increases the number of potential global suppliers by reverse auctions
	• Puts new rivals in the global competitive arena
Weaken government	• Makes it easier for customers to by-pass customs and tax levies
barriers to open trade	• Puts pressures on government to harmonise standards and policies
	• Gives customers more incentives to lobby their governments to align with more customers
	• Friendly regulations

want to maximize their global presence involves structuring relationships and information flow so that the right parties can obtain the information at the right time. In all these views, IT and e-business initiatives play critical roles in the strategy of global competition, especially in regard to their global supply chain application.

Before the advent of the new information and e-business technologies of the past decade and before easy access to global information systems became available to companies, customers and suppliers had to make major decisions with little information on which to base them. With the global e-business solutions, buyers and suppliers of all sizes can now easily track the status arid current location of their orders around the world. Before this proliferation of global e-business capability was available, small and midsize companies, especially, might have found themselves left out of the countless new business opportunities in an exploding global economy.

Obviously, small and midsize companies do not possess the sizable resources usually reserved for the biggest global companies in the world. At the same time, those that will succeed in the future understand that the Internet and e-business technology are invaluable, indispensable business tools that need to be harnessed and crafted into a company's overall strategies. To ensure success on the new global business frontier, business leaders from these companies must do what they've always had to do: formulate and implement ideas, tactics, and strategies. Now, they must do this at a much higher level—at a global level—to enable their companies to survive and prosper in the new global marketplace.

DEVELOPING GLOBAL E-BUSINESS STRATEGY

The greatest challenge for all businesses that want to truly maximize their global presence centers on structuring relationships and the flow of information so that the right parties—customers, suppliers, employees, etc.—can obtain it at the right time and at the right place. In this view, e-business and IT initiatives play critical roles in forging a successful global company. This is especially true for small and midsize businesses.

Many companies, however, large and small, wrongly believe e-business and IT will harvest big rewards by merely overlaying computers on top of traditional work processes. These companies fail to understand that e-business and IT work best when they are used to transform those same traditional processes as well as the entire corporate culture. The most successful companies specifically focus on ways that e-business and IT can add value to existing business systems by gaining improved and increased efficiencies. Such a mind-set and resulting strategy affords a small and midsize company the ability to develop entirely new business capabilities and processes to then forge the company's global presence.

Globally savvy companies and their managers view projects, as well as the business overall, from a global perspective. Striving to overcome cultural challenges, regional, national, and personal differences are subrogated to the overall global good of the company to maximize results for the entire organization. Leaders of these companies realize that success depends on the unrestricted flow of information throughout their global business network, which then comes together in the right place and at the right time. For these companies, this doesn't happen by chance. It's a function of its global company culture, and at its core, it is this culture that drives the global organization and, in turn, its global business success. Now, more than ever, e-business technology is driving culture and this new culture is driving globalization.

E-business Strategy: Manifestly Global

The new digital economy is manifestly global—a global phenomenon, yet truly globalized e-businesses are the exception. Even the largest companies on the planet still have a ways to go before they can claim total globalization. Globalization of a company's e-business processes or its Internet presence is not a simple task. It engages a variety of complex issues, and language translation is just the beginning. Failure to sufficiently tackle e-business globalization can isolate entire markets and jeopardize relationships between a company and the marketplace. Moreover, it has the potential to erode and destroy a company's business on a regional or global scale. *A* cogent and inclusive e-business globalization strategy can ensure a company's place in the new borderless digital economy, enabling businesses of all sizes to exploit a new world of opportunities.

A global marketplace awaits all business, with all the attendant customers, consumers, competition, and suppliers that this entails. This is an exciting time for business, indeed, but also a potentially dangerous time. Companies of all sizes too often are blinded by the promises of the new global economy. Herein lays the seductive danger of the Internet and its creation of e-business. Harvesting the Internet's potential rewards requires more than just making a company Internet-enabled. Companies that want to offer their products and services to the world and successfully compete in the new global marketplace must fundamentally change the very way they think about doing business. In this new global, digital world, the axiom, "change or die," has never been more appropriate.

Global E-business Strategy: Key Components

Communications. Global business is about adapting a company's products and services to meet the varied expectations of markets ?round the world. A company must also adapt and customize its communications to customers, consumers, suppliers, and others around the world. There exists no common formula to achieve either of these in business today.

Further complicating matters, developing a successful global e-business strategy demands cautious and thorough consideration of linguistic, cultural, economic, and legislative differences in markets around the world. In the past, only the largest companies attempted to create a truly global presence. Companies incapable of competing at this level simply confined themselves to a domestic market, or to a very limited subset of international markets. The Internet and the advent of e-business fundamentally rewrite the rules by wiping out distance, dramatically reducing the barriers of entry to the electronic marketplace, and inciting an atmosphere of hypercompetition on a global level.

Change or die. The global companies must discard their previously successful strategies or face real danger. Large and small, new and old businesses similarly must struggle with the challenges of how to best conduct business in the new, global digital world.

In the past, businesses adapted their products simply by translating the language on their packaging and their user instructions or by simply changing electrical connectors and voltage to meet local market requirements. Simple language translation or minimal, basic product modifications are not the solutions today.

Business globalization is likewise not simply including existing local cultural and business nuances into a collective global melting pot. A global e-business strategy with its message streaming along the Internet will have to simultaneously provide localized communications to both internal and external users in dozens of different markets while adhering to exacting performance requirements—all this as it processes real-time content changes. Few companies, if any, have mastered this.

The following information will provide companies of all sizes, and most of all, small and midsize companies, a practical road map or template to use as they develop their own global e-business strategy. This information should serve as a checklist of the most critical activities required to successfully deploy a global e-business strategy for any company. The level and depth to which a company will need to go depends largely on the size of the company, the resources it has available, and its vision and aspirations to become truly global.

Global E-business Strategy and Business Plan Development

Any company's globalization strategy can be tremendously enhanced with an effective e-business strategy. To develop a successful e-business globalization strategy, companies of all sizes must first: clearly articulate their overall business and e-business strategies; Second, possess a keen knowledge of their target markets (countries)', considering: geography, demographics, economic conditions, internal country politics, the political situation between home and target countries, home and target countries' legal requirements, and Internet readiness. Third, carefully select target markets (countries), groups of markets, etc. Finally, plan to establish a company and/or brand identity in target markets. Also, regardless of the degree of complexity of the company's global e-business strategy, some common traits typically emerge with most, if not all, e-business sites. Specifically, these include: (i) Visitors to multiple-language sites remain on the site almost twice as long as they do with English-only language sites, (ii) Business users are three times more likely to buy when the site is in their own local language and (iii) Customer service costs decrease when instructions on the site are in the customer's own local language.

Market Selection

A company should prioritize and rank the markets (countries) that may be targeted in its global business strategy. As with all business, developing a global e-business strategy requires that a company know its targeted customer groups very well.

If a company already conducts business in specific markets or if a market is a new high-priority target market, the firm must determine if these markets meet a set of strategic screening criteria. Criteria to be considered are as follows:

For automatic inclusion:

i) Markets already accounting for significant company revenue
ii) Markets where there already is a large e-business presence
iii) Markets with large physical presences or strategic regional importance (e.g., Brazil in South America, United Kingdom in Europe)

For automatic exclusion:

i) Markets not a significant source of current revenue
ii) Markets not a significant source of future revenue
iii) Markets whose local laws do not support the necessary intellectual property rights or copyrights
iv) Markets that are subject to trade embargoes or other internationally imposed sanctions

For markets that do not clearly fall into either of the categories of automatic inclusion or exclusion, a more detailed analysis should be conducted. A rating and ranking mechanism should be developed to prioritize these remaining markets. Any mechanism that is developed should rate and rank markets based on key economic, strategic, or business criteria. Criteria for detailed analysis should include: First, economic viability: current market size, potential market size, current market penetration, potential market penetration, current market revenue and profit, potential market revenue and profit, presence or absence of local business and/or brand alliances, and the presence or absence of direct and/or indirect competition; Second, internet preparedness: current Internet penetration, rate of current and forecasted Internet growth, projected Internet pentration, Internet usage (e.g., willingness to conduct business/purchase online), and, internet infrastructure capabilities; finally, the business capability: size of in-market business presence, experience with company/product brand localization, and the existing language translation capabilities.

Establish Localization/Regionalisation Parameters

A company must establish a set of cultural expectations regarding how a local e-business and Internet presence should perform for each market that a company selects. Based on these local expectations, parameters should then be selected for each market. Sometimes, localization parameters need not apply across all selected markets, but rather they may be applied across a common group of markets in a homogeneous region (e.g., the Middle East). In this case, a regional approach to establishing localization parameters may be more appropriate. Parameters to be considered are: company and/or product/service brand(s), information architecture, visual design, application functionality, content, and the, business processes.

Establish Globalization Parameters

Once a company has set its localization and regionalisation parameters it can establish its globalization parameters. The firm must consider relevant factors from each market. To the extent that any localization feature can be applied on a globalized level, localized or regionalized parameters may then influence and otherwise determine specific globalization parameters. Also, not all localization or regionalisation parameters may need to be addressed in the final set of globalization parameters. In some cases, it may be more cost-effective to localize or regionalize some systems without globalizing them. Parameters that should be globalized include: languages, writing systems, currencies, weights and measurements, calendars, time zones, time measurements, and postal and telephone systems.

Languages and phonetic systems. Language is one of the primary differentiators for many cultures. The importance of language clearly makes language-related functions prime targets in implementing global e-business strategy. This is no simple task, however. Languages are extremely diverse, and they change very rapidly.

There are currently 6,700 living languages in the world, but only 435 of these languages are in commercial use. Of all spoken languages, the top 15 in the world together account for 49.5 percent of all the languages spoken by the world's total population.

Writing and ideogrammatic systems. Writing systems have a major impact on the way information is presented. Direction of script varies significantly between writing systems. The direction of Latin script is from left to right, top to bottom. The direction of Japanese scripts is generally from top to bottom, right to left, although there can be a mixture of directions on a single page.

Not only does the direction of script vary between systems, but the method used to sort words differs as well. The Latin writing system sorts words and letters using a process based on a fixed sequence called alphabetical order (A to Z). The Japanese hiragana writing system arranges the syllables in the order they appear in a famous Buddhist poem. The Chinese hanzi writing system orders symbols by the number of brush strokes it takes to draw them.

Currencies. Currency is involved in most commerce, and thus is another prime target of global e-business. Many potential customers in markets around the world expect to purchase goods using their own currencies. While offering them this service is desirable, it can also expose an organization to considerable risk if not handled correctly.

Currency conversion rates fluctuate on a very short time scale because of trading in global currency markets. This fluctuation makes setting fixed prices in different markets difficult to coordinate. The Internet makes this form of arbitrage even easier.

Weights and measurement systems. Commerce often involves the exchange of fixed quantities of goods or materials that meet certain dimensional specifications. Thus, it is important to consider internationalizing weights and measures. The International System of Units (SI), more commonly referred to as the metric system, is effectively the global standard for measurement. A few markets still cling to old systems: At this time, only three markets—Myanmar, Liberia, and the United States—have not adopted the SI standard as their official system of weights and measures.

The United States is the only industrialized nation that does not mainly use the metric system in its commercial and standards activities, but acceptance is increasing in science, medicine, government, and many sectors of industry in the United States.

Calender systems. Calendars, especially in a global e-business context, are useful in determining holidays, shipment dates, or the date on which a transaction took place. Calendars, like writing systems, come in several varieties. Each calendar determines the number and names of days and months in the year, including when leap years occur.

Three calendar types and at least ten calendars are in daily use around the world. Following are the three calendar types with examples of each:

1. Solar—based on the yearly solar cycle. Examples: Gregorian, Julian, Ethiopic, Coptic, Modern Hindu
2. Lunar—based on the cycle of the moon. Example: Islamic
3. Lunisolar—that attempt to reconcile the cycles of both the sun and moon. Examples: Chinese, Hebrew, Old Hindu

These differences can lead to significant confusion when converting from one calendar to another is required. With today's information technology, the task of reconciling the different calendar systems can be made simpler.

Time zones. Specification of time zones is important for standard time measurement, and could be highly relevant in computer transactions. There are 24 international time zones, and markets set their local time according to the time zone they are in and the time zones adopted by their trading partners and neighbors.

All markets define their own local time in terms of hours ahead or behind Greenwich Mean Time (GMT), up to a maximum of 11 hours ahead or behind. The situation is complicated by the fact that many markets observe daylight saving time, usually hours ahead or behind local time. This is determined at the market level, with different markets beginning and ending daylight saving on different dates (e.g., the U.S. and Canada versus Europe). Individual markets may also vary the start and end dates of daylight saving from year to year, further complicating matters.

Time measurement Systems. For certain types of e-business systems, the measurement of accurate time is crucial. This is especially true when systems comprise multiple components distributed geographically. The management of time can become a significant hurdle. Coordinating multiple clocks and managing time changes to and from daylight saving time across multiple time zones requires considerable planning. While these problems may be new to many commercial organizations, they have been recognized and solved by scientific and military institutions.

An example illustrating the need for highly accurate time coordination is in the financial and commodities markets. Most financial and commodity market maker systems that provide auctions also require accurate time synchronization so auctions can close exactly when required and bids can be "time-stamped" with the correct time. Time stamps are also very useful in many cryptographic protocols, where time is intimately connected with the exchange of messages.

Postal systems. The Universal Postal Union (UPU), with headquarters in Bern, Switzerland, is a specialized institution of the United Nations that regulates the postal services of its member countries. The postal addressing systems outline the elements that form the basis for proper postal addressing. These elements ensure the correct wording of addresses and guarantee the quick and efficient handling of letter-post items.

Postcodes can also be used to validate text addresses. Software systems are available that can derive a postcode from a text address and a text address from a postcode. These systems are usually only available with delivery code systems. They require large supporting databases and must be updated frequently to account for new addresses and codes.

Telephone dialing systems. Telephone dialing codes are another means for geographic location; they are quite useful for communication as well. From the standpoint of globalisation, it is important to understand the relevant international standards for telecommunications, and also the degree of local variation in the way countries handle telephone numbers.

KEY ATTRIBUTES OF A SUCCESSFUL GLOBAL E-BUSINESS STRATEGY

Irrespective of any individual company-specific parameters (globalisation, localization/ regionalisation), company size, industry or markets targeted, a successful global e-business strategy should possess three key attributes: flexibility, adaptability, and controllability.

Flexibility. Localization/regionalisation parameters that may apply in one market may not apply in another. Globalization parameters that are critical to support a single major market may undermine the overall strategy and render it cost-ineffective. Typically, most companies find there is no single, correct solution, and that any global e-business strategy will have its tradeoffs. In the end, any viable globalization strategy chosen must be flexible across targeted markets.

Adaptability. Everything in the world of business and financial markets changes. International and national politics and laws change, sometimes daily. So, too, does the Internet; and changes seem to be accelerating each year. Any chosen global e-business strategy must be able to adapt to the many changes that have become part of everyday business life, especially on a global level.

Controllability. To ensure the success of any global e-business strategy, a company must exert a high degree of control to implement a stable and manageable global business organization and its resulting structures. This is especially critical when localizing business processes, for local management will likely be charged with implementing and managing market-specific e-business functions.

Cost-Benefit Analysis

Once a company has determined all the criteria with which to establish its global e-business strategies, it must then conduct a cost-benefit analysis to determine the economic viability of the chosen strategies. When analyzing costs, companies must consider both the implementation costs as well as the costs of re-engineering any business processes, ongoing systems maintenance costs, training costs/etc. Once these costs are determined, they can then be weighed against the strategic and economic benefits offered by extending the company's, global reach into targeted markets.

Strategy and Business Plan Optimization

If the cost-benefit analysis reveals anything in the global e-business strategy that may be economically viable, a company should consider either adding or removing markets from the mix, modifying some market-specific localization parameters, or adjusting some of its globalization parameters. For example, the cost of globalizing language and writing systems for the Chinese market may be too high, while localization or regionalisation is more viable.

Depending on what parameters will be adjusted, added, or removed, it will likely be necessary to review both sets of localized/ regionalized and globalized parameters. Following each series of adjustments, a new cost-benefit analysis should be conducted and the viability of the global e-business strategy reassessed.

Once optimized, the cost-benefit analysis should yield a global e-business strategy that will include: prioritized list of markets to be targeted; parameters to be localized within the targeted markets; requirements mapping of localization and /or regionalisation of selected business processes that may be necessary; parameters to be globalized within various business systems; and estimation of costs and benefits of the global e-business strategy. Table-2 lists the organisational requirement for e-business.

GLOBAL E-BUSINESS STRATEGY IMPLEMENTATION

Once a company has successfully developed and optimized its global e-business strategy, it must develop and execute an implementation plan. Key components of any such implementation plan should include the following:

i) Localization/regionalisation of business processes as required
ii) Globalization of business processes as required
iii) Globalization of appropriate global parameters as required
iv) Localize globalized parameters within selected markets
v) Localize nonglobalised parameters within selected markets

TABLE-2

Organisational Requirements for e-Business

Transparency	• Integrity and consistency of information • Clear data and procedures
Sharing culture	• Horizontal as well as vertical exchange of information • External partners have access to data-bases • No 'silos'
Process integration	• All management processes are compatible with each other to facilitate information flow
Pooled co-ordination	• Ability to have different department working together instantaneously instead of sequentially • Ability to bundle different parameters in real time • Sequential co-ordination too time-consuming
Real-time commitment	• Ability to make decisions quickly • No time for hierarchical checking
Horizontal processes	• Hierarchical communication and decision processes inefficient

Typically, a phased approach is taken regarding these implementations, with the most strategic markets being implemented first. At the same time, some implementation tasks may be undertaken concurrently with others in selected markets. The ultimate methodology selected by a company will depend on its chosen strategy and the specific challenges presented in each case.

Cultural Adaptability of Global Technology Implementation

Standardized technologies alone won't guarantee successful global e-business operations. The most successful global organizations properly manage multilingual and multicultural implementations of applications and data. Because every successful global e-business implementation must employ components of the technology that require these multilingual and multicultural services and support, companies that specialize in translation, localization, and cultural practices are thriving as part of the global e-business solution. A rudimentary search on the Internet will yield scores of such companies prepared and ready to assist any size company to achieve the desired level of multilingual and multicultural needs that any company may have.

The need to translate and localize foretells that the true challenges in implementing global e-business systems still center on culture, not in the deployment of new technology. In short, everyone can be given the same applications, but ensuring that those applications are used consistently to benefit the company is much more difficult.

By drastically reducing the importance of proximity, the new technologies change people's perceptions of community. The Internet connects people and companies across borders with exponentially growing ease, while separating them from natural and historical associations with nations. Doing business globally filters through many levels of the information technology, local practices, and corporate culture. The more sensitive corporate leadership is toward language and cultural differences, the more an organization is able to improve and add value to its global e-business initiatives. Overall company cultures, particularly in local company offices around the world deeply influenced by their individual market cultures, will need to change their mind-sets to make that shift.

Culture—the amalgam of tradition, relationships, and values—shapes business practices and processes in widely varying ways. Cultural differences often make it hard to obtain consensus and collaboration, and not what the "technology of the day" is. The divide between culture, technology, and knowledge can be enormous. To close this divide, successful global organizations of all sizes and cultures realize that a clear understanding of their own company and its home market culture as well as the culture of others is urgently needed.

Cultural Communications in Global E-business Strategy

Cultural differences can make a large impact on the interpretation of visual design. What is considered a cutting-edge design in one culture can appear rude and unprofessional in another. Common interpretations of visual design simply cannot be assumed when working internationally. By their nature, visual messages are often more ambiguous and open to interpretation than is the written word.

Colours. Colours are a part of most people's everyday worlds. We attach a great deal of significance to them, whether we realize it or not. The meanings attached, however, and even the words we use to describe them, vary between cultures. For example, Japanese do not differentiate between green and blue. In the Netherlands, blue connotes quality, and in China, red has negative connotations. Different interpretations of colour abound throughout the world.

Image. Images are also interpreted differently across cultures and locations. It is very difficult for a central organization to make appropriate choices about local imagery. Apart from the obvious case where images include text, images themselves often contain cultural assumptions. Images must be made locally appropriate; what appears as an innocuous pictogram of the thumbs-up signal (representing approval) is, in fact, an offensive gesture in some cultures. A car shown driving down the right side of the road would contradict experience in several markets, thus disrapting the intent of a carefully built design.

Colours, images, and text combine to create a graphical interface, and changes to any one of these elements can impact the entire visual design. Text translation can cause significant expansion in the length of text that, in turn, may create a negative impact on a visual design. Substantial modification of text can disrupt the flow of information and qualitatively change the look and feel of an interface. Careful localization of text helps preserve the original intent and spirit of a visual design.

Cultural assumptions affect function in a way similar to information architecture and visual design. As a result, the function of a system may have to be localized to meet cultural requirements. For instance, the concept of the shopping cart on a commercial Web site does not translate for all cultures. The supermarket as a standard for a commercial experience is justified only when most customers experience supermarkets as a regular part of their daily life. Only then will they know what to expect when confronted with the Internet shopping cart.

If an application offers a negative or confusing experience to a user with a different set of cultural expectations, it is no longer useful and thus fails in its intent. Before creating any content (words, images, audio, or video), a company with an Internet presence must first develop a content strategy that articulates the voice and tone of its brand. This strategy ensures that the content is consistent and compelling, and that it properly communicates the message of the brand.

As is the case with information architecture and visual design, the local focus of content must account for subtle and not-so-subtle cultural variations. For example, localizing the audio portions of a Web site requires not only translating the audio into the appropriate language, but accounting for dialect and pronunciation differences. The localization of text requires a similar attention-to idiomatic expressions, differences in usage, and culturally specific grammatical conventions.

Language. Language translation is an art, not a science. Literal translation is almost never sufficient. At best, it can produce stilted approximations of the original and, at worst, it can erode a brand's credibility by being unintentionally amusing or even insulting to the target audience and others.

Ensuring text is carefully reviewed by a native speaker is essential even when the text is not ostensibly being translated into another language. In Spain the verb *to take* is perfectly acceptable, while in Mexico it is considered crude. At first glance, a manufacturer may believe that the American version of a product catalog can be reused in all English-speaking markets. This may be the case; the catalog would probably still be understandable. If local language usage is not taken into account, however, it might also cause serious brand erosion. In effect, this means that language and market are inseparable. For example, American, British, Australian, Canadian, and South African English should be treated as separate languages. Each market has its own language variation that must be handled individually.

Another factor to consider when localizing text is that translation can have a significant, even damaging, effect on visual design and information architecture. When text is translated, the amount of space required to hold that contiguous block of text can change dramatically. On the average, English increases by 30 percent when it is translated to other European languages, and can increase by 400 percent in extreme cases.

Finally, the organisational attributes may sometimes conflict with local cultures. Table-3 contrasts Internet cultural requirements with typical Asian corporate culture. The challenge for the global firm is to overcome these culture differences among their employees, suppliers, customers and partners to make Web transactions effective.

TABLE-3

Internet Managerial Culture Versus Managerial Culture

Transparency	• Partial, and multiple information • Lack of clear procedures
Sharing culture	• Vertical information sharing • Clannic retention
Process integration	• 'Siloed' processes
Pooled co-ordination	• Top-down processes, otherwise sequential processes
Real-time commitment	• Several checks, vertically organised
Horizontal processes	• Hierarchical

QUESTIONS

1. What is global e-business? What are the effects of the internet on globalisation?
2. Discuss the key components of global e-business strategy.
3. Describe the key features of a successful global e-business strategy.
4. How would you develop a global e-business strategy.
5. Explain the organisational requirements for implementing global e-business strategy.
6. Distinguish between internet managerial culture and managerial culture.

REFERENCES

Booz Alien & Hamilton, *Competing in the Digital Age: How the Internet Will Transfer Global Business.* New York: EIU, 1999.

Cairncross, Frances, *The Death of Distance: How the Communications Revolution Will Change Our Lives.* London: Orion Business Books, 1998.

De Meyer, Arnoud, Soumitra Dutta and Sandeep Srivastana, *The Bright Stuff: How Innovative People and Technology Can Make the Old Economy New.* London: Financial Times/Prentice-Hall, 2002.

Evans, Philip and Thomas Wurster, *Blown to Bits.* Boston, MA: Harvard Business School Press, 2000.

Hartman, Amir and John Sifonis, *New Ready: Strategies for Success in the Net Economy.* New York: McGraw-Hill, 2000.

Liatuad, Bernard and Mark Hammond, *e-Business Intelligence: Turning Information into Knowledge into Profit.* New York: McGraw-Hall, 2000.

Porter, Michael, 'Strategy and the Internet', *Harvard Business Review,* March-April 2001, pp. 63-78.

Sanders, Matthew, 'Global e-Commerce Approaches Hypergrowth', *The Forrester Brief,* 18 April 2000a. Forrester Research, Inc., 400 Technology Square, Cambridge, MA 02239.

Sanders, Matthew, 'Sizing Global Online Exports', *The Forrester Report,* November 2000b. Forrester Research, Inc., 400 Technology square, Cambridge, MA 02239.

Sharrard, Jermey, 'Global Online Trade Will Climb to 18 per cent of Sales', *The Forrester Brief,* 21 December 2001. Forrester Research, Inc., 400 Technology Square, Cambridge.

Subramanian, Rangan and Adner, Ron, 'Profit and the Internet: Seven Misconceptions', MIT *Shan Management Review,* Summer 2001, pp. 44-53.

Truong, David, 'E-Business Networks', *The Forrester Report,* April 2000a. Forrester Research, Inc., 400 Technology Square, Cambridge, MA 02239.

Truong, David, 'Brokered Partner Integration', *The Forrester Report,* April 2000b. Forrester Research, Inc., 400 Technology Square, Cambridge, MA 02239.

Yip, George S., 'Global Strategy in the Internet Era', *Business Strategy Review,* 11(4), 2000, pp. 1-14.

Unit IV

17

DESIGNING GLOBAL ORGANISATIONAL STRUCTURE AND CONTROL

INTRODUCTION

Globalisation has arrived in the world, but not in most of the world's organisations. To explore this, we need to identify the different trends that are influencing globalisation and examine the extent to which these are affecting the way in which organisations operate. It is also important to understand the linkages between global industries and markets as the nature of a global and transnational strategy will be influenced by industry and market characteristics. The chapter explores the determinants of organisational structure, the alternative organisational structures available to international organisations, introduces recent alternative configurations, and examines the complex interrelationships between global strategy and the organisation and control issues associated with its implementation.

CAUSE OF GLOBALISATION

The causes of globalistion are, like their effects, complex. Although globalisation is itself regarded as a relatively recent phenomenon, its roots can be traced back to many of earliest civilisations. Egyptians, Phoenicians, Greeks and Romans were all heavily involved in trade across national boundaries. Yet the roots of globalisation really lie in the eighteenth, nineteenth and twentieth centuries. It is major technological, economic, social and political forces, some recent and others more distant, which have caused businesses to become internationalised and then globalised. All of these forces are closely linked to each other and are largely interdependent (Figure-1).

Globalisation of Industries

The globalisation of industries is linked, but different in nature, to the globalisation of markets. Whereas market globalisation is centred on customer needs, industry globalisation centres on the ability of businesses to configure and co-ordinate their productive or value-adding activities globally and across national boundaries. A business can choose to disperse all its activities around the world or to disperse some activities and concentrate others in locations which possess specific advantages. Globalised

FIGURE-1

FORCES LEADING TO GLOBALISATION

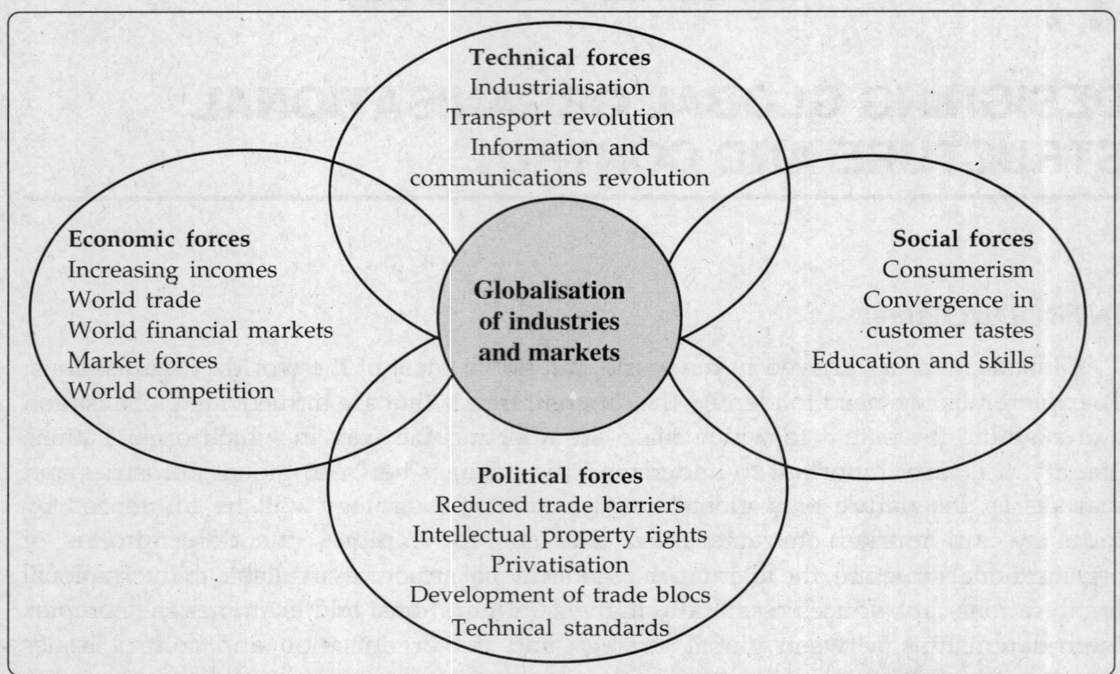

industries are characterised by worldwide competition, opportunities for economies of scale and scope, rapid technological change, common technical standards and favourable trading conditions. A global industry is capable of serving fragmented markets by producing products or services which are adapted to meet local requirements. In most cases, however, global industries serve markets which are themselves increasingly global.

Globalisation of Markets

Markets are defined by customers and their needs. The extent to which a market is global will depend upon the extent to which customer needs for a product or service are similar throughout the world. It may well be true that customer needs are becoming increasingly homogeneous with respect to certain products and services. Despite this trend, the market is far from global and, even as it becomes more global, there is unlikely to be the standardisation of products. In fact, customers are likely to demand a variety of products previously associated with a variety of countries.

This demand for variety is a consequence of the fact that globalisation has made customer needs more informed and sophisticated. They demand more varied and complex products and services, rather than the standardised offerings which many predicted would become the norm. It was also predicted that global customers would be more price conscious. This may be the case but they are often more conscious of quality, technical features and design than price. In serving seemingly global markets, the business must be alert to the similarities in customer needs but also to the differences and to the increasing complexity of their requirements.

Technological Forces

Industrial Development

The technological origins of globalisation lie in the industrial revolution, beginning in the late eighteenth century and continuing into the nineteenth and twentieth centuries.

Industrialisation marked the beginning of the factory system and mass production of goods. It marked the beginning of 'a new pattern of geographical specialisation'. The continued development of mass production techniques underlies the globalisation of industries and the concentration of activities in certain locations but this has also been dependent upon other global forces. Mass production also contributed to the development of mass markets and, ultimately, to global markets. As mass production forced prices down, the global attractiveness of certain products increased.

Improved Transportation

Development in transportation is the second technological force without which globalisation could not have taken place. The development of railway networks throughout the world, and the impact of steam and diesel power on shipping provided the means for moving materials and finished goods around the world. This opened national markets to international products on a previously unknown scale, at the same time as reinforcing the benefits of concentrated manufacturing. Air travel has played a major role in the globalisation of businesses both by allowing managers to travel quickly anywhere in the world and by allowing consumers to travel widely, giving them experience of products and services which were previously denied to them.

Improved Information Management

The most recent technological development, which arguably completes the jigsaw of globalisation, is that of what has been called the information 'revolution'. Developments in information and communications technology have had major impacts directly on the advance of globalisation itself and on its underlying forces. Global communications, like the telephone, the fax, the internet and electronic mail, have made it possible for businesses to co-ordinate their activities throughout the world. Global communications, like satellite television, have also played a major role in creating global customer needs, increasing awareness of products and brands across the globe.

As well as contributing directly to globalisation of industries and markets, all three groups of technological developments have played a major role in bringing about the economic, political and social changes which have also contributed to globalisation.

Social Forces

Rising levels of income, coupled to the boom in consumer credit, have contributed to worldwide consumerism. Demand for consumer goods and services has increased beyond recognition in post-war years. This has been most evident in the case of motor vehicles, consumer electronics products like televisions, hi-fis, video recorders, telephones and home computers, and white goods like washing machines and refrigerators.

Such products are closely associated with increasing affluence and also with converging consumer tastes and wants. Technological developments have played a major role in converging consumer tastes. Travel, satellite television and global advertising have all assisted in developing global markets. Improvements in education and training have also contributed to technological progress and to rising levels of productivity throughout the world which have helped to give rise to the globalisation of production.

Political and Legal Forces

Increasing world trade and globalisation have also resulted from reducing barriers to international trade. Under the provisions of the World Trade Organisation (WTO) and its predecessor, GATT (the General Agreement on Tariffs and Trade), barriers to trade have fallen substantially in post-war years, although progress has been uneven. Trading blocs (sometimes called *customs unions)*, like the European Union and the North American Free Trade Area, have also played a major role in fostering the inter-country trade which is the forerunner of global business.

The increasing legal recognition of intellectual property rights in most countries of the world has played a major part in protecting global products and brands. There have been similar moves to secure acceptance of similar technical standards throughout the world which are particularly important to the development of global consumer electronics products.

Many governments have taken steps to reduce their levels of intervention in economic matters. Privatisation has become commonplace alongside reductions in taxation and government spending. In Eastern Europe the collapse of communism has opened up markets which were previously closed to international trade. This increasing prevalence of market forces over government regulation has helped to reduce the political barriers to globalisation.

Economic Forces

Competition in many industries and markets has become increasingly global as the role of governments diminishes and free market forces are allowed to play a more significant role. In addition, the increasing volume of world trade has gone hand in hand with rising income levels in the major First World economies. Both are interdependent and are also closely associated with technological and political developments. Increasing levels of income have created the demand for global products and services. Finally, the finance for world trade has been made available through the development of world financial markets between which transactions charges have been made insignificant by technological developments.

ESSENTIALS OF ORGANISATIONAL STRUCTURE: KEY VARIABLES

Organisational structure concerns the shape adopted by the business in the pursuit of its strategic objectives. For international businesses, the importance of structure is brought into focus because of the distances between the various parts and the need to co-ordinate activities between them. Structures are usually distinguished according to two variables: i) the height and width of the structure; ii) the extent to which hierarchical management is observed.

'Height' and 'Width' of Structures

'Height' refers to the number of layers that exist within a structure. Larger organisations are higher than smaller ones. The guide to how high an organisational structure should be depends upon the complexity of the tasks that a proposed strategy entails. A small, single-site manufacturer will typically be involved in competing in one industry, sometimes with a single product type. This scenario is much less complex than a transnational chemical company that competes in many national markets, in several product types and with a high dependence on research and legal regulations.

Height facilitates the engagement of specialist managers in the middle of an organisation who can oversee and direct the many activities that some large organisations are involved in. Not all organisations have this requirement and it would be more appropriate for such organisations to have a flatter structure. Companies with a high requirement for specialist professional staff often have several layers of management (thus increasing their height) and accordingly, civil engineering consultancies, accountancy firms, chemical and specialist engineering companies often have this feature.

The 'width' of organisational structures refers to the extent to which the organisation is centralised or decentralised. A decentralised organisational structure is one in which the centre elects to devolve some degree of decision-making power to other parts of the organisation. A centralised organisation is one in which little or no power is devolved from the centre. In practice, a continuum exists between the two extremes along which the varying extents of decentralisation can be visualised (see Figure-2). Transnational businesses tend towards the right-hand side of the continuum.

FIGURE-2

THE CENTRALISATION-DECENTRALISATION CONTINUUM

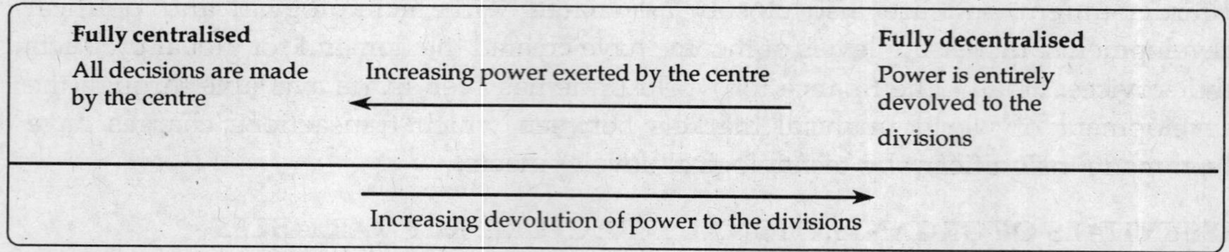

As with the height of structures, there is a trade-off between the costs and benefits of width. The advantages of centralisation are mainly concerned with the ability of the centre to maintain tighter direct control over the activities of the organisation. This is usually more appropriate when the organisation is smaller and engages in few product or market segments. Some degree of decentralisation is advantageous when the organisation operates in a number of markets and localised specialised knowledge is an important determinant of overall success.

Hierarchical Configuration of Structures

It would be wrong to assume that all organisations observe a strict form of structural hierarchy. Strict hierarchy is not always an appropriate form of organisation, especially when it cannot be automatically assumed that seniority guarantees superior management skill.

In some contexts, formal hierarchy is entirely appropriate in implementing strategy. In others, however, allowing employees to act with some degree of independence can in fact enable the organisation to be more effective in its various spheres of activity. The use of matrix structures, for example, can result in the organisation being able to carry out many more tasks that a formal hierarchical structure. Many companies go 'half way' in this regard by seconding employees into special task forces or cross-functional teams that are not part of the hierarchical structure, and which act semi-independently in pursuit of their brief.

BASIC APPROACHES TO THE FORMATION ORGANISATIONAL STRUCTURE

There are two basic approaches to the formation of organisational structure, the *contingency approach* and the *configuration approach*. According to the contingency approach, the structure of an organisation will depend upon factors like the nature of its 'business and its strategy, its size, the geographical span of its activities, its age and history and the nature of its environment. Rather than adopting a contingency approach, it is sometimes better to base structure on a configuration approach. Factors like spans of control, the need for formalisation, centralisation or decentralisation, and planning systems should be logically configured into internally consistent groupings. It is argued that excellent' organisational performance depends upon strategy, systems, culture (shared values), skills, leadership, staff and structure. As these organisational features are interdependent, each was thought to play an important part in determining the others so that structure will be affected by strategy, systems, culture etc. Equally, structure will help to shape strategy, culture and systems. It is therefore evident that there are many complex factors shaping the structure of organisations.

Contingency Approach

Contingency theory (as it relates to organisational structure) suggests that the most important determinants of organisational structure will include a number of factors. The key point with contingency theory is that the structure adopted (which may be a domestic or internationalised business) will depend upon several determining factors:

The Nature of the Business

Businesses whose value-adding activities are largely repetitive, and which may be centred on a production line, are likely to adopt hierarchical structures with centralised decision making. Hierarchical structures are better suited to standardisation of procedures. Organisations whose activities are diverse, creative or innovative are more likely to be based upon flatter structures which encourage horizontal communication and devolve decision making powers.

The Environment of the Organisation

The more dynamic, turbulent and complex the environment, the more adaptable the organisation will usually need to be. In these circumstances, decision making is likely to be decentralised so as to increase responsiveness. On the other hand, it is argued that organisations will tend to centralise decision making under conditions of extreme environmental hostility. In the international environment, a market which is globally homogeneous will permit greater centralisation of authority while diversity of market conditions will increase the need for local responsiveness and will require decentralised decision making.

The Global Strategy of the Business

When a business has a globally standardised strategy its structure will tend to concentrate power at the centre as this facilitates global co-ordination and integration of activities. A strategy which is centred upon local responsiveness will require devolution of power to local managers. A transnational strategy, combining global co-ordination with local responsiveness, will require a complex structure allowing a degree of global control to be combined with the ability to respond locally. Developments in information and communications technology have made possible new organisational structures designed to achieve these dual, but somewhat conflicting, objectives.

The Age and History of the Organisation

The older organisations and businesses in mature industries tended to have more formalised structures. Few structures are designed 'from scratch' and consequently, most structures evolve alongside the business itself. Accordingly, a small, new organisation will have little need for a formal or complex structure but as an organisation grows, the need for formalisation and the observance of hierarchy increases.

The Size of Business and Limitations of Span of Control

Larger organisations have more formalised and complex structures with greater specialisation of tasks and clearly defined methods of communication. Tasks will be clustered into related groupings and the relationships between these groupings will be well established. The size of any cluster of activities will be dictated by the limitations of a manager's effective span of control (i.e. the number of subordinates he or she can directly control). Activities are often typically grouped by functional area so that marketing-and sales-related activities will be grouped together, and activities like recruitment, training and payroll are often grouped under the banner of human resources management.

The Level of Technology in the Organisation

Information and communications technology (ICT) has widened the potential span of control of an individual manager, making possible flatter organisational structures. Similarly, ICT makes it possible to centrally co-ordinate activities while simultaneously allowing decentralisation of decision making assisting local responsiveness. Before the advent of ICT, most international businesses operated on a multinational basis — allowing considerable autonomy to national subsidiaries because it was almost impossible to co-ordinate activities across boundaries with such constraints upon effective communication.

The Geographical Span of Activities

The greater the geographical span of an organisation's activities, the greater the need for formalisation and complexity of structure. Again, ICT has increased the ability of organisations to increase the geographical span of their activities. Developments in telecommunications, like satellite and cable technology, have been critical in allowing businesses to integrate and manage their activities on a worldwide basis.

The Culture of the Organisation

The values, attitudes and beliefs of the members of the organisation will play an important part in moulding organisational structure. Most successful organisations have a clear statement of their mission and purpose. This statement must be thoroughly understood throughout the organisation, and it must be credible. It makes changing the culture of an organisation a less difficult task. Direct doctrine is frequently used to disseminate the message of an organisation's purpose and mission. If managers stress this doctrine, a company will be full of believers and ringleaders who can help form the culture of the organisation. The target of integration is the members. Therefore, it is important for a global company to have a clear statement of its mission and goals, so that the employees will be on the same track as the company. New members who fail to socialise and acculturate tend to be rejected by group members. Therefore, it is important to screen new members in an effort to ensure that their values and beliefs will be compatible with those that exist in the group. Thus a creative organisation like a software house or an advertising agency will often have a flexible structure (less observance of hierarchy) whereas a production-based manufacturing company is likely to have much more precisely defined and formalised groupings of activities with a much firmer observance of hierarchy. Organisational culture also often has its origins in the national culture of the country of origin of the business. The organisational culture of many Japanese businesses, for example, is often strongly influenced by values, attitudes and beliefs like loyalty and obedience which are prominent features of traditional Japanese society.

Leadership and Leadership Style

Larger organisations with strong leadership will tend to adopt structures which concentrate power at the centre of the organisation. Smaller organisations have structures which spread from the leader at the centre. There will also be a close relationship between leadership style and organisational culture.

Configuration Approach to Organisational Design

The configuration of an organisation must take account of the following design parameters:

i) *job specialisation* — to logically divide up the tasks of the organisation;
ii) *behaviour formalisation* - standardisation of work processes;
iii) *training* — instructional programmes to provide employees with the skills and knowledge to do their jobs;
iv) *indoctrination* — to inculcate organisational norms in workers;
v) *unit grouping* — according to (i) business function (e.g. marketing, finance, production etc.) and (ii) market served. These may conflict with each other as grouping by business function centres on the efficiency of the processes of the organisation while grouping by market increases organisational flexibility but encourages duplication (so, in turn, reducing efficiency);
vi) *unit size* — the number of positions contained in a single unit of the business;
vii) *planning and control systems* — used to plan and control the activities of the organisation;

viii) *liaison and integrating devices* — devices like task forces and committees can integrate the units of the business. The logical conclusion of such devices is a matrix structure;

ix) *the need for centralisation or decentralisation* — the extent to which it is necessary or desirable to diffuse decision making power.

In addition, it is important to consider both horizontal and vertical communication requirements and systems within the organisation. In an international business unit grouping, planning and control systems, integrating devices, the need for centralisation or decentralisation and indoctrination are particularly important. The way in which units are grouped is one of the most significant decisions to be made in the design of international organisations. It is not simply a decision between grouping by functional area or by market, but rather how to integrate the two. The structures of global organisations must also take account of the need to co-ordinate and integrate geographically dispersed activities, at the same time as making possible local responsiveness where and when it is required. The matrix and the transnational are alternative forms of organisation which attempt to resolve these conflicting requirements.

There is no ideal organisational structure. There are several commonly found types of structure which incorporate the parameters above and which reflect the range of internal and external factors influencing the evolution of organisation structure.

TYPES OF GLOBAL ORGANISATIONAL STRUCTURE

A well-developed international decision-making system is a continuing source of international strategic management. The quality of the decisions that management makes will influence the successes of strategic management. The traditional measurement is not the right measurement; if it were, there would be no need for decisions. The companies must take their products abroad. They must recognise that global considerations have to be a part of their future plans. They must create new markets and new products if they want to be competitive in the international market. This can be done through joint ventures, mergers, and acquisitions. Companies have to learn to think globally without sacrificing local markets.

Conventional formal organisational structures (e.g., the international division; organisations segmented by function, product, market, or geography; or matrix structure) inherently lack the information processing capacity and responsiveness that are required to be successful in a complex business environment. Successful companies purposely developed their informal organisation to enhance their information processing capacity and responsiveness. Of the traditionally defined formal organisational structures, the matrix structure provides a well-defined basis for decisions on a broad range of influences. Table-1 provides a range of alternative organisational structures. Each structure has its own inherent strengths and weaknesses.

International Structures

Export Departments

The establishment of a separate export department to control and co-ordinate foreign sales is most frequently found in companies in the early stages of internationalisation where foreign production is minimal and foreign markets are supplied mainly through domestic production and exports. The creation of a separate export department allows a greater degree of control and co-ordination of the export drive by concentrating knowledge of foreign markets in a single department and by ensuring that foreign sales are included in the planning process.

TABLE 1

Types of Transnational Organisational Structure

International structures	*Characteristics*
Export department	Responsibility for foreign sales transferred from domestic product divisions to a separate export department reporting directly to the Group CEO
Mother—daughter structure	Parent company acts as holding company for largely autonomous foreign subsidiaries. Subsidiary management report directly to CEO, but on an informal and personal basis. Subsidiaries are granted substantial operating freedom subject to satisfactory performance evaluation
International divisional structure	Responsibility for all foreign operations transferred to a separate international division based at the corporate centre. Foreign subsidiaries report directly to the international centre
Global structures	
Functional	Responsibility for foreign operations allocated to functional line managers at the centre. Foreign subsidiaries report directly to functional executives at the centre (production; marketing; human resources; finance etc.)
Product	Responsibility for foreign operations allocated to product divisions based at the centre. Foreign subsidiaries report directly to product divisions
Geographic/regional	Responsibility for foreign operations allocated to area executives. Foreign subsidiaries report directly to geographic/ regional division based at the centre or abroad
Matrix	Responsibility for foreign operations divided between product and geographic divisions. Foreign subsidiaries report directly to both product and geographic centres

Export departments, however, suffer from two main weaknesses. *First*, conflicts of interest may arise between domestically-orientated product divisions and the export department regarding the relative importance of foreign as opposed to domestic sales. The export department will be dependent on domestic product divisions for both products and technology. Since the latter are mainly concerned with domestic sales, less attention may be devoted to enhancing foreign markets. *Second,* export departments are ill-suited to further foreign market expansion through licensing, subcontracting and FDI because of the lack of expertise in managing foreign operations as opposed to foreign sales. Largely because of the second of these disadvantages, most export departments are relatively short-lived. Continued foreign market expansion through FDI has led most international businesses to replace their export departments with international divisions.

Mother-Daughter Structures

This type of structure is particularly suited to two types of international enterprise. *First,* new foreign investors, where foreign operations are not of crucial importance to the parent company. *Second,* businesses with extensive foreign direct investments, but limited central resources, as with some European businesses. The main advantage of the mother-daughter structure is that it encourages subsidiary innovation and motivation by substituting subsidiary autonomy for centralised control. Its main disadvantage, on the other hand, is the lack of global planning and co-ordination of activity.

International Divisional Structures

The international division provides a focal point for the growing foreign involvement of the company (through FDI) by concentrating international knowledge and expertise in a single division. This allows greater control and co-ordination of foreign operations as well as ensuring that the interests of foreign subsidiaries are taken into account in the corporate planning process. On the negative side, however, the same conflict of interest evident between domestic product divisions and export departments will also exist in the relationship between the former and the international division. International divisions are also usually short-lived in most international companies. Indeed, the very success of the international division in stimulating FDI may sow the seeds of its own destruction. The continued foreign expansion of the company through FDI will result in the need for closer control and planning of foreign activities by the parent company. This has led most international organisations to replace their international divisions with global structures aimed at providing a greater degree of co-ordination and integration of their worldwide activities. Such global structures may be organised on functional, product or geographical lines of responsibilities.

An international work group is an informal group that sets its own goals based on the cultural values or beliefs of its members. The group is familiar with and has studied the value of the host country culture in the context of production-oriented tasks. This because it is a unit of organisation for any but the simplest of tasks.

These groups form naturally when people work together, and there is no way to prevent them short of prohibiting the same people from working together on a day-today basis in the same place at the same time. Therefore, managers have little choice but to accept these groups and manage them to work to their benefit.

These groups tasks of management have three main functions: (1) to influence the behavior of the group so as to be consistent with the goals of the organisation, (2) to influence the formation and composition of groups, and (3) to co-ordinate interaction and interdependencies in the group. The best way to control group membership is through a screening process for all new members of the organisation. It is, therefore, important to find people who will commit to the goals and mission and be part of organisational team.

Global Structures

Functionally-based Structures

The global functional organisation allows tight control over specific functions worldwide, which may be of particular importance to businesses whose competitive strengths lie in superior technology, marketing or personnel practices. Such advantages, however, are often outweighed by the disadvantages of this type of structure. *First*, co-ordination of functions is difficult, leading to the potential separation of, for example, production and marketing. *Second*, subsidiaries will be reporting to several different divisions at the corporate centre, resulting in the duplication of effort and a possible breakdown of communications. *Finally*, the structure is unsuitable for multi-product or geographically dispersed organisations. As a consequence of such disadvantages, most international companies have incorporated functional responsibilities within global divisions based on product or geographical lines.

Product-based Structures

Under the global product organisational structure, product divisions at the corporate centre are given worldwide responsibilities for their own products and services, including both functional and geographical responsibilities. The global product structure is particularly suited for global businesses with diverse product lines, when products go to a variety of end-users, and when a high degree of technology capability is required. Organisation by product may also permit significant economies of scale to be achieved through the co-ordination and integration of production in different countries. It also allows the business to respond quickly to the actions of competitors. The principal weaknesses of global product divisions relate to the lack of emphasis placed on international or geographical planning. Global product divisions may be staffed by executives with particular product expertise but with limited knowledge of international/geographic markets. Thus, the emphasis of the division may be on the domestic market to the detriment of foreign markets. Similarly, the lack of international knowledge may create difficulties in assessing changes in environmental and political conditions in overseas markets, leading to lost opportunities for expansion. Finally, co-ordination and integration of the subsidiary companies in a particular geographical area is difficult to achieve under global product divisions.

Geographicl Regionally-based Structures

The problems associated with the lack of regional co-ordination can be overcome by adopting global regional/geographic structures. Under this structure, subsidiary companies (regardless of product line) report directly to corporate executives responsible for a particular geographical area. Each area division has both product line and functional responsibilities for all operations within its area. Such area divisions may be based at the centre. More commonly, however, separate regional headquarters will be established in the relevant areas.

Various reasons for the establishment of such offices identified are listed below:

- i. *pooling of resources*—the provision of specialist staff support to operating divisions;
- ii. *product rationalisation*—it management of product integration on a European basis;
- iii. *size of reporting structures*—to reduce the number of subsidiaries reporting directly to the patent company;
- iv. *day-to-day control*—to exert greater operating control over subsidiaries than is possible from a distant parent company;
- v. *management development*—the regional headquarters is used to develop a cadre of highly trained managers with global orientations;
- vi. *unification of external relations*—the consolidation of public relations efforts.

The global regional/geographic structure is particularly suited for international companies with narrow product lines but with geographically dispersed operations. The structure allows co-ordination and integration of activities within particular regions, as well as allowing greater responsiveness to local or regional market conditions. The concentration of knowledge of particular regions within a separate division may allow scope for the further development of the organisation's operations in that area. Many global businesses have established separate regional head offices for Europe since the development of the Single Market. The weaknesses of the global regional/geographic structure relate to the lack of integration of product lines and the possible duplication of functional and product specialists at each regional headquarters.

The Matrix Structure

The matrix structure in a domestic company is a relationship between function and project, or projects when the employee has a dual responsibility. The matrix structure is often suggested for firms operating under a complex environment. The design of multinational corporations is found to resemble some of the characteristics of the matrix structure. The majority of the focus or dual focus and information is found in the informal structure of the organisation. Liaison structures and other mechanisms are typically employed in these organisations. These mechanisms can be identified as: i) Hiring managers with a strategic perspective; ii) Developing informal channels of communication; iii) Using committees and task forces staffed with people from different areas; iv) Improved articulation of corporate objectives; v) A reward system that enforces the desired adaptation behaviors; and vi) Role models among corporate executives who emphasise cooperation These mechanisms are examples of how an emphasis on responsiveness and information processing can be achieved in the informal structure of an organisation. Successful firms in a highly complex environment optimise their performance by consciously and purposely using both the formal and informal structures, which are characterised by the following: i) a hierarchical structure based on legitimate power; ii) subunits are independent in some dimensions but are linked to the central organisation; iii) actions among the various units of the organisation are co-ordinated through adaptation

DEVELOPMENT OF GLOBAL AND TRANSNATIONAL STRUCTURES

In order to preserve the strengths of each of these international structures and to overcome their disadvantages, many global businesses adopted global matrix structures which attempted to co-ordinate and integrate worldwide functional, product and area responsibilities. Under this structure, responsibility for foreign operations is divided between global product and regional divisions with subsidiary managers reporting to two bosses (thus confusing the hierarchy of the organisation). Co-ordination and integration of product and area responsibilities is achieved through frequent interchanges between the product and regional divisions and through the CEO. The drawbacks of the global matrix structure are that it can be difficult to manage because of conflicts of interest between product and regional groupings. Decision-making procedures are also complex because decision-making is a group process.

The link between corporate strategy and corporate structure is firmly established if a company's product/market strategy changes organisational structure too to support implementation of the new strategy. These patterns of development may be noted in the structures of many multinational businesses. When only a limited range of products are sold abroad, and when foreign sales are only a small proportion of sales, many companies initially manage their overseas activities through an international division. Organisations which then broaden the range of products offered abroad tend to establish a worldwide product division. Those which expand sales abroad without broadening product range will often do so by establishing an area division structure. When sales abroad reach a high percentage of total sales and a broad range of products are offered for sale then businesses often opt for a matrix structure. Figure-3 shows that in international structure stages, development through path 1 or path 2 will culminate in the development of a global matrix structure. However, the extent to which global

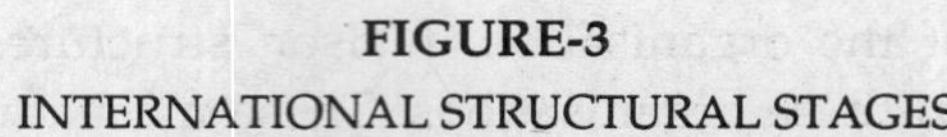

FIGURE-3

INTERNATIONAL STRUCTURAL STAGES

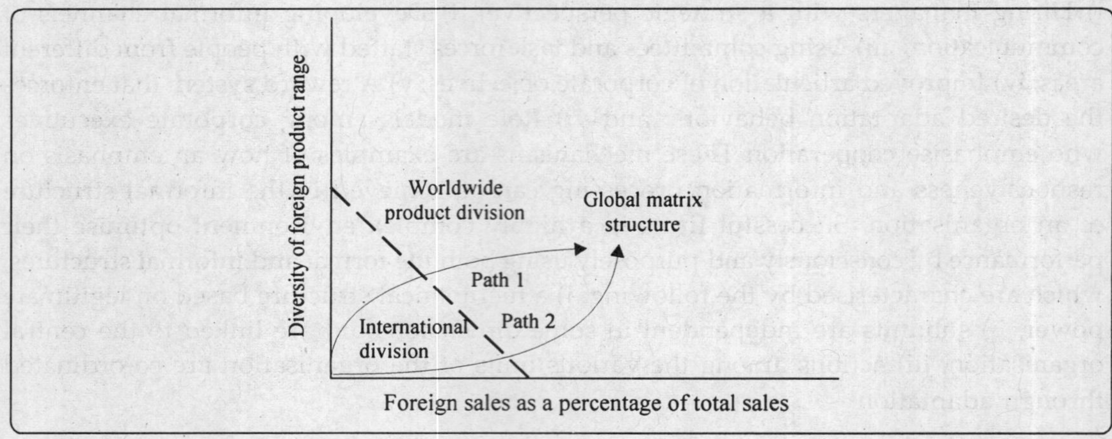

matrix structures provide a solution to the complex organisation and control problems of transnationals has been the subject of extensive debate.

At some point in the internationalisation process, the introduction of global structures becomes necessary to achieve co-ordination and integration of geographically dispersed activities. One possible approach to this situation is the global matrix structure which is one means of achieving global co-ordination and local responsiveness.

One of the key benefits of a matrix structure is that co-ordination and integration of activity on a global scale can be achieved through global product divisions. Local responsiveness can be achieved through global regional or geographic structures. Thus, global matrix structures, which combine both product and geographic divisions, can achieve both global co-ordination and national responsiveness simultaneously. The main advantage of matrix compared to strict hierarchical structures is that they are able to accommodate managers with worldwide (product) responsibilities for particular businesses and country managers responsible for specific area markets. However, many companies which had previously adopted matrix structures have now abandoned them. This is because of the problems inherent in managing through such structures which include: overlapping responsibilities; reporting duplication with managers reporting to two or more bosses, often with conflicting objectives; survival of the fittest with one decision-making centre emerging as dominant; excessive time spent on reaching compromise decisions; duplication of information, communications and activities; and, increased administrative costs.

The key organisational task, therefore, is not to design ever more elegant and complex structures but to capture individual capabilities and motivate the entire organisation to respond co-operatively to a complicated and dynamic environment. To achieve this, the traditional organisational sequence which emphasises organisational anatomy (formal structure), physiology (communications and decision processes), and psychology (corporate beliefs and norms that shape managers' perceptions and actions) should be reversed. Rather than searching for the 'dear' organisational anatomy (structure), the first task is to alter organisational psychology; then to enrich communications and decision processes through improvements in organisational physiology. Only then these changes should be consolidated and confirmed by realigning organisational anatomy through changing the formal structure. The companies which respond most successfully to the complexities of the global business environment are those which emphasise the need to change organisational psychology in the broad corporate beliefs and norms that shape managers' perceptions and actions. These changes can be reinforced by changing organisational physiology by enriching and clarifying communications and decision processes. Only then should these be consolidated by realigning organisational anatomy, i.e. the formal structure (see Figure-4).

Industries have changed from being international, multinational or global to being 'transnational'. In such an environment, organisations themselves must become transnational. Successful international corporations must 'optimise efficiency, responsiveness and learning simultaneously in their worldwide operations'. The difficulty is achieving 'a three way balance of organisational perspectives and capabilities among product, function and (geographical) area'.

The issue is not whether to be globally integrated *or* locally responsive but how to be *both* simultaneously. Authoritative global corporate management is required to integrate activities and ensure global efficiencies are obtained. Corporate managers must determine the overarching strategy of the organisation, stress the interdependence of its functional and geographical parts, and co-ordinate its activities. The development and transfer of core competences requires capable functional management. Functional managers must facilitate learning and innovation within each domain of the business. Strong geographical management is required to ensure local responsiveness to national and regional markets. Local managers, in turn, must develop locally-determined competences which must then contribute to company-wide competences. Only a multidimensional organisation can provide these three strands of management simultaneously.

Accordingly, the transnational is multidimensional by ensuring that tasks are systematically *differentiated* by treating different businesses, functions and areas differently; and by allowing them to be organised differently: relationships between the different parts of the business are based on *interdependence* rather than independence; *co-ordination and co-option* of differentiated and interdependent organisational units are achieved through shared vision and integrative mechanisms.

Creating a transnational is more concerned with creating a organisational culture based on a global vision, emphasising differentiation and co-ordination, rather than a

FIGURE-4

ORGANIZATIONAL CONFIGURATION

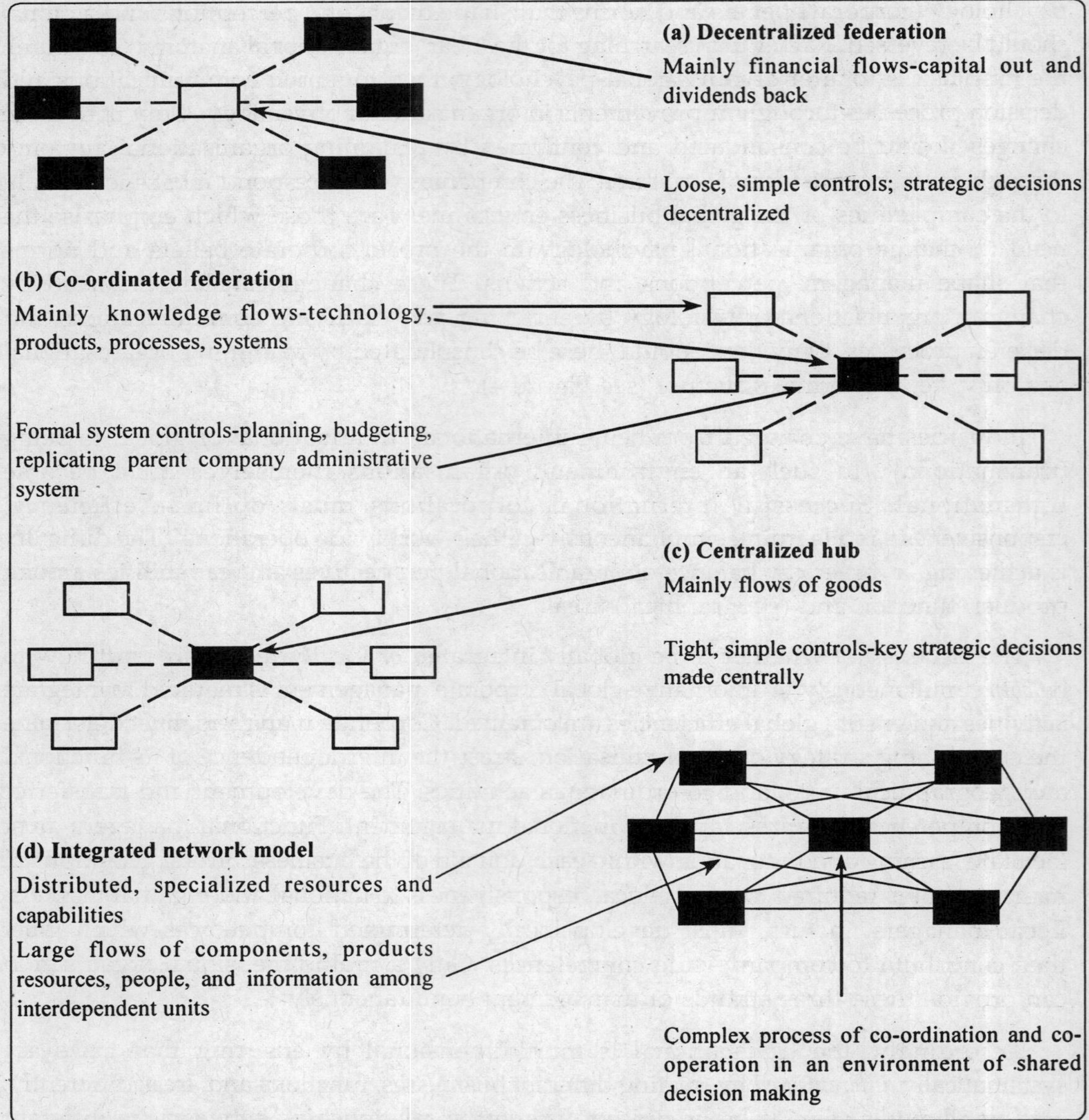

specific structure which incorporates tight controls. Transnationals possess integrated networks with three major characteristics: *multidimensional perspectives; distributed, interdependent capabilities; flexible integrative processes.*

Multidimensional Perspectives

The cultural diversity and increasing volatility of the international business environment have increased the need for organisations to sense and respond to environmental changes. This depends on developing strong global, subsidiary and functional management without domination by any one of these groups. Strong subsidiary management is required to identify the changing needs of local customers. Strong global management, is required to respond to the global strategies of competitors and to co-ordinate an appropriate response. Strong functional management is required to provide focus for areas of organisational knowledge and to ensure its transfer among units of the organisation.

Distributed, Interdependent Capabilities

In devising its response to changes in the environment, a transnational seeks to avoid the problems of other international configurations. The global centralised hub makes it difficult to respond to diverse local demands while the decentralised federation results in duplication, inefficiency and barriers to organisational learning. Within a transnational it is not seen as necessary to centralise activities which require global scale or specialised knowledge. Global scale can be achieved by making a local plant into a global production centre serving all the company's worldwide markets. A particular research and development centre can become the centre of excellence for the whole business. A local marketing group with proven expertise may be given the role of developing a global marketing strategy for a particular product. In this way the company becomes an *integrated network* of distributed but interdependent capabilities which benefit the whole organisation.

Flexible Integrative Processes

Once the network of distributed and integrated capabilities has been created alongside the management groups which represent the multiple perspectives of the organisation's environment, then flexible integrative management processes are required which integrate these diverse perspectives and capabilities. These processes must be flexible to allow differentiated operating relationships, adaptable operating relationships and functional decision-making roles which can change over time in response to changing circumstances.

This flexible integration is achieved by three separate but interdependent management processes.

i) *Centralisation* — which is sensitive to the groups within the organisation but allows senior management to intervene in certain decisions to ensure co-ordination.

ii) *Formalisation* - which allows different parts of the organisation to have influence on key decisions.

iii) Socialisation — which is a set of cultural norms and procedures which provides the framework for delegated decision making in the context of the overall organisation.

There is no prescribed structure for a transnational. Rather there are a set of principles which guide the managers of global businesses in the design and configuration of their organisations. These principles assist in achieving simultaneous global co-ordination and local responsiveness, alongside organisational learning and competence building.

DECISION-MAKING AND CONTROL IN INTERNATIONAL BUSINESS

Decentralisation and Control

The issue of decision-making within the transnational is closely related to the organisational structures. In traditional multinationals, for example, decision-making is largely decentralised at the level of the foreign subsidiary. In global structures, on the other hand, greater centralisation of decision-making may be expected although this will vary between different businesses and across functional areas. In a transnational corporation the issue is how to combine centralisation and decentralisation so as to achieve global co-ordination and local responsiveness.

Too much centralisation may prevent the utilisation of local initiative and have an adverse effect on the motivation of local management. Over-centralised decision-making may also result in a lack of adaptation to local market needs and may create political problems with host country governments. Decentralising certain decision-making to the local subsidiary may overcome many of these difficulties. By granting subsidiary autonomy the transnational may encourage the use of local initiative and the flexibility of the subsidiary to changes in local market conditions. Pressures on the corporate centre are also reduced as are the potential tensions with host country governments. The identification of a 'local' image may also be important in a number of industries. National units can develop new products and new techniques locally which can then be used throughout the transnational.

Centralisation of some decision-making may be necessary to achieve the benefits of global co-ordination through global economies and efficiencies. In the transnational model this centralised decision-making would include representation of different local, functional and business areas rather than only central management. Typically the centre of any organisation is concerned with establishing its overall vision, mission and its broad strategy. At the same time, within a transnational the centre plays an important role in co-ordinating activities, improving efficiency through benchmarking and setting standards, promoting innovation, and encouraging a learning and interdependent culture.

Evaluating Performance

Performance evaluation within the transnational serves a number of functions: i) ensuring the co-ordination and integration of strategy. Global and local strategy are integrated; ii) assisting in the internal benchmarking of performance. This acts as a mechanism to spread best practice throughout the organisation; iii) ensuring a realistic level of profitability. Performance of parts of the organisation may be measured against some target variable (e.g. actual profit, return on investment etc.); iv) early identification or problems, failure to meet targets provide early warning system in order that corrective action may be taken; v) resource allocation. Limited resources channelled into areas of highest return; vi) The performance evaluation system provides essential information on the operations of the different parts of the business; vii) long-run planning. Information acts as an input into strategic planning; viii) motivation. Performance evaluation used to motivate management in different parts of the organisation; and, finally, ix) communications. Performance evaluation—stimulates discussion between different parts of the organisation regarding performance, problems, long-run trends etc.

While each of these functions may be important the three most important functions performed by the evaluation procedure are: *ensuring subsidiary profitability; identifying potential problems; facilitating resource allocation.*The importance of these three objectives varies with the nature of the international involvement of the company. Large, geographically-dispersed, transnational emphasised the problem identification and resource allocation roles, while early internationalises emphasise profitability as an objective.

In terms of the actual performance measures used, the transnational has the same alternatives available as a domestic company including return on investment, income/ profit contribution, market share, cash flow measures etc. The use of these measures, however, is usually more difficult in an transnational due to exchange rate variations, differences in accounting procedures, variations in national inflation rates and tax rates, transfer pricing and restriction on remittances

Country-centred strategies (geographically-dispersed operations with minimum co-ordination) imply an organisational structure which is country-responsive, such as a geographic divisional structure, with considerable decision-making autonomy being devolved to the local subsidiaries. On the other hand, in geographically-dispersed but highly co-ordinated businesses, the need for global planning, and co-ordination will be reflected in the organisational structure which will be based on factors like global product, geographic or matrix systems. This, in turn, will depend on the company's product range and its geographical spread of activities. Similarly, authority over a range of both strategic and operational decisions will be transferred to a higher level in the organisation which has a global perspective. Decision-making, therefore, will be highly centralised, with a hierarchical chain of command between subsidiary and parent. Performance evaluation within such organisations will serve several functions relating to resource allocation, problem spotting and planning, in addition to the short-run measurement of subsidiary profitability.

QUESTIONS

1. Discuss the nature of international organization design. Explain the initial impacts of international business activity on organization design.
2. Why do international firms need to develop a unique organization design rather than simply model themselves after other firms?
3. Why is a global matrix design almost always transitional in nature? What are its strengths and weaknesses?
4. Do managers of international firms need to approach organization design differently from their counterparts in domestic firms? Why or why not?

REFERENCES

1. Bartlett, C.A. and Ghoshal, S. *Transnational Management: Text, Cases and Readings in Cross-Border Management*, R.D. Irwin, Homewood. 1995.
2. Brooke, M.Z. and Remmers, H.L. *The Strategy of Multinational Enterprise.* Pitman, London, (1976).
3. Davidow, W. and Malone, M. *The Virtual Corporation*, Harper Business, London, 1992.
4. Johnson, G. and Scholes, K. *Exploring Corporate Strategy*, Prentice Hall, Englewood Cliffs 1999.
5. Mintzberg, H. *Mintzberg on Management: Inside Our Strange World of Organisations*, The Free Press, New York. 1984.
6. Mintzberg, H., Quinn, J.B. and Ghoshal, S. *The Strategy Process* (Revised European Edition), Prentice Hall, Englewood Cliffs, *1998.*
7. Mullins, L. (WK) *Management and Organisational Behaviour*, Pitman, London. 1996.
8. Peters, T. and Waterman, R. *In Search of Excellence*, Harper and Row, New York. 1982.
9. Porter, M.E. Changing patterns of international competition, *California Management Review*, 28(2), Winter, 1986.

18

GLOBAL KNOWLEDGE MANAGEMENT

INTRODUCTION

In today's global economy, knowledge moves around the world at a faster and faster rate. Indeed, *via* digital means, some types of knowledge can be moved quickly and at virtually no cost. Networking and connectivity developments such as internet bring the 'global village' ever nearer. Information/knowledge has led to intensity efficient production; many factory workers use their heads more than their hands. MNCs must develop their strategies by tapping into the repositories of knowledge that exist in all parts of their organisations. However, this knowledge is context dependent: the more valuable the knowledge, the more difficult it is to replicate in other parts of the organisation. Moreover, innovation is critical for competitiveness. The knowledge source for innovation cannot be exclusively in the home country. Firms must find and exploit valuable knowledge from inside and outside their organisations in all the geographic markets in which they operate. In this chapter we explore how that knowledge can be managed and transferred in the global organisation.

Global economy, described as one in transition to a 'knowledge economy' or an 'information society', needs rewriting the rules and practices that determined the success of 20th century in today's interconnected world where resources such as know-how are more critical than other economic measures. Knowledge, like money, has velocity: the more it gets used, the greater the potential effect. In order to generate extraordinary value for shareholders, a company has to learn better than its competitors and apply that knowledge throughout its businesses faster and more widely than they do. No matter where the knowledge comes from, the key to reaping a big return is to leverage that knowledge by replicating it throughout the company so that each unit is not learning in isolation. The wonderful thing about knowledge is that it is inexpensive to replicate if one can capture it. The reality is that there are significant transactional difficulties associated with exploiting organisational knowledge. Quite simply, organisational knowledge is hard to capture, transfer, and make usable. Because knowledge is embedded in organisational structures, processes, procedures, and routines, it is not easy to separate it from the context in which it has been created. In addition, when knowledge is tacit, it is difficult to transfer without moving the people who have the knowledge.

ORGANISATIONAL KNOWLEDGE

Organisational knolwedge differs in many respects from other firm assets. *Firstly*, unlike assets such as raw materials, plants and equipment, and buildings, knowledge is not depleted (and does not depreciate) during production. Additional use will probably enhance knowledge. *Secondly*, knowledge can be possessed by multiple "owners" simultaneously. *Thirdly*, Knowledge is embedded and cumulative. *Fourthly*, knowledge transfer cannot easily be governed by contracts. *Finally*, giving value to knowledge is problematic and few companies have adequate systems to measure knowledge.

For organisational knowledge to be valuable, it must be usable at some point in the future. Value is derived from use, and as the more knowledge is used, the more valuable it may become. Knowledge is an asset that differs from traditional hard or tangible assets, and the difference is a function of its nature. Knowledge is cognitive perceptions as well as the skills and expertise embodied in products or services. Knowledge can be directed into two types: *information* and *know-how*. Information, or knowledge of what something means, includes facts, axiomatic propositions, and symbols. Know-how, or awareness of how to do something, is the accumulated practical skill or expertise that allows a person to do something smoothly and efficiently. A simpler, and perhaps more useful, view is that organisational knowledge creates the capacity for repeatable action by the organisation's members. In other words, people link the knowledge to a meaningful application within the organisation. The notion of repeatable is important because nonrepeated and idiosyncratic pieces of knowledge are not valuable; organisations are interested in reusable knowledge. This distinction separates organisational knowledge from facts that have little value for the organisation.

Tacit and Explicit Knowledge

The distinction between tacit and explicit organisational knowledge is a critical one. Tacit knowledge is intuitive and unarticulated, and not capable of being verbalized. It is knowledge that has been transformed into habit and made traditional, in the sense that it becomes "the way things are done around here." Tacit knowledge is highly context specific and has a personal quality, which makes it difficult to formalize, communicate, and transfer. For example, tacit knowledge may originate from an organisational story or unique experience. From that experience, such as an organisation's establishing its first international subsidiary or overcoming significant geographic barriers to market entry, personnel may have developed unique knowledge about international markets. If this knowledge is not written down, if it exists solely in the heads of these individuals, then the knowledge is tacit. Should those individuals leave the organisation, the knowledge would be lost.

In contrast to tacit knowledge, explicit knowledge is knowledge that is transmittable in formal, systematic language and may include facts and symbols. Examples of explicit knowledge are a document describing how to connect the components of a personal computer or direction on how to utilize an e-mail system. Explicit knowledge can be codified or articulated in manuals, computer programs, training tools, and so on. For example, much of the success of McDonald's can be attributed to the company's ability to articulate and codify its process of fast-food delivery to ensure consistent quality around the world. Some of the company's more recent problems can perhaps be attributed to the fact that competitors also understand the McDonald's process and have improved upon it. As a result, making knowledge explicit is a double-edged sword: on one hand, explicit knowledge can be transferred and replicated easily; on the other hand, it is much more subject to competitive spillover and appropriation than tacit knowledge.

A key challenge for organisations is to convert tacit knowledge to explicit knowledge. There is a need to identify various dimensions of organisational knowledge, including complex *versus* simple, teachable versus not teachable, and observable in use *versus* not observable in user. For all these dimensions, it is important not to create a false dichotomy. Knowledge exists along a spectrum, and the end-points are mainly descriptive devices. Although the distinction between tacit and explicit is important, it does not allow us to consider any gray areas. Thus, explicit and tacit knowledge types can be classified on a continuum that ranges from the explicit knowledge embedded in specific products and processes to the tacit knowledge acquired through experience and use, and embodied in individual cognition and organisation routines. Tacit, personal knowledge has little value until it can be converted into explicit knowledge that organisational members can share. However, this conversion process risks imitation by other firms. Therefore, firms must be cognizant of the tradeoff between the need to share and transfer knowledge internally and the risk of exposing the knowledge to competitors.

KNOWLEDGE MANAGEMENT

Knowledge management and the ability to create, transfer, assemble, integrate, and exploit knowledge assets are critical for a firm's success. It is much more than managing the flow of information. It means nothing less than setting knowledge free to find its own paths. It means fueling the creative fire of self-questioning in organisations. This means thinking less about knowledge management and more about knowledge partnering. Knowledge management involves processes such as sharing individual knowledge and its evolution to a collective state, embedding new knowledge in products and services, and transferring knowledge across organisational boundaries. The success of knowledge management depends on whether that new knowledge improves organisational actions or creates the basis for new action.

To be successful in a global knowledge economy, organisations must not only process information but also create new knowledge. For the MNC, the source for new knowledge should be the world. This means that all units of a global firm should bear responsibility for finding and capturing new knowledge. In turn, headquarters must recognize that its local bases are real assets in discovering knowledge and that knowledge-transfer mechanisms must be established to ensure that local knowledge is not relegated to a peripheral role. The successful knowledge management ensures that the various subunits of the firm are capable and willing to seek opportunities to create, share, and transfer knowledge.

Organisational Knowledge Transfer

The concept of knowledge transfer has its roots in technical information-processing research, where the primary focus has been on the storage and retrieval of knowledge. However, information-processing approaches tend to assume that a common language underpins the transfer process. There are the difficulties in transferring knowledge across boundaries. Individuals involved in knowledge transfer are often reluctant to abandon existing knowledge for something new, or novel. When these individuals must communicate across boundaries, the circumstances are often viewed as novel because there is no common language or context. Individuals can differ in their cognitive knowledge and specialization, language, social norms and identities, and type of sense-making used to analyze problems. When the circumstances are novel, knowledge transfer becomes sticky and prone to failure. Knowledge that is deeply embedded in the context in which it was created tends to be resistant to both movement and receipt. For example, information about doing business in a foreign market is a combination of tacit and explicit knowledge that is usually quite difficult to extract from its foreign-market context. As a result, firms often rely on local partners for assistance in entering new markets. Even after establishing themselves as viable competitors in the local market, organisations may be unable to acquire and transfer the local knowledge, which means that local partners may become permanently necessary. In addition, knowledge rooted in organisational values and cultures can be difficult to transfer in a manner that leads to a desired change.

The transfer of organisational knowledge can occur through a variety of mechanisms: personnel movement, training, communication and personal relationships, observation, transfer of goods and services, patents, scientific publications, presentations, and interactions with suppliers and customers. Regardless of the method used, the transfer manifests itself through changes in the degree of knowledge or the performance of the recipient unit. As a framework for understanding these different mechanisms, there is a need to distinguish between moving knowledge itself and modifying the knowledge of the recipient unit. That is, when knowledge itself is moved it must be adapted to a new context. The knowledge can be moved by transferring the people possessing that knowledge or by moving the tools in which the knowledge is embedded. In technology-based alliances such as licensing agreements, knowledge transfer may be a quite straightforward movement of software, product design, or manufacturing systems. If the knowledge is moved via people, the transfer will be most successful when the knowledge is not overlay complex and when the individuals have the ability to influence those receiving the knowledge.

For knowledge modification at the recipient to occur, there must be intensive social interactions involving managers at various organisational levels, along with consensus building among the managers involved. Alternatively, if knowledge at the recipient end is not modified or no consensus on the value of the knowledge is reached, the transfer of context-specific knowledge will be difficult. There is evidence that knowledge transfer is facilitated by intensive communication and social interaction. Indeed, knowledge transfer has been described as individuals within one organisation communicating on specific problems and procedures with individuals from another organisation. Through communication, managers can develop an understanding of the value of knowledge and how an existing knowledge base needs to be modified to absorb new knowledge.

The ability to transfer knowledge is a primary source of a firm's competitive advantage and growth. MNCs that can effectively tap into their various pockets of valuable knowledge have the potential to outperform competitors that rely on one-way knowledge flows from headquarters to subsidiaries. Not too long ago, it was rare for an MNC to think much about knowledge transfer from subsidiaries to headquarters or from subsidiary to subsidiary. More typically, a U.S. or European firm either acquired or established a subsidiary as the means of market entry. In many cases, local production was necessary to avoid tariffs and other barriers. If the business was acquired, it would usually be left alone, aside from the introduction of headquarters' policies. If the subsidiary were a greenfield site, the headquarters would transfer the appropriate knowledge based on how things were done in Europe or the United States. In the case of a manufacturing subsidiary, the transferred knowledge would consist primarily of product design and manufacturing technology. When Japanese firms began to aggressively enter new markets in the 1960s, their internationalization model resulted in the term *transplant*, which is applied to the replication of a home-country production model in a new geographic market. The Japanese MNCs rarely acquired firms, preferring to transfer their own management systems to the new markets.

In most instances, the knowledge transfer models used in the previous century can be called *projection models:* the knowledge was projected from headquarters to the distant realms of the corporate empire. Under the right conditions, the projection model can work quite well. One of those conditions is that the firm projecting its knowledge should have a clear and sustainable advantage with few threats from other firms in its global markets. Obviously, firms of this sort are few and far between. As a result, firms in today's competitive environment must exploit their total knowledge resources and abandon the idea that the headquarters or a primary subsidiary has the most valuable knowledge. Increasingly, firms are tearing down the boundaries that prevent knowledge from crossing borders and cultures.

Keeping valuable knowledge isolated in geographic areas no longer makes sense in the global automobile industry. Organisational knowledge has value when it can be used in repeatable applications. This suggests that organisations should be constantly searching for new applications for existing knowledge and also for new knowledge outside their boundaries. The difficulty is that very often what might be repeatable in one organisation is foreign, different, and highly suspicious to another organisation, or even to another division of the same organisation.

Transferring Knowledge in MNCs: MNC must transfer knowledge between various parts of the organisation. Various approaches used for successful knowledge transfer involve a significant commitment of resources. Three approach to transfer knowledge are: *First,* in the *headquarters commissioned and executed approach,* the home office sets the tone for knowledge-management initiatives and provides technology solutions and support, training, and policies and procedures. Standardization of interfaces, procedures, and policies was the overriding principle. This approach is found in companies with standardized global products and services, and is used to take advantage of economies of scale. For example, this approach might be used by a software company designing a new marketing strategy. Since the software is technically the same in each geographic market, a common approach to marketing may make sense (although that will depend on many factors, such as whether the target is an individual consumer or an enterprise). *Second,* the *headquarters commissioned and regionally executed approach* involves headquarters initiation and broad guidelines and policies. The regional centers then execute the knowledge transfer. In this case, the regional centers are major hubs in each continent where the organisation operates. This approach allows tailored solutions for meeting regional requirements and is common for organisations involved in global consulting efforts and manufacturing. Headquarters sets the knowledge-management initiatives, objectives, and tools; the regional centers are allowed to customize aspects of the management such as language and interface mechanisms. *Third, regionally commissioned and locally executed approach,* the vision and initiatives for knowledge management come from the regional offices. The impetus for regional involvement is recognition of a need to exchange knowledge on a frequent and local basis. Each office in a region can execute knowledge transfer to achieve the goals and policies it has set. The benefit of this approach is speed, while the downside is that knowledge transfer is confined to a region and globalization of these efforts may not happen.

The most typical example of global knowledge management in MNCs is knowledge sharing along functional lines, such as marketing or operations. This type of knowledge sharing is often referred to as *the sharing of best practices.* If firms are committed to capturing knowledge, they must create innovative collaborative mechanisms to support the generation and transfer of the knowledge. If knowledge creation and transfer efforts receive only limited and sporadic attention, the payoffs will also be minimal.

Knowledge activists play a key role in ensuring that knowledge gets transferred. The more complex and valuable the knowledge to be gained, the greater the role that innovative and entrepreneurial knowledge activists will play in the transfer. There are knowledge activists who start off as lonely voices and over time founded a community of shared understanding. Within this community, there was a mutual understanding based on practice and experience that allowed the knowledge to transfer easily. But until the community has sufficient critical mass, changing the traditional knowledge base is bound to be difficult.

There are a variety of potentially effective knowledge-transfer mechanisms, including people transfers, training programs, and interpersonal relationships. The choice of mechanism depends on the type of knowledge involved and the transfer objective. Some explicit knowledge can be transferred quite easily, although often companies mistakenly believe knowledge is explicit and then discover it is otherwise. GM initially thought that videotapes of the Toyota production system would support knowledge transfer. It took a few years to realize that the most valuable knowledge could not be transferred without some face-to-face interaction, such as training, teaching, visits, and on-the-job experience. The company also learned that it was necessary to supplement the personal transfer with specific learning assignments and training.

The complexity of the knowledge significantly increases the difficulties of acquiring that knowledge. Social interaction between partners in a joint venture is critical for knowledge to be transferred. Knowledge acquisition is enhanced when the knowledge is related to what is already known and when there is a common language for interpreting experience. Unrelated knowledge is difficult to acquire and may have limited value. Within a community, there is mutual understanding based on practice and experience that allows knowledge to move easily. But between communities, as in the case of alliance partners, there are different standards, different priorities, and different evaluating criteria that must overcome for knowledge to move. Likewise, unrelated knowledge is difficult to transfer and may have limited value to the recipient because there is no common language for understanding and integrating that knowledge. For unrelated knowledge to become valuable, modification of the knowledge at the recipient may be necessary.

As knowledge gets transferred and put to use, its value increases and the network of individuals using the knowledge also expands, which creates further opportunities to exploit the knowledge. In a sense, the transfer of best practices, especially home-country practices, is often about replication, not innovation, although the best practices themselves may be improved upon by the recipient. A different knowledge-transfer situation occurs when the MNC uses local knowledge as the basis for product innovation. Two ways to leverage locally embedded knowledge are local-for-regional and regional-for-global.

Very few local innovations become global without active corporate management because local managers are generally not in a position to impact global operations and strategy. The *local-for-regional approach* is the exploitation of local innovation for regional application. The *regional-for-global approach* involves mobilization of regional knowledge on a global basis. When this happens, innovation often occurs at the local level and then the regional office helps identify its greater potential application. The regional office bridges the gap between innovations developed in local units and strategy creation by headquarters in the home country. The regional office identifies the potential for innovation, then implements the procedures for extracting the relevant knowledge and diffusing it throughout the global MNC network. In this way, the regional office acts as a knowledge broker for the rest of the organisation.

LEVERAGING KNOWLEDGE RESOURCES GLOBALLY

In today's global economy, organisations are not only processing information but also creating new information and knowledge. For the MNC, the source for new knowledge should be the world. Every business is essentially an information business. For example, a manufacturer of automobiles must be aware of demand and supply patterns, technology developments, changes in sources of supply for inputs, inventory levels, trends among its loyal customers, and its after-sales service record. Information is what makes value chains and supply chains work. By extension, it is entirely possible to separate information from the physical aspects of the manufacturing process. For example, although an inventory of raw materials encompasses a range of goods that have monetary value, the process of inventory management relies on information about that inventory rather than the physical inventory itself. Thus, it is possible to manage and control inventory from a distant location using personnel who may never see the goods themselves. Similarly, at the customer end, market research, customer demographics, and customer support are all examples of processes that are rich with an information component.

Separating the physical component from the information component allows organisations to rethink, reengineer, and reconfigure their value chains to maximize added value. For example, Ventura, based in India, will deploys its call-center operations in Mumbai and Yorkshire to handle the contract. Client Logic uses its centers in New Delhi and Derby to do the same. This is a classic illustration of an organisation's ability to separate the information aspects of its business from its core processes.

Creating a Knowledge-Oriented Culture

There is little doubt that for the MNC, knowledge exploitation is critical for long-term success and thus will become even more important in the future. The projection model the knowledge projected from headquarters to subsidiary as the MNC's sole means of transferring knowledge is a dying concept. Thus, a key question for MNCs is how to create a knowledge-oriented culture. An initial step is to understand the barriers to knowledge transfer and learning.

One barrier to knowledge transfer is the nature of knowledge itself. Valuable knowledge is context dependent. Successful transfer of context-dependent knowledge cannot occur until the knowledge source and recipient units are aligned regarding the value and potential impact of that knowledge on the organisation. When knowledge is embedded in a unique culture and/or context, its transfer becomes difficult. When knowledge is embedded, particular problems arise. The knowledge is not available in simple, unitized packages that can be bought for cash. For one organisation to secure embedded knowledge from another, its personnel must have direct, intimate, and extensive exposure to the social relationships of the other organisation.

A second barrier to knowledge transfer is the not-invented-here syndrome. Managers and organisations tend to be highly resistant to knowledge that originates outside their sphere of activity and understanding. What should firms do to overcome the liabilities of the not-invented-here syndrome? The first step is to assess the degree to which the firm is knowledge oriented. This requires the identification of several questions that managers should ask about their organisations: How good is the company at uncovering opportunities for knowledge transfer among different parts of the company? How enthusiastic are the subsidiaries to share knowledge with other units? How eager are the subsidiaries to learn from other parts of the company? How good is the company at codifying the innovations generated by the subsidiaries? Has the company built efficient communication mechanisms for sharing the codified know-how across locations? How good is the company at keeping codified knowledge proprietary to the company? Has the company built effective mechanisms (e.g., people transfer, face-to-face interchange) for the transfer of tacit knowledge across locations?

A second step to consider is the organisation culture and the need for a global knowledge orientation. The successful companies: Steal with pride (i.e., "great artists steal") and copy with passion; think about competition from a global perspective; recognize that the periphery of the organisation has valuable knowledge; recognise that learning and knowledge transfer rarely happen spontaneously; firms willing to invest in learning; develop cosmopolitan managers who understand that headquarters does not have all the answers; people movement should not be one way: people should be moved to and from subsidiaries; and finally, develop a culture in every part of the organisation that says "Here is not better than there."

TABLE 1

Leveraging Subsidiary Knowledge

1. Assess and value subsidiary knowledge
   i) What are the core competencies of the MNC's subsidiaries?
   ii) What specific knowledge does the subsidiary have that could enhance the competitive strategy of other parts of the company?
   iii) What are the core subsidiary skills relevant for product/markets in other parts of the firm?
   iv) Are the subsidiary skills and capabilities relevant to the strategy and capabilities of other parts of the firm?
2. Determine subsidiary knowledge accessibility
   i) Is learning and knowledge transfer a priority for local managers?
   ii) Do you have easy geographic access to the subsidiary operations?
   iii) Is there any reason why access to knowledge in subsidiaries is restricted?
3. Evaluate the tacitness and ease of transfer for knowledge of interest
   i) Is the local knowledge tacit or explicit?
   ii) Where in the subsidiary does the knowledge reside?
   iii) Is the knowledge strategic or operational?
   iv) Does the company understand what it is trying to learn, how the knowledge can be used in other parts of the organisation, and the ease (or difficulty) of knowledge transfer?
4. Establish knowledge connections between subsidiaries
   i) Do headquarters managers visit subsidiaries on a regular basis? Do local managers visit headquarters?
   ii) Has a systematic plan been established for managers to move between subsidiaries and the headquarters?
   iii) Have subsidiary initiatives been incorporated into headquarters strategic plans and do local managers participate in parent strategic planning discussions?
   iv) What is the level of trust between headquarters and local managers?
5. Draw on existing knowledge to facilitate learning
   i) Have the managers seeking to learn from each other worked together in the past?
   ii) Are experiences with other subsidiaries being used as the basis for managing current learning opportunity?
   iii) Are they open-minded about knowledge that does not have immediate short-term applicability?
6. Ensure that headquarters and local managerial cultures are in alignment
   i) Is subsidiary knowledge viewed as a threat or as an asset by headquarters managers?
   ii) Is there agreement at the headquarters on the strategic rationale and value for sharing knowledge between various parts of the organisation?
   iii) In the subsidiaries, do managers understand the importance of the headquarters learning objective?

The questions in Table 1 are designed to help MNC managers identify and leverage valuable subsidiary knowledge. It is based on the assumption that every subsidiary has valuable knowledge that should be shared with other parts of the organisation. The challenge is to identify the most valuable knowledge and then develop a process for capitalizing on it.

Offshore operations are 'old wine in the new bottles.' The migration of jobs with a strong service or knowledge component is quite consistent with the progress of globalization and the disaggregation of value chains. Thus, the phenomenon can hardly be thought of as a radical departure from the way global business is conducted or has been conducted for centuries. Just as China, Taiwan, and Mexico were recipients of manufacturing jobs from U.S. companies seeking more favourable labour and production costs, India, Hungary, South Africa, and the Philippines are witnessing significant inflows of service and knowledge jobs given their attractive cost position. However, although the reasons underlying the migration of knowledge and service jobs parallel earlier waves in manufacturing, the driver of this shift is quite different. It is the transition to knowledge-based competition in most of the industries that has in large part fuelled this change.

The prominent country destinations for value-added functions with a relatively high knowledge quotient and back-office processes that entail analytical skills have some fundamental similarities. All of these countries offer a qualified labour pool with strong technical skills, high fluency in English, a reliable Internet infrastructure, and competitive labour costs. India, for example, has twice the number of technical graduates as does the United States and has recently accelerated the number of graduates in technical disciplines.

The plentiful supply of technical graduates in these countries has helped meet the shortage of such talent in the developed world. Countries such as India and China have a relatively well established educational infrastructure that emphasizes analytical skills and numerical ability. India has the added advantage of an education system geared to English as the main language of instruction, making its graduates ideal candidates to take charge of MNC back-office processes. Although the same could be said for South Africa, Ireland, and a few other English-speaking locales, the wage rates in those countries are much higher and, hence, may not offer a value proposition as enticing.

Classical theories of foreign trade, such as those of absolute and comparative advantage, were predicated on the immobility of key resources such as labour and physical-factor endowments (e.g., availability of raw materials). Since these critical factors of production could not be moved, buyers seeking to take advantage of these resources established operations in countries where the resources were plentiful. But for knowledge-based industries, this reasoning doesn't apply, since knowledge workers (such as computer programmers and systems analysts) can migrate to companies in developed countries where their skills are in demand. Thus, many companies have recruited significant specialized labour resources in countries such as India and China. Having breached the mobility barrier, companies now can locate headquarters, design, manufacturing, and other elements of business almost anywhere feasible. Developments in technology, especially the growing sophistication of telecom networks, have allowed organisations to access knowledge resources in faraway locations without a need to physically transplant such resources to the home country. Companies such as Microsoft and Intel, which have relied on foreign talent for engineering and development services, now operate full-fledged knowledge centers and research facilities overseas, linking these outputs to home-country sites through real-time communication networks. This not only allows them to take advantage of low-cost skilled labour elsewhere but also to leverage time differences to maintain a continuous work flow spanning a 24-hour day.

The decentralization of business processes and knowledge creation offers enormous benefits that transcend mere cost savings (although these savings are quite critical). McKinsey researchers estimated in 2004 that a U.S. software programmer costs the company $60 per hour while her counterpart in India costs only $6—a labour cost advantage that even the most fiercely nationalistic firms would find extremely hard to overlook. McKinsey also found that while about 16 percent of the work in IT services is done remotely, away from the location where the services are consumed, only about 6 percent of software engineering is currently done remotely and only 1 percent of banking services. McKinsey suggests that as much as half of the work in these industries could be moved abroad. Other service industries are also ripe for significant change, including legal services, market research, architecture and drafting, construction design, and insurance.

The urge to move activities offshore is, in significant part, driven by cost pressures and the need to stay competitive and maximize shareholder value. Beyond direct cost savings, the less visible benefits of using offshore locations include: access to better-skilled manpower; the potential to generate cost savings at home to fund expansion; redeployment of home-office personnel to more higher value-added jobs; the ability to stay competitive in markets where price pressures are significant; an improvement in the range and responsiveness of customer-centric activities; the ability to offer 24-hour service; and, the ability to offer better jobs for people in emerging markets.

DECISION PARAMETERS IN CREATING AN OFFSHORE STRATEGY

Decentralization decisions that involve knowledge-based resources or the intellectual capital of the company are often extremely difficult to make. They are inextricably linked with strategic, operational, political, legal, social, and financial considerations.

They transcend the simple logic of monetary gains and differential cost advantages. Since intellectual capital is the lifeblood of all organisations, these decisions have to take into account issues such as privacy, security, potential loss of vital competitive information, political hazards, and infrastructure-related risks that routine manufacturing outsourcing decisions may not entail. Beyond the typical considerations of cost, quality, and ability to deliver, the outsourcing decision will be impacted by the need for secrecy and limited access in order to avoid leakage of competitive information, infrastructure reliability, exposure to political hazards, and legal considerations. The characteristics of the process to be migrated, such as transferability, criticality of the business function, extent of client contact entailed, and need to maintain competitive control all impact knowledge-offshoring decisions. Table 2 offers an example of the types of decision parameters involved in grafting an offshore strategy. For ease of illustration, the dimensions have been divided into external and internal parameters. External parameters relate to location-specific aspects and, hence, are largely beyond the domain of influence of an individual company, while internal factors relate to parameters that aré controllable by the company.

TABLE 2

Decision Parameters in an Offshore Strategy

External Decision Parameters	*Internal Decision Parameter*
i) Country location—access, time zone	i) Business function characteristics such as criticality of the function, frequency of the process, and need for competitive control
ii) Nature of host government policies toward businesses	ii) Ability to manage the public relations issues that accompany large-scale job transfers to other countries
iii) Stability of host government	iii) Previous experience with foreign ventures especially from a project management perspective
iv) Corporate tax laws and the legal institutional framework	iv) Prior experience with vendor selection and management in foreign locations
v) Patent protection and enforcement	v) Availability of managerial manpower internally to spearhead the move to offshore
vi) Hiring and firing practices—incidence of labour unions	vi) Commitment of senior management to an offshore strategy
vii) Infrastructure—transportation, communications, accessibility	vii) Ability to implement organisational structures and reporting relationships to maximize the benefits of an offshore strategy ranging from knowledge acquisition and learning to cost containment and quality enhancement
viii) Labour pool characteristics including cost, education level, skill level, trainability, availability, and size of the pool	
ix) Language proficiency—level of familiarity with the dominant language that will be used to transact business	
x) Cultural compatibility in terms of social characteristics as well as work behaviors	
xi) Level of familiarity with professional management approaches	

Determinants of the Ideal Processes and Functions That May Be Offshored

There are several process- and function-related parameters that must be weighed in determining the optimal mix of activities that can be decentralized. Although there is a wide array of services that can be obtained through arms-length relationships with service providers in low-wage countries, it is imperative that the decentralization decision be driven by sound business logic. Typically such an analysis will encompass the dimensions: (i) Criticality of the business process or function to overall value creation (ii) Extent of direct client contact that the function entails. (iii) Frequency of transactions. (iv) Extent of managerial intervention required by the process or function. (v) Extent of competitive control that is required over the process. (vi) Ease of transferability of the function or process.

The criticality of a business function refers to the extent to which the function plays a central role in an organisation's day-to-day decision making. In a manufacturing firm, functions such as inventory management and production scheduling are critical functions that have a crucial bearing on the implementation of operational strategies. Thus, such functions might inherently be difficult to process at distant satellite locations, cost benefits notwithstanding. On the other hand, industries such as consumer electronics and telecommunications equipment have largely outsourced their manufacturing activities. When this process began, many observers doubted the wisdom of outsourcing manufacturing, since it was believed that manufacturing was a core activity. Now, some years later, it is widely accepted within these industries that manufacturing activities remain critical but can be adequately performed by contract manufacturers.

The extent to which a function closely depends on direct client contact is also an important factor driving the decentralization decision. Functions and processes that require frequent client contact, such as many marketing and sales-related processes, typically will not lend themselves to offshoring. In many of these functions, it is feasible to identify processes that do not require intensive client interface; for example, processes related to customer relationship management entailing the analysis of data could easily be outsourced while the actual customer interface cannot.

The frequency of the transaction is a crucial determinant of the economic benefits of offshore processing. In organisations such as airline companies, financial services companies, or banking institutions, there are many high-frequency business process transactions that are quite routine, such as processing airline tickets and reconciling corporate accounts. These routine transactions require very little managerial intervention, thus such functions often benefit from the significant cost savings that arise from offshore processing. Once the basic processes and control systems are in place, the actual country site where the processing takes place is fairly inconsequential. Thus, almost all the major airline companies have significant back-office operations in countries such as India, where routine functions are handled cost-effectively. In addition, some airlines like British Airways have set up independent processing companies that offer services to other airlines.

Competitive control is another primary determinant of the potential for offshore success. Since many offshore ventures are structured as arms-length or contractual partnerships, they carry all the complexities of traditional firm relationships, including the risk of loss of competitive information. The incidence of information leakage is accentuated by the context within which offshoring is pursued. Typically, the countries where much of this work takes place lack adequate legal infrastructures, raising significant questions about the protection of intellectual property and data privacy. In circumventing this potential risk, some firms have sought to establish wholly owned subsidiaries to undertake offshore functions like back-office operations. However, this decision is one that obviously has significant economic implications, calling for a disciplined cost versus benefits analysis.

Offshore Decision: Location, Structure, and Ownership

Once the decision to offshore has been made and the offshore functions identified, the organisation has to plan its entry strategy. The three major decisions at this stage involve (a) the location where the offshored functions will be performed, (b) the organisation structure that will be deployed to maintain oversight of the functions, and (c) the nature of ownership that the organisation seeks to exercise over the operations. Although these three decision points address different facets of the process of moving functions to other locations, they are not mutually independent. For example, the choice of ownership structure could be determined by the specific country location being considered and vice versa. The control structure will likewise be influenced by the ownership structure and the location. Thus, given their contingent nature, these decisions must converge on a set of mutually feasible options.

Near-Shore versus Far-Shore

A fundamental choice that organisations confront when outsourcing knowledge functions is between near-shore and far-shore locations. Near-shore locations typically are closer to headquarters and, hence, more politically and socially palatable to its target audience and immediate community than far-shore locations (although not always; moving from Germany to Poland or Hungary is short in miles but often long in attitude). There could be added advantages of cultural similarities that might dampen concerns about the management problems that usually arise in arms-length transactions. For example, companies headquartered in the United States often choose Canada for some of their call-center operations, given their heightened sensitivity to the political and social backlash from far-shore operations in locations such as India. While this choice might help the company maintain an even keel with respect to public relations, it could quite easily have a negative impact on the organisation's bottom line, especially because the wage differentials between the United States and Canada are not as significant as those between the United States and China or India. The near-shore option might also offer the benefit of maintaining closer control over quality-of-work processes and forge closer relationships with headquarters. However, the closer the two countries are in terms of economics and geography, the greater the likelihood that they will share constraints such as manpower access, infrastructure limitations, and the like. The far-shore option, on the other hand, brings several advantages, such as lower labour costs and a better skilled labour pool. The disadvantages are in the immense coordination challenges, management of multiple cultures, and the political and social storms that recur periodically. Table-3 presents the major advantages and disadvantages of near-shore and far-shore locations.

Many organisations pursue a blend of near-shore and far-shore locations. Their choice is invariably driven by the nature of the function being outsourced and the pressures for leveraging cost efficiencies. The "right source" options emerge from a careful evaluation of the costs, benefits, constraints, and challenges associated with the array of location choices measured against key facets of the function targeted for offshoring.

TABLE 3

Major Advantages and Disadvantages of Near-Shore versus Far-Shore Location Options

Near-Shore	*Far-Shore*
i) Easier for organizations to pursue in light of potential backlash against the migration of jobs	i) Far-shore locations offer significant advantages in labor cost, access of skilled manpower, and overall operations costs
ii) Cultural similarities with the near-shore location might help minimize operational problems, especially in customer contact functions	ii) Since far-shore locations do not share many similarities with the home base, it is likely that business risk factors will not co-vary
iii) Might be a better option for projects and functions that are by definition loosely defined and require frequent intervention	iii) Some far-shore locations such as China and India have qualified and technically competent workforces, making it feasible to hire people with advanced skill sets at relatively lower costs; this improves output quality
iv) Carries a reduced perceived business risk given potential similarities in economic, legal, and social systems	iv) The control and coordination costs could be prohibitive if they entail significant intervention from the home base on an ongoing basis
v) Coordination and control become easier due to geographic proximity	v) Might be less suitable for evolving projects that do not have clear work specifications
vi) Might be cost-effective in terms of travel and hands-on contact time spent by headquarters personnel	vi) Managing a culturally different workforce often poses additional challenges that limit the ability to implement a unified headquarters system of beliefs and practices.
vii) Might not be able to leverage significant cost savings since the costs of doing business may not be substantially different across locations	

Structuring an Offshore Entity

Structuring an offshore entity to take over routine business processes is a complex manoeuvre. It entails aligning organisational goals and strategies with on-the-ground realities. While some organisations prefer to structure their offshore knowledge operations as wholly owned subsidiaries, others prefer either an arms-length relationship established through a third-party vendor or an intermediary or alliance relationship. While each choice comes with its own advantages and disadvantages, the decision on structure is usually driven by the specifics of the function or process.

Establishing *de novo* operations in the form of a wholly owned subsidiary provides the obvious advantages of control over the operation, an ability to implement corporate policies and procedures, and some safeguards against poor work quality. On the other hand, an arms-length relationship or an alliance helps overcome local obstacles such as managing a local workforce, handling cultural differences, and overcoming local regulatory roadblocks, all of which require considerable experience and learning for a newcomer to do on its own. For example, organisations such as GE, Microsoft, and Intel have chosen the de novo approach in India. Others such as Cisco Systems, Lloyds TSB, and Barclays have chosen to partner with third-party vendors to execute their offshore strategy in the same country.

Another option for structuring offshore operations involves a variation on the conventional partnership arrangement with a third-party vendor. Unlike the conventional partnership arrangement, whereby contract services are performed by the vendor at preset fees and charges, the new form includes an element of risk and revenue sharing. For example, Wipro, the Indian offshore service provider, develops software products for its telecommunications network management clients for a development fee that includes a proportion of revenues generated by the sale of these products. This seems a unique way by which the embattled telecommunications companies can sustain new product innovation without bearing all the risks associated with such complex product-development ventures. The upside for the third-party vendor is the potential to leverage its captive access to low-cost labour and technological expertise and to ride the wave of success should the product balloon into a major innovation.

Wholly Owned Subsidiaries versus Contractors

While the intensity of management challenges faced in a wholly owned venture could indeed differ from those presented in a contractual partnership, it is very likely that the crucial aspects of handling a diverse workforce, ensuring service quality, and managing virtually will remain prominent. The proximity of the offshore operation and the nature of the company's relationship with the offshore operation are among the two most crucial variables. A fully owned offshore facility will offer the best potential for close operational control and quality monitoring, allowing the company to imprint its value systems and belief structures on its employees in far-flung locations. However, this does not always happen on it own. For example, when Siemens set up a regional development facility in India to leverage native software talent and a low-cost labour pool, it launched a fully owned venture. Despite implementing the best project management practices that had distilled from years of experience with 16 other global development centers the company found that its learning curve was rather steep. Siemens had to patiently solve significant cultural, technical, and motivational problems, as well as deal with government regulations to make Bangalore a productive node in its network. It took over five years for the process of acculturation and resource acquisition to run its course before the center was able to take independent responsibility.

The benefits of using a third-party provider to orchestrate the migration of process from home office to offshore facility are manifold. These independent service providers are likely to be entrenched in the local economy and well versed in navigating the cultural, political, and economic realities. For example, many companies find that employee retention is a significant management challenge. The competitive labour market not only drives wages constantly upward but also gives rise to routine poaching of trained talent. Thus, retaining employees requires a careful blend of compensation and development opportunities challenging enough to hold employee interest. Independent providers are experts, in these matters and have significant advantage over de novo operators. In the fierce political debate over the migration of jobs to emerging countries, some companies feel it in their best interests to stay out of the debate by using independent providers to handle the business, circumventing political fallout at least in the short term. The independent service provider functions much like any other contract vendor of goods and services. Indeed, a new genre of intermediary companies has emerged to counsel multinational firms on the process of leveraging benefits from offshore processing. Some of the world's largest consulting companies, such as IBM and Accenture, are already major players in this area.

The key downside to using an independent service provider is the risk of loss of competitive information. While contracts can be structured to ensure that adequate controls are in place, there is no fail-safe method to prevent competitive information from falling into the hands of competitors. There is also the very real possibility that increased reliance on contracted offshore services could ultimately damage the innovative capacity of the organisation and undercut its ability to add value in any meaningful manner. Table 4 summarizes some of the key costs and benefits of using a wholly owned approach and a contracted provider approach.

Successfully Managing Offshore Relationships

Whether the arrangement is a wholly owned subsidiary, a contracted partnership in the form of a vendor, or a third-party services intermediary, managing an offshore relationship requires some unique skills and competencies. Geographic distance, cultural dissimilarity, and variations in employee skills at the offshore location make for a challenging management environment. When offshore facilities take on the routine tasks of fundamental business processes, they need to be integrated into the organisational network on a real-time basis. Decisions to be made in one part of the network rely on

TABLE 4

Key Costs and Benefits of a Wholly Owned Model and a Contracted Provider Model

Wholly Owned	*Contracted Provider*
i) Offers the best possible level of competitive control over operations	i) Offers the quickest solution to entering the offshore labor market in order to gain cost benefits with the least amount of project gestation time
ii) Internalizes all the cost benefits associated with offshoring since it eliminates intermediary margins	ii) Leverages the expertise of the provider that is likely to include an in-depth understanding of important dimensions such as local labor market conditions, skills availability, and regulatory restrictions
iii) Allows the firm to establish its own value structure and belief system over the offshore facility to ensure a seamless migration between home office and the subsidiary	iii) Builds on the experience curve and learning advantages that the contract provider would have already internalized
iv) Provides excellent channels to ensure that output quality meets established standards and complements the process with a well-tested system of checks and balances developed at the home office	iv) Offers some limited protection from the negative public relations fallout that invariably accompanies the migration of knowledge-based jobs to offshore locations
v) Could provide global career development opportunities that transcend subsidiary borders—an important tool in increasing employee retention	v) Provides flexibility in ramping up and scaling down operations on an "as needed" basis, a prospect that would be difficult in the case of a wholly owned subsidiary model
vi) Normally takes a longer period of time to realize cost benefits since the startup will require substantial coordination costs	vi) The firm that is buying contracted services needs to be able to enforce contracts in emerging markets should there be a leakage of competitive knowledge, often a very costly proposition
vii) Often a challenge to establish home office norms (e.g., policies and procedures)	vii) Long-term reliance on the contract provider model has to be limited to noncore functions, forcing the firm to forgo cost and quality benefits that could arise by outsourcing some of the core functions
viii) Often challenging to maintain reasonable levels of employee retention in a market that is very competitive and where noncompete contract clauses are not easily enforceable	

data originating in a different part of the network, and most often in real time. Take the example of Lufthansa, the German flagship carrier that processes most of its ticketing functions in India. The Indian facility maintains all information systems pertaining to routes, seat availability, and fares. Managers in Lufthansa's Frankfurt office routinely scan the data to make decisions regarding projected passenger and revenue yields on the thousands of daily departures, adjusting fares to make sure that optimum yields can be realized. Thus, the geographically distant offices need to perform their functions in a synchronous manner calling for management skills that transcend geographic, cultural, and technological boundaries. Thus, success turns on the ability of the managers to marshal virtual teams. *Virtual teams* are new entities that sprang up with the advance of offshore outsourcing. These teams encompass members who may or may not work for the same company, who may or may not belong to the same culture, who may or may not possess the same functional skills. Yet this geographically dispersed network has to be closely choreographed to ensure that organisational objectives are met. Apart from the usual demands originating in geographic and cultural diversity, a new set of challenges arises: these networks often involve members of third-party organisations such as specialized service providers. Leadership of virtual teams consequently demands a blend of skills ranging from persuasion and technological competence, to the ability to manage high levels of ambiguity and cross-cultural communication.

BEST PRACTICES IN LEVERAGING OFFSHORE LOCATIONS

Organisations that compete at the frontiers of globalization are quickly beginning to understand the need to access knowledge-based advantage across borders. What typically started out as routine back-office processing, as in the case of GE, has blossomed into a research and development center in India that develops most of GE's proprietary software systems, performs significant design functions in areas ranging from aerospace to medical imaging, and processes much of GE's routine accounting transactions. The experiences of Microsoft and Intel, among others, have been quite similar. Synthesizing some of these experiences into best practices offers insights into approaches to handle offshore knowledge-based functions.

Successful companies have shown that there is considerable value in thinking about outsourcing and offshoring along strategic lines rather than as tactical moves to match prevailing demands for increased efficiency and cost-effectiveness. American Express, for example, has been using offshore facilities in India for business process transactions for over a decade. This exposure evolved into operating call centers both in both near-shore and far-shore locations and using of a blend of independent service providers and wholly owned facilities to man age its critical software development projects. Much of the company's success has been predicated on careful strategic analysis of the value fundamentals of offshoring. This helps the firm guard against what could sometimes be a herd response to what others have done.

Analysis must supersede expediency. The analysis must encompass exhaustive cost versus benefits estimates that account for all real and imputed costs, such as the costs of coordination, travel, and use of expatriate managers over seas. Although most organisations factor in obvious costs such as wages and benefits, they often do not factor in the largely invisible costs of coordination. The benefits that can be expected, such as improved quality levels in output, cost savings, reduction in development cycle time, and so on, must also be appropriately captured. A thoughtful audit of skills and competencies required for successfully moving some business processes offshore is a key milestone. This audit includes detailed analyses of the strength of the local talent pool and productivity comparisons. The evaluation of intended strategy, along with a comprehensive analysis of costs and benefits, will help address issues relating to ownership structure and questions of wholly owned facilities versus using contracted services.

For offshoring to be successful, the quality of the overall package (i.e., error-free work, ironclad guarantees of privacy, etc.) has to be superior. Similar to the widely adopted standards in most manufacturing industries, global standards have emerged in knowledge operations as well. Clear articulation or objectives and expectations should shape the work undertaken by the offshore facility. This process involves setting realistic goals for the offshore facility and ensuring that the resources required for meeting those goals are readily available. There must be a strong commitment from senior management to the offshore strategy as a prerequisite for success. Often this commitment takes the form of in-person visits, cross-company meetings, and communiques from top management about the role of the offshore facility in the overall strategy of the organisation. The deployment of resources must be matched with a robust monitoring system of checks and balances to optimize the use of off-shore resources. It is a necessity to periodically examine the fundamental logic behind the offshore venture to make sure that the rationale fits new market realities that might have emerged. This should encompass the often difficult questions of cost of delivered services, especially for in-house operations compared to market prices. This disciplined comparison with market prices focuses the organisation on the value proposition of its offshore facilities.

Thus, the decision to decentralize functions with a large knowledge component is mostly based on country-specific considerations that leverage the unique location-specific characteristics to add superior value to the function. Much like the decentralization of manufacturing processes, the decentralization of knowledge-based processes is valuable only when the benefits outweigh the costs. Although there has been a remarkable trend toward greater levels of offshore activity in recent years, some analysts believe that the costs often outweigh the benefits. They cite the costs associated with rectifying error-prone processes and software products, the costs of travel to far-off locations to ensure smooth progress, and the significant adjustments to large time-zone differences—all take a toll on home operations and often lead to costs that exceed promised benefits. However, the trend to shift processes offshore is unlikely to abate anytime soon since lower costs and reasonable quality are powerful lures.

To be successful in leveraging offshore activities, firms are institutionalising the following best practices: i) Articulating a clear, defensible strategic rationale (both short and medium term) for engaging offshore facilities in moving knowledge-based functions and processes. ii) Providing a comprehensive assessment of costs and benefits that explicitly accounts for hidden transaction costs, such as the deployment of expatriate managers or the use of special coordination devices. These assessments also include a realistic estimation of the benefits in terms of cost savings, new knowledge acquisition, and enhanced output quality. iii) Choosing between wholly owned and contracted provider models on basis of strategic need rather than expediency and cost consideration. iv) Cultivating excellent partnering skills, cross-border management skills, and virtual teaming skills among employee cadres across all levels of the organisations that are likely to be come into contact with offshore operations. v) Setting clear and explicit goals and expectations for the offshore facilities while providing the resources needed to accomplish the assigned tasks. This calls for a comprehensive audit of skills and competencies and the creation of long-term staffing plans and career development paths. vi) Creating adequate monitoring systems that are not too onerous but at the same time rigorous enough to provide a snapshot of performance and progress on an ongoing basis. The system must offer enough flexibility for local management to demonstrate initiative within the broad contours of expectations articulated by the home office.

While offshoring has generated substantial controversy and anti-globalization activists excoriate companies for using offshore locations, the reality is that most industries and value-chain activities remain solidly non-global. As the global economy is reduced to an 'electronic village', the net result is that goods and services can be developed, bought, sold, and in many cases even delivered over electronic networks. Electronic commerce offers many advantages in terms of costs savings, efficiencies and market reach over traditional physical methods. Today's knowledge economy differs from the traditional economy in several key respects: (i) The economics is not of scarcity, but rather of abundance. Unlike most resources that deplete when used, information and knowledge can be shared, and actually grow through application; (ii) The effect of location is diminished. Using appropriate technology and methods, virtual marketplaces and virtual organizations can be created that offer benefits of speed and agility, of round the clock operation and of global reach; (iii) Laws, barriers and taxes are difficult to apply on solely a national basis. Knowledge and information 'leak' to where demand is highest and the barriers are lowest; (iv) Knowledge enhanced products or services can command price premiums over comparable products with low embedded knowledge or knowledge intensity; (v) Pricing and value depends heavily on context. Thus the same information or knowledge can have vastly different value to different people at different times; (vi) Knowledge when locked into systems or processes has higher inherent value than when it can 'walk out of the door' in people's heads; and (vii) Human capital - competencies - are a key component of value in a knowledge-based company, yet few companies report competency levels in annual reports. In contrast, downsizing is often seen as a positive 'cost cutting' measure.

These characteristics, so different from those of the physical economy, require new thinking and approaches by policy makers, senior executives and knowledge workers alike. To do so, though, requires leadership and risk taking, against the prevailing and slow changing attitudes and practices of existing institutions and business practice.

The evolving knowledge economy has important implications for policy makers of local, regional and national government as well as international agencies and institutions e.g.: Traditional measures of economic success must be supplemented by new ones. Economic Development policy should focus not on 'jobs created' but rather on infrastructure for sustainable 'knowledge enhancement' that acts as a magnet for knowledge-based companies; Develop regulation and taxation for information and knowledge trading at international level, looking to future knowledge-based industries rather than traditional industries; Stimulate market development through new forms of collaboration may be *on market development (rather than product development) and encourage participation by collaboration across national boundaries using electronic knowledge networking methods.* In the global knowledge economy, focusing many businesses are now realizing the role of knowledge and are creating knowledge management programmes and appointing CKOs (Chief Knowledge Officers). Such responses should be part of a coordinated effort that recognizes the importance of knowledge to their business bottom line. They are *developing* new measures of corporate performance based on knowledge and for this they are providing a technology infrastructure to enhance knowledge creation and sharing. They are also encouraging the sharing of knowledge through effective Internet setting and business practices. However, the main challenges facing policy makers and business leaders are: i) It is difficult to 'go it alone'. Stakeholders, especially employees and business partners must share similar views for your own initiatives to succeed; (ii) Alone recognition and reward systems usually do not sufficiently recognise recognizee contributions. They are linked to performance measures of the traditional economy; (iii) Measures of return on investment are done using traditional accounting methods, thus investments in knowledge enhancing activities need strong advocates at senior levels.

Few businesses have recognized the full scope of performance improvements that globalization makes possible. Globalization creates opportunities to enhance performance, and that firms can save enormous money by globalising their value chains. To do this, firms must use global assets effectively and efficiently, and they must understand the benefits and risks associated with building a global value chain. Moreover, firms that do not exploit these opportunities will be left behind.

QUESTIONS

1. Discuss the concept of knowledge transfer.
2. Critically examine the key costs and benefits of a wholly owned model and a contracted provider model.
3. Distinguish between tacit and explicit organisation knowledge. Discuss the transactional difficulties associated with exploiting organisational knowledge.
4. What are the main decision parameters in an offshore strategy?
5. Discuss to major advantages and disadvantages of near-shore *versus* far-shore location options.

REFERENCES

Andrew C. Inkpen, "Creating Knowledge through Collaboration," *California Management Review 39*, no. 1 (1996), pp. 123-140.

Christopher A. Bartlett and Sumantra Ghoshal, *Managing across Borders: The Transnational Solution* (Boston: Harvard Business School Press, 1989); and Bruce Kogut and Udo Zander, "Knowledge of the Firm, Combinative Capabilities, and the Replication of Technology," *Organisation Science 3* (1992): 383-397.

David J. Teece, "Strategies for Managing Knowledge Assets: The Role of Firm Structure and Industrial Context," *Long Range Planning 33* (2000): 35-54.

Diana Farrell, "Beyond Offering: Assess Your Company's Global Potential," *Harvard Business Review 82* (December 2004): 82-88.

Eric D. Darr and Eric R. Kurtzberg, "An Investigation of Partner Similarity Dimensions on Knowledge Transfer," *Organisational Behavior and Human Decision Processes 82* (2000) : 28-44.

Gunnar Hedlund and Ikujiro Nonaka, "Models of Knowledge Management in the West and Japan," in *Implementing Strategic Processes: Change, Learning, and Cooperation*, ed. Peter Lorange, Bala Chakravarthy, Johna Roos, and Andrew Van de Ven (Oxford: Blackwell, 1993), pp. 117-144.

Ikujiro Nonaka, Hirotaka Takeuchi and Hiro Takeuchi, *The Knowledge-Creating Company: How Japanese Companies Create the Dynamics of Innovation* (New York: Oxford University Press, 1995).

Joesph L. Badaracco, *The Knowledge Link* (Boston: Harvard Business School Press, 1991), p. 98.

Kazuhiro Asakawa and Mark Lehrer, "Managing Local Knowledge Assets Globally: The Role of Regional Innovation Relays," *Journal of World Business 38* (2003): 31-42.

Kevin Desouza and Roberto Evaristo, "Global Knowledge Management Strategies," *European Management Journal 2], no.* 1 (2003): 62-67.

Khozem Merchant, "GE Champions Indian's World Class Services," *Financial Times*, June 3, 2003, p. 11.

Linda Argote and Paul Ingram, "Knowledge Transfer: A Basis for Competi-tive Advantage in Firms," *Organisational Behavior and Human Decision Processes* 82 (2000): 150-169.

Paul A. Carlile, "Transferring, Translating, and Transforming: An Integrative Framework for Managing Knowledge across Boundaries," *Organisation Science* 15 (2004): 555-568.

Pete Engardio, Aaron Bernstein, and Manjeet Kripalani, "The New Global Job Shift," *Business Week*, February 3, 2003, pp. 50-58.

Peter J. Buckley and Martin J. Carter, "A Formal Analysis of Knowledge Combination in Multinational Enterprises," *Journal of International Business Studies 35* (2004): 371-384.

Phillip A. W. Kaser and Raymond E. Miles, "Understanding Knowledge Activists' Successes and Failures," *Long Range Planning 35* (2002): 9-28.

Sydney G. Winter, "Knowledge and Competence as Strategic Assets," in *The Competitive Challenge*, ed. David Teece (Cambridge, MA: Ballinger Publishing, 1987), pp. 159-184.

Thomas H. Davenport, David W. De Long, and Michael C. Beers, "Successful Knowledge Management Projects," *Sloan Management Review* 39; no. 2 (1998): 43-57.

Verna Allce, *The Knowledge Evolution: Expanding Organisational Intelligence* (Boston: Butterworth-Heinemann, 1997).

Yves L. Doz, Jose Santos, and Peter Williamson, *Global to Metanational: How Companies Win in the Knowledge Economy* (Cambridge, MA: Harvard Business School Press, 2001).

19

CROSS-CULTURAL MANAGEMENT

INTRODUCTION

The art of managing cultural interfaces has become an everyday business challenge at every organisational level. Myriad of cultures more than a rainbow of racial colours or an ethnic babble of languages, representing new challenge of globalisation, provide an opportunity to take a radically different approach : one that embraces diversity in ways that allow business to grow and profit from the many dramatically difficult cultural qualities that characterise most of communities and organisations. Diversity - as a world, as nations, region, communities, as professions and businesses — can be turned to advantage. And, in the 21st century, the ability to communicate and collaborate among racial, national, corporate and functional "tribes" will provide an essential competitive code.

WHAT IS A CULTURE?

By culture we mean the whole set of social norms and responses that condition a population's behaviour. It is these that make one social environment different from another and give each a shape of its own. The basic discipline that is most relevant here is cultural anthropology. Cultural anthropologists have devoted a great deal of time and effort to definitions of culture, arguing what should or should not be included.

Culture is acquired and inculcated. It is the set of rules and behaviour patterns that an individual learns but does not inherit at birth. For every society these norms and behavioural responses develop into a different cultural pattern that gets passed down through the generations with continual embellishment and adaptation; but with its own focus on aspects that are most highly developed.

For much cultural conditioning, the individual is unaware of the learning. The subtle process of inculcating culture through example and reward or punishment is generally much more powerful than direct instruction, and the individual unwittingly adopts the cultural norm. This process of learning a cultural pattern, called *enculturation*, conditions individuals so that a large proportion of their behaviour fits the requirements of their culture and yet is determined below the level of conscious thought.

CULTURE AND COMMUNICATION

A language is inextricably linked with all aspects of a culture, and each culture reflects in its language what is of value to the people. Culture is largely inculcated through languages - spoken or written. Language, then, becomes the embodiment of culture. It may even condition what we look for and therefore see whereas communication involves translation from one language into another, the problems of ascertaining meaning that arise within one culture are multiplied many times. But translation is not simply a matching of words with identical meanings. It involves interpretation of the cultural patterns and concepts of one country in terms of the patterns and concepts of another.

Communication does not always take the form of language. All behaviour communicates and each culture may differ in the way it experiences and uses time, space, relationships, and a variety of other aspects of culture. The use of time may convey quite different meanings in different cultures. To be 30 minutes late for an appointment with a business associate may be the height of rudeness in culture A but in culture B it may be early and unexpectedly reliable. Different messages may be conveyed by the amount of notice given for a meeting, the time of departure, invitations to future commitments, or the way in which a party agrees to the order of discussion at the meeting.

Operating difficulties can arise when workers from an agrarian peasant society are required to accept the kind of scheduling of time and routine essential for efficient industrial operations. In most agrarian societies, work is not equated with time and is not regularly and precisely scheduled. Instead, work is geared to seasonal emergencies, climatic time schedules or deadlines will evoke a positive response in certain cultures and a negative response in others.

In a similar way, the use of space conveys different meanings. The distance one person stands away from another indicates the degree of relationship or interest and can dramatically influence what is said. Different cultures have different norms for the appropriate distance for a given type of interaction. Middle Easterners and Latin Americans, for example, stand much closer than Western Europeans. The size of an office in relation to other offices conveys a great deal about the status of an American executived. In the Arab world, the size and location of an office are poor indicators of the importance of the person who occupies it.

ADJUSTING TO CULTURAL DIFFERENCES

The international firm has a special need for cultural sensitivity and adjustment. It has an existence outside each local culture in which it operates and many of its actions, such as cross-national transfers of old products or standard company practices, may represent a local innovation. And in many cases, the international firm may encounter unexpected problems because it is an unwitting agent for transplanting aspects of one culture into another.

The experienced international enterprise will try to accept the values of local culture patterns and seek to work within the accepted behaviour patterns and customary goals that underlie these beliefs, in preference to substituting those of another culture pattern. As a general rule, national sensitivities tolerate less deviation from local standards by foreign firms than by native companies.

Three important general classes of business adaptation are product individual and institutional. The degree of necessary adjustment ranges from none or token to comprehensive. Adaptation is defined as the achievement of business goals with a minimum of problems and setbacks due to the various manifestations on cultural conflict.

Adjustment of the multinational enterprise is needed at two levels — the national and the multinational. The issues at the national level might be characterised as bicultural. The situation is largely of a "we and they" type. The manager of a subsidiary must be aware of possible conflicts between local conditions and the cultural assumptions underlying the business practices being imported. Essentially these problems are two sided, and management personnel of subsidiaries must be the bridge between the local situation and the international enterprise.

At the multinational level, or more specifically at global or regional headquarters, the international enterprise must coordinate and integrate business activities that are operating in many different cultural environments. Managers must deal with many languages and across many cultures. The problems are both horizontal — across many cultures — and vertical — between each subsidiary and headquarters. And the organisational structure and policies of the global enterprise must facilitate communications and the implementation of policies across many cultures in order to achieve global goals.

METHODOLOGY FOR CULTURAL ASSESSMENT

The impact of cultural differences on international business makes quite clear the need for skills in cultural assessment on the part of the international manager. The manager may never become an expert cultural anthropologist in addition to being a management specialist, but should at least develop skills in assessing the key cultural elements that will have a direct bearing on effectiveness as a manager.

There is no one method to adopt in making cultural assessment as a basis for specific business decisions. Business problems cover such a wide range that the methods used may extend from a narrow depth study of respectivity to a new management practice, though to broad assessment of a society's attitudes to spending.

Approaches for Assessing Cultural Differences

The most common approach to cultural assessment is a partial approach confined to studying particular aspects of a culture. Partial approaches are less powerful than comprehensive approaches that endeavour to identify and classify an entire range of cultural differences. The immense number of elements that can vary between cultures, however, makes overall approaches extremely unwieldy and costly to use. A compromise, often used by social anthropologists, is to compose a word picture of some constrained slice of behaviour in the culture being examined, emphasising, as would an artist, the more significant elements in the subject. Examples of such word pictures would be a description of a day in the life of a typical consumer, or the motivation and thinking leading an employee to instigate a major confrontation with another worker.

In examining cultural patterns, the manager should be aware of similarities as well as differences. Cross-cultural analysis for international business tends to emphasise differences because they are likely to create business problems. But to err perceiving more differences than actually exist can also cause serious difficulties. Further, the observed cultural patterns may be representative of a national group yet not applicable to everyone in the group. What is usually being discussed is a modal pattern, and considerable variation from the mode will exist within a group or a subset of the group. In fact, for some cultural characteristics there may be a wider range within a given society than between societies. The manager should be careful always to define the limits of the group that is of interest and still be prepared to allow for individual differences.

Approaches for Assessing Culture Change

A cultural assessment may be either static or dynamic. A static assessment serves only to identify the differences in variables between cultures. A dynamic assessment seeks to indicate which variables will change and perhaps in what order and with what speed. For the international manager, the identification of what changes will be readily accepted and what will be rejected can mean the differences between success and failure.

Two approaches may be helpful in mapping culture changes as a basis for business decisions. The first is a mapping of the way any change is expected to diffuse through the culture. The second is a mapping of the decision-making and influence process for the key individuals to be affected by the change at each stage. Such mappings make quite explicit the assumptions that are held about the change process and frequently provide a necessary framework against which to specify actual research questions. Without some mapping of these two processes, any quantification on which to base a decision to introduce the change should hardly be soundly based.

Avoiding Cultural Bias

In all cases requiring cross-cultural assessment the problem of cultural bias will be present. Everyone tends unwittingly to bias their view of other cultures by unconscious acceptance of their own cultural conditioning. It takes a great deal of discipline to force the mind to see things that one's own culture ignores or places in low value.

Cultural bias can be reduced through the development of culturally sensitive management. Specific attempts to eliminate what is called the "self-reference criterion" (SRC), however, can be built into cultural analysis of overseas operations. The problems are first defined in terms of the cultural traits, habits, or norms of the home society, and then redefined, without value judgements, in terms of the foreign cultural traits, habits and norms. The difference between these two specifications indicates the likely cultural bias, or SRC effect, which can then be isolated and carefully examined to see how it influences the concept of the problem. Following this examination, the problem is redefined with the bias removed. Such an approach can be used for a wide variety of business problems. Its value lies in forcing managers posing the problem to make very specific the assumptions held about the cultural elements affecting the problem and to question whether they hold for another culture.

PARTIAL CULTURAL ASSESSMENT : SOME KEY ASPECTS

Some key cultural aspects, fundamental to the way in which business is managed and yet vary greatly among cultures, are :

Attitudes Toward Work and Achievement

The dominant view in a society toward wealth and material gain can have significant bearing on the types, qualities and numbers of individuals who pursue enterpreneurial and management careers as well as on the way workers respond to material incentives. In most countries, wealth tends to be considered desirable and the prospect of material gain operates as a significant motivation. But there are societies where a workers will be on the job until he earns a certain amount of money and then be absent until these earnings are exhausted.

Variations among cultures in the dominant views toward achievement and work, which can be a vital determinant of management performance and productive efficiency have been the subject of considerable research under the rubric of "achievement motivation". The achievement motivation of an individual refers to a basic attitude toward life, namely, the willingness of an individual refers to a basic attitude toward life, namely, the willingness to commit oneself to the accomplishment of tasks considered by the person to be worthwhile and difficult. An achievement-motivated person makes accomplishment an end in itself. Tangible rewards are not rejected but they are not essential.

Measures of achievement motivation have been devised, and desires for achievement within different countries compared. Also, experiments have been undertaken in various countries on the effectiveness of techniques in changing achievement motivations. Achievement motivation is the prime factor in managerial success.

Attitudes Toward the Future

Some of the principal differences among cultures lie in assumptions and attitudes relating to man's ability to influence the future. For example, an assumption that people can substantially influence the future underlies much of management philosophy. Long-range planning becomes a worthwhile investment because of confidence that planning can influence what is to happen. In cultures where other attitudes prevail, management practices based on such assumptions are not likely to be effective. On the other hand, care must be taken not to overgeneralise. Despite a general view that Moslem cultures are fatalistic, it is found Arab executives most amenable to planning, quoting a saying in the Moslem Hadith that admonishes man first to think and plan ahead then put his trust in God. Some Moslem peasant groups may indeed be fatalistic, but this is probably not an irrational attitude on their part. For peasants operating at base subsistence level it may be a just estimation of the enormous and discouraging weight of the chancy factors that condition the success of their efforts.

Whatever the explanation for varying attitudes, the critical issue for business operations is whether individuals believe that events will occur regardless of what they do and whether they can help shape future outcomes significantly. The self-determination or 'master of destiny' attitude is generally qualified by the accompanying view that future aspirations must be realistic and that hard work is necessary to achieve future goals.

Patterns of Decision Making

Reliance on objective analysis in decision making varies greatly among cultures. In U.S. business, decisions are supposed to be based on objective analysis of facts, and all persons who can contribute relevant information are expected to do so. Such a norm leads to large collections of data and the development of impersonal decision-making techniques.

In other societies, the personal judgement of a senior executive may be the accepted basis for a decision. A request that the executive can explain or give the rationale for his decision would be interpreted as a lack of confidence in the executive's judgement. Furthermore, it may be considered inappropriate for a senior executive to seek facts and consult others — especially juniors — on matters on which the senior is already presumed to be wise. In such cultures, hierarchical, emotional, and mystical considerations, rather than objective analyses, may dominate.

Attitudes Toward Authority

The dominant view of authority in a society may range from an autocratic system at one extreme to a democratic-participative system at the other extreme. In autocratic systems, managerial decisions would typically be highly centralised with little delegation of authority. At the other extreme, managerial authority would be shared with subordinated and workers and considerable decentralisation in decision making would be typical of business enterprises.

It is not possible to say which forms of managerial authority along the continuum are best in terms of efficiency or in achieving other business goals. The forms vary greatly from country to country. Whatever authority system prevails in a given country, the international enterprise will have to relate its management patterns to the expectations and traditions of local employees.

Authority systems are also highly relevant to marketing. It is important to know whether purchasing decisions within buying units are typically decentralised or reserved for the top-echelon executives. In negotiating with governments, the international manager will have to know whether decision authority resides with low-level bureaucrats or must be handled at the highest level of government bureaucracy.

Expression of Disagreement

Differences among societies in frankness of expression and tolerance for personal differences affect interpersonal relations. In Far Eastern cultures it is traditional to value politeness over blunt truth. The Japanese business executive finds it inappropriate to say no in many situations. In dealing with an American, the Japanese may make all kinds of barely favourable noises and them may be say, "I'll think about the matter". The Japanese has actually told the American no, but it is entirely possible that the American thinks that the answer was yes, and later imagines that the Japanese was being deceptive.

In many Latin American countries, frankly expressed differences in view do not easily fit the culture. If a person expresses criticisms of a policy in order to improve the quality of decision making, such statements are likely to be interpreted as personal attacks. If a subordinate disagrees with the boss, the boss will most certainly feel insulted. Persons in subordinate positions are expected either to present information or judgements that support the ideas of senior officials or be silent.

Responsibility to Family

In some countries, businessmen operate as individuals independent of family. In others, some version of the extended family prevails. Under this pattern large numbers of near as well as quite distant relatives are encompassed in a system of shared rights and obligations. All members of this group are interdependent, and it is the responsibility of the leaders to see that the economic resources are available to satisfy the needs of each member of the group. Among Arab executive, the use of personal (family and friendship) ties and connections is not only widespread, but is also an important and necessary means of doing business. This approach is in direct contrast with the reliance upon official, institutional, or formal business channels for conducting business affairs. In the Arab world the use of such personal ties and connections is evident in a wide range of activities. Typical examples that were provided by the executives include : (a) expediting and getting a work-permit, a passport or a visa, and generally bypassing or expediting most governmental formalities and paperwork; (b) obtaining referrals or employment and (c) knowing about, negotiating and eventually securing a multi-million dollar business contract. For the Arab executive, there is a powerful incentive to use personal (family and friendship) ties instead of institutional or formal channels in getting things done. This is particularly due to the inefficiency and sometimes the absence of institutional systems and procedures; and partly due to the importance of family and friendship ties which are usually more powerful than institutional rules and procedures.

Strong and extended family ties can result in what has been characterised as patrimonial management. Ownership and key positions in a business enterprise are held by family members. Nepotism is generally dominant in the full range of employment decisions, and business goals are oriented toward family interests and aspirations. Such patrimonial management has the advantage of encouraging teamwork, loyalty and mutual interest. Family codes can enforce morality in financial and other matters, and family loyalty attracts and holds managers in situations where the supply of qualified managers is limited.

The extended family situation also has drawbacks. It emphasises nepotism rather than competence. It can vitiate the will to work by limiting personal incentives. Family business may be run like an authoritarian household with little concern for considerations other than family goals. And family enterprises may suffer from a lack of invigorating ideas and innovations that can come from outsiders. Even where the family is not dominant within an organisation, top executives in countries in which extended family is important may expect and be expected to behave as head of a family.

Family patterns can be extremely important from the standpoint of marketing as well as general management. In Western societies, the husband and wife typically share decision making on family purchases, with children and other members of the family having a secondary vote. In the extended family, the family patriarch holds the key decision-making position, although this is declining with the monetization of the economy, the demise of family enterprises, and an increase in geographic and social mobility.

Social Structure

A final category of cultural elements can be grouped under the general heading of social structure. It includes such variables as interclass mobility, determinants of status, and patterns of education. Few societies in the world assume that all men are equal. Instead, societies have traditional systems of ranking individuals and groups. Relative positions in the social hierarchy are based on ethnic, cultural, educational and linguistic differences, as well as on economic position. Sometimes traditional and social structures are fairly rigid, such as the caste system of India. Sometimes the distinctions are more fluid and considerable interclass mobility is the rule. In most countries of the world, there is a distinction between the elite, who have political and economic control of the country, and the relatively underprivileged peasant groups.

Two aspects of social structure are a special concern to the international enterprise - interclass mobility and the status assigned by a society to individuals who engage in business occupations. If a rigid social structure prevents a substantial number of individuals from moving into the ranks of management or other responsible business positions, managerial effectiveness is likely to be constrained in many, if not most, business activities. If the status assigned to business pursuits is low in the social structure, it will be difficult to attract adequate numbers of competent persons to business positions.

COMPREHENSIVE CULTURAL ASSESSMENT

The international manager may have neither the time nor the need to build a comprehensive picture of a particular culture. Yet familiarity with ways to conceptualise the overall culture can provide the manager with a checklist of elements that are important for particular business problems but likely to be overlooked. Two such approaches, both two-dimensional will be briefly outlined here.

Edward Hall presents his map of culture as a two-dimensional matrix composed of 10 aspects of human activity, which he calls Primary Message Systems. These are shown in Figure-1.

FIGURE-1

PRIMARY MESSAGE SYSTEMS OF EDWARD HALL'S THE SILENT LANGUAGE

Primary message system	*Depicts attitudes and cultural rules for:*
1. Interaction	The ordering of man's interaction with those around him, through language, touch, noise, gesture and so forth.
2. Association	The organisation (grouping) and structuring of society and its components.
3. Subsistence	The ordering of man's activities in feeding, working and making a living.
4. Bisexuality	The differentiation of roles, activities, and function along sex lines.
5. Territoriality	The possession, use and defense of space and territory.

6. Temporality	The use, allocation and division of time.
7. Learning	The adaptive process of learning and instruction.
8. Play	Relaxation, humour, recreation and enjoyment.
9. Defense	Protection against man's environment including medicine, warfare and law.
10. Exploitation	Turning the environment to man's use through technology, construction and extraction of materials.

Source: Adapted from Edward T. Hall, The Silent Language (Garden city, N.Y. : Doubleday, 1959), pp. 61-81.

While each aspect can be examined alone, Hall shows how a grasp of the complex interrelationships of a culture can be obtained by commencing with any of the 10 aspects and studying its intersection with each of the others. In a matrix there will be two intersections of each pair of aspects.

For a direct application of Hall's matrix to international business, take the example of a large manufacturer of toys and games assessing opportunities in a new country. The firm will be directly engaged in the play aspect of the new culture, and it is certain that the cultural patterns with respect to play will differ from those the firm is currently dealing with. Use of Hall's matrix would raise 18 categories of questions about play patterns in the new culture (see Figure-2). Stemming from the interaction of play with the remaining primary message systems, the first two categories would ask about interaction of play and about play in interaction, the second two would ask about the associations — that is, organisations involved in play and games involving associations, and so on. It must be clear from the questions raised within 18 categories that the map does not magically produce the right answers or even the right questions. This is simply one structured approach to investigating how a new culture may differ.

FIGURE-2

A BUSINESS APPLICATION OF EDWARD HALL'S MAP OF CULTURE

Intersections of play and other primary message systems	*Sample questions concerning cultural patterns significant for marketing toys and games*
1. Interaction/play	How do people interact during play as regards competitiveness instigation or leadership?
2. Play/interaction	What games are played involving acting, role playing or other aspects of real-world interaction ?
3. Association/play	Who organises play and how do the organisation patterns differ ?
4. Play/association	What games are played about organisation; for example, team competitions and games involving kings, judges or leader-development rules and penalties ?
5. Subsistence/play	What are the significant factors regarding people such as distributors teachers, coaches, or publishers who make their livelihood from games ?
6. Play/subsistence	What games are played about work roles in society such as doctors, nurses, firemen ?
7. Bisexuality/play	What are the significant differences between the sexes in the sports, games and toys enjoyed ?

8.	Play/bisexuality	What games and toys involve bisexuality; for example, dolls, dressing up, dancing ?
9.	Territoriality/play	Where are games played and what are the limits observed in houses, parks streets, schools, and so forth ?
10.	Play/territoriality	What games are played about space and ownership; for example Monopoly ?
11.	Temporality/play	At what ages and what times of the day and year are different games played?
12.	Play/temporality	What games are played about and involving time; for example, clocks, speed tests ?
13.	Learning/play	What patterns of coaching, tuition and training exist for learning games?
14.	Play/learning	What games are played about and involving learning and knowledge; for example, quizzes ?
15.	Defense/play	What are the safety rules for games, equipment and toys ?
16.	Play/defense	What war and defense games and toys are utilised ?
17.	Exploitation/play	What resources and technology are permitted or utilised for games and sports; for example, hunting and fishing rules, use of parks, cameras vehicles, and so forth ?
18.	Play/exploitation	What games and toys, about technology or exploitation are used; for example scouting, chemical sets, microscopes ?

UNDERSTANDING CULTURE CHANGE

Acceptance and Resistance to Change

A characteristic of human culture is that change does occur, although it may not be rapid or without resistance. The manager operating cross-culturally therefore needs an understanding of what aspects of a culture will resist and how those will differ among cultures, how the process of change takes place in different cultures, and what the speed of change will be.

There are two seemingly contradictory forces within cultures. On the one hand, people attempt to protect and preserve their culture with an elaborate set of sanctions and laws invoked against those who deviate from their norms. On the other hand, the environment within which a culture exists is continually changing and a culture must change in order to ensure its own continuity. Where a culture comes into contact with other cultures, this same dichotomy exists. There is, on the one hand, an ingrained belief, called *ethnocentrism,* that the ways of one's own culture are superior to those of other cultures, and on the other hand, a realisation that a culture must be competitive if it is to retain its own identify.

These conflicting forces make some elements of culture highly resistant to change. Others immediately fall to innovations, even though some of them may give an impression that they are immutable. *How can these elements be differentiated?*

Edward Hall classifies cultural aspects into formal, informal and technical, based primarily on differences in the way the cultural norm is learned, the culture's level of awareness of the norm and the response to a deviation from the norm.

Formal rules are at the core of the culture and really determine its essence. They are taught through example and admonition as rules for which there is either right or wrong, with clear indication of when a mistake has been made. There is a formal awareness of the norm and a great deal of emotion if the norm is violated. Most societies, for example, have a formal rule that there should be no enjoyment from hurting others physically or from seeing them hurt. The rule is made clear from early childhood and penalties are imposed for breaking it.

Informal rules are not taught so directly. Usually the learner picks them up by imitation and is unaware of learning them. The society is generally unconscious of the rules, and if one is violated, there would be only an expression of anxiety or some informally learned reaction. The average child does not receive direct instruction in how to play but is left to observe others and to do likewise. If the child attempts to dominate playmates, for example, the playmates will very likely develop ways of excluding the child. Thus, by experience rather than direct instruction, the child learns how to behave in groups.

Technical rules are usually taught by instruction in a logical and coherent manner. These are at the highest level of awareness as they are verbalised, reasoned, and explicit. Few emotions are attached to the violation of a technical rule. Breaking a rule by adopting a different training approach for an athletic sport, for example, would occasion intellectual interest but little emotion.

The aspects falling into each category differ from culture to culture. If we continue with a sporting example, for instance, we might find that the English regard acceptance of the referee's rulings as a fundamental principle of sportsmanship — a formal rule that would produce an emotional response from most of the population if they were confronted with a direct violation. On the other hand, the Germans may have a clear set of technical rules for when and how to object to rulings, while Americans adopt an informal approach that objections should be made as and when justified. Any aspect of culture could be compared between cultures in this way.

Attitudes toward change clearly differ for each of the three classes. Formal rules would be held with great tenacity, change very slowly, and be particularly resistant to any attempt to force change from outside. Informal rules can change more easily. There is room for more deviation by individuals and imitation can be selective in one direction or another. Change comes most easily with technical rules, because they are readily observed, talked about, transmitted, and accepted at a more or less rational level. The key to culture change seems to lie in the informal system. In a complex and changing environment, imitation of others will not be perfect. When some of the variants that emerge seem to work better than others, they are copied and eventually develop as technical rules.

Technical changes are most likely to deal with details of an activity — for example, the introduction of a new type of a motor. But a series of changes in technical rules, initially consonant with the existing formal systems can cause more fundamental changes in the formal and informal systems. Technical and informal rules seem to surround each part of the formal system, and when these supports are removed, formal rules may eventually give way. This may explain why some parts of a culture reject change persistently only to collapse later on. Hall illustrates this sort of phenomena with the change in attitude toward premarital chastity in the United States. Changes in women's social life, education, career patterns, and dress habits, and the widespread use of the private car removed many technical supports to the formal rule. After resisting change for many years, the rule eventually changed very rapidly.

Not all the new elements that evolve from within a culture, or are introduced from outside, are adopted by the culture. They have to fall on fertile ground in the sense that there is perception of the need for the change and a broad acceptance of it. The social structure of the society and those who introduce the change or are aware of it will thus be important factors in its acceptance. Cultures also tend to develop a particular interest in some parts of their system — called a *cultural focus*. A culture is more likely to develop and adopt changes in those areas on which it places this emphasis. Conversely, less important areas will change less and there will be lower tolerance for change in them. The Arabs, for example, have regarded the "fellahin" engaged in agriculture as of very low status and have adopted few agricultural innovations in comparison with Israelis who accord agriculture high status and reward successful agricultural innovation with almost national fame.

Social Dynamics of Culture Change

It is as important for the international manager to identify the roles different people will play in the change process as it is to identify what cultural aspects will resist change. Cultural change implies change in the pattern of behaviour of the individuals adhering to that culture. The other in which persons with different characteristics adopt an innovation and the influences that affect their decision are thus of particular importance. The field of diffusion studies has a great deal to say about these.

Adopters of any innovation are conventionally classified into five groups, according to the order in which they adopt the innovation, as follows :

Adopter category	
Innovators	First 2.5%
Early adopters	Next 13.5%
Early majority	Next 34%
Late majority	Next 34%
Laggards	Remaining 16%

The idea behind this classification is that common characteristics may be identified for the adopters of each stage.

"Innovators" are regarded by themselves and by others as deviants from the norms of their culture or subculture. They tend to have a characteristic venturesomeness and to have seem more of other cultures than later adopters. One study of firms commencing export activity showed almost all the innovators to have international background. "Early innovators" tend to have a higher position in the social hierarchy than innovators and to rate high as opinion leaders. They may have a considerable influence on later adopters. The "early majority" seems to be characterised by their capacity for deliberation. They do not adopt until other respected persons have done so, seldom emerging as leaders. Contrasted with this, the dominant value of the people who make up the "late majority" is skepticism. They tend to wait until the weight of public opinion strongly favours the innovation before they proceed. "Laggards" tend to be older, to be suspicious of innovations, and to take the past and tradition as their point of reference.

Associated with the study of diffusion, and particularly relevent for cultural change, is the concept of an adoption process. This is conceived as a set of five mental stages through which an individual passes from first hearing about an innovation until he finally adopts it. These are (1) awareness, (2) interest, (3) evaluation, (4) trial and (5) adoption. Studies of each of these stages and the information and influence sources important at each stage have provided some significant generalisations about adoptions. It has been found that impersonal sources of information tend to be most influential at the awareness stage, and personal sources tend to be most influential at the evaluation stage. Commercial change agents, that is, advertising and selling, seem to be more important at the trial stage than at any other stage. In the earlier stages of the process nonlocal sources of information tend to be most important. But in the later stages local sources take the command position. These findings may be very significant for firms planning the introduction of products into new cultural environments.

Social-class identification by groups within a culture can also affect the diffusion of an innovation. A social class, however defined, is likely to exhibit some common variants of the overall national culture, particularly if its members are grouped in the same living environment. One landmark study suggests that the cultural norms of a social class at the particular time were a significant factor in the acceptance or rejection of a particular innovation. The pattern of interaction and influence that leads to adoption or rejection may also be largely carried on within one social class. Changes may thus not trickle down the social scale with each class striving to copy classes above it. The international businessman must be prepared, therefore, to observe what happens within social groups as well as across a society as a whole.

PROMOTING CULTURE CHANGE

In many situations, management will not passively adapt to the ever-changing patterns of cultural differences within which it operates but will endeavour to induce change in some aspect of a local culture. The most common targets for active attempts to induce change in this way are consumer buying patterns and employee work patterns. In most cases the attempt will be based on actual observation of the success of a culture change in another situation and will not stem merely from a management desire to "move ahead". Culture transplants are more likely to be successful when an actual example of a similar culture change already exists.

The international enterprise may promote change, but it is the members of the foreign culture who have to accept change. The general strategy, therefore, must be to discover the ways and incentives characteristic of the culture that are likely to result in acceptance. The comparative business literature is replete with examples of unsuccessful attempts to induce cultural change. Yet the success stories are numerous also, and they provide considerable encouragement for the likely success of well designed and well-informed efforts to promote cultural change. Some of the elements that should be considered in deciding how the attempt to promote change to be carried out are :

Building on the Old

Unless they produce dramatic benefits, the easiest way to have innovations accepted is to make sure they present no open conflict with traditional values and customs and to graft into them. Medicine is one field in which problems have often occurred. In societies that have continued to rely on folk-medical practices, it has frequently been effective to relate new Western medical products to irrational traditional beliefs. Use of existing power and influence structures is also recommended. For instance, strategies that involve using existing power or influence structures such as midwives to disseminate birth-control pills or faith healers to distribute condoms do not cause a loss of pride or dignity among these often highly regarded individuals. To the contrary, their status, which is a source of their pride, is reinforced and enhanced.

Identifying the Rational

The straightforward approach of presenting information and rational argument assumes that individuals are guided by reason. Such a strategy, called a reeducative strategy is the most neutral of all strategies, and can be effective in many situations. Firms providing training and technical help to customers as part of their sales approach are adopting this sort of strategy. Nevertheless, education is a slow process, and what is rational to the protagonist of the change might not be what the change target believes is rational. Rationally, after all, does not exist independently of the objectives that are adopted. An individual's actions to protect an established status position against change may be very rational.

Avoiding the Unknown

When the full nature of a change and its outcome are unknown, uncertainty and anxiety abound for those who perceive they may be affected. Resistance to the change then builds up as a protection against the unknown. The promoter of change should thus take great care to specify exactly what the change is and how it will work. Even prior to this stage, the development of awareness of the need for change may be desirable. Conceivably, an innovation may be brought about simply through providing the necessary tools with which to recognise the problem.

Recognising the Influence of Others

The attitudes of individuals toward change are influenced by those around them. Individuals may change because of a desire for recognition by others, prestige, or to emulate others with more status than themselves. If an individual is asked to change behaviour in a way that will not be supported by others of significance to that individual, then the change is unlikely to come about. The introduction of a change may have more chance of success, therefore, if its promoter works through opinion leaders who will influence each others.

Providing Support

Anything new is likely to require further changes in using it. A change should not be introduced and dropped. It should be supported until it is thoroughly operational. Examples abound of modern equipment lying abandoned in the fields, factories, homes and offices because of lack of instruction on use or maintenance.

Compensating the losers. It is often argued that when a net gain results through change, nobody loses. In more cases than not, however, there will be net costs to some party affected. Measures to protect those affected adversely, from economic loss or from decreases in personal status and dignity, can go a great way toward smoothing the adoption of innovations. Firms within single nations have developed policies of compensating workers for adopting changes in technology. So, too, in multinational corporations will there is be increased demands to compensate employees hurt economically by innovations, even though the same innovations have already been adopted in other parts of the multinational organisation.

INTERNATIONAL BUSINESS AS A CHANGE AGENT

A final topic related to the cultural components of the international business environment is the role of international business as a change agent. Here we are referring to the cultural fallout as well as the deliberately promoted cultural changes. The concept of international business as a change agent usually has a favourable connotation in business circles and refers to such benefits as the transfer of technology and management skills, the training of workers, and the social and economic modernisation effects in the host country. All of these features of international business are generally assumed to be positive and desirable contributions to the countries in which international business activity takes place. But as the social scientists have observed, cultural change can have both positive and negative aspects for the members of a given society.

Some cultural changes for which international enterprises can claim credit are consistent with the goals of national leaders who are enxious to modernise and industrialise their society. The nature or the pace of other changes can provoke negative reactions to the international enterprise by government leaders or groups in the society. Because it is an agent of change, whether or not the change is intentional, the international enterprise should attempt to anticipate the changes for which it might be held responsible and the full chain of results from changes it is promoting. Such anticipation requires the international executive to construct a model or description of the changing society.

QUESTIONS

1. Describe the primary characteristics of culture.
2. Explain Hofstede's primary findings about differences in cultural values.
3. Describe the major cultural clusters and their use to international business people.
4. Discuss the various element of culture and provide examples of how they influence international business.
5. Critically examine the behavioral factors influencing countries' business practices.
6. What strategies can a company follow to get host cultures to accept the innovations it would like to introduce? How can it avoid misrepresenting its intent?
7. Almost all opportunities associated with global business are emerging very rapidly. Those who are 'selling' the change, or those who discover its advantages, may be inclined to focus on the positive aspects of potential change rather than explore the negatives as well. What examples of this are evident to you? Analyze the problems you see with adopting these perspective without questioning them.
8. Global business culture is emerging because the cultural mechanisms within nation-states are not able to address and manage the problems societies face in a globally interdependent world. What national cultural mechanisms have failed? What are the problems societies face in a globally interdependent world? How and why are businesses involved in solving these problems?
9. Describe an organization's structure, processes, and people practices that show the organization is consistent with the culture of the nation where it is located or globally. What are the additional problems and opportunities of cultural globalisation?
10. Discuss how religious and other values affect the domestic environments in which international businesses operate.

REFERENCES

Bhalla, V.K., "International Economy : Liberalisation Process", Anmol Publications Pvt. Ltd., 1993.

Bhatt, M.C. and K.L. Dalal, "Indian enterprises abroad: A study", Indian Council for Research on International Economic Relations, 1989, 80 p.

Grilli, E. and J. Riedel, "The East Asian Growth Model : How General Is It ? 1993. Paper prepared for conference on "Sustaining the Development Process", Canberra : Australian National University.

Hall, Edward T.: *The Silent Language* , Doubleday, Garden City, New York : 1959

Harbison, F. and Charles A. Myers :*Management in Industrial World* McGraw-Hill, New York, 1959

Katz,Daniel and Robert I. Khan: *The Social Psychology of Organisations*, John Wiley & Sons, New York, 1962

Kumar, Nagesh, "Intangible assets, internationalization and foreign production: Direct investments and licensing in Indian manufacturing", Weltwirtschaftliches archiv. 123 : 325-345, 1987.

Lall, Rajiv B., "Multinationals from the third world : Indian firms investing abroad", Delhi, Oxford University Press, 1987, 122 p.

Lall, Sanjaya, "India" in John H. Dunning (ed.) Multinational enterprises, economic structure and international competitiveness, Chichester, John Wiley and Sons, 1986, pp. 309-335.

Lall, Sanjaya, "The new multinationals : the spread of Third World enterprises", Chichester, John Wiley and Sons, 1983, 268 p.

Lewis, Oscar: Five Families: Mexican case study in the culture of poverty Basic Books ,New York ,1959

Martinussen, John., "Transnational corporations in a developing country : The Indian Experience", New Delhi, Sage Publications, 1988, 228 p.

Muna A. Farid: *The Arab Executive*, Macmiillan Press Ltd., 1980

Nair, Ronald Arun, "The role of India's foreign investment laws in controlling activities of multinational corporations", Syracuse Journal of International and Commerce, 14, 519-553, Spring 1988.

Negandhi, Anant R., "Indian foreign investment policies" in W. Teng and N.T. Wang (eds.) Transnational corporations and China's open door policy, Lexington, Lexington Books, 1988, 352 p.

Oman, Charles (ed.), "New Forms of overseas investment by developing countries : the case of India, Korea, and Brazil", Paris, OECD, 1986, 183 p.

Porter, M.E., 1985, "Competitive Advantage", New York: McMillan Press.

___________, 1989, "The Competitive Advantage of Nations", New York, The Free Press.

United Nations, ESCAP/UNTEC Joint Unit on Transnational Corporations from developing Asian economies : host country perspective. (ST/ESCAP/605), UNCTC Publication, Series B, No. 12, Bangkok, 1988, 581 p.

20

CORPORATE GOVERNANCE

INTRODUCTION

Corporate governance refers to the top management process that manages and mediates value creation for, and value transference among, various corporate claimants (including society at large), in a context that simultaneously ensures accountability towards these claimants. Corporate governance practices and regulations significantly impact the structure of societies. Corporate governance has implications for many aspects of corporate practice and the general business environment, including: the roles and responsibilities boards and top management; board committee structure and makeup (audit, compensation, etc.); management compensation and rewards; the market for corporate control; the relations among firms, shareholders, and creditors; employee and union relationship with firms; the behaviour of the firm under financial distress; types of corporate financing and payouts; and social responsibility etc.

THE NATURE OF CORPORATE GOVERNANCE

In recent years corporate governance has taken on new importance. Every firm must by governed in a manner that takes into account the interests of various stakeholders and ensures that the firm remain a profitable, going concern. Successful governance practices are a mix of those required by law and those chosen by the firm's board and management, who act as the agents of the shareholders. The legally imposed governance mechanisms are closely linked to, and often altered by, the political process. For example, the recent wave of corporate scandals United States resulted in the Sarbanes-Oxley Act of 2002, which imposed new rules on public companies, such as a requirement to reveal off-balance-sheet arrangements and restrictions on the use of pro formal accounting.

At the heart of any corporate governance system is the issue of separation of ownership and control. In the typical modern corporation in the major developed economies, the providers of capital are not the managers of the firm. How do the capital providers ensure that they get their money back after giving it to the firms? As a starting point, contracts can be signed between the capital providers and the managers that specify what the managers can and cannot do. However, complete contracts that can accurately predict future contingencies cannot be written for complex organizations. As a result, managers end up with substantial control rights over how to manage the firm and how to allocate value to investors and other stakeholders. To ensure that managers minimise their self-interested behaviour, various governance mechanisms are designed and imposed by legislation. For example, the requirement that financial statements be prepared using generally accepted financial principles is intended to provide comparative financial data and a scorekeeping record. Strict reporting standards exist for firms traded on the world's major stock exchanges. For managers themselves, incentive contracts can be designed that link managerial behaviour with compensation (although incentive contracts can create new problems of opportunism and private benefits, as demonstrated by the use of stock options in the 1990s).

CORPORATE GOVERNANCE MECHANISM

Corporate governance mechanisms differ as between different countries. The governance mechanism in each country is shaped by its political, economic and social history as also by its legal framework. The governance practices adopted in any country reflect national ethos and value systems adopted in that country over a long period of time. For most of the countries the corporate form of organisation did not evolve and emerge through a natural business process. It has been an alien concept transplanted from another soil. Hence different countries have assimilated it in their own way. In view of this, a pertinent question arises as to whether it is possible to have a set of universally accepted corporate governance standards. In the beginning most of the countries found the company to be merely a convenient form of organisation that enabled entrepreneurs to raise money from a large number of investors for funding their growing business or new ventures especially if they are large.

Given the differing social and business value systems of individual countries, assimilation process of the philosophy of the corporate form of organisation was not necessarily similar in different countries. Interestingly, however, in most of the countries, current managements of business entities generally enjoy a special status *vis-a-vis* the shareholder community. Most of the common shareholders also do not revolt immediately if the existing management tries to perpetuate its control over a business entity so long as the management does not grossly mismanage it. Shareholders start agitating only when they perceive that the company is being highly mismanaged and that the shareholder value is getting destroyed.

Despite the differences in the shareholder philosophies across different countries in regard to corporate governance mechanisms there is no denying of the fact that good governance needs to be encouraged among all the corporate as well as the non-corporate entities. This should hold good in respect of both private and public sector entities. With appropriate variations, the sound principles and practices of corporate governance should also be made applicable to public sector units, banks and financial institutions. The basic objective is to ensure/encourage adoption of good governance mechanisms and practices as they make it possible for more efficient use of economic resources and protection of the interests of shareholders and the society at large. Increasing globalisation is generating highly competitive business climate across all the countries. It is in this context that there is a pressing need to identify best corporate governance standards which facilitate countries like India to prepare themselves to face global competition more effectively.

While multilateral organisations like the World Bank and the Asian Development Bank have evinced keen interest in the subject of corporate governance, the intellectual lead in this area has been given by the OECD in evolving a set of cogent principles of corporate governance. Being an inter-governmental organisation of the industrially developed nations of the world, OECD has come out with a set of clearly defined principles, which it hopes, will be useful to all countries irrespective of their stages of development, legal systems, institutional frameworks, and traditions. The main objective of the OECD in drafting these Principles is to assist both its member governments as also non-member governments to bring about suitable improvements in their legal, institutional and regulatory framework for facilitating good corporate governance regimes. OECD considers that the principles evolved by it contain essential elements that should normally form an integral part of all good corporate governance regimes.

TABLE 1

OECD Principles of Corporate Governance

The corporate governance framework should:

1. Protect shareholders' rights.
2. Ensure the equitable treatment of all shareholders, including minority and foreign shareholders. All shareholders should have the opportunity to obtain effective redress for violation of their rights.
3. Recognize the rights of stakeholders as established by law and encourage active cooperation between corporations and stakeholders in creating health, jobs, and sustainability of financially sound enterprises.
4. Ensure that timely and accurate disclosure is made on all material matters regarding the corporation, including the financial situation, performance, ownership, and governance of the company.
5. Ensure the strategic guidance of the company, the effective monitoring of management by the board, and the board's accountability to the company and the shareholders.

Source: Organization for Economic Co-operation and Development, *Principles of Corporate Governance* (1999).

While the basic focus of the OECD Principles is on publicly traded companies it is hoped that they will serve, as a useful instrument to improve corporate governance in non-traded companies including state owned enterprises. The logic is that there is considerable synergy "between economic efficiency and corporate governance". If the quality of corporate governance is to be improved in any country the major initiative, no doubt, should preferably come from the corporate sector, both private and public. All the same, the acceptability of well-spelt out corporate governance principles and the willingness of the corporate sector to adopt them would be significantly better if such principles are well supported by an influential international organisation like the OECD.

At the national level, however, it is equally important that the legal, regulatory and institutional environment should be sufficiently conducive. In the Indian context it means that the Companies Act, the Securities Contracts Regulation Act and the rules formulated thereunder should make it obligatory for the corporate sector to adopt good governance practices. There are some areas where suitable strengthening of the policy framework is necessary. For instance, in the area of accounts, adoption of international accounting standards to ensure full disclosure and consolidated accounts would be desirable.

In this context it may be worthwhile to take note of the doubts raised by some about the relevance or applicability of the OECD Principles to all countries irrespective of their cultural and historical background. It is argued that the OECD Principles may not be highly suitable for some of the Asian countries as these are drafted keeping in view the situation of the OECD countries. However, this argument does not seem to be fair in view of the explicit recognition of these factors by the OECD before formulating its governance principles. In the Preamble to the Principles, OECD says, *"There is no single model of good corporate governance. At the same time, work carried out in Member countries and within the OECD has identified some common elements that underlie good corporate governance. The Principles build on these common elements and are formulated to embrace the different models that exist"*. This statement is a clear indication of the fact that the OECD principles do not rely on the template of any particular country. They are framed by picking up the best elements of good corporate governance as noted in different countries, which have varied historical and cultural backgrounds, different legal systems, institutional frameworks and traditions. Good governance standards that contribute to creation of higher shareholder value and encourage greater economic efficiency need not therefore be country specific. Adoption of the OECD principles would be in the best interests of all countries which are seriously trying to integrate themselves in the emerging more competitive global economy as most of the member countries give effect to the commitments given by them under the Word Trade Organisation (WTO) agreements. It is therefore, not appropriate to maintain that the operational framework of the OECD principles has been designed to suit basically the developed free market economies and not countries like India, which is still in the process of integrating with the global economy.

THE KEY CONSTITUENTS

Board of Directors

The board of directors consists of shareholder-elected representatives. The primary functions of the board of directors are to hire the chief executive officer and to oversee management and company performance. Recent developments have redefined the responsibilities of a member of the board of directors and what is involved in managing a corporation. These developments are changing the relationship between the board of directors and management in many different ways. The board of directors is becoming more liable for its decisions than ever before.

Laws governing the operation of a multinational corporation (MNC) differ in each country. Because of the expansion of MNCs, there has been an increased focus on the issues of governance in these corporations. Each country has its own set of laws concerning the board of directors. Some of these laws are ambiguous, but where there is limited liability, MNCs are required to have a body to oversee the company and to protect the interests of the stockholders.

The board of directors should set policies and oversee management. However, the Chairman plays a major role in the decisions made by the board of directors. Directors must realise that their job is not to satisfy the Chairman but instead to satisfy the stockholders. The board should be a check on management. The owners of the company should be represented by the directors. That has ceased to happen at lots of companies where management dominates the board. The role of the board is not to be a contender against management. Its role is to help management.

The directors need to be aware at all times of what is going on in the company they represent. If board members believe that the firm is not performing up to their expectations, and that it is top management's responsibility, then the board should probably dismiss the Chairman. The mere presence of dissenting expectations and attributions within the Board increases the likelihood for dismissal.

In India, in accordance with Companies (Amendment) Act, 2000 the Chairman like other Directors of the Company is also responsible for the compliance of the legal requirements. The Act has casted certain obligations on the Directors by including a provision for Director's Responsibility Statement to be annexed to the Director's Report. The Director's Responsibility Statement contains: i) That in the preparation of the annual accounts, the applicable accounting standards had been followed along with proper explanation relating to material departures; ii) That the directors had selected such accounting policies and applied them consistently and made judgments and estimates that are reasonable and prudent so as to give a true and fair view of the state of affairs of the Company at the end of the financial year and of the profit or loss of the Company for that period; iii) That the directors had taken proper and sufficient care for the maintenance of adequate accounting records in accordance with the provisions of the Act for safeguarding the assets of the Company and for preventing and detecting fraud and other irregularities; iv) That the directors had prepared the annual accounts on a going concern basis. This will ensure that the Directors have taken steps to safeguard the assets of the Company. In addition, a public company will have small shareholder directors if: the paid-up capital of ₹ 5.00 crores or more; one thousand or more small shareholders may have at least one Director elected by such small shareholders in the manner as maybe prescribed; Small shareholders means a shareholder holding shares of nominal value of ₹ 20000/- or less.

A person shall not be capable of being appointed Director of a Company if he is already a Director of a Public Company which (i) has not filed annual accounts and annual return for any continuous three financial years commencing on after 01/04/1999 or (ii) has failed to repay its deposits or interest or redeem its debentures on due date or pay dividend and such failure continuous for one year or more. Any such director shall not be eligible to be appointed as a director of any other Public Company for a period of 5 years from the date on which such Public Company in which he is a director failed to file annual accounts and annual returns or has failed to repay its deposits/interest or redeem its debentures on due date or pay dividend. Further, no person can be director of more than 15 Companies. In calculating the quantum of 15 directorship, the Companies excluded are: i) a Private Company which is neither a subsidiary nor a holding Company of a Public Company; ii) an Unlimited Company; iii) an association not carrying on business for profit or which prohibits the payment of dividend; and iv) a Company in which such person is only an Alternate Director i.e. Director who is only qualified as such during the absence or incapability of some other Director.

Management

The management comprises the Chief Executive, Executive-directors and the key managers of the company, involved in day-to-day activities of the company. The over-riding aim of management is to maximise shareholder value without being detrimental to the interests of other stakeholders. The management however, is subservient to the board of directors are must operate within the boundaries and the policy framework laid down by the board. While the board is responsible for ensuring that the principles of corporate governance are adhered to and enforced, the real onus of implementation lies with the management. It is responsible for translating into action, the policies and strategies of the board and implementing its directives to achieve corporate objectives of the company framed by the board. It is therefore essential that the board should clearly define the role of the management. The management should carry out the following functions by: i) Assisting the board in its decision making process in respect of the company's strategy policies, code of conduct and performance targets, by providing necessary inputs; ii) Implementing the policies and code of conduct of the board; iii) Managing the day to day affairs of the company to best achieve the targets and goals set by the board, to maximise the shareholder value; iv) Providing timely, accurate, substantive and material information, including financial matters and exceptions, to the board, board-committees and the shareholders; v) Ensuring compliance and all regulations and laws; vi) Ensuring timely and efficient service to the shareholders and to protect shareholder's right and interest; vii) Setting up and implementing an effective internal control system, commensurate with the business requirement; viii) Implementing and comply with the Code of Conduct as laid down by the board; and ix) Co-operating and facilitating efficient working of board committees.

As a part of the disclosure related to management, the management discussion and analysis report should form part of the annual report to the shareholders. Management discussion and analysis should include discussion on the following matters within the limits set by the company's competitive position: industry structure and developments; opportunities and threats; segment-wise or product-wise performance; outlook; risks and concerns; internal control systems and their adequacy; discussion on financial performance with respect to operational performance; and material development in human resources/industrial relations front, including number of people employed. Infact, good corporate governance casts an obligation on the management in respect of disclosures. The disclosures must be made by the management to the board relating to all material financial and commercial transactions, where they have personal interest, that may have a potential conflict with the interest of the company at large (for e.g. dealing in company shares, commercial dealings with bodies, which have shareholding of management and their relatives etc.)

Shareholders

The shareholders are the owners of the company and as such they have certain rights and responsibilities. But in reality companies cannot be managed by shareholder referendum. The shareholders are not expected to assume responsibility for the management of corporate affairs. A company's management must be able to take business decisions rapidly. The shareholders have therefore to necessarily delegate many of their responsibilities as owners of the company to the directors who then become responsible for corporate strategy and operations. The implementation of this strategy is done by a management team. This relationship therefore brings in the accountability of the boards and the management to the shareholders of the company. A good corporate framework is one that provides adequate avenues to the shareholders for effective contribution in the governance of the company while insisting on a high standard of corporate behaviour without getting involved in the day to day functioning of the company.

The General Body Meetings provide an opportunity to the shareholders to address their concerns to the board of directors and comment on and demand any explanation on the annual report or on the overall functioning of the company. It is important that the shareholders use the forum of general body meetings for ensuring that the company is being properly stewarded for maximising the interests of the shareholders. This is important especially in the Indian context. It follows from the above, that for effective participation shareholders must maintain decorum during the General Body Meetings.

The effectiveness of the board is determined by the quality of the directors and the quality of the financial information is dependent to an extent on the efficiency with which the auditors carry on their duties. The shareholders must therefore show a greater degree of interest and involvement in the appointment of the directors and the auditors. Indeed, they should demand complete information about the directors before approving their directorship.

Stakeholder versus Shareholder Debate

There has been numerous debates between stakeholder and shareholder approaches to corporate governance Notwithstanding what is legally required by the firm, the orientation of top management to one or the other approach can have important consequences for the actual governance practices used in a company. These debates have been described in terms such as "contracts versus communities," or "private property versus public," or "the firm as a social entity versus a private profit-seeking enterprise." In recent years this debate has intensified. From a global perspective, the debate is often pitched as the "Anglo-American view versus the European/Japanese view." In reality, all corporate governance systems must be responsive, at some level, to all stakeholders. It is simplistic to say, as critics of different national systems often do, "American corporate governance is too shareholder oriented" or "continental European systems are too stakeholder oriented than another. Following are some of the underlying philosophical issues on which corporate governance mechanisms have been built as the basis for understanding governance from a global perspective.

The stakeholders of a firm include its employees, customers, shareholders, creditors, suppliers, officers, board members, communities, and society at large. The stakeholder approach to corporate governance rejects the idea of maximizing a single objective function and argues that the corporation should be viewed as an entity that has citizenship responsibilities. The stakeholder view professes that the purpose of the corporation is to create and distribute wealth to all the primary stakeholders. In doing so, no stakeholder group should be favoured over another. The role of management is not restricted to carrying out shareholder responsibilities; it is also to respond to citizenship responsibilities on behalf of all constituencies. Thus, stakeholder management is a never-ending task of balancing and integrating multiple relationships and multiple objectives.

Shareholder sovereignty is bound to flounder. It is a fair weather model that works well only in times of prosperity. Top management of the future will need to balance the three dimensions i.e., objective functions] of the corporation: as an economic organization, as a human organization, and as an increasingly important social organization.

A stakeholder-oriented governance system means that in its decision making, management must take into account the core values of a possibly very diverse group of stakeholders. Management must balance these core values and establish relationships with the various stakeholders. In contrast, a shareholder-maximization approach has a much narrower perspective. A shareholder-oriented governance system views the corporation as a shareholder value-maximizing economic entity and emphasizes various elements: contractual exchanges; the role of law to promote contractual freedom; discipline forced by the invisible hand; a market for corporate control; and competition in product, labour, and capital markets. U.S. corporate governance in the last few decades has shifted to an emphasis on shareholder primacy. Accordingly maximizing shareholder value as the objective function will lead to decisions that enhance outcomes for multiple stakeholders. Several supporting arguments are:

1. Maximizing shareholder value maximizes the value of the whole firm, and thus the value of the pie to *all* its claimants.
2. Maximizing shareholder value provides the most appropriate incentives for managers to take risks.
3. More than one objective function makes governing difficult, if not impossible.
4. It is easier to make shareholders out of stakeholders, rather than vice versa.
5. All major stakeholders other than shareholders have protection through contracts and the legal system.

In establishing corporate governance practices for a firm, top management must balance what is legally required and what makes sense given the nature of the business, competitor practices, the makeup of the stakeholder set, the corporate values, and so on. This is not an easy task. Regardless of management's orientation, the stakeholder versus shareholder debate is not an either/or issue. Firms must be pro-stakeholder because if they are not, they will lose their access to capital, suppliers, communities, employees, and so on. Nevertheless, managers do have discretion in how value is transferred to the various stakeholders, and it is this value transference that creates enormous controversies, and occasionally disasters, for the various stakeholder groups.

CORPORATE GOVERNANCE MODELS

The Traditional Model

The traditional model of corporate governance, which is the prevalent model in the

United States, holds that shareholders' property rights are paramount. The shareholders, or owners of the corporation, elect the board of directors. The board acts as an intermediary between the owners and the management of a corporation. The board appoints the officers who run the corporation on a daily basis. Management exercises its authority over the firm's employees in order to achieve the corporate objectives.

In theory, the stockholders exercise their legal right by voting at an annual stockholder meeting. The stockholders evaluate management's corporate performance and then elect their representatives to sit on the board of directors. The board selects the officers of the corporation to run the business on a daily basis and meets periodically with management to resolve the issues that need stockholder approval. The board also oversees management to ensure that the stockholders' interests are looked after. Management chooses the employees necessary to run the business and accomplish the corporate goals and objectives.

It is clear that in this type of organisation, the main emphasis is on the stockholders' interests. Management is more concerned with production and their own rewards. Employees are concerned with wages and benefits. This model relies on the ability of the CEO to run the company efficiently and effectively. Even though the traditional corporate statutes require that the business affairs of a corporation be managed by the board of directors, in practice the board rarely performs either as management or policymakers of a corporation. The reality is that ownership of most major U.S. corporations is so dispersed that most stockholders hold an amount of stock that is too small to make any difference. They think of themselves as investors rather than owners of the corporation. When they do not make enough return on their investments, they prefer to sell their stock because they have little power to effect change individually.

The Codetermination Model

Codetermination is a two-tiered system in which there is a division between supervision and management. This system originated in Germany and has spread to many European countries.

The codetermination, or European, model maintains that both capital and labour should be represented in the process of corporate governance. Representatives of both ownership and the employees comprise the board of directors. One practical version of this model promotes a two-tiered structure, with a supervisory board and a management board. The supervisory board oversees the operation, and the management board is involved with daily operation of the corporation. The supervisory board has ultimate authority in that it can select and dismiss members of the management board.

The major feature of this system is not that it creates two levels of administration where only one existed before or that it recognises management as a separate organ, but that it makes a clear distinction between those who manage and those who monitor.

This results in a system of checks and balances which avoids conflicts of interest.

Who monitors the upper tier in a two-tiered board? Here, the implication is that the supervisory tier does not need external supervision, because it consists of two distinct interests—the shareholders' and the workers' representatives—and that each side will not let the other get away with anything unprofessional. Mining and steel corporations fall under a special code of regulation. In these industries, the formula was and still is equal representation for shareholders and for employees, plus one additional neutral outside member acceptable to both sides. Some critics of the two-tiered system are skeptical of its motivation. They believe that it is put into effect primarily to ensure that worker representatives are not elected to the essential management body of a company. Some companies in Germany have gotten into trouble due to the inability of their boards of directors to provide effective measures to influence the governance process. Lack of ability, information, and authority gives the board little opportunity to effectively monitor management's performance in corporate affairs.

Other Models

In the stakeholder model of corporate governance, all constituencies that have a direct stake in the performance of a corporation are represented in the governance process. The constituents include more than just the employees and owners. The interests of all stakeholders are taken into account when employees, major customers, major suppliers, major creditors, environmentalists, bankers, and other affected parties are represented on the board of directors of a corporation. Objectives are achieved by balancing the often-conflicting interests of the different constituents. The participation of these various stakeholder groups in the governance process ensures that a wide range of interests will be taken into account in corporate decision making.

The American Law Institute (ALI) has proposed an independent board of directors whose function is to monitor as opposed to manage. Under the ALI proposals, the board would focus on auditing functions, reviewing management, operations, staffing, and execution, to assess the competency of the CEO and senior' staff of an organisation. The monitoring board would actually be a new level of top management. In addition to the monitoring board, the ALI recommends an audit committee, a nominating committee, and a compensation committee. Table-2 presents the comparison of corporate governance models with ALI proposals.

There are broadly three models of corporate governance observed in the developed and the newly industrialising countries. At one end of the spectrum we have the widely discussed "outsider model" of the US and UK. The main feature of this model is the separation of control from ownership arising from widely dispersed equity ownership among large number of institutional and innumerable small shareholders. Consequently, the control of corporate units vests with professional managers. This is also referred to as the principal-agent model where the shareholders (the agents) entrust the task of running the company to managers (the principals) who are in effective control of the company. Growing importance of the economies of scale and scope has necessitated the birth of large firm with its distant shareholders and professional management. This has given rise to the agency problem viz., how to ensure that the managers function in the interests of the shareholders and the stakeholders.

TABLE 2

Comparison of Corporate Governance Models with American Law Institute Proposals

Traditional model	*Codetermination (European) model*	*Stakeholder model*	*ALI proposals*
Stockholders (owners)	Capital and labour	Social, political, and economic interests	Independent monitoring by board of directors
Board of directors	Supervisory board	Stakeholder participation in board of directors	Audit committee
Officers and managers	Management board	Management	Nominating committee
Employees	Management	Employees	Compensation committee

Both the UK and the US have a long tradition of equity ownership by individuals. During the last five to six decades these countries have witnessed emergence of a large number institutional shareholders like mutual funds, pension funds and insurance companies that have come to hold ever increasing proportion of equity. Since there is a clear separation of control from ownership in these countries the primary objective of their regulatory and legal frameworks is to encourage and facilitate corporate governance systems that protect interests of the widely dispersed shareholders.

In contrast to this outsider model we have two types of "insider models", the European model and the East Asian model. The European continent represents one type of insider model, although there are several versions of it in different European countries as also in different sectors of a given country. The main feature of the European insider model is that a small relatively compact group of shareholders (who maintain relatively longer term and stable relationship among themselves) are able to exercise control over corporate entities. The countries in which such an insider model is common are the ones that have witnessed less institutionalisation of equity holdings than the Anglo-American outsider model. These countries also reflect much higher dependence of the corporate sector on banks as a source of finance. Generally, the corporate entities also have much higher levels of debt-equity ratios. Table-3 presents the use of these models on corporate governance in various countries.

TABLE 3

The Spread of Better Governance Beyond the United States

	Traditional model	*Codetermination model*	*Other models*
Owners	Stockholders	Stockholders and labour	Stockholders with direct interest
Overseers	Board of directors	Supervisory board	Board stakeholder and management representative
Daily operations	Management	Management	Management
Users	United States Great Britain Japan France Turkey	Germany Sweden	Theory

The typical East Asian form of corporate governance model embodies a purer version of the insider model where "the founding family" generally holds majority of the controlling shares, directly or through other holding companies, most of which in turn may be controlled by the founding families. The main difference between the European and the pure East Asian version is that, in the East Asian case, close knit families are generally the controlling entities. The East Asian insider model is therefore far simpler version of the European insider model. The European insider model, on the other hand, is characterised by a variety of controlling forms including one interesting form where the controlling shareholders are backed by complex shareholder agreements. Countries with predominantly insider form of organisations are more tolerant of their activities even when such activities are not fully in the interests of the common shareholders.

ISSUES RELATED TO CORPORATE GOVERNANCE

Corporate governance structures play an important role in determining FDI decisions of state-owned MNCs raising concerns in host economies. There is a significant diversity in the behaviour of state owned enterprises (SOEs) around the world as State-owners differ in their interest and political systems. Even SOEs owned by the same State differ, for instance in their mission, technologies, industry and market context. SOEs may have multiple objectives - for instance, political, social, or cultural, or income re-distribution. Many of them were created originally to pursue public policy objectives. These aspects complicate the understanding (in comparison with private companies) of how SOEs operate, the way they are governed and how their relationship with the State plays out.

At a general level, the development of SOEs as MNCs is influenced by the political and economic underpinnings of the country of origin. *First,* it is important to distinguish between countries where free market policies or interventionism are preponderant. *Second,* State-owned MNCs' internationalization process may be influenced by the level of development of the country. The less developed a country, it can be argued, the more the State will tend to intervene in SOE management as SOEs become an important tool for the country's development. In some cases the government might hinder FDI by SOEs, as this could reduce their contribution and role (e.g. social, industrial) in the domestic economy; however, in other cases, the State might be willing to support FDI by SOEs as this may help to build economies of scale and/or further develop the competitive position of the firm and that of the home country. *Third,* influencing the possibilities and modalities of SOEs' internationalization are specific government industrial, technological, financial, social and foreign policies.

Thus, it is important to distinguish between cases where the link to the State might either hinder or support SOEs' FDI and performance:

i) Government as hindrance to internationalization (e.g. in Italy, where there has been repeated concern about the potential effects of SOEs' internationalization on local unemployment rates).

ii) Government as supporter of internationalization (e.g. China's "Go Global" policy, GCC countries' economic diversification policy the Republic of Korea's Overseas Investment Policy Package, and South Africa's outward FDI policies

iii) Government as indifferent to SOE internationalization, but with general support and with greater regard to developmental impact (e.g. Vattenfall (Sweden) in Africa).

In general terms it is argued that the extent to which SOEs are free of, or subject to, government involvement in operational and management matters (including FDI) is critical. Active government participation in SOEs is often regarded as a limit to good economic performance. However, if the degree of autonomy is very high, the SOE could behave just like a private firm, and this may impact on its original mission and public policy role. This situation suggests that although a certain level of State intervention can be good for SOEs' performance, including international diversification, too much State intervention might be detrimental.

The level and mode of FDI by SOEs is also influenced by host country policies that regulate inward FDI. State-owned MNCs might be perceived either favourably or unfavourably, depending on conditions and the attitude of the host country. For example, there are persistent claims of "unfair" competition by State-owned MNCs, as well as concerns about State-owned MNCs as instruments of foreign policy. Partly in response, host countries - particularly in the developed world -have over the past few years focused attention on developing legal frameworks and processes to provide the necessary instruments for identifying and preventing deemed adverse consequences arising from State-owned MNC investments (e.g. Australia, Canada).

However, there are also countries with more favourable attitudes concerning FDI by foreign SOEs. For instance there are cases in which two States, because they do not yet have established political ties, perceive FDI by their SOEs as a step - among others - towards establishing a closer relationship between them. Examples include the case of Malaysian State-owned MNCs such as Petronas and some African countries, in which investments were often fostered by the Government of Malaysia. There are also cases in which, because of the already existing strong ties between States, FDI by SOEs is perceived as further strengthening these ties. Their international business operations became part of ODA packages.

Typical potential corporate governance concerns regarding State-owned MNCs are related to their objectives arising from State ownership (which may diverge from the commercial norms), a perceived lower level of transparency, potentially inexperienced boards of directors, and poor relationships with other shareholders and stakeholders. As many SOEs may have no public reporting requirements, and relevant information may only be available to the State, this hinders monitoring, limits accountability and, under some conditions, may create opportunities for corruption.

In light of this situation, the future policy agenda that host governments may wish to deal with revolves around the core differences between State-owned and private MNCs, and focuses on alleviating these concerns: i) National security concerns are particularly prominent when State-owned MNC activity increased. It is argued that sometimes their investments would endanger the national security position of any host country. For instance, an acquisition of port management businesses in six major United States seaports in the United States by DP World (UAE) in 2006 came under close scrutiny, be-cause of fears of compromising port security. Political resistance ultimately forced DP World to divest these assets. Explicitly defining and reaching an agreement (between the State and SOE governance) on SOE objectives can help reduce concerns in both host and home countries, clarify management goals, improve performance monitoring, and reduce opportunism. ii) Competition concerns may be voiced where foreign investment is deemed a threat to national core industries and "national champions", but they may also be raised in the con-text of knowledge and technology transfer issues. A recent controversial case that failed for these reasons concerned a proposed second deal in 2009, in the mining industry, which otherwise would have led to the Aluminum Corporation of China (Chinalco), China's State-owned metals group, purchasing more stake in Rio Tinto (Australia/United Kingdom), a leading global mining company. iii) Concerns over governance and social and environmental standards might become more prominent in the future for host countries as investments from State-owned MNCs increase, although such concerns are already being voiced with regard to extractive industries and agriculture. To improve transparency, SOEs are also expected to comply with high standards of accounting and auditing. In reality, less than one-fifth, or 119 firms, of 653 State-owned MNCs in UNCTAD's database subscribe to the United Nations' Global Compact, and only 3 per cent (or 17 firms) use the Global Reporting Initiative (GRI) standards, compared to 60 per cent in both initiatives for the world's top 100 MNC. The OECD has pre-pared guidelines regarding provision of an effective legal and regulatory framework.

Also, from the perspective of home countries, there are concerns regarding the openness to investment from their State-owned MNCs. Given the current absence of any broader consensus on the future rules of engagement of State-owned MNCs as sources of FDI, it is critical that home and host economies determine and define more clearly the rules and regulations under which State-owned MNCs pursue their investment activities.

CONVERGENCE OF STANDARDS

Different corporate governance systems are gradually converging in the direction of a broadly unified corporate governance model. Such a governance model is likely to embrace many common elements, which are an integral part of the market oriented governance system of the US and the UK. The process of convergence in corporate governance is gathering momentum due to growing international integration of financial markets, including that in India. As the inflow of direct and portfolio foreign investment increases there will be demands to address the concerns and requirements of foreign investors in regard to corporate governance standards and practices. Among the several key criteria used by the global investors for evaluating investment proposals, good corporate governance generally ranks very high on their value chain. Companies, which are highly transparent and attach considerable importance to good corporate governance standards, invariably command a high premium in the capital markets because the investment appraisal exercise of such companies becomes more dependable and meaningful.

Companies that intend to raise equity from international markets and list them on global stock exchanges like New York Stock Exchange or NASDAQ would not get better valuation unless they are able to project a good image of themselves. The quality of corporate governance including the disclosure standards adopted by companies seeking capital from global markets becomes crucial for attracting greater investor interest from active global markets. Major institutional investors, in particular, demand that companies should respect good norms of governance and those in management control should respect rights of minority shareholders. Companies should make special attempt to be transparent in regard to the various norms adopted by them in their governance mechanisms. Therefore, due importance is being given by several companies to adoption of higher standards of corporate governance, including appointment of important board committees such as the audit committee, remuneration committee, and appointment/nomination committee.

Globalisation of product markets and deregulation of domestic financial markets are acting as additional pressure points on companies to adopt good governance practices. So long as companies operate mainly in the domestic market, which often restricts competition through regulatory measures and also protects them from foreign competition through trade and tariff barriers there is hardly any pressure on the companies to adopt more efficient production systems or good governance practices. During the last decade economic climate in most of the countries including India is undergoing rapid transformation. Indian economy is increasingly getting deregulated. With growing liberalisation in the entry conditions for foreign direct investment since 1991, product markets are becoming increasingly competitive. As a part of the phased compliance to the WTO requirements, Government has been continually bringing down the average level of import duties and removing quantitative restrictions on imported goods. Consequently, competition from foreign producers is becoming more intense as the days pass. To survive in the emerging highly competitive environment, domestic producers will have to adopt production technologies and governance systems and practices that are conducive to efficiency and bringing down unit costs of production.

Firms that operate in highly competitive market conditions of the global market would have to remain much more open and alert to new ideas for improving productivity levels and adopting better corporate governance standards. Good corporate governance is not a pre-condition for developing a strong competitive position in the market and achieve higher productivity and profitability levels. Empirical studies on the subject do not conclusively prove one-to-one relationship between good corporate governance and higher productivity or profitability levels. It may be noted that sound corporate governance may be one of the necessary but not sufficient conditions to realise improved profitability and operational efficiency. Good corporate governance may not be of much help if the strategic direction of the company is wrong, if the management falters in implementing a good strategy, or if the institutional and legal structures of a country hinder rather than encourage efficiency. It should, however, be noted that good governance does help companies to gain respect among customers, suppliers, and investor community. Companies with good governance engender trust and confidence among all those who have business or investment relationship with them. It is expected that globally competitive forces would induce greater convergence in corporate governance standards across different countries. The more dynamic and forward-looking firms will be the early ones to introduce, on their own, good corporate governance practices that help in improving their acceptability to the foreign investor community. The rate of progress in this area, however, would largely depend on the leadership role played by the government of each country. The governments, which are keen to strengthen competitive advantage of their industries, should hasten the process of reforming their legal, regulatory, and institutional framework so that business entities are encouraged to adopt/imbibe improved corporate governance practices.

IMPLICATIONS FOR INTERNATIONAL BUSINESS MANAGEMENT

There are many implication of corporate governance in international markets, three of which are discussed here. The first implication is concerned with the recruitment and selection of international managers. American-based MNCs may find it difficult to compete in the international market without acquiring and developing international managers. In addition to possessing all the qualities that make a good manager in a domestic corporation, these managers must also be mobile, receptive, and at ease in cultures other than their own. Emphasis should be placed on selection rather than just training. Belief in worker participation is not intuitive; rather, it develops over a period of time. This implies the need for a responsible policy, which is sensitive to other cultures, in recruiting international managers. The failure of many MNCs can be attributed to a lack of understanding and conflicts in decision making. This means that a MNC can be successful in international markets only if the orientation and values of its overseas managers are consistent with the values of the local society. In other words, a MNC should blend with a culture and not conflict with it. Familiarity with and sensitivity to a host country are prerequisites for a successful operation.

The second implication is related to human resource planning in the international arena. People with appropriate skills and knowledge are a scarce commodity. For many years, MNCs have tended to rely on expatriate managers for overseas assignments. Unfortunately, experience indicates that this policy is usually costly and inappropriate. A long-term perspective for the recruitment and development of indigenous personnel to assume managerial responsibility is imperative and should not be left to chance. Furthermore, developing international managers gives a MNC a competitive edge and can strengthen its position in a market.

The third implication relates to maximising a company's resources for success. What can a company do to ease into a foreign culture? A subsidiary board should he chosen carefully and should include nationals from the host country. This board can be helpful in creating a spirit of friendship between the home and host countries.

It is almost a truism that the adequacy and the quality of corporate governance shape the growth and the future of any capital market and economy. The concept of corporate governance has been attracting public attention for quite some time in India.

The progressive firms in India have voluntarily put in place systems of good corporate governance. Internationally also, while this topic has been accepted for a long time, the financial crisis in emerging markets has led to renewed discussions and inevitably focussed them on the lack of corporate as well as governmental oversight. The same applies to recent high-profile financial reporting failures even among firms in the developed economies. Focus on corporate governance and related issues is an inevitable outcome of a process, which leads firms to increasingly shift to financial markets as the pre-eminent source for capital. In the process, more and more people are recognising that corporate governance is indispensable to effective market discipline. This growing consensus is both an enlightened and a realistic view. In an age where capital flows worldwide, just as quickly as information, a company that does not promote a culture of strong, independent oversight, risks its very stability and future health. As a result, the link between a company's management, directors and its financial reporting system has never been more crucial. As the boards provide stewardship of companies, they play a significant role in their efficient functioning.

Studies of firms in India and abroad have also shown that markets and investors take notice of well-managed companies, respond positively to them, and reward such companies, with higher valuations. A common feature of such companies is that they have systems in place, which allow sufficient freedom to the boards and management to take decisions towards the progress of their companies and to innovate, while remaining within a framework of effective accountability. In other words they have a system of good corporate governance.

Strong corporate governance is thus indispensable to resilient and vibrant capital markets and is an important instrument of investor protection. It is the blood that fills the veins of transparent corporate disclosure and high-quality accounting practices. It is the muscle that moves a viable and accessible financial reporting structure. Without financial reporting premised on sound, honest numbers, capital markets will collapse upon themselves.

Another important aspect of corporate governance relates to issues of insider trading. It is important that insiders do not use their position of knowledge and access to inside information about the company, *and* take unfair advantage of the resulting information asymmetry. To prevent this from happening, corporates are expected to disseminate the material price sensitive information in a timely and proper manner and also ensure that till such information is made public, insiders abstain from transacting in the securities of the company. The principle should be *'disclose or desist'*. This therefore calls for companies to devise an internal procedure for adequate and timely disclosures, reporting requirements, confidentiality norms, code of conduct and specific rules for the conduct of its directors and employees and other insiders. For example, in many countries, there are rules for reporting of transactions by directors and other senior executives of companies, as well as for a report on their holdings, activity in their own shares and net year to year changes to these in the annual report. The rules also cover the dealing in the securities of their companies by the insiders, especially directors and other senior executives, during sensitive reporting seasons. However, the need for such procedures, reporting requirements and rules, also goes beyond corporates to other entities in the financial markets such as Stock Exchanges, Intermediaries, Financial institutions. Mutual Funds and concerned professionals who may have access to inside information.

THE FUTURE OF CORPORATE GOVERNANCE

Globally, stockholders are finally demanding that they be heard. Shareholders are increasingly asserting themselves and are calling for reforms in how companies are being run. The current wave of proxy battles at annual meetings is a sign of shareholder discontent. Big investors are demanding international standards of corporate behavior, accounting clarity, and disclosure. Boards of directors have been sued and found liable for their actions (or nonactions). Shareholders in some companies have had a hand in the dismissal of the Chairman and other management. Globally the agency theory has become a popular framework for studying governance issues. Agency theory implies a well known trade-off between risk bearing efficiency and incentive efficiency. The unit of analysis in an agency model is the relationship between a principal and client; and the focus of the theory includes causes and consequences of goal divergence between the two parties. An agency problem is said to exist when an agent has established goals which conflict with those of a principal. *Golden parachutes, poison pills, excessive level of executive compensation, and wealth-diluting mergers and acquisitions are generally viewed as symptoms of agency problem.* Such problems are likely to occur when a key-decision maker has a minimal financial interest in the outcome of his decision. In spite of the agency problems created by the separation of ownership and control, ownership dispersion may be optimal for large companies because individuals cannot bear the large risks involved.

Due to diffused ownership in publicly held firms, the board of directors serves as the proxy for individual shareholders, and is responsible for representing their interests. Growing number of directors have based their decisions on capital asset pricing model (CAPM) which assumes that investors are perfectly rational. If they are irrational, are businesses making the wrong choices?

Financial markets' evaluation of risk determines the way the firms invest. What if the markets are wrong? Financial theorists have found that beta *is not* much use for explaining changes in share prices. There appears that to sustain competitive advantage in the future, the companies will have to focus less exclusively on shareholder and financial measures of success and more on all their shareholder relationships and a broader range of measurements. The companies that have high book-to-market ratios tend to earn excess returns over longer periods, even after adjusting for the risks that are associated with beta. The book-to-market effect must capture an extra risk factor so that managers incorporate it into their hurdle rates. The new alternative hurdle rate may be labelled as New Estimator of Expected Return (NEER). Beta can be the right measure of risk provided it captures an asset's fundamental risk—that is, its contribution to the market basket's risk. Then it will often make sense for directors to pay attention to it even if investors are somehow failing to.

Often, but not always, at the heart of NEER has a critical distribution between—*(a)* boosting a firm's long-term risk value, and *(b)* trying to raise its share price. If investors are rational, these are same things: any decision that raise long-term value will instantly increase the share price as well. But if investors are making predictable mistakes, the board must choose. For instance, if the board wants to increase today's share price—perhaps because the members (directors) want to sell their shares, or to fend off a takeover attempt—the members must usually stick with the NEER approach, accommodating investors' misperceptions. But if they are interested in long-term value, they should usually continue to use beta. Showing a flair for marketing, is far-sighted alternative to NEER is the fundamental asset risk (FAR) approach.

Recent developments in the theory of finance will no doubt irritate many company bosses, who are fond of denouncing their investors' myopia. Such developments go to the heart of corporate governance. How should legitimate power be exercised? Who is accountable, who is responsible to whom and for what? Such questions have not been asked seriously since the corporate concept was first invented in 19th century. There are signs that the concept of the corporation itself is under attack.

Significant changes are taking place in corporate regulation around the world. Some countries have rewritten their business and company law, others are in the process. Securities regulators have also become more demanding and, through the work of the International Organisation of Securities Commissions, there have been a move towards global convergence in regulation. Stock exchange listing rules are being extended and tightened up almost everywhere, although the arguments between the need for corporate control and the costs of regulation and reduction of business freedom remain. The move towards the adoption of international accounting standards in many countries is also changing the governance scene. Increasing recognition is beginning to dawn that the crucial issues are not really about board structures, company regulation or even shareholder power: they are about the processes, perceptions and powers of directors.

Should shareholders be conceived with director compensation? Historically, compensation has not been a major factor. Directors accept board membership, not for income, but for the opportunity to learn how other companies operate and the prestige value derived from an identification with other impressive firms. Busy executives seek directorship to cultivate a reputation for expertise. Such reputation building is most credible when the direct payments to outside directors are small. A substantial increase in director pay may reflect a general trend to subvert or co-opt board members so as to create a 'rubber stamp' board. This approach to substantially compensate directors may be described as a way to guarantee director loyalty or as "If I'm there for them, they'll be there for me". How can a firm pay for exceptional directors without unintentionally buying a passive board? One design strategy for directors pay is to set a low base component, but with a substantial bonus. A counterpart to this is the mix between an annual retainer and per meeting fees. Making much of the director's compensation contingent on meeting fees is likely to facilitate board attendance, and psychologically, it reminds the directors of their role (i.e. a source of advice at meetings versus a figurehead). A related issue concern pay-for-performance, paying directors with firm equity. Although such equity holdings may represent only a small portion of an outsider director's personal wealth, such stock serves as a powerful symbolic reminder of the board's fiduciary responsibilities.

Can a firm's size be a primary factor in setting director pay? It is argued that emphasis on size may create the wrong incentives for directors as this practice is likely to invite top executives and board members to pursue mergers and acquisitions which may not be in the firm's best interests. Size alone cannot measure the requirements of and contributions by a firm's board. For example, is the business environment simple or complex, stable or changing, a monopoly or heavily competitive? Are directors with the necessary expertise scarce or readily available? Will the board be evaluating many strategic decisions, or none? So, rather than focussing on size, director compensation practices should reflect the effort put forth by the board.

The corporate governance mechanism introduced in buy-outs and buy-ins are argued to provide an effective means for reducing the problems associated with the agency costs of control. The governance mechanism in both buy-outs and buy-ins involve a integrated combination of managerial equity holdings, commitments to serve external funding and monitoring of active investors. The essential difference in the governance mechanism in buy-outs and buy-ins lies in the nature of equity ownership. Buy-outs involve significant equity ownership by incumbent management whereas in buy-ins new equity owning managers enter the firm from outside. Managers are thus, in principle, highly incentivised in both cases. However, the inside-outside distinction raises potential governance problems both in relation to the effect of managers on performance but also in relation to the other elements of the overall governance structure.

In principle, in buy-outs the incentives for incumbent management are enhanced and weak monitoring by diffuse shareholders or head office is replaced by a more focussed system. Similarly, in buy-ins it may be expected that gains to investors will be obtained from turning around underperforming companies through the replacement of inadequate management and governance by new entrepreneurs and active investors. However, it is important to recognise that incoming managers, in particular, are faced with potentially severe asymmetric information and adverse selection problems. Whilst incumbent managers may know the real internal state of affairs, incoming managers may only identify problems fully after they have completed the transaction. To the extent that these problems lead managers (and their investors) to misjudge the situation a deal and accompanying of financial structure may be agreed which is inappropriate and possibly unviable. As a result, the control mechanism introduced by the commitment to meet the cost of serving external finance may lead to sub-optimal decisions.

Financial institutions are also faced with an adverse selection problem in that they are unable to gauge the manager's performance in the enterprise prior to deal completion. They, too, also have to rely on imperfect information about the true state of affairs in making their investment decisions. These issues raise crucial problems in the potential effectiveness of post-transaction monitoring by institutional investors. Some of the difficulties in monitoring are common across all types of investment, but buy-ins also have special problems. Venture capitalists are faced with problems in screening for good quality entrepreneurs and target companies. Not only is there evidence that the entrepreneurial characteristics of entrepreneurs in buy-outs and buy-ins are significantly different, but it may also be more difficult for venture capitalists to judge the ability of an incoming entrepreneur to manage a company than it is in respect of one who is already in place.

Changes in corporate governance are certainly occurring. In the case of troubled buy-outs and buy-ins, the extent and nature of action by financial institutions may depend crucially upon their judgment as to the cause of poor performance, the prospects, for the success of restructuring action of cost-reward relationship involved in such actions. It is possible to identify two general types of problem cases: *Living Dead and Good Rump. Living Dead* investments, which essentially involve enterprises where the business collapses with little prospect of turnaround, may be written down to a very low but realist valuation so that it then does not matter significantly whether the institution is able to sell the business or not. However, such investments still risk involving a disproportionate amount of monitoring and control, especially if the buy-outs or buy-ins are small. Moreover, it may be difficult for the venture capitalist to implement changes in such companies where management typically have a majority of the equity until a pressure point arises which cannot be relieved by other funding sources. Active efforts may be made either to solicit an offer from a trade buyer (even for a nominal sum) or, more likely, to persuade management to buy-out the institution's interest. When sales do occur, because the possibility of a turnaround may still exist, which would potentially produce significant gains on a nominal purchase price, institutions may include 'non-embarrassment clause' to participate in future gains.

The second category, 'Good Rump' is distinguishable from the first in that these firms are viewed as capable of being turned round but the effects of restructuring have yet to be seen. Such cases may be underperforming because of general sectoral problems. In both cases the nature of the restructuring to be undertaken in order to turn-round the business may be problematical and be heavily influenced by whether the institutions are controlling shareholders or not. A problem of enforcing restructuring is that it may be difficult to agree with other parties what form it should take. In a smaller buy-outs and buy-ins, since management are usually important majority shareholders, great care is needed in taking action with the principal strategy typically being to produce a consensus on necessary action. It may, though, be difficult for institutions to agree with such managers over asset disposals or deferrals of capital expenditure programmes. Greater difficulties in restructuring may be anticipated in the case of management buy-ins, especially when faced with a relatively weak market and with limited resources as an independent company. However, undertaking due diligence as an outsider may be as much a problem in larger companies as it is in smaller private companies, despite possible differences in levels of information disclosure and sophistication of internal management systems.

Larger management buy-ins may be able to bear extensive restructuring and it may be economical for institutions to invest the effort to undertake it, whereas the possibilities may be very limited for smaller cases. The need to reimburse large amounts of outside funding may leave little scope for rescuing a weakening marketing position. Moreover, competitors perceiving the relative weakness of the company may take the opportunity to mount a competitive attack. These problems are likely to be exacerbated in adverse market conditions and when predicated asset sales are difficult to achieve.

The governance problem applicable to both buy-outs and buy-ins is the effort-cost-reward trade-off. The development of hybrid buy-ins/buy-outs and institutional buy-outs represent important market responses to the governance problems which may arise in pure management buy-ins. Although investors may adopt a stance of being close monitors or not, irrespective of the nature of transaction, there is a need for flexible approach to governance under which the forms adopted take account of the specific circumstances of a particular enterprise.

With continued globalisation, corporate governance practices around the world will evolve, with increased harmonisation likely to proceeds global shifts. The international business managers should be familiar with international corporate governance. Increasingly, companies are appointing foreign CEOs and directors. The important reasons for the companies to look for foreign directors are: (i) The corporate cultures of global firms are becoming as global as their businesses. The board has to be able to oversee and understand cross-cultural dimensions and handle diverse organizations; (ii) Global corporations have global citizenship responsibilities and require directors who understand local citizenship issues; (iii) Cross-border mergers and acquisitions and strategic alliances are becoming common for all leading companies. The board needs to be able to oversee and lead these investments with an understanding of local and global factors; and the (iv) Global companies need access to foreign capital. The global makeup of a board helps create and maintain the confidence of foreign investors and helps ensure appropriate investor communication to these groups.

For international business managers, corporate governance will, in all probability, take on greater meaning as country practices evolve and more of the world's economic activity is conducted through markets and firms rather than states. When firms rather than states are involved in economic activity, all stakeholders will expect that value creation and transference is fair and that managers are held accountable for their actions. In the absence of an environment that allows fairness and accountability to flourish, firms will be reluctant to invest. Thus, managers involved in international competition should view knowledge of international governance as an essential element of global strategy. Most strategic decisions will be impacted by corporate governance practices. For example, a company contemplating an acquisition will require an understanding of takeover law in the jurisdiction of interest. More important, the company will need to understand how the various stakeholders will respond to the takeover. If layoffs will be necessary to achieve cost synergies, are they possible? Are there labour unions that can block takeovers or make life difficult in the postmerger period? How will related companies and local communities react? What rights do minority shareholders have? How are takeovers communicated to shareholders? What political issues are involved in the proposed acquisition? In the developed-country economies, these questions can be answered more or less unambiguously but in emerging markets, there will likely be a high degree of ambiguity and uncertainty regarding specific laws, their interpretation, and the degree to which the laws may or may not be enforced or enforceable. Thus, a solid understanding of the principles of corporate governance will help managers navigate the legal, regulatory, and cultural waters to design and implement appropriate corporate governance practices.

QUESTIONS

1. Describe the nature of corporate governance.
2. Explain the corporate governance mechanism.
3. Discuss the main implications of corporate governance for international business management.
4. Critically examine the future of corporate governance in an increasingly interdependent world economy.
5. Discuss the main components of corporate governance.
6. Critically examine the traditional model and the codetermination model of corporate governance.

REFERENCES

Abbass F. Alkhafaji, *A Stakeholder Approach to Corporate Governance: Managing in a Dynamic Environment* (New York: Quorum Books), 1989.

Adolf A. Berle and Gardiner C. Means, *The Modem Corporation and Private Property* (New York: Macmillan), 1932, pp. 89-93.

Bhalla, V.K., *Corporate Governance: Agency Costs and the Politics of Finance*, Chartered Secretary, January, 1997.

Bleicher, K., "Corporate Governance Systems in a Multinational Environment: Who Knows What's Best?" *Management International Review*, 3: 4-15, 1986.

J.W. Fredrickson, D.C. Hambreck, and S. Baumron, "A Model of CEO Dismissal," *Academy of Management Review*, 13: 255-270, 1988.

Joseph Moson, "Directions in the United States and European Corporate Governance," paper presented at the AACSB Conference on Business Environment and Public Policy, Summer 1979, pp. 1-2.

Mace, M.L., *Director: Myth and Reality*, by the President and Fellows of Harvard College Press, Boston, 1971, pp. 78-79.

Melvin Eisenberg, *The Structure of the Corporation: A Legal Analysis* (Boston: Little, Brown), 1976, pp. 14-18.

Robert J. Larner. *Management Control and the Large Corporation* (New York: Dunellen), 1971, pp. 9-24.

Rogene A. Buchholz, *Business Environment and Public Policy Implications for Management and Strategy*, 4th edition (Englewood Cliffs, N.J.; Prentice-Hall), 1992, pp. 241-270.

S.P. Sherman, "Pushing Corporate Boards to Be Better," *Fortune*, p. 18, July 1988.

21

INTERNATIONAL BUSINESS ETHICS

INTRODUCTION

Today's business world presents many complex ethical challenges and continually demands that may be chosen among often apparently contradictory sets of values—and all of this take place in a very tough, highly competitive economic climate. Corporate codes of conduct and education in ethics are both important elements of a successful programme aimed at increasing ethical behaviour in the workplace. An even more important aspect, however, may be the values of a company's leaders. The most visible evidence of attention to ethical concerns is manifest in the many changes in corporate policy and decision making. This would indicate that corporate managers are placing greater emphasis on ethical criteria in their strategic planning. Ethics has become, and will continue to be, an important component in every business decision, whether domestic or international. This chapter reviews frameworks of international business ethics and demonstrates the philosophical, social, political and organizational theories adopted in this programme and how they apply to business. The approach emphasizes self-awareness, using case study analysis, experiential exercises, reflective questioning and discussion.

VALUE AND ETHICS

Value and ethics are often claimed to be the fundamental basis of good business behavious. The word *ethics* comes from the Greek word *ethos,* which means character. The business ethics is a code, where every-one conforms to a norm, which varies from business to business. In other words, ethics is a conception of right and wrong in relation to human behaviour. *Ethics* can be defined as reflecting on the question 'What ought I (we) do?'. In business, as in any context, this question is about making a decision and commitment to a course of action based on principles and beliefs. The concept of 'ought' is normative. It is not descriptive. It rather seeks to determine what 'ought' or 'should' mean in a specific situation. The notions of should and ought represent personal responsibility that is associated with the responsibility an dividual fills as a result of their role in an organizational a certain time and place. In other words, *ethics can be defined as the planned attempt to follow society's accepted norms, standards, and expectations that ought to govern human conduct and the values worth pursuing in life.* Thus, the attempt is systematic and hence goes beyond what each reflective person tends to do in his daily life in making sense of his moral experience, organising it, and attempting to make it coherent and unified. Ethics concerns itself with human conduct, which is taken here to mean human activity.

Morality is a term used to cover those practices and activities that are considered "right" or "wrong," the rules which govern those activities, and the values that are pursued or followed in operation and practice. The morality of a society is related to its modes (the customs accepted by a society or group as being the right and wrong ways to act) as well as its laws, which add legal prohibitions and sanctions to many activities considered to be immoral.

Business ethics first appeared in the 16th century. Before the 16th century, according to Christian theology, work was a curse and the pursuit of money was not moral. At the time, religion played an important role in society, with strong influence on both individuals and government. Because of the church's view, there was no need for business ethics, so businessmen did what they wanted. The Protestant Revolution paved the way for business ethics by making financial success moral.

A number of factors continue to contribute to the increasing role and importance of ethics in business. Some of these factors include such as the practices in the manufacture or representation of goods and services that jeopardise product safety are unethical and will not he tolerated. Companies conducting international business will be subject to different standards of ethical behavior in different countries. Certain practices that might be acceptable in one country might not be ethical in another. Therefore, multinational corporations need to fully understand the environment and expectations of their host countries. In today's global economy, domestic companies will be forced to compete with companies from abroad, and this increased competition will raise ethical issues and considerations.

Economic exploitation of the environment by manufacturers, real estate developers, transportation companies, and a variety of other industries will not be tolerated. Such unethical and illegal activities will receive increasing attention and criticism, forcing companies to consider the environmental impact of business decisions.

In addition, the diversity of the work force will produce a number of ethical challenges for business in the future. These challenges range from equality in hiring, promotion, and compensation to the way businesses provide benefits in such areas as medical care.

Much discussion in business ethics centres round the resolution of ethical dilemmas. These involve the prospect of 'bad consequences' when, no matter which choice is selected, some ethical principles are likely to be violated. For example, the reduction of an organization's workforce in order to avoid collapse has to be balanced against the hardships imposed on redundant employees. Corporations in a globalized world increasingly confront such dilemmas. Some cognitive dissonance may be reached to rationalize their decision and ease malcontents in the management tea. The management may justify their actions because they base their judgement and place trust in economists' arguments that freed labour will transfer to other jobs and continue to add value to society.

Values can be identified as one of the bases for determining 'right action'. The values defined and described by a society, an organization, or held by an individual are likely to be reviewed to determine an appropriate policy or action. They will emerge from a number of viewpoints - moral philosophy (e.g., distributive justice), a political or social framework (beliefs, underpinning democracy), or cultural heritage (values emerging from a Christian or Confucian understanding).

Why be Ethical?

There are many arguments for and against business ethics. The main argument for is that if management followed good business ethics, there would be no need for government intervention. When the private sector does not maintain adequate ethical standards and/or when it does not respond to new ethical issues, government will continue to intervene by enacting legislation that can result in civil and criminal penalties for unethical practices. The outcome of this legislation will be regulations that have a widespread effect on all industries, from manufacturing, to service, to health care, to transportation.

An argument against business ethics is the free market theory, which states that if the market is left alone and everyone pursues his or her own self-interests, the good of society will follow as the end result. Another argument against is that business operates according to a special set of ethical principles which differ from society's.

THE CODE OF CONDUCT

The code must be more than a document hanging on a wall—it must become ingrained in the corporate culture. To achieve results, the CEO and those around him or her must be openly and strongly committed to ethical conduct and give constant leadership in tending and renewing the values of the organisation. This commitment is communicated in a variety of ways, including speeches, directives, company publications, policy statements, and, most importantly, actions.

The importance of understanding the values and traditions of host countries is essential, for doing business overseas. It is important for managers to evaluate the significance of particular practices in their organisations and the way they should he applied in different cultural settings. The code of conduct must be communicated by top management to all members of the organisation, along with their commitment to enforce the code. It is important to make sure that expatriates are aware of the consequences of violating the code of conduct to the company as well as society at large.

No longer is profit the only justifiable motive for business activity. A long-term focus is both the best and the only way to go. Doing what is right is its own reward. *Ethical behavior builds trust, trust builds confidence, and confidence builds profitable business relationships with customers, suppliers, investors, employees, creditors, and the general public.*

Ethics codes are more than just rules and regulations; they embody basic values and epitomise corporate culture. The most significant benefit of having an ethics code is its ability to set a highly responsible tone for the organisation. In the long-term focus, higher ethical standards may translate into higher profits.

An important aspect of an organisation communicating its commitment to its employees is the issuance of a corporate code of ethics. However, some of the codes of conduct are merely conflict of interest statements. Although such statements are relevant to a company's ethical policy, they do not constitute a code of ethics as the term is understood, and when they are broadly stated, employees are able to dismiss them as cosmetic. Although no code will cover all situations, some form of written document that sets forth principles of conduct for the whole organisation will serve to help and guide the judgments and consciences of employees as they make specific decisions. It is also important that these codes communicate clear expectations.

Petrick and Quinn identified different orientations to business ethics. They have developed a model which creates a typology of organizations, using two variables - flexible/control oriented and internal/externally focused. This enabled them to define four types of businesses which coincide with four orientations to business ethics. Table-1 summarizes their model.

TABLE -1

Petrick and Quinn's Business Ethics Orientation Model

Organization Type	*Business Ethics Orientation*
Flexible and internally focussed	Virtue ethics
Control oriented and internally focused	Deontology
Control oriented and externally focused	Teleology
Flexible and externally focused	Systems ethics

Virtue Ethics

Virtue ethics is often associated with personal ethics. This approach, drawn from Aristotles notions relating to a good life is commonly identified with individual decision-making and behaviour. It involves questions such as 'How should I act to become the person I want to be?' or 'How should I behave to lead *a good life?'* These questions are commonly framed in terms of personal values and morality - the aspects of personality or character that drive one to behave in a 'virtuous' way. They were defined by Aristotle as 'habits' to be cultivated in order to be worthy of the status of 'citizen'. The refined practice of such habits would lead to *eudemonia*, the happiness of a 'good life' pursued by all.

This orientation to ethics has an individualistic focus. Robert Solomon has reinterpreted ethics for contemporary secular societies where many choose to pursue a professional career in business. In this context, ethical considerations, including the pursuit of personal identity and satisfaction, involve responsibilities associated with being an employee. Solomon, an American business ethicist, reworked Aristotle's original virtue ethics to be applicable in an organizational setting, adapting the six dimensions to the moulding of the 'character' of an employee, manager or executive, rather than the citizen role to which Athenians aspired. The new virtue ethics are community, holism, role identity, excellence, judgement and integrity.

Community

Working individuals join organizations. These in turn provide income, status and a sense of identity. Organizations are 'communities' or 'sites of mutual interdependency' that fit within society. By agreeing to 'belong' to them, and signing on as an employee, individuals become responsible for preserving that community. Allegiance to one's community is an element of personal identity and pride. Some individuals move from country to country, community to community and business to business. They may derive identity and pride by maintaining their network of contacts and learning. Career progression may require individuals to pursue job titles as a form of personal identity.

Role Identity

This dimension of virtue ethics encourages each individual to consider organizational role identity, and its associated duties, before choosing to act. Individuals are paid to fulfil specific duties and their associated responsibilities. Consider the different roles played by accounting, information technology, human resource management and marketing within a company. To be effective, each employee must behave as required to fulfil specific role requirements. There may be role conflicts either between role fulfilment within an organization or between one's role as an employee and for example that of a parent, sibling or citizen.

Excellence

To act 'virtuously' in an organization, individuals must do their best and seek to excel, not merely comply at the lowest lowest level. In *Search of Excellence*, the organizations are able to survive, and even thrive, in a competitive environment. As a personal philosophy, it encourages individuals to be fully and creatively engaged in their work.

Holism

This dimension requires each individual to recognize and apply core human values. These include respect for life and the rights of strangers to the decisions they make in their working lives. Holism encourages managers and decision makers to treat the rights and needs of their employees, suppliers and customers as respectfully as they would those of their family and friends.

Judgement

The ability to judge effectively is an essential business 'virtue'. It is a product of upbringing, education and professional development. Managers and decision makers are continually required to master facts and approaches so that they may make sound judgements. Solomon sees this as the 'linchpin of all the virtues' because it seeks to balance and mediate conflicts.

Integrity

Solomon regards integrity as the ability to demonstrate 'courage under fire', where people display the ability to act properly when core principles are threatened. In the context of the individual's corporate duties and responsibilities, integrity is demonstrated when someone knows whether to 'conform' to organizational demands or to 'rebel' against them. Managers possessing integrity in this sense will make the hard decisions, will be prepared to face up to difficult situations and will acknowledge ethical dilemmas.

Virtue ethics, as identified above, reflects an approach that is most appropriate in organizations where flexibility is required and personal autonomy is high. The types of organizations that strongly emphasize virtue ethics are likely to be consulting firms and accounting and law practices. Virtue is a powerful and pertinent area of ethical analysis for senior executives - CEOs and board members. Corporate scandals and collapses often are associated with organizations whose senior managers seemed to disregard the concerns outlined above in virtue ethics.

Deontology

Deontology is the arena of ethics associated with seeking to answer the question 'Is it right?' and searches for 'rightness'. Traditionally, deontology has involved reference to a set of principles, defined 'rights', duties, or obligations. In a business sense, it has become associated with adherence to appropriate rules and regulations and their associated processes. Hence, an organization that emphasizes a deontological approach to 'right' behaviour is likely to be, in Petrick and Quinn's terms, control oriented and internally focused - such as a hospital, a prison, or a bank. Such organizations have a clear and well defined understanding of their principles and are able to manage and create 'ethical' behaviour because they create guidelines on how the principles should be upheld and implemented. Examples include: hospitals making people well;

governments agencies that protect society; and, the financial institutions that manage depositors' funds prudentially.

In this context categorical imperative is another example of deontology. According to this perspective, one can determine 'right action' by reflecting on whether or not that behaviour should be universally applied. This could be determined by referring to three 'laws':

1. 'act as if the maxim of thy action were to become by thy will a universal law of nature';
2. 'act that you use humanity, whether in your own person or in the person of any other, same time as an and, never merejyas a means';
3. 'act that we may think of ourselves as legislating irnrvers laws through our maxims'.

Thus, the determination to act in a certain way is based on the judgement that the decision taken would become a moral obligation for every person facing the same circumstances, based on the respect due to every human being. In the business context, categorical imperative can help resolve questions about whether to purchase goods made by indentured labour or that cause environmental damage. The corporate directors recognize that the implications of decisions reached should be monthly and universally compelling.

Roles and responsibility ~ principles and process The increased reliance on regulation as a means of improving corporate governance recently has given deontological approaches greater and wider prominence. There are two significant reasons for this increased recognition. Firstly, with globalization and the growth of multinational corporations, initiatives have emerged to regulate and control business behaviour. Responses range from aspiration based principles to regulate MNC activities through home country legislation such as anti-corruption legislation or the laws prohibiting corporations from engaging in corruption in foreign countries. The aim is to raise awareness and thus discourage business managers from undertaking activities incompattible with good business and social justice around the world. Secondly, since the corporate collapses in 2000-2001 (Enron, World Com, Parmalat and Arthur Andersen) several different countries have passed legislation to encourage directors and executives to act more 'ethically'.

Teleology

Teleology is the study of the end or purpose of things. In the ethical context, it involves the pursuit of the best outcome. The question involves the notion of 'good' understood as the best possible result of an action or decision. It is a term derived from the two Greek words, *telos.* meaning 'purpose or end' and *logos,* meaning 'word'. It is often seen in terms of individualism from two perspectives - first, the 'self, often known as ethical egoism - 'what is best for me' and second, the 'other' - altruism, 'what is best for the other(s)'. Teleology can also relate to 'the group' - utilitarianism, 'what is best for all of us'. In other hand an ethical action is that which produces 'the greatest good for the greatest number'. This way of conceptualizing ethics is also known as consequentialism. Emphasis is on 'What are the consequences of my/our actions?'

In business, much decision-making is concerned with outcomes such as how to improve profitability, how to increase sales, how to make products that consumers want or need. The goal-oriented focus of many business decisions corresponds with teleology. Business managers tend to be comfortable with this approach

Tensions emerge when business decisions have different impacts on stakeholders, especially when they create winners and losers. Executives continually have to make decisions that must be balanced in terms of their outcomes. Those who understand teleological analysis and practice it, consciously taking account of the impact on all stakeholders, are likely to be seen as ethical decision makers. Those who are unable to foresee the inevitable 'unintended consequences' of decisions are more likely to be tripped up by unwanted and unexpected ethical dilemmas.

Conversely, considerable tension in organizations can emerge because managers are conscious of outcomes. Decisions, that seen 'too hard' may be shelved. The drive for self-preservation may mean that people seek to avoid responsibility because of their awareness of inevitable 'bad' outcomes. Often 'good' managers, those who can 'just do it', are those prepared to make 'the tough choices'. Equally, the situation in which they find themselves may permit them to direct actions of others that they themselves wouldn't undertake. The question of who has responsibility for the strategy and who is responsible for 'getting the job done' may be divorced. This can permit a level of cognitive dissonance to creep into the decision-making process and commitment to tasks. Given that business demands that decisions must be made, when they are made 'consciously' and recognize all consequences, the chance of balanced outcomes is increased. Anticipated tangible results of actions may be assessed using decision-making tools such as cost/benefit analysis or SWOT analysis. Hence, this approach to ethics is appropriate when organizations undertake strategic planning, risk assessment and performance monitoring and evaluation. It is also directly connected to stakeholder theory.

Systems Ethics

As business systems and processes become more complex and supply chain networks enable improved organizational performance, a systemic approach to ethics has also become more necessary. This area involves ways that an organization develops and maintains its ethical culture. The approaches covered by virtue ethics, deontology and teleology together combine to develop an appropriate and effective ethical culture. This approach is described as the formulation of an integrity system for an organization. It is a relatively new field of organizational development that is increasing in importance as establishments either works jointly in different countries and regions.

Systems ethics can be seen from both an internal and external perspective. Internal systems relate to the development, within organizations, of: codes of conduct; clear structures and systems which encourage ethical behavours; ethics training and development for both managers and executives; ethics monitoring and reporting; and 'whistleblower' protection. External system within countries relate to: effective legal systems; appropriate public service agencies which encourage integrity in public policy; well developed oversight agencies, that protect the rights of the public in both the public and private sectors.

Another theme of systems ethics relates to the increased economic and social significance of multinational corporations. A more holistic notion of systems theory considers the interaction between economic, socio-cultural and environmental systems both locally and globally. This ethical approach to organizations involves themes such as corporate social responsibility, sustainability and 'triple bottom line' analysis.

ETHICAL ASPECTS OF FREE MARKET SYSTEMS

Although there is no free competition in the marketplace, the issue of competition is still the most important element that can be used to distinguish between the free market and the command market. Thus, the ethical aspects of competition could be used to explain the case of free market ethics for several reasons. Competition is supposed to be a mechanism for the free market production and distribution of goods and services that people want. Competition in the economic order has supported and furthered rivalry as an essential cultural characteristic of a free market society. Most activities of the free market can be viewed as a competitive contest in which people engage to provide products and services for a profit as has been noted by many researchers.

The Main Sources of Free Market Ethics

In addition to the economic nature of the free market system, there are some roots to ethics in such a market. Three widely accepted sources of ethics in a free market are market ethics, the Protestant ethic, and the liberty ethic. These three ethics set the stage for the Industrial Revolution and the accompanying growth in business. During this period, the industrial capitalist was allowed to run free—to build giant corporations, exploit workers, and engage in fiercely competitive practices for profit and economic expansion.

Market Ethics

The ethics of the free market system were set through the writings of Adam Smith. In *The Wealth of Nations*, Smith's message was in tune with a growing number of would-be entrepreneurs seeking academic rationalisation for their views. England thus found in Smith's writings a market ethic—an economic sanction for the private initiative rather than mercantilism, competition rather than protection, innovation rather than economic stagnation, and self-interest rather than state interest—as a motivating force.

The Protestant Ethic

In *The Protestant Ethic and the Spirit of Capitalism*, Max Weber set forth a connection between the Protestant ethic and capitalism. The Protestant ethic, sometimes called the work ethic, had its beginning in biblical times. Saint Paul stated, *"If any one will not work, let him not eat."* Martin Luther later provided additional religious sanction for work and achievement. There is, however, another widely held point of view of the Protestant work ethic, as stated by Rogene Buchholz:

> The Protestant ethic not only had behavioral implications, as Weber and others have pointed out; it also had ideological implications in providing a moral legitimacy for capitalism. As an ideology, the Protestant ethic served to legitimise the capitalism system by providing a moral justification for the pursuit of profit and distribution of income that are a part of the system.

The Liberty Ethic

According to the writings of John Locke, the liberty ethic placed man in a participatory role in government, encouraged private property, discouraged rule by dictatorial whims, and introduced more freedom and individualism in all spheres of life. The liberty ethic has encouraged the rise and applicability of the other two types of ethics. As Carroll stated: that the postulates of economic freedom (the market ethic) and the sanctions of individual rewards for worldly efforts (the Protestant ethic) can operate freely only in a political system that is conducive to individual liberty.

ETHICAL DECISION-MAKING IN BUSINESS: AN INTEGRATED APPROACH

Ethics in the broadcast sense provides the basic condition of acceptance for any activity. The ethics of a game or sport both implies its purpose and specifies rules of fair play. In the same vein, it is also argued that the ethics of business is the ethics of a game, which is different from the ethics of religion or society, since business has its own characteristics as a game—a game that demands both a special strategy and an understanding of its special ethics. Furthermore, the business game is also considered as a poker game, in which certain rules govern the ethical behavior of managers within a company. The rules of the business game are the state laws and the strategies within these laws that constitute the atmosphere of business behavior. Consequently, business should have the right to follow any approach to achieve its objectives within this atmosphere, regardless of the approach used, since no violation of the rules of the game occurs, as in the case of poker.

However, there are three parallels between poker and business strategy: in the option to enter the game, in the demand to interpret, and in the resultant uncertainty in the mind of the opponent. These similarities between business and poker might be clearly observed in bidding strategy which implies inverted signaling intended to create uncertainty in the mislead opponents. Hence, in poker, one correctly distrusts others, ignores claims of friendship, and knows that cunning, deception, and concealment of strengths, weaknesses, and intentions are vital.

What is universal about these examples is that these managers, each functioning on a different corporate level, are concerned with one thing—getting the job done. Most companies give numerous awards for achievement and accomplishment, for sales, for growth, for longevity and loyalty, but there are no medals in the business world for honesty, compassion or truthfulness. However, the comparison of business to poker is unfair and inaccurate since business is too important an area of human endeavour to be regarded as a game. Others consider the idea to condone unethical business practices and say that a business executive cannot separate the ethics of his or her business from the ethics of his or her home life. With regard to the parallels which have been considered between business and poker, some argue that the argument, by analogy of course, does not demand complete parallels. All decisions may be decisions of strategy, but not all decisions need be in terms of a noncooperative zero-sum game. In business, one could participate as one of a group, or even as one of a society, and a cooperative solution, as defined, means that the individual player can gain more by cooperation than he or she could by going it alone. Finally, it must be noted that if business fails to raise the moral level of its practices, it invites eventual reprisals from the public and government.

The conclusion here is that the free market system has two major objectives: to produce the goods and services that consumers want and to distribute the outcome of the production process among those who participate in the process. Each of these objectives has at least one main criterion for evaluation. The main criterion for the production function should be efficiency, which means to produce goods of high quality at a low cost. The main criterion for the distribution function should be justice.

If each criterion is applied to its relevant function, one might say that, from the production point of view, the free market system is still the most efficient system in the world as compared to other systems, such as a command system or mixed economy system. However, no system can have a full degree of efficiency. However, from the disruption of outcome, the free market system fails to fit the criterion of justice among groups of society; rather, it creates a large job of the inequality situation compared to other market systems.

An appropriate approach to making ethical decisions takes all perspectives into account. All ethical theories are interrelated. If applied in isolation they cease to be effective. Personal values and behaviour, principles and processes, impacts and outcomes and overall systems must all be considered before making business decisions. In response to the basic initial question 'What ought to be done?', the subsidiary questions, could be considered in sequence, starting from those related to virtue ethics. This highlights the need to recognize the micro, personal ethical position, through the organizational impact, to systemic considerations and social/environmental implications. Depending on the situation, the sequence could start at either the individual end (virtue ethics) or from the worldview perspective. If managers followed this process of analysis, they are likely to diminish the risk of making short term decisions which threaten sustainability.

Personal values and behaviour, principles and processes, impacts and outcomes and overall systems must all be considered before making business decisions. In response to the basic initial question 'What ought to be done?', the subsidiary questions, noted in Figure 1, could be considered in sequence, starting from those related to virtue ethics. This highlights the need to recognize the micro, personal ethical position, through

FIGURE 1
A DECISION-MAKING DIAGRAM

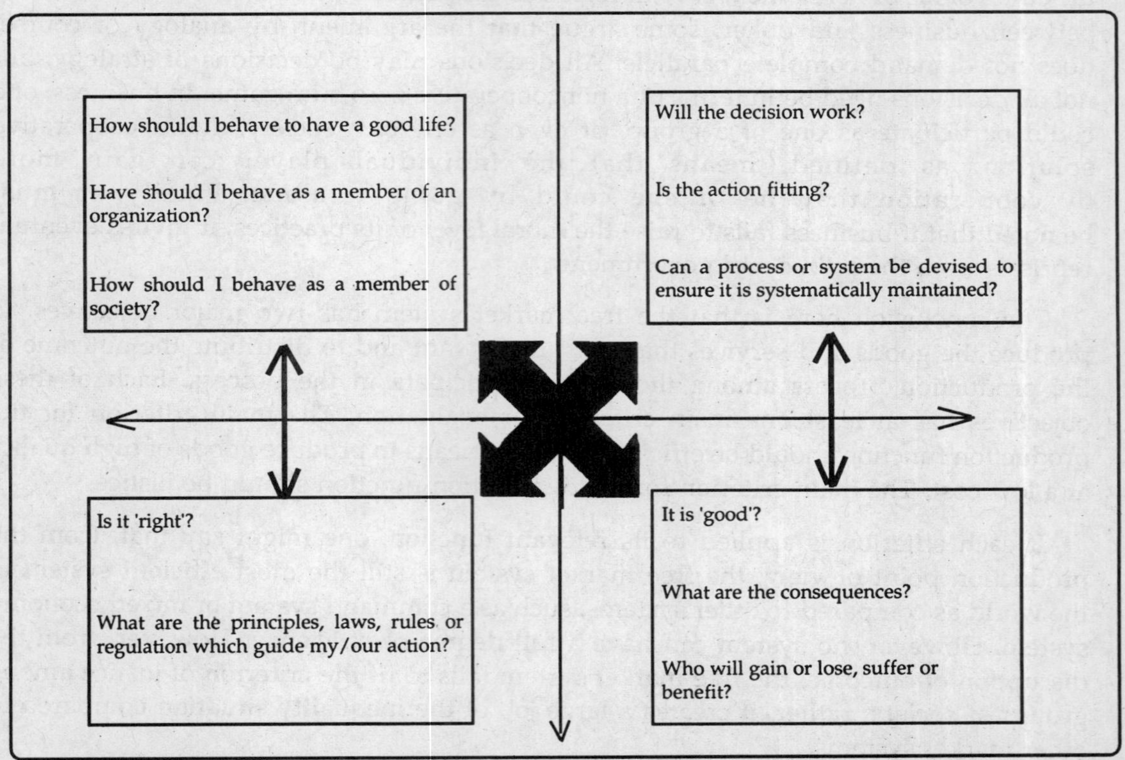

the organizational impact, to systemic considerations and social/environmental implications. Depending on the situation, the sequence could also start at either the individual end (virtue ethics) or from the world view perspective. If managers followed this process of analysis, it would likely decrease the risk that stems from short-term decisions that are not sustainable social or when economical consequences are not foreseen.

Stakeholder Theory

Stakeholders are increasingly recognized by corporations as influencing relates to good business ethics.

The concept of 'stakeholder engagement' describes the interaction of an organization with members of a number of groupings. These include those who have a direct economic relationship as well as those who have an indirect involvement and interest in the entity's activities. Stakeholders are characterized in two groups, namely, primary (direct) and indirect (secondary); Primary-Directare are financial investors; shareholder/security holders; Banks and other finance providers; employees - management/non-management; customers and suppliers; government bodies such as the taxation department and business or corporate regulation agencies. Indirect Social are: local cornrnumties represented by local and state government agencies and lobby groups; regional, national and global communities, represented by non-government organizations (NGOs), lobby groups etc. and Indirect Environmental; government agencies such as environmental protection and planning authorities; and non-government bodies representing environmental interests NGOs, research institutes, etc.

Business most commonly considers direct stakeholders. Such interests may be represented by others, for example, directors acting on behalf of shareholders. The interests of direct stakeholders can be positively influenced by an organization's actions. Consequently, while seeking to ensure protection, they are keen to see business in a positive way. However, the environment and the community are more likely to limit or control the impact of business growth.

In the past these interests often have been ignored or negatively affected by business decisions. For this reason the environment is often referred to as the 'silent stakeholder'. Advocates often act on behalf of social or environmental threats, especially those posed to future generations. The growing power and concern of such people or groups has forced business managers to become increasingly sensitive to critics portrayed as primarily 'negative' influences, who oppose their decisions. Decision makers who apply stakeholder theory may come to realize that negotiating with those stakeholders who could frustrate their business purpose is as important as gaining support from, say, financial backers.

FIGURE 2

A STAKEHOLDER MAP

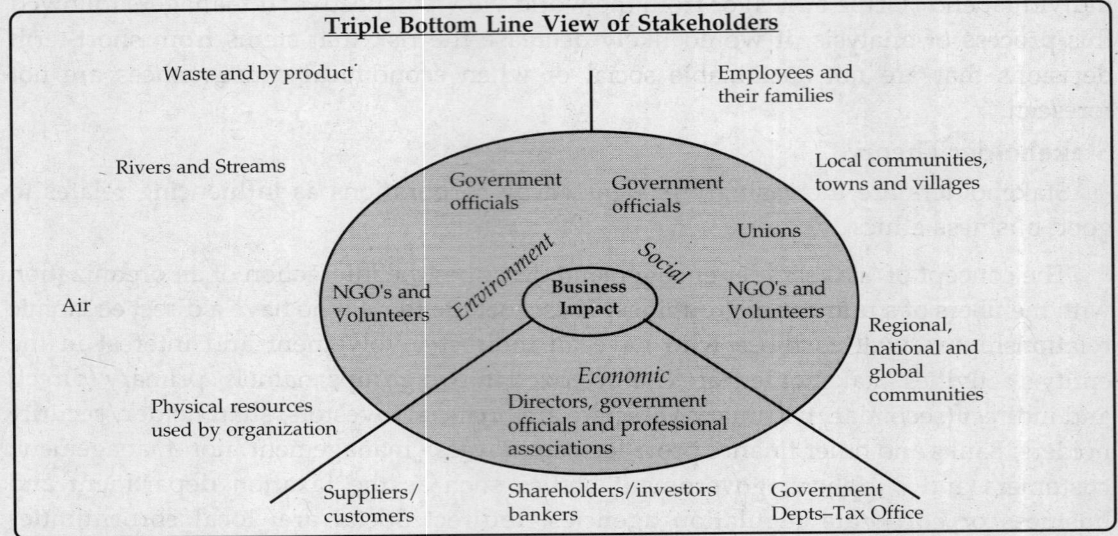

The Figure 2 identifies the relationships between a business and its stakeholders. Whilst the stakeholders in the outer circle both can be direct and indirect, those relating to the social and environmental considerations tend to be represented by advocates.

Sustainability, Corporate Social Responsibility (CSR) and the 'Triple Bottom Line'

Traditionally businesses 'accounted for their actions' by producing annual financial reports. Such documents show the economic impact - companies' profits or losses and their status in terms of assets and liabilities at a given point in time. Growing concerns about the social and environmental impact of business and the sustainability of current patterns of production and consumption have increased the demands that business must take a broader view of its impact. As such there have been growing calls for corporations, especially those operating globally, to incorporate social and environmental, as well as economic, responsibility as part of their mission.

Such concerns led to the concept of the 'triple bottom line', namely that businesses should report on their social and environmental activities and the financial 'bottom line'. Such disclosure has proved difficult and little headway has been made to introduce standards for reporting such broad scale data. However, there is a growing recognition of the need, and the feasibility, for CSR as a basis of ensuring sustainability.

FIGURE 3

A SUSTAINABILITY DIAGRAM

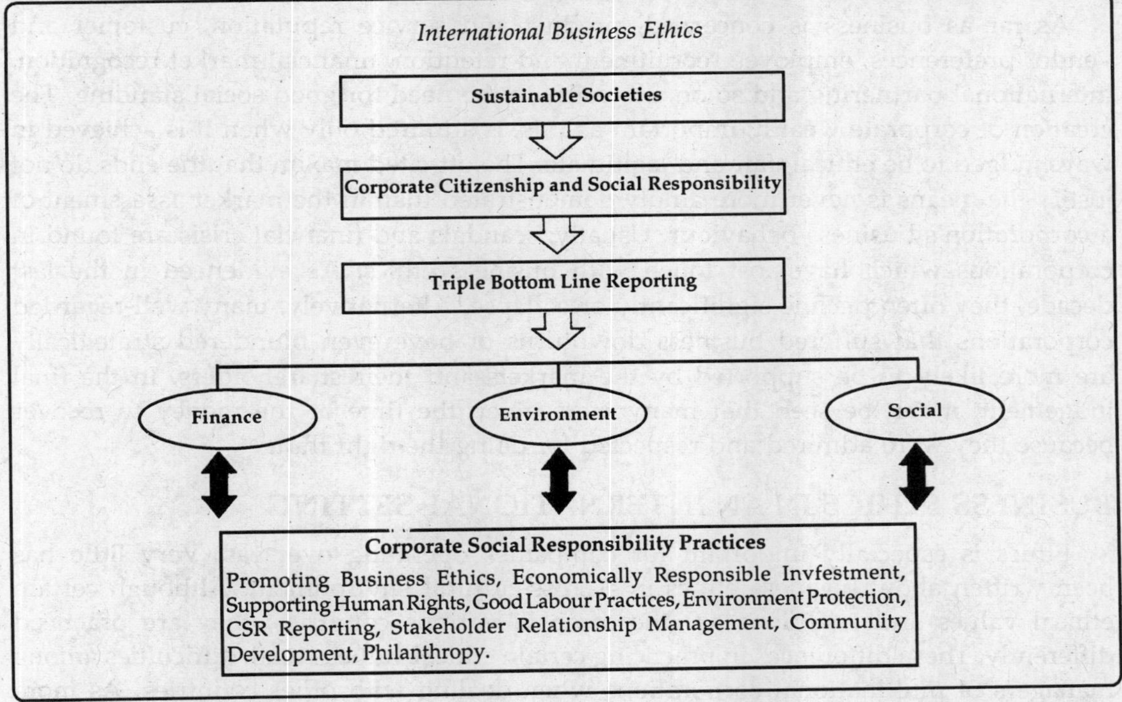

Figure 3 identifies the relationship between the concepts of the triple bottom line, corporate social responsibility and sustainability.

In the final analysis, ethics is essential for individuals, business corporations and well functioning societies. People who maintain high standards of personal ethics are often noted as those who are able to 'sleep well' - they are confident and happy that their behaviour is well founded and will not lead to future dilemmas. This notion is often related to the 'sunshine test' which suggests that an action or decision should be avoided if its disclosure would lead to embarrassment or shame.

Organizations known for their high standards of ethics often are identified as those people are proud to work for. In that sense they become 'employers of choice'. Most employees prefer to work for ethical organizations and are attracted to them. They are likely to be easier and more pleasant places to work in as the behaviour of others usually is predictable and based on socially accepted norms.

When ethical behaviour becomes the norm in societies are inevitably more harmonious, predictable and enjoyable environments to live in. Each citizen leads a 'good life'. Social capital is high and people enjoy high levels of social trust. Businesses function effectively and people are able to develop positively and to their best ability in such environments.

As far as business is concerned, product and service reputation, customer and vendor preferences, employee recruitment and retention, financial market recognition, international partnering and so on, all testify to the need for good social standing. The creation of corporate wealth, important as it is, is admired only when it is achieved in ways judged to be ethical, fair and legitimate. The oft-cited maxim that the ends do not justify the means is never more amply demonstrated than in the market assessment of a corporation's business behaviour. Usually, scandals and financial crisis are found in corporations which have lost touch with business ethics. As evidenced in the last decade, they often decline significantly or collapse. Alternatively, many well-regarded corporations that suffered business downturns or have even blundered strategically are more likely to be supported by the markets and their shareholders. In the final judgement, it can be seen that many were given the time or the money to recover because they were admired and respected for doing the right thing.

BUSINESS ETHICS IN AN INTERNATIONAL SETTING

Ethics is especially important for companies operating overseas. Very little has been written about business ethics in a cross-cultural environment. Although certain ethical values and traditions are the same in various countries, they are practiced differently. These differences in practicing certain ethical values create difficulties among managers of multinational corporations when dealing with other countries. As more corporations move into the global arena, dilemmas related to ethical values and traditions are becoming increasingly common. Scant attention has been given to understanding the differences in the processes used by people in different cultures to evaluate ethical situations. The differences in cognitive process and values are a good starting point for understanding intercultural differences. The issue of business ethics across cultures is difficult to address because it must deal with understanding how individuals from different cultures approach ethical issues and how differences in their approach affect the criteria by which they judge the ethical acceptability of a situation.

Many multinational corporations have developed codes of conduct to help their employees deal with different value settings. However, these codes deals with broad corporate relations with the government, ,in particular political contributions, foreign government bribes, and the integrity of financial records. They rarely cover specific ethical positions on a significant number of issues.

NEGOTIATING ACROSS CULTURES

International business negotiations face enormous cultural barriers, as illustrated by the difficulties that Westerners have had in negotiating business agreements with other cultures. When people from two different countries of origin try to negotiate on political or commercial issues, they have to understand and acknowledge any ethical dilemmas that might occur. These standards of conduct and moral judgment on any issue are the basis for deciding the outcome. One negotiator might misinterpret the message and views of another, which can cause an argument and create distrust. Basic concepts are fairness, dependability, friendship, and timeliness.

There are two models of negotiating, as presented by Solomon and Bertrand: the linear model, which relates to Chinese culture, and the encompassing model, which is said to be more descriptive. The first stage of the linear model (Figure 4) is the discussion of *principles* or broad goals. In the culture of China, this stage is emphasised so that foreigners understand the commitments they make. The second stage deals with bargaining *positions*, or what each has to offer and wants to obtain. The third stage clarifies *details*. The fourth and final stage is *implementing* the process.

FIGURE 4

THE LINEAR MODEL OF NEGOTIATION

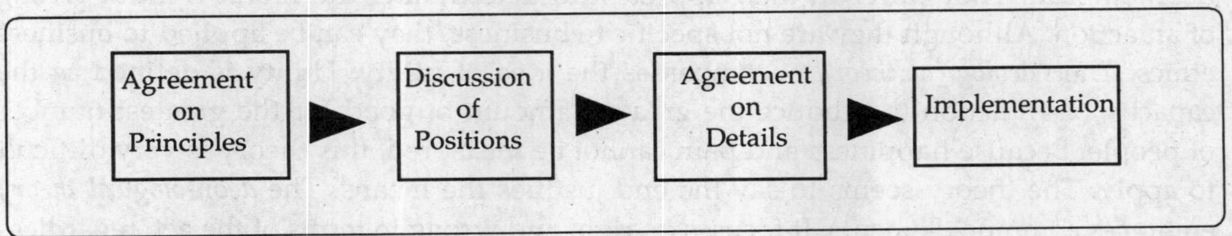

The encompassing model (Figure 5) includes the same stages but emphasises the degree to which each stage is presented. The Chinese base their negotiations on enhancing their national goals, which include promoting national development, growth, and enhancement of life in China. The Chinese expect Western firms to sacrifice their goals if necessary in order that the Chinese may achieve their goals.

FIGURE 5

THE ENCOMPASSING MODEL OF NEGOTIATION

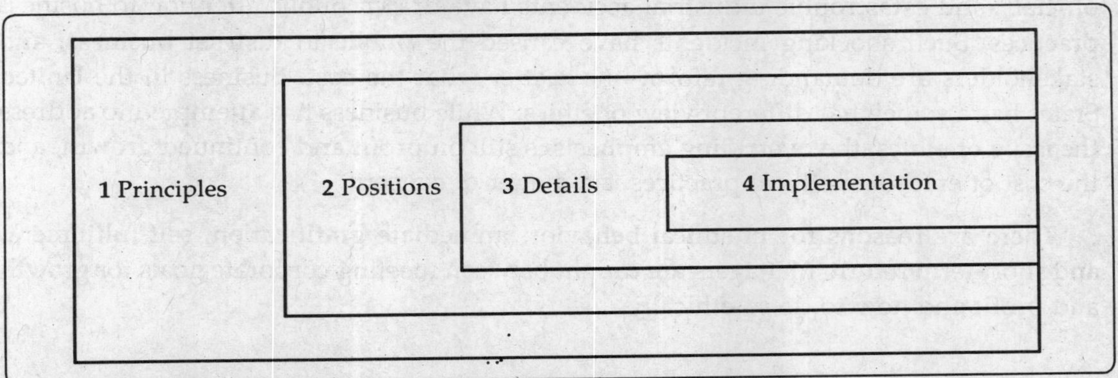

Western firms base their negotiations on such corporate goals as product quality, profit, and enhancing shareholder value. Sacrificing corporate goals would deny corporate responsibility, which is the main reason for negotiating.

Cultural barriers present ethical dilemmas in negotiating between cultures. Misinterpreted messages and views can create arguments and feelings of betrayal between participants. A particular problem may never be resolved, but it should at least be recognised during the process of negotiation.

GLOBAL STRATEGY ISSUES AND ETHICS

Everyone knows that honesty is the best policy, that good triumphs over evil, that the man or woman with a reputation for fair dealings will prosper, and that those who maximise profit are perfectly honest. However, there are probably more examples where the opposite is true.

Ethical principles are derived from two major theories: the teleological and the deontological. They differ in their approach to determining the moral right or wrong of an action. Although they are not specific to business, they can be applied to business ethics. The *teleological theory* encompasses the idea of utility. Utility is defined as the capacity of an action to produce the greatest amount of good for the greatest number of people. Because happiness and pain cannot be measured, this theory is very difficult to apply. The theory seems to say the end justifies the means. The *deontological theory* embraces common elements. It focuses on right and wrong in terms of the act, regardless of outcome. The value of an act is in the motive. Right or wrong is determined on the basis of duty, honesty, and fairness.

A number of events have caused Americans to distrust big business. Watergate and political kickbacks in a number foreign countries added to the negative perceptions. Polls indicate that public confidence in heads of corporation is as low as 15% and that the general public and business executives see a decline in ethical behavior in the United States. Recent scandals such as insider trading, Watergate, payments to foreign officials, and catastrophic industrial accidents have drawn public attention to business practices. Such shocking incidents have caused the public to distrust business, and stakeholders are demanding reform—no matter what the cost. Business in the United States has a somewhat different view of ethics. While business has attempted to address the issue of ethics, the overriding emphasis is still on profit and continued growth, and the cost of enforcing ethical practices is a matter of concern.

There are reasons for unethical behavior: immediate gratification, self-fulfillment, and short-term return. Managers are caught between meeting corporate goals for growth and profit and how to do so ethically.

Individuals new to an organisation are governed by corporate norms. By the time someone reaches the top, he or she is well entrenched in the norms of the organisation. It seems to be a world where treachery pays, power is abused, and dishonesty is tolerated. According imply the moral advantages are simple. Concepts of trust and more broadly of virtue would be empty if bad faith and wickedness were not financially rewarding. If wealth naturally followed straight dealings we would only need to speak about conflicts between the long term and the short, stupidity and wisdom, high discount rates and low. We would worry only about others' good sense, not about their integrity. It is the very absence of predictable financial reward that makes honesty a moral quality we hold dear.

Power has the ability to do both great harm and tremendous good. People do business with someone they do not trust if it suits their purpose or accept a deal because it is too good to pass up. Sometimes the powerful leave others no choice but to play ball. Ethical questions fall into gray areas, and because competition has intensified, it seems plausible that more individuals will be pressured into seeing how far they can stretch the rules. Therefore, it is probably a good idea to ask the following questions when making any decision: Is it fair? Will I feel good about it?

To quote Ivan Boesky, "Greed is all right, by the way. I want you to know that. I think greed is healthy. You can be greedy and still feel good about yourself." Mr. Boesky was feeling very good about himself, and then he was indicted for insider trading. Insider trading is the use of confidential information, not available to the general public, to make capital gains in the market. Boesky cut a deal with the SEC. In exchange for allowing the SEC to tap his phone for two months, and testifying against any individuals or firms indicted as a result of the conversations, he agreed to put $50 million in escrow for the benefit of investors hurt by his illegal trading. He also agreed to pay the U.S. Treasury a $50 million fine. He was barred from the investment business in the United States for life and faced a five-year jail term. He was also permitted to dump $440 million of his portfolio onto the market before the SEC went public with his indictment.

Regardless of one's orientation as to the appropriate corporate objective, even Milton Friedman would agree that business must be conducted while conforming to the basic rules of society, which are embodied in law and in ethical custom. The problem and challenge for MNEs is to define what is meant by "basic rules of society." There will always be gray areas not defined by laws or regulations, or where laws differ from country to country, or where laws and practices diverge. In some countries, there may be a complete absence of laws in areas such as pollution and environmental protection.

Because of these gray areas, MNEs face ethical considerations that vary from one market and geographic region to another. A list of ethical issues that may confront

MNEs is shown in Table-2. The list is far from exhaustive and is connected to a wide range of strategic and managerial decisions. Some of these issues have become highly public in the past few years, such as the safety and compensation practices of manufacturing plants in emerging markets that supply MNEs. Ethical considerations also tend to be connected to the political mood of the day. For example, the decision to move a company's headquarters outside a country for tax reasons may become politically charged while in the past that decision has gone largely unnoticed. Other ethical considerations are more subtle, but not necessarily less strategic. In China, gift giving can play a key role in solidifying trust and understanding with potential customers, suppliers, government officials, and so on. Many MNEs forbid gift giving in their home market—what happens when they go to China? Is gift giving in China morally acceptable because it is part of Chinese culture and morally unacceptable in the United States because it is not part of the U.S. culture?

While there will always be disagreements about the meaning of what is morally and ethically appropriate, in most societies the boundary between ethical and unethical business practices is reasonably clear. Obviously, illegal actions are not morally acceptable. When the boundary is not clear, or the law has not yet been established, or when firms go against what is publicly acceptable, governments may have to step in.

TABLE 2

Typical Questions of Ethics Confronting Multinational Enterprises (MNEs)

1. Should a firm do business in a country in which the government may be violating human rights?
2. Should a firm market a product in a country or region that lacks adequate consumer protection, product liability laws, and certain penalties for unlawful behaviors?
3. If a firm makes a product that has potentially harmful side effects when used improperly, should that firm market its product in a country where a high level of illiteracy is likely to mean that some customers will be unable to follow directions for safe product usage?
4. Should a firm have a responsibility for end-user behaviour that may not be legal?
5. Should a firm use bribery in a country where corruption is widespread?
6. Should a firm pay facilitation fees to ensure that goods clear customs in a timely manner?
7. Should a firm follow local laws in areas such as employee safety and environmental protections?
8. How should female employees be treated in countries where the rights of women are not equal to those of men?
9. Should MNEs use tax avoidance strategies, such as moving the head office to a lower tax regime in order to reduce taxes?
10. Should an MNE do business with *a* firm that engaged in actions that would *be* illegal in the home country of the MNE but are legal in another jurisdiction?

When a firm crosses an international border, there is a need to develop new understanding of ethical norms and it must learn about the new market or society. As a starting point, it should be easy to say that firms should avoid illegal activities when doing business in new markets. Unfortunately, the legal environment in countries such as China is murky at best, and what is legal or illegal is often far from clear. Moreover, laws in many countries are not transparent and seem to be almost a moving target. When shifting from the rule of law to the more ambiguous notion of ethical custom, it is easy to see why international managers often struggle to make the "right" decision. What may be legal and culturally acceptable in the home country may be illegal and culturally unacceptable in the new market. In a country like India, the rule of law may be clearer than in China because of the British legal heritage. However, India's different religions, languages, geographies, and cultural traditions impose many challenges in determining what is culturally acceptable. What is a norm in one part of the country may be a major violation of acceptable behaviour in another region. Moreover, the ancient India exists in tandem with a modern government and regulatory environment characterized by red tape and bureaucracy.

The question of whose morals and whose ethical standards rule confronts MNEs as soon as they cross a border. For example, the issue of environmental laws and regulations is highly controversial. In the debate about the merits of free trade, those against free trade often argue that firms take advantage of lax environmental standards in emerging markets (in other words, firms export their pollution and garbage to less developed nations). Most MNEs will publicly promise to obey all applicable laws and regulations in the countries in which they operate. However, what if the environmental regulation is weak or nonexistent? In this case, MNEs need to make decisions about which environmental laws to uphold: those of the home country, those of the country in which a subsidiary is located, or those of a third country? If the environmental laws of one country are not very stringent, it could be cheaper for the subsidiary to produce in that country. But, is it ethically acceptable to knowingly operate a manufacturing facility in an emerging market that creates more pollution than a similar plant in, say, the United States or Germany.

So does an MNE have a moral and ethical responsibility to ensure a safe, fair, environmentally sustainable, and legal working environment in emerging markets when local laws are silent or less stringent than other countries? Addressing this question can lead one into a philosophical debate involving relativism, objectivism, and pluralism. Ethical relativism holds that morality is relative to the norms of one's culture. That is, whether an action is right or wrong depends on the moral and cultural norms of the society in which it is practiced. Ethical objectivism suggests that there is a single universal standard of ethical truth against which all behaviors can be measured. That is, what is ethical behaviour in one society should also be followed in another society. Ethical pluralism is, in a sense, somewhere between relativism and objectivism. The core claim of ethical pluralism is that there may be multiple correct answers to ethical questions of right and wrong. The obvious question is, what is the basis for finding the correct answers and how is this much different from relativism?

In an attempt to deal with the vexing issue of international business ethics, a pluralistic framework has been developed and applied to global ethics. The framework, called *integrative social contracts theory,* is based on the argument that firms must understand the transcultural value implications of their actions. The framework incorporates the concept of norms of behaviour against which an MNE's actions can be plotted. Hypernorms are principles that exist in all cultures, such as fundamental human rights. Consistent norms are more culturally specific but likely consistent with most cultures. Moral free space involves norms that are inconsistent with at least some legitimate norms found in other economic cultures. Illegitimate norms are those that are clearly inconsistent with hypernorms.

Although this framework does not completely eliminate the question of whose values to follow, it does suggest that firms must never resort to *"When in Rome do as the Romans do"* behaviour, nor should they insist that *"We have one set of ethical values that we employ wherever we do business."* For those actions that do not clearly fall within the hypernorm category, managers have to be creative. Cultures are different, which means that those making ethical decisions must respect the right of other cultures to shape their own societal values. MNE managers will often experience moral tensions and dilemmas; this should be viewed as the natural way of global business and not something that must be avoided. For example, in Singapore the concept of maternity leave exists but is not well developed, and many business-people (men and women) are openly dismissive of the idea that women should have guaranteed job security after taking time off to have a baby. In Sweden, a country with one of the most generous maternity-leave policies in the world, women can get up to 96 weeks of leave at 80 percent of their salary. Should a Swedish company operating in Singapore offer the same maternity-leave benefits as in Sweden? This issue would appear to fall within both the consistent norm and moral free space areas. While short maternity leave in Singapore is generally considered reasonable, the Swedish model would be seen as excessive and unfair to employers.

The actions and decisions of many firms have ethical dimensions. From a global strategy perspective, a particularly important decision deals with the product markets and geographic regions in which a firm competes, or seeks to compete. From an international ethics perspective, the question of *"Where should a company do business?"* has various subquestions, such as *"Should a firm do business in a country in which the government may be violating human rights or should a firm market a product in a country or region that lacks adequate consumer protection, product liability laws, and certain penalties for unlawful behaviors?'* More generally, when ethical standards in one country are different from the norms of behaviour in the home market, global firms face three basic choices:

1. The firm can avoid doing business in that particular country.
2. The firm can enter the country, maintain its home market standards, and risk being at a competitive disadvantage to firms that follow the prevailing norms.

3. The firm can change its standards and play the game the way the locals do, following an argument such as *"What is corruption to one person may be the norm for the other."*

In an attempt to clarify MNEs' responsibilities to their host nations, Richard DeGeorge suggested moral guidelines for MNEs, such as "Multinationals should do no intentional direct harm. (See table-3.) It is unlikely that too many people would oppose these guidelines in principle. However, they raise practical questions about how a firm could measure and account for harm, development, cooperation, and other suggested outcomes.

TABLE 3

Richard DeGeorge's Seven Moral Guidelines for Multinational Enterprises (MNEs) Competing in Emerging Markets

- Multinationals should do no intentional direct harm.
- Multinationals should produce more good than bad for the host country.
- Multinationals should contribute by their activity to the host country's development.
- Multinationals should respect the human rights of their employees.
- To the extent that local culture does not violate ethical norms, multinationals should respect the local culture and work with and not against it.
- Multinationals should pay their fair share of taxes.
- Multinationals should cooperate with the local government in developing and enforcing just background institutions (i.e., laws, government regulations, consumer groups, labour unions).

Source: Richard DeGeorge, *Competing with Integrity in International Business* (New York: Oxford University Press, 1993).

Formal Corporate Ethics Programs

Given the wide array of ethical challenges created by globalization, the MNE's use of formal and informal structures in its management of ethical issues is an important consideration. A formal corporate ethics programs will usually include some or all of the following elements:

i) Formal ethics codes that articulate a firm's expectations about ethics

ii) Ethics committees charged with developing ethics policies, evaluating company or employee actions, and/or investigating and adjudicating possible violations

iii) Ethics communication systems to provide a means for employees to report abuses or obtain guidance

iv) Ethics officers or ombudspersons charged with coordinating policies, providing ethics education, or investigating allegations

v) Ethics training programs aimed at helping employees to recognize and respond to ethical issues disciplinary processes to address unethical behaviour

The problem with advice on global ethics is that it often appears either too oriented toward the MNE or hopelessly impractical. Thus, rather than offering advice we will conclude by saying:

i) All major strategic decisions have social, political, and ethical consequences.

ii) The corporation is not just an economic actor and all managers operating in the international arena will have to make decisions that involve more than just economic analysis.

iii) Although Milton Friedman says "stay within the rules of the game," it is not always clear what the rules are or who sets the rules or when the rules change.

iv) Just as innovation and creativity are the foundation of strategic choices with respect to product, markets, and customers, innovation and creativity will inevitably be necessary to manage global ethical challenges.

Over the period, internationalization influenced the role of ethics in MNEs since there is a positive relationship between the internationalization of a firm and its top executives' visible concern for ethical issues. Internationalization appears to heighten executives' concern to see that ethically proper behaviour occurs. In this both formal and informal controls play a role in managing ethical issues. In making strategic decisions about the global marketplace, firms must be prepared to grapple with issues that are absent from or less prevalent in their domestic markets, such as bribery, child labour and workplace safety issues, human rights violations, intellectual property theft, product liability and customer safety questions, and questionable environmental practices.

Given the broad range of potential situations that firms can encounter in international markets, a normative approach identifying specific business practices that qualify as ethically proper cannot capture the reality of global competition. For a code of conduct to meet the expectations of the various involved parties, four elements that must be present are:

1. Be economically viable for the MNE
2. Address substantive issues that are of importance to the various MNE stakeholders
3. Engage important stakeholders in the formation and implementation
4. Have specific measurable performance standards

The large corporation, and especially the multinational corporation, must become an active agent for social change. As a dominant institution in society, the corporation must assume its rightful place and contribute to shaping the public agenda instead of simply reacting to policy changes advocated by others. With continued globalization, MNEs will increase their share of world economic output, putting the largest MNEs in a unique position to impact people's lives.

QUESTIONS

1. Why be ethical? Discuss the Petrick and Quinn's business ethics orientation model.
2. Explain the concept of Deontology.
3. Discuss the concept of the good corporate citizen, and how business in different countries perceives its responsibility for social issues.
4. How ethical norms change in response to economic and political factors, and vary across cultures?
5. Discuss the concept of teleology.
6. Discuss the problems of ethical decision making within modern organizations and across cultures.
7. Critically examine the ethical aspects of free market systems.
8. Discuss an integrated approach to ethical decision-making in business.
9. How would you negotiate across cultures? What are the ethical issues involved in negotiating across culture which MNEs face?
10. Discuss the global strategy issue and ethics.
11. Where should a company do business? Should a firm do business in a country in which government may be violating human rights or should a firm market a product in a country or region that lacks adequate consumer protection, product liability laws, and certain penalties for unlawful behaviours?

REFERENCES

Adams, Jane, "A Job You Can Believe In," *New Woman*, pp. 90-94, March 1991.

Andrews, Kenneth R., "Ethics in Practice," *Harvard Business Review*, p. 102, September-October 1989.

Aristotle (2000), *Nihomachean Ethics,* in ed. Cohen, S.M., Curd, P. and Reeve, C.D.C. *Readings in Ancient Greek Philosophy* (Cambridge, MA: Hackett), pp. 577-86.

"Assuring America's Competitive Preeminence," *Business America*, pp. 3-12, March 2, 1987.

Berney, Karen, "That Ethical Edge," *Reader's Digest*, pp. 177-180, April 1988.

Bowers, E., "Confusion and Lost Sales Are the Payoffs from Foreign Bribery Act," *Iron Age*, p. 33, March 1, 1982.

Cook, J.M. and T.P. Kelley, "The Foreign Corrupt Practices Act Has Made the Internal Accounting Controls of Public Companies a Matter of Law," *Journal a/Accountancy*, pp. 56-64, January 1979.

Elkington, J. (1998), *Cannibals with Forks: The Triple Bottom Line of 21st Century Business* (Gabriola, BC: New Society Publishers).

"Foreign Corrupt Practices Act of 1977," *United States Code Congressional and Administrative News* (95th Congress First Session 1977, Vol. 1, 91 Stat., Public Law 95-213 IS. 3051), pp. 1494-1500, 1977.

Lieber, J., "Bribery is Back," *New Republic*, pp. 7-9, September 30, 1981.

Lissakors, K., "Don't Help Bribery Make a Comeback," *Washington Post, p.* C7, July 3, 1988.

"Misinterpreting the Antibribery Law," *Business Week*, p. 150, September 3, 1979.

Odiotne, George S., "Ethics for the Nineties," *Manage*, pp. 8-14, 33, April 1988.

Peters, T. and Waterman, R. (1982), *In Search of Excellence: Lessons from America's Best-Run Companies* (New York: Harper Collins).

Petrick, J.A. and Quinn, J.F. (1997), *Management Ethics: Integrity at Work* (Thousand Oaks, CA: Sage Publications).

Sandroff, Ronni, "How Ethical is American Business?" *Working Women*, pp. 113-116, September 1990.

Solomon, R.C. (1993), 'Corporate Roles, Personal Virtues, Moral Mazes: An Aristotelian Approach to Virtue Ethics', in Coady, A. and Sampford, C. (eds) *Business, Ethics and the Law* (St Leonards, NSW: Federation Press), pp. 24-51.

22

SOCIAL RESPONSIBILITY OF AN INTERNATIONAL FIRM

INTRODUCTION

Corporate social responsibility (CSR) encompasses an array of meanings and intended applications that have undergone substantial modifications over time. These are important to note and understand because they influence the dialogue between governments, business and other civil society groups. The same term, or its variations may carry different implications among various parties regarding the legitimacy, obligations and impact of corporate social responsibility standards. All societal groups are expected to perform certain roles and functions that can change over time with a society's own evolution. Expectations related to business enterprises, and particularly MNCs, are undergoing unusually rapid change due to the expanded role these enterprises play in a globalising society. *Should this expansion of action, space and rights be accompanied by an increase in corporate responsibilities?* In the international context, this question attracts particular attention because MNCs are one of the principal drivers of globalisation. They are also seen to be the most important beneficiaries of the liberalisation of investment and trade regimes, with rising influence on the development of the world economy and its constituent parts. The concept of "social responsibility" captures the search for an answer to this question. It implies that firms have obligations that go beyond what countries require individually, and agreements prescribe internationally. Hence, discussions relating to MNC social responsibility standards and performance therefore comprise an important component of efforts to develop a stable, prosperous and just global society.

CORPORATE SOCIAL RESPONSIBILITY STANDARDS

CSR standard can be contained in binding 'hard law' instruments, such as national laws and regulations, or in voluntary non-binding 'soft law' instruments. Over recent years, CSR standards have expanded in both number and form in a complex, multilayered, multifaceted and interconnected universe of standards. While it would be difficult to provide an exhaustive account of every such standard and initiative, the universe of

CSR standards can be categorized as follow according to the organization that created them.

Intergovernmental Organization Standards

Universal principles as recognized by international declarations and agreements are the source of the most prominent and authoritative CSR standards. The three main sources of these international instruments are the United Nations, the ILO and the OECD. Three of the leading standards in this category are:

- United Nations declarations and instruments: one of the most prominent examples is the UN Global Compact: launched in 2000, this is an initiative of the UN Secretary General's office to translate the most relevant UN declarations into 10 guiding principles for enterprises (box 1).
- ILO conventions and declarations: there are 188 ILO conventions, the most relevant for MNC operations being the Tripartite Declaration of Principles concerning Multinational Enterprises and Social Policy ("MNE Declaration") (first adopted in 1977, latest revision in 2006) and the Declaration on Fundamental Principles and Rights at Work (1998) (also known as "Fundamental Labour Standards").
- The OECD Guidelines on Multinational Enterprises ("OECD Guidelines"). The 42 adhering governments are fewer in number than the signatories of UN and ILO conventions, but they include large developed economies whose corporations accounted for 70 per cent of FDI in 2010.

BOX 1

The 10 Principles of the UN Global Compact

Human Rights

Principle 1: Businesses should support and respect the protection of internationally proclaimed human rights; and

Principle 2: make sure that they are not complicit in human rights abuses.

Labour Standards

Principle 3: Businesses should uphold the freedom of association and the effective recognition of the right to collective bargaining;

Principle 4: the elimination of all forms of forced and compulsory labour;

Principle 5: the effective abolition of child labour; and

Principle 6: the elimination of discrimination in respect of employment and occupation.

Environment

Principle 7: Businesses should support a precautionary approach to environmental challenges;

Principle 8: undertake initiatives to promote greater environmental responsibility; and

Principle 9: encourage the development and diffusion of environmentally friendly technologies.

Anti-Corruption

Principle 10: Businesses should work against corruption in all its forms, including extortion and bribery.

Source: www.unglobalcompact.org.

The standards of the UN and its specialized agencies, including the ILO, along with the Guidelines of the OECD, cover the fundamental issues of CSR. In each of the categories of standards reviewed below, it is common to find references to these major intergovernmental organization standards. In addition to the three most commonly noted standards above, there is a large number of relevant intergovernmental organization standards and conventions emanating from the UN (and its specialized agencies, including the ILO) and the OECD.

Multi-stakeholder Initiative Standards

Multi-stakeholder initiatives (MSIs) are "crosssectoral partnerships created with a rule-setting purpose, to design and steward standards for the regulation of market and non-market actors". These partnerships contain a mix of civil society, business, labour, consumers and other stakeholders. MSI standards most often address non-product-related process and production methods (PPM), i.e. issues related to how a product is produced, such as the environmental or social aspects of certain production methods. Although MSI standards are mostly developed by civil society and business actors, they often make reference to the normative frameworks of international soft law instruments.

A unique MSI is the International Organization for Standardization (ISO), a non-governmental organization whose members are national standard-setting bodies. ISO standards are widely recognized by international institutions (e.g. the WTO) and national governments. In 2010, ISO launched the ISO 26000 standard "Guidance on Social Responsibility", which serves as a significant reference point for defining the terms of "social responsibility".

Industry Association Codes and Individual Company Codes

An industry-specific code typically involves the adoption of a code jointly developed by the leading companies within an industry, to address social and/or environmental aspects of supply chains and international operations. There are thousands of individual company codes in existence, and they are especially common among large MNCs: more than three-quarters of large MNCs from both developed and developing countries have policies on social and environmental issues. About half of MNC codes that apply to value chains make reference to one or more intergovernmental organization standards.

The universe of voluntary CSR standards consists of a multitude of standards, each differing in terms of source, functions, addressees, and interrelationships, and each yielding influence and impacting on development in different ways. The proliferation of these standards has resulted in a number of systemic challenges related to standardsetting and standard implementation.

CHALLENGES WITH EXISTING STANDARDS: KEY ISSUES

Gaps, Overlaps and Inconsistencies

Gaps between standards exist in terms of subjects covered and industry focus. The OECD Guidelines cover a broad range of responsible business practice, from human rights to taxation. However, they are negotiated by a more limited number of member States, compared to UN and ILO instruments. The ILO MNE Declaration focuses more specifically on employment practices and human rights, but applies to a larger group of member States that are directly addressed, alongside employers, workers and MNCs, to observe the MNE Declaration. Subject matter gaps exist among MSIs, as many standards focus either on the environment or on social issues, but not often to the same extent on both.

An emerging trend among MSIs is the inclusion of social issues within environmental standards. Subject matter gaps can also include standards that focus on specific outcomes (e.g. minimum wage compliance) versus standards that focus on "process rights" (e.g. labour rights). Gaps also exist in industry focus, with not all industries (or parts of the value chain) being the subject of a standard. While the absence of a standard may reflect a gap that has yet to be filled, it can also represent either an area that does not necessarily require a standard, or where a standard is not considered the most appropriate way to address existing problems.

Gaps also exist in uptake among companies as uptake is driven by the concerns of consumers, media, and investors. CSR standards are primarily adopted by those companies that are most exposed to such concerns. While the adoption of standards by large MNCs can create a cascade effect that pushes sustainability across the value chain, this does not necessarily have a uniform impact on all members. Indeed there may be a tendency for some standards to favour concentration at different levels and to crowd out small enterprises and producers. Nevertheless, as leading firms adopt and implement CSR standards, they set a benchmark for best practice against which other firms are measured.

Among individual company standards, there can be both a high degree of overlap in the issues covered (e.g. labour practices, environment, human rights, bribery), and a high degree of inconsistency in detailed operational guidelines. As most companies refer to major intergovernmental organization standards for key issues, this reduces inconsistencies in the general subjects covered, but since many intergovernmental organization standards lack detailed micro-level operational guidance, companies are left to innovate these details themselves. The resulting inconsistencies mean that suppliers can be faced with differing requirements, adding complexity and higher compliance costs. The rise of industry-specific standards can help to alleviate this situation.

In some industries, more than one MSI or industry association standard exists. This can cause confusion among companies, often leading them to opt for multiple certifications to ensure that all relevant issues have been addressed. MSIs are increasingly working together towards alignment between standards that address the same subject or the same industry.

Inclusiveness in Standardsetting

The credibility of a standard is linked to the inclusion of a sufficiently broad range of stakeholders in the standard-setting process. Company codes and industry association codes are often challenged as being less credible because of the limited involvement of outside stakeholders. The intergovernmental organizations are perceived as authoritative standard-setters because they reflect international consensus. The popularity of MSI standards is due largely to their inclusive cross-sectoral process. Addressing the challenge of inclusiveness also means addressing the often limited participation of developing country stakeholders in CSR standard-setting processes, which arises out of resource constraints.

Relationship between Voluntary CSR Standards and National Legislation

Voluntary CSR standards can complement government regulatory efforts; however, where they are promoted as a substitute for labour, social and environmental protection legislation, or where CSR standards are not based on national or international rules, then these voluntary standards can potentially undermine, substitute or distract from governmental regulatory efforts.

Reporting and Transparency

Despite tremendous growth in CSR reporting in recent years among MNCs of developed and developing countries, such reporting continues to lack uniformity, standardization and comparability. A number of initiatives promote a standardized CSR reporting framework. While uptake of such frameworks among companies is growing rapidly, it nevertheless remains relatively low and even among companies adopting a voluntary CSR reporting framework, implementation of the framework can be selective and incomplete.

Compliance and Market Impact

A critical challenge is to ensure that companies voluntarily adopting a standard actually comply with the standard. Failure to demonstrate compliance can lower the standard's credibility and market impact. The compliance promotion mechanisms embodied in existing CSR standards range from none, to reporting requirements and redress mechanisms, to proactive mechanisms such as audits, factory inspections, etc.

(Table 1) The major intergovernmental organization standards contain compliance mechanisms, including the UN Global Compact (the "integrity measures" and the "communication on progress"), the ILO MNE Declaration (the "interpretation procedure"), and the OECD Guidelines ("the specific instance procedures" and the system of "National Contact Points"). MSI standards and industry association standards often have certification or accreditation programmes which typically include inspections/ audits, corrective action programmes, reporting and consumer labelling schemes. To enhance credibility, many MSIs have separated their standards-setting process from the certification process, relying increasingly on professionalized third parties for the monitoring and auditing processes. The dynamic nature of the field of CSR standards also includes significant practices of "ratcheting-up" compliance mechanisms over time, e.g. adding new standards, tightening up inspection procedures, adding complaints procedures.

TABLE 1

Compliance Mechanisms of Selected International CSR Standards

Source of standard	*Proactive mechanisms (audits, inspections)*	*Reporting requirements/ redress mechanisms*	*No formal compliance mechanisms*
Intergovernmental Organization		• UN Global Compact • OECD Guidelines • ILO Tripartite Declaration	
Multistake-holder/NGO	• ISO14000 • MSC • FSC • FLA RSPO • SA8000 • 4C Assoc.		• ISO 26000 • GRI
Company/ Industry association	• C.A.F.E. Practices • Leather Working Group • BSCI • International Council of Toy Industries		• EICC • Pharmaceutical Industry Principles for Responsible Supply Chain Management

Source: UNCTAD.

While compliance promotion mechanisms can be an integral part of a standard, they can also be associated to a standard by third parties. Many intergovernmental organization standards are key references for some of the certifiable standards of the MSI. In this way, company compliance with "soft law" intergovernmental organization standards can be driven by other CSR standards with proactive compliance mechanisms.

A challenge associated with certification schemes and audits is that they may impose a higher burden on companies, and thus lead to lower rates of adoption of the standard, and reduced market impact. Conversely, a lack of compliance mechanisms can lead to high rates of voluntary adoption of the standard, but low, unclear and/or immeasurable rates of implementation. However, a number of MSI and industry association codes employ proactive compliance mechanisms and are nonetheless having a significant impact, with some influencing more than half of the global market for the industry in question (Table 2).

TABLE 2

Impact of Selected MSI and Industry Association CSR Standards and Individual Company Codes

Standard	*Compliance mechanisms*		*Market impact*
	Certificat-ion/ Audits	*Public reporting*	
		Multi-stakeholder initiative standards	
Forest Stewardship Council	Yes	Annual Report, Audit Results	Covers 11% of global forests used for (1993) productive activities
ISO14001	Yes	Annual Report	As of December 2009, 223,149 organizations in 159 countries are (1996) certified to ISO 14000
SA8000	Yes	Annual Report	Over 1.4 million workers are employed in over 2,400 SA8000 certified (1997) facilities in 65 countries, across 66 industrial sectors
Marine Stewardship Council (1997)	Yes	Annual Report, Audit Results	Covers 6% of global landed fish
Fair Labor Association (1998)	Yes	Annual Report, Audit Results	Covers 75% of the athletic footwear industry
Fair Wear Foundation (1999)	Yes	Annual Report Audit Results	FWF affiliates in 2009 sourced from a total of 1,153 factories, with an estimated total of 300,000 workers (growth rate of 60% in the last 3 years)
UTZ CERTIFIED (1999)	Yes	Annual Report	Covers 5% of global coffee production
4C Association (2004)	Yes	Annual Report with performa-ance data of member companies	Covers 30% of global coffee production
Roundtable on Sustainable Palm Oil (2004)	Yes	Audit Results	Covers 8% of global palm oil production
		Industry association codes	
Business Social Compliance of Initiative (BSCI) Code of Conduct (2002)	Yes	Annual Report	11,200 suppliers audited according to the BSCI code conduct and 4,000 suppliers trained in 9 different countries
International Council of Toy Industries (ICTI) Code of Conduct (2004)	Yes	Biennial Report	75% of the global toy business is committed to only source from suppliers certified by ICTI in the future
Leather Working Group Principles (2005)	Yes	No	The working group covers 10% of the global leather production
		Individual company codes	
Nike	Yes	Yes	31% of the global market for athletic footwear; through its supplier code of Supplier code of conduct conduct Nike influences the conditions of more than 800,000 employees in 700 factories in 45 countries

Adidas Supplier code of conduct	Yes	Yes	22% of the global market for athletic footwear; through its supplier code of conduct Adidas influences the conditions of more than 775,000 employees in 1,200 factories in 65 countries

Source: UNCTAD, based on data from MSI, industry associations, companies and FAO.

With global market shares ranging between 5 and 10 per cent for some standards (such as the Marine Stewardship Council (MSC) and the Forest Stewardship Council (FSC)), the "proof of concept" phase has been passed; the challenge now is how to achieve widespread uptake of these standards. This is particularly so in highly fragmented industries, where adoption by many companies would be required to cover a large market share. In less fragmented industries, even individual company codes can have a significant impact.

Concerns about Possible Trade and Investment Barriers

There are unresolved questions about whether social and environmental standards, especially nonproduct- related PPM standards, could potentially become barriers to trade and investment. It is not clear under WTO rules whether non-product PPM standards are covered by the WTO's Technical Barriers to Trade (TBT) agreement or other WTO agreements (e.g. sanitary and phytosanitary measures; Agreement on Government Procurement). Outside of the TBT agreement, there was the "shrimp-turtle" case from the late 1990s, where environmental regulations in the United States led to an import ban for shrimp-exporting countries that did not use turtle-safe harvesting practices (which had already been introduced by the United States fishing industry on the basis of consumer demands).

Similarly, it is possible for CSR standards to create barriers to (inward and outward) investment for companies that are unable to meet the requirements of the standards. In Guatemala, for example, forestry companies without FSC certification are prohibited from operating within the Mayan Biosphere reserve, and in Denmark, only companies meeting the Government's CSR standard qualify for outward investment assistance. In both cases, the challenge is to distinguish where the use of a standard constitutes a legitimate application, and where it constitutes an abuse of protectionist intent. For example, the use of CSR standards can become a form of protectionism if they are applied in a discriminatory way, differentiating between companies by national origin. It is important therefore to monitor the application of CSR standards and to identify discriminatory practices where they arise. Voluntary CSR standards may be less susceptible to challenge through WTO trade agreements, and less prone to questions of investment protectionism, since there is no requirement that firms must follow them. For example, a voluntary standard pertaining to organic foods gives firms the option of using the approach adopted in the standard, but does not require that firms use this standard as a condition of market entry. In this way, voluntary CSR standards may be less problematic than mandatory requirements, in terms of achieving public policy objectives. That said, voluntary standards alone can create a risk of neglect and indifference on the part of firms. The balance between mandatory and voluntary standards is delicate, but legitimate restrictions based on objective criteria of necessity and proportionality are permitted under trade and investment agreements. Equally, the State's right to regulate may create legitimate restrictions on investors and their investments in the interests of public policy and economic development. Thus the challenge is to maintain an appropriate balance between mandatory and voluntary standards.

Challenges for Suppliers (Particularly SMEs) in Developing Countries

The proliferation and application of CSR codes poses a series of serious challenges for suppliers, particularly SMEs in developing countries. Challenges include, inter alia: (i) the use of international standards that exceed current regulations and common market practices in the host country; (ii) the existence of diverging and sometimes conflicting requirements from different MNCs; (iii) the capacity constraints of suppliers in under-standing and applying international standards in their day-to-day operations; (iv) an overload of multiple on-site inspections and complex reporting procedures; (v) consumer and civil society concerns about technical or quality standards for products and for marketing, in addition to suppliers' existing challenges in meeting them; and (vi) competitiveness concerns for firms that bear the cost of fully complying with CSR standards relative to other SMEs that do not attempt to fully comply.

Suppliers that operate in countries that are categorized by MNCs as "high-risk sourcing zones" are subject to particularly strong scrutiny from their customers. These suppliers are more frequently subject to CSR assessments, such as self-evaluation questionnaires and monitoring or auditing processes. Because most suppliers serve multiple customers, they often need to undergo multiple social audits throughout the year. This is especially challenging, because each auditor or purchasing company has its own factory evaluation checklist, differing in specificity, length, requirements and topics addressed.

An additional structural challenge results from the fact that the purchasing practices and the CSR practices of many MNC buyers remain independent of one another. As a consequence, suppliers receive messages that are sometimes at odds (i.e. CSR demands vs. price, quality and delivery-time demands). In the absence of greater coordination among companies to harmonize CSR codes and simplify evaluation processes, and within companies to align CSR with other more conventional business demands, SMEs face the burden of a large number of audits and the challenge of meeting sometimes contradictory policies on CSR and purchasing.

Almost all companies expect their suppliers to implement "corrective action plans" to address deficiencies identified during audits, yet these plans are often inadequate for creating long-lasting change in a supplier's operation. Some companies have begun to create supplier development programmes with a CSR focus. However, most only offer such programmes to their key suppliers, which are often large companies in their own right, leaving SMEs without direct support.

To fill the gap left by the private sector, various civil society and governmental stakeholders have engaged in supplier development programmes for SMEs. However, such programmes are still limited in number and scope. Where they exist, they are mostly initiated, funded and implemented by development agencies, intergovernmental organizations or civil society, with very limited involvement of local governments. The main challenges with externally funded programmes are scalability (i.e. how to apply them to a broader group of companies) and sustainability (i.e. how to ensure the programmes can continue over the long term). To address these challenges, some stakeholders are calling for government action in CSR capacity-building. Most national governments, however, have not yet mainstreamed CSR into their SME and supplier development programmes.

RECENT DEVELOPMENTS IN CORPORATE SOCIAL RESPONSIBILITY

Recent developments influencing the application of social responsibility concepts to international business derive from many different sources that comprise the stakeholders of MNCs, as well as from the corporations themselves. The major new development, at least in developed countries, is a proliferation of groups representing general public or specific issue interests that utilise a wide array of public pressure tactics, intermingled with instances of more direct dialogue, to promote an activist view of MNC duties towards an expanding agenda of social responsibility objectives. An expanding number of private enterprises are creating and/or revising individual statements of business principles or codes, although this group would still constitute only a small percentage of the total MNC community. Collective business organisations have adopted a mixed approach. Some sectoral groups actively responded to social responsibility pressures with industry-specific initiatives, while most organisations take a more cautionary approach, with the notable exception of a new statement on environmental principles. Governments continue to use international organisations to promote guidelines or codes of conduct on issues or in sectors in which international consensus is insufficient to support more precise legal standards. Only occasionally do national governments individually endeavour to develop MNC social responsibility initiatives.

INCREASED ACTIVITIES BY CIVIL SOCIETY GROUPS

A major development, particularly evident over the past decade, is the expanding number, range, coordination and activism among parts of civil society on issues relating to MNC social responsibility. Although some groups organise around very specific products, such as tobacco or nuclear energy, most activism focuses on a relatively small set of major issue themes that are then exemplified and addressed in terms of specific products, companies or events. The issues most prevalent over the past decade involve labour rights and working conditions, the environment and human rights, reflecting primarily a developed country perspective on MNC social responsibility. Some groups choose to focus principally on one of these areas, such as Greenpeace on the environment or Amnesty International on human rights. Others, such as religious organisations or other socially-directed institutional investors, may be active across a spectrum of social issues. Although most groups originate in the developed countries and draw their most involved membership from that base, an increasing number of organisations is emerging in developing countries as well. Where interests and perspectives are shared, groups may forge ties internationally through affiliated networks, conferences, newsletters and an exponential growth in relatively inexpensive Internet linkages. In fact, the emergence of the Internet is virtually unparalleled in its impact, both on increasing international communication among elements of civil society and on facilitating these groups' outreach to media channels that can focus instant attention on MNC activities worldwide.

BUSINESS RESPONSES

The business community remains generally cautious regarding international initiatives that call for expansive new commitments to MNC social responsibility obligations. However, the diverse membership of general business organisations makes it difficult to reach a consensus among various industries on a common position that reflects the interests and needs of the full business community. As with some intergovernmental institutions comprised of diverse country members, organisational dynamics can either stall action or drive it towards a lowest common denominator position.

Many individual companies adopt their own codes of conduct that address social responsibility issues, sometimes drawing on an industry code or a set of international business principles. These codes of conduct have been adopted for a variety of reasons, ranging from the personal interest and beliefs of the chief executive officer to explicit expectations voiced by important governmental or other public interest groups. Often MNC code development is reactive, sparked by instances of perceived misconduct by a firm or others in its industry. Sometimes firms are proactive yet still defensive, formulating codes designed to head off possible public criticism. Among the most common factors that impel MNCs to promulgate individual codes are the following: firms, or their business associates, have received criticism for their practices; the industry is "high risk" in terms of exposure to or involvement with recognised social responsibility issues; the company has a "high-profile" name or product brand whose reputation and image is commercially important; and the firm's sales are vulnerable to organised customer boycotts or other commercial sanctions.

Although most corporate codes appear to be associated with past or potential public criticism, backed by possible commercial sanctions for misdeeds, positive inducements can also play a role. For some corporations, proactive corporate social responsibility is perceived as good business. Individual codes can serve to enhance the corporate image and, quite possibly, bottom-line profitability as well. Corporations may explicitly advertise their compliance with evolving social responsibility standards to gain favourable public recognition, particularly on environmental issues.

The increased activities of civil society groups require changes in the way business responds to the expectations stakeholders put forward regarding the companies' behaviour. In fact, companies see themselves confronted with increasing demands as to their accountability to, and interaction with, groups of civil society. For many years, corporations were generally trusted to be good corporate citizens without any particular activities required to prove this proposition right. Over the past 20 to 30 years however, companies have been increasingly confronted with demands from NGOs in many (especially developed) countries to provide evidence on their activities and impacts in different social responsibility areas. Some companies responded to this charge by drafting codes of conduct, others by preparing special reports on issues pertaining to social responsibility (including environmental or social reports). But this is no longer enough: companies are now more and more asked to establish systematic and independent monitoring and auditing processes to demonstrate how corporate principles and policies are implemented in daily business practices. In a further step, some companies are intensifying their interaction with stakeholders on social responsibility issues by actively soliciting stakeholders views on issues over which conflicts may arise or have already occurred. This process can be encapsulated in a four-step sequence:

i) the "trust me"- phase, in which companies did not face any expectations going beyond the respect of law and order;

ii) the "tell me"- phase in which companies were asked to give an account of their companies principles and impacts regarding certain social responsibility issues;

ii) the "show me"- phase, in which companies are asked by civil society to actually demonstrate that they adhere to their principles and standards; and

iv) the "join me"- phase, in which companies are asked to involve actively and interact with, stakeholders in the process of solving problems pertaining to social responsibility.

At present, companies can be found at different stages of the model. Many have not paid much attention to social responsibility issues, however. Those that have, do not necessarily respond in the same way to civil society expectations as individual companies find themselves under different pressures and, accordingly, respond differently. Still, there appears to be an overall trend that indicates that companies are putting more resources into responding to social responsibility demands and into interacting with civil society groups on issues pertaining to social responsibility.

POLICY OPTIONS

Governments can play an important role in creating a coherent policy and institutional framework to address the challenges and opportunities presented by the universe of CSR standards. In this regard, some governments are beginning to apply CSR standards to the architecture of corporate governance and international trade and investment. This approach aims to promote best practice in corporate compliance with national laws and international agreements in order to maximize the sustainable development impact of MNCs. A number of policy options follow.

(a) Supporting CSR Standards Development

Governments can encourage and support the development of CSR standards, including through the provision of material support, technical expertise, and mobilizing the participation of relevant stakeholders. For example, the 4C Association is a sustainability standard for the coffee industry, initiated by the Government of Germany and implemented by the German development agency. With support from the Government of Switzerland and other public and private sector representatives, the 4C Association has become an influential industry standard.

Governments can support the development of national certifiable management system standards (MSSs). This approach provides enterprises with a certifiable standard to distinguish themselves in the area of CSR. Recent years have seen the creation of a number of national CSR MSSs, including standards in Brazil and Mexico in 2004, Portugal in 2008, Spain in 2009, and the Netherlands and Denmark in 2010. In some cases these national MSSs are based on or aligned with ISO standards. As national CSR MSSs proliferate, there may be increased interest in an international CSR MSS.

(b) Applying CSR to Public Procurement Policy

Governments can consider applying CSR standards to their purchasing policies, to promote good business practices on more environmentally friendly products, while being careful to avoid discriminatory practices that would be a form of protectionism. The Government of China, for instance, maintains a "green list" of environmentally friendly products which should be given preferential treatment in public procurement. The Government of Germany has made a commitment to purchase only wood and wood products that are verified as coming from legal and sustainable sources, and accepts the FSC certification as verification of this. The Netherlands also has a sustainable procurement policy; the Government of Switzerland is in the process of developing such a scheme; and the Government of the United Kingdom has laid out a strategy ("Government Sustainable Procurement Action Plan") and has already committed to source fish for its public institutions (e.g. schools) exclusively from MSC-certified suppliers.

While applying CSR standards to procurement policies can help promote the uptake of such standards by companies, it can also negatively affect the competitive position, and hence operations, of companies – especially those from poorer countries – that have limited capacity to adhere to such standards.

(c) Building Capacity

One factor that can lead to low uptake of standards is a lack of knowledge, skills and capabilities at various stages of a value chain. Thus, implementation of standards often requires a capacity-building component. This is part of creating "shared responsibility" within a value chain (which involves MNCs providing assistance to suppliers), as opposed to what critics call "offloading responsibility" (wherein the compliance burden falls solely on developing country suppliers that may have little capacity for meeting CSR standards).

Developing country governments wishing to promote standards in their countries can partner with donor States to deliver capacity-building initiatives and technical assistance to local industry and regulatory bodies. A project between the Government of Bolivia and USAID, for example, promotes FSC certification in the Bolivian forestry industry. This has included capacity-building for companies that are willing to be certified, and assistance linking certified companies with export markets. As a result of this programme, Bolivia now has the largest area of FSC-certified tropical forest in the world. In Gambia, the Ministry of Fisheries works in partnership with USAID to obtain MSC certification for the country's fisheries. Governments can further strengthen CSR capacity-building by engaging in the exchange of best practice at international forums, such as UNCTAD.

(a) Promoting CSR Disclosure and Responsible Investment

To enhance transparency and comparability of CSR practices, a number of stock exchanges – especially in emerging markets – have employed stock exchange listing rules to promote the uptake of CSR reporting to facilitate responsible investment practices. In close cooperation with national policymakers, the Malaysian stock exchange, for example, has made CSR reporting mandatory for all listed companies, and the Shanghai Stock Exchange in China has published the Shanghai Environmental Disclosure Guidelines, with which listed companies are urged to comply.

An alternative to developing a national CSR reporting framework is to adopt an existing framework developed by an international initiative. The Johannesburg Stock Exchange in South Africa, for example, requires companies to use the GRI guidelines in preparing sustainability reports. Using a common framework like this can promote international comparability between reports. Policymakers interested in promoting an internationally harmonized approach to CSR reporting and encouraging responsible investment, including in the area of "impact investing" (box 2), can work together through forums such as UNCTAD's ISAR working group56 and/or the Sustainable Stock Exchanges initiative.

BOX 2

Impact Investing: Achieving Competitive Financial Returns While Maximizing Social and Environmental Impact

Over time, responsible investment has become a multitrillion dollar industry. Responsible investing has various themes. It can be focused on negative screens that prohibit investment in firms that manufacture or promote certain products and services. It can also be focused on shareholder advocacy and positive environmental, social and governance (ESG) screens, to target investment in particular companies. "Impact investing" takes this a step further. It is the explicit incorporation of social, environmental and developmental objectives into the fabric of business and financial models. It is based on the fundamental belief that it is possible for investors to achieve competitive financial returns and social change simultaneously.

The potential range of impact investment opportunities remains largely unknown. According to an estimate the impact investments could reach between $500 billion and several trillions over the next decade. To illustrate the magnitude of opportunities in impact investing, a few examples are given below.

To address climate change, the International Energy Agency estimates that $1.3 trillion in investment will be required to halve greenhouse gas emissions from the energy sector by 2050. Another $41 trillion is needed by 2030 to modernize infrastructure systems worldwide. Water infrastructure, at $23 trillion, is the largest portion of this investment. McGraw Hill Construction estimates that the green building market will more than double worldwide to between $96 and $140 billion by 2013. Further, according to the World Resources Institute, the 4 billion people with annual incomes below $3,000 constitute a $5 trillion global consumer market. Moreover, the 1.4 billion people with per capita incomes between $3,000 and $20,000 represent an even larger $12.5 trillion market globally.

Despite the enormous potential of impact investing, there are critical gaps in understanding the market conditions necessary for success, together with inadequate policy and regulatory frameworks, and limited knowledge of financial models that sufficiently incorporate environmental, social and developmental factors into valuations and alpha forecasts.

Through its "20ii " Investing with Impact" initiative, the United States Department of State will work with UNCTAD, the OECD, and other institutions to address these gaps and galvanize sources of private capital to tackle high priority social and environmental challenges.

Source: Contributed by the United States Department of State, in collaboration with Harvard University's Initiative for Responsible Investment.

(e) Moving from Soft Law to Hard Law

Governments can consider adopting some of the existing CSR standards as part of regulatory initiatives, turning hitherto voluntary standards (soft law) into mandatory requirements (hard law). For example, organic food standards originated in most countries as voluntary standards from civil society or industry associations, but today are usually regulated under national legislation. This model allows governments to use the dynamic space of voluntary standards as a laboratory for future government regulations.

Another option is a mixed "public–private regulatory regime", wherein regulatory initiatives ensure compliance with standards developed by civil society and/or the private sector. In Sweden, for example, State-owned enterprises are required to prepare reports using the GRI standard. In Guatemala, the Government has made FSC certification mandatory for forestry firms operating in the Mayan Biosphere reserve. This approach can be useful for preserving the dynamism and aspirational nature of many multi-stakeholder standard-setting processes, while adding uniformity of implementation through regulation.

(f) Strengthening Compliance Promotion Mechanisms Among Intergovernmental Organization Standards

Governments could consider further strengthening the compliance promotion mechanisms of existing intergovernmental organization standards. As noted above, many intergovernmental organization standards already have some compliance promotion mechanisms in place. These organizations periodically review the efficacy of such instruments, including their redress mechanisms. In the case of the UN Global Compact, for example, the UN Joint Inspections Unit recently recommended that the UN "reinforce the implementation of the Integrity Measures and accountability in implementing the ten principles".

(g) Applying CSR to Investment and Trade Promotion and Enterprise Development

Governments could play an active role in promoting socially and environmentally sustainable inward and outward investment, while avoiding discriminatory practices that would be a form of protectionism. Governments can consider offering incentives for investments in sustainable industries (e.g. renewable energy) or for compliance with CSR standards. For example, the Brazilian National Economic Development Bank has introduced a code of ethics, based on intergovernmental organization standards, to which all of its clients must adhere. Similarly, the Government of Denmark requires companies receiving financial support from the Danish Industrialization Fund for Developing Countries (IFU) to comply with IFU's CSR policy. Some governments are also providing incentives through preferential trade agreements. For instance, the European Union has complemented its General System of Preferences (GSP) with the "GSP Plus" scheme, which offers additional tariff reductions for developing countries that have ratified and implemented 27 key international conventions related to CSR practices (e.g. the ILO Core Conventions). Care has to be taken, however, to ensure that those countries that do not a priori fulfil the criteria receive the required technical assistance in order to do so, and hence may benefit from such initiatives, in line with their overall development priorities and strategies.

(h) Introducing CSR into the International Investment Regime

Governments can also consider introducing CSR into the international investment regime. While CSR specific clauses do not currently feature prominently in IIAs, a small but growing number of agreements, especially recent FTAs with investment chapters, include such provisions. While this process has its origins in the mid-1990s, specific references to CSR started appearing more recently. Today, three Canadian FTAs with investment provisions61 refer to CSR in the preamble and contain substantive provisions. For example, Article 816 of the Canada- Colombia FTA, the earliest of these references, states that:

> *"each Party should encourage enterprises operating within its territory or subject to its jurisdiction to voluntarily incorporate internationally recognized standards of corporate social responsibility in their internal policies, such as statements of principle that have been endorsed or are supported by the Parties. These principles address issues such as labour, the environment, human rights, community relations and anti-corruption. The Parties remind those enterprises of the importance of incorporating such corporate social responsibility standards in their internal policies."*

In addition, the preambles of the European Free Trade Association's 2009 FTA with Albania and 2010 FTA with Peru refer to CSR-related issues. While BITs by EU member States do not include CSR clauses, the European Parliament has called for the inclusion of a CSR clause in every future FTA investment chapter concluded by the EU.

Finally, a few countries have included innovative CSR provisions in their model agreements, referring to specific corporate contributions, such as human capital formation, local capacity-building, employment creation, training and transfer of technology. However, the implementation of CSR provisions in "real" IIAs remains to be seen.

While it is difficult to assess their impact on conditions "on the ground", such clauses nevertheless serve to flag the importance of CSR in investor–State relations, which may also influence the interpretation of IIA clauses by tribunals in investor–State dispute settlement cases, and create linkages between IIAs and international CSR standards. Again, care has to be taken to ensure that increasing consideration of CSR does not open the door to justifying policy interventions with undue protectionist purposes.

(i) Effective Promotion of CSR Standards in Global Supply Chains

To ensure continued growth and international competitiveness, SME suppliers in developing countries need support to cope with the challenges presented by CSR codes. Ways and means of providing such support include the following four:

i) *National governments and international organizations should mainstream CSR issues into national enterprise development programmes.* CSR has become a commonplace demand in most industries, yet SMEs in developing countries are rarely provided the tools they need to address this challenge. Policymakers should therefore consider promoting training on environmental management, human resource management, and occupational safety and health.

ii) *National governments and international organizations should do more to assist enterprises with operational guidance for international standards.* Because most private codes of conduct refer to international standards, it is necessary to provide more practical guidance on how to implement these standards on the factory floor.

iii) *MNCs should be encouraged to harmonize their CSR codes at the industry level and to streamline application procedures.* Suppliers today can be subject to multiple audits or factory inspections per year. Most of these inspections are largely redundant, with different buyers asking the same questions. Initiatives such as the Supplier Ethical Data Exchange can help rationalize supplier inspections, promote sharing of information among buyers, harmonize reporting practices and generally reduce unnecessary burdens on suppliers. Policymakers should encourage and support such initiatives.

iv) *MNCs should be encouraged to integrate CSR policies into purchasing policies, with the aim of ensuring that suppliers are effectively motivated and supported to meet all the demands being placed on them.* There is a need for greater policy coherence within MNCs. For example, purchasing policies on price and delivery time, on the one hand, and CSR policies on pay and excessive overtime hours, on the other, need to have some degree of alignment to avoid mutual exclusivity. Private CSR policies that are not fully aligned with private purchasing policies send mixed signals and can create situations in which compliance becomes impossible.

Consumer and civil society concerns are driving CSR, raising the bar for market entry for developing-country suppliers. Meeting these demands will require an upgrade of management skills. Governments can assist through capacity development programmes and by strengthening national institutions that promote compliance with labour and environmental laws. Countries that equip their SMEs with the capacity to meet CSR codes will create new opportunities for their enterprises in global supply chains.

All in all, investment policies – at both the national and the international level – are developing in a constantly changing economic environment with evolving political goals. Whereas in the past the focus was very much on investment liberalization and quantitative growth, policy concerns are nowadays more about how to make FDI instrumental for qualitative and inclusive growth, how to find the "right" balance between investment liberalization and regulation for the public good, and how to harness CSR in this context. This raises considerable challenges in terms of how best to calibrate FDI, how to promote responsible investment and how to improve the international investment regime. For this, the governments have a range of policy options for promoting CSR. Pioneering examples in both developing and developed countries suggest that it is time to mainstream CSR into national policies and international trade and investment regimes, while devising mechanisms for addressing unintended consequences and preventing possible protectionist abuses. While there are a number of policy implications, the various approaches already underway are increasingly taking the form of a combination of regulatory and voluntary instruments that work together to promote responsible business practices. Two critical components of this mix will be improved CSR reporting by companies (to better inform future policy development), and strengthened capacity-building programmes (to assist developing country enterprises to meet international best practice in this area).

QUESTIONS

1. What is meant by 'social responsibility' in relation to the modern company? In what ways does it represent a departure from stakeholder theories?
2. Should global expansion of the companies action, space and rights be accompanied by an increase in social responsibility?
3. Describe the scope and context of corporate social responsibility.
4. Critically examine the corporate responsibility standards. In what way the government can play an important role in creating a coherent policy and institutional framework to address the challenges presented by the universe of CSR standards.
5. What do you understand by global corporate citizenship? Discuss the international aspects of corporate social responsibility.
6. Discuss the perceptions of business, civil society and government toward the corporate social responsibility.
7. Critically examine the recent developments in the field of corporate social responsibility.

REFERENCES

Beauchamp, Tom L. and Norman E. Bowie (eds.): *Ethical Theory of Business*, Prentice-Hall, 1983.

Carroll, Archie B.: *Business and Society: Ethics and Stackholder Management*, South-Westen Publishing Company, 1989.

————, (ed.) *Managing Corporate Social Responsibility*, Little, Brown and Company, 1977.

Hoffman, W.M. and J.M. Moore (ed.): *Business Ethics: Readings and cases in Corporate Morality*, McGraw-Hill, 1984.

Nelson, J.: "Labour, gender and economic/social divide" *International Labour Review*, 137, 1, (Geneva; ILO), 1998.

Ostensson, O.: *The Stackholder: interest and Objectives*, (Geneva: UNCTAD), 1999.

Sivalingam, G.: The Economic and social impact of export processing zones: The case of Malaysia, (Geneva: ILO), 1994.

23
SUSTAINABLE DEVELOPMENT

INTRODUCTION

Sustainable development (SD) is founded on the premise that human well-being should advance without irreparable harm to ecosystems and the vital services they provide, without depleting essential resources, and without posing risks to future generations. The importance of SD had been realized by United Nations and for that a conference was scheduled in Stockholm in 1972, devoted exclusively to this cause. And in same year, UN founded the U.N. Environment Programme. But the Programme on sustainable development ran strong resistance because of economic difficulties. For the important relationship between well-being and environmental commitment, the U.N. General Assembly created a World Commisson on the Environment under Prime Minister Brundtland of Norway. The Commisson on the Environment submitted the final report called *Our Common Future* in 1987. The Commission defined sustainable development as *development that meets the needs of the present, without compromising the ability of future generations to meet their own needs.* The concept of *needs,* in particular the essential needs of the world's poor, to which overriding priority should be given; the idea of limitations imposed by the state of technology and social organizations, and on the environment's ability to meet present and future needs.

CONCEPT OF SUSTAINABLITY AND SUSTAINABLE DEVELOPMENT

Sustainability is the concept of delicately balancing the economic prosperity of an organization, its environmental performance, and its social equity in a way, that gives the organization an edge over its competitors. Businesses operate in an increasingly heterogeneous environment, including globalization and trade, increasing transparency, unprecedented innovation and change, changing legislation, and a market shift towards SD. Creating a sustainable future, economically, socially and environmentally requires, all organizations and individuals to rethink on how to use resources, how to interact, and what to achieve, so that future generations are able to meet their own needs.

Sustainability is traditionally defined as the capacity of an eco-system to endure. Exploiting the carrying capacity of the planet wantonly, impoverishes future generations.

The word *wantonly* is critical, because world could add to future capital by innovating new models of production and consumption. This is what has enabled homo-sapiens to thrive on this planet, and take gigantic leaps despite monumental natural handicaps.

The idea of sustainable development has evolved over the last four decades with a proliferation of its interpretation in terms of vision, values and principles. Sustainable development, an important concept concerning business activity, is the result of realization that any business conducted with the core motive of profit maximization for the shareholders, in disregard of societal and environmental concerns is bound to fail in the long run. However, this traditional concept of business has come a long way since the famous economist and Nobel Laureate, Milton Friedman proclaimed in 1970. In 1984, Edward Freeman introduced the stake holder theory and argued that socially responsible activities helped business in build in strong relationship with stakeholders, and that management must pursue actions that are optimal for a broad class of shareholders rather than those that serve only to maximize shareholder interests. In 1989, Kenneth Andrews exhorted corporate to focus corporate power to objectives that are possible but sometimes less economically attractive than socially desirable. In 1998, John Elkington introduced the concept of Triple Bottom line to emphasize that a company's performance is best measured by the economic, social and environmental impact of its activities. Thus, in microeconomic sense, organizational sustainability interfaces with economics through the social and ecological consequences of economic activities, undertaken by a firm in pursuit of fulfilling its avowed goal, mainly concentrating on maximization of shareholders' wealth.

Sustainable means endurable. The focus of sustainability ranges from the total carrying capacity (sustainability) of plane ecosystems, countries municipalities, individual lives, individual goods and services, and so on. However, a universally accepted definition of sustainable development remains elusive, because it is expected to achieve multifarious phenomena. Most sustainability frameworks incorporate considerations of environmental, economic and social impact. Some sustainability frameworks ever assess those impacts a time dimension, which incorporates short term to long term, and considers impacts along the lifecycle, from supply, production, use, and fate, including impacts on future generations. Part of the problem is that the sustainability framework is dynamic, and evolutionary. In order to be effective, it must be multi-dimensional and multi-scalar. A multi-scalar place-based approach, which recognizes that values are a function of people, culture and Maslowian circumstances. Companies struggling to move from the "why" to the "how" of sustainability, must recognize that the goal of achieving sustainability should be global, at the system-level; however implementation, in most cases, must occur at a more local level.

CORE PRINCIPLES FOR INVESTMENT POLICY-MAKING FOR SUSTAINABLE DEVELOPMENT

With the global population approaching 7 billion, world today is consuming resources at a rate greater than the earth's ability to replenish them. If the whole world consumed at the rate that UK does, we would need three planets. If we consumed at the rate of the US, we would need five. Nearly 16% of the world population lives in India but India has only 4% of world's water resources. This is crisis that has the potential to derail the economic and social development of the country, and impact the health and livelihoods of people across the county.

The sustainability principles are to : Conserve, protect, and where needed, restore the productivity and diversity of nature (ecological processes and structure), to levels necessary to maintain ecological health (within special focus on key areas such as riparian areas, floodplains, wetlands, native plant habitats etc.).; Phase-out the use and emission into nature of toxic minerals, metals and fossil fuels and synthetic persistent bio-accumulating toxic materials and substances while phasing-in the use of renewable energy and naturally occurring, non-toxic materials and substances in production processes, goods and services; Eliminate waste through reduction at the source and enhanced reuse, remanufacturing and recycling internally within and externally between agencies, institutions and business; Increase the efficiency by which natural resources and energy are extracted, processed and used; ; and, finally, Enhance business development, economic competitiveness, job creation, fairness in the distribution of resources to meet basic human needs, public safety, health care and education consistent with the principles above.

Corporate sustainability is the capacity of an enterprise to maintain economic prosperity in the context of environmental responsibility, entails the creation of sustainable competitive advantage by means of building the capacity of a firm to add value through the product it produces or services it renders, and ensuring its operation ad infinitum in a socially and environmentally just and equitable modus operandi. The capacity depends on the degree of human ingenuity and innovation. In fact, the cornerstones of sustainability are innovation, engagement, transparency and accountability. Innovation needs clash of ideas, and acceptance of dissent, as a value enhancer. This requires a culture, where people can freely discuss contrarian viewpoints. It is only through diversity and difference that ideas are generated and innovation is stimulated. Disclosure is a prerequisite for trust, and key to successful team work and synergy. Corporate Sustainability Strategy not only embeds the principles of sustainability into an organization but also, makes sustainability part of the corporate DNA. The sustainability roadmap is charted and measured in terms of costs, revenues and reputation. A successful organization is a creative organization. In a successful organization, innovation is sustainable and on-going, rather than a process characterized by succession of "boom and bust" events. A creative organization is "led," rather than "managed." A sustainable innovative organization must be fluid and "organic", almost biological in nature to foster the constant creativity vital for the success of a modern organization. A degree of security and stability is essential to "incubate" creativity. In the fiercely competitive 21st century marketplace, innovative is essential for survival. An organization is to assess and quantify sustainability's impact in all key areas, including : Value chain (production, supplier selection process, logistics); Products and services (materials, packaging, pricing strategies); Organization structure (governance, sales and marketing, finance); Talent management (recruiting, performance management); and, Culture (leadership, change management).

Businesses should support inclusive growth and equitable development and recognize the challenges and social economic development faced by India, and build upon the development agenda that has been articulated in the government policies and priorities. The central strategic query of sustainable well-being and progress of the larger whole of life by partnering with other stakeholders of the organization like the employees, customers, suppliers and the community and also, wherever necessary, with competitors, in a mutually beneficial and complementing partnership. Building Sustainability would involve: i) CSR The heart of Corporate Governance, Integrity, Quality & Social Responsibility; ii) Sensitizing Human Resource for environment & sustainability needs;iii)HR strategies to create a sustainable world class organization; iv) Governance for environmentally sustainable future; v) Transforming strategy to scale up green Growth solutions; vi) Maintaining climate change concerns in economic development models; vii) Driving Sustainable business through green economy; and, finally, viii) Sustainability strategy – Post Rio+20 & Beyond.

Business need to integrate sustainability into their operating processes, logistics, and premises. It may involve introducing new products and services, which are more sustainable. Top leadership has to believe and walk the talk, staff and other stakeholders need to hear their leaders explain regularly what responsibility and sustainability means for the business. Why it is important, and how it is integrated with business purpose and strategy. Managers need to be sensitized to, and have good antennae for risks and opportunities, associated with sustainability and business impacts on society.

Sustainable sourcing is vital to business in the long-term. Companies must take responsibility for their extended value chains, which go beyond their own direct impact of factories, offices and transport. They must look both upstream and downstream to maximize the opportunities available. Leading responsible growth also means broadening access, and participation in the supply chain. It means looking at all suppliers, big and small. But the challenge is not just to source, manufacture and distribute our products sustainably; it is as important, if not more, to motivate consumers around the world to be part of this agenda.

The core principles towards sustainable development aim to guide the development of national and international investment policies To this end, the policy-makers translate the challenges of investment policy-making into a set of "design criteria" for investment policies. They call for integrating investment policy in overall development strategies, enhancing sustainable development as part of investment policies, balancing rights and obligations of States and investors in the context of investment protection and promotion, including CSR in investment policy-making, and encouraging international cooperation on investment-related challenges.

The design of the Core Principles has been inspired by various sources of international law and politics. Some of these instruments have importance for the entire set of the Core Principles as they relate – to various degrees – to sustainable development. Several other international instruments relate to individual Core Principles. These core principles for investment policy-making for sustainable development are presented in Box-1.

BOX-1

Area	*Core Principles*
1 Investment for	• The overarching objective of investment policy-making sustainable development is to promote investment for inclusive growth and sustainable development.
2 Policy coherence	• Investment policies should be grounded in a country's overall development strategy. All policies that impact on investment should be coherent and synergetic at both the national and international levels.
3 Public governance and institutions	• Investment policies should be developed involving all stakeholders, and embedded in an institutional framework based on the rule of law that adheres to high standards of public governance and ensures predictable, efficient and transparent procedures for investors.
4 Dynamic policy-making	• Investment policies should be regularly reviewed for effectiveness and relevance and adapted to changing development dynamics.
5 Balanced rights and obligations	• Investment policies should be balanced in setting out rights and obligations of States and investors in the interest of development for all.
6 Right to regulate	• Each country has the sovereign right to establish entry and operational conditions for foreign investment, subject to international commitments, in the interest of

	the public good and to minimize potential negative effects.
7 Openness to investment	• In line with each country's development strategy, investment policy should establish open, stable and predictable entry conditions for investment.
8 Investment protection and treatment	• Investment policies should provide adequate protection to established investors. The treatment of established investors should be non-discriminatory.
9 Investment promotion and facilitation	• Policies for investment promotion and facilitation should be aligned with sustainable development goals and designed to minimize the risk of harmful competition for investment.
10 Corporate governance and responsibility	• Investment policies should promote and facilitate the adoption of and compliance with best international practices of corporate social responsibility and good corporate governance.
11 International cooperation	• The international community should cooperate to address shared investment-for development policy challenges, particularly in least developed countries. Collective efforts should also be made to avoid investment protectionism.

These Core Principles are grouped as follows:

- Principle 1 states the overarching objective of investment policy-making.
- Principles 2, 3 and 4 relate to the general process of policy development and the policy-making environment as relevant for investment policies.
- Principles 5 through 10 address the specifics of investment policy-making.
- Principle 11 refers to cooperation in investment related matters at the international level.

ANNOTATION TO THE CORE PRINCIPLES

Principle 1: Investment for Sustainable Development

This overarching principle defines the overall objective of the Investment Policy Framework for Sustainable Development. It recognizes the need to promote investment not only for economic growth as such, but for growth that benefits all, including the poorest. It also calls for the mainstreaming of sustainable development issues – i.e. development that meets the needs of the present without compromising the ability of future generations to meet theirs – in investment policy-making, at both the national and international levels.

Principle 2: Policy Coherence

This principle recognizes that investment is a means to an end, and that investment policy should thus be integrated in an overarching development strategy. It also acknowledges that success in attracting and benefiting from investment depends not only on investment policy "stricto sensu" (i.e. entry and establishment rules, treatment and protection) but on a host of investment-related policy areas ranging from tax to trade to environmental and labour market policies. It recognizes that these policy areas interact with each other and that there is consequently a need for a coherent overall approach to make them conducive to sustainable development and to achieve synergies. The same considerations apply with respect to the interaction between national investment policies and international investment rule-making. Successful experiences with investment for development often involved the establishment of special agencies with a specific mandate to coordinate the work of different ministries, government units and policy areas, including the negotiation of international investment agreements (IIAs).

Principle 3: Public Governance and Institutions

The concept of good public governance refers to the efficiency and effectiveness of government services, including such aspects as accountability, predictability, clarity, transparency, fairness, rule of law, and the absence of corruption. This principle recognizes the importance of good public governance as a key factor in creating an environment conducive to attracting investment. It also stresses the significance of a participatory approach to policy development as a basic ingredient of investment policies aimed at inclusive growth and fairness for all. The element of transparency is especially important, as in and by itself it tends to facilitate dialogue between public and private sector stakeholders, including companies, organized labour and nongovernmental organizations (NGOs).

Principle 4: Dynamic Policy-making

This principle recognizes that national and international investment policies need flexibility to adapt to changing circumstances, while recognizing that a favourable investment climate requires stability and predictability. For one, different policies are needed at different development stages. New factors may emerge on the domestic policy scene, including government changes, social pressures or environmental degradation. International dynamics can have an impact on national investment policies as well, including through regional integration or through international competition for the attraction of specific types of foreign investment. The increasing role of emerging economies as outward investors and their corresponding desire better to protect their companies abroad drives change in investment policies as well.

The dynamics of investment policies also imply a need for countries continuously to assess the effectiveness of existing instruments. If these do not achieve the desired results in terms of economic and social development, or do so at too high a cost, they may need to be revised.

Principle 5: Balanced Rights and Obligations

Investment policies need to serve two potentially conflicting purposes. On the one hand, they have to create attractive conditions for foreign investors. To this end, investment policies include features of investment liberalization, protection, promotion and facilitation. On the other hand, the overall regulatory framework of the host country has to ensure that any negative social or environmental effects are minimized. More regulation may also be warranted to find appropriate responses to crises (e.g. financial crisis, food crisis, climate change).

Against this background, this core principle suggests that the investment climate and policies of a country should be "balanced" as regards the overall treatment of foreign investors. Where and how to strike this balance is basically an issue for the domestic law of host countries and therefore requires adequate local capacities. International policies vis-à-vis foreign investors likewise play a role and – if not carefully designed – might tilt the balance in favour of those investors. The principle does not mean that each individual investment related regulation of a host country would have to be balanced.

Principle 6: Right to Regulate

The right to regulate is an expression of a country's sovereignty. Regulation includes both the general legal and administrative framework of host countries as well as sector- or industry-specific rules. It also entails effective implementation of rules, including the enforcement of rights. Regulation is not only a State right, but also a necessity. Without an adequate regulatory framework, a country will not be attractive for foreign investors, because such investors seek clarity, stability and predictability of investment conditions in the host country.

The authority to regulate can, under certain circumstances, be ceded to an international body to make rules for groups of states. It can be subject to international obligations that countries undertake; with regard to the treatment of foreign investors this often takes place at the bilateral or regional level. International commitments thus reduce "policy space". This principle advocates that countries maintain sufficient policy space to regulate for the public good.

Principle 7: Openness to Investment

This principle considers a welcoming investment climate, with transparent and predictable entry conditions and procedures, a precondition for attracting foreign investment conducive for sustainable development. The term "openness" is not limited to formal openness as expressed in a country's investment framework and, possibly, in entry rights granted in IIAs. Equally important is the absence of informal investment barriers, such as burdensome, unclear and non-transparent administrative procedures. At the same time, the principle recognizes that countries have legitimate reasons to limit openness to foreign investment, for instance in the context of their national development strategies or for national security reasons.

In addition, the issue of "openness" reaches beyond the establishment of an investment. Trade openness can be of crucial importance, too; in particular, when the investment significantly depends on imports or exports.

Principle 8: Investment Protection

This principle acknowledges that investment protection, although only one among many determinants of foreign investment, can be an important policy tool for the attraction of investment. It therefore closely interacts with the principle on investment promotion and facilitation (Principle 9). It has a national and an international component. Core elements of protection at the national level include, inter alia, the rule of law, freedom of contract and access to courts. Key components of investment protection frequently found in IIAs comprise the principles of non-discrimination (national treatment and most-favoured-nation treatment), fair and equitable treatment, protection in case of expropriation, provisions on movement of capital and effective dispute settlement.

Principle 9: Investment Promotion and Facilitation

Most countries have set up promotion schemes to attract and facilitate foreign investment. Promotion and facilitation measures often include the granting of fiscal or financial incentives, and the establishment of special economic zones or "one- stop shops". Many countries have also set up special investment promotion agencies (IPAs) to target foreign investors, offer matchmaking services and provide aftercare.

The principle contains two key components. First, it stipulates that in their efforts to improve the investment climate, countries should not compromise sustainable development goals, for instance by lowering regulatory standards on social or environmental issues, or by offering incentives that annul a large part of the economic benefit of the investment for the host country. Second, the principle acknowledges that, as more and more countries seek to boost investment and target specific types of investment, the risk of harmful competition for investment increases; i.e. a race to the regulatory bottom or a race to the top of incentives (with negative social and environmental consequences or escalating commitments of public funds). Investment policies should be designed to minimize this risk. This underlines the importance of international coordination.

Principle 10: Corporate Governance and Responsibility

This principle recognizes that corporate governance and CSR standards are increasingly shaping investment policy at the national and international levels. This development is reflected in the proliferation of standards, including several intergovernmental organization standards of the United Nations, the ILO, the IFC and the OECD, providing guidance on fundamental CSR issues; 5 dozens of multi- stakeholder initiatives; hundreds of industry association codes; and thousands of individual company codes. Most recently, the UN Human Rights Council adopted a resolution endorsing the Report of the Special Representative of the Secretary- General on the issue of human rights and transnational corporations and other business enterprises.

Principle 11: International Cooperation

This principle considers that investment policies touch upon a number of issues that would benefit from more international cooperation. The principle also advocates that particular efforts should be made to encourage foreign investment in LDCs. Home countries can support outward investment conducive to sustainable development. For a long time, developed countries have provided investment guarantees against certain political risks in host countries or offered loans to companies investing abroad. The Multilateral Investment Guarantee Agency (MIGA) provides investment insurance at the international level. The principle builds upon examples of countries that have started to condition the granting of investment guarantees on an assessment of social and environmental impacts.

The importance of international cooperation also grows as more and more countries make use of targeted investment promotion policies. Better international coordination is called for to avoid a global race to the bottom in regulatory standards, or a race to the top in incentives, and to avoid a return of protectionist tendencies.

More international coordination, in particular at the regional level, can also help to create synergies so as to realize investment projects that would be too complex and expensive for one country alone. Another policy area that would benefit from more international cooperation is investment in sensitive sectors. For example, recent concerns about possible land grabs and the crowding out of local farmers by foreign investors have resulted in the development by the FAO, UNCTAD, the World Bank and IFAD of Principles for Responsible Investment in Agriculture (PRAI).

SUSTAINABLE DEVELOPMENT AND INDIA

India's journey on the path of sustainable development has so far been marked both by reasons for celebration and introspection. The right place to begin the story would be the 1980s and early 1990s, which mark the beginning of economic reforms, catalyst for India's phenomenally faster growth rates since, and coinciding with a time when countries around the world acknowledged and started addressing the increasing environmental concerns, such as at the Earth Summit in Rio in 1992. India's faster gross domestic product (GDP) growth over the last two decades has been unprecedented; but at the same time India's rankings in terms of the human development index (HDI) as well as indices measuring environmental sustainability are yet to fully reflect this growth. However, it would be a mistake to downplay the enormous progress made, as India has followed a much more conscious path of sustainable development with impressive results on the ground.

The key environmental challenges have become sharper in the past two decades. The 2009 State of the Environment Report by the Ministry of Environment and Forests (MOEF) clubs the issues under five key challenges faced by India, which are climate change, food security, water security, energy security, and managing urbanization. Climate change is impacting the natural ecosystems and is expected to have substantial adverse effects in India, mainly on agriculture on which around 58 per cent of the population depends for livelihood, water storage in the Himalayan glaciers which are the source of major rivers and groundwater recharge, sea-level rise, and threats to a long coastline and habitations. Climate change will also cause increased frequency of extreme events such as storms, floods, and droughts. These in turn will impact India's food & water security problems. India also faces the critical challenge of meeting its rapidly growing energy demands. It currently depends on around 80 per cent imports for its crude oil requirements. A large section of the rural population is still not connected to the grid or efficient modern cooking fuel sources, and India's per capita energy consumption of 439 kg of oil equivalent is far below the world average of 1688 kg. The energy poverty of the household sector is indicated not only by the low penetration of electricity into the sector, but also by its primary dependence on traditional inefficient fuel for cooking and lighting.

SCIENCE AND ECONOMICS OF CLIMATE CHANGE

The atmosphere carries out the critical function of maintaining life-sustaining conditions on earth. The sun radiates solar energy on earth and a large part of this energy, about one-third is radiated back into space, the balance being absorbed by the surface and atmosphere. GHGs like carbon dioxide (and water vapour re- emit some of this heat to the earth's surface. If they did not perform this useful function, most of the heat energy would escape, leaving the earth cold and unable to support life. In this manner the atmosphere creates a natural greenhouse effect which helps sustain life on earth.

With climate change, the type, frequency, and intensity of extreme events, floods, and droughts are expected to increase. Thus climate change represents additional stress on ecological and socioeconomic systems that are already facing tremendous pressure due to rapid economic development. Hence, addressing climate change is a major challenge in terms of policies and resources needed to address it at domestic and international levels.

Science suggests that the impacts of climate change are serious and broad ranging, with economics implying that they interact with other market failures and economic dynamics, giving rise to complex policy issues. To put it briefly, climate change is a global externality associated with the emission of GHGs, which has long, persistent and, beyond a level, irreversible effects. These emissions impose a cost on both the present and future generations, which are not fully recouped from the emitters of these emissions. Hence, there is need for policy intervention as markets alone fail to account for these failures.

This forms the starting point for the international climate change negotiating regime, suggesting a need for globally coordinated policy action as the incremental impact of a ton of GHG on climate change is independent of where in the world it is emitted, and because the nature of GHG emissions is such that it affects the environment with a lag. This characteristic shapes some important features of climate change policy framework, namely historical responsibilities and inter- and intra-generational equity. The requisite policy hence should balance the distribution of outcomes within and across generations. Every effort for conservation must be carried out early to protect our future generations by providing them with a better quality of life including productive resources for the future. Along with this we also have to safeguard our reasonable interests and concerns as environmental issues cannot be delinked from our efforts to provide the present generation with the basic necessities and a better quality of life. Also, there has to be a cooperative endeavour to protect the climate and environment along with development imperatives. Put together, combating climate change ultimately boils down to a complex economic policy issue with very difficult choices involving rates of economic growth, volumes of emission, probable increase in temperature, and adverse impacts and costs of addressing climate change.

Sustainable development is a difficult balancing act in countries with low incomes. Society has to simultaneously accomplish three things with trade-offs: improve economic well-being with social justice for the present generation, yet manage with more restrained use of land, air, forest, energy, and water resources, and protect future generations. The choices are more difficult in developing countries because they affect people's livelihoods. Such a 'stewardship' to succeed therefore needs to respond to people's needs, share information on choices and costs, and ensure participation and ownership.

India has done well on all such counts of stewardship over the past decades. Economic reforms since the 1980s have accelerated growth and incomes. Social well-being has improved broadly, as measured by gains in life expectancy. India has stepped up protection of its natural environment such as forests. Its particular development path has relied on fast-growing services–a low emissions-intensity path with accelerated literacy and education promising a better future. While India could have done even better, much has been accomplished. The reasons behind such progress are undoubtedly strong institutional underpinnings: democratic participation, constitutional protection of social justice, and a steady accretion of environmental laws and regulations, multiple actors, markets, and expanding government programmes and policies.

India will nevertheless need to save and spend even more to meet its objectives of economic well-being with environmental sustainability, while continuing to reduce its carbon intensity of growth. This is possible and doable. New institutional challenges are being posed by more intense pressures on land and agriculture, rapid urbanization, the quality of public services, public environmental health, and deteriorating air and water. Differential prices, incentives, regulations, and taxes will need to be supportive, especially on energy, to help shift to a more efficient and equitable development path. New non-carbon, renewable energy sources and technologies will be crucial, mostly led by the private sector. Social justice will require stepped- up public spending on energy access and other elements of the eight National Missions.

Turning to the global context, India has voluntarily endeavoured to reduce the energy intensity of its growth path by 2020. It is well on the way to accomplishing that goal. However, the global community needs to act on its commitment to equity and fair burden sharing: reducing the massive gaps in per capita emissions between rich and poor countries and enhanced financing for massive adaptation and mitigation efforts in developing countries—so that developed countries do not end using up all the carbon space at the cost of the developing world.

Another challenge from India's perspective lies in preparing itself for enhanced actions on the transparency of its mitigation actions arising from the new regime of International Consultation and Analysis (ICA) and ensuring, in future negotiations, a space for equitable access of developing countries to atmospheric resources and guarantee against punitive actions embedded in the domestic legislation of developed countries. India will also need to institute necessary domestic mechanisms for effectively participating in and benefitting from the arrangements for advancing technology and forestry-related actions.

Climate change is a global phenomenon that we have to address in a spirit of cooperation taking into account the historical responsibilities and capabilities of countries. World seems to hit the limits of sustainability, whichever direction we depart from today's untenable status quo. Culture, philosophical and religious beliefs, as well as moral values, seem to exhibit the same suspense. Clear logic of self-destruction is abundant in these areas, but no proof of inevitable and unavoidable failure: i) We reverberate to multiple challenges to human sustainability: economic, environmental, epidemiological, demographic, cultural and moral with little certainty in outcomes, or what we can do about these challenges. ii) To know whether there might be limits to sustainability, one would need a good working definition of firstly sustainability, and also limits. iii) Limits suggest a boundary in space, time, or "psychic space" and sustainability seems to suggest both the static concept of "no change", as well as a more dynamical concept of "change", consistent with the continued capacity of a system to support the kind of activity that leads to the change. iv) The real question for humanity is about the limits to sustainability, "what pace of destructive change is acceptable for humanity's purpose?" and "how can humanity ensure that change is managed to remain within that acceptable pace?" v) The concept of sustainable development should be open to the cultural and geographical differences, sensible to the different local contexts. In many of the industrialized countries, there is a strong need to focus on sustainability; on the other hand in the developing part of the world there is a strong need for further economic growth. Consequently, in efforts to find the limits to sustainability, we are faced with need for dualism in recommendations to the political system. As a responsible and enlightened member of the international community, India showed flexibility along with other developing countries towards the success of the Durban Conference. At Durban, the world recognized India for its spirited defence of the interests of developing countries. India ensured that the objectives of social and economic development and poverty eradication will not be compromised in any way, whether upto 2020 or in the post 2020 arrangements that are to be negotiated and finalized by 2015. It is hoped that the developed countries will reciprocate the flexibility shown by India at Durban by addressing the concerns of developing countries on all outstanding issues. The negotiations should not prejudge the agreed outcomes. The legal nature of the outcomes under the Durban Platform shall be determined not by form but by their substance. Therefore each action in this context must be seen from the perspective of the most underprivileged. The entire global community has to work towards this issue. More than a question of an agreed or a binding commitment it is more importantly a question of the division of fair responsibilities among nations considering historical responsibilities, development processes, the objective of poverty eradication, and capacities to provide resources of different countries.

QUESTIONS

1. Discuss the concept of sustainability and sustainable development.
2. Explain the science and economics of climate change. What are the main principles of sustainability?
3. "Corporate sustainability is the capacity of an enterprise to maintain economic prosperity in the context of environmental responsibility, entails the creation of sustainable competitive advantage by means of building the capacity of a firm to add value through the product it produces or services it renders, and ensuring its operation ad infinitum in a socially and environmentally just and equitable modus operandi. The capacity depends on the degree of human ingenuity and innovation". Comment.

4. Critically examine the core issues for investment policy making for sustainable development.
5. What are the main issues engaging governments and corporation in relation to sustainable development in India?
6. Explain the issues involved in formulating an environmental policy and competitiveness in a globalised economy.
7. What improves environmental performance? How can a MNC combine environmental management with eco-efficiency?
8. Critically examine the impact of foreign direct investment (FDI) on the environment in host developing countries.
9. What are the pressures on governments to pursue national objectives in environmental protection and how can these be reconciled with global objectives?

REFERENCES

Adams, J.: Environmental Policy and Competitiveness in a globalised economy: Conceptional issue and a review of the empirical evidence, in OECD, *Globalisation and Environment: Preliminary Perspectives*, Paris : OECD) 1997.

Asian Development Bank (ADB) : *Environment and Development: A Pacific Island Perspective* (Manila: ADB), 1992.

Barton, J.R.: "Environmental regulation and business strategies in the E.U. iron and steel industry, in *Proceedings of the Environmental Regulation and Business Strategies in the EU iron and steel Industry* (Leeds: University, of Leeds), 1998.

Christmann, P.: "Environmental strategies of multinational companies: determinants and effects on competitive advantage (globalisation), (Los Angeles: University of California), 1997.

Dasgupta, A., H. Hettige, and D. Wheeler : *What improves environmental performance? Evidence from Mexican Industry"* (Washington, D.C.: The World Bank), 1998.

Eriksen, J. and M. Housen: "Environmental aspects of Denish direct investment: managing the environment in on open economy," Occasional paper No. 2 (Copenhagen: Copenhagen Business School), 1999.

Grossman, R. and A. Krueger: *Economic Growth and Environment*, NBER Working paper No, 4634 (Cambridge, MA : NBER), 1994.

Low, P. (ed.), *International Trade and Environment*, (Oxford: Oxford University Press), 1998

Pearson, C.: *Multinational Corporations, the Environment of the Third World*, Duke University Press, 1987.

Repetto, R.: *Jobs, competitiveness and Environmental Regulation: What are the real issues?* World Resource Institute, 1995.

Vogel, D. : *Trading up: Consumers and Environmental Regulations in a Global Economy*, Harvard University Press, 1995.

Xing, Y and C. Kolstad : *"Do lax environmental regulations attract foreign investment? University of California, 1997*

Zarsky, L.: *Havens, halos and spaghetti: untangling the evidence about foreign direct investment and the environment"* (Paris : OECD), 1999.

Unit V

24

GLOBALISATION AND HUMAN RESOURCE DEVELOPMENT

INTRODUCTION

Globalisation through international production creates scope for MNCs and foreign firms to play a role in the generation and upgrading and of human resources the building up of skills in host countries. In the new economic order an increasing proportion of the world's labour force is engaged in activities that compete with or are linked — through international trade and international production — to activities taking place in other countries. This means that national labour markets are becoming increasingly interdependent. Maintaining or increasing employment and its quality in a particular country requires that its labour markets must be responsive not only to changes related to development and growth within the country, but also to changing conditions worldwide. The role and impact of MNC activities in these respects varies, however, according to the type or motivation of FDI, the industries in which MNCs invest, the strategies they adopt, and host country conditions. They also depend significantly on the policies of host countries on FDI for increasing employment quantity, improving employment quality and strengthening human resource capabilities and for minimising any negative effects that FDI may have in these respects.

MNCs STRATEGIES AND THEIR IMPLICATIONS FOR GENERATING EMPLOYMENT AND BUILDING SKILLS

MNCs, like other enterprises, combine labour and other factors of production to generate goods and services. The quantity and quality of employment generated within a firm — regardless of whether it is a MNC or not — depend mainly upon the industry group to which it belongs, the production activities in which it is engaged, and its size. The activity in which a firm is engaged, and the technological parameters of that activity determine the capital-, labour- and knowledge-intensities of its production, although there is usually a range of technological options and hence combinations of labour with capital that are available to producers to choose from, depending upon, among others, relative factor costs. The size of a firm, on the other hand, determines whether a large or small amount of labour is employed, given the combination of labour, capital and knowledge that are required to produce one unit of output. It also determines the extent to which a firm can invest in training and the building up of skills.

While these determinants of the volume and nature of employment are the same for all firms, there are some factors that suggest that the behaviour, practices and role of MNCs with respect to employment and skills upgrading may differ in some respects from those of other firms. These include the larger size and greater technological sophistication of many MNCs, the competitive pressures under which they operate, and their ability to deliver, by means of FDI, non-tradable goods and (especially) services. Among other things, because of their size, many MNCs are employers of larger total numbers of workers than uni-national firms in the same industries. At the same time, because of their technology-intensity and competitive behaviour, they are likely to generate smaller numbers of jobs than other firms of equal output size.

The principal difference between MNCs and other firms, however, is that MNCs distribute their production activities and, hence, employment, between their internationally dispersed facilities. The distribution of employment by size and quality among different locations depends upon several factors. It depends upon the MNC's motivations for and strategies with respect to international production and on the locational advantages of different countries. It also depends upon labour market conditions in host and home countries, including the availability and cost of labour of various skills and capabilities.

While FDI of all types involves employment in host countries, some FDI is motivated specifically by considerations directly related to the employment of skilled or unskilled labour. Resource-seeking and efficiency-seeking FDI in manufacturing and services is often made with the specific objective of accessing low-cost labour for labour-intensive production or taking advantage of relatively abundant supplies of educated and skilled workers. For market-seeking FDI, on the other hand, the availability and cost of labour or skilled human resources is not the main consideration in the choice of location, although it is likely to be one of several secondary factors that determine the investment location decision.

Given the broad motivations that underly MNCs' decisions regarding FDI, their strategies and the resulting organisational structures of their international production activity affect in a number of ways the intra-firm distribution of employment among home and host countries:

i) Under a "stand-alone" strategy, in which a MNC replicates in its foreign affiliates much of the value-chain of the parent firm (with the exception, typically, of technology development and finance that are retained at headquarter operations), affiliates in host countries perform the tasks necessary for production to service the host-country and/or neighbouring markets. Accordingly, most of the employment of labour necessary for host country production occurs in the foreign affiliates. Indeed, if foreign affiliate sales replace exports from the home country, that may be accompanied by a reduction of employment in the home country facilities within the MNC systems. Replacement of actual or potential employment in parent firms by that in foreign affiliates does not, of course, occur if the foreign investment is motivated by high tariffs or other restrictions on the home country's exports. It also does not occur where FDI is the only means of serving foreign markets, as for many services that by their very nature require proximity between the provider and the customer.

ii) Under a "simple integration" strategy, in which a MNC locates one or a few elements of its value chain in its foreign affiliates, the latter undertake — typically with technology obtained from the parent firm — a limited range of activities to supply their parent firms with specific inputs or products that they are in a more competitive position to produce. Simple integration does not involve reproducing the parent firm's occupational structure in foreign affiliates; rather, it introduces a complementary hierarchy of occupations within a MNC system across different locations. Employment quantity and quality in a host country depend upon the nature of the locational advantages that attract FDI.

iii) Under "complex integration" strategies, each MNC affiliate specializses in a product, process or function integrated with those of other units within the MNC's regional or global network of integrated international production. Deeper integration of this kind provides efficiency gains for a MNC and could result in a smaller system-wide workforce for a given output size than the other two strategies mentioned: specialisation and consolidation of business functions in various locations have a rationalising effect on total firm employment when compared, for example, to the replication of value-adding activities in all host locations as in a stand-alone strategy, or limited specialisation among locations as under simple integration strategies. Employment quantity in different locations depends upon the role assigned to the parent firm or a particular affiliate within the network.

The motivations and strategies of individual MNCs — each with its firm-specific advantages, including, among others, those arising out of its international production networks— interact with the locational advantages of particular host countries to determine how much FDI the latter attract, in what industries, and of what kind. Simultaneously, they determine the size and quality of employment and the potential for skills upgrading directly in foreign affiliates. Different organisational forms and structures have different implications and potentials in these respects. In addition to these direct effects, there are indirect effects on employment and related skills building that occur through competition, production linkages and multiplier and accelerator effects of income generated by FDI. Moreover, MNC strategies and behaviour with respect to investment and, hence, employment, human resource management, and investment in skills formation change in response to changes in global, regional or country-specific conditions affecting their competitive positions and profit opportunities. Globalisation and increased global competition are leading MNCs to shift towards more complex corporate strategies and integrated international production structures. These involve a greater geographical dispersion of MNC activities, increasing coordination and specialisation of the activities of individual affiliates, and greater importance being attached to created assets in making locational decisions. Host developing countries can, by taking MNC strategies and changes therein into account, harness the potential of FDI to generate employment and, in particular, create jobs of good quality and impart skills to the workforce under conditions prevailing at any given time. They can, moreover, induce MNCs to sustain their employment- generating investments, upgrading the quality of employment they provide by moving into higher value-added production, and increasing the training and skills available to human resources in foreign affiliates and local enterprises linked to them.

FDI EMPLOYMENT AND SKILLS IN HOST DEVELOPING COUNTRIES

Employment Generation

FDI generates employment in host countries directly and indirectly. Foreign affiliates of MNCs employ people in their mines, plantations, manufacturing plants and service establishments (direct employment). They also cause employment to be created in enterprises that are suppliers, subcontractors or service providers to them; the latter include domestic firms as well foreign affiliates of other MNCs, some of which may be established because of associated investments attracted to the country by the demand for their products or services from original investors (indirect employment). Foreign affiliates also indirectly create employment by adding to output and incomes and thereby, further investment. Other things remaining the same, inward FDI thus has both direct and indirect effects that add to employment generation in a host country.

These positive effects may, however, be offset by a loss of employment caused by MNC activities. Such effects may also be direct or indirect. If FDI enters a host economy through mergers and acquisitions (M&As), it may lead to significant labour shedding in the acquired firms — the newly created foreign affiliates — as they restructure their activities in line with the objectives underlying the M&As. Moreover, FDI could, under certain conditions, crowd existing firms out of business, creating unemployment for their workers. It may also induce local competitors to shed employees, either by reducing the local firms' production due to a decreased share of the market or because of efforts by local firms to increase their efficiency and competitiveness by downsising their labour force.

The balance of these various effects is difficult to assess and is likely to vary among host countries and industries. Effects may also vary over time. A short-term loss of employment may be more than offset by longer-term gains if FDI raises the competitiveness, efficiency and export-orientation of domestic firms, thereby raising their production levels, or stimulates the establishment of new local or foreign supplier firms. On the other hand, if FDI is footloose, or adversely affects local enterprise development or holds back technology upgrading, the long- term employment and skill effects may reverse short-term gains or worsen short-term losses. Since it is difficult to specify the counterfactual — what would have happened if an investment had not taken place — the final effect is uncertain. However, a closer look at the nature of direct and indirect effects under various conditions, and empirical evidence throw further light on how and to what extent FDI may affect employment generation in host developing countries.

The direct and indirect effects of FDI on employment generation in host economies depend upon several factors. A few of them deserve particular attention while considering the effects in developing host economies.

i) The direct employment effects differ by the mode of entry of FDI. If investment is in greenfield sites (new production facilities), it generates new demand for workers. Entry through M&A, on the other hand, not only does *not* create new demand for workers but may lead to labour shedding, either immediately or with a time lag. In developed countries, where M&As are the major made if entry for FDI, they almost invariably lead to lay-offs, at least initially in developing countries, the effects are less clear. Some M&As salvage moribund enterprises and contribute to conserving employment. Others could reduce total employment in the host economy by dismissing labour or by out-competing local firms. Whether or not employment subsequently rebounds depends on a host of factors, including productivity, multiplier and growth effects.

ii) Employment generation by MNC's depends upon the size of FDI in general and especially that of FDI in labour- or human-resource intensive activities. Given labour-market conditions, this depends on the trade and industrial policies of a host economy. Countries with abundant low-cost labour that establish export-oriented trade regimes and an environment conducive for FDI can promote significant employment generation by attracting export-oriented activities. As the early experience of East and South-East Asia, and subsequent experience in China show, simple processing activities for exports in foreign affiliates create large numbers of jobs, initially at low wages and requiring low skills. Whether this employment is sustainable over time depends on several factors, including whether technologies and skills in affiliates are deepened and improved as wages rise. Countries with import-substituting regimes can also stimulate employment generation by attracting FDI, especially when their markets are large; however, employment growth in market-seeking foreign affiliates in such regimes tends to slow over time if high levels of protection are maintained and lead to technological lags or constrict economies of scale. In general, a competitive environment that places fewer barriers to the entry of new firms tends to generate more sustainable growth in output and employment. However, much depends upon how competitive conditions are introduced: a sudden shift to competitive structures carries the possibility of widespread labour-shedding resulting in unemployment that could take time to resolve; for example, in some Latin American countries, liberalisation led to a dramatic shift towards capital- intensive industries and methods, and high unemployment levels.

As developing countries move towards more liberal trade and industrial regimes, their ability to sustain employment in tradable goods and services depends partly on how quickly these activities can be restructured to face international competition. It also depends on whether new FDI flows in: while large domestic markets remain a strong magnet for FDI, the growth of employment in the new global context depends increasingly on host economies' competitive capabilities. Thus, growth of employment resulting from FDI in the tradables sector is increasingly likely to be concentrated in economies that can support rapid restructuring and efficient new production activities. However, given the growing importance of the services sector, both because of shifting consumption patterns as incomes grow and because of the growing importance of producer — including infrastructure — services in production, the potential for FDI to contribute to sustained employment growth in non-tradable service activities, such as finance, trade, tourism and utilities, should not be overlooked.

iii) A third important factor that shapes the capacity of host economies to attract employment generating FDI is the quality of the labour force: the level and composition of skills available, and the training potential of managers technicians and workers. In some developing economies, the authorities have pursued ambitious and comprehensive education policies that have resulted in skill levels well above the developing country averages. Some of the best outcomes in terms of skill formation are found where governments and enterprises have worked together to improve the training system. Singapore, for example has used focused training programmes effectively, not just for upgrading the industrial structure but also for attracting high-quality FDI.

iv) Finally, the efficiency of the labour market and the quality of labour market institutions, such as labour laws, unionisation and industrial relations in a host economy have an important role to play in the extent and manner of employment generation in foreign affiliates. If labour cannot move easily to new jobs or enter new types of employment arrangements, or if information on job opportunities is not transparent and accessible, investment may not result in commensurate employment opportunities. Similarly, if there is labour market segmentation by gender, ethnicity or other factors, investments are likely to create less employment or upgrade it less efficiently than where labour markets work well. On the other hand, where labour markets are open and well organised, and where industrial relations function smoothly and facilitate communications and exchange of information, they can serve to channel employment opportunities and stimulate ideas on how to upgrade skills *as* well as employment and working conditions. Thus, well-functioning institutions and appropriate regulations that ensure an efficient, fair and equitable functioning of labour markets are a precondition for harnessing FDI to employment generation.

Employment Quality

Because of their size, technological sophistication and origin principally in developed countries, MNCs are often expected to be better employers than domestic firms. Foreign affiliates are expected to offer higher remuneration and superior conditions of work, investing more in training and imparting more modern skills to their workers. On the other hand, recognising that MNCs, like all private enterprises, are driven by the profit motive, some observers, including trade unions, have concerns regarding the possibilities for MNCs to exploit their advantage of mobility over labour, which is largely location-bound, to squeese wages and labour standards and indirectly induce governments to weaken their regulation of labour markets. These concerns are reinforced by layoffs and resort to informal employment caused by privatisation and by the implementation of structural adjustment programmes in some developing countries, and by the decline in real wages that has taken place following trade and investment liberalisation in several countries and economic crises in some, even if the decline in wages is not directly related to FDI. The experiences of many developed countries in which employment has become increasingly casual and precarious (through, for example, part-time work and short-term contracts with insufficient protection against lay-offs) have also reinforced concerns regarding the consequences for employment quality. At the same time, both governments and unions are increasingly conscious of the potential benefits that FDI and MNC operations might contribute in a globalising world towards upgrading employment quality provided that institutions for labour representation and collective bargaining are in place. Plugging into the international production and distribution networks of MNCs can be an effective way of accessing new skills and technologies. This, in turn, can be helpful to introducing better work practices and upgrading employment.

Again, in general, the workforce directly employed in foreign affiliates enjoys higher remuneration and more favourable conditions of work than that employed in domestic firms in host countries. This applies not only to developed countries but also to developing countries. This tendency reflects a number of factors.

i) Foreign affiliates tend to be more concentrated in higher capital-, skill- and marketing- intensive industries than national firms, and productivity in such industries is generally higher than in others. In developing countries, there are also pronounced disparities between foreign and domestic firms in size, technology and production organisation, (even within the same industry), explaining the prevalence of intra-industry wage differentials.

ii) World-market oriented foreign affiliates need a reliable workforce to meet quality-control standards and production schedules. In particular, when affiliates are part of global networks of interdependent producers, quality and efficiency dictate the need for a well-trained, stable and experienced workforce. Affiliates in such industries tend to take root in the host environment and offer good wages, benefits and work conditions. They also have high sunk costs for training, infrastructure and supplier systems. By offering attractive inducements, foreign affiliates can induce capable workers to join and to remain with them, and reduce the risk of production errors and delays. These inducements are likely to be especially costly in countries' in which local skilled labour and managers are scarce and where there is a cultural bias in favour of domestic firms among prospective employees. Wage differentials *vis-a-vis* domestic firms are also likely to be particularly large where the affiliate has invested in generic skills that workers can transfer to other firms. In the case of such skills, foreign affiliates may also offer higher wages in an effort to poach experienced workers from other firms.

iii) The size and visibility of many MNCs may make them more prone than smaller domestic firms to unionisation and union pressure, as well as national or international action concerning standards of employment.

Notwithstanding the general tendency towards higher wages in foreign affiliates than in domestic firms in similar activities, wages in the former in low value-added activities based on simple technologies are low. In particular, affiliates in labour-intensive assembly operations in EPZs offer low remuneration, often lower than that in the larger enterprises operating in the main host economy, and/or catering to the domestic market. In fact, low labour costs are the competitive advantage sought by these MNCs in investing in certain industries or certain locations, such as EPZs. Locating in EPZs may even, in some cases, place affiliates outside the normal wage norms or laws. Firms in such Low-skill industries also tend to be footloose and have little incentive to upgrade the skills and capabilities of their employees. An important consideration, as far as employment quality is concerned, is how rapidly workers can move out of these kinds of jobs into more remunerative occupations. This would require technological and industrial capacity building and boosting trade competitiveness in some higher-value-added industries in which countries might have dynamic comparative advantage. Needless to say, real wages paid by MNCs in developing countries are generally much lower than those paid in developed countries. These differences are explained in part by differences in labour market conditions as regards supply, and also in part, by differences in labour productivity; generally, productivity in manufacturing in developing countries tends to be roughly 40 to 50 per cent of that in the same industry in developed countries. Notably, wages for low- or unskilled workers are much lower in labour-abundant developing countries than in developed (or for that matter, developing) home countries where labour supplies are less plentiful. It is precisely this wage differential — which is, of course, related to the restrictions on the mobility of labour across borders — that attracts FDI in labour-intensive activities to developing countries. However, labour productivity in some labour-intensive activities is unlikely to differ much between countries, regardless of the level of development, but wages paid by affiliates in developing countries may be at times far lower than warranted by productivity differences.

With respect to terms and conditions other than remuneration, working conditions and employment standards in foreign affiliates, in general, are not less favourable than those of comparable national employers; often, they rate better than the average in local firms. In particular, large, well-established and visible MNCs are likely to comply with international standards and not to undercut the labour standards *of* their host (and home) countries. They apply corporate labour standards uniformly across MNC systems to reap economies of scale, develop marketing advantages or win shareholder approval. In addition, their brand-name products are often subject to intense scrutiny where consumer groups or NGOs are sensitive to labour-standard or health issues. They adhere to minimum-wage, working hours, overtime and compensation regulations, and regulations regarding the provision of health services or leave, as they seek to attract and retain qualified workers and protect their reputations. Many of the larger MNCs from developed countries are likely to be found in this group. However, other affiliates, especially those driven by cost saving and who produce for the lower end of the market, are often more lax. This is also related to the fact that some host governments may relax requirements on employment standards, and exempt some investors from the labour laws applicable in the host economy, as is the case in some EPZs.

Upgrading Skills

Sustaining and upgrading employment increasingly requires the workforce to be multi- skilled and reasonably mobile, and to be able to assume wider responsibilities than under traditional systems of management and work division. Employability in the new context needs the upgrading of skills on a continuous basis, often with changing specialisation. As technology cycles become shorter, therefore, flexible lifetime learning becomes an essential part of skill formation.

The level and evolution of workforce skills in an economy depend directly on the following factors: i) pre-employment formal (primary, secondary or tertiary) education; ii) pre-employment formal and informal vocational or industrial training; iii) formal vocational training during employment, either by the employer or by outside institutions; iv) skills acquired informally by experience and learning — so-called "tacit" skills; v) specialised training offered for workers who have to upgrade or change occupational group (or wish to); vi) "lifetime learning" offered by different parts of the education system.

There is a complex interaction between these different modes of skill formation, in particular between the general education system and enterprise-financed training. Firms, including MNCs, always undertake some form of training, at the minimum to ensure that technologies in use are deployed efficiently. However, the decision to invest in more advanced forms of training depends on the returns they expect, their time horizon, and the extent of competition they are exposed to. The profitability of training also depends upon the skills provided by the education system, the prospects of retaining trained workers or the "appropriability" of returns to training investments.

Firms, regardless of ownership, have greater incentives to offer advanced training where they can build on employees' general and cognitive skills, that is where the education base is strong. Otherwise, the expected economic returns of further training will be low and firms will invest only in minimal operational training, mostly on the job. Similarly, where firms are protected from competition, particularly from international competition, they are less inclined to invest in advanced or up-to-date training. The issue of the "appropriability" of investments in skill formation is a problem that applies particularly to the creation of general, transferable skills that allow employees to move to better paid jobs in other firms. (Skills that are firm- specific do not earn commensurately high wages elsewhere).

MNCs can contribute to skill upgrading by investing directly in training in their affiliates. They can also induce or support local firms, notably their suppliers and buyers, to do so as well. They can influence local competitors or unrelated firms that emulate their practices. They can interact with training institutions to improve courses and teaching materials. They can induce the government or industry associations to set up new training facilities. They may attract or induce training institutions from their home countries to set up similar establishments in host countries.

All firms train their employees on the job. Some also invest in formal training, within the firm or in specialised training institutions. MNCs tend to be more aware than other firms of the benefits of training and have well-developed routines, systems and materials for training. They tend to use advanced technologies and management systems that call for more intensive training. They can transfer trainers across countries, and send employees to different parts of the MNC system (and to suppliers) for training. MNCs in the same industry sometimes collaborate in offering training courses to each other's employees and to employees of suppliers.

Like other firms, MNCs are reluctant to invest in training if they cannot earn a sufficient return and a large part of the benefits of their efforts accrues to other firms. There is a range of options that firms can choose to remedy these problems. For instance, an enterprise can offer a premium for loyalty whereby wages or other benefits increase more than proportionately when employees stay with a firm, or give incentives in the form of promotion for successful trainees. It can offer bonded training where it provides training only if employees contract to stay on for a designated period after the completion of the training.

The role of MNCs in skill building differs by sector, industry, or even product line, and among host countries. For instance, some MNCs may start with training employees in low-skill categories and go on to invest in further training them over time as their wages rise and more complex technologies are used. In others, however, rising labour costs and technological upgrading may not converge. For example, in the case of FDI in export-oriented activities where heir advantage depends primarily on low wages and simple technologies, MNCs may just move on to other locations as wages rise. Or, MNCs may be in more complex activities but may not find it economical to use more advanced technologies because the cost of training is significantly higher than that of relocating to countries with better skill endowments. In these cases, the host economy may be in a "low-skill trap" where its competitiveness depends on keeping wages low (and providing little education to the workforce); this allows it to produce only low-technology products. In turn, firms have little inducement to invest in skill upgrading because their employees lack the educational base to make training effective. The only way out of this trap is for the government to raise basic skill levels and to persuade firms to invest more in training their employees.

Large firms in developed countries, transnational or otherwise, have accumulated extensive expertise in enterprise-provided training. As employee skills have become more significant as competitive assets, they have increased their investment in training. Foreign affiliates are generally better equipped to provide training than local firms in developing countries. Affiliates are more aware of training needs and have established systems to recognise and reward skill formation. They have access, through the MNC system, to training budgets, departments and personnel, as well as training materials and facilities in other affiliates or headquarters. However, in developing host countries, the level of skills of workers and the intensity of training in affiliates provide a mixed picture. In MNCs investing abroad to utilise their technological advantages, skills and training both in management and on the shop floor tend to be better than in uni-national and local firms. In MNCs investing to take advantage of low-cost labour, the average skill levels may be lower, and relatively little may be invested in further training. Even in low-wage operations, however, export-oriented investments must have high standards of quality and delivery, and so need good skills at supervisory, technical and managerial levels. To some extent, such skills and capabilities can be obtained through frequent visits and other forms of intra-firm cooperation for skills transfer to developing country affiliates. In the long run, however, building up local capabilities can be cost-effective for firms as well as skills-enhancing for the host country.

MNCs react to the availability of skills in host economies by raising technological content and upgrading their investments, in turn contributing to skill upgrading. They provide training on a general level; they also undertake advanced training and work with industry associations, suppliers and governments. However, the extent of training and collaboration is much higher in countries with advanced educational systems, and in technology-intensive activities for export markets.

The issue for developing countries that host foreign affiliates exporting unprocessed, low-value commodities or low-skill manufactures is to enter the virtuous circle of skill upgrading, higher value-added activity and greater better-quality FDI. *How can they change the skill mix and ensure that skilled workers find employment commensurate with their skills, and better remunerated, while moving up from their established base of competitiveness in low-skill activities? How can they draw upon the resources offered by MNCs to upgrade their human-capital base while keeping their economy cost-competitive and attractive?*

POLICY IMPLICATIONS

The employment-generating potential and the role that inward FDI might play in upgrading employment and building the skills base of an economy depend primarily on the amount and type of FDI that a country receives and the strategies of the MNCs involved in making the investments based on their primary objectives with reference to employment, government policies can be grouped into two sets: those related to employment creation and those related to employment and skills upgrading. These can be further divided into policies that work directly and those that work indirectly to influence FDI and MNCs. The former typically include policies that explicitly focus on FDI and are in the domain of investment-promotion agencies or similar government-run or para-statal agencies. Most policies, however, work indirectly by enhancing the labour market environment and institutions, industrial relations, and the skills quality and mix of human resources. They include, for example, the measures available under trade, industrial, competition and infrastructure policies. They also include various measures and incentives for promoting the development of local firms — potential partners for FDI and competitors of foreign affiliates. In a long-term perspective, they comprise policies related to science and technology and human resource development policies. By affecting the composition of industries, supplier chains and linkages, and the quality and regional distribution of employment in a host economy, these policies have a bearing on the amount and type of employment generated by inward.

Employment Creation

If the objective is to increase the quantity of employment generated within host economies by MNCs, the menu of options for governments includes the following measures:

i) Governments can take measures that increase FDI inflows generally. Investment in greenfield plants is likely to create additional employment — provided local enterprises are not crowded-out of the market. Investment by means of M&As can help conserve existing employment and, over time, help it to expand.

ii) Governments can target certain types of "employment-intensive" FDI. Since different industries feature different direct and indirect employment effects, a case can be made for pro-active market-friendly policies or careful selective intervention.

iii) Fiscal incentives may be provided to encourage employment generation by foreign affiliates. These may take the form of tax deductions or transfers such as subsidies on inputs, or preferential loans.

iv) To even-out employment among regions, wage tiers differentiated by districts might be applied, provided that a collective bargaining mechanism is involved in establishing such systems of graded minimum wages. These may serve to attract FDI into economically depressed or remote areas. The effects of such wage policies are mixed, however, since the choice of investment location is driven primarily by productivity and labour quality, as well as other factors unrelated to labour costs, rather than nominal wages.

v) Another increasingly popular policy measure that is relevant for efforts to induce FDI in order to increase employment is to provide industrial parks where the basic industrial infrastructure is put at the disposal of firms under guarantee that services in the park will be reliable and of good-quality. In addition, EPZs are measures that have a long tradition and have in general included the availability of amenities required for industrial production.

Upgrading Employment and Skills

If the objective is to upgrade the quality of the labour force, governments nave several options regarding workforce training and education, including measures directed at foreign affiliates:

i) Governments can rely on the public education system. They can launch schemes to provide specific forms of training for activities they wish to promote. However, many developing country governments are constrained by limited budgets and prefer to reserve resources for primary education. In such cases, publicly-run training programmes may be weak and inefficient, since salaries and equipment are meager, so that qualified instructors are not available. One remedy is to use official development assistance to implement training programmes. There is, however, still a problem in that it is difficult for governments to anticipate the precise training needs to correspond to the FDI attracted and the jobs generated over time.

ii) Governments can initiate public-private training partnerships to complement publicly-funded or MNC-based training. In such partnerships, governments and MNCs, or their affiliates in the host country concerned, can each seek to influence employment effects in accordance with their respective priorities, while sharing the financial burden of training. For this modalities of sharing could be to provide public premises free of cost but require participating affiliates to cover trainers' salaries and building-maintenance costs, and to supply training materials and equipment.

iii) Governments can foster employee-training programmes by companies, including foreign affiliates. A combination of levies and grants for training is one instrument that is widely used. To encourage affiliates to offer training, it can allow double deduction for expenses incurred in-house, or for the costs of sending employees to training programmes. Another fiscal measure is to penalise firms that invest too little in training.

iv) Skills audits are yet another technique. Governments undertake surveys among affiliates and supplier firms to ascertain their current and projected training needs, and register the skill requirements of prospective investors. This information then needs to be channelled to the appropriate training institutions. A combination of such tools has allowed a number of governments to succeed in creating a "training culture" — an environment where the value of continuous skills upgrading is generally appreciated — thereby enhancing a country's reputation as a suitable location for skills-intensive investment. Providing recognition to affiliates that have been especially active in the realm of employee training and certifying course content and achievement, are other measures to foster company-based training.

v) Governments can rely on private institutions for certain purposes. Private education may outperform public education, particularly in vocational training, if governments face resource constraints for purchasing the equipment needed for apprenticeships and vocational training.

The above measures refer to human resources development for workers at the shop- floor level. An equally important element in attracting FDI that will upgrade employment is to ensure that MNCs find professionals and provide local training as well. This includes technicians and engineers; plant, personnel and sales managers; accountants and market analysts. A number of policy instruments can be used for this purpose. Payroll taxes can be calibrated financially to benefit local employment or a large share of high-skill employment, expatriate or local. A longer-term strategy is for governments to train actively, or arrange for the training of, local professionals. Tertiary education in areas such as engineering and management can be provided publicly — with host government assistance or through official development assistance — or commercially. Parallel with that, conditions with respect to the share of local staff in affiliates' management can be negotiated with investor MNCs, or incentives such as rebates on wage- based taxes can, again, be offered.

If governments choose to attract commercial providers of professional training and education, they might need to adapt their regulatory framework with respect to foreign participation in educational services. This might mean allowing entry of certain types of professional training institutions run by foreign entities or more actively, granting tax incentives to them. MNCs may have a special interest here — as users of such services for their employees, or as providers of education services.

INDUSTRIAL RELATIONS

Whether a government is primarily concerned with generating a large number of jobs, or moving an increasing number of workers into higher-quality jobs requiring more skills and paying good wages, the industrial relations regime has a strong role to play. The type of institutions, laws, and standards in place with respect to trade unions and their collective bargaining rights, and labour-management relations vary greatly among countries and regions. The differences among countries are often influenced more by socio-cultural factors than by strictly economic ones. Regardless of how labour and management interact with each other, stable and reliable relations and collective bargaining frameworks are necessary both for MNCs and their affiliates to function effectively and for host country employment objectives to be met. Where industrial relations are unstable, tense or frail, both FDI and employment are likely to be fraught with problems.

Many foreign affiliates recognise, and have bargained with, trade unions for decades. Others do not, either because their workforce has not insisted on such relations or because management has resisted or suppressed union organisation. In looking for a pattern in trade union relations with MNCs, it is clear that the dominant influence is the prevailing industrial relations system in the country concerned. The "nationality", or home country, of a MNC is also important, but there are plenty of examples of foreign affiliates following the norms of the country in which they are located rather than the norms of their home country. However, there are signs of change both in management thinking about relations with trade unions and in union strategies for addressing the need to represent workers in companies that are planning and acting with a global perspective.

This global perspective is reflected in increasing international contracts among trade unions. These contacts seems to be more common in firms in which national-level union management relations are widespread and an international dimension is a logical step for both sides.

As a result of these various interlocking trends, the dialogue between unions and MNCs is becoming increasingly complex and sophisticated. It is also no longer restricted by national boundaries and has an international character that is likely to evolve still further. The question of whether unions and MNCs are "enemies or partners" is becoming harder to answer and perhaps obsolete. Antagonistic relations tend to be publicised more frequently than the more subtle forms of contact and dialogue over issues of common concern.

Good industrial relations can serve to enhance employment and further the goal of upgrading employment quality and skills in foreign affiliates. Their merit is to facilitate communications, and to accommodate constructive negotiations which can bridge the conflicting objectives of governments, MNCs and their affiliates, and the representatives of labour. Functioning industrial relations are a prerequisite if severe imbalances are to be avoided; they are thus in the best interests of domestic development as well as long-term FDI.

QUESTIONS

1. Discuss the importance of people to various management processes and functional areas.
2. Critically examine the companies' alternatives for recruitment, selection, compensation, development, and retention of international managers.
3. Identify the advantages and disadvantages of various groups of personnel and discuss the mix of personnel from an international perspective.
4. Characterise the nature of human resource management in international business.
5. Describe basic human resource issues involving nonmanagerial employees.
6. Critically examine the MNCs strategies and their implications for generating employment and building skills.
7. Discuss for international firms conduct performance appraisals and determine compensation for their expatriate managers.

REFERENCES

Bhalla, V.K.,"International Economy: Liberalisation Process", Anmol Publications, 1993.

Bhatt, M.C. and K.L. Dalal, "Indian enterprises abroad: A study", Indian Council for Research on International Economic Relations, 1989, 80 p.

Harbison, F. and Charles A.Myers: *Management in Industrial World* McGraw-Hill,New York, 1959

Katz, Daniel and Robert I. Khan, *The Social Psychology of Organisations*, John Wiley & Sons,New York, 1962

Kotabe, Masaaki and Michael R. Czinkota (1992) "State Government Promotion of Manufacturing Exports: A GAP Analysis," *Journal of International Business Studies*, 4, 637-58. (See chapter 8.)

Lall, Rajiv B., "Multinationals from the third world: Indian firms investing abaord", Delhi, Oxford University Press, 1987, 122 p.

Lall, Sanjaya, "India" in John H. Dunning (ed.) Multinational enterprises, economic structure and international competitiveness, Chichester, John Wiley and Sons, 1986, pp. 309-335.

Martinussen, John.,"Transnational corporations in a developing country: The Indian Experience" New Delhi, Sage Publications, 1988, 228 p.

Negandhi, Anant R., "Indian foreign investment policies" in W.Teng and N.T. Wang (eds.) Transnational corporations and China's open door policy, Lexington, Lexington Books, 1988, 352 p.

Oman, Charles (ed.), "New Forms of overseas investment by developing countries: the case of India, Korea, and Brazil", Paris, OECD, 1986, 183 p.

Porter, M.E., 1985, "Competitive Advantage", New York: McMillan Press.

Seringhaus, Rolf F.H. and Philip J. Rosson (1990) *Government Export Promotion: A Global Perspective*. London: Routledge.

United Nations, ESCAP/UNTEC Joint Unit on Transnational Corporations from developing Asian economies: host country perspective. (ST/ESCAP/605), UNCTC Publication, Series B, No. 12, Bangkok, 1988, 581 p.

25

GLOBALISATION, MARKETS FOR WORKERS AND LABOUR

INTRODUCTION

The ongoing globalisation of the labour market has drawn increasing attention from policymakers and the media, particularly in the advanced economies. There has been increasing flows of migrants across borders, through both legal and informed routes. The most asked question is whether the addition of this unprecedentedly large pool of labour from emerging market and developing countries is adversely affecting compensation and employment in the advanced economies. How rapidly has the global labour supply grown, and which channels of labour globalisation have been most important? To what extent can recent trends in labour shares and labour compensation in advanced economies be explained by the changing global labour supply relative to other factors such as technological change and labour market reform? Has the impact been different in skilled and unskilled sectors? What policies can help the advanced economies meet the challenges of further labour market globalisation? To this end, policies should seek to improve the functioning of labour markets; strengthen access to education and training; and ensure adequate social safety nets that cushion the impact on those adversely affected, without obstructing the process of adjustment.

GLOBALISATION OF LABOUR

A first question to address is how the opening up of China, India, and the former Eastern bloc countries, together with ongoing demographic developments, has affected the global labour supply. This is not easy to answer because much depends on the assumptions made about how much of a country's labour force is in, or could potentially compete in, the global market. One simple approach is to weigh each country's labour force by its export-to-GDP ratio. By this measure, the effective global labour supply quadrupled between 1980 and 2005, with most of the increase taking place after 1990. East Asia contributed about half of the increase, due to a marked rise in working-age population and rising trade openness, while South Asia and the former Eastern bloc countries accounted for smaller increases. While most of the absolute increase in the global labour supply consisted of less-educated workers (defined as those without higher education), the relative supply of workers with higher education increased by about 50 percent over the last 25 years, owing mostly to advanced economies, but also to China.

Advanced economies can access this increased pool of global labour both through imports of goods and services and through immigration. Trade has been the more important channel and has grown more rapidly, not least because immigration remains highly restricted in most countries. A similar picture emerges for developing and emerging market countries, where the export-to-GDP ratio is in general much higher than the ratio of emigrants to the domestic labour force. Nevertheless, immigration has expanded significantly over the past two decades in some large European economies (Germany, Italy, and the United Kingdom) and in the United States. The share of immigrants in the U.S. labour force is now close to 15 percent and hence comparable to the share of imports in GDP. Elsewhere the share of immigrants is still substantially less than the share of imports in GDP, but it is not negligible.

Focusing on trade, the share of developing country products in the manufacturing imports of advanced economies has doubled since the early 1990s. This owes much to China. Developing countries have also been capturing an increasing share of world markets. At the aggregate level, however, trade is a win-win game. As China, India, and the Eastern bloc countries have opened up, world markets and opportunities to export have expanded considerably for advanced economies and developing countries alike. Developing countries' imports have been growing faster than those of advanced economies and the share of advanced economies' exports going to developing countries has been rising (though not as rapidly as the share of developing countries in their own imports).

The strong export dynamism of emerging market and developing countries is in skilled as well as unskilled products: developing countries' share in world exports of skilled goods and services has been on the rise in recent years. China has led the way, reflecting its very strong growth and a move toward more skill-intensive goods in its export basket. India's export basket is also changing rapidly toward skill-intensive services, but the country's weight in world trade remains small.

One category of trade that has received much attention in recent years is trade in intermediates. The reduction of barriers to cross-border trade and capital flows, combined with technological progress in transport and communication, has made it easier for firms to move parts of their production to less costly foreign locations—a process referred to as offshore outsourcing or, more simply, offshoring. Nevertheless, and contrary to some popular perceptions, offshored inputs, which account for about half of total imports (the rest being imports of final products), have grown somewhat more slowly than total trade. Moreover, the scale of offshoring is still quite limited in the overall economy.

The manufacturing sector has been most affected by offshoring because it is more tradable. The rise in offshoring in advanced economies has been driven mostly by imports of skilled rather than unskilled inputs. Several factors may help explain this finding. *First,* in line with advanced economies' comparative advantage in skill-intensive production, goods traditionally produced in unskilled sectors (e.g., textiles) are more likely to be imported as final goods rather than intermediates. The share of imported intermediates in total imports of unskilled products is lower than the comparable share for skilled products, at 37 percent and 68 percent, respectively Sectors involved in the rise in the imports of intermediaries are electronic equipment; other machinery and equipment; and chemical, rubber, and plastic products. It should be noted, however, that offshoring is likely to involve the least skill-intensive stages of production in these skilled sectors. *Second,* the bulk of advanced economies' imports (of both final and intermediate products) still comes from other advanced economies and likely includes more skilled rather than unskilled products. *Third,* the global supply of labour with higher education has increased relative to labour with lower education.

How Has the Globalisation of Labour Affected Workers in Advanced Economies? The rapid growth of the global labour supply and its manifestation through increasing exports of emerging market and developing countries leads to the question of how these trends have affected workers in advanced economies. With exports from emerging market and developing countries being intensive in labour, especially unskilled labour, traditional trade theory would predict that the integration of these countries into the world economy would exert downward pressure on the wages (corrected for productivity) of workers in advanced economies. Hence, the share of national income received by labour— the so-called labour share—would be expected to decline. To see this, it is worth noting that the labour share can be expressed as the ratio of labour compensation per worker to average worker productivity.

Nevertheless, workers in advanced economies could still be better off if the positive effects from enhanced trade and productivity on the economy's income (the size of the total "pie") are larger than the negative effect on the share of this income that accrues to labour. It has been argued that the productivity-enhancing effect from trade in intermediates could be even larger than from trade in final goods because, in addition to a competition effect for producing sectors, trade in intermediates also reduces the cost of production of using sectors. The global pool of labour can be accessed by advanced economies through imports and immigration. Trade is the more important and faster-expanding channel, in large part because immigration remains very restricted in many countries. Contrary to popular perceptions, the intensity of offshoring of the production of intermediates is still small in the overall economy, although the manufacturing sector is more affected because of its greater tradability. Imports of offshored intermediates have also been growing somewhat more slowly than total trade.

The integration of workers from emerging market and developing countries into the global workforce has produced important benefits for advanced economies. Export opportunities have expanded considerably. It has provided access to cheaper imported goods and has enabled companies to operate more efficiently. This has boosted productivity and output, and contributed to rising real labour compensation. For emerging market economies, the ongoing integration of labour into the global marketplace has benefited workers, with manufacturing wages rising rapidly. Nevertheless, labour globalisation has negatively affected the share of income accruing to labour in the advanced economies (the labour share). It is, however, only one of several factors that have affected the labour share over the past two decades. Rapid technological change—especially in the information and communications sectors— has had a bigger impact, particularly on the labour share in unskilled sectors.

Against this background, the increasing globalisation of labour and ongoing technological changes raise important challenges for policymakers in the advanced economies. They must seek to harness the benefits that the growing pool of global labour is creating. This means continuing along the path of trade liberalization, while ensuring that domestic economies are sufficiently flexible to be able to adjust and respond to the pressures of globalisation. At the same time, it is important to be fully cognizant of adjustment costs, and policies do need to support those people who are negatively affected by labour market globalisation and technological changes. In broad terms, policies need to respond along three dimensions:

i) *Improve the functioning of labour markets.* Steps to reduce tax wedges to enable workers to take home a larger proportion of their gross pay and to ensure that unemployment benefit replacement rates do not deter workers from seeking employment have helped a number of countries adjust to the pressures of globalisation. The duration of unemployment benefits and the work availability requirements are also important. Moreover, policies that increase the flexibility of the economy and thereby enable workers to move more easily from declining to expanding areas of the economy help the process of adjustment.

ii) *Improve access to education and training.* Developing workers' skills is necessary for keeping up with rapid technological change and for continuing innovation. Skilled sectors have been better able to adapt to changing conditions caused by the ICT revolution than unskilled sectors. Further, countries that started adopting ICT and training workers in this area earlier experienced less decline in their labour share. Workers must also be ready to compete with the growing pool of skilled workers in emerging markets, especially those in Asia. Beyond increases in spending on education and training, the quality of this spending is crucial.

iii) *Ensure adequate social protection for workers during the adjustment period.* This includes providing adequate income support to cushion, but not obstruct, the process of change, and also making health care less dependent on continued employment and increasing the portability of pension benefits in some countries. The latter would also enhance the flexibility of the economy by facilitating the move of workers from declining sectors to expanding sectors. Whether measures specifically targeted at workers who have been displaced by international trade are desirable is less clear. The fact that these workers may face special hurdles reintegrating into the labour market as they are often older and less educated, and their skills are specific to declining industries or occupations, argues in favour of such measures. Also, minimizing losses for such workers may increase support for the international economic integration process. However, it may be difficult (even conceptually) to differentiate between job losses caused by globalisation and those caused by other factors, since most labour markets are characterised by high rates of turnover and year-to-year earnings variability. If trade-displaced workers are treated more generously, including, for instance, by being provided supplementary wage subsidies, such compensation should be structured to avoid dulling incentives to search actively for new jobs.

FOSTERING A SKILLED AND HEALTHY WORKFORCE

Governments around the world share the goal of having more and better jobs for their citizens. The public policies affecting the labour market play a critical role in this effect people to jobs. And there is room for improvement in most countries. Though regulation of labour markets is usually intended to help workers, but can also be a significant constraint on firms. Ill-considered regulations can discourage firms from creating more jobs and contribute to a swelling of the informal economy. When this is the case, some workers may benefit, but the unemployed, the low-skilled, and those in the informal economy will not be among them. The government needs to facilitate allocation of labour to its most productive use while helping workers cope with labour mobility. Technological progress that leads to higher productivity and economic growth improves working conditions and wages, but it can also result in more rapid changes to firms and industries. In modern economies, many firms are created and destroyed each year—about 20 percent in many countries— involving 10-20 percent of the workforce.

People's skills and health affect their ability to participate in society, escape poverty, cope with economic and natural risks, and contribute to productivity increases and growth. The availability of skilled and healthy workers also shapes the decisions of firms to adopt new technologies, expand, or enter new markets. Education improves health through greater awareness and access to information. The links between education, health, and growth can create virtuous circles: good education and health enable growth, which in turn promotes further investment in them. The circles can also be vicious: poor education and health reduce incentives for productive investment and entrepreneurship, which limits the resources for enhancing education and health.

Investment climate improvements interact strongly with education. A sound investment climate strengthens the incentives for individuals to obtain more education. This is best exemplified by the major surge in returns *to* education in the formerly centrally planned economies during their transition to market systems. Similar patterns have emerged in other countries. The link between investment in human capital and growth is mediated by the way education services are delivered and skills are allocated in the economy. But investment climate improvements almost always increase the demand for human capital. As firms have more opportunities and better access to new technologies, they demand more skilled workers and have stronger incentives to engage in growth-enhancing activities, raising both the private and social returns to education.

Skilled workers are needed to adopt new technologies because they are better at dealing with changes. This is true for different types of firms and different levels of technological development. Technology transfers by multinational firms, and technology adoptions by local firms, require a minimum of human capital and training. New technologies generally require significant organisational changes, which are also handled better by a skilled workforce. Even among self-employed farmers in low-income countries, having at least primary education enables them to use more efficient production techniques.

Skill constraints are a common problem for firms in developing countries. The constraints are especially severe for firms planning to innovate and expand. For firms that consider a lack of skilled workers to be a "major" or "very severe" constraint are those upgrading their production processes. Those firms are also more inclined to invest in training their workforce. While large firms have the capacity to organise internal training for their workforce, smaller firms often do not.

High levels of formal education are not needed for all firms or activities. Lack of availability of workers with tertiary education may be more of a constraint for firms in higher value-added manufacturing and services than for those in less complex industrial processes. For some activities, language proficiency may be important. For example, a large English-speaking population has helped India attract "back-office" services for foreign firms. In many cases education to provide basic literacy and numeracy skills can be complemented by on-the-job or vocational training to enhance the productivity and hence potential wages of workers.

In creating a skilled force, the Governments can help in a variety of ways. Public funding can improve the equity of the education system by opening opportunities to those who could not otherwise afford it. Many traditional approaches focused on providing funding through public educational institutions. Newer approaches direct resources through individuals so that they have greater choice, with the resulting competitive pressure on providers sharpening the incentives to be efficient and responsive. Options for providing such support include income-contingent loans and voucher schemes of various kinds.

CRAFTING INTERVENTIONS TO BENEFIT ALL WORKERS

Governments intervene in worker-firm relations on three main fronts. They intervene in the wage-setting process, they regulate working conditions, and they control the hiring and firing of workers. These interventions are theoretically justified by the (perceived or effective) inability of laissez-faire conditions to deliver efficient and equitable outcomes. Efficiency arguments stress information problems and a need to improve the matching of labour demand with supply. There may also be equity arguments if there is unequal bargaining power between employers and workers, discrimination against vulnerable groups, or incomplete or imperfect insurance of workers against risks.

Beyond the core labour standards—the minimum framework for a sound labour market —government interventions need to strike a balance between several interests. It has been common to portray the tension as primarily between the interests of firms and workers. But this ignores the broader range of interests involved. Workers in the informal economy and the unemployed can have very different interests from those currently employed in the formal economy. And consumers and potential recipients of tax-funded services also have a stake in the outcome. Where the balance between these interests is struck will be influenced by social preferences in each country. But as in other areas of government intervention, approaches can deviate from the socially optimal level because of factors such as rent-seeking by particular interest groups and a failure to adapt approaches to local circumstances. Indeed, as in other areas of regulation, labour regulation in many developing countries mimics or exceeds that in developed countries, benefits only part of the population because of widespread informality, and imposes a disproportionate burden on those firms that do comply.

How labour market interventions influence the opportunities and incentives for firms to invest productively, create jobs, and expand? It is argued that the labour regulations can be a major or severe constraint on firm operations in many developing countries. Regulations can reduce incentives to make new investments, adjust the organisation of work to take advantage of new technologies or opportunities, or hire more workers. Some curtailment of those incentives can be justified by social goals beyond those reflected in the core labour standards including, for example, the promotion of workplace safety. But ill-conceived approaches can exacerbate poverty by contributing to unemployment and swelling the size of the informal and unprotected economy. If a society's goal is to advance the interests of all workers— rather than just those who currently benefit from regulated employment—governments need to confront these difficult and often sensitive tradeoffs.

Striking a balance between promoting job creation by firms and protecting existing jobs or workers is particularly contentious during periods of economic reforms—when the long-term benefits of increased employment and wages are often clouded by short-term concerns for the job and wage security of those affected during the transition. Successful reforms bring about higher wages and better working conditions—as well as higher employment and lower unemployment and informality in the long run. There are, however, short-term costs due to changes in job characteristics and greater labour mobility in a modern, productive economy. This reinforces the importance of looking at labour market policies in the context of broader strategies, including efforts to foster a more skilled and adaptable workforce and to help workers cope with change.

Governments can take following three steps to ensure labour market interventions benefit all workers:

Encouraging Wage Adaptability

Governments intervene in the wage-setting process by establishing rules for wage bargaining and for industrial relations. These interventions can reduce negotiation costs if they do not reinforce the monopoly power of the parties or impose rigidities in wage adjustments. Many governments also set wage floors in an attempt to reduce the number of working poor, but setting the floors too high can reduce the jobs available for low-skilled workers and the opportunities for low-tech firms to emerge in the formal sector.

Wage Bargaining Benefits from a Dear Policy Framework

The dialogue between freely elected (and representative) associations of workers and employers can reduce uncertainty and transaction costs and improve information flows. Collective bargaining offers a platform for involving both employers and workers in discussions with government about structural reforms. Consider the tripartite negotiations to promote macroeconomic and structural reforms.

However, in industries where regulation shelters firms from competition, unions are likely to bargain for a share of the rents. An unstable political environment also tends to reduce incentives for unions to "invest" in wage restraint in exchange for expected better economic outcomes in the future. High union wage premiums and bigger drags on productivity are indeed found in countries and sectors lacking competitive pressure.

Enhancing Wage Adaptability

Governments can foster wage adaptability by promoting pluralism of representation in wage bargaining. They can also reinforce the links between wage agreements and firm performance either through improving coordination among social partners or through more decentralised negotiations.

(i) Improving Coordination

Some developed countries with a tradition of collective bargaining have reinforced coordination among the different levels of wage negotiation (national, sectoral, firm). In some of them, nationwide agreements now fix only the basic wage increase, leaving to the firm-level negotiation further increases consistent with a firm's performance. Unions have also been part of the design and implementation of large structural changes in many countries.

(ii) Decentralising Negotiations

Following the experience of developed countries, some emerging and transition economies have reinforced wage responsiveness by shifting wage bargaining to the firm. Unionisation is low in newly created private firms, especially small ones, and wage bargaining mostly takes place at the firm level. The reformed wage-bargaining system has resulted in increasing direct negotiation by relaxing the collective negotiation process, introducing voluntary arbitration as an alternative to state administrative decisions, and eliminating state approval of agreements. The reform also increased collective autonomy by protecting the unions' right to registration, and strengthened union pluralism by allowing more than one union to exist in a firm.

(iii) Reassessing Minimum Wages

The main goal of setting minimum wages is to promote decent jobs and reduce poverty among workers. But its effectiveness in many developing countries is questionable. Minimum wages represent a high proportion of the average wages in these countries, and any further increase shifts the wage distribution upward, punishing rather than helping the workers intended to be supported—young, low-skilled, and female workers. When enforcement is weak, as is often the case, a hike in the minimum wage encourages even more under-reporting of wages and strengthens incentives for firms and jobs to remain in the informal economy.

The minimum wage cuts the lower end of the wage distribution and makes firms and jobs with low productivity levels unviable, at least in the formal sector. The level of the minimum wage affects firms, jobs, and income distribution: i) In developed countries minimum wages tend to be relatively low (although in some cases may approach 50 percent of the median wage) with only a modest impact on low-tech firms and the employment of low-productivity workers. ii) In several low-income countries minimum wages are close to, if not higher than, the average income per capita. At these levels many private firms, especially those in low-tech activities, cannot afford to comply. The poor continue to work in informal activities for only a fraction of the mandated minimum wage. iii) In middle-income countries, the minimum wage is generally about half the median in the formal sector. Its coverage and enforcement tend to be low, but its impact on low-productivity firms and jobs can be large.

Noncompliance with the minimum wage is also concentrated among the most vulnerable workers. Youths and other workers lacking skills or work experience may have little chance of being hired at the minimum wage when it is set much higher than their productivity potential. In backward areas the national minimum wage may be close to the underlying local average wage, severely affecting labour demand from small and medium firms that rely largely on low-skilled workers. Despite low compliance, the minimum wage can act as a strong pay signal for the informal sector, implying that hikes in the minimum wage can have distributional implications that go beyond the formal sector—the income of the low-paid might increase in both segments of the economy, but their employment prospects might declined.

Given these effects, a growing number of countries are reassessing minimum wages to expand opportunities for low-skilled workers and encourage formalisation. They have done so mainly by reducing indexation of the minimum wage and by having lower subminimal for some groups (young workers) or for subnational labour markets.

Ensuring Workplace Regulations Reflect a Good Institutional Fit

Promoting health and safety conditions in the workplace, regulating working time, and encouraging paid leave have been major achievements in all societies. As in most other areas, improvements in working conditions in developed countries evolved gradually, hand in hand with more general economic progress. Attempting to apply the same or higher standards to countries at earlier stages of economic development and with weaker enforcement capacity often leads to poor or even perverse results.

Improving workplace safety is an important objective for all countries, and well-designed regulation can help to achieve this goal. But safety or other regulations will have limited impact if they or other features of labour regulation have the effect of keeping firms or workers in the informal economy where workers usually lack any statutory protection. Stronger enforcement efforts can help in some cases. When regulations are out of step with local realities, however, there will be tradeoffs between providing high levels of protection for workers that enjoy regulated employment and expanding protection and opportunities to a broader group of workers.

Regulations affecting working hours and paid leave can involve similar tradeoffs. Many developing countries have adopted far-reaching regulations on these subjects—in some cases going beyond what is on the books in most developed countries. Even among countries at similar stages of development, the differences in regulations can be large, with significant effects on labour costs and on the ability of firms to accommodate fluctuations in demand.

These regulations can benefit workers in the formal sector and, by promoting better working conditions and motivation, can contribute to productivity. Beyond any potential productivity effect, however, the impact on firms' incentives to create jobs depends on who bears the costs. The evidence suggests that wages do not fully adjust to compensate for the additional costs of these benefits. For example, in Latin America, firms bear up to 50 percent of the costs of nonwage benefits, thus reducing firms' potential for expansion and job creation. These effects would not be a source of concern if they reflected the rational choice of workers to trade off not only lower earnings, but also some unemployment, for better working conditions. When this is not the case, workplace regulations reduce wages below what poor workers would be willing or able to accept. They can also encourage unregulated and unprotected employment.

Indeed, workplace regulations have long suffered from poor compliance in many developing countries. And while recent progress toward global integration is sometimes thought to result in a lowering of standards experience suggests that this is not necessarily the case

Balancing Employment Stability with Firms' Need to Adjust the Workforce

Probably the most contentious government intervention in the labour market is the regulation of the hiring and firing of workers— generally referred to as employment protection legislation. Regulatory intervention may be justified to protect workers from arbitrary action and to provide some stability in employment, which can be particularly important in the absence of effective social safety nets. To the extent job protection leads to long-lasting work relationships, it may also encourage firms to provide training.

But as elsewhere, governments need to balance these potential benefits against the likely costs. By affecting the cost of workforce reorganisation, employment protection legislation can strongly influence the cost of doing business, especially the opportunities and incentives for firms to adopt new technologies and to expand. Modern economies require a continuous process of firms' retooling and firm turnover to channel resources to their most productive uses.

Regulating Hiring and Firing

The protection offered to regular workers and the conditions for temporary employment vary considerably across countries. Firms in many countries regard employment protection legislation as a significant obstacle to their expansion. When asked to evaluate eight areas of regulation for the burden imposed on the operation and growth potential of their businesses, firm managers ranked labour regulations as the major or second most important obstacle in many countries. There is also a close correlation between managers' perceptions of labour regulations and the stringency of such regulations from a more objective standpoint. Impact on firms onerous regulations can affect firms' spending on innovation, the entry of new firms, their average size, and the incidence of informality.

(i) Cost of Doing Business and Exploiting Technological Opportunities

Onerous hiring and firing regulations raise the cost of workforce reorganisations required by new vintages of technology, reducing incentives for firms to innovate and adopt new technologies. Evidence from developed countries suggests that stricter rules are associated with lower research and development (R&D) expenditure and tend to tilt specialisation away from high-tech industries. For example, one cross-country study suggests that by reforming their labour rules to the OECD average, developed countries with very strict employment regulations could reduce their productivity gap with the technological leader by about 20 percent. Similar reforms in developing countries could yield even larger productivity gains, given the greater potential for catchup by adopting technologies available in international markets.

(ii) Creative Destruction

Onerous regulations also have repercussions on the turnover of firms in the market. Because new firms are often better at harnessing new technologies than incumbent firms, stringent regulations reduce the potential for productivity gains. The countries with more flexible hiring and firing rules experience significantly higher entry rates of small firms (but not microenterprises, often exempt from such regulations or managing to avoid them). Stringent rules also tend to discourage foreign direct investment (FDI), especially in countries where rules are opaque and enforcement is uncertain.

(iii) Self-employment and Informality

Onerous labour regulations are associated with larger proportions of self-employed, informal firms, and small firms. Firms facing high labour adjustment costs either remain very small—and more or less informal and thus exempt from employment regulations—or move to a higher scale or to more capital-intensive technologies, in both cases reducing the incidence of hiring and firing costs on total expected adjustment costs. In Russia many large firms have circumvented strict regulations by pushing workers to leave the firm voluntarily, through wage arrears, prolonged administrative leaves, reduced hours, and other forms of deteriorating working conditions. With no future in the firm and no source of income, many workers eventually quit.

To the extent stringent regulations reduce the potential for firm expansion and job creation in the formal sector, they also reduce workers' access to decent jobs. More job stability for some workers often implies fewer job opportunities in the formal sector. So it is not surprising that stricter employment laws are not associated with a more equal labour market. If anything, income disparities tend to be greater in countries with stricter regulations.

Reducing Labour Adjustment Costs and Formalising work Relations

Reforming government have adopted two main strategies to reduce labour adjustment costs. The first focuses on reducing the burden of adjustment for workers hired under regular employment contract by bringing standards more in line with international norms. A second strategy focuses on liberalising fixed-term or temporary contracts. But liberalising temporary contracts, while leaving in place strict regulations on regular contracts, reinforces the inequality in the labour market. Firms will have stronger incentives to hire more workers at the entry level and employ them for a limited period, without giving them a regular position thereafter. This increases job turnover but not necessarily overall employment or productivity, because the additional hires will be accompanied by additional layoffs at the end of the temporary contracts, and there will be little or no development of internal human capital.

The effects of reforming labour regulations are likely to differ depending on initial conditions and on the sequencing of the reforms in product and labour markets. For example, stringent employment protection legislation can influence the outcomes of trade liberalisation by shifting more jobs to the informal economy. Colombia's trade liberalisation was associated with increased informal employment in industries with the largest tariff cuts, but once labour market reforms were introduced, this pattern was reversed. Similarly, Indian states with less stringent labour regulations experienced stronger growth in the formal sector after trade liberalisation than those with stricter labour regulations.

HELPING WORKERS COPE WITH CHANGE

Investment climate improvements that help create a modern, productive economy facilitate the reallocation of labour across firms and sectors in response to changes in technology, demand, and other conditions. While this reallocation of labour benefits society as a whole, workers may need to change jobs several times in the course of their working lives. This has long been a feature of work in the informal economy, but can be painful for workers who have grown accustomed to more stable employment in protected industries. Helping workers cope with these changes not only benefits the individuals concerned, but can also enhance economic efficiency insofar as it enables better matches between worker abilities and the requirements of new jobs. It can also reduce resistance to investment climate improvements. In many developing countries, inadequate or nonexistent social insurance mechanisms mean that unemployed workers cannot afford to remain without income and are forced to accept the first job that comes their way, even if it is not a good or productive one.

Improving government policies in these areas requires three interrelated actions:

Helping Workers Cope with Large-Scale Restructurings

There is often strong pressure to compensate groups directly threatened by structural reforms, such as workers in previously protected industries. Typically not poor, these groups are very vocal and could represent concentrated opposition to reforms that benefit society as a whole. Providing one-time compensation to them may be a socially efficient way to allow reforms to move ahead.

Workers affected by large-scale dismissals can also face particular difficulties. They may be specialised in activities that may not be highly demanded in the broader economy, and may be concentrated in specific locations, making it more difficult to regain employment locally. This was the case for most transition economies, where many one-company towns and certain rural areas experienced a collapse in labour demand and major surges in unemployment and underemployment.

The traditional approach to dealing with large dismissals is to promote voluntary departures with generous severance pay. This can reduce worker opposition and the social impact of restructuring or downsizing. The challenge is to set severance pay at a level that will be acceptable to workers yet be financially feasible. Setting severance pay at too high a level can lead to high short-term costs and the adverse selection of the best employees leaving first. It can also slow or even stop the process of firm restructuring.

Governments can also provide specific retraining programmes to help workers regain employment, but when these programmes operate in a context of weak labour demand it is difficult to identify the best training curricula and to motivate workers to participate. In many cases a small proportion of eligible workers takes these courses, which often come too late, after workers have already left. To make schemes more effective, early intervention and effective targeting are essential, as are efforts to tailor approaches to local circumstances. Particularly when labour demand is weak, removing impediments to job creation through investment climate improvements plays a critical role.

Reinforcing Social Insurance to Promote Labour Mobility

A variety of strategies can be adopted to help workers cope with the income risks associated with external or domestic shocks as well as the demands of a more flexible labour market. Sound macroeconomic policies and public support for education are the best risk prevention instruments. Social protection programmes can also mitigate the impact of risks while encouraging efficient labour reallocation and entrepreneurship. Even when public resources to finance these schemes are limited, as in the case of most developing countries, much can be done to improve their effectiveness by reinforcing insurance principles and better targeting.

The policy mix best suited to each country depends on the factors driving economic insecurity and the cost-effectiveness of alternative options. However, international experience highlights the importance of four broader measures:

(i) Reducing Economic Volatility

Many developing countries remain vulnerable to external shocks. When a negative aggregate shock hits the economy, capital— often the most mobile factor of production—tends to leave the country, while labour tends to bear the brunt of the adjustment in either real wage cuts or unemployment and underemployment. Export diversification can reduce exposure to large fluctuations in external demand, and deeper capital markets and stronger financial systems can help mitigate the impact. The welfare benefit from reducing macroeconomic volatility in developing countries can be substantial.

(ii) Moving Away from Procyclical Fiscal Policy

The exposure of workers to shocks is compounded by the fact that governments often lack the discipline to promote countercyclical financing for social programmes. Many governments tend to adopt an expansionary fiscal stance in good times and a contractionary stance in bad. Mounting budget deficits in recessions thus create pressures to reduce public spending on social protection (among other things) just when the need for it is increasing. Greater fiscal discipline and better diversification of the fiscal revenue base are essential to ensuring resources are available to cushion the necessary labour adjustment process.

(iii) Removing Market Distortions

Beyond macroeconomic policies, the most effective strategy for risk prevention and mitigation is to develop a sound investment climate where firms have opportunities and incentives to invest productively and create jobs. Investment climate improvements allow for stronger job creation in the formal sector and expand tax resources available for social programmes. Improving the operation of financial markets also expands opportunities for firms to insure themselves against temporary shocks without resorting to wage or employment cuts.

(iv) Supporting Workers' Adaptability

In addition to improving the coverage and quality of education, governments can improve the ability and willingness of workers to move to more productive and rewarding jobs by supporting training, counseling, and placement services. While the effectiveness of these programmes is mixed, especially in countries with limited administrative capacity, when well-targeted they can complement skill enhancements and income support measures.

These broader measures can be accompanied by social insurance schemes. Beyond enhancing the welfare of the unemployed, these schemes improve the investment climate by facilitating the allocation of labour to more productive uses and encouraging entrepreneurship. They do so in three main ways. *First*, they can stimulate riskier but more productive jobs, industries, and portfolio choicest. Second uninsured shocks that reduce individual consumption below the threshold needed to maintain productivity can give rise to "dynamic poverty traps." This happens when families are forced to sell productive assets needed to support their microenterprises or other ventures. *Third*, unemployment-related benefits can provide resources to increase the effectiveness of the job search or to enter self-employment.

Expanding and improving social insurance schemes can involve reinforcing self-insurance among workers in the formal economy through severance pay arrangements and increasing the pooling of risks across workers.

Reinforcing Self-insurance Among Formal Workers

Mandatory severance pay provisions are the main form of insurance against unemployment for workers in the formal sector in most developing countries. Generally easy to administer, the provisions exchange resources in the event of unemployment for an "insurance premium." Whether the severance pay premium is paid by the workers or not has implications for the overall labour costs for firms and hence their incentive for hiring workers in the first place. Even when workers bear the costs, the schemes offer only a limited pooling of unemployment risk because they are firm-specific and because benefits generally evolve with job tenure rather than the risk of unemployment.

Severance pay provisions also suffer from noncompliance in many countries, increasing worker resistance to leaving a job. Required disbursements of severance payments tend to increase when financial resources are lacking because the firm is experiencing difficulties—and the resources may simply not be available if the firm goes bankrupt. Noncompliance looms particularly large among small firms and among low-skilled workers who have few alternative instruments to smooth consumption. To tackle these, shortcomings, some countries have introduced pre-funding or brought payments more in line with international norms.

Increasing the Pooling of Risks Across Workers

Experience in developed countries suggests that unemployment insurance benefits are the next natural step to pooling unemployment risks and facilitating efficient labour allocation Following this model, most transition countries have introduced unemployment insurance schemes since the early 1990s. The schemes have been the main source of income for workers affected by labour reallocation during the transition. The clear welfare gains for workers affected by job losses need to be weighed against the costs of these schemes, including their impact on economic efficiency. Both the costs and the impact depend largely on the ability to monitor eligibility requirements to minimise moral hazard and make sure that workers have incentives to actively search for a new job. Effective enforcement is difficult in developing countries, which generally have weak public employment services or none, coupled with a large informal economy that offers many opportunities for undeclared paid work. Even when countries have the required administrative capacity, unemployment benefits should provide only a fraction of the previous wage—and they should be short-lived—to provide incentives for recipients to seek a new job.

Reaching Out to Workers in the Rural and Informal Economies

Most of the programmes, however, fail to reach workers in the rural and informal economies, which in many developing countries account for the majority of the population. They typically rely on support from employers or private transfers to cope with income losses. Rural employers often pay workers a fixed wage when they are employed, regardless of seasonal and other fluctuations in demand, or provide loans workers who face unexpected expenses. Given the informality of the employment arrangement, employers have a lot of discretion. Poor households also rely on their own savings and private transfers to cope with shocks.

These forms of private risk-coping provide only limited help to poor and informal workers, and can force people to resort to unproductive strategies including selling productive assets, withdrawing children from school, and cutting back medical expenditures. The most promising strategy for improving their situation is through investment climate improvements that expand job opportunities in the formal economy and contribute to greater tax revenues to fund the provision of education and other services. But governments can also complement private risk-sharing with targeted public support. Three main strategies have been adopted in developing countries that can also contribute to better investment conditions: workfare programmes, social funds, and conditional cash transfers.

(i) Workfare Programmes as Social Protection Schemes

In South Asia workfare programmes started as "food-for-work" schemes, in which workers were paid for their labour with food aid from donor countries. Workfare programmes have gradually moved to "cash for work," operated by a variety of agencies, including local and state governments and non-governmental organisations (NGO). They are increasingly viewed as insurance—not emergency—programmes for informal and rural workers. The schemes generally transfer income to poor households by providing unskilled manual workers with short-term employment on projects such as road construction and maintenance, irrigation infrastructure, reforestation, and soil conservation.

Workfare programmes have often smoothed consumption and kept poor people in contact with the labour market. Well-designed programmes build much-needed infrastructure and so reduce the tradeoff between public spending on income transfers and on development. The Maharashtra Employment Guarantee Scheme in India, operating for more than three decades, has created considerable irrigation, infrastructure, and rural roads in the state of Maharashtra. Workfare programmes have also helped many small private contractors emerge and grow.

A key feature of successful workfare programmes is the ability to target participants through self-selection processes. In Argentina the Trabajar programme kept the wage rate below the minimum wage, encouraging the poor to self-select into the programme. In the Philippines, in contrast, the programme wage was much higher than the agricultural market wage, attracting a substantial number of non-poor into the programme. Self-selection of participants can be accompanied by targeting to the poorest areas to ensure that programmes also promote local development. In South Africa a demand-driven approach to the allocation of funds for workfare programmes in the mid-1990s was found to favour more developed and better connected communities at the expense of some of the neediest communities.

(ii) Social Funds to Improve Opportunities—and the Investment Climate—in Poor Areas

Social funds in developing countries now absorb close to $10 billion per year in foreign and domestic financing. Social funds offers a fairly positive assessment of their effectiveness in providing income support and promoting local development. Spending has been highly progressive, with poor districts and poor households receiving more per capita support than wealthier districts or households. Schools and health centres that received funds have enjoyed equal or greater access to staff and inputs and greater participation by local communities than other institutions. The effects on poor households can also be sizable. Investments in school infrastructure were estimated to have increased primary enrollment rates.

(iii) Conditional Cash Transfers to Preserve Human Capital and Health

Conditional cash transfers are another way to combine income support with local development. They belong to a family of transfer programmes that combine close targeting with capital accumulation by making income support conditional on either basic needs triggers, such as utility offset payments (in some transition economies), or behavioural changes, such as the continued school enrollment of children or attendance at health clinics. They typically address chronic poverty rather than idiosyncratic risks of job loss.

The focus of conditional cash transfers on human capital formation makes them suitable to address poverty and local development at the same time. As with any transfer programme, conditional cash transfers can be problematic when the increased demand for services is not met by increased supply (schools or clinics) or when the targeting is not sufficiently robust.

QUESTIONS

1. Discuss the special considerations involved in managing a cross-cultural workforce.
2. Critically examine the effect of international operations on collective bargaining.
3. Often individuals are the first to feel the impact of globalisation as jobs are created and disappear. In terms of the job, the impact is experienced as organizations strive to become more adaptable, perhaps replacing traditional management principles with unfamiliar ones. Changes like these change opportunities to work and the environment of work. For the individual these changes may seem personal when in fact they reflect a bigger force called globalisation . What changes in job opportunities do you foresee in the next five years, and how will they affect work options?
4. Discuss how firms recruit and select managers for international assignments.
5. What advantages and disadvantages do you see for organizations becoming 'stateless' from the perspective of the enterprise, 'stateless' from the perspective of nations, and 'stateless' from the perspective of the individual employed by the 'stateless' firm?

REFERENCES

Addison, John T., and Paulino Teixeria (2001). *The Economics of. Employment Protection.* Bonn Institute for the Study of Labour Discussion Paper 381.

Agemor, Pierre (1996). "The Labour Market and Economic Adjustment". IMF Staff Papers 43 (2): 261-335.

Aidt, Toke, and Zafiris Tzannatos (2002). Unions and Collective Bargaining-Economic Effects in a Global Environment, Washington, D.C.: World Bank.

Besley, Timothy, and Robin Burgess (2004). Can Labour Regulation Hinder Economic Performance? Evidence from India". Quarterly Journal of Economics 1191): 91-134.

Bresnaahan, T.F., E. Brynojolfsson, and L.M. Hitt (2002). Information Technology, Workplace Organisation and the Demand for Skilled Labour: Firm-Level Evidence. " Quarterly Journal of Economics 117 (1): 339-76.

Blown, D.K. (2000). ' International Trade and Core Labour Standards: A Survey of Recent Literature," Paris, OECD, Occasional Papers 43.

Calmfors, Lars (1993). "Centralisation of Wage Bargaining and Macroeconomic Performance: A Survey:" OECD Economic Studies 21:161-91.

Chen, Martha Alter, R. Jhabvala, and F. Lund (2002). Supporting Workers in the Informal Economy: A Policy Framework, Geneva: I L O.

Coleman, James S. (1998). "Social Capital in the Creation of Human Capital," American Journal of Sociology 94. (Supplement): 95-120.

Djankov, S., R.L. Porta, F. Lopez-de. Silanes, A-Shleifer and J. Botero (2003). "The Regulation of Labour", Cambridge Mass: NBER, Working Paper Series 9756.

Freeman, Richard (1994). A Global Labour Market? Differences in Wages Among Countries in the 1980, Washington, D.C., World Bank.

Kugler, Adriana, and G. Pica (2003) Effect of Employment Protection and Product Market Regulation on the Indian Labour Market." Bonn, Germany: Institute for the Study of Labour, Discussion Paper 948.

Nestoriak, Nicole (2004). Endogenous Technology and Local Labour Market Skill". University of Maryland.

Nicoletti, G., and S. Serapetta (2003). Regulation, Productivity and Growth: OECD Evidence, Economic Policy 18 (36): 9-51.

Pissarides, Christopher (2000). Human Capital and Growth: A Synthesis Report, Paris: OECD Development Centre, Technical Paper, 168.

Rawling, Laura B., Lynne Sherburne-Benz, and Julie Van Domelen (2003). Evaluating Social Funds: A Cross-Country Analysis of Community Investments. Washington, D.C.: World Bank.

Rawling. Laura B., and Gloria M. Rubio (2002). Evaluating The Impact of Conditional Cash Transfer Programmes: Lessons from Latin America, Washington. D.C.: World Bank.

Tabor, Steven R. (2002). "Assisting the Poor with Cash: Design and Implementation of Social Transfer Programmes". Washington, D.C., World Bank Social Protection Discussion Paper Series 223.

26

GLOBAL MANAGER

INTRODUCTION

Globalisation creates opportunities for new entrepreneurs as well as for established businesses around the world but it also presents challenges and threats that yesterday's business managers did not have to deal with. The concern for the global manager is the accelerated rate at which this shift is occuring. They have to decide how best to expand into a foreign market. For success in the global economy, it seems pretty clear that a global manager is going to have a repertoire comprising a comprehensive knowledge base and a well-developed set of relational and cross-cultural skills. Manager of the future will have to require knowledge along with an ability to take action. *Should they export to that market from their home base, should they invest in production facilities in that market, producing locally to sell locally; or should they produce in a third country where the cost of production is favourable and export from that base to other other foreign markets and perhaps to their home market?* Managers have to decide whether and how to customise their product offerings, marketing policies, human resource practices, and business strategies to deal with national differences in culture, language, business practices, and government regulation. And managers have to decide how to deal with the threat posed by efficient foreign competitors entering their home market. Some of the substantive issues facing managers in a diversified global business include: integrating large international acquisitions, understanding the meaning of preference and accountability in a globally integrated system of product flows, building and managing a world-wide logistics capability; developing country-specific corporate strategies that take into account the political as well as economic imperatives, forming and benefiting from collaborative arrangements around the world; and, balancing the pressures for global integration and local demands.

The global manager will have to master more than concepts and theories; he or she will also have to command new skills. The purpose of this chapter is to identify and describe the skill set of the global manager.

REQUISITE SKILLS AND CHARACTERISTICS OF GLOBAL MANAGERS

To think globally really requires an alteration of mind-set. Thinking globally means extending concepts and models from one-to-one relationships to holding multiple realities and relationships in one's head simultaneously, and acting skillfully on this more complex reality. The shift means that even if one has a regional responsibility, say, as marketing manager for Central and South America, it is likely that more will be required than an understanding of Latin cultures and a capacity to speak Spanish and Portuguese. To illustrate, many of the executive traits now and in the future are presented in Exhibit-1.

EXHIBIT - 1

Executive Traits Now and in the Future

Now	*The Future*
All knowing	Leader as learner
Domestic vision	Global vision
Predict future from past	Intuits the future
Caring for individuals	Caring for institutions and individuals
Owns the vision	Facilitates vision of others
Uses power	Uses power and facilitation
Dictates goals and methods	Specifies processes
Alone at the top	Part of an executive team
Values order	Accepts peradox of order amidst chaos
Monolingual	Multicultural
Inspires the if boards, shareholders	Inspire the trust of owners, customers, and employees

This exhibit encompenses many of the particular skills required by global managers. Global expansion enables a company to add value by transferring core skills overseas, using global volume to cover product development costs, realising economies of scale from global volume, and configuring value-creation functions in locations where value-added is maximised. Companies pursuing a global strategy can gain cost economies by integrating manufacturing, marketing, and competitive strategies across national boundaries, but they must give up a certain degree of responsiveness to national conditions. A purely global strategy is appropriate when the pressures for global integration are high and the pressures for local responsiveness are low, as is the case in the electronic components industry.

ROLE OF GLOBAL MANAGER

To achieve the benefits of globalisation , the manager of a worldwide business need to recognise when industry conditions provide the opportunity to use global strategy levers. These managers, for the success in business, must be equipped with knowledge about business and technical matters, social, political and economic system, and culture, and ability to define and solve problems in the face of uncertainty; implementation skills; and a keen sense of how and when previous experience is relevant in new cultural settings. There has been tremendous increase in the demand for global managers in recent years since large number of joint ventures are prevailing in developing countries. Life as the head of a joint venture is characterised by a unique tension inherent to this particular organisational form. Doubie parenting exacerbates the difficulties and challenges that are a normal part of managing internationally, and also create new ones.

The role of the joint venture global manager differs from that of global manager in a wholly-owned subsidiary. His task is more complicated in a variety of ways: with essentially two bosses and two sets of expectations, he must simultaneously accommodate the interests of two partners. He often faces a great deal of ambiguity in terms of defining both parents' criteria of success and must deal with issues of commitment and communications between the two parents. At the same time he has less job security—if either parent of the board of directors disapproves of him, he may well have to move.

Amongst all these disadvantages, the joint venture global manager does have several things to look forward to. He has two sets of resources and skills with which to work. He can often produce at better economies than competitors in the developing countries by gaining quality and technical expertise from the MNC and knowledge of the local economy, politics and culture from the local partner. The role of the joint venture global manager is to balance these opportunities and risk and make them work for him. Achievement of this difficult task can make for a successful venture. Exhibit-2 provides a brief overview of the role joint venture global manageras compared to that of the general manager of a wholly-owned subsidiary (WOS) in a foreign country and a wholly-owned subsidiary in its home country.

To manage in an environment constrained by present company control practices in developing countries, joint venture global managers generally have less autonomy than they want to think they have. In particular, joint ventures' board of directors play a major role in the decision-making process, greater than in the joint ventures operating in developed countries. An explanation for this is that in developing countries, in addition to the level of uncertainty and the foreign parent's desire to be in control, there is a lack of managerial depth and the board of directors constitutes a mechanism for transferring the parents' expertise.

Control refers to the process through which a parent company assures that the way a joint venture is managed conforms with its own interest. From a JVGM's perspective, an understanding of the parents' control practices serves two purposes. First, it helps to map the boundaries of authority within which one is expected to operate; second, it helps to identify opportunities for independence (areas of freedom from parent authority or involvement).

EXHIBIT-2

Role of the Global Manager (GM): Three Perspectives

1	2	3
As they apply to GM of WOS in a DC[1]	*As they apply to GM of WOS in an LDC*	*As they apply to GM of JV in the LDC*
Interpersonal roles		
1. Figurehead roles —represents the organisation on ceremonial occasions	As in column 1; however additional legal requirements in each country necessitate greater emphasis in this role	As in column 2 plus increased number of occasions due to ceremonial situations relating to two nationalities
2. Liaison role —interacting with other managers and groups outside the organisation unit	Very prominent; must also frequently interact with government officials; may have problems if GM is an expropriate and working/dealing with nationals outside organisational unit	As in column 2
3. Leader role —establishing relationships with subordinates (motivating, supervising) and exercising formal authority within the organisational unit	More complex than in 1; may find it difficult to motivate and supervise nationals due to different values and ethics, etc.	Increased complexity compared to 2; must do this with expatriates and nationals likely from different countries; hence, must understand how to motivate people from other countries
Information roles		
1. Monitor role —receiving and collecting information from both inside and outside the organisational unit	Outside information-searching may be harder for an expartriate in an LDC than a DC; dealing with subordinates who are nationals may be hard	This is more easily done here as JVGM and managers may have access to information from two organisations
2. Disseminator role —transmitting information to members within the organisational unit	Can talk to nationals, but general manager is usually an expartriate, therefore may have communication breakdown	General manager usually national himself, hence role is easier

3. Spokesman role —informing those outside the organisational unit	Again, due to being expartriate, often difficult to do	Being national, it would be easier to do; however more groups (partners) for information to be conveyed to
Decision-related roles		
1. Innovator role —initiating change	Easier than JVGM due to need to convince only one superior; more complex than in 1 since physical distance means GM cannot rely on others	Very prominent role; must convince both parents and the board of directors (BOD)
2. Resource allocation —deciding where effors and energies will be directed	Similar to 1; not too difficult since there would be one set of objectives to achieve rather than conflicting goals as in 3	Very difficult due to two sets of resources and expectations
3. Negotiator role —dealing with situations involving negotiations on behalf of the organisation	Due to being expatriate may be difficult; as well, presence in an LDC environment may complicate negotiations	Perhaps the primary skill required of the JVGM
4. Disturbance handler role —taking charge when crises arise and the organisation is threatened	Handles individually; support from direct superior if need be, but as above	Has other influences (both parents and BOD) which complicate the decision

Parent companies have been found to exercise control through both positive and negative mechanisms. A parent uses positive and negative mechanisms. A parent uses positive control when it is in a position to influence activities or decisions in a way consistent with its own expectations and interests. It uses negative control when it is in a position to prevent decisions or activities it does not agree with from being implemented (Exhibit-3). Negative mechanisms such as a veto right over major decisions are particularly useful to parents in a minority shareholder position.

How do global managers Respond to These Challenges? As global managers learn how to live and manage under double parenting, they are to develop an agenda of their own which differs in an important way from that of their parents. While managers from parent companies tend to decide on the joint venture's success based on how will the joint venture meets their own expectations, the global managers' judgement is based on the avoidance of bad relationships between the parties involved. In other words, managers in the parent companies tend to use indicators centered on

EXHIBIT-3

Positive and Negative Control Mechanisms

Positive	*Negative*
Ability to make specific decisions	Board
Ability to design:	Executive committee
1) Planning process	Approval required for:
2) Appropriation requests	1) Specific decisions
	2) Plans, budgets
Policies and procedures	3) Appropriation request
	4) Nomination JVGM
Ability to set objectives for JVGM	Screening/no objection of parent before ideas are discussed with other parent
Contracts: management, technology transfer, marketing, supplier	
Participation in planning or budgeting process	
Parent organisation structure	
Reporting structure	
Staffing	
Training programme	
Staff services	
JVGM bonus tied to parent results	
Ability to decide on future promotion of JVGM (and other joint venture managers)	
Feedback: strategy/plan budgets, appropriation requests	
JVGM participation in parent's worldwide meetings	
Relations with JVGM: phone calls, meetings, visits	
Staffing parent with someone with experience with joint venture	
MNC level in the LDC	
Informal meetings with other parent	

the idea of achieving specific results, while global managers tend to use indicatorscentered on the idea of preventing bad relationships from developing. The following quotes capture the essence of the global managers' concern:

> *GM 1: 'If the joint venture is able to accomplish a desired result without too much "noise" it is a sign for future prosperous relationships.'*

> *GM 2: 'For the joint venture to be successful I have to grow, to achieve the objectives set by the company and maintain the leadership position and build a trust relationship between the partners.*

GM 3: 'A good indication of the success of the joint venture is that one parent has been able to run the joint venture without interference from the other parent.'

In cases where the global manager is a national of the host country, an important item on the agenda is the joint venture's contribution to the country's economic and social development. Nationalistic concerns appear to play a more important role in developing countries than in developed countries and are noted in joint ventures staffed with national top managers, be they appointed by the local or the multinational parent.

Parent's vs Joint Venture's Interests

In case of joint ventures, the global managers tend to see their allegiance to the joint venture first and to the parents second. This applies to the vast majority of global managers whether they come from one parent or not. When trying to resolve differences between the parents. They find that the joint venture's interests should be placed first and the parent's second.

Essentially global managers want to stay away from situations where one parent is perceived to win and the other to lose over a specific issue.. It the global manager tries to satisfy one parent more than the other, or if he is perceived to do so, sooner or later he is going to erode his credibility and jeopardise his working relationship with the partner who feels discriminated against.

When managers refer to a joint venture's interest, they implicitly conceptualise a criterion of what is good or bad for the joint venture. This criterion may be operationalised in a number of ways, depending on the manager, the joint venture, the circumstances in which it is used. etc. For instance, one manager may decide that when facing a choice, the alternative which is expected to yield the highest profit has to be selected (assuming the joint venture is considered as a profit centre). Meanwhile, in one of the joint ventures which has been assigned a common set of objectives by its parents, a manager may decide that anything consistent with these objectives is in the best interest of the joint venture.

When the joint venture has been assigned a set of agreed-upon objectives, or is considered as a profit centre, by its two parents, it is easy to decide what is in the best interests of the joint venture. However, it is important to recognise that the joint venture's interests are a reflection of the parents' interests who define them: they are not independent. The separation between the joint venture's and a parent's interests occurs when the joint venture intends to carry out an activity which is consistent with its interests. The typical example given by managers is when an MNC parent wants the joint venture to cut exports to foreign countries it can serve through a wholly-owned plant which has temporary overcapacity. In this case what is in the best interest of the joint venture is not longer in the best interest of the parent and conversely. Here the joint venture's position is well understood. It was originally defined (or at least agreed upon) by the parent itself.

In cases where the joint ventures does not have a specific set of objectives assigned, managers use the term 'joint venture's interest' to refer to undefined, non-explicit objectives that the joint venture would strive for were it an independent company (e.g. increase market share, maximise profits). In this sense the joint venture's interests are not necessarily a reflection of the parent's interests; they are simply a concept, an ideal, that managers feel useful as a means of settling a conflict between the two parents. They suggest that rather than seeing one partner win and the other lose over a specific issue, it might be better to see the joint venture win, even if in practice it is the same thing.

Global Managers' Time Orientation

The global managers' concern with preventing major clashes between and/or with the parents prompts them to be very prudent with the short-term impact of their decisions. As shown in Exhibit-4, global managers are short-term oriented while there is no such clear pattern for managers from the parent companies.

By holding global managers accountable through such close scrutiny, managers from parent companies inevitably trigger the global managers' short-term orientation. It does not mean that global managers are not concerned with the long-term health of the joint venture, but that when trade-offs have to be made, the short-term considerations carry the greatest weight in decision-making. Not all global managers are alike, though global managers with limited-term contracts (two-to-three years) have not surprisingly, a shorter time orientation than global managers with longer-term contracts.

THE GLOBAL MANAGER AS DIPLOMAT: FACILITATING COMMITMENT, TRUST AND COMMUNICATION

Commitment is one of the key variables associated with the success of joint ventures—something the global manager must be concerned with. There are four levels of commitment relevant to joint ventures: 1) commitment to international business; 2) commitment to joint ventue success; 3) commitment to the particular joint venture; and 4) commitment to the particular venture partner.

The trust-communication-commitment characteristics are truly integrated. By developing and maintaining an open communication system with the joint venture and with the partner, the parent is able to: 1) understand the joint venture's problems better and offer better solution; 2) become aware of changes occurring in the joint venture business or in its partner's expectation; 3) keep in touch with its partner, hence showing commitment to the joint venture and contributing to a trust relationship.

EXHIBIT-4

TIME ORIENTATION OF THE PARTNERS INVOLVED IN THE JOINT VENTURES AS REFLECTED IN THEIR MAIN CRITERIA OF SUCCESS

	JV MNC parent	*Local parent*	*JVGM*
1.	*Long term* Optimise long term shareholder's value through consistent real growth in earnings	*Short term:* Yearly growth rate Operating efficiency	*Short term:* Sales and profit growth Profit margin on net sales
2.	*Short term* Profitability Growth	*Long term:* Growth Joint venture as a tool to diversify parent's portfolio in hotel business	*Short-term:* Growth Profitability Successful middleman
3.	*Long term* Market share growth Search for opportunities in	*Short term:* Meet budgets Long term: Develop growth potential	*Short term:* Meet budgets
4.	*Short term:* Profits, growth and quality of their own brand	*Short term:* Operating results *Long term:* Profits Growth Future prospects	*Short term:* Avoid conflicts Achieve plan
5.	*Short term:* Return on net assets Dividends Business runs smoothly	*Short term:* Profitability Auto financing	*Short term:* Successful diplomat Long term: Growth
6.	*Long term:* Build long term profit base Achieve strategic plan Identification of future growth opportunities	*Short term:* Contribution to parent through transfer prices	*Short-term:* Monthly results Profit ROI
7.	*Short-term:* Achieve mission ROI Dividends	*Long-term:* Protection against erosion of money Fiscal benefits Mission (growth and exports)	*Short-term:* Maintain peace between partners Achieve plan (1 Year)
8.	*Short-term* Achieve mission ROI Dividends Operating results *Long-term:* Successful	*Short-term* Short-term growth in sales and profit	*Short-term:* Operating results *Long-term:* Maintain leadership Maintain trust between partners

implementation of strategy		
9. *Long-term* Volume growth Market share Vehicle to look for opportunities	*Short-term:* Profitability Supplies from joint venture information on market *Long-term:* Future growth	*Short-term:* Meet budgets Profitability
10. *Short term:* Profits	*Short-term:* Dividends	*Short-term:* Growth Profitability
Long-term: Enhance parent reputation	*Long-term:* Build asset base	

The global managers in joint ventures are is often the center of all the interaction between the two partners. By understanding the importance of open communication to a trusting relationship and how it achieves a higher level of commitment from the partners, the global manager of a joint venture as diplomat can strive to open barriers that may be blocking this profitable cycle.

In order to cope with the political and interpersonal constraints of their job, global managers must show great sensitivity to the parent companies' differences in culture, management style and expectations. Being under the scrutiny of two or more parents, they have to reconcile the achievement of their personal and career objectives with the parents' objectives and with the unique strategic and operating imperatives of running a company in an LDC.

Since a distinct advantage of a joint ventures over a wholly-owned subsidiary is its access to the skills and resources of two parents, the global manager has an implicit opportunity to use this advantage to his benefit. However, a potential limitation is that the need for parent support is generally crucial in the early stages of a joint venture, at a time when the global manager has not yet built his network with the parents.

Managers in parent companies should be prepared to staff joint ventures in developing countries with local managers. This is all the more important when there is a tendency in MNCs to insist on providing management personnel to the joint venture. This is frequently the case of very large MNCs which tend to duplicate their managerial systems and processes in their foreign subsidiaries, or for companies which have little or no experience in developing countries and/or with joint ventures. In these two sets of circumstances the rationale for appointing expatriates is the belief that it reduces uncertainty by facilitating communications with the joint venture and the parent and by appointing as joint venture managers individuals whose managerial style and practice are known. However, such practice does not recognise that the skills and knowledge required to manage a joint venture successfully in a developing countries are very different from those developed in managing wholly-owned subsidiaries and/or in developed countries. For example, dealing with the local elites, business people, politicians and the local partner is highly subtle exercise in diplomacy which may prove more important than the ability to run an operation effectively.

In order to avoid surprises, to understand the operating context of the joint venture, to be able to ask the 'right' questions and to interpret the answers, managers in parent companies need to manage their relationships with the global manager in a joint venture on the one hand and with the partner(s) on the other hand. In joint ventures, a relationship is something which is built over time, not something which is there when one needs it.

QUESTIONS

1. Discuss the role of global manager as diplomat as they are to facilitate commitment, trust and communication.
2. Evaluate issues that arise when companies transfer managers abroad.
3. Explain the unique qualifications of international managers.
4. Discuss the drawbacks of a global strategy.
5. "Globalisation is a process". Do you agree? What are specific managerial skills required by a global manager?
6. Will globalization make it more or less possible for small firms to participate in business? In what ways does globalization create similar changes for any size firm? What are the key differences between large and smaller firms that make each more and less adaptive to globalization?
7. If the traditional domestic mindsets are the Indian norm, but the emerging global mindset is the wave of future, what will be the implications for you as a manager? What type of skills do you need to develop to think according to a more global mindset? What changes will you need to make in the way you currently think and work?

REFERENCES

Alder, Lee and Hlavcek, James D. *Joint ventures for product innovation*, American, New York, 1976.

Baetz, Mark C. and Beamish, Paul W., *Strategic management: Canadian cases*, Richard D. Irwin, Homewood, Illinois, 1987.

Caves, Richard E., *Multinational enterprise and economic analysis*, Cambridge University Press, Cambridge, Massachusetts, 1982.

Hennart, Jean-Francois, *A theory of multinational enterprise*, University of Michigan Press, Ann Arbour, 1982.

Kolde, E.J. *The multinational company*, Lexington Books, Toronto, 1974.

Vaupel, James W. and Curhan, Joan P., *The world's multinational enterprises*, Harvard University Press, Boston, Massachusetts, 1973.

Williamson, Oliver E., *Markets and hiearchies: analysis and anti-trust implications — a study in the economic of internal organisations*, Free Press, New York, 1975.

Unit VI

27

INTERNATIONAL MARKETING

INTRODUCTION

Global, political, and economic liberalization trends created tremendous business opportunities and challenges for international marketers. The opening up of new markets in Eastern Europe and a tendency toward economic liberalisation in the developing world have spawned new business opportunities. Similarly, the emergence of regional trading blocs in the form of the EU (European Union), the NAFTA (North American Free Trade Agreement), and MERCOSUR (Mercado Comun del Sur) have necessitated reorganisation in the production and marketing strategies of firms. The changes in strategy include serving different markets from one production source or the shifting of production facilities for greater efficiency.

However, the global financial crisis in the latter half of the 2008 provided a significant reality check on the wisdom of globally integrated strategy development. Wildly fluctuating exchange rates make it difficult for multinational companies to manage globally integrated but geographically scattered activities. Indeed, many companies are scurrying to speed steps toward making their procurement, manufacturing, and marketing operations in localisation strategy. MNCs have moved to build an international production system less vulnerable to currency fluctuations by investing in local procurement and local marketing.

ROLE OF MARKETING IN GLOBAL AND TRANSNATIONAL STRATEGY

With the internationalisation of business, MNCs face increased competition at home from both foreign and domestic competitors and internationally as the MNC seek to enter new markets. In developing a competitive strategy, firms utilise the marketing process to identify, create and deliver products or services that are in demand and that customers are willing to buy. To perform successfully, global marketing strategy is to analyse the extent of globalisation of various aspects of the market environment like similarities and differences in consumer tastes, cultural similarities and differences, technical standards, levels of income, legislation, availability of advertising media etc.

International marketing interests operating simultaneously in different environments, coordinating international activities, and learning from the experiences gained in one country to make marketing decisions in other countries. In the overall global corporate strategy, marketing is seen as an important source of value added which perform three significant roles. First, *Market configuration,* which refer to the location of various marketing activities through the world (geographically concentrated or dispersed). Second, *market coordination,* which refers to the extent of standardisation or adoptation of the marketing mix globally. Third, the *strategic role of marketing*, especially the link between marketing and the other value-added activities of the company, e.g., design, technology development, manufacturing etc. Within the framework adopted, marketing is seen as fulfilling the following roles in the over all global strategy of the business: (i) identifying and making recommendations about future trends and opportunities in the markets where the company is already active; (ii) identifying and making recommendations about new marketing opportunities; (iii) providing estimates of the marketing resources (budget) needed to exploit these opportunities; (iv) developing and implementing marketing strategies which are consistent with the overall strategic direction of the company in global markets. Important competitive advantages can be derived, however, by concentrating certain marketing activities globally, when conditions permit, including the production of promotion material; central sales force; central service support; centralised training and global advertising.

There are a number of ways in which geographically-dispersed marketing activities can be co-ordinated to gain competitive advantage including: performing marketing activities using similar methods across countries; transferring marketing know-how and skill from country to country; sequencing of marketing programmes across countries; and, integrating the efforts of various marketing groups in different countries. Finally the greatest leverage from taking a global view of marketing is its links to other upstream and support activities in the value chain. In particular, global marketing can allow significant economies of scale and learning in production and research and development, through uniform products for global markets.

Broadening of the marketing concept, to include strategic as well as operational decisions, has resulted in an overlap between marketing and strategic management; and has generated considerable controversy over the role and position of marketing in corporate strategy. Global marketing strategy, an essential element of an overall transnational strategy, should be both customer and competitor-based and should be both globally and locally orientated. Today, customer needs, and therefore markets, are becoming increasingly global for many goods and services, but the extent of globalisation varies considerably from market to market. Even in a market where customer needs are similar on a global basis there may be elements of the marketing mix (this being the considerations over product design, price, place, i.e. segment, and promotion) which must be varied locally.

A global marketing strategy and the associated marketing mix must take account of the following factors in the market environment:

i) *Customer needs*— the extent to which they are global or to which there are specific local needs;
ii) *culture*—the products, brand names or advertising may have to be varied on a local basis to account for regional cultural differences;
iii) *language*—may require local variations in packaging, labelling, brand name and advertising;
iv) *technology*—the level of technology in a country or differing technical standards may require variations in product;
v) *legal factors*—may demand variations in packaging, advertising, product features and so on.

GLOBAL MARKETING STRATEGIES

An important feature of global marketing strategy is the co-ordination and integration of marketing on a worldwide basis in the pursuit of global competitive advantage. Three main phases in the evolution of global marketing with each stage presenting new strategic challenges and decision priorities to the firm are:

Phase One: Phase one represents the initial stage of international market expansion where the main strategic decisions facing the business include the choice of country to enter, the mode of entry adopted and the extent of product standardisation or adaptation.

Phase Two: Once the company has established a 'beachhead' in a number of foreign markets, it then begins to seek new directions for growth and expansion, thus moving to phase two of internationalisation. The focus in this stage is mainly on building market penetration in countries where the company is already located. In consequence, the expansion effort is mainly directed by local management with marketing strategy being determined on a country-by-country or nationally responsive basis.

Phase Three: It is the third evolutionary phase which is the most important in the context of global marketing. In phase three the business moves towards a global orientation. The country-by-country approach to marketing is replaced by one in which markets are viewed as a set of interrelated and interdependent entities. These are increasingly integrated and interlinked worldwide and co-ordination and integration of global marketing becomes essential to fully exploit the competitive advantages to be derived from the company's global scope. There are two key strategic thrusts in phase three. *First,* the drive to improve the efficiency of worldwide operations through co-ordination and integration. This will cover both marketing activities such as product development, sourcing and management. Standardisation of product lines globally, for example, will facilitate the development of a globally integrated production and logistics network. The *second* key strategic thrust is the search for global expansion and growth opportunities. This will involve a range of activities including opportunities for transferring products, brand names, marketing ideas, skills and expertise between countries; the identification of global market segments and target customers; and worldwide product development aimed at global markets.

A shift in focus from the evolution towards global marketing is reflected in Figure-1. The focus is now more on the competitive marketing strategies of international businesses, identifying four generic international competitive marketing strategies.

FIGURE - 1

GENERIC INTERNATIONAL MARKETING STRATEGIES

Scope		High	Low
	Global	Global high share strategy	Global niche strategy
	National	National high share strategy	National niche strategy

Configuration of activities

Global High Share Strategies

These strategies involve pricing, promotion, product and other elements of the marketing mix being geared towards high volume segments of global markets. The essence of global high share strategies is the worldwide co-ordination of company resources behind global objectives. The global scope of marketing creates opportunities for competitive advantage through lower costs and economies of scale; providing a global service; international sourcing; experience transfers; promoting an international corporate image; global resource focus; and improving the risk/return characteristics of the company's international business portfolio.

Global Niche Strategies

These involve specialisation by product, technology, stage of life cycle, market segment etc. and avoid head-on competition with companies pursuing global high share strategies.

National High Share Strategies

These involve the use of nationally based competitive advantages, with marketing and production geared towards achieving high volume and lower costs relative to other national competitors.

National Niche Strategies

These involve specialisation on a national scale to avoid competition with both global and national high share companies.

Only the first two of these marketing strategies can be classified as being global. A more comprehensive coverage of the main components of global marketing can be traced in the development of a global marketing strategy which involves four main stages: defining the global marketing mission; the global segmentation strategies; the competitive-market positioning strategy; the global marketing mix strategy.

Global Marketing Mission: The global marketing mission defines the major target markets to be attacked, the way these markets are to be segmented and the competitive position to be adopted in each market. In other words, the mission establishes the general parameters within which global marketing strategy decisions are made.

Segmentation Strategies: In terms of global segmentation strategies, the three main alternatives identified are: i) *global market segments*—where markets are segmented according to variables which largely ignore national boundaries, e.g. demographic, buying practices, preferences etc. The strategy concentrates on identifying similarities in customer needs across countries rather than emphasising country/cultural differences. ii) *national market segments*—which involves serving the same market segments in multiple markets but on a national basis. Segmentation is on the basis of geography/nationality which emphasises cultural differences rather than similarities between countries; iii) *mixed market segments*—which is largely a combination of the first two. Some national markets may be of a sufficient size to warrant individualisation. Others may be clustered into similar market segments.

Deciding on Competitive Position and Marketing Mix: Once the broad segmentation strategy has been established, the global company must decide on its competitive position within each market and its marketing mix strategy. A global marketing strategy must be part of a global business strategy. Global strategy will be appropriate when customer needs are globally common, there are global customers and channels, and when marketing is globally transferable. In addition, cost drivers are likely to favour a global approach to marketing by creating economies of scale and scope. There are also competitive advantages of global marketing, through, for example, global branding. However a marketing strategy adopted should not be global in every detail, rather one which is global where there are evident advantages and local where necessary.

So global marketing is not a blind adherence to standardisation of all marketing elements for its own sake, but a different, global approach to developing marketing strategy and programmes that blends flexibility with uniformity. In essence, a global or transnational marketing strategy is concerned with devising a strategy which is global in scope and which is globally co-ordinated. The extent of globalisation of each element of the strategy will be dependent upon the transnational strategy of the organisation, the relative advantages of globalisation or localisation based on factors such as customer needs. (Table-1) shows that the potential advantages and limitations of global marketing strategy.

TABLE 1

Advantages of global marketing	*Comments*
Unit cost reduction	Consolidation of the global marketing function, economies of scale, experience curve economies, dilution of R&D and other fixed costs etc.
Improved quality of products and programmes	through concentration on key marketing activities, uniform products etc.
Enhanced customer preferences	Through global customer knowledge of products, global availability, global serviceability etc.
Increased competitive leverage	By focusing resources and unifying the approach to competition
Risk reduction	Through reduced dependency on local demand, wider access to capital
Global knowledge and information transfers	transfer of experience, practice, etc.
Limitations of global marketing	
Company-specific factors	For example, lack of resources, lack of global orientation, higher costs of co-ordination
Environment factors	Linguistic, cultural, technological and legal factors
Market factors	Customer need differences, channel differences etc.
Product factors	Over-standardisation can result in products which satisfy nobody
Responsiveness	Over-centralisation reduces responsiveness

Segmentation Basis

The traditional approach to international marketing segmentation was to segment a market on a country basis to take account of national differences in demand conditions. A different approach for segmenting international markets, more compatible with the requirement for global marketing co-ordination, may be to make customers and their needs the basis for segmentation. It has the advantage of being consumer orientated, while allowing global co-ordination of marketing, since it focuses on similarities rather than differences across groups of consumers in different countries. The basis of this approach is the 'strategically equivalent segmentation' (SES) of consumers. This is the identification of transnational segments of consumers, with similar needs, who will respond similarly to a given marketing mix. Four main stages are involved in identifying SES: (i) *the criteria to be used in segmenting markets*—develop qualifying and determining dimensions; (ii) *country screening*—using qualifying dimensions to narrow down the list of countries as viable entry candidates; (iii) *identifying market segments in each country*—develop microsegments in each qualified country; (vi) *measuring segments*—develop factor score representation of microsegments and clustering analysis for SES.

The initial stage is the identification of qualifying criteria for identifying market segments (e.g. age, sex, income etc.). This is followed by country screening to identify the relative size of the segments in each country. After these filtering processes to identify which segments in which countries are to be targeted, the target market segment is then aggregated across countries to provide the total market. The major advantage of this approach is that it permits a business to adopt a global marketing strategy in strategically equivalent segments without assuming the complete cultural convergence of countries.

Market Positioning

Issues involved in global marketing positioning can be identified, *first*, in market positioning which refers to the competitive position of a product in the market, for example, market leader; strong number two etc; *second*, in product positioning which refers to the attributes of a product in comparison with other products or to consumer needs. These two types of positioning can occur at two levels; first, the marketplace and second, in the consumer's mind. The first emphasises the importance of competition; the second, customer orientation. A combination of these alternatives gives the model shown in Table-2. The importance of this to global marketing is that different positioning strategies can be adopted in different country markets in terms of market and product position.

Advantages of uniform position have to be weighed against the advantages of differentiated positioning. Businesses adopting the same positioning strategy in all market have adopted a *global positioning strategy* while those that vary position across markets are said to have adopted a *mixed positioning strategy*.

TABLE 2

	Market position (competitive standing)	*Product position (profile attributes)*
Measurements—marketplace	Market share	Comparison of attributes
Consumers mind	Reputation	Image (perceptual map)
Possible positions	Leader (lion)	Product category
	Challenger (tiger)	Price / quality vector
	Leaper (frog)	Main features
	Nicher (groundhog)	
	Follower (ant)	
	Imitator (mouse)	
Possible strategies	Enlarge	Reinforce
	Concur	Reposition
	Advance	
	Protect	
	Withdraw	

Global Marketing Management

The adoption of global marketing strategies involving co-ordination and integration of worldwide marketing raises a large number of important issues concerning global management of the marketing mix. Four main categories of marketing mix strategy based upon the global segmentation and positioning strategy of the business are presented in Figure 2. These four options for marketing strategy are:

i) *ideal global marketing strategy*—the marketing of a standard product to a global market segment using uniform marketing programmes;
ii) *ideal national marketing strategy*—the marketing mix is specifically tailored to meet the requirements of each national market;
iii) *hybrid I marketing strategy*—the standardisation of products but the adaptation of other elements of the marketing mix to reinforce the product strategy;
iv) *hybrid II marketing strategy*—the standardisation of one key element of the marketing mix but the adaptation of others.

FIGURE 2

THE GLOBAL MARKETING STRATEGY MIX

Product strategy			
	Global product	*Hybrid* I marketing strategy	Ideal global marketing strategy
	National product	Ideal national marketing strategy	Hybrid II marketing strategy
		National market segments	*Global market segments*
		Segmentation strategy	

Any elements of the marketing mix can be standardised or varied as part of a global marketing strategy, according to the requirements of the global market. The extent of standardisation and customisation of marketing strategy will depend upon the competences of the business, the nature of its products, the nature of its markets and the importance of cultural, legal, technological and other factors.

Global Products

A company's products define its business. Pricing, communication, and distribution policies must fit the product. A firm's costumers and competitors are determined by the products it offers. They can have a major impact on performance of the whole business in global markets. Product represent the most visible aspect of the company in foreign markets. Product design, quality, performance etc. have a very significant effect on the global image and reputation of the company. In addition, other elements of the global marketing mix (pricing, promotion and distribution) need to be designed and developed on the basis of product decisions.

A wide range of decisions need to be taken in the area of global product policy including: *product range decisions* concerning the number, range and type of product sold throughout the world; *new product development* for global markets including the process of research and development; *global product diffusion and adoption* concerning the rate of transfer and acceptance of new products in different markets; *managing the international product life cycle* which may be at different stages in different markets; *product standardisation or differentiation* questions; *generic product strategies* which may be based on core competences and associated cost leadership, differentiation, hybrid or focus; *packaging, branding, after-sales service* etc. decisions.

Global Branding

A brand is defined as *a name, term, sign, symbol, mark, lettering or design (or any combination thereof) intended to differentiate a product form its competitors.* Successful branding strategies can be an important source of competitive advantage in some marketplaces by differentiating the product from those of competitors, maintaining product quality and image, achieving strong brand loyalty and sustained consumer commitment, and erecting barriers to entry. Brands tend to be most important in consumer rather than industrial or intermediate markets. Whereas brands tend to cultivate confidence amongst consumers in FMCG (fast-moving consumer goods) or consumer durables sectors, intermediates such as petrochemicals, energy, aggregates and other industrial goods tend to be brought much more on the basis of technical specification or price.

The advantages of successful branding will be particularly important in global marketing given the intensity of the competitive environment in consumer goods sectors. One of the most important issues in branding for global markets is the choice between global or multiple country brands, that is whether a standardised global brand is sold worldwide or whether the brand is adapted to local market differences.

There are several advantages to be gained from a global brand name. Brand names are often associated with consumer perceptions of quality, reliability, performance and other positive product features. Perhaps the most important advantage, therefore, is the positive perception that consumers have of products associated with the brand name. Other major advantages to be derived from global branding are marketing efficiency through economies of scale, promotion of a global image and reputation, and global consumer loyalty.

The extent of global branding, however, is constrained by several factors including: *legal constraints*—in some developing countries, for example, foreign brands may be either banned or taxed more heavily; *language and cultural factors*—which may lead to misleading connotations of certain brand names, requiring brand adaptation; *consumer homogeneity*—the extent to which global branding is possible obviously depends on the extent of consumer homogeneity between markets—the extent of 'converging commonality'; *counterfeiting*—this is one of the most serious problems faced by global branders.

Key Branding Decision

The strategic decisions facing companies in global branding are: *first, whether to brand or not to brand*—which depends on whether the product has salient attributes which can be differentiated; *second, whether to use the manufacturer's own brand or the distributor's/retailer's private brand; third, whether to use global or local brands*— which depends on the extent of inter-market differences; *fourth, whether to use single or multiple brands* in the same market. These decisions are summarised in Figure-3. The main advantages and disadvantages of each of these strategic options are listed in Table-3. The figure and table should be considered in conjunction with each other as they assist in the brand decision making process. Particular attention should be paid to the advantages and disadvantages of worldwide branding. The framework can be used as the basis of analysis of the branding strategy of a particular business in global markets.

Though some doubts have been expressed on the significance of brand names as a means of attracting customers. Some oft he doubts are the result of research which targeted general consumers rather than consumers from the segments where brands are known. In any case, a successful brands can still be built and that brand building must involve: *getting lean*—pruning weak brands and concentrating resources on successful and potentially successful brands; *investment*—particularly in product innovation; and *listening*—to consumers and understanding their needs.

It is evident that the decision to brand globally or locally is not simple. Many business therefore adopt a hierarchy of global, regional and local brands to combine the benefits of global and local branding.

Global Pricing

Pricing Decisions

Like branding and advertising, *price* is an important element of a global marketing strategy. While price is heavily influenced by the overall strategy of the business, there is a need to ensure that it is sensitive to local market conditions. Price determination in international marketing is significantly more complex than in domestic marketing as a result of factors such as variations in market demand and competitive conditions abroad, transport and distribution costs, tariffs and other government price controls, exchange rate fluctuations etc. The need to integrate pricing with global strategy suggests that there should be global co-ordination of pricing policy, but the need to be locally responsive suggests variation in pricing.

FIGURE 3
BRANDING DECISIONS

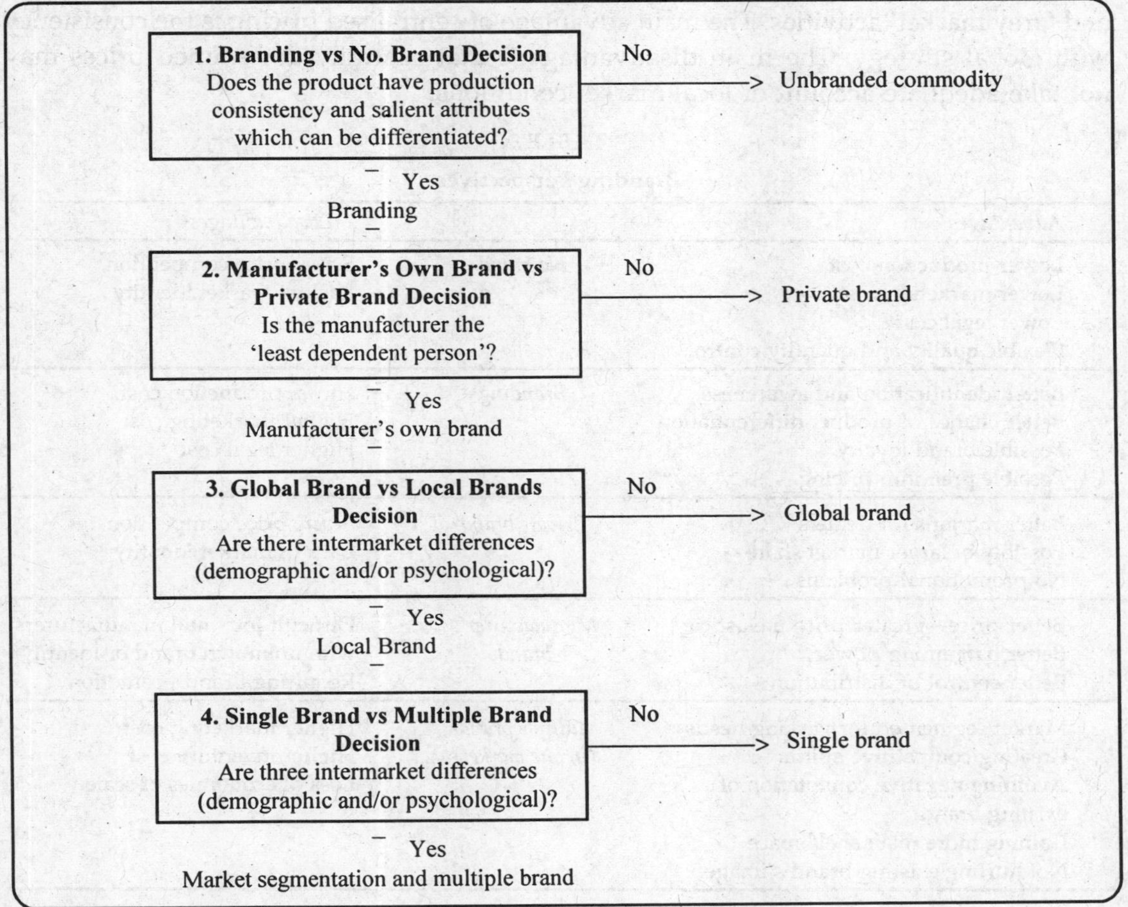

One of the most important price-related decisions in global marketing is the need for pricing policy to be developed within the context of the company's overall strategic objectives in global markets and this is a powerful argument in favour of centralised co-ordination of pricing decisions. At the same time, however, prices need to be responsive to local environmental and market conditions in different countries and this favours a decentralised approach, with pricing decisions being the responsibility of foreign subsidiaries. Decentralising pricing decisions, on the other hand, may lead to inter-subsidiary price competition.

The advantages and disadvantages of alternative pricing strategies are important to consider. Highly decentralised pricing has the advantage of being full responsive to local market conditions. The main disadvantage is that decentralised prices may not be consistent with the overall global market objectives of the company and may encourage inter-subsidiary price competition. This, in turn, may lead to opportunities for arbitrage and 'grey market' activities. The main advantage of centralised pricing is the consistency with global strategy. The main disadvantage is that centrally determined prices may not take adequate account of local market conditions.

TABLE 3

Branding Perspectives

Advantages		*Disadvantages*
Lower production cost Lower marketing cost Lower legal cost Flexible quality and quantity control	*No brand*	*Severe* price competition Lack of market identity
Better identification and awareness Better chance of product differentiation Possible brand loyalty Possible premium pricing	*Branding*	*Higher* production cost Higher marketing cost Higher legal cost
Better margins for dealers Possibly of larger market share No promotional problems	*Private brand*	*Severe* price competition Lack of market identity
Better price—greater price inelasticity Better bargaining power Better control of distribution	*Manufacturer's brand*	Difficult for small manufacturers with unknown brand or identity Requiring brand promotion
Market segmented for varying needs Creating competitive spirits Avoiding negative connotation of existing brand Gaining more retail shelf space Not hurting existing brand's image	*Multiple brands (in one market)*	Higher marketing cost Higher inventory cost Loss of economies of scale
Marketing efficiency Permitting more focused marketing Eliminator of brand confusion Good for product with good reputation (halo effect)	*Single brand (in one market)*	Assuming market homogeneity Existing brand's image hurt when trading up/down Limited shelf space
Meaningfull names Local identification Avoidance of taxation on international brand Quick market penetration by acquiring local brand Allowing variations of quantity and quality across markets	*Local brands*	Higher marketing cost Higher inventory cost Loss of economies of scale Diffused image
Maximum marketing efficiency Reduction of advertising costs	*Worldwide brands*	Assuming market homogeneity Problems with black and grey markets

Elimination of brand confusion	Possibility of negative connotation
Good for culture-free product	Requiring quality and quantity consistency
Good for prestigious product	LDC's opposition and resentment
Easy identification/recognition for international travellers	Legal complications
Uniform worldwide image	

There are two intermediary situations between the two extremes of centralised, uniform pricing and decentralised, local market pricing. *First*, centralised pricing policy with decentralised price determination. Under this strategy each national subsidiary is responsible for determining its own prices, but overall pricing policy is determined centrally. This may include decisions regarding rates of return to be achieved; market share and product positioning objectives etc. *Second*, prices may be determined decentrally but only within clearly defined limits laid down by the corporate centre.

Cross-subsidization is an important and controversial issue in global pricing. This occurs when a transnational or global company uses profits made in one country to subsidize prices elsewhere to gain market share. Thus, some Japanese companies have been accused of using surplus profits made in the protected Japanese market to subsidise prices on entry into the US and European markets leading to accusations of 'dumping' (such as in the case of some semiconductors).

Three alternative approaches to global pricing listed before are presented in table-4.

i) *Standard world pricing*—uniform pricing throughout the world.

ii) *Market differentiated pricing*—prices are customised for each market.

iii) *Dichotomous pricing*—standardised foreign prices separate from the domestic market price structure.

TABLE 4

Pros and Cons of Different Pricing Strategies

	Advantages	*Disadvantages*
Standardised world pricing	Simple Equitable Removes possibility for arbitrage	Lack of responsiveness to local economic and demand conditions
Market differentiated pricing	Market responsiveness	Creates opportunities for arbitrage and 'grey marketing'
Dichotomous pricing		Worst of both words

Subject to central co-ordination, a market differentiated approach should be adopted in many cases, because environmental factors affecting prices often vary significantly from market to market; pricing policy should be used proactively to achieve local market goals; the advantages of price uniformity are generally small; may of the drawbacks of price differentiation can be anticipated and managed.

Transfer Pricing

The question of transfer pricing is an important and controversial one in global marketing. Transfer prices are the prices charged on intra-group trade. It occurs when there is a movement of parts, components, machinery, technology etc. from one part of the global business network to another. The flow of goods and services is one-way; the flow of payment for these goods/services is the other way. The question then arises—what price is to be charged on such intra-group trade? **Four main approaches** to transfer pricing are: *transfer at direct cost; transfer at direct cost plus apportioned overhead and margin; transfer at a price derived from end market prices; transfer at an 'arm's-length price,' i.e. a price which would have been negotiated by unrelated parties.*

The crucial issue here is that international business can derive a number of benefits from the manipulation of internal transfer prices. These include reduced tax liability; circumventing restrictions on profit repatriation; reducing exchange risk; and avoidance of import tariffs. The global tax liability of the business can be reduced by shifting declared profits from high tax to low tax countries. One way of achieving this is to manipulate transfer prices in order to increase the profits of subsidiaries in low tax countries. Similarly, restrictions on profit repatriation may be overcome by 'overcharging' subsidiaries for goods and service transfers. Thus, money may be remitted from the country as payment for goods and services rather than as profits. In the same way, foreign exchange risk can be mitigated by manipulating transfer prices to siphon funds from countries where local currency depreciation is expected. Again, where import tariffs are charged as a proportion of the value of goods, these can be reduced by artificially reducing the value of imports to subsidiaries through manipulating transfer prices. Finally, transfer pricing is also important in relation to management of exchange rate risk.

Global pricing must be consistent with transnational strategy and with other elements of marketing strategy. Just as other elements of strategy can be standardised or localised, so can pricing. This allows the benefits of global strategy to be combined with those of local flexibility.

Global Promotion

Marketing Communications

Global promotion is defined here to include all forms of marketing communications that seek to influence the buying behaviour of existing and potential customers including advertising, personal selling, direct mail, point-of-sale displays, literature, publicity and word of mouth communications. Marketing texts have referred to these promotions as above-line (media promotions), below-line (more focused non-media promotions) and direct selling.

The major *objectives* of global promotion, as with domestic marketing, are, *to enhance the company's image vis-a-vis its competitors and/or to inform, educate, and influence the attitudes and buying behaviour of the individuals, companies, institutions, and/or government agencies that make up a target market.*

Despite sharing the same objectives, global promotion is far more complex than domestic promotion due tot he complexity of the global environment, i.e., the extent of standardisation of global promotion; the ways in which global promotion is organised and controlled (centralisation versus decentralisation); management of global promotion campaigns; and the role and growth of global advertising agencies.

Standardisation of Global Promotion

One of the most important factors constraining global advertising standardisation is the relationship between the centre and subsidiary managers. The main obstacle to global advertising and the reason so many global campaigns fail is not because of cultural differences around the world, but rather because of inter-personal relationships between foreign subsidiaries and corporate headquarters, i.e. the 'not invented here' syndrome which can create subsidiary opposition to centrally-designed campaigns. A concise summary of arguments for and against standardisation of global advertising is given in Table-5.

Organisation and Control of Promotions

Organisation and control issues, therefore, are central to the debate on global advertising and they have been well covered in the literature. Centralisation of advertising decisions allows for greater co-ordination and integration of world wide promotion with the associated benefits listed in Table 6. Decentralisation, on the other hand, will allow greater flexibility and responsiveness to local market needs.

The extent to which a business standardises global promotion is governed by several external and internal factors. The major external factors are: (i) *language differences* which may affect the translation of the advertising message and the appropriateness of trade names, brands, slogans etc.; (ii) *cultural differences* which may affect behaviour patterns, values, tastes, fashions etc.; (iii) *social differences* especially the general attitude of society towards advertising; (iv) *economic differences* including the stage of development of the country and its effects on education, levels of literacy, possession of radio, TV etc.; (v) *competitive differences* and the promotional campaigns of competitors; (vi) *promotion infrastructure differences*—the relative importance of different promotion channels can vary significantly between countries as between TV, radio and the media; and, finally, (vii) *legal and regulatory controls* including codes of practice and legislation can vary considerably.

The most important internal factors are the overall global strategy of the business and the relationship between headquarters executives and foreign subsidiary management. The scope for global promotion is far greater when transnational strategy places greater emphasis on co-ordination of activities rather than when a locally responsive approach is adopted. Similarly, the greater the degree of centralised control, the greater the standardisation of promotion. When decision-making power is decentralised then there is greater scope for local variations in promotion.

TABLE 5

Global Advertising Standardisation

Arguments in favour of standardisation	*Arguments against standardisation*
Costs saving through economies of scale in promotion	The heterogeneity of countries in terms of culture, mentality and product usage
Promotion of uniform brand and corporate image	The 'not invented here' syndrome, i.e. the desire of each country to create its own campaign
Utilisation of global media	Differences in the media scene
Simplified promotional planing through uniform objectives and simplified co-ordination and control	Legal and regulatory constraints
Maximum use of good ideas, transmission of know-how and continuous exchange of ideas	Competitive position in different markets
The tendency for global business to be centrally managed	Product may be at different stages of its life cycle in different countries
Better use of management abilities and resources	Danger of being regarded as a foreign enterprise
Universal guidelines and quality standards	Higher co-ordination costs which need to be balanced against economies of scale
Better access to stored know-how and experience of other countries and improved ways of identifying global opportunities	

The choice of promotional strategy is, of course, not a simple choice between total standardisation and complete local adaptation. As with other aspects of transnational strategy, it is more likely that a company will adopt an approach which combines a high degree of uniformity with local variations. In relation to the decision as to the extent to which promotion should be centralised or decentralised, three broadly identified alternative options are listed below:

(i) *the centralised organisation*—centralisation of all promotional decision-making at corporate headquarters;

(ii) *the decentralised organisation*—decentralisation of promotional decision-making;

(iii) *the mixed organisation*—combining elements of centralised and decentralised promotional decision-making.

Several factors will influence the choice between these three alternatives: (i) *corporate and marketing objectives*—where global objectives predominate, promotion will tend to be centralised; (ii) *the uniformity of the product*—the greater the uniformity of the product, the greater the centralisation of promotion; (iii) *the appeal of the product or brand*—where this is widespread, decentralisation will be increased; (iv) *legal constraints*—decentralisation may be necessary to take account of different national regulations; (v) *cultural aspect*—may dictate decentralisation; (vi) *socio-economic conditions*—different tastes, habits and preferences may require decentralisation; and finally, (vii) *the competitive situation*—where this differs from country to country promotional decisions will need to be at least partially decentralised.

Existing decision-making processes in global businesses vary considerably. Companies adopting global strategies will be significantly more centralised in promotional decision-making than nationally responsive ones. Generally speaking, however, the two extremes of complete centralisation or complete decentralisation are rare in practice, with most businesses adopting a variation of the mixed organisation.

Generally, corporate (at the centre) staff are responsible for developing the core promotional objectives and core campaigns; and for providing advice and expertise to foreign affiliates. Decisions regarding the detailed implementation of core campaigns in foreign markets are often best left to subsidiary managers to achieve local flexibility. Certain local decisions, however, may still require the ultimate approval of the parent company. Further, in examining the role of corporate headquarters in global advertising, a distinction may be drawn between the professional and management role. The former refers to the role of headquarters in creating and placing advertising. The later refers to the importance of ensuring co-operation between headquarters and subsidiary and for evaluating campaign effectiveness. The main responsibilities of the centre included product/brand positioning and effect measurement. Foreign subsidiaries, on the other hand, were mainly responsible for media planning and media buying. Decisions which were jointly determined by both headquarters and foreign subsidiaries included advertising agency selection; concept development; execution; and marketing research. The role of corporate headquarters in global advertising is summarised in Figure-4.

The Management of Global Promotional Campaigns

Strategic issues in promotion planning may be distinguished from management issues. The six main strategic issues are: (i) *the market segment*—at which at promotion is directed—in global marketing this refers mainly to the territorial boundaries or geographical scope of the campaign whether national, regional or global; (ii) *the objectives of the promotion campaign*—where a distinction can be made, for example, between building a global brand and increasing market share in a particular country; (iii) *the message(s)*—communicated and whether this should be the same across countries; (iv) *The allocation of expenditure*—tot he campaign and the total budget; (v) *the allocation of the total budget*—across promotional mix elements—media, geographical areas, products and over time; and finally, (vi) *procedures for monitoring the performance*—of the campaign.

The major managerial issues involved in implementing a campaign include: (i) *the organisation and control dimension*—as discussed in the previous section; (ii) *choosing an advertising agency*—where alternatives include using a domestic agency; using an agency with branches overseas; using local agencies in foreign markets; or some combination of these alternatives. The choice between these alternatives will be influenced by three broad categories of factors including: (a) corporate factors such as the extent of the company's internationalisation, organisational structure, and standardisation policy; (b) market-specific factors such as sociocultural, economic and legal differences; and, (c) characteristics of the agency itself including its market coverage, quality and reputation.

FIGURE-4

THE ROLE OF CORPORATE HEADQUARTERS IN GLOBAL ADVERTISING

(a) Professional Role

i) Positioning
ii) Strategy development
iii) Creative concept development and judgement
iv) Assisting local management in selecting the right target groups
v) Giving an insight into the degree to which specific products and product attributes must be emphasised in local campaigns or in adapted campaigns
vi) Providing an insight into what kind of advertising is most effective in which country
vii) Selecting the media types to be used, both locally and internationally
viii) Drawing up procedures for reporting and internal communication between subsidiaries and head office
ix) Cultivating a feeling for cultural differences and thus increasing the possibilities of standardising a creative approach
x) Evaluating international media
xi) Co-ordinating advertising research and measurement of effect

(b) Management Role

i) Providing worldwide planning systems including worldwide production outlines or guidance
ii) Organising worldwide co-ordination of local advertising plans
iii) Setting global budgets, dividing them according to region or country, evaluating country budgets and checking whether they meet the company's requirements
iv) Assisting with the selection of local advertising managers
v) Developing documentation systems for registering successful multinational campaigns in order to help local subsidiaries developing their own campaigns
vi) Selecting advertising agencies (local, multinational or global)
vii) Evaluating agency relationships and remuneration arrangements

Steps in planning worldwide advertising identified are listed below:

(i) *Situation analysis*—analysis of the forces influencing promotional decisions including organisational structure, brand portfolio, the extent of standardisation, market share abroad and brand positioning.

(ii) *Marketing communications strategy and objectives*—whether a brand is to be developed globally or multi-locally.

(iii) *Deciding on the target groups*—identifying similar market segments in each country

(iv) *Setting the total communications budget*—whether it is set centrally or locally, determine the basis upon which the budget is determined, e.g. based on past experience, objectives etc.

(v) *The message*—the choice between standardised and locally varied.

(vi) *The means of communication and their integration*—choices on sales, promotion, PR, media advertising, sponsorship and the interrelationships between these methods.

(vii) *Centralised or decentralised control of the means of communication*—decisions governing who controls promotion.

(viii) *Budget allocation*—between different promotional media and communications channels.

(ix) *Organisation and implementation*— of the strategy including managing agency arrangements.

(x) *Control and evaluation*—measuring the effectiveness of the campaign in each country.

Choosing an Advertising Agency

The globalisation of business and the attention focused on the opportunities for global promotion has resulted in a rapid internationalisation of the advertising industry itself. Since the mid-1980s, internationalisation of the advertising industry has accelerated at an unprecedented rate, with the emergence of a number of global, 'mega'-agencies. This has mainly been a consequence of the wave of cross-border mergers and acquisitions which have swept the industry in recent years.

The rapid internationalisation of the advertising industry and the emergence of global, 'mega'-agencies can be attributed to three main causes.

1. *Globalisation*—with acceptance of the premise of 'converging commonality', the opportunities for global promotion have become apartment. To exploit such opportunities, agencies have established geographically dispersed subsidiaries throughout the world—sometimes through establishing new branches, but more commonly through mergers and acquisition.

2. *The benefits of size*—closely related to the advantages of globalisation, are the benefits of size. Global, 'mega'-agencies, due to their size and geographical scope, can exert considerable influence over media groups, and can achieve considerable economies of scale in operations.
3. *Synergy*—a third factor in the emergence of global, 'mega'-agencies has been the view that substantial benefits can be derived from the provision of an integrated undertaking communications service to clients. Thus, most of the rapidly expanding agencies have diversified their operations to include not only advertising and promotion but also other services including public relations, market research, consultancy, design, executive recruitment etc.

Think globally, act locally is still the dominant strategy of international advertisers but with a slight revision: *think globally, act regionally*. This implies that global headquarters has a central role to play in ensuring a globally consistent message while regional managers must have the autonomy to adapt advertising to local markets.

ICT and Global Marketing

It has been claimed that commercialisation of the WWW will revolutionise the study and practice of international marketing. Certainly the Internet has the potential to revolutionise many aspects of global marketing and strategy. Three main strategic applications of the internet in the context of internationalisation are: *a communications tool* supporting network relationships with overseas customers (actual and potential), agents, distributors, suppliers etc.; *a low cost export market research resource; a global marketing and promotions tool* through the design and effective marketing of company web sites and the development of integrated Internet supported strategies.

The Internet is potentially useful to both large and small companies operating in or wishing to enter global markets. It is a valuable tool for communicating both with customers and with other businesses. It is inexpensive to use and is therefore of particular value to small and medium sized enterprises wishing to operate internationally. Table-6 summarises the most significant effects of the internet on global marketing strategies.

TABLE 6
Effects of Internet on Global Marketing

	Effect	*Comment*
1.	Improved global communications with customers	The web allows businesses greater opportunity to communicate directly with their customers all over the world
2.	Improved global communications with other businesses	Suppliers and distributors all over the world can be contracted electronically. Materials etc. can be globally sourced via the web at low cost.

3.	Improved internal communications	The internet can be used to provide cheap and quick worldwide internal communications within a global business.
4.	Improved corporate image	The web site of a business can be used to present its corporate image.
5.	Finding new global customers	New customers can be attracted by the company's web site. Additionally new customers can be approached directly via the web on a worldwide basis
6.	Reduced market entry costs for small business	Small businesses were often deterred from entering global markets on the basis of the costs of market research, agents charges etc. The internet has reduced these costs substantially
7.	Global price standardisation	Marketing on the internet increases the advantages of and need for global price standardisation.
8.	Global market niche strategies	Niche markets can be accessed through groups on the web. Customers are also more able to access specialist services and products by searching the web
9.	Global marketing research tool	Access to information sources available on the internet
10.	Reduced importance of traditional marketing intermediaries	Agents etc. will be of less value to businesses entering international markets

One thing is certain: the impact of the internet on global marketing has increased and will increase further, particularly amongst small- and medium-sized enterprises. As we have seen, it is likely to influence global promotion, pricing, logistics and distribution and, indeed, permeates most aspects of global marketing. Managers in global businesses must assess the potential role of the internet in their global marketing strategies.

QUESTIONS

1. Discuss the role of marketing in global and transnational strategy.
2. Discuss the techniques for assessing the market sizes for given countries.
3. Discuss the major international considerations within the marketing mix: product, pricing, promotion, branding, and distribution.
4. Contrast practices of standardized *versus* differentiated marketing programmes for each country in which sales are made.
5. What are some of the fundamental issues that must be addressed in international advertising?
6. Are the four P's of international marketing of equal importance to all firms? What factors might cause some to be more or less important than others?
7. Discuss the effects of internet on global marketing.
8. The ethnocentric approach and the geocentric approach both suggest standardization of the marketing mix. What is the difference between these two approaches, if both lead to standardization?
9. Discuss the role of corporate headquarters in global advertising.

REFERENCES

Becker, H. and Thorelli, H. (eds.): Strategic planing in international marketing, in: *International Marketing Strategy*, Pergamon Press, New York, 1980.

Dox, Y. *Strategic Management in Multinational Companies*, Pergamon Press, New York, 1986.

Hamill, J. Global marketing, in: Baker M.J. (ed): *Perspective on Marketing Management*, 2, John Wiley, New York, 1992.

Keegan, W.J., Five strategies for multinational marketing, in: Thorelli, H. and Becker, H. (eds), *International Marketing Strategy*, Pergamon, New York, 1980.

Kotabe, M. and Helsen, K., *Global Marketing Management*, John Wiley, New York, 1998.

Leontiades, J. *Multinational Corporate Strategy: Planning for World Markets*, Lexington Books, Lexington, 1985.

Ohmae, K., *The Borderless World: Power and Strategy in the Inerlinked Economy*, Collins, London, 1990.

Toyne, B. and Walters, P.G.P., *Global Marketing Management: A strategic Perspective*, Allyn and Baco Boston, 1993.

Yip, G. *Total Global Strategy*, Prentice Hall, Englewood Cliffs, 1992.

28

EXPORT MANAGEMENT

INTRODUCTION

Countries engage in international trade for a variety of reasons. Exports are special because they can affect currency values and the fiscal and monetary policies of governments, shape public perception of competitiveness, and determine the level of imports a country can afford. Abroad, exports augment the availability and choice of goods and services for individuals, and improve the standard of living and quality of life. On the level of the firm, exports offer the opportunity for economies of scale. By broadening its market reach and serving customers abroad, a firm can produce more and do so more efficiently, which is particularly important if domestic sales are below break-even levels. As a result, the firm may achieve lower costs and higher profits both at home and abroad. Through exporting the firm benefits from market diversification, taking advantage of different growth rates in different markets, and gaining stability by not being overly dependent on any particular market. Exporting also lets the firm learn from the competition, makes it sensitive to different demand structures and cultural dimensions, and proves its ability to survive in a less familiar environment in spite of higher transaction costs. All these lessons can make the firm a stronger competitor at home. Finally, since exporting is only one possible international marketing strategy, it may well lead to the employment of additional strategies such as direct foreign investment, joint ventures, franchising or licensing—all of which contribute to the growth and economic strength of the firm, and, on an aggregate level, to the economic security of a nation.

STAGES OF EXPORT INVOLVEMENT

A systematic evaluation of export promotion programmes mandates identification of firms' export-related skills and needs for improvement. Various alternatives exist to differentiate firms and their level of export expertise. Given the increase research attention the export activities of firms have received, segmentation schemes abound. Some authors, for example, have focused on managerial attitudes. Other scrutinised the size of the firm, its service orientation, or differentiated between sporadic and regular exporters. Since firms' export involvement is a gradual learning process, which develops from a series of incremental decisions and over time draws some firms into the international market, export stages may be shown to segment most successfully between firms to evaluate the classification of firms by stage of export involvement.

Table-1 summarises the stages of internationalisation or export involvement. Although the number of discrete stages differs across the classification schemes, the description of the evolutionary pattern of export involvement is essentially identical. Therefore, a five-stage model may be employed by the produce exporter and the export traders. The major difference between the producer-exporter and the export trader is that the latter has the opportunity to buy products from (or act as an agent for) different producers in the same or different industries. In this respect, an export trader shares many of the same characteristics as an import trader. The "ownership advantages" of export traders typically lie in knowledge of markets in par-ticular countries or in knowledge of worldwide markets for particular products. They are also market connectors and face the same problems as pure importers once they have linked domestic producers with buyers in export markets.

In the early stage of export involvement, the internationalisation process is a consequence of incremental adjustments to the changing conditions of the firm and its environment, rather than a result of its deliberate strategy. Such a pattern is due to the consequence of greater uncertainty in international business, higher costs of information, and the lack of technical knowledge about international marketing activities.

Some firms progress to a more involved stage of internationalisation once three conditions are satisfied. *First*, the management of the firm obtains favourable expectations of the attractiveness of exporting based on experience. *Second*, the firm has access to key resources necessary for undertaking additional export-related tasks. Such availability of physical, financial, and managerial resources is closely associated with firm size. Particularly, small firms may have few trained managers, and little time for long-term planning as they are preoccupied with day-to-day operational problems, and consequently find it difficult to become involved in exporting. *Third*, management is willing to commit adequate resources to export activities. A high level of export commitment is evident in various ways, such as (1) existence of an export department or personnel, (2) development of direct export channels, and (3) frequent executive trips to foreign markets.

The long-term commitment of the firm to exporting depends on how successful management is in overcoming various barriers encountered in export activities. These barriers can be distinguished from those faced by firms in the earlier stage of internationalisation. An experienced exporter has to deal with difficulties in maintaining and expanding export involvement. These difficulties include import/export restrictions, cost and availability of shipping, exchange rate fluctuations, collection of money, and development of distribution channels, among others.

TABLE-1

Stages of Export Involvement

Stage 1: Partial interest in exporting	**Would fill an unsolicited export order, but make no effort to explore the feasibility of exporting**
Stage 2: Exploring exports	**Actively explore the feasibility of exporting, but currently exporting less than 5% of total sales**
Stage 3: Experimental exporter	**Exporting on an experimental basis to countries that are geographically close or that share a culture similarity, export sales represent a volume greater than 5% of total sales**
Stage 4: Experienced exporter with limited scope	**Experienced exporter with an export sales level greater than 5% of total sales, that adjusts export offerings optimally with changes in the foreign environment (e.g. exchange rates., tariffs, etc.) although still only exports to countries that are geographically close or have a similar culture**
Stage 5: Experienced exporter	**Experienced exporter with an export sales level greater than 5% of total sales, currently exploring the feasibility of exporting to additional countries that are farther away than previous exports, or have a very different culture**

Overall, favourable experience appears to be a key component in moving firms along the internationalisation continuum. To a large degree an appropriate measure of favourableness for firms consists of profits. An increase in profits due to a certain activity is likely to increase management's interest in such activity. Since profits are largely the compensation for the risk incurred by the firm, degrees of profitability should vary with the amount of risk taken, in order to produce similar levels of profit.

In the context of internationalisation, one should be able to compare degrees of profitability of domestic operations with those of international operations. Since international activities tend to involve greater distances, more complexity, and new factors, such as currency exchange rates, they are likely to be seen by firms as resulting in greater uncertainty. Such a rise in uncertainty is likely to lead to a perception of greater risk, which in turn requires compensation through higher degrees of profitability. In order for a firm to be enticed into international business rather than domestic expansion, international operations must produce at least the same level of profit as domestic activities. Therefore, the degree of profitability of international operations must be higher than of domestic operations.

A PERSPECTIVE ON EXPORT PROMOTION

Even though exports are important, in times of tight budget constraints and competing public priorities, it is important to ask why firms should be enticed into exporting through the use of public funds. Given the motivation of business activity by profit, one could argue that the profit opportunities for exporters should be enough of an incentive to motivate firms to export.

The Export Development Process

To explore this issue, it is helpful to understand the export development process within the firm. Typically, firms evolve along different stages to become experienced exporters. These stages start out with a firm being uninterested in things international. Management frequently will not even fill an unsolicited export order. Should such orders or other international market stimuli continue over time, however, a firm may move to the stage of export awareness, or even export interest. Management will begin to accumulate information about foreign markets and may consider the feasibility of exporting. At the export trial stage, the firm is likely to fill selected export orders, serve few customers, and expand into countries that are geographically close or culturally similar to the home country. At the export evaluation stage, firms consider the impact of exporting on overall corporate activities. If expectations placed in exporting are not met, the firm is likely to discontinue its export efforts and either seek alternative international growth opportunities or restrict itself to the domestic market. If the evaluation is positive, the firm will, over time, move on to become an export adapter, make frequent shipments to many customers in more countries, and incorporate international considerations into its planning.

In each one of these stages, firms have different concerns. For example, at the awareness level, firms worry mainly about information on foreign markets and customers. At the interest stage, firms become concerned about the mechanics of exporting. During the export try-out, communication, logistics, and the sales effort become key problems. At evaluation time, government regulations and financing take on greater importance. In the adaptation stage, service delivery and control are major issues.

This process of internationalization may be short-circuited at any stage if the results of export operations are not seen as favorable. Such a decision may be incorrect if the firm has not really given export operations the same attention that it has given domestic markets. Conversely, a firm may have no choice but to start at some more advanced stage. The domestic market may be too small to support any operations at all, much less a scale-efficient one. Increasingly, however, the evolution of the international trading environment has forced more and more firms at a faster and faster pace through these stages of internationalization to become full-fledged export marketers. Table-2 summarizes many of the key conceptual issues for each of the major export stages according to various features.

Here, it may be pointed that managing imports has received relatively little attention in international marketing or international business. Yet for every export, there is an import. And arm's-length importing still represents the majority of imports. However

TABLE-2

Conceptual Issues Emerging from Export Development Models

Model Features	Export Stages		
	Pre-Engagement	*Initial*	*Advanced*
(i) Facilitators and Inhibitors: Managerial characteristics	A number of objective and subjective managerial parameters might act as inhibitors in the firm's export engagement. of firms in export activities.	Certain managerial characteristics, such as cosmopolitan, multilingual and educated management, might facilitate the involvement	Management quality and dynamism is an important facilitator in advanced export operations,
Management style	The firm's management style applies only to the domestic business situation and it is rather institutionalized and structured. tend to become more formalized, continuous, and structured.	The decisionmaker approaches export marketing in a rather informal, disjointed, and unplanned manner.	With the establishment of appropriate systems and processes relating to foreign business, decision-making styles
Organizational determinants	Certain organizational determinants might prevent the engagement of the firm in foreign operations.	Some organizational factors. particularly those relating to the firm's competitive advantages, might facilitate the engagement of the firm in international operations.	The firm capitalizes on differential advantages, such as possession of unique products, competitive prices, and technological intensiveness, to gain a foothold in foreign markets.
Organizational resources	There is typically a limited number of corporate resources that are used exclusively for domestic, operations.	The firm gradually commits small amounts of financial, human, and allied resources to international operations, due to the high uncertainty prevailing in foreign markets.	An increasing amount of organizational resources is released to export operations, but their allocation is based upon real market conditions and strategic preferences.

cont...

Model Features	Export Stages		
	Pre-Engagement	*Initial*	*Advanced*
(ii) Information needs and acquisition:			
Information requirements	There is limited or no knowledge about export operations: firms actively seeking to export want and, information about foreign market possibilities.	The firm has limited experience and knowledge about exporting therefore, seeks information of a more experiential and general nature.	As the firm gains more experience and exposure to export activities, it searches for more objective and specific information,
Information acquisition	Lack of information about exporting results in high levels of uncertainty in international markets compared to the domestic market	The availability of information about export business and foreign marketing practices is still limited, thus creating considerable uncertainty. markets.	The firm gradually obtains more export-related information, particularly of an experiential nature, leading to reduced levels of uncertainty regarding overseas
(iii) Stimuli and barriers:			
Stimulating forces	The nonexporting firm is not responsive to various export stimuli to which it is exposed due to managerial, organizational, or environmental constraints.	The firm is more likely to be motivated in international business by reactive and external factors, exemplifying passive and tactical thinking toward exporting.	The export stimulation of the firm is more likely to occur due to proactive and internal factors, indicating an aggressive and strategic approach to international business.
Barrier factors	The would-be exporter is exposed to a number of export barriers, the most important being its inability to locate/analyze foreign markets.	The firm experiences obstacles that are related mainly to difficulties in understanding the mechanics and day-to-day activities of exporting.	Export obstacles are associated mainly with strategic marketing issues and external constraints in foreign markets,
(iv) Market selection, entry/expansion:			
Market selection	The firm deals exclusively with the domestic market from where it might choose to serve specific segments.	The firm selects few countries that are more psychologically close to its home business and, therefore, easier and less costly to penetrate.	The firm gradually expands its foreign operations to a greater number of host countries that are psychologically more distant

cont....

Model Features	Export Stages		
	Pre-Engagement	Initial	Advanced
Entry mode	The firm uses only domestic distribution methods since its goods are sold exclusively in the home market	The firm enters foreign markets via indirect export methods, such as export merchants, trading companies, resident buyers, and export agents.	The firm distributes its products to overseas markets using direct export methods, such as agents, distributors, and sales branches.
Market expansion	The firm is likely to undergo an extraregional expansion, that is, expansion within regions of its own country base. market focus.	Limited corporate resources, fear of the unknown, and other barriers are responsible for the firm adopting a concentrated foreign	As the firm acquires more resources, seeks to exploit more foreign opportunities, and gains expertise in handling export problems, it spreads to a large number of markets.
(v) Marketing strategy:			
Marketing control	The firm maintains full or partial control over the elements of the marketing mix, because it deals xclusively with the domestic	The firm is highly dependent on overseas buyers' guidelines and actions with regard to product, pricing, distribution, and promotional requirements in foreign markets.	The firm gradually internalizes and ultimately gains full control of the elements of the export e marketing mix strategy, market.
Marketing adaptations	The firm's marketing strategy is relatively standardized as it deals exclusively with local customers.	The firm is more likely to adopt more standardized export marketing strategies.	Considerable adaptations in the elements of the marketing mix are likely to take place, particularly as regards products and promotion.

Source: L. C. Leonidou and C. S. Katsikeas, 'The Export Development Process: An Integrative Review of Empirical Models," *Journal of International Business Studies*, Vol. 27, No. 3, 1996, pp. 532-33.

from the perspective of the importer, the export framework presented earlier cannot simply be turned inside out. As Table-3 points out, the assumed importer behaviors associated with the relevant export decisions are not identical with actual importer behavior. An importer assesses the comparative and competitive advantages of producers outside the home market; assesses the evolving demand and supply characteristics of the home market to look for gaps in markets or segments of markets that these producers' products could fill; assesses the impediments to connecting producers abroad with buyers in the home market and the factors that might facilitate this linkage; and assesses the channels of distribution that might be used to link producers abroad with buyers in the home market. An importer could either have the objective to resell the imported products (an import marketer) to other buyers or to use these products as raw or semifinished materials, or as components in its own final products (an import purchasing manager).

TABLE-3

Understanding Importer Behavior

Relevant Export Decisions	*Assumed Importer Behavior*	*Actual Importer Behavior*
Export initiation	• Exporters export to importers.	• "Global" importers recruit, select, train exporters.
	• Importers lured into importing when exporters offer better deals.	• Buyers forced into importing when existing vendors failed to meet task-requirement and nontask expectations.
Export targeting	• Importers search the world for best exporters.	• Importers search heuristically to minimize cognitive effort and risk.
	• Best vendors included in choice set via screening analysis.	• Choice set limited by accessibility in bilateral search and discovery.
	• Best importers always available, "out there"; no deadline in targeting.	• Search terminated when "good enough" vendor found,
Export entry	• Vendor evaluation is transaction-based, process objective, and analytical.	• Vendor evaluation is relationship-based, previous association important.
	• Vendor evaluation compensatory, all relevant factors considered.	• Vendor evaluation judgmental based on available info, and cognitive heuristics.
	• Best vendor chosen on the merits of export proposal (bid).	• Qualified vendor chosen for non-task-related benefits.
	• Export strategy based on 4Ps.	• More than 4Ps at work.

Export management	• Exporters are the prime movers of international trade.	• World markets are increasingly "buyer's markets"; much international exchange is buyer-coordinated importing rather than producer-initiated exporting.
	• Importers implement export strategy formulated/supported by exporters.	• Importers have strategies of their own.
	• Export marketing decision controlled by exporters.	• Importers may take control of export marketing decisions in importer-led international exchange.

Source: N. Liang and A. Parkhe, "Importer Behavior: The Neglected Counterpart of International Exchange," *Journal of International Business Studies*, Vol. 28, No. 3, 1997, p. 523.

Pure importers usually have an "ownership advantage" related to the domestic market in which they operate, such as knowledge of the domestic market, ownership of or access to the channels of distribution, or expertise in evaluating government regulation of imports, or business practices in the domestic market. Importers typically possess one of two other ownership advantages: knowledge and expertise in operations in one or more foreign countries or knowledge and expertise in the production capabilities of some product or range of products worldwide. The knowledge of domestic conditions allows importers to create value for producers abroad relative to the value they could access by exporting directly to buyers in the domestic economy. Knowledge of production capabilities worldwide allows them to create value for domestic producers (for imported inputs) and domestic retailers relative to the value they would receive if they tried to search out these products for themselves.

Pure importers are market connectors; they create value through linking producers abroad to buyers in the domestic market. If they do not continue to create value after the initial link has been made, producers abroad may begin to sell directly to the buyers in the domestic market. Similarly, purchasers in their domestic market will make direct connections with producers abroad.

A Divergence of Profit and Risk

As a firm moves through these stages, unusual things can happen to both risk and profit. In light of the gradual development of expertise, the many concerns, and a firm's uncertainty with the new environment it is about to enter, management's perception of risk exposure grows. In its previous domestic expansion, the firm has gradually learned about the market, and therefore managed to have its risk decline. In the course of international expansion, the firm now encounters new factors such as currency exchange rates and their vagaries, greater distances, new modes of transportation, new government regulations, new legal and financial systems, new languages, and cultural diversity. As a result, the firm is exposed to increased risk. At the same time, due to the investment needs of the exporting effort, in areas such as information acquisition, market research, and trade financing the immediate profit performance may deteriorate. Even though international market familiarity and diversification effects are likely to reduce the risk below the previous "domestic only" level, and increase profitability as well, in the short and medium term, managers may face an unusual and perhaps unacceptable situation—rising risk accompanied by decreasing profitability. In light of this reality, and not knowing whether there will be a pot of gold at the end of the rainbow, many executives either do not initiate export activities or discontinue them. A temporary gap in the working of market forces seems to exist. Government export assistance can help firms over this rough patch to the point where profits increase and risk heads downward. Bridging this short-term market gap may well be the key role of export assistance; and the major justification for the involvement of the public sector. Figure-1 illustrates this process.

FIGURE-1

PROFIT AND RISK DURING EXPORT INITIATION

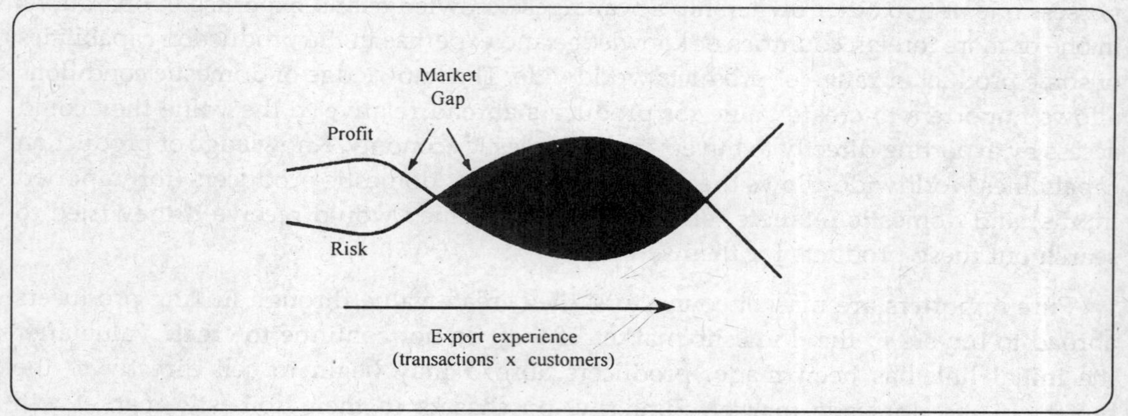

Linkages Among Assistance Components

If export assistance and promotion are to be rendered, it becomes important to consider how budgets and efforts should be expended in order to be most effective. Figure 2 provides a structural perspective of the linkage between export assistance, the firm, the international market and, eventually export performance. The firm is separated into its organisational and its managerial dimensions. Organisational key determinants of business and export success are size, human and financial resources, technology, service and quality orientation, information system, research capabilities, market insights and connections, and the firm's capabilities to manage regulations. The managerial characteristics that research has most closely linked to export success are education, international exposure, expertise, international orientation, and commitment. These

FIGURE-2

EXPORT ASSISTANCE AND PERFORMANCE—A STRUCTURAL MODEL

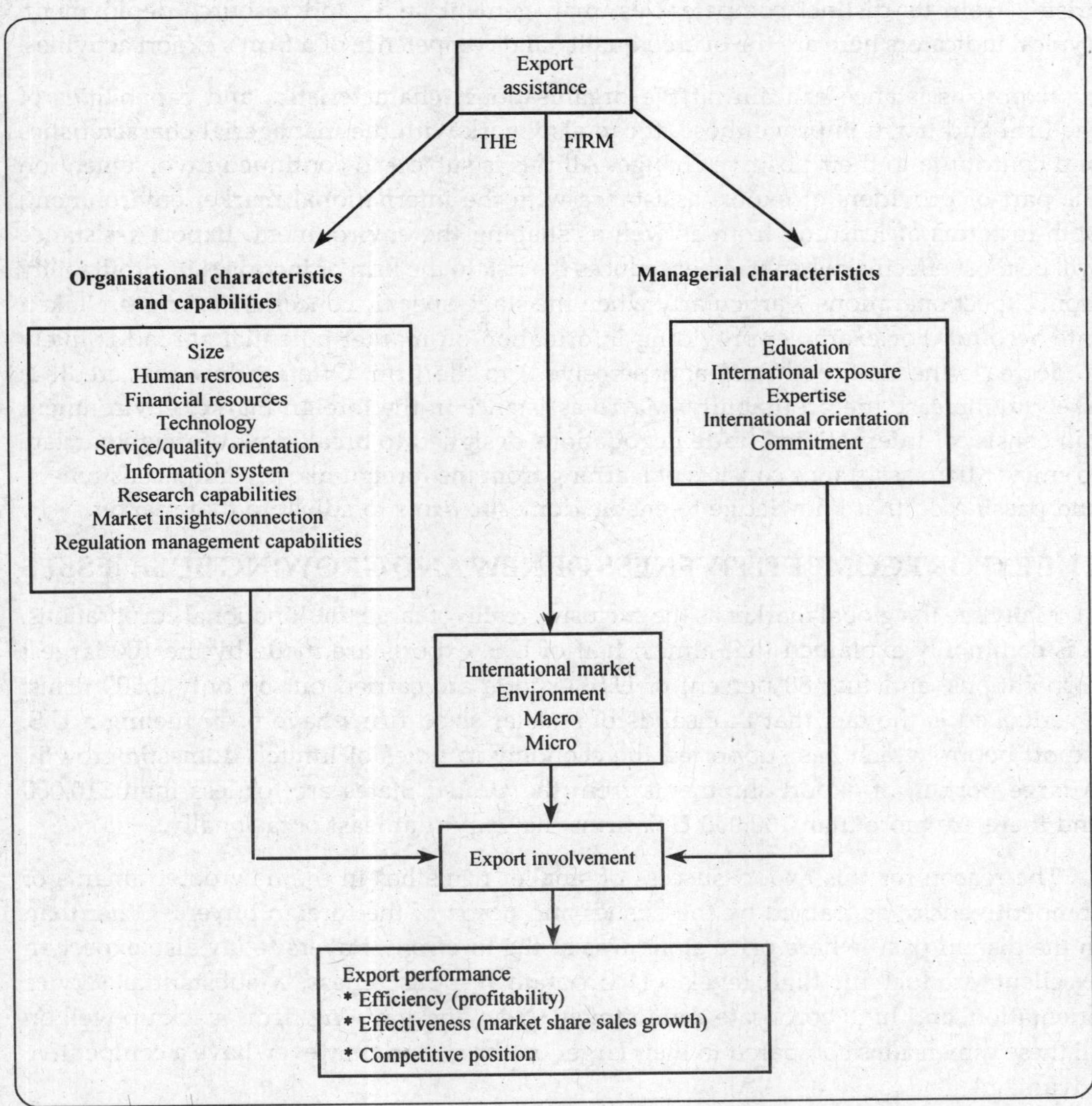

corporate dimensions, subject to the opportunities and constraints of the international market environment, determine the degree of the firm's export involvement. This involvement in turn will result in export performance, which can be measured in three different ways. Efficiency refers to the relationship between corporate input employed and the resulting outputs achieved. Typically, efficiency is measured through the proxy of export profitability. Effectiveness refers to relative business success when compared to other competitors in the market, and is often measured in terms of market share and export sales growth. Competitive position addresses the (overall strength of a firm arising from its distinct competencies, management style, and resource deployment. Typical indicators here are the overall quality and competence of a firm's export activities.

Export assistance can aim at the organisational characteristics and capabilities of the firm and try to improve those. It can also work with the managerial characteristics and contribute to their positive change. All this is subject to continued involvement on the part of providers of export assistance with the international market environment, both in terms of learning from as well as shaping the environment. Export assistance will be most effective when it either reduces the risk to the firm or increases its profitability from expect operations, particularly when the stage-specific concerns of firms are taken into account. For example, providing information on market potential abroad is likely to decrease the risk (both real and perceived) to the firm. Offering low-cost credit is likely to increase the profitability. Macro assistance in the foreign market environment can consist of international trade negotiations designed to break down foreign barriers to entry. Micro assistance consists of learning from the foreign market and its customers, and passing on that knowledge to enable domestic firms to adjust to that market.

THE EXPORT COMPETITIVENESS OF NEW AND GROWING BUSINESSES

Many see the global market as the exclusive realm of large, multinational corporations. It is commonly explained that almost half of U.S. exports are made by the 100 largest corporations, and that 80 percent of U.S. exports are carried out by only 2,500 firms. Overlooked is the fact that thousands of smaller sized firms have been fueling a U.S. export boom, which has supported the economy in times of limited domestic growth. A large portion of export shipments from the United States are for less than $10,000 and there are more than 100,000 U.S. firms that export at least occasionally.

The reason for this export success of smaller firms lies in the new determinants of competitiveness, as framed by the wishes and needs of the foreign buyers. Other than in the distant past, where price alone was at the forefront, buyers today also expect an excellent product fit, high levels of corporate responsiveness, a substantial service orientation, and high corporate commitment. New and growing firms stack up well on all these dimensions compared to their larger brethren, and may even have a competitive advantage.

Take the issue of product fit. In today's era of niche marketing, where specialisation rather than mass production is prized, the customisation of operations is often crucial, In a large corporate system, changes are often subject to delays as various layers of management are consulted, costs recalculated, and multiple communication levels exercised. In a smaller operation, procedures can more easily be adapted to the special needs of the customer or to local requirements.

Smaller firms can offer clearer lines of accountability since the decision maker can be more visible and responsive to the customer. During negotiations, or later on, if something does not go according to plan, the customer knows who to contact to fix the problem. Smaller firms are better equipped to handle exceptions. Since international sales situations have high variability, either in terms of the timing or the nature of the sale, a smaller firm can provide a more flexible framework for the decision process. Exceptions can be handled when they occur rather than after waiting for concurrence from other levels of the organisation. Smaller firms offer their customers better inward and outward communication linkages, which are direct between the provider of a service or product and its user. The result is a short response time. If a special situation should arise, response can be immediate, direct, and predictable to the customer, providing precisely those competitive ingredients that reduce risk and costs.

Smaller firms also have the most to gain from the experience curve effects of exporting. Each time cumulative output of a firm doubles, the costs on value added decrease. Due to the small original base, it is much easier for a new or growing business to double cumulative output and reap the resulting benefits than it is for a large established firm. Most importantly, once a small firm goes international, it usually does so with the full commitment of the owner and top management. The foreign customer therefore knows that this is activity which has management's heart and soul behind it. In today's times where we are moving, on a global level, away from transaction marketing and toward relationship marketing, such a perception may be crucial in providing the winning edge.

COPING WITH OBSTACLES

All these advantages do not remove the existing obstacles to international market prosperity. Smaller firms in particular tend to encounter five types of export-related problem areas. One of these concerns logistics—arranging transportation, determining transport rates, handling documentation, obtaining financial information, coordinating distribution, packaging, and obtaining insurance. Another one consists of legal procedures and typically covers government red tape, product liability, licensing, and customs/duty issues. The servicing of exports is a third area, where the firm needs to provide parts availability, repair service, and technical advice. Sales promotion is a fourth area; firms need to cope with advertising, sales effort, and the obtaining of marketing information. The fifth problem area concerns foreign market intelligence, which covers information on the location of markets, trade restrictions, and competition overseas.

These obstacles, both real and perceived, often prevent firms from exporting. Many managers often see only the risks involved in exporting rather than the opportunities that the international market can present.

BOOSTING EXPORT COMPETITIVENESS

In a globalising world, export success can serve as a measure for the competitiveness of a country's industries. Changing pattern of world trade shows that the technological context of export competitiveness is changing rapidly. There is a consistent trend for exports of technology-intensive products to grow faster than others. Manufactured exports as a whole expand far more rapidly than primary products. Within manufactured exports, growth rises with technological complexity. As a consequence, there are large changes in trade share by technological category. Complex (high- and medium-technology) manufactured products are the most dynamic element in world trade. In the 50 fastest-growing manufactures in world trade, they account for over 60 per cent. The leading four are all high-technology electronics products; together they accounted for one third of the value of dynamic exports in 1995 and for 37 per cent of the growth in value since 1980. High—and medium-technology products in the group accounted for three-quarters of the total value of dynamic exports and just under half of all manufactured exports in 1995. This trend has continued beyond 1995.

What does this mean for export competitiveness? Markets for technologically complex products are growing faster than those for other products because of the higher income elasticity of demand and greater scope for product innovation and productivity increases. Thus, it is easier for a country to sustain export growth if it can establish a competitive position in these products rather than in traditional resource-based or simple labour-intensive products. It is still possible to grow rapidly in slow-growing product groups, by specialising in dynamic products or by expanding market shares. Some low-technology products face slow demand growth and technological change, but enjoy rapid trade growth because of rapid relocation of production from high- to low-wage countries. This is the case, for example, with recent growth of exports of clothing and footwear. However, growth is likely to slow as the restructuring process matures. More importantly, a competitive position in such products is vulnerable to easy entry by new, lower-wage competitors. The simultaneous entry of several producers can create a glut and considerably lower prices. It is possible to establish more secure, high-value niches by entering high-quality segments, but this is difficult. It requires advanced technological and marketing capabilities, and until now largely remains the preserve of industrialised countries and established traders. Export success among developing countries has been concentrated in a few countries. The comparative advantage of most developing countries lies traditionally in primary commodities and unskilled-labour-intensive manufactures. Over time, as they grow and accumulate capital and skills, and wages rise, their competitive base has to change. They have to upgrade their primary and labour-intensive exports into higher value-added items, and they have to move into new, more advanced, export-oriented activities. Both require greater inputs of skill and technology. Countries can attain these objectives in several ways: by improving and deepening the capabilities of domestic enterprises, by tapping into TNC networks as conduits for trade, or by attracting FDI into export activities and upgrading these activities over time. These strategies may be complementary or alternatives. In most cases they are found together, but different countries deploy different combinations of domestic enterprise-led and FDI-led export development. Neither strategy is easy. Export sustainability requires that developing countries push into these segments, but also that they diversify into more complex, dynamic products as much as they can. Diversification has another important benefit: low-technology products generally offer limited scope for learning and beneficial technological spillovers in comparison to complex products. Thus, export dynamism has large overlaps with industrial and technological deepening.

Past strategies of protected import substitution have often held developing economies back from exploiting fully their initial endowments or creating new skill- or technology-based advantages. Trade and investment liberalisation can stimulate both. But it may not suffice by itself. Developing countries face pervasive market, structural and institutional deficiencies that can diminish or abort a vigorous response to market signals. It is necessary to calibrate trade liberalisation to the pace at which supply capabilities can develop, and to develop the requisite skill, capital, technology, and other capabilities. Otherwise, a leap into the world of technology- or skill-based competitiveness and growth may prove impossible or exceptionally difficult.

It is not easy for developing countries to launch new exports. They face problems in reaching world levels of productivity and quality. It is costly to collect information about consumer needs and designs or the requirements of industrial firms (where they are exporting intermediate products). Delivery and effective marketing are also difficult. These problems rise with the technical complexity and differentiation of a product. The easiest segments to enter involve simple production processes with low skill needs, no scale economies, undifferentiated products and stable technologies. The most difficult involve complex processes with high learning and skill requirements, rapidly changing technologies, large economies of scale or scope, branded products and after-sale servicing needs. These difficulties notwithstanding, developing countries need to make every effort to enter export markets. TNCs can help in this effort.

ROLE OF FDI IN BUILDING EXPORT COMPETITIVENESS

TNCs impact on export competitiveness in a variety of ways, both positively and negatively. Their greatest potential contribution lies in difficult technology- and marketing-intensive products, where they have the largest ownership advantages over other firms. There are, of course, different kinds of TNCs. The large globalised firms from industrial countries can promote exports best in complex or branded products. TNCs from developing countries or smaller firms from industrial countries might promote exports of simpler or less marketing-intensive products, or increase regional exports. The pattern of manufacturing export success in the developing world is highly skewed. A small number of countries dominate manufactured export activity, with concentration level rising by level of technological sophistication. While there are differences in specialisation, the same economies appear in the list of top exporters of most product categories.

1. Technology and Trade Patterns

Reflecting TNC strategies and host country conditions, the role of TNCs in manufactured exports, disaggregated by different technological categories, has varied among countries and over time.

Low-technology Activities

TNCs from developed countries played a critical role in the initial stages in stimulating labour-intensive exports from developing countries; TNCs from developing countries become more important in later stages. The evolution differed by host region and country, largely reflecting the growth of local capabilities. International production involving labour-intensive activities, led by clothing, started in the 1960s, when developed countries eased their import barriers and facilitated offshore processing by granting tariff privileges. Declining transport costs and the liberalisation of FDI regimes made the process economical. The developing countries that attracted export-oriented FDI had low-cost semiskilled labour. But they also had more: attractive fiscal incentives, export-oriented production facilities like export processing zones (EPZs) and infrastructure, and, in the successful cases, a cadre of skilled technicians and managers.

Medium and High-Technology Activities

The export role of FDI, particularly by TNCs from developed countries, has understandably been larger in complex industrial activities. Again, this role has varied by country, and has been especially important in three types of activities: *offshore assembly, mature infant industries* and *large-scale processing of natural resources for exports.*

a) *Offshore assembly* for export is concentrated in electrical and electronic industries, with some activity in automotive and other engineering products. The activity tends to have low local content and take place in EPZs, in relative isolation from the domestic economy of host countries. While its determinants—low labour costs—are similar to those of low-technology export-oriented activities, high-technology activity differs in its organisation. It is predominantly a part of integrated TNC systems (making subcontracting to independent local firms difficult); advanced technological functions and processes remain in the home countries. These systems have developed complex specialisation patterns, with assembly facilities being set up in emerging newly- industrialising economies, more advanced facilities in mature newly-industrialising economies, and design in home countries.

b) The second type of complex export-oriented activity involves *mature infant industries* and is an outgrowth of import substitution, from industries being restructured because of economic liberalisation. In most large import-substituting economies with a large foreign presence, such as Mexico and Argentina, TNCs lead the export surge. The most striking example is the automotive industry, now the single largest manufactured exporter from Latin America.

c) The third type of TNC activity involves *large-scale processing of natural resources* for export. Unlike earlier resource-extracting activities that had little local value added, this activity involves large new world-class plants, high levels of local skills and tight integration into international networks.

Given the advanced technological, manufacturing and marketing capabilities required, few developing economies have important local exporters of sophisticated manufactures. The main exceptions are the Republic of Korea and Taiwan Province of China. They pursued relatively autonomous technological strategies and built up the skill base to enable export competitiveness. As local enterprises acquired competence and government policies increasingly favoured national ownership, the direct role of TNCs diminished. Their indirect role, particularly via licensing or original equipment manufacture arrangements, continued. As local firms grew and became international competitors, it became harder for them to obtain technology from TNCs. Independent R&D then became vital in order to copy, absorb and create technology; the leading firms set up large research and design departments and invested heavily in innovation. More recently, they have begun to use strategic alliances with leading foreign TNCs to expand their technology base. All in all, the autonomous strategy has given these economies much greater local content in sophisticated manufacturing and industrial depth.

However, this skilful mix of strategy has succeeded in only a few cases — most countries have been unable to meet the skill, information and bureaucratic demands of this strategy to mount efficiently the range and depth of policies needed for domestic capacity-building. Furthermore, under the new rules of the game, the scope for industrial policies that favour domestic capacity-building is diminishing. A number of the tools used for example by the Asian newly- industrialising economies are no longer permitted today for advanced developing countries, or are difficult to apply. Technologies are changing much faster and production systems are more integrated, and are raising the barriers of entry into sophisticated markets. In the future, developing countries may well use TNCs more to move into advanced export activity, either through FDI or by tapping into TNC distribution systems.

Indeed, elsewhere in the developing world, for complex products, an FDI-assisted export strategy has been more common than local enterprise-led export strategies. A substantial proportion of such manufactured exports from developing countries comes from foreign affiliates, and a significant part of this takes the form of intra-firm trade. An FDI assisted export strategy can provide rapid entry into complex activities, along with continuous access to new technologies and close integration into global markets and networks. The result can be impressive export growth; indeed, the relocation of labour-intensive processes in high technology activities has been a major factor in the recent export growth and diversification in the developing world.

However, this strategy is not without costs and risks. Most exports start at the bottom of the skill and technology ladder. The risk is that an erosion of competitiveness (as wages rise or technologies change) follows a burst of exports based on low-wage advantages. Unless the country improves its skill, technology, supplier and infrastructure base, the FDI-assisted route can run out of steam; the creation of backward linkages is particularly important here. As with domestic firm-based strategies, therefore, the upgrading of local factors and institutions becomes vital under FDI-assisted strategies once inherited advantages reach their limit. The only difference may be that the static base of competitive advantage lasts longer under an FDI assisted strategy.

It would be wrong, therefore, to consider the two policy approaches - domestic-enterprise based *versus* TNC-assisted export drives - as mutually exclusive. Indeed, both have worked as far as exports are concerned. In many instances they are mutually supportive. A strong base of local capabilities can attract higher quality, technologically more advanced FDI, with greater local linkages and spillovers. Over time, a more rapid growth of local skills and capabilities can induce faster and greater upgrading of affiliate activities. The competitiveness of the domestic industrial sector can benefit from a stronger TNC presence and competition. A large, export-oriented TNC base can stimulate greater competence in local firms and provide stronger direct links to global markets and technologies. As local firms grow in competence, they can themselves go transnational, or enter strategic alliances with other TNCs.

2. Expanding Market Access for Exports

Foreign affiliates have several potential advantages over local firms in developing host countries in accessing and serving foreign markets. Assuming identical production costs, therefore, they can export more from a host economy than their local counterparts in products where such marketing advantages are significant. Affiliates draw an advantage from the very fact of being part of a TNC system and hence being able to use the system's physical distribution network or exploit their parent firms' links with customers. The parent company may have strong links with buyers in importing countries; such links are important in getting orders of customised industrial products or projects (e.g. capital goods, specialised components or turnkey plants). Again, these are difficult for new entrants to replicate. Foreign affiliates also face lower transaction costs and have other marketing advantages in exporting than do local firms. They have access to established brand names, warehousing, transport facilities and marketing links, trade finance and channels overseas. Affiliates often can use established brand names which are particularly important in differentiated consumer products. Competing local firms face a severe handicap in having to sell unbranded products, unless they are able to invest the large sums needed to develop independent brands (and the distribution and servicing they require), or a TNC is willing to franchise or license the use of its brand. Both can happen. Some developing country firms have gained the size and spread to build up global brands, but they are few and primarily from advanced newly-industrialising economies. TNCs allow independent firms to sell under their brands, under *original equipment manufacture* (OEM) arrangements, as in electronics, or under international subcontracting, as in clothing.

A number of foreign affiliates are parts of integrated international production systems. Such systems can be of two types (or their combination): different stages of production located in different countries, or different components each sourced from several countries. The first system entails different processes at different levels of technology, spread over countries according to factor costs and capabilities. The second involves distribution of similar production activities across affiliates in countries with similar capabilities. In the latter case, production facilities are distributed geographically to diversify risk, reap scale economies or meet government demands (say, to achieve a rough balance in trade or maintain employment). For instance, automobile firms spread their engine and component manufacture over several countries. While it is possible for non-affiliates to export via such networks, the transaction and coordination costs of participation can be high. The costs rise with the complexity of a network, sophistication and proprietary value of technology, frequency of changes, and speed of response required. Consequently, TNCs are unlikely to involve independent firms deeply in such networks unless the product is simple and standardised, or the independent firm is a specialised supplier of long standing.

Finally, foreign affiliates may have easier access to developed country markets, or face lower tariffs there, because of lobbying by parent companies. One important form of access is favourable treatment of offshore processing (with duties imposed only on value-added overseas). This is favoured by TNCs seeking to relocate labour-intensive processes in low wage areas to maintain competitiveness. The growth of *maquiladora* exports from Mexico, for instance, owes greatly to such treatment by the Government of the United States. TNCs in many developed countries press for provisions of this sort, while trade unions in the home countries tend to oppose them to prevent the "export of jobs".

Being part of TNC systems can also have costs for export competitiveness. Affiliates have to conform to sourcing and location patterns imposed by the parent firm. They are more prone than domestic firms to source inputs as imports from overseas. This may be from other affiliates in the TNC network, or from established suppliers based in the home country or third countries. A high import propensity of affiliates is observed in both low- and high- technological industries - in the former, since affiliates are often limited to processing imported inputs; in the latter, because affiliates' production is capital-intensive or requires sophisticated inputs not available locally. Import intensity can be high in some services industries as well, notably in tourism. Here, one observes problems of leakages, especially in the case of luxury tourism under franchises in low-income developing countries. Capital and consumption goods not available locally are imported, and profits remitted, thus cutting into the export earnings generated.

Where the parent firm has a regional or global strategy (many do not), affiliates cannot choose whether to export, or, if they do, which markets to serve. TNCs do not encourage competition among affiliates. Where they have affiliates in different markets, they may prohibit competing exports. The process of deep integration then takes a different direction. Infact, there is a possibility that, in a liberalised world, TNCs may centralise production in a few larger-scale facilities. This can boost exports from affiliates that become such bases, but lower or eliminate exports from others, converting them into sale or final-assembly bases. Only to the extent that the process is cumulative, will successful affiliates will deepen their capabilities and pull further ahead of others. In these circumstances, local firms may actually do better than affiliates operating as part of a TNC network because they are not subject to such market access decisions. However, to take advantage of their freedom they must have the technological and marketing capabilities to match TNC competitors.

The role of TNCs in export markets is large and growing. In fact, to support their competitive positions, successful national exporters themselves tend to go transnational, investing in developing as well as developed countries. Firms linked to TNCs tend to follow them overseas with supporting production facilities. With growing liberalisation and globalisation, such trends will intensify. This does not necessarily mean that the same set of TNCs from the same home countries will benefit and increase their dominance of world trade. The identity of competitive firms is constantly changing, and increasing numbers will hail from developing countries. Their market shares are, of course, difficult to predict. But a portfolio of locational assets will be increasingly important for their international competitiveness, and hence will lead to the further growth of developing country export-oriented FDI.

3. Building Dynamic Comparative Advantages

Many developing host countries expect TNCs to be agents for the creation of dynamic comparative advantage, particularly in the export of manufactured products. Dynamism can take many different forms, depending on the nature of the host economy and the time-frame considered. In the short term, it can mean moving up to the next level of technological complexity: for a developing country with unprocessed primary exports and endowments of unskilled labour, dynamism means the launching of simple manufactured exports. For countries established in simple exports, it means the shift to higher value added products using relatively simple technologies. For those with a more diverse base of exports, it means entry into high technology products, and so on. In the long term, dynamism means not just the shift up the skill and technology scale in particular activities, but also *deepening the content* of export activity and *building the capacity* to sustain such a shift across a range of tradable activities in response to changing world demand and technologies. This means, in turn, that export activity needs to lead to greater local content in terms of labour, resources and intermediate products, more complex technological functions (design and development), and more intense linkages with the local technology system.

There are several reasons why countries may expect TNCs to dynamise their comparative advantage in all these cases. TNCs are considered well placed—relative to local firms—to provide the tangible and intangible assets needed to transform existing resources, skills and technical competence to world levels. They are believed to be better able to overcome the cost of marketing overseas, providing the information, marketing, brand name and other assets needed to generate exports. Over time, they can keep up more readily with changing technologies and shifting demand in different markets. At the same time, developing countries worry that TNCs transfer the technologies and skills that use their existing resources and capabilities, but do not do enough to upgrade or deepen them.

Both perceptions can be valid—the extent depends on the specific country context. TNCs *can* dynamise comparative advantage, but only where the host economy is able to mount the right policies and improve the base of capabilities that investors draw upon. Or, they also may not provide the dynamic benefits that comparable local firms doThe technological deepening of foreign affiliates, their local linkages and their spillover benefits may be less than those of comparable local firms. However, this is only so where comparable local firms exist in activities undertaken by foreign affiliates, or where a country is able to mount the policies needed to enable local firms to develop the necessary capabilities. Generalisations are difficult. What is possible is to review existing, often patchy, data on the contribution of TNCs to export activity and qualitative evidence on its upgrading in particular countries.

A useful indicator to start with is the share of foreign affiliates in merchandise exports. The evidence shows large differences in these shares across a number of countries, reflecting their locational advantages as export bases. Countries with a low level of FDI (such as Japan) or with low locational advantages have very low shares. Countries with a large FDI presence and strong locational advantages such as close proximity to, and integration with, a large market (Canada), or input cost advantages (Hungary, Singapore, Malaysia and China), have high shares. The shares of foreign affiliates in exports can also vary greatly by industry, as exemplified by a comparison of the Czech Republic and Hungary. Such variations in foreign affiliate shares in national exports are to be expected. They reflect differences in the amount and type of FDI a country receives and the relative export competence of domestic enterprises and foreign affiliates.

Important questions arise relating to the export performance of TNCs in a more dynamic setting. *How do they react as technology changes and wages and other costs rise in a developing host country, making it uneconomical as an export site? Do they dynamise comparative advantage by upgrading facilities and local capabilities or do they move their facilities to cheaper locations?*

Both outcomes are possible. Which happens depends on the industry, the technology and host-country factors. From the perspective of TNCs, the main considerations are the rate at which costs are rising, the possibility of offsetting this by improved technology and the cost of implementing that technology, weighed against the costs of relocating. Relocation costs depend on the sunk costs. Operations for which sunk costs tend to be low and technical change incremental--simple activities with low costs of training and so on--tend to relocate rather than dynamise capabilities in their original location. This is often (but not always) the case with such activities as clothing and footwear. By contrast, industries with high sunk costs tend to "stick", unless the technological change is so drastic that it either becomes economical (despite sunk costs) to relocate or it is not possible to use new technology at the old location. Apart from that, the capacity of affiliates to absorb new technologies plays a role, as do efforts by governments to retain and upgrade investment. Shifting comparative advantage due to technological upgrading may explain the changing export propensities of United States foreign affiliates. Over time, their export propensities have declined in some regions (e.g. Asia) and risen in others (e.g. Latin America). This may reflect that, in Asia, the rising cost of producing simpler export-oriented products in which most Asian countries had a comparative advantage at an earlier stage has not yet been offset by increased competitiveness in more technology-intensive products.

The upgrading of comparative advantage is not a discrete "either/or" decision. There are many possible levels of upgrading, depending on the ability of a host economy to provide the capabilities needed. For instance, TNCs can train employees, but only if the base of formal qualifications needed is present. They can develop the skills for advanced product design locally only if enough design engineers are available. They can import more advanced equipment, but only if local staff can be trained at reasonable cost to use it at world levels of efficiency. Importing skilled personnel can relax the skill constraint temporarily, but this is an expensive solution that can only be used for a small number of high level tasks. Therefore, building up a strong education base that facilitates skills upgrading is indispensable.

FDI can also act as catalyst for the restructuring of domestic firms, directly in those linked to TNCs, or indirectly by intensified competition between domestic firms and foreign affiliates. This is particularly the case in growing industries, e.g. software in India. But countries cannot rely on TNCs alone to advance restructuring. In the textile and clothing industry, for example, where subcontracting arrangements with TNCs are predominant, the availability of a wide range of potential subcontractors in different host countries means that a subcontractor may be cut out of export markets at short notice. The limited relationships that exists between subcontractors and TNC buyers, and the absence of links with the ultimate clients, make it difficult for domestic firms to build dynamic comparative advantages and restructure their activities. However, firms that develop a sustained relationship with buyers can move up the value chain, even to the point where they can develop their own brand names. In general, judging from the experience of Asian newly-industrialising economies, successful restructuring in the textile and clothing industry in developing countries require substantial effort by local firms, backed by government support, to improve their capabilities (including through outward FDI into low-cost locations), learn (including from TNCs) how to compete in international markets, and develop their own marketing channels.

Restructuring by TNCs also implies that small or relatively inefficient import substituting affiliates may have to be wound down, or merged with larger, more viable firms, as affiliates are exposed to world competition. The economic determinants of these processes have been noted: the level of capabilities in existence, the distance from competitive frontiers and the efficacy of policies and institutions to support upgrading. The larger the distance, and the less adequate the policy measures to improve factors - or, to provide direct aid to restructuring firms or areas as done extensively in developed countries - the greater the likelihood of there being losers. Strategic factors include a INC's view of a particular location in its global and regional operations, its assessment of country risk, the competitive pressures it faces and its technological strengths and weaknesses.

The interaction of these factors causes continuous changes in the location of activities and sourcing of supplies by TNCs. For instance, in the automobile industry, TNCs are shifting their plants and suppliers across countries in line with changing locational advantages as well as corporate strategies. Corporate strategic differences aside, the response of TNCs is likely to be similar to that of other firms. However, for obvious reasons, it is likely to be more rapid and definitive.

ISSUES RELATED TO THE ROLE OF FDI IN BOOSTING EXPORT COMPETITIVENESS

There are several sets of policy issues related to the role of FDI in boosting export competitiveness in developing countries. Some of the main issues for different groups of developing countries are:

i) For countries with strong national innovation systems and exports led by national enterprises, the main issues include the following: Can their enterprises and institutions continue to cope with the rapid pace of technical change and keep up with world technology frontiers? *Can they move from imitation and absorption to genuine innovation? Can they keep ahead of emerging competition from cheaper countries and make inroads into markets held by the more advanced industrial countries? What role should inward FDI play in maintaining export competitiveness? How should national enterprises relate to TNCs, both as competitors and as potential collaborators?*

ii) For countries that have entered areas of dynamic comparative advantage assisted by TNCs, the issues relate to sustainability and upgrading. *Can they continue to attract TNCs that source high-technology products as their wages rise and cheaper competitors appear? How can they induce higher local content and technological depth in local affiliate operations? How can they ensure beneficial spillovers from TNCs to local firms? More generally, how can they strengthen their national innovation systems to ensure that they graduate to sustained growth in sophisticated manufacturing by both TNCs and local firms?*

iii) For countries that have attracted FDI into low technology export activity but have failed to diversify their export base or to move into higher value products, the main issues concern broadening the competitive base. *How much can they upgrade their exports into less vulnerable, more value added products within the low technology groups? How can they diversify into more complex activities? How can they attract TNCs into a different set of activities and build more advanced domestic skills and capabilities?*

iv) For countries that have built up sizeable industries behind protective walls but have not made the transition to dynamic export growth by either foreign or local enterprises, the issues relate to the incentive regime and industrial restructuring. *What is the best way to liberalise in order to build upon the existing base of capabilities and make the FDI regime competitive? How can existing industries be reoriented and upgraded to become export competitive? How can foreign affiliates be induced to integrate their operations better into their parent companies' global operations? How can new export-oriented FDI be attracted, initially to a range of activities and over time to higher technology activities? What role can TNCs play in restructuring domestic firms? What can be done to re-gear the national technology system to international competitiveness?*

v) For countries with weak industries, marginalised in export growth and FDI, the issues relate to their ability to attract FDI and to stimulate industrial growth in general. *How can they improve their investment climate and attract manufacturing FDI? What is the best way to create the basic skills and institutions needed to promote learning in simple industrial activities and diversify production from the primary sector? How can they attract investments, as a first step, into the low technology activities becoming uncompetitive in more advanced developing countries? What needs to be done to upgrade traditional SMEs to participate in manufactured export activity?*

In view of the objective of enhancing export competitiveness, a common set of preconditions and issues runs through all of these groups. The preconditions encompass prudent macroeconomic management - especially of the exchange rate - and an institutional environment conducive to exporting. The common issues relate to liberalising FDI and trade regimes; attracting export-oriented FDI and upgrading TNC activity; and strengthening domestic skills, capabilities and institutions. Each of these has a vital role to play in realising the role of FDI in generating and upgrading exports. The precise nature of the policy problems differ, however, according to the level of national capabilities and development, the nature of the policy regime and the form of participation in TNC networks.

The *first* set of policy measures relates to liberalisation. The new institutions and rules of international trade and especially the nature of technological change suggest that globalisation will continue. In this new context, the way to raise productivity and living standards lies in greater participation in international investment and trade - albeit with due preparation to ensure that liberalisation does not lead to economic devastation or technological stagnation. The pace of liberalisation has to be calibrated to ensure that domestic capabilities improve and the productive structure is upgraded. The rules of the game may provide sufficient flexibility to developing countries to manage this calibration, but taking advantage of them needs careful preparation and market-friendly strategies. In this situation, governments face several options to increase trade competitiveness.

This liberalisation process has, however, not been uniform. A number of countries have opted to use protection, because full-fledged liberalisation could create problems for the survival of domestic industries. In such policy situations, selective liberalisation might be a way to reconcile efforts to attract export-oriented FDI with the need to protect particular economic activities or industries. Selective liberalisation can take various forms, for example, EPZs - which limit trade and investment liberalisation to a spatially-confined area; bonded-warehouse and duty drawback systems - which exemp export-oriented industries from domestic tariffs; and gradual tariff phase-outs over period of time - which allow an economy to shield selectively certain products industries considered strategic. Governments might also pursue a policy of "tra neutrality". The objective of this policy is to eliminate any anti-export bias (to the extent that it exists) whereby exporters may be buying inputs at prices above world prices, but can only sell their output at world prices. Trade neutrality might serve to attract export-oriented FDI.

The *second* policy issue is that of attracting FDI by targeting investment conducive to export competitiveness and upgrading. Again, a variety of measures are available. Where an investment promotion agency exists, it could gear at least part of its activities to this objective. Targeting as a policy instrument may be particularly effective if it has top-level government support and where it is incorporated into a cohesive overall policy framework. The more concrete elements of targeting range from systematically providing comprehensive information on industries with export-potential (e.g. databases on local firms and their capabilities, ideally made available through the Internet), to active research and investment promotion.

A special effort, for example, could be made to draw FDI into industries in which the host country has a revealed comparative advantage (RCA), i.e. where its exports of a product are growing faster than exports of that product worldwide. If this can be combined with attracting TNCs that have a competitive edge in that product and in world trade, a virtuous cycle could be in the making. Targeting initiatives might also seek out TNCs from developing countries, for example SMEs, that are active in particular export niches or which serve as specialised supplier industries to global exporters. With the growth of FDI from developing countries, it can become an important reservoir of capital and other assets, and may facilitate access into new markets. This might require Governments to review their FDI regulatory framework to see whether it is not biased against nontraditional TNCs.

The *third* issue for policy consideration is that of domestic capacity. Strengthening domestic enterprises, as well as the skills, capabilities and institutions on which they rely is probably the single most important long-term element for a successful export-oriented policy. This is so regardless of the role FDI plays in export activity: reliance ɔn TNCs does not eliminate the need to invest in domestic capabilities. The entry of NCs can complement and catalyse domestic resources; it cannot substitute for them. foster the creation of backward linkages and to increase the share of value added in host economy, countries - developed and developing - have used local content ements. Such requirements are subject to provisions of the Agreement on Trade- Investment Measures. Developing countries have also used export performance ents to encourage the export orientation of foreign affiliates.

ic capacity-building also calls for measures to support local export-oriented ɔat can serve as a magnet for FDI; nurturing efficient supplier networks is ɔsure. Governments can, for example, initiate training programmes for domestic companies to upgrade their product quality and productivity or they can enlist the assistance of the TNCs engaged in the export sector for this training. Indonesia and Malaysia, for example, have had successful programmes in which TNCs in the export sector have conducted training courses for domestic companies in supplier industries. Targeted incentives might include incentives for creating specific skills required by a particular export industry which can yield large dividends in dynamising the export structure. The skilful use of incentives, and investment in skills and supply capabilities, can also induce sequential investment into the upgrading of affiliates.

Strengthening export competitiveness and upgrading is not merely an issue of *domestic* policy for host developing countries. These countries cannot reach full export competitiveness as long as developed countries restrict access to their markets. Many developed countries have tariff regimes that are characterised by tariff escalation for processed goods locking out potential suppliers - and in the process deterring potential foreign investors in those industries. Similarly, restrictions on certain industries have hampered the development of competitive industries in developing countries that would have a comparative advantage, given their natural resource and labour endowments (e.g. the Multifibre Agreement). In other industries - such as tropical beverages and some categories of vegetables or fruit - tariff peaks make it difficult for developing countries to develop export markets.

In a broader context, an efficient rule-based multilateral trading system is of critical importance to developing countries. WTO membership, and the capacity to follow up on implementation, are important since a number of policy instruments of that Organisation have a direct bearing on the impact of FDI on export competitiveness and upgrading. These concern, in particular, domestic content, and trade-balancing requirements and restrictions on exports. They are contained in the Agreement on Trade-related Investment Measures. It requires WTO members to notify the use of instruments contained in the TRIMs illustrative list. Developing countries can seek extension of these transitional periods, taking into account the individual development, financial and trade needs of the country concerned. Indeed, given that some developing countries have found these measures useful, proposals have been made to extend the transitional period. Active and skilful participation by developing countries can help ensure that the review of the TRIMs Agreement accords with their development interests. As the multilateral trade environment is being developed further, the links between trade and FDI need to be assessed carefully by developing countries as they formulate their agenda. The ability to conduct complex investment discussions and negotiate international investment agreements is increasingly important for determining the role that FDI can play in boosting the export competitiveness of developing countries. To build a more sustainable and dynamic export base, countries have to use proactive policies. They also need to improve their human capital and capabilities in order to attract higher quality investment. This allows them to attract more sophisticated activities and functions from foreign investors and to strengthen domestic enterprises as direct exporters and as suppliers to TNCs. Only the development of a local capability base will allow countries to plug into the dynamic segments of export activity. TNCs can, in turn, help in the further development of domestic capabilities, leading to a virtuous circle of rising incomes, higher-quality FDI and dynamic competitiveness in trade.

SOME POLICY IMPLICATIONS

It is important to recognise the linkages between these efforts and the need for them to occur simultaneously. Otherwise there will be more results like the ones obtained from the U.S.—Japan wood products initiative. In this particular case, U.S. trade negotiations with Japan were conducted for more than a decade, so that more U.S. solid wood products could enter the Japanese market. High-level meetings, ongoing negotiations, government financial support, and industry demonstration projects were to achieve that goal. Japanese building codes and product certification procedures were changed and tariffs were lowered. The Foreign Agricultural Service spent more than $17 million to promote U.S. wood-product sales to Japan. The result? Canadian lumber companies are the leading wood exporters to the Japanese market. There were only marginal increases in U.S. exports and export-related jobs.

There are reasons for this outcome. U.S. products were not tailored to the Japanese market. Japanese builders prefer post-and-beam construction, which requires 4X4 inch lumber and 3 ´ 6 foot modules to match the standard tatami mats that cover floors. But U.S. companies were either unaware of those requirements or unwilling to meet them. Instead, the U.S. producers focused on the standard 2 ´ 4 products used in the United States, even though only 7 per cent of new homes in Japan use that standard. In effect, U.S. negotiators and companies focused their energies on increasing the U.S. presence in the smallest part of the market, rather than pursuing the biggest market. This focus was the result of trying to sell what is produced, rather than producing what foreign customers want to buy. In addition, some of the U.S. firms that did enter the Japanese market did so with only limited enthusiasm and commitment. In contrast to the Canadian firms, many companies paid little attention to product quality and appearance and did not deliver after-sales service. Few firms translated their product information into Japanese or wrote manuals describing the new type of construction. Those U.S. companies that did try to vigorously pursue the new market encountered major problems in obtaining information about specific market requirements. They also had trouble adjusting their production processes to meet Japanese product specifications and obtaining financing to pay for new equipment and larger export inventories. Without these resources, their efforts were severely handicapped.

A well-intended approach may not achieve its deserved success if the focus rest on the wrong opportunities, the needs of customers are not sufficiently taken into account, firms are unable to unwilling to adjust to market requirements, and the linkages between all these components are not taken into account. The crucial dimensions that should guide export assistance efforts, in particular where new and growing business are concerned, are:

1. CLARITY OF PURPOSE

Agreement needs to be reached on what export assistance is to achieve. Some of the objectives currently competing with each other are global fairness, the opening of world markets, and economic activity and jobs in the domestic market. Public funds are too scarce, as is our capacity to negotiate, and our capability to achieve negotiation success—to invest funds and government attention solely to right wrongs or for the sake of fairness. There needs to be explicit recognition of the fact that the times are over when a country used to open foreign markets simply for the well-being of the world. Though it might be a delightful side effect to also see had nations' trade increase under the WTO.

Clarification is also needed for the time frame involved. Given a short-term orientation, emphasis on a temporary increase in the export sales will be most desirable. A more long-term orientation will concentrate efforts on introducing more and new firms to the global market.

2. TIGHTNESS OF FOCUS

Export assistance needs to achieve either a specific reduction of risk or an increase in profits for firms It should be concentrated primarily in those areas where profit and risk inconsistencies produce market gaps, and be linked directly to identifiable organisational or managerial characteristics that need improvement. Otherwise, assistance supports only exports that would 'ave taken place anyway Such a focus, of course, requires the implementation of evaluation criteria and measurement mechanisms, which determine the effectiveness of export assistance. However, for policy purposes, such measurement should not be based on the firm's export performance which is mainly controlled by the corporation. Rather, the measurement should he based on the export involvement of the firm, focusing on the number of customers transactions, and countries served.

3. COORDINATION OF APPROACHES

Coordination must occur both within and outside the government. Within government, it will be crucial to set overall effectiveness priorities and to trade off export assistance programmes across agencies. Otherwise, an economic sector with relatively low employment effects could consume resources in an over proportionate fashion while priority industries would suffer from insufficient support. Externally, export assistance must be directly linked to domestic industries to ensure that the policy gains abroad can be taken advantage of by firms. Doing so must include collaboration for both product and process technologies, which now play a crucial role in attaining global competitiveness, similar to the much supported field of science. For example, the issue of quality performance can well become the focus of a cooperative effort throughout an entire industry, its suppliers, and customers alike. Rather than concentrate only on the well-entrenched industries, it is particularly important here to include a focus on sunrise industries.

4. EMPHASIS ON STRENGTHS

Within government, export assistance should emphasise those areas where government can bring a particular strength to bear—such as contacts, prowess in opening doors abroad, or information

5. TARGETING OF CRUCIAL FACTORS

Export assistance is likely to have the greatest impact when it serves the needs of companies programmes. Therefore, the government should start out by analysing the current level of international involvement of the firm and then deliver assistance appropriate to the firm's needs. For example, help with after sales service delivery is most appropriate for firms at the adaptation stage; firms at the awareness stage worry much more about information and mechanics. Assistance must also take foreign market conditions and foreign buyer preferences into account, and communicate the resulting constraints and opportunities to domestic firms. It is easier to sell what is in demand.

6. BOLDNESS OF VISION

In spite of the need to improve ongoing programs, there should be a spark of boldness which goes beyond ensuring that things are done right, but checks whether one can do more right things. One could, for example, think about domestic and international efforts to set standards for technology and quality. One could go beyond products in such an effort and also include services and agriculture. One could even include the grading of enzymes, meats, hormones, and other products developed by biotechnology firms. There could be efforts to develop the domestic mentoring services of a senior executive corps to provide much needed international experience to new and growing firms. Or one could think about the development of a national forfeiting institution to be of major assistance in handling the financial and documentation aspects of exporting.

QUESTIONS

1. Discuss the stages of export involvement or internationalisation.
2. Describe forms of exporting and the types of intermediaries available to assist firm in exporting their goods.

3. Discuss the profit and risk involved during export initiation.
4. Explain the key elements in formulating the export and import strategies.
5. Critically examine the conceptual issues emerging from export developing models.
6. Critically examine the policy issues related to the role of FDI in boosting export competitiveness in developing countries.
7. How do MNCs react as technology changes and wages and other costs rise in a developing host country, making it uneconomical as an export site? Do they dynamise comparative advantage by upgrading facilities and local capabilities or do they move their facilities to cheaper location?

REFERENCES

Czinkota, Michael R. and Ilkka A Ronkainen (1993) *International Marketing,* 3rd edn. Fort Worth: The Dryden Press.

Kotabe, Masaaki and Michael R. Czinkota (1992) "State Government Promotion of Manufacturing Exports: A GAP Analysis," *Journal of International Business Studies,* 4, 637-58. (See chapter 8.)

Seringhaus, Rolf F.H. and Philip J. Rosson (1990) *Government Export Promotion: A Global Perspective.* London: Routledge.

United States General Accounting Office (1993) *Agricultural Marketing: Export Opportunities for Wood Products in Japan Call for Customer Focus.* Washington, D.C.: Government Printing Office, May.

United States General Accounting Office (1992) *Export Promotion: U.S. Programmes Lack Coherence.* Washington D.C.: Government Printing Office, March.

29

NON-EQUITY MODES (NEMs) OF INTERNATIONAL PRODUCTION: FRANCHISING AND LICENSING

INTRODUCTION

Franchising and licensing used to be regarded as a second-rate method of entry into a foreign market. They were considered to be neither here nor there, in the way exporting is here and a fully owned subsidiary is there. But that is changing, even for the large companies, as they examine more closely the net risk-adjusted advantages in different markets. It is of even greater interest to smaller or medium-sized firms that lack the capital, management, or experience to go in and make an investment in a foreign market. In short, franchising and licensing may be the most attractive entry methods because of the nature of the market or because of the resources or strategy of the firm, and this will be determined by the market analysis and the self-audit of the firm's own resources. Moreover, it can be quite rewarding financially technical assistance, engineering fees, a management contract, quality control, profit form sales of bulk materials or specialised machinery, and of course, royalties on sales.

But, although licensing is a relatively easy form of entry, it is controversial mainly because, overall, the transfer of technology is from the richer economies to the poorer nations that don't have the resources to develop or buy their own technology, or whose markets are so small they won't justify doing it. It used to be that the control and management of capital was the most controversial aspect of international operations, but recently the control and cost of technology has come to the fore, especially as the foreign-exchange shortages of many countries have highlighted all foreign payments and particularly licensing fees that are often for intangible or invisible assets. So, although licensing is low-risk entry strategy, it has to be evaluated carefully to avoid the danger of licensing when one should not and not licensing when one should. Most of the large companies pick and choose between different strategies in different situations. Some companies do nothing except licensing. It is necessary, therefore, to take a look at the circumstances that make licensing the only or preferred entry method.

FRANCHISING

In many ways franchising is equivalent to licensing with some of the technical assistance, quality control, or supply factors included. In this case it is not just license to use a technology, a trademark, or a trade name; there are also requirements on how the technology or trademark is used. The most common franchises are in fast-food restaurants, hotels and motels, car rentals etc. Internationally, the most famous are in fast food and car rental. Operations and procedures are supposed to be standardised.

Generally, a franchising arrangement involves a much greater support system than licensing. For the franchisor, product image is a valuable asset, and this has to be maintained in each market. This may require a continual supply of inputs and machinery as well as the advertising and promotional materials around which the international image or trade name is build. To reach the desired standards of service, technical assistance is usually supplied in areas like quality control, operating procedures, and, of course, marketing. Franchising also goes beyond licensing by often providing financial support, and it often moves from being a franchising operation to a joint venture with the local partner. As with exporting and licensing, franchising can be a first step into a market because it involves limited risk, but there is usually a high correlation between the degree of risk and the level of control and profits. The move into joint ownership with the local partner may occur if financial support is converted into equity and if the franchisor sees the joint venture as a much more profitable way to go.

Finding a suitable franchising partner may be more difficult than to find one in licensing because what is being transferred is a whole system of doing business, rather than a license to produce or manufacture a product, something that the local partner is likely to have competence in the first place. That is why most well-known franchise operations are in areas like fast food, car rentals, and hotel and motel management. They didn't require much capital, and the skills are fairly easily transferable because many of them are mechanical duplications of a single process. If one moves into the more technical service areas like real estate, accounting, or advertising, it is much more difficult to enter by franchising because much more sophisticated skills are required and regulations and accepted procedures differ so much form country to country. Nevertheless, franchising is not monolithic throughout the world. The marketing expertise of the major franchisors is far too sophisticated to allow a procedure that works in one country to interfere with sales in another. Changes are made in local markets to comply with that country's regulations, for example in the use of certain ingredients.

The risks associated with franchising are essentially the same as those found in licensing, the biggest being loss of control and the creation of a competitor. This may be one of the main reasons for the move nationally and internationally toward equity participation in the franchise. This gives greater control and makes the licensee the potential competitor and the licensor's new partner. The entry method, therefore has to be continually evaluated. Licensing or franchising may be most suitable as a first step in the market, but the company may see later that to remain in it in a worthwhile way or to get bigger returns, for that it is to move into partial or sole ownership. Usually , the most attractive franchising areas are in consumer-type products where the capital outlay is not large.

FRANCHISE SYSTEM IN THE WORLD

Worldwide sales of franchised enterprises reached nearly $2.5 trillion in 2010 (Table-1), of which the value of cross-border franchising was around $330-350 billion. The share of international franchising varies significantly by country. In most developed markets domestic franchising accounts for 80-90 per cent of the total, but franchising has reached maturity in some major emerging markets as well. In Brazil, for example, foreign franchise chains represent only around 10 per cent of the total, all of the top 10 chains being domestic franchises. However, initial growth of franchising in developing markets is often driven by international franchise operators. In most African markets, except for South Africa, international franchisors account for 80 per cent or more of the total, and in emerging markets such as Mexico, the Russian Federation and Turkey, the rate is still between 30 and 40 per cent.

The franchising formula is found in different sectors, and takes different forms. The most important franchising sectors are retail (including high-street retailing as well as grocery), restaurants (often quick-service restaurants), hotels, business services, as well as a diverse range of other services sectors, from education to personal care services. In developed countries the share of higher value added services tends to be higher; in the United States, for example, business and personal services account for 37 per cent of the total franchising sector. By contrast, in developing countries, micro-franchising (mostly one-person businesses) and lower value added services are more common. For example, in South Africa the most important franchising sector is quick-service restaurants, with a share of almost 25 per cent of franchised systems, followed by retail (also a limited value added sector) with 22 per cent. Similarly, in India the leading sector is retail, with a share of 32 per cent, followed by quick-service restaurants with 16 per cent.

Most large global franchising operators (franchisors) originate in developed countries, whether they are international retailers expanding through franchise networks, luxury brands expanding internationally on the high street, in shopping malls and at airports, or restaurants transplanting their successful formulas to new markets as consumers develop an "international taste". The top 15 global franchisors by number of outlets are all United States firms, apart from one company each from Japan, Canada and the United Kingdom. Most of these 15 firms are fast-food chains such as McDonald's

(United States) and Pizza Hut (United States). The remaining companies out of this group are essentially convenience stores or hotels, including 7-Eleven (Japan) and Intercontinental (United Kingdom).

TABLE-1

Franchise Systems[a] in the World, 2010

Region/Economy	*Frranchise systems*	*Number of outlets (Thousand)*	*Sales ($ billion)*	*Employees (Thousand)*	*Cross-border (Per cent)[b]*
World	30 000	2 640	2 480	19 940	15
Developed economies	12 200	1 310	2 210	12 400	10
Europe	7 700	370	340	2 830	20
Japan	1 200	230	250	2 500	5
United States	2 500	630	1 480	6 250	5
Developing/transition economies	17 400	1 330	270	7 540	30
Africa	1 600	40	30	550	70
Latin America and the Caribbean	3 800	190	70	1 810	20
Asia	11 200	1 070	170	4 810	25
South-East Europe and the CIS	800	30	5	370	50

Source: UNCTAD estimates, based on a joint UNCTAD/World Franchise Council survey of national franchise associations.

a. A franchise system consists of all the franchised units and units managed by the franchisor itself that operate under the same banner and business format, for example the McDonald's franchise system.

b. Refers to the share of cross-border outlets in the total number of outlets.

Global franchise chains are frequently widely dispersed, with many franchisees in developing countries. For example, KFC (United States) has franchisees in about 110 countries globally, of which some 75 are developing economies; the equivalent numbers for Holiday Inn are over 100 and 80. The choice of location is driven by market size, which is reflected in the top franchising country locations.

LICENSING

Most companies decide to go the licensing road because of the characteristics of the market itself. Some firms may look at the market and because of the difficulties of the other more conventional forms of entry may decide to pass it up altogether. But if the world is the marketplace, that is not sufficient reason because licensing may be both possible and rewarding. The characteristics of the market that will indicate that licensing is the road to go include the following:

1. The market has low-volume potential, cannot be served by exports, but could generate extra revenues from royalties and fees.

2. It is impossible to export either because of trade restrictions or the inability of importers to get the foreign exchange to cover the cost of finished imports. Of course, this may also mean difficulty in getting foreign exchange for royalties or other fees, but these sums are likely to be considerably less than the cost of imported goods.
3. Competition in the market has made the products too expensive. This may be because of high domestic production costs, the location of facilities far away from a port, or the transportation costs involved in getting the product to a distant market.
4. The risk may be too high for an equity investment, or it may be too high relative to the resources at the company's disposal.

Other factors related to the company may determine that licensing is the best way for it to go even if other forms of entry are suitable as far as the market itself is concerned. Some of these factors may be:

1. The company needs immediate cash flow and a foreign manufacturer can begin production much faster than the company could if it made a direct investment.
2. The company does not have the resources now to manufacture for the market or invest in it, but it wants to recovery some of its R and D costs or to generate a stream of incremental income.
3. The company want to protect its technology or patent from being copied in certain countries, so it officially license somebody to use it. Although its patent or trademark is registered, it may have protection for only one year in foreign countries, and after that somebody else may be able to exploit the asset. So, the only recourse might have is to license somebody to produce in order to protect its rights.
4. The company may have a good product and attractive markets, but the modification required in the product are too many or too expensive for it to incorporate. But, it may not be so for a licensee who has a line of similar products.
5. Finally, although the market is attractive and the risk is manageable, it cannot afford to go in directly because of lack of capital, management skills, or experience. If there is a large difference in the operating environment between what the company is used to and what exists and even if it has the capital, it might decided that since it does not have the experience and it could use the licensing arrangement as a stepping stone to a larger involvement at a later date.

WHAT'S IN IT FOR THE LICENSEE?

Like an agent or distributor agreement, the licensor/licensee contract has to be rewarding to both sides. The licensor chooses this method of entry because it suits him or her. But the licensor has to make sure that the licensee needs him for the long term. Some of the reasons the licensee is willing to pay for the technology are:

1. He or she is an entrepreneur who see the potential for the product or product line in the market and is eager to cash in on it.
2. He or she has been the agent or the distributor of the company and wants to graduate into manufacturing, a goal that in certain circumstances could coincide with the company.
3. He or she is already producing other items, has excess capacity, and wishes to use it.
4. He or she needs to update and keep up to date in technology in order to compete. In areas of production where technology is changing rapidly, it is extremely costly to get the most advanced know-how, and if there is free trade outdated technology is a recipe for going out of business.
5. Licensing may be the least costly way to get into production for the licensee just as it may be the least costly entry method for the licensor.

Although all of these are valid reasons for a foreign firm to get the company's technology, but it still need to look beyond them to other qualifications that are also required. Look out for the following:

1. Can the firm get a production license? This may be difficult, even if the firm is already in production. Special permission may be required. It could be a great waste of time to begin negotiations, come to an agreement and then find the partner is not authorised to produce the product.
2. Does the licensee have the production facilities or access to facilities to produce the goods?
3. If the partner is a manufacturer, has he or she the skills or resources to market the product? If the manufacturer is already producing other goods, he or she probably has a distributor network. On the other hand, if the distributor or somebody with no manufacturing experience is going into manufacturing does he or she have the required skills? Generally, the company does not want a manufacturer who cannot sell its goods or a distributor who cannot manufacture them. So, technical competence as well as marketing and management skills are important.

THE LICENSING AGREEMENT—THE MOST IMPORTANT COMPONENTS

In negotiating a licensing agreement, there are five particularly important guidelines for the licensee.

1. Clearly define what is being licensed. The technology package may have only one element, namely, a secret process or know-how. Or it may be quite complex involving not only know-how, but specialised equipment, secret ingredients, and a trademark. The total package may also include assistance in quality control, management, and marketing. A careful, detailed description of exactly what is covered by the agreement will close loopholes and prevent misunderstandings in the future. The more complex the package, the greater the control the licensor has. If all the company is licensing the trademark or know-how that can be easily adapted, the licensee may develop the capability of getting on quite well without the licensor or even of becoming a major competitor.
2. Specify exactly what territories are covered by the agreement. Obviously, the licensor does not want the licensee competing with him or her in another country where the licensor is supplying the market directly or through another channel. So the licensor needs limit the licensee's freedom to sell wherever he or she wants to sell.
3. Ensure high quality production. Since the licensor's brand name or its reputation for quality or for the safety of the product may be a large part of its asset. To safeguard it the licensor may have to be sure of high-quality production. This is particularly important in an exclusive agreement, where the licensee alone can use the technology within the market because now the licensor has no other recourse, and a poor or second-rate product could lead to loss to trademark rights. Depending on the product, the licensor may visit the plant for inspection prior to signing an agreement, it may insist on the presence of its own technical experts, or it may specify the use of certain types of machinery or raw materials. In products where there is a safety factor involved like health products, electric tools, or foodstuff it will have to insist on high-quality standards and regular inspections to ensure they are maintained.
4. Make sure valuable licensed asset remains secret or under the licensor's control. Obviously, if it were in the public domain it would be of little value, so in a licensing agreement the licensor will need to protect the confidentiality of what transferring, not only for the duration of the agreement, but for a number of years afterwards. In practice, the confidentiality clause will be limited to information or knowledge that could not be discovered by any other means. Obviously, information that licensee already knows or that a third party reveals cannot be bound to secrecy.
5. Insist on a minimum performance clause in the contract. Essentially, this is to protect the licensor from a non-performing partner who has its asset tied up in an agreement but doesn't use it. If the licensor is depending on royalties on sales, it will have no income.

Outline of the Licensing Agreement

The following outline is presented to prepare the licensor for all the areas that need to be covered before signing an agreement. It is the equivalent of a checklist, each component of which will require a decision. Of course, the agreement itself will require legal help, a knowledge of local laws, and considerable attention to detail, but the major decisions are business decisions that the licensors will have to make.

A. Formal Provisions

The first clause identifies the parties, their locations, what the licensor has to offer under license, and the date of the agreement.

B. Definition of Terms

This is an extremely important section because the clarity and preciseness established here will govern all that follows, and perhaps of more importance, it will prevent misunderstandings in the future. Definitions cover such areas as the licensed patent, what technology is involved, on what basis royalties are paid, and what law governs the agreement.

C. License Grant

This covers who is the licensor, who is the licensee, what is being lincensed, whether if exclusive or not, sublicensing, and other conditions of use.

D. Royalties and Other Payments

This covers questions such as method of payment, currency of payment, royalty percentage, sales base, premarketing payments, minimum payments, and payment for any of the technical assistance, management, marketing, or other assistance provided.

E. Grant Backs

This refers to the right of access to new developments of the technology discovered by the licensee.

F. Patent Enforcement and Maintenance

This refers to the need to protect the secrecy of what the licensor transferring not only for the duration of the agreement but for a number of years afterwards.

G. Assignability

This clause clarifies the extent or limits of assignability to successors of the party involved or to a third party.

H. Effective Date Duration and Termination

This clause describes the length of the contract, terms of renewal, and conditions of termination by either the licensor or licensee.

I. The Report Clause

The clause outlines the accounting required by the licensor to ensure accurate payment by the licensee and the right of the licensor to audit the reports.

J. Governing Law and Arbitration

This may be quite a complicated area because the laws of two different nations may conflict in area such as antitrust. Arbitration outlines the specific disputes that are to be arbitrated, who the arbitators will be, and how decisions will be reached.

K. Confidentiality

This covers the need by the licensor to protect his or her know-how or trade secret.

L. Force Majeure Clause

This lists the uncontrollable circumstances under which the licensor or licensee will be exempted from responsibility for nonconformance. This include such extraordinary events as earthquakes, revolutions, or accidents and might even include items like strikes, equipment breakdowns, or interference by the government.

M. Notice

These specify where notices are to be sent, how they are to be sent and on what date they become effective.

In straightforward licensing agreement royalty revenues as a percentage of sales is the usual method of payment. Depending on the value of the licensed technology, trademark, or patent the percentage on sales usually runs in the range of 3 per cent to 7 per cent. The second clause of the agreement is very important because it clearly defines the base on which the percentage will be established. Are discounts allowed, or commissions to agents or distributors? Who pays taxes or expenses associated with faulty products or warranties? Usually all of these are deducted from gross sales and royalties are paid on net receipts from sales.

A very important factor is the question of minimum payments. This is to motivate the licensee to promote and market the product so that a minimum sales target is reached. In case of developing countries it is important to specify the currency of payment and alternative payment methods in the event there are currency or the government limits future payments. Such an alternative might be an equity share in the licensee firm, a step that would move you in the direction of a joint venture.

GLOBAL ROYALTIES AND LICENSE PAYMENTS

International licensing spans a wide range of industries and activities, touching on nearly every step of many industries' global value chains. UNCTAD estimates that cross-border NEM-related licensing resulted in sales of $340-360 billion in 2010. NEM-related licensing has grown steadily since 1990, registering a steady 10 per cent average annual growth rate as measured by estimated sales up to 2008, although there was a decline in 2009 because of the financial and economic crisis. Balance of payments statistics suggest that licensing activity directed at developing markets increased markedly in the past decade, though developed economies continue to dominate. Global royalty payments are indicative of licences received (and hence the location of NEM partners to TNCs) and, on this basis, developing and transition economies now pay out roughly a quarter of global royalty fees (Table-2). The geographical dispersal of licensees (based on royalty payments) is wide, although South, East, and South-East Asia comprised nearly 70 per cent of the total from developing and transition economies in 2009, followed by Latin America and the Caribbean, South-East Europe and the CIS, Africa, and West Asia. Within each region there is a high concentration of licensing activity in a few countries, e.g. South Africa and Egypt in Africa; Brazil and Argentina in Latin America; and Turkey in West Asia. This is slightly less the case for East, South and South-East Asia, with Singapore, China and Taiwan Province of China most licensing partners.

TABLE-2

Royalties and Licence Payments by Selected Developing and Transition Cconomies, 2005, 2008, 2009

(Billions of Dollars)

Region/Economy	*2005*	*2008*	*2009*
World	143.4	204.2	197.4
Developed economies	113.1	153.5	149.2
Developing and transition economies	30.3	50.7	48.2
Africa	1.6	2.5	2.5
South Africa	1.1	1.7	1,6
Egypt	0.2	0.3	0.3
Nigeria	0.1	0.2	0.2
Latin America and the Caribbean	3.3	6.5	6.1
Brazil	1.4	2.7	2.5
Argentina	0.7	1.5	1.5
Mexico	0.1	0.6	0.5
Chile	0.3	0.5	0.5
Asia and Oceania	23.1	35.8	34.4
West Asia	0.5	1.1	1.0
Turkey	0.4	0.7	0.6
Iraq	0.0	0.4	0.3
South, East and South-East Asia	22.7	34.7	33.5
Singapore	9.3	12.5	11.6

China	5.3	10.3	11.1
Taiwan Province of China	1.8	3.0	3.4
Thailand	1.7	2.6	2.3
India	0.7	1.5	1.9
South-East Europe and the CIS	2.3	5.9	5.2
Russian Federation	1.6	4.6	4.1
Ukraine	0.4	0.8	0.6
Croatia	0.2	0.3	0.2

Source: UNCTAD, based on IMF's balance-of-payment statistics.

SOME PITFALLS TO AVOID

Usually there is little or no capital investment made by the licensor. So the possibility of losing equity or being expropriated does not arise. But that does not mean an absence of all risk. It is just that the risks are of a different kind. Perhaps the greatest danger is the loss of the company's valuable asset, namely, a patent or brand or trademark. Of course, the company will try to avoid this in the written contract, but in many countries that does not give full protection, especially if the licensee has the full knowledge and ability to produce the product. This is why licensors with an easily duplicated technology hold back specific components of the product that only they can supply. But even then, the product can be imitated and a brand name or trademark used, as for instance, when bottles of black liquid are sold as "Koca Kola."

Another danger is the loss of control of marketing, quality, and product image. Again, these factors can all be covered in the agreement, but it may be difficult to do anything about them in practice if the company find itself with the wrong licensee. Then they can be alleviated by technical assistance, management support, and quality control programmes provides. As in most such arrangements, a lot will depend on the working relationship of the parties involved. If things go badly, the company's brand name may be splashed on inferior products, and it may be getting little revenues because sales are low and there is poor market performance by the licensee.

Beware of creating a competitor. What happens if the licensee in Brazil begins to export to Venezuela where the company have a lucrative direct export market? Or if, after the license runs out, he or she continues to manufacture and faces head on in foreign markets or worse still in its own domestic market? In the license agreement the company can try to prevent all of this by restricting the licensee's sales to a specific territory and by requiring the manufacturer to stop producing after the contract ends. But it is easier said than done. Unlike a direct investor who can stop capital flow or cause a reduction in employment, the company has little leverage especially when the agreement runs out. In many countries an appeal to the courts will drag on and is unlikely to gain the company anything in the long run except legal fees. Depending on the nature of the manufacturing process, it may be able to maintain a satisfactory level of control by supplying components or ingredients not easily obtained elsewhere. If the company does not have such leverage, an alternate means of control is to be able to come up with improvements in the technology or know-how that it is licensing so that the licensee needs it.

Another risk is associated with payment. If the company supplying components or technical or management assistance of any kind, the problems and methods of payment are the same as of dealing with payments for exports. A letter of credit is the usual means of payment. The biggest problem arises with royalties on sales, the usual means of compensation of the licensor. Two problems can arise here. First, revenues may be low if the marketing effort is poor; second, the company may have difficulty getting the royalties converted and out of the country. One of the disadvantages of licensing is that royalties are not large in the first place, usually 3 to 7 per cent of sales, but if sales are low or foreign exchange is restricted, it may have given up a valuable asset and gotten very little in return. These problems can be overcome by, for example, requiring a minimum royalty payment independent of sales volume or by accepting payment in the form of part ownership of the licensee's business, in which case the company moving into a joint venture.

Although royalties from sales may be low compared with profits form exports or returns form direct foreign investment, there is the potential for increased income flows form the licensee for other services. A lot will depend on the nature of the business. Some large companies enter a licensing agreement not for the royalties on sales but for the revenues earned from supplying essential inputs into the manufacturing process. For the smaller or medium-sized firm and for firms selling technology or pure know-how, opportunities for incremental income can come from a variety of services supplied with the technology package. For example, the licensee may need licensor to design and assist in the construction of the manufacturing plant. He or she may need the in starting it up, operating it, and training local counterpart personnel. The licensor may be able to procure or sell his own equipment to be used in producing the goods. The licensee may also require management and marketing assistance to effectively penetrate the market. Obviously, the licensee will be willing to pay for some or all of these services if it is profitable for him or her. In case where to licensor's major source of income comes from supplying components of the product, he may have to supply some of these services free of charge. This is especially true of services related to quality control where product image is of importance to this and other markets. The licensee is likely to regard that as licensor's concern and not something for which he or she should have to pay.

In providing these ancillary services to the licensee, the licensor may include them under the general licensing contract, but in general, it is much better to have them separate. As soon as the licensee reaches the minimum level of competence in an area, he or she is likely to want to take over the function and terminate the technical assistance or management agreement. If there are two separate agreements, the important and long-term licensing one will not be affected and will not have to be renegotiated, a process that can be long and drawn out in the first place. Anyway, any technical assistance contract is likely to be of shorter duration than a desirable licensing agreement. But this does not mean that it is not worthwhile. On the contrary, fees and services associated with the start-up of the project and its continuing functioning could make this method of entry much more attractive than if the royalties on sales alone were considered.

QUESTIONS

1. What is international licensing? What are the advantages and disadvantages of licensing?
2. Discuss the basic issues in international licensing.
3. Evaluate the costs and benefits associated with joint ventures.
4. When would a company use overseas (import) distributor and / or dealer network? When would the use of import agents be appropriate? What are some of the pitfalls in using either import distributors or import agents? What are the alternatives when a company is committed to exporting and not to manufacturing abroad?
5. Describe the pros and cons of turnkey arrangements, wholly owned subsidiaries, and joint ventures.
6. Discuss the advantages and disadvantages of licensing agreements from the point of view of licensors and licensees.
7. Explain how smaller companies can gain by working through trading companies.
8. What factors could cause you to reject an offer from a potential licensee to make and market your firm's products in a foreign market.
9. Discuss the most important components of a licensing agreement.

REFERENCES

Adler, Lee and Blavacek, James D., *Joint ventures for product innovation,* Amacom, New York.

Aharoni, Yair, *The foreign investment decision process,* Harvard University Press, Boston, Massachusetts, 1966.

Baetz, Mark C and Beamish, Paul W., *Strategic Management: Canadian Cases,* Richard D. Irwin, Homewood, Illionois, 1987.

Buckley, Peter J. and Casson, Mark, *The future of the multinational enterprise,* Macmillan, London, 1976.

——, *The economic theory of the multinational enterprise,* St Martin's Press, New York, 1985.

Caves, Richard E. *Multinational enterprise and economic analysis,* Cambridge University Press, Cambridge, Massachusetts, 1982.

Friedmann, Wolfgang G. and Beguin, J.P., *Joint international business ventures,* Columbia University Press, New York, 1971.

——, and Kalmanoff, George, *Joint international business ventures,* Columbia University Press, New York, 1961.

Hennart, Jean-Francois, *A theory of multinational enterprise,* University of Michigan Press, Ann Arbour, 1982.

Konde, E.J., *The multinational company,* Lexington Books, Toronto, 1974.

Matthews, Geoffrey J. and Morrow, Robert, Jr., *Canada and the world: an atlas resource,* Prentice-Hall, Scarborough, Ontario, 1985.

Walmsley, John, *Joint ventures in Saudi Arabia,* Graham and Trontman, London, 1979.

30

JOINT VENTURES

INTRODUCTION

A joint venture can be described as the participation of two companies in the ownership, management, and control of a third enterprise designed to benefit. Indeed, it may not be a bad definition if we say that setting up a good joint venture is like having a model child. It brings credit to its parents, contributes to their well-being and is effectively under their direction and control. A bad joint venture is like a delinquent teenager; its problems often arise from the fact that there are two parents, giving different commands, leading to a loss of control and maybe even a divorce both. It as the offspring of a marriage of convenience of two independent parents that might have preferred to serve the market in some more desirable way that was not possible. Unlike the most American and European countries which prefer to fully control through any kind of direct investment, the Japanese have taken a the route of international strategic alliances through joint venture by keeping a low profile, and yet, in effect, controlling the enterprise.

JOINT VENTURES: DIFFERENT COUNTRIES, DIFFERENT PARTNERS

Usually the choice facing a company entering a foreign market is to form a joint venture with a local firm. This may be done out of preference or necessity. It is done out of preference if the foreign company believes that, all things being considered, this is the best way of entering and being successful in this market. It is done out of necessity if it is the only way. For example, some countries will not allow a 100 per cent ownership of a subsidiary and many other limit foreign ownership on certain fields. The choice then is to forego the market altogether or to enter a joint venture. Other countries follow the policies whereby 51 per cent of the capital had to be in the host hands for a certain period of time. But, if partnership with a local company is the most common form of joint venture, it is important to get the detailed information on following ten questions to calculate expected returns, detailed information on many factors. This information can be summarised in the following ten questions:

1. *What are the costs to the company?*
2. *What are the benefits to the company?*
3. *What percentage of ownership do the company require?*
4. *Who are the potential partners of the company and what have they to offer?*
5. *Does ownership distribution reflect what the company's partner has to offer?*
6. *How does value a partner's assets, such as knowledge of the local environment or political and financial contacts?*
7. *Will the contribution of each partner change over time?*
8. *Is this reflected in the ownership structure?*
9. *How much control do the company need?*
10. *What restrictions does the local government impose?*

We will now take a closer look at each one of the questions to elaborate on what the company needs to look for in each.

1. The company immediate costs can be broken down under financing required, technology supplied, supplies required, and very important, the management and marketing time that will be taken up by the joint venture, especially in the start-up period. But there are other costs, for example, the lost of exports now being sent to the market or the loss of the most economic use of resources caused by a loss of control.

2. The benefits will primarily be from increased sales in the new market and possibly from increased sales in nearby regional markets with preferential trading arrangements. There will be associated benefits to the parent, for example, dividends, interest payments, and payments for any other assistance like management, marketing, or technical assistance.

3. Once the company calculated the costs and the benefits, it can determine its expected returns. But, perhaps of more importance, its can decide what percentage ownership of the joint venture its requires to justify its contribution. In many countries what it can own will be limited by law, but under the upper limit there may be a wide range and its share of that should reflect its contribution to the joint venture.

4. Screening distributors, agents, and licensees to get the right one for the company is serious business, but most of the time a mistake may be undone. With a joint venture the stakes are much higher and questions of control are much more important. A mistake here is going to be costly. The company needs to go through a systematic screening process to determine the right fit for its goals. In practice, the number of candidate firms will not be that great because it is likely to be looking for a very specific set of requirements, like, for instance, experience in producing or marketing a similar product line. And it will have at its disposal all of the information. If the

company is already active in this market, it probably is familiar with the operations of the best candidates.

In the case of government restrictions on local private ownership the company does not have much choice; it can join with the state agency responsible for that area of production or operation. Choosing the right partner presumes the company has some kind of profile of what it wants and the company knows the assets it requires to complement it own in the joint venture. For example, the company may require existing production facilities because it wants a quick start-up. The company may require a certain level of financing or a marketing network in place. The more detailed its requirements are the easier it will be to narrow down its choice. Apart from the company's profile, the partner may have special assets. For instance, the firm may have a multilingual sales force in a country with many dialects. Or it may have developed high-level political and financial contacts that will ease the operations of the venture.

5. Distribution of ownership is a crucial element in a successful joint venture because it has a large impact on the distribution of payments and on control. The basic rule is that each partner should be getting out of the joint venture rewards proportionate to what they are putting in. One problem is that contributions may vary over time, and the distribution of ownership remains rigid. For example, some of the contributions of the local partner, such as knowledge of the market or of the work force, are important at the beginning but become less significant as the joint venture itself gains experience. The danger is that the contributions of the partners go out of the balance without a change in benefits, and the result is dissatisfaction or even joint-venture divorce.

6-8. Putting a value on some of the assets of the local partner is a difficult job. How, for instance, does a company quantify something like a knowledge of the local market? Although such a valuation will be a rather crude measurement, it should be done. More important, all contributions of both partners should be quantified over time so that benefits accruing to each partner can also be adjusted over time. It is not just the local partner's contribution that may decrease in importance. The company may have very important contributions to make up front, for example, technology, money, or machinery, but they may cease as the joint venture develops its own skills or ability to finance itself out of its own profits. If significant changes in the contribution of each partner are likely to occur after the start-up of the joint venture, then the benefits should be adjusted accordingly. If it is not possible to adjust them by the distribution of ownership, it may be possible to rectify an imbalance by payments for management time or technical assistance or increased dividends.

9. How much control the company needs what level of control it requires, and in what areas is a question that is obviously related to the earlier questions on what contributions each partner makes and how ownership is distributed as well as how

independent its product makes the company. Important areas of control can be outlined as follows:

i) Which partner is responsible for which management positions? Obviously, this is a controversial area due to the sensitivity and power of certain positions, for example, the financial manager.

ii) Who selects and appoints the management?

iii) How are the earnings and profits of the joint venture going to be used? The local partner may want to expand and diversify the joint venture. The company may want profits to be distributed to the parents.

iv) How are prices determined for machinery, supplies, or other inputs supplied by a partner?

v) Who makes key decisions on new products, expansion, financial structure, hiring, and the amount of advertising?

The amount of control the company needs will obviously have an impact on the earlier question: *What kind of partner does it want?* If the company is interested in high levels of control in most areas here outlined, it may decide to disperse ownership through several partners, or it may choose dummy-type firms, with little bargaining power, or silent partners. On the other hand, if it wants a real operating joint venture and it want to make good use of local skills, it will choose a partner that may lessen its control but who will be involved actively in strategic business decisions and will make a significant contribution to a successful venture. The company may even decide to pick a public-sector partner, and again there are several kinds. Many countries like Brazil have enterprising profit-conscious public or semi-public companies that would be active joint venture partners. Many in other countries are more politicised and stagnant, with overweighted managements, too many employees, and high overheads.

10. The local government may restrict the company's options in a joint venture. The most significant limits may be on ownership and requirements to place indigenous managers in key positions. The ownership limits may be general, limiting the degree of ownership any company may have in any industry. Or they may be specific to certain industries, like telecommunications.

GROWING TREND TOWARDS JOINT VENTURES

On a worldwide basis, the use of JVs continues to grow each year. There are various explanations for this rising trend in the number of JVs:

i) *Deregulation.* Many countries continue to deregulate industries and invite foreign competition, often in the form of alliances.

ii) *Strengthening of intellectual property law.* In the past firm have been reluctant to enter new markets in industries such as pharmaceuticals and biotechnology for alliances because offer of losing intellectual property (IP) to partners. In various countries, the strengthening of IP laws has alleviated that fear, increasing the willingness of foreign firms to collaborate.

iii) *Globalisation.* The continuing spread of global ideas, concepts, and competition creates ever increasing pressure on firms to globalise; alliances are a fast-response competitive weapon.

iv) *Innovation in alliance design.* New types of alliances are constantly being invented, thus increasing the range of strategic choices that firm have for forming alliances.

v) *Strategic importance of speed.* Speed and time to market continue to mandate the need for fast competitive response.

vi) *Increased skills in alliance management and alliance exit.* Relative to a decade ago, firms are, on average, much more sophisticated in alliance management (both entry and exit). As opposed to the ad hoc approaches that used to characterise alliance management, many firms have learned, often from bitter experience, that alliance cannot succeed without effective alliance management process.

vii) *Easier communication across long distances.* The interest has greatly simplified the ability of firms to communicate with distant international alliance partners.

viii) *Unbundling of the value chain or "skeleton companies with brains."* As firms continue to focus on core activities, alliances play a key role in allowing them to participate in noncore activities without a wholesale exit from these activities.

EQUITY JOINT VENTURES AND THE THEORY OF THE MULTINATIONAL ENTERPRISE

The term joint venture covers a broad array of possible interfirm relationships. The 'classic' equity joint venture is formed when two or more distinct firms (the parents) pool a portion of their resources in a separate jointly owned organisation. In the case of two-partner joint ventures, the equity stake may be equal or one partner may hold the majority. An equity joint venture could be formed *via* greenfield (i.e., new plant, new employees, etc.) or *via* a divisional merger whereby the parents contribute an existing division to the joint venture.

Non-equity joint venture involve no exchange of equity and no new company is formed. There are many variation on nonequity joint ventures, including: licensing and technology exchange, joint R&D, joint product development, and joint distribution or marketing. New forms of non-equity joint ventures are being created all the time. Unlike equity joint-ventures, nonequity relationships are easier to form and dissolve, and they typically involve less complex corporate governance and partner management issues. On the negative side, nonequity relationships often suffer from unclear strategic objectives and a lack of equity signals that the joint ventures may be temporary.

In addition to the equity and the non-equity joint ventures, there may be minority joint ventures. In this category of joint venture, one parent makes a minority investment in the other, and under this umbrella variety of deals are made. Minority equity joint ventures are used quite frequently in industries with high technological uncertainty, such as telecommunication, software, and biotechnology. In these instances a minority equity alliance can be a hedge, in that the larger firm may have an option to later purchase a majority equity stake in its smaller partner. Minority equity joint-ventures are also used when there are government restriction on fall acquisition.

JOINT VENTURES AND THE THEORY OF INTERNALISATION

Internalisation theory was developed to provide an economic rationale for the existence of MNCs. By definition these firms establish local operations as a means of serving a foreign market rather than engaging in arm's-length transactions with market intermediaries. The theory posits that due to the transaction costs which must be borne as a result of conducting business in imperfect markets, it is more efficient (less expensive) for the firm to use internal structures rather than market intermediaries to serve a foreign market. These market imperfections arise from two environmental conditions: uncertainty and a small number of market agents. When these conditions coexist with two sets of human factors, opportunism, and bounded rationality, then the costs of writing, executing and enforcing arm's-length complex contingent claims contracts with market intermediaries are greater than the costs of internalising the market. In other words, a firm facing a complex, unpredictable business environment and having a few potential channel members to utilise would be more profitable performing the distribution function itself when there was a strong likelihood market agents would try to take advantage of the firm's lack of complete knowledge and the firm was unable to specify all possible future transaction contingencies.

In order to justify the utilisation of international JVs within the internalisation framework two necessary conditions must be shown to exist: the firm possesses a rent-yielding asset which would allow it to be competitive in a foreign market; and joint venture arrangements are superior to other means for appropriating rents from the sake of this asset in the foreign market.

The attractiveness of joint ventures is a function of both the revenue-enhancing and cost-reducing opportunities they provide the MNC. However, according to internalisation theory in its present formulation, firms would have a strong economic incentive always to avoid joint-venture arrangements since these are regarded as being inferior to wholly owned subsidiaries (WOSs) in allowing the firm to maximise the returns available on its ownership-specific advantages. The value of the foreign local partners' assets would apparently be insufficient in any conceivable situation to offset the strategic risks and transactions costs faced by the MNC in exploiting its ownership-specific assets. Yet this solution to the problem of imperfect markets assumes that management has the ability to organise an internal market and that a joint venture cannot be structured in such a way as to maintain both the bargaining and maladaptation costs inherent in such arrangements at acceptable levels. Thus, in its current state of development, internalisation theory focuses primarily on the situation where WOS and arm's length transactions are the only alternatives available to deal with market-disabling factors of opportunism, bounded rationality, uncertainty and small numbers.

However, the JVs which conform to certain preconditions and structural arrangements can actually provide a better solution to the problems of opportunism, small numbers dilemma and uncertainty in the face of bounded rationality than wholly-owned subsidiaries. Although there would be costs associated with writing, executing and enforcing pricing agreements and use restrictions regarding the transfer of the enhanced revenue potential of its assets as a result of forming a JV. As well, rents can exceed those available through wholly-owned subsidiaries due to the potential synergistic effects of combining the MNC's assets with those of the local partner.

One of the most significant transactional contingencies faced by MNCs considering a joint venture would apparently by provoked by the problem of opportunism. Yet even opportunistic behaviour is not necessarily an inevitable aspect of inter-firm behaviour although he suspects such situations would be uncommon. Infact in situations where a joint venture is established in a spirit of mutual trust and commitment to its long-term commercial success, opportunitistic behaviour is unlikely to emerge. This is similar to the concept of mutual forbearance, where agents on a reciprocal basis, deliberately pass up short-term advantages. With a foundation of trust the partner, and particularly the MNC, would be more willing to exercise the tolerance and perseverance necessary to see the joint venture through its difficult times. Problems could be effectively dealt with by the MNC without damaging the long-run viability and efficiency of the joint venture arrangement. In these circumstances the effective management of opportunism would depend far more on managerial perspicacity and persistence than on company lawyers masterminding complete contingent claims contracts. Furthermore, if these positive attitudes are reinforced with supporting inter-organisational linkages such as mechanisms for the division of profits, joint decision-making processes and reward and control systems, the incentives to engage in self-seeking pre-emptive behaviour could be minimised. Under such circumstances, then, opportunism is not likely to obtain as the parties would be able to pursue their own self interest without a need to resort to guile. They could negotiate a shared perception of the relative value of their respective contributions over time and establish a mutually acceptable division of profits in a vigorous yet open fashion. Their attention could be directed toward long-term joint profit maximisation since there would be no need to make pre-emptive claims on profit streams. Consequently the partners could take the long view for investment purposes while simultaneously adjusting to changing market circumstances in an adaptive sequential manner.

A small numbers situation, particularly when combined with opportunism, would normally result in serious transactional difficulties for the firm. In the case of joint ventures, even if initially there are several local firms from which to select a suitable partner, a small numbers condition could obtain if the firm wished to change the terms of the agreement at a later date and seek a new partner. Having some experience with the MNC, the initial local partner will clearly enjoy cost advantages over firms not selected at the outset. The option of switching partners is, therefore, not optimal for the MNC. However, in the absence of local partner opportunism, this small numbers situation could present much less serious transactional difficulties than normally might be expected. Moreover, by establishing those inter-organisational linkages, to it is possible to manage many of the types of difficulties associated with exchange between bilateral monopolists regarding individual or joint maximisation of profits. There will be much less incentive to secure gains by strategic posturing and the interests of the joint venture can be promoted. Thus, under certain conditions, the small numbers dilemma can be effectively dealt with in a joint venture.

The problem of uncertainty can also be handled efficiently within some international joint ventures. In the absence of opportunism and small numbers disabilities there are strong incentives for the parties to pool their respective resources. By doing so it is possible for the MNC to economise on the information requirements of foreign investment. The MNC can provide firm-specific knowledge regarding technology, management and capital markets while the local partner can provide location-specific knowledge regarding host country markets, infrastructure and political trends. By pooling and sharing information through the mechanism of a joint venture the MNC is able to reduce uncertainty at a lower long-term average cost than through pure hierarchical or market approaches. Because the parties would have little incentive to behave opportunistically the derivative condition of information impactedness due to uncertainty and opportunism would to arise. Although bounded rationality would continue to be a problem, a pure hierarchical mode of transacting would not represent a superior solution to this problem alone. The low costs associated with opportunism, small numbers, uncertainty and information impactedness in joint ventures under the conditions specified above would render this mode of transacting the most efficient means of serving a foreign market.

Theoretically, although they have advantages over the market and wholly-owned subsidiaries in certain circumstances, there are limits to the relative efficiency gains provided by joint ventures. *First,* they can suffer from the same goal distortions as hierarchies. The MNC can become biased towards the maintenance of its initial arrangements with the joint-venture partner without considering the long-term profit or cost implications. However, several approaches to ensuring that profitability goals are not subordinated to other considerations or that the joint- venture mode of transaction is not uncritically preserved can be taken. For instance, profitability goals can be maintained by giving the general manager an equity position in the joint venture. This provides a strong incentive for him to ensure that profits are earned in the joint venture itself and are not unequally siphoned to' one partner over the other. Mechanisms can also be established which prevent either partner having total control over distribution or final selling price. Clearly, the lower the price to the distributor, the greater the profit that the distributing partner does not have to share. As well, management fees (usually paid to the MNC) can be tied to the productivity, profitability of the joint venture and the length of management contracts can be held to a relatively short time period. Not tying the joint ventures to a single source of supply, particularly if it is one of the partners, can help ensure that procurement biases are minimised. Finally, a conscious effort can be made to ensure that the total income derived from the joint venture by each partner, even if the mechanisms for doing so differ, are approximately equal. Infact, many overseas ventures are being formed as a mix of direct investment, licensing and trade. The joint venture partner may be compensated by a package involving some return on equity investment, royalties, technical services and management fees, and/or margins on components or finished product traded with the joint ventures.

Ensuring the joint venture arrangement is not uncritically maintained requires explicit recognition by both parties that: a partner may resort to guile at some point (even if this was absent in his behaviour at the outset, if the absolute number of locally available managers increases, the need for a foreign partner and his ability to supply management resources may he reduced); and while the foreign partner may possess the requisite knowledge about the local economy, politics and culture at the outset he may not continue to put forth the effort necessary to maintain this knowledge. Commitment to the success of joint ventures often varies over time. From the MNC's perspective the level of ongoing commitment may be a function of who in the firm helped set up the joint venture and his current status with the company.

The risk of leakage of proprietary knowledge also serves to limit the efficiency gains available through joint-venture arrangements. Leakage can occur in one of two major ways: a local employee may decide to resign and use the knowledge acquired in the joint venture to establish a competing firm (type I); or the local partner may decide to dissolve the arrangement and use the knowledge gained through the joint venture as a basis for continuing to serve the local (and possibly a foreign) market through his own organisation (type 2). Type-1 leakages are especially hard to prevent particularly if the employee concerned recognises the personal trade-offs involved and is willing to live with some limitations such as being forced to serve a single market. Type 2 leakages are often easier to control because the negative consequences for the local partner can be quite significant. Pirating the MNC's existing technology will normally mean that the local partner loses access to export markets, ongoing technological developments, trademarks, marketing skills and possibly specialised raw materials. Moreover depending on how the original agreement was structured, his pirating of technology might even be construed as a form of industrial espionage. Presumably the threat of lawsuits would act as a disincentive. Certainly there is, however, a dilution of complete control with industrial espionage Leakage, therefore, is a problem in joint ventures and its costs lo serve to limit the efficiency gains joint ventures offer markets and hierarchies.

Notwithstanding the potential for technology leakage, what seems often to be overlooked by management in the overall economic evaluation of joint ventures is that even though the start-up costs of wholly-owned subsidiaries may be substantially lower, the long-term average costs may be much higher than joint ventures due to the very significant cost associated with dependent efforts to overcome a lack of knowledge about the local economy, politics and culture.

OWNERSHIP AND RELATIONSHIP-CENTERED APPROACHES TOWARDS JOINT VENTURES

International joint venture activity has been increasing in recent years both in terms of frequency and strategic importance. In spite of the rising popularity of joint ventures (JVs), there is significant dissatisfaction with their performance This is intuitively inconsistent and indicates that though firms perceive the need for JVs they find them difficult to manage. Considering their increasing popularity, it is important to address this inconsistency.

A major cause for dissatisfaction with JVs is that a dual hierarchy, arising as a result of shared ownership, results in a high potential for conflict. Conflicts of interest due to divergent objectives and operational asymmetries may adversely affect a firm's flexibility in decision making and its ability to coordinate globally. This hampers the efficient conduct of its operations. One approach towards overcoming the difficulties inherent in managing JVs is oriented primarily towards the issue of formal control through ownership. This approach may be referred as the ownership-centered approach. It suggests that a wholly owned subsidiary provides the firm with the desired flexibility to coordinate activities globally and facilitates decision making through more direct means of control, such as hierarchical fiat, available as a result of ownership. In this way, it avoids the problem of managing conflict in JVs. This may be referred as unambiguous control

Another approach focus more closely on the social dimension within which the relationship is embedded in order to attain the desired flexibility. This approach referred to as the trust-centered approach, revolves primarily on the notion of trust and related issues such as reciprocity, commitment and mutual forbearance. Hère, ownership and control are not viewed as commensurate with one another. This ownership-centered approach tends to neglect the social context surrounding the JV relationship. This prevents the exploitation of the full potential benefits of shared resources, and hampers recognition of the potential for effective reduction of the costs inherent in shared ownership through nurturing the social quality of the relationship. Furthermore, it also hinders the attainment of coordination efficiencies. These efficiencies are facilitated by a mutual orientation towards one another, which is based on trust. Furthermore, a cooperative attitude manifests itself in a higher level of flexibility within the relationship. These arguments suggest that, even in the case of majority ownership the dominant partner would be better off paying attention to the venture's social relations and gradually building up trust since forcing decisions by virtue of sheer ownership would be a pyrrhic victory and ultimately threaten the venture.

Although the focus differs, the common factor underlying birth the ownership-centered and the trust centered approaches is the objective of flexibility and efficiency in the conduct of the operation. One emphases the attainment of flexibility and efficiency through hierarchical relations while the other emphasises this through social relations. Given this commonality of interest it would be useful to understand how the two approaches inform one another. That this has not been done may reflect the different orientations of the two approaches. Ownership-centered approaches are outcome oriented, relatively static and do not address the critical role of social phenomena in interorganisational relationships. Furthermore, ownership-centered approaches are primarily investigating phenomena from within a more structural framework An overemphasis on the structural features of interorganisational exchange results in a neglect of important process issues which add value to the exchange.

TRUST AND ITS ROLE IN JOINT VENTURE RELATIONSHIPS

The Structural and Social Dimensions of Trust

In order to explore the dynamics of trust in explaining the tolerance for JV relationships, it is important to understand what trust is and why actors would have a trusting orientation towards each other. Trust is based on a set of mutual expectations or anticipations regarding each other's behaviour and each actor's fulfillment of its perceived obligations in light of such anticipation. Trust does not mean the "naive belief in the honesty of other actors but rather the probability of violation of implicit or explicit agreements". In other words, trust is the perceived likelihood of the other not behaving in a self-interested manner.

Trust has two components—the structural and the social—each of which reinforces the other. The structural component refers to the complementarity of the resources contributed. Synergy through resource complementarity provides the value added and the consequent inducement to contribute toward the relationship.

With regard to the social component, the quality of the relationship has a strong impact on the nature and value of exchange within it. Trust, arising from the perception of long-term equity within the relationship, is essential for continued benevolent exchange. This perception of equity, by increasing overall goal congruence, induces behaviour in the interest of the relationship and reduces the need for monitoring. Trust is especially important in situations of uncertainty since, in its presence, less stringent contracting can occur in the expectation that the social dimensions of the relationship will occasion mutually desirable behaviour. Where performance is difficult to measure, as in the team production characteristic of many JVs, trust becomes critical to the relationship since performance need not be so directly measurable in a situation of mutual trust and commonality of interests.

The pattern of interaction provides the social "glue" within which economic exchange occurs. By providing the motive to cooperate and the mutual orientation that determines which action is in the best interest of the relationship, a regime of trust induces reciprocity and coordinates action. Investment in building trust through mutually oriented actions can then be interpreted as the creation of a stock of goodwill from which an actor can draw when the need arises. Such action also signals a commitment to the relationship. It conveys a long-term intent and creates reciprocal obligations. Such reciprocal obligations encourage flexibility within the relationship, although an approximate balance is required over the longer term for its sustenance. Here, each round of interactions need not be equally satisfactory to both parties provided that, on average, both actors are satisfied by the general pattern of interaction within the relationship over time. Since overall goal congruence facilitates the tolerance of both partial goal conflict and temporary periods of inequity within the relationship, trust creates flexibility within a relationship and has efficiency implications. It reduces friction and is "the behavioural lubricant that can improve a system's operating efficiencies.

It is important to recognise the difference in orientation between the structural and social dimensions of trust within a relationship. For the former, the incentive to abstain from behaving in a self-interested manner, i.e. to mutually forbear, is that it would be costly to do otherwise. Here, both firms are in a mutual hostage situation. Opportunistic behaviour would deplete the potential value added arising from the partners' complementarities to the detriment of both parties. On the other hand, from the social perspective, mutually oriented behaviour is more positive in nature and occurs not to prevent value depletion but to enhance the relationship's value. The two together lower the perceived probability of opportunistic behaviour or, conversely, increase trust.

The structural dimension is essential for the creation of the relationship but not sufficient for its continuation. It is necessary since, unless both parties are benefiting from the relationship, it is inherently unstable. It is not sufficient for two reasons. Firstly, a weak social foundation undermines the potential value of the synergy that can be gained by two firms pooling their assets together, since contributions become much more tentative. The partners would also tend to discount the future stream of benefits from the operations more heavily. Furthermore, the cost of the operation increases since greater expectation of opportunism by a partner causes the other to bear higher costs of installing safeguards against opportunism. A breakdown of the regime of trust and a consequent increase in uncertainty therefore weakens the mutual orientation and diminishes the perceived value of the relationship, making it unsustainable. Secondly, contributions cannot be continuously evenly matched. This is where the social dimension stabilises the relationship. It cements the relationship and provides the tolerance through the social "glue" to tide over temporary periods of disequilibrium.

A strong social foundation enhances the potential value of the synergy that can be gained by two firms pooling complementary assets. Where the structural basis of trust is weak, the relationship becomes unstable. The social basis of trust does not play the role of a "super glue" to patch together of inequity. It makes the relationship more resilient and, consequently, durable. The critical notion here is that inequity is often temporary, and the durability of the relationship is dependent on the social quality within which it is embedded. Therefore, during a period of flux in a relationship, the social aspect of trust acts to prevent a hasty or premature rupture that would sacrifice significant potential future benefits. In other words, the band of tolerance for inequity is wider in the presence of more deeply embedded social relations.

However, the social basis of trust is not adequate in and of itself. There is difference between the existence of compatible capabilities and the willingness to provide them, with both being critical to the success of a relationship. These, are parallel to the structural and social aspects of a relationship. The social aspects facilitate the attainment of the objectives of the collaboration through more sustained and higher quality inputs and lower conflict and coordination costs. Therefore, investment in trust-building becomes important. The underlying synergistic potential, however, lies in the structural aspects. Generally, there is a high correlation between the motivation underlying the formation of JVs and partner complementaries, even amongst partners where there had been a history of successful cooperation. This suggests that, just as the structural component is necessary but not sufficient, neither are the social aspects sufficient in and of themselves. The two do not substitute for one another but rather supplement and reinforce one another.

Proposition 1: The structural component of trust is necessary but not sufficient for the sustained continuation of interfirm relationship.

Proposition 2: The social component of trust is necessary but not sufficient for the sustained continuation of interfirm relationships.

Proposition 3: A relationship will be more durable when the social component is strong than when it is weak.

Proposition 4: Where the structural component is equally strong, differences in the social foundation underlying relationships will result in different rates of stability.

A trustful relationship does not just happen. It evolves gradually over time through repeated successful interaction and has to be carefully nurtured through various forms of hard and soft commitments. A major implication of this is that creating a foundation of trust is a slow, time-consuming and expensive process requiring a significant investment of resources—financial, temporal and managerial. In this regard, the structural and social components of trust have the potential for a positive feedback effect upon one another. As mentioned, successful interfirm cooperation requires a relationship that has both a potential for synergistic creation of value and a more mutually oriented behaviour in order to tap and enhance this potential. This value outcome provides the ability or means to invest in the value creation process while the social component provides the willingness to do so.

Proposition 5: Interfirm relationships characterised by both a strong structural and a strong social component of trust will be characterised by a greater investment in trust-building expenditures than those relationships that are not so characterised.

The presence of both components of trust is therefore important. The positive feedback effect between the two components of the relationship, by influencing the ability or means and the willingness to invest in the relationship, builds resilience into a relationship and strengthens it by making it more self-sustaining

An effective collaboration smoothens the interface between partners and is characterised by trust and understanding. In this way, it confirms the partners' importance to one another. A couple of prominent examples are illustrative. One is the GE-Snecma JV. Originally brought together by product-market complementarities in jet engine technology, this JV enjoyed strong top-level commitment. When lower level personnel in GE would attempt to engage in self-interested behaviour, these issues were always resolved at a higher level in the spirit of the partners mutual commitment. Success in the initial phase of the relationship resulted in continued cooperation over a family of engines that has lasted to the present. Such cooperation has been facilitated by a demonstration of flexibility over the duration of the relationship. For example, in order to be fair, GE and Snecma have periodically readjusted their contractual revenue-sharing formula due to unexpected changes in inflation and exchange rates. This is not to suggest that the relationship has not been occasionally stormy. However, due to their structural complementarities and the social quality of the relationship, the arrangement has survived these moments. Such conflict, if handled properly, plays a positive role in that it tests the resolve and strengthens the resilience of the relationship.

Infact such conflict results in better "real" relationships and provides the to deal with dynamic environments characterised by uncertainty without destroying the commitment to the venture. Another example is the collaboration between Boeing, the dominant partner, and a Japanese consortium for the development of jet aircraft. The two sides needed one another to share massive development costs and to realise synergies between the design experience of Boeing and the manufacturing efficiencies of the Japanese. In this venture the Japanese had to undertake a significant degree of risk in terms of loss of income should the expected sales of the 757 fail to materialise. When this happened, Boeing allocated some work on other planes as a compromise gesture, even though there was no contractual commitment to do so This gesture of integrity created a level of good will that facilitated resolution of later conflicts.

Application to the JV

Partner commitment and compatibility is a critical issue in JV relationships. The ownership arrangements are riot as important for successful JV performance as the similarity of outlook and objectives, i.e. compatibility. Greater compatibility increases the probability of balance between inducements and contributions with temporary imbalances being smoothed by trust. Greater compatibility manifests itself in greater commitment to the JV, which enables broader "bands of tolerance" and makes the partners more flexible with respect to the JV's operations. In such cases, they would be more willing to accept minority ownership, adapt products to local markets, accept the partner's personnel in important positions, adapt systems to accommodate the partner's needs, etc. Such ventures are characterised by a greater allocation of time and effort towards trust-building and knowledge transfer greater interaction through more regular meetings and visits, and an open communication system, all of which results in clear mutual expectations and enables more efficient coordination

A positive correlation between commitment and need for the both dimensions of trust in a JV relationship. The former addresses the mutual complementarities which underlie the structural dimension of trust while the latter addresses the social aspects, where the existence of commitment mitigates the desire for formal control measures. The extent of concern over control reflects the nature of a firm's attitudes toward the partner's contributions, with lower concern being symptomatic of a more positive evaluation of the relationship and a lower tendency to act solely in one's own interest. Such a positive evaluation, and consequent commitment, is facilitated by a high level of structural compatibility between the partners' inputs. Positive attitudes result in a greater ability to tap and benefit from partners' resources.

It is not necessary that wholly owned subsidiaries are more efficient than JVs is not necessarily true. Depending on the nature of resources needed, the initial stock of commitment and the interaction between these two factors, JVs can be both a revenue enhancing and a more efficient mode of organising. In this respect, mutual need for the partner's resources makes shared ownership more conducive towards encouraging participation while the presence of commitment curbs the transaction costs arising from opportunism, small numbers bargaining and uncertainty, and also facilitates information sharing. Under these conditions, the additional costs faced in the management of JVs can be contained at a level where benefits are greater than the costs. Development of the relationship over time leads to lower costs of transacting.

Arguments against the use of JVs due to the associated problems of coordination and control imply that internalisation would solve these problems. However, this does not recognise that headquarter subsidiary relationships are also mixed-motive, similarly characterised by independent and interdependent interests. Accordingly, depending on the role and strengths of different subsidiaries, the multinational firm faces governance problems and related costs in control and coordination of different operations, even when fully owned. Therefore, the assumption of such a direct inverse relationship between ownership and coordination and control costs is questionable, and it would be more appropriate to approach the issue in a comparative manner, where the coordination and control costs of JVs are compared with those of wholly owned subsidiaries.

The incremental costs of managing JVs arise partially from the costs of maintaining safeguards against the possibility of self-seeking behaviour arising from divergent objectives. As noted above, ownership-centered approaches inadequately recognise the scope for reduction of opportunistic behaviour which is available through addressing the social context of the relationship. A positive social dynamic between partners is important, since it facilitates the building of trust within, a relationship. It is argued that where a relationship is value laden due to its social properties it can manifest the advantages of hierarchies. Neither pure market nor pure hierarchical relations are critical for sustaining a relationship: *trust is.*

The argument that nurturing the social dimension increases flexibility and tolerance, especially in a situation of ambiguity, is especially relevant in entities such as JVs, which involve team production by two actors contributing their respective inputs for mutual benefits. Here, the observation of dissatisfaction with the JV's performance in cases where one partner had greater than two avenues over the other for earning income is significant. This shows that the perception of equity within the relationship does not automatically arise from the formal aspects of ownership. The alignment of incentives through the sharing of ownership is not adequate to ensure desirable action by the partner. Through income earning avenues like royalties for technology supplied, monopoly over the supply of inputs, management fees etc., the multinational firm can capture the bulk of the value added prior to the formal sharing of gains through the ownership structure. Therefore the critical issue is not that of the formal distribution of the residual income in line with the percentage of equity ownership but rather, that of equity and fairness with respect to the process of the relationship itself. This perception of equity is important to encourage mutually oriented action, beyond the very minimum under the terms of the agreement. Without it, the base of trust would be violated.

In this regard, statement that JVs are a mixture of contract and commitment is relevant. Here, the critical initial decisions are agreed to contractually in the negotiation phase, but sustenance of the relationship is based on trust and commitment. This commitment develops through interaction, and results in a trust-based relationship that more closely resembles an internalised mode than a contractual one. This implies a shift from control through the ownership structure to influencing behaviour through interaction and the nurturing of relationships.

The need for control is positively correlated with lack of information which then heightens the level of risk perceived by an actor and consequently affects the choice of governance structure. A successful pattern of interaction results in not only a trustful orientation, where relationship-specific routines as a result of greater experience with each other facilitate coordination and lower the proclivity to be opportunistic, but also greater knowledge about each other as a result of a more open sharing of information. This lowers information asymmetries and consequent scope for opportunism and perceived risk. This then lowers the perceived probability of opportunism and, combined with a lower perceived necessity for maintaining safeguards, explains why a successful cooperative history was found to be the most important criterion in the selection of JV partners.

REVISITING THE MULTINATIONAL FIRM'S TOLERANCE FOR JOINT VENTURES

Product and Market Standardisation Strategies

The extent of ownership has always been a critical issue in multinational operations. The market or product standardisation strategies occurring in the mature stages of an industry when there is greater homogeneity of tastes and stiffer competition, are characterised by pressures to lower both production and administrative costs through consolidation and rationalisation. This increases the desirability of tighter coordination between units and, by centralising the locus of decision making, results in a lower tolerance for JVs. JVs increase the potential for friction and adversely effect the flexibility in decision making required for overall system optimisation. In other words, strategies requiring centralised control result in a more cautious attitude towards JVs. On the other hand, a strategy based upon product diversification or market expansion results in a higher tolerance for JVs since, when a firm's resources are allocated towards introduction of new products rather than cost minimisation and strategic coordination, JVs provide a desirable complementarity.

These arguments can be interpreted in a different light. JVs by definition are more complicated to manage because of dual hierarchies. One way to manage the greater potential for friction is to influence the social context of interaction, As mentioned earlier, creating a foundation of trust is a slow, time-consuming and expensive process. Creation and sustenance of trust requires both structural compatibility as well as the willingness to invest in the relationship to enable more effective realisation, on a continual basis, of the potential benefits of such compatibility. The requirements for investment in trust-building are greater in the formative period of a relationship in order to absorb the initially higher costs of creating commitment, including any possible losses from self-interested behaviour in the initial stages. However, once the foundation has been secured, extraordinary expenditures for relationship sustenance are minimal, though normal expenditures are still necessary to enable continued enhancement and realisation of value from the relationship.

One principal source of resources for investment into the relationship is above-normal returns. Greater competition during the more mature stages of an industry, when firms pursue standardised strategies, makes the attainment of above normal returns difficult. This is not the case in an earlier stage characterised by less competition. This argument addresses the issue of scarcity and munificence of environments where, in lean environments characterised by more intensive competition and dissipation of excess rents, there is less slack and coordination and cost minimisation become more important. Furthermore, in cases where the scope of the operation is global, as is often the case in world-wide consolidation and rationalisation strategies, while the JV partner is strictly local, coordination at a more centralised level is preferred by the multinational firm and communication flows at a local level are largely of an implementing nature. The weaker structural foundation, due to relatively insubstantive inputs from the local unit results in lower commitment towards building a long-term stable relationship. Therefore, both the structural and the social basis of the relationship are undermined. In such environments, firms are less able to undertake, and less tolerant of, the investments necessary' for trustbuilding in JVs.

Product Diversification

With respect to product diversification, it may be pointed that most product diversification strategies are to be in related products. The product diversification strategies involve uncertainty for multinational firms since these firms are usually product-oriented and lack the market orientation that is equally important for the success of such strategies. These strategies require greater decentralisation and flexibility to adapt to local market, which increase the tolerance for JVs. In such cases, the need for complementary resources is greater than the cost of reduced levels of control. The provision of an ownership stake in recognition of the partner's contribution is expected to provide incentives to the partner to act in the interest of the JV.

The argument was made earlier, however, that a mere ownership stake is not sufficient in a JV, and needs to be supplemented by a belief or trust that each partner is acting in the best interest of the relationship. A perception of equity, aside from the ownership structure, is all the more important in strategies of related product diversification. This is because the relatedness makes it difficult for the value of the firm's contribution to be accurately measured and reflected in a contract, since shared activities are difficult to disentangle and cost separately. This increases coordination costs and opportunities for conflict.

In a situation characterised simultaneously by the desirability of the partner's contributions and greater scope for conflict, investment in trust-building expenditures is critical in order to exploit more effectively the synergies due to product-market complementarities. Under related diversification strategies, economies of scope arising from the relatedness between products result in more efficient utilisation of firm resources. Such economies are unlikely to be available in the case of single or unrelated products where there is little scope for sharing costs across activities. Moreover, first-mover advantages of new product introduction into new markets provide scope for initial monopolistic rents. This first-mover advantage is further enhanced in the case of JVs oriented towards local markets of limited capacity. All these factors enable the firm to undertake the investments necessary' to create and realise a more sound relationship with their JV partners.

Product Innovation

The product innovation strategies, being dominated by fears of technology leakage, free riding and problems of technology pricing, are characterised by a desire for greater control This resulted in a strong apprehension regarding JVs and a preference for subsidiaries over JVs.

Product innovation strategies are characterised by a high degree of uncertainty due to the technological and task complexity and the uncertainty of returns. Furthermore, product innovation mostly occurs in the early stages of the product life cycle when the environment is more volatile and the routines less codified. Greater complexity and a more volatile environment in these stages lower firms' ability to respond to situations through a fixed set of routines, and consequently increases the scope for conflict. This lowers the tolerance for decision making through JVs. In situations characterised by such uncertainty and ambiguity, the contract would be increasingly incomplete, consequently heightening the firm's concerns regarding opportunistic behaviour by a partner. In such situations, a high level of trust would be required to mitigate such concerns. The resources required, whether temporal, managerial or financial, for creating such a high level of trust would make the firm reluctant to enter into a locally oriented JV, which provides limited scope to generate a sufficiently high level of gain. Furthermore, as in the case of product and market standardisation strategies, a local partner's contribution is not so significant. This weakens the commitment toward building a long-term stable relationship. All these factors undermine the relationship and result in a lower tolerance for JVs.

The highest tolerance for JVs invested when the strategy and the scope of the operation was local in nature. Here, both partners were able to make valued contributions. Where the JV is such that the local partner does not make a significant contribution, there is little incentive to enter into a JV except for defensive or passive reasons, such as financing needs or benefits of local identity. Here, the partner's contribution is valued more as a convenience than a contribution, resulting in little commitment on both sides and a greater incentive to free ride by the local partner. Furthermore, any opportunistic behaviour by the local partner is less likely to be tolerated by the multinational, since the asset contributed by the partner to the venture is not so firm-specific. In other words, a small numbers situation does not exist, resulting in a lack of incentive to nurture the relationship and, simultaneously, little patience for shirking and free riding by the local partner. A weak structural foundation and such a negative social atmosphere lowers tolerance for JVs and makes sustenance of the relationship improbable. This further explains the low tolerance for JVs in the case of product innovation, marketing standardisation, and production rationalisation.

Ability to Manage Change

Thus, the scope of a particular operation, deriving from the multinational firm's strategy, is critical to the tolerance for JVs. JV instability may be at it height in line with changes in strategy and accompanying changes in structure, though there are differences in the lags between the change and the instability, as well as differences instability rates. For example, with increasing significance of international operations and other exogenous environmental changes, like demand convergence and technological developments, a shift from a decentralised strategy through an international division to a more centralised one through worldwide product divisions or geography-based regional structures resulted in a lack of tolerance for existing JVs and consequent increase in failure rates.

This can be understood more clearly when one considers the nature and pattern of interaction within a relationship, rather than its institutional properties, which are critical for the efficient conduct of an activity. Trust is a dynamic concept and the structural and social aspects underlying the relationship strongly influence the nature and pattern of interaction. A major cause of conflict in JVs is that the relative contributions and comparative advantages of the venture partners change continually, whether due to exogenous events or due to internal dynamics, for example differential rates of learning by both partners. This influences the evaluation of a firm's contributions.

Regarding finding of a peak in JV instability, the change in strategic scope or purpose of the operation and concomitant change in structure and systems changed the nature and desirable pattern of interaction within the relationship. The perceived propensity for trust or opportunism depends upon the nature and pattern of interaction. In this case, the need for strategic coordination and control of the operation increased and the locus of strategic decision making moved to a supranational level. Consequently, the role of the local operation changed from a relatively substantive one to that of an implementor, where the erstwhile contributions of the JV partner are less valued, reducing the structural bonding properties of the relationship. In other words, the structural foundation of the relationship became weakened in a manner creating not a temporary but a long-term disequilibrium. Furthermore, increased interdependence among various units under such closely coordinated strategies increased the negative externalities of self-interested behaviour. In a relationship with a more tightly coordinated and interdependent system, where the structural foundation of the relationship is weakened and, simultaneously, there is a greater potential for negative externalities, the potential for, and probability of self-interested behaviour is perceived to be higher, i.e. lower trust. This in turn influences the evaluation of the relationship and destabilises it, since there is a lack of correspondence between the incentive or payoff structure and the new reality. Such a correspondence between the relatively inflexible incentive system and the variable importance of partners' respective inputs is difficult to maintain, and is a major source of strain in the relationship.

Structural changes in firm complementarities can therefore strain a relationship and consequently influence tolerance for JVs. Where the basis for such conflict is long-term structural disequilibria in contributions, the bonding properties of the social dimension become inadequate. Clearly, there are limits to trust. At the same time, the underlying social properties of the relationship would be manifest in different degrees of flexibility in managing these strategic disjunctures, and would be reflected in differences in lags before failure and differential survival and failure rates in the face of similar strategic changes.

The above discussion of the peaking phenomenon suggests that comparative costs need to be evaluated not just against another governance structure, for instance a subsidiary versus a JV, but also with regard to costs within the same form before and after a change in strategy that alters the scope or purpose of the activity to be undertaken. It is worth mentioning, however, that where the social foundation of a relationship is strong, a demise of one venture due to structural weaknesses need not equate with the end of the relationship between two actors. There are numerous instances of partners being engaged in multiple partnerships, simultaneous or sequential, which have been built around a successful cooperative history. Here the relationship, the process and not the outcome, is viewed as a value-bearing asset in its own right.

The ability to build and maintain trust is a critical component of understanding tolerance for JVs. Clearly, however, there are differences in actors' abilities to invest in trust building expenditures and to pursue a cooperative strategy. In the presence of significant size asymmetries, it is easier for a larger firm, being less dependent on the venture, to nurture a positive atmosphere. This is due to both a higher tolerance for losses, in case of opportunistic behaviour, and to the normally higher stakes and greater vulnerability of the smaller partner. Such would be the case in many of the multinational operations. Similarly, a well-diversified firm has a greater ability to make trust-building gestures, since resources from other activities can both be tapped for investment in trust building as well as provide the firm with the buffering capacity to absorb violations of trust in any single activity. This is much more difficult for firms with more limited sources of income based on a single critical sphere of activities. This reinforces the fact that undiversified firms pursuing functional strategies have a lower tolerance for JVs.

So, the simultaneous popularity of international JVs and dissatisfaction with their performance indicates that need for greater attention to, and a more sophisticated understanding of, the process of governing them. *Relationship management* is increasingly important in today's business environment where the forces of global competition and technological dynamism compel even the strongest firms to enter collaborative relationships in order to remain competitive.

CREATING SUCCESSFUL STRATEGIC INTERNATIONAL ALLIANCES

The cliche "same bed, different dreams" is often evoked to describe the reality of alliance management. This phrase gives the impression that alliance partners should expect problems in their alliance efforts. The international alliances can be challenging to manage and, in some instances, lead to serious partner conflict and painful termination. There are several issues that are unavoidable when it comes to alliance management:

i) *Alliances involve uncertainty and ambiguity.* This uncertainty and ambi-guity add to the managerial challenge and are one of the main reasons alliances involve significant coordination costs.
ii) *The partner relationship will evolve in ways that are hard to predict.*

iii) Alliances are formed for strategic reasons and as strategies and competitive environments evolve, so must alliances.

iv) *Alliances remain vulnerable to many types of destabilising factors regardless of the strategic logic underpinning their formation.*

v) *Today's ally may be tomorrow's rival.* Successful companies never forget that their new partners may be out to disarm them.

vi) *The partners will eventually go their separate ways.* All alliances eventually will end, which means firms must be realistic in considering alliance longevity.

Apart from the unavoidable issues, there are two additional issues or risks that can be circumvented:

i) *Alliances do not have to be very difficult and expensive to manage.* Alliances can involve significant managerial time, especially when a firm has little experience in managing alliances or when the prior experience between the partners is limited. However, the last decade has seen growing competencies in alliance management. As firms gain experience with alliances and build effective control systems, these partnerships do not have to be viewed as expensive and difficult to manage. See Table-1 for a list of key questions that should be considered in a strategic alliance development process.

TABLE 1

Strategic Alliance Development Process

A strategic alliance development process should include a series of checkpoints that must be satisfied before the process moves forward. The process should be designed to ensure that key questions are posed and debated as the alliance moves through the formation process. The questions that should be addressed during strategic alliance development include:

- Are there clearly understood and agreed-upon objectives before alliance formation?
- How will the alliance be integrated with the parent firm's strategy?
- Will there be cultural compatibility and organisational fit between the partners?
- Does the alliance leverage the complementary strengths of the partners?
- Will an exit strategy be defined upfront?
- Is there a monitoring process for new alliances?
- Have all the partnering risks been identified and accounted for?

Properly implemented, a systematic alliance development process will ensure that:

- Projects are strategic to the firm.
- Projects meet financial objectives.
- Projects move quickly through required corporate approval processes.
- Project risks and challenges are identified and understood by all parties involved in the alliance formation process.

ii) *Core competencies will not necessarily be appropriated by your partner— that is, "sleeping with the enemy."* As alliances do create competitive risks and there are enough cases of knowledge theft the companies must be aware of these risks. Fortunately, a firm can take a few easy steps to protect intellectual property in strate-gic alliances (see Table-2).

TABLE 2

Protecting Intellectual Property in Strategic Alliances

Steps that an alliance partner can take to help protect its intellectual property from par appropriation include the following:
1. Anticipate partner's learning intent and learning ability.
2. Design the joint tasks to "wall off' certain aspects of the business.
3. Transfer older technologies to the alliance.
4. Locate the alliance close to the facilities of the parent to provide easier monitoring
5. Limit the number of managers a partner can contribute to the alliance.
6. Limit personnel transfers from the alliance to the partner organization.
7. Limit the number of partner visitors to the alliance.

To create successful alliances, firms should consider various issues after an alliance has been identified as a possible strategic option but before negotiations begin. These issues, if properly dealt with, provide the foundation for creating viable collaborative relationships. Table-3 provides a list of questions that should be addressed in order to consider all the issues. The questions in table-3 are generic in the sense that they should be asked for any proposed alliance. If a firm cannot answer these questions, it is not ready to enter alliance negotiations. Alternatively, the answers may suggest that an alliance is not the best course of action. Of course, the answers to the questions are contingent on various factors, including the firms involved, the nature of the proposed alliance, the anticipated impact on firm strategy, and the collaborative experience of the firms involved. After an alliance is formed, firms need to regularly review the alliance and ask some fundamental questions about performance and partner interactions. These questions include: Is the strategic logic of the alliance grounded in reality? What will each partner gain and how will the alliance continue to create value? Do the partner firms pursue a set of mutually beneficial and agreed-upon goals? Has a climate of openness between the partners been established? Do the firms understand your partner's competitive position? Do the partners contribute more than money and contribute on a continuing basis [technology, products, ideas, etc.]? All partners need an incentive to remain in the alliance. Are the partners equally committed to remaining in the alliance? Will there be managerial continuity between the partners? Are the partners willing to review and readjust the governance systems? Don't assume that degree of ownership equals control. Are the alliances performance measures consistent with the alliance strategic intent? Is the expectation of alliance longevity realistic? Are exit provisions well thought out?

TABLE 3

Key Planning Issues for the Success of Joint Venture

Mutual Value Creation

- Have both short- and long-term collaborative objectives been clearly established? Will an alliance help to achieve those objectives?
- Will the alliance negotiation be focused on joint economic success and mutual value creation or will it lead to a one-sided outcome?
- What will happen if an agreement cannot be reached in your alliance negotiations? Besides an alliance, what are the options for achieving strategic objectives?

Initial Partner Knowledge

- What does the firm really know about its partner and its ability to work together? What are the partner's strengths and weaknesses? How much experience and success does the firm have with alliances?
- Has the prior experience with the potential partner created a strong level of interfirm trust? Can that trust play a key role in current negotiations and will the individual managers who built the trust be involved in the planned alliance?
- Is the partner a competitor or likely to become a competitor at some point in the future? What role will your firm's knowledge play in determining whether or not the partner becomes a competitor?

Risk

- How much risk is the firm willing to bear? What are the implications if the alliance is terminated and the business is sold to the partner?

Essential Terms

- Has the firm you clearly determined the issues that are nonnegotiable? Is the firm willing to compromise on these issues in the case of unique collaborative opportunities?

Individuals' Roles

- Does the firm the role that its counterpart negotiators will play in the future alliance?
- Will these individuals be the managers the firm have to work with when the alliance is formed? Or will a new set of managers be assigned to operational roles?
- Does the firm's counterpart negotiators have personal incentives associated with a successful alliance negotiation?
- Will operational managers be involved in the negotiations? Have these managers initiated the potential alliance?
- What will the alliance top management team look like? Will the partner have any objections to the firm's choice of managers? Based on the relationship between partner and the competitive environment the alliance faces, what skills should the alliance managers have?

Alliance Governance and Trust

- Do both parties understand that successful alliances will undergo a series of transitions as the partners learn more about each other and competitive dynamics shift?
- Do venture partners recognize that the alliance negotiation is a means to an end? No matter how well the alliance is negotiated, issues of organizational fit and implementation will be critical in contributing to alliance success.
- Do all partners understand the importance of flexibility in the negotiation process and the contractual agreement?

Cross-Cultural Issues

- Are the managers who will be involved in the negotiation and venture management familiar with the national culture of the partner? If not, are there other internal or external advisors who can be consulted?
- Is the partner skilled in cross-cultural management?

Flexibility and Review

- Is review time built into the alliance formation and negotiation plan?

Source: Andrew C. Inkpen and Kou Qing Li, "Joint Venture Formation: Planning and Knowledge Gathering for Success," *Organizational Dynamics* 27, no. 4 (1999): 33-47.

JVs are often shaped in highly uncertain settings and involve partners with different and often competing agendas. There may be a failure to develop clear performance measures, for various reasons: unfamiliarity with alliance measurement, unwillingness to deal with partner conflict over performance issues, asymmetric views on performance measurement, multiple constituencies with input in the performance issues, and unclear managerial responsibility for alliance outcomes. Therefore, JVs managers keep must keep the following three factors in mind when considering alliance performance measurement:

1. JVs should be evaluated using a combination of factors: objective measures, such as financial performance (ROI, cost structure, process improvements) and market share; subjective measures, such as relationship between the partners, alliance stability, and technological learning; and survival of both the partnership and the alliance business.
2. The weight of each measure should vary over time. In newly formed JVs, objective measures should be discounted. In older JVs, objective measures will receive greater attention.
3. The weight of each measure should be consistent with the strategic intent of the JV. If the intent is market share or profits, strategic measures may be discounted. Finally, subjective measures will always be difficult to assess.

It is a mistake to equate longevity with success. Longevity can be a rough indicator of success. As long as alliance serve the strategic objectives of the venture, the alliance should be safeguarded, nurtured, and kept alive. Therefore, managers involved in alliance must be prepared to critically assess performance and recognize when performance is poor and unlikely to improve. However, when alliances fail to fulfill their promise or outlive their usefulness because partner objectives have been accomplished, they must be terminated.

Mutual value creation is the foundation for successful alliance management. Many international alliances survive and prosper for many years, with both sides becoming more competitive in a win-win relationshipip. While some alliances may result in a zero-sum game of winners and losers, if alliances are to be an integral element of global strategy, firms should seek partners with whom they can achieve an effective working relationship that links complementary assets. In the international arena, national culture adds a dimension to the challenge of partner selection and building successful alliances. But it is important to remember that cultural differences do not arise just from differences in nationality. All alliances involve the combining of organizational cultures that may be vastly different. Firms that are skilled in alliance management recognise that successful collaboration requires a commitment to the collaborative task and a willingness to tolerate some ambiguity and flexibility. When properly managed, alliances create the foundation for global opportunities that may be difficult or impossible to exploit independently.

QUESTIONS

1. Describe and explain the similarities and differences between strategic alliances and joint venture agreements.
2. Discuss the various forms of Joint Ventures.
3. Describe the ownership and relationship—centered approaches toward joint venture.
4. Explain the trust and its role in joint venture relationships.
5. Discuss the use of strategic alliances within the environment of antitrust activity by governments to maintain open and competitive markets.
6. What are the important ingredients in creating a successful joint ventures?

REFERENCES

Alder, Lee and Hlavcek, James D. *Joint ventures for product innovation*, American, New York, 1976.

Aharoni, Yair, *The foreign investment decision process*, Havard University Press, Boston Massachusetts, 1966.

Baetz, Mark C. and Beamish, Paul W., *Strategic management: Canadian cases*, Richard D. Irwin, Homewood, Illinois, 1987.

Caves, Richard E., *Multinational enterprise and economic analysis*, Cambridge University Press, Cambridge, Massachusetts, 1982.

Friedman, Wolfgang Ga. and Begiun, J.P., *Joint international business ventures in developing countries*, Columbia University Press, New York, 1971.

———, and Kalmanoff, George, *Joint international business ventures*, Columbia University Press, New York, 1961.

Hennart, Jean-Francois, *A theory of multinational enterprise*, University of Michigan Press, Ann Arbour, 1982.

Janger, Allen R., *Organisation of international joint ventures*, The Conference Board, New York, 1980.

Kolde, E.J. *The multinational company*, Lexington Books, Toronto, 1974.

Minttzberg, H. *The nature of managerial work*, Prentice-Hall, Englewood Cliffs, New Jersey, 1980.

McMillan, C.H. and St Charles, D.P., *Joint ventures in eastern Europe: a three-country comparison*, C.D. Howe Research Institute, Montreal, 1974.

Newbound, Gerald D., Buckley, Peter J. and Thurwell, Jane C. *Going international*, John Wiley and Sons, Toronto, 1978.

Rugman Alan M. *Internatioal diversification and the multinational enterprise*, D.C. Health, Lexington< Massachusetts, 1979.

United Nations *Manual on the establishment of industrial joint-ventures agreements in developing countries*, UN, New York, 1971.

Vaupel, James W. and Curhan, Joan P., *The world's multinational enterprises*, Harvard University Press, Boston, Massachusetts, 1973.

Williamson, Oliver E., *Markets and hiearchies: analysis and anti-trust implications — a study in the economic of internal organisations*, Free Press, New York, 1975.

31

MANAGING THE MULTINATIONAL CORPORATIONS

INTRODUCTION

Multinational corporations have existed since the beginning of overseas trade. They have remained a part of the business scene throughout history, entering their modern form in the 17th and 18th centuries with the creation of large, European-based monopolistic concerns such as the British East India Company during the age of colonization. Multinational concerns were viewed at that time as agents of civilization and played a pivotal role in the commercial and industrial development of Asia, South America, and Africa. By the end of the 19th century, advances in communications had more closely linked world markets, and multinational corporations retained their favorable image as instruments of improved global relations through commercial ties. The existence of close international trading relations did not prevent the outbreak of two world wars in the first half of the twentieth century, but an even more closely bound world economy emerged in the aftermath of the period of conflict.

In more recent times, multinational corporations have grown in power and visibility, but have come to be viewed more ambivalently by both governments and consumers worldwide. Indeed, multinationals today are viewed with increased suspicion given their perceived lack of concern for the economic well-being of particular geographic regions and the public impression that multinationals are gaining power in relation to national government agencies, international trade federations and organizations, and local, national, and international labor organizations.

Despite such concerns, multinational corporations appear poised to expand their power and influence as barriers to international trade continue to be removed. Furthermore, the actual nature and methods of multinationals are in large measure misunderstood by the public, and their long-term influence is likely to be less sinister than imagined. Multinational corporations share many common traits, including the methods they use to penetrate new markets, the manner in which their overseas subsidiaries are tied to their headquarters operations, and their interaction with national governmental agencies and national and international labor organizations.

WHAT IS MULTINATIONAL CORPORATION?

The term 'multinational' is widely used today, the phrase is still subject to varying interpretations practitioners and researchers use the terms 'international', 'supranational', 'global', 'transnational', and 'multinational' interchangeably. While some writers have a clear idea of what constitutes a MNC, others have vague notions. To some multinational corporations are *business entities* that operate in more than one country. The typical multinational *corporation* or MNC normally functions with a headquarters that is based in one country, while other facilities are based in locations in other countries. In some circles, a multinational corporation is referred to as a multinational enterprise (MBE) or a multinational corporation (MNC).

The exact model for an MNC may vary slightly. One common model is for the multinational corporation is the positioning of the executive headquarters in one nation, while production facilities are located in one or more other countries. This model often allows the company to take advantage of benefits of incorporating in a given locality, while also being able to produce goods and services in areas where the cost of production is lower. Another structural model for a multinational organization (MNO) is to base the *parent company* in one nation and operate subsidiaries in other countries around the world. With this model, just about all the functions of the parent are based in the country of origin. The subsidiaries more or less function independently, outside of a few basic ties to the parent. A third approach to the setup of an MNC involves the establishment of a headquarters in one country that oversees a diverse conglomeration that stretches to many different countries and industries. With this model, the MNC includes affiliates, subsidiaries and possibly even some facilities that report directly to the headquarters.

The economic definition emphasizes the ability of owners and their managerial agents in one country to control the operations in foreign countries. There is a frequent confusion that equates the ability to control with the flow of capital across national borders. It is recognized widely that capital flow is not the distinguishing characteristic of a multinational corporation. Capital can flow from one country to another in expectation of higher rates of return. However, this flow may be invested in the form of bonds, or in equity amounts too insignificant to grant control to foreign owners. In this case, this type of investment is treated as a 'portfolio' investment. The central aspect of 'direct investment' is the ownership claim by a party located in one country on the operations of a foreign firm or subsidiary in another. The multinational corporation is, thus, the product of foreign direct investment that is defined as the effective control of operations in a country by foreign owners.

The economic definition, however, does not capture the importance of the multinational corporation as the organizational mechanism by which different social and economic systems confront each other. The multinational corporation, because usually it develops in the cultural and social context of one nation, exports its organizational baggage from one institutional setting to another. In this regard, it plays a powerful role as a mechanism by which to transfer organizational knowledge across borders. However, while being foreign implies that it might serve the valuable role of importing new practices, its foreign status also implies that its practices are likely to conflict with existing institutions and cultural norms. Moreover, since multinational corporations are often large, they pose unusual challenges to national and regional governments who seek to maintain political autonomy and yet are often anxious to seek the investment, technology, and managerial skills of foreign firms.

There are, thus, economic and sociological definitions of the multinational corporation that differ, and yet complement, each other. In the economic definition, the multinational corporation is the control of foreign activities through the auspices of the firm. In the sociological definition, the multinational corporation is the mechanism by which organizational practices are transferred and replicated from one country to another.

HISTORY OF MNCs

The multinational corporation is defined in some sense arbitrarily by where frontiers are drawn. In ancient Greece, these frontiers were the borders among city-states. In imperial Rome, the new administrative units of an expanding empire and its external boundaries defined the borders. Political borders correspond only approximately to the distribution of cultural and ethnic dispositions. The history of the multinational corporation is tied closely to the origins of trade in and between cultural communities, and these communities remain important in many sectors in the modern economy.

Early trade was often characterized by the difficulty of transacting across borders. Trading has always instigated from the unequal and varied distribution of resources across geographies. The trading of salt was an important factor in most continents and still can be found in rather ancient forms in east Africa. Towns, such as Salzburg, owed their origins to their fortuitous access to salt mines.

This unequal distribution incited traders to travel long distances and undergo unusual risks for the hope of gain. The dilemma is quite apparent. How can markets for trade develop between distant cultures? Indeed, there is good evidence that early trading was quite precarious. Brown notes that Hermes was not only the god of messengers but also of theft and trade. He was often worshipped at borders, marking the place of trade. Herodotus describes the practice of the 'silent trade' of goods at boundary markings in which one party would deposit their goods at the border, the second party would later deposit a corresponding offer. The original party might accept this bid, take the goods, and leave their initial offer. Clearly, only a strong demand for unusual foreign goods could sustain such a treacherous institution of transaction.

Not surprisingly, Curtin doubts the accuracy of this account. Instead, he stresses the importance of ethnic groups, such as the Gujarati or overseas Chinese, or the force of imperialism and military power as ways in which 'cross-cultural trading' was permitted to develop. But such solutions remained fragile, with foreign enclaves and ethnic groups subject to local hatred and military rule often confronting competition from other powers.

Yet, trade persisted through the centuries. Indeed, the demand for foreign goods was so strong that incredible profits could be realized by international trade. Since transportation was poor, and technology to hold inventories rudimentary, an agent in the right spot at the right time could earn fortunes. And in this laid the great problem. For in times of great demand, prices could rise astronomically, as Braudel documents in his history of material life. With such distances between the agent and the principal in the exporting country, an agent could easily, and often did, disappear with the profits.

The early solutions were many and provide insight into one of the great properties of the multinational corporation: its ability to organize transactions within its own organizational boundaries. Great fairs were one solution, where principals met their customers in one place. But fairs were intermittent and often distant from final markets. The further development of Roman commercial law during the medieval and Renaissance periods strengthened the liability of the principal and also legal recourse in principal-agent conflict. However, the application of law between two parties in different legal jurisdictions has always been a difficult form of dispute resolution. In his study of the Jewish Magrebi traders of the twelfth century, Greif places considerable emphasis upon the value of membership in ethnic 'trading communities.' Since ethnic enclaves in foreign sites could monitor the activities of agents, principals could be informed of malfeasance. Agents could then be excluded from future contracts within the community, thus deterring dishonest behavior. Partnerships were also another way in which agents were also bonded to the firm.

However, another solution was the company, a word whose roots come from the Latin meaning 'with bread' which implies the familial origins of this business organization. The company permitted in time the investing of capital in its ownership by outsiders in promise of future dividends. The capital might be raised for a single voyage or, eventually, could be maintained in the company in the form of stock ownership. With the evolution of limited liability law in the nineteenth century, and the diminished role of the state in restricting the growth of the joint stock company, this organizational form expanded rapidly in many European countries as well as in the United States. Along with the growth of equity markets, the financial resources to invest overseas became more available due to advances in the banking system and also in bond markets. Indeed, the great capital needs of the railway industry created an international market for the sale and purchase of railroad bonds. However, international loans and bonds were risky and it was not uncommon for sovereign governments to default, including state governments within the United States.

The increasing wealth of western countries, along with constraints on the speed by which national industries could absorb new loans, encouraged massive foreign investments by the end of the nineteenth century and early twentieth century. This was a period of globalization in terms of the percentages of capital outflows to total capital accumulation. Great Britain is estimated to have exported some 25 percent of its capital prior to World War I and French capital exports were often greater. This capital went to countries hungry to finance their industrial expansion, including the newly industrializing countries of Russia and especially America.

The British were unusual in directing a considerable amount of their outward capital flows in the form of direct investments. A great deal of this investment went into their colonies. Prior to the mid-1800s, companies operating overseas engaged largely in wholesale operations; they did not run factories, operate mines, or own agriculture. The British direct investments were, thus, different than before, as British came to own and run local operations. Moreover, the British invested in South and North America.

The 'free-standing' company, as labeled by Wilkins, was a peculiar form of investment that was quite prominent in many British colonies. This firm raised capital in the domestic financial market where its administrative office was located, but it operated no domestic activities. All operations were overseas. This form of company represents the advantage of western countries in being able to raise capital from efficient financial markets. However, it posed the same problem as facing the medieval agent relationship, namely, how could foreign investors be confident that they would recover profitably their investments if the assets were located overseas, often in countries with very poor legal infrastructures? Wilkins found that oversight occurred through the executive boards of the companies, where prominent people located in the home market faced the loss of reputation if the company should prove to be dishonest.

The United States offers an unusual case. A rapidly growing country, it imported more capital than it exported up to World War I. However, whereas it imported largely portfolio investments, its outward flows were dominated by foreign direct investments. In other words, American companies showed an early penchant for expanding overseas. The Singer Company built within two decades of its founding a large factory employing thousands of workers in Scotland. Oil companies, Kodak, Westinghouse, Ford, and mining and agricultural companies all invested overseas. Companies in oil, mining, and agriculture often invested in poorer markets where there were resources to be found. These early investors were often involved inextricably in the politics of the foreign governments, and the American military itself intervened aggressively numerous times in the Caribbean, Mexico and Central America, and South America. As in the British case, the history of American direct investment occurred in the context of an expanding military presence of the home government. Moreover, since many of these countries were poor, the multinational corporations responded to the demands of the host nation, especially in the form of concessionary contracts, to provide public services, e.g., hospitals, roads, and power. This complicated legacy of the early history of the multinational corporation created hostility on the part of the local population that persisted throughout most of the twentieth century.

It is important to underscore that the multinational corporation usually evolved in the context of specific national institutions. As many others have pointed out, the multinational corporation is a growing firm whose organizational borders have spilled across borders. Moreover, since this large firm is usually tied to a larger domestic network of suppliers and customers, its expansion overseas is accompanied by the co-investments of these other members. This is a pattern seen in American investments in the United Kingdom in the 1950s and repeated by Japanese multinational corporations investing in the United Kingdom in the 1980s and 1990s.

Chandler noted that these multinational corporations reflected the national characteristics of management. In comparing the cases of the largest firms in the United Kingdom, Germany, and the United States, Chandler found that differences in managerial capabilities, reflecting national institutions, explain their success and failure patterns. He particularly criticized the managerial capabilities of British firms, a point not shared by some British historians (Hannah). But more importantly, Chandler's thesis assumed that size itself constituted the realization of scale and scope economies instead of the outcome of success and growth. This observation is especially important for understanding the lack of large multinational corporations in Italy or in Taiwan, both of which have very successful small firm economies but do not have multinational corporations comparable to other countries of similar levels of economic wealth. Yet, both countries are relatively wealthy and successful, and their many small companies have achieved high rates of exporting. Even in the case of the United States, the evidence implies that American firms, large and small, came to Europe, riding on the back of the national organizing principles of standardization in work methods (Kogut). Chandler's larger point of the effect of national systems on firm capabilities is largely accepted; his belief that large firms reflect better management because they achieve scale is disputed far more.

ORGANIZATION OF MULTINATIONAL CORPORATIONS

The national origins of the multinational corporation influence their subsequent organizational evolution. In the United States, the great post-World War II expansion of multinational corporations coincided with the diffusion of their adoption of the multi-divisional structure. Indeed, the refinement of 'organizational technologies' permitted American firms to manage their rapidly growing operations on a worldwide basis.

The young American multinational corporation began with little knowledge and experience of the foreign market. Initial foreign sales are exports executed within the existing organizational structure. These structures could be functional (e.g., organized by production and sales) or divisional (e.g., organized by geographic area or product division). As foreign sales increased, an international division was created to make the sale and to provide customer support. In consequence, the domestic organizational unit would sell to the international division its products at an internal 'transfer price.' As this price was set by the domestic market, it was unlikely to reflect the competitive conditions in the foreign country. Moreover, the products were often not designed to the tastes of foreign demand. Because of this internal conflict, the American multinational corporation would replace the international division by transferring responsibilities to area divisions (e.g., Europe, Asia-South America) or to product divisions. While these structures diminished the internal conflict, they ran the hazard that the divisional managers across areas did not cooperate or that managers across product divisions tended to fall back upon focusing on the home market.

European firms grew up in a different environment. Europe was a highly unstable continent during the twentieth century, with significant political and economic conflicts. Borders sometimes changed, and they also marked the necessity to pay commercial duties. The gradual creation of the European Union in the last third of the twentieth century eliminated tariffs and lessened national differences. This history marked their firms. The organizational technologies in most of these countries were quite different to those found in the United States. Holding company structures were common, banks or other financial institutions played powerful roles in ownership and cross holdings, and firms were tied together in complex financial webs. These structures, often called 'mother-daughter' organizations, reflect the linguistic terms used in northern Europe to describe headquarters and subsidiary. These mother-daughter structures consisted often of a headquarters that held a portfolio consisting of ownership control over dozens of companies, many of them in the same sector but located in different countries. Reporting relationships among these companies and headquarters was less formal than found in American companies, and control was often exercised through the movement of managers who were lifetime employees. These structures were often seen as inefficient, especially compared to the size and organization of American multinationals that were investing rapidly in Europe at this time. European critics called for the restructuring of European firms and industry along American lines.

The structure of Japanese companies reflected also their historical origins. In Japan, the trading company performed an extraordinary role in the exports during the first two-thirds of the twentieth century. These companies started primarily as wholesalers, but over time developed their own industrial companies located in Japan and eventually overseas. Though the forced imposition of American antitrust law after World War II disrupted these patterns, trading companies and other affiliated company networks, called *keiretsu,* reconstituted the earlier pattern of constellations of domestic companies competing in home and, through their trading companies, in foreign markets. As in the American and European cases, Japanese firms varied in their internal structures, with functional and even factory-based organization being the predominant structures. Still, a dominant trend emerged over time as the role of trading companies declined, especially for the exportation of industrial and high technology goods. This trend consisted of the appendage of an international division to the existing structure.

These different national structures confronted an increasingly more globally integrated environment in the course of the twentieth century. This environment posed the classic organizational problem of balancing integration and differentiation. For the multinational corporation, this problem posed itself as meeting the demands to achieve global scale against the needs of national markets and governments. Given different national principles of organizing the activities of multinational corporations, there was not a rapid convergence to a global structure. The growth of multinational corporations, especially in Europe, was stymied by these traditions. Continuing national differences and the failure to develop harmonized European corporate law deterred the emergence of pan-European multinational corporations. Many of the most important cross-European mergers failed initially within a decade lnstead. American multinational corporations, less bound by these separate national traditions, were able to create integrated European strategies.

Nevertheless, it was in Europe where new organizational structures developed to resolve the conflict between integration and differentiation. Multinational corporations from smaller countries offered the laboratory experiments that influenced the evolution of multinational corporations from larger nations. Because of the small size of many European countries, large firms in Sweden, Switzerland, and the Netherlands quickly became multinational corporations, and these corporations had far more assets and employees outside their home countries than within. Over the course of the last two decades of the twentieth century, organizational structures developed, labeled as transnational corporations, that distributed global responsibilities to national subsidiaries, created global teams and projects, and encouraged the transfer of 'best practices' across borders.

MNCs FROM EMERGING MARKETS

Multinational companies from the emerging world are a relatively new phenomenon.

Emerging Markets Multinationals (EM-MNCs) have become important in almost every industry. India's Infosys and TCS have become two of the world's leading information technology companies. China's Haier is the fourth-largest maker of home appliances in the world, and its ZTE is on its way to becoming one of the world's top five manufacturers of telecommunications equipment and systems.

According to the United Nations Conference on Trade and Development (UNCTAD), multinationals in emerging economies accounted for only 0.4 percent of world outward foreign direct investment (FDI) in 1970. That share grew to 15.8 percent by 2008.Alone, emerging nations in Asia and Oceania accounted for 11.9 percent of world outward FDI in 2008; among these nations, China has seen the most dramatic and continuous growth.

Recent trend of multinationals from emerging countries shows that firms from emerging countries are very heterogeneous in terms of their origin, maturity, position in the value chain and strategy. This suggests a variety of drivers for internationalization. Such huge heterogeneity makes it difficult to generalize about how EM-MNCs are similar or dissimilar to more traditional multinationals. EM-MNCs do not usually possess strong global brands or cutting-edge technologies that place them close to the technology frontier. Rather, they often acquire established brands to become well-known—such as the Tata Group of India, which acquired the automobile manufacturers Jaguar and Land Rover—or acquire firms that already developed proprietary technology. However, this does not mean that they do not possess ownership advantages. One view is that EM-MNCs expand to other countries in order to obtain new advantages to serve as a further springboard for inter-nationalization. One of these advantages is the ability to adapt products developed elsewhere to domestic markets, gaining greater production efficiency by using inputs more efficiently or by using more labor and less capital, or by reducing overhead costs. Some EM-MNCs have advantageous access to resources and markets, and also have "adversity advantages," that is, the ability to survive poor infrastructure, corrupt bureaucracies, regulatory uncertainties and weak educational institutions all of which hamper multinational from advanced economies that operate within emerging economics.

HOW MULTINATIONALS CAN GAIN TRACTION IN EMERGING MARKETS

The growth of the world's emerging markets may no longer be a surprise, but the sheer scale of their transformation still has the ability to shock. Recent McKinsey Global Institute research demonstrates the size of the opportunity presented by emerging markets: annual consumption of $30 trillion by 2025. That is not a typo. China and India, the two biggest emerging markets, are experiencing economic acceleration 10 times that of Europe's industrial revolution—on 100 times the scale. It represents the biggest opportunity in the history of capitalism.

And yet, multinational companies are failing to compete successfully in these energetic emerging markets. In 2010, annual consumption in emerging markets was $12 trillion, or about 32% of the world's total. (And by 2025, about 50% of the world's economic growth will be driven by cities such as Ahmedabad, Calcutta, Manila and Wuhan.) But among 100 of the world's largest companies headquartered in developed economies, just 17% of total revenue comes from emerging markets—about half the "natural share" these global organizations could be expected to hold.

Even though such internationals work from small bases as they build operations in emerging markets, their average annual revenue growth remains barely half that achieved by incumbent emerging-market players. There is a fundamental disconnect between the way companies from developed economies should operate in emerging markets and the way they actually do.

So what can be done? There is no easy answer, of course; these emerging markets are complex and present a range of challenges. But there are three broad fronts across which companies must develop their capabilities to succeed in emerging markets.

First, they must carefully choose their opportunities and focus on cities. Existing size and strength offers no guarantees, and companies should take advantage of the wealth of data now at their disposal to target specific consumers in specific geographies and cities in very specific ways. For example, two of China's biggest cities — Guangzhou and Shenzhen — are in the same province and just two hours apart. Yet Guangzhou residents are mostly born locally, speak Cantonese, and spend their leisure time at home with family and friends. More than 80% of Shenzhen residents are migrants, most speak Mandarin and spend their leisure time away from home. A provincewide approach — let alone a countrywide one, will not work.

Second, once companies commit to expand, they must do so aggressively. In general, companies from emerging markets invest more, and more often, than their counterparts in the developed world: between 1999 and 2008, emerging-market companies paid out half as much in dividends, but invested much more in fixed assets. Companies in emerging economies choose to generate wealth for shareholders not by paying dividends, but by aggressively reinvesting capital to spur growth. Newcomers will have to adjust their definitions of success accordingly.

Finally, companies must be persistent. Capturing the emerging-market opportunity is a long-term effort: management processes and structures may need to be changed, and new models adopted. Be prepared to compete on your own turf as well, and soon: companies from emerging markets also are increasingly succeeding within developed economies. Actually, the companies from emerging markets achieve superior revenue growth pretty much everywhere, leaving established multinationals struggling to both capture emerging-market growth and defend against new competitors in traditional markets. They do this by getting exactly these basics right: they carefully identify opportunities, invest appropriately and stick with it.

For established multinationals. this should hardly be radical. Today, however, too few of them appear to be heeding these lessons. However, even a tiny slice of the biggest opportunity in the history of capitalism is something worth grasping.

AN INTEGRATED STRATEGY OF MNCs

The multinational corporation (MNC) is the first institution in human history to plan on a global scale. Its purpose is to organise and integrate economic activity around the world in order to maximise profit. In fact, the revenues of these transnational corporations exceed the gross national product of many of the countries in which they operate. Its failures and successes are measured through growth in global profit and market share. International trade usually benefits all parties involved. The basic assumption in such trade is that the growth of the whole strengthens the welfare of all. The overall focus is increased efficiency. International companies now have significant influence on world productivity and technological advancement. Their influence has grown so vast that it affects all aspects of society. Furthermore, the average rate of growth of the most successful MNCs is two to three times higher than that of most advanced countries.

Manufacturing firms usually follow a four-step process to enter the international environment: (1) A corporation exports goods requested by foreign customers. (2) A firm initiates marketing activities abroad. (3) A firm establishes other functional activities overseas, such as manufacturing. Firms in this stage are called **multinationals**. (4) A firm is characterised by widespread operation and is no longer identified with just one particular country. Firms in this stage are called **transnationals**.

Going International

Modern corporations are trying to grain and advantage over their competitors. Most are finding that a good way to do so is through the complex process of going international. By going international, corporations can extend their product lines to other cultures. They can also save money on labour costs by taking advantage of the lower standard of living in some countries. One big advantages of doing business in foreign countries, particularly developing countries, is that high unemployment rates provide inexpensive and vast labour pools. This helps companies to generate more capital and, therefore, bring in more revenue. These countries are ideal for industrial companies in labour-intensive industries. Many U.S. manufacturing firms have found that they incur lower input costs by locating their manufacturing facilities outside the

United States and thus can export their products at lower prices than if those same products were manufactured at home. The *maquiladora* in Mexico is a case in point; by sending parts to Mexican plants for assembly, manufacturers can save on labour costs. By going international, a company can make and save money simultaneously, depending on the geographic area.

Several factors both influence the decision to go international and make the move feasible. The ever-pressing need to get ahead of the competition may be a good reason to go abroad. In underdeveloped nations, labour is inexpensive, which means that a company pays less to get the same job done. Another reason for going abroad is rapid expansion, in an effort to keep up with product demand. A home-based company may be expanding rapidly, but not rapidly enough to keep up with market demand. An overseas facility can satisfy such demand. A final reason for going international is the absence of trade barriers vital to many economies throughout the world. This trend is reflected in the increased efforts of many countries to promote international trade.

Strategy Formulation

Objectives and strategies are formulated by considering mission, strategic policy, and information. When a firm operates outside its home country, its strategic objectives and overall strategy change. To adjust its strategy to its various environments, a firm can implement a number of options. Depending on the type of change required, it can choose either expansion or expansion and diversification. However, a firm that chooses expansion as its strategy to achieve corporate development and efficient use of existing resources for higher profits will soon find that it needs to diversify to maintain systematic growth. In the diversification strategy, a firm has two alternatives for expansion:

1. **Geography** (the international route): A strategy is prepared to weight the pros and cons of developing foreign markets and the implications of the decision.
2. **Product**: A firm can choose a move into a new business as an alternative to going international or as a way to enter foreign markets. A company can also purchase another business that operates in a foreign environment.

The stages of strategy formulation can be categorised as follows: (1) decision preparation stage (also called long-term planning), (2) matching stage (also called intermediate-term planning), and (3) implementation stage (also called short-term planning). In the preparation stage, strategists gather questions and ideas and develop ways to measure and determine feasibility. Other activities include establishing a more objective view of the company's future and setting policies to aid in achieving corporate objectives. It also involves the preparation of a timetable for supplementary decisions. The strategists at this stage plan for the efficient use of corporate resources to the greatest possible advantage and design a system to manage the constant flow of information. When the basic decisions about strategy have been made, a corporation is ready to undertake the next step. The matching stage involves the development of systematic guidelines to forecast opportunities and threats, along with setting deadlines to measure progress and establishing mechanisms to cope with possible problems. The strategists develop a structure for international logistics to purchase raw materials and distribute products. Then the strategists select methods to integrate and compromise between the company's resources and the design of the decision system. In the third stage, tasks and available machinery are assigned to each operating unit for implementation. Other activities in this stage include developing efficient inventory procedures, financial practices, and the flexibility to accommodate delays when a part of the program runs late.

MNCs are highly dependent on a strategic advantage, as are most organisations. Many multinational firms key in on the superiority of some resource, such as capital, labour, or technology. Capitalising on an advantage can compensate for a weakness. Strategy formulation gives a company a competitive advantage in that it improves quality and reduces costs. It also facilitates innovation through open lines of communication among team members.

A key factor for success in going multinational is a strong integrated strategy. *An integrated strategy should always include costs and margins.* A corporation that wants to be strong in the international arena must consider competitive advantage. In a long-range strategic plan, it would be senseless to operate an international subsidiary whose costs exceed its profits. The same is true in integrated strategy.

Two assumptions are connected with a successful multinational integration strategy: (1) integration provides a MNC with an advantage over its competitors and (2) an organisation can trade off some proceeds of its competitive advantage with host governments. Once these assumptions have been implemented, a company must pay close attention to economies of scale and the economic situation in the countries to which it expands.

Another function of integration is supplier partnership, which facilitates better communication with suppliers and can prove to be valuable in product design.

Implementing an integrated strategy usually requires several compromises with the host country. These usually involve sharing the economic benefits of the new subsidiary or branch of the MNC. Laws and regulations, whether domestic or international, also need to be considered, because they differ from country to country.

An integrated strategy should also consider customer needs and tastes, which vary from culture to culture. An integrated strategy allows a company that is going international to adjust its product line to suit a variety of customers and cultures. It also allows room for improvements, such as new distribution channels, for optimal international commercial practices.

A strong integrated strategy includes logistic management, which is the central operational task. Logistic strategy analysis must start with economic factors, because the production-marketing system exists to implement the resource transmission capabilities rooted in these factors. The major factors are economic differentials and the efficiencies available through a unified global system. However, analysis based on economic factors must be modified by other influences, including government actions and corporate characteristics. Logistics strategy for a MNC has three main goals:

1. To efficiently transmit resources so as to maximise their flow in a natural direction as determined by economic differentials and government actions.
2. To utilise the potential and make maximum use of the special advantages of a MNC as a global organisation
3. To effectively implement resource transmission, with special regard to communication as a critical factor.

MNCs use logistics systems to keep production balanced and to check inconsistencies in the schedules of integrated plants. At monthly meetings, key managers and company experts schedule production, lines and corporate goals for the upcoming month. A key topic is generally inventory control.

Unfortunately, many companies fail due to inconsistencies. Decisions in the expansion of an integrated system are more complicated than the daily operations of a domestic corporation. Efficiency of operation and flexibility of supply must be carefully monitored on a daily basis. The number of integrated plants should be kept at a limited or optimal level in order to avoid unnecessary complexities. For example, when Volkswagen invested in the United States, it did not realise the magnitude of the risk involved. First, the cost of labour was extremely high. Then, when the dollar rose dramatically, the cost of operation was affected by the exchange rate, which made the integration obsolete. Integration strategies and logistic play an important role in the expansion process, not only for U.S.-based companies but for growing companies throughout the world.

HOST COUNTRY CONTROLS AND REGULATIONS

Companies must adhere to different rules in international marketing, and, therefore, strategies must also be altered. Indeed, the governments of different countries impose different regulations on MNCs, in varying degrees. Host countries often restrict the following:

i) **Ownership:** Host countries typically require that a local firm own a majority or controlling interest;

ii) **Employment:** Almost all host countries demand that certain managerial and technological positions he held by host country nationals;

iii) **Profits and fees:** Profits and fees are typically set at some maximum level;

iv) **Internal debt capital:** Internal debt capital is often set according to a preestablished formula;

v) **Training and development:** Insistence on training and development for host country nationals is common;

vi) **Host country markets:** Most host countries demand development of their exports;

vii) **Technological bases:** Most host countries seek technology-based industries rather than extractive industries.

Setting objectives is also significantly affected by a multinational environment because: growth may he legislatively limited; efficiency may be held to an undesirably low level by extra costs as dictated by governments; use of resources may be set at specified levels; contribution to owners (profits) is usually set at arbitrary levels; contribution to customers may be modified to meet government-established levels; contribution to employees focuses on technical training and often includes guaranteed employment as opposed to true development; contribution to society is stressed by the government's involvement in all areas.

A basic strategy of Japanese companies is to diversify early in their history. U.S. firms do not diversify quite as early, and European firms tend to diversify later still. Japanese companies pay closer attention than any other country to quality in production. Japanese management philosophy is oriented toward the group or team. In virtually all countries, negotiation with the government is becoming increasingly more critical than it has in the United States and Canada. While objectives and strategies will vary, *the basics of strategy are the same*. The differences in the basic strategies of MNCs can be traced to cultural/historical factors.

DESIGNING STRATEGY

Whether to globalise, and how to globalise, have become two of the most burning strategy issues for managers around the world. Many forces are driving companies around the world to globalise by expanding their participation in foreign markets. Almost every product market in the major world economies has foreign competitors. Trade barriers are also falling. Maturity in domestic market is also driving companies to seek international expansion.

Companies are also seeking to globalise by integrating their worldwide strategy. Such global integration contrasts with the multinational approach whereby companies set up country subsidiaries that design, produce, and market products or services tailored to local needs. This multinational model (also described as a "multidomestic strategy") is now in question. Several changes seem to increase the likelihood that, in some industries, a global strategy will be more successful than a multidomestic one. One of these changes is the growing similarity of what citizens of different countries want to buy. Other changes include the reduction of tariff and nontariff barriers, technology investments that are becoming too expensive to amortise in one market only, and competitors that are globalising the rules of the game.

Companies want to know how to globalise - in other words, expand market participation - and how to develop an integrated worldwide strategy. As depicted in Figure-1, three steps are essential in developing a total worldwide strategy:

FIGURE-1

TOTAL GLOBAL STRATEGY

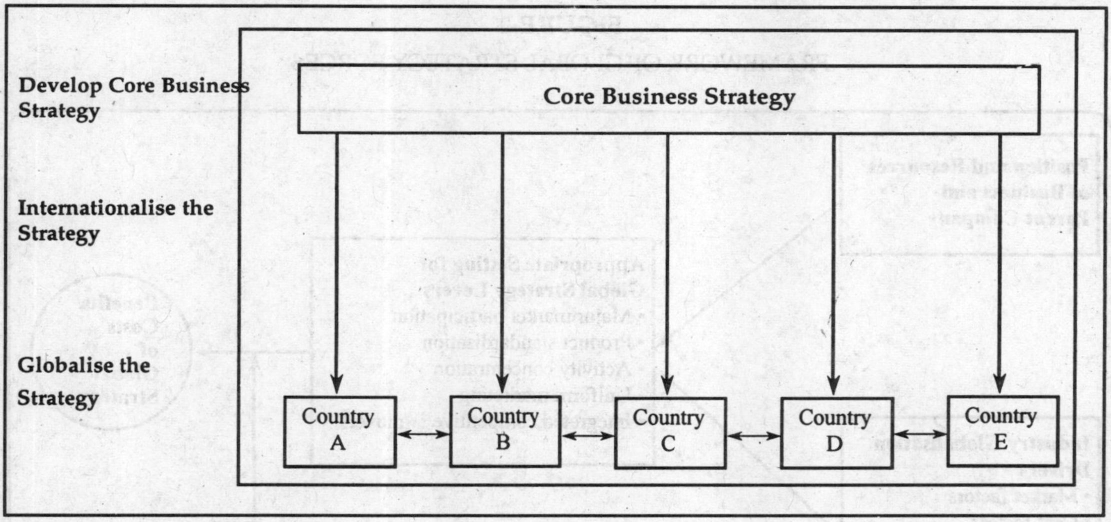

i) Developing the core strategy - the basis of sustainable competitive advantage. It is usually developed for the home country first.

ii) Internationalising the core strategy through international expansion of activities and through adaptation.

iii) Globalising the international strategy by integrating the strategy across countries.

Multinational companies know the first two steps well. They know the third step less well since globalisation runs counter to the accepted wisdom of tailoring for national markets. *How might a global strategy work and directs manager toward opportunities to exploit globalisation. What are the drawbacks and costs of globalisation?* Figure-2 lays out a framework for thinking through globalisation issues.

Industry globalisation drivers (underlying market, cost, and other industry conditions) are externally determined, while global strategy levers are choices available to the worldwide business. Drivers create the potential for a multinational business to achieve the benefits of global strategy. To achieve these benefits, a multinational business needs to set its *global strategy levers* (e.g., use of product standardisation) appropriately to industry drivers, and to the position and resources of the business and its parent company. The organisation's ability to implement the strategy affects how well the benefits can be achieved.

What is global strategy?

Setting strategy for a worldwide business requires making choices along a number of strategic dimensions. Table-1 lists five such dimensions or "global strategy levers"

FIGURE-2

FRAMEWORK OF GLOBAL STRATEGY FORCES

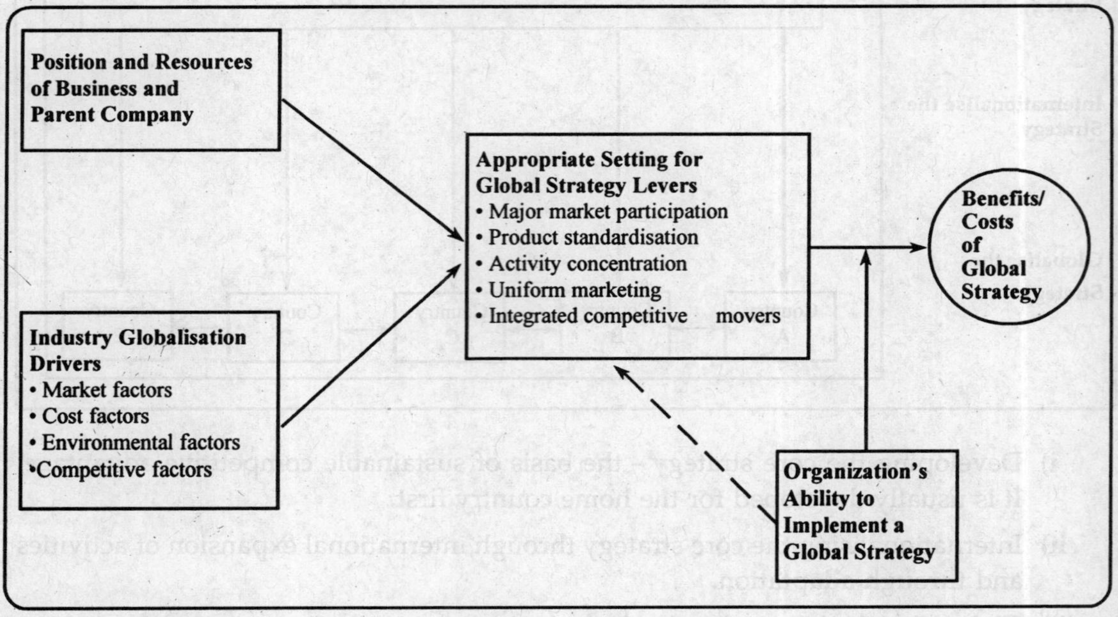

and their respective positions under a pure multidomestic strategy and a pure global strategy. Intermediate positions are, of course, feasible. For each dimension, a multidomestic strategy seeks to maximise worldwide performance by maximising local competitive advantage, revenues, or profits; a global strategy seeks to maximise worldwide performance through sharing and integration.

TABLE-1
GLOBALISATION DIMENSIONS/GLOBAL STRATEGY LEVERS

Dimension	*Setting for pure multidomestic strategy*	*Setting for pure global strategy*
Market Participation	No particular pattern	Significant share in major markets
Product Offering	Fully customised in each country	Fully standardised worldwide
Location of Value-Added Activities	All activities in each country	Concentrated—one activity in each (different) country
Market Approach	Local	Uniform worldwide
Competitive Moves	Stand-alone by country	Integrated across countries

Market participation

In a multidomestic strategy, countries are selected on the basis of their standalone potential for revenues and profits. In a global strategy, countries need to be selected for their potential contribution to globalisation benefits. This may mean entering a market that is unattractive in its own right, but has global strategic significance, such as the home market of a global competitor. Or it may mean building share in a limited number of key markets rather than undertaking more widespread coverage. A pattern of major share in major markets is advocated in Ohmae's USA-Europe-Japan "triad" concepts. In contrast, under a multidomestic strategy, no particular pattern of participation is required - rather, the pattern accrues from the pursuit of local advantage.

Product offering

In a multidomestic strategy, the products offered in each country are tailored to local needs. In a global strategy, the ideal is a standardised core product that requires minimal local adaptation. Cost reduction is usually the most important benefit of product standardisation. Levitt has made the most extreme case for product standardisation. Others stress the need for flexibility, or the need for a broad product portfolio, with many product varieties in order to share technologies and distribution channels. In practice, some multinationals have pursued product standardisation to a greater or lesser extent: Differing worldwide needs can be met by adapting a standardised core product.

Location of value-added activities

In a multidomestic strategy, all or most of the value chain is reproduced in every country. In another type of international strategy - exporting - most of the value chain is kept in one country. In a global strategy, costs are reduced by breaking up the value chain so each activity may be conducted in a different country. One value chain strategy is partial concentration and partial duplication. The key feature of a global position on this dimension is the strategic placement of the value chain around the globe.

Marketing approach

In a multidomestic strategy, marketing is fully tailored for each country, being developed locally. In a global strategy, a uniform marketing approach is applied around the world, although not all elements of the marketing mix need be uniform. Similarly, a product that serves a common need can be geographically expanded with a uniform marketing programme, despite differences in marketing environments.

Competitive moves

In a multidomestic strategy, the managers in each country make competitive moves without regard for what happens in other countries. In a global strategy, competitive moves are integrated across countries. The same type of move is made in different countries at the same time or in a systematic sequence: a competitor is attacked in one country in order to drain its resources for another country, or a competitive attack in one country is countered in a different country. Perhaps the best example is the counter-attack in a competitor's home market as a parry to an attack on one's own home market. Integration of competitive strategy is rarely practised, except perhaps by some Japanese companies. For instance, Bridgestone Corporation, the Japanese tire manufacturer, tried to integrate its competitive moves in response to global consolidation by its major competitors - Continental AG's acquisition of Gencorp's General Tire and Rubber Company, General Tire's joint venture with two Japanese tire makers, and Sumitomo's acquisition of an interest in Dunlop Tire. These competitive actions forced Bridgestone to establish a presence in the major U.S. market in order to maintain its position in the world tire market. To this end, Bridgestone formed a joint venture to own and manage Firestone Corporation's worldwide tire business. This joint venture also allowed Bridgestone to gain access to Firestone's European plants.

BENEFITS OF A GLOBAL STRATEGY

Companies that use global strategy levers can achieve one or more of these benefits: *cost reductions; improved quality of products and programmes; enhanced customer preference; and increased competitive leverage.* (see Table-2)

Cost reduction: An integrated global strategy can reduce worldwide costs in several ways. A company can increase the benefits from economies of scale by *pooling production or other activities* for two or more countries. Understanding the potential benefit of these economies of scale, Sony Corporation has concentrated its compact disc production in Terre Haute, Indiana, and Salzburg, Austria. A *second* way to cut costs is by *exploiting lower factor costs* by moving manufacturing or other activities to low-cost countries. This approach has, of course, motivated the recent surge of offshore manufacturing, particularly by U.S. firms. *Thirdly,* the global strategy can also cut

TABEL 2

GLOBAL STRATEGY LEVERS AND GLOBALISATION BENEFITS.

	Benefits				*Major Drawbacks*
Global Strategy Levers	*Cost Reduction*	*Improved Quality of Products and Programs*	*Enhanced Customer Preference*	*Increased Competitive Leverage*	*All Levers Incur Coordination Costs, Plus*
Major Market	Increases volume for economies of scale		Via global availability, global servicetability and global recognition	Advantage of earlier entry Provides more sites for attack and counter-attack, hostage for good behaviour	Earlier or greater commitment to a market than warranted on own merit
Product Standardisation	Reduce duplication of development efforts Allows concentration of production to exploit economies of scale	Focuses development and management resources	Allows consumers to use familiar product while abroad Allow organisations to use some product across country units.	Basis for low-cost invations of markets	Less responsibe to local needs
Activity Concentration	Reduces duplication of activities Helps exploit economies Exploits differences in country factor costs Partial concentration allows flexibility vs. currency changes, and vs. bargaining parties	Focuses effort Allows more consistent quality control		Allow maintenance of cost advantage independent of local conditions	Distance activities from the customer Increases currency risk
Uniform Marketing	Reduce design and production costs of marketing programmes	Focuses talent and resources Leverages scares, good ideas	Reinforces marketing messages by exposing customer to same mix in different countries	and marketing	Reduces adaptation to local customer behaviour environment
Integrated competitive Moves				Provides more options and leverage in attack and defense.	Local competitiveness may be sacrificed

costs by *exploiting flexibility.* A company with manufacturing locations in several countries can move production from location to location on short notice to take advantage of the lowest costs at a given time. Dow Chemical takes this approach to minimise the cost of producing chemicals. Dow uses a linear programming model that takes account of international differences in exchange rates, tax rates, and transportation and labor costs. Finally, an integrated global strategy can also reduce costs by *enhancing bargaining power.* A company whose strategy allows for switching production among different countries greatly increases its bargaining power with suppliers, workers, and host governments.

Improved quality of products and programmes: Under a global strategy, companies focus on a smaller number of products and programmes than under a multidomestic strategy. This concentration can improve both product and programme quality. Global focus is one reason for Japanese success in automobiles. Toyota markets a far smaller number of models around the world than does General Motors, even allowing for its unit sales being half that of General Motors's. Toyota has concentrated on improving its few models while General Motors has fragmented its development funds.

Enhanced customer preference: Global availability, serviceability, and recognition can enhance customer preference through reinforcement. Soft drink and fast food companies are, of course, leading exponents of this strategy. Many suppliers of financial services, such as credit cards, must have a global presence because their service is travel-related. Manufacturers of industrial products can also exploit this benefit. A supplier that can provide a multinational customer with a standard product around the world gains from worldwide familiarity. Computer manufacturers have long pursued this strategy.

Increased competitive leverage: A global strategy provides more points from which to attack and counterattack competitors. In an effort to prevent the Japanese from becoming a competitive nuisance in disposable syringes, Becton Dickinson, a major U.S. medical products company, decided to enter three markets in Japan's backyard. Becton entered the Hong Kong, Singapore, and Philippine markets to prevent further Japanese expansion.

DRAWBACKS OF GLOBAL STRATEGY

Globalisation can incur significant management costs through increased coordination, reporting requirements, and even added staff. It can also reduce the firm's effectiveness in individual countries if overcentralisation hurts local motivation and morale. In addition, each global strategy lever has particular drawbacks. For instance, a global strategy approach to *market participation* can incur an earlier or greater commitment to a market than is warranted on its own merits. Many American companies are struggling to penetrate Japnese markets, more in order to enhance their global competitive position than to make money in Japan for its own sake. Again, a *product standardisation* can result in a product that does not entirely satisfy *any* customers. When companies first internationalise, they often offer their standard domestic product without adapting it for other countries, and suffer the consequences. For example, Procter & Gamble stumbled when it introduced Cheer laundry detergent in Japan without changing the U.S. product or marketing message (that the detergent was effective in all temperatures). After experiencing serious losses, P&G discovered two instances of insufficient adaptation. *First,* the detergent did not suds up as it should because the Japanese use a great deal of fabric softener. *Second,* the Japanese usually wash clothes in either cold tap water or bath water, so the claim of working in all temperatures was irrelevant.

Uniform marketing can reduce adaptation to local customer behaviour. A globally standardised product is designed for the global market but can seldom satisfy all needs in all countries. For instance, Canon, a Japanese company, sacrificed the ability to copy certain Japanese paper sizes when it first designed a photocopier for the global market. Further, the *activity concentration* distances customers and can result in lower responsiveness and flexibility. It also increases currency risk by incurring costs and revenues in different countries. Recently volatile exchange rates have required companies that concentrate their production to hedge their currency exposure. Moreover, *integrated competitive moves* can mean sacrificing revenues, profits, or competitive position in individual countries, particularly when the subsidiary in one country is asked to attack a global competitor in order to send a signal or to divert that competitor's resources from another country.

Finding the Balance

The most successful worldwide strategies find a balance between overglo balizing and underglobalising. The ideal strategy matches the level of strategy globalisation to the globalisation potential of the industry. In Figure both Business *A* and Business *C* achieve balanced global and national strategic advantage. Business *A* does so with a low level of strategy globalisation to match the low globalisation potential of its industry (e.g., food products). Business *C* uses a high level of strategy globalisation to match the high globalisation potential of its industry (e.g., computer equipment). Business *B* is at a global disadvantage because it uses a strategy that is less globalised than the potential offered by its industry. The business is failing to exploit potential global benefits such as cost savings via product standardisation. Business *D* is at a national disadvantage because it is too globalised relative to the potential offered by its industry. The business is not tailoring its products and programmes as much as it should. While there is no systematic evidence, it seems that far more businesses suffer from insufficient globalisation than from excessive globalisation. Figure-3 is oversimplified in that it shows only one overall dimension for both strategy and industry potential. A global strategy has major dimensions and many subdimensions. Similarly, the potential of industry globalisation is multidimensional.

FIGURE-3

GLOBALISATION POTENTIAL OF INDUSTRY *Vs.* GLOBALISATION STRATEGY

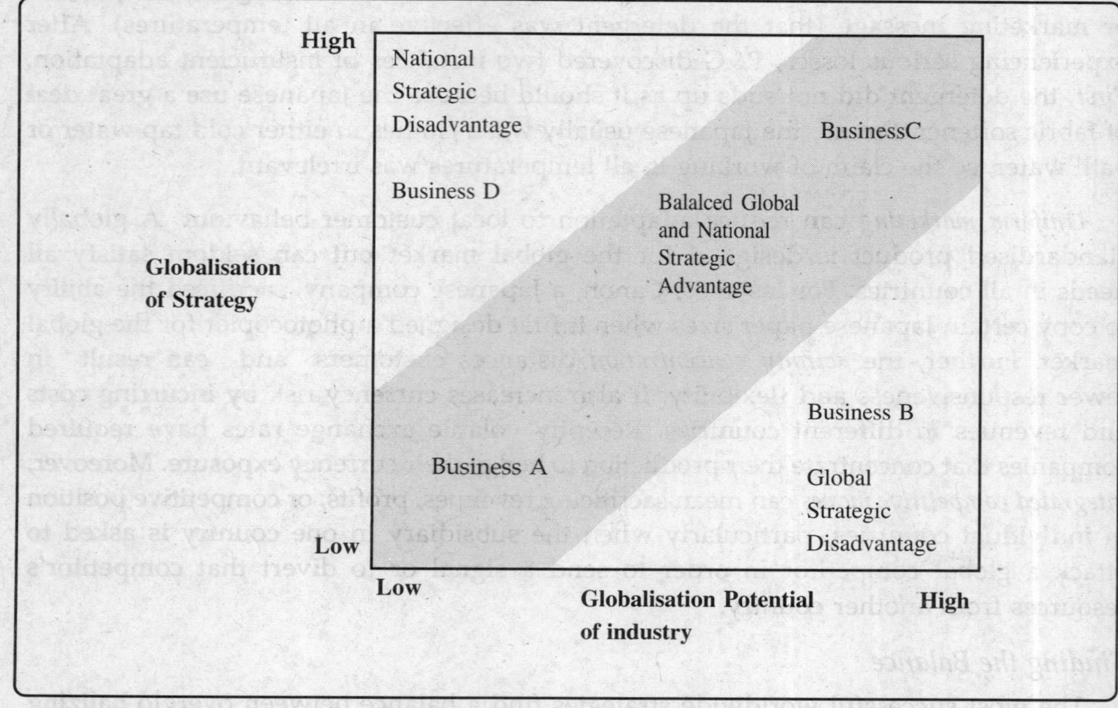

IMPLEMENTING GLOBAL STRATEGY

The *zeitgeist* of the new millennium will be the spirit of free economic competition and co-evolution between nations. Nations peopled by highly educated, open-minded, driven entrepreneurs who create productive enterprises through constant innovation and fast imitation will flourish. Such nations must also be led by progressive politicians who understand that central to their economic policy is the fostering of progressive knowledge about design and manufacturing processes.

Global Enterprise is awaiting a new day, anticipating the encounter with its international competitors. *Global Enterprise* is visualised as being capable of outmaneuvering its predecessor, the international corporation, by reading to market demands more efficiently and effectively. Multinational corporations identify themselves in terms of such barriers as national borders and sociocultural differences; their customers are domestic markets, and they allocate products according to the preferred tastes of each country. The reward and control structures of multinational corporations are oriented more toward the growth of domestic markets than the growth of the world as a market.

Unlike the multinational corporation, the global enterprise does not limit itself to the boundaries imposed by national markets and views the whole world as its market. Instead of running subsidiaries under the control of a centralised management structure, the global enterprise is a decentralised system, composed of various management, manufacturing, marketing, resource, and financial nodes. The nodes are structured to operate with full efficiency and effectiveness. The manager of each node is given the latitude and authority to adapt the operation to local conditions and, occasionally, to contact counterpart nodes to resolve problems directly. At the name implies, a multinational corporation should be well positioned to become a global enterprise. A small but growing number of companies that are not multinationals may, however, be better positioned to become a global enterprise because they already have the flexible, efficient structure that many multinationals lack.

For a company that would aspire to become a global enterprise, the time to make the transition is now. Those that wait will not be prepared to face new forms of competition on a truly global scale. How long will it take for the leadership of a country to change its geopolitical diplomacy and trade policy to the new reality? These organisations of the future will be knowledge based, evolving through a painful trial-and-error process. Strategy-structure research indicates that numerous firms have failed by clinging to the old ways, looking to their formal structures to provide the necessary organisational capacity to compete in a complex global business environment. This same research is beginning to provide hints of the practices that organisations are finding successful in this environment. These practices emphasise the information processing capability necessary for the knowledge transfer that permits optimisation of responsiveness and efficiency. They also look to self-direction and self-control by task-oriented individuals and teams.

The effective implementation of global decisions is a challenge that top-level managers face. Top management must understand the concept of due process and make a serious attempt to implement it in the decision-making process. There are additional problems to contend with. The collapse of appraisal and control capability, the eroding power of the head office, and the decline in common values and expectations are among the serious issues confronting managers. Managers also have to go beyond their normal duties and be creative in their decision making.

Managers of multinational concerns must have a broad understanding of the cultural and political environments in which they are doing business. Careful business management is critical in international markets, where the possibility of both loss and gain is high and many complex factors can affect the outcome. All management functions should be followed along with an integrated strategy. Despite the complexities, the promise for multinationals is high, not only in monetary terms, but also in the accumulation of knowledge and new business ideas.

It is in the context of informal work groups that we can best understand the motivation and behavior of both individuals and teams. Behavior is shaped by the norms of a group which, in turn, are shaped by the values and beliefs of its members. It is obvious that if the behavior of these informal work groups is to be consistent with the strategies and goals of a firm, the values and beliefs of Its members must also reflect that congruity.

Managers can directly control the shape of the formal organisation and can do many things to influence both the shape of the informal organisation and its culture. A few of these things have been outlined here, and the subject is abundantly covered in the literature on motivation and group behavior. The difficult task for managers is to forfeit direct control of parts of the organisation in order to achieve enhanced organisational capability. Through the use of authority, managers can substitute for direct control the indirect control that can be derived only from managing the culture.

So how might a country become number one? The primary responsibility for determining how a nation competes with other nations rests with the managers and owners of industry. They decide whether to implement new production strategies and training policies, to invest in new equipment, to launch research projects, or introduce new products. Their decisions, which cannot be dictated by government, will shape the competitiveness of industry— and, ultimately, the standard of living of workers. The government cannot dictate corporate policy, but it can influence and support research and training to help owners, managers and engineers learn to make ever better decisions about whether to implement new production strategies and training policies, to invest in new equipment, to launch research projects, or introduce new products. If the primary responsibility rests with managers to make excellent decisions, then the primary responsibility of government should be to do everything it can to help firms help themselves improve the quality of their managerial decision making and develop the nation's "powers of production."

The most effective way of increasing the global competitiveness of firms is to improve the management of innovation in products and processes. The best way of improving such skills is for the governments to energise the market for production and management process skills in four ways: i) making the *market* for process skill learning more efficient through higher quality market information; ii) encouraging a better supply of process management skills through very focused public-private sector education and research initiatives; iii) encouraging more demand among firms for higher process skills through tax incentives; and iv) encouraging innovations in learning and training by designing processes and technology to match the skills of workers, rather than vice versa.

DIFFUSION OF ORGANIZATIONAL KNOWLEDGE

In its evolution the multinational corporation is not without serious contradictions.

Evolving from its national context, the multinational corporation employs large numbers of employees of diverse nationalities and ethnicities. Westney notes that a subsidiary is, thus, caught between the institutional pressures to conform to the company norms and values, as well as to the cultural and social influences of its local national environment. At the heart of the evolution of the multination corporation, thus, lies the tension between national institutions and the fragile emergence of a global culture.

The international evolution of the organizational structures of multinationals mirrored, the broader diffusion of organizational technologies in the home market. The initial investments by a firm took place, often, on the basis of opportunity and the extension to familiar countries. Much like the ethnic trading communities dating back to the earliest times, the inexperienced multinational corporation preferred countries that are culturally similar to what their managers know at home. In these countries, they often established foreign enclaves where their expatriate managers could live in the simulated familiarity of their home environments.

The relevance of the second definition of foreign direct investment as the transfer of organizational knowledge is critical to understanding the powerful conflicts posed by the multinational corporation. The multinational corporation, competing often on superior technologies and managerial capabilities as a conduit of knowledge across borders. Some kinds of technologies can be purchased on markets and the flow of licensing payments attached to the sale of the right to use a technology constitutes a nontrival flow in international balance of payments. Technology can also flow by the movement of people.

There exists an international market for managers and skilled workers. However, some knowledge is embedded in organizations and can only be transferred as an organization across borders. The issue is more than whether knowledge is tacit or explicit, for this pertains to the knowledge held by individuals too. The central feature of the diffusion of knowledge by the multinational is that it transfers the knowledge of how to organize and how to coordinate people and across divisions. These organizing principles then provide the capabilities for the firm to achieve quality, speed products to the market, or lower costs. For this the multinational corporation is required, which through its own activities or in joint ventures with host companies, transfers the organizational knowledge.

It is important to *realize* that once this transition period passed, the multinational corporation and multinational service firms, such as those engaged in consulting, banking, and advertising, had permanently and historically changed the global economy. No longer was the flow from the US to Europe, or from one ethnic community to another. The network of connections developed by the multinational corporation permitted the flow of ideas and practices among and between countries. Thus, whereas it took half a century for American practices to diffuse to Europe, the introduction of quality circles from Japan happened within a decade or two of their original innovation. In Europe, Japanese innovations were often diffused by American firms, including consulting companies.

However, this image of the free flow of knowledge needs to be strongly conditioned on the continuing importance of national institutions. Nations consist of defined cultures and economic and social institutions, such as unions, financial systems, and religious values. These institutions interact and their complex interactions causally influence behaviors. For example, the German system of centralized bargaining, enterprise clubs, strong banks, and social welfare has, until recent times, composed a national configuration of institutions that influences the capabilities of resident firms to be able to manufacture high quality goods for export markets. The introduction of Japanese and American teams confronts in Germany the presence of existing work councils. These councils are fairly rigid features of the German environment. Since Japanese methods may not be effective without teams as complementary factors in organization, this institutional refusal can effectively deter the diffusion of these methods. In short, national organizing principles are embedded in the wider social institutions. Inconsistency between these institutions and principles, then, is an empirical question of the bargaining strength of vested powers.

While formulating global strategy, multinationalism in complex organisations has yet to be precisely defined. There is considerable disagreement among internationalists over a satisfactory meaning of multinationalism. Given this lack of consensus, it is not surprising that multiple classification schemes, such as the one described in Figure-4 are currently in vogue.

Objective indices, consisting of both structural and performance measures, are usually readily visible and hence quantifiable. The number of overseas offices, foreign languages spoken in the head office, and certain other indices are sacredly held by some observers as the best indicators of a company's true commitment to international business. Controversy, of course, rages over the validity of these supposedly objective measures of multinationality. *Is a company, for instance, with operations in seven countries really any less multinational than another that operates in ten countries?* Probably not. So no matter how useful structural and performance indices are, critics argue that they are not the only definitions of multinationalism, nor are they sufficient ones.

Some of the difficulty in measuring multinationalism with objectives indices can be solved by a combination of various measures. No single criterion of multinationality, such as ownership or the number of nationals overseas, is sufficient and external and quantifiable measures, such as the percentage of investment overseas or the distribution of equity, are useful but not enough.

FIGURE-4

DEFINITION OF MULTINATIONALISM

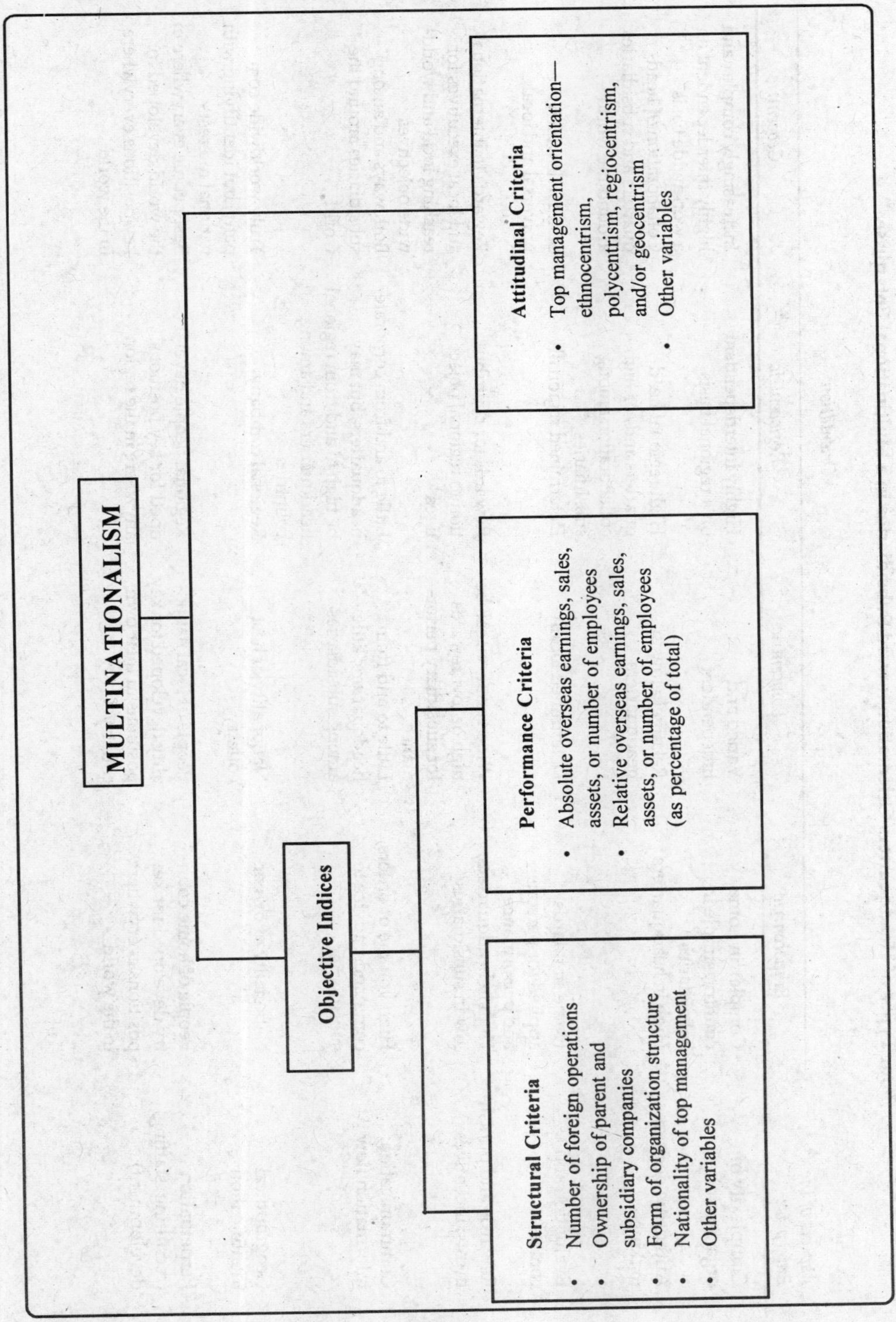

EXHIBIT 2

Four Types of Headquarters Orientation toward Subsidiaries in a Multinational Enterprise

Aspects of the Enterprise	*Orientation*			
	Ethnocentric	*Polycentric*	*Regiocentric*	*Geocentric*
Complexity of organisation	Complex in home country, simple in subsidiaries	Varied and independent	Highly interdependent on a regional basis	Increasingly complex and highly interdependent on a worldwide basis
Authority; decision making	High in headquarters	Relatively low in headquarters	High regional headquarters and/or high collaboration among subsidiaries	Collaboration of headquarters and subsidiaries around the world
Evaluation and control	Home standards applied for persons and performance	Determined locally	Determined regionally	Standards which are universal and local
Rewards and punishments; incentives	High in headquarters; low in subsidiaries	Wide variation; can be high or low rewards for subsidiary performance	Rewards for contribution to regional objectives	Rewards to international and local executives for reaching local and worldwide objectives
Communication; information flow	High volume of orders, commands, advice to subsidiaries	Little to and from headquarters; little among subsidiaries	Little to and from corporate headquarters, but may be high to and from regional headquarters and among countries	Both ways and among subsidiaries around the world
Geographical identification	Nationality of owner	Nationality of host country	Regional company	Truly worldwide company, but identifying with national interests
Perpetuation (recruiting, staffing, development)	People of home country developed for key positions everywhere in the world	People of local nationality developed for key positions in their own country	Regional people developed for key positions anywhere in the region	Best people everywhere in the world developed for key positions everywhere in the world

The more one penetrates the living reality of how decisions are made in a MNC, the more weight must be given to how executives think about doing business around the world. *How do they decide who will get important foreign assignments? Analyse various overseas market opportunities? Select a joint-venture partner in a foreign country?* Underlying these key decisions are home-country attitudes and beliefs regarding which persons or ideas are competent and trustworthy (foreigners versus compatriots). These attitudes, outlined in Exhibit-2, can be labeled ethnocentric, polycentric, regiocentric, and geocentric.

Ethnocentrism refers to a preference for putting home-country people in key positions everywhere in the world and rewarding them more handsomely for work, along with a tendency to feel that this group is more intelligent, more capable, or more reliable. Ethnocentrism is often not attributable to prejudice as much as to inexperience or lack of knowledge about foreign persons and situations. This is not too surprising, since most executives know far more about employees in their home environments. As one executive put it, *At least I understand why our own managers make mistakes. With out foreigners, I never know. The foreign managers may be better. But if I can't trust a person, should I hire him or her just to prove we're multinational?*

The board and top management in the headquarters and affiliated companies are from the home country and have been indoctrinated with the home-country experience. People feel more comfortable with others of similar background, say these managers. Of course, these same attitudes are visible when other vital decisions—like the selection of an overseas banking relationship—are made. Ethnocentric attitudes are universal and no doubt quite resistant to change.

Polycentrism is the attitude that cultures of various countries are quite dissimilar, that foreigners are difficult to understand, and that they should be left alone as long as their work is profitable. In justifying a decision, headquarters executives of such a company might say: *Let the Romans do it their way. We really don't understand what's going on there, but we have to have confidence in them. As long as our foreign managers earn a profit, we want to remain in the background.* Local nationals in a polycentric organisation occupy virtually all the key positions in their respective local subsidiaries and appoint and develop their own people. Home-country personnel are kept out of these countries. Headquarters, with its holding-company attitude, is manned by home-country nationals who try not to interfere in the territory of each local managers. This low-profile approach of headquarters is justified on managerial and political grounds. Local managers are viewed as having high, if not absolute, sovereignty over their people.

The *regiocentric* attitude sees advantages in recruiting, developing, appraising, and assigning managers on a regional basis. Such a personnel policy is viewed as supportive of functional rationalisation on a more-than-one-country basis. For example, a single European production facility may serve several markets. A regional advertising campaign may be launched by Italian, French, British, and German managers with a European orientation. Candidates for positions in European subsidiaries are brought to regional headquarters in Brussels, London, Paris, or Geneva. Despite the continued nationalism of European countries, a European team is established with a Eurocentric view.

The *geocentric* attitude is evidenced in the attempt to integrate diverse regions through a global systems approach to decision making. Headquarters and subsidiaries see themselves as parts of an organic worldwide entity. Superiority is not equated with nationality. Executives convey in their key decisions the attitude that the distinctive competence of the truly multinational firm is its capacity to optimise resource allocation on a global basis. Good ideas come from any country and go to any country within the firm.

The geocentric approach is not the ideal for all firms with international interests. In practice, it poses a major challenge, given the persistent ethnocentric and polycentric pressures that generally characterise the home and foreign environment of a multinational enterprise.)

The EPRG Profile

The extent to which a worldwide firm exhibits ethnocentrism, polycentrism, regiocentrism, and geocentrism in its key decisions may be thought of as its EPRG profile. No doubt many factors—ranging from the background of the chief executive officer to the firm's history in international business—influence the firm's level of multinationalism. But importantly, all four attitudes usually are demonstrated in varying degrees. It would be both naive and incorrect to state that a firm is ethnocentric or that its product line is geocentric. Most MNCs probably evolve from ethnocentrism to polycentrism (and later, in some geographical areas, to regiocentrism) and finally to geocentrism.) Certainly for those firms intent on international expansion, this appears to be the favoured course. But any company—if highly motivated to multinationalise (for instance, with the arrival of a globally minded chief executive officer)—may proceed directly from ethnocentrism to geocentrism. For various reasons (say, the retirement of the same executive), the enterprise may reverse direction from geocentrism back to regiocentrism, polycentrism, or ethnocentrism. Thus, there are several routes to multinationalism.

Stakeholder influences on the EPRG profile, of course, are also considerable. In our present era, this evolution is not so clear. While the geocentric approach may be fostered by organisational changes, such as developing worldwide product divisions that regard the domestic market as just another market, the effect of the external stakeholders on the firm's profile is significant. For example, the ethnocentric approach may be increased by home-government behavior, such as taxation policies on overseas profits or support of defense-related R&D, or by intense pressures from labour unions in times of economic recession and unemployment. The chief executive officer (CEO) may feel the need to pay more attention to the stakeholders of the corporate headquarters than to those from abroad. And since the ownership of most MNCs is mononational, this can also be a basis for legitimising the ethnocentric approach.

FIGURE-5
DIRECTIONS OF MULTINATIONALISM

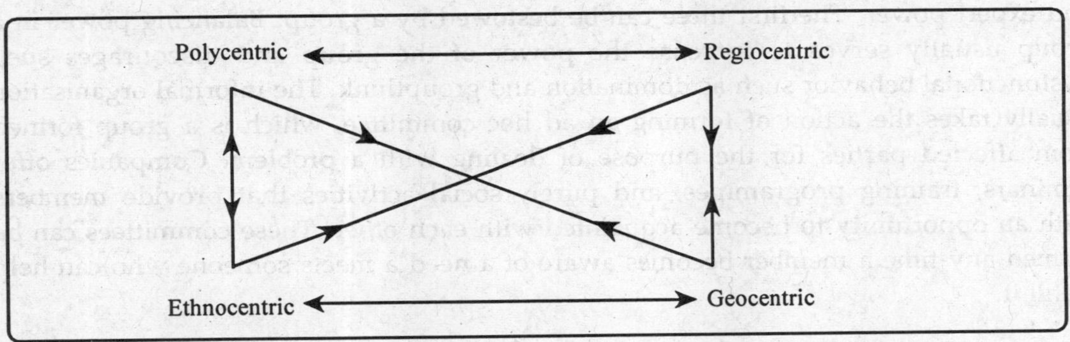

Stakeholder influences on the EPRG profile, of course, are also considerable. In our present era, this evolution is not so clear. While the geocentric approach may be fostered by organisational changes, such as developing worldwide product divisions that regard the domestic market as just another market, the effect of the external stakeholders on the firm's profile is significant. For example, the ethnocentric approach may be increased by home-government behavior, such as taxation policies on overseas profits or support of defense-related R&D, or by intense pressures from labour unions in times of economic recession and unemployment. The chief executive officer (CEO) may feel the need to pay more attention to the stakeholders of the corporate headquarters than to those from abroad. And since the ownership of most MNCs is mononational, this can also be a basis for legitimising the ethnocentric approach.

In the era of unilateral regulation, however, pressures from the host-country stakeholders and local-country managers may be in the polycentric direction. Where host-country laws forbid reduction of the working force without permission; where engineering standards are determined locally; and where, on occasion, the government is customer, competitor, and joint-venture partner, the vectors toward polycentrism are considerable. So, whatever the orientation, stakeholder pressures on the firm's multinational profile must be carefully assessed.

Establishing appropriate interdependencies is important because they play a large role in determining the shape of the information organisation. They are also a major contributor in motivating members of the organisation. If these interdependencies are mismanaged, friction will result. Reciprocal interdependence refers to establishing relationships between both individuals and groups in which goal accomplishment for one is dependent on goal accomplishment of the other.

The informal organisation has a greater ability to use the power to detect and respond to change than the formal organisation. Use of power is the ability to influence others. Politics is the use of power toward some goal. There are five sources of power: reward power, coercive power, legitimate power, referent power (based on respect), and expert power. The first three can be bestowed by a group. Balancing power in a group usually serves to increase the power of the group and discourages such dysfunctional behavior such as domination and groupthink. The informal organisation usually takes the action of forming an ad hoc committee, which is a group formed from affected parties for the purpose of dealing with a problem. Companies offer seminars, training programmes, and purely social activities that provide members with an opportunity to become acquainted with each other. These committees can be formed any time a member becomes aware of a need a meets someone who can help fulfill it.

An informal work group is an example of a human network, which is a system of individuals connected by some common interest. These networks offer the opportunity to expand influence and information across a larger area. They also help to form communication channels with the formal organisation.

Enhancing the ability of an organisation through the development of its informal structure can add to the ability of the organisation to process information and respond to the rapidly changing demands of the international business environment. It can also add to the ability of the informal organisation to engage in dysfunctional behaviour if the goals of its members are not consistent with the goals of the formal organisation.

ECONOMICS AND POLITICS OF MULTINATIONAL CORPORATIONS

Since the multinational corporation is definitionally equivalent to foreign direct investment, theories of foreign direct investment must account for why one country invests in another and why this investment is carried out within organizational boundaries of a firm. In distinguishing between portfolio and direct investment, Hymer noted that firms operate at a disadvantage in foreign markets and hence they must have an offsetting competitive advantage to compete overseas. These advantages for overseas investments are the same ones that allow a firm to compete and grow in the home market. These observations have important implications. The first is that direct investment is the growth of the firm across borders and hence the firm expands internationally on what it has learned at home. This observation is the basis for the evolutionary theory of the firm. The second observation that Hymer made is that firms that expand overseas, because they have competitive resources, are also likely to be large and to belong to oligopolistic industries.

In these observations, we can understand the ambivalence expressed in popular and policy debates regarding the multinational corporation. Competition among multinational corporations often is the extension of their home domestic and oligopolistic rivalry that spills across national borders. In many global industries, the same company names dominate each country's list of the largest firms inside their national frontiers. No matter if it is China or India, Singapore or Mexico, the same multinational corporations will be found in the local oligopolistic industries (e.g., consumer goods or automobiles). Because they are large even in their home markets, investments by multinational corporations can have a large impact on a host country.

As a consequence, the multinational corporation has often been the subject of debates concerning national sovereignty and welfare. In recent decades, acquisitions have generally been the primary way by which multinationals invest in wealthy foreign countries, where the vast proportion of direct investment is concentrated. Given the size of a multinational corporation and occasional national importance of the targeted acquisition, even wealthy countries frequently evidence discomfort, if not out-right public hostility, to multinational investments. Moreover, multinational corporations are sometimes the vehicles for foreign policies of their home or host country.

Multinational corporations are especially problematic in developing countries. By definition, developing countries are relatively poor, thus both in need of capital and yet concerned over their loss of independence. As discussed above, the history of multinational corporations in developing countries is marked by its origins in policies of imperialism and colonialism. Especially in Latin America, where a school of thought labeled *Dependencia* has been influential, the concern over dependence on the United States resulted in efforts to curb the power of the multinational corporations by restricting the amount of equity ownership a foreign firm could hold in a domestic company or by prohibiting investment in certain sectors.

The other side of the coin is that multinational corporations bring investment and technology to the foreign country. Vernon hypothesized that innovations start in wealthy countries. As the market is saturated and as oligopolistic rivalry increases, multinational corporations are pushed out from their home markets to expand abroad in new markets and to locate less expensive places. Thus, Vernon seized both sides of the debate, recognizing the value of the transfer of technology but also emphasizing the oligopolistic nature of multinational investment.

It is, in fact, difficult to draw simple conclusions regarding the relationship of foreign investment and national growth. Countries such as Singapore, Malaysia, and Thailand have encouraged foreign direct investment actively. The growth in China's coastal sector is indisputably linked to the massive investments by multinational corporations. However, historically Japan and Korea have pursued more cautious policies regarding investments by multinational corporations. In these countries, the state has often negotiated the terms for entry by multinational corporations, sometimes requiring licensing to domestic competitors as a price. The efficacy of such policies for these countries is much disputed. However, for many other countries, the intervention of the government in demanding licenses unquestionably leads to internal corruption and to insufficient domestic competition.

There are many channels by which a country can absorb foreign technology and managerial techniques. Most of the evidence shows, however, that prohibitions on the in-flows of direct investment can be very costly for many countries. With their domestic industries still to be developed, a developing country requires substantial investment. Some countries, primarily in Asia, have been able to achieve very high savings rates to finance their industries without direct investment. Moreover, high savings rates, plus political stability, create growth, and growth attracts foreign portfolio capital. A poor country that prohibits foreign direct investment but does not have high rates of saving is entirely dependent upon portfolio capital. The history of debt and currency crises convinced many poor countries that foreign direct investment was a preferable means of attracting capital, because it could not be easily pulled out of a country on short-notice in response to a financial crisis.

However, multinational corporations also respond to the volatility in the global market. This volatility derives from changes in exchange rates, politics, and productivity. Once having achieved sufficient experience and having established subsidiaries around the world, the multinational corporation might choose to close a plant in one location and open plants in new locations. Of course, such actions might provoke a response by labor, but historically, labor has been organized by national, not by international, organizations. Yet, there is also the possibility that locations lose some kinds of plants but gain more sophisticated investments. Some regions and countries pull multinational investments. It has long been noticed that foreign direct investment among developed countries flows to high cost locations. Regions such as Silicon Valley, Baden-Wuertemberg, and Singapore attract multinational investments not because wages are low, but because productivity levels are high and workers are well trained. In many cases, developing countries have given rise to their own multinational corporations acting in the region and sometimes globally. In this sense, the multinational corporation acts as a training center in the developmental strategies of emerging economies.

The peculiar conflict in the world economy is the growing trend toward economic integration without a concomitant growth in global political and social institutions to regulate and arbitrate this trend. Multinational corporations are rapidly adopting advanced information technologies to increase the efficiency and capabilities of their operations. Valuable information, such as software or financial services, is transmitted digitally.

Governments are often unable to tax the value of these services or control their content. Moreover, information technologies, often supported by private telecommunication networks, permit for example, a unit in US to control the manufacturing operations located in India. Digital technologies permit a high degree of integration and, in the short run, aggravate the gap between countries that are rich and those that are poor and do not have the infrastructural capabilities. However, these technologies are beginning to have profound effects on some regional economies. In parts of China, India, Israel, and elsewhere, advanced satellite transmission transmits digitally encoded work between their sites and other organizational units of multinational corporations located elsewhere. Whereas before the Indian engineer from Bangalore might have tried to migrate to the US to bring his human capital to a more attractive labor market, the increasing wages and job prospects in India are encouraging many to stay at home and participate digitally in the world economy.

These trends have unclear effects on multinational corporations. They permit more easily the development of projects that are in continual development, as work passes from one unit to the next as the day advances. They also allow more easily the coupling of less expensive labor in one country with more expensive skilled labor in another.

At the same time, the origins of the multinational corporation laid in its ability to organize labor on a worldwide basis on principles other than ethnic and cultural identities. This organization has never been without cost and risk. The growth of a world digital economy permits alternative ways by which labor can cooperate and be coordinated on a world basis. The intriguing question at this point in history is whether the multinational corporation, though still a vital presence in the world economy, nevertheless will recede relatively in importance as information technologies reduces the meaning of geographic distance.

QUESTIONS

1. Define multinational corporations (MNCs) and also critically examine the economics and politics of MNCs.
2. Discuss the evolution of multinational corporations (MNCs). What are the challenges posed by emerging market multinational corporations (EM-MNCs) in recent times to the MNCs from developed countries ?
3. Discuss the organisational evolution of MNCs and also explain the contradiction in their evolution.
4. How can multinational companies (MNCs) gain traction in emerging markets ?
5. Discuss an integrated strategy of MNCs to enter the international market. What are the strategic issues by faced mangers around the world to be considered while designing global strategy.
6. What is global strategy ? Discuss the main global strategy levers. Explain the benefits and costs of global strategy.

REFERENCES

Barton, Daniel F., Jr., Erich Bloch, and Mark S. Mahomey. "Multinationals." *Challenge*, September-October 1994.

Braudel F. (1973) *Capitalism and Material Life, 1400-1800* (trans. Kochan M). Harper and Row, New York.

Brown N.O. (1969) *Hermes the Thief: The Evolution of a Myth*, 2nd edn. University of Wisconsin Press, Madison, WI.

Buckley P.J., Casson M. (1976) *The Future of the Multinational Enterprise.* MacMillan, London.

Cantwell J. (1989) *Technological Innovations and Multinational Corporations.* Blackwell, London.

Caves R.E. (1974) Causes of direct investment: Foreign firms. Shares in Canadian and United Kingdom manufacturing industries. *Review of Economic Statistics* 56: 79-93.

Chandler A.D. (1990) *Scale and Scope: The Dynamics of Industrial Capitalism.* Belknap Press, Cambridge, MA.

Channon D.F. (1973) *The Strategy and Structure of British Enterprises.* Harvard University, Boston.

Choucri, Nazli. "The Global Environment and Multinational Corporations." *Technology Review*, April 1991.

Curtin P.D. (1984) *Cross-cultural Trade in World History*. Princeton University Press, Princeton, NJ.

Dobbs, Lou. "The Myth of Insourcing." *U.S. News & World Report*, 3 May 2004, 56.

Francis, Diane. "The New Love Affair with Transnational." *Maclean's*, 20 December 1993.

Greif A. (1989) Reputation and coalitions in medieval trade: Evidence on the Maghribi traders. *Journal of Economic History* 39: 857-82.

Hannah L. (1999) Marshal's 'trees' and the global 'forest': Were 'Giant Redwoods' different? In: Lamereaux N R, Raff D M G, Temin P (eds.) *Learning by Doing in Markets, Firms, and Countries.* University of Chicago Press, Chicago pp. 253-86.

Hatfield, John. "At the Mercy of the Monsters." *CA Magazine*, September 1998.

Hymer S. (1976) The international operations of national firms: A study of direct investment. Ph.D. thesis, Massachusetts Institute of Technology.

Jane, Wills. "Taking on the CosmoCorps?" *Economic Geography*, April 1998.

Jones G. (1993) *British Multinational Banking, 1830-1990.* Oxford University Press, New York.

Kogut B 1992 National organizing principles of work and the erstwhile dominance of the American multinational corporation. *Industrial and Corporate Change* 1: 285-325.

Lall S. (1983) *The New Multinationals: The Spread of Third World Enterprise.* Wiley, Chichester, UK.

Martinelli A. (1975) Multinational corporations, national economic policies and labor unions. In: Lindberg L, Alford R, Crouch C, Offe C (eds.) *Stress and Contradiction in Modern Capitalism.* Heath, Lexington, MA pp. 425-43.

Robinson R.D. (1964) *International Business Policy*. Holt, Rinehart, and Winston, New York.

Soskice D. (1990) Wage determination: The changing role of institutions in advanced industrialized countries. *Oxford Review of Economic Policy 6:* 36—61.

Streeck W. (1995) German capitalism: Does it exist? Can it survive? In: Crouch C, Streeck W (eds.) *Modern Capitalism or Modern Capitalisms?* Pinter, London.

Suzuki Y. (1991) *Japanese Management Structures, 1920-1980.* St. Martin's Press, New York

Tsang, Eric W.K. "Intel-nationalization as a Learning Process: Singapore MNCs in China." *Academy of Management Executives*, February 1999.

Unit VII

32

INTERNATIONAL FINANCIAL MANAGEMENT

INTRODUCTION

Multinational corporations have become central actors of the world economy and, in linking foreign direct investment, trade, technology and finance, they are a driving force of economic growth. Since global finance has become a reality, financial capital is one of the most fungible assets to cross national boundaries. The determinants of the way in which transnational corporation acquire, organise and manage those assets is of critical importance, not only to the success of those corporations, but also to the development and industrial restructuring of nation states. Thus the range of enterprises for which the practice and theory of international financial management is relevant is much more inclusive than the traditional concepts of the multinational corporation (MNC), which is defined typically as a firm having a substantial portion of its activities and assets deployed in different countries. The concept relevant for financial management comprises all firms that are involved in international business, directly or indirectly, to such an extent that the managerial process must take into account the complexities of a *multimarket, multicurrency environment*. The objective of international financial management is the same as that of domestically oriented financial management i.e. the maximisation of the value of the firm. The differences arise because of the term's exposure to international and multinational environments. The xmon thread of international aspects of financial management is found in the following: What aspects of the issue are peculiarly international, and what opportunities does a firm have by virtue of its being international? The clues to an answer lie in the basic understanding of the management of the cross border financial assets and liabilities and cash flows. The task of international financial manager is to make the best possible tactical decision that the market has to offer on liabilities, within the strategic funding constraints set by currency denomination, maturity, and capital structure.

THEORETICAL DEVELOPMENTS IN THE INTERNATIONAL FINANCIAL MANAGEMENT

From the perspective of international corporate financial management, the definition of international business and—by implication—the international firm, is quite comprehensive: it includes all business activities on which management must make financial decisions, taking into account simultaneously: (1) the conditions prevailing in *two or more financial markets*, (2) regulatory and institutional *barriers* to the international movement of funds, and (3) the changes in the *exchange rates* of national monies. To illustrate, instead of taking into account one set of national tax rules, one rate of inflation, one set of interest rates, one integrated system of money and capital markets and the assorted institutions, management must now take into account the complex interactions of at least two tax systems, two interest rate structures, and two sets of financial institutions when making decisions. Obviously, this entails additional complications and risks. However—and this represents the other side of the coin—management has available more alternatives and, therefore, better opportunities to attain the firm's objectives: to enhance the value of the business enterprise by minimising the cost of funds and the risk to the firm. From a corporate perspective, the most important theoretical developments in international financial management can be captured by concentrating on the following areas:

The Foreign Exchange Markets

Foreign exchange is simply a *payment or a deposit* in some national currency (or artificial currency) that is exchanged for a payment in another currency. Doing business across national boundaries means dealing with more than one currency and therefore involves exchange risk. *Exchange risk* is the additional systematic risk to a firm's flows arising from exchange rate changes. The three main types of foreign exchange-risk management which are of special interest to MNCs fall under the heading of *economic, transaction* and *translation*—exposure management. The foreign exchange economic exposure is defined as the likelihood that the net present value of a firm's future cash flows will change due to an unexpected change in exchange rates. When exchange rates change unexpectedly, a transnational corporation's sales volume, price and costs are likely to be affected.

Effort by the firm to manage exchange rate changes are really the macroeconomic version of what is happening at the macroeconomic level. International economics literature is rich in discussions of how countries adjust to exchange rate changes. For example, the concept of a "real (inflation-adjusted) exchange rate" is well understood in economics literature and by government policy makers. However, neither economic exposure nor the real effective exchange rate are well understood by top management. Instead, they often assume that any foreign exchange issue is the responsibility of the treasurer or financial vice president. In reality, managing economic exposure is best accomplished by internationally diversifying sales, production and financing by currency. These are strategic decisions that must be approved by top management and the board of directors, as well as by the financial officers.

International Financial Markets

The capital markets of the world consist of sources of finance, and uses for finance, in a number of different countries. Each of these is a capital market on its own. Since national capital markets are of very different stages of development and size and depth, they have very different prices and availability of capital. Hence, the international financier has great opportunities for *arbitrage*—finding the cheapest source of funds, and the highest return, without adding to risk. And because markets are imperfectly linked, the means and channels by which foreigners enter domestic capital markets, and domestic sources or users of funds go abroad, are the essence of this aspect of international financial management. The other aspect is the fact that domestic claims and liabilities are denominated in national currencies. These must be exchanged for one another for capital to flow internationally; since relative values depend on supply and demand, the international financier faces *exchange risk*. Finally, the past few decades have seen a new phenomenon: the separation of *currency of denomination* of assets and liabilities from *country of jurisdiction*. This removal of currencies from their home countries is the *Euromarket* phenomenon.

Exhibit-1 illustrates *the three sets* of markets—home, foreign and Euromarket—faced by every investor or borrower, plus the fourth market, the foreign currency market, which must be crossed as one enters the world of finance. Each country has more or less imperfect linkages with every other country and with the Euromarket, both the segment in its own currency and Euromarket segments in other currencies. The *linkages of each country with its Euromarket* segment are very important, since domestic and Euromarket instrument are close substitutes and no foreign exchange market comes between them. The *links among segments of the Euromarket* are also very important, since no national controls come between them—in other words, linkages within the Euromarket are perfect, being differentiated only by currency of denomination. They are linked through the *spot* and *forward foreign exchange markets*.

This scheme provides a picture of the contents herein *as* well as that of the environment of international finance. International finance is thus concerned with:

Domestic capital markets and their linkages with Euromarkets and other domestic markets.

Euromarkets and their linkages' with other Euromarkets and domestic markets.

Foreign exchange markets that link domestic markets and Euromarkets in different currencies.

The *techniques* of borrowing, investing, moving; and exchanging funds internationally: international financial management.

EXHIBIT-1

Markets of International Finance

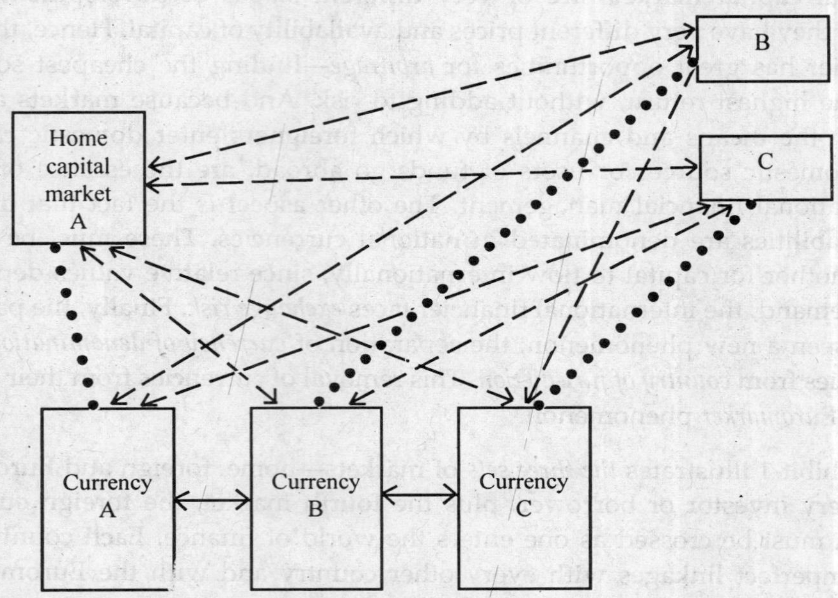

Key: Solid lines, prefect linkages; dotted lines, partial linkages; arrow, foreign exchange linkages.

Domestic Capital Markets and Their Linkages

The *international role* of a capital market and the *regulatory climate* that prevails are closely related. Appropriate regulation can and does make markets more attractive (e.g., by minimising the risk of losses through fraud, through conflicts of interest, and through a lack of adequate disclosure). However, the dividing line between regulatory measures that improve markets and those that have just the opposite effect is very thin. When governments pursue other objectives, such' as *credit allocation* according to political criteria, or when they discriminate against non-residents, markets can quickly become inefficient. The result is that both foreign and domestic market participants use markets in other jurisdictions.

Foreign Financial Markets

Most of the savings and investments of a country take place in that country's domestic financial market. However, many financial markets have extensive links abroad-—domestic investors purchase foreign securities and invest funds in foreign financial institutions. Conversely, domestic banks can lend to foreign residents, and foreign residents can issue securities in the national market or deposit funds with resident financial intermediaries. These are the *traditional foreign markets* for international financial transactions.

The significant aspect of traditional foreign lending and borrowing is that all transactions take place under the rules, usances, and institutional arrangements prevailing in the respective national market. Most important, all these transactions are directly subject to public policy governing foreign transactions in a particular market. To illustrate, when savers purchase securities in a foreign market, they do so according to the rules, market practices, and regulatory precepts that govern such transactions in that particular market. The same applies to those who invest their funds with foreign financial intermediaries.

Likewise, foreign borrowers who wish to issue securities in a national market must follow the rules and regulations of that market. Frequently, these rules are *discriminatory* and *restrictive*. The same is true with respect to financial intermediaries; the borrower who approaches a foreign financial institution for a loan obtains funds at rates and conditions imposed by the financial institutions of the foreign country and is directly affected by the authorities' policy towards lending to foreign residents.

The Euromarkets and Their Linkages

Eurocurrencies—which are neither currencies (they are deposits, loans, or securities) nor are they necessarily connected with Europe—represent the separation of currency of denomination from the country of jurisdiction.

Banks and clients make this separation simply by locating the market for credit denominated in a particular currency outside the country where that currency is legal tender (i.e. the locus is in a jurisdiction that offers a more hospitable regulatory climate for such transactions).

To illustrate, markets for dollar-denominated loans, deposits, and securities in jurisdictions other than in the United States effectively avoid U.S. banking and securities regulations. These markets are referred to as "Euro" or, more properly, as "external" markets in order to indicate that they are not part of the domestic or national financial system. Thus the essence of this classification criterion is the nature of regulation. Differences in interest rates, practices and regulations that exist between domestic and external markets arise primarily from the extent to which regulatory constraints are different.

As in the domestic markets, the Euromarket consists of *intermediated funds* and *direct funds*. Intermediated credit in channel through banks is called the "Eurocurrency market". Direct credit—in particular, bonds—can be arranged by banks but it represents the direct liability of the borrower. The Eurobond market is such a market.

Exhibit-2 summarises the three-tiered structure of capital markets. Capital markets consist of:

A *domestic market,* usually with special and unique aspects and institutions stemming from historical and regulatory differences.

A *foreign segment* attached to the national market, where non-residents participate as suppliers and takers of funds, frequently playing both roles simultaneously, but always under the specific conditions, rules and regulations established for foreign participants in a particular national market.

An *external segment* that is characterised by being in a different political jurisdiction, with only the currency used to denominate the financial claims being the essential link to the national market.

As a result, the various external markets have more features in common with each other than with the respective national markets. Therefore, they are properly discussed as a common, integrated market where claims denominated in different currencies are exchanged.

International business is subject to *capital and credit controls.* International managers should know how to respond to governments' attempts to restrict the movement of funds into or out of countries and to manipulate the allocation of funds in domestic capital markets.

EXHIBIT - 2

International Credit Markets

A Schematic Presentation

	National		International
Credit Channel	Domestic	Foreign	Euro
Intermediated (banks)			
Direct (securities markets)			
	Internal		External

The multinational enterprise, by virtue of its foreign origin and international character, has special *monopolistically held advantages* that enable it to create and take advantage of imperfections in markets for factors, products and financial capital.

As the last suggests, much of what international financial management is about is taking advantage of the international firm's ability to exploit market imperfections. The crux of this is the ability to distinguish between situations where market imperfections truly exist and those where the profit opportunities have been eliminated by the workings of the market. A prime example is in the foreign exchange forecasting area—in currency markets that are likely to be efficient, no gain is to be had from exchange rate forecasting. The task is therefore to judge where the markets are inefficient and where the firm has a special advantage.

In general, where the market works the firm is better off accepting market prices as signals rather than searching out additional information. A framework against which market imperfections can be judged is corporate funding decisions. From the standpoint of the individual operating unit, for example, a foreign affiliate that is typically in the legal form of a subsidiary and undertakes the asset commitment, two basic alternatives present themselves. First, funds can be obtained from within the corporate group. This includes the use of the affiliate's own funds through a reduction of cash or the liquidation of other assets. Alternatively, funds can be obtained from either the parent or one of the sister affiliates who use their own resources. Second, funds can be obtained from outside sources, either directly, from the financial markets, or via the parent and other affiliates.

Cost of Capital

A number of transnational corporations have been able to lower their cost of capital by raising funds in international capital markets and by cross-listing on foreign stock exchanges. As a result of the efforts of those firms to internationalise their cost of capital, segmented capital markets have gradually become more integrated and international portfolio investment has flourished. In addition, the investors may purchaser the shares of firms which are resident in segmented capital markets. This could further lower the cost of capital of transnational firms.

If capital markets are partially segmented, investors cannot gain the full benefit from international portfolio diversification, and firms cannot fully lower their cost of capital by selling their securities to foreign investors. A national capital market can be segmented because of government interference and/or because of investor perceptions. An example of government interference is restrictions on the free movement of capital, either by limiting what domestic securities foreign investors can buy, or by limiting what foreign securities domestic investors can buy. Other examples are discriminatory tax policies, rationing of foreign exchange, and policies which increase transactions costs in domestic securities markets. Investor perceptions are shaped by the quality of financial disclosures, familiarity with foreign securities markets and institutions, alternative portfolio possibilities, foreign exchange risk and political risk.

If a country's capital market is segmented, investors resident in that country may not be able to hold an efficient internationally diversified portfolio, and firms resident in that country may not enjoy the lowest possible cost of capital. However, with the proper strategies, transnational firms may be able to raise their funds abroad and gain an international pricing of their securities even though their home market remains segmented. On the other hand, firms which are too small to tap international capital markets are forced to continue to accept the higher cost of capital typical of their domestic markets.

The "small firm" bias is even more of a deterrent when it comes to interesting international equity investors in holding the shares of a small firm. Most institutional investors are very concerned about their ability to sell as well as to buy a firm's shares. The market for shares in a small firm is perceived as being illiquid, whether that firm is transnational or domestic.

To what extent can the shares of a transnational corporation serve as a substitute for investors who wish to diversify their portfolios internationally but cannot find or purchase the shares of firms which are resident in segmented capital markets? Considerable evidence exists to suggest that transnational firms should have a lower cost of capital than their domestic counterparts. Because of that, they may receive a higher valuation by investors who are using their shares for international diversification into segmented markets that they cannot tap themselves. Listing on foreign securities exchanges has a favourable liquidity effect because more investors are available to buy the limited number of a firm's shares outstanding. Tapping foreign markets is also a way for firms which are resident in segmented markets to escape the lower valuation of their shares in that market. Normally a firm must be transnational, or at least extremely visible abroad, to succeed in attracting a significant following of foreign investors.

Financial Structure

Modigliani and Miller launched the great debate about whether or not an optimal financial structure for a firm exists. Their original contention was that, under certain very restrictive assumptions about perfect competition, financial structure was irrelevant. They later modified this assertion by recognising that the tax advantages of debt biases the firm towards a much higher use of debt. Later theorists suggested that agency and bankruptcy costs place an upper limit on the desirable portion of debt.

The "traditionalists" always felt that an optimal debt ratio exists in the form of a U-shaped cost of capital curve. As a firm takes on debt, the weighted average cost of capital is reduced due to the tax advantages of debt; but when the debt ratio becomes too high, agency and bankruptcy costs, as well as the reticence of lenders, raises the cost of capital. Therefore, the optimal debt ratio is a flat range at the bottom of the U-shaped cost of capital curve.

Capital structure decisions are particularly important when financial structure decisions dealing with leverage (or gearing) must be made. To the extent that any priorities can be established among the complex, interrelated steps of a funding decision in MNC, such strategic considerations probably take first place. Of course, the reason why the debt/equity ratio matters so much is that it determines the financial risk of the enterprise, because of the contractually fixed nature of payments to debt holders, returns to the owners of equity will fluctuate more in response to given, unanticipated fluctuations of operating returns the higher the proportion of debt relative to equity. Thus a positive partial relationship between the risk of equity returns and leverage ratios can be documented. Because of nontrivial default costs one can also find that a firm's leverage ratios and enterprise risk are negatively related. The interaction between the tax shield provided by debt and the various costs associated with default provide the theoretical support for an optimal capital structure. And to the extent that these factors are influenced by environmental factors such as tax laws and factors affecting the cost and probability of bankruptcy, one finds significant country factors in the capital structure of MNCs based in various countries.

This rationale is often mistakenly applied in the analysis of funding decisions involving individual, wholly owned affiliates. What is usually overlooked is the fact that such wholly owned affiliates of MNC's have a distinct and separate debt/equity ratio only if the parent is prepared to allow the affiliate in question to default on its debt without coming to its rescue. On the other hand, as long as the rest of the MNC group has a *legal* (loan guarantees) or an effective *moral obligation* to prevent the affiliate from defaulting—even if this threatens the survival of the remainoer of the group—the individual affiliate has *no independent debt/equity ratio.* Its true leverage ratio is equal to that of the consolidated group.

Since virtually all MNC's feel obliged to their wholly owned (and sometimes even partially owned) affiliates, simply because they cannot afford to lose their financial respectability, the debt/equity ratio of the affiliate is determined by purely institutional factors. Most prominent among such are (i) *Statutory laws,* which prescribe a required minimum equity level in many countries; (2) *tax laws,* which often treat interest payments differently than payments on equity (dividends): (3) *exchange control regulations,* which are usually less restrictive when interest payments are concerned: (4) expropriation risk, *which can be lessened if the parent expects to default on its local debt in the specific case that the lending institutions have also been taken over by the government in question, or the lending institutions are state-owned already.*

Thus the debt/equity decision for foreign affiliates is either a purely legal one—as opposed to a financial decision—or it involves *strategic questions of ownership* to the extent that third-party investors, local or otherwise, own a part of the affiliate's equity.

When it comes to making debt/equity decisions for the parent, or rather the group as a whole, a very difficult issue arises: which market's standards will govern its "acceptable" debt/equity ratio? For domestic firms, the answer is usually quite clear. In different national capital markets, certain target debt/equity ratios have been established by market forces for different kinds of firms. These acceptable debt/equity ratios are influenced by the nature of the firm. To illustrate, public utilities, whose operating risk is relatively low, are permitted to have a much higher proportion of debt before the market begins to penalise these enterprises by increasing the required rate of return on equity or the interest on their debt relative to for example, capital goods producers, whose return on assets is very much subject to the vagaries of the business cycle. The problem for the multinational firm is that different national markets differ quite a bit in terms of standards for acceptable debt/equity ratios, and to the extent that MNCs sell their equity or borrow funds in many countries they must choose a reference market.

Theoretically, this question is largely unsolved because empirical work in finance has not sufficiently progressed to answer the question. "Precisely how are financial assets priced internationally?" That is, which is a more correct approximation of reality, that markets are separated or that they are integrated? In practice, most MNCs do not have to face this problem head on because the great bulk of the equity is usually held by investors of a national market whose standards dominate the applicable debt/equity ratio. However, as more and more companies make an effort to broaden their stockholder base internationally (e.g., by listing their stock on the exchanges of two or more countries) this issue will become more and more acute.

Next to capital structure decisions, the issue of *debt denomination* is probably the most important strategic aspect of the funding decision. In the absence of specific and identifiable market imperfections, currency decisions cannot be made on the basis of financial market factors alone. They must be coordinated with an analysis of the impact of *currency fluctuations* on the firm's operating cash flows (i.e., *corporate exchange risk*).

Intracompany Transfers

The problems encountered in the financial structure decision of a multinational firm and its individual affiliates turn up again when tactical questions of funding international operations are being considered. By their nature MNCs have complicated legal structures, such as that depicted in Exhibit-3.

Of course, Exhibit-3 is a schematic presentation only and in reality an almost infinite number of combinations are possible. For financial management, this raises the question as to which one of the entities should contract with providers of funds. In respect to equity, this is almost invariably the parent company, especially if the firm has a policy of maintaining wholly owned affiliates. With respect to debt, however, there are many possibilities. And unless the answer to the question is. "The same affiliate that needs the funds," another decision must be made right away—how to move the funds through the various corporate entities to their final destination. In turn this decision is directly related to yet another question: In what legal form and in which currency should funds be injected in the affiliate that acquires productive assets?

EXHIBIT-3

Legal Structure of a Multinational Corporation

Having affiliates in many financial markets provides the MNF with opportunities to *minimise the cost of funds* for the corporation by borrowing wherever the effective cost is least. In practice, however, there are serious constraints that limit these opportunities. After all, it is because of the government restrictions, and to a certain extent institutional arrangements, that the cost of funds in various markets will not be equalised through direct arbitrage.

The only real advantage that the MNC has in this respect is that it can somewhat more easily circumvent such restrictions because of its particular structure of centrally coordinated, but legally separate entities. To illustrate, many countries have tight controls on direct lending to borrowers abroad. Theoretically, then, a multinational firm can get around this restriction by having its local affiliate borrow the funds and subsequently transfer them in some form to its parent or sister affiliates. Governments, of course, are aware of such operations, too, and they have usually issued all kinds of rules and regulations to prevent such international *intracorporate transfers of funds.* However, if these regulations were written and administered too tightly, they would strangle international trade and investment. Thus firms usually have some leeway in transferring funds, although their flexibility is much more limited than is usually implied by critics of multinational firms.

In an integrated MNC, where each affiliate has dealings with the others, transfer of funds can usually be effected because most are simply necessary to run the operation, regardless of the existence of restrictions. Thus the question is not one of whether or not to shift funds among the MNC's affiliates, but how much and in which direction. This also highlights the fact that it is often impossible to determine the "correct" arm's length transaction, not only for government but even the corporate controller. To illustrate, economists and accountants still argue about correct cost allocation, transfer prices, and interest charges in multidivision operations that are closely integrated. Interestingly, many financial executives in multinational firms point to the fact that their ability to move funds within the corporate family is severely restricted not only by government, but by the disadvantage of distorting their internal control system.

That MNC's do have some freedom to move funds internationally is simply based on the fact that funds flows can be effected in very many ways, as depicted in Exhibit-4.

EXHIBIT-4

Financial and Real Flows in the Multinational Firm

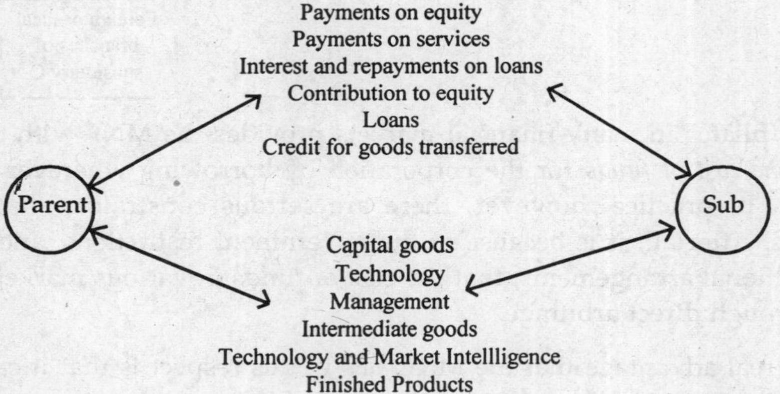

Analytically, it is very important to generalise on a point that is made above in respect to the debt/equity ratios: Intracompany transfers of funds do not give rise to any change in the cost of funds or the risk of the multinational firms as such. These transfers have an impact only in terms of taxes, exchange controls, and other regulatory aspects. The cost of funds and financial risk is affected only when there is a change in the kind or amount of *outside sources of funds.* Thus the determinants of such inside transactions are to be found in tax and regulatory matters only.

While all this sounds very complex—and in reality it is complex because of all the environmental factors that impinge upon the decision (tax effects, exchange regulations, financial market regulations and practices, banking relations, etc.)—the basic conceptual framework is quite simple and can be summarised as follows. If an MNC requires additional funds, it can raise these funds directly or through any one of its affiliates. The conditions on which the funds are obtained from outside sources (i.e., debt vs. equity, short-term vs. long-term funding, currency of denomination, and restrictive covenants) will have an impact on the basic cost of funds and the financial risk faced by the group as a whole. And it is these relationships that determine the weighted average cost of funds that must be minimised.

Capital Budgeting

Capital budgeting for a foreign project uses the same discounted cash-flow techniques as are used to evaluate domestic projects. In a true transnational corporation, all projects, foreign and domestic, compete on an equal footing for a piece of the capital budget. However, the analysis of a foreign project is considerably more complex than for a domestic project for the following reasons:

i) Parent cash flows must be distinguished form project cash flows. Each of these two types of flow contributes to a different view of value.

ii) Parent cash flows often depend on the form of financing. Thus cash flows cannot be clearly separated from financing decisions, as is done in domestic capital budgeting.

iii) Remittance of funds to the parent must be explicitly recognised because of differing tax systems, legal and political constraints on the movement of funds, local business norms, and differences in how financial markets and institutions function.

iv) Cash flows from affiliates to parent can be generated by an array of non-financial payments, including payment of license fees and payments for imports from the parent.

v) Differing rates of national inflation must be anticipated because of their importance in causing changes in competitive position, and thus in cash flows over a period of time.

vi) The possibility of unanticipated foreign exchange rate changes must be remembered because of possible direct effects on the value to the parent of local cash flows, as well as an indirect effect on the competitive position of the foreign affiliate.

vii) Use of segmented national capital markets may create an opportunity for financial gains or may lead to additional financial costs.

viii) Use of host government subsidised loans complicates both capital structure and the ability to determine an appropriate weighted average cost of capital for discounting purposes.

ix) Political risk must be evaluated because political events can drastically reduce the value or availability of expected cash flows.

x) Terminal value is more difficult to estimate because potential purchasers from the host, parent, or third countries, or from the private or public sector, may have widely divergent perspectives on the value to them of acquiring the project.

Since the same theoretical capital budgeting framework is used to choose among competing foreign and domestic projects, a common standard is critical. Thus all foreign complexities must be quantified as modifications to either expected cash flow or the rate of discount. Although in practice many firms make such modifications arbitrarily, readily available information, theoretical deduction, or just plain common sense can be used to make less arbitrary and more reasonable choices.

Though some inputs were made to introduce the complexities of capital budgeting for a foreign project into the corporate finance literature of the late 1960s, but it was many years before mainline financial theories considered the problem worthy of further study. It was suggested that a foreign project be evaluated from the viewpoint both of the parent firm and of the foreign project itself. In order to be acceptable, a project should pass muster on both counts. Further, the financial cash flows must be considered rather than just operating cash flows since project cash flows were not necessarily immediately available to the parent. Moreover, when they would be repatriated in the future, contingent tax and foreign exchange cost could be expected. In addition, an allowance for political and foreign exchange risks should be made by charging cash flows the cost of a programme of uncertainty absorption, whether or not is actually carried out. Uncertainty could be absorbed by purchasing more *information,* borrowing most of the investment locally, buying, hedging and investment insurance if available and negotiating the environment with the host-country government. Arbitrarily raising the discount rate for a foreign project was rejected because that does not take account of the actual amounts at risk, or for variations in the degree of risk of the project over time. It should be noted, however, that capital budgeting was at an early stage of acceptance even for domestic projects. During the 1970s, capital budgeting for foreign projects attracted a respectable number of scholars' attention to expand the analysis to include more variables, in particular, the tax treatment of foreign income, the risk of expropriation, blocked hinds, inflation and segmented capital markets. They advocated that all foreign risks should be incorporated as adjustments to cash flow rather than adjusting the discount rate.

In 1985, Lessard contributed an adjusted present-value approach to foreign project evaluation. The main difference between this approach and the traditional one lies in its separation of contractual and non-contractual cash flows. For example, the tax advantages of debt are treated separately and explicitly as is the effect of expropriation, exchange risk and other foreign complexities. The present value of each of these components can be determined separately, perhaps even with different discount rates to reflect varying risks, and then all the resulting present values are added together. The main advantage of this approach is its simplicity because it breaks up a complex simulation into more manageable prices. Its main disadvantage is that a whole generation of managers has finally learned capital budgeting in the traditional manner, and it is difficult for them to simultaneously learn both the foreign complexities and a new approach to analysis.

INTERNATIONAL FINANCIAL MANAGEMENT AND IMPERFECTIONS IN FINANCIAL MARKETS

The equilibrium relationships and market linkages provide a point of departure for decision making. One can think of the expected relationships—in particular, the *unbiased forward rate* theory—as providing *market-based forecasts* of the exchange rate and other conditions.

Such forecasts can be used as a *benchmark* against which to judge the firm's own ability to forecast or to exploit market imperfections. Given the market-based forecasts, one can distinguish three situations, each with distinct implications for the currency aspects of financial planning:

1. *When the financial markets in question are reasonably efficient, and financial planners know of no systematic biases or constraints on market rates, then market-based forecasts should be accepted as valid.* Under these conditions, which probably hold for most financial decisions involving the U.S. and major international financial markets, no expected gain will result from manipulating the timing or currency of borrowing or investing, and financial management's energies should be directed toward matching borrowings and investments with the timing and currency of the funds needed or generated by the firm's operations. The use of market-based forecasts then implies planning for the deviations, or forecasting errors, that will probably occur.

> Specifically, what one wants to know is how cash flows from operations (return on assets) will change for any given deviation of the interest or exchange rate from the value predicted. As long as the return on assets is contractually fixed and denominated in a particular currency, as would be a portfolio of bonds or loans, the analysis is quite straightforward. A rise in interest rates will cause a proportional fall in the value of such a fixed-interest portfolio; a given fall in the exchange rate will lead to an equal drop in the dollar value of the portfolio. Protecting the value of such assets, therefore, requires funding the liabilities of the firm in the same currency and maturity as the assets.

This *efficient market financial planning framework* assumes the market's forecasts unbiased predictions of future exchange rates. Often, specific market imperfections will not allow this assumption to hold. The next two situations consider the Implications of such biases.

2. *When the term structure of interest or exchange rates deviates in a systematic way from the market's actual expectations because of government controls, or because of other specific market imperfections, financial management has profit opportunities.* The exploitation of these opportunities requires first, a flexible legal and operational structure, and second, *an* explicit trade-off function that permits management to decide whether the gains are worth the increase in risk and the exploitation of market imperfections might involve.

Government controls tend to be always partial, never comprehensive. The reason is simple; controls on all borrowing or lending, and all international transfers of funds, would cause economic activity to come to a grinding halt. Therefore, with regulations permitting certain transactions, and funds being fungible, international firms with diverse legal structures and a multitude of intercompany links usually are in a privileged position to *exploit the financial windfalls that government distortions provide* by keeping interest rates low and preventing exchange rates from adjusting to market pressures.

3. *When the market-based forecasts deviate from forecasted rates, not because of* market *imperfections but because the firm has some proprietary information or unusual forecasting ability, then financial managers should act on their forecasts only when the risks of doing so are offset by the expected gains.* When financial planners can confidently answer the questions, "Why do we believe we can predict interest or exchange rates better than the market"? Their focus should be on the proper perspective on the risks involved in speculative actions, and on a rapid response to opportunities when action is warranted.

Few financial managers can consistently resist the temptation to base financing decisions on their own judgements rather than those of the market. In most cases little harm is done, for unless the firm really goes out on a limb, position and negative forecasting errors tend to cancel out over time. But the mark of a good financial manager is not a knack for occasionally outguessing the market's forecasts, but rather an ability to obtain the highest return on invested assets, for a given level of risk, and the best long-run terms and conditions on debt, irrespective of the tend of interest rates or exchange rates. It is important for the integrity of the financial management process to keep these aspects of the function strictly separate. Otherwise, the inability of financial management out perform the markets tends to be hidden in the results of the risk management function.

The imperfections and linkages of domestic financial markets, Euromarkets, and foreign exchange markets provide both risks and opportunities for the international financial management. Management attention should be concentrated on those markets and channels in which the firm has a competitive advantage, and should rely on banks, partners, and markets themselves to do what they can do more cheaply and efficiently. In the area of foreign exchange risk management, the market's forecasts of future exchange rates are readily available in the form of the forward exchange rates. On the other hand, where financial managers feel they have a peculiar advantage in financial markets, resulting from the firm's legal structure, geographical locations, or because of an unusual forecasting ability, then the timing, maturity, and currency of borrowing and investment decisions should be based on the firm's own forecasts whenever the expected gains justify the risks.

ROLE OF THE INTERNATIONAL FINANCIAL MANAGER

The chief tasks of the international financial manager are summarised as under:

Forecasting the financial environment—prices, inflation rates, interest rates and exchange rates.

Management of assets—from cash management to international capital budgeting, at home and abroad, in domestic and foreign currencies.

Management of liabilities—borrowing relationships and decisions, in domestic and foreign currencies and markets, short-term and long-term.

Exchange risk management—measuring the effect of exchange rate changes on balance sheets, income, and cash flows, and managing these risks.

Performance evaluation and control—accounting for outsiders, the tax authorities, and for management, and doing so across countries and currencies without distortion.

Sounds like a Herculean agenda? Yes, but domestic financial markets are complex too, and many of the techniques are transferable. The place to start learning about international financial markets is therefore to gain a basic understanding of what and how financial markets operate affect the value of the firm.

ECONOMIC FRAMEWORK OF INTERNATIONAL FINANCIAL MANAGEMENT

Much of received international financial management doctrine consists of techniques for borrowing, investing, or hedging decisions in one currency or another work only under certain macroeconomic conditions, and the rules of thumb do not apply under other, quite plausible, conditions. In order to see how a number of the techniques of international finance are applicable under conditions of disequilibrium, the economic

EXHIBIT-5

Disequilibrium Conditions

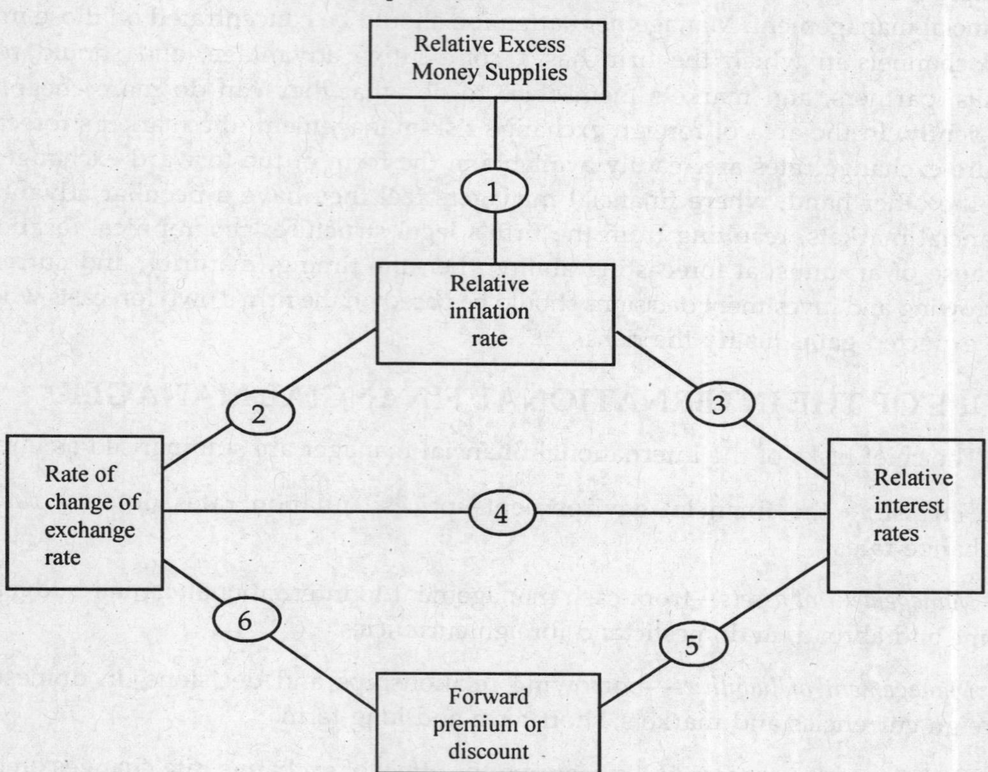

framework showing the linkages among prices, exchange rates, interest rates, and other variables is to be decision-making.

Many interpreted, Exhibit-5 shows the international differences in the extent to which the growth of the money supply exceeds the growth of real income result in international differences in inflation rates. Through the purchasing power parity relationship the inflation rate differential causes a corresponding rate of change of the exchange rate. If the foreign exchange market is efficient, the forward exchange rate equals the market's expected future exchange rate. Hence, the expected rate of change of the exchange rate equals the forward premium or discount, which in turn equals the interest rate differential while the interest rate differential equals the expected inflation rate differential.

These six relations are stated more explicit:

1. Inflation rate = rate of growth of money supply—rate of growth of real gross national product (too much money chasing too few goods).

2. Rate of change of exchange rate = Inflation rate differential (Purchasing power parity theory).
3. Interest rate = "Real " interest rate + Expected inflation rate (Fisher effect: one country).
4. Expected rate of change of exchange rate = Interest rate differential (International Fisher effect).
5. Forward exchange premium or discount = Interest rate differential (Interest rate parity theorem).
6. Forward premium or discount = Expected rate of change of exchange rate (unbiased forward rate theory).

Clearly, the "equilibrium" world only provide a useful point of departure. If all the relationships hold, then the firm is not subject to economic exposure, since interest rates anticipate currency value changes and prices of real goods adjust to offset exchange rate changes. Because the forward rate equals the market-expected future spot rate, the expected cost of hedging is zero; but hedging is also of little value.

QUESTIONS

1. Discuss the main theoretical development in the international financial management.
2. Discuss the role of the international financial manager.
3. What is the economic framework of international financial management?
4. "The imperfections and linkages of domestic financial markets, Euromarkets, and foreign exchange markets provide both risks and opportunities for the international financial manager." Comment.
5. Discuss the effect of market segmentation on a corporation's cost of capital.
6. If domestic securities are inaccessible to foreign investors would they commands super-risk premium?
7. Discuss the effects of international operations on the market value of the multinational firm.

REFERENCES

Bhalla, V.K., International Financial Management, Anmol Pub., 2010.

Eiteman, D.K., and A.K. Stonehill, Multinational Business Finance, Addison-Wasley, 1989.

Folks, W.R., Jr., and R.A. Aggarwal: International Dimensions of Financial Management, PWS-Kent 1987-88.

Lessard, D.R., International Financial Management, John Wiley & Son, N.Y. 1985.

Madura, J., International Financial Management, West Publishing, 1986.

Rodriguez, R.M., and E.E. Carter, International Financial Management, Printice-Hall, 1984.

Waston, J.F., and B.W. Sorge, Guide to International Financial Management McGrew-Hill, 1977.

33

FOREIGN INVESTMENT

INTRODUCTION

Flows of finance, information, skills, technology, goods and services between countries are increasing rapidly. In a world of intensifying competition and accelerating technological change, this complementary and catalytic role of these flows can be very valuable. Globalisation - which links countries closer than ever before with each other - reinforces this need. Since globalisation has its dangers, countries need to prepare their own capabilities to harness its potential, including through foreign investment. Foreign investment on its own cannot counteract the marginalisation of developing countries. This chapter examines the role of foreign capital movement, channels of capital flows, cross-country experience on capital flows and, in particular, the role of capital controls in stabilising the growth process.

ROLE OF FOREIGN INVESTMENT

Foreign capital in the growth process generally yields conflicting results. Conventionally, the standard analysis of growth accounting in an open economy encounters an apparent contradiction between "export-led growth" on the one hand, and "capital-flow induced growth" on the other, even though in reality both strategies could be operationalised simultaneously to strengthen the growth process. The apparent contradiction arises from the macro-economic identity which suggests that while a surplus in the external goods and services account—reflecting the result of an export-led growth strategy—could increase GDP, that would tantamount to no role for net external financing as the country must neessarily save more than it can invest, leading to net capital outfolws. The underlying assumption behind this assessment is that an export-led growth strategy can stimulate growth only by generating a surplus in the external goods and services account. The actual external resource transfer process and the stages over which the importance of each form of transfer changes can explain how a developing country could simultaneously benefit from both export-led and capital-flow-induced growth strategies. This two-gap approach justifies the role of foreign capital for relaxing the two major constraints to growth. In the neo-classical framework, however, capital neither explains differences in the levels and rates of growth across countries nor can large capital flows make any significant difference to the growth rate that a country could achieve. In the subsequent resurrection of the two-gap approach, the emphasis was generally laid on the preconditions that could make foreign capital more productive in developing countries. The important preconditions comprised presence of surplus labour and excess productive demand for foreign exchange. With the growing influence of the new growth theories in the second half of the 1980s that recognised the effects of positive externalities associated with capital accumulation on growth, the role of foreign capital in the growth process assumed renewed importance. In the endogenous growth framework, the sources of growth attributed to capital flows comprise the spillovers associated with foreign capital in the form of technology, skills, and introduction of new products as well as the positive externalities in terms of higher efficiency of domestic financial markets, improved resource allocation and efficient financial intermediation by domestic financial institutions. Since the spillovers and externalities associated with different forms of foreign capital could vary, a pecking order approach to the composition of capital flows is often pursued which helps in prioritising the capital flows based on the growth enhancing role of each form of capital.

The dominant view on what drives cross-border capital flows is that marginal productivity of capital is higher in a country where capital is scarce. If marginal productivity of capital widely differed across countries, then in the presence of capital flows shortfalls in domestic saving should not constrain investment. The seminal finding that domestic saving and investment rates are highly correlated, however, indicated that the degree of capital mobility across countries may not be high. The marginal productivity of capital in India was 58 times that of the United States as obtained through the standard estimation of Cobb-Douglas production functions. India, however, could never attract enough foreign capital to take advantage of the productivity differentials. Unlike the wide differences in estimated productivity of capital, however, real interest rates - a measure of real return received by the investors - turned out to be much less divergent across countries in reality. Capital markets could be imperfect, preventing capital flows from being driven by productivity differentials. Incremental investment would be more productive in countries with skilled workforce and well developed physical infrastructure. Thus, the presence of internal growth supportive factors appear important, not only for attracting higher private foreign capital but also for enhancing the growth inducing effects of such foreign capital. The importance of internal growth supportive factors is amply demonstrated by the extremely lopsided pattern of private capital flows to the emerging markets. About 12 emerging markets account for more than 80 per cent of the total private flows to all emerging markets.

The role of relative prices and profitability of investment has been offered as an alternative explanation to the Feldstein and Horioka puzzle. The presence of factors such as technology and human capital can induce growth and attract capital flows to strengthen a virtuous cycle and show deviations from the Feldstein and Horioka findings. Corrected for relative prices (*i.e.*, at domestic price of capital instead of at international price), the dispersion of the marginal product of capital across countries could be small. Disincentives to capital formation in the form of high prices of capital goods could also lower growth. Cross-country experience shows that high-income countries are generally more open to capital flows and more open economies benefit from capital flows if the internal sources of growth are strong and their past growth record is satisfactory.

CHANNELS OF FINANCIAL FLOWS

Capital flows have followed a boom-bust patterns, notwithstanding the large regional and compositional variations. The main channels through which capital flows take place are discussed below:

FOREIGN DIRECT INVESTMENT (FDI)

Capital flows in the form of FDI flows have been widely believed to be an important source of growth in recent year. FDI is the process whereby residents of one country (the source country) acquire ownership of assets for the purpose of controlling the production, distribution and other activities of a firm in another country (the host country). The International Monetary Fund's *Balance of Payments Manual* defines FDI as "an investment that is made to acquire a lasting interest in an enterprise operating in an economy other than that of the investor, the investor's purpose being to have an effective voice in the management of the enterprise". The United Nation's 1999 *World Investment Report* (UNCTAD, 1999) defines FDI as "an investment involving a long-term relationship and reflecting a lasting interest and control of a resident entity in one economy (foreign direct investor or parent' enterprise) in an enterprise resident in an economy other than that of the foreign direct investor (FDI enterprise, affiliate enterprise or foreign affiliate)". The term "long-term" is used in the last definition in order to distinguish FDI from portfolio investment, FDI does not have the portfolio investment characteristic of being short term in nature, involving a high turnover of securities.*

* The common feature of these definitions lies in words like "control" and "controlling interest", which represent the most important feature that distinguishes FDI from portfolio investment, since a portfolio investor does not seek control or lasting interest. There is no agreement, however, on what constitutes a controlling interest, but most commonly a minimum of 10% shareholding is regarded as allowing the foreign firm to exert significant influence, either potentially or actually exercised, over the key policies of the underlying project. Many firms are unwilling to carry out foreign investment unless they have 100% equity ownership and control. Others refuse to make such investments unless they have at least majority control (that is, a 51% stake). In recent years, however, there has been a tendency for indulging in FDI cooperative arrangements where several firms participate and no single party holds majority control (for example, joint ventures).

Classification of FDI

FDI can be classified from the perspective of the investing firm and from the perspective of the host country (the recipient of FDI). *From the perspective of the investor,* it is possible to distinguish among *horizontal FDI, vertical FDI* and *conglomerate FDI.* Horizontal FDI is undertaken for the purpose of horizontal expansion to produce the same or similar kinds of goods abroad (in the host country) as in the home country. Hence product differentiation is the critical element of market structure for horizontal FDI. More generally, horizontal FDI is undertaken to exploit more fully certain monopolistic or oligopolistic advantages such as patents or differentiated products, particularly if expansion at home were to violate anti-trust laws. Vertical FDI, on the other hand, is undertaken for the purpose of exploiting raw materials (backward vertical FDI) or to be nearer to consumers through the acquisition of distribution outlets (forward vertical FDI).

From the perspective of the host country, FDI can be classified into (i) *import-substituting* FDI, (ii) *export-increasing FDI and* (iii) *government-initiated FDI.* Import-substituting FDI involves the production of goods previously imported by the host country, necessarily implying that imports by the host country and exports by the investing firm will decline. This type of FDI is likely to be determined by the size of the host country's market, transportation costs and trade barriers. Export-increasing FDI, on the other hand, is motivated by the desire to seek new sources of input, such as raw materials and intermediate goods. This kind of FDI is export-increasing in the sense that the host country will increase its exports of raw materials and intermediate products to other countries, where the investing firm and its subsidiaries are located. Government-initiated FDI may be triggered, for example, when a government offers incentives to foreign investors in an attempt to eliminate a balance of payments deficit.

FDI may also be classified into expansionary and defensive types. *Expansionary FDI* seeks to exploit firm-specific advantages in the host country. This type of FDI has the additional benefit of contributing to sales growth of the investing firm at home and abroad. On the other hand, *defensive FDI* seeks cheap labour in the host country with the objective of reducing the cost of production.

FDI may take one of *three forms: greenfield investment, cross-border mergers and acquisitions (M&As),* and *joint ventures.* Greenfield investment occurs when the investing firm establishes new production, distribution or other facilities in the host country. Typically, host countries prefer greenfield investment because of the job-creating potential and value-added output. FDI may occur via an acquisition of, or a merger with, an established firm in the host country (the vast majority of M&As are indeed acquisitions rather than mergers). This mode of FDI has two advantages over greenfield investment: (i) it is cheaper, particularly if the acquired project is a loss-making operation that can be bought at a low price; and (ii) it allows the investor to get quick access to the market. Firms may be motivated to engage in cross-border acquisitions to bolster their competitive positions in the world market by acquiring special assets from other firms or by using their own assets on a larger scale. A large number of M&As fail in the sense that the firms engaging in this activity do not produce better results in terms of share prices and profitability than those firms that do not indulge in this activity.

FDI can also take the form of joint ventures either with a host country firm or with a government institution, as well as with another company that is foreign to the host country. One side normally provides the technical expertise and its ability to raise finance while the other side provides valuable input through its local knowledge of the bureaucracy as well as local laws and regulations.

Determinants of Foreign Direct Investment

A number of theories have been put forward to explain FDI. Series of hypotheses on which various theoretical models built to explain FDI have been critically examined below:

FDI depends on the rate of return on the underlying project

The differential rates of return hypothesis represents one of the first attempts to explain FDI flows. This hypothesis postulates that capital flows from countries with low rates of return to countries with high rates of return move in a process that eventually leads to the equality of *ex ante* real rates of return. The hypothesis obviously assumes risk neutrality, making the rate of return the only variable upon which the investment decision depends. Risk neutrality in this sense implies that the investor considers domestic and foreign direct investments to be perfect substitutes, or in general that direct investment in any country, including the home country, is a perfect substitute for direct investment in any other country.

One problem with the differential rates of return hypothesis is that it is not consistent with the observation that countries simultaneously experience inflows and outflows of FDI. This is because a rate of return differential implies capital flows in one direction only, from the low-rate country to the high-rate country, and not vice versa. There is, obviously, something missing in this hypothesis. Furthermore, the validity of the differential rates of return hypothesis can be questioned on theoretical grounds. First of all, multinational firms may indulge in FDI for reasons other than profit, particularly in the short run and medium run. For example, the objective may be to maximise sales revenue in accordance with the market penetration objective. Or the objective may not be purely financial, but rather logistical and operational, such as the desire to circumvent trade barriers. In general, multinational firms are faced with a multiplicity of objectives for their international operations, and these objectives are likely to change with the passage of time. More importantly, however, risk aversion implies that the FDI decision does not only depend on return but also on risk. Finally, the differential rates of return hypothesis does not explain why a firm indulges in FDI rather than portfolio investment.

FDI depends on return and risk

When the assumption of risk neutrality is relaxed, risk becomes another variable upon which the FDI decision is made. If this proposition is accepted, then the differential rates of return hypothesis becomes inadequate, in which case we resort to the diversification (or portfolio) hypothesis to explain FDI. The choice among various projects is therefore guided not only by the expected rate of return, but also by risk. The same idea of reducing risk via diversification that is relevant to portfolio investment is used here. Because of risk aversion, a rate of return differential will not induce capital flows in one direction until the differential disappears via arbitrage. Rather, capital mobility will be constrained by the desire to minimise or reduce risk, which is achieved via diversification.

FDI depends on market size

The volume of FDI in a host country depends on its market size. This hypothesis is particularly valid for the case of import-substituting FDI. As soon as the size of the market of a particular country has grown to a level warranting the exploitation of economies of scale, this country becomes a potential target for FDI inflows. The rationale for the hypothesis that firms increase their investment in response to their sales is based on neoclassical domestic investment theories.

One way to test the market size hypothesis is to find out whether or not the share of FDI of a given country going to a group of host countries is correlated with the individual income level of the host country. The empirical studies using this testing approach seem to support the hypothesis that higher levels of sales and the host country's income are positively related to FDI.

Size does matter, according to a survey by A.T. Kearney, the results of which were summarised in the 17 February 2000 issue of *The Economist*. This survey is based on the views of 135 executives of the world's 1000 largest companies who gave marks on a scale of 0-3 for the likelihood of investing in a particular country. The top three countries favoured for investment turned out to be the USA, China and Brazil. Mexico was ranked sixth, whereas India was ranked seventh. Needless to say, the ranking of countries from the top to the bottom of the list did not exactly match the ranking of countries in terms of size, because of the influence of other determinants of FDI. For example, Japan was twentieth, whereas the UK was fourth.

FDI can be explained in terms of firm-specific advantages

When a firm establishes a subsidiary in another country it faces several disadvantages emanating from differences in language, culture and the legal system as well as other inter-country differences. If, in spite of these disadvantages, a firm engages in

FDI, it must have some advantages arising from intangible assets such as a well-known brand name, patent-protected technology, managerial skills and other firm-specific factors. It is, therefore, firm-specific advantages that explain why a firm can compete successfully in a foreign market. This hypothesis, however, does not explain why a firm chooses to invest in country A rather than country B.

FDI is triggered by the need for internalisation

According to the internalisation hypothesis, FDI arises from efforts by firms to replace market transactions with internal transactions. For example, if there are problems associated with buying oil products on the market, a firm may decide to buy a foreign refinery. These problems arise from imperfections and failure of markets for intermediate goods, including human capital, knowledge, marketing and management expertise. The advantages of internalisation are the avoidance of time lags, bargaining and buyer uncertainty. The internalisation hypothesis explains why firms use FDI in preference to exporting and importing from foreign countries. It also explains why they may shy away from licensing. Because of the significant time lags and transaction costs associated with market purchases and sales, firms replace some of the market functions with internal processes (that is, with intra-firm transactions).

FDI exists because of the international immobility of factors of production

According to the location hypothesis, FDI exists because of the international immobility of some factors of production such as labour and natural resources. This immobility leads to location-related differences in the costs of factors of production. One form of location-related differences in the costs of factors of production is the locational advantage of low wages. Thus, the level of wages in the host country relative to wages in the home country is an important determinant of FDI. This is why countries like India attract labour-intensive production (such as footwear and textiles) from high-wage countries. It is also why multinational firms wanting to establish production facilities in North America choose Mexico in preference to Canada.

Locational advantages do not only take the form of low wages, as they are also applicable to other factors of production. For example, a firm may indulge in FDI by building a factory in a country where it is cheap to generate hydroelectric power. Similarly, a factory could be located near a copper mine in the host country if copper is an important input in the production process. This is a locational advantage because significant savings can be made on the cost of shipping copper from where it is produced to where it is used. Apart from these savings, the firm can avoid delays in the delivery of copper shipments arising from the time it takes to ship the metal and the red tape that may be involved in this operation. In general, the location hypothesis emphasises the importance of unavoidable government constraints such as trade barriers. Capital may also be the underlying factor of production, particularly if capital markets are segmented. The idea here is that FDI flows to countries where the cost of capital is low.

The eclectic theory

The eclectic theory results from the integration of the industrial organisation hypothesis, the internalisation hypothesis and the location hypothesis without being too precise about how they interrelate. The eclectic theory aims at answering the following two questions. First, if there is demand for a particular commodity in a particular country why is it not met by a local firm producing in the same country or by a foreign firm exporting from another country? Second, suppose that a firm wants to expand its operations, why does it not do so via other means, which include (i) producing in the home country and exporting to the foreign country; (ii) expanding into a new line of business within the home country; (iii) indulging in portfolio investment in the foreign country; and (iv) licensing its technology to foreign firms that can carry out the production.

Suppose that there is demand for a particular product in which a particular domestic firm has an ownership advantage. What happens depends on the internalisation and locational advantages. If there are no internalisation gains, the firm will license its ownership advantage to another firm, particularly if locational factors favour expansion abroad. If there are internalisation gains and if locational factors favour home expansion, the firm expands at home and exports. And, if there are internalisation gains and if locational factors favour foreign expansion, FDI will take place.

The role of the product life cycle

According to the product life cycle hypothesis, products go through a cycle of initiation, exponential growth, slowdown and decline. The hypothesis postulates that firms indulge in FDI at a particular stage in the life cycle of the products that they initially produce as innovations.

FDI takes place as the cost of production becomes an important consideration, which is the case when the product reaches maturity and standardisation. FDI is thus a defensive move to maintain the firm's competitive position against its domestic and foreign rivals. The product life cycle hypothesis predicts that the home country where the innovative product first appears switches over time from an exporting to an importing country.

The role of oligopolistic reaction

The oligopolistic reaction hypothesis postulates that FDI by one firm triggers a similar action by other leading firms in the industry in an attempt to maintain their market shares. An implication of the oligopolistic reaction hypothesis, which is incompatible with some stylised facts, is that the process of FDI is self-limiting, since the invasion of each other's home market leads to an increase in competition and a decline in the intensity of oligopolistic reaction. Moreover, this hypothesis also fails to identify the factors that trigger the initial investment.

The role of internal financing

Internal financing refers to the utilisation of profit generated by a subsidiary to finance the expansion of FDI by a multinational firm in the same country where the subsidiary operates. The internal financing hypothesis postulates that multinational firms commit a modest amount of their resources to their initial direct investment, whereas subsequent expansions are financed by reinvesting the profits obtained from operations in the host country. It therefore implies the existence of a positive relationship between internal cash flows and investment outlays, which is plausible because the cost of internal financing is lower. The hypothesis seems to be more appropriate for explaining FDI in developing countries for at least two reasons: (i) the presence of restrictions on the movement of funds, and (ii) the rudimentary state and inefficiency of financial markets.

The effect of exchange rates

The currency areas hypothesis postulates that firms belonging to a country with a strong currency tend to invest abroad, whereas firms belonging to a country with a weak currency do not have such a tendency. In other words, countries with strong currencies tend to be sources of FDI, whereas countries with weak currencies tend to be host countries or recipients of FDI. This hypothesis is based on capital market relationships, foreign exchange risk and the market's preference for holding assets denominated in strong currencies. It is arguable that a multinational firm in a hard currency area is able, based on reputation, to borrow at lower rates than local firms in a country that has a soft currency. In essence, the crucial assumption is that there is bias in capital markets, which arises because an income stream located in a country with a weak currency is associated with foreign exchange risk. Hence the view arises that a strong currency firm may be more efficient in hedging foreign exchange risk. In this context, market imperfections may further explain the effect of exchange rates since a weak currency is likely to be associated with FDI inflows owing to informational imperfections in the capital market and that these imperfections make the cost of external financing higher than the cost of internal financing.

Changes in exchange rates are theoretically bound to have an effect on FDI. *First* of all, depreciation of the domestic currency makes domestic assets more attractive for foreigners while foreign assets become more expensive for residents in the home country. Thus FDI inflows will increase. This explains the increase in FDI in the US as a result of the depreciation of the US dollar that started in March 1985. But this argument can be dismissed as follows. In a world with mobile capital, risk-adjusted expected returns on all international assets will be equalised. For this equality to hold, depreciation of the domestic currency will result in a rise in the prices of domestic assets. The question that arises here is that if foreigners can buy domestic assets with an appreciating currency, why can't domestic residents with access to global capital markets borrow the foreign currency and take advantage of the situation just like the foreign investors? Still, it may be argued that "the view that exchange rates are irrelevant to FDI is at odds with more than just casual empiricism.

The effect of exchange rates on FDI may be ambiguous because the latter is affected by both the level and variability of exchange rates. Moreover, the effect of the level of the exchange rate depends on the destination of the goods produced. If the investor aims at serving the local market then FDI and trade are substitutes, in which case appreciation of the currency of the host country attracts FDI inflows. Alternatively, if FDI is aimed at re-exports then FDI and trade are complements. In this case appreciation of the currency of the host country reduces FDI inflows through lower competitiveness. The effect of exchange rate variability also depends on the objective of FDI. If the investor aims at serving the local market then exchange rate variability encourages FDI. If, however, the objective is to re-export then this benefit vanishes.

Diversification with barriers to international capital flows

For international diversification to be carried out through firms, two conditions must hold: (i) there must exist barriers or costs to portfolio flows that are greater than those associated with direct investment, and (ii) investors must recognise that multinational firms provide diversification opportunities that are unavailable otherwise. It has been found that there is a systematic relationship between the extent of international involvement and excess market value. This relationship gets stronger in periods characterised by the presence of barriers to capital flows.

The role of political risk and country risk

Lack of political stability discourages inflows of FDI. Political risk arises because unexpected modifications of the legal and fiscal frameworks in the host country may change the economic outcome of a given investment in a drastic manner. For example, a decision by the host government to impose restrictions on capital repatriation to the investor's home country will adversely affect the cash flows received by the parent company.

The role of tax policies

Domestic and foreign tax policies affect the incentive to engage in FDI and the means by which it is financed. Tax policies affect the decisions taken by multinational firms via three channels. *First*, the tax treatment of income generated abroad has a direct effect on the net return on FDI. *Second*, the tax treatment of income generated at home affects the net profitability of domestic investment and the relative profitability of domestic and foreign investment. *Third,* tax policies affect the relative cost of capital of domestic and foreign investment.

While simple intuition might suggest that higher taxes should discourage both foreign and domestic investments but in reality at has been found that increased taxes boost inward FDI. The general equilibrium effects on asset returns combined with a careful consideration of foreign tax systems reveals reasons for foreign investors to increase their investments in response to high taxes in the host country.

The effect of trade barriers

FDI may be undertaken to circumvent trade barriers, such as tariffs, because FDI can be viewed as an alternative to trade. This means that open economies without many restrictions on international trade should receive less FDI flow. The surge in FDI in countries like Mexico and Spain is partly attributed to the desire of multinational firms to circumvent the trade barriers imposed by NAFTA and the EU. Sometimes, the threat of protectionism by the host government triggers FDI.

NATIONAL FDI POLICY FRAMEWORK

National policies are key for attracting FDI, increasing benefits from it and assuaging the concerns about it. Those policies have to be seen in the broader context of the determinants of FDI, among which economic factors predominate (table-1). Policies are decisive in preventing FDI from entering a country. But once an enabling FDI regulatory framework is in place, the economic factors become dominant. Even then, the regulatory regime can make a location more or less attractive for foreign investors and for maximizing the positive development effects of FDI, while minimizing negative ones.

Countries seek FDI to promote their growth and development. With its package of tangible and intangible assets, FDI can contribute directly and indirectly to building national capabilities. The growing appreciation of the benefits of FDI reflects several factors. Concessional aid is declining, and various financial crises have created a preference for long-term and more stable capital inflows. Access to innovative technologies is more important. And some of the earlier fears about FDI may have been exaggerated, given the economic benefits that many developing countries have drawn from FDI. Many governments are now more confident in dealing with MNCs. And MNCs have learned to be more responsive to the concerns and priorities of host countries.

The best way of attracting and drawing benefits from FDI is not always passive liberalization (an "open door" policy). Liberalization can help get more FDI, but alone it is not enough. Attracting FDI in a highly competitive market for investment now requires stronger locational advantages and more focused efforts at promotion. Getting FDI in technologically advanced or export-oriented activities is even more demanding.

TABLE I

Host country determinants of FDI

Host country determinants

I. Policy framework for FDI

- economic, political and social stability
- rules regarding entry and operations
- standards of treatment of foreign affiliates
- policies on functioning and structure of markets (especially competition and M&A policies)
- international trade and investment agreements
- privatization policy
- trade policy (tariffs and non-tariff barriers) and coherence of FDI and trade policies
- tax policy

II. Economic determinants

III. Business facilitation

- investment promotion (including image-building and investment-generating activities and investment-facilitation services)
- investment incentives
- hassle costs (related to corruption, administrative efficiency, etc.)
- social amenities (bilingual schools, quality of life, etc.)
- after-investment services

Type of FDI classified by motives of TNCs	Principal economic determinants in host countries
A. Market-seeking	• market size and per capita income • market growth • access to regional and global markets • country-specific consumer preferences • structure of markets
B. Resource/ asset-seeking	• raw materials • low-cost unskilled labour • skilled labour • technological, innovatory and other created assets (e.g. brand names), including as embodied in individuals, firms and clusters • physical infrastructure (ports, roads, power, telecommunication)
C. Efficiency-seeking	• cost of resources and assets listed under B, adjusted for productivity for labour resources • other input costs, e.g. transport and communication costs to/from and within host economy and costs of other intermediate products • membership of a regional integration agreement conducive to the establishment of regional corporate networks

Having attracted foreign investors into a country, policies are crucial to ensure that FDI brings more benefits. Policies can induce faster upgrading of technologies and skills, raise local procurement, secure more reinvestment of profits, protect the environment and consumers and so on. They can also help counter the potential dangers of FDI—say, by containing anticompetitive practices and preventing foreign affiliates from crowding out viable local firms or acting in ways that upset local sensitivities.

Free markets do not always ensure efficient and equitable outcomes, particularly in developing countries with weak markets and institutions. Hence, the need for policy intervention. The groundwork for making markets work well—sound legal systems, clear and enforceable rules of the game, responsive market institutions, a vibrant domestic enterprise sector and the like—has to be laid down by the host country government. But even then, the strategic objectives of MNCs may not match the development goals of host governments. Policies need to bring them more in line with those goals.

The list of market failures and policy responses is long. The basic point here is that, in the real world of imperfect markets, governments have a major role. They can influence FDI in many ways with varying degrees of intervention, control and direction.

Developed countries have moved towards "market-friendly" policies—pursuing sound macro management, having stable and non-discriminatory rules on business entry and exit, promoting competition, building human capital, supporting innovation and so on. But even the most market-friendly countries have not given up promotional measures to attract foreign investors. Several use sophisticated promotion techniques as well as large grants and subsidies to target particularly valuable investments.

Developing countries are also trying to attract FDI and increase the benefits from it. And they, too, are moving towards market-friendly policies. But they have to be careful doing so, since their market structures are weaker and their development needs more pressing. That is why they are more concerned about preserving their national policy space for investment, to be able to use the policy instruments that can address their special needs.

The discussion here focuses on three objectives—attracting FDI, benefiting more from it and addressing concerns about MNCs. Some objectives and measures overlap, but they are considered separately for convenience.

Attracting Investment

Countries can attract FDI in many ways. They can simply liberalize the conditions for the admission and establishment of foreign investors without doing much more. They can promote FDI inflows in general, without trying to attract particular kinds of investment—say, according to their technology content. Or they can promote FDI more selectively, focusing on activities, technologies or investors. Measures are often used together—by leaving most activities open to foreign investors, creating a better investment climate generally and putting special effort into bringing in particularly desirable investment.

The economic attractiveness of a country for FDI depends primarily on its advantages as a location for investors of various types. Market-seeking investors look for large and growing markets. Resource-seeking ones look for ample natural resources. And efficiency-seeking ones look for a competitive and efficient base for export production.

More general factors affect all prospective host economies: political stability, a sound macroeconomic framework, welcoming attitudes to foreign investment, adequate skills, low business transaction costs, good infrastructure and the like (Table 1).

Given these factors it is still useful to use promotional policies to attract investors, particularly as competition for FDI mounts and investors become choosier. The information for basing investment decisions is not perfect, and subjective perceptions matter. Good marketing can make a difference (of course, only if other conditions are in place). And it is possible for host countries to create conditions that make investments more viable (rather than simply marketing what they already have). This may simply involve removing constraints to foreign affiliate operations. But it may also involve creating new skills, infrastructure or support institutions.

How much promotion is needed depends on the kind of FDI and the basic attractions of a host economy. A large and dynamic economy needs to promote itself less than a small and less dynamic one. The bulk of the massive inflows into China are not the result of active FDI promotion. And promotion can only go so far. If the economic base is weak or unstable, no amount of persuasion will attract large and sustained FDI inflows.

The main ways countries have sought to attract FDI and the key sensitive issues that arise in international investment agreements (IIAs) are:

(i) *Reducing obstacles to FDI* by removing restrictions on admission and establishment, as well as on the operations of foreign affiliates. The key issues here are how investment is to be defined for liberalizing entry or offering protection (direct and portfolio capital flows may be treated differently) and what kind of control should be exercised over FDI admission and establishment.

(ii) *Improving standards of treatment of foreign investors* by granting them non-discriminatory treatment vis-a-vis domestic or other foreign investors. The key issue here is what degree of national treatment should be granted to foreign affiliates once they are established in a host country.

(iii) *Protecting foreign investors* through provisions on compensation in the event of nationalization or expropriation, on dispute settlement and on guarantees on the transfer of funds. A key issue here is how far the right to expropriate or nationalize extends (especially to what extent certain regulatory actions of governments constitute takings of foreign property). Another is the acceptability of the kind of dispute settlement mechanisms available to foreign investors and countries. Third is what restrictions, if any, are acceptable on the ability of governments to introduce capital controls to protect the national economy.

(iv) *Promoting FDI inflows* through measures that enhance a country's image, provide information on investment opportunities, offer location incentives, facilitate FDI by institutional and administrative improvements and render post-investment services. Host countries do most of this, but home countries may also play a role. The key issues here relate to the use of financial, fiscal or other incentives (including regulatory concessions) and the actions that home countries can take to encourage FDI flows to developing countries.

The general trend is to reduce obstacles, create investor-friendly settings and promote FDI. But the nature and balance of policies applied by countries varies. Why? Because locational advantages differ. Because the cost of some measures is much higher than others. And because governments differ in their perceptions of how best to attract FDI.

Benefiting more from FDI

Attracting FDI may not be enough to ensure that a host country derives its full economic benefits. Free markets may not lead foreign investors to transfer enough new technology or to transfer it effectively and at the depth desired by a host country. But policies can induce investors to act in ways that enhance the development impact—by building local capabilities, using local suppliers and upgrading local skills, technological capabilities and infrastructure. The main policies and measures used for this include:

(i) *Increasing the contribution of foreign affiliates to a host country through mandatory measures.* The objective is to prescribe what foreign affiliates should do to raise exports, train local workers or transfer technology. The key issue here relates to the use of performance requirements.

(ii) *Increasing the contribution of foreign affiliates to a host country by encouraging them to act in a desired way.* The key issue here, as in attracting FDI, is using incentives to influence the behaviour of foreign affiliates. (Incentives may be tied to performance requirements). Particularly important here is enticing foreign affiliates to transfer technology to domestic firms and to create local R&D capacity.

Countries are learning that foreign affiliate activity can be influenced to enhance host country benefits only if they strengthen their capabilities. New technologies can be diffused in a host economy only if the skill base is adequate or if domestic suppliers and competitors can meet MNC needs and learn from them. Export activity can grow only if the quality of infrastructure so permits. Governments need to mount policies to build domestic capabilities, drawing on foreign affiliates and their parent firms in this effort. And again home countries can help in various ways through measures of their own. Indeed, even MNCs can try to increase the benefits to host economies.

FOREIGN PORTFOLIO INVESTMENT (FPI)

Portfolio capital has emerged as the key channel for integrating capital markets worldwide. Investment in equity provides returns in two firms: dividends and capital appreciation. Foreign equity investment is preferred even if it offers lower dividend yield and rate of capital appreciation than domestic equity investment if the foreign currency appreciates by more than the sum of dividend yield differential and the capital appreciation rate differential. Notice, however, that at the time when the decision concerning the choice is made, the value of these variables are unknown, so the decision should be made on their expected or *ex ante* values.

There are five alternative investment vehicles for foreign equity investment, which will be described in turn.

Direct purchase of securities in overseas markets

The firm carrying out the purchase or sale of foreign securities must have a branch or correspondent securities firm authorised to deal on the foreign stock exchange. When a firm buys individual foreign stocks, it would be exposed to four different kinds of risk: (i) country risk, which relates to economic and political events that have adverse effects on price or the liquidity of the market; (ii) foreign exchange risk, which results from fluctuations in exchange rates; (iii) systematic risk, or market risk, which is the risk that cannot be eliminated via diversification; and (iv) unsystematic risk, which refers to the variability of the return on a single security.

The use of American Depository Receipts (ADRs)

An ADR is a receipt issued by a US bank certifying that the bank holds an equivalent number of shares issued by a foreign company. Securities brokers provide the market-making function in ADRs. The market price of an ADR (in US dollar terms) is the price of the underlying security in foreign currency terms multiplied by the exchange rate adjusted for the number of shares included in one ADR (say, ten). ADRs have two advantages over the direct purchase of equities: (i) avoidance of foreign exchange transaction costs; and (ii) ability to trade the foreign securities during regular stock market trading hours of the investor's stock market.

Single country funds

Single country funds trade the shares of companies of a single country. The majority of country funds have a closed end status. A closed end fund issues a given number of shares that are traded on the stock exchange as if the fund were an individual stock by itself. Unlike the shares of an open-end fund, shares of a closed-end country fund cannot be redeemed, and the underlying net asset value is set at the home market of the fund. The share value of a fund may very well diverge from the underlying net asset value in the fund's home market. The difference is known as the premium/ discount.

International funds

International funds trade the shares of foreign companies belonging to several countries. The risk related to international funds is called "modified systematic risk" (international diversification reduces risk below the level of risk experienced in most or all national markets).

Global funds

Unlike international funds, global funds also trade domestic shares. In the USA, international funds are defined to include no more than 24% in US securities, whereas global funds have 50% These funds are issued by large organisations. They tend to be cost-effective in that they sell and redeem shares at net asset value.

International long-term portfolio investment is investment in long-term securities (bonds and equity) denominated in various currencies. The secondary equity markets of the world (also called stock markets or share markets) serve two purposes by providing marketability and equity valuation. Investors or traders who buy shares from the issuing firm in the primary market may not want to hold them indefinitely: the secondary market allows share owners to reduce their holdings of unwanted shares and purchasers to get the shares. Firms will have a difficult time attracting buyers in the primary market without the marketability provided through the secondary market. Competitive trading in the secondary market establishes fair market prices for existing issues.

Foreign portfolio investment is different from domestic portfolio investment in many respects. Some of these differences arise because of: i) The differences in risk and perceptions of risk, including business risk, economic risk and liquidity risk. Furthermore, international investment is subject to foreign exchange risk; ii) the differences in market mechanisms, which can be an obstacle to investment. For example, some markets are illiquid, whereas others are characterised by a concentration of activity. Furthermore, some stock exchanges do not have a trading monopoly, and there are invariably differences in the settlement and how long it takes. Typically, there are some differences in transaction costs and government regulation; iii) the differences in the availability and quality of available information, including disclosure; and finally iv) the (a) differences in accounting standards, which arise from lack of agreement on the objectives of financial standards; (b) different requirements under the company laws of individual countries; (c) differences in tax laws; and (d) differences in the development of the local professional bodies. Specific differences in accounting standards pertain to consolidation practices, disclosure, foreign exchange accounting, auditing and accounting for inflation.

International portfolio management may be conducted by following one of three approaches. The first is passive indexation, whereby international fund managers concentrate on a large number of large capitalisation share issues belonging to leading market indices. The second is the tactical asset management strategy which is based on a broad economic analysis of the leading market indices. The third is the global approach, which is based on measuring risk, return and correlation in terms of the investor's base currency.

Passive management has its theoretical support in the efficient market hypothesis. If the market has priced securities according to all available information, and if the market responds to newly arriving information in a rational manner, then it may be difficult, if not impossible, to outperform the market. Active management, on the other hand, requires considerable analysis and forecasting. The forecaster must provide detailed forecasts of the (i) national economic trends and their influence on each national market in terms of risk and return; and (ii) industrial trends on a worldwide basis, together with their implications for risk and return of specific company shares on a worldwide basis.

There is also modified active management, which requires a basic amount of forecasting for risk return and correlation of the securities or the national indices. Based on this information set, an efficient frontier can be estimated and used as a basis for portfolio selection and construction.

EXTERNAL AID

At the G-8 meeting in Gleneagles, Scotland, in 2005, world leaders pledged a large increase in official development assistance to low-income countries. The objective was to help poor countries achieve the Millennium Development Goals agreed upon at the Millennium Summit of the United Nations in 2000. The promised surge in aid flows is a unique opportunity to fight poverty on a large scale; however, it raises some macroeconomic challenges that need to be addressed to ensure that aid flows have the most beneficial impact.

Aid Flews Are Volatile

Aid flows to poor countries are often large and very volatile in last decade, about 40 poor countries experienced net aid inflows {excluding debt relief) above 10 percent of GDP. This compares with net private capital flows to emerging markets, which in the past two decades have generally been less than 5 percent of GDP. Moreover, annual changes in net aid flows can be huge, easily exceeding 10 percent of GDP and even more than 20 percent of GDP for a handful of countries. Moreover, recent research shows that aid is volatile and unpredictable even in countries that follow reasonable policies. Such volatility poses particular macroeconomic challenges to policymakers in low-Income countries, which often suffer from weak public expenditure management, shortages of skilled workers, undiversified production structures, and shallow financial markets.

Challenges in Macroeconomic Managing of Aid Flows

The problem of managing large aid inflows has several dimensions. *First,* the volatility and unpredictability of aid can complicate public expenditure management. It would be highly damaging if spending on recurrent expenditures (such as in the health and education sectors) had to be adjusted upward and downward on an annual basis because of aid fluctuations. Moreover, sustained periods of large aid inflows could weaken efforts in mobilising domestic revenues, resulting in significant public financing gaps when aid is phased out. *Finally,* institutional constraints (such as weak capacity to manage and monitor public expenditure, or even corruption) may limit the capacity to quickly absorb large amounts of aid effectively.

Another key macroeconomic concern arises when large aid flows are spent on goods and services produced in the domestic economy, which can push up the price of nontraded goods relative to the price of traded goods (the real exchange rate), resulting in a loss of competitiveness in export-oriented, high-value-added sectors. This phenomenon is often called *Dutch disease.* As an example, consider the case in which aid is spent on hiring skilled workers, such as nurses, doctors, and teachers. Because skilled workers are in short supply, their wages quickly go up. As a result, wages of educated people in manufacturing industries and other sectors also increase, hurting exporters who can-not pass on their higher costs to customers.

Policies to Mitigate the Side Effects of Aid

Generally aid-recipient countries are often reluctant to let the real exchange rate appreciate as aid flowed in. In some countries, the fiscal authority simply did not spend the aid in the year it was received, while the central bank accumulated foreign exchange reserves (Ethiopia and Ghana). In other countries, the fiscal authority increased spending in line with the surge in aid, while the monetary authority tried to prevent real exchange rate appreciation by sterilizing the monetary expansion associated with the increase in public spending (Mozambique, Tanzania, and Uganda).

Gradually phasing in a spending buildup so as to limit the strain on domestic capacity and sterilizing the monetary expansion associated with aid spending both amount to temporarily saving part of the aid in the form of international reserves and can mitigate Dutch disease problems and other side effects of aid. Indeed, these policy responses eased the aggregate demand and real appreciation pressures associated with aid inflows. However, policies aimed at redistributing aid resources over time for the purpose of managing the macroeconomic consequences of large aid flows pose specific challenges. In poor countries, shallow financial markets may make it difficult to execute sterilization operations in the bond markets and result in a burden on banks, for example, through higher reserve requirements. Sterilization policies could also lead to an undesired increase in interest rates and crowding out of private investment.

As a general principle, countries receiving aid should aim at spending it over time as part of their poverty reduction strategy. However, in the short term, saving part of volatile and unpredictable aid flows in the form of international reserves can be justified from both a public finance and a macroeconomic management perspective. *First*, from a public finance perspective, if a temporary spurt of aid is all spent when it arrives (as was often the case in the past), a subsequent sharp drop in aid receipts could prompt the need for either a costly retrenchment of spending or recourse to higher domestic financing of expenditures, which could lead to loss of monetary control and inflation In contrast, saving part of temporary aid surges would help avoid excessive reliance on domestic financing and prevent an unsustainable buildup of expenditure. On the whole, effective medium-term budgeting requires that: aid-recipient countries smooth recurrent expenditures, so that all programmes undertaken are funded while providing for key lumpy expenditures. *Finally*, to prevent aid dependency, periods of sustained large flows should not diminish efforts to mobilize domestic revenues.

From a macroeconomic management perspective, saving part of temporary increases in aid flows reflects the need to smooth aggregate consumption and to balance demand against supply. Building reserve buffers to self-insure against future negative shocks is particularly important in countries that have low reserve coverage of imports and are subject to frequent exogenous shocks (such as terms-of-trade shocks and droughts). Saving part of aid to smooth spending paths may also be necessary when a country's absorptive capacity is weak and when there are risks of loss of competitiveness from Dutch disease.

In choosing aid spending and absorption paths, policymakers in recipient countries should take into account country specifics such as macroeconomic stability, current and projected improvements in absorptive capacity, the risks of Dutch disease, and debt sustain-ability. Given the challenges associated with achieving optimal aid spending paths through macroeconomic policy adjustments, donors would contribute to a more effective use of aid by committing to coordinated multi year aid disbursements tailored to country-specific circumstances. In this perspective, the 2005 Paris Declaration on Aid Effectiveness is a welcome step in improving aid predictability.

COMMERCIAL DEBT CAPITAL

Commercial debt capital includes a whole range of sources of foreign capital where the overriding consideration is commercial, *i.e.* risk adjusted rate of return. External commercial loans could include bank loans, buyer's credit, supplier's credit, securitised instruments such as Floating Rate Notes and Fixed Rate Bonds, and commercial borrowings from the private sector window of multilateral financial institutions.

INTERNATIONAL FINANCIAL FLOWS AND THE INDIAN ECONOMY: OPPORTUNITIES AND CHALLENGES

In the pre-first World War period spanning the 19th century and the early 20th century, London was the pre-eminent financial centre, and many of today's developed countries were developing then. This period saw a great expansion of private investment in developing countries, notably in the United States (US), Canada and Australia. It also stretched to Argentina, Brazil, Mexico and India. The capital flows to developing countries took two main forms: bond issues by various levels of public administration and foreign direct investment (FDI)

In the interwar period, in the 1920s the US emerged as a major lender. Consequently, New York emerged as a key center for international lending up until the Great Depression of 1929. The interwar period was also marked by extensive defaults. Latin America was affected by the abrupt halt in foreign lending. In the immediate post-Second World War period there was virtually no borrowing by developing countries in the world capital market. Private portfolio investment and bank lending resumed only in the 1960s. By the 1980s, private capital flows had picked up substantially. This is the period when the Latin American debt crisis erupted reflecting macroeconomic imbalances arising out of high budget deficits and overvalued exchange rates. Later, the East Asian Economies were faced with a currency crisis in 1997 even though they had good macroeconomic fundamentals. The infirmity emanated primarily from huge short-term external borrowings by banks and corporates

A common thread running through the debt crises is that in almost all the episodes, waves of lendings were followed by a sudden stop or reversal of capital flows resulting in distress in the borrowing countries. *What lessons did the Emerging and Developing Economies (EDEs) learn from these crises?* Though gross capi al flows to EDEs accelerated in the 2000s, but for the interruption in 2008 due to the global financial crisis, their external balance sheets showed greater resilience. This is reflected in changes in the components of international investment positions (IIPs) of major EDEs. The external liabilities of EDEs once were mainly debt. Now FDI and portfolio equity together dominate the stock of their liabilities. The advantage of FDI and portfolio equity flows over pure debt flows is that there is risk sharing between the lender and borrower in the case of the former. Moreover, FDI flows tend to be more stable than other forms of capital flows.

Gross capital inflows to EDEs rose over eight fold from US$ 200 billion in 1999 to over US$ 1,700 billion in 2007, just before the crisis in 2008. While FDI increasing steadily remained the most stable component, the acceleration was dictated by portfolio and other investment. During the crisis the gross portfolio investment inflows to these economies dropped sharply from about US$ 420 billion in 2007 to a low of about US$ 10 billion in 2008.

The long-term trend in capital flows indicates that the peaks in capital flows are often followed by sudden fall. In the 2000s, net capital flows to EDEs peaked to 4 per cent of their GDP just before the global financial crisis in 2008

The sudden reversal that the EDEs had to face during the crisis of 2008 despite their good fundamentals and improved external liabilities position brought to the fore various questions on capital controls again. Capital flows have interfered with the simultaneous management of fixed/managed exchange rate peg and inflation targets – a phenomenon known as Mundell's 'Impossible Trinity'. For EDEs with flexible exchange rates, volatility of the exchange rate and the loss of trade competitiveness prompts central banks to occasionally intervene in the foreign exchange market. This increases domestic liquidity with its inflationary consequences if left unsterilised. But sterilisation has quasi-fiscal costs.

Against this backdrop, the issue of capital controls, especially the imposition of financial transactions tax, some form of Tobin Tax, is being widely debated among policy makers in multilateral forums like the G-20, and the IMF as well as in academic circles

Significantly, the Bretton Woods institutions have relaxed their earlier position on capital controls. The IMF's own Independent Evaluation Office found that during the 1990s the Fund clearly encouraged capital account liberalisation in its bilateral policy advice to member countries. The Fund's multilateral surveillance also emphasised the benefits to developing countries of greater access to international capital flows. But following the 2008 crisis, in a policy note in February 2010 the IMF noted 'circumstances in which capital controls can be a legitimate component of the policy response to surges in capital flows'. The World Bank also recognised that 'capital controls might need to be imposed as a last resort to help mitigate a financial crisis and stabilise macroeconomic developments.' The G-20 recognised in October 2011 that 'to maintain financial stability, capital controls may be adopted or reversed as destabilising pressures abate'.

INTERNATIONAL FINANCIAL FLOWS MANAGEMENT IN INDIA

India's capital account liberalisation began in a substantive sense in 1991 following a severe balance of payments (BoP) crisis. The analytical foundations for reforms were provided by three reports: Report of the High Level Committee on Balance of Payments (Chairman: C. Rangarajan, 1991) and the two reports on Capital Account Convertibility (Chairman: S.S. Tarapore, 1997 and 2006). These reports, inter alia, suggested: (i) encouragement to private capital inflows; (ii) shift from debt creating to non-debt creating flows, (iii) a shift within the debt inflows from short-term to long-term debt, (iv) emphasised on monitoring of external commercial borrowings, and (v) gradual liberalisation of outflows

The capital account liberalisation in India was considered as a process rather than an event. The sequencing of the process was conditional on underlying domestic macroeconomic fundamentals and sustainability of the balance of payments (BoP). Considerable progress has since been made as reflected in the volume and variety of capital flows without undermining the stability of external account.

India's status with regard to capital account liberalisation could be seen in terms of its policy stance towards capital transactions by residents and non-residents on the one hand and by the underlying instruments of cross border flows on the other. Nonresidents have been provided considerable extent of convertibility whereas permission to residents to undertake capital account transactions across borders is relatively restrained. Moreover, distinction is made not only between residents and non-residents but also between different categories of residents.

Residents

If residents are classified into corporates, financial institutions and individuals, the regime is most liberal in the case of corporates followed by financial intermediaries and individuals. Corporates and financial intermediaries are permitted to raise equity resources through American Depository Receipts (ADRs)/Global Depository Receipts (GDRs) and are allowed to borrow through debt instruments from abroad. External Commercial Borrowings (ECBs) could be raised under both automatic and approval routes subject to quantity as well as price restrictions. Under automatic route, eligible borrowers in industry, infrastructure sector and NBFCs (excluding micro finance companies) can now borrow upto US$ 750 million in a year. For borrowing above this stipulation prior approval is required. There is an all-in-cost ceiling currently ranging between 350 basis points and 500 basis points over 6 month LIBOR for loans with minimum maturity of 3 years to more than 5 years. Banks can borrow upto 50 per cent of their unimpaired Tier I capital. Apart from inflows, corporates are allowed to invest abroad in overseas joint or wholly owned subsidiaries up to 400 per cent of their net worth. Banks can invest overseas up to 25 per cent out of their demand and time liabilities in India. Indian mutual funds can invest abroad within overall aggregate limit of US$ 7 billion. Individuals can remit an amount equivalent to US dollar 200,000 in a year under liberalised remittance scheme.

Non-residents

Non-resident corporates and financial intermediaries can invest in domestic companies and instruments across sectors subject to some instrument-wise and sector-wise conditions. For portfolio investment, they need to register themselves with the SEBI. Recently, Qualified Foreign Investors (QFI) including individuals and groups or associations have also been permitted to invest directly in the equity market in India after meeting the stipulated norms including Know Your Customer (KYC).

The deteriorating external financing conditions also rendered Indian firms' access to external commercial borrowings and trade credits somewhat difficult. The resilience shown by FDI inflows, however, reflects the continued confidence in the Indian economy as a long-term investment destination. There was massive decline in net capital flows from US$ 106.6 billion in 2007-08 (8.8 per cent of GDP) to US$7.2 billion (0.6 per cent of GDP) in 2008-09. The decline was mainly due to net outflows under portfolio investment including foreign institutional investments (FIIs), American depository receipts (ADRs)/global depository receipts (GDRs) (US$ 14.0 billion), banking capital including NRI deposits (US$ 3.2 billion) and short-term trade credit (US$ 1.9 billion). However, notwithstanding these adverse developments, the resilience of FDI inflows (US$ 17.5 billion in 2008-09) reflected the growing perception of India as one of the favourite long-term investment destinations.

All the components under net capital flows, except loans and banking capital, showed improvement during April-September 2009 from their levels in the corresponding period of the previous year. In banking capital, net inflows under non-resident deposits remained higher during April-September 2009 as compared to their previous year's level. Net inward FDI into India remained buoyant at US$ 21.0 billion during April-September 2009 (as against US$ 20.7 billion in April-September 2008) reflecting the continuing liberalization and better growth performance of the Indian economy. During this period, FDI was channeled mainly into manufacturing (21.4 per cent) followed by communication services (12.8 per cent) and the real estate sector (12.6 per cent). Net outward FDI of India at US$ 6.8 billion in April-September 2009 remained at almost the same level as that of the corresponding period of 2008-09. Due to the large inward FDI, the net FDI (inward minus outward) was marginally higher at US$ 14.1 billion in April-September 2009.

The net external commercial borrowings (ECBs) inflow remained lower at US$ 0.7 billion in April-September 2009 than the US $ 3.2 billion in April-September 2008. Banking capital (net) amounted to US$ 1.1 billion in April-September 2009 as compared to US$ 5.0 billion in April-September 2008. Among the components of banking capital, NRI deposits witnessed higher net inflows of US$ 2.9 billion in April-September 2009 as compared to US$ 1.1 billion in April-September 2008. Short-term trade credit recorded

Instruments

In terms of instruments, inflows to India are subject to a hierarchy of preferences with direct investment preferred over portfolio flows, rupee denominated debt preferred over foreign currency debt and medium and long-term debt preferred over short-term debt.

As regards, non-debt flows, the overall approach has been to substantially liberalise FDI flows so as to meet domestic investment requirements and raise growth potential of the economy. However, keeping in view socio-economic implications, FDI is prohibited in certain sectors, viz., lottery business, chit funds, nidhi companies, tobacco products, agriculture and plantation, and activities/sectors not open to private sector investment, e.g., atomic energy and railway transport other than mass rapid transport systems.

Apart from direct investment, non-residents can acquire equity stakes through portfolio investment as well. Portfolio investment could be made by the entities which are registered with the SEBI as Foreign Institutional Investors (FIIs). FIIs do not need prior approval as long as they are within the sectoral and individual limits. There are no restrictions on repatriation of equity investments.

With regard to debt flows, policy levers comprise both quantity and price based prudential prescriptions. There is a ceiling on the extent of FII investment in sovereign debt (US$ 15 billion) and corporate debt (US$ 45 billion) and there is also a withholding tax. ECBs flows under both the automatic and approval routes are moderated by interest rate ceilings and those under the automatic route through an additional quantity ceiling. In addition, there are end use and minimum maturity restrictions of 3 years for ECB. However, trade credit is available for short-term with quantity and price restrictions.

Foreign Currency denominated Non-Resident Indian (NRI) deposits are regulated through an interest rate ceiling linked to LIBOR/SWAP rate of the corresponding currency. However, rupee denominated NRI deposits have recently been deregulated with the condition that interest rate on those should not be more than the rate offered on domestic deposits of comparable maturities. There is no restriction on repatriation of NRI deposits.

TRENDS IN CAPITAL FLOWS TO INDIA

In the period leading up to the crisis, the capital account was dominated by debt creating flows. For example, in 1990-91, debt creating flows constituted about 97 per cent of capital inflows. In the debt creating flows, there was a large component of external assistance. However, this scenario changed substantially following the BoP crisis that triggered wide ranging reforms.

The period since 1991-92 can be seen in three phases on the basis of our economic performance based on economic growth: Phase I (1992-93 to 2002-03) when India's

Stronger recovery in India, ahead of the global recovery along with positive sentiments of global investors about India's growth prospects, encouraged a revival in capital flows during 2009-10. The turnaround was mainly driven by large inflows under the FIIs and short-term trade credits. The gross capital inflows at US$ 345.7 billion during 2009-10 were 10.2 per cent higher than the US$ 313.6 billion in 2008-09, while gross capital outflows at US$ 292.3 billion were lower by 4.8 per cent from US$ 306.9 billion in 2008-09. As a result, net capital flows at US$ 53.4 billion (3.8 per cent of GDP) were much higher during 2009-10 as compared to US$ 6.8 billion (0.5 per cent of GPD in 2008-09.

Both inward as well as outward FDI showed declining trend in 2009-10 vis-a-vis 2008-09. The inward FDI declined by 12.4 per cent to US$ 33.1 billion in 2009-10 from US$ 37.8 billion in 2008-09. Similarly outward FDI declined by 19.6 per cent from US$ 17.9 billion in 2008-09 to US$ 14.4 billion 2009-10. Consequently, the net FDI (inward FDI minus outward FDI) was marginally lower at US$ 18.8 billion in 2009-10, as compared with US$ 19.8 billion in 2008-09. The FDI was channelled mainly into manufacturing followed by constructional financial services and the real estate sector.

Portfolio investment witnessed net inflow of US$ 32.4 billion in 2009-10 as against a net outflow of US$ 14.0 billion in 2008-09. The attractive domestic market conditions facilitated net FII inflows of US$ 29.0 billion in 2009-10 (as against net outflows of US$ 15.0 billion in 2008-09). At US$ 3.3 billion, the ADRs/GDRs remained at the same level in 2009-10 as in 2008-09. Net ECBs slowed down to US$ 2.8 billion (US$ 7.9 billion in 2008-09) mainly due to increased repayments.

The net short-term trade credit to India increased significantly to US$ 7.6 billion in 2009-10 from net outflows of US$ 2.0 billion a year earlier, reflecting international confidence in domestic importers. After recording net inflows under non-resident deposits during the first three quarters, there were outflows during the last quarter of the 2009-10. Overall net non-resident deposits inflows stood lower at US$ 2.9 billion during 2009-10 as compared to US$ 2.9 billion during 2009-10 as compared to US$ 4.3 billion during 2008-09.

Net capital inflows increased significantly during 2010-11, mainly due to FII inflows, short-term trade credits and ECBs. The net surplus in the capital account in the first quarter of 2010-11 exceeded the levels of the previous two quarters, as well as the financing need in the current account. There was a compositional shift across different components of capital flows. Foreign investment, which used to be a major constituent of the capital account, showed some moderation, mainly due to the slowdown in Foreign Direct Investment (FDI) inflows. Net inflows by FIIs were also lower during the April-June, 2010-11. FIIs, which were traditionally investing in equity market, started diversifying towards debt markets. The attraction of the debt market could be attributed

Capital Flows

(US$ billon)

Component	*2011-12*				*2012-13*		
	Q1	*Q2*	*Q3*	*04*	*Q1*	*Q2*	*Q3*
	Avarage of montnly flows						
1	*2*	*3*	*4*	*5*	*6*	*7*	*8*
FDI in India	2 4.1	33.1	4 2.3	51.5	62.0	7 3.4	81.9*
FDI by India	1.0	1.0	0.6	1.0	0.7	0.5	0.9*
FIls	0.8	-0.5	0.6	4.7	-0.6	2.6	3.3
ADRs/GDRs	0.1	0.1	0.03	0.01	0.03	0.03	0.0
ECB	1.0	1.6	-0.3	0.8	0.1	0.5	1.3
NRI	0.4	0.9	1.1	1.6	2.2	0.9	0.9*

*: October— November

During the 11-year period 1992-2003, capital inflows to India resumed to an annual average of US$ 8.6 billion. There was a significant shift in favour of equity which accounted for over 54 per cent of capital inflows. Within equity, the FDI component was dominant. In the debt component, NRI deposits were dominant. During the 5-year period 2003-08, there was a sharp increase in capital inflows to an annual average of US$ 45 billion. The composition of inflows continued to be towards equity, though its share moderated slightly to 53 per cent. However, within equity there was a shift towards portfolio investment. The debt flows were dominated by trade credit and external commercial borrowings.

During the recent 4-year period of 2008-12, net capital inflows moderated to an annual average of US$ 39 billion. Initially, the adverse impact of the global financial market turmoil and liquidity problems on India's BoP was felt in terms of reversal of FIIs inflows and decline in long-term and short-term debt flows. A positive development was, however, turnaround in NRI flows and resilience of FDI inflows in the face of reversal of capital flows, reflecting the attractiveness of India as a long-term investment destination. The capital account balance moderated during April-December 2008 mainly due to higher gross capital outflows coupled with lower gross capital inflows.

to the rising interest rate environment in India and the near zero interest rate conditions in advanced countries over an extended period. Strong domestic demand along with the rising interest rate differentials also led to higher net inflows of External Commercial Borrowings (ECBs) during the quarter. Short-term trade credit to India recorded a large net inflow of US$ 5.6 billion in the first quarter of 2010-11 (as against a net outflow of US$ 1.5 billion during the corresponding quarter of 2009-10) in line with the increase in imports associated with strong domestic economic activity and improved conditions in the global financial markets. Banking capital recorded inflows of US$ 4.0 billion during the quarter, mainly due to overseas foreign currency borrowings of banks and net inflows under NRI deposits. Debt flows during the quarter at about US$12 billion accounted for almost 64 per cent of total net capital flows.

In 2010-11 both gross inflows of US$ 499.4 billion outflows of US$ 437.4 billion under the capital account were higher than gross inflows of US$ 345.8 billion and outflows of US$ 294.1 billion in the preceding year. In net terms, capital inflows increased by 20.2 per cent to US$ 62.0 billion (3.7 per cent of GDP) in 2010-11 vis-a-vis US$ 51.6 billion (3.8 per cent of GDP) in 2009-10 mainly on account of trade credit and loans (ECBs and banking capital). The Non-debt flows or foreign investment comprising FDI and portfolio investment (ADRs/GDRs and FIIs) on net basis decreased by 21.4 per cent from US$ 50.4 billion in 2009-10 to US$ 39.7 billion in 2010-11. Decline in foreign investment was offset: by the debt flows component of loans and banking capital which increased by 130.3 per cent from US$ 14.5 billion in 2009-10 to US$ 33.4 billion in 2010-11.

Inward FDI showed a declining trend while outward FDI showed an increasing trend in 2010-11 vis-a-vis 2009-10. Inward FDI declined from US$ 33.1 billion in 2009-10 to US$ 25.9 billion in 2010-11. Sector-wise, deceleration during 2010-11 was mainly on account of lower FDI inflows under manufacturing, financial services, electricity, and construction. Country-wise, investment routed through Mauritius remained the largest component of FDI inflows to India in 2010-11 followed by Singapore and the Netherlands. Outward FDI increased from US$ 15.1 billion in 2009-10 to US$ 16.5 billion in 2010-11. With lower inward FDI and rise in outward FDI, net FDI (inward minus outward) to India stood considerably lower at US$ 9.4 billion during 2010-11 (US$ 18.0 billion a year earlier).

Net portfolio investment flow witnessed marginal decline to US$ 30.3 billion during 2010-11 as against US$ 32.4 billion in 2009-10. This was due to decline in ADRs/GDRs to US$ 2.0 billion in 2010-11 from US$ 3.3 billion in 2009-10, even though FII inflows showed marginal increase to US$ 29.4 billion in 2010-11 from US$ 29.0 billion in 2009-10. Other categories of capital flows, namely debt flows of ECBs, banking capital, and short-H1 of 2010-11 as compared to USS 9.5 billion during H1 of 2009-10.

Risk aversion in the global financial markets has slackened the pace of capital flows to India. FDI inflows remained robust averaging US$ 4.9 billion per month during April-August 2011 but moderated to US$ 3.2 billion per month during September-November 2011. Pick up in FII flows has been mainly on account of investment in debt instruments. Several measures have been undertaken to improve inflows of external commercial borrowings (ECBs) and NRI deposits. While inflows on account of NR(E)RA and NRO accounts were higher during April-December 2011, the same on account of FCNR (B) accounts were negative. ECBs and FCCBs by Indian companies due for redemption in Q4 of 2011-12 are estimated to be less than US$ 4 billion. Recognising the global macro-economic and financial market conditions, the Reserve Bank raised all-in-cost ceiling on ECBs. The increase in the all-in-cost ceiling, and emphasis on bringing immediately the proceeds of the ECBs meant for rupee expenditure in India, augur well for raising overseas borrowings and financing the CAD. Also, greater flexibility has been given to banks in mobilising nonresident deposits by further deregulating interest rates on NRE and NRO accounts.

Although recent measures by the European Central Bank and other central banks may have eased financing conditions for banks in the euro area, deleveraging by some European banks has begun to affect cross-border lending to the emerging markets. Therefore, actual ECB inflows in the coming quarters would largely depend on risk perception of European banks. If risk aversion persists in the global financial markets, there might be some implications for cost of obtaining external funding.

The exacerbation in CAD during 2011-12 led to depletion of reserves notwithstanding improved capital flows. Since Q1 of 2012-13, concerns about the growth and financial health of euro area countries have further intensified. In addition, signs of weakness in the US and China have also made investors more cautious and driven up global financial market volatility. These factors, combined with weakening domestic macroeconomic conditions, led to a net FII outflow of US$ 1.7 billion in Q1 of 2012-13. Concerns about the domestic business environment appear to be weighing on FDI inflows as well. NRI deposits, however, have picked up. Since concerns about the growth outlook for AEs seem to have prompted investors to reconsider the resilience of emerging market growth as well, the outlook for capital flows to EDEs including India remains subdued. The second quarter of 2012-13 witnessed a turnaround in FII flows. While in Q1 of 2012-13, FIIs disinvested in the equity segment that were partially offset by their net investments in the debt segment, FII investments in Q2 improved distinctly in both segments. There was a surge in portfolio inflows after the reform measures were initiated in mid-September 2012, with net FII investment of over US$ 5.5 billion in a month and a half. FDI flows to India moderated to US$ 10.7 billion during April-August 2012 compared with US$ 19.6 billion during April-August 2011.

While net inflows under FDl moderated somewhat during April-November 2012, net inflows by foreign institutional investors (FII) have shown a significant uptrend. Net FII inflows during 2012-13 (up to January 18} at US$ 18.8 billion were significantly higher than during the corresponding period of the previous year (US$ 7.6 billion), thus providing temporary comfort for financing of CAD (Table 1). Besides improved global liquidity and sentiment, robust FII inflows were largely the outcome of improved perception about the domestic economy, driven by recent reforms announced by the government since September 2012. These reforms include, inter alia, liberalised FDl norms for the retail, insurance and pension sectors, a roadmap for fiscal consolidation and an increase in FII limits in the corporate and government debt markets. The FII Investment limits in government Securities and corporate bonds were raised by US$ 5 billion each, taking the total investment limit in domestic debt (including corporate debt for infrastructure) to US$ 75 billion, while the increased limit may enhance debt inflows, they do not provide a solution to CAD financing on a sustainable basis.

Much of the recent FII Investment under the G-sec limits has flown into short term T-bills, enhancing the refinancing risks to external debt. On the other hand, a range-bound currency after a bout of depreciation has made the Indian equity market attractive for FIIs. Going forward, the implementation and acceleration in domestic reforms would be critical for sustained equity flows to the economy. Though the risk aversion in global markets declined during the previous quarter, the flows could be volatile given the euro area risks.

Benefitting from higher interest rates and a weakening rupee, non-resident Indians (NRIs) nearly doubled their deposits with banks in India during April-November 2012 compared with the corresponding period of 2011-12. Net flow through external Commercial borrowings (ECBs) was higher during Q3 of 2012-13 compared to previous quarter, despite high principal repayments made by the Indian corporate sector. ECBs were mainly raised for the import of capital goods, new projects and the redemption of FCCBs.

India's outward FDI peaked from US$ 2.2 billion in 2004-05 to US$ 19.4 billion in 2008-09 before moderating somewhat to US$ 16.5 billion in 2010-11. This underscores maturing of India's capital account liberalisation process which has encouraged two-way flows. How did this rising trend and shift in composition of capital flows impact the BoP? Table 3 presents the relative share of debt and equity flows since 1990-91.

TABLE 3

Relative Share of Debt and Equity in Capital Flows

(in per cent)

	Crisis Year		*Period Average*		
	1990-91	*1991-92*	*1992-93 to 2002-03*	*2003-04 to 2007-08*	*2008-09 to 2010-11*
1. Equity	1.5	3.0	54.0	52.8	62.6
1.1 Net FDI	1.4	2.9	28.0	17.2	31.2
1.2 Portfolio Investment	0.1	0.1	26.0	35.6	31.4
2. Debt	98.5	97.0	46.0	47.2	37.4
2.1 External Assistance	30.7	68.9	8.8	2.5	6.4
2.2 External Commercial Borrowings	31.4	33.2	16.5	22.9	14.0
2.3 NRI Deposits, net	21.4	6.6	21.0	5.2	6.6
2.4 Short Term Trade Credits	15.0	-11.7	-0.3	16.6	10.4

Note: Equity Debt composition of Capital Accounts excludes other capital.

What key conclusions can we draw from a review of international financial flows and our BoP developments in India over the past two decades since the crisis of 1991?

First, global capital flows now increasingly show a two-way movement between EDEs and advanced economies. However, EDEs remain vulnerable to volatility and sudden stops in capital flows. This is because EDEs have limitation in borrowing in their own currencies in international capital markets, a phenomenon known as *'original sin'*. This is evident from the recent crisis. The epicenter of 2008 crisis was the US but capital flows to EDEs, including India, was severely affected. Now the epicenter has shifted to Europe but capital flows to EDEs continues to be impaired.

Second, considerable lessons seem to have been learnt by EDEs from their past experience debt and currency crises, particularly from the Latin American debt crisis of the 1980s and the East Asian currency crisis of 1997. This has reinforced the hierarchy of capital flows with a preference by EDEs for equity flows. This is also reflected in a discernible shift in the composition of capital flows to EDEs in favour of equity, particularly FDI.

Third, capital flows to EDEs depend on push factors emanating from low interest rate and lack of investment opportunity in advanced economies as well as by pull factors emanating from strong economic fundaments and growth prospects in the recipient country. Particularly, stable flows like FDI are guided more by pull factors.

Fourth, availability of foreign capital is not an unmixed blessing. While it alleviates domestic resource constraints, it could also destabilise the economy in two ways: one, excess capital inflows could result in asset price inflation and loss of competitiveness through over valuation of exchange rate; two, sudden outflow on risk aversion could trigger a currency crisis.

Fifth, the earlier dominant view was tilted towards unfettered capital movement. But, following the recent global financial crisis of 2008, there is explicit recognition – even by multilateral bodies such as the IMF, World Bank and the G20 – that capital controls may be desirable under certain circumstances.

Sixth, India's external sector policy had always believed in some form of management of capital account with a preference for equity inflows, though there is now international recognition of this policy. This policy of cautious opening of the capital account has served India well as reflected in the stability of its BoP since the 1991 crisis. The composition of its capital account has shifted from almost entirely debt to predominantly equity.

Seventh, notwithstanding relative stability of our BoP, some stress has developed post-2008 global financial crisis as capital inflows have moderated in the face of expanding current account deficit. This is reflected in worsening of some of the vulnerability indicators of the external sector. India's dependence on private capital inflows to finance current account deficit has increased. Moreover, India has to factor in uncertainties in the global financial markets. These developments call for vigorous domestic policy reforms with a greater emphasis on trade competitiveness and energy security so as to enhance the pull factor for FDI.

QUESTIONS

1. "New Economic Policy has encouraged the India has encouraged the India companies to explore the euro-market." Comment.
2. Discuss the importants of the NRI investments and Deposits in capital inflows.
3. Comment on the recent steps taken by the Government of India to attrack foreign portfolio investment.
4. Discuss the emerging trends and policy developments on foreign portfolio investments.
5. Critically examine the external commercial borrowings (ECBs) as an additional source of funding for corporate finance.
6. Discuss the special deposit schemes designed to attract the funds from non-residents.
7. Discuss the role of foreign capital in growth process. Why has it generally yielded conflicting results?
8. Critically examine the recent measures taken by the countries worldwide to improve their investment climate.
9. "Foreign direct investment has different implications for the host and recipient countries as compared to other capital flows." Discuss.

10. Discuss the economic rationale to attract foreign investment. What is the effect of these incentives on investment decisions?
11. "Liberalisation of national policy frameworks is one of the key driving force of globalisation." Comment.
12. Critically examine the main determinants of foreign direct investment (FDI).
13. "Foreign Direct Investment (FDI) exists because of the international immobility of the factors of production." Do you agree?
14. Discuss the role of strategic and long-term factors in the foreign capital movement.
15. Discuss the alternative vehicles for foreign equity investment.
16. Critically examine the factors which led to the spectacular growth in foreign portfolio investment since 1990s.
17. Critically examine the macroeconomic consequence of large and volatile aid flows. How should these challenges be addressed to ensure that aid flows have a beneficial impact?

REFERENCES

1. Butler, W.F., and E.C. kavesh. *How Business Economists Forecast,* part 3. Englewood Cliffs, N.J.: Prentice-Hall, 1966.
2. Cardarelli, Roberto, Selim Elekdag, and Subir Lall, 2009, "Financial Stress, Downturns, and Recoveries," IMF Working Paper 09/100 (Washington: International Mon- etary Fund).
3. Cashin, Paul, C. John McDermott, and Alasdair Scott, 2002, "Booms and Slumps in World Commodity Prices,"*Journal of Development Economics,* Vol. 69 (October 1), pp. 277–96.
4. Chen, Nai-fu, R. Roll, and S.A. Ross, "Economic Forces and the Stock Market." Working Paper Ser. B-73, University of California at Los Angeles, December 1983.
5. Claessens, Stijn, Giovanni DellfAriccia, DenizIgan, and Luc Laeven, 2010, "Lessons and Policy Implications from the Global Financial Crisis," IMF Working Paper 10/44 (Washington: International Monetary Fund).
6. Eichengreen, Barry, 2007, *Global Imbalances and the Lessons of Bretton Woods* (Cambridge, Massachusetts: MIT Press).
7. Gooding, Arthur E., "Quantification of Investors' Perceptions of Common Stocks: Risk and Return Dimensions," *Journal of Finance* 30, no. 5 (December 1975): 1301-1316.
8. Gray, William S. III. "The Anatomy of a Stock Market Forecast." *Journal of Portfolio Management* 16, no. 1 (Fall 1989).
9. Keran, Michael W. "Expectations, Money, & the Stock Market," *Review.* Federal Reserve Bank of St. Louis, Jan. 1971.
10. Moor, Roy E. "The Use of Economics in Investment Analysis," *Financial Analysts Journal.* Nov.-Dec. 1971.
11. Moore, Geoffrey H., and Julius Shiskin. *Indicators of Business Expansions and Contractions.* National Bureau of Economic Re-search, 1967.
12. Schwert, William: "Stock Market Volatility," *Financial Analysts Journal.* May-June 1990, pp. 23-34.
13. Siegel, Jeremy J. "Does It Pay Stock Investors to Forecast the Business Cycle?" *The Journal of Port-folio Management* 18, no. 1 (Fall 1991).
14. Spigelman, Joseph H. "What Basis for Superior Performance?" *Financial Analysts Journal,* May-June 1974, p. 32.

15. Tobin, James: " Liquidity Preference as Behavior towards Risk." *Review of Economic Studies*, February 1958. pp. 65-85.

16. Various Issues of Economic Survey(GOI)

17. Wagner, Jerry, Steven Shellans and Richard Paul, "Market Timing Works Where It Matters Most... in the Real World," *Journal of Portfolio Management* 18, no. 4 (Summer 1992).

18. Williams, Arthur: *Managing Your Investment Manager*, Dow Jones-Irwin, New York, 1990.

34

INTERNATIONAL MERGERS, ACQUISITIONS AND DIVESTITURES

INTRODUCTION

International mergers and acquisitions (M&As) are being sought by a growing number of companies looking to foster dynamic corporate development. These savvy businesses are reaching across international borders and trade barriers to target viable M&A prospects. M&As are the predominant forms of internalisation expansion, and growth. However, the reasons for, and the full extent of, the worldwide growth of cross-border M&As have not yet been fully explored, nor have the implications of this shift in the preference of MNCs regarding the choice of entry mode for expanding internationally been considered in a systematic fashion.

DEFINITIONS AND CLASSIFICATIONS

A firm can undertake FDI in a host country in either of two ways: greenfield investment in a new facility, or acquiring or merging with an existing local firm The local firm may be privately or state owned: privatisations involving foreign investors count as cross-border M&As, which entail a change in the control of the merged or acquired firm. In a cross-border merger, the assets and operations of two firms belonging to two different countries are combined to establish a new legal entity. In a cross-border acquisition, the control of assets and operations is transferred from a local to a foreign company, the former becoming an affiliate of the latter. Figure-1 presents the structure of cross border M&As.

To the extent that both greenfield investment and cross-border M&As place host country assets under the governance of MNCs — and, hence, contribute to the growth of an international production system — there is no reason to distinguish between them. Both involve management control of a resident entity in one country by an enterprise resident in another. To the extent, however, that the assets placed under MNC control are newly created in the case of greenfield FDI, and existing assets are transferred from one owner to another in the case of cross-border M&As, then there is

FIGURE 1

THE STRUCTURE OF CROSS-BORDER M&As

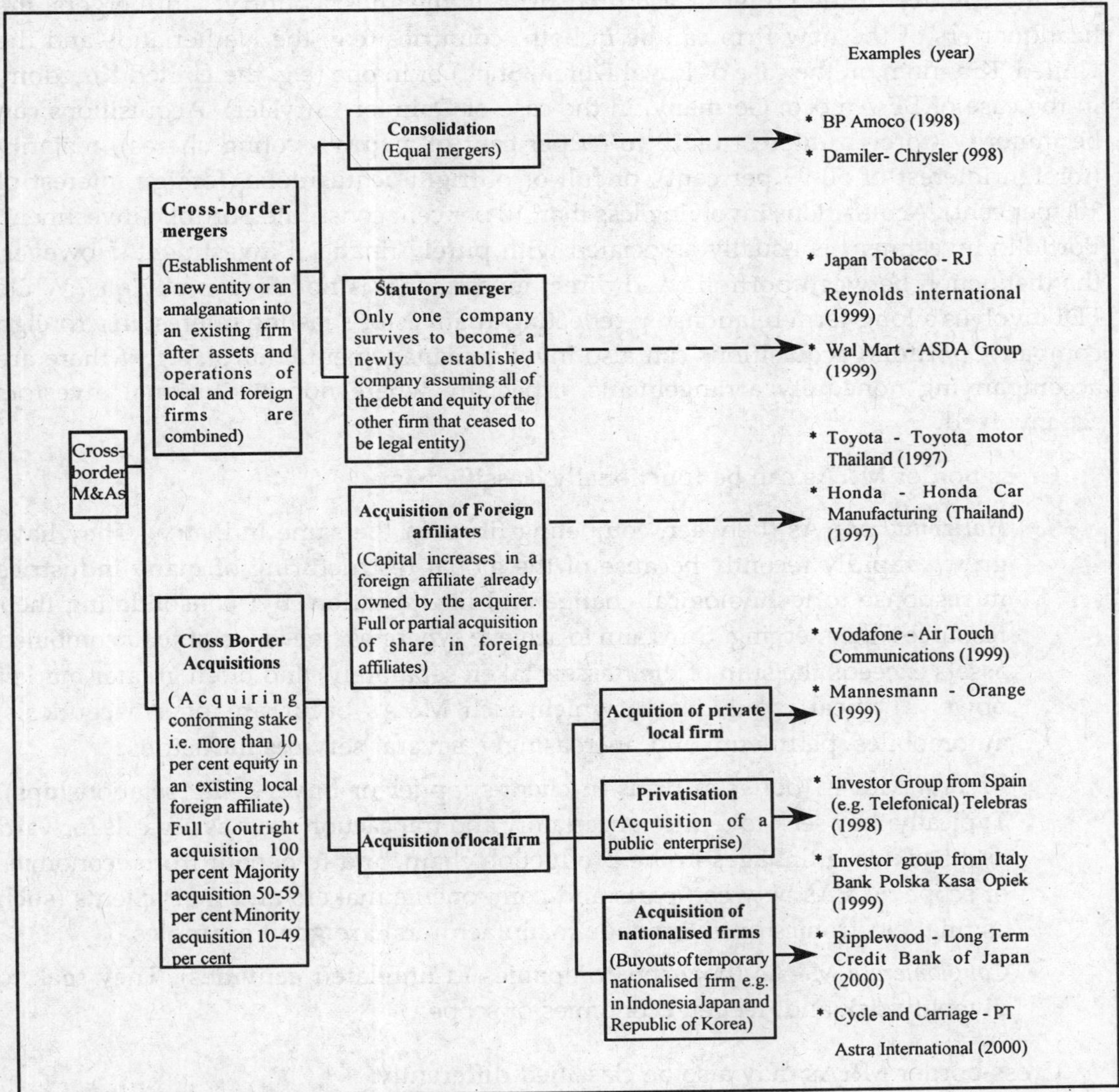

Source: UNCTAD.

a. The key diference between statutory mergers and full acquisitions lies in the fact that a new legal entity is established in the former case, but not in the latter. These two forms, however, may otherwise be treated as identical.

reason to consider them separately. The normal definitions of FDI apply to entry through M&As as well. The country of the acquirer or purchaser is the "home country" and the country of the target or acquired firm is the "host country". In mergers, the headquarters of the new firm can be in both countries (e.g. the Netherlands and the United Kingdom, in the case of Royal Dutch/Shell) or in one (e.g. the United Kingdom, in the case of BP-Amoco; Germany, in the case of Daimler-Chrysler). Acquisitions can be minority (foreign interest of 10 to 49 per cent of a firm's voting shares), majority (foreign interest of 50-99 per cent), or full or outright acquisitions (foreign interest of 100 per cent). Acquisitions involving less than 10 per cent constitute portfolio investment. Portfolio investment is usually associated with purely financial investment. However, the distinction between portfolio and direct investments is not always obvious. While FDI involves a long-term relationship reflecting an investor's lasting interest in a foreign company, portfolio acquisitions can also involve management control, e.g. if there are accompanying nonequity arrangements, especially where non-institutional investors are involved.

Cross-border M&As can be functionally classified as:

- *Horizontal* M&As (between competing firms in the same industry). They have grown rapidly recently because of the global restructuring of many industries in response to technological change and liberalisation. By consolidating their resources, the merging firms aim to achieve synergies (the value of their combined assets exceeds the sum of their assets taken separately) and often greater market power. Typical industries in which such M&As occur are pharmaceuticals, automobiles, petroleum and, increasingly, several services industries.
- *Vertical* M&As (between firms in client-supplier or buyer-seller relationships). Typically they seek to reduce uncertainty and transaction costs as regards forward and backward linkages in the production chain, and to benefit from economies of scope. M&As between parts and components makers and their clients (such as final electronics or automobile manufacturers) are good examples.
- *Conglomerate* M&As (between companies in unrelated activities). They seek to diversify risk and deepen economies of scope.

Cross-border M&As may also be classified differently:

- M&As can be driven primarily by short-term financial gains, rather than strategic or economic motivations such as the search for efficiency. Typical examples include deals where buy out firms and venture capital companies acquire other firms.
- Friendly M&As can be distinguished from those that are hostile. In friendly M&As, the board of a target firm agrees to the transaction. (This does not

exclude the possibility that, initially, the management of the target firm was against the transaction.) Hostile M&As are undertaken against the wishes of the target firms, i.e. the boards of the latter reject takeover/merger offers. Regardless of whether hostile M&As involve bidding by several prospective acquirers, the price premium tends to be higher than in friendly transactions. Over a period, the target companies have developed various defence mechanisms, including *"poison pills"*, selling off *"crown jewels"* and calling in *"white knights"* to avoid becoming a target (see Box-1).

BOX-1

Poison Pills and Other Defence Mechanisms

Companies adopt various measures to avoid takeovers. Poison pills are used by companies that fear hostile takeovers to ensure that a bid, if successful, will trigger events that will significantly reduce the value of the firm. For instance, *flip-in* poison pills allow all existing holders of target company shares to buy additional shares at a bargain price. *Flip-over* poison pills allow holders of common stock to buy (or holders of preferred stock to convert into) the acquirer's shares at a bargain price. This defence measure has been installed in many companies, in particular United States companies. Although it is not certain how much poison pills alone have contributed to the low number of hostile takeovers, they have forced raiders to negotiate with the board of target firms to agree to a fair market price for the acquired firms's shares.

Another type of defense mechanism is when a target company warns an acquirer that, in the event of a successful takeover, the entire management team will resign at once, leaving the company without experienced leadership.

Other measures include selling off "crown jewels" (dilute the intention of the acquirer by selling the assets of a target frim to a third party); and calling in "white knights" (find a more preferable firm and ask it to acquire the target firm).

WHY DO FIRMS ENGAGE IN CROSS-BORDER M&As?

Why are firms increasingly engaging in cross-border M&As when undertaking FDI? Although cross-border M&As represent one mode of FDI entry into foreign locations, the received literature on international production can only partly explain this phenomenon. Indeed, the "OLI paradigm" — the most prominent explanation of FDI — does not distinguish between different modes of entry and was formulated primarily in reference to greenfield FDI (box 2). Thus, it is useful to consider first the basis reasons for M&As in general, and for cross-border M&As in particular.

1. MOTIVATIONS FOR CONDUCTING M&As

To explain why firms may prefer to grow via M&As rather than through organic growth, two factors stand out as being particularly important: *speed* and *access* to proprietary assets.

BOX–2

The OLI Paradigm and Cross-border M&As

The OLI paradigm (Dunning, 1993). addresses *three questions* related to FDI:

Which firms undertake FDI? Firms investing abroad must possess specific proprietary or ownership ("O") advantages to overcome the extra costs of operating in a different, less familiar environment. These advantages are generally costly to create, but can be transferred to new locations at relatively low cost. The analysis of "O" advantages draws on industrial organisation, resource based, evolutionary and management theories, with advantages residing mainly in firm-specific technology, brand names, privileged access to factor or product markets or superior technological or management skills. Initial "O" advantages allow firms to grow and invest abroad, but size and international spread can, in turn, feed back and provide new advantages (accessing capital markets and information, spreading risks and so on). In some cases, firms may go overseas to supplement or enhance their existing "O" assets ("asset-seeking" FDI) seeking synergies between their own strengths and those of foreign firms or institutions.

Where do firms choose to exploit their advantages, in the home country (by exports) or abroad, and in which foreign locations? They select sites with location ("L") advantages that best match the deployment of their "0" assets. The analysis of "L" advantages draws on trade and location theory, the main factors determining comparative costs being factor and transport costs, market size and characteristics, and government policies (e.g. stability, predictability, tariffs, taxes and FDI regulations). Asset-seeking FDI is drawn to locations with strong technological, educational or information creation activities.

Why do firms choose to internalize their advantages by direct investment in preference to selling them to other firms? The analysis of internalisation ("I") draws on transaction-cost theories of the firm, and centres on the feasibility of and returns to contracting the sale of intangible advantages to other firms. The most valuable and new advantages tend to be internalized, since these are the most difficult to price and contract over time. The more mature ones are easier to price, less" subject to uncertainty and less valuable to the owner: these are licensed more readily. Internalisation can also explain vertical FDI, where a particular process or function is located abroad by MNCs to serve its production system (rather than subcontracted to independent suppliers). Transaction-cost analysis can also help explain why it is difficult or costly to contract independent firms for such arrangements, particularly in technology-intensive or strategic activities.

While the paradigm does not explicitly distinguish between different modes of FDI entry, the origins of the paradigm were more in greenfield investments than M&As. On the "ownership" side, the original thesis on which it draws explained the growth of United States companies in terms of an industrial organisation analysis of barriers to entry in setting up new facilities (Hymer, 1960). The extension made to multi-plant operations again was conceived in terms of firms setting up new plants. The "internalisation" analysis was based upon work explaining how firm boundaries were drawn in terms of the costs of hierarchical control (internalisation) versus market control (externalisation) of their assets. The implicit setting was the expansion of firms by the building of new facilities rather than the joint internalisation of assets by different firms involved in M&As. With regard to international investment in developing host countries, the analysis was entirely conducted in terms of greenfield FDI. Until recently, cross-border M&As in these countries were rare.

It is therefore useful to consider OLI factors specifically for M&As, and to distinguish mergers from acquisitions (table-1). Mergers are taken to involve firms of roughly similar size and capacity that jointly internalize their "ownership" advantages to gain economies of synergy, size and scope. Acquisitions are taken to involve larger, more powerful or better capitalized firms taking over smaller or weaker ones, and using this to gain speedy access to the latter's "ownership" and "locational" assets. The OLI factors can be considered separately for the three main types of M&As (horizontal, vertical and conglomerate), bearing in mind that horizontal transactions account for nearly two-thirds of cross-border M&A activity.

TABLE 1

The OLI Paradigm and Cross-border M&As

Type	*Horizontal*	*Vertical*	*Conglomerate*
Mergers	*O:* Both firms have O advantages complementing each other in scale, synergy, finance or market power. *L:* Standard location factors are not relevant where two MNCs merge their global production systems. *I:* Both firms seek to gain economies of scale by internalizing joint advantages. Joint internalisation differs from "internalisation" in usual OLI terms, but determinants (transaction costs in some sense) are similar. Mergers provide a much faster way of exploiting each other's advantages.	*O:* Both firms have O advantages that complement each other in different processes of the production chain. *L:* As with greenfield FDI, but also see horizontal mergers. *I:* Merging firms both seek to gain security, information, finance or market power, and to reduce transaction costs.	*O:* Both firms have O advantages in unrelated activities that may have economies of scope, but not technological complementarity. A merger is thus not based on O advantages in the usual sense; it may just involve access to finance. *L:* Mainly market size/growth or prospects of capital appreciation, not location advantages in the OLI sense. *I:* Merging firms seek a larger capital base or economies of scope, but are not internalizing their O assets to save on transaction costs.
Acquisitions	*O:* Acquiring firms tend to have greater O advantages than acquired firms, or seek specific new O advantages (technology, contacts, etc.). *L:* As with greenfield FDI, except that many L advantages are "embodied" in the acquired firm. *I:* As with greenfield FDI, acquiring firms strengthen their competitive positions by internalisation.	*O:* Acquiring firms have a stronger financial or managerial base that allows them to acquire vertically linked firms abroad. *L:* As with horizontal acquisitions. *I:* As with greenfield FDI, acquiring firms strengthen their competitive positions by internalisation.	*O:* Acquiring firms have greater financial and/or managerial resources, but no O advantages in the usual sense. *L:* Mainly market size and growth and prospects of capital appreciation, not location advantages. *I:* Acquiring firms seek diversification or economies of scope, but are not internalizing in an OLI sense.

Cross-border M&As and their characteristics call for an adaptation of the conventional analysis. The fact that M&As allow investors much faster access to, or offer new, ownership advantages accounts partly for their growing use in the current international competitive environment. The internalisation factors are also different in that there is *joint* internalisation, particularly in M&As between similar firms. In addition, the traditional OLI paradigm does not take into account non-economic, explanations, such as personal motivations of managers or corporate responses under strategic interdependence. The traditional OLI analysis of locational factors is thus not particularly relevant in explaining mega mergers between

MNCs, pooling not only their ownership-specific advantages, but also the global locational advantages of their worldwide production networks. The framework can still be applied to acquisitions by more advanced firms of less advanced ones — and so to FDI flows from developed to developing countries or economies in transition.

Speed is crucial. M&As often represent the fastest means of reaching the desired goals when expanding domestically or internationally. For example, when time to market is vital, the takeover of an existing firm in a new market with an established distribution system is far more preferable to developing a new local distribution and marketing organisation. For a latecomer to a market or a new field of technology, M&As can provide a way to catch up rapidly. Enhanced competition and shorter product life cycles accentuate the necessity for firms to respond quickly to opportunities in the economic environment, preferably before competitors move. The pressure of time and the feeling of urgency are highlighted in the observations often made in the information technology (IT) industry today that, in the new economy in which we live, a year has only 50 days, or in the business slogan that *Speed is our friend— time is our enemy*. While erstwhile planning may have taken place in five-year intervals, the watchword today is *"plaction"*— plan and act at once.

The second main motivation for firms to merge with or acquire an existing company, rather than to grow organically, is the *quest for strategic assets*, such as R&D or technical know-how, patents, brand names, the possession of local permits and licences, and supplier or distribution networks. Ready made access to proprietary assets can be important because, by definition, they are not available elsewhere in the market and they take time to develop.

Such assets may be crucial to advance a firm's *static* advantages, i.e. its income-generating resources and capabilities at a given moment in time, or to strengthen its *dynamic* advantages, i.e. its ability to sustain and increase the income-generating assets over time. To take just one example of where the need for speed — the alternative between "build" or "buy" — and the search for proprietary assets came together: the main reason for the Indian company Tata Tea to acquire Tetley Ltd. in the United Kingdom was to obtain access to a global brand name and a global distribution network; reaching the same objective through organic growth would have been more or less impossible. To quote Tata Tea's Vice-Chairman who engineered the acquisition: *For us to develop a global market in the time frame we had in mind, the acquisition of Tetley, with its brand name and distribution system, was the only option.*

These two main advantages of M&As interact with a number of other driving forces, which play out differently in different industries and markets, and which often simultaneously affect the decision to undertake M&As. Many of the driving forces listed below can also motivate FDI in general, but, when speed enters the picture, they tend to favour M&As, as the objectives sought for can be realized more quickly:

i) The ***search for new markets and market power*** is a constant concern for firms. Where domestic markets are saturated, in particular, foreign ones beckon. High transaction costs associated with arm's-length transactions involving intangible assets may explain why firms possessing ownership specific capabilities often prefer to exert direct control (instead of exporting or licensing) when exploiting them in new geographical locations or industry segments. Through M&As, firms can quickly access new market opportunities and develop critical mass without adding additional capacity to an industry. By taking over an existing company, immediate access to a local network of suppliers, clients and skills can be obtained. This motivation is of particular importance for cross-border M&As as the need for knowledge about local conditions increases when leaving the home market. Beyond this, and especially in markets characterized by oligopoly, M&As can also be motivated by the pursuit for market power and *market dominance.* Especially in the case of horizontal M&As, the motivation can well be the search for oligopolistic positions; in addition, consolidated market control may provide opportunities for anti-competitive practices and increased barriers to entry.

ii) Anticipated ***efficiency gains** through synergies* are probably the most cited justification for M&As. Synergies can be static (cost reduction or revenue enhancement at a given point in time) or dynamic (e.g. innovation-enhancing) in character. Examples of the former kind of synergies include the pooling of management resources (one head office instead of two), revenue enhancement by using each others' marketing and distribution networks, purchasing synergies (greater bargaining power), economies of scale in production leading to cost reductions, and the avoidance of duplication of production, R&D or other activities. Dynamic synergies may involve the matching of complementary resources and skills to enhance a firm's innovatory capabilities with long-term positive effects on sales, market shares and profits. The search for static synergies may be particularly important in industries characterized by increased competitive pressure, falling prices and excess capacity, such as in the automotive and defence industries. Meanwhile, dynamic synergies may be crucial in industries experiencing fast technological change and that are innovation-driven, such as in information technology and pharmaceuticals. The efficiency-through-synergy motive is present for both domestic and cross-border M&As. However, the scope for rationalisation and improving company performance by achieving an international specialisation of the value chain can be particularly high in the case of cross-border investments that allow firms to locate different activities in places with appropriate mixes of locational advantages.

iii) In a globalizing economy, ***greater size*** can be a crucial parameter, particularly in operations requiring economies of scale, large expenditures for R&D and the expansion of distribution networks for example. Size in itself can also make it more difficult to be taken over and, therefore, can have a protective' function. Large size can furthermore create financial, managerial and operational synergies that reduce the operational vulnerability of firms. Sheer size normally means lower-cost access to investible funds as there are economies of scale in capital raising. Information asymmetries between corporate insiders and investors can make internal financing more favourable. A company can use its internal capital market by letting cash rich divisions with few profitable projects finance capital expenditures in cash poor divisions with better growth opportunities. Another advantage of size is that larger firms with multiple operations across geographical locations and segments can have an advantage in the collection and adoption of new information and innovation. The size motive can apply to both domestic and cross-border M&As.

iv) A fourth driver behind M&As is the desire for risk reduction (operational risks, foreign exchange risks, etc.) through product or geographical market ***diversification***. Firms may make cross-border M&As on the basis that industry returns across countries may be less correlated than within an economy. By acquiring foreign companies, a firm may be able to circumvent tariff and non-tariff barriers and thereby lower the level of uncertainty. As intensified global competition and rapid technology development have led firms to focus on their core activities, however, the product diversification motive has become less important although geographical diversification plays a role.

v) There can be important ***financial motives*** behind M&As. Stock prices do not always reflect the true value of a firm. A potential acquirer can, for example, value a company's anticipated earnings stream higher than current shareholders do. Bad management of a firm, imperfections in the capital market and major exchange rate realignments may provide short-term capital gains to be made by acquiring an undervalued firm, or affect the timing of planned M&As. Such motivations are particularly important in the case of portfolio-type M&As and in economies with poorly developed capital markets or in financial crisis. In addition, some M&As are undertaken partly for tax considerations, e.g. to exploit unused tax shields.

The ***personal gains (or behavioural)*** explanation argues that corporate managers pursue their own self-interest, especially where corporate governance is weak (a manifestation of what economists have denoted the principal-agent problem). They may seek expansion or empire building to enhance executives' power, prestige, job-security or remuneration, even when this is not technically efficient or in the interest of shareholders. They can also be under the pressure of financial markets — especially where double-digit growth rates are considered the norm — to show high growth and profit rates; M&As can provide the easiest route in this respect, compared to organic greenfield investment growth. Individual managers may also overestimate their ability to manage acquisitions and think that they are especially well equipped to make a merger-deal work.

The factors discussed so far basically apply to both domestic and cross-border M&As. While all factors are important to consider when explaining why firms undertake cross-border M&As, it is seldom only one factor that is decisive. In fact, mergers occur for a myriad of reasons, and in any given case, several different motives may simultaneously influence the merging parties' behavior.

2. *CHANGES IN THE ECONOMIC ENVIRONMENT*

So far the principal basic motivations for undertaking cross-border M&As have been examined. But the acquisition behaviour of firms is also greatly affected by changes in the economic and regulatory environment and, when it comes to cross-border M&As, by the international economic and regulatory environment. Some of the major changes — as regards technology, the regulatory framework and capital markets — that have taken place in the past decade and that have facilitated cross-border M&As and, indeed, encouraged firms to pursue them are discussed below:

a. Technology

The rapid pace of technological change has intensified competitive pressures on the world's technology leaders. Consequently, the costs and risks of innovation have risen in most industries, as has the need to incorporate continuously new technologies and management practices. Firms thus need more efforts to maintain innovative leads, to find new areas of technological leadership, and to keep up with new knowledge and shorter product-life cycles. In an environment characterized by rapid technological change and rising expenditures for risky R&D projects, many firms feel compelled to enter into cross-border M&As as a way of sharing the costs of innovation and accessing new technological assets to enhance their innovatory capabilities. M&As allow firms to do this quickly. Such asset-seeking FDI by MNCs from developed (and increasingly from developing) countries is a rising form of FDI. It is likely to become more common as intangible, knowledge-based assets and access to a pool of skilled people and work teams become more important in the world economy.

But technological developments also have other implications. Some of the most important changes relate to the new information and communication technologies. They enable a better management of operations distributed worldwide, and provide new ways of organizing contacts within and between firms as well as with consumers. The use of electronic commerce, for example, makes it possible to restructure the supply chain and reduces the costs of reaching large consumer markets. By lowering transport, information-access and communication costs, technical progress has dramatically shrunk economic space. One result is more intense competition, as foreign competitors may be able to deliver goods and services more cheaply, technologies are diffused more rapidly and information is more broadly available. Another, however, is that MNCs can compete more effectively. They can communicate better across their international production systems, transfer goods and personnel across borders more cheaply and break up production and management processes to locate sub-processes in different countries to minimize cost. Even between different headquarters operations — finance, strategy, R&D, design, marketing — locational links are being loosened, as some MNCs place some of these operations in dispersed sites.

Technological change thus has an impact on the size of firms, reduces costs and facilitates better management of far-flung transnational operations. It allows new management systems to be applied more effectively across the globe, and makes globally integrated production systems more feasible and cost-effective. Cross-border M&As play a critical role in allowing MNCs to set up and expand these systems to develop a portfolio of locational assets. As a result, too, MNCs gain more experience in "digesting" acquired enterprises into existing corporate systems which, in turn, makes the M&A route more enticing than before.

b. Changes in the Policy and Regulatory Environment

If the crucial role of technology makes asset-seeking FDI "more important and technological changes have facilitated the operation of international production systems, changes in the policy and regulatory environment during the past decade have provided more space for these systems to expand, including through M&As. Key here are the liberalisation of FDI and trade regimes, regional economic integration, privatisation and the deregulation of various industries.

(i) Policies on FDI and Cross-border M&As

The liberalisation of FDI regimes has continued apace, typically on a unilateral basis. Most countries are now trying to attract direct investment, not just by removing restrictions, but also through active promotion and by providing high standards of treatment, legal protection and guarantees. Of the 1, 035 FDI regulatory changes between 1991 and 1999 in over 100 countries in all regions, 974 went in the direction of facilitating FDI inflows. Examples of such changes relevant to M&As include the removal of compulsory joint venture requirements, restrictions on majority ownership and authorisation requirements. The international regulatory framework has also been strengthened, especially through the conclusion of bilateral investment protection and double taxation treaties. Multilateral agreements support these trends. For instance, WTO agreements limit the use of certain investment-related measures that affect trade, like local content requirements on MNCs, and certain types of export requirements. World Bank and IMF programmes encourage countries to adopt more open, transparent and welcoming regimes towards foreign investors.

As FDI regimes typically apply to both greenfield investment and cross-border M&As, the latter have also been facilitated by FDI policy liberalisation in developed and developing countries. Generally, most laws dealing with FDI do not explicitly make a distinction between greenfield investment and M&As. When industries are removed from closed lists, both forms of FDI are typically permitted; and when restrictions on foreign ownership are removed, majority acquisitions of domestic firms are also allowed. Within this overall trend, however, a number of host countries have various policy instruments to deal with cross-border M&As, including special authorisation requirements for cross-border M&As under their FDI laws, as e.g. in Malaysia, Canada and, until recently, New Zealand and Sweden. Some countries also have instruments to screen cross-border M&As for particular purposes, e.g. national security considerations. Moreover, governments may reserve the right to approve some proposed investment projects and reject or modify others to preserve important public interests. Furthermore, when governments screen FDI projects, it may well be that more greenfield proposals have been approved than M&As; but as the relevant bodies do not normally publish their results and reasoning, no precise conclusions are possible. Finally, governments have sometimes kept "golden shares" in privatized companies in order to be able to preserve essential strategic interests; golden shares have been used to veto undesirable further changes in ownership and control of the privatized company.

(ii) Other Changes in the Regulatory Environment

Trade liberalisation gathered pace in the 1990s with the conclusion of the Uruguay Round. The cumulative effect has been a radical change in the signals and competitive setting for international investors. Firms now face more intense competition at home as well as abroad.

The formation of regional free trade areas has facilitated both greenfield investment and cross-border M&As in several ways. Regional trade agreements enlarge the size of the immediately accessible market for firms, and so attract foreign investors to serve them by setting up new facilities. They can enhance market transparency and, if they link national currencies, lower the costs of cross-border transactions. If they incorporate investment agreements, they make M&As more feasible. From a MNC perspective, the need to establish a local presence is particularly strong if an integrating area sets up high common external tariffs; but even low external barriers to trade can be a powerful magnet in rich or expansive regional markets. The formation of the European Community, for instance, provided a major stimulus to inward FDI and promoted restructuring by national, regional (intra-EU) and cross-border (non-EU) M&As. The initial impetus was greatly strengthened by the creation of a single market and, more recently, the launch of the Euro, which adds to competitive pressures and to the restructuring of previously segmented markets. Increased competition underlines the role of rapid responses by companies, thus favouring cross-border M&As in particular. Regional trade agreements in the developing world, like ASEAN in South-East Asia and MERCOSUR in Latin America, are stimulating similar restructuring, even if the markets involved are not as large and the integration processes less intense.

In parallel with trade liberalisation and regional integration processes, there has been widespread *privatisation* and *deregulation* of activities, most notably in such service industries as telecommunications, transportation, power generation and financial services. These changes have provided another stimulus to M&As in general and cross-border ones in particular. Privatisation programmes in many developing countries and economies in transition have increased the availability of domestic companies for sale. In fact, the combination of privatisation and deregulation has created a number of new MNCs. Previously state-owned utility companies, for example, facing new competitive pressures at home, have responded by becoming dynamic international investors. In Europe, activities that have long been strongly homebound, like water supply, power generation, rail transports, telecommunications, and airport construction, are now populated by transnational operators. The first wave of expansion (with foreign participation in privatisation) is being followed by further consolidation and restructuring, with M&As again set to play a vital role.

(iii) Changes in Capital Markets

Cross-border M&As have been facilitated by changes in world capital markets. The liberalisation of capital movements, new information technology providing instant information across the globe, more active market intermediaries, and new financial instruments have had a profound impact on M&A activity worldwide. Whereas the liberalisation of capital markets since the mid-1980s had already greatly facilitated the growth of cross-border M&As, most developed countries now have completely liberalized their capital accounts, with virtually unrestricted facilities for cross-border loans and credits, foreign currency deposits and portfolio investment. More recently, financial transactions have also been substantially liberalized in many developing countries.

In addition, the increased use of cross-border M&As mirrors changes in the market for corporate ownership. The number of available targets, both among publicly listed and non-listed firms, is rising. Financial advisors have been expanding their operations and are more widely presenting potential "deal opportunities" to prospective clients. The bulk of the major cross-border deals are handled by a small number of large deal makers, most of which are based in the United States. The growing demand for acquisition targets is adding to a sense of urgency. Meanwhile, corporate executives are also under increased pressure from the stock market to participate actively in the global restructuring process to seize potential opportunities. This combines with new ways of financing major transactions. The liberalisation of foreign equity ownership has facilitated M&As based on stock swaps rather than cash deals. Major M&As have also been facilitated by the rise of stock markets and ample liquidity in capital markets, which has allowed firms to raise large amounts of money through banks and bond issues. This was accentuated by the introduction of the single European currency, which has created a liquid market in European corporate bonds. Companies are increasingly issuing Euro-denominated bonds to refinance debt and to raise money for takeovers.

For example, the rise of the Euro-denominated corporate bond market and the underlying Euro-syndicated loan market greatly facilitated Olivetti's acquisition of Telecom Italia.

c. A Secular Trend

M&As are part of a process of regional and global restructuring, in which actions by national and international policy-makers trigger responses by firms and vice versa. While this process is far from complete and its incidence is highly uneven, its direction is quite clear. The major changes that have simultaneously taken place in the international business environment have profoundly affected the setting in which firms are operating and have provided new and expanded business opportunities, as well as risks.

The advent of the internet has added to this as it stimulates M&A activity between "old economy" and "new economy" firms in search of opportunities and as it may lead firms to try to find new solutions to some of the problems to which M&As have traditionally represented the solution. An example is the business-to-business exchanges, which may be akin to functional mergers.

In this new and continuously evolving environment, the key strategic issue for firms becomes how to survive and prosper, knowing that there is a market for firms and that sanctions await them if they fail to deliver growth and profits. One such sanction is to be taken over. All the basic motivations for firms to undertake cross-border M&As then combine to become key elements in the overarching strategic goal to defend and develop competitive positions. Cross-border M&As are growing so rapidly in importance precisely because they provide firms with the fastest way of acquiring tangible and intangible assets in different countries, and because they allow firms to restructure existing operations nationally or globally to exploit synergies and obtain strategic advantages. In brief, cross-border M&As allow firms rapidly to acquire a portfolio of locational assets, which has become a key source of competitive strength in a globalizing economy

The fact that a considerable part of the current expansion of M&A activity consists of major deals in industries in which a limited number of companies dominate the market, leading to a consolidation at the regional or global level, suggests that strategic interactions among the leading firms also play an important role. Indeed, under conditions of strategic interdependence and uncertainty, once the established equilibrium is disturbed by the move of a major player (say, to acquire a foreign company) it can be expected to have a strong impact on key competitors and to trigger a chain reaction of countermoves at both domestic and international levels by rivals anxious to protect their positions. By pursuing a merger or acquisition, management minimizes the largest possible regret, which occurs when *ex post* successful moves by other players have not been imitated, or when they themselves become a target for a takeover. Thus, even firms reluctant to pursue this course may be forced into it for fear of becoming an acquisition target themselves. Such pre-emptive actions can be intended to create "strategic comfort" rather than shareholder value or economic wealth. Moreover, if they do not move quickly enough, there may be fewer desirable partners left. By moving, however, they will help amplify a merger wave that has just started.

SO HOW TO SUCCEED?

The most basic principle is to be crystal clear about the logic of the deal. However wrapped up in sonorous stuff about synergy, plenty of mergers begin with sheer executive boredom. For the executives at the top, running a company can be dull. Organic growth, in a mature market, is grindingly slow. Doing deals is easier—hire ire a bunch of investment bankers and set them to work-and much more exhilarating. A chief executive spends perhaps five years in the top job: the surest way to make a mark in so short a time is to buy something big. Quite apart from the surge of adrenalin, it brings the gratifying attentions of investment bankers, and makes a splash on the financial pages. Brokers are pleased: now your share price will move—one way or another-and so they will make money. Testosterone, vanity and greed are poor ingredients for successful merging.

FIGURE-2

THE DRIVING FORCES OF CROSS-BORDER M&AS

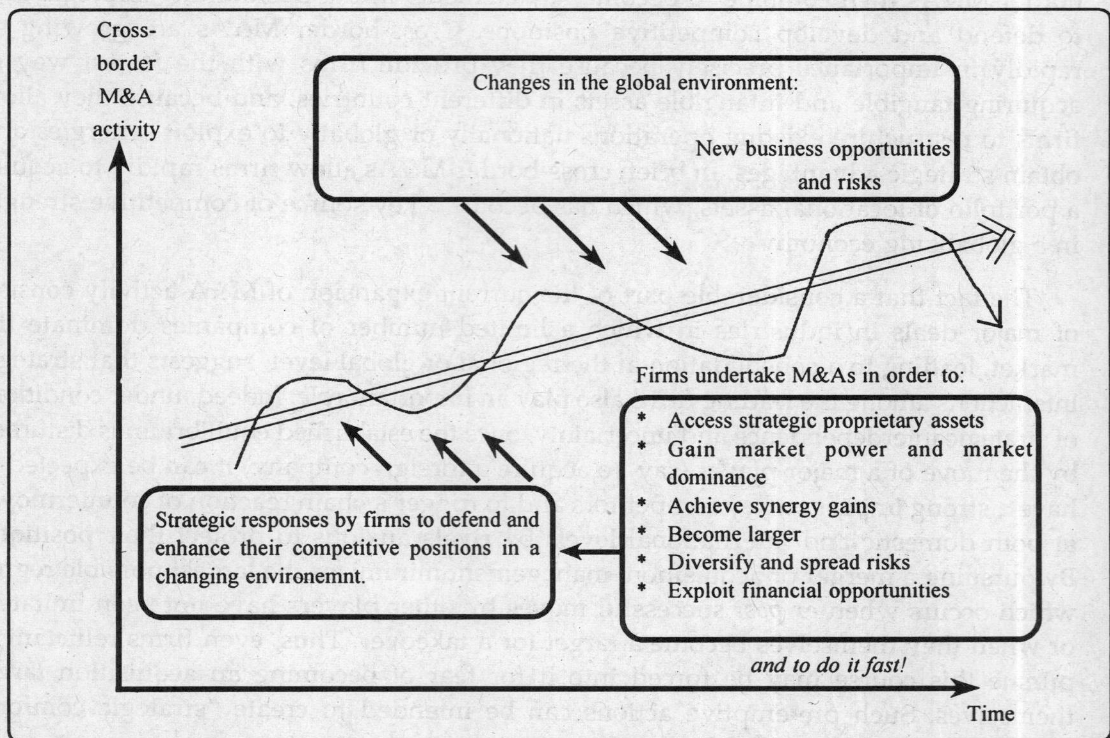

So is the fear of looking foolish, or of being left behind. All too many boards are carried away by a terror that they will be bought before they can buy. Even when the initial courtship sows doubts, too few decide, that it is better to break off the engagement and return the presents than to go through with the wedding. That decision is even harder to make when everyone else is pairing off: copycat mergers-where one big deal is hastily followed by others in the same industry-seem especially prone to problems.

Instead, look for similarities. That does not mean only a good business fit, vital though that it. Nor does it require similarity of size: mergers of equals seem to be especially tricky, perhaps because they disrupt two strong corporate cultures, and they often throw up intractable problems of leadership. More important is similarity of outlook. One of the most successful mergers in pharmaceuticals, between Sandoz and Ciba Geigy to form Novartis, was between two firms whose closeness of approach was the greater for being based in the same Swiss town (and doubtless run by executives who had done national service together).

Even more crucial, concentrate on the marriage, not the wedding. Doing a deal involves delicate compromises. A whole consulting industry thrives by advising companies on post- merger integration, a salvage operation to recover something from the wreckage of impossible promises and ill-considered goals. Companies that agree on a clear strategy and management structure before they tie the knot stand a better chance of living happily ever after.

And once a merger is agreed, put a managerial heavy-weight in charge, full-time, of making it work. This is more essential than ever when a merger is the product of weakness rather than strength, as so many of today's art. Such deals will succeed mainly by cutting capacity, which may mean product lines or branches, but almost always means jobs. To push through these cuts quickly, explaining them to bewildered and resentful employees, is often the hardest part of making a merger succeed, when the investment bankers have taken their cheques and moved on, that is the job the managers are left with.

RECENT TRENDS AND CHARACTERISTICS OF CROSS-BORDER M&AS

Firms may enter host economies through greenfield investments or M&As. The choice of mode is influenced by industry-specific factors. For example, greenfield investment is more likely to be used as a mode of entry in industries in which technological skills and production technology are key. The choice may also be influenced by institutional, cultural and transaction cost factors, in particular, the attitude towards takeovers, conditions in capital markets, liberalization policies, privatization, regional integration, currency risks and the role played by intermediaries (e.g. investment bankers) actively seeking acquisition opportunities and taking initiatives in making deals.

The value of private equity-sponsored cross-border M&As increased by 14 per cent to $122 billion in 2010, compared to $107 billion in 2009 after two years of consecutive decline (Table 1). At the same time, the corresponding number of cross-border M&As reached a record high, with 2,050 deals completed.

The factors behind the increase in FDI by private equity funds are largely related to the stabilization of macroeconomic conditions. Also, investors were looking for yields, in a declining interest rate environment. Positive trends were supported by stronger private equity activity in emerging markets. Thus 31 per cent of FDI by private equity firms, amounting to $38 billion, was directed to developing and transition economies in 2010, up from 26 per cent in 2009. This rise reflects the increasing interest of private equity firms in developing country firms and venture capital business, which provide better business opportunities than before.

TABLE 1

Cross-border M&As by Private Equity Firms, 1996–May 2011
(Number of deals and value)

	Number of deals		*Value*	
Year	*Number*	*Share in total (%)*	*$ billion*	*Share in total (%)*
1996	932	16	42	16
1997	925	14	54	15
1998	1 089	14	79	11
1999	1 285	14	89	10
2000	1 340	13	92	7
2001	1 248	15	88	12
2002	1 248	19	85	18
2003	1 488	22	109	27
2004	1 622	22	157	28
2005	1 736	20	207	22
2006	1 698	18	271	24
2007	1 917	18	457	27
2008	1 785	18	322	25
2009	1 993	25	107	19
2010	2 050	22	122	17
2011	591	17	91	20

Source: UNCTAD, cross-border M&A database (www.unctad. org/fdistatistics).

Note: Value is on a gross basis, which is different from other M&A tables based on a net value. The table includes M&As by hedge funds. Private equity firms and hedge funds refer to acquirers as "investors not elsewhere classified". This classification is based on the Thomson Finance database on M&As.

Despite stronger private equity-sponsored cross-border M&As in 2010, their value is still more than 70 per cent lower than the peak level in 2007. The volume share of private equity in total cross-border M&As fell from 19 per cent in 2009 to 17 per cent in 2010. The relative contribution of private equity funds to total FDI contracted by nearly 40 per cent from 2004, its peak year, to 2010.

A more benign global economic environment should see fundraising and investment picking up in 2011, also bolstering a more positive outlook for private equity-sponsored FDI. Private equity investors were estimated to have held nearly a trillion dollars of uninvested capital at the beginning of 2010, including reserves for future use, that could result in a surge in volume of cross-border M&As in 2011.

On the supply side, there are now more opportunities. There are two factors. First, companies owned by private equity firms are becoming targets for other private equity firms. The relative performance of these secondary buyouts (i.e. buyouts of private equity invested firms) is only slightly lower than that of primary buyouts: this is because the former can be executed faster than the latter in issuing IPOs (initial public offerings), and because secondary buyouts entail a lower risk profile. Second, private equity firms are now seeking smaller firms, and are engaged in smaller-scale buyouts. This is an area to which private equity firms have not paid much attention in the past, yet one where many attractive firms are to be found.

M&As IN INDIA

Indian companies—owing to health performance, strong management capabilities and access to competitive financing—have seen a spurt in the cross-border merge and acquisition (M&A) activity. As they go beyond borders to acquire foreign assets to serve global markets, the total value of M&A deals in India has grown at a compounded annual growth rate of around 28 per cent during 2002-06. Most of this growth has come over the last 2 years, with the value of M&A deals increasing from US$7.5bn in 2004 to US $2.14bn in 2006. The number of cross-border deals from India in 2006 grew much faster than domestic deals. Last years the M&A deals in India stood at 480 with a total value of about $20.3bn. Of these, more than half, or 266, were cross-border deals (value $15.3bn). Of the 480 M&A deals, only 40 head a deal value of over US $100 mn. The domestic, inbound and outbounds deals increased in the range from 26%-42%. The share of domestic, inbound and outbound deals were more or less stable, with domestic deals having a share of 44% inbound deals 16% and outbound deals 40%.

From 1995 to August 2006, the largest proportion of outbound acquisition has been in North America, accounting for 32% of total outbound deals. This was followed by Europe that accounted for 29% of total deals. Europe is now emerging as the prime destination for Indian companies making acquisitions abroad.

Tata Steel's acquisition of the Anglo Dutch steel maker Corus at a price of US $12.1bn has already set the trend. Hindalco's announcement of acquisition of Novelis for $ 6 bn has further fuelled this trend. Vodafone's deal of US $11.1bn for Hutchison's stake in telecom operator Hutchison-Essar spells the trend for inbound investment. However, outbound deals from India have had a sectoral trend with Pharma companies being particularly aggressive in scouting for opportunities abroad, going to the top of M&A league with total deal of a little over $2.2bn. The other sector that has take the leads is the IT Sector. In the energy sector, ONGC's acquisition of equity stakes in a couple of oil blocks in Columbia and Brazil as also Suzlon Energy's acquisition of Hansen led the M&As deals. Overall M&As were on the rise in 2007 . Both the inbound and outbound M&As increased dramatically and the deals crossed $100 billion. But the constant growth in M&As activities witnessed a fall by a third in 2008 due to bearish capital markets and credit lockup .The average valuation of Indian deals declined by 9%,while the BSE increased by 4.6%. The share of Indian National deals in the total number slightly increased by 2%. The increase in national deals was relatively modest in the context of global downturn. The share of Indian cross-border deals also declined ,but was still high with 66%. With respect to industry number, it was noted that most deals had taken place in the consumers, industrials, materials and high technology sectors. By value most important sectors have been energy& power, healthcare, industrials and materials. With respect to the number of transactions, almost all sectors have experienced a decline with the notable exceptions of real estate, healthcare, energy & power, high technology, and consumer products, services and staples have increased. Cross-border deals dominated the list of top deals in 2008. Only one out of the 15 deals a share buyback, taking advantage of lower valuations.

M&As activities, which were in vogue in the pre-economic crisis meltdown period, hit rock-bottom after the collapse of Lehman Brothers in September 2008. During January-March 2009, the inbound M&As deals,which had the maximum share in total M&As deal during October-December 2008, contracted by a whopping 85.28%. The outbound M&As deals shrunk 48.62 % as the number of deals declined from 28 in October-December 2008 to 16 in January-March, 2009. The aggregate M&As deals size plunged more than 70%in the first quarter of 2009. The number of deals also declined from 58 to 45 during the period. The total number of deals announced during the first half of 2009 stands at 123, with total value of $4.93 billion.Though recovery talk is doing the rounds but companies are still apprehensive about using their reserves to acquire other businesses and assets. Second half of 2009-10 is expected to kickstart inbound M&As activities in view of the strong financial position of domestic companies and robust demand in sectors like telecom, pharma and capital goods.

DIVESTURE ANALYSIS

Even after MNC's accept/reject decisions are made, they should be reassessed at various times. Some foreign projects that have been rejected may become acceptable as a result of a reduction in the MNC's cost of capital, increased host government incentives, improved economic conditions in the host country, or more favourable projections of exchange rates. Foreign projects that have been implemented must be assessed to determine whether they should be continued or divested.

Indian government unveiled a road map for the *big bang* disinvestments programme in major Central Public Sector Undertakings (CPSUs) for 2009-10, indicating that nearly 60 CPSUs, including SAIL, BSNL, COAL INDIA,for selling government stake. The government also announced that NTPC and Rural Electrification will make their follow-on public offer (FPO) within the fiscal along the Satluj Vidyut Nigam,which is expected to come out with an initial offer (IPO) to offload 10% stake.

M&As AND GREENFIELD INVESTMENT: A COMPARISON

The corporate motivations for M&A deals vary and so do the effects of cross-border M&As for countries. The private and public costs and benefits of cross-border M&As can also diverge significantly. Viewed from a host country's standpoint, cross-border M&As are one form of FDI inflows, along with greenfield investments. These two types of inward FDI are often compared in their desirability for host countries. It is argued that, other things being equal, greenfield FDI is more desirable than M&A FDI, since the former immediately and directly adds to the existing industrial capacity in host countries, whereas the latter merely transfers ownership of local assets from domestic to foreign interests. This may be true as far as the immediate impact is concerned, and greenfield FDI is normally preferred by host countries for this reason. In addition to this short-term capital stock effect, however, there are a host of possible long-term effects that also need to be taken into account in evaluating the relative merits of these two kinds of FDI.

Capital Formation

Greenfield FDI is, by definition, investment in new productive facilities. Hence, assuming that no viable domestic investment will take place in the absence of such FDI, it immediately adds to the stock of capital in the host country. Furthermore, it is necessarily accompanied by the transfer of foreign MNCs' intangible assets such as technology and managerial skills, which are internalised/ embodied in their greenfield projects, assets that enable foreign MNCs to stay competitive relative to host country firms in the latter's own backyard. Greenfield projects are thus likely to result in new capital formation, both physical and human.

In contrast, M&As may not lead to capital formation in the short run. The immediate effect is merely an asset transfer from a host country owner to a foreign MNC. But the acquirer may carry out modernisation and capacity expansion (perhaps as a condition of the deal, as is usually the case with privatised state properties in developing countries and Central and Eastern Europe) or induce other related investments (perhaps other related FDI undertaken by suppliers). New incremental or supplementary capital formation may then eventually occur in the form of both sequential and associated FDI which is larger than the original purchase. Furthermore, if the acquired firm would otherwise have gone bankrupt, thereby decreasing the capital stock involved, the M&A may have been instrumental in maintaining or revitalising a host country's capital formation There is, of course, the danger that the acquisition may have been undertaken for the sole purpose of eliminating competition by eventually closing down the acquired firm.

Employment and the Tax Base

Just as with capital accumulation, greenfield FDI immediately creates new jobs (assuming again the absence of credible domestic investment). M&As would have no such positive employment effect in the short run. In fact, job reduction may ensue if an acquisition involves a troubled high- cost firm that needs to be restructured and slimmed down. In the long run, however, if a MNC turns an acquired firm into a successful unit as part of its corporate network, employment may rise.

In general, the tax base is likely to expand more favourably under greenfield FDI than through M&As for the very reason that new business units are created by the former as additional taxable entities. For this reason, in their eagerness to create employment opportunities and expand the tax base, host governments are generally more interested in attracting greenfield FDI than in seeing existing local firms sold off to foreign MNCs It is thus no surprise that special incentives are often given to greenfield FDI.

Nonetheless, it is conceivable that an acquired firm will end up contributing as much or more to the local tax base, depending on whether it might have gone bankrupt in the absence of the acquisition or on the effectiveness with which it handles new infusions of capital and technology under foreign ownership.

Structural Diversification

From a host country's point of view, FDI is desirable in part because it may bring new assets (e.g. industrial knowledge) in new fields, thereby contributing to industrial diversification in the local economy. Since M&As mostly involve transfers of existing productive assets, they are not likely to help a host economy diversify into new industrial activities, unless the acquired firm itself later diversifies. If the acquired units become integrated with the foreign MNCs' corporate systems, however, they may have an opportunity to move into new fields. Besides, there is no guarantee that greenfield FDI necessarily opens up new industrial sectors, although the chances of structural diversification are probably greater in greenfield FDI than in M&As.

Competition

Market competition is desirable because it stimulates and improves efficiency, resulting in lower prices for consumers. Greenfield FDI can enhance local competition if its superior assets/market power are harnessed in such a way as to prevent predatory practices and to attract competitors. In contrast, while M&As will not generate new competition in the short run, they can maintain the level of competition that prevailed before, if the acquired firms might have gone out of business in the absence of a deal. In addition, if a new owner revitalises a moribund local firm, local competition will be revitalised as well. On the other hand, if the acquiring firm were pan of a small number of firms at the global level, the takeover might reduce global competition as well as competition in the host country.

Political and Cultural Considerations

Since M&As involve the transfer of ownership of a local productive activity and assets, a national security issue arises when local assets (e.g. technology) have military applications and can thus damage national security if they fall into foreign hands. Greenfield FDI does not directly pose this problem but some greenfield ventures may be aimed at monitoring local technological progress. Similar considerations apply with respect to national sentiment and culture. For example, some countries may consider the broadcasting or film-making industry a cultural industry critical to the preservation of national traditions. It all depends upon the nature of the industry involved, the market power of the new entrant, and the characteristics of the host countries themselves.

Liquidity

FDI is often welcomed because it brings liquidity, whether in the form of foreign exchange at the national level or in the form of needed funds at the company level. Liquidity is usually a priority for any country that experiences a balance-of-payments crisis and is in dire need of foreign exchange. In terms of national liquidity considerations, greenfield FDI and M&As are equally desirable alternatives.

In developed countries with flexible exchange rates, however, this 'foreign reserves" rationale hardly exists. Only a company-level need for liquidity may arise. For example, founders may want to sell because they wish to retire or some young start-up ventures may reach a point where they need additional capital. Here, obviously, greenfield FDI is not an alternative to M&As from the point of view of the individual enterprise.

In some developing countries, on the other hand, the sales of local businesses to foreign firms can become important, precisely because both the governments and the local firms are desperately in need of liquidity. Partial M&A deals may also occur to secure a minimum level of liquidity.

Supplementary Resources

Both M&As and greenfield FDI can bring in some critical supplementary resources such as new managerial, production and marketing techniques that are lacking in host countries. The new owners of local firms may apply new techniques to make their acquired businesses profitable. M&As are also often motivated by the desire to capture synergies by combining sets of corporate assets between the deal-making parties; the intra-corporate supplementing of local assets with foreign assets is a possibility unique to cross-border M&As. The Daimler-Chrysler merger and the VW-Rolls Royce merger are examples. Synergy-creating M&As certainly add to both the host and home countries' stock of resources and may bring both public and private benefits.

Similarly, greenfield FDI is likely to transplant supplementary resources at the national level, since the ownership-specific advantages they internalise are supposed to be superior to their local counterparts if such FDI is to succeed. Hence, the upshot is an augmentation of the host country's resource base. A prime example of such greenfield FDI is NUMMI (New United Motor Manufacturing Incorporated), a joint venture between GM and Toyota, in the United States, which has served as a learning conduit for GM in flexible manufacturing.

In contrast, an M&A may not involve any transfer of new resources from the acquiring foreign firm. It may even cause a reverse transfer, particularly if the new owner's intention is to siphon off knowledge from the acquired firm to the new owners, as is the case with some asset-seeking FDI. In such a case, an M&A results in the draining of resources (e.g. technology) from host countries.

So which is better from a host country's point of view? "It all depends" is the appropriate answer. Depending upon specific circumstances and the policy priorities of host countries, one or the other may be preferable. At the individual firm level, M&As can enable local firms directly to become parts of transnational corporate systems with a number of competitiveness-enhancing advantages. This source of gain is important, especially when dealing with distressed, non-performing local businesses. They require immediate and direct transfusions of new capital and supplementary resources at the firm level In fact, when it comes to distressed local business units, whether privately or publicly owned, the requirement is simply a buyer, whether foreign or domestic. These units need to be sold off, if not entirely then at least partially, for they have to be acquired by or merged into other firms if they are to avoid their ever-accumulating losses or debts and eventual demise. They need transfusions of both new capital and new managerial resources to survive and prosper. In many cases, these existing businesses cannot be purchased and upgraded by domestic firms, simply because they may themselves be short of capital and deficient in technological resources. In these cases, foreign firms may be the only possible suitors.

QUESTIONS

1. What are the important considerations in evaluating the long-run impact of a merger or the combined firm on earnings per share? Why may a long-run view change a merger decision?
2. Often in merger-especially in conglomerate merger-tax considerations are a key motive for a

business combination. Why and in what situations may the acquisition of a firm with a tax-loss carryforward be quite acceptable?

3. Can a merger with a large, stable company serves as an effective way to raise capital for a growth oriented smaller company?
4. Is the public interest served by an increase in merger activity? Give arguments both pro and con.
5. Are the negotiations for merger agreements more difficult if the firms are in different industries or in the same industry? If they are about the same size or quite different in size? If the ages of the firms are about the same or if they are very different? Why?

REFERENCES

Chudnovsky, Daniel, B.; *The Globalisation of Multinational Enterprise Activity and Economic Development*, Macmillan; London, 1999.

Dunning, John H.: *The Globalisation of Business*, Routledge: Harrow, 1993.

Lall, Sanjaya: *Learning from the Asian Tigers: Studies in Technology and Industrial Policy*, Macmillan, London, 1996,

Jameson, F., and Miyoshi, M. (Ed.): *the Cultures of Globalisation*, Duke University, Press, 1998.

Porter, M.: *The Competitive Advantage of Nations*, Free Press : New York, 1990.

Rodrik Dani: "Has Globalisation Gone Too far?" *Institute of International Economics*, Washington, D.C.,1997.

Yeates, A.J.: "Just how big is a global production sharing?" Working Paper No. 53 (Geneva: ILO), 1998.

35

COUNTRY RISK ANALYSIS

INTRODUCTION

Country risk is exposure to a loss in cross-border lending, caused by events in a particular country. These events must be, at least to some extent, under the control of the government of that country; they are definitely not under the control of a private enterprise or individual. The risk of foreign lending is quite different from the risk of foreign direct investment, and so is the approach to the assessment of the risk. As most large banks and other institutions are exposed to both types of risk there is a case for making a clear distinction between the two by reserving the term "country risk" for the risk of foreign lending. Thus, a loan in U.S. dollars to a Bahamian borrower by the Nassau branch of a foreign bank is exposed to country risk, whereas the branch itself (the building, furniture, equipmen, cash in hand, goodwill, ability to conduct business) is exposed to the risk of foreign direct investment.

WHAT IS AT RISK?

All cross-border lending in a country-whether to the government, a bank, a private enterprise or an individual-is exposed to country risk. Country risk is thus a broader concept than sovereign risk, which is the risk of lending to the government of a sovereign nation. Further, only events that are, at least to some extent, under the control of the government, can lead to the materialization of country risk. A default caused by bankruptcy is country risk if the bankruptcy is the result of the mismanagement of the economy by the government, it is commercial risk if it is the result of the mismanagement of the firm. An interesting case is that of natural calamities. If they are unforeseeable, they cannot be considered as country risks. But if past experience shows that they have a tendency to recur periodically-such as typhoons in Southeast Asia-then the government can minimize their effects. Prudent analysts also make allowance for them in their assessment of country risk. "Control by the government" is understand in the broad sense. If the government can to some extent control at least the impact of an adverse development, even though it cannot control the event itself, the possibility of that event is country risk.

COUNTRY RISK: POLITICAL, SOCIAL AND ECONOMIC RISKS

The most frequent events that can lead to the materialization of country risk can be classified as:

Political Components

War, occupation by foreign power, riots, disorders caused by territorial claims, ideological differences, conflict of economic interests, regionalism, political polarization, etc. are the many of the critical factors of country risk analysis of political nature. Table-1 includes both domestic and international factors. The list is certainly not exhaustive. Depending on the particular type of project for which the country risk analysis is being performed, the analyst should consider more specific subcategories in some of these areas and some other important categories.

TABLE-1

Political Factors Affecting Country Risk

I. DOMESTIC

A. The Political System

1. Its Basic Strength
2. Its resiliency—capacity for change without disruptive conflict

B. The Group in Power

1. Philosophy
2. Policies
3. Government officials
   a. Ability and number of qualified officials
   b. Willingness and capability for making tough decisions
4. Strength ,capability of implementing plans

C. Opposition Groups

1. Strength
   a. Likelihood of system dirupting conflictarisng from within the country
2. Philosophy of strong opposition groups

D. The Government System

1. Efficiency
2. Red tape
3. Flexibility
4. Responsiveness

II. INTERNATIONAL

A. Likelihood of system disrupting conflict arising from outside the country

1. Due to country's own problems
2. Due to treaty or other obligations

B. Relations with major trading partners

C. Relations of the company's home country with other countries

Socio-Cultural Components

When a company operates in a foreign country ,it must consider the possible effects of many socio-cultural variables such as civil war, riots, disorders caused by tribal strife, unequal income distribution, union militancy, religious divisions, antagonism between social classes, etc. Table-2 covers most of the major types of the socio- cultural variables, but many more can be important, especially for specific types of investments.

TABLE-2

Socio -Cultural Factors Affecting Country Risk

I. DOMESTIC

A. Social Groups

1. Homogeneity of population
   a. Ethnic
   b. Religious
   c. Linguistic
   d. Class
2. Extent of cohesiveness or divisiveness

B. General psychology of population work ethic

C. Unemployment

D. Political activism of population

E. Extent of social unrest

1. Strikes
2. Riots
3. Insurgency

II. INTERNATIONAL

A. Cross-border ties

a. Ethnic
b. Religious
c. Linguistic
c. Historical

B. Cross-border antagonism

a. Ethnic
b. Religious
c. Linguistic
c. Historical

Economic Components

Economic factors e.g. a long-term slowdown in GNP growth, strikes, rapid rise in production costs, fall in export earnings, sudden increase in food or energy imports, etc. can obviously be of great importance in determining the degree of country risk confronting a foreign company. Table-3 outlines many of the most important of these variables.

TABLE-3

Economic Factors Affecting Country Risk

I. DOMESTIC
A. Economic growth, investment trends
B. Cyclicality of economy, economic diversification
C. Inflation
a. Monetary policy
b. Fiscal policy, budget deficits
D. Strength of local financial markets ,portion of total investment financed locally

II. INTERNATIONAL
A. Balance of payments
B. International trade
1. Importance of trade in GNP
2. Stability of trade earnings
    a. Diversity of exports
    b. Elasticity of export demand
    c. Elasticity of import demand
        i. capital equipment
        ii. necessities
            —Degree of self- reliance in food
            —Reliance on imported energy
        iii. luxuries
3. International trade ties, proximity to major markets
4. Extent of trade controls

C. International capital
1. Currency
    a. Strength
    b. Stability
    c. Quality of exchange markets
    d. Depth of exchange markets
    e. Extent of controls over exchange markets
2. Debt
    a. Total
    b. Short -term as share of total
    c. Debt service ratio
    d. Debt-service schedule
3. International Financial Resources
    a. International reserves
    b. International borrowing capacity
        i. History of debt repayment
        ii. Credit rating
    c. Autonomous capital inflows
4. Share of total investment financed from abroad

Among economic events, recession is an interesting case. If it is worldwide, and the government applies the appropriate counter cyclical policies, it is not country risk. But if it is caused in a country by inept government policies, or if it is aggravated by such policies, it is country risk.

In this sense one can speak about political, social and economic risks. But these refer to the nature of the event that may cause a loss and they apply to all borrowers in a country; lending to a private corporation, for instance, is certainly subject to political risk. But political risk is a narrower concept than country risk, since country risk also includes social and economic risks.

The risk of direct investment abroad is usually called political risk because it is mostly caused by political events. It may also be called environmental risk or even country risk. Is this the same kind of risk as the risk of lending abroad-which is this book is called country risk? What are the differences and similarities?

In principle the difference is hardly significant. Changing only a few words in the definition of country risk, one can define the risk of direct investment abroad as exposure to a loss of a real asset or business abroad as well as to a loss by a business abroad, caused by events that are, at least to some extent, under the control of the government of the host country but definitely not under the control of the owners of the asset or managers of the business.

In practice, however, there are at least six considerable differences regarding what is at risk, the time period of the exposure to the risk, the kind of events that can lead to its materialization, the probabilities of materialization, the options to avoid or minimise the risk, and the need to evaluate it.

In the case of both lending and direct investment abroad, an asset and the income produced by that asset are at risk. However, in the case of a loan, the asset is money and which directly produces income in the form of interest. In the case of direct investment - apart from the goodwill - the asset is real (plant and equipment), and the income is generated through the production and sale of goods and/or services. It is thus the plant and equipment, and the ability to use them for the production and sale of goods and/or services which are at risk (See Table - 4).

TIME HORIZON

Loans are made from one day to a maximum of 10-12 years, and country risk evaluation encompasses these periods. It is extremely rare to contemplate a direct investment for less than five years. This is thus the minimum time horizon for risk assessment. The maximum is around 30 years, for example for oil exploration, plantations, or mining.

PROBABILITY OF LOSSES

There are significant differences in the kind of situations that can lead to the materialization of risks and in the probability of losses. When it lends to the private sectoı without government guarantee, the lender's concern are similar to those of the direct investor. The major exceptions are expropriation and indigenization which are only of minor concern to a lender. For unguaranteed private debt, the probability of capital losses and losses of earnings is also similar to that of the direct investor.

TABLE - 4

Risk of Lending and Risk of Direct Investment Abroad

	Lending	Direct investment
What is at risk?	Money Ability of debtor to service the debt	Real assets and money Ability of plant to produce and/or sell product
Maximum time horizon	12 Years	30 Years
What can go wrong?	Destruction of debtor's assets interruption of production	Destruction of subsidiary's assets interruption of production
	(Caused by war, revolution, occupation by foreign power, natural calamities, disorders, strikes)	
	Major concern in case of unguaranteed private debt where it can result in partial or complete write-off claim. Rarely leads to the write-off of public sector debt. With regard to disorders and strikes, only if they are countrywide do they affect the public sector's debt servicing ability.	Major concern. May result in partial or complete write-off of assets, severe losses of income, and bankruptcy.
	Expropriation, indigenization of debtor's assets	Expropriation, indigenization of subsidiary
	Minor concern only in case of unguaranteed private debt. New owner normally honours obligations of previous owner.	Major concern. May result in substantial capital losses as well as loss of expected earnings.
	Impossibility of transferring funds	Impossibility of repatriating capital and/or remitting earnings
(Because of imposition of exchange controls by government)		
	Major concern only in case	Major Concern. of unguaranteed private debt.
	Fall of earnings, bankruptcy of debtor	Fall of earnings, bankruptcy of subsidiary
(Caused by mismanagement of the economy, credit squeeze, long-term slowdown in GNP growth, strikes, rapid rise in production costs, etc.)		
	Major concern but only in case of unguaranteed private debt	Major concern only if the plant produces mainly for the market of the host country

cont...

Deterioration of the balance of payments of debtor/host country Overextension in external borrowing by debtor/host country (These can be caused by a great number of political, social & economic factors)		
	Major concern in case of public debt. Concern in case of unguaranteed private debt only in as exchange controls-see above.	Concern only in as much as it can lead to exchange controls-see above. much as it can lead to
Probability of losses	Could be significant-for both capital losses and losses of expected earnings - in case of unguaranteed private debt. In case of public debt, probability of capital loss is negligible. That of expected earnings could be higher but it is usually less than in case of unguaranteed private debt.	Could be significant for both capital losses and losses of expected earnings.
Reaction to identified risk		
Before loan is granted, investment effected	Grant the loan or not grant it.	Go ahead with the project as planned; cancel the project; redesign the project to minimize the impact of perceived risk.
After the loan has been granted, investment effected	Virtually no possibility of minimizing the risk of outstanding loans.	Adoption of suitable strategies to minimize risk.
Need for risk evaluation	There is an international financial market and a market consensus on country risk. The lender can perform close to the market average, without country risk evaluation, just by following the market. Risk evaluation is needed only if the lender (a bank) wants to perform above the market average.	There is no international market for direct investment and no market consensus on political/environmental risk. The direct investor has to do its own risk evaluation.

Country risk of loans to the public sector differs considerably from the risk of foreign direct investment, with respect to the situations that can lead to its materialization and the probability of capital and income losses. Taking into account the share of unguaranteed private loans in total commercial bank lending abroad, one can conclude that less than 50 percent of bank lending faces country risk similar to the risk faced by foreign direct investment.

REACTION TO RISK

Once a particular risk has been identified there are considerable differences in the options of a lender and direct investor. Assuming that for the individual bank the spread (fee for financial intermediation and compensation for risk taking) is given, the bank has only two options: to take the risk and go ahead with the loan, hoping for the best, or not to lend. Between these two extremes the potential direct investor has the additional option of redesigning the project to minimize in advance the impact of the risk. For instance, if there is the risk that the government of the host country will introduce legislation to prevent temporary redundancies, the project can be redesigned to sub-contract part of the work.

The difference in this respect is even more important if the risk is identified after the loan has been granted or the direct investment effected. The bank can do virtually nothing to minimize the risk of outstanding loans; it can only hope for the best. (It can, of course, refrain from making new loans, but this is a different matter.) Again, the direct investor can adopt suitable strategies to minimize the risk.

NEED FOR RISK EVALUATION

The need or compulsion to evaluate country risk (political risk, environmental risk) is not quite the same in the cases of lending and direct investment. Country risk assessment is a complex, tedious and costly exercise. A respectable body of opinion holds that the benefits do not justify the costs. The argument runs on the following lines:

The spread is a fee for financial intermediation and leaves a small profit margin which should cover non-interest costs plus a reward for risk taking. The fee itself does not change from one loan or one country to another. If the risk is perceived to be nil or negligible, the spread is say 3/8 percent. If the spread is more than 3/8 percent, the excess is the reward for risk taking. This reward varies, according to the market's perception of the risk, from one country to another and, within the same country, from one borrower to another.

The international financial market is near-perfect, so the argument goes, in the sense that no individual borrower or individual bank can influence the spread. Given the efficiency and speed with which information is gathered and transmitted, knowledge is near-perfect on the market. It follows that the collective unbiased risk evaluation of the marketplace, based on the best available information and reflected in the spread, cannot be surpassed in accuracy by any individual bank. Assessment of country risk is thus an exercise in futility: "The market knows best."

Events of the last decade have demonstrated that, just as the stock market, the international financial market can in the short term be disastrously wrong in its collective evaluation of country risk. Like stock market analysts in their evaluation of a company's long term prospects, individual banks can be ahead of the market in their evaluation of country risk if they have insight based on information and its interpretation as well as analytical ability superior to the market average. The purpose of country risk evaluation is to improve the individual bank's performance relative to the market average. If the bank can in the short term assess country risk more accurately than the market and can anticipate changes in the risk situation ahead of the market, it can move into countries where the risk is better than the market's perception, or where the bank perceives an improvement before its competitors, it can fund at the most favourable rates, and have smaller losses and wider average spreads than its competitors.

An individual bank can be right where the market is wrong because:

i) The market is probably less perfect than it has been thought previously. If so, spreads may not reflect an unbiased market consensus of country risk.

ii) The individual bank can have a superior insight regarding particular countries' conditions.

iii) Even without such insight, the bank can use superior techniques and develop a superior analytical ability.

At least six qualifications are required for proper assessment of country risk:

i) Conceptual awareness of factors that have a bearing on country risk.

ii) Analytical ability to assess how these factors interact in affecting debt servicing ability. (It is not enough to be aware that high and/or accelerating inflation is likely to affect debt servicing ability adversely, it is also important to know how this may happen.)

iii) In-depth knowledge of the country under scrutiny: its political and economic structure, the institutional and regulatory framework, recent political and economic developments, economic policies, strength and determination of the government to implement policies, etc.

iv) Specialized expertise to predict political variables.

v) Familiarity with economic forecasting techniques to make short and long-term projections of relevant variables: real GDP growth, inflation, balance of payments, external debt, debt service payments.

vi) Experience and skills to draw conclusions regarding debt servicing ability from observed and predicted variables, and combine these into a risk rating.

The acquisition of these qualifications requires considerable learning, training and experience. Few individuals are likely to combine all the qualifications, so country risk evaluation should be the result of cooperation, drawing on all the available expertise within, and accessible to, the bank, and should under no circumstances be left to amateurs.

EXTERNAL DEBT

Debt servicing ability can be fairly accurately forecast in short term. Uncertainty tended to increase over time, and so may the perception of the risk. The reverse may, occasionally, also be true. If, for example, a company experiences liquidity problems that are perceived to be only temporary, a short-term loan carries a higher risk than a five-year loan with a two-year grace periods.

Type of Borrower

A government is generally a better risk than the private sector because:

i) There is no transfer risk. Exchange restrictions, which create the transfer risk, are imposed by, and do not apply to, the government.

ii) The number of events or situations that may lead to the materialization of a risk is smaller than for a private borrower.

iii) In case of renegotiation the new terms will probably be less unfavourable to the bank than in the case of renegotiation of a loan to private borrower. A private corporation under financial stress will strive for conditions that will enable it to stay in business. A government is not under similar constraints because countries do not go out of business, however great their financial difficulties. Moreover, because this is known, the renegotiating country still has some credit standing left to worry about, together with its international prestige in the broader sense. Such considerations do not usually affect the negotiating position of a company.

iv) The probability of the materialization of the risk is less (although there may be exceptions to this rule). This assumptions is based on the fact that government can take measures that are not within the reach of company management to avert debt servicing difficulties. They can raise income through increasing taxes, and foreign exchange earnings thoroughly appropriate policy action; they can also count on other governments and international organizations to provide assistance.

Within the private sector, banks are probably better risks than non-banks because:

i) in some countries they can count on central assistance;

ii) interbank loans are usually for short terms, and can thus be recovered fairly rapidly after the flashing of the danger signal.

Purpose of the Loan

In principle, a balance of payments loan is a better risk than a budget loan to finance current government consumption. The latter, by definition, increases external indebtedness without increasing productive capacity upon which the servicing of the debt depends. This is not necessarily true for balance of payments loans.

The risk of a development loan is usually lower than that of a straight balance of payments loan (although most balance of payments loans are nowadays disguised as development loans). Almost be definition, a development loan contributes to the improvement of the country's debt servicing ability in the long term. A balance of payments loan, again by definition, implies an already precarious liquidity position. This may or may not improve, depending on external factors beyond the country's control and upon the government's ability and willingness to make good use of the time to improve its economic situation.

If the viability of a project can be assessed with greater accuracy than the viability of an economic development plan, then project financing is a better risk than development finance.

Within project financing, a project that generates its own foreign currency earnings will be a better risk than projects to improve the infrastructure or to create productive capacity to serve the domestic market.

Because there is no international market for direct investment there is no market consensus of political or environmental risk. The direct investor is on its own, and has to do its own risk evaluation. Direct investors have a much longer time horizon than lenders, but they are mainly concerned with a limited number of political variables. This is why they usually refer to the political risks of foreign investment. Lender's time horizons are much shorter but when they lend to the public sector, they have to look at all the political, social and economic variables that may affect a country's debt servicing ability. This is why they find the term political risk too restrictive and prefer country risk.

Differences in time horizons and in concerns mean that country risk evaluation from the point of view of direct investors is of limited use to lenders and vice versa. Some countries may be good risks for setting up a plant but not quite so good for commercial bank lending; the reverse may be true for others. More importantly, differences in time horizons and concerns require different approaches and techniques for risk evaluation.

CLASSIFICATION OF COUNTRY RISK

Much of the conceptual confusion that surrounds country risk arises from the different criteria according to which risks can be classified. These include:

i) by the side of the balance sheet which is exposed to risk, whether assets or liabilities;

ii) in case of assets, by type of asset which is at risk: loans (country risk) vs. direct investment;
iii) geographically: Austrian, Brazilian, Chilean, etc. risk;
iv) within each country, by the nature of events that may lead to its materialization: political, social, economic, etc.;
v) regarding country risk, by type of borrower: government (or sovereign) risk, private sector risk, corporate risk, individual risk;
vi) for each type of borrower, by the action taken by the borrower that causes a loss: repudiation, default, renegotiation, rescheduling, etc;
vii) for each of these, by degree, i.e. high, low, moderate risk.

Classification by Action Taken by Borrower

Among the various classifications, the type of action taken by the borrower is probably the most important.

Repudiation or Default

In this case, the debtor notifies the creditor that he will definitely cease making any further service payments because he cannot or does not want to pay (default), or because he does not recognize the debt (repudiation). As the distinction between repudiation and default has little relevance to the lender, and because repudiation is extremely rare, we are concerned here only with default. Default as defined here is quite different from the widely used term of "technical default".

Renegotiation

Renegotiation here indicates that the lender will receive less than originally agreed because the interest rate is lowered, the spread narrowed and/or because part of the principal will not be repaid. Refinancing not covered by a penalty clause has similar consequences to the lender.

Rescheduling or Moratorium

This implies that the terms of the loan are lengthened either because annual repayments of principal are lowered and spread over a great number of years than originally agreed (rescheduling) or because there will be a grace period for the repayment of principal (moratorium). The interest (or spread) remains the same as originally agreed.

There may be an opportunity loss if the lender could have relent the principal at a higher interest rate or wider spread had it been repaid as originally scheduled. There may alternatively be an opportunity gain, if the market has become more liquid in the meantime.

There will also be a loss of convenience as the schedule of the actual cash flow will be different from that of the expected cash flow. There are extra administrative costs, such as the cost of negotiating the rescheduling or the moratorium. This is usually the only measurable loss that the lender suffers as a result of rescheduling or moratorium, but even that may be recovered through a one percent penalty interest on rescheduled amounts.

Technical Default

Technical default arises when the borrower fails to meet one or several terms for debt service payments because of, for example, temporary inability (or unwillingness) to pay, administrative delays, or inefficiency. The accent is on the word "temporary" : usually there is little doubt that the debtor will eventually meet his debt servicing obligations. Usually he also pays interest-sometimes at a penalty rate-on service payments due. In that case the impact from the lender's point of view is similar to that of a moratorium: there is a possibility of opportunity loss and there will be a convenience loss as well as the extra costs incurred in prompting the debtor to meet his debt servicing obligations.

Transfer Risk

If prohibitive exchange restrictions have been imposed by the government, it may become impossible to transfer payments. This type of country risk can only materialize for private borrowers; if the government cannot service its own debt because it does not have the required amount of foreign exchange, the risk would come under default, renegotiation, rescheduling, moratorium or technical default.

A so-called improductive loan-a loan that is not serviced-may be a case of technical default or transfer impossibility. Depending upon how the issue is eventually resolved, it may also belong to any of the other categories.

Geographical Location of Risks

To which country does the risk of a given loan belong? The answer to this question is not always obvious, although it is relevant not only to the assessment of country risk but also to the setting of country exposure limits.

The risk of a loan is usually located in the country of domicile of the borrower. But if the loan is guaranteed, should it be the country of the guarantor? What about "brass plate" domiciles, where the head office is legally domiciled in a tax haven and the assets of the company are elsewhere?

As a general rule, the risk should belong to the country on which the principal protection as to the repayment of the loans depends. The risk of each loan can only be located after careful scrutiny of the overall situation, covering safeguards against loss and country jurisdiction.

The Development of Country Risk Evaluation

As sovereign lending increased, international divisions appended a one or two-page factsheet to each loan proposal or request for increase of exposure limit that went to the board for approval. These were modeled on the factsheets that accompanied requests for commercial loan approvals in domestic banking, including factors such as size, population, GNP, type of government, main exports and imports, and main trading partners.

INTERNATIONAL COMPARISON

A cross country comparison of external debt of twenty most indebted developing countries, based on data from the World Bank's 'International Debt Statistics, 2013' which contains the debt numbers for the year 2011 and has a time lag of two years, showed that in 2011 India was in fourth position in terms of absolute external debt stock after China, the Russian Federation and Brazil. The ratio of India's external debt stock to gross national income (GNI) at 18.3 per cent was the third lowest with China's being the lowest at 9.4 per cent (Table 5). In terms of the cover of external debt provided by foreign exchange reserves, India's position was seventh highest at 81.1 per cent.

TABLE 5
International Comparison of Top Twenty Developing Debtor Countries, 2011

Sl. No.	*Countries*	*Total external debt stock*	*Total debt to GNI (per cent) (US$ million)*	*Short-term to total external debt (per cent)*	*Foreign exchange reserves to total debt (per cent)*
1	2	3	4	5	6
1	China	685,418	9.4	69.6	467.3
2	Russian Federation	542,977	31.1	12.9	83.6
3	Brazil	404,317	16.6	10.4	86.7
4	India	334,331	18.3	23.3	81.1
5	Turkey	307,007	40.1	27.3	25.5
6	Mexico	287,037	25.2	17.9	50.2
7	Indonesia	213,541	26.0	17.9	49.9
8	Ukraine	134,481	83.3	24.3	22.6
9	Romania	129,822	72.3	22.9	33.1
10	Kazakhstan	124,437	77.9	7.2	20.2
11	Argentina	114,704	26.3	14.5	37.7
12	South Africa	113,512	28.4	16.6	37.5
13	Chile	96,245	41.0	17.8	43.6

14	Malaysia	94,468	34.8	46.3	139.5
15	Thailand	80,039	24.0	56.2	209.1
16	Colombia	76,918	24.3	14.1	40.8
17	Philippines	76,043	33.6	9.2	88.5
18	Venezuela	67,908	21.8	24.6	14.6
19	Pakistan	60,182	27.3	4.2	24.1
20	Vietnam	57,841	49.1	17.2	23.4

Source: World Bank's International Debt Statistics 2013.

Note: Countries are arranged based on the magnitude of debt presented in Column 3 in the Table.

India's external debt stock at end-March 2012 stood at US$ 345.4 billion (₹ 1,765,333 crore) recording an increase of US$ 39.5 billion (12.9 per cent) over end-March 2011 level of US$ 305.9 billion (₹ 1,365,929 crore). Component-wise, long-term debt increased by 10.9 per cent to US$ 267.2 billion at end-March 2012 from US$ 240.9 billion at end-March 2011, while short-term showed an increase of 20.3 per cent to US$ 78.2 billion from US$ 65.0 billion at end-March 2011. India's external debt stock increased by about US$ 20.0 billion (5.8 per cent) to US$ 365.3 billion at end-September 2012 over the level at end March 2012. The rise in external debt is largely due to higher NRI deposits, short-term debt and commercial borrowings. NRI deposits alone accounted for 42.1 per cent of the rise in total external debt at end-September 2012 over the level of end March 2012, while short-term debt and commercial borrowings together accounted for 52.6 per cent of the rise in debt during the period.

The maturity profile of India's external debt indicates the dominance of long-term borrowings. Long-term external debt at US$ 280.8 billion at end September 2012 accounted for 76.9 per cent of the total external debt, while the remaining 23.1 per cent was short-term debt. Long-term debt at end September 2012 increased by US$ 13.6 billion (5.1 per cent) over the level at end-March 2012, while short-term debt increased by US$ 6.3 billion (8.1 per cent). Within long-term, components such as commercial borrowings, NRI deposits and multilateral borrowings taken together, accounted for 62.1 per cent of total external debt at the end of September 2012 while other long-term debt components (viz. bilateral borrowings, export credit, IMF and rupee debt) accounted for 14.8 per cent of total external debt (Table 6).

The currency composition of India's total external debt shows that the share of US dollar denominated debt continued to be the highest in external debt stock at 55.7 per cent at end September 2012, followed by Indian rupee (22.9 per cent), Japanese yen (8.6 per cent), SDR (8.1 per cent) and euro (3.2 per cent). The currency composition of Government (sovereign) debt indicates pre-dominance of SDR denominated debt (36.6 per cent), which is attributable to borrowing from International Development Association (IDA) i.e., the soft loan window of the World Bank under the multilateral agencies and

SDR allocations by the IMF. The share of US dollar denominated debt was 26.2 per cent followed by Japanese yen denominated (19.3 per cent), Indian rupee (14.3) and euro (3.6). At end-September 2012, Government (sovereign) external debt was US$ 81.5 billion. It accounted for 22.3 per cent of India's total external debt. Non Government external debt amounted to US$ 283.9 billion which was 77.7 per cent of total external debt at end-September 2012.

TABLE 6

Composition of External Debt (per cent of total external debt)

Sl. No.	*Component*	*March 2011 PR*	*March 2012 PR*	*June 2012 PR*	*September 2012 QE*
1	2	3	4	5	6
1	Multilateral	15.8	14.6	14.3	13.9
2	Bilateral	8.4	7.7	7.8	7.6
3	IMF	2.1	1.8	1.7	1.7
4	Export credit	6.1	5.5	5.5	5.2
5	Commercial borrowings	28.9	30.4	29.9	29.8
6	NRI deposit	16.9	17.0	17.5	18.3
7	Rupee debt	0.5	0.4	0.3	0.4
8	Long-term debt (1 to 7)	78.8	77.4	76.9	76.9
9	Short-term debt	21.2	22.6	23.1	23.1
10	Total external debt (8+9)	100.0	100.0	100.0	100.0

Source: Ministry of Finance and RBI.

PR: Partially Revised.

QE: Quick Estimates.

Over the years, India's external debt stock has witnessed structural change in terms of composition. The share of concessional in total debt has declined due to shrinking share of official creditors and the Government debt and the surge in non-concessional private debt. The proportion of concessional in total debt declined from 42.9 per cent (average) during the period 1991-2000 to 28.1 per cent in 2001-2010 and further to 13.2 per cent at end-September 2012. The rising share of nongovernment debt is evident from the fact that such debt accounted for 65.6 per cent of total debt during the decade of 2000s, vis-a-vis 45.3 per cent in 1990s. Non-Government debt accounted for over 70 per cent of total debt in the last five years and stood at 77.7 per cent at end-September 2012.

The key external debt indicators are presented in Table-7. India's foreign exchange reserves provided a cover of 80.7 per cent to the total external debt stock at end-

September 2012 vis-à-vis 85.2 per cent at end-March 2012. The ratio of short-term external debt to foreign exchange reserves was at 28.7 per cent at end-September 2012 as compared to 26.6 per cent at end-March 2012. The ratio of concessional debt to total external debt declined steadily and worked out to 13.2 per cent at end-September 2012 as against 13.9 per cent at end-March 2012.

TABLE 7

India's Key External Debt Indicators (Per Cent)

Year	*External debt (US$ billion)*	*Total external debt to GDP*	*Debt-service ratio*	*Foreign exchange reserves to total external debt*	*Concessional debt to total external debt*	*Short-term external debt* to foreign exchange reserves*	*Short-term external debt* to total debt*
1	2	3	4	5	6	7	8
1990-91	83.8	28.7	35.3	7.0	45.9	146.5	10.2
1990-91	83.8	28.7	35.3	7.0	45.9	146.5	10.2
1995-96	93.7	27.0	26.2	23.1	44.7	23.2	5.4
2000-01	101.3	22.5	16.6	41.7	35.4	8.6	3.6
2005-06	139.1	16.8	10.1#	109.0	28.4	12.9	14.0
2006-07	172.4	17.5	4.7	115.6	23.0	14.1	16.3
2007-08	224.4	18.0	4.8	138.0	19.7	14.8	20.4
2008-09	224.5	20.3	4.4	112.1	18.7	17.2	19.3
2009-10	260.9	18.2	5.8	106.8	16.8	18.8	20.1
2010-11	305.9	17.5	4.3	99.6	15.5	21.3	21.2
2011-12	345.4	19.7	6.0	85.2	13.9	26.6	22.6
2012-13							
end-June 2012 PR	348.8	-	5.9	83.1	13.5	27.8	23.1
end-Sept. 2012 QE	365.3	-	-	80.7	13.2	28.7	23.1

Source: Ministry of Finance and RBI.

Notes: Not worked out for the broken period. PR : Partially Revised QE-Quick Estimates.

*: Short-term debt is based on original maturity.

#: Works out to 6.3 per cent, with the exclusion of India millennium deposits (IMDs) repayments of US$ 7.1 billion and prepayment of US$ 23.5 million. Debt-service ratio is the proportion of gross debt service payments to external current receipts (net of official transfers).

India's external debt has remained within manageable limits as indicated by the external debt to GDP ratio of 19.7 per cent and debt service ratio of 6.0 per cent in 2011-12. The active external debt management policy of the Government of India has helped in containing rise in external debt and maintaining a comfortable external debt position. The policy continues to focus on monitoring long and short-term debt, raising sovereign loans on concessional terms with longer maturities, regulating external commercial borrowings through end-use, all-in-cost and maturity restrictions; and rationalizing interest rates on non-resident Indian deposits (Box 1).

BOX 1

Risks in Foreign Currency Borrowings

Corporate borrowers in India and other emerging economies are keen to borrow in foreign currency to benefit from lower interest and longer terms of credit. Such borrowings however, are not always helpful, especially in times of high currency volatility. During good times, domestic borrowers could enjoy triple benefits of (i) lower interest rates, (ii) longer maturity and (iii) capital gains due to domestic currency appreciation. This would happen when the local currency is appreciating due to surge in capital flows and the debt service liability is falling in domestic currency terms. The opposite would happen when the domestic currency is depreciating due to reversal of capital flows during crisis situations, as happened during the 2008 global crisis.

A sharp depreciation in local currency would mean corresponding increase in debt service liability, as more domestic currency would be required to buy the same amount of foreign exchange for debt service payments. This would lead to erosion in profit margin and have mark-to-market implications for the corporate. There would also be 'debt overhang' problem, as the volume of debt would rise in local currency terms. Together, these factors could create corporate distress, especially because the rupee tends to depreciate precisely when the Indian economy is also under stress, and corporate revenues and margins are under pressure.

In this context, it is felt that one of the factors contributing to faster recovery of Indian economy after the 2008 global crisis was the low level of corporate external debt. As a result, the significant decline in the value of rupee did not have major fallout for the corporate balance-sheets. Foreign currency borrowings, therefore, have to be contracted carefully, especially when no 'natural hedge' is available. Such natural hedge would happen when a foreign currency borrower also has an export market for its products. As a result, export receivables would offset, at least to some extent, the currency risk inherent in debt service payments. This happens because fall in the value of the rupee that leads to higher debt service payments is partly compensated by the increase in the value of rupee receivables through exports. When export receivables and the currency of borrowings is different, the prudent approach is for corporations to enter currency swaps to re-denominate asset and liability in the same currency to create natural hedge. Unfortunately, too many Indian corporations with little foreign currency earnings leave foreign currency borrowings unhedged, so as to profit from low international interest rates. This is a dangerous gamble for reasons described above and should be avoided.

POLITICAL RISK ANALYSIS

The most common error of the early country risk evaluations was the separate assessment of political risk and economic risk. Some country risk analysts also included attitudinal risk, business risk, financial risk, and other separately evaluated risks. It was not yet clear that country risk always refers to a financial phenomenon: the inability to make payments because of the unavailability of hard currency. Business risk may be synonymous with commercial or corporate risk, in which case it is not country risk; or it may be simply the country risk of unguaranteed loans to private enterprises. Gradually, country risk analysts came to realize that country risk materializes through the interaction of political and economic developments. It requires a comprehensive approach and cannot be broken down into separate political and economic evaluations. In particular, political developments rarely have a direct impact on debt servicing ability; they usually work through the economy. Table - 8 shows two examples of this process.

TABLE - 8
Interaction of Political and Economic Factors

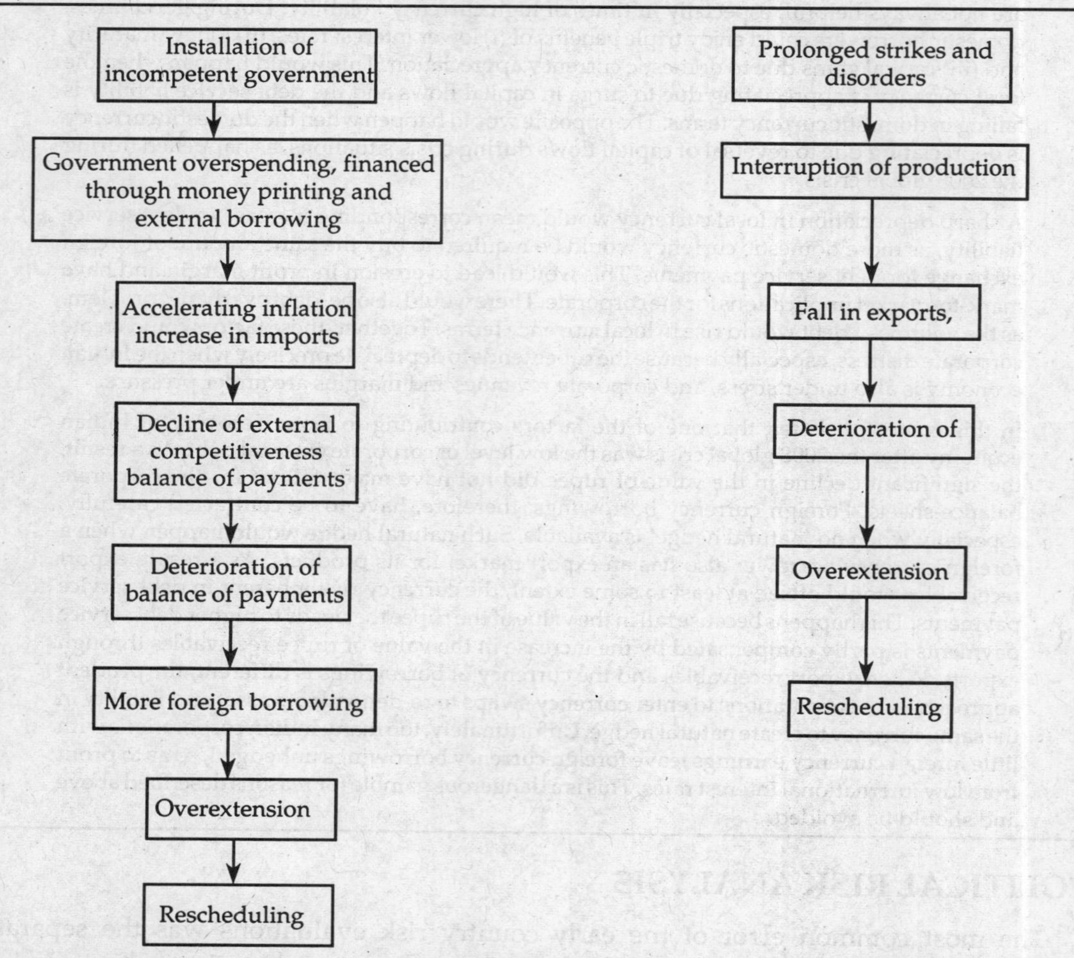

The first principle for the international manager should be "The world is my market place, and I can do business anyplace". Or, in the words of the old Chinese proverb "Whether the cat is black or white makes no difference as long as he catches mice". The second principle is that you yourself are the best judge of foreign risk. Of course, there are services and consultants who can assist, but ultimately it is your product, your company, and your money that is involved. To make no decision because of unfamiliarity is a no-go decision and in the long run may turn out to be just as costly as another 'go' decision that failed.

All corporate strategic planning depends on certain assumptions regarding national political conditions. Through its legislative power, government is able to influence and change the national business environment, including regulations affecting the firm's ability to compete and even the ownership of company assets.

Politics and government are particularly significant to the strategy of multinational companies. Because such companies operate within the jurisdiction of more than one government, the probability that their plans will be affected by some form of government initiative is increased. Their international mobility means that they have a certain degree of choice regarding their political environment. Unlike the domestic firm whose operations are limited to its country of origin, the strategic choice open to multinational firms includes national location and hence government. The political environment itself becomes a variable, part of management's strategic decision making. The foreign ownership links of the multinational enterprise place it in a special category in the eyes of host governments. Even though it may be incorporated under local national laws, it is classed as a foreign firm, and this often means that it is subject to special regulations and government actions not applied to domestic firms.

The practical result of these characteristics is reflected in the high priority that most multinationals place on their relations with government, and with good reason. History has shown that even the smaller nation-states are able to assert major influence and expropriate the assets of some of the world's largest multinational firms. Although such takeovers are the exception rather than the rule, they serve to underline the distinction between economic and political power. All companies derive their authority from and are dependent on government. Recognition of this fact does not imply that they are without resources in managing their relationships with government.

In its broadest sense, political risk refers to government-associated change that might adversely affect the firm's operations or assets. The term risk stems from the fact that such predictions are probability statements, estimates as to the likelihood of certain events, based on available evidence.

Although readily defined in principle, in practice there may be differences of opinion on the dividing line between events that constitute risk and those that do not. All firms, both domestic and those with foreign operations, are routinely involved with government actions and change that affect their business. Changes in taxation, industry regulations on safety and pollution, company law, and manufacturing standards may affect some firms adversely, but they are so much a part of the normal business of government that as long as their impact is minor and they are not directed at foreign firms, management tends to think of them as part of the firm's normal business activity. At the other extreme are certain events, such as nationalization and expropriation of company assets, that clearly qualify as potential political risks.

In practice, political risk is defined more narrowly to refer to government associated hazards of doing business in foreign countries. Table -6 presents a typology of such political risk. Category 1 contains those events that, being less visible and less associated with threat or force, are not always identified under the heading of political risk. Nevertheless, they merit close attention since they may have a major impact on the firm. These include special taxes falling on the products, profits, or assets of foreign firms and discrimination in government sales or purchases. Price controls have been imposed by some government on certain products of multinational firms, particularly drugs and medicines. Quite a few multinationals have found that excessive bureaucratic requirements or "red tape" represent a major obstacle to their international operations. Indigenization of management refers to government programs aimed at increasing the proportion of local nationals in the management of the firm's operations in that country.

Indigenization of capital refers to government pressure on the multinational to award an ownership stake in its operations (within the country in question) to local national investors. Finally, there are the more obvious risks associated with the loss of company assets. Note that the ordering of the risk indicated in Table - 9 does not necessarily indicate their importance on impact on the firm. Certain types of tax discrimination or price control may have a greater impact and be considered far more important than, for example, indigenization of capital or restrictions on repatriation of funds.

The purpose of political risk forecasting is to anticipate the likelihood of future events. Political risk forecasts fall into two distinct categories: predictions about evolutionary change, which unfolds with only minor deviation within the existing political system, and forecasts aimed at predicting major discontinuities in the political system itself.

Evolutionary Political Change

The emphasis here is on understanding and interpreting the existing political system, its likely future actions and directions of change. Valuable assistance toward this end may be obtained through the use of outside experts. Former political figures, diplomats, and specialized consulting firms are used by multinational companies to supplement their own efforts. However, many of the most important judgments are those that require internal knowledge of the firm, its specific circumstances and future plans, and how these may be expected to interact with future government actions. Ultimately political forecasts of this type will rely heavily on the ability of the company's own management to interpret future change in three areas: the firm's political leverage with the host government, the relationship of the firm relative to the host government's objectives and strategy, and internal change within the host government.

TABLE-9
Typology of Political Risk

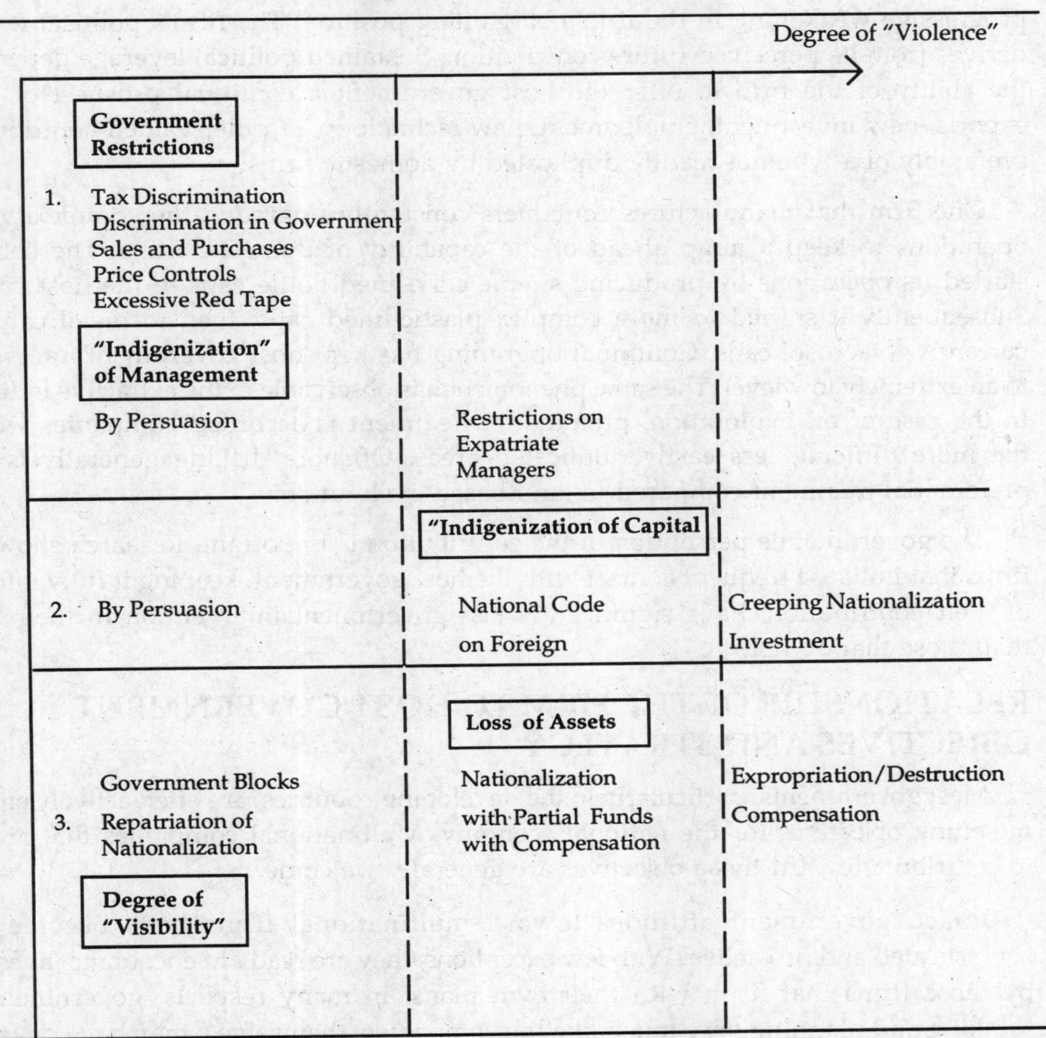

Degree of "Violence" →

Government Restrictions 1. Tax Discrimination Discrimination in Government Sales and Purchases Price Controls Excessive Red Tape **"Indigenization" of Management** By Persuasion	Restrictions on Expatriate Managers	
2. By Persuasion	**"Indigenization of Capital** National Code on Foreign	Creeping Nationalization Investment
Government Blocks 3. Repatriation of Nationalization **Degree of "Visibility"**	**Loss of Assets** Nationalization with Partial Funds with Compensation	Expropriation/Destruction Compensation

Forecasting Political Risk

The basis of the agreement between the firm and the host government begins to change as soon as the company commits itself to the country in question. Once the investment is made and the company's facilities are in place, the firm's original bargaining position is sharply altered. Its chief bargaining lever, the freedom to commit its resources to another part of the world, has disappeared. Host governments are not unaware of this fact. The original agreement between firm and government has been aptly characterized by Raymond Vernon as an "obsolescing bargain." Unless the firm is able to forward additional contributions, in the form of prospective new investment or future contributions in the way of new technology, there will be a tendency toward progressive weakening in the firm's bargaining position. The firm's political leverage derives from its perceived future contribution. Sustained political leverage depends on the ability of the firm to offer the host government a continual prospect of future exports, new investment, employment, new technology, or other valued contributions, preferably of a type not readily duplicated by domestic firms.

One firm that manufactures containers constantly upgraded the complexity of its operations to keep a jump ahead of the capability of domestic firms. The company started its operations by producing simple cork-lined bottle caps in the host country. Subsequently it shifted to more complex plastic-lined caps, then to metal cans, and currently to aerosol cans. Continual upgrading has kept host government intervention to an extremely low level. The same phenomenon is observable in the extractive industries. In the case of oil exploration, preferential treatment is accorded companies working the more difficult, less easily duplicated areas. Offshore drilling generally is given preferential treatment compared to land-based exploration.

The government's perception of the contribution is important. Research shows that firms that initiated frequent contact with the host government, keeping it fully informed of their contribution, have significantly less government intervention in their affairs than those that do not.

RELATIONSHIP OF THE FIRM TO HOST GOVERNMENT OBJECTIVES AND STRATEGY

Most governments, particularly in the developing countries, are often actively engaged in setting objectives for the national economy. Multinational companies that are seen to contribute toward those objectives are generally welcome.

Infact, government attitudes toward multinational firms have become more sophisticated and pro-active. With few exceptions, they are ready to encourage investment by those firms that fit in with their own plans. In many respects, governments are thinking and planning very much like the companies themselves; they have developed strategies for attracting and managing multinational companies.

Identifying and understanding the host government's strategy is an important aid in forecasting its actions. Although no two countries will have precisely the same strategy toward foreign direct investment, it is possible to describe a number of national groups that have certain similarities in their general strategic approach toward multinationals.

Indigenous Industrialisations

A large number of developing countries are primarily interested in the contribution that multinational firms can make to the development of domestic companies and industries. Government policies are developed to ensure that foreign direct investment is largely owned and managed by nationals of he host country. A high priority is placed on the transfer of technology to national firms.

Leapfrog

Countries such as Singapore, Taiwan, Hong Kong, South Korea, and others aggressively seek international foreign direct investment to achieve a level of industrialization associated with the more advanced industrial countries. Favorable tax and other incentives (including production facilities in tariff-free zones) are provided for foreign investors, particularly companies that can contribute to the development of the country's technological and management skills. Government pressure to shift the ownership and management of multinational subsidiaries is absent or minimal.

Infant Industries

Japan is the prime example of this strategy, directed primarily at sheltering domestic companies from competition against foreign investors until they are judged able to complete effectively. Until relatively recently, incoming foreign investment was subject to severe restrictions. Only a few select firms, generally in high technology areas, were allowed into the country on the basis of 100 percent ownership. Most foreign companies that were permitted to invest did so on the basis of minority joint ventures, under the watchful eye of the government. Since the early 1970s, there has been a gradual lifting of such restrictions. They are formally terminated in 1980, though the government continues to influence the foreign investment climate.

Open Door

Foreign investors are offered equal treatment with national firms, but there is no particular drive by the central government to encourage or prohibit such investment. There are very few countries falling into this category, perhaps because foreign direct investment is a relatively minor segment of the economy.

Systematic Screening

Most countries today are selective about the type of firms that are encouraged or discouraged from establishing themselves within their boundaries. They have developed highly systematic procedures for selecting and monitoring such companies. Based on far-reaching investigations of the impact of foreign investment on the national economy, countries screen potential candidates to select those companies with attributes considered desirable and in the national interest. The screening criteria are subject to change in line with the government's economic objectives.

Change Within the Home Government

Evolutionary political change within the present system of government becomes a certainty with the passage of time. Political parties and the members comprising the national government will alter as a result of elections or other provisions for succession. Political attitudes and policies also will change in response to economic and other developments.

Japan at one time exercised stringent control over foreign investors entering the country. Industries open to foreign firms and the degree of foreign ownership were controlled in line with government strategy. Over time the country's economic situation has improved so dramatically that most of these restrictions have gradually been lifted. In other cases, the reverse happened. The 1983 fall in oil prices forced Nigeria to take measures to curtain imports and import-sensitive industries.

Forecasting internal evolutionary political change requires a close knowledge of the political pressures for change shaping the course of the current government and its likely successors. Inevitably the analysis will extend beyond the purely political. It will include cultural, economic, and institutional considerations and their influence on political events. There is no substitute for close, preferably personal, knowledge and on-the-spot contact with political trends, leaders, and institutions.

Discontinuous Change in the Political System

Major change in the political system, such as the overthrow of the established government through revolution, is viewed by some as the major source of political risk. This type of change strikes at the very foundations of the assumptions underlying all of the firm's plan and poses a threat to its continued existence in that country. There is, admittedly, an element of irrationality in viewing all such change as inevitably negative. It may be argued that every major change is bound to benefit some, even if adversely affecting others. Nevertheless, it is understandable that management would seek advance notice of impending political discontinuity and also that it would perceive such change as introducing the possibility of major adverse political events. Perhaps it would be more accurate to describe such forecasts as concerned with predicting the stability of political systems and the probability that the present rules of the game might be changed. In making such forecasts, companies rely on both subjective and quantitative assessments.

The traditional method of forecasting political change relies on expert opinion. The firm may seek the subjective judgment of people who are well informed on the national political situation, but there are obvious hazards in this approach. Experts have been proved wrong before. More to the point is conscious or unconscious bias. For example, if the expert is a member of, or closely associated with, the national government, he or she may have personal reasons for wanting to encourage foreign direct investment to help stabilize and improve the national economy. Similarly, the company's own managers will not be without individual biases. Line managers, with everything to gain from new expansion within their own jurisdiction, are known for their optimism.

Nevertheless, this approach can be effective, especially where the government structure is more a matter of personalities than established constitutional practice, as in the Middle East. This "old hands" approach can be useful in appraising the objectives and personalities of the country's current leadership, the strengths and weakness of competing political groups, and the likelihood of new legislation.

Checklists, as shown in Table - 10, are used to assist in the interpretation of political system and potential change.

TABLE -10

Checklist of Political Risk Indicators

Political Environment	*Foreign Pressures*
Form of government	Threat of war
History of government stability	Military related violence
Party fractionalization	Diplomatic crises Party political platforms
Trade disputes Volatility of electorate	External threats to supplies
Popular support of ruling party	Alliances Role of military
Attitude to foreign companies	*Economic Pressures*
Legal system	Per capita income
Treaties on tax and investment	Economic crises
State companies	Balance of payments
Religious or ethnic splits	Inflation rate
Internal Stability	Exchange rate volatility
Riots	Controls on repatriation of capital
Public demonstrations	National debt
Political strikes	Income distribution
Purges	Wealth distribution
Assassinations	
Government crisis	
History of military coups	

Expert opinion can also be sampled on a large scale, such as with the use of Delphi techniques. A number of consulting firms that advise on political events employ a panel of experts to assess political stability. The Delphi method of using a panel of experts in successive iterations is supposed to move opinion toward a consensus view that is superior to individual estimates.

More recently, there has been a growing emphasis on quantitative methods to forecast discontinuous political change. Although they must be considered promising (and their use growing), they are still considered somewhat experimental.

In principle, the employment of such methods is not unlike the use of leading business indicators used to forecast economic change. In forecasting discontinuous political change, the objective is to arrive at a probability estimate of political upheaval through the use of certain measurable events that act as lead indicators. The variables selected are usually those thought to be causally related with drastic political change. The reasoning here is that measurable change in these variables will precede discontinuous political change.

Hans Schollhammer has developed a quantitative model that uses measures of certain causal factors to forecast political change (defined as government executives transfers and executive adjustments). The causal factors are of two types. Political causal factors include quantitative estimates of national riots, armed attacks, deaths from domestic violence, government sanctions, defense expenditures and fractionalization among political parties. Another set of measures has reference to economic causal factors, such as average per capita income, national income distribution, capital formation (as a percentage of GNP), per capita education expenditures, and available food supply measured in terms of calories per capita. Quantitative measures for these factors over time were assembled for sixty countries and adjusted for differences in population size. A statistically significant relationship was found between these factors and political change.

Both methods have weaknesses. The more mechanical approach of the quantitative techniques is unlikely to capture unique characteristics and subtle changes in mood that may shed light on particular national situations. The expert opinion approach is subject to the problems already noted together with the fact that it is unlikely to be consistent across different national territories where assessment includes to be consistent across different national territories where assessment includes more than one country. Inevitably there will be numerous cases where the decision is not clear-cut. In these marginal cases, it may make sense to use both methods. In the words of one executive.

Rummel and Heenan conclude that political change is influenced by domestic instability, foreign conflict, political climate, and economic climate. In assessing these headings, they advocate an integrated approach combining quantitative analysis and expert qualitative judgments.

MANAGING POLITICAL RISK

Although there is little a firm can do to influence national political change, this is far from suggesting that management has no power to mitigate or otherwise manage the effects of political change, whether evolutionary or discontinuous.

One method is the premium for risk approach, a form of self-insurance that the firm implements by requiring a higher rate of return in countries considered exceptionally risky. Although this is one of the best-known and most widely used methods, there are a number of hedging strategies that are often more effective. These are discussed in two categories: hedging strategies that the firm can take prior to investment in a given country and those available to it after investment. These categories are subdivided into measures internal to the firm and those that depend on passing the risk to external agencies. Table-11 summarises these methods.

TABLE - 11

Hedging Strategies

Before Investing

- Internal hedging
    - Minimization of local equity
        - Local borrowing
        - Local equity (joint ventures)
        - Management contract
    - International integration
        - Production integration
        - Marketing integration
        - International supply sourcing
        - External hedging
    - Government insurance
    - Private insurance
    - Host government guarantees

After Investing

- Internal hedging
    - Good citizen policy
    - Increase in technical contribution
    - Negotiation and arbitration
- External hedging
    - Private insurance
    - International investment codes
    - Divestment

BEFORE INVESTING

Minimising Local Equity

An obvious way to hedge against loss is to minimize the firm's equity investment in the country. Local borrowing not only limits the company investment subject to political risk, it has the important further benefit of creating allies, local lenders who have a vested interest in the success of the firm. Furthermore, it reduces the firm's exposure to foreign exchange risk since locally generated earnings can be used to repay local capital and interest payments denominated in the same currency.

Minimizing the company's equity stake can also be achieved through local equity participation-that is, forming a joint venture with local shareholders. Participation of local shareholders will also help to build links with the local community and provide the benefit of local management advice and knowledge. Where there are local indigenization programs in effect, participation of local equity shareholders is a prerequisite rather than an option.

Equity risk may be eliminated altogether through a management contract that compensates the firm for management services provided. No company investment in ownership of facilities is involved.

International Integration

If the company established in the foreign territory is dependent on raw materials, technical skills, machinery, management, or other inputs from abroad, the government will have to think seriously before taking any measures that jeopardize the flow of such supplies. A strategy of international integration builds interdependence between the company facility in question and links with facilities in other countries. Peru's Velasco regime omitted Chrysler from its extensive program of foreign company takeovers. The Peruvian plant manufactured only some 50 percent of the Chrysler product; the remainder was imported from Chrysler plants in Detroit, Brazil, and Argentina. The Peru plant could not be operated without cooperation from Chrysler plants in these countries. Integrating production internationally with supplier plants in other countries effectively preempted a successful takeover.

The protective effect of international integration can also by achieved through control of corporate output, such as markets for the firm's products. For many years, the international oil companies operating in the Middle East were relatively immune from government takeovers because of their control over the market for petroleum products. Nationalization of the oil wells was of limited use unless the government also had the means to dispose of their production profitably.

Another form of international integration on the output side can be implemented through the use of international trademarks and brand names. Increasingly companies are able to register their international brand names under protective legislation in a wide number of countries. Should a government expropriate the national production facilities of a such firm, the company in question is still in a position to refuse to allow the government the right to use its brand names in other countries. This would significantly reduce the value of such assets to the expropriating government. Perhaps with this in mind, the Mexican government passed a law in 1976 that required manufacturing firms to use a local trademark in all advertising and packaging.

External Hedging

In his research into the hedging strategies for French multinationals, Bernard Marois found that the risk-reducing strategy preferred by most firms was to try to shift political risk to an external agency. Several means are available for this type of hedging.

Government and Private Insurance

Many governments in the industrial countries provide various forms of insurance for companies that invest abroad, particularly if the investment is made in the developing countries. Private insurance provided by such firms as Lloyds of London is also available to cover certain types of political risk. In both cases, whether the insurance is public or private, there are insurance premiums. The insurance covers only some portion of the assets lost by the firm in the country in question. It does not cover opportunity cost.

Host Government Guarantees

Another frequently used method is the use of host government guarantees, agreements arrived at between the firm and the host government prior to investment (when the firm's bargaining power is highest) guaranteeing certain provisions in writing. These may cover tax concessions, provisions for compensation in the event of expropriation, and other contingencies. They serve as an additional protective measure, though management will be aware that the governing power of the country will, at any time, have both the power and the authority to repudiate such agreements. This does not mean that they are without value. Many governments with an eye to the future credibility of their statements will not take such action lightly.

AFTER INVESTING

After the firm has committed itself to a particular national territory, its bargaining power is usually diminished, but is by no means without measures to influence government actions that might be against its interests.

Good Citizen Policy

Corporate behavior conforming to what is usually referred to as a good citizen policy is one of the most popular prescriptions for avoiding adverse political initiatives. A good citizen policy as applied to the behavior of a foreign firm refers to corporate initiatives such as the following:

1. Prompt Response to Both the Letter and Spirit of Host Government Requests

These may not always be a matter of legal requirement. Governments frequently will exhort companies to embark on various measures judged to be in the national interest on a voluntary basis, such as hiring handicapped workers, purchasing goods and components from national suppliers, and setting high standards of safety.

2. Contribution to National Goals

In all countries, there will be certain recognized national goals that the government hopes to forward. These may include increased exports, building up the national technological base, and developing new products. Identifying where and to what degree the company can contribute toward such goals without sacrificing its own interests is a matter of management discretion.

3. Contribution to National Welfare

This refers to company support of educational institutions, hospitals, latest development and other programs that contribute to the general national welfare.

4. Developing a Corporate Image

A company that seeks to be recognized as a good citizen will be interested in projecting an acceptable corporate image. This is as much a matter of what it does not do as much as anything else. It is possible for any foreign firm to accentuate its international links to the point where they irritate and aggravate public relations. Especially in the developing countries, a low profile is frequently an important part of being a good citizen. Nevertheless, many firms that have qualified as good citizens have been the subject of government takeovers.

Increase in Technical Contribution

The strategy of systematic and planned increase in the firm's contribution to national technological capability is closely related to the previous point. The increased importance of technology and its near universal pursuit by government, together with the perception of the multinational as a technology transfer agent, means that the firm that can present itself in this light to the host government is in a powerful bargaining position. Negotiation and Arbitration. For the multinational firms, entry into the host country in most cases will have been the subject of negotiations with the host government. Particularly in cases involving large-scale foreign investment or investment in sensitive areas, such as those related to national defense, communications, and natural resources, normally there will have been detailed discussions between the firm and the host government in arriving at the complex arrangements and commitments that comprise the final agreement governing the conditions of entry. In the developing countries, negotiations between the investing company and the host government will apply to virtually all cases of foreign investment.

Both the company and the host government will have a degree of flexibility in terms of the entry conditions that are considered acceptable. The final agreement reflects an area where the interests of the two parties overlap, that is, an area of mutually acceptable terms and conditions of entry.

In the case of major political change, the firm's position in the country and its relationship with the new government may have to be renegotiated. In the event of such change, prudent management will seek to establish whether such new negotiations are called for. Negotiations with the new government regarding proposed initiatives that threaten the firm can prove effective in minimizing or avoiding loss. The multinational firm inevitably will have certain bargaining counters, such as possible new investment, continued licensing of technology and the use of trade names, and provision of overseas outlets. Presented to government tactfully and effectively, these can significantly improve the company's position.

Where such negotiations fail, third-party arbitration is a possibility. Although relatively rare, the greater involvement of international agencies in developing codes of conduct for both companies and host governments offers the hope that this will become a more realistic option in the future.

Private Insurance

Even after the firm has committed its resource, it can resort to private insurance schemes to hedge against future loss. The insurance premium will be proportional to the threat of asset loss.

Investment Codes

An increasing number of international organizations are attempting to promulgate international codes providing reciprocal guarantees between multinational companies and host governments. Organization involved in such efforts include the United Nations, the International Monetary Fund, and the OECD. As yet such codes have had limited validity. However, there is hope and even expectation that in the future they may provide for international investment the sort of regulatory framework and grievance procedures currently provided for international trade.

Multilateral Investment Guarantee Agency, a member of the World Bank Group, which commenced operations in April 1988 to promote private foreign direct investment for economic development in its member countries, is expected to play an important role in: (1) Guaranteeing investments made by foreign investors against political risks in developing member countries; (ii) Producing promotional and advisory services to assist member countries in creating an alternative climate for private foreign direct investment. MIGA is a legally distinct entity from the Bank or the IFC and has its own Executive Board.

Divestment

Voluntary divestment of national assets can prove a valuable device in reducing the damage caused by government takeovers that are inevitable. Planned well in advance, divestment can be effective in extricating the firm from a situation that is no longer tenable with a minimum of damage.

The firm's ability to adjust to the constraints and conditions imposed by national government depend on its ability to anticipate and interpret political change. This refers to change within the existing political system as well as change in the system itself. Even where political developments appear to be moving against the firm, a number of hedging strategies are available that can prove effective in reducing or eliminating loss.

Outside expert opinion and forecasts may assist management in its projection and interpretation of political change. But in the final analysis, the objective will be to determine the impact of such change on the firm's own particular situation and prospects (generalizations about sweeping national political change are only a means to this end). This indicates that many of the key decisions concerning such change and the firm's reaction to it will require the judgment of internal company management.

The guideline make up the essence of what you need to know and do in political risk analysis are: i) Don't eliminate any market any place without a systematic look at it; ii) Package and present your project so that the benefits to the country are easily seen by all; iii) Remember in most cases you don't have to worry about confiscation or destruction but rather than the smaller changes that make doing business more costly, iv) Remember political systems are always changing, which means you have continually to monitor sources of risk; v) Know why they may be picking on you, your product, or your services, or in other words know your specific sources of risk; vi) Don't be a passive observer. You can influence the outcome of the pressures and minimise the risks in several ways; and finally, vii) Be flexible. As they say in the East, when the wind blows north the bamboo bends northward; when the wind blows south, the bamboo bends southward. And the bamboo survives a long time.

QUESTIONS

1. What is country risk? What are the socio-cultural factors affecting country risk?
2. Define political risk and discuss the concept and its assessment and management.
3. What characteristics of a company do you think make it more vulnerable to political risk?
4. Describe the criteria used for classification of country risk. What are the economic factor affecting country risk?
5. Discuss the risk of lending and direct investment abroad.
6. Would you expect political risk assessment to be more common and more formalized in companies today than in the past ? Why or why not?
7. Why should there be any risk evaluation? Explain the interaction of political and economic factors in country risk analysis.
8. Outline the political risk process that enables a company to estimate the degree of risk that exists in a given situation and then decide how to deal with that risk in an international context.

REFERENCES

Abuaf, Niso, "Foreign exchange options; the leading hedge". Midland Corporate Finance Journal, 5 (Summer 1987) pp. 51-58.

Agmon, Tamir, and Donald Lessard, "Investors recognition of corporate international diversification", Journal of Finance, 32 (September 1977), pp 1049-1055.

Babbeim, David F., "Determining the optimum strategy for hedging currency exposure", Journal of international Business Studies, 14 (Spring/Summer 1983), pp 133-39

Bachman, Heinr B., "Industrialised Countries' Policies Affecting Foreign Direct Investment in the Last two Decades, The World Bank/MIGA, 1991.

Bhalla, V.K.: Foreign Investment and New Economic Policy, Anmol Publications Pvt. Ltd. 1994.

———, International Economy: Liberalisation Process Anmol Publications Pvt.. Ltd. 1993.

Brewer, Thomas L., "The Prospects for Foreign Direct Investment", In Lars Oxelheim, ed. The Global race for Foreign Direct Investment in the 19905, 1993.

Choi, Frederick D.S., Howard D Lowe, and reginald C Worthley, "Accountors Accountaints, and standard No. 8" Journal of International Business Studies, 9 (Fall 1978) PP 81-87

Cohn, Richard A., and John J. Pringle, "Imperfections in international financial markets: implications for risk premia and the cost of capital to firms", Journal of Finance, 28 (March 1973), pp 59-66

Collins, J Markham, and William S, Sekely, "The relationship of head- quarters, country, and industry classification to financial structure". Financial Management 12 (Autumn 1983) pp 45-51

Dornbush, Rudiger: "Expectations and exchange rate dynamics", Journal of Political Economy, M (December 1976), pp 1161-1176.

Eaker, Mark R., "Denomination decision for multinational transaction" Financial Management, ((Autumn 1980) pp 23-29.

Fry, M. 1992. "The Role of Foreign Direct Investrnent in South Asia", World Bank Working Paper. Washington D.C.: IBRD: South Asia Region.

Germany J. David, and John E, Morton "Financial innovation and deregulation in foreign industrial countries", Federal Reserve Bulletin, 71 (October 1985) pp 743-753.

Hughes John S., Dennis E. Logue and Richard J Sweeney. "Corporate international diversification and market assigned measures of risk and diversification" Journal of Financial and Quantitative Analysis, 10 (November 1975) pp 627437

Ibbotson Roger C., Richard C. Can, and Anthony W, Robinson, "International equity and bond returns" Financial Analysis Journal 38 (July-August 1982) pp 61-83.

Jacque, Laurent L., "Managements of foreign exchange risk: a review article" Journal of International Business Studies 12 (Spring/ Summer 1981) pp 81-101

Lall, Rajiv B., "Multinationals from the third world: Indian firms investing aboard", Delhi, Oxford University Press, 1987, 122 p.

Lall Sanjaya, "The new multinationals : the spread Of Third World enterprises", Chichester, John Wiley and Sons, 1983, 268 p.

Lee Kwang Chul, and Chuck C.Y. Kwok, "Multinational corporations vs. domestic corporations: international environmental factors and determinants of capital structure". Journal of International Business Studies, 19 (Summer 1988), pp 195-217.

Lessard, Donald R., "International portfolio diversification: A multivariate analysis for a group of Latin American countries", Journal of finance , 28 (June 1973) pp 619433.

———, "Finance and global competition: Exploiting financial scope and coping with volatile exchange rates",. Midland Corporate Finance Journal, 4 (Fall 1986) pp 6-29

Levich Richard M., "Tests of forecasting models and markets efficiency in the international money market", in Jacob A Frenkel and Harry G, Johnson, eds. The Economics of Exchange Rates (Reading Mass Addison-Wesley, 1978), pp 129-158

Modigliani Franco and Merton Miller, "The cost of capital, corporation finance and the theory of investment" American Economic Review XLVIII (June 1958) pp 261-297

Oblak Davei J. and Roy L. Helm Jr., "Survey and analysis of capital budgeting methods used by multinationals" Financial Management, 9 (Winter 1980) pp 3741.

Rodriguez, Rita M., "Corporate exchange risk management: theme and aberrations", Journal of Finance, 36 (May 1981), pp. 427-439

Rutterford, Janette, "An international perspective on the capital structure puzzle", Middland corporate Finance Journal, 3 (Fall 1985), pp 60-72

Shapiro, Alan C., and David P. Rutenberg, "When to hedge against devaluation", Management Science, 20 (August 1974), pp 1514- 1530.

Solnik, Bruno H., "Note on the validity of the random walk for European stock market capital structure", Journal of Finance, 28 (December 1973) pp 1151-1159.

Stanley, Marjorie and Stanley Block, "An empirical study of management and financial variables in influencing capital budgeting decisions for multinational corporations in the 1980s," Management International Review 23 (1953), pp 61-71.

Stapleton, Richard C., and Marti Subrahmanyam. "Market inperfections, capital market equilibrium, and corporation finance", Journal of Finance, 32 (May 1977), pp 307-319.

Stonehill, Arthur, and Thomas Stizel, "Financial structure and multinational corporations", California Management Review, 12 (Fall 1969).

Primo Braga, C.A. and Alexender Yeats, How Minilateral Arrangements May Affect the Post-Uruguay Round World", Working Paper, The World Bank, 1992..

Rana, P.B. 1988, "Recent Trends and Issues on Foreign Direct Investment in Asian and Pacific Developing Countries:. Asian Development Bank Staff Paper, No.41.

Ramstetter, E.D., ed., 1991, "Foreign Direct Investment in Developing Economies in Asia and the Pacific in the 19905", Honolulu and Washington: East-West Center, HAS, UNDP.

Riedel, J., 1990, "Intra-Asian International Trade and Direct Investment", Asian Development Review 9, No.1, 1991.

Safadi Raed and Alexender Yeats, "The North American Free Trade Agreement - Its Effect on South Asia", Working Paper, International Economics Department, The World Bank, March 1993.

Siddharthan, N.S., "In-house R and D, imported technology, and firm size : lessons from Indian experience", The Developing Economies, 26 : 212-221, September 1988.

Solamano, A., "Adjustment Lending and Private Investment Response", The World Bank, Country Economics Department, 1991.

Stoever, William A., "Foreign collaboration policy in India : A review", Journal of Developing Areas 23, 485504, July 1989.

Thomas, M., 1991, "Foreign Direct Investment Flows to Developing Countries: 1980-89", Washington, FIAS.

United Nations, ESCAP/UNTEC Joint Unit on Transnational Corporations from developing Asian economies : host country perspective. (ST/ESCAP/605), UNCTC Publication, Series B, No.12, Bangkok, 1988, 581 p.

Wheelwrigh, Steve, "Applying decision theory to improve corporate management of currency-exchange risks", California Management Review, 17 (Summer 1975), pp 41-49.

36

BALANCE OF PAYMENTS

INTRODUCTION

The balance of payments is a comprehensive record of economic transactions of the residents of a country with the rest of the world. The record is so prepared as to provide meaning and measure to the various components of the country's external economic transactions. Thus, it aims at presenting an account of all receipts and payments on account of goods exported, services rendered and capital received by residents of the country and goods imported, services received and capital transferred by residents of the country.

THE CONCEPT OF BALANCE OF PAYMENT

The balance of payments record the *flow* of economic transactions between the *residents* of a given country and the *residents* of other countries during a certain *period of time.* In other words, it is a statistical statement for a given period showing (a) transactions in goods, services and income between an economy and rest of the world, (b) changes of ownership and other changes in that economy's monetary gold. Special Drawing Rights (SDRs) and claims on the liabilities to the rest of the world, capital transfers and (c) unrequited transfers and counterpart entries that are needed to balance, in the accounting sense, any entries for the foregoing transactions and changes which are not mutually offsetting.

The 'economy' referred to above is conceived as comprising economic entities that have a closer association with a given territory than with any other territory. Such an economic entity is called a resident. Balance of payments of a given economy will record an economic entity's transactions with the rest of the world, if the entity is a resident of the economy, or any economic entity's transactions with the given economy if the entity is considered a non-resident.

An economic entity which is not a resident entity by the above criterion, is a non-resident. The resident economic entities are classified into three categories. They comprise (i) general government and individuals, (ii) enterprises and (iii) private non-profit making bodies serving individuals. The 'general government' includes all departments, establishments and bodies of Central, State and Local Governments located in the territory of a given economy and also includes embassies, consulates, military establishments and other entities of general government located elsewhere. The latter institutions are treated as residents of that economy because firstly, they are extra-territorial to the economy where they are physically located and secondly, they have a closer affinity with the government they represent. Similarly, embassies, consulates, etc., of foreign countries located in the given economy are treated as residents of the foreign economy and hence a non-resident for the given economy. The conceptual basis relevant for determining the resident status of an individual is whether he is regarded to have been involved in the productive and consumptive process of a given economy with some degree of permanence. The rule of thumb generally adopted for recognition of permanence is a stay for one year or more. This implies that persons visiting the territory of an given economy and staying there for a year or more are to be treated as residents while those visitors who stay for less than a year would be treated as non-residents. Exception to this rule is the given economy's diplomatic or consular representatives and other government personnel stationed abroad. These persons are treated as residents of the given economy and not of the economy where they stay, irrespective of length of their stay. 'Enterprises' include all enterprises engaged in (a) the production of goods and services, (b) transactions in land, etc., or (c) leases, rights, etc., on a commercial or equivalent basis, within the territory of a given economy. 'The private non-profit making bodies serving individuals' are treated on whose territory they are functioning.

The 'transaction' referred to above is an economic transaction. A transaction presupposes two parties or transactors. An economic transaction takes place when something is exchanged between one party and another for economic value. There are, however, few exceptions to the rule that there must be two parties to every transaction. One such exception is a transaction between a branch and its office, as a branch has no separate legal existence. Similarly, when a migrating individual transfers his assets from the old country to the new country, no two parties are involved in the movement of resources. The latter example also serves as an exception to the rule that an economic transaction provides for *quid pro quo*. This is a one sided transaction. Such a transaction is known as an 'unrequited transfer'.

Transactions that enter balance of payments are usually between a resident and a non-resident. A notable exception to this are transactions in gold between a Central Monetary Authority and other residents, both being 'residents'. Certain transactions involving claims on and liabilities to the rest of the world also get covered here even if they are between two residents or between two non-residents. The transactions relating to claims on and liabilities to the rest of the world involve financial flows and these flows are recorded under different economic sectors under capital account. A sale of foreign exchange by the central bank to a commercial bank (both residents) in the same country would be recorded as a reduction in the foreign assets of the official sector matched by a corresponding increase in banking sector's foreign assets. The other types of transactions which form part of balance of payments are the 'unrequited transfers' referred to above and imputed transactions for undistributed income of direct investment enterprises attributable to direct investors.

Allocation (or Cancellation) of Special Drawing Rights (SDRs)

The allocation or cancellation of SDRs by the IMF involves the creation or extinction by the IMF of reserve assets which form part of a country's holdings of official reserve assets. The allocation of SDRs results in increase (debit) in SDR holdings while cancellation results in decrease (credit). The SDR holdings is a component of official reserve assets. In the balance of payments, the offsetting entry to increase in SDR holdings is provided by the item allocation (credit) while cancellation (debit) serves as an offsetting entry to decrease in SDR holdings.

Monetisation/Demonetisation of Gold

Gold is both a commodity and a financial asset. When it is held by the Central Monetary Authority (in India, it is the Reserve Bank of India), as a part of its international reserves, it is treated as a financial asset and it referred to as monetary gold. When it is held by any other party including the government, it is treated like any other commodity. When the Central Monetary Authority acquires gold with a view to strengthening its international reserves, from a non-monetary sector, either from a resident or from a non-resident, it is referred to as monetisation of gold. Demonetisation refers to the reverse transfer of gold from monetary sector to non-monetary sector. It occurs when the Central Monetary Authority releases monetary gold from the holdings of official reserve assets for non-monetary purposes.

Unrequited Transfers

The unrequited transfers cover gifts, grants, migrants' transfers, taxes, etc. where one transactor provides something of an economic value to another without a *quid pro quo* i.e., anything in return. The country receiving the grant or gift neither transfers nor promises to transfer anything in exchange. The lack of economic values on one side is compensated for by an entry which is referred to unrequited transfers. In India's balance of payments, the term 'transfers' is used in the same sense as unrequited transfers.

Migrants' transfers represent a particular type of unrequited transfer. When a person migrates from an economy to a new economy, the property (real and financial resources) owned by the migrant also gets transferred to the new economy. As this is a one sided transaction, it is treated as an unrequited transfer. In principle, this transaction includes all the migrants' property whether or not it accompanies him.

Undistributed Income Attributable to Direct Investors

Retained earnings of an enterprise are owned by its equity holders. The retained earnings are reinvested in the enterprise. That part of such earnings which is attributable to non-resident equity holders need to be recorded in balance of payments. Such retained earnings/reinvested earnings are conceived as a payment of income to the foreign investor and a simultaneous reinvestment of that income by the foreign investor in the same enterprise. In the balance of payments statistics, such retained earnings attributable to direct investors are recorded as a component of foreign investment income receipts/payments in the current account matched by an outflow/inflow of direct foreign investment in the capital account.

Double Entry System of Recording

The balance of payments is built on double entry system of book-keeping. Similar to that used in business accounting. This is an internationally accepted convention for balance of payments compilation. Transactions in a double entry accounting system are recorded in pairs of credit and debit entries of equal value. In an accounting sense, therefore, a country's balance of payments is always in balance. As most of the entries in the balance of payments refer to transactions which have economic values, the counterpart entries for credits or debits are automatically paired.

Valuation

As every transaction has a credit and a debit aspect due to adoption of double entry recording assumes significance. If they are not valued at the same price, the balance of payments statement would not balance. Need for uniform valuation arises *firstly* because the credit and debit aspects are often derived independently from separate sources. *Secondly*, without the uniform valuation system, different items in the balance of payments cannot be compared with each other. *Thirdly*, balance of payments statements of different countries will not be comparable unless every country adopts a uniform valuation procedure. The IMF has, therefore, recommended in the *Balance of Payments Manual* that "market prices" be used for valuing transactions.

Generally, the value of merchandise transactions recorded in India's balance of payments represents the actual price paid through the banking channel, as required under the *Exchange Control Manual* of the Reserve Bank of India. However, it may not always be possible to value transactions at market price. For example, valuation of issue of shares against import of machinery and technical know-how may not be at the market price. Transactions between a branch and its parents office may not necessarily be at a market price. Further, exports could be undervalued or imports overvalued. Alternatively, exports could also be overvalued (to take advantage of export incentives) or imports undervalued (to benefit from import duty on lower base value). In all such cases, it may not be possible to ascertain the market price. In the case of non-merchandise items, transactions are recorded in balance of payments at the price reported by transactors to authorised dealers while putting through the financial transactions.

Another aspect of the valuation of merchandise transactions is that both exports and imports are to be valued f.o.b. at the customs frontier of the exporter's country. In India's balance of payments statistics, exports are valued on f.o.b. basis at the port of shipment. In the case of imports, they are valued on c.i.f. basis, which also covers cost of insurance and freight borne by the importer, as it is not possible to segregate cost of shipment services.

Still another problem arises in regard to valuation of transactions originally denominated in foreign currencies. Such transactions are to be converted into domestic currency at the market rates of exchange prevailing on the date of transaction.

Timing

In order to avoid discrepancies in the two sides of balance of payments statements, both sides of the transaction that may be registered using different data sources, are required to be recorded in the same period in the balance of payments statistics. In accordance with this principle, the uniform time of recording the current account transactions is conceived of as the time when legal ownership of goods of services change. In the case of capital account transactions, by convention, the change of ownership takes place at the time when transactions are effected through banking channel.

DIFFERENCE BETWEEN BALANCE OF PAYMENTS DATA AND CUSTOMS DATA

There have all along been differences in the data on merchandise trade between the balance of payments statistics published by the Reserve Bank of India (RBI) and the customs data on trade published by the Directorate General of Commercial Intelligence and Statistics (DGCI&S). The RBI figures, particularly of imports, tend to be higher than those of the DGCI&S. These differences arise due to differences in coverage, valuation and timing.

Coverage: For various reasons, the coverage of transactions in the two sets of data are not the same. For example, the RBI data cover exports by parcel post fully while these exports are not fully covered by the DGCI&S. Similarly, trade with Nepal and Bhutan is covered by the DGCI&S while it is not covered under the RBI data as India does not maintain a balance of payments record in respect of Nepal or Bhutan.

Valuation: Relates mainly to the conversion procedure adopted in the two sets of data for converting trade data invoiced in foreign currencies into rupees. In the RBI data, both for exports and imports, values in foreign currencies are converted at average exchange rate for the respective month, while in the DGCI&S data they are converted at rates notified by the Ministry of Commerce which are revised as and when there occurs a change of five per cent or more in the exchange rate of the rupee.

Timing: Differences in timing between the two sets of figures arise because a given set of transactions does not enter the two records at the same time. In the customs data, exports are recorded on the basis of shipment of goods while imports are recorded on the basis of arrival of goods and their clearance from the customs. In the RBI data, exports are booked on the basis of GR/PP original forms which are export declarations (although they are adjusted for short and shut-out shipments). There is always a timing difference of around three to four weeks between the export declarations and actual shipment of goods in respect of those declarations. In the RBI data imports are booked on the basis of payments made, i.e., when exchange is sold to the importers or transferred to the foreigners. Payment for goods and the arrival of goods may not take place at the same time.

Additional factors accounting for the difference, which are specific to imports, are given below:

(a) Lead in Payment

In regard to suppliers' credits and import of machinery and equipment on a cash payment basis, importers are required to make advance payments of 10-15 per cent. These are covered in the RBI data as import payments, while in the DGCI&S statistics, imports of such capital goods will be booked only when these arrive in the country. In a period of rising imports, this may cause a lead in payments for imports.

(b) Ships and Aircrafts

Payments made for the acquisition of mobile equipment (such as ships and aircrafts) are fully covered in the RBI data, while in the DGCI&S data, till recently, they were covered if and when they arrived at the Indian customs frontiers. Thus, value of ships acquired at foreign shipyards, kept abroad for repairs, etc., or used for carrying goods in international waters, are not included in the DGCI&S data. However, these data are now being compiled by the DGCI&S and presented as Appendix.

(c) Defence Stores

For security reasons, customs (DGCI&S) statistics do not cover import of items of defence stores while the RBI data cover the same as these imports are paid for and the RBI data on imports are based on payments made.

(d) Imports Under External Assistance and Commercial Borrowings

In regard to the payments for imports under the above borrowings, imports are recorded in the RBI data at the time when payments are made to suppliers. In the DGCI&S data, such imports are reflected at the time when the goods arrive into the country. This also causes a lead in payments in RBI data.

(e) Further, *imports not requiring customs clearance* are not covered in the DGCI&S data, while they would get reflected in the RBI data if they are paid for.

INTERNATIONAL ECONOMIC LINKAGES

The analytical framework that links the international flow of goods, services, and capital to domestic economic behaviour consists of a set of basic *macroeconomic accounting identities*. These basic identities linking national economic activity with balance-of-payments account shows that a nation produces more than it spends will save more than it invests, export more than it imports, and wind up with a capital outflow. A nation that spends more than it produces will invest more than it saves, import more than it exports, and wind up with a capital inflow. Exhibit-1 show the macroeconomic accounting identities that links domestic spending and production to savings, consumption, and investment behaviour, and hence to the current-account and capital-account balances. By manipulating the equation shown in Exhibit-1, we can identify the nature of links between the Indian economy and the world economy and assess the effects on the domestic economy of international economic policies, and vice versa.

EXHIBIT-1

Basic Macroeconomic Accounting Identities: Linking National Economic Activity with Balance-of-Payments Accounts

	National Product (Y)	–	Total spending (E)
Minus	Spending for Consumption	minus	Spending for consumption
=	National Saving (S)	—	Investment in new real assets (I_d)
=	Net foreign investment, or net increase in claims on foreigners and official reserve assets, e.g., gold (I_d)		
	National products (Y)	—	Total spending (E)
minus	Spending on domestic goods and services		minus Spending on domestic goods and services
=	Export of goods and services (X) – Import of goods and services (M)		
=	Balance on current account		
=	(Balance on capital and official reserves accounts)		

$$Y - E = S - I_d = X - M = I_f$$

COPING WITH THE CAPITAL INFLOWS: ADJUSTMENT MIX POLICY

In recent years, capital inflows to some developing countries have increased sharply. This increase in capital inflows has provided much needed financing to increase the use of existing capacity and to increase investment level. Though it appears paradoxical but *too much* capital inflows to developing countries is a matter of concern because of the macroeconomic and other related effects that capital inflows could have on the recipient countries. Indeed, capital inflows could potentially be a problem if they are of a short-term nature and highly volatile. This type of inflow, also called hot money, is usually attracted by some imperfections or policy mistakes that create a large gap between domestic and expected devaluation-augmented foreign interest rates. This type of inflow could create undue instability in inflation rates and in the nominal and real exchange rates. If there are imperfections in capital markets and hysterisis type of effects in the export and import competition sectors, or real bankruptcy and reallocation costs, then these fluctuations could have important economic costs.

Not surprisingly, in many countries the economic authorities try to discourage hot money by lifting the imperfections that encourage them in the first place, or by controlling the side effects of capital inflows through different types of government intervention. Capital inflows of a more cyclical variety could also create cyclical fluctuations in the real exchange rate. The later could create difficulties to the tradable sectors and to overall macroeconomic management. This type of flow creates problems similar to the traditional Dutch disease problem of a mineral discovery.

What can be done to deal with the side effects of Capital Inflows? Many countries have tried to gain access to international capital flows while simultaneously protecting the macroeconomic situation from a large real appreciation and/or acceleration of inflation. To deal with these potential problems caused by capital inflows, countries can use either indirect methods, direct methods, or both.

Direct Methods

If capital inflows (due to their size or composition) are considered to create macroeconomic problems and are motivated by imperfections in the domestic financial markets, countries may try to eliminate the distortion causing the capital inflow. A type of distortion that encourages short-term capital inflows is, for example, keeping a high domestic interest rate while at the same time offering free currency risk protection through a swap facility at the central bank. Offering free deposit insurance at domestic commercial banks, along with a high domestic interest rate and a fixed nominal exchange rate, may also cause an increase in capital inflows.

Short-term speculative capital inflows (hot money) could also result from a restrictive monetary policy that accompany an expansionary fiscal policy. In the latter case, changing the policy mix toward a more restrictive fiscal policy and a less restrictive monetary policy by reducing domestic interest rates to a level closer to the sum of international interest rates and the expected rate of devaluation (that is, getting closer to the interest rate parity condition) reduces the incentives for the type of capital inflows that respond mainly to interest rate differentials and/or to the expectation of a future drop in domestic interest rates, that is, bank loans and portfolio investment.

If the ultimate cause of the increase in capital inflows could not be dealt with, and the country is concerned with the macroeconomic effects of capital inflows, it could try direct methods to control their size. Direct methods consist of imposing restrictions on capital inflows in order to reduce their amount. Measures include ceiling on foreign borrowing, minimum reserve requirements on foreign loans, and ceiling on foreign direct investment. The authorities could also try to reduce the size of the inflows through taxation of the flows with a Tobin-type interest rate equalisation tax. This measure works only in the short run as it is very difficult to have effective ways to control capital flows in the long run.

Indirect Methods

Indirect methods comprise the following:

i) Intervention.

Intervention is the purchase of foreign currency by the central bank in order to support the nominal exchange rate. It can be of two types: *sterilised* and *nonsterilised*. In the case of sterilised intervention, the central bank also carries out open market operations to mop up the liquidity created by the initial purchase of foreign exchange. The sterilisation could also be done by imposing other restrictions that work through a reduction in the money multiplier—such as an increase in commercial banks' required reserves or a ceiling in total commercial effect of the purchase of foreign currency (that is, limits the increase in the money supply). However, the room in this area is limited by the degree of substitution between foreign and domestic assets. In a fixed exchange rate or preannounced nominal exchange rate regime, the more open the capital account is and the higher the degree of substitution between domestic and foreign assets is, the less effective is this policy. This policy also usually increases the quasi-fiscal deficit of the central bank. In countries with a level of output close to the potential output, nonsterilised intervention is usually implemented with another policy to restrain aggregate demand.

ii) Fiscal Adjustment

A restrictive fiscal policy is intended to have a macro effect and a composition effect. The first effect *(ceteris paribus)* attempts to counteract for the increase in aggregate demand created by capital inflows. The second effect helps to keep a higher real exchange rate than otherwise, as government consumption is most likely more intensive in tradable goods than private expenditures.

iii) Current Account Liberalisation

The liberalisation of the current account helps to ease the pressure on the domestic economy by shifting consumption toward tradable (that is, importable and exportable) goods. Like a restrictive fiscal policy, it has a composition effect and helps to keep a higher real exchange rate than otherwise possible.

iv) Capital Outflow Liberalisation

The liberalisation of capital outflows may induce domestic investors, to take their capital abroad. This may partially compensate for the effects of capital inflows.

v) Move Toward a Floating Exchange Rate System

By moving closer to a floating exchange rate regime, such as widening the band in a target-zone exchange-rate system, the exchange-rate risk faced by market participants increases. Therefore, there will be less interest in bringing short-term capital inflows.

USES OF THE BALANCE OF PAYMENTS

In recent years, the balance of payments has emerged as a major branch of economic enquiry. The interest in this subject is, in part, a reflection of the complex payments problems of the postwar years and, in part, the result of a greater appreciation of the implications of national economic measures of the external financial position of a country. Developments in the balance of payments are, therefore, of special concern to all those interested in the formulation of correct national economic policies.

The practical uses of a balance of payments statement are many. Apart from lending precision to a country's external transactions, it gives an idea of the historical influences governing the balance of payments. Data presented over a period of time provide a reliable basis for estimating the kind of relationship that exists between the balance of payments and the national income, and help to provide answers to such other questions as the seasonal and cyclical trends, and regional features of the transactions. The usefulness of a balance of payments statement as a guide to monetary, fiscal, trade and other policies cannot, therefore, be over-emphasised. A decision to raise the Bank Rate, for instance, inevitably involves an examination of the balance of payments. A tax measure on exports or on imports may affect the balance of payments similar to direct regulations of trade. Public investment policies too, have an important bearing on, and are, therefore, framed with reference to balance of payments. A decision to expand the capacity of an export industry has necessarily to be based, *inter alia,* on the foreign exchange earnings of the industry. Similarly, development of facilities for foreign tourists requires a knowledge of their expenditure patterns and the contribution of tourism to the economy of the country providing the facilities. The balance of payments also assists in assessing a country's ability to pay for current goods and services and of its credit-worthiness to borrow abroad and repay the loans.

A major contribution to the development of standard compilation techniques for balance of payments statistics came from the International Monetary Fund, a specialised agency of the UN operating in the monetary and exchange field. India is one of the members of the IMF. Among the various obligations imposed by the membership of the institution is one which requires every member to submit periodic reports on the balance of payments to the IMF. To facilitate a consistent system of international reporting, the IMF, has also developed a "Balance of Payments Manual."

Compilation of balance of payments was not entirely a new technique to India. During the per-war years, India had, in fact, compiled certain estimates of balance of payments for the use of the League of Nations which had assumed responsibility for the dissemination of data on the international transactions of the individual countries before the setting up of the IMF. In the pre-war estimates of India's balance of payments, a large part of the invisible transactions remained unrecorded and the compilations lacked certain essentials of a modern balance of payments statement. A systematic compilation of India's balance of payments commenced only in 1948 for meeting the growing official demands for statistics in this field and for fulfilling the country's obligations to the IMF.

There is an obvious relationship between the balance of payments and the national income, since the latter, providing as it does a measure of a country's total economic transactions, includes also the activities of the residents transcending the national boundaries. The contribution of the balance of payments to, or its draft on the flow of national income will equal the difference between the exports and imports of goods and services. Other relationships between the balance of payments and the national income have also been gaining increasing attention in recent years. Mention may be made here, in passing, of such relationships as the propensity to import, the income elasticity of imports, the foreign trade multiplier and the foreign trade accelerator. In the context of the development that has been planned in India, studies of these relationships would gain in importance.

BALANCE OF PAYMENT: RECENT TRENDS IN INDIA

Emerging market economies like India were not significantly affected by the global financial crisis in the initial stages, which had set in around August 2007. In fact, the initial effect of the global financial crisis was positive, as India received huge Foreign Institutional Investment (FII) inflows of US$ 22.5 billion during September 2007 to January 2008, as against US$ 11.8 billion during April-July 2007. This contributed to the debate on "decoupling", where it was believed that the emerging economies might remain largely insulated from the crisis and provide an alternative engine of growth to the world economy. The argument was proved unfounded as the global financial crisis intensified and spread to emerging economies through capital and current account routes of the balance of payments (BoP).

The global crisis began to impact emerging market economies through slowing down and reversal of capital flows. The portfolio flows to India (net) turned negative due to sale of equity stakes by Foreign Institutional Investors (FIIs) to replenish overseas cash balances. This had knock-on effect on the stock market and the exchange rates through creating a supply-demand imbalance in the foreign exchange market.

India's external sector exhibited resilience during the global financial crisis of 2008. The balance of payments however has been under increasing stress recently. Exports have declined while imports have not fallen significantly, resulting in increasing trade and current account deficits. Though capital flows are bridging the gap, the nature of portfolio capital may lead to greater potential financial fragility and also rupee volatility. India's growing external exposures can also be attributed to the increasing integration of the Indian economy with the rest of the world, which is reflected in both current and capital account transactions. The combined share of exports and imports of goods increased from 14.2 per cent of GDP in 1990-91 to about 43.0 per cent in 2011-12. Two way external sector transactions (i.e, gross current account plus gross capital account flows) have risen from 30.6 per cent of GDP in 1990-91 to about 108.0 per cent in 2011-12. Therefore, while the globalization of Indian economy has helped raise growth, it has also meant greater vulnerability to external shocks.

Table 1 shows that India's balance of payments continued to be under stress. This is reflected in the higher current account deficit in H1 (April-September) of 2012-13 than the corresponding period of the previous year, mainly due to worsening of trade deficit reflected in sharper decline in exports than the imports and lower invisibles surplus. The net capital flows in absolute term, were also lower during H1 of 2012-13 vis-a-vis the corresponding period of 2011-12.

TABLE 1

Balance of Payments : Summary (US$ million)

Sl. No.	*Item*	*2007-08*	*2008-09*	*2009-10*	*2010-11[PR]*	*2011-12[P]*	*2011-12 H1 (April-Sept. 2011)PR*	*2012-13 H1 (April-Sept. 2012)P*
1	2	3	4	5	6	7	8	9
I.	Current Account							
	1. Exports	166,162	189,001	182,442	256,159	309,774	158,202	146,549
	2. Imports	257,629	308,520	300,644	383,481	499,533	247,739	237,221
	3. Trade Balance	-91,467	-119,519	-118,203	-127,322	-189,759	-89,537	-90,672
	4. Invisibles (net)	75,731	91,604	80,022	79,269	111,604	53,103	51,699
	A Non-factor Services	38,853	53,916	36,016	44,081	64,098	30,409	29,572
	B Income	-5,068	-7,110	-8,038	-17,952	-15,988	-7,587	-10,510
	C Transfers	41,945	44,798	52,045	53,140	63,494	30,281	32,637
	5. Goods and Services Balance	-52,614	-65,603	-82,187	-83,241	-125,661	-59,128	-61,100
	6. Current Account Balance	-15,737	-27,914	-38,181	-48,053	-78,155	-36,433	-38,973
II	Capital Account							
	Capital Account Balance	106,585	7,395	51,634	63,740	67,755	43,490	39,989
	i. External Assistance (net)	2,114	2,439	2,890	4,941	2,296	640	15
	ii. External Commercial Borrowings (net)	22,609	7,861	2,000	12,160	10,344	8,388	1,726
	iii. Short-term debt	15,930	-1,985	7,558	12,034	6,668	5,940	9,511

iv. Banking Capital (net)]	11,759	-3,245	2,083	4,962	16,226	19,714	14,899
of which:							
Non-Resident Deposits (net)	179	4,290	2,922	3,238	11,918	3,937	9,397
v. Foreign Investment (net)	43,326	8,342	50,362	42,127	39,231	17,087	18,608
of which:							
A FDI (net)	15,893	22,372	17,966	11,834	22,061	15,741	12,812
B Portfolio (net)	27,433	-14,030	32,396	30,293	17,170	1,346	5,796
vi. Other Flows (net)	10,847	-6,016	-13,259	-12,484	-7,008	-8,278	-4,769
III Errors and Omission	1,316	440	-12	-2,636	-2,432	-1,338	-653
IV Overall Balance	92,164	-20,080	13,441	13,050	-12,831	5,719	363
V Reserves change							
[increase (-) / decrease (+)]	-92,164	20,080	-13,441	-13,050	12,831	-5,719	-363

Source: RBI. PR : Partially Revised. P : Preliminary.

Current Account

The current account of the BoP includes all the transaction (other than those in financial items) involving exchange of economic value which takes place between resident and non-resident entities. During 2011-12, exports crossed the US$ 300 billion mark for the first time. The rate of growth however, declined to 20.9 per cent to US$ 309.8 billion against 40.5 per cent (US$ 256.2 billion) in 2010-11. Exports at US$ 158.2 billion performed well in first half (H1–April-September 2011) of 2011- 12 vis-a-vis exports of US$112.0 billion in H1 of 2010- 11. There was, however, significant deceleration in exports during second half (H2- October 2011 – March 2012) of 2011-12 to US$ 151.6 billion (US$ 144.2 billion in H2 of 2010-11). This was on account of deterioration in global trading conditions reflecting weakening of world demand inter-alia caused by euro zone crisis. Imports valued at US$ 499.5 billion, recorded 30.3 per cent increase in 2011-12 over US$ 383.5 billion in 2010-11. The growth in imports during 2011-12 was mainly due to higher growth in imports of petroleum, oil and lubricants (POL), gold and silver and machinery. Oil imports grew by about 47 per cent, while gold and silver registered a growth of 49 per cent in 2011-12. Imports of oil and precious metal (gold and silver) together accounted for nearly 45 per cent of total imports in 2011-12. The trade deficit increased to US$ 189.8 billion (10.2 per cent of GDP) in 2011-12 as compared to US$ 127.3 billion (7.4 per cent of GDP) during 2010-11. Higher growth in imports than exports was responsible for the widening of the trade deficit in 2011-12.

The net invisible balances showed significant improvement, registering 40.7 per cent increase to US$ 111.6 billion during 2011-12 from US$ 79.3 billion in 2010-11, due to increase in invisibles receipts while invisible payments witnessed a decline. The invisible receipts increased by 15.1 per cent to US$ 219.2 billion in 2011-12 as compared to US$ 190.5 billion during 2010-11, mainly driven by services exports (comprising travel, transportation, insurance, Government not included elsewhere (GNIE), software and non-software), which recorded a growth of 14.2 per cent during 2011-12 (as against of 29.8 per cent in 2010-11). Invisibles payments decreased by 3.2 per cent to US$ 107.6 billion during 2011-12 (US$ 111.2 billion during 2010-11), mainly reflecting lower services payments.

Services exports increased to US$ 142.3 billion in 2011-12 from US$ 124.6 in 2010-11. Though the increase in services exports was broad-based, it was more prominent in case of insurance, transportation, travel and software services. Receipts on account of software services witnessed a rise, mainly on account of improved efficiency and diversified exports destinations. Software receipts at US$ 62.2 billion, accounting for nearly 43.7 per cent of total services receipts, showed an increase of 17.1 per cent in 2011-12. Payment on account of services imports witnessed a decline from US$ 80.6 billion in 2010-11 to US$ 78.2 billion in 2011-12, primarily on account of decline in the imports of business and software services.

Among other components of invisibles, transfers, mainly representing private transfers (secondary income as per BPM 6) recorded a significant increase while income (primary income as per BPM 6) showed a decline. Net private transfer receipts, which basically comprise remittances from Indians working overseas increased by 18.9 per cent to US$ 66.1 billion in 2011-12 from US$ 55.6 billion in the previous year. Increase in private transfers could be attributed to depreciation of rupee in the recent period. In contrast, income (net) showed an outflow of US$ 16.0 billion albeit marginally lower than the preceding year. Overall, gross invisible receipts, showed a sharp rise of 15.1 per cent in 2011-12. Invisible payments declined by 3.2 per cent to US$ 107.6 billion in 2011-12 from US$ 111.2 billion in 2010-11. The decline in payments was mainly on account of lower imports of software and business services and investment income payments. Net invisible balance as per cent of GDP improved to 6.0 per cent in 2011-12 from 4.6 per cent in 2010-11.

The Goods and Services deficit (i.e. Trade Balance plus Services) increased substantially by 51.1 per cent to US$ 125.7 billion (6.7 per cent of GDP) during 2011-12 as compared to US$ 83.2 billion (4.9 per cent of GDP) during 2010-11. The CAD widened to its highest ever level both in absolute terms as well as a proportion of GDP in 2011-12. The CAD in 2011-12 at US$ 78.2 billion was 4.2 per cent of GDP as compared with US$ 48.1 billion or 2.8 per cent of GDP in 2010-11.

In the first Half (H1 - April-September 2012) of 2012-13, there was a steep decline in exports to US$ 146.5 billion, registering a 7.4 per cent decline over US$ 158.2 billion in H1 of 2011-12. Commodity-wise data show that growth in exports of engineering goods, petroleum products, textile products, gems & jewellery and chemical & related products were severely affected as the demand conditions in key markets like the US and Europe continued to remain sluggish. During H1 of 2012-13, EU accounted for nearly 27 per cent of the total decline in merchandise exports, followed by Singapore (19 per cent), China (13 per cent) and Indonesia (6 per cent). Lower growth in export oriented Asian economies caused by setbacks to the global recovery has clearly weighed on India's external demand from these economies. Detailed analysis is given in the chapter on international trade. Like exports, there was decline of 4.2 per cent in imports to US$ 237.2 billion in H1 of 2012-13 from US$ 247.7 billion during the corresponding period in previous year. The steep fall in exports than that in imports was responsible for widening of trade deficit to US$ 90.7 billion (10.8 per cent of GDP) in H1 of 2012-13 vis-à-vis US$ 89.5 billion (9.9 per cent of GDP) in H1 of 2011-12.

During H1 (April-September 2012) of 2012-13, net surplus under invisibles showed a decline of 2.6 per cent as outflows on account of payments under invisibles increased considerably. Growth in invisible receipts decelerated to 4.7 per cent, mainly due to lower growth in exports of services, private transfers and decline in investment income. Lower growth in exports of software services accompanied by decline in exports of travel, transport and insurance services led to a growth of 4.3 per cent in service exports in H1 of 2012-13, substantially lower than 22.7 per cent in the corresponding period of 2011-12. Lower growth in receipts under invisibles was also caused by lower growth in private transfers and decline in income receipts. Within income receipts, investment income declined by 19.1 per cent to US$ 3.5 billion during H1 of 2012-13 reflecting the lower level of interest rates abroad. In contrast to lower growth in receipts under invisibles, payments under invisibles recorded an increase of 12.3 per cent in H1 of 2012-13, as against a decline of 0.8 per cent in H1 of 2011-12. In particular, payment on account of business services showed a sharp increase as compared with a decline in H1 of 2011-12. Investment income payments rose by 17.6 per cent to US$ 14.5 billion during H1 of 2012-13 on account of rising external liabilities. Net secondary income receipts, which primarily comprise private transfers, increased by 8.2 per cent to US$ 32.9 billion during H1 of 2012-13 compared to US$ 30.4 billion a year ago. During H1 of 2012-13, net invisible balance declined to US$ 51.7 billion (6.2 per cent of GDP) from US$ 53.1 billion (5.9 per cent of GDP) in H1 of 2011-12.

Goods and Services deficit at US$ 61.1 billion in H1 of 2012-13 recorded an increase of 3.4 per cent from US$ 59.1 billion during H1 of 2011-12. India's CAD worsened further in H1; CAD was US$ 39.0 billion (4.6 per cent of GDP) during H1 of 2012-13 as compared to US$ 36.4 billion (4.0 per cent of GDP) in H1 of 2011-12. Besides global factors, the increase in the CAD to GDP ratio was also because of slower GDP growth and its contraction in dollar terms due to the depreciation of rupee (Box 1).

BOX 1

Impact of Euro Zone Crisis on Current Account

The unfolding of euro zone crisis, the austerity measures in advanced economies, recession in many euro zone countries, risk on/ risk off behaviour of investors and the uncertainty surrounding the future of euro zone have adversely affected the global economy.

The fallout for the Indian economy has been a sharp deceleration in exports and a slowdown in GDP growth. Import demand however has remained resilient because of the continued high international oil prices that did not decline, unlike what happened after the Lehman meltdown of September, 2008. The high value of gold imports, driven mainly by the 'safe haven' demand for gold that has led to a sharp rise in prices, contributed to the high import bill and widening of the trade deficit.

The trade deficit, as a result, increased to US$ 189.8 billion in 2011-12, which was 10.2 per cent of the GDP. With invisible surplus of US$ 111.6 billion (6.0 per cent of GDP), the current account deficit widened to record 4.2 per cent of GDP. This is unlike the situation during the 2008 crisis, when the high trade deficit of 9.8 per cent of GDP in 2008-09, was partly offset by an invisible surplus of 7.5 per cent, lowering CAD to 2.3 per cent of GDP.

The signs of strain on BoP continued in the first half of 2012-13 (April-September 2012) with the trade deficit of US$ 90.7 billion increasing to 10.8 per cent of GDP and CAD of US$ 39.0 billion at 4.6 per cent of GDP. The high CAD has had implications for rupee volatility and business confidence in the economy. A positive development is that high CAD has lately been financed by capital inflows, which explains why the downhill movement of rupee, witnessed till July 2012, has been largely arrested. There has however been high dependence on volatile portfolio flows and external commercial borrowings.

This makes capital account vulnerable to a 'reversal' and 'sudden stop' of capital, especially in times of stress.

As per the latest data available from the Ministry of Commerce, exports of US$ 214.1 billion during April-December 2012, registered a decline of 5.5 per cent over export of US$ 226.6 billion during the same period in 2011-12. Imports of US$ 361.3 billion recorded a marginal decline of 0.7 per cent during April-December 2012 over the figure of US$ 363.9 billion during the corresponding period of previous year. As a result of steeper decline in exports than imports, trade deficit increased by 7.2 per cent to US$ 147.2 billion during April-December 2012 as compared to US$ 137.3 billion in April December 2011.

Capital Account and Financial Account

The capital account comprises capital transfers receivable and payable between residents and non-residents and the acquisition and disposal of non-produced non-financial assets between residents and nonresidents. The financial account records transactions relating to financial assets and liabilities and that take place between residents and non-residents. Some of the major components of financial accounts include direct investment, portfolio investment, financial derivates (other than reserves) and employees stock options, other investments, reserve assets (monetary gold), equity and investment fund shares, debt instruments and other financial assets and liabilities.

The overall balance on the financial account is called net lending/net borrowing depending on the outflow or inflow of resources. The capital account showed a small outflow of US$ 0.06 billion in 2011-12 vis-à-vis inflow of US$ 0.04 billion in 2010-11. In the first half of 2012-13, there was also an outflow of US$ 0.5 billion. During 2011-12, both gross inflows of US$ 478.8 billion and outflows of US$ 411.1 billion under the capital account (old format) were lower than those of US$ 503.7 billion and US$ 439.9 billion in the preceding year 2010-11. However, net inflows of US$ 67.8 billion under the capital account (bifurcated into capital account and financial account under BPM6) were moderately higher than that of US$ 63.7 billion in 2010-11. This was primarily on account of a revival in FDI flows to India, a surge in NRI deposits and higher overseas borrowings by banks. However, there was a decline in inflows under FII investments, ADRs/ GDRs, external assistance, ECBs and short term trade credit. Risk on/risk off behaviour significantly influenced capital flows (Box 2) to India.

BOX 2

Risk on/Risk off Behaviour and Capital Flows to India

The main fallout of euro zone crisis is global uncertainty. This has led to investors' alternating between risk-on/risk-off behaviour, with consequent implications for surge and reversal of capital to emerging economies. A risk-on, prompted by new policy initiatives, creates a favourable disposition towards emerging economy investment, leading to surge in FIIs flows and vice versa.

While change in investor attitude is generally observable in the long-run, the fallout of euro zone crisis has been quick shift between risk-on/risk-off behaviour that has immediate implications for capital flows. An additional factor has been quantitative easing in the US. This increases the supply of liquidity in the system and together with low interest environ and better growth prospects in emerging economies, contributes to increase in capital flows.

A closer look at the global risk-on/off events and FII flows to India shows strong correlation between such events and surge and reversal of capital. For example, the US credit rating downgrade in early August 2011, together with worsening of euro crisis, created a risk-off environment. As a result, there was net withdrawal of FII investment of US$ 3.7 billion during August-October, 2011.

The Long Term Refinancing Operation (LTRO) of European Central Bank that injected more than euro 1 trillion in the banking system in two tranche in December, 2011 and February, 2012 again created a risk-on environ. As a result, there was a net FII inflow of US$ 16.9 billion during December 2011-February 2012. The investor euphoria soon evaporated as the euro crisis worsened and the spectre of Greek exit loomed. Consequently, the investor behaviour again became risk-off, leading to net FII outflow of US$ 2.3 billion during March-June 2012.

The investment climate began improving in July, 2012 with (i) announcement by European Central Bank President that the euro would be saved at all cost; (ii) proposal to set-up Banking Union in the euro zone; (iii) launch of permanent European Stability Mechanism and (iv) launch of QE3 in US. The resulting risk-on atmosphere has seen a net FII inflow of US$ 10.8 billion during July-October, 2012.

Even though the FDI to India (inward FDI) of US$ 33.0 billion in 2011-12 was significantly higher than US$ 29.0 billion in the preceding year, net inflows on account of portfolio investments at US$ 17.4 billion were lower as compared to US$ 31.5 billion in 2010-11 reflecting trend towards risk aversion among FIIs due to global economic uncertainty. Rise in inward FDI reflected flows received under BPReliance deal of US$ 7.0 billion in 2011-12. Sectorwise, manufacturing, construction, financial services, business services and communication services received significant amount of inflows. Country-wise, investment routed through Mauritius remained, as in the past, the largest component, followed by Singapore and the UK. FDI by India (i.e., outward FDI) in net terms moderated by 37.0 per cent to US$ 10.9 billion in 2011-12 compared to US$ 17.2 billion a year ago. Sector-wise, moderation in outward FDI was observed in agriculture, hunting, forestry & fishing, financial insurance, real estate & business services, manufacturing and wholesale, retail trade, restaurants & hotels. Furthermore, sectors, viz. financial, insurance, real estate & business services and manufacturing continued to account for more than 50 per cent of total outward FDI during 2011-12. Net FDI (inward FDI minus outward FDI) at US$ 22.1 billion in 2011-12 showed a significant increase of about 87.0 per cent as against US$ 11.8 billion in 2010-11.

Among the debt creating capital flows, net flows under NRI deposits of US$ 11.9 billion surged more than three-fold in 2011-12 vis-à-vis US$ 3.2 billion in 2010-11 because of the higher interest rates prevailing in India. Net flows under external commercial borrowing and trade credit showed a decline in 2011-12 vis-à-vis 2010-11. In net terms, capital inflows increased moderately by 6.4 per cent to US$ 67.8 billion (3.6 per cent of GDP) in 2011-12 as compared with US$ 63.7 billion (3.7 per cent of GDP) during 2010-11. Since net capital inflows were inadequate to finance the higher CAD recorded during 2011-12, there was a net drawdown of foreign exchange reserves to the extent of US$ 12.8 billion during the same period.

Both gross inflows of US$ 219.5 billion and outflows of US$ 179.5 billion under the financial account were lower in H1 of 2012-13 as compared with gross inflow of US$ 246.4 billion and outflow of US$ 202.9 billion in the same period a year ago. In net terms also, financial inflows declined to US$ 40.0 billion in H1 of 2012-13 as against US$ 43.5 billion in H1 of 2011-12. As regards the pattern of capital inflows during H1 of 2012-13, there has been a mixed trend. Inward FDI to India at US$ 16.2 billion during H1 of 2012-13 decreased by 26.0 per cent compared to US$ 21.9 billion in H1 of 2011-12. Outward FDI by India was US$ 3.4 billion in April-September 2012 as against the US$ 6.1 billion in April-September 2011. The net FDI (inward minus outward) to India was US$ 12.8 billion during first half of 2012-13 vis-avis US$ 15.7 billion during the corresponding period of previous year. However, recent measures taken by Government regarding liberalisation of FDI limits are likely to improve investment sentiment and to boost FDI flows into the Indian economy. Scope for further liberalization of FDI norms however remains (Box 3).

BOX 3

Liberalization of FDI Norms

Foreign Direct Investment (FDI) is preferred to the foreign portfolio investments primarily because FDI is expected to bring modern technology, managerial practices and is long term in nature investment. The Government has liberalized FDI norms overtime. As a result, only a handful of sensitive sectors now fall in the prohibited zone and FDI is allowed fully or partially in the rest of the sectors.

Despite successive moves to liberalize the FDI regime, India is ranked fourth on the basis of FDI Restrictiveness Index (FRI) compiled by OECD. FRI gauges the restrictiveness of a country's FDI rules by looking at the four main types of restrictions viz. foreign equity limitations; screening or approval mechanism; restrictions on the employment of foreigners as key personnel; and operational restrictions. A score of 1 indicates a closed economy and 0 indicates openness. FRI for India in 2012 was 0.273 (it was 0.450 in 2006 and 0.297 in 2010) as against OECD average of 0.081. China is the most restrictive country as it is ranked number one with the score of 0.407 in 2012 indicating that it has more restriction than India. As there is moderation in FDI inflows to India in the current fiscal vis-à-vis last year it is imperative therefore to rationalize FDI norms further.

At present, defence sector is open to FDI subject to 26 per cent cap. It also requires FIPB approval and is subject to licensing under Industries (Development & Regulation) Act, 1951 and guidelines on FDI in production of arms & ammunition. Within the 26 per cent cap, FII is also permissible subject to the proviso that overall cap is not breached. India needs to open up the defence production sector to get access and ensure transfer of technology. The existing FDI policy for defence sector provides for offsets policy. The offsets policy has been revised recently but its direct and indirect benefits have not had visible impact on the domestic defence industry. There is a strong case for a hike in the 26 per cent FDI limit in the defence production sector. By beginning to produce defence goods that advanced countries currently produce, there is scope for productivity improvement, strengthening of manufacturing, generation of employment and lowering of imports in the country.

There is need to review increasing of FDI cap in insurance and public sector banks. By raising cap to 49 per cent in the insurance sector, there is scope for substantial growth in the coming years. Competition and adoption of best practices could strengthen this sector, reduce the premium and expand the services to the vast untapped rural India. This sector could be one of the major sources of long-term investment in infrastructure. Similarly, FDI limit in public sector banks could be increased to 26 per cent. Further, there is also a need to review existing approval mechanisms, operational restrictions and conditions in other sectors to attract foreign investment.

Net portfolio flows including FIIs showed a quantum jump to US$ 5.8 billion during H1 of 2012-13 as against US$ 1.3 billion in H1 of 2011-12. Among debt creating flows, NRI deposits remained robust at US$ 9.4 billion in H1 of 2012-13 (US$ 3.9 billion in H1 of 2011-12) but net flows under ECBs declined sharply by about 80.0 per cent to US$ 1.7 billion during H1 of 2012-13 from US$ 8.4 billion in H1 of 2011-12. However, unlike in H1 of 2011-12, net flows under trade credit showed an increase of nearly 60 per cent to US$ 9.5 billion during April-September 2012 as against US$ 5.9 billion during the corresponding period of 2011-12. Net accretion to reserves (on a BoP basis) during H1 of 2012-13 at 0.4 billion was substantially lower as compared to US$ 5.7 billion in H1 of previous year.

As per the latest available information on capital inflows, FDI flows to India stood at US$ 22.2 billion during April-December 2012, which is 22.1 per cent lower than US$ 28.5 billion during April-December 2011. Up to December 2012, net FII flows amounted to at US$ 16.0 billion (US$ 2.7 billion during the corresponding period of 2011-12). FII flows in recent months witnessed improvement, reflecting the impact of various reform measures announced by the Government.

QUESTIONS

1. Discuss the concept of balance-of-payments. Critically examine the various methods of compilation of statistics of balance-of-payments.
2. Why should a government concern about the increase in capital inflows?
3. Discuss the analytical framework that links international flow of goods, services, and capital to domestic economic behaviour.
4. Distinguish between balance of trade and balance of payments. Discuss the macroeconomic and other related effects of capital inflows.
5. Discuss some of the selected key economic indicators of Indian external sector and fastest growing export and import commodities.
6. Differentiate between balance of payment data and customs data. Discuss the international environment factors which carries potential downside risks for the balance-of-payments outlook.
7. Dissuss the various uses of the balance of payments in economic enquiry.
8. Discuss the rationale of policy adjustment mix to capital inflows.

REFERENCES

Agmon Tamir, and Donald Lessard, "Investor recognition of corporate international diversification", *Journal of Finance*, 32 (September 1977), pp.1049- 1055

Bhalla, V.K., *Managing International Investment and Finance*, Anmol Publication Pvt. Ltd., New Delhi, India, 1997.

———, International Economy: Liberalisation Process, Anmol Publication Pvt. Ltd., New Delhi, India, 1993.

Caves, R.E., and R.W. Jones, *World Trade and Payments*, Little, Brown, Boston: 1981.

Eaker, Mark R., "Denomination decision for multinational transactions", *Financial Management*, 9 (Autumn 1980), pp.23-29.

Eiteman, David K., Arthur I. Stonehill and Michael H. Moffett, *Multinational Business Finance*, sixth edition (Reading, Mass., Addison-Wesley, 1992), pp.493-494.

Gray, Peter H.: *International Trade, Investment, and Payments*, Houghton Mifflin, Proston, 1979

Grubel, Herbert G., "Internationally diversified portfolios: welfare gains and capital flows", *American Economic Review*, 58 (December 1968), pp. 1299-1314.

Lee, Wayne Y., and Kanwal S. Sachdeva, "The role of the multinational firm in the integration of segmented markets", Journal of Finance, 32 (May 1977), pp.479-492.

Root, F.R., *International Trade and Investment*, South-Western, 1984.

Walter, I., and K. Areskog, *International Economics*, John Wiley, N.Y., 1981.

37

MANAGING EXCHANGE RATE AND FOREX RESERVES

INTRODUCTION

The global financial crisis has had severe fall out for the economies worldwide. Almost every single economy now faces deceleration of varying magnitude in economic growth, increased unemployment, increased fiscal burden, heightened currency volatility and so on. The real sector developments are gloomy and challenging; but evolution of the price process in the financial markets worldwide during this period is truly interesting. Prior to the onset of the financial crisis, there was optimism all around; risks were underpriced and prices of all assets were moving heavenwards. As soon as the crisis broke out, markets crashed and prices bottomed out. The response of the monetary and fiscal authorities worldwide was swift and overwhelming. Consequently, the markets recovered sooner than expected, which however was short-lived as the Euro problem – the root of which lie partly in inherent structural problems of the union but also partly in the post-crisis fiscal response, threw the market into fresh turmoil that is yet to be resolved. The chapter focus is on management of foreign exchange rate and forex reserves.

DEFINITION OF FOREIGN EXCHANGE MARKET

The foreign exchange market is the market where one currency is traded for another. This market is somewhat similar to the over- the-counter market in securities. The trading in currencies is usually accomplished over the telephone or through the telex. With direct dialing telephone service anywhere in the world, foreign exchange markets have become truly global in the sense that currency transactions now require only a single telephone call and take place twenty-four hours per day. As banks end their regular business day in San Francisco and Los Angeles, they open in Singapore, Hong Kong, Sydney and Tokyo, and by the time the latter wind down their regular business day, banks open in London, Paris, Zurich, Frankfurt, and Milan; and before the latter close, New York and Chicago banks open. The different monetary centres are connected by a telephone network and video screens and are in constant contact with one another, thus forming a single international foreign exchange market. However, the currencies and the extent of the participation of each currency in this market depend on local regulations which vary from country to country.

MARKETS AND MARKET PARTICIPANTS

From ladder of transactions the participants can be identified in foreign exchange markets. At the base, or at the first level, are traditional users (such as tourists, importers, exporters and investors, who exchange domestic currency for foreign currencies and vice versa) as well as traders and speculators (individuals, investment managers, and corporate treasurers who trade currencies seeking short-term profits by betting on the direction of changes in their relative price). At the next or second level are the commercial banks, which act as clearing house between users and earners of foreign exchange. At third level are foreign exchange brokers, through whom the nation's commercial banks even out their foreign exchange inflow and outflows among themselves (the so-called interbank or wholesale market). Finally, at the top is the nation's central bank which acts as a seller or buyer of last resort when the nation's total foreign exchange earnings and expenditures are required. When the market rate of the currency reaches the upper lines ("upper intervention point") of the band, the central bank of that country must increase sales of its currency in exchange for other currencies. Similarly, the central bank must sell foreign exchange and buy its own currency when the market rate reaches the "lower intervention point".

FOREIGN EXCHANGE TRANSACTIONS

The most common type of foreign exchange transaction involves the payment and receipt of the foreign exchange within two business days after the day the transaction is agreed upon. The two-day period gives adequate time for the parties to send instructions to debit and credit the appropriate bank accounts at home and abroad and complete requirements under the forex regulations. This type of transaction is called a *spot transaction,* and the exchange rate at which the transaction takes place is called the *spot rate.* Besides spot transaction, there are *forward transactions.* A forward transaction involves an agreement today to buy or sell a specified amount of a foreign currency at a specified future date at a rate agreed upon today (the forward rate). The typical forward contracts is for one month; three months; or six months, with three months being most common. Forward contracts for longer periods are not as common because of the great uncertainties involved. However, forward contract can be renegotiated for one or more periods when they become due.

The equilibrium forward rate is determined at the intersection of the market demand and supply forces of foreign exchange for *future delivery.* The demand for and supply of forward foreign exchange arise in the course of hedging, from foreign exchange speculation, and from covered interest arbitrage.

FOREIGN EXCHANGE MARKET: A THREE-TIER STRUCTURE IN INDIA

The growing depth of the Indian forex market reflects essentially the result of the implementation of a number of recommendation of various study group. At present, the foreign exchange market in India is a three-tier structure comprising (a) the Reserve Bank at the apex, (b) Authorised Dealers (ADs) licensed by the Reserve Bank, and (c) customers such as exporters and importers, corporates and other foreign exchange earners. Apart from these main market players, there are foreign exchange money changers who bring buyers and sellers together but are not permitted to deal in foreign exchange on their own account. The ADs are governed by the guidelines framed by the Foreign Exchange Dealers Association of India (FEDAI). Dealing in the foreign exchange market include transactions between ADs and the exporters/importers and other customers, transactions among ADs themselves transactions with overseas bank and transactions between ADs and the Reserve Bank.

EXCHANGE RATE MANAGEMENT

The task of determining appropriate exchange rate and market intervention policies in extremely difficult for central banks all over the world. Though in principles, and in theory, there is a strong case for either freely floating exchange rates (without intervention) or a currency board type arrangement of fixed rates but in practice, however, because of the operational realities of foreign exchange markets, most countries have adopted intermediate regimes of various types including crawling pegs, fixed rates within bands, managed floats with no pre-announced path, and independent floats with market intervention moderating the rate of change and preventing undue fluctuations. By and large, most countries have some variety of "managed" floats and central banks intervene in the market periodically.

The exchange rate policy is guided by the broad principles of careful monitoring and management of exchange rates with flexibility, while allowing the underlying demand and supply conditions to determine the exchange rate movements over a period in a orderly manner. Subject to this predominant objective, intervention by the RBI in the foreign exchange market is guided by the objectives of reducing excess volatility, preventing the emergence of destablizing speculative activities, maintaining adequate level of reserves and developing an orderly foreign exchange market.

VOLATILITY IN THE FOREX MARKETS

Volatility is an unavoidable feature of all financial markets and heightened volatility in the forex market that we witness today is neither unprecedented nor unexpected.

All economic agents with currency risk will have to frame a conscious risk management policy to cope with the impact of the volatility on their cost, revenue and profit. Even as the Reserve Bank strives to maintain orderly conditions in the forex market, certain behavioral issues that tend to accentuate volatility have to be understood by all market participants and factored into their response and risk management strategy

India, around the onset of the crisis, inundated with capital flows and the Rupee had appreciated. It had touched a high of 39.27 in Nov 2007. As the crisis unfolded, the trend reversed and Rupee started depreciating and reached 52.06 in March 2009. The Rupee started correcting soon and for almost two years between Nov 2009 and Aug 2011, remained range-bound at 44-47 levels. Overall the movement of the exchange rate in 2011-12 indicates that the average monthly exchange rate of rupee against the US dollar depreciated by 10.6 per cent from ₹ 44.97 per US dollar in March 2011 to ₹ 50.32 per US dollar in March 2012. Similarly, on point-to-point basis, the average exchange rate of rupee (average of buying and selling rate of FEDAI) depreciated by 12.7 per cent from ₹ 44.65 per US dollar on 31 March 2011 to ₹ 51.16 per US dollar on March 30, 2012. The monthly average exchange rate of rupee vis-a-vis pound sterling, euro and Japanese yen also depreciated in 2011-12. The monthly average exchange rate of rupee vis-a-vis pound sterling depreciated by 8.7 per cent from ₹ 72.71 per pound sterling in March 2011 to ₹ 79.65 in March 2012. Similarly, monthly average exchange rate of rupee depreciated by 5.3 per cent from ₹ 62.97 in March 2011 to ₹ 66.48 in March 2012 against the euro and against the Japanese yen by 9.9 per cent from ₹ 54.98 per 100 Japanese yen in March 2011 to ₹ 61.03 per 100 Japanese yen in March 2012.

On an annual average basis, rupee depreciated against major international currencies in fiscal 2011-12. The annual average exchange rate of rupee was ₹ 45.56 per US dollar in 2010-11 that depreciated by 4.9 per cent to ₹ 47.92 per US dollar in 2011-12. Similarly, the annual average exchange rate of rupee in 2010-11 was ₹ 70.87 per pound sterling, ₹ 60.21 per euro, and ₹ 53.27 per 100 Japanese yen which depreciated by 7.2 per cent to ₹ 76.38 per pound sterling, 8.6 per cent to ₹ 65.88 per euro and 12.3 per cent to ₹ 60.73 per 100 Japanese yen respectively in 2011-12.

The sharp fall in value of rupee can be explained by the supply-demand imbalance in the domestic foreign exchange market on account of slowdown in FII inflows, strengthening of US dollar in the international market due to the safe haven status of US Treasuries and heightened risk aversion and deleveraging due to the euro area crisis that impacted financial markets across emerging market economies. Apart from the global factors, there were several domestic factors that have added to the weakening trend of the rupee, which include increasing current account deficit, high inflation (Box 1). In order to reduce the volatility of exchange rate value of the rupee, the RBI intervened in the foreign exchange market through sale of US dollars amounting to US$ 20.1 billion in 2011-12. Further, in view of the sharp depreciation of the rupee in

2011-12, the RBI announced various policy measures that were aimed at curbing speculative behaviour of banks and corporate in the foreign exchange market. A number of steps were also taken to facilitate capital flows and boost exports to augment supply of foreign exchange.

BOX 1

Reasons for High Volatility in Rupee Exchange Rate

The rupee has experienced unusually high volatility in the past few months. The currency touched the low of ₹ 57.22 per US dollar on 27th June, 2012, before appreciated to ₹ 51.62 per US dollar on October 05, 2012. It again began declining thereafter and has since been in the range of ₹ 53-54 per US dollar. Such volatility has introduced a measure of uncertainty in the domestic market and has impacted business confidence.

The rupee has been under pressure since August 2011, when US sovereign rating was downgraded and the euro zone crisis escalated. The currency went steadily downhill till the end of July, 2012, except for intermitted respite and appreciation in January-February 2012, mainly due to European Central Banks Long Term Refinancing Operation (LTRO) that injected more than euro 1 trillion in three-year loans to banks and created a risk-on environment.

The rupee fell due to decline in exports on account of euro-zone crisis and widening of trade deficit, as imports remained resilient due to high oil prices and gold imports. The widening of trade deficit to 10.2 per cent of GDP in 2011-12 had upset the supply-demand balance in the domestic foreign exchange market, placing downward pressure on the currency. The trade deficit has remained high at 10.8 per cent of GDP in the first six months of the current financial year (April-September 2012), with current account deficit at 4.6 per cent of GDP.

Improved capital flows in recent months, particularly FII flows, however have dampened the downward pressure on the rupee. Such an increase in portfolio flows is partly due to the risk-on behaviour of investors, following series of policy initiatives in the euro zone that lowered the `tail risk' of euro zone disintegration. The launch of quantitative easing (QE3) by the US Federal Reserve further helped the process. Capital flows have also been attracted by the confidence -inducing effects of major policy reforms that have been announced recently. The resulting increase in capital flows has more than balanced the widening current account deficit in recent months, curbing the rupee slide. Volatility however remains high because of high share of FII flows in total capital flows, and the week-to-week variation in such flows.

Another contributory factor is the fluctuation in the dollar exchange rate vis-a-vis other international currencies. Since bulk of global trade is invoiced and settled in US$ and most capital flows are denominated in US dollar, the volatility in the value of US dollar exchange rate in the international market has an immediate impact on rupee-US dollar exchange rate. Thus, the fall in the US dollar exchange rate in the international market leads to rupee appreciation, unless offset by widening trade deficit/ changes in the volume of capital flows and vice-versa.

In the current fiscal, the exchange rate value of rupee has so far undergone many ups and downs. The monthly average exchange rate of rupee per US dollar mostly remained in the range of ₹ 54-56 per US dollar except in the month of April 2012 when the rate was ₹ 51.81 and ₹ 53.02 in October 2012. In the first quarter of current fiscal 2012-13, monthly average exchange rate of rupee showed depreciating trend, going down by 2.9 per cent in April 2012, 4.9 per cent in May and 2.8 per cent in June 2012 over the previous month. In the month of June 2012, the rupee touched all-time low of ₹ 57.22 per US dollar (RBI's reference rate) on June 27, 2012 indicating 10.6 per cent depreciation over ₹ 51.16 per US dollar on March 30, 2012. In the second quarter of 2012-13, monthly average exchange rate of rupee has appreciated by 1.0 per cent in July 2012 and 1.7 per cent in September 2012 over the previous month, while in the month of August 2012 it has marginally depreciated by 0.1 per cent. In the third quarter, it appreciated by 3.0 per cent in October 2012 and 0.2 per cent in December 2012 while in month of November 2012 it depreciated by 3.2 per cent over the previous month level.

The Government of India and the RBI have taken a number of steps to boost exports and facilitate capital inflows so as to reduce external vulnerability. Under the Annual Supplement 2012-13 to Foreign Trade Policy 2009-14, the Government has announced initiatives to boost exports. The government has further liberalised FDI policy, including allowing foreign direct investment in multibrand retail. Other measures to boost capital inflows include a hike in FII investment in debt securities (both corporate and Government), enhancement of all-in-cost ceiling for external commercial borrowings (ECBs) between 3-5 year maturity, higher interest rate ceiling for foreign currency non-resident deposits, deregulation of interest rates on rupee denominated NRI deposits, and administrative steps to curb currency speculation.

Domestic policy measures for attracting FDI, coupled with the announcement of quantitative easing by the US Federal Reserve and Bank of Japan in September 2012 contributed to increase in capital inflows to India leading to strengthening of the rupee. Besides, the RBI sold nearly US$ 3.1 billion during 2012-13 (April-December 2012). As a result, the rupee recovered to ₹ 51.62 per US dollar on October 05, 2012. However, since the second week of October 2012, rupee again showed depreciating trend on account of concerns relating to high CAD and the demand for dollars from oil importing firms and continued uncertainty in the global financial markets. In December 2012, rupee remained range bound (₹ 54.20-55.09 per US dollar) as FIIs continued to be largely buoyant except on December 21, 2012 when rupee touched a low of ₹ 55.09 per US dollar. The month-wise exchange rate of the rupee against major international currencies and the RBI's sale/purchase of foreign currency in the foreign exchange market during 2012-13 are shown in Table 1.

TABLE 1

Exchange Rates of Rupee Per Foreign Currency and RBI's Sale/Purchases of Dollar in the Exchange Market during 2012-13

Month	*Average exchange rates (₹ per foreign currency)*[a] US Dollar	Pound sterling	Euro	Japanese Yen[b]	RBI Net sale (-) / purchase (+) (US$ million)
1	2	3	4	5	6
2011-12 (annual average)	47.9190 (-4.9)	76.3809 (-7.2)	65.8761 (-8.6)	60.7257 (-12.3)	(-) 20,138
March 2012	50.3213 (-2.3)	79.6549 (-2.5)	66.4807 (-2.1)	61.0259 (2.8)	
2012-13 (monthly average)					(-) 3123.0
April 2012	51.8121 (-2.9)	82.9119 (-3.9)	68.1872 (-2.5)	63.7934 (-4.3)	-275.0
May 2012	54.4736 (-4.9)	86.7323 (-4.4)	69.6991 (-2.2)	68.3286 (-6.6)	-485.0
June 2012	56.0302 (-2.8)	87.1349 (-0.5)	70.3087 (-0.9)	70.6743 (-3.3)	-50.0
July 2012	55.4948 (1.0)	86.5173 (0.7)	68.2520 (3.0)	70.2809 (0.6)	-785.0
August 2012	55.5594 (-0.1)	87.3444 (-0.9)	68.8750 (-0.9)	70.6814 (-0.6)	-452.0
September 2012	54.6055 (1.7)	87.8663 (-0.6)	70.1263 (-1.8)	69.9084 (1.1)	- 10.0
October 2012	53.0239 (3.0)	85.2128 (3.1)	68.7522 (2.0)	67.2305 (4.0)	- 95.0
November 2012	54.7758 (- 3.2)	87.5374 (- 2.7)	70.3665 (- 2.3)	67.6032 (- 0.6)	- 921.0
December 2012	54.6478 (0.2)	88.1910 (- 0.7)	71.6671 (- 1.8)	65.2805 (3.6)	-50.0

Source: RBI.

Notes: a. Per 100 Yen; Figures in parentheses indicate appreciation (+) and depreciation (-) over the previous month/year in per cent. Figures may not tally due to rounding off.

b. FEDAI market indicative rates. Data from May 2012 onwards are RBIs reference rates,

It may be noted that a depreciating exchange rate in 2012-13 is not specific to India. The currencies of other emerging economies, such as Brazilian real, Argentina peso, Russian rouble, and South Africa's rand also depreciated against the US dollar reflecting the increased demand for dollar as a safe haven asset in the wake of sovereign debt crisis in the euro zone and due to uncertain global economic environment. On a point-on-point basis between March 30,2012 and December 28, 2012, the Argentina peso has depreciated by 10.9 per cent, Brazilian real by 10.5 per cent, South African rand by 9.7 per cent, Indian rupee by 6.7 per cent, Indonesian rupiah by 5.1 per cent and Russian rouble by 3.4 per cent.

NOMINAL EFFECTIVE EXCHANGE RATE AND REAL EFFECTIVE EXCHANGE RATE

Nominal rupee depreciation, while having some adverse effects such as greater imported inflation, is also useful over time in offsetting higher domestic inflation and ensuring Indian exports remain competitive. The nominal effective exchange rate (NEER) and real effective exchange rate (REER) indices are used as indicators of external competitiveness of the country over a period of time. NEER is the weighted average of bilateral nominal exchange rates of the home currency in terms of foreign currencies, while REER is defined as a weighted average of nominal exchange rates, adjusted for home and foreign country relative price differentials. REER captures movements in cross-currency exchange rates as well as inflation differentials between India and its major trading partners and reflects the degree of external competitiveness of Indian products. The RBI has been constructing six currency (US dollar, euro for euro zone, pound sterling, Japanese yen, Chinese renminbi and Hong Kong dollar) and 36 currency indices of NEER and REER.

The 6-currency trade-based NEER (base: 2004-05=100) depreciated by 9.6 per cent between March 2011 and March 2012 and by 8.0 per cent between March 2012 to December 2012. As compared to this, the monthly average exchange rate of rupee depreciated by 10.6 per cent between March 2011 and March 2012, while in current fiscal it depreciated by 7.9 per cent against the US dollar from ₹ 50.32 per US dollar in March 2012 to ₹ 54.65 per US dollar in December 2012. The 6-currency trade-based REER (base: 2004-05=100) of the Rupee depreciated by 5.5 per cent from 115.97 to 109.59 between March 2011 and March 2012. During 2012- 13 so far (up to December 2012), the 6 currency index of 104.56 showed depreciation of 4.6 per cent over March 2012 index of 109.59 largely reflecting depreciation of rupee in nominal terms (Table 2).

US Dollar Exchange Rate in International Market

In so far as international currencies are concerned, the US dollar appreciated by 2.2 per cent against the pound sterling, 6.0 per cent against the euro, and 0.8 per cent

TABLE 2

Indices of NEER and REER of the Indian Rupee (Six-Currency Trade-based Weights) Base 2004-05 (April-March) = 100

Month average	*NEER*	*Appreciation (+)/ depreciation (-) NEER over previous period/month*	*REER*	*Appreciation (+) depreciation (-) REER over previous period/month*
1	2	3	4	5
March 2011	90.29	115.97		
March 2012	81.60	-9.6	109.59	-5.5
2012-13				
April 2012 (P)	79.24	-2.9	107.57	-1.8
May 2012 (P)	76.10	-4.0	104.12	-3.2
June 2012 (P)	74.67	-1.9	102.24	-1.8
July 2012 (P)	75.95	1.7	104.16	1.9
August 2012 (P)	75.53	-0.6	104.76	0.6
September 2012 (P)	75.67	0.2	105.75	0.9
October 2012 (P)	77.55	2.5	107.86	2.0
November 2012 (P)	75.33	- 2.9	105.11	- 2.5
December 2012 (P)	75.05	- 0.4	104.56	- 0.5

Source: RBI. P: Provisional.

against the Japanese yen during between March 2011 and March 2012. However, it depreciated by 4.2 per cent against Australian dollar during the same period. In current fiscal (up to end-December 2012), the US dollar appreciated by 0.7 per cent against euro, 1.4 per cent against Japanese yen and 0.6 per cent against Australian dollar between March 2012 and December 2012. However, US dollar depreciated by 2.0 per cent against pound sterling (Table 3).

TABLE 3

Exchange Rate of US Dollar against International Currencies

Month/Year	*USD/ GBP*	*USD/Euro*	*JPY/USD*	*USD /AUD*
1	2	3	4	5
March 2010	1.5082	1.3543	90.8850	0.9095
March 2011	1.6168	1.3999	81.7936	1.0102
March 2012	1.5817	1.3201	82.4348	1.0543
US$ Appreciation (+) / Depreciation (-) (March 2011- March 2012) in percent	2.22	6.04	-0.78	-4.18

2012-13				
April 2012	1.6009	1.3162	81.4895	1.0350
May 2012	1.5906	1.2800	79.7084	0.9982
June 2012	1.5564	1.2526	79.3214	0.9986
July 2012	1.5589	1.2276	78.9830	1.0293
August 2012	1.5713	1.2400	78.6648	1.0468
September 2012	1.6119	1.2871	78.1678	1.0401
October 2012	1.6083	1.2975	78.9686	1.0293
November 2012	1.5966	1.2820	80.7920	1.0412
December 2012	1.6144	1.3109	83.5778	1.0477
US$ Appreciation (+) /Depreciation (-) (March 2012-December 2012) in percent	-2.03	0.70	1.39	0.63

Source: Reserve Bank of India. Note: Exchange rate is based on monthly average.

ISSUES INVOLVED IN INDIAN RUPEE DEPRECIATION AND VOLATILITY

There are two issues involved here – depreciation and volatility. As far as depreciation is concerned, the facts are well known. India has always had current account deficit which has increased significantly during the past few years in view of strong petroleum prices, increased gold imports coupled with strong gold prices and deceleration in the growth of exports on the back of faltering or even falling growth in most of the developing/developed countries which also happen to be the major trading partners. On the other hand, autonomous capital flows also seem to have slowed down because of several factors including global risk aversion, slowdown of investment in the Indian economy and several structural issues including inadequate infrastructure. In such a situation Rupee exhibiting a depreciating bias is no surprise. A depreciating currency is often seen to act as an instrument for correction of imbalances in the BoP. However, a sharp depreciation within a short period of time has a destabilising impact inasmuch as it provokes panic reaction amongst market participants which apart from leading to sub-optimal economic decision making further accentuates the price process. While the policy response to structural as well as exogenous factors that lead to mismatch between inflows and outflows and consequent depreciation (or appreciation) of the currency take time to yield results, Reserve Bank has a mandate to maintain orderliness in the foreign exchange market.

In forex markets, volatility essentially means unpredictability. Unpredictability not only of the extent of change over any given time period but also the direction of change. It affects all as the decisions are to be taken today that will fructify at a future point in time. Because all financial prices are inherently forward looking in the sense that they incorporate the participants' future view, it is no wonder that volatility is their most important attribute. It is further complicated by the fact that usually future view is informed by past experience. It may be interesting to recall that in 2007-08 when Rupee was at 39 levels, informed participants were forecasting 35-36 levels by the end of 2008 and very recently, during end-June this year, when Rupee reached 57, market was looking at 58-60 or even 60-65 as inevitable. It is to be emphasised that when economic agents take decision based on such a view of the future, it certainly does not bode well either for them or for the economy as a whole. This raises a related issue. If we accept that market makers/analysts who often are in a position to influence the market sentiment tend to be either euphoric or despondent, what is the accountability if their forecasts turn out to be widely wrong but meanwhile some participants in the market do get taken in by these forecasts and their decisions then turn out to be sub-optimal or inappropriate?

Thus, it needs to be recognised that increased volatility in the financial markets has become a way of life- a kind of new normal-and it has to be accepted as such. Capital account liberalisation during last few decades and enormous increase in the scale and variety of cross border financial transactions has increased the magnitude of exchange rate movements, particularly in the emerging market economies. Of course, volatility may be moderate for some stretch of time – recall that in 2006 people were seeking explanations for low volatility in the forex market – and heightened at other times, as now. The question is: *What should be the response to volatility?* For ease of exposition, may be discussed the issue in the context of two sets of market participants. The real sector agents – exporters, importers, foreign currency borrowers and so on and the banks or authorised dealers.

Real Sector or Real Culprits?

First, the real sector. In view of the extant capital account restrictions, exposure of residents to assets denominated in foreign currency (other than overseas direct investment) is marginal. Whenever a contract is denominated in a foreign currency, the contracting party faces uncertainty in its cost or revenue and ultimately profit on account of fluctuations in the exchange rate. It is to be particularly emphasised in the case of exporters, who in the face of stiff global competition and absence of any significant pricing power, have to reckon with rather thin margins which can be easily eroded because of fall in the value of the foreign currency before the payment is received. The same applies to importers as well when they are handicapped by incomplete pass-through of the increase in their input cost. The foreign currency borrower, who has to carry the exposure for a much longer period than the exporter or the importer, can find his cash flows and the bottom line seriously impaired because of depreciation of the home currency.

How do the corporates manage this risk? There are basically two routes available: non-hedging techniques and hedging techniques. Non-hedging techniques include:

(a) Settlement of transaction through advance payment, which though beneficial for an exporter, carries a cost for the importer and is impossible for a borrower. Even for the exporter, it is doubtful, in how many cases an exporter can demand and obtain advance payment without the risk of losing the order.

(b) Invoicing in the home currency has been discussed a great deal in recent times, which, however is quite sometime away before it can be effectively implemented. In the current state of global slowdown declining exports, exporters simply are not in a position to dictate terms.

Now, when it comes to hedging , are the corporates taking a well- deliberated and calculated call? To this , 'no' would have to be the answer in most cases. The reason is obvious. The rupee was rock solid in the range of 44 to 46 for about 2 years from 2009 to 2011. That lulled the corporates into a sense of complacency that nothing can go wrong. They started believing that this is the eternal range for rupee. A good bit of sales talk from various analysts (and some bankers too) convinced then that hedging is an unwarranted cost imposed on the business when the rupee is so well-behaved. It is like saying that life insurance is of no value since you are alive today !! This is where the answer to the earlier question comes in. If India is a high inflation country in comparison to the US, then the classical theory of foreign exchange states that rupee has to depreciate against the dollar to the extent of inflation differential. But there seems to have been an optimism among the corporates that the rupee will continue to be stable even if India is a high inflation country and that the financing of the CAD will never be a problem since India will continue to attract flows!

Over the years, a wide range of derivative products have been made available to enable those with foreign currency exposure to effectively manage their risk. The products include forwards, options and futures. The OTC forex markets and the Currency Futures are two different market segments for the same product. Both are governed by two different regulatory framework in terms of requirement of underlying, delivery and the extent of position taking by participants. We can no doubt have competing market segments as competition will bring in more efficiency. But, how can the competition be fair when the playing fields are completely asymmetric? This is an important issue warranting further public debate. But it need to be underscore the fact that exchange rate is a critical macro-economic variable particularly for countries having capital controls, perhaps no less sacrosanct than the policy interest rates which are targeted by the central banks, the world over. We also need to bear in mind that excessive overshooting and volatility in such a critical variable can have adverse financial stability implications. There is a paramount need for aligning these market segments, perhaps with a road map over an acceptable time span. One of the motivations for introduction of derivative products like exchange traded futures or options was to enable the small and medium enterprises to access the derivative market at competitive cost. But the use of these products depends on the agents themselves. But, unfortunately, even these hedging instruments have become weapons in the hands of corporates to trigger market instability. Whether it is past-performance based booking or cancellation and rebooking, or EEFC accounts, the corporate deemed these instruments as unfailing profit channels rather than flexible operational tools to manage real- life business events. These instruments have a tendency to exacerbate volatility in the markets and create a constant undercurrent of instability. That is why Reserve Bank had to step in to moderate volatility and cushion the rupee fall.

EXCHANGE RATE RISK MANAGEMENT FRAMEWORK

What should determine the use of the derivative products by the agents? Like in case of any risk, currency risk requires identification, measurement and management. It is important therefore that a firm should have a comprehensive framework for risk management and the decision to hedge or not to hedge should flow out of a conscious assessment of risk and the costs and consequences of entering a zero, partial or full hedge. The potential downside of any hedging strategy has to be recognised. Take the case of a forward contract, the most direct and commonly used hedge. An exporter, who had sold his receivables forward at a particular level, stands to makes a notional loss in comparison with an unhedged position if the foreign currency appreciates beyond the contracted level. Similar is the case when an exporter, anticipating a fall in the value of the foreign currency, sold his receivables forward only to find the trend reverse, as happened in 2007-08. Exporters cancelling forward contracts and importers rushing to cover their exposure are a common phenomenon we see when the Rupee depreciates.

There is a fallacy of composition involved here. What is a good strategy for one may not remain so if everybody adopts the same strategy. After all, a forward contract in essence shifts the demand from one point in time to another. If everyone adopted hedging strategy in anticipation of Rupee decline at a future point of time, the Rupee decline will happen now and here. The point is that the hedging strategy should be part of a well-conceived risk management framework built around assessment of risk and risk appetite. Having bought certainty through a hedge, the agent should be free to concentrate on his chosen line of activity without bothering about the potential gain or loss on account of currency movement. Having bought a car insurance, one should not regret that no accident has taken place.

As present, the fear of mark-to-market losses, inhibits many firms from hedging activity that their risk assessment and appetite would warrant. However, the objective of accounting is to faithfully reflect the true economic essence of business affairs. If accounting rules stand in the way of agents' adopting a hedging strategy that economic rationale hold optimal – on the basis of information available at the time, then perhaps there is a need to take a relook at this inconsistency.

What should be the optimal role of banks in a volatile situation. The banks are market makers in foreign exchange not only in the interbank market but also in relation to their clients. Obviously therefore they have to carry a position. By 'position', it is meant trading position involving rupee as one of the currency. The need for this position arises from the fact that without this – inventory, as it were – banks would not be in a position to serve their clients efficiently. *What should be the magnitude of this position?* Naturally, this would depend upon the nature of their clientele, size of their need and the volume of business. It is natural that like all traders, a forex dealer will also be tempted to profit from shortage by building up a hoard. Therefore, to align incentives of the forex dealers with the larger public purpose, there are constrained to impose restrictions on positions, knowing well that such restrictions may impair liquidity in the market. Because a trading position is a risky market exposure, obviously it has to be limited by availability of commensurate capital for the purpose. But that does not mean that if you have capital, you can take as large a position as you want, irrespective of your needs. Not in the present regime, not at times of volatility.

The banks' responsibility to ensure appropriateness of the product for the client is not merely to satisfy a regulatory mandate nor is it motivated by altruism. Foreign exchange business in India is a part of relationship banking and it is in the banks' interest that clients do not end up taking unwarranted risk through ill-understood and inappropriate hedging products. In this context, an important issue is of , ensuring inclusion in forex transactions. Today, the large number of SME customers in India are not getting fair rates for their hedging transactions. This is a serious missed opportunity and calls for some serious cooperative efforts among the banks to offer finer rates to the SME Clients who today feel that what they are faced with is a 'rip off'. It may be argued that it has been the age old practice that rates are often way off the normal distribution for smaller transactions. But sincere effort to change set thoughts and practices can always be made.

MANAGING FOREIGN EXCHANGE RESERVES

The foreign exchange reserves has received renewed interest in recent times in the context of increasing globalisation, acceleration of capital flows and integration of financial markets. The debt-banking-financial crises in several countries have also necessitated the need for an international financial architecture in which the management of foreign exchange reserves has emerged as one of the critical issues.

Contextually, the subject of foreign exchange reserves may be broadly classified into two inter-linked areas, *viz.*, the theory of reserves and the management of reserves. The theory of reserves encompasses issues relating to institutional and legal arrangements for holding reserve assets, conceptual and definitional aspects, objectives for holding reserve assets, exchange rate regimes and conceptualisation of the appropriate level of foreign reserves. In essence, a theoretical framework for reserves provides the rationale for holding foreign exchange reserves. Reserve management is mainly guided by the portfolio management consideration, i.e., how best to deploy foreign reserve assets subject to statutory stipulations? The portfolio considerations take into account *inter alia*, safety, liquidity and yield on reserves as the principal objectives of reserve management. The institutional and legal arrangements are largely country specific and these differences should be recognised in approaching the critical issues relating to both reserve management practices and policy-making.

MOTIVES FOR HOLDING FOREIGN EXCHANGE RESERVES

The motives for holding reserves may be broadly classified under three categories, viz, transaction, speculative and precautionary. International trade gives rise to currency flows, which are assumed to be handled by banks driven by the transaction motives. Similarly, speculative motives is left to individuals or corporates. Central banks reserves, however, are characterised primarily as a last resort stock of foreign currency for unpredictable flows, which is consistent with precautionary motives for holding foreign assets. Precautionary motive for holding foreign currency, like the demand for money, can be positively related to wealth and the cost of covering unplanned deficit, and negatively related to the return from alternative assets. Furthermore, foreign exchange reserves are instruments to maintain or manage the exchange rate, while enabling orderly absorption of international capital flows. Official reserves are mainly held for precautionary and transaction motives keeping in view the aggregate of national interests, to achieve balance between demand for and supply of foreign currencies, for intervention, and to preserve confidence in the county's ability to carry out external transactions.

The objectives for maintaining reserves are: (i) maintaining confidence in monetary and exchange rate policies; (ii) enhancing capacity to invervence in foreign exchange markets; (iii) limiting external vulnerability by maintaining foreign currency liquidity to absorb shocks during times of crisis including national disasters or emergencies; (iv) providing confidence to the markets, including credit rating agencies, that external obligations can always be met (thus reducing the overall costs at which foreign exchange resources are available to all the market participants); and (v) adding to the comfort of the market participants, by demonstrating the backing of domestic currency by external assets.

FOREIGN EXCHANGE RESERVE ACCUMULATION

Foreign exchange reserves are an important component of the balance of payments and an essential element in the analysis of an economy's external position. Rapid reserve accumulation has significant implications for a central bank's balance sheet. While capital inflows—particularly portfolio inflows - have often been seen as temporary (perhaps justifying intervention), current account surpluses tend to endure and have persistent effects on the exchange rate. Moreover, there has been a tendency among investors and currency traders to identify persistent current account surpluses with an appreciation of the long-run equilibrium exchange rate. Resisting this may cause even larger capital inflows, potentially perpetuating a vicious circle of increased appreciation pressure and yet more intervention. Box-2 presents a stylised version of a monetary authority's balance sheet. Its assets consist of foreign currency and domestic assets; its liabilities comprise currency, bank reserves (taken together as monetary liabilities), its own securities, other liabilities (taken together as non-monetary liabilities) and equity capital. Of these, currency is largely determined by the public's demand for cash balances. Equity capital represents government transfers to the central bank (plus accumulated profits and losses). The remaining liabilities are within the control of the central bank.

An injection of equity capital in order to finance reserve accumulation would not result in monetary expansion, provided that the government did not finance this by drawing on deposits or using an overdraft facility at the central bank. Without increased equity capital, and assuming other things (i.e. the demand for cash) equal, the accumulation of reserves requires financing in some form. One simple measure of such a financing need is the excess of foreign currency reserves over currency in circulation. Up until the late 1990s, such a financing gap was either small or negative in many developing countries. In other words, forex reserve assets and currency in circulation were of a similar order of magnitude. However, the gap has widened appreciably over the past five years as a percentage of GDP in many emerging market economies, especially in Asia. In many countries, such a gap is also large in relation to the stock of public debt securities.

BOX-2

A central bank's Balance Sheet

Assets	*Liabilities*
Net foreign assets	Monetary liabilities
Net domestic assets	• Currency
	• Bank reserves
	Non-monetary liabilities
	• Central bank securities
	• Others
	Equity capital

As intervention takes place, the central bank can finance this gap by issuing domestic monetary liabilities (typically commercial bank monetary reserves). Should these increased monetary reserves be allowed to put downward pressure on the short-term interest rate (unsterilised intervention), bank credit would tend to expand and inflationary pressures would eventually mount. If central banks have a target for the short-term rate (usually the policy rate), they would attempt to offset increases in bank reserves through changes in other balance sheet items (usually selling domestic assets or issuing their own securities) over which they have control (sterilised intervention).

Challenges from Sterilised Intervention

Fully sterilising reserve accumulation can be challenging. Even when fully sterilised, intervention can have other unwelcome implications that can limit its usefulness as a policy instrument. The four possible and unwelcome implications are:

(i) The Fiscal Costs of Intervention

An earlier presumption was that intervention by central banks, in countries where local interest rates were well above international levels, entailed large carrying costs, and it was often these rising costs which led to policy reversals in the past. Nonetheless valuation losses do not reduce the central bank's ability to intervene (i.e. to sell local currency to limit further appreciation), nor do they reduce the purchasing power of its foreign currency reserves in terms of foreign goods. To the extent that the private sector and the government are net borrowers in foreign currency, appreciation reduces their net debt burden. Valuation losses might matter, however, if they were to undermine a central bank's credibility or independence.

(ii) Future Monetary Imbalances

The long-term effectiveness of sterilised intervention in dealing with excess liquidity depends on the instruments used for sterilisation and which sector ends up holding such paper. Large-scale reserve accumulation typically raises the underlying liquidity position of the banking system. This can be partly neutralised by selling long-term government bonds to banks. If such bonds are then sold to non-banks, sterilisation can be thought to be reasonably complete: households or non-bank firms lower their holding of monetary assets and increase that of non-monetary assets such as government bonds.

(iii) Financial Sector Imbalances

Intervention to prevent a rise in the exchange rate can accentuate macroeconomic and financial imbalances. There are several possible channels for this. Increased bank lending resulting from partial or ineffective sterilisation could finance excessive investment in certain sectors such as property markets. Such effects could also be associated with a persistently low inflation and low interest rate environment. Another possible channel is that expectations of future currency appreciation could attract large short-term capital inflows, pushing up equity prices. Such an effect could be reinforced by perception of a one-way currency bet, leading to increased currency substitution and unhedged foreign currency borrowing.

There are no simple indicators to show how far exchange rates might have become misaligned, or the extent to which investor expectations about future exchange rate movements might have been influenced, by continued sterilised intervention. Nevertheless, real exchange rates have not risen significantly in many countries with large and persistent current account surpluses. In some cases, real effective exchange rates are actually below what they were at the beginning of the decade, when current account surpluses were small.

(iv) Implications for Financial Intermediation

The difficulties experienced in sterilising large-scale intervention can lead to recourse to non-market instruments to drain excess liquidity, which may have adverse implications for the financial system. Prolonged sterilised intervention could alter the behaviour of banks: easy profits from large holdings of treasury securities could weaken pressures on banks to become more efficient. Moreover, large-scale issuance of sterilisation-related debts might also hamper the development of a private bond market, as a large supply of risk-free government and central bank paper crowds out private sector issuance. In contrast, in countries where the stock of initial public debt securities is relatively low, the issuance of sterilisation-related debt could actually help develop a domestic bond market.

INTERNATIONAL RESERVES AND OPTIMALITY

The policy of accretion to reserves to meet the transactions and precautionary needs generally involves both financial and economic cost to the country. In the absence of any unique definition of the opportunity cost, one comes across several interpretations in the literature, the applicability of which depends on the particular economic context. When an economy is both foreign exchange and saving constrained, the opportunity cost could be the rate of return on domestic investment (assuming that the foreign exchange used to finance unsatiated investment demand would have fetched the return on domestic investment). When an-economy is only foreign exchange constrained, the opportunity cost could be in terms of foregone consumption. When an economy is not foreign exchange constrained *(i.e.,* all productive forex demand are met before the reserves are built up), the opportunity cost would depend on the difference between the cost of borrowing and the return on reserve assets. If high cost borrowings are used to build reserves on which modest returns are obtained because of the emphasis on safety and liquidity of reserve assets, such reserve build-up policies may prove more costly. Another form of cost—often known as the quasi-fiscal cost - arises from the higher rate of return on domestic assets vis-a-vis foreign assets, Since sterilised intervention gives rise to an offsetting change in the domestic asset holding of a central bank when its foreign assets increase, the overall profits arising from the total asset portfolio of the Central Bank's balance sheet may decline. As a result, the profits transferred—to the Government-which represents a major source of non-tax revenue for the Government may decline. For countries operating with large fiscal imbalances, such a decline in non-tax revenue could prove more costly, forcing a higher mobilisation of tax revenue or a cut in expenditure that may affect growth and development.

The development of money demand theory along, the lines of optimal inventory control or buffer stock model provides a natural theoretical benchmark for the study of optimal reserve accumulation and has spurred a large body of empirical literature in the late 1960s and early 1970s. Heller used a cost-benefit approach and stressed that the issue is one of choosing an optimal level of reserves at which the central bank minimises the total expected cost i.e., the sum of the adjustment cost that is incurred when reserves reach some lower bound and the opportunity cost. Heller's estimation indicated that optimal reserves are directly proportional to the variability of exports and are inversely related to the opportunity cost variable (defined as foregone earnings or economic welfare). Frankel and Jovanovic and Landell-Mills also found a negative relationship between the demand for reserves and its opportunity cost. Flood and Marion, however, did not find any, relationship between reserves and opportunity cost. The sign of the propeinsity to import has also turned out to be ambiguous in the literature. Several studies have found an inverse relationship, while some others found a positive relationship between import propensity and reserves. While the inverse relationship between reserves and the propensity to import has been interpreted as the extent of adjustment to an external shock, the direct relationship is an indicator of the degree of openness. Eaton and Gersovitz formally introduced the concept of transactions demand for reserves. In addition to the 'conventional' variables, Ben-Bassat and Gottlieb introduced risk of default or sovereign risk into the assessment of precautionary demand for reserves. Lane and Burke adopted a broad approach to identify the potential determinants of reserves and found: (i) trade openness to be the most important variable along with financial deepening; (ii) smaller and more volatile industrial countries hold larger reserves than their larger, less volatile counterparts; and (iii) more indebted developing countries had smaller reserve ratios. The traditional determinants identified in the empirical literature on foreign exchange reserve holdings are presented in Box-3.

BOX-3

Determinants of the Demand for Reserves

Variables	*Description*
Scalar variable	Imports, per capita income, GDP, population
Propensity to import	Marginal/average propensity to import
Variability measure	Exports, imports, terms of trade, receipts, payments, nominal effective exchange rate, balance of payments, reserves
Opportunity cost	Marginal product of capital (MPK) or in the absence of MPK, per capita output (as an inverse proxy for marginal product of capital), marginal utility of

consumption, rate of interest on borrowing from abroad, net foreign indebtedness, the government bond yield, the spread between the government bond yield and short-term international interest rates, marginal productivity of social capital, one-year deposit rate.

Analytically and empirically, reserve holding appears to be an under-researched area. Clear standard methodologies have yet to evolve on this subject. However, relatively high demand for international reserves by countries in Far East and relatively low demand by some other countries has attracted attention. Aizenman and Marion recently showed that for 125 developing countries, reserve-holding over 1980-1996 period could be predicted by the size of international transactions, their volatility, the exchange rate arrangement and political- considerations. Sovereign risk and fiscal liabilities led to relatively large precautionary demand for reserves.

Aizenman and Marion showed that there has been a structural break in the equation for the demand for reserves in several Asian countries that were affected by crisis in 1997. Using a standard estimating equation, they found that over the period 1960-96, their model over-predicted the reserve holdings of countries such, as China, Taiwan, Hong Kong, South Korea and Singapore implying thereby that their reserves were low in relation to what was estimated as desirable in the model. Out of sample forecasts of desirable levels generated for 1997-99, however, under predicted the reserve holding (i.e., actual reserves holdings exceeded the predicted desirable level). Such a result has to be assessed in the context of the overall change in policy stance of the emerging market economies in the aftermath of the financial crisis that viewed high reserves as an appropriate policy of "self-insurance".

In India, the determinants of reserve holdings appear to have changed considerably and evolved over the recent years with the gradual opening up of the capital account. The substantial growth in reserves since 2001-02 has generated a debate regarding the cost of holding reserves. While the cost of reserves is secondary to properly meeting the overall objective behind holding reserves, it is important to note that in India, in the last few years, almost the whole addition to reserves has been made without increasing the overall level of external debt, which has hovered around US $ 100 billion during the previous five years. The increase in reserves largely reflects higher remittances, quicker repatriation of export proceeds and non-debt flows. Even after taking into account foreign currency denominated NRI flows (where interest rates are linked to LIBOR), the financial cost of additional reserve accretion in India in the recent period is low.

MONETARY IMPACT OF FOREIGN EXCHANGE RESERVES

While the reserve build up policies of the emerging market economies like India reflect the importance of appropriate reaction to the vastly altered conditions prevailing at both national and global levels, high reserve policies also entail several other implications, particularly for monetary management and in terms of the quasi-fiscal costs, both of which poses different type of challenge to the policy makers.

Cross-country experiences of surges in capital inflows indicate that in the context of the limited capacity of the economy to absorb capital flows in the form of higher productive investment and the resultant implications for the exchange rate, monetary authorities often intervene in the foreign exchange market to absorb the surplus in the market and thereby avoid nominal appreciation of the exchange rate. A non-sterilised (or partially sterilised) intervention can, however, cause a sharp rise in the monetary base and hence higher inflation. Real appreciation resulting from higher inflation could erode external competitiveness; lower interest rates could also fuel lending and consumption boom, that can potentially lead to a sharp deterioration in the current account balance and culminate in a possible currency crisis. When the conflict between the policy objectives of checking nominal appreciation and limiting inflation emerges, central banks attempt to counter inflation through sterilised intervention, which by nature appears money supply neutral.

Among the instruments available for sterilisation, recourse to open market operations (OMOs) is particularly effective if inflows are temporary and there exists a near perfect elastic demand for domestic government securities. However, if the demand for government securities is not perfectly elastic in view of the limited absorptive capacity of market participants and the underdeveloped nature of the financial markets, OMOs can cause domestic interest rates to rise, nullifying the impact of sterilisation as higher interest rates could attract larger capital inflows. Sterilisation typically involves exchanging high-yielding domestic assets for low-yielding foreign assets and, therefore has quasi-fiscal costs. The degree of effectiveness of sterilised intervention would therefore depend on: (i) the sensitivity of domestic interest rates to OMOs and (ii) the degree to which foreign capital flows respond to such interest rate variations. The combined effect, which is captured through the estimated "offset coefficient", indicates that the value of the coefficient may range between 0 and (-) 1, with values close to zero indicating "effectiveness of sterilisation" and values close to (-) 1 indicating "ineffective sterilisation". Sterilisation induced increase in interest rates, however at times, may be more than offset by the change in the stance of monetary policy. When capital flows are persistent and sterilisation proves ineffective cross-country studies show that countries often attempt a few options available to them. These include: fiscal adjustment, easing of restrictions on capital outflows, accelerated trade liberalisation, lower interest rates on foreign currency deposits, prepayment of costly debt, adoption of new sterilisation techniques such as" foreign exchange swaps, switching of government deposits from the banking system to the central bank, imposition of taxes on domestic assets purchased by foreigners, fixing of ceilings on foreign borrowings by domestic residents, and recourse to indirect capital controls, such as variable unremunerated reserve requirements on certain categories of foreign borrowing. In the Indian case, capital flows have had a softening effect on interest rates and positive effect on broad money growth.

Capital inflows have served the twin purpose of meeting India's domestic investment-saving gap and the need for reserve accretion consistent with the standard indicators of reserve adequacy. Nonetheless, the surge in capital flows often poses a challenge to the conduct of monetary and exchange rate policy. As a result of large accretion to reserves resulting from surges in capital flows in the face of low domestic absorption, there has been a substantial increase in net foreign exchange assets (NFA) of the Reserve Bank. There is hardly any formal analysis available for emerging market economies (including India) to evaluate the monetary impact of large capital flows econometrically. One way to assess the impact is to simulate the emerging monetary condition in counterfactual scenarios where reserve accretion is placed at lower levels. For this purpose, an interest rate reaction function has been estimated that relates domestic interest rate to its possible determinants like inflation, output and capital flows along with a conventional money demand equation in terms of income and interest rate. Controlling for the impact on interest rates from the accretion to reserves, the counterfactual path generated through a simulation exercise under lower reserves accumulation points towards a perceptible monetary impact of reserves in terms of higher broad money demand.

In the period of surge in capital flows and significant accretion to foreign exchange reserves with the monetary authority, the literature points to the emergence of newer channels of monetary expansion, especially, if there is a disassociation between the growth of broad money and reserve money. In India, notwithstanding a fall in reserve money growth broad money grew almost at the same level in the two decades, which may be symptomatic of such a disassociation. There is an attempt to explore the likely mechanism that characterises the underlying process of monetary expansion. It is suggested that had there been a lower reserve accumulation with the RBI, the interest rate would perhaps have been higher, thus, possibly signifying that the liquidity effect of reserve accumulation would have outweighted the sterlization effect in the Indian context. Composition of reserve money expansion has shifted from domestic assets to foreign assets reflective of the surge in capital flows, accumulation of reserves and sterilisation operations of the Reserve Bank. Sterilisation operations have so far been successful in arresting reserve money growth to levels where the inflationary potential of capital flows has been kept in control. However, future concerns on monetary management may arise, among others, from the following factors: (i) need to ensure sufficient stock of Government securities at the hands of the Reserve Bank for sterilisation operations of the required magnitude; (ii) the absorption capacity of the financial system for Government securities once the credit demand picks up; and (iii) the upward drift in money multiplier arising partly from fall in currency-deposit ratio and CRR has sustained higher growth of broad money in the face of declining reserve money growth. With financial liberalisation and market-determined interest rates, there is evidence that innovations to money multiplier emanate from interest rates and other macroeconomic variables (such as growth) apart from the conventional proximate determinants. To the extent that these newer determinants of money multiplier are not entirely under the control of the monetary authority, it poses a challenge for the Reserve Bank to manage the emerging monetary conditions.

FOREIGN EXCHANGE RESERVES IN INDIA

The guiding objectives of foreign exchange reserves management in India are similar to those of many central banks in the world. The demands placed on the foreign exchange reserves may vary widely depending upon a variety of factors including the exchange rate regime adopted by the country, the extent of openness of the economy, the size of the external sector in a country's GDP and the nature of markets operating in the country. Even within this divergent framework most countries have adopted the primary objective of reserve management as preservation of the long-term value of the reserves in terms of purchasing power and the need to minimise risk and volatility in returns. India is not an exception in this regard. While safety and liquidity constitute the twin objectives of reserve management in India, return optimisation becomes an embedded strategy within this framework.

STATUTORY PROVISIONS AND MOVEMENT OF RESERVES

The Reserve Bank of India Act, 1934 provides the overarching legal framework for deployment of the foreign currency assets (FCA) and gold defining the broad parameters in respect of currencies, instruments, issuers and counterparties. The essential legal framework for reserves management is provided in sub-sections 17 (6A), 17(12), 17(12A), 17(13) and 33 (6) of the above Act. In brief, the law broadly permits the following investment categories:

(i) deposits with other central banks and the Bank for International Settlements (BIS);

(ii) deposits with foreign commercial banks;

(iii) debt instruments representing sovereign/sovereign-guaranteed liability with residual maturity for the debt papers not exceeding 10 years;

(iv) other instruments / institutions as approved by the Central Board of the Reserve Bank in accordance with the provisions of the Act; and

(v) dealing in certain types of derivatives.

RBI has framed appropriate guidelines stipulating stringent criteria for issuers /

counterparties / investments with a view to enhancing the safety and liquidity aspects of the reserves.

GROWTH IN FOREIGN EXCHANGE RESERVES

India's foreign exchange reserves comprise foreign currency assets (FCA), gold, special drawing rights (SDRs) and reserve tranche position (RTP) in the International Monetary Fund (IMF). The level of foreign exchange reserves is largely the outcome of the Reserve Bank of India (RBI) intervention in the foreign exchange market to smoothen exchange rate volatility and valuation changes due to movement of the US dollar against other major currencies of the world. Foreign exchange reserves are accumulated when there is absorption of the excess foreign exchange flows by the RBI through intervention in the foreign exchange market, aid receipts, interest receipts and funding from the International Bank for Reconstruction and Development (IBRD), Asian Development Bank (ADB), International Development Association (IDA) etc.

Foreign currency assets are maintained in major currencies like the US dollar, euro, pound sterling, Canadian dollar, Australian dollar and Japanese yen etc. Both the US dollar and the euro are intervention currencies, though the reserves are denominated and expressed in the US dollar only, which is the international numeraire for the purpose. The movement of the US dollar against other currencies in which FCA are held, therefore impacts the level of reserves in US dollar terms. The level of reserves, denominated in US dollars declines when US dollar appreciates against major international currencies and vice versa. The twin objectives of safety and liquidity have been the guiding principles of foreign exchange reserves management in India with return optimization being embedded strategy within this framework.

Beginning from a low level of US$ 5.8 billion at end-March 1991, India's foreign exchange reserves increased gradually to US$ 25.2 billion by end-March 1995, US$ 38.0 billion by end-March 2000, US$ 113.0 billion by end-March 2004 and US$ 199.2 billion by end-March 2007. The reserves stood at US$ 314.6 billion at end-May 2008 before declining to US$ 252.0 billion at the end of March 2009. The decline in reserves in 2008-09 was inter alia a fallout of the global crisis and strengthening of the US dollar vis-à-vis other international currencies. Foreign exchange reserves increased to US$ 279.1 billion at end-March 2010, mainly on account of valuation gain as the US dollar depreciated against most of the major international currencies. In fiscal 2010-11, the reserves again showed an increasing trend, reaching US$ 304.8 billion at end-March 2011. In fiscal 2011-12, they reached all-time high of US$ 322.0 billion at end-August 2011. However, they declined thereafter and stood at US$ 294.4 billion at end-March 2012. Details of foreign exchange reserves, component wise, since 1950-51 in rupee and US dollar are given at Appendix 6.1 (A) and 6.1 (B).

In 2012-13, the reserves increased marginally by US$ 0.4 billion from US$ 294.4

billion at end-March 2012 to US$ 294.8 billion at end September 2012. Of this total increase, US$ 0.3 billion was on BoP basis and US$ 0.1 billion was on account of valuation effect. A summary of changes in the foreign exchange reserves since 2007-08, with a breakdown into increase / decrease on BoP basis and valuation effect is presented in Table-4.

TABLE 4

Summary of Changes in Foreign Exchange Reserves (US$ billion)

Sl. No.	*Year*	*Foreign exchange reserves at the end of financial year (end March)*	*Total Increase (+)/ decrease (-) in reserves*	*Increase/decrease in reserves on a BoP basis*	*Increase/decrease in reserves due to valuation effect*
1	2	3	4	5	6
1	2007-08	309.7	110.5	92.2 (83.4)	18.3 (16.6)
2	2008-09	252.0	- 57.7	-20.1 (34.8)	- 37.6 (65.2)
3	2009-10	279.1	27.1	13.4 (49.4)	13.7 (50.6)
4	2010-11	304.8	25.7	13.1 (51.0)	12.6 (49.0)
5	2011-12	294.4	- 10.4	- 12.8 (123.0)	2.4 (-23.0)
6	2012-13 (up to Sept. 2012)	294.8	0.4	0.3 (75.0)	0.1 (25.0)

Source: RBI.

Note: Figures in parentheses indicate percentage shares of total change.

In the current fiscal, foreign exchange reserves on month-on-month basis remained in the range of US$ 286.0 billion (at end-May 2012) to US$ 295.6 billion (at end-December 2012). At end December 2012, reserves stood at US$ 295.6 billion, indicating a marginal increase of US$ 1.2 billion from US$ 294.4 billion at end-March, 2012. At this level, reserves provided about seven months of import cover. Issues relating to build up of foreign exchange reserves are summarized in Box 4.

BOX 4

Building up Foreign Exchange Reserves

The distinction between convertible and non-convertible currencies is important for emerging economies, as most transactions with the rest of the world are in convertible currencies like US dollar, euro, pound sterling, yen, Swiss Franc etc. The need for increasing the availability of convertible currency for self-insurance has also been behind the race to build-up foreign exchange reserves (FER) in emerging economies after the Asian Crisis of 1997. Such FER accumulation, however, is constrained by the fact that it is possible only in times of currency appreciation.

Following the BoP crisis of 1990-91 that was essentially due to depletion of foreign exchange reserves, there was a conscious effort by the RBI to build up FER. This was done through buying foreign currency in the market during periods of surge in capital flows. As a result,

FER levels increased from US$ 5.8 billion in 1990-91 to US$ 314.6 billion at end May 2008. The RBI is however following a hands-off policy in foreign exchange market after the 2008 global crisis, with intervention limited to curbing excess rupee volatility. As a result, during 2009-10 and 2010-11, when rupee was appreciating due to increase in capital flows, there was virtually no intervention to build up FER.

The sharp decline in rupee in 2011-12 however led the RBI to inject foreign exchange to the extent of US$ 20.1 billion to stem the rupee slide. The pressure on currency has continued in the financial year 2012-13 because of the ongoing euro-zone crisis. The import cover of FER, as a result, has declined from 14.4 months of imports in 2007-08 to 7.1 months in 2011-12. There are costs to intervention. The main cost is the release of corresponding rupee liquidity, when RBI intervenes in the market to buy foreign exchange. This may stoke inflation, which may not appeal in the current inflationary situation.

Past experience however shows that measures like Market Stabilization Scheme (MSS) have been effective in draining excess liquidity from the system. Countries like China and Turkey use cash reserve ratio (CRR) for the same purpose. The cost of a particular policy, however, has to be weighed against the benefits, which are manifold. First, intervention to buy FER during surge in capital leads to build-up of reserves, which provides self-insurance against external vulnerability. Second, the higher reserve levels restore investor confidence and may lead to an increase in foreign direct and portfolio investment flows that spurs growth and helps bridge the current account deficit. Third, in a scenario of high trade and CAD, as in India, allowing the currency to appreciate through non-intervention during times of surge in capital, could have further negative fallout for the BoP by making exports less competitive and imports cheaper. Lastly, buying foreign exchange provides more ammunition for intervention when the currency is declining, which could potentially lower currency volatility.

Foreign Currency Assets (FCAs)

FCAs are the major constituent of India's foreign exchange reserves. FCAs increased by US$ 1.7 billion from US$ 260.7 billion at end March 2012 to US$ 262.4 billion at end-December 2012. In line with the principles of preserving the long-term value of the reserves in terms of purchasing power, minimizing risk and volatility in returns and maintaining liquidity, the RBI holds FCAs in major convertible currencies instruments. These include deposits of other country central banks, the Bank for International Settlements (BIS) and top-rated foreign commercial banks, and in securities representing debt of sovereigns and supranational institutions with residual maturity not exceeding 10 years, to provide a strong bias towards capital preservation and liquidity. The annualized rate of return, net of depreciation, on the multi-currency multi-asset portfolio of the RBI has shown declining trend over the years. It declined from 4.2 per cent in 2008-09 to 2.1 per cent in 2009-10, 1.7 per cent in 2010-11 and further to 1.5 per cent in 2011-12.

Foreign Exchange Reserves of Other Countries

India continues to be one of the largest holders of foreign exchange reserves. Country-wise details of foreign exchange reserves reveal that India is the eighth largest foreign exchange reserves holder in the world, after China, Japan, Russia, Switzerland, Brazil, Republic of Korea and China P R Hong Kong (Table-5) at end-December 2012.

TABLE 5
Foreign Exchange Reserves of Some Major Countries

Sl. No.	*Country*	*Foreign exchange reserves (end Dec. 2012) (US$ billion)*
1	2	3
1	China	3310.0[a]
2	Japan	1304.1
3	Russia	538.6
4	Switzerland (November 2012)	531.7
5	Brazil	373.1
6	Republic of Korea (November 2012)	326.2
7	China P R Hong Kong (November 2012)	305.2
8	India	295.6[b]
9	Germany (November 2012)	259.4
10	France (November 2012)	211.0
11	Italy	185.6
12	Thailand	184.2

Source: IMF

a: As per PBC, at end-December 2012, China's foreign exchange reserves stood at US$ 3.31 trillion (source: http:/www.pbc.gov.cn).

b: RBI

In additional foreign exchange reserves of Taiwan are shown at US$ 403.2 billion (Q4) as per The Economist January 31, 2013.

RISK MANAGEMENT AND FOREIGN EXCHANGE RESERVES

Sound risk management is an integral part of efficient foreign exchange reserves management. The strategy for reserves management places emphasis on managing and controlling the exposure to financial and operational risks associated with deployment of reserves. The broad strategy for reserve management including currency composition and investment policy is decided in consultation with the Government of India. The risk management functions are aimed at ensuring development of sound governance structure in line with the best international practices, improved accountability, a culture of risk awareness across all operations and efficient allocation of resources for development of in-house skills and expertise. The risks attendant on deployment of reserves, *viz.*, credit risk, market risk, liquidity risk and operational risk and the systems employed to manage these risks are discussed below:

Credit Risk

Credit risk is defined as the potential that a borrower or counterparty will fail to meet its obligation in accordance with agreed terms. The Reserve Bank has been extremely sensitive to the credit risk it faces on the investment of foreign exchange reserves in the international markets. Investments in bonds/treasury bills, which represent debt obligations of highly rated sovereigns and supranational entities, do not give rise to any substantial credit risk. Placement of deposit with BIS and other central banks is also considered credit risk-free. However, placement of deposits with commercial banks as also transactions in foreign exchange and bonds/treasury bills with commercial banks/investment banks and other securities firms give rise to credit risk.

Credit risk has been in focus since the onset of the credit crisis in the US financial markets and its contagion effect on other economies leading to global financial crisis during the second half of 2008 and during 2009. The Reserve Bank continues to apply stringent credit criteria for selection of counterparties. Credit exposure *vis-a-vis* sanctioned limit in respect of approved counterparties is monitored continuously. Besides, the financial strength of counterparties is constantly under watch. The basic objective of such an on-going exercise is to assess whether counterparty's credit quality is under potential threat.

Market Risk

Market risk arises on account of exchange rate and interest rate movements. These are detailed as under:

Currency Risk

Currency risk arises due to uncertainty in exchange rates. Decisions are taken regarding the long-term exposure on different currencies depending on the likely movements in its exchange rate and other considerations in the medium and long-term (e.g.., maintenance of major portion of reserves in the intervention currency, the approximate currency profile of the reserves in line with the changing external trade profile of the country, benefit of diversification, etc.). The decision making procedure is supported by reviews of the strategy on a regular basis.

Interest Rate Risk

The crucial aspect of the management of interest rate risk is to protect the value of the investments as much as possible from the adverse impact of the interest rate movements. The interest rate sensitivity of the reserves portfolio is identified in terms of benchmark duration and the permitted deviation from the benchmark. The focus of the investment strategy revolves around the overwhelming need to keep the interest rate risk of the portfolio reasonably low with a view to minimising losses arising out of adverse interest rate movements, if any. This approach is warranted as reserves are viewed as a market stabilising force in uncertain environment.

Liquidity Risk

Liquidity risk involves the risk of not being able to sell an instrument or close a position when required without facing significant costs. The reserves need to maintain a high level of liquidity at all times in order to be able to meet any unforeseen and emergency needs. Any adverse development has to be met with reserves and, hence, the need for a highly liquid portfolio is a necessary constraint in the investment strategy. The choice of instruments determines the liquidity of the portfolio. For example, in some markets, treasury securities could be liquidated in large volumes without much distortion to the price in the market and, thus, can be considered as liquid. In fact, excepting fixed deposits with the foreign commercial banks and the central banks and securities issued by supranationals, almost all other types of investments are in highly liquid instruments which could be converted into cash at short notice. The Reserve Bank closely monitors the portion of the reserves which could be converted into cash at a very short notice to meet any unforeseen / emergent needs.

Operational Risk and Control System

In tune with the global trend, considerable attention is paid to strengthen the operational risk control arrangements. Key operational procedures are documented. Internally, there is total separation of the front office and back office functions and the internal control systems ensure several checks at the stages of deal capture, deal processing and settlement. There is a separate set-up responsible for risk measurement and monitoring, performance evaluation and concurrent audit. The deal processing and settlement system is also subject to internal control guidelines based on the principle of one point data entry and powers are delegated to officers at various levels for generation of payment instructions. There is a system of concurrent audit for monitoring compliance in respect of all the internal control guidelines. Further, reconciliation of accounts is done regularly. In addition to annual inspection by the internal machinery of the Reserve Bank for this purpose and statutory audit of accounts by external auditors, there is a system of appointing special external auditors to audit the dealing room transactions. The main objective of the special audit is to ensure that risk management systems and internal control guidelines are adhered to. There is a comprehensive reporting mechanism covering significant areas of activity / operations relating to reserve management. These are being provided to the senior management periodically, *viz.*, on daily, weekly, monthly, quarterly, half-yearly and yearly intervals, depending on the type and sensitivity of information. The Reserve Bank uses SWIFT as the messaging platform to settle its trades and send financial messages to its counterparties, banks with whom *nostro accounts* are maintained, custodians of securities and other business partners.

Going forward, capital inflows to India during 2010-11 are expected to be stronger driven by both push and pull factors. While the push factors for surge in capital inflows include excess global liquidity accompanied by low interest rates leading to search for higher yield, the pull factors include the buoyant growth prospects, favourable interest rate differential and relaxation of ECB norms for 3G spectrum. Higher expected capital inflows, however, may exert pressures on asset prices and exchange rate.

India has followed a consistent policy on allowing capital inflows in general and on capital account management in particular. RBI position is that capital account convertibility is not a stand alone objective but a means for higher and stable growth. Indian economy should traverse towards capital convertibility along a gradual path - the path itself being recaliberated on a dynamic basis in response to domestic and global developments. In other words, continue to move towards liberalizing our capital account, but to revisit the road map to reflect the lessons of the crisis.

Among the components of capital flows, India prefer long term flows to short-term flows and non-debt flows to debt flows. The logic for that is self-evident. The policy on equity flows has been quite liberal, and in sharp contrast to other EMEs which liberalized and then reversed the liberalization when flows became volatile, India's policy has been quite stable.

Historically, India has used policy levers on the debt side of the flows to manage volatility. Contrary to popular perception, the policy is to use both quantity and price based variables to moderate debt flows. There is a ceiling on the extent of FII investment in sovereign and corporate debt (quantity variable) and there is also a withholding tax (price variable). External commercial borrowings (ECB) by corporates come in through both an automatic route and an approval route. ECB flows under both the automatic and approval routes are moderated by interest rate ceilings (a price variable) and those under the automatic route through an additional ceiling on total quantity (quantity variable). Non-Resident Indians (NRI) deposits are monitored through an interest rate ceiling, a price variable.

Although India does not have a deliberate strategy of building up reserves for self-insurance, the reserves got built up as a result of relatively flexible exchange rate policy. The reserves so built up have been used to contain volatility in the event of capital flows reversals.

QUESTIONS

1. Discuss the forex market structure in India.
2. Discuss the recent developments in the forex markets in India and other emerging economies. How has US dollar exchange rate moved in international market vis-a-vis other key currencies since March 2010.
3. Distinguish between the nominal effective exchange rate (NEER) and real effective exchange rate (REER). Critically examine the recent times indices of NEER and REER of the Indian rupee.
4. What are the reasons for high volatility in rupee exchange rate in recent times ?

5. Is real sector a real culprit of four market volatility ?
6. Discuss the concept of volatility in the forex market ? What should be the response to the volatility ?
7. Critically examine the renewed interest in recent times in foreign exchange reserves in the context of increasing globalisation, acceleration of capital flows and integration of financial market.
8. Comment on the changing composition of the foreign exchange reserves in India.
9. Critically examine the forex market turnover during the post-reform period.
10. Discuss the motives for holding foreign exchange reserves. Is foreign exchange reserves build-up **immical ????** to growth?
11. Discuss the challenges posed by the surge in capital flows to the conduct of monetary and exchange rate policy.
12. Critically examine the determinants of the demand for foreign exchange reserves.

REFERENCES

International Monetary Fund, *Exchange Rate Volatility and World Trade,* Occasional Paper 28 Washington, D.C.: IMF, July 1984).

J. M. Boughton, *The Monetary Approach to Exchange Rates: What Now Remains?* Essays in International Finance, No. 171 (Princeton, N.J.: Princeton University Press, International Finance Section, October 1988).

J.A. Frankel, "Tests of Monetary and Portfolio Balance Models of Exchange Rate Determination," in J.F.O. Bilson and R. C. Marston, eds., *Exchange Rate Theory and Practice* (Chicago: University of Chicago Press, 1984), pp. 239-260.

J.A. Frenkel, "Flexible Exchange Rates, Prices, and the Role of "News': Lessons from the 1970s," *Journal of Political Economy,* August 1981, pp. 665-705.

J.F.O. Bilson and R. M. Martson, eds., *Exchange Rate Theory and Practice* (Chicago: University of Chicago Press, 1984).

J.F.O. Bilson, "Exchange Rate Dynamics," in J.F.O. Bilson and R. Marston, eds., *Exchange Rate Theory and Practice* (Chicago: University of Chicago Press, 1984).

J.F.O. Bilson, "The Monetary Approach to Exchange Rate: Some Empirical Evidence," *IMF Staff Papers,* 1978, pp. 48-75.

K. K. Lewis, "Puzzles in International Financial Markets," in G. Grossman and K. Rogoff, eds., *The Handbook of International Economics,* Vol. Ill (Amsterdam: North-Holland, 1995), pp. 1913-1971.

K. Rogoff, "Monetary Models of Dollar/Yen/ Euro Nominal Exchange Rates: Dead or Alive?" *The Economic Journal,* November 1999, pp. 655-659.

M. Mussa, *Exchange Rates in Theory and Practice,* Princeton Essay in International Finance No. 179, Princeton, N.J., Princeton University Press, December 1990.

M. Mussa,"The Theory of Exchange Rate Determination," in J.F.O. Bilson and R. C. Marston, eds., *Exchange Rate Theory and Practice* (Chicago: University of Chicago Press, 1984), pp. 13-78.

M. Obstfeld and A. C. Stockman, "Exchange Rate Dynamics," in R.W Jones and P. B. Kenen, eds., *Handbook of International Economics,* Vol. II (Ams-terdam: North-Holland, 1985), pp. 917-977.

N. C. Mark,"Exchange Rates and Fundamentals: Evidence on Long-Horizon Predictability," *Amer-ican Economic Review,* March 1995, pp. 201-218.

R. Dornbusch, "Currency Depreciation, Hoard-ing and Relative Prices," *Journal of Political Econ-omy*, July-August 1973, DO. 893-915.

R. Dornbusch, "Expectations and Exchange Rate Dynamics," *Journal of Political Economy*, December 1976, pp. 1161-1176.

R. MacDonald, "Exchange Rate Behavior: Are Fundamentals Important?" *The Economic Journal*, November 1999, pp. 673-691.

R. Mundell, *International Economics* (New York Macmillan, 1968, chs. 9,11, and 15.

R.. M. Levich, "Overshooting in the Foreign Exchange Market," Occasional Paper, No. 5 New York: Group of Thirty, 1981).

38

INDIA'S FOREIGN TRADE

INTRODUCTION

The foreign trade of different countries, consisting of importing and exporting commodities of different countries in the aggregate constitutes international trade. Foreign trade in India includes all imports and exports to and from India. At the level of central government it is a administered by the ministry of commerce and industry. The focus of the chapter is on the India's merchandise trade performance in recent times. It also analyses disaggregated commodity-wise and direction-wise details of India's foreign trade.

DEFINITION OF FOREIGN TRADE

Foreign trade is exchange of goods and services between countries. The inclination for one country to trade with another is based in large part on the idea of comparative advantage—which says that any country, no matter how technologically disadvantaged it might be, can always find some sort of good that will let it enter the game of foreign trade. In this sense, foreign trade is just an extension of the production, exchange, and consumption that's a fundamental part of life. The only difference with foreign trade is that producers and consumers reside in separate countries. The nature, level of development, and significance of foreign trade are determined by the specific mode of production. International division of labour is the basis of foreign trade.

TYPES OF FOREIGN TRADE

Foreign Trade can be divided into following three groups :-

1. *Import Trade :* Import trade refers to purchase of goods by one country from another country or inflow of goods and services from foreign country to home country.

2. *Export Trade :* Export trade refers to the sale of goods by one country to another country or outflow of goods from home country to foreign country.

3. **Entrepot Trade** : Entrepot trade is also known as Re-export. It refers to purchase of goods from one country and then selling them to another country after some processing operations.

NEED AND IMPORTANCE OF FOREIGN TRADE

Following points explain the need and importance of foreign trade to a nation.

1. Division of labour and specialisation

Foreign trade leads to division of labour and specialisation at the world level. Some countries have abundant natural resources. They should export raw materials and import finished goods from countries which are advanced in skilled manpower. This givés benefits to all the countries and thereby leading to division of labour and specialisation.

2. Optimum allocation and utilisation of resources

Due to specialisation, unproductive lines can be eliminated and wastage of resources avoided. In other words, resources are channelised for the production of only those goods which would give highest returns. Thus there is rational allocation and utilization of resources at the international level due to foreign trade.

3. Equality of prices

Prices can be stabilised by foreign trade. It helps to keep the demand and supply position stable, which in turn stabilises the prices, making allowances for transport and other marketing expenses.

4. Availability of multiple choices

Foreign trade helps in providing a better choice to the consumers. It helps in making available new varieties to consumers all over the world.

5. Ensures quality and standard goods

Foreign trade is highly competitive. To maintain and increase the demand for goods, the exporting countries have to keep up the quality of goods. Thus quality and standardised goods are produced.

6. Raises standard of living of the people

Imports can facilitate standard of living of the people. This is because people can have a choice of new and better varieties of goods and services. By consuming new and better varieties of goods, people can improve their standard of living.

7. Generate employment opportunities

Foreign trade helps in generating employment opportunities, by increasing the mobility of labour and resources. It generates direct employment in import sector and indirect employment in other sector of the economy. Such as Industry, Service Sector (insurance, banking, transport, communication), etc.

8. Facilitate economic development

Imports facilitate economic development of a nation. This is because with the import of capital goods and technology, a country can generate growth in all sectors of the economy, i.e. agriculture, industry and service sector.

9. Assitance during natural calamities

During natural calamities such as earthquakes, floods, famines, etc., the affected countries face the problem of shortage of essential goods. Foreign trade enables a country to import food grains and medicines from other countries to help the affected people.

10. Maintains balance of payment position

Every country has to maintain its balance of payment position. Since, every country has to import, which results in outflow of foreign exchange, it also deals in export for the inflow of foreign exchange.

11. Brings reputation and helps earn goodwill

A country which is involved in exports earns goodwill in the international market. For example, Japan has earned a lot of goodwill in foreign markets due to its exports of quality electronic goods.

12. Promotes World Peace

Foreign trade brings countries closer. It facilitates transfer of technology and other assistance from developed countries to developing countries. It brings different countries closer due to economic relations arising out of trade agreements. Thus, foreign trade create a friendly atmosphere for avoiding wars and conflicts. It promotes world peace as such countries try to maintain friendly relations among themselves.

INDIA's MERCHANDISE TRADE

India's merchandise trade increased exponentially in the 2000s decade from US$ 95.1 billion in 2000-1 to US$ 620.9 billion in 2010-11 and further to US$ 793.8 billion in 2011-12. India's share in global exports and imports also increased from 0.7 per cent and 0.8 per cent respectively in 2000 to 1.7 per cent and 2.5 per cent in 2011. Its ranking in the leading exporters and importers improved from 31 and 26 in 2000 to 19 and 12 respectively in 2011. While India's total merchandise trade as a percentage of the gross domestic product (GDP) increased from 28.2 per cent in 2004-5 to 43.2 per cent in 2011-12 as per provisional estimates, India's merchandise exports as a percentage of GDP increased from 11.8 per cent to 16.5 per cent during the same period.

INDIA'S EXPORT GROWTH

Bolstered by the measures taken by the government to help exports in the aftermath of the world recession of 2008 and also the low base effect, India's export growth in 2010-11 reached an all time high since Independence of 40.5 per cent. Though it decelerated in 2011-12 to 21.3 per cent, it was still above 20 per cent and higher than the compound annual growth rate (CAGR) of 20.3 per cent for the period 2004-5 to 2011-12. After registering very high growth of 56.5 per cent in July 2011, export growth started decelerating with a sudden fall to single digits in November 2011 as a result of the emerging global situation and then to negative figures from March 2012. Monthly export growth rates in 2012-13 (April-December) were negative except for a marginal positive growth in April 2012. For three months in 2012-13, exports declined YOY by double digits with the largest decline recorded in July 2012 at -15.1 per cent. In January, 2013, there is a marginal positive growth of 0.8 pe cent.

Export Growth and Exchange Rate Changes

Export growth in dollar terms was negative at -4.9 per cent in 2012-13 (April-January), compared to 21.3 per cent growth in 2011-12 (full year). In rupee terms, it was positive at 9.1 per cent, though here too, there was a deceleration from the 28.3 per cent in 2011-12 (full year).

India's export growth has almost continuously been above world export growth in the 2000s decade and in 2011. One issue that has been a topic of debate is whether India's export growth rate is dependent on world growth/trade or exchange rate. There is a strong correspondence between India's export growth and world export growth. This is clearly visible in 2009 when there was a big dip in both world exports and India's exports. The relationship between changes in real effective exchange rate (REER) and India's export growth is not however as clear-cut as that with world trade.

Trade Quantums and Unit Values

The very high export growth rate in rupee terms in 2010-11 is due to the high increase in both volume and unit value indices from the very low base of the previous year (Table 1). While crude materials inedible except fuels and manufactured goods contributed to the high increase in unit values, machinery and transport equipment, mineral fuels, lubricants and related materials, and manufactured goods classified chiefly by materials and food and food articles contributed to the high rise in volumes. The 28.3 per cent export growth in rupee terms in 2011-12 was due to the high growth in the unit value index of 20.2 per cent besides the 8.9 per cent growth in the volume index. While the high growth in the unit value index is due to growth in chemicals and related products (41.2 per cent), inedible crude materials other than fuels (41 per cent), and mineral fuels and related materials (36 per cent), growth in the quantum index of exports is mainly due to growth in food and food articles (35.9 per cent) machinery and transport equipment (28.0 per cent) and miscellaneous manufactured articles (16.8 per cent). A dissection of country-wise export quantum indices shows that the high growth in this index in 2011-12 is due to the high export quantum growth to Japan (26.8 per cent), Belgium (26 per cent), Bangladesh (20.9 per cent), and the UK (17 per cent).

TABLE 1

Trade Performance: Growth in Quantum and Unit Value Indices

(Annual per cent change)

	Exports				*Imports*				*Terms of Trade*	
	Rupee terms	*US$ terms*	*Quantum*	*Unit Value*	*Rupee terms*	*US$ terms*	*Quantum*	*Unit Value*	*Net*	*Income*
2001-2	2.7	-0.6	0.8	1.0	6.2	2.9	4.0	2.8	-2.1	-1.7
2002-3	22.1	20.3	19.0	2.9	21.2	19.4	5.8	14.3	-9.8	7.8
2003-4	15.0	21.1	7.3	7.5	20.8	27.3	17.4	3.1	3.6	10.4
2004-5	27.9	30.8	11.2	14.9	39.5	42.7	17.2	18.9	-3.5	8.0
2005-6	21.6	23.4	15.1	6.1	31.8	33.8	16.0	14.0	-6.0	8.1
2006-7	25.3	22.6	10.2	13.7	27.3	24.5	9.8	15.1	-1.3	8.7
2007-8	14.7	29.0	7.9	5.1	20.4	35.5	14.1	1.9	2.6	10.9
2008-9	28.2	13.6	9.0	16.9	35.8	20.7	20.2	13.8	2.5	11.3
2009-10	0.6	-3.5	-1.1	1.0	-0.8	-5.0	9.9	10.0	12.3	11.1
2010-11	35.2	40.5	15.2	13.8	23.4	28.2	8.0	13.0	1.1	16.7
2011-12	28.3	21.3	8.9	20.2	39.3	32.3	-20.9	74.9	-27.2	-20.7
2012-13a	9.1	-4.9	-	-	14.5	0.0	-	-	-	-

Source: Directorate General of Commercial Intelligence and Statistics (DGCI&S). a April-January.

Note: Quantum and unit value indices of exports and imports are with new base (1999-2000=100).

Contrary to general belief, the high import growth (in rupee terms) in 2011-12 was not due to quantum increase but due to high unit value increase (74.9 per cent), with growth in quantum of imports even being in negative figures at - 20.9 per cent in 2011-12. The unit value index of imports registered unusually high growth of 74.9 per cent in 2011-12 mainly due to growth in unit values of two high weighted items, machinery and transport equipment (169.2 per cent) due to a sharp rise in prices; and mineral fuels, lubricants, and related materials (28.9 per cent) due to the rise in price of crude petroleum and products. The high negative quantum growth of imports was mainly due to fall in quantum of machinery and transport equipment (- 52 per cent) which had become costlier and manufactured goods classified chiefly by materials (- 7.9 per cent).

The net barter terms of trade in 2011-12, which measures the unit value index of exports as a proportion of unit value index of imports, declined to - 27.2 per cent due to the high growth in the unit value index of imports while growth in the unit value index of exports was moderate. Income terms of trade, reflecting the capacity to import, declined for the first time after 2001-2 by 20.7 per cent, indicating a very unfavourable terms of trade situation for India. In 2001-2, the fall was very marginal with the relevant component of the indicator also showing marginal increases.

EXPORT PERFORMANCE OF INDIA AND EDEs: A COMPARISON

The share of the select Emerging and Developing Economies (EDEs) in the US$ 18 trillion world exports in 2011 has increased to a sizeable 41 per cent with a change in share of 15.6 per cent over 2000. If the four newly Industrialized Asian Economies namely, Singapore, Hong Kong, Taiwan and Republic of Korea are also included then the share would be 50.5 per cent. The performance of China is spectacular with its share in world exports increasing by 6.6 percentage points between 2000 and 2011, comprising 42.4 per cent of the total increase in EDEs share over this period, while India's rise in share of 1 percentage point constitutes only 6.5 per cent of the total increase. However, China's export growth rate at 20.3 per cent in 2011 was substantially lower than that of India. India's export growth rate of 33.8 per cent in 2011 over and above the 37.3 per cent growth of 2010 is one of the highest in the world.

India's share in world merchandise exports which started rising fast from 2004, reached 1.5 per cent in 2010 and 1.7 per cent in 2011. It declined marginally to 1.6 per cent in 2012 (January-October), mainly due to its relatively negative export growth of - 5.1 per cent compared to world export growth of - 0.2 per cent (Table 2). In contrast China's share increased to 11.2 per cent in 2012 (January -October) with a positive export growth of 7.9 per cent.

TABLE 2

Export Growth and Share in World Exports : India and Other Select Countries

	Value (US$ billion)	*Growth rate %*				*Share in world exports (%)*				*change in shares*
		CAGR	*Annual*							
	2011	*2000-09*	*2010*	*2011*	*2012 (Jan-Oct.)*	*2000*	*2010*	*2011*	*2012 (Jan-Oct.)*	*2011/2000*
EDEs	7400	12.3	28.8	24.9	1.8	25.4	39.2	41.0	41.7	15.6
of which										
China	1899	19.1	31.3	20.3	7.9	3.9	10.4	10.5	11.2	6.6
Russia	522	12.5	32.0	30.4	3.1	1.7	2.7	2.9	2.9	1.2
Mexico	350	3.6	29.8	17.3	7.0	2.6	2.0	1.9	2.1	-0.7
India	303	16.3	37.3	33.8	-5.1	0.7	1.5	1.7	1.6	1.0
Malaysia	228	5.4	26.2	14.8	-0.6	1.5	1.3	1.3	1.3	-0.3

Brazil	256	12.0	32.0	26.8	-5.2	0.9	1.3	1.4	1.3	0.6
Thailand	226	9.2	28.6	15.9	0.8	1.1	1.3	1.3	1.3	0.2
Indonesia	201	6.9	32.1	26.9	-6.2	1.0	1.0	1.1	1.0	0.1
South Africa	97	8.5	30.7	18.5	-9.8	0.5	0.5	0.5	0.5	0.1
NIAEs*										
Korea, Republic	557	8.6	29.0	19.3	-1.3	2.7	3.1	3.1	3.0	0.4
Hong Kong	429	5.2	22.5	9.9	1.4	3.2	2.6	2.4	2.4	-0.8
Singapore	410	7.8	30.4	16.4	0.3	2.2	2.3	2.3	2.3	0.1
Taiwan	308	3.6	34.8	12.2	NA	2.3	1.8	1.7	NA	-0.6
World	18033	7.7	22.0	19.4	-0.2	100.0	100.0	100.0	100.0	-

Source: Computed from IMF, International Financial Statistics, January 2013.

Note: * Newly Industrialized Asian Economies, NA : Not Available.

Latest monthly growth rates of exports and imports of some of India's major trading partners have been low or negative. The EU's import growth has been negative for most of the months in 2012. There has been a slight but unsteady pick-up in import growth in the last two or three months in countries like the US, Hong Kong, and Singapore and in December 2012 in China.

INDIA's IMPORT GROWTH

After recovering in 2010-11 from the previous year's fall, India's merchandise imports increased further to US$ 489.2 billion with a growth of 32.3 per cent in 2011-12. This was due to the increase in growth of petroleum, oil, and lubricant (POL) imports by 46.2 per cent and non-POL imports by 26.7 per cent. POL imports (with a share of 31.7 per cent in India's total imports) registered a high growth mainly due to increase in import price of the Indian crude oil import basket by 31.5 per cent in 2011-12 as against 22 per cent in 2010-11.

BOX 1
Gold Imports and Policy Measures

India is one of the largest importers of gold in the world, with import growth of 11.2 per cent in terms of quantity and 39.0 per cent in terms of value during 2011-12. Gold is the second major import item of India after POL and constitutes 11.3 of its imports in 2011-12 in value terms. The rise in imports of gold is one of the factors contributing to India's high trade deficit and CAD in 2011-12, forming 30 per cent of its trade deficit. The RBI in its draft report of the Working Group to Study 'Issues Related to Gold Imports and Gold Loans by NBFCs in India' has stated that if gold imports in India had grown by 24 per cent (an average of growth in world gold demand during past three years) instead of 39 per cent in 2011-12, the CAD would have been lower by approximately US$ 6 billion and the CAD-GDP ratio would have been 3.9 per cent instead of 4.2 per cent. Globally, the demand for gold is rising, mainly due to demand from emerging economies like China and India. The major source countries for import of gold include Switzerland, responsible for 52 per cent of the total imports by India of raw gold during 2011-12 (which has led to an unfavourable bilateral balance of trade for India), followed by the UAE (17.6 per cent), and South Africa (11.5 per cent). The rise in gold imports is due to many factors.

The love of Indians for the yellow metal is well known. India is one of the largest consumers of gold in the world with consumption increasing from 721.9 tonnes in 2006 to 933.4 tonnes in 2011 and 612 tonnes in the first three quarters of 2012, accounting for around 27 per cent of world gold consumption in 2011, and 26.4 per cent in 2012 (total of first three quarters). As per the Annual Report 2011-12 of the Ministry of Mines, domestic production of gold is estimated at only 2.8 tonnes in 2011-12 and can meet around 0.3 per cent of the demand. This has inevitably led to its import. Gold is also used for trading/investment. Net retail investment constitutes 39.2 per cent of the India's total gold consumption in 2011 and 32.5 per cent during the first three quarters of 2012 in terms of quantity. As stated in the RBI report, one of the major components of gold demand in recent years has been investment demand at global level. Rising gold prices in recent years have not deterred the acquisition of gold in India, implying that investment in gold is becoming price inelastic. India also imports gold for manufacturing purposes and exports a portion of it as jewellery. In the case of export of gold jewellery, the major export destinations include the UAE (57.9 per cent), Hong Kong (14.1 per cent), and the USA (12.0 per cent).

International gold price movements which have been volatile in recent years also have a bearing on the value of the country's gold imports. During the 2000 to 2012 period, international gold prices have grown at a CAGR of 16.2 per cent. In 2011-12 they increased by 23.4 per cent though they moderated to 4.3 per cent during April-November 2012 over the corresponding period in the previous year. Even with this moderation, gold prices were at a high level of US$1721 per troy ounce in November 2012 and currently at US$ 1672.3 per troy ounce (as on 5th February 2013). As stated by the RBI report, volatility in international gold prices in recent quarters is positively skewed, implying that it provides fewer large losses and a greater number of larger gains. The worsening global situation has also led to a rise in purchase of gold as a safety metal and a further rise in its price. Fluctuations in international gold prices get automatically reflected in India's gold prices along with the markup due to duties and taxes. Substantial increase in gold prices seems to have fuelled positive price expectations also contributing to sharp rise in the value of gold imports in recent years.

To restrict the rising trend in gold imports which is adversely affecting India's balance of payments, measures were and are being taken by the government. In Budget 2012-13, import duty on standard gold and platinum was raised from 2 per cent to 4 per cent and non standard gold from 5 per cent to 10 per cent. On 21 January 2013, the Import duty on gold and platinum was increased from 4 per cent to 6 per cent. It has also been proposed to provide a link between the Gold ETF (Exchange Traded Fund) and Gold Deposit Scheme with the objective of unfreezing or releasing a part of the gold physically held by mutual funds under Gold ETFs and enabling them to deposit the gold with banks under the Gold Deposit Scheme. The value of gold imports during April-December 2012 declined by 14.7 per cent to US $ 38.02 billion and quantity of imports fell by 11.8 per cent compared to same period of previous year. Total gold consumption has also declined by 23 per cent during the first three quarters of 2012. While the supply of gold through organized channels can be constricted, there is need to be vigilant regarding gold inflows through unauthorized channels. Ultimately, the best way to reduce gold imports in a sustainable way will be to offer the public financial investment opportunities that generate attractive returns.

This means bringing down inflation as well as expanding the range of investments investors have easy access to.

Source: Compiled from reports and data of the RBI, EXIM Bank of India and the Gems and Jewellery Export Promotion Council.

POL import volume growth decelerated from 14.9 per cent in 2009-10 to 3.7 per cent in 2010-11 and 3.5 per cent in 2011-12. International oil prices (Brent) which reached a high of US$ 132.47/bbl in July 2008 declined sharply to US$ 40.35 /bbl in December 2008, following the global recession. From 2009 onwards, oil price has been increasing with intermittent volatility, reaching US$ 125.33/bbl in March 2012 and falling marginally with volatility in the following months. Currently Brent oil price is hovering around US$110/bbl.

Gold and silver imports (with a share of 12.6 per cent in India's total imports) grew by 44.5 per cent in 2011-12. Gold imports alone accounted for 91.7 per cent of the total imports of gold and silver. In 2011-12, gold imports grew by 38.8 per cent in value and 11.2 per cent in volume terms. Non-POL non-bullion imports increased by 23.3 per cent in 2011-12 compared to 29 per cent in 2010-11.

At US$ 406.9 billion imports in 2012-13 (AprilJanuary) registered a growth of 0.01 per cent. During 2012-13 (April-December), POL imports at US $ 125.2 billion grew by 12.8 per cent. Non-POL imports at US $ 239.8 billion declined by 5.1 per cent and gold and silver imports at US $ 39.3 billion declined by 14.7 per cent. Non-POL and non-bullion imports which basically reflect the imports of capital goods needed for industrial activity and imports needed for exports declined by 3.0 per cent.

TRADE DEFICIT

Trade deficit (on customs basis) reached a peak of US$ 184.6 billion in 2011-12 from US$ 118.6 billion in 2010-11 with the highest growth of 55.6 per cent since 1950-1. Moderate export growth and high import growth, particularly in POL imports due to high prices and high gold and silver imports, led to the highest-ever trade deficit in India since 1950-1, contributing to a high current account deficit (CAD) of 4.2 per cent of GDP.

The trade deficit of US $ 167.2 billion for 2012-13 (April-January) was 7.9 per cent higher than the US $ 154.9 billion in 2011-12 (April- January). While POL imports grew by 46.2 per cent in 2011-12, POL export growth was relatively lower at 34 per cent due to lower growth in the quantum of POL exports by 3.8 per cent, resulting in net POL imports increasing to US $ 99.3 billion in 2011-12. In 2012-13 (April-November), though POL import growth moderated to 11.7 per cent, POL export growth was negative at -7.3 per cent which was also due to the decline in the volume of POL exports by - 0.9 per cent. As a result the share of net POL imports in total imports increased to 23.5 per cent in 2012-13 (April-November) compared to 20.3 per cent in 2011-12 (whole year).

TRADE COMPOSITION

EXPORT COMPOSITION

Compositional changes in India's export basket have been taking place over the years. While the share of primary products in India's exports fell over the years from 16 per cent in 2000-1, in 2012-13 (April-November) it regained the share of 16 per cent mainly due to the export of agricultural items like rice and guar gum meal. The share of manufacturing exports fell drastically from 78.8 per cent in 2000-1 to 66.1 per cent in 2011-12 and further to 64.5 per cent in 2012-13 (April-November) mainly due to the fall in shares of traditional items like textiles and leather and leather manufactures even though the share of engineering goods and chemicals and related products increased. Share of gems and jewellery fell marginally. Share of petroleum, crude & products exports, which also include refined items, increased from 4.3 per cent in 2000-1 to 18.3 per cent in 2011-12 and 18.6 per cent in 2012-13(April-November).

The destination-wise exports of major items to the major trading partners from 2009-10 to 2012-13 (April-November) show great changes in the composition of exports to USA and China (Table 3). In the case of India's exports to the USA, the share of exports of primary products has increased from 6.8 per cent in 2009-10 to 21.3 per cent in 2012-13 (April-November), mainly due to the rise in share of agriculture and allied products, while the share of manufactured goods in India's exports to the USA has fallen from 89.1 per cent to 74.2 per cent during the same period. This decline has been mainly due to the fall in growth rates of exports of textiles and gems and jewellery. In the case of India's exports to China, the share of primary products has fallen from 65.7 per cent in 2009-10 to 38.4 per cent in 2012-13 (April-November) due to the fall in share and growth rate of ores & minerals. The share of manufactures in India's exports to China has increased from 32.2 per cent to 58.0 per cent during this period, mainly due to the rise in share of engineering goods, textiles, and chemicals and related products. In the case of India's exports to the EU, there has been a marginal rise in the share of primary products and petroleum products and a fall in the share of manufactured goods.

TABLE 3

Composition of Exports by Major Markets

	Percentage share						*Growth rate**				
	2000-01	*2009-10*	*2010-11*	*2011-12*	*2011-12 (Apr.-Nov.)*	*2012-13 (Apr.-Nov.)*	*2009-10*	*2010-11*	*2011-12*	*2011-12 (Apr.-Nov.)*	*2012-13 (Apr.-Nov.)*
I Primary products											
World	16.0	14.9	13.2	15.2	13.3	16.0	3.8	23.9	39.8	37.2	11.2
USA	9.4	6.8	8.0	14.5	11.9	21.3	-13.5	52.8	149.5	123.7	101.6
EU	13.1	8.6	8.2	9.7	9.0	9.9	-5.7	22.2	33.8	38.3	-2.0
China	45.2	65.7	51.6	55.2	49.5	38.4	26.9	4.7	24.8	7.0	-42.1

others	18.9	13.1	11.7	13.1	11.7	14.9	-1.7	31.7	35.7	41.9	17.5
(a) Agri. & allied products											
World	14.0	10.0	9.7	12.4	10.7	14.0	1.1	36.1	53.9	60.8	21.1
USA	9.0	5.8	7.1	13.7	11.0	20.4	-12.1	58.7	165.7	139.3	107.3
EU	11.9	7.1	7.1	8.1	7.6	8.7	-6.4	27.7	30.4	37.9	1.3
China	18.9	14.8	16.8	26.5	20.4	17.8	122.8	50.6	84.2	79.1	-35.0
others	16.8	11.3	10.2	12.0	10.7	13.8	-3.3	33.8	41.9	54.2	18.9
(b) Ores and minerals											
World	2.0	4.9	3.4	2.8	2.6	2.0	9.9	-1.3	-0.4	-14.3	-29.6
USA	0.4	1.0	0.9	0.8	0.9	1.0	-21.1	18.5	24.4	22.0	29.2
EU	1.3	1.5	1.2	1.6	1.4	1.2	-2.5	-3.5	54.6	40.7	-20.4
China	26.3	50.9	34.8	28.7	29.1	20.6	12.8	-8.7	-3.7	-16.6	-47.2
others	2.2	1.8	1.5	1.1	1.0	1.1	9.6	18.6	-7.4	-23.7	1.9
II Manufactured goods											
World	78.8	67.2	69.0	66.1	66.9	64.5	-5.9	44.2	16.2	27.7	-10.4
USA	90.6	89.1	87.4	81.4	83.3	74.2	-8.7	27.0	27.9	35.2	-0.2
EU	86.8	73.2	72.1	74.9	73.9	72.6	-15.4	25.8	18.6	34.4	-12.8
China	54.6	32.2	42.4	39.2	42.3	58.0	29.5	75.4	7.8	4.3	2.3
others	71.4	65.1	67.8	63.5	64.4	60.8	-2.5	53.4	13.6	25.7	-12.6
(a) Textiles incl. RMG											
World	23.6	10.5	9.1	8.7	8.6	8.7	-1.2	21.3	16.9	29.1	-6.4
USA	27.2	18.4	17.1	14.1	13.7	12.0	-7.6	20.2	13.0	19.2	-1.7
EU	29.2	18.5	16.3	16.3	15.7	14.4	-6.7	12.1	14.6	36.6	-18.7
China	9.3	1.8	2.8	4.1	3.7	8.6	47.0	104.2	68.5	51.4	73.6
others	20.2	7.4	6.4	6.2	6.3	6.5	6.2	27.1	17.9	27.3	-4.0
(b) Gems & jewellery											
World	16.6	16.2	16.1	14.7	14.9	15.4	3.7	39.6	10.8	38.6	-4.0
USA	29.3	24.2	20.8	19.5	22.3	18.0	2.8	11.7	28.5	52.7	-9.4
EU	11.5	6.7	6.8	9.2	9.2	7.1	-26.2	31.4	52.9	90.8	-31.5
China	0.0	3.8	0.5	0.7	0.7	0.7	-41.4	-81.0	42.8	25.0	-25.5
others	14.4	19.2	19.5	16.6	16.4	18.0	10.7	49.1	3.6	30.5	1.5
(c) Engineering goods											
World	15.7	18.2	19.8	19.2	19.2	19.3	-18.7	53.0	17.3	15.8	-6.4
USA	13.4	17.1	20.2	19.8	20.5	17.1	-33.9	53.0	34.5	37.9	-6.6
EU	14.0	20.8	20.9	21.0	20.8	21.5	-25.1	28.6	14.6	26.3	-8.4
China	9.9	12.4	25.8	18.8	20.7	24.4	63.6	177.9	-14.8	-21.3	-11.9
others	17.5	18.2	18.9	18.6	18.4	18.9	-15.8	53.2	19.3	14.6	-5.2
(d) Chemicals & related products											
World	10.4	12.8	11.5	12.2	11.8	13.7	0.9	26.0	28.6	35.4	7.4

USA	5.7	17.2	17.7	16.9	15.9	17.2	7.4	33.2	30.9	28.9	21.1
EU	9.7	12.5	12.8	14.1	13.6	15.1	-11.8	30.9	25.6	36.6	-1.2
China	15.5	10.2	9.4	11.1	12.1	15.5	40.8	23.3	37.7	48.5	-4.5
others	12.4	12.4	10.4	10.9	10.6	12.4	1.7	22.9	28.2	35.6	8.0
(e) Leather & leather mnfrs											
World	4.4	1.9	1.6	1.6	1.6	1.7	-5.5	16.3	22.6	36.0	-2.8
USA	3.7	1.5	1.4	1.3	1.3	1.4	-17.8	17.4	26.6	29.3	20.8
EU	11.4	6.3	5.5	5.8	5.9	5.8	-2.1	12.6	20.2	39.7	-12.5
China	1.1	0.4	0.5	0.7	0.7	1.1	-2.2	55.5	65.2	74.3	12.9
others	1.6	0.7	0.6	0.6	0.6	0.7	-9.9	24.8	24.2	26.4	12.8
(f) Handicrafts including carpet handmade											
World	2.8	0.5	0.5	0.4	0.4	0.4	-10.6	35.7	-12.9	-6.7	7.4
USA	6.0	1.5	1.6	1.2	1.2	1.3	-14.6	40.4	2.4	14.6	16.5
EU	4.4	1.1	1.0	0.7	0.7	0.8	-7.5	8.4	-12.1	-3.8	-2.9
China	0.3	0.1	0.0	0.1	0.1	0.1	106.9	-40.9	40.1	16.3	-2.4
others	0.8	0.2	0.3	0.2	0.2	0.2	-13.1	80.1	-29.2	-27.9	8.5
III Petroleum, crude & products											
World	4.3	15.8	16.5	18.3	18.7	18.6	2.3	47.1	34.0	54.3	-7.3
USA	0.0	2.3	3.7	3.5	4.5	3.7	180.3	110.9	30.1	139.9	-8.0
EU	0.0	16.9	18.8	15.0	16.5	17.0	45.4	42.7	-9.4	19.2	-8.7
China	0.0	0.8	5.3	6.3	8.6	3.2	-8.4	745.2	38.1	608.2	-72.2
others	8.1	19.9	19.4	23.5	23.3	23.5	-3.9	43.6	47.0	59.4	-6.5
Total exports											
World	100.0	100.0	100.0	100.0	100.0	100.0	-3.5	40.5	21.3	32.7	-7.0
USA	100.0	100.0	100.0	100.0	100.0	100.0	-7.6	29.5	37.4	43.9	12.2
EU	100.0	100.0	100.0	100.0	100.0	100.0	-8.4	27.9	14.1	31.4	-11.2
China	100.0	100.0	100.0	100.0	100.0	100.0	24.2	33.3	16.8	12.4	-25.4
others	100.0	100.0	100.0	100.0	100.0	100.0	-3.4	47.2	21.3	33.3	-7.6

Source: Computed from DGCI&S data. * Growth rate in US dollar terms.

Notes: 1. RMG stands for ready-made garments.

2. Share in a particular item means share of each country in total exports of India to that country.

3. Totals may not add up mainly due to some unclassified items.

The reason for India's export growth in 2012-13 (April-November) being more negative than in 2009-10 in the aftermath of the global recession can be seen from India's commodity-country export performance. India's exports to EU and China have been more negative during the recent global slowdown than in 2009-10, while its performance to USA has been better for most of the sectors except gems and jewellery.

The performance of India's exports to EU of textiles and readymade garments, gems and jewellery and ores: and to China of manufactures, engineering goods, chemicals gems and jewellery and ores was worse off in 2012-13 (April-November) compared to 2009-10. India's POL export growth to all major markets also decelerated in 2012-13 (AprilNovember) compared to 2009-10. Thus, the Euro Zone crisis and the Chinese slowdown have affected India's exports more during the recent slowdown than in 2009-10.

Export Diversification

In 2011, India had a global export share of 1 per cent or more in 53 out of a total of 99 commodities at the two-digit harmonized system (HS) level. While noticeable changes can be seen in India's market diversification, the same is not the case with its export basket diversification (Box 2).

BOX 2

Market vs Product Diversification

India has been fairly successful in diversifying its export markets from developed countries like the US and Europe to Asia and Africa, which has helped to a great extent in weathering the global crisis of 2008 and the recent global slowdown (Table 1.1).

Table 1.1: Region-wise Share of India's Exports:

		2000-1	*2005-6*	*2011-12*	*2012-13 (Apr.-Nov.)*
1)	Europe	25.9	24.2	19.0	18.7
2)	Africa	5.3	6.8	8.1	9.6
3)	America	24.7	20.7	16.4	19.5
4)	Asia	37.4	46.9	50.0	50.4
5)	CIS & Baltics	2.3	1.2	1.0	1.3

Source: Computed from DGCI&S data.

However, in terms of product diversification a lot more needs to be done as can be seen from the following:

- In the top 100 imports of the world at the four-digit HS level in 2011, India has only 6 items in the top 50; it has only 5 items with a share of 5 per cent and above and 18 items with a share of 2 per cent and above (Table 1.2), with 6 new items with high export growth (India) entering the list and 3 going out of the list in 2011 compared to 2010. The new items are medicaments consisting of mixed or unmixed products for therapeutic use; other articles of iron and steel; men's or boys' suits, ensembles; cruise ships, excursion boats, ferry-boats, cargo ships, barges and similar vessels; cane or beet sugar and chemically pure sucrose in solid form; and maize.

Table 1.2: Export Items of India with 2 Per Cent and Above Share in Top 100 World Imports at Four-Digit Level

Rank# World 2011	*HS4*	*Items*	*India share in world 2011*	*Growth rate in India (Export)*	*2011 World (Import)*
2	2710	Petroleum oils and oils obtained from bituminous minerals, etc.	6.7	49.0	39.4
7	3004	Medicaments consisting of mixed or unmixed products for therapeutic use	2.1	36.0	5.7
11	2601	Iron ores and concentrates, including roasted iron pyrites	2.3	-32.3	37.8
14	7102	Diamonds, whether or not worked, but not mounted or set.	23.8	44.7	14.7
34	7403	Refined copper and copper alloys, unwrought	3.2	-53.7	12.2
39	8803	Parts of goods of heading no. 88.01 or 88.02.	3.5	45.4	1.2
51	6403	Footwear with outer soles of rubber	3.1	23.0	9.2
52	6204	Women's or girls' suits, ensembles, jackets, blazers, dresses	4.9	34.8	9.2
55	7210	Flat-rolled products of iron or non-alloy steel	2.8	0.8	12.2
56	7113	Articles of jewellery and parts thereof, of precious metal	28.5	83.6	13.4
61	2902	Cyclic hydrocarbons.	4.4	47.8	27.8
68	7326	Other articles of iron or steel.	2.0	97.9	13.9
69	3902	Polymers of propylene or of other olefins, in primary forms.	2.8	46.0	17.3
72	6203	Men's or boys' suits, ensembles, jackets, blazers, trousers, etc.	2.3	31.5	16.4
92	6109	T-shirts, singlets & other vests, knitted or crocheted	6.0	22.1	12.1
97	8901	Cruise ships, excursion boats, ferry-boats, cargo ships, barges, and similar vessels	2.2	40.0	-25.8
99	1701	Cane or beet sugar and chemically pure sucrose, in solid form.	6.0	123.1	20.1
100	1005	Maize	3.4	103.1	34.1

Source: Computed from UN Comtrade data extracted on 9 January 2013.

Note: # Rank is in top 100 world imports.

- India has a very high export share in world imports in the case of only two four-digit HS items, jewellery and diamonds. While India can increase its shares further in the other 16 items given in the table, there are many other simple items in the top 100 world imports with high demand where India has developed its competence. Most of the items come under the three Es, electronic, electrical, and engineering items and some textiles items. Greater focus on these items could lead to a perceptible increase in India's share of exports in world imports.

Source: Internal study, Economic Division, Department of Economic Affairs.

IMPORT COMPOSITION

There have been some significant compositional changes in India's import basket in recent years. The share of POL imports increased from 28.7 per cent in 2010-11 to 31.7 per cent in 2011-12 (with a very high growth rate) and 34.6 per cent in 2012-13 (April-November). The share of gold and silver imports increased from 9.3 per cent in 2000-1 to 12.6 per cent in 2011-12 with a high import growth rate of 44.5 per cent. However, in part due to policy measures like raising import duty on gold, there was a moderation in gold and silver imports in 2012-13 (April-November) with its share falling to 10.5

per cent following a negative growth of - 20.4 per cent. The import share of pearls, precious and semiprecious stones also fell sharply in 2011-12 to 6.1 per cent following a negative growth of -13.3 per cent and further to 4.1 per cent in 2012-13 (AprilNovember), with a high negative growth rate of - 32.3 per cent. Another important development is related to the share of capital goods imports which increased from 10.5 per cent in 2000-1 to 13.6 per cent in 2010-11 and further to 14.1 per cent in 2011-12, declining thereafter to 11.9 per cent in 2012-13 (April-November) following a negative growth rate of - 6.5 per cent. Among capital goods, the import shares of all items machinery except electrical and machine tools, transport equipment, project goods, and electrical machinery fell, clearly signaling a slowdown in industrial activity. The share of electronic goods, which includes both consumer electronics and capital goods, also fell in 2012-13 (April-November) (Table 4).

TABLE 4

Commodity Composition of India's Imports

Commodity Group	*Percentage Share*					*CAGR*	*Growth Ratea*			
	2000-01	2010-11	2011-12	2011-12 (Apr.-	2012-13 Nov.)	2000-01 to 2009-10	2010-11	2011-12	2011-12 (Apr.	2012-13 -Nov.)
I. Food and allied products, of which	3.3	2.9	3.1	3.1	3.5	22.7	2.2	44.4	38.0	11.6
1. Cereals	0.0	0.0	0.0	0.0	0.0	24.3	15.8	-34.2	-46.6	6.8
2. Pulses	0.2	0.4	0.4	0.4	0.4	38.3	-23.1	27.2	11.3	9.2
3. Edible oils	2.6	1.8	2.1	2.1	2.5	17.2	19.0	57.7	55.3	18.0
II. Fuel, of which	33.5	30.9	37.4	34.3	38.0	21.0	22.4	59.7	52.3	9.8
4. POL	31.3	28.7	31.7	30.7	34.6	21.0	21.6	46.2	50.6	11.7
III. Fertilizers	1.3	1.9	2.4	2.3	2.2	29.0	4.8	72.1	32.2	-6.8
IV. Capital goods, of which	10.5	13.6	14.1	12.6	11.9	26.1	19.2	36.9	25.6	-6.5
5. Machinery except electrical & machine tool	5.9	7.0	7.2	6.7	6.3	24.4	24.0	35.8	28.2	-5.8
6. Electrical machinery	1.0	1.0	1.0	1.0	0.9	22.7	25.1	33.1	26.6	-5.5
7. Transport equipment	1.4	3.1	3.0	2.5	2.3	36.4	-0.9	31.8	13.1	-8.3
V. Others, of which	52.5	49.6	49.0	47.6	44.3	19.3	43.2	30.8	29.6	-7.6
8. Chemicals	5.9	5.2	5.1	5.0	5.1	19.5	29.6	31.8	24.3	1.1
9. Pearls, precious, semi-precious stones	9.7	9.3	6.1	6.1	4.1	14.0	116.9	-13.3	4.3	-32.3
10. Gold & silver	9.3	11.5	12.6	13.0	10.5	23.0	43.0	44.5	59.2	-20.4
11. Electronic goods	7.0	7.1	7.1	7.0	6.5	21.6	28.4	31.7	22.2	-7.7
Total imports	100.0	100.0	100.0	100.0	100.0	21.5	28.2	32.3	36.2	-0.8

Source:Computed from DGCI&S data.

a Growth rate in US dollar terms

DIRECTION OF TRADE

There has been significant market diversification in India's trade. Region-wise, while India's exports to Europe and America have declined, its exports to Asia and Africa have increased. However, in 2012-13 (April- November), the share of India's exports to the USA increased to 13.5 per cent. Within Asia, while the share of North East Asia (consisting of China, Hong Kong, Japan) and ASEAN (Association of South East Asian Nations) fell from 14.8 per cent and 12.0 per cent in 2011-12 to 13.1 per cent and 10.3 per cent respectively in 2012-13 (April- November), there was a noticeable rise in the share of West Asia-GCC (Gulf Cooperation Council) countries from 14.9 per cent in 2011-12 to 17.7 per cent in 2012-13 (April- November).

In 2012-13 (April- November), compared to 2000-01, the share of India's imports from Europe has declined to 16.7 per cent from 27.6 per cent, while that from Asia has increased substantially to 61.1 per cent from 27.7 per cent. The share of America in India's imports also increased to 11.5 per cent from 7.9 per cent. India's top 15 trading partners have nearly 60 per cent in share in its trade with the top three contributing nearly half of this share. While Iran and UK are out of this top 15 list in 2011-12, Iraq and Kuwait are the new entrants. The musical chairs for the top slot among the top three trading partners seems to be continuing with the USA relegated to third position in 2007-8 from first, UAE relegated to second position from first in 2011-12 by China, and China in turn relegated to second position by the UAE in 2012-13 (April-November). The final word for 2012-13 is not yet out as the USA is inching closer to China with its share increasing by around one percentage point and that of China falling.

At 10 per cent in 2011-12 India's trade deficit as a per cent of GDP is one of the highest in the world. Export-import ratios reflecting the bilateral trade balance (Table-5) show that among its top 15 trading partners, India had bilateral trade surplus with

TABLE 5
India's Trade Share and Export-Import Ratio with Major Trading Partners

Sl. No.	Country	Share in total trade					Export/Import ratio[a]				
		2009-10	2010-11	2011-12	2011-12 (Apr-Nov.)	2012-13 (Apr-Nov.)	2009-10	2010-11	2011-12	2011-12 (Apr-Nov.)	2012-13 (Apr-Nov.)
1	China	9.09	9.50	9.52	9.62	8.95	0.38	0.36	0.31	0.29	0.23
2	UAE	9.31	10.72	9.03	8.99	9.74	1.23	1.03	1.00	0.98	0.92
3	USA	7.82	7.30	7.46	7.29	8.23	1.15	1.26	1.42	1.42	1.51
4	Saudi Arabia	4.50	4.04	4.63	4.57	5.43	0.23	0.23	0.18	0.17	0.28
5	Switzerland	3.27	4.11	4.22	4.30	3.50	0.04	0.03	0.03	0.03	0.04
6	Singapore	3.01	2.73	3.21	3.30	2.53	1.18	1.38	1.96	1.85	1.75
7	Germany	3.37	3.00	3.05	3.02	2.75	0.52	0.57	0.49	0.50	0.48

8	Hong Kong	2.70	3.18	2.97	3.09	2.53	1.67	1.10	1.21	1.09	1.51
9	Indonesia	2.51	2.52	2.68	2.69	2.50	0.35	0.57	0.46	0.38	0.34
10	Iraq	1.61	1.56	2.48	2.49	2.73	0.07	0.08	0.04	0.03	0.07
11	Japan	2.22	2.21	2.32	2.19	2.29	0.54	0.59	0.52	0.46	0.47
12	Belgium	2.09	2.32	2.22	2.21	1.91	0.62	0.67	0.69	0.71	0.52
13	Kuwait	1.93	1.96	2.21	2.02	2.38	0.09	0.18	0.07	0.08	0.06
14	Korea RP	2.57	2.29	2.20	2.20	2.30	0.40	0.36	0.33	0.35	0.29
15	Nigeria	1.86	2.08	2.19	2.19	2.14	0.19	0.19	0.18	0.18	0.20
	Total of 15 Countries	57.84	59.50	60.40	60.16	59.91	0:56	0.55	0.51	0.49	0.50
India's trade		100.00	100.00	100.00	100.00	100.00	0.62	0.68	0.62	0.62	0.58

Source: Computed from DGCI&S data.

Note: a. A coefficient of export and import ratio between 0 and 1 implies that India's imports are greater than exports and if the coefficient is greater than one, India exports more than what it imports.

four countries in 2011-12, viz. the UAE, USA, Singapore, and Hong Kong. In 2012-13 (AprilNovember), India's trade balance with the UAE has turned slightly negative while it has improved further with the USA and Hong Kong. Another important trend is the growing trade deficit of India with China and Switzerland, increasing from US$ 28 billion and US$24.1 billion in 2010-11 to US$ 39.4 billion and US$ 31.3 billion respectively in 2011-12. In 2012-13 (April-November), the export-import ratio with China worsened further to 0.23 from 0.31 in 2011-12.

QUESTIONS

1. Define the term foreign trade. What are the different types of foreign trade ?
2. Discuss the need and importance of foreign trade to a nation.
3. Critically analyse the developments in the India's merchandise trade in recent times.
4. Compare the export performance of India and the Emerging Developing Economics (EDEs).
5. Discuss the change in the trade composition of India's foreign trade.
6. Is there a significant diversification in India's trade ? Discuss the major changes in the direction of trade in recent time.

REFERENCES

Chandra R., S. Pohit, A.V. Deerdorff and R.M. Stern: *Analysis of India's Policy Reforms'* World Development, Vol. 21(2), March, 1999.

Easter, W.R., Islam and J.E. Stiglitz: Shaken and Stirred: Volatility and Macroeconomic Paradigms for Rich and Poor Countries; *Michael Brund Memorial Lecture,* Buenos Aires, World Bank Document,.1999.

Government of India: *Report of the Committee on Import-Export Policies and Procedure* (Chairman: P.C. Alexander), New Delhi, 1978.

Krishna, P. and D. Mitra: *Trade Liberalisation, Market Discipline and Productivity Growth: New Evidence from India,* Journal of Development Economics, Vol. 56, 1998.

Sharma A. and P.K. Mehta: *Indian Exports and European Union,* in R. Kapila and U. Kapila (ed.) Economic Development in India, Vol. 2, Academic Foundation, Delhi, 1998.

39

INDIA'S FOREIGN TRADE POLICY

INTRODUCTION

Policy makers have increasingly come to realisation that it is very difficult to isolate domestic economic activity from international market events. Dramatic effect of the closer global economic linkage has put on the enormous responsibilities. As more parts of a domestic economy are exposed to international shifts and changes, these parts are simultaneously becoming less controllable. The same interdependence that has made countries more affluent has also left them more vulnerable. The formulation of a new foreign trade policy with an objective to use it as an economic and foreign policy tool reflects the change in the perception towards the external sector and its role in the overall strategy of development. The chapter discusses some of the important features of the changes in India's trade policy.

TRADE DEVELOPMENT EFFORTS IN INDIA

In the post-war period, several developing countries pursued import substitution-led development strategies. Poor growth resulting from such strategies, however, led to policy reorientation in the early 1960s. While one set of countries started giving more incentives for the export sector even while persisting with a moderate form of import substitution (for instance, Brazil, Argentina and Mexico), another set of countries made a more fundamental shift in favour of outward orientation (for instance Korea, Singapore and Taiwan) (Balassa, 1989). The Indian development strategy recognised the significance of liberal trade policy in the early 1980s, which was manifested in the form of a number of important recommendations made at that time by several Committees. The notable ones focused on a shift in emphasis from control to deregulation through simplification in import licensing system (Alexander Committee, 1978), clear recognition of dynamic comparative advantages associated with export growth (Tandon Committee, 1980), the need to harmonise foreign trade policies with other macroeconomic policies, advantages of an export-led growth strategy, a phased reduction in effective protection (Abid Hussain Committee, 1984) and the need to discourage inefficient import substitution (Narasimham Committee, 1985). Notwithstanding these concerns, the trade regime continued to be characterised by a licensing system which together with a high tariff structure protected the economy from external competition. In addition, the trade performance was constrained by restrictive foreign investment policies (RBI, 1999).

The process of trade liberalisation, however, gathered momentum only during the 1990s in the aftermath of the external payments Crisis. The policy measures undertaken aimed at making domestic industry cost-efficient by enhancing efficiency in resource use under international competition, which was expected to derive a better export performance in the long-run. The major trade policy changes in the post-1991 period included simplification of procedures, removal of quantitative restrictions, and substantial reduction in the tariff rates as also their dispersion as recommended by the Tax Reforms Committee, 1992 (Chairman: Raja J. Chelliah). Furthermore, the reach of the export incentives was broadened, extending the benefits of various export-promotion schemes to a large number of non-traditional and non-manufactured exports. Following the announcements in the Export Import (EXIM) policies, various changes were effected such, as the removal of quantitative restrictions, strengthening the export production base, removal of procedural bottlenecks, technological upgradation and improvement of product quality. Various steps were also taken to promote exports through multilateral and bilateral initiatives, including identification of thrust areas and focus regions. The policy stance also marked a move away from the provision of direct export subsidy to indirect promotional measures. India also took several policy initiatives at the multilateral levels for tariffication of the non-tariff barriers. As per India's commitment to the World Trade Organisation (WTO), India agreed to the phased removal of all balance-of-payments (BoP) related quantitative restrictions by end-March 2001.

FOREIGN TRADE POLICY

For India to become a major player in world trade, an all encompassing, comprehensive view needs to be take for the overall development of the country's foreign trade. While increase in exports is of vital importance, the imports need to be facilitated which are required to stimulate economy. Coherence and consistency among trade and other economic policies is important for maximizing the contribution of such policies to development. Thus, while incorporating the existing practice of enunciating an annual Exim Policy, it is necessary to go much beyond and take an integrated approach to the developmental requirements of India's foreign trade.

Objectives

Trade is not an end in itself, but a means to economic growth and national development. The primary purpose not the mere earning of foreign exchange, but the stimulation of greater economic activity. The Foreign Trade Policy is built around two major objectives. These are: (i) To double India's percentage share of global merchandise trade within the next five years; and (ii) To act as an effective instrument of economic growth by giving a thrust to employment generation.

Strategy

These objectives are proposed to be achieved by adopting, among others, the following strategies:

(i) Unshackling of controls and creating an atmosphere of trust and transparency to unleash the innate entrepreneurship of our businessmen, industrialists and traders.

(ii) Simplifying procedures and bringing down transaction costs.

(iii) Neutralizing incidence of all levies and duties on inputs used in export products, based on the fundamental principle that duties and levies should not be exported.

(iv) Facilitating development of India as a global hub for manufacturing, trading and services.

(v) Identifying and nurturing special focus areas which would generate additional employment opportunities, particularly in semi-urban and rural areas, and developing a series of 'Initiatives' for each of these.

(vi) Facilitating technological and infrastructural upgradation of all the sectors of the Indian economy, especially through import of capital goods and equipment, thereby increasing value addition and productivity, while attaining internationally accepted standards of quality,

(vii) Avoiding inverted duty structures and ensuring that domestic sectors in India are not disadvantaged in the Free Trade Agreements/Regional Trade Agreements/Preferential Trade Agreements that India enters into in order to enhance our exports.

(viii) Upgrading infrastructural network, both physical and virtual, related to the entire Foreign Trade chain, to international standards.

(ix) Revitalising the Board of Trade by redefining its role, giving it due recognition and inducting experts on Trade Policy.

(x) Activating Indian Embassies as key players in export strategy and linking Commercial Wings abroad through an electronic platform for real time trade intelligence and enquiry dissemination.

SALIENT FEATURES

1. Special Focus Initiatives

With a view to doubling India's percentage share of global trade within 5 years and expanding employment opportunities, especially in semi urban and rural areas, certain special focus initiatives have been identified for the agriculture, handlooms, handicraft, gems & jewellery, leather and marine sectors.

2. Promotional Measures

Box-1 presents the some of the trade promotional measures.

BOX-1
Trade Promotional Measures

Assistance to States for Infrastructure Development of Exports (ASIDE)

Scheme for Assistance to states for Infrastructure Development of Exports (ASIDE) is formulated to encourage State Governments to participate in promoting exports, and is administered by Department of Commerce (DoC). Objectives of ASIDE include: (i) Developing infrastructure such as roads connecting production centers with ports, (ii) Setting up of Inland Container Depots (ICD) and Container Freight Stations (CFS), (iii) Creation of new State level export promotion industrial parks / zones, (iv) Augmenting common facilities in existing zones, (v) Equity participation in infrastructure projects, (vi) Development of minor ports and jetties, (vii) Assistance in setting up of common effluent treatment facilities, (viii) Stabilizing power supply, and (ix) Any other activity as may be notified by DoC.

Market Access Initiative (MAI)

MAI scheme, intended to provide financial assistance for medium term export promotion efforts with sharp focus on a country / product and is administered by DoC. A whole range of activities can be funded under MAI scheme. These include, amongst others, (i) Market studies, (ii) Settingup of showroom / warehouse, (iii) Sales promotion campaigns, (iv) International departmental stores, (v) Publicity campaigns, (vii) Brand promotion, (viii) Registration charges for pharmaceuticals and (ix) Testing charges for engineering products. Each of these export promotion activities can receive financial assistance from Government ranging from 25% to 100% of total cost depending upon activity and implementing agency.

Marketing Development Assistance (MDA)

MDA Scheme is intended to provide financial assistance for a range of export promotion activities implemented by Export Promotion Councils (EPCs), ITAs on a regular basis every year. The scheme is administered by DoC. Assistance includes, amongst others, participation in (i) Trade Fairs and Buyer Seller meets abroad or in India, and (ii) Export promotion seminars. Financial assistance with travel grant is available to exporters traveling to Latin America, Africa, CIS region, ASEAN counties, Australia and New Zealand. In other areas, financial assistance without travel grant is available.

Meeting Legal Expenses for Trade Related Matters

DOC would provide financial assistance to deserving exporters on recommendation of EPCs for meeting cost of legal expenses for trade related matters.

Towns of Export Excellence (TEE)

A number of towns have emerged as dynamic industrial clusters contributing handsomely to India's exports. It is necessary to grant recognition to these industrial clusters with a view to maximizing their potential and enabling them to move higher in value chain and tap new markets. Hence, selected towns producing goods of ₹1000 crore or more are notified as based on potential for growth in exports. However for TEE in Handloom, Handicraft, Agriculture and Fisheries sector, threshold limit is to be ₹250 crores. Recognized associations of units will be able to access funds under MAI scheme for creating focused technological services. Common service providers in these areas shall be entitled for *EPCG* scheme. Further such areas will receive priority for assistance under ASIDE scheme.

Brand Promotion and Quality

Central Government aims to encourage manufacturers and exporters to attain internationally accepted standards of quality for their products. Central Government will extend support and assistance to Trade and Industry to launch a nationwide programme on quality awareness and to promote total quality management.

Test Houses

Central Government will assist in modernisation and upgradation of test houses and laboratories to bring them at par with international standards.

Quality Complaints/ Disputes

Regional Sub-Committee on Quality Complaints (RSCQC) set up at Regional Offices of this Directorate shall investigate quality complaints received from foreign buyers.

Trade Disputes Affecting Trade Relations

If it comes to DGFT notice or he has reason to believe that an export or import has been made in a manner that (i) is gravely prejudicial to trade relations of India with any other country; and/or (ii) is gravely prejudicial to interest of other persons engaged in exports or imports; and/or (iii) has brought disrepute to the country; DGFT may take action against such exporter or importer in accordance with FT (D&R) Act, Rules and Orders made there under and foreign trade policy.

Export and Trading House (ETH)

Merchant as well as Manufacturer Exporters, Service Providers, Export Oriented Units (EOUs) and Units located in Special Economic Zones (SEZs), Agri Export Zones (AEZs), Electronic Hardware Technology Parks (EHTPs), Software Technology Parks (STPs) and Bio-Technology Parks (BTPs) shall be eligible for ETH status. ETH holder shall be eligible for following facilities: (i) Authorisation and Customs clearances for both imports and exports on self-declaration basis; (ii) Fixation of Input-Output norms on priority within 60 days; (iii) Exemption from compulsory negotiation of documents through banks. Remittance / Receipts, however, would be received through banking channels; (iv) 100% retention of foreign exchange in Exchange Earner's Foreign Currency (EEFC) account; (v) Enhancement in normal repatriation period from 180 days to 360 days; (vi) Exemption from furnishing of Bank Guarantee (BG) in Schemes under FTP; and (vii) SEHs and above shall be permitted to establish Export Warehouses, as per DoR guidelines.

Services Exports

Services include all 161 tradable services covered under GATS where payment for such services is received in free foreign exchange.

Registration Cum Membership Certificate (RCMC) for Service Providers

Software exporters shall register themselves with Electronics and Software EPC. Exporters of 13 specific services are required to register themselves with services EPC. Other service exporters shall register themselves with Federation of Indian Exporters Organisation (FIEO). Government shall promote establishment of Common Facility Centres for use by home-based service providers, particularly in areas like Engineering & Architectural design, Multimedia operations, Softwarre developers etc., in state and District-level towns, to draw in a vast multitude of home-based professionals into services export arena.

Served from India Scheme (SFIS)

SFIS's objective is to accelerate growth in export of services so as to create a powerful and unique 'Served from India' brand, instantly recognized and respected world over. All Service providers who have a total free foreign exchange earning of at least ₹ 10 Lakhs in preceding financial year shall qualify for Duty Credit scrip. For Individual Service Providers, minimum would be ₹ 5 Lakhs. All service providers (except Hotels, Restaurants and other service providers in Tourism Sector) shall be entitled to Duty credit scrip equivalent to 10% of free foreign exchange earned during proceeding financial year. Free foreign exchange earned through International Credit Cards and other instruments as permitted by RBI for rendering of service shall also be taken into account for Duty Credit scrip.

Hotels of one-star and above (including managed hotels) and heritage hotels approved by Department of Tourism (DoT) and other service providers in tourism sector registered with DoT shall be entitled to duty credit scrip equivalent to 5% of free foreign exchange earned during proceeding financial year. Stand-alone restaurants will be entitled to duty credit equivalent to 10% of foreign exchange earned by them in preceding financial year.

Duty credit scrip may be used for import of any capital goods including spares, office equipment and professional equipment, office furniture and consumables; that are otherwise freely importable under ITC (HS). Imports shall relate to any service sector business of applicant. Utilization of Duty credit scrip earned shall not be permitted for payment of duty in case of import of vehicles, even if such vehicles are freely importable under ITC (HS). In case of hotels, golf resorts and stand-alone restaurants having catering facilities. Duty Credit scrip may also be used for import of consumables including food items and alcoholic beverages. Entitlement / goods (imported / procured) shall be non transferable (except within group company and managed hotels) and be subject to actual user condition.

Vishesh Krishi and Gram Udyog Yojana (VKGUY): Special Agriculture and Village Industry Scheme

The objective of VKGUY is to promote exports of (i) Agricultural produce and their value added products; (ii) Minor forest produce and their value added variants; for exports w.e.f. 1.4.2004 (iii) Gram Udyog products, for exports w.e.f. 01.04.2006; and (vi) Forest based products, for exports w.e.f. 01.04.2007.

Duty credit scrip benefits are granted with an aim to compensate high transport costs. Exporters, of products shall be entitled for duty credit scrip equivalent to 5% of FOB value of exports (realized in free foreign exchange). However, Duty credit scrip benefits shall be granted only at a reduced rate of 3.5% of FOB value of exports (realized in free foreign exchange) in such cases where exporter has availed benefits under FTP for import of Agriculture Inputs (other than catalysts, consumables and packing materials) relating to export item under this scheme. However, following exports shall not be taken into account for duty credit scrip entitlement: (a) (i) Export of imported goods covered under FTP; (ii) Exports through transshipment, meaning thereby that exports originating in third country but transshipped through India; (b) Deemed exports; (c) Exports made by SEZ units; and (d) Items, which are restricted or prohibited for export under export policy in ITC (Hs). Further, all status holders shall be incentives with duty credit script equal to 10% of FOB value of agricultural exports which can be used for duty free import / procurement of capital goods related to infrastructure meant for agro-processing to promote agricultural exports. This would be in addition to prevailing benefits in other administered by ministry of agriculture and others for infrastructure development for agriculture, agricultural items and agro-processing activities like : (i) Cold storage units including controlled atmosphere (CA) and modified atmosphere (MA) stores, pre-cooling units and mother storage for onions etc. (ii) Pack houses (including facilities for handling, grading, sorting and packaging etc.), and (iii) Reefer Van / Containers. Assessment of applicant's proposal would be done with respect to past export performance and on a first come first served basis.

Focus Market Scheme (FMS)

Objective of the FMS is to offset high freight cost and other externalities to select international markets with a view to enhance export competitiveness in these countries. Exporters of all products through EDI enabled ports to notified countries shall be entitled for duty credit scrip equivalent to 2.5% of FOB value of exports for each licensing year commencing from 1st April, 2006. However in the additional markets notified shall be entitled for duty credit scrip on exports w.e.f. 1.4.2007. Following exports shall not be taken into account for computation of entitlement: **a)** (i) Export of imported goods covered under FTP; (ii) Exports through transshipment, meaning thereby that exports originating in third country but transshipped through India; **b)** Export turnover of SEZ units or supplies made to such units or SEZ products exported through DTA units; **c)** Deemed Exports; **d)** service Exports; **e)** diamonds and other precious, semi precious stones; **f)** Gold, silver, platinum and other precious metals in any form, including plain and studded Jewellery; **g)** Ores and concentrates, of all types and in all forms; **h)** Cereals, of all types; **i)** Sugar of all types and in all forms; **j)** Crude / Petroleum oil & crude / Petroleum based products covered under ITC HS codes of all types and in all forms; and **k)** Items which are restricted or prohibited for export under export policy in ITC (HS).

Focus Product Scheme (FPS)

Objective 7th FPS is to incentives export of such products, which have high employment intensity in rural and semi urban areas, so as to offset infrastructure inefficiencies and other associated costs involved in marketing of these products. Exports of notified products through EDI enabled ports to all countries shall be entitled for duty credit scrip equivalent to 1.25% of FOB value of exports for each licensing year commencing from 1st April, 2006. However, additional products notified / clarified shall be entitled for duty credit scrip on exports w.e.f. 1.4.2007. The exports made by EOUs / EHTPs / BTPs who do not avail direct tax benefits / exemption shall be eligible, provided the same is not covered earlier. But the exports not be taken into account for computation of entitlement in case of exports through transhipment, meaning thereby that exports originating in third country but transhipped through India; and export turnover of SEZ units or supplies made to such units or SEZ products exported through DTA units; and deemed exports.

High Tech Products Export Promotion Scheme

The objective is to incentive export of High technology products. Exports of notified high tech products through EDI enabled ports to all countries, shall be entitled for duty credit scrip equivalent to 10% of incremental growth in exports of notified products put together (realized in free foreign exchange) for current year (i.e., 2007-08 over previous year (i.e., 2006-07) for each licensing year commencing from 1st April, 2007. For this, the computation would be an following basis: (i) Exports of notified products taken together. (ii) FOB value realized (as reflected in BRC / FIRC). (iii) Applicant with 'nil' exports in base year shall not be eligible.

Duty credit scrip shall not exceed ₹ 15 crore for an exporter for all shipments done in a licensing year put together, for which benefit is being claimed under this scheme. Following shall not be counted for entitlement. (i) Export of imported goods covered under FTP; (ii) Exports originating in third country but transshipped through India; (iii) Exports of SEZ units or SEZ products exported through DTA units; and (iv) Deemed Exports.

Finally, there are certain common provisions for schemes under promotional measure except where specifically provided for instance, additional customs duty/excise duty paid in cash or through debit under duty credit scrip shall be adjusted as CENVAT credit or duty drawback as per DoR rules, except under SFIS. However, Government reserves right in public interest, to specify export products or services or exports to such countries, which shall not be eligible for computation of entitlement. Further Government reserves right to change ceiling on duty credit scrip. Similarly, Government may also notify goods which shall not be allowed for import under Duty Credit scrips. Utilization of Duty Credit Scrip for imports from a port other than port of registration shall be allowed under Telegraphic Release Advice (TRA) facility as per DoR notification. Duty Credit Scrip may be used for import of inputs or goods including capital goods, provided same is freely importable under ITC (HS). Duty Credit scrip and items imported against it would be freely transferable, except under SFIS.

For a shipment, benefit under any one of schemes can alone be claimed, at exporter's option. Utilization of Duty Credit scrip shall be permitted for payment of duty in case of import of capital goods under lease financing in terms of provision of FTP. Transfer of export performance from one to another shall not be permitted. Thus, a shipment bill containing name of applicant shall be counted in export performance / turnover of applicant only if export proceeds from overseas are realized in applicant's bank account and this shall be evidenced from Bank Realisation Certificate (BRC) / Foreign Exchange Inward Remittance Certificate (FIRC).

3. Duty Exemption and Remission Schemes

Duty exemption schemes enable duty free import of inputs required for export production. Duty Exemption Schemes consist of (a) Advance Authorisation and (b) Duty Free Import Authorisation (DFIA). A Duty Remission Scheme enables post export replenishment / remission of duty on inputs used in export product. Duty remission schemes consist of (a) Duty Entitlement Passbook Scheme (DEPB) and (b) Duty Drawback (DBK) Scheme. Goods exported under Advance Authorisation / DFIA / DEPB may be re-imported in same or substantially same form subject to DoR specified conditions.

Value addition (VA) (Except for Gems and Jewellery Sector) shall be:-

$$VA = \frac{A-B}{B} \times 100,$$

Where:

A = FOB value of export realised / FOR value of supply received.

B = CIF value of inputs covered by authorisation, plus any other imported materials used on which benefit of DBK is claimed.

Advance Authorisation Scheme

An Advance Authorisation is issued to allow duty free import of inputs, which are physically incorporated in export product (making normal allowance for wastage). In addition, fuel, oil, energy, catalysts which are consumed / utilised to obtain export product, may also be allowed DGFT, by means of Public Notice, may exclude any product(s) from purview of Advance Authorisation. Duty free import of mandatory spares upto 10% of CIF value of Authorisation which are required to be exported / supplied with resultant product are allowed under Advance Authorisation.

Advance Authorisation can be issued either to a manufacturer exporter or merchant exporter tied to supporting manufacturer(s) for (i) Physical exports (including exports to SEZ); and/ or (ii) Intermediate supplies; and /or (iii) supply of goods to the categories mentioned in (iv) supply of 'stores' on board of foreign going vessel / aircraft subject to condition that there is specific SION in respect of item(s) supplied.

In addition, in respect of supply of goods to specified projects mentioned in FTP, an Advance Authorisation can also be availed by sub-contractor to such project provided name of sub contractor(s) appears in main contract. Such Authorisation can also be issued for supplies made to United Nations Organisations or under Aid Programme of the United Nations or other multilateral agencies and paid for in free foreign exchange.

Advance Authorisations are exempted from payment of basic customs duty, additional customs duty, education cess, anti-dumping duty and safeguard duty, if any. However, imports for supplies will not be exempted from payment of applicable antidumping and safeguard duty, if any. Advance Authorisation and / or materials imported thereunder will be with actual user condition. It will not be transferable even after completion of export obligation. However, Authorisation holder will have option to dispose off product manufactured out of duty free inputs once export obligation is completed.

Advance Authorisations necessitate exports with a positive value addition. Exports to SEZ Units / supplies to Developers / Co-developers, irrespective of currency of realization, would also cover. For physical exports for which payments are not received in freely convertible currency, same shall be subject to value addition. In case of Authorisation for import of Tea, minimum value addition under Advance Authorisation shall be 100%. Similarly, in case of spices, duty free import of spices shall be permitted only for value addition purposes like crushing / grinding / sterlization or for manufacture of oils and oleoresins and not for simple cleaning, grading, re-packing etc. and minimum value addition shall be 15%.

Free of Cost Supply by Foreign Buyer

Facility of Advance Authorisation shall also be available where some or all inputs are supplied free of cost to exporter by foreign buyer.

In such cases, for calculation of VA, notional value of free of cost inputs along with value of other duty-free inputs shall be taken into consideration. However, if all inputs are supplied free of cost, exporter shall also have option to follow provision prescribed by DoR. Further, any firm / company registered with BIFR or any firm / company acquiring a unit, which is under BIFR shall be allowed Export Obligation Period (EOP) extension as per rehabilitation package prepared subject to approval of BIFR or 5 years if not specified, without payment of composition fee. Above provisions apply also to SSI units as per rehabilitation scheme of concerned State government.

GEMS and Jewellery

Exporters of gems and Jewellery can import/procure duty free inputs for manufacturing. Exporters may obtain Replenishment (REP) Authorisations from and this replenishment authorisation may also be for consumables. An exporter (with turnover of ₹ 5 crores annual export for last three years) may export cut & polished diamonds (each of 0.25 carat or more) abroad to any of the specified agencies / laboratories with re-import facility at zero duty within 3 months as per DoR guidelines. Exporters of gold/silver/platinum jewellery and articles thereof may import their essential inputs such as gold, silver, platinum, mountings, findings, rough gems, precious and semi-precious stones, synthetic stones and unprocessed pearls etc. in accordance with the procedure specified in this behalf. Nominated agencies are MMTC Ltd, Handicraft and Handloom Export Corporation (HHEC), State Trading Corporation (STC), the Project and Equipment Corporation of India Ltd (PEC), Premier Trading House under FTP and any other agency authorised by RBI. Exporters (except EOU/units in SEZ) may obtain gold silver/platinum from nominated agency(s). A bank authorised by RBI is allowed export of gold scrap for refining and import standard gold bars as per RBI guidelines. Following items, if exported, would be eligible for facilities: (a) Gold jewellery, including partly processed jewellery and articles including medallions and coins (excluding legal tender coins), whether plain or studded, containing gold of 8 carats and above; (b) Silver jewellery including partly processed jewellery, silverware, silver strips and articles including medallions and coins (excluding legal tender coins and any engineering goods) containing more than 50% silver by weight; (c) Platinum jewellery including partly processed jewellery and articles including medallions and coins (excluding legal tender coins and any engineering goods) containing more than 50% platinum by weight.

Value Addition (VA) for gems and jewellery sector would be calculated as under:

$$VA = \frac{A-B}{A} \times 100,$$

where

A = FOB value of the export realised / FOR value of supply received.

B = Value of inputs (including domestically procured) such as gold / silver / platinum content in export product plus admissible wastage along with value of other items such as gemstone etc. Wherever gold has been obtained on loan basis, value shall also include interest paid in free foreign exchange to foreign supplier.

An advance authorisation may be granted for duty free import of: (a) Gold of fineness not less than 0.995 and mountings, sockets, frames and findings of 8 carats and above; (b) Silver of fineness not less than 0.995 and mountings, sockets, frames and findings containing more than 50% silver by weight; (c) Platinum of fineness not less than 0.900 and mountings, sockets, frames and findings containing more than 50%

platinum by weight. Advance Authorisation holder may obtain gold / silver / platinum from nominated agencies in lieu of direct import.

Diamond Imprest Authorisation for import of cut and polished diamonds including semi processed diamonds, half cut diamonds, broken in any form, for mixing with cut and polished diamonds or for export as it is, may be issued for export of cut and polished diamonds and shall carry an EO. An exporter of cut & polished diamonds who is status holder may be issued an Authorisation for import of cut & polished diamonds upto 5% of preceding year's export performance of cut & polished diamonds.

Nominated agencies and their associates, with approval of DoC, and others, with approval of Gem & Jewellery EPC (GJEPC), may export gold / silver / platinum jewellery and articles thereof for exhibitions abroad. In case of exports through Foreign Post Office (including via Speed Post), value of jewellery parcels shall not exceed US$50000 and 20 kg. by weight. Private / Public Bonded Warehouses may be set up in SEZ /Domestic Tariff Area (DTA) for import and re-export of cut & Polished diamonds, cut & polished coloured gemstones, uncut & unset precious & semi-precious stones, subject to achievement of minimum VA of 5%. Firms and companies dealing in purchase / sale of rough or cut and polished diamonds / precious metal jewellery plain, minakari and / or studded with / without diamond and / or other stones with a track record of at least 3 years in import or export of diamonds / coloured gemstones / diamond and coloured gemstones studded jewellery / plain gold jewellery and having an average annual turnover of ₹ 5 crore or above during preceding three licensing years may also carry out their business through designated Diamond Dollar Accounts (DDA).

Dollars in such accounts available from bank finance and / or export proceeds shall be used only for (i) Import / purchase of rough diamonds from overseas / local sources; (ii) Purchase of cut and polished diamonds, coloured gemstones and plain gold jewellery from local sources; (iii) Import / purchase of gold from overseas nominated agencies and repayment of dollar loans from the bank; and (iv) Transfer to Rupee Account of exporter. A non DDA holder is also permitted to supply cut and polished diamonds to DDA holder, receive payment in dollars and convert same into Rupees within 7 days. Cut and polished diamonds and coloured gemstones so supplied by non-DDA holder will also be counted towards discharge of his export obligation and / or entitle him to replenishment Authorisation.

4. Export Promotion Capital Goods (EPCG) Scheme

EPCG scheme allows import of capital goods for pre-production, production and post-production (including CKD / SKD thereof as well as computer software systems) at 5% Customs duty subject to an export obligation equivalent to 8 times of duty saved on capital goods imported under EPCG scheme to be fulfilled in 8 years. In case of agro units, and units in cottage or tiny sector, import of capital goods at 5% Customs duty shall be allowed subject to fulfillment of export obligation equivalent to 6 times of duty saved on capital goods imported in 12 years. For SSI units, import of capital goods at 5% Customs duty shall be allowed subject to fulfillment of export obligation equivalent to 6 times of duty saved on capital goods in 8 years and total investment in plant and machinery after such imports does not exceed SSI limit. However, in respect of EPCG Authorisations with a duty saved amount of ₹ 100 crores or more, export obligation, shall be fulfilled in 12 years. In case CVD is paid in cash on imports under EPCG, incidence of CVD would not be taken for computation of net duty saved provided the same is not Cenvated.

Capital goods shall include spares (including refurbished/ reconditioned spares), tools, jigs, fixtures, dies and moulds. Second hand capital goods without any restriction on age may also be imported under EPCG scheme. However, import of motor cars, sports utility vehicles/all purpose vehicles shall be allowed only to hotels, travel agents, tour operators or tour transport operators and companies owning / operating golf resorts subject to condition that: (i) total foreign exchange earning from hotel, travel & tourism and golf tourism sectors in current and preceding three licensing years is ₹ 1.5 crores or more. (ii) duty saved amount on all EPCG Authorisations issued in a licensing year for import of motor cars, sports utility vehicles / all purpose vehicles shall not exceed 50% of average foreign exchange earnings from hotel, travel & tourism and golf tourism sectors in preceding three licensing years. (iii) vehicles imported shall be so registered that the vehicle is used for tourist purpose only. However, parts of motor cars, sports utility vehicles / all purpose vehicles such as chassis etc. cannot be imported under EPCG Scheme. Spares (including refurbished / reconditioned spares), tools, spare refractories and catalyst for existing plant and machinery shall be allowed to be imported subject to an export obligation equivalent to 8 times of duty saved to be fulfilled in 8 years.

To create modern infrastructure in retail sector, concessional duty benefits under EPCG scheme shall be extended for import of capital goods required by retailers having minimum area of 1000 sq meters. Such retailer shall fulfill export obligation i.e., 8 times of duty saved in 8 years.

EPCG scheme covers manufacturer exporters with or without supporting manufacturer(s) / vendor(s), merchant exporters tied to supporting manufacturer(s) and service providers. Import of capital goods shall be subject to Actual User condition till export obligation is completed. Following conditions shall apply to the fulfillment of the export obligation: (i) Export obligation shall be fulfilled by export of goods, manufactured / services rendered by the applicant. Export obligation shall be, over and above, the average level of exports achieved by applicant in preceding three licensing years. Such average would be the arithmetic mean of export performance in last 3 years. Export obligation may also be fulfilled by exports of group company / managed hotel which has EPCG Authorisation. However, in such cases, additional export obligation imposed shall be over and above average exports achieved by unit / company / group company / managed hotel in preceding three years. For this purpose, average would be based on previous export of goods and services put together. (ii) Shipments under Advance Authorisation, DFRC, DFIA, DEPB or Drawback scheme would also count for fulfillment of EPCG export obligation. (iii) Export obligation can also be fulfilled by supply of ITA-1 items to DTA provided realization is in free foreign exchange. (iv) Exports shall be physical exports. However, deemed exports shall also be counted towards fulfillment of export obligation alongwith usual benefits. Royalty payments received in freely convertible currency and foreign exchange received for R&D services shall also be counted for discharge under EPCG. Payment received in rupee terms for port handling shall also be counted for export obligation discharge. (v) Foreign exchange counted towards fulfillment of export obligation (over and above the average) shall not be eligible for incentives / rewards under promotional measures / schemes.

Any firm / company registered with BIFR or any firm / company acquiring a unit, which is under BIFR shall be allowed EO extension as per rehabilitation package subject to approval of BIFR or 12 years if not specified. These provisions apply also to SSI units as per rehabilitation scheme of concerned State government. Legal Under Taking (LUT) / Bond or 15% BG (as applicable) may be given for EPCG Authorisation granted to units in Agri Export Zones provided EPCG Authorisation is taken for export of primary agricultural product(s) or their value added variants.

A person holding an EPCG Authorisation may source capital goods from a domestic manufacturer. Such domestic manufacturer shall be eligible for deemed export benefit Such domestic sourcing shall also be permitted from EOUs and these supplies shall be counted for purpose of fulfillment of positive Net Foreign Exchange (NFE) by said EOU. In case of direct imports, export obligation shall be reckoned with reference to actual duty saved amount. In case of domestic sourcing, export obligation shall be reckoned with reference to notional Customs duties saved on FOR value.

EPCG Authorisation holders can opt for Technological Upgradation of existing capital good imported under EPCG Authorisation. Conditions governing Technological Upgradation of existing capital goods are: (i) Minimum time period for applying for Technological Upgradation of existing capital goods imported under EPCG is 5 years from Authorisation issue-date. (ii) Minimum exports made under old capital goods must be 40% of total export obligation imposed on first EPCG Authorisation. (iii) Export obligation would be refixed such that total export obligation mandated for both capital goods would be sum total of 6 times of duty saved on both the capital goods, to be fulfilled in 8 years from new authorisation issue-date,(iv) Facility for technological Upgradation shall be available only once and the minimum imports to be made shall be at least 10% of the existing investment in plant and machinery by applicant.(v) Capital goods to be imported must be new and technologically superior to earlier CG.

To incentivise fast track companies with a view to accelerate exports, in cases where Authorisation holder has fulfilled 75% or more of export obligation (including average level of exports) in half or less than half the original export obligation period specified, remaining export obligation shall be condoned.

Export Oriented Units (EOUs), Electronics Hardware Technology Parks (EHTPs) Software Technology Parks (STPs) and Bio-Technology Parks (BTPs)

Units undertaking to export their entire production of goods and services (except permissible sales in DTA), may be set up under the Export Oriented Unit (EOU) Scheme, Electronic Hardware Technology Park (EHTP) Scheme, Software Technology Park (STP) Scheme or Bio-Technology Park (BTP) Scheme for manufacture of goods, including repair, re-making, reconditioning, re-engineering and rendering of services. Trading units are not covered under these schemes.

Export and Import of Goods

(a) An EOU / EHTP / STP / BTP unit may export all kinds of goods and services except items that are prohibited in ITC (HS). Export of Special Chemicals, Organisms, Materials, Equipment and Technologies (SCOMET) shall be subject to fulfillment of the conditions indicated in ITC (HS).

Procurement and supply of export promotion material like brochure / literature, pamphlets, hoardings, catalogues, posters etc. upto a maximum value limit of 1.5% of FOB value of previous years exports shall also be allowed.

(b) An EOU / EHTP / STP / BTP unit may import and/or procure from DTA or bonded warehouses in DTA / international exhibition held in India without payment of duty all types of goods, including capital goods, required for its activities, provided they are not prohibited items of import in the ITC (HS). Any permission required for import under any other law shall be applicable. Units shall also be permitted to import goods including capital goods required for approved activity, free of cost or on loan / lease from clients. Import of capital goods will be on a self certification basis. Goods imported by a unit shall be with actual user condition and shall be utilized for export production.

(c) State Trading regime shall not apply to EOU manufacturing units.

(d) EOU / EHTP / STP / BTP units may import / procure from DTA without payment of duty certain specified goods for creating a central facility. Software EOU / DTA units may use such facility for export of software.

(e) An EOU engaged in agriculture, animal husbandry, aquaculture horticulture, pisciculture, viticulture poultry or sericulture may be permitted to remove specified goods in connection with its activities for use outside bonded area.

(f) Gems and jewellery EOUs may source gold / silver / platinum through nominated agencies on loan / outright purchase basis. Units obtaining gold / silver / platinum from nominated agencies, either on loan basis or outright purchase basis shall export gold / silver / platinum within 90 days from date of release.

(g) EOU / EHTP / STP / BTP units, other than service units, may export to Russian Federation in Indian Rupees against repayment of State Credit / Escrow Rupee Account of buyer subject to RBI clearance, if any.

(h) Procurement and export of spares / components upto 1.5% of FOB value of exports may be allowed to same consignee / buyer of export article within the warranty period.

Second hand capital goods, without any age limit, may also be imported duty free. Further, an EOU / EHTP / STP / BTP unit may, on the basis of a firm contract between parties, source capital goods from a domestic / foreign leasing company without payment of customs / excise duty. In such a case, EOU / EHTP / STP / BTP unit and domestic / foreign leasing company shall jointly file documents to enable import / procurement of capital goods without payment of duty.

EOU / EHTP / STP / BTP unit shall be a positive net foreign exchange earner except for sector specific where a higher value addition shall be required. NFE Earnings shall be calculated cumulatively in blocks of five years, starting from commencement of production. On approval, a Letter of Permission (LoP) / Letter of Intent (Lol) shall be issued by Development Commissioner/designated officer to EOU / EHTP / STP I BTP unit. LoP / Lol shall have an initial validity of years by which time unit should have commenced production. Its validity may be extended further up to 3 years by competent authority. However, proposals for extension beyond six years shall be considered in exceptional circumstances, on a case-to-case basis by BOA. Once unit commences production, LOP / LOI issued shall be valid for a period of 5 years for its activities. This period may be extended further by DC for a period of 5 years at a time.

Investment Criteria

Only projects having a minimum investment of ₹ 1 Crore in Plant & Machinery shall be considered for establishment as EOUs. This shall, however, not apply to existing units and units in EHTP / STP / BTP, Handicrafts / Agriculture / Floriculture / Aquaculture / Animal Husbandry / Information Technology, Services, Brass Hardware and Handmade jewellery sectors. Board of Approval (BoA) may also allow establishment of EOUs with a lower investment criteria.

DTA Sale of Finished Products/Rejects/Wastes/Scrap Remnants and By-products

Entire production of EOU / EHTP / STP / BTP units shall be exported subject to following Units, other than gems and jewellery units, may sell goods upto 50% of FOB value of exports subject to fulfillment of positive NFE on payment of concessional duties. Within entitlement of DTA sale, unit may sell in DTA its products similar to goods which are exported or expected to be exported from units. No DTA sale at concessional duty shall be permissible in respect of motor cars, alcoholic liquors, books, tea (except instant tea), pepper & pepper products, marble and such other items as may be notified from time to time. Such DTA sale shall also not be permissible to units engaged in activities of packaging / labeling / segregation / refrigeration / compacting / micronisation / pulverization / granulation / conversion of monohydrate form of chemical to anhydrous form or vice-versa. Sales made to a unit in SEZ shall also be taken into account for purpose of arriving at FOB value of export by EOU provided payment for such sales are made from Foreign Exchange Account of SEZ unit. Sale to DTA would also be subject to mandatory requirement of registration of pharmaceutical products (including bulk drugs).

For services, including software units, sale in DTA in any mode, including on line data communication shall also be permissible up to 50% of FOB value of exports and / or 50% of foreign exchange earned, where payment of such services is received in foreign exchange.

Gems and jewellery units may sell upto 10% of FOB value of exports of the preceding year in DTA subject to fulfillment of positive NFE. In respect of sale of plain jewellery, recipient shall pay concessional rate of duty as applicable to sale from nominated agencies. In respect of studded jewellery, duty shall be payable as applicable.

Unless specifically prohibited in LoP, rejects within an overall limit of 50% may be sold in Domestic Tariff Area (DTA) on payment of duties as applicable to sale under on prior intimation to Customs authorities. Such sales shall be counted against DTA sale entitlement. Sale of rejects upto 5% of FOB value of exports shall not be subject to achievement of NFE.

Scrap / waste / remnants arising out of production process or in connection therewith may be sold in DTA on payment of concessional duties as applicable within overall ceiling of 50% of FOB value of exports. Such sales shall not, however, be subject to achievement of positive NFE. There shall be no duties / taxes on scrap / waste / remnants in case same are destroyed with permission of Customs authorities. By-products included in LoP may also be sold in DTA subject to achievement of positive NFE on payment of applicable duties. Sale of by-products by units not entitled to DTA sales shall also be permissible on payment of full duties.

EOU / EHTP / STP / BTP units may sell finished products, except pepper and pepper products and marble which are freely importable under FTP in DTA against payment of full duties provided they have achieved positive NFE.

In case of units manufacturing electronics hardware and software, NFE and DTA sale entitlement shall be reckoned separately for hardware and software. In case of DTA sale of goods manufactured by EOU / EHTP / STP / BTP, where basic duty and CVD is nil, such goods may be considered as non-excisable for payment of duty. In case of new EOUs, advance DTA sale will be allowed not exceeding 50% of its estimated exports for first year except pharmaceutical units where this will be based on its estimated exports for first two years.

Following supplies effected from EOU / EHTP / STP / BTP units to DTA will be counted for fulfillment of positive NFE: (a) Supplies effected in DTA to holders of Advance Authorisation /Advance Authorisation for annual requirement / DFIA under duty exemption / remission scheme / EPCG scheme. (b) Supplies effected in DTA against foreign exchange remittance received from overseas. (c) Supplies to other EOU / EHTP / STP / BTP / SEZ units provided that such goods are permissible for procurement. (d) Supplies made to bonded warehouses set up under FTP and / or under section 65 of Customs Act and free trade and warehousing zones, where payment is received in foreign exchange. (e) Supplies of goods and services to such organizations which are entitled for duty free import of such items in terms of general exemption notification issued by MoF. (f) Supply of services (by services units) relating to exports paid for in free foreign exchange or for such services rendered in Indian Rupees which are otherwise considered as having been paid for in free foreign exchange by RBI. (g) Supplies of Information Technology Agreement (ITA -1) items and notified zero duty telecom / electronic items. (h) Supplies of accessories tags, labels, printed bags, stickers, belts, buttons or hangers to DTA Unit for export.

An EOU / EHTP/ STP/ BTP unit may export goods manufactured/software developed by it through another exporter or any other EOU / EHTP / STP / SEZ unit subject to: (a) Supplies from DTA to EOU / EHTP / STP / BTP units will be regarded as "deemed exports" and DTA supplier shall be eligible for relevant entitlements besides discharge of export obligation, if any, on the supplier. Notwithstanding the above, EOU / EHTP / STP / BTP units shall, on production of a suitable disclaimer from DTA supplier, be eligible for obtaining entitlements. For claiming deemed export duty drawback, they shall get Brand Rates wherever All Industry Rates of Drawback are not available. (b) Suppliers of precious and semi-precious stones, synthetic stones and processed pearls from DTA to EOU shall be eligible for grant of Replenishment authorisations, (c) In addition, EOU / EHTP / STP / BTP units shall be entitled to following. (i) Reimbursement of Central Sales Tax (CST) on goods manufactured in India. Interest on delay in refund of CST would be paid, as notified. (ii) Exemption from payment of Central Excise Duty on goods procured from DTA on goods manufactured in India. (iii) Reimbursement of Duty paid on fuels from domestic oil companies as per Drawback rate notified by DGFT from time to time. (iv) CENVAT Credit on service tax paid.

Other entitlements of EOU / EHTP / STP / BTP units are: (a) Exemption from Income Tax as per Section 10A and 10 B of Income Tax Act. (b) Exemption from industrial licensing for manufacture of items reserved for SSI sector. (c) Export proceeds will be realized within 12 months. (d) Units will be allowed to retain 100% of its export earning in the EEFC account. (e) Units will not be required to furnish bank guarantee at the time of import or going for job work in DTA, where units has (i) a turnover of Rupees 5 crores or above; (ii) units is in existence for at least three years; and (iii) unit is having an unblemished track record. (g) 100% FDI investment permitted through Automatic Route similar to SEZ units.

Inter-Unit Transfer

Transfer of manufactured goods from one EOU / EHTP / STP / BTP unit to another EOU / EHTP / STP / BTP unit is allowed with prior intimation to concerned Development Commissioner and Customs authorities following procedure of in bond movement of goods. Transfer of manufactured goods shall also be allowed from EOU / EHTP / STP / BTP unit to a SEZ Developer or Unit following procedure prescribed in SEZ Rules, 2006. Capital goods may be transferred or given on loan to other EOU / EHTP / STP / BTP / SEZ units with prior intimation to concerned Development Commissioner and Customs authorities. Goods supplied by one unit of EOU/EHTP/STP/BTP to another unit shall be treated as imported goods for second unit for payment of duty, on DTA sale by second unit.

Sub-Contracting

EOU / EHTP / STP / BTP units, including gem and jewellery units, may on the basis of annual permission from Customs authorities, subcontract production processes to DTA through job work which may also involve change of form or nature of goods, through job work by units in DTA. These units may subcontract upto 50% of overall production of previous year in value terms in DTA with permission of Customs authorities.

EOU may, with annual permission from Customs authorities, undertake job work for export, on behalf of DTA exporter, provided that goods are exported directly from EOU and export document shall jointly be in name of DTA / EOU. For such exports, DTA units will be entitled for refund of duty paid on inputs by way of Brand Rate of duty drawback. Duty free import of goods for execution of export order placed on EOU by Foreign Supplier on jobwork basis would be allowed subject to condition that no DTA clearance shall be allowed. Further, subcontracting of both production and production processes may also be undertaken without any limit through other EOU / EHTP / STP / SEZ / BTP units on the basis of records maintained in unit. In addition, subcontracting of part of production process may also be permitted abroad with approval of Development Commissioner. Scrap / waste / remnants generated through job work may either be cleared from job worker's premises on payment of applicable duty on transaction value or destroyed in presence of Customs / Excise authorities or returned to unit. Destruction shall not apply to gold, silver, platinum, diamond, precious and semi precious stones.

Sale of Unutilised Material

In case an EOU / EHTP / STP / BTP unit is unable to utilize goods and services, imported or procured from DTA, it may be (i) transferred to another EOU / SEZ / EHTP / STP/BTP unit or (ii) disposed off in DTA with approval of Customs authorities on payment of applicable duties and submission of import authorisation, or (iii) exported. Such transfer from EOU / EHTP / STP / BTP unit to another such unit would be treated as import for receiving unit.

Capital goods and spares that have become obsolete / surplus, may either be exported, transferred to another EOU / EHTP / STP / BTP / SEZ or disposed of in DTA on payment of applicable duties. Benefit of depreciation, as applicable, will be available in case of disposal in DTA. No duty shall be payable in case capital goods, raw material, consumables, spares, goods manufactured, processed or packaged, and scrap / waste / remnants / rejects are destroyed within Unit after intimation to Customs authorities or destroyed outside Unit with permission of Customs authorities. Destruction shall not apply to gold, silver, platinum, diamond, precious and semi precious stones. In case of textile sector, disposal of left over material / fabrics upto 2% of cif value or quantity of import, whichever is lower, on payment of duty on transaction value may be allowed, subject to certification of Central Excise / Customs officers that these are leftover items.

Disposal of used packing material will be allowed on payment of duty on transaction value.

Reconditioning Repair and Re-engineering

EOU / EHTP / STP / BTP units may be set up with approval of BoA to carry out reconditioning, repair, remaking, testing, calibration, quality improvement, up-gradation of technology and re-engineering activities for export in foreign currency.

Replacement/ Repair of Imported/Indigenous Goods

General provisions of FTP relating to export / import of replacement / repair of goods would also apply equally to EOU / EHTP / STP / BTP units. Cases not covered by these provisions shall be considered on merits by DC.

Goods sold in DTA and not accepted for any reasons may be brought back for repair / replacement, under intimation to concerned jurisdictional Customs / Excise authorities.

Goods or parts thereof on being imported / indigenously procured and found defective or otherwise unfit for use or which have been damaged or become defective subsequently may be returned and replacement obtained or destroyed. In the event of replacement, goods may be brought back from foreign suppliers or their authorized agents in India or indigenous suppliers. However destruction shall not apply to precious and semi precious stones and precious metals.

Exit from EOU Scheme

With approval of DC, EOU units may opt out of scheme. Such exit shall be subject to payment of Excise and Customs duties and industrial policy in force. If unit has not achieved obligations, it shall also be liable to penalty at the time of exit. In the event of a gem and jewellery unit ceasing its operation, gold and other precious metals, alloys, gem and other materials available for manufacture of jewellery, shall be handed over to an agency nominated by DoC at price to be determined by that agency. An EOU / EHTP / STP / BTP unit may also be permitted by Development Commissioner, to exit on payment of duty on capital goods under the prevailing EPCG Scheme as a one time option. This will be subject to fulfillment of eligibility criteria under that Scheme and standard conditions.

Unit proposing to exit out of EOU scheme shall intimate DC and Customs and Central Excise authorities in writing. Unit shall assess duty liability arising out of debonding and submit details of such assessment to customs and Central Excise authorities. Customs and Central Excise authorities shall confirm duty liabilities on priority basis. After payment of duty and clearance of all dues, unit shall obtain "No Dues Certificate" from Customs and Central Excise authorities. On the basis of "No Dues Certificate" so issued by the Customs and Central Excise authorities, unit shall apply to DC for final debonding. In case there is no proceeding pending under FT (D&R) Act, DC shall issue final debonding order within a period of 7 working days. Between "No Dues Certificate" issued by Customs and Central Excise authorities and final debonding order by DC, unit shall not be entitled to claim any exemption for procurement of capital goods or input. Unit can however, claim Advance Authorisation / DEPB / Duty Drawback. Since the duty calculations and dues are disputed and take a long time, a BG / Bond / Installment processes backed by BG shall be provided for expediting the exit process.

In cases where a unit is initially established as DTA unit with machine procured from abroad after payment of applicable import duty or from domestic market after payment of excise duty and unit is subsequently converted to EOU, in such cases removal of such capital goods to DTA after debonding would be without payment of duty. Similarly, in cases where a DTA unit imported capital goods under EPCG Scheme and after completely fulfilling export obligation gets converted into EOU, unit would not be charged customs duty on capital goods at the time of removal of such capital goods in DTA when debonding.

An EOU / EHTP / STP / BTP Unit may also be permitted by Development Commissioner to exit under Advance Authorization as a one time option. This will be subject to fulfillment of positive NFE criteria.

Conversion

Existing DTA units, may also apply for conversion into an EOU / EHTP / STP / BTP unit, and Income Tax benefits under Section 10A and 10B will be available for plant, machinery and equipment already installed.

Existing EHTP / STP units may also apply for conversion / merger to EOU unit and vice-versa. In such cases, units will remain in bond and avail exemptions in duties and taxes as applicable.

5. Special Economic Zones (SEZ)

The Government of India had announced a SEZ scheme in April, 2000 with a view to provide an internationally competitive environment for exports. The objectives of SEZs include making available goods and services free of taxes and duties supported by integrated infrastructure for export production, expeditious and single window approval mechanism and a package of incentives to attract foreign and domestic investments for promoting export-led growth.

In order to give a long term and stable policy framework with minimum regulatory regime and to provide expeditious and single window clearance mechanism, the Special Economic. Zones Act, 2005 has been brought into effect along with the Special Economic Zones Rules, 2006 from 10 February 2006.

The Act and the Rules together aim to provide a single self contained legislation governing the operations of SEZs and replaces the hitherto applicable legislations and rules governing the operations of SEZ in India.

Under the Act, SEZ could be set up either jointly or severally by the Central Government, State Government, or any person (including a private or public limited company, partnership or proprietorship): for manufacture of goods; or for rendering services: or as a Free Trade and Warehousing Zone. The Act provides for certain fiscal incentives to developers of SEZ and units established in SEZs.

Key Fiscal Incentives for Developers/SEZ Units-Indirect Tax Incentives

Developer and the SEZ unit shall be entitled to the following exemptions drawbacks and concessions:

(i) exemption from customs duty on goods imported into the SEZ by the developer or SEZ Unit: to carry on the authorised operations;

(ii) exemption from customs duty on goods exported from the SEZ by the developer or SEZ Unit to any place outside India;

(iii) exemption from excise duty on goods brought from Domestic Tariff Area ("DTA") to the SEZ by the Developer or SEZ unit to carry on the authorized operations;

(iv) drawback or such other benefits (as may be admissible from time to time) on goods brought from the DTA into a SEZ by the Developer or unit to carry on the authorized operations;

(v) exemption from service tax on taxable services provided to a Developer or Unit to carry on the authorized operations in a SEZ. However, there is no specific service tax exemption on services provided by a Developer of an SEZ or a SEZ Unit. Exemption, if any, would be as per the service tax legislation;

(vi) exemption from the securities transaction tax in case the taxable securities transactions are entered into by a non-resident through the International Financial Services Centre ("IFSC"}

(vii) exemption from levy of Central Sales Tax on the sale or purchase of goods by the Developer or SEZ unit if such goods are meant to carry on the authorized operations;

(viii) Local sales tax/ VAT exemption or concession on supply of goods to an SEZ Developer or Unit or sale of goods by an SEZ Developer or Unit is subject to the respective sales tax/ VAT legislation of the state in which the SEZ is set up.

The Central government has prescribed the manner, terms and conditions subject to which above exemptions/ concessions would be available.

Removal of goods into DTA is subject to prescribed conditions and on payment of applicable customs duties as levied on importation of such goods into India.

Fiscal Incentives-Income Tax Incentives of SEZ Units

1. Tax Holiday for SEZ units engaged in Manufacture or providing services: A new section 10AA has been inserted in the IT Act by SEZ Act, 2005 which provides that the units in SEZ which start manufacturing or producing articles/ things or which start providing services on or after April 1, 2005 will be eligible for a deduction of 100 percent of export profit for the first five years from the year in which such manufacture/provision of services commences and 50 percent of the export profits for the next five years. Farther, for the next five years a deduction shall be allowed of upto 50 percent of the profit as is debited to the profit and loss account and credited to the Special Economic Zone Reinvestment Reserve Account (subject to conditions).
2. Tax Holiday for Offshore Banking units in SEZ: A deduction In respect of certain incomes would be allowed under the new section 80LA, to scheduled banks or foreign banks having an Offshore Banking unit in SEZ or to a unit of IFSC. The deduction shall be for 100 percent of income for five consecutive

years beginning from the year in which permission/ registration has been obtained under the Banking Regulation Act or the SEBI Act or any other relevant law and 50 percent of income for next five years.

3. Interest received by non-residents and not ordinary residents on deposits made with an Offshore Banking Unit on or after April 1, 2005 shall be exempt from tax.
4. Exemption from Minimum Alternate Tax ("MAT"): Income arising or accruing on or after April 1, 2005 from any business carried on, or services rendered by SEZ unit would be exempt from MAT under section 115JB.
5. Exemption from Capital Gains: Capital gains arising on transfer of assets (machinery, plant, building, land or any rights In buildings or land) on shifting of the Industrial undertaking from an urban area to any SEZ would be exempt from capital gains tax.

The exemption would be allowable if within one year before or three years after such transfer: machinery or plant is purchased for the purposes of business of industrial undertaking in SEZ by the assessee; assessee has acquired land or building or has constructed building for the purposes of business in SEZ; the original assets are shifted and establishment of the industrial undertaking is transferred to SEZ; and other specified expenses are incurred. The amount of exemption for capital gams would be restricted to the costs and expenses incurred in relation to all or any of the purpose, mentioned above.

Fiscal Incentives: Income Tax Incentives for SEZ Developers

1. Tax holiday for SEZ developers: A new section 80-IAB has been Introduced in the IT Act vide SEZ Act, 2005 whereby a deduction of 100 percent of profits derived from the business of developing SEZ (notified on or after Apr 1 l, 2005) would be available to developer of SEZ for any 10 consecutive years out of 15 years beginning from the year in which SEZ has been notified.
2. Exemption under section 10 (23G) that was available to infrastructure capital fund or a cooperative bank on interest and long term capital gains investment had been extended to investment made by SEZ developers qualifying for tax holiday under section 80-IAB of the IT Act. However, this exemption has been withdrawn with effect from assessment year 2007-08.
3. Exemption from Dividend Distribution Tax ("DDT"): No DDT would be payable by a developer of SEZ on dividend declared, distributed or paid on or after April l, 2005 out of current: income.
4. Exemption from MAT: Any income earned on or after April 1, 2005 by a SEZ developer would be exempt from MAT under section 115JB of the Act.

During 2005-06, exports from functioning SEZs, which are mainly the former EPZs were around US$5 billion. At present 1,016 units are in operation in these SEZs providing direct employment to over 1.79 lakh persons (about 40 per cent of whom are women). Private investment by entrepreneurs for establishing units in these SEZs is of the order of about ₹ 3163 crore.

After the SEZ Act and SEZ Rules came into effect on February 10, 2006, formal formal approvals have been granted for setting up of 579 SEZs, of which 384 have been notified. Of the total employment provided to 9,45,990 persons in SEZs as a whole, that to 8,11,286 persons is incremental employment generated after February 2006 when the SEZ Act came into force. This is apart from the million mandays of employment created by the developer for infrastructure activities. While in 2010-11 physical exports from SEZs were worth ₹ 3,15,867.85 crore, in 2011-12 the figure had gone up ₹ 3,64,477.73 crore in 2011-12, registering a growth of 15.4 per cent. The total physical exports from SEZs in the first half of the current financial year have been to the tune of ₹ 239628.78 crore approximately, registering a growth of 36 per cent over exports in the corresponding period of the previous year. The total investment in SEZs till 30 September 2012 was ₹ 2,18,795.41 crore approximately, including ₹ 2,14,759.90 crore in the newly notified zones. As per the provisions of the SEZ Act 2005, 100 per cent FDI is allowed in SEZs through the automatic route. A total of 160 SEZs are exporting goods and services. Of this 93 are IT/ ITES, 17 multi-product and 50 other sector-specific SEZs. The total number of units in these SEZs is 3308.

6. Free Trade & Warehousing Zones (FTWZ)

The Free Trade & Warehousing Zones (FTWZ) shall be a special category of Special Economic Zones with a focus on trading and warehousing. The objective is to create trade-related infrastructure to facilitate the import and export of goods and services with freedom to carry out trade transactions in free currency. The scheme envisages creation of world-class infrastructure for warehousing of various products, state-of-the-art equipment, transportation and handling facilities, commercial office-space, water, power, communications and connectivity, with one-stop clearance of import and export formality, to support the integrated Zones as 'international trading hubs'. These Zones would be established in areas proximate to seaports, airports or dry ports so as to offer easy access by rail and road.

Proposals for setting up of FTWZs may be made by public sector undertakings or public limited companies or by joint ventures in technical collaboration with experienced infrastructure developers. The proposals shall be considered by the Board of Approval in the Department of Commerce. On approval, the developer will be issued a letter of permission for the development, operation and maintenance of such FTWZ.

In a FTWZ, Foreign Direct Investment would be permitted up to 100% in the development and establishment of the zones and their infrastructural facilities. But the proposal must entail a minimum outlay of ₹100 crores for the creation and development of the infrastructure facilities, with a minimum built up area of five lakh sq. mts.

The developer shall be permitted to import duty free such building materials and equipment as may be required for the development and infrastructure of the zone. Such equipment and materials as are sourced from the DTA shall be considered as physical exports for the DTA suppliers. Once it has developed the FTWZ, the developer shall also be permitted to sale/lease/rent out warehouses/workshops/office-space and other facilities in the FTWZ to traders/exporters. The developer shall itself or through suitable special purpose arrangements, ensure a reliable mechanism for the proper maintenance of the common facilities and security of the FTWZ.

FTWZ scheme envisages duty free import of all goods (except prohibited items, arms and ammunitions, hazardous wastes and SCOMET items) for ware housing. As far as bond towards customs duty on import is concerned, the units would be subject to similar provisions as are applicable to units in SEZs. Such goods shall be permitted to be re-sold/re-invoiced or re-exported. Re-export shall be permitted without any restrictions. However export of SCOMET items shall not be permitted except with the permission of Inter-Ministerial Committee. Further these goods shall also be permitted to be sold in the DTA on payment of customs duties as applicable on the date of such sale. Payment of duty will become due only when goods are sold/delivered to DTA and no interest will be charged as in the case of bonded warehouses.

Packing or/re-packing without processing, and labeling as per customer or marketing requirements could be undertaken within the FTWZ. The maximum period that goods shall be permitted to be warehoused within the FTWZ will be two years, after which they shall necessarily have to be re-exported or sold in the DTA. On expiry of the two year period, customs duties as applicable would automatically become due unless the goods are re-exported within such grace period, not exceeding three months, as may be permitted.

The Units set up under FTWZ are entitled for Income Tax exemption as *per* 80 IA of the Income Tax Act; (ii) Exemption *from Service* Tax. (iii) Free foreign exchange currency transactions would be permitted, (iv) Other benefits mutatis mutandi as applicable to units in SEZs.

Units in FTWZs shall be net foreign exchange earners. Net foreign exchange earning shall be calculated cumulatively for every block of five years from the commencement of warehousing and/or trading operations as per formula, applicable for SEZ units.

7. Deemed Exports

"Deemed Exports" refers to those transactions in which goods supplied do not leave country and payment for such supplies is received either in Indian rupees or in free foreign exchange. Following categories of supply of goods by main / sub-contractors shall be regarded as "Deemed Exports" under FTP, provided goods are manufactured in India:

(a) Supply of goods against Advance Authorisation / Advance Authorisation for annual requirement/ DFIA;

(b) Supply of goods to EOUs or STPs or EHTPs or BTPs;

(c) Supply of capital goods to holders of Authorisations under EPCG Scheme;

(d) Supply of goods to projects financed by multilateral or bilateral agencies / funds as notified by Department of Economic Affairs (DEA), MoF under International Competitive Bidding (ICB) in accordance with procedures of those agencies / funds, where legal agreements provide for tender evaluation without including customs duty; Supply and installation of goods and equipment (single responsibility of turnkey contracts) to projects financed by multilateral or bilateral agencies / funds as notified by DEA, MoF under ICB in accordance with procedures of those agencies/funds, which bids may have been invited and evaluated on the basis of Delivered Duty Paid (DDP) prices for goods manufactured abroad;

(e) Supply of capital goods, including in unassembled / disassembled condition as well as plants, machinery, accessories, tools, dies and such goods which are used for installation purposes till stage of commercial production and spares to extent of 10% of FOR value to fertilizer plants;

(f) Supply of goods to any project or purpose in respect of which the MoF, by a notification, permits import of such goods at zero customs duty;

(g) Supply of goods to power projects and refineries not covered in (f) above;

(h) Supply of marine freight containers by 100% EOU (Domestic freight containers-manufacturers) provided said containers are exported out of India within 6 months or such further period as permitted by customs;

(i) Supply to projects funded by UN agencies; and

(j) Supply of goods to nuclear power projects through competitive bidding as opposed to ICB.

Deemed exports shall be eligible for any / all of following benefits in respect of manufacture and supply of goods qualifying as deemed exports subject to terms and conditions as; (i) Supply of goods against Advance Authorisation/Advance Authorisation for annual requirement / DFIA. (ii) Deemed Export Drawback (iii) Exemption from terminal excise duty where supplies are made against ICB. In other cases, refund of terminal excise duty will be given. However, the benefits of deemed exports shall be available under (d), (e) (f) and (g) only if the supply is made under procedure of ICB

RECENT TRADE POLICY MEASURES

The government has announced many trade policy measures in the Annual Supplement to Foreign Trade Policy (FTP) released on 5 June 2012. Many measures were also taken by the government in Union Budget 2012-13 and the RBI in its monetary and credit policies during the course of the year to help exports (Box 2).

BOX 2

Some important trade policy measures

Budget Related

- Imports of equipment for initial setting up or substantial expansion of fertilizer projects fully exempted from basic customs duty of 5 per cent for a period of three years up to 31 March 2015; and basic customs duty on some watersoluble fertilizers and liquid fertilizers other than urea reduced from 7.5 per cent to 5 per cent and from 5 per cent to 2.5 per cent.
- Concessional import duty available for installation of mechanized Handling Systems and Pallet Racking Systems in mandis or warehouses extended for horticultural produce.
- Full exemption from basic customs duty for coal-mining projects.
- Basic customs duty on plant and machinery imported for setting up or substantial expansion of iron ore pellet plants or iron ore beneficiation plants reduced from 7.5 per cent to 2.5 per cent.
- Full exemption from basic customs duty of 5 per cent for automatic shuttle-less looms and reduction in basic customs duty on wool waste and wool tops from 15 per cent to 5 per cent.
- Basic customs duty increased on standard gold bars; gold coins of purity exceeding 99.5 per cent and platinum from 2 per cent to 4 per cent and on non-standard gold from 5 per cent to 10 per cent.

Credit Related

- In November 2011, the RBI increased the all-in cost ceilings for External Commercial Borrowings (ECBs) increased to 350 basis points (bps) over 6-months Libor/Euro Libor/Euribor for a maturity period between three and five years and 500 bps over 6-months Libor/Euro Libor/Euribor for a maturity period more than five years. Accordingly the all-in cost ceiling on trade credits has also been increased to 350 bps over 6-months Libor/Euro Libor/Euribor until 31 March 2013.
- With effect from 5 May 2012, banks were allowed to determine their interest rates on export credit in foreign currency with the objective of increasing the availability of funds to exporters.
- On 18 June 2012, the RBI enhanced the eligible limit of the export credit refinance (ECR) facility for scheduled banks (excluding regional rural banks [RRB]) from 15 per cent of the outstanding export credit eligible for refinance to 50 per cent, with effect from 30 June 2012. The objective was to provide additional liquidity support to banks of over Rs 300 billion. The rate of interest charged on the ECR facility was retained at the prevailing repo rate under the liquidity adjustment facility (LAF).
- The 2 per cent Interest Subvention Scheme, earlier meant only for handlooms, handicrafts, carpets, and SMEs, was extended on 1 April 2012 to 31 March 2013 for labour-intensive sectors also, viz. toys, sports goods, processed agricultural products, and readymade garments. This was further extended upto 31 March 2014 and 134 tariff lines of engineering goods were also included in the scheme.

Foreign Trade Policy Measures in 2012-13

- Incentive on Incremental Exports: Incentives to be granted on incremental exports made during the period JanuaryMarch 2013 over the base period January-March 2012. The incentive to be granted to an Importer and Exporter Code (IEC) holder at the rate of 2 per cent on incremental growth of exports made to the USA, Europe, and Asian countries during this particular quarter, i.e. January-March 2013.
- Export Promotion Capital Goods (EPCG) Scheme: Zero Duty EPCG Scheme extended up to 31t March 2013 and its scope enlarged. Export obligation under this scheme to be 25 per cent of the normal export obligation for export of products from north-eastern states and export of specified products through notified Land Customs Stations of the north-eastern region provided additional incentive to the extent of 1 per cent of Free on Board (FOB) value of exports.
- Support for Export of Green Technology Products: To promote exports of 16 identified green technology products, export obligation for manufacturing of these products under the EPCG Scheme reduced to 75 per cent of the normal export obligation.
- Support for Infrastructure for the Agriculture Sector: Status holders exporting products under ITC (HS) Chapter 1 to Chapter 23 (both inclusive) are getting Duty Credit Scrip equivalent to 10 per cent of FOB value of agricultural products so exported. Import of 14 specified equipments have now been notified in Appendix 37 F for setting up of pack-houses besides import of capital goods and equipment for cold storage units, pack-houses, etc.
- Incentives for Promoting Investment in Labour-intensive Sectors: Status holders issued status holders incentive scrip (SHIS) to import capital goods for promoting investment in upgradation of technology of some specified labourintensive sectors like leather, textile & jute, handicrafts, engineering, plastics and basic chemicals. Up to 10 per cent of the value of these scrips will be allowed to be utilized to import components and spares of capital goods imported earlier.
- Market and Product Diversification: Seven new markets have been added to the Focus Market Scheme (FMS) and seven to the Special Focus Market Scheme (Special FMS). Forty-six new items have been added to the Market Linked Focus Product Scheme (MLFPS). The MLFPS has been extended till 31 March 2013 for exports to the USA and EU in respect of items falling under Chapter 61 and Chapter 62. Around 100 new items have been added to the Focus Product Scheme (FPS) list. Three new items have been added to the Vishesh Krishi and Gram Udyog Yojana (VKGUY). Additional measures announced as trade facilitation measures by widening and deepening of export incentives under chapter 3 of FTP in December, 2012 to be made effective from 01.01.2013. These include addition of 5 new markets to FMS, one new market to Special FMS, 62 new items to MLFPS and 102 new items to FPS.
- Simplification of Procedures: Import under advance authorization (AA) permitted at any of the Electronic Data Interchange (EDI) ports, irrespective of the EDI port in which the AA has been registered. There would be no requirement of Telegraphic Release Advice (TRA). Export shipments from Delhi and Mumbai through post, courier, or e-Commerce to be entitled for export benefits under the FTP.
- New 'e-BRC' Initiative: A major EDI initiative the 'e-BRC' launched which would herald electronic transmission of foreign exchange realization from the respective banks to the Directorate General of Foreign Trade (DGFT) server on a daily basis. The exporter will not be required to make any request to the bank for issuance of a bank export and realization certificate (BRC).

Policy for Promoting State-wise Exports

The top five states in India's exports in 2011-12 were Maharashtra, Gujarat, Tamil Nadu, Andhra Pradesh, and Karnataka, accounting for 63.4 per cent of India's exports. While in 2011-12, these five states had high robust growth (except Gujarat with 5.5 per cent growth) in 2012-13 (April-November) all of them had negative growth. In fact all the other states in the top 15 except Odisha had positive growth in 2012-13 (April-November) with Kerala, Rajasthan, and Punjab having high export growth in 2012-13 on top of robust growth in 2011-12. Export growth of Haryana was also relatively high in 2012-13 (April-November) though it was low in 2011-12.

The Assistance to States for Developing Export Infrastructure and Allied Activities (ASIDE) Scheme provides assistance to state governments / union territory (UT) administrations for creating appropriate infrastructure for development and growth of exports. The budget outlay for financial year 2012-13(R.E.) under the ASIDE scheme is ₹ 655.5 crore of which ₹ 573.22 crore has been sanctioned/ released till the end of January 2013. The outlay has two components: state (80 per cent of the total outlay) and central (20 per cent of the total outlay). Statewise allocation under the state component of ASIDE shows that the top five states in terms of allocation in 2012-13 are Gujarat, Maharashtra, Tamil Nadu, Karnataka, and Andhra Pradesh which are also the top five states in India's exports. Among the northeastern states, those with significant allocation are Assam, Meghalaya, and Tripura.

QUESTIONS

1. Discuss the various trade policy measures initiated in India to promote trade.
2. Critically examine the duty exemption and remission schemes.
3. Discuss the export promotion capital goods (EPCG) scheme
4. Do you think Special Economic Zones (SEZ) scheme has provided an internationally competitive environment for exports?
5. Explain the Free Trade and Warehousing Zones (FTWZ) scheme. Has it been able to achieve its objective by creating trade related infrastructure to facilitate the import and export of goods and services?

REFERENCES

Chandra R., S. Pohit, A.V. Deerdorff and R.M. Stern: *Analysis of India's Policy Reforms'* World Development, Vol. 21(2), March, 1999.

Easter, W.R., Islam and J.E. Stiglitz: Shaken and Stirred: Volatility and Macroeconomic Paradigms for Rich and Poor Countries; *Michael Brund Memorial Lecture,* Buenos Aires, World Bank Document,.1999.

Government of India: *Report of the Committee on Import-Export Policies and Procedure* (Chairman: P.C. Alexander), New Delhi, 1978.

Krishna, P. and D. Mitra: *Trade Liberalisation, Market Discipline and Productivity Growth: New Evidence from India,* Journal of Development Economics, Vol. 56, 1998.

Sharma A. and P.K. Mehta: *Indian Exports and European Union,* in R. Kapila and U. Kapila (ed.) Economic Development in India, Vol. 2, Academic Foundation, Delhi, 1998.

40

FINANCING OF INTERNATIONAL TRADE

INTRODUCTION

Financing international trade is a complex process, involving many variables, ranging from corporate policy and marketing strategy to exchange risk and general borrowing conditions. The reason behind this complexity is that trade involves two countries with *different currencies* and *jurisdictions.* In addition, payments must be made *at a distance* and *across time,* so the exporter, the importer, or both need credit during part or all of the period from the initial manufacture of goods by the exporting firm to the time of the final sale and collection by the importer. The main objective of a good corporate export financing policy should be financing the greatest possible amount of sales with the greatest possible management simplicity and with minimal risk.

International trade financing, one of the oldest functions of international business, is also one of the least glamorous. Nevertheless, for the majority of firms engaged in international business, export financing forms the core of international finance. While the techniques are standardised, the range of applications is as varied as the content and destinations of a nation's exports, and things can easily go wrong. Among the potential problems are that of *exchange risk,* the problem of *inadequate information* regarding financial strength of foreign customers. And the problem of *special financing sources,* and costs. In addition, many of the less-developed nations have strict and sometimes unpredictable *exchange controls* on remittance and convertibility of hard currencies. The export financing manager must develop experience in handling all of these details in addition to the extensive, often tedious, documentation needed for the transfer of goods and payments internationally.

These obstacles aside, the exporter can count on readily available support and expertise from major commercial banks. Moreover, it is almost every government's policy to promote exports in order to improve the balance of payments and increase employment. Various countries have programme to assist the exporter, whether in the financing of trade or in managing the different risks involved. The Indian government is no exception. There are several government programmes available to promote exports, whether directly or indirectly through supporting the private sector by extending the much needed credits. The purpose of this chapter is to analyze the *international trade phase* for a domestic firm that begins to import goods and services from foreign suppliers and to export to foreign buyers.

TRADE FINANCING: THE FLOW OF GOODS AND THE FLOW OF FUNDS

Trade financing shares a number of common characteristics with the traditional value chain activities conducted by all firms. All companies must search out suppliers for the many goods and services required as inputs to their own goods production or service provision processes. A global firm's purchasing and procurement department must determine whether each potential supplier is capable of producing the product to required quality specifications, producing and delivering in a timely and reliable manner, and continuing to work with the firm in the ongoing process of product and process improvement for continued competitiveness. All must be at an acceptable price and payment terms. As illustrated in Exhibit 1, this same series of issues applies to potential customers, because their continued business is equally critical to firm's operations and success.

EXHIBIT 1

Financing Trade: The Flow Chart

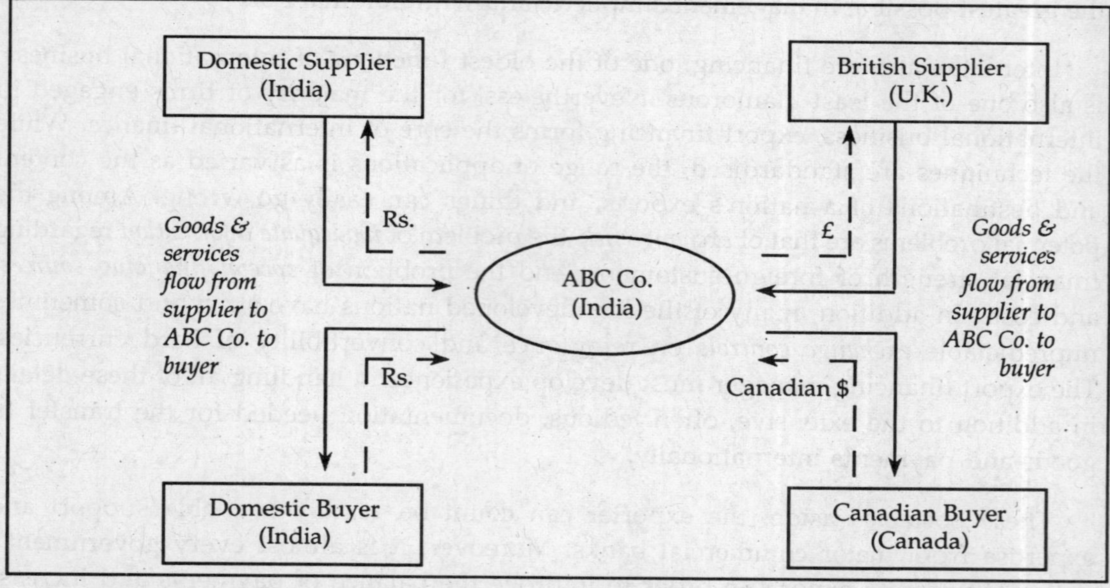

The nature of the relationship between the exporter and the importer is critical to understanding the methods for import-export financing utilized in industry. Exhibit-2 provides an overview of the three categories of relationships: *unaffiliated unknown*, *unaffiliated known*, and *affiliated*.

EXHIBIT-2

Alternative International Trade Relationships

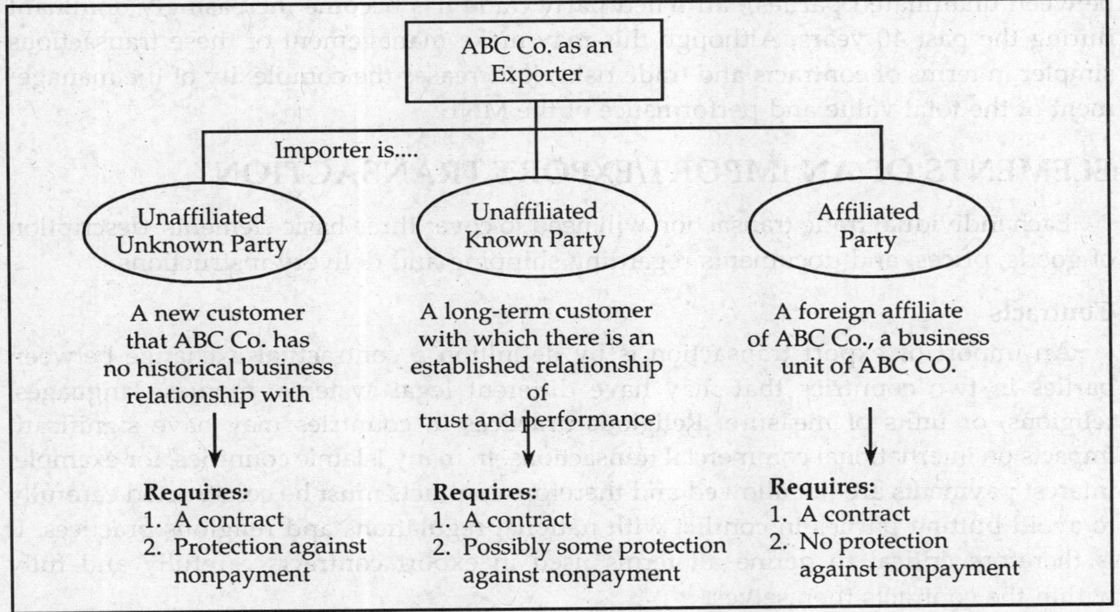

- A foreign importer with which the firm has not previously conducted business would be considered *unaffiliated unknown*. In this case the two parties would need to enter into a detailed sales contract, outlining the specific responsibilities and expectations of the business agreement. The firm would also need to seek out protection against the possibility that the importer would not make payment in full in a timely fashion.
- A foreign importer with which the firm has previously conducted business successfully, would be considered *unaffiliated known*. In this case the two parties may still enter into a detailed sales contract, but specific terms and shipments or provisions of services may be significantly looser in definition. Depending on the depth of the relationship, the firm may seek some third-party protection against noncompletion or conduct the business on an open account basis.
- A foreign importer that is a subsidiary business unit of the firm, such as the firm Brazil, would be an *affiliated party* (sometime referred to as *intrafirm trade*). Because both businesses are part of the same MNE, the *most* common practice would be to conduct the trade transaction without a contract or protection against nonpayment. This is not always the case, however. In a variety of international business situations it may still be in the firm's best interest to detail the conditions for the business transaction and possibly to protect against any political or country-based interruption to the completion of the trade transaction.

The composition of global trade has changed dramatically over tne past few decades. Whereas for centuries international trade was dominated by interfirm trade (transactions between unaffiliated parties), affiliated party trade has become increasingly dominant during the past 40 years. Although this may make management of these transactions simpler in terms of contracts and trade risks, it increases the complexity of the management of the total value and performance of the MNE.

ELEMENTS OF AN IMPORT/EXPORT TRANSACTION

Each individual trade transaction will need to cover three basic elements: description of goods, prices, and documents regarding shipping and delivery instructions.

Contracts

An import or export transaction is by definition a contractual exchange between parties in two countries that may have different legal systems, monies, languages, religions, or units of measure. Religious practices in countries may have significant impacts on international commercial transactions. In many Islamic countries, for example, interest payments are not allowed and therefore contracts must be constructed carefully to avoid putting parties in conflict with national regulations and religious practices. It is therefore critical to define all terms used in export contracts carefully and fully within the contracts themselves.

All contracts should include definitions and specifications for the quality, grade, quantity, and price of the goods in question. Definitions should be complete and should not use abbreviations. Whenever possible, terms such as "ton" should be defined further to include quantities if possible (2,000 or 2,200 pounds, for example). References in the contract to published prices or catalogs with associated descriptions are often helpful, as are product, blueprints or diagrams that include any engineering or other technical details related to expected product qualities and characteristics.

Prices

Price quotations can be a major source of confusion. Price terms in the contract should conform to published catalogs, specify whether quantity discounts or early payment discounts are in effect (and how they are calculated), and state whether finance charges are relevant in the case of deferred payment, transportation charges, insurance fees, or specific surcharges or fees relative to the countries in question.

Documents

Documentation covers a variety of issues of particular importance from a financial management perspective. An importer wishing to take possession of goods at a dock, airport, or any other point of delivery and clear them through customs, must possess certain customs and shipping documents. These typically include *bills of lading, commercial invoices, insurance policies, consular invoices,* and *packing lists*.

- A *bill of lading*, or *B/L*, is issued to the exporter by a common carrier transporting the merchandise. It will be described more fully later in this chapter.
- A signed *commercial invoice* is issued by the exporter and contains a precise description of the merchandise. Unit prices, financial terms of sale, and amount due from the importer are indicated, as are shipping conditions related to charges, such as "FOB" (free-On board), "FAS" (free alongside), "CFR" (cost and freight), or "CIF" (cost, insurance, freight).
- *Insurance documents* must be as specified in the contract of sale and must be issued by insurance companies or their agents. The insurance may be issued to the exporter, who must then endorse the policy to "the importer, or it may be issued in the name of the importer. Insurance must be of types and for risks specified in the letter of credit.
- *Consular invoices* are issued in the exporting country by the consulate of the importing country to provide customs information and statistics for that country and to help prevent false declarations of value. The consular invoice may be combined with a certificate of origin of the goods.
- *Packing lists* may be required so that the contents of containers can be identified, either for customs purposes or for importer identification of the contents of separate containers. In addition, an *export declaration* prepared by the exporter to assist the government in the preparation of export statistics may be required.

Shipping Deadline

Most importers insist on a specified deadline or time interval by which the shipment will be made. If the goods in question are particularly time-sensitive (such as products for seasonal sale), remedies will be included in the sales contract for failure to meet time commitments.

Payment Instructions

Which of the parties—the exporter or the importer—is to pay such charges as freight, insurance, import duties, handling fees, taxes, etc., must be specified carefully in the sales contract. The currency in which all payments are to be made between importer and exporter must also be specified clearly. The payment terms state whether cash is to be paid in advance, whether letters of credit are required, and what documents need- to be presented against payment, consignments, or payment on open account. These terms must be detailed in the sales contract.

Packaging and Marking

Depending on the nature of the goods, proper packaging may be critical to preserving and protecting items being shipped. Proper markings on the inner and outer boxes and containers are needed to conform with customs regulations in countries. These markings typically include clear and conforming invoices of the value of all items for import duty calculation and payment purposes.

Warranties, Guarantees, and Inspections

Assurances regarding the performance or qualities demonstrated by the goods from the exporter may also be included in the sales contract. This may include not only protection against product defects and proper performance, but protection against any consequential damages from defective parts or performance. In some cases the importer may wish to have the right to inspect the goods before paying (and even the right to inspect the goods while being manufactured before shipping). These stipulations should of course be delineated in the sales contract.

Included in documents may be *certificates of analysis,* required to ascertain that certain specifications such as weight, purity, or sanitation have been met. These conditions may be required by health or other officials of the importing country—especially in the case of foods and drugs—or they may be insisted on by the importer as assurance that it is receiving what it ordered. The certificates may be issued by government or private organizations, as specified in the letter of credit.

INTERNATIONAL TRADE RISKS

In order to understand the risks associated with international trade transactions, it is helpful to understand the sequence of events in any such transaction. Exhibit-3 illustrates, in principle, the series of events associated with a single export transaction.

From a financial management perspective, the two primary risks associated with an international trade transaction are *currency risk* (currency of denomination of payment) and *risk of noncompletion* (timely and complete payment). Exhibit-3 illustrates the traditional business problem of credit management: The exporter quotes a price, finalizes a contract, and ships the goods, losing physical control over the goods based on trust of the buyer or the promise of a bank to pay based on documents presented. The risk of default on the part of the importer is present as soon as the financing period begins, as depicted in Exhibit-3.

In many cases the initial task of analyzing the credit worth of foreign customers is similar to procedures for analyzing domestic customers. If a firm has had no experience with a foreign customer but that customer is a large, well-known firm in its home country, the firm may simply ask for a bank credit report on that firm. The firm may also talk to other firms that have had dealings with the foreign customer. If these investigations show the foreign customer (and country) to be completely trustworthy, the firm would likely ship to them on open account, with a credit limit, just as they would for a domestic customer. This is the least costly method of handling exports because there are no heavy documentation or bank charges. However, before a regular trading relationship has been established with a new or unknown firm, the firm must face the possibility of nonpayment for its exports or noncompletion of its imports. The risk of nonpayment can be eliminated through the use of a letter of credit issued by a creditworthy bank.

EXHIBIT-3

The Trade Transaction Time Line and Structure

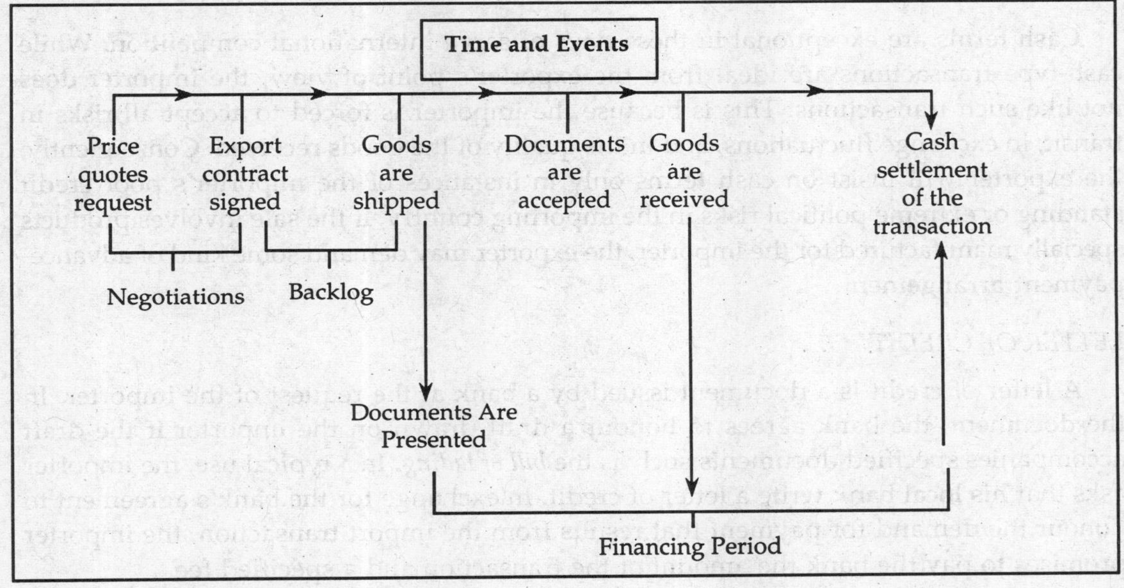

PAYMENT METHODS FOR INTERNATIONAL TRADE

In any international trade transaction, credit is provided by either the supplier (exporter), the buyer (importer), one or more financial institutions, or any combination of these. Supplier may have sufficient cash flow to fund the entire trade cycle, beginning with the production of the product until payment is eventually made by the buyer. This form of credit is known as *supplier credit*. In some cases, the exporter may require bank financing to augment its cash flow. On the other hand, the supplier may not desire to provide financing, in which case the buyer will have to finance the transaction itself, either internally or externally, through its bank. Banks on both sides of the transaction can thus play an integral part in trade financing.

CASH TERMS

Cash terms may be either COD or CBD. COD terms mean cash on delivery of the goods and CBD terms mean cash before delivery of the goods. Under either COD or CBD terms, the exporter does not extend credit. Although credit risk does not exist under either terms, COD terms are accompanied by the risk that the importer may refuse the shipment while CBD terms avoid all risk. Under CBD terms, the exporter may insist on cash at the time of order or he may specify the time of cash payment prior to shipment. Another possible arrangement is that a part of the payment is made at the time of order, that progress payments are made between the time of order and the time of shipment, and that the final payment is made just before the release of the goods to a common carrier.

Cash terms are exceptional in these days of serve international competition. While cash-type transactions are ideal from the exporter's point of view, the importer does not like such transactions. This is because the importer is forced to accept all risks in transit, in exchange fluctuations, and in the quality of the goods received. Consequently, the exporter will insist on cash terms only in instances of the importer's poor credit standing or extreme political risks in the importing country. If the sale involves products specially manufactured for the importer, the exporter may demand some kind of advance-payment arrangement.

LETTER OF CREDIT

A letter of credit is a document issued by a bank at the request of the importer. In the document, the bank agrees to honour a draft drawn on the importer if the draft accompanies specified documents such as the *bill of lading*. In a typical use, the importer asks that his local bank write a letter of credit. In exchange for the bank's agreement to honour the demand for payment that results from the import transaction, the importer promises to pay the bank the amount of the transaction and a specified fee.

The letter of credit is of advantage to both exporters and importers because it facilitates International trade. It gives a number of benefits to exporters. *First,* they sell their goods abroad against the promise of a bank rather than a commercial firm. Because banks are usually larger and better credit risks than most business firms, exporters are almost completely assured of payment if they meet specific conditions. *Second,* they can obtain funds as soon as they have such necessary documents as the letter of credit and the bill of lading. When shipment is made, the exporter prepares a draft on the importer in accordance with the letter of credit and presents it to his local bank. If the bank finds that all papers are in order, it advances the funds, the face value of the draft less fees and interest.

Although its major beneficiaries are exporters, the letter of credit also gives a number of benefits to importers. First, it assures them that the exporter will be paid only if he provides certain documents, all of which are carefully examined by a bank. If the exporter is unable or unwilling to make proper shipment, recovery of the deposit is much easier from the bank than from the exporter. Second, the letter of credit enables the importer to remove the commercial risk for the exporter in exchange for other considerations. Thus, the importer can bargain for better terms such as a lower price.

Moreover, it is comparatively cheaper to finance the goods under a letter of credit than by borrowing. Letter of credit will be described in greater detail later in this chapter.

DRAFTS

A draft or a bill of exchange is an order written by an exporter that requires an importer to pay a specified amount of money at a specified time. Through the use of drafts, the exporter may use its bank as the collection agent on accounts that the exporter finances. The bank forwards the exporter's drafts to the importer directly or indirectly (through a branch or a correspondent bank) and then remits the proceeds of the collection back to the exporter.

A draft involves three parties: the drawer or maker, the drawee, and the payee. The drawer is the person or business who issues the draft. This person is ordinarily the exporter who sells and ships the merchandise. The drawee is the person or business against whom the draft is drawn. This person is usually the importer who must pay the draft at maturity. The payee is the person or business to whom the drawee will eventually pay the funds. If the draft is not a negotiable instrument, it designates a person or bank to whom payment is to be made. Such a person, known as the payee, may be the drawer himself or a third party such as the drawer's bank. However, this is generally not the case because most drafts are a bearer instrument. Drafts are negotiable if they meet a number of conditions. (I) They must be in writing and signed by the drawer-exporter. (2) They must contain an unconditional promise or order to pay an exact amount of money. (3) They must be payable on sight or at a specified time. (4) They must be made out to order or to bearer. If a draft is made out to order, the funds involved should be paid to the person specified. If it is made out to bearer, the funds should be paid to the person who presents it for payment.

There are two types of drafts: *sight drafts* and *time drafts*[1]. A sight draft is payable on demand to the drawee-importer. A time draft is payable a specified number of days after presentation to the drawee. When a time draft is presented to the drawee, the drawee or his bank accepts it. This acceptance acknowledges in writing the drawee's obligation to pay the sum indicated on the face of the draft. When drafts are accepted by the importer, they become trade acceptances. When drafts are accepted by the bank, they become bankers' acceptances.

1. Drafts are also classified as clean or documentary. Unlike a documentary draft, a clean draft does not require any other document. When a clean draft is used in trade, the exporter usually sends the shipping documents directly to the buyer. Clean drafts are sometimes used when multinational companies ship the goods to their own subsidiaries, because matters of trust and credit are not important. However, most international trade transactions involve documentary drafts which require various shipping documents.

Because bankers' acceptances are highly marketable, the exporter can sell them in the market or discount them at his bank. Whenever they are sold or discounted, the seller adds his endorsement on the back of the draft. In the event of the importer's failure to pay at maturity, the holder of the draft will have recourse for the full amount of the draft from the last endorser.

There are a number of reasons why drafts are used in foreign trade. (1) They provide written evidence of obligations in a comprehensive form. (2) They allow both the exporter and the importer to reduce the cost of financing and to divide the remaining costs equitably. (3) They are negotiable and unconditional. That is, drafts are not subiect to disputes which may occur between the parties involved.

CONSIGNMENTS

Goods for export may be consigned to the exporter's own agent (subsidiary), an independent agent, or an import house. Assume that an exporter in India ships to an importer in London, 100 cases of quart bottles on a consignment basis. Because the exporter pays all the expenses connected with the shipment, the importer incurs no expenses at the time this shipment is delivered to this warehouse. Actually, the 100 cases of bottles are still the exporter's inventory. Thus, if the importer should fail, the exporter can demand that all the unsold bottles be returned to him.

Let us further assume that this consignment arrangement involves a ten per cent commission on all bottles sold. If the importer sold all the 100 cases at ₹ 2000 per case, he would deduct his commission of ₹ 20,000 (100 × ₹ 2000 × .10) and remit to the exporter a dollar draft for ₹ 1,80,000.

Consignment to the independent agent or the import house raises most of the same problems encountered in open account transactions. Under a *consignment* arrangement, the exporter ships the goods to the importer while still retaining actual title to the merchandise. The importer has access to the inventory, but does not have to pay for the goods until they have been sold to a third party. The exporter is trusting the importer to remit payment for the goods sold at that time. If the importer fails to pay, the exporter has limited recourse, since there is no draft involved and the goods have already been sold. As a result of the high risk, the consignment method is seldom used except by affiliated and subsidiary companies trading with the parent company. Hence, this type of operation is usually confined to companies working very closely together and between companies that completely trust each other.

CREDIT TERMS

Most importers are not required to pay for goods before or on delivery but are allowed a short deferment period before payment is made. During this period, the exporter extends credit to the importer. There are three types of trade credit: *open account*, *notes payable*, and *bankers' acceptances/ trade acceptances*.

Open account credit does not require the importer to sign a formal debt instrument to evidence the amount that he owes the exporter. The importer simply charges his purchases, much in the same fashion that domestic retail stores extend credit to their customers. Then the importer's account is carried on the books of the exporter like any other receivables. This arrangement places the entire financial burden upon the exporter. Because banks usually refuse to advance against accounts receivable, it ties up large amounts of the exporter's capital. In addition, with this arrangement the exporter assumes the risks of foreign exchange blockage and buyer default. Therefore, open account terms are extended only to trusted customers in countries that have no foreign exchange or political problems.

In some export transactions, promissory notes are employed instead of open account credit. In this case, the importer is requested to sign a note that evidences his debt to the exporter. Thus, this arrangement makes the importer recognise his debt formally. The note calls for the payment of the obligation at some future date.

Bankers' acceptances are time drafts or bills of exchange drawn on, and accepted by the importer's bank (drawee bank). By accepting the draft the drawee bank assumes an unconditional obligation to pay a specified (face) amount at the draft's maturity to a bona fide holder. In effect, bankers' acceptances at the draft's maturity are guarantees of the debt by the importer's bank. Bankers' acceptances are negotiable instruments and, since the bank's name backs the instrument, they are discountable. These features allow the exporter who receives a bankers' acceptance in lieu of immediate payment to realise cash on the sale immediately by selling the acceptance, at a discount, to either the drawee or any other bank. Or, if the exporter does not need cash immediately, the acceptance can be held until the maturity date and then presented to the drawee bank for payment.

Banker's acceptances can be created under a letter of credit, in which case a number of shipping documents must be submitted by the exporter to the drawee bank. There are also so-called clean acceptances, which do not require a presentation of the shipping documents to the accepting bank: in this instance the importer must have an acceptance agreement with the bank, which entitles the importer to request the issuance of bankers' acceptances.

Trade acceptances are similar to bankers' acceptances but instead of being drawn on and accepted by the importer's bank they are drawn on and accepted by the importer, who, by this acceptance, promises to pay to the holder in due course the face amount of the acceptance at the specified maturity date. Trade acceptance and bankers' acceptances are negotiable. They cannot, however, be discountable if the importer on whom it is drawn is not well known and regarded in the market.

A trade acceptance is a form of short-term financing common in almost all foreign trade activities. In fact, it is the largest source of short-term funds for importers. Under this method of financing, the exporter draws a draft on the importer ordering him to pay the draft at some specified future date. The exporter will not release the goods until the importer accepts the draft. When the importer accepts the draft, it becomes a trade acceptance.

An exporter can specify the credit terms under which he is willing to extend with a foreign export sale. The degree of competition has a strong impact on the actual terms. The exporter may be compelled to grant 60 or 90 day credit even if he would like to be paid immediately after shipment. The shortest credit term is extended when the exporter draws a sight draft on a correspondent bank of the importer's bank. Payment is made to the exporter on demand when the draft arrives at the importer or his bank. Longer credit terms are achieved when the exporter draws a time draft, which specifies the time period after presentation when the funds must be paid.

When a time draft is employed in foreign trade, the exporter may carry the credit for his own account or refinance it through a local bank. Under the latter arrangement, the letter of credit ordinarily specific who will pay the expenses of financing. Although these expenses may be paid by the exporter or the importer, the ultimate choice depends largely upon the conditions of competition at the time of the transaction.

TRADE FINANCING METHODS

Most international trade involves a time lag between the date of shipment and when payment is made. Although some international transactions are of course paid for in cash up front, such advance payment is as rare internationally as it is domestically. For transactions between unrelated parties, however, financing is usually needed. Many other international trade transactions are between different units of the same multinational enterprises.

A bank can finance goods in transit, as well as goods held for sale, based on the three key documents, without exposing itself to questions about the quality of the merchandise or other physical aspects of the shipment. The bank in effect promises to pay the exporter on behalf of the importer, and receives reimbursement from the importer at some agreed-upon date. The bank thus acts like a trusted intermediary between the two parties.

LETTER OF CREDIT (L/C)

Introduced earlier, the *letter of credit, (L/C)*, is a bank's conditional promise to pay issued by a bank at the request of an importer (the applicant/buyer), in which the bank promises to pay an exporter (the beneficiary of the letter) upon presentation of documents specified in the L/C. An L/C reduces the risk of noncompletion, because the bank agrees to pay against documents rather than actual merchandise. The relationship between the three parties can be seen in Exhibit-4.

An importer (buyer) and exporter (seller) agree on a transaction and the importer then applies to its local bank for the issuance of an L/C. The importer's bank issues an L/C and cuts a sales contract based on its assessment of the importer's creditworthiness. The bank might require a cash deposit or other collateral from the importer in advance. The importer's bank will want to know the type of transaction, the amount of money involved, and what documents must accompany the draft that will be drawn against the L/C.

EXHIBIT-4

Parties to a Letter of Credit (L/C)

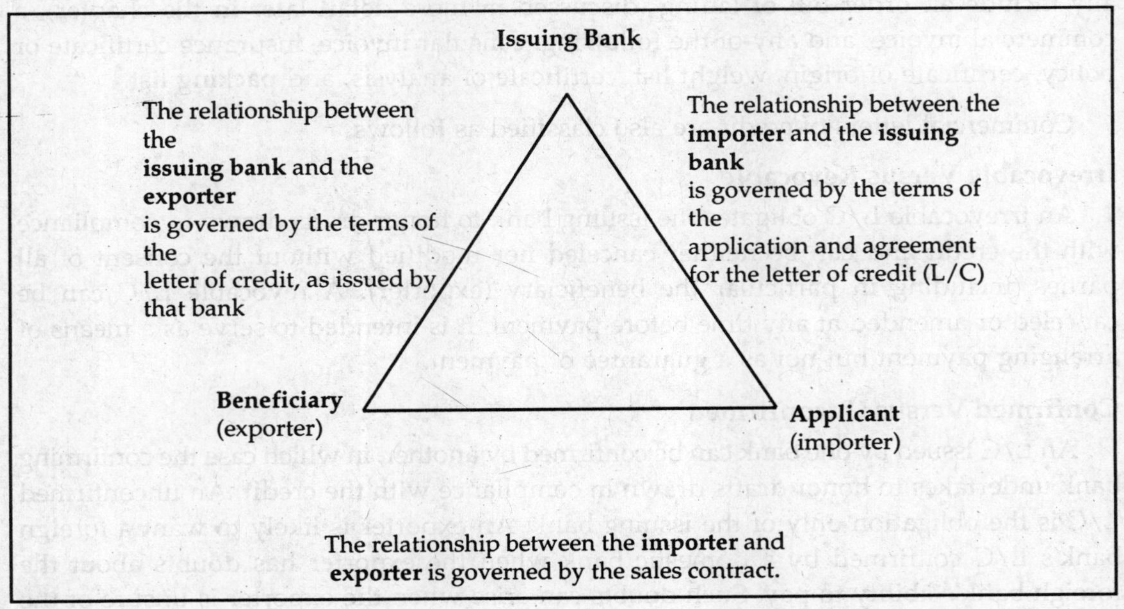

If the importer's bank is satisfied with the credit standing of the applicant, it will issue an L/C guaranteeing to pay for the merchandise if shipped in accordance with the instructions and conditions contained in the L/C.

The essence of a L/C is the promise of the issuing bank to pay *against specified documents*, which must accompany any draft drawn against the credit. The L/C is not a guarantee of the underlying commercial transaction. Indeed, the L/C is a separate transaction from any sales or other contracts on which it might be based. To constitute a true L/C transaction, all of the following five elements must be present with respect to the issuing bank:

1. The issuing bank must receive a fee or other valid business consideration for issuing the L/C.
2. The bank's L/C must contain a specified expiration date or a definite maturity.
3. The bank's commitment must have a stated maximum amount of money.
4. The bank's obligation to pay must arise only on the presentation of specific documents, and the bank must not be called on to determine disputed questions of fact or law.
5. The bank's customer must have an unqualified obligation to reimburse the bank on the same condition as the bank has paid.

Most commercial letters of credit are *documentary*, meaning that certain documents must be included with any drafts drawn under their terms. Required documents usually include an order bill of lading (discussed in more detail later in the chapter), a commercial invoice, and any of the following: consular invoice, insurance certificate or policy, certificate of origin, weight list, certificate of analysis, and packing list.

Commercial letters of credit are also classified as follows.

Irrevocable Versus Revocable

An irrevocable L/C obligates the issuing bank to honor drafts drawn in compliance with the credit and can be neither canceled nor modified without the consent of all parties, including in particular the beneficiary (exporter). A revocable L/C can be canceled or amended at any time before payment; it is intended to serve as a means of arranging payment but not as a guarantee of payment.

Confirmed Versus Unconfirmed

An L/C issued by one bank can be confirmed by another, in which case the confirming bank undertakes to honor drafts drawn in compliance with the credit. An unconfirmed L/C is the obligation only of the issuing bank. An exporter is likely to want a foreign bank's L/C confirmed by a domestic bank when the exporter has doubts about the foreign bank's ability to pay. Such doubts can arise when the exporter is unsure of the financial standing of the foreign bank, or if political or economic conditions in the foreign country are unstable.

Advantages and Disadvantages of Letters of Credit

The primary advantage of an L/C is that it reduces risk—the exporter can sell against a bank's promise to pay rather than against the promise of a commercial firm.

The exporter is also in a more secure position as to the availability of foreign exchange to pay for the sale, since banks are more likely to be aware of foreign exchange conditions and rules than is the importing firm itself. If the importing country should change its foreign exchange rules during the course of a transaction, the government is likely to allow already outstanding bank letters of credit to be honored for fear of throwing its own domestic banks into international disrepute. Of course, if the L/C is confirmed by a bank in the exporter's country, the exporter avoids any problem of blocked foreign exchange.

An exporter may find that an order backed by an irrevocable L/C will facilitate obtaining pre-export financing in the home country. If the exporter's reputation for delivery is good, a local bank may lend funds to process and prepare the merchandise for shipment. Once the merchandise is shipped in compliance with the terms and conditions of the credit, payment for the business transaction is made and funds will be generated to repay the pre-export loan.

The major advantage of an L/C to the importer is that the importer need not pay out funds until the documents have arrived at the bank that issued the L/C and after all conditions stated in the credit have been fulfilled. The main disadvantages are the fee charged by the importer's bank for issuing its L/C, and the possibility that the L/C reduces the importer's borrowing line of credit with its bank. It may, in fact, be a competitive disadvantage for the exporter to demand automatically an L/C from an importer, especially if the importer has a good credit record and there is no concern regarding the economic or political conditions of the importer's country.[2]

---

2. The landscape of trade finance in Asia is changing. Given the proliferation of electronic and online facilities, traditional trade finance resources such as the letter of credit (L/C) stand to be replaced, perhaps totally, in a very short time frame. More important, banks and companies need to change their business mind set in order to accomodate the different type of financing arrangements required by the e-commerce business model. Tai Kah Chye, vice president and Asia Head of e-commerce trade and supply chain at JP Morgan, sums up the shift of balance: "The emergence of e-commerce technologies continues to capture the headlines in trade financing. Whilst it is true that e-commerce is not a substitute for financing, it is nonetheless fundamentally changing the way that trade financing has been conducted in the past."

Although the L/C is the most conventional trade finance tool, and one that still has a function in the region, its level of usage has declined in some Asian countries. Notes Wenyir Lu, senior vice president and general manager at bank SinoPac in Taiwan: "In Taiwan, the use of L/C has declined from 50%-60% of total trade transactions three years ago to below 30% today." The main reason for the drop in L/C usage in countries like Taiwan, Hong Kong, and Singapore is the long processing time: negotiating an L/C (from the time of shipment to the time of presentation by the issuing bank) can take over 20 days.

It's easy to pick electronic and online application service providers in the market. One is Bolero, a service launched in late 1999 and jointly owned by SWIFT and the Through Transport Club. By standardizing the architecture through which electronic documents are exchange, Bolero acts as a third-party authenticator of messages, allowing trading parties and banks to excahnge documents with confidence. This means the entire L/C cycle can be processed electronically, with greater speed and with less fraud. See "The LC Goes On-Line," *Asimoney*, February 2001, pp. 72-76.

BANKERS' ACCEPTANCES

When a draft is accepted by a bank, it becomes a bankers' acceptance. As such it is the unconditional promise of that bank to make payment on the draft when it matures. In quality the bankers' acceptance is practically identical to a marketable bank certificate of deposit (CD). The holder of a bankers' acceptance need not wait until maturity to liquidate the investment, but may sell the acceptance in the money market, where constant trading in such instruments occurs.

The first owner of the bankers' acceptance created from an international trade transaction will be the exporter, who receives the accepted draft back after the bank has stamped it "accepted." The exporter may hold the acceptance until maturity and then collect. On an acceptance of, say, ₹ 10,00,000 for six months the exporter would receive the face amount less the bank's acceptance commission of 1.5% per annum:

Face amount of the acceptance	₹ 10,00,000	
Less 1.5% per annum commission for 6 months	-3,500	(.015 x 6/12 x ₹ 10,00,000)
Amount received by exporter in 6 months	₹ 9,92,500	

Alternatively, the exporter may "discount"—that is, sell at a reduced price—the acceptance to its bank in order to receive funds at once. The exporter will then receive the face amount of the acceptance less both the acceptance fee and the going market rate of discount for bankers' acceptances. If the discount rate were 10% per annum, the exporter would receive the following:

Face amount of the acceptance	₹ 10,00,000	
Less 1.5% per annum commission for 6 months	-7,500	(.015 x 6/12 x ₹ 10,00,000)
Less 10% per annum discount rate for 6 months	50,000	(.10 x 6/12 x ₹ 10,00,000)
Amount received by exporter at once	₹ 9,42,500	

The discounting bank may hold the acceptance in its own portfolio, earning for itself the 10% per annum discount rate, or the acceptance may be resold in the acceptance market to portfolio investors. Investors buying bankers' acceptances provide the funds that finance the transaction.

The *securitization* of export receivables for financing trade is an attractive supplement to bankers' acceptance financing. A firm can *securitize* its export receivables by selling them to a legal entity established to create marketable securities based on a package of individual export receivables. An advantage of this technique is to remove the export receivables from the exporter's balance sheet because they have been sold without recourse.

The receivables are normally sold at a discount. The size of the discount depends on four factors:

1. The historic collection risk of the exporter
2. The cost of credit insurance
3. The cost of securing the desirable cash flow stream to the investors
4. The size of the financing and services fees

Securitization is more cost effective if there is a large value of transactions with a known credit history and default profitability. A large exporter could establish its own securitization entity. While the initial setup cost is high, the entity can be used on an ongoing basis. As an alternative, smaller exporters could use a common securitization entity provided by a financial institution, thereby saving the expensive setup costs.

BILL OF LADING (B/L)

The third key document for financing international trade is the *bill of lading*, or *B/L*. The bill of lading is issued to the exporter by a common carrier transporting the merchandise. It serves three purposes: a receipt, a contract, and a document of title.

As a receipt, the bill of lading indicates that the carrier has received the merchandise described on the face of the document. The carrier is not responsible for ascertaining that the containers hold what is alleged to be their contents, so descriptions of merchandise on bills of lading are usually short and simple. If shipping charges are paid in advance, the bill of lading will usually be stamped "freight paid" or "freight prepaid." If merchandise is shipped collect—a less common procedure internationally than domestically—the carrier maintains a lien on the goods until freight is paid.

As a contract, the bill of lading indicates the obligation of the carrier to provide certain transportation in return for certain charges. Common carriers cannot disclaim responsibility for their negligence through inserting special clauses in a bill of lading. The bill of lading may specify alternative ports in the event that delivery cannot be made to the designated port, or it may specify that the goods will be returned to the exporter at the expo ter's expense.

As a document of title, the bill of lading is used to obtain payment or a written promise of payment before the merchandise is released to the importer. The bill of lading can also function as collateral against which funds may be advanced to the exporter by its local bank .prior to or during shipment and before final payment by the importer.

Characteristics of the Bill of Lading

Bills of lading are either *straight* or *to order. A straight bill of lading* provides that the carrier deliver the merchandise to the designated consignee only. A straight bill of lading is not title to the goods and is not required for the consignee to obtain possession. Because a straight bill of lading is *not* title, it is not good collateral for loans. Therefore, a straight bill of lading is used when the merchandise has been paid for in advance, when the transaction is being financed by the exporter, or when the shipment is to a subsidiary.

An *order bill of lading* directs the carrier to deliver the goods to the order of a designated party, usually the shipper. An additional inscription may request the carrier to notify someone else of the arrival. The order bill of lading grants title to the merchandise only to the person to whom the document is addressed, and surrender of the order bill of lading is required to obtain the shipment.

The order bill of lading is typically made payable to the order of the exporter, who thus retains title to the goods after they have been handed to the carrier. Title to the merchandise remains with the exporter until payment is received, at which time the exporter endorses the order bill of lading (which is negotiable) in blank or to the party making the payment, usually a bank. The most common procedure would be for payment to be advanced against a documentary draft accompanied by the endorsed order bill of lading. After paying the draft, the exporter's bank forwards the documents through bank clearing channels to the bank of the importer. The importer's bank, in turn, releases the documents to the importer after payment (sight drafts), after acceptance (time drafts addressed to the importer and marked D/A), or after payment terms have been agreed upon (drafts drawn on the importer's bank under provisions of a L/C).

FACTORING

When an exporter ships goods before receiving payment, the accounts receivable balance increases. Unless the exporter has received a loan from a bank, it is initially financing the transaction, and it must monitor the collections of receivables. Since there is a danger that the buyer will never pay at all, the exporting firm may consider selling the accounts receivable to a third party, known as a *factor*. In this type of financing, the exporter sells the accounts receivable without recourse. The factor then assumes all administrative responsibilities involved in collecting from the buyer and the associated credit exposure. As one would expect, the factor performs its own credit approval process on the foreign buyer before purchasing the receivable. For providing this service, the factor usually purchases the receivable at a discount and also receives a flat processing fee.

Factoring provides several benefits to the exporter. *First,* by selling the accounts receivable, the exporter does not have to worry about the administrative duties involved in maintaining and monitoring an accounts receivable accounting ledger. *Second,* the factor assumes the credit exposure to the buyer, so the exporter does not have to maintain personnel to assess the creditworthiness of foreign buyers. *Finally,* the sale of the receivable to the factor provides immediate payment and improves the exporter's cash flow.

Since it is the importer who must be creditworthy from a factor's point of view, *cross-border factoring* is often used. This involves a network of factors in various countries who assess credit risk. The exporter's factor contacts a correspondent factor in the buyer's country to assess the importer's creditworthiness and handle the collections of the receivable. Factoring services are usually provided by the factoring subsidiaries of commercial banks, commercial finance companies, and other specialised finance houses.

FORFAITING

Because capital goods are often quite expensive, an importer may not be able to make payment on the goods within a short time period. Thus, longer-term financing may be required here. The exporter could be able to provide financing for the importer but may not desire to do so, since the financing may extend over several years. In this case, a type of trade finance known as forfaiting could be used. Forfaiting refers to the purchase of financial obligations, such as bills of exchange or promissory notes, without recourse to the original holder, usually the exporter. In a forfait transaction, the importer would issue a promissory note in favour of the exporter to pay for the imported capital goods. The term generally ranges from three to seven years. The exporter would then sell the notes, without recourse, to the forfaiting bank. In some respects, this is similar to factoring, in that the forfaiter (or factor) assumes responsibility for the collection of payment from the buyer and the underlying credit risk and country risk. Since the forfaiting bank assumes the risk of nonpayment, it should asses the creditworthiness of the importer as if it were extending a medium-term loan. Forfait transactions are normally collateralised by a bank guarantee or letter of credit issued by the importer's bank for the term of the transaction. Since financial information is usually difficult to obtain on the importer, the forfaiting bank places a great deal of reliance on the bank guarantee as the collateral in the event the buyer fails to pay as agreed. It is this guarantee backing up the transaction that has fostered the growth of the forfait market, particularly in Europe, as a practical means of trade finance.

Forfaiting transactions can be denominated in most currencies. For some larger transactions, more than one bank may be involved. In this case, a syndicate is formed wherein each participant assumes a proportionate share of the underlying risk and profit. A forfaiting firm may decide to sell the promissory notes of the importer to other financial institutions willing to purchase them. However, the forfaiting firm is still responsible for payment on the notes in the event the importer is unable to pay

COUNTERTRADE

The term countertrade denotes all types of foreign trade transactions in which the sale of goods to one country is linked to the purchase or exchange of goods from that same country. Some types of countertrade, such as barter, have been in existence for thousands of years. However, only recently has countertrade gained popularity and importance. The growth in various types of countertrade has been fueled by large balance of payments disequilibriums, foreign currency shortages, and developing countries' debt problems, and stagnant worldwide demand. As a result, many multinationals have been confronted with countertrade opportunities, particularly in Asia, Latin America, and Eastern Europe. The most common types of countertrade include barter, compensation, and counter purchase.

Barter represents the exchange of goods between two parties without the use of any currency as a medium of exchange. Most barter arrangements are one-time transactions governed by one contract.

In a *compensation* or clearing-account arrangement, the delivery of goods to one party is compensated for by the seller's buying back a certain amount of product from that same party. The transaction is governed by one contract, and the value of the goods is expressed in monetary terms. The buy-back arrangement could be for a fraction of the original sale *(partial compensation)* or more than 100 per cent of the original sale *(full compensation)*. An example of compensation would be the sale of phosphate from Morocco to France in exchange for purchasing a certain percentage of fertiliser. In some countries, this is also referred to as an industrial cooperation arrangement. Such arrangements often involve the construction of large projects, such as power plants, in exchange for the purchase of the project's output over an extended period of time. For example, a hydroelectric plant was sold by Brazil to Argentina in exchange for Brazil's purchase of a percentage of the plant's output over a long-term contract.

The term *counter purchase* denotes the exchange of goods between two parties under two distinct contracts expressed in monetary terms. Delivery and payment of both goods are technically separate transactions.

The countertrade market is still developing. The primary participants are governments and multinationals, with assistance provided by specialists in the field, such as attorneys, financial institutions, and trading companies. The transactions are usually very complex and large. Many variations of countertrade exist, and the terminology used by the various market participants is still forming. Nonetheless, despite the economic inefficiencies of countertrade, it has grown in significance and is used by the experienced traders and governments.

EXPORT FINANCE IN INDIA

As the process of internationalisation of national economies gathers momentum, promotion of external trade assumes added importance. External trade opens up vast opportunities in terms of access to the global supply market and having the world as the potential market for exports, with the trade barriers being progressively brought down. Countries that can attune their policies to the demands of global forces can alone benefit from the new trends. Many countries that had, hitherto, instituted import-substitution regimes, obviously, need to reform their trade policies quite substantially. Although the export promotion drive in India had begun in early 70s, the import-substitution policy continued due to the scarcity of funds for the required imports. The Economic Reforms Process initiated in mid 1991 focussed initially on liberalising the Export Import Policy regime with equal importance being given to the simplification and rationalisation of the procedural system. Since finance being the back-bone of trade, whether domestic or international, Reserve Bank of India has taken various steps to ensure free flow of financial assistance to export sector at lower rates of interest.

Banks, being the main source of finance, are encouraged in several ways to extend export finance, to achieve the objectives of the foreign trade policy. Though export credit is not formally categorised as a priority sector credit by RBI, banks have to achieve a minimum floor level of export credit at 10% of each bank's net bank credit. Further it is of greater significance to banks since the credit is being extended to one of the vital sectors of the economy and serves the process of economic development, which is a national objective. In order to compensate the banks for extending export finance at lower rates of interest and encourage them to extend more liberal finance, various measures are taken. These include liberal export refinance by Reserve Bank of India (RBI) and Export/Import Bank of India (Exim Bank) and credit guarantee coverage facilities by Export Credit Guarantee Corporation of India Ltd. (ECGC).

Reducing export finance to be a critical area of reforms, commercial banks and other financial institutions in India have been constantly coming up with new schemes for financing different stages of export activity. Under the Post Shipment Credit Denominated in Foreign Currency (PSCFC) scheme introduced with effect from January 1, 1992, exporters can avail of post-shipment credit denominated in foreign currency and pay interest at internationally competitive rates. The rates, however, continued to be administered by the RBI. The LIBOR (London Inter Bank Offered Rate) linked Export Bills Discounting/Rediscounting (EBD/R) scheme introduced subsequently in October '93 effectively deregulated interest rates at the post-shipment stage. This was a landmark step. It was soon followed by the effective deregulation of interest rates at the pre-shipment stage as well with the launching of Pre-shipment Credit in Foreign

Currency (PCFC) scheme in November '91. The scheme enables exporters to finance both domestic and imported inputs of exportable goods at interest rates linked to LIBOR. Normally, the credit period in the export financing schemes run by commercial banks is restricted upto 180 days. Thus, the cost of short-term export finance in India now compares favourably with that in other competing countries, provided the finance is taken in foreign currency. However, this facility is generally available only at designated offices of banks. Most of the small exporters at upcountry centres still have to manage with relatively expensive rupee finance. Letting interest rates being determined by market forces rather than artificially by any direct or indirect subsidy may enable all exporters to benefit from lowering of interest rates. It is also seen that export credit on deferred payment terms is more expensive in India because of the weak government support to export credit agencies like the ECGC and the EXIM Bank. It appears that ECGC is constrained from effectively discharging its intended role in the development of exports due to inadequate budgetary support. (On the other hand, a number of foreign insurance companies are waiting to enter the huge Indian insurance sector). It may be worthwhile to explore the possibility of allowing the foreign insurance companies to enter India on condition of undertaking certain level of export insurance commitments as part of their overall insurance exposures in India.

The Exim Bank offers credit mainly on deferred term basis. Exim Bank has designated special lending programmes for export oriented units and units in export processing zones. Forfaiting, which enables exporters to convert credit sales to cash sales without recourse, is the latest addition in its lending programmes. However, a policy push is required to make it a big success.

As far as adequacy of credit is concerned, the RBI has given very clear directives to banks to ensure that they must meet the needs of exporters fully. However, this would become possible only if banks start taking decisions based on the past track records rather than on the exporters' capacity to offer security. Modern techniques like factoring and forfaiting should be developed to facilitate financing the export ventures of small and new exporters who find it difficult to secure L/C backed contracts. Likewise, in the area of project exports too, forfaiting would prove helpful in making adequate credit available.

Procedural bottlenecks and obstacles is another vital area of concern. There are considerable delays in appraising and sanctioning of finance and other facilities. Top priority must, therefore, be accorded to upgradation of technology. The increasing complexities arising from the availability of export credit in foreign currencies, multi-currency accounting and managing floating interest rate exposures make it imperative for banks to switch over completely to computerised book-keeping and accounting. Simultaneously, the communication channels need to be strengthened to ensure speedy realisations and credit of export proceeds as also for advising export letters of credit, dissemination of other relevant information, etc. Further, it may be necessary to create a credit rating agency exclusively for exporters if banks have to successfully implement the lending guidelines that require a new proposal for export finance to be cleared within 45 days, a request for review/renewal of credit facilities within 30 days and a request for adhoc facility within 15 days.

It may also be necessary to increase the range of services for exporters such as increasing the period of suppliers' credit from 180 days to one year, permitting exporters to tie up lines of credit with branches of Indian and foreign banks abroad with provisions to repay the borrowings within one year, extending finance for market development and business travel to small and medium size exporters to help them in their marketing efforts, increasing the number of branches offering special services to exporters, financing against duty drawback receivables, allowing overseas buyers to maintain interest bearing deposit accounts in India, permitting exporters to book forward cover for exports based on their average exports rather than on the basis of firm orders in hand, permitting exporters direct access to forex markets rather than through authorised dealers as at present, making the Exchange Earners' Foreign Currency (EEFC) account fully convertible, etc. A review of some financing schemes is also called for. For example, there does not seem adequate logic for continuing with the Post-shipment Credit Denominated in Foreign Currency (PSCFC) scheme after the introduction of the Export Bill Discounting/ Rediscounting (EBD/R) scheme. Similarly, the- Foreign Currency Account (FCA) scheme for exporters has become almost completely redundant especially, after the expansion of the size of Exchange Earners' Foreign Currency (EEFC) account scheme with which exporter can now release foreign exchange currency by them even beyond 1 year provided they justify its wealth.

Export finance is broadly classified into two categories, depending upon at what stage of export activity the finance is extended namely:

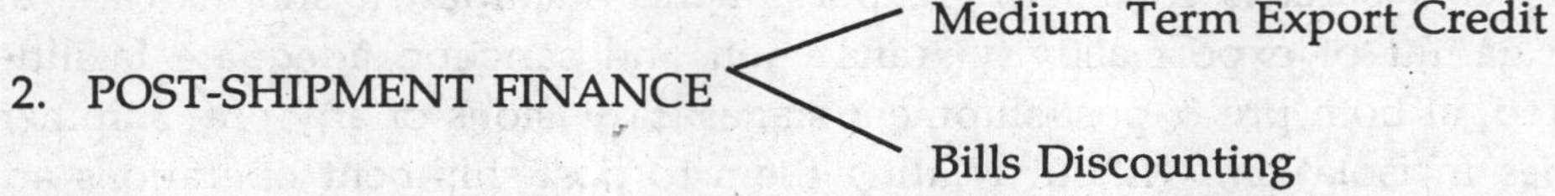

Financial assistance extended to the exporters, prior to shipment of export, goods, falls within the scope of pre-shipment finance. Financial assistance extended after the shipment of export goods falls within the scope of post-shipment finance.

Export finance (both at pre-shipment and post-shipment stages) in India is governed by and large by RBI directives and FEDAI rules. Since export finance is related to foreign trade, knowledge of the trade policy, procedures and directives of Export Trade Control authorities, international trade practices, particularly those of International Chamber of Commerce (ICC) Paris and the pulse of local as well as international markets is very much essential. Government of India has set up a vast network of institutional infrastructure to strengthen and subserve the objective of export promotion. Information regarding functional areas of these institutions will also help bankers very much.

Export finance is made available at concessional and liberal terms, as it is specifically aimed at serving a vital national cause. A banker extending such finance is expected to be prudent and judicious. Further, the exports being a part of external sector of the economy, is subject to several rules and regulations directly and indirectly. Thus, it casts an additional responsibility on the lending banker, who has to keep in view all such rules and regulations, in addition to usual principles of lending, while financing exports.

Some of the general lending guidelines to banks relating to export finance are:

1. Export Finance proposals should be expeditiously disposed off so that timely and adequate credit is made available to exporters. The applications for credit limits for export sector are to be disposed off, within the time frame given below:
   (a) Sanction of fresh/enhanced credit limits 45 days
   (b) Renewal of existing limits30 days
   (c) Sanction of adhoc limits 15 days
2. Banks should adopt a flexible approach to export lending and norms of lending. At the same time, it is their responsibility to see that exporters do not misuse this concessional and liberal finance. It should be strictly "PURPOSE ORIENTED & NEED BASED".
3. Whenever a bank is considering export finance facilities, it should view the entire gamut of export activity transaction and sanction adequate facilities required, at both pre & post-shipment stages. Provisions of any pre- shipment facilities in isolation, without relating them to post-shipment operations and requirements (should not be restored to). Preferably, all requisite facilities should be considered at the same time as a package deal. This is in view of the interwoven links and regulations.
4. Banks must keep in view the past performance of exporters and future potential, while assessing the credit proposals. In the case of new exporters, their experience in domestic market in dealing with the relative commodities and other background factors must be taken into consideration.

5. Banks must keep a close watch on the end-use of finance and timely fulfillment of export orders.
6. RBI has allowed several relaxations in respect of export lending, including relaxations of credit norms. Some of them are listed below:
   (a) While computing the overall working capital gap/maximum permissible bank finance (MPBF), banks can exclude export receivables out of such computation process and export sales finance limits can be assessed and sanctioned separately, over and above the permissible bank finance.
   (b) Wherever exporters are unable to bring in additional contribution (margin) in respect of additional credit facilities required for specific export transactions, banks can waive such additional contribution required from exporters.
   (c) If borrowing units have substantial export activity and the bank has identified excess finance as per applicable methods of lending in respect of such units and decides to convert such excess finance into WORKING CAPITAL TERM LOAN (WCTL), any excess finance in respect of pre- shipment finance limits should be carved out separately on notional basis, so that, on such WCTL concessional rates of interest as applicable to export finance can be levied.
   (d) Banks are free to decide the levels of holding of individual items of inventory and receivables which should be supported by bank finance, after taking into account the production/processing cycle of the industry in question, as also other relevant factors. (This will apply to all categories of borrowers).
   (e) Additional credit needs of exporters arising out of firm orders/confirmed letters of credit (and which are not taken into account while fixing the regular credit limits) should be met in full, even if sanction of such additional credit limits exceed MPBF.

TRADE CREDIT: THE CURRENT SCENARIO IN INDIA

Trade credit is a critical component of global trade. Internationally active firms rely extensively on trade credits. As per a recent WTO study using quarterly country-level data of export credit insurers from the Berne Union for the period 2005 to 2011, a 1 per cent increase in trade credit granted to a country leads to a 0.4 per cent increase in real imports of that country. This effect does not vary between crisis and non-crisis periods. Thus both availability and cost of trade credit are important in the current environment of financial uncertainties when the banking system is likely to be tempted to reduce exposure to cross-border banking.

Reflecting improved global financial conditions, the gross inflow of short-term trade credit (up to 1 year) to India reached ₹ 392,526 crore during end September 2012, which represented a year-on-year increase of 24.6 per cent (but a quarter-on-quarter decline of 1.1 per cent in Q2 of 2012-13). Inflow of trade credit in H1 of 2012-13 at US$ 57.6 billion was 14 per cent higher than in 2011-12 and growth in outflow of trade credit was lower at 7.7 per cent. As a result, net trade credit grew by 60.1 per cent in H1 of 2012-13 and stood at US$ 9.5 billion as compared to the decline of 14.4 per cent in H1 of 2011-12.

TABLE 1

Export Credit

Outstanding as on	*Export credit*	*Variations (Per cent) (₹ Crore)*	*Export credit as per cent of NBC*
24 Mar. 2000	39118	9.0	9.8
23 Mar.2001	43321	10.7	9.3
22 Mar. 2002	42978	-0.8	8.0
21 Mar. 2003	49202	14.5	7.4
19 Mar. 2004	57687	17.2	7.6
18 Mar. 2005	69059	19.7	6.3
31 Mar. 2006	86207	24.8	5.7
30 Mar. 2007	104926	21.7	5.4
28 Mar. 2008	129983	23.9	5.5
27 Mar. 2009	128940	-0.8	4.6
26 Mar. 2010	138143	7.1	4.3
25 Mar. 2011	168841	22.2	4.3
23 Mar. 2012	181852	7.7	3.9
30 Nov. 2012	185803	4.7*	3.7

Source: RBI.

Notes: * Variation over 18 November 2011.

NBC: Net Bank Credit.

Data pertain to all scheduled commercial banks excluding regional rural banks (RRBs) availing of export credit refinance from the RBI.

Export credit has been decelerating since 2011-12. In 2012-13 (up to 30 November 2012), it has grown by 4.7 per cent over end-March 2012 compared to 7.7 per cent in full FY 2011-12. Export credit as a per cent of net bank credit which was at 9.8 per cent as on 24 March 2000 has been decelerating almost continuously over the years. It further decelerated in 2012 to 3.7 per cent as on 30 November 2012 (Table-1).

QUESTIONS

1. Show how export-import transactions are closely related to receivables and inventory management for the multinational firm. In particular, explain the link between the choice of an invoicing currency and the credit decision.
2. Are the L/C and banker's acceptance instruments that are exclusively used in financing foreign trade? Why are these two instruments especially adapted to foreign trade? State the advantages that each instrument provides for the exporter and importer in a typical foreign trade transaction.
3. Why have major capital goods exporting countries found it necessary to establish government export financing programmes, instead of relying on banking and other private financing facilities? Does EX-IM Bank subsidise India exports?
4. Distinguish between factoring and forfaiting as techniques for managing receivables arising from exports. Which particular situations lend themselves best to forfaiting?
5. Explain why so many international transactions require international trade credit faciliated by commercial banks.
6. What is the purpose of a letter of credit? What are the major types of L/C's?
7. Why might different documentation be used for an export to a non-affiliated foreign buyer who is a new customer as compared to an export to a nonaffiliated foreign buyer to whom the exporter has been selling for many years?
8. For what reason might an exporter use standard international trade documentation (letter of credit, draft, order bill of lading) on an intrafirm export to its parent or sister subsidiary?
9. What reasons can you give for the observation that intrafirm trade is now greater than trade between nonaffiliated exporters and importers?
10. Explain the difference between a letter of credit (L/C) and a draft. How are they linked?
11. Identify each party to a letter of credit (L/C) and indicate its responsibility.
12. Most letters of credit are irrevocable. The bank must honor drafts drawn in accordance with the L/C. However same letter of credit are revocable. Why would a recoverable letter of credit be used?
13. Why would an exporter insist on a confirmed letter of credit?
14. How may an exporter use a letter of credit to extend credit to an importer?
15. Can a banker's acceptance be sold to another party? Since it does not pay interest, why would a person buy it? Who guarantees payment?
16. Discuss the steps taken by the RBI to extend export finance to achieve the objective of the foreign trade policy.
17. Discuss the impact of the global financial crisis on trade credit.
18. Discuss the measures taken by the international institutions selected to trade financing during world recession.

REFERENCES

Exim Bank: *Transaction Costs of Indian Exports: An Analysis*, 1999.

Government of India: *Economic Survey* (various issues), Ministry of Finance, New Delhi.

——: *Report of the Committee on Import-Export Policies and Procedure* (Chairman P.C. Alexander), New Delhi, 1978

ITPO: *Indian Export Bulletin* (various issues).

Reserve Bank of India: *Report on Currency and Finance*, 1999-2000.

World Bank: *Country Economic Memorandum of India*, Washington, D.C., 1996.

Unit VIII

41

THE INTERNATIONAL MONETARY SYSTEM

INTRODUCTION

Towards the end of World War II the governments of the leading trading nations of the free world decided that the chaotic financial conditions of the inter-war period could not be tolerated after the war had ended. An International Monetary and Financial Conference of the United and Associated Nations was convened at Bretton Woods, New Hampshire on I July 1944. The main goal of the architects of the Bretton Woods system was to establish an international economic order that would prevent another political and economic collapse. This new order under the leadership of the United States aimed to prevent a return to economic nationalism by fostering free trade and high level of international interaction.

INTERNATIONAL MONETARY FUND (IMF)

The prime goal of the IMF agreed at Bretton Woods was to assist its members in resolving short-term balance or payments problems under a regime of fixed exchange rates, thus permitting the orderly expansion of international trade. The Fund was created as an international institution to supervise and promote an open and stable international monetary system. The purposes of the International Monetary Fund are stated in Article I of the IMF's constitutive document. These are:

(i) To promote international monetary cooperation through a permanent institution which provides the machinery for consultation and collaboration on international monetary problems.

(ii) To facilitate the expansion and balanced growth of international trade, and to contribute thereby to the promotion and maintenance of high levels of employment and real income and to the development of the productive resources of all members as primary objectives of economic policy.

(iii) To promote exchange stability, to maintain orderly exchange arrangements among members, and to avoid competitive exchange depreciation.

(iv) To assist in the establishment of a multilateral system of payments in respect of current transactions between members and in the elimination of foreign exchange restrictions which hamper the growth of trade.

(v) To give confidence to members by making the general resources of the Fund temporarily available to them under adequate safeguards, thus providing them with opportunity to correct maladjustments in their balance of payments without resorting to measures destructive of national or international prosperity.

(vi) In accordance with the above, to shorten the duration and lessen the degree of disequilibrium in the international balance of payments of members.

ORGANISATIONAL STRUCTURE

The IMF, organisational structure is set out in its Articles of Agreement, which entered into force in December, 1945, The Articles provide for a Board of Governors, an Executive Board, a Managing Director, and a staff of international civil servants.

The *Board of Governors,* the highest decision-making body of the IMF, consists of one governor and one alternate for each member country. The governor, appointed by the member country, is usually the minister of finance or the central bank governor. The Board of Governors has delegated to the Executive Board all except certain reserved powers. It normally meets once a year.

The *Executive Board* (the Board) is responsible for conducting the business of the IMF. It is composed of 24 directors, who are appointed or elected by member countries or groups of countries. The Managing Director serves as its chairman. Meeting several times a week, the Board deals with a wide variety of policy, operational, and administrative matters, including surveillance of members' exchange rate policies, provision of IMF financial assistance to member countries, and discussion of systemic issues in the global economy.

Selected by the Executive Board, the IMF's *Managing Director* serves as the head of the organisation's staff. Under the Board's direction, the Managing Director is responsible for conducting the ordinary business of the IMF. The Managing Director serves a five-year term and may be reelected to successive terms.

The *International Monetary and Financial Committee of the Board of Governors* (formerly the Interim Committee of the Board of Governors on the International Monetary System) is an advisory body composed of 24 IMF governors, ministers, or other officials of comparable rank and represents the same constituencies as the IMF's Executive Board. It normally meets twice a year, in April or May and at the time of the Annual Meeting of the Board of Governors in September or October. Among its responsibilities are to guide the Executive Board and to advise and report to the Board of Governors on issues related to the management and adaptation of the international monetary and financial system— including sudden disturbances that might threaten the international monetary system—and on proposals to amend the IMF's Articles of Agreement.

The *Development Committee* (the Joint Ministerial Committee of the Boards of Governors of the World Bank and the IMF on the Transfer of Real Resources to Developing Countries) also has 24 members— finance ministers or other officials of comparable rank—and generally meets at the same time as the International Monetary and Financial Committee. It advises and reports to the Boards of Governors of the World Bank and the IMF on development issues.

FUNCTIONS OF THE IMF

The Fund is designed to perform three important roles in the international monetary system. *First,* to regulate the financial relations of its members. This regulatory function includes an element of rule supervision and law enforcement with respect to exchange rates and balance of payments restrictions. *Secondly,* to provide financial assistance to members experiencing balance of payments difficulties. The Fund has acted as a lender of the last resort to countries with chronic payments problems. The regulatory and financial roles are closely entwined with access to the Fund's resources being made dependent on following the code of conduct devised by the Fund. *Thirdly,* to act as a consultative organ. The IMF's role is to create a climate in which governments are persuaded to dismantle exchange controls and to permit free trade and the free movement of capital.

Although 28 of the 44 nations represented at the Bretton Woods Conference can be classified as underdeveloped, these countries exerted minimal influence on the negotiations and the final outcome. The negotiations at Bretton Woods reflected the prevailing distribution of political and economic power in the international system. The deliberations were based around the plans developed by John Maynard Keynes (UK) and Harry Dexter White (US). American hegemony ensured that the final agreement bore a greater resemblance to the White Plan than the Keynes Plan. The developing countries were in a subordinate position and closely linked through imperial ties to the leading European states. Nevertheless, some developing countries, notably India, attempted to influence the final outcome of the conference. India called on the IMF to *assist in the fuller utilisation of the resources of the underdeveloped countries* and was supported in this request by Ecuador. An amended version of this request which called for *the development of the resources and productive power of all member countries with due regard to the needs of the economically backward countries* also failed. The developed countries insisted that development was within the terms of reference of the World Bank and not the IMF. Thus from the outset the concern of the Fund was with short-term balance of payments financing and not development.

This has led to charges that the IMF is anti-development and sacrifices development for stability. The Fund's retort is that a stable economic environment is a necessary prerequisite for the achievement of economic development. It has been argued, however, that since the Articles of Agreement of the IMF acknowledged the 'development of the productive resources of all members' as a salient objective, this is an indication that some importance was given to the special problem of development. However, this rather cursory reference to development, when taken in the context of the Fund's overall approach at its inception, which was to treat countries in an undifferentiated manner, did not suggest that the Fund would be sensitive to the special needs of the developing countries.

This review of the origins of the IMF shows that the main purposes of the Fund at its inception were to foster international cooperation and promote stability. Economic development was not a prime goal of the international regime established at Bretton Woods. The efforts of the Third World states to increase their participation in the international monetary system led them to demand changes in the IMF. The concerted campaign by the developing countries for a recognition of their particular interests has, to date, achieved limited success.

RECENT STRUCTURAL CHANGES IN THE IMF

Quotas: Capital Base

The IMF is a financial cooperative, in some ways like a credit union. Each member of IMF is assigned a quota, based broadly on its relative size in the world economy, which determines its maxdimum contribution to the IMF's financial resources. Upon joining the IMF, a country normally pays up to one-quarter of its quota in the form of widely accepated foreign currencies (such as the U.S. dollar, euro, yen or pund sterling) or Special Drawing Rights (SDRs). The remaining three-quarters is paid in the country's own currency.

Quotas are reviewed at least every five years. The 1998 quota review led to a 45 percent increase in IMF quotas. The reviews concluded in January 2003 and January 2008 resulted in no change in quotas. Initial ad hoc quota. The increase in 2006 as the first step in a two-year programing of reforms raised quotas by another 1.8 percent. As part of the quta and voice reform process, further ad hoc quota increases were approved by the Board of Governors on April 28, 2008, which raise quotas by 9.55 percent (with an overall increase under the reform of 11.5 percent.)

Gold Holding

The Fund's gold holdings amount to about 103.4 million ounces making the Fund the third largest official holder of gold in the world. However, the IMF's Articles of Agreement strictly limit its use. If approved by an 85 percent majority of voting power of member countries, the IMF may sell gold or may accept gold as payment by member countries; but the IMF is prohibited from buying gold or engaging in other gold transactions.

IMF's Lending Capacity

IMF can use its quota funded holdings of currencies of financially strong economies to finance lending. The IMF's Executive Board selects these currencies every three months. Most are issued by industrial countries, but the list also has included currencies of lower income countries such as Botswana, China, and India. The IMF's holdings of these currencies, together with its own SDR holdings, make up its own usable resources. If needed, the IMF can supplement its own usable resources by borrowing.

The amount the IMF has readily available for new (non-concessional) lending is indicated by its one-year forward commitment capacity. This is determined by its usable resources, plus projected loan repayments over the subsequent twelve months, less the resources that have already been committed under existing arrangements, less a prudential balance

Borrowing Arrangements

The IMF maintains two standing multilateral borrowing arrangements—the New Arrangements to Borrow (NAB) and the General Arrangements to Borrow (GAB)—with a total borrowing capacity of SDR 34 billion (about $50 billion). If the IMF believes that its forward commitment capacity might fall short of its members' needs—for example, in the event of a major financial crisis—it can activate these arrangements. Their renewal was approved in 2007 for another five years starting in 2008.

In February 2009, the IMF signed a bilateral borrowing agreement with Japan to temporarily bolster its capacity to support members during the current global economic and financial crisis. Under this agreement Japan committed to lend up to US$100 billion (about SDR 68 billion) to the IMF. Supplementary resources available under this loan will help ensure that the Fund can continue to provide timely and effective balance of payments assistance to its members.

Economic Surveillance

The main job of the IMF is to promote international monetary cooperation and economic and financial stability in member countries and at the global level as a basis for sustained economic growth, which is essential for raising living standards and reducing poverty. Promoting macroeconomic and financial stability is partly a matter of avoiding economic and financial crisis, which can destroy jobs, slash incomes, and cause great human suffering. But it is also a matter of avoiding large swings in economic activity, high inflation, and excessive volatility in exchange rates and financial markets. Any of these types of instability can increase uncertainty and discourage investment, impede economic growth, and erode living standards.

A dynamic market economy necessarily involves some degree of instability, as well as gradual structural change. The challenge for policy-makers is to minimize instability without hampering the ability of the economic system to raise living standards through higher productivity, efficiency, and employment.

Types of Surveillance

Country

The IMF holds consultations, normally once a year, with each member country about its economic policies. These "Article IV consultations," which are required under the IMF's Articles of Agreement, focus on the member's exchange rate, fiscal, and monetary policies; developments in its balance of payments and external debt; the influence of the country's policies on its external accounts; the international and regional implications of its policies; and the identification of potential vulnerabilities.

As financial markets around the world have become more integrated, IMF surveillance has become increasingly focused on capital account, financial, and banking sector issues. Institutional issues, such as central bank independence, financial sector regulation, corporate governance, and policy transparency and accountability, have also become more important to IMF surveillance in the wake of financial crises in emerging market countries and in the context of member countries making the transition from planned to market economies.

Regional

To supplement country consultations, the IMF examines policies pursued under regional arrangements, such as in the Central African Monetary and Economic Union, the Eastern Caribbean Currency Union, the Euro Area, and the West African Economic and Monetary Union. In addition, the IMF is paying more attention to issues of common interest to countries in given regions (for example, in Central America, the Middle East, Pacific Island countries, and sub-Saharan Africa).

Global

In addition to country and regional surveillance, the IMF monitors global economic conditions, countries' economic policies in the global context, and developments in international capital markets. In this surveillance work, the IMF also assesses the global effects of major economic and financial developments, including in such areas as oil markets and trade.

Conditionality

When the IMF provides financial support to member countries, it must be sure the members are pursuing policies that will improve or eliminate their external payments problems. The explicit commitment that members make to implement corrective measures in return for the IMF's support is known as "conditionality." This commitment also ensures that members are able to repay the IMF in a timely manner, which in turn allows the IMF's limited pool of financial resources to be made available to other members with balance of payments problems. IMF financing, and the important role it plays in helping a country secure other financing, enables the country to adjust in an orderly way without resorting to measures that would harm its own or other countries' prosperity.

Over the years, the IMF has developed a number of loan instruments, or "facilities," that are tailored to address the specific circumstances of its diverse membership (See Box-1).

BOX-1

How the IMF lends: Terms and conditions of financial facilities

STAND-BY ARRANGEMENT AND EXTENDED FUND FACILITY

STAND-BY ARRANGEMENT (1952)

Addresses balance of payments difficulties that are short term; the arrangement is typically 12–18 months with a legal maximum of 3 years.

Access limits: Annual: 100 percent of quota; cumulative: 300 percent of quota for all use of IMF resources in the General Resources Account.

Maturities (expected repayment)/(obligatory repayment): 2¼–4 years/3¼–5 years.

Charges: Basic rate of charge + level-based surcharges of 100 basis points on amounts above 200 percent of quota and 200 basis points on 300 percent of quota.

Conditions: Member adopts policies that provide confidence that its balance of payments difficulties will be resolved within a reasonable period.

Cumulative access: Above 25 percent of quota is subject to stricter conditions (known as upper credit tranche conditionality).

Phasing and monitoring: Quarterly disbursements contingent on observance of performance criteria and other conditions.

EXTENDED FUND FACILITY (1974)

Provides longer-term assistance in support of structural reforms that address longer-term balance of payments difficulties.

Access limits: Annual: 100 percent of quota; cumulative: 300 percent of quota for all use of IMF resources in the General Resources Account.

Maturities (expected repayment)/(obligatory repayment): 4½–7 years/4½–10 years.

Charges: Basic rate of charge + level-based surcharges of 100 basis points on amounts above 200 percent of quota and 200 basis points above 300 percent of quota.

Conditions: Member adopts 3-year programme, with structural agenda, and provides annual detailed statement of policies for the next 12 months.

Phasing and monitoring: Quarterly or semiannual disbursements contingent on observance of performance criteria and other conditions.

SPECIAL LOANS

SUPPLEMENTAL RESERVE FACILITY (1997)

Provides short-term assistance to members with balance of payments difficulties related to a sudden and disruptive loss of market confidence. Available only as a supplement to a regular arrangement.

Access limits: None; this facility is available only when access under an associated regular arrangement would otherwise exceed either annual or cumulative limit.

Maturities (expected repayment)/(obligatory repayment): 2–2½ years / 2½–3 years.

Charges: Basic rate of charge + 300 basis points rising to a maximum of 500 basis points after 2½ years.

Conditions: Programme under an associated arrangement, with strengthened policies to address a loss of market confidence.

Phasing and monitoring: Facility available for one year; front-loaded access with two or more disbursements.

COMPENSATORY FINANCING FACILITY (1963)

Covers a shortfall in a member's export earnings and services receipts or an excess in cereal import costs that is temporary and arises from events beyond the member's control.

Access limits: Maximum 45 percent of quota for each element—export shortfall and excess cereal import costs—and a combined limit of 55 percent of quota.

Maturities (expected repayment)/(obligatory repayment): 2¼–4 years / 3¼–5 years.

Charges: Basic rate of charge; not subject to surcharges.

Conditions: Usually available only when a member already has a Stand-By Arrangement or when its balance of payments position, apart from its export shortfall or import excess, is otherwise satisfactory.

Phasing and monitoring: Typically disbursed over a minimum of six months and in accordance with the phasing provisions of the arrangement.

EMERGENCY ASSISTANCE

Natural disasters (1962): Provides quick, medium-term assistance to members with balance of payments difficulties related to natural disasters.

Postconflict (1995): Provides quick, medium-term assistance for balance of payments difficulties related to the aftermath of civil unrest or cross-border armed conflict.

Access limits: 25 percent of quota, although larger amounts can be made available in exceptional cases.

Maturities (expected repayment)/ (obligatory repayment): No early repayment expectation / 3¼–5 years.

Charges: Basic rate of charge; not subject to surcharges; possibility of interest subsidy for low-income countries if resources are available.

Conditions: Reasonable efforts to overcome balance of payments difficulties and focus on institutional and administrative capacity building to pave the way toward an upper credit tranche arrangement or an arrangement under the Poverty Reduction and Growth Facility. The conditions for emergency postconflict assistance also include that IMF support would be part of a concerted international effort to address the aftermath of the conflict.

Phasing and monitoring: Typically none.

LOANS FOR LOW-INCOME MEMBERS

POVERTY REDUCTION AND GROWTH FACILITY (PRGF) (1999)

Provides longer-term assistance for deepseated, structural balance of payments difficulties; aims at sustained, povertyreducing growth.

Access limits: 140 percent of quota; exceptional maximum, 185 percent.

Maturities (expected repayment)/(obligatory repayment): No early repayment expectation / 5½–10 years.

Charges: Concessional interest rate: ½ of 1 percent a year; not subject to surcharges.

Conditions: Based on a Poverty Reduction Strategy Paper prepared by the country in a participatory process, and integrating macroeconomic, structural, and poverty reduction policies.

Phasing and monitoring: Semiannual (or occasionally quarterly) disbursements contingent on observance of performance criteria and completion of reviews.

EXOGENOUS SHOCKS FACILITY (ESF) (2005)

Approved but not yet fully funded. Would provide policy support and financial assistance to low-income countries facing exogenous shocks (such as commodity price changes, natural disasters, and trade disruptions caused by events in a neighboring country). Available to countries eligible for the PRGF but without a PRGF-supported programme in place; ESF programmes would be one to two years in length.

Access limits: 25 percent of quota; cumulative access limit of 50 percent of quota.

Maturities (expected repayment)/ (obligatory repayment): No early repayment expectation / 5½–10 years.

Charges: ½ of 1 percent a year; not subject to surcharges.

Conditions: Poverty reduction strategy must be in place, and comprehensive economic programme must be formulated.

Phasing and monitoring: Semiannual or quarterly disbursements contingent on observance of performance criteria and, in most cases, completion of a review.

Non-concessional loans are provided through four main facilities: Stand-By Arrangements (SBAs), the Extended Fund Facility, the Supplemental Reserve Facility, and the Compensatory Financing Facility. Low-income countries may borrow at a concessional interest rate through the Poverty Reduction and Growth Facility (PRGF) and, if hit by a shock beyond their control, through the Exogenous Shocks Facility (ESF). The ESF is designed for countries without a PRGF supported programme or with a Policy Support Instrument (PSI) programme. An on-track PSI could provide the basis for rapid access to ESF financing if a shock occurs, although access would not be automatic. Members recovering from natural disasters and armed conflicts can also request emergency assistance from the IMF—possibly at concessional rates for low income countries.

When a member does not face a pressing balance of payments need, it may treat an IMF arrangement as precautionary, which provides the right—conditional on implementation of specific policies—to make drawings should the need arise. In recent years, the largest number of loans has been made through the PRGF. The largest amount of funds is provided through SBAs, however. In the context of the IMF's medium-term strategy further consideration is being given to a possible new instrument to provide high- access contingent financing for emerging market economies that have strong macroeconomic policies, sustainable debt, and transparent reporting but remain vulnerable to shocks.

Non-concessional facilities are subject to the IMF's market related interest rate, known as the "basic rate of charge." This rate of charge is based on the Special Drawing

Right (SDR) interest rate, which is revised weekly tu take into account changes in short-term interest rates in the major international money markets. Large loans carry an interest rate premium, or "surcharge." The amount that a country can borrow varies with the type of loan and is expressed as a multiple of the country's IMF quota. To finance an exceptional balance of payments need, the IMF may also lend beyond the access limits. The IMF encourages early repayment of loans. Although it has a standard repayment obligations schedule, members are expected to repay according to a faster schedule when possible.

Conditionality in IMF Lending

When a country borrows from the IMF, its government commits to strengthening its economic and financial policies—a requirement known as conditionality. Conditionality provides assurance to the IMF that the borrower will use the loan to resolve its economic difficulties and be able to repay promptly, so that the funds become available to other members in need.

In recent years, the IMF has streamlined the conditions attached to its financing. The IMF's Board adopted revised guidelines in September 2002 emphasizing the need to focus conditionality on the key macroeconomic objectives and policy instruments and to promote stronger national ownership of policy programmes. A recent review suggested that conditionality has indeed become more focused and that fewer programmes now stop prematurely.

The policies to be adopted by users of IMF resources should not only resolve the immediate balance of payments problem but also lay the basis for sustainable economic growth over the longer term by achieving broader economic stability—for example, measures to contain inflation, reduce public debt, or strengthen financial systems. Policies may also address structural impediments to healthy growth—such as price and trade liberalization or improvements in governance.

Together, these policies constitute a member country's "policy programme," which is described in a letter of intent or a memorandum of economic and financial policies that accompanies the country's request for IMF financing. The specific objectives of a programme and the policies adopted depend on the country's circumstances. However, the overarching goal in all cases is to restore or maintain balance of payments viability and macroeconomic stability while setting the stage for sustained, high-quality growth.

How is Compliance Assessed?

Most IMF loans feature phased disbursements. This allows the IMF to verify that a country is continuing to adhere to its commitments before successive installments are disbursed. Programme monitoring relies on several different tools:

(i) **Prior actions** are measures that a country agrees to take before the IMF's Executive

Board approves a loan or completes a programme review (see below). Such measures ensure that the programme has the necessary foundation to succeed or is put back on track following deviations from the agreed policies. Prior actions could include, for example, adjustment of the exchange rate to a sustainable level, elimination of price controls, or formal approval of a government budget consistent with the programme's fiscal framework.

(ii) **Performance criteria** are specific conditions that have to be met for the agreed amount of credit to be disbursed. There are two types of performance criteria: quantitative and structural. ***Quantitative criteria*** typically refer to macroeconomic policy variables such as international reserves, monetary and credit aggregates, fiscal balances, or external borrowing. For example, a programme might include a minimum level of net international reserves, a maximum level of central bank net domestic assets, or a maximum level of government borrowing. ***Structural criteria*** are used for structural measures that are critical to the success of the economic programme. These vary widely across programmes but could, for example, include specific measures to improve financial sector operations, reform social security systems, or restructure key sectors such as energy.

(iii) Quantitative criteria may be supplemented with **indicative targets**. These are often set for the later months of a programme and are then turned into performance criteria, with appropriate modifications, as economic trends firm up.

(iv) **Structural benchmarks** are used for measures that cannot be monitored specifically enough to be performance criteria, or for small steps in a critical reform process; breach of these would not individually warrant an intetruption of IMF financing.

(v) Another important monitoring tool is the **programme review**, which serves as an opportunity for a broad-based assessment by the Executive Board of progress toward the programme's objectives. Reviews are used to discuss policies and introduce changes that may be necessary in light of new developments. In some cases, a country might request a waiver for a breached performance criterion—for example, when its authorities have already taken measures to correct the deviation.

Conditions for IMF financial support may range from general commitments to cooperate with the IMF in setting policies, to the formulation of specific, quantified plans for financial policies. IMF financing from its general resources in the "upper credit tranches" (that is, where larger amounts are provided in return for implementation of remedial measures) is disbursed in stages. The IMF requires a "letter of intent" or a "memorandum of economic and financial policies," in which a government outlines its policy intentions during the period of the adjustment program; the policy changes it will make before the arrangement can be approved; performance criteria, which are objective indicators for certain policies that must be satisfied on a quarterly, semiannual, or in some instances monthly basis in order for drawings to be made; and periodic reviews that allow the Executive Board to assess whether the member's policies are consistent with the program's objectives.

Transparency at the IMF

The IMF has also focused on improving its own accountability by establishing in 2001 the Independent Evaluation Office and by increasing over the past decade the transparency of its operations and decision making. The IMF has become a more open and accountable institution and a major source of information for the general public and capital market participants while preserving its role as confidential advisor to its member countries.

Technical Assistance and Training

The IMF provides technical advice and training to help strengthen the design and implementation of macroeconomic and financial sector policies in member countries and boost the institutional capacity of their governments. Sound economic policy-making and implementation require know-how and effective government institutions. Many developing countries, in particular, need help to build up expertise in economic management and advice about what policies, reforms, and institutional arrangements are appropriate and have worked well elsewhere. The IMF gives priority to providing assistance where it complements and enhances its other key activities—surveillance and lending.

SPECIAL DRAWING RIGHTS (SDRs): AN INTERNATIONAL RESERVE ASSET

The SDR is an international reserve asset created by the IMF in 1969 to supplement members' existing reserve assets—official holdings of gold, foreign exchange, and reserve positions in the IMF. Since 1970, the IMF has allocated a total of SDR 21.4 billion to its members in two series of allocations. The SDR is also the unit of account for IMF operations and transactions and serves a similar function in a number of other international and regional organisations and international conventions. To a limited extent, it has also been used to denominate financial instruments created outside the IMF by the private sector (private SDRs).

As value of the SDR—determined daily based on basket of major international currencies—tends to be more stable than that of any single currency in the basket. Movements in the exchange rate of any one component currency will tend to be partly or fully offset by movements in the exchange rates of the other currencies.

The basket is reviewed every five years to ensure that the currencies included in it are representative of those used in international transactions and that the weights assigned to the currencies reflect their relative importance in the world's trading and financial systems. Since 1981, the currencies of five countries— France; Germany, Japan, the United Kingdom, and the United States—have been included in the basket because these five countries have the largest exports of goods and services. With the introduction of the euro on January 1, 1999, the currency amounts of the deutsche mark and the French franc were replaced with equivalent amounts of euros.

In the last review of the SDR valuation and interest rate baskets, the SDR is the sum of the values of the following accounts of each currency.

U.S. dollar 0.577

Euro 0.426

Japanese yen 21.0

Pound sterling 0.0984

The decision on the amount of each currency in the SDR valuation basket is the final step implementing the results of the latest review of the method of valuing the SDR. Previously, the IMF had determined that the composition of the SDR basket and the weights assigned each currency would be 45 per cent for the U.S. dollar, 29 per cent for the euro, 15 per cent for the Japanese yen, and 11 per cent for the pound sterling. The precise amounts of each currency were determined so that the value of the new and existing SDR baskets were the same on the last working day (December 29, 2000) before the new basket came into effect (January 1, 2001). The actual share of each currency in the valuation of the SDR on any particular day depends on the market values on that day of the fixed amounts of each currency in the basket.

USE OF SDRs

IMF members may use SDRs in a variety of voluntary transfers. Transactions are facilitated by arrangements between the IMF and 12 member countries that are prepared to buy or sell SDRs for one or more freely usable currencies, provided that their SDR holdings remain within certain limits. These arrangements have helped to ensure the liquidity of the SDR system. In addition, SDRs can be used in such operations as forward purchases and sales and in swaps, to settle financial obligations, to make loans and donations, and as security for the settlement of financial obligations.

Members may also use SDRs to discharge their financial obligations to the IMF in the General Resources Account. These obligations mainly take the form of charges levied on members' use of IMF resources, repurchases (repayments), and quota subscriptions. The IMF transfers SDRs from the General Resources Account to members primarily for purchases (drawings); remuneration on members' creditor positions; and repayments of, and interest payments on, IMF borrowing.

WORLD BANK

Like the IMF, the World Bank was created at Bretton Woods in July 1944, the culmination of wartime discussions between the United States and the United Kingdom on the shape of the post-World War II international economic order. The flank that emerged was essentially an American creation. The IMF was established to provide funds for short-term balance of payments relief and the role of the International Bank for Reconstruction and Development was the provision of longer-term finance for the development of productive resources. The initial priority of the IBRD, which opened for business on 25 June 1946, was reconstruction. Box-2 provides the basic difference between these two international twins.

BOX-2

The IMF and the World Bank—What's the Difference?

The IMF and the World Bank were conceived at the Bretton Woods conference in July 1944 to strengthen international economic cooperation and to help create a more stable and prosperous global economy. Although these goals have remained central to both institutions, their mandates and functions differ, and their work has evolved in response to new economic developments and challenges. The IMF promotes international monetary cooperation and provides member countries with policy advice, temporary loans, and technical assistance so they can establish and maintain financial stability and external viability, and build and maintain strong economies. The IMF's loans are provided in support of policy programmes designed to solve balance of payments problems—that is, situations in which a country cannot obtain sufficient financing on affordable terms to meet international payment obligations. Some IMF loans are relatively short term and funded by the pool of quota contributions provided by its members. Others are for longer periods, including concessional loans provided to low-income members on the basis of subsidies financed by past IMF gold sales and members' contributions. In its work in low-income countries, the IMF's main focus is on how macroeconomic and financial policies can contribute to laying a basis for sustainable growth and poverty reduction. Most IMF professional staff are economists.

The World Bank promotes long-term economic development and poverty reduction by providing technical and financial support, including by helping countries reform particular sectors or implement specific projects—for example, building schools and health centers, providing water and electricity, fighting disease, and protecting the environment. World Bank financial assistance is generally long term and is funded both by member country contributions and through bond issuance. World Bank staff have qualifications that embrace a broader range of disciplines than those of IMF staff.

The IMF and the World Bank collaborate in a variety of areas, particularly in supporting governments in implementing poverty reduction strategies in low-income countries, providing debt relief for the poorest countries, and assessing the financial sectors of countries. The two institutions hold joint meetings twice a year.

The Bank that emerged from the Bretton Woods conference was mainly conceived in terms of the economic problems of the immediate post-war period. It was the tasks of reconstruction rather than the challenge of development which ranked uppermost in the minds of its major proponents. The developing countries attending the conference were concerned that if too high a priority was placed on reconstruction limited resources would be available for development. The Latin American countries therefore proposed that in the Articles of Agreement equal emphasis should be given to reconstruction and development. The United States conceded the inclusion of development functions in the Articles of Agreement so that Latin American countries would agree to join the IMF, access to the Bank's lending being tied to membership of the Fund. It was decided that the resources and facilities of the Bank shall be used exclusively for the benefit of members with equitable consideration to projects for development and projects for reconstruction alike. Nevertheless, the provision of capital for reconstruction of the war-damaged economies dominated the concerns of the organisation. It was envisaged that the flank would fulfil its role in reconstruction largely by channelling US private investment to Europe through its guarantee of these loans. In the absence of private investment on reasonable terms the Bank was mandated to provide finance for investment purposes out of its own financial resources.

IDA, IFC AND MIGA

As its mission has expanded, the World Bank has cueted these affiliated organisation: International Development Association (IDA), International Finance Corporation (IFC) and Multilateral Investment Guarantee Agency (MIGA). The IDA established in 1960 as the soft-loan affiliate of the IBRD has its own constitution but shares the same offices and staff as the IBRD. In organisational terms the IDA is an 'elaborate fiction.' Though Membership is open to all members of the IBRD, but some IBRD members have chosen not to join the IDA. The IDA is essentially an instrument for resource transfer. The criteria for project selection, scrutiny of projects, implementation and financial and economic rates of return are identical to the IBRD but IDA credits are reserved for developing countries not capable of borrowing from the IBRD. Some countries, the so-called 'blend countries' are eligible for both IDA credits and IBRD loans. Eligibility for IDA loans—called credits-is based on per capita national income. IDA loans are interest-free but carry an annual service charge of 0.75 per cent. The maturity on an IDA credit is 35 to 40 years with a grace period of 10 years. Unlike the IBRD, the IDA is almost wholly dependent on member countries for its finances. The primary source of funding comes directly from grants made by its members in three-yearly replenishments. Further, income accrues from transfers of IBRD income from its retained profits, repayment of principal and special supplementary contributions from members. The dependence of the IDA on the industrialised countries for the periodic replenishment of its resources makes it vulnerable to the changing development assistance priorities of these countries and ensures the existence of a permanent negotiating process between the Bank and donor governments.

The IFC, founded in 1956, is legally a separate entity from the Bank although membership in the IFC is not open to non-members of the IBRD. Membership of the IFC stood at 146 in 1992. The IFC has its own legal and operating staff but draws on the Bank for administrative and other services. The IFC functions like an investment bank. It participates directly in equity as well as loan investments. It participates only in private ventures and its loans are not dependent on government guarantees.

Created in 1988, the MIGA offers investment insurance to mitigate political risk through its guarantee programme and provides promotional and advisory services 10 assist member countries in their efforts to attract or retain direct foreign investment. MIGA is a legally distinct entity from the Bank or the IFC and has its own Executive Board.

REFORM THE INTERNATIONAL MONETARY SYSTEM

The outbreak of the current crisis and its spillover in the world have confronted us with a long-existing but still unanswered question, i.e., what kind of international reserve currency do we need to secure global financial stability and facilitate world economic growth, which was one of the purposes for establishing the IMF? There were various institutional arrangements in an attempt to find a solution, including the Silver Standard, the Gold Standard, the Gold Exchange Standard and the Bretton Woods system. The above question, however, as the ongoing financial crisis demonstrates, is far from being solved, and has become even more severe due to the inherent weaknesses of the current international monetary system.

Theoretically, an international reserve currency should first be anchored to a stable benchmark and issued according to a clear set of rules, therefore to ensure orderly supply; second, its supply should be flexible enough to allow timely adjustment according to the changing demand; third, such adjustments should be disconnected from economic conditions and sovereign interests of any single country. The acceptance of credit-based national currencies as major international reserve currencies, as is the case in the current system, is a rare special case in history. The crisis again calls for creative reform of the existing international monetary system towards an international reserve currency with a stable value, rule-based issuance and manageable supply, so as to achieve the objective of safeguarding global economic and financial stability.

I. The outbreak of the crisis and its spillover to the entire world reflect the inherent vulnerabilities and systemic risks in the existing international monetary system. Issuing countries of reserve currencies are constantly confronted with the dilemma between achieving their domestic monetary policy goals and meeting other countries' demand for reserve currencies. On the one hand, the monetary authorities cannot simply focus on domestic goals without carrying out their international responsibilities; on the other hand, they cannot pursue different domestic and international objectives at the same time. They may either fail to adequately meet the demand of a growing global economy for liquidity as they try to ease inflation pressures at home, or create excess liquidity in the global markets by overly stimulating domestic demand. The Triffin Dilemma, i.e., the issuing countries of reserve currencies cannot maintain the value of the reserve currencies while providing liquidity to the world, still exists.

When a national currency is used in pricing primary commodities, trade settlements and is adopted as a reserve currency globally, efforts of the monetary authority issuing such a currency to address its economic imbalances by adjusting exchange rate would be made in vain, as its currency serves as a benchmark for many other currencies. While benefiting from a widely accepted reserve currency, the globalization also suffers from the flaws of such a system. The frequency and increasing intensity of financial crises following the collapse of the Bretton Woods system suggests the costs of such a system to the world may have exceeded its benefits. The price is becoming increasingly higher, not only for the users, but also for the issuers of the reserve currencies. Although crisis may not necessarily be an intended result of the issuing authorities, it is an inevitable outcome of the institutional flaws.

II. The desirable goal of reforming the international monetary system, therefore, is to create an international reserve currency that is disconnected from individual nations and is able to remain stable in the long run, thus removing the inherent deficiencies caused by using credit-based national currencies. Though the super-sovereign reserve currency has long since been proposed, yet no substantive progress has been achieved to date. Back in the 1940s, Keynes had already proposed to introduce an international currency unit named "Bancor", based on the value of 30 representative commodities. Unfortunately, the proposal was not accepted. The collapse of the Bretton Woods system, which was based on the White approach, indicates that the Keynesian approach may have been more farsighted. The IMF also created the SDR in 1969, when the defects of the Bretton Woods system initially emerged, to mitigate the inherent risks sovereign reserve currencies caused. Yet, the role of the SDR has not been put into full play due to limitations on its allocation and the scope of its uses. However, it serves as the light in the tunnel for the reform of the international monetary system.

A super-sovereign reserve currency not only eliminates the inherent risks of credit-based sovereign currency, but also makes it possible to manage global liquidity. A super-sovereign reserve currency managed by a global institution could be used to both create and control the global liquidity. And when a country's currency is no longer used as the yardstick for global trade and as the benchmark for other currencies, the exchange rate policy of the country would be far more effective in adjusting economic imbalances. This will significantly reduce the risks of a future crisis and enhance crisis management capability.

III. The reform should be guided by a grand vision and begin with specific deliverables. It should be a gradual process that yields win-win results for all. The reestablishment of a new and widely accepted reserve currency with a stable valuation benchmark may take a long time. The creation of an international currency unit, based on the Keynesian proposal, is a bold initiative that requires extraordinary political vision and courage. In the short run, the international community, particularly the IMF, should at least recognize and face up to the risks resulting from the existing system, conduct regular monitoring and assessment and issue timely early warnings.

Special consideration should be given to giving the SDR a greater role. The SDR has the features and potential to act as a super-sovereign reserve currency. Moreover, an increase in SDR allocation would help the Fund address its resources problem and the difficulties in the voice and representation reform. Therefore, efforts should be made to push forward a SDR allocation. This will require political cooperation among member countries. Specifically, the Fourth Amendment to the Articles of Agreement and relevant resolution on SDR allocation proposed in 1997 should be approved as soon as possible so that members joined the Fund after 1981 could also share the benefits of the SDR. On the basis of this, considerations could be given to further increase SDR allocation.

The scope of using the SDR should be broadened, so as to enable it to fully satisfy the member countries' demand for a reserve currency. SDR, which is now only used between governments and international institutions, could become a widely accepted means of payment in international trade and financial transactions. Further the use of the SDR in international trade, commodities pricing, investment and corporate book-keeping should be actively promoted. This will help enhance the role of the SDR, and will effectively reduce the fluctuation of prices of assets denominated in national currencies and related risks. In addition, financial assets denominated in the SDR to increase its appeal should be created. The introduction of SDR-denominated securities, which is being studied by the IMF, will be a good start. Moreover, to improve the valuation and allocation of the SDR, the basket of currencies forming the basis for SDR valuation should be expanded to include currencies of all major economies, and the GDP may also be included as a weight. The allocation of the SDR can be shifted from a purely calculation-based system to a system backed by real assets, such as a reserve pool, to further boost market confidence in its value.

IV. Entrusting part of the member countries' reserve to the centralized management of the IMF will not only enhance the international community's ability to address the crisis and maintain the stability of the international monetary and financial system,

but also significantly strengthen the role of the SDR: Compared with separate management of reserves by individual countries, the centralized management of part of the global reserve by a trustworthy international institution with a reasonable return to encourage participation will be more effective in deterring speculation and stabilizing financial markets. The participating countries can also save some reserve for domestic development and economic growth. With its universal membership, its unique mandate of maintaining monetary and financial stability, and as an international "supervisor" on the macroeconomic policies of its member countries, the IMF, equipped with its expertise, is endowed with a natural advantage to act as the manager of its member countries' reserves.

The centralized management of its member countries' reserves by the Fund will be an effective measure to promote a greater role of the SDR as a reserve currency. To achieve this, the IMF can set up an open-ended SDR-denominated fund based on the market practice, allowing subscription and redemption in the existing reserve currencies by various investors as desired. This arrangement will not only promote the development of SDR-denominated assets, but will also partially allow management of the liquidity in the form of the existing reserve currencies. It can even lay a foundation for increasing SDR allocation to gradually replace existing reserve currencies with the SDR.

QUESTIONS

1. Discuss the organisational structure and function of International Monetary System
2. Define the principle of "conditionality" as applied by the IMF. Is the IMF still applying this principle under the current international monetary system? Why do a large number of countries find it difficult to accept the IMF prescription as a cure for their ailments?
3. "Quotas define members' voting and borrowing rights with IMF." Discuss.
4. Discuss the response of the IMF/World Banks to the Third World's demands.
5. Discuss the evolution of the IMF/the World Bank. Critically examine the role and ideologies of the IDA, IFC and MIGA institution.
6. Discuss the cooperative efforts to strengthen the international monetary system.
7. Discuss the social dimensions of IMF-supported programmes.
8. "The IMF is a financial co-operative, in some ways like a credit union." Do you agree?
9. Discuss the use of SDRs as an international ıeserve asset.
10. Critically examine the IMF's sources of supplementary financing.
11. Critically examine the IMF financing facilities and policies to help members to correct balance of payments problems in a manner that promotes sustained growth.
12. Describe and explain the operation of the World Bank. Discuss how can it be used by multinational companies seeking overseas business opportunities.
13. Describe and explain the operation of the internatioıal Monetary Fund. Discuss how can it be used by multinational companies in planning trade and investment strategies.

REFERENCES

Barman, Abheek (1998), "What Happened to Asia?", *The Economic Times.* January 30,1998 p. 6.

Bhalla, V.K.: International Economy :Liberalisation Process (1993).

————, International Monetary Cooperation: European Monetary Reform (1992).

Bilson, John P.O. "Rational expectations and the exchange rate", in Jacob A. Frenkel and Harry G., Johnson, eds., The Ecionomics of Exchange Rates (Reading, Mass,. Addision-Wesley, 1978), pp. 75-96.

Burton, John, (1998), "Seoul Fires Warning Shot Over Chaebol", *Financial Times.* Jan.22, 1998 p. 6.

Cohn, Richard A., and John J. Pringle, "Imperfections in international financial markets: implications for risk premia and the cost of capital to firms", Journal of Finance, 28 (March 1973), pp. 59-66.

Dufey, Gunter and lan H. Giddy, "International Financial Planning: the use of market-based forecasts", California Management Review, 21 (Fall 1978) pp. 69-81.

Eiteman, David K.m, Aurhur I Stonehill and Michael H. Moffett, Multinational Business Finance, sizthe edition (Reading, Mass Addison-Weslety. 1992), pp. 493-494.

Fidler, Stephen (1998), "Chilean Lessons for Asian Crisis", *Financial Times.* Jan. 14, 1998 p. 3. Financial Times (1998), "The Origins of the Asian Crisis", *Financial Times.* Jan. 17,1998 p. 14.

"Finance and global competition: Exploiting financial scope and coping with volatile exchange rates",. Midland Corporate Finance Journal, 4 (Fall 1986) pp. 6-29.

George, Abraham M,. "Cash flow versus accounting exposures to currency risk", California Managbement Review 20 (Summer 1978) pp. 50-55.

Lee Wayne Y., and Kanwal S. Sachdeva. "The role of the multinational firm in the integration of segmented markest" Journal of Fuinaiice 32 (May 1977) pp. 479-492.

Lessard, Donald R., "International portfolio diversification:. A multivariate analysis for a group of latin american countrier", Journal of finance, 28 (June 1973) pp. 619-633.

Sachs, Jeffrey; Aaron Tornell and Anres Velasco (1996),"The Collapse of the Mexican Peso: What Have We Learned?", *Economic Policy - A European Forum,* vol.22, April 1996, pp. 15-63.

Stapleton, Richard C., and Marti Subrahmanyam. "Market inperfections. capital market equilibrium, and corporation finance", Journal of Finance, 32 (May 1977), pp. 307-319.

Wheelwright, Steve, "Applying decision theory to improve corporate management of currency-exchange risks", California Management Review, 17 (Summer 1975), pp. 41-49.

42

EUROPEAN MONETARY SYSTEM

INTRODUCTION

Economic and Monetary Union (EMU) in Europe can be described as an unprecedented, imaginative and successful model for economic integration. The objectives initially pursued by European integration -ensuring peace and prosperity in what had historically been a conflict-ridden part of the world— have thus far been fulfilled. This is proof of how successful the European Union (EU) has been in adjusting to the manifold challenges of its more than 50-year history. Such is its attractiveness that there are now many non-EU countries eager to join EMU.

HISTORICAL OVERVIEW

A cursory glance at European history over the past few decades clearly shows that progress in European integration has been a lengthy and gradual process with many obstacles, detours and setbacks on the way. The first attempts at European integration were in the economic field with the setting up of the European Coal and Steel Community (ECSC) in 1951. This institution had already had a supranational High-Authority which was consistent with the desire for political integration to go beyond purely economic relations. This goal was even more evident in the Treaty on the Establishment of the European Defence Community (EDC), signed in 1952. At the same time, plans to establish a European Political Union were being drafted. However, these initiatives ended abruptly in the summer of 1954 when the French National Assembly failed to ratify the Treaty on EDC. This refusal reflected the underlying mood that it was not the right moment to move towards political union. However, this period of disappointment was soon forgotten, thanks to the strong desire of the leading political figures in Europe of the time to learn from the past by concentrating on economic integration in the future.

The Treaty of Rome (1957) created the European Economic Community, which proved to be a success, as evidenced by the number of applications to join and the subsequent enlargement from the original six members. The Single European Act (SEA) of 1986 and the Single Market (1992) were further milestones in the economic integration process.

The removal of all barriers to transactions, stemming from the completion of the Single Market, almost concluded the contribution which economics alone could make to the process of European integration. Thereafter, further integration obviously had to focus on the creation of new institutions. This step was brought about by the Maastricht Treaty after it was signed in 1992. Indeed, it bears the title "Treaty on European Union" and the preamble underlines, first of all, the resolve to "mark a new stage in the process of European integration".

The most significant contribution of the Maastricht Treaty was the establishment of a clear deadline for the start of EMU, in addition to provisions to establish the European System of Central Banks (ESCB). The Maastricht Treaty also provides for a common foreign and security policy and for co- operation in the fields of justice and home affairs, albeit in a general and non- committal way. In other words, with the ratification of the Maastricht Treaty, the citizens of the EU adopted an imaginative model for rather modest political integration coupled with full economic integration to include the introduction of a new single currency and a single monetary policy for the entire area.

ORGANISATION OF THE EUROPEAN SYSTEM OF CENTRAL BANKS (ESCB)

The European System of Central Banks (ESCB) is composed of the European Central Bank (ECB) and the national central banks (NCBs) of all EU Member States. The "Eurosystem" is the term used to refer to the ECB and the NCBs of the Member States which have adopted the euro. The primary objective of the Eurosystem is to maintain price stability by performing following basic tasks: (i) to define and implement the monetary policy of the euro area; (ii) to conduct foreign exchange operations; (iii) to hold and manage the official foreign reserves of the Member States; and (iv) to promote the smooth operation of payment systems. The Eurosystem contributes to the smooth conduct of policies pursued by the competent authorities relating to the prudential supervision of credit institutions and the stability of the financial system.

The Eurosystem is independent. When performing Eurosystem-related tasks, neither the ECB, nor an NCB, nor any member of their decision-making bodies may seek or take instructions from any external body. The Community institutions and bodies and the governments of the Member States may not seek to influence the members of the decision-making bodies of the ECB or of the NCBs in the performance of their tasks. The Statute of the ESCB makes provision for the following measures to ensure security of tenure for NCB governors and members of the Executive Board: (i) a minimum renewable term of office for governors of five years; (ii) a minimum non-renewable term of office for members of the Executive Board of eight years (it should be noted that a system of staggered appointments was used for the first Executive Board for members other than the President in order to ensure continuity); and (iii) removal from office is only possible in the event of incapacity or serious misconduct; in this respect the Court of Justice of the European Communities is competent to settle any disputes.

THREE STAGES TOWARDS EMU

In June 1988 the European Council confirmed the objective of the progressive realisation of economic union. 'Delors Report' proposed that EMU should be achieved in three discrete but evolutionary steps. And on the basis of the Delors Report, the European Council decided in June 1989 that the first stage of the realisation of economic and monetary union should begin on 1 July 1990—the date on which, in principle, all restrictions on the movement of capital between Member States were abolished. For the realisation of Stages Two and Three, it was necessary to revise the Treaty establishing the European Economic Community (the "Treaty of Rome") in order to establish the required institutional structure. To this end, Treaty on European Union which was agreed in December 1991 and signed in Maastricht on 7 February 1992.

The establishment of the European Monetary Institute (EMI) on 1 January 1994 marked the start of the second stage of EMU and with this the Committee of Governors ceased to exist. The two main tasks of the EMI were:

i. to strengthen central bank co-operation and monetary policy co- ordination; and
ii. to make the preparations required for the establishment of the European System of Central Banks (ESCB), for the conduct of the single monetary policy and for the creation of a single currency in the third stage.

On December 1995 the European Council agreed to name the European currency unit to be introduced at the start of Stage Three, the "euro", and confirmed that Stage Three of EMU would start on 1 January 1999. And, on 1 January 1999 the third and final stage of EMU commenced with the irrevocable fixing of the exchange rates of the currencies of the 11 Member States initially participating in Monetary Union and with the conduct of a single monetary policy under the responsibility of the ECB.

What did the creation of the euro mean for exchange rate policy? Prima facie, the answer is straightforward. Having a single currency automatically implies having a single exchange rate and thus also a single exchange rate policy. Yet the repercussions of EMU go beyond these "automatic" consequences.

INTERNATIONAL ROLE OF THE EURO

For much of the post-war period, the United States' role in world output and trade, its macroeconomic stability and financial market depth, and network externalities clearly favoured the US dollar as the leading reserve currency. Then in the 1990s European monetary union (EMU) triggered a debate about the potential for the euro to challenge the US dollar. Some argued that the dominant role of the dollar would not wane, while others suggested that the use of the euro would come to match that of the dollar.

The school of thought which concluded that the euro would not challenge the dollar stressed the uncertainties surrounding the impact of EMU in the light of two considerations. *First,* history and empirical work have highlighted the relevance of the advantages of incumbency. Network externalities lend inertia and path dependence to the development of reserve currency status. *Second,* the institutional structure, and in particular the lack of supervisory and regulatory authority of the ECB, was likely to have a negative influence on the euro's prospects as a reserve currency. The attractiveness of the US dollar as a reserve currency derived from the existence of a deeper and more liquid markets in US Treasury securities, and in particular in treasury bills, compared to euro markets. This situation was unlikely to change. Further, the role of domestic and cross-border trade in euro-denominated assets and the current obstacles to the full integration of euro area government bond markets are an important factor limiting the international role of the euro. Moreover, at least for the functions of unit of account and means of payment, two international currencies would be inefficient and contrary to the rationale for having an international currency. This situation can be compared to one where an international airline gives its pilots, who now universally communicate in English, the option of communicating, or not communicating as the case would be, in their own languages. Hence, the emergence of the euro as a significant international currency is not likely to happen. This point is perhaps inspired more by a analogy of adopting the dollar as an international currency and the situation where two individuals from two different countries meet and decide to communicate in the language of the larger country. This is more clearly a sound argument for the medium of exchange function than the store-of-value role. In the last case, diversification arguments can be invoked in the name of the individual investor if not the system as a whole.

By contrast, the second school of thought is of the view that the euro's role would match that of the dollar a decade after monetary union. This is based on the relative size of the euro area economy and its importance in global trade, as well as a view that EMU would spur the growth of euro area financial markets. It has also been argued that the euro would benefit from monetary stability, grounded on the Maastricht treaty. However, a significant role for the euro would require a protracted current account deficit of the euro area. The euro would eventually have a role comparable to that of the dollar, since an international investor should diversify to hedge their exposure to macroeconomic risks, resulting in a "multiplicity" of reserve currencies. The euro will challenge the dollar as the world's leading international reserve currency on the strength of the relative size of the economy and financial markets. The euro may surpass the dollar as the leading international reserve currency by 2020, if the United Kingdom and other non-euro area EU members join EMU by 2020, or the recent depreciation trend of the dollar persists into the future.

EURO AS A RESERVE CURRENCY

Well developed financial markets are a necessary condition for a currency to play a role as a reserve currency. The introduction of the euro greatly improved the functioning of euro financial markets. The common currency and associated efforts to harmonise institutional structures led to a reduction in transactions costs as well as a decline in country-specific macroeconomic risks. Indeed, the development of euro financial markets is often seen as the most tangible benefit of European monetary union.

Roles and Determinants of a Reserve Currency

An international currency is one which is used by non-residents as a medium of exchange, store of value and unit of account. While in principle these roles can be fulfilled by different currencies, historically the international currency that has dominated as a medium of exchange has also served as the main store of value.

Composition of Official Reserves

At present, though the official reserve assets are gradually being diversified, the currency composition has not changed as much as the instrument composition. Reserve managers have steadily reallocated their portfolios towards higher yielding, higher risk instruments. However, this reallocation has not been accompanied by a significant shift out of US dollars. The euro's share of reserves is higher today than it was immediately prior to monetary union, but it is still well below the US dollar's share and below even the share of euro legacy currencies in the 1980s and early 1990s.

The mechanical effect of exchange rate movements contributed to fluctuations in the US dollar's share but were certainly not the only explanation. The large swings in quantity shares, after controlling for exchange rate movements, suggest that reserve management decisions and differing paces of reserve accumulation across countries were also important driving factors. Asian reserve managers respond asymmetrically to valuation effects, increasing their purchases of US Treasury securities in response to capital losses by more than they reduce their purchases in response to capital gains. Moreover, the Asian reserve managers react more strongly to interest rate changes than to exchange rate change.

Role as a Medium of Exchange

The most important role of a reserve currency is as a medium of exchange. This is linked to the monetary authorities' choice of the currency in which to intervene in foreign exchange markets. The choice of intervention currency is influenced, at least in part, by liquidity conditions in foreign exchange markets. When intervening to influence a bilateral exchange rate, it is sometimes more effective to do so in a third, more heavily traded currency.

While the euro seems to be as liquid as its predecessor currencies, it is unclear whether the euro has become more or less liquid compared to the US dollar. The results of the most recent Triennial Survey of Foreign Exchange and Derivatives Markets show that, in April 2004, the euro entered on one side of 37% of all foreign exchange transactions, more than the Deutsche mark in 1998 but less than all euro constituents taken together in 1998. Most of this difference can be explained by the disappearance of intra-EMS foreign exchange trading. The dollar's share in foreign exchange markets edged down from 94% in 1998 to 89% in 2004, while the yen's share doubled from 10% to 20%. Dollar/euro was by far the most traded currency pair in 2004, capturing 28% of global turnover. It was followed by dollar/yen with 17% and dollar/sterling with 14%.

The choice of intervention currency is also influenced by liquidity conditions in asset markets. Reserve managers typically invest the bulk of their reserves in instruments with limited market and credit risk. For example, EMU increased the attractiveness of diversifying reserves from dollars into euros by creating the second largest government securities market in the world. At the end of 2005, the outstanding stock of debt securities issued by euro area central governments totalled $4.7 trillion . By comparison, the outstanding stock of US Treasury securities equalled $4.2 trillion. However, size alone is not sufficient to tip the balance in favour of the euro. After all, the Japanese government securities market has grown to be by far the largest, yet the proportion of reserves held in yen-denominated instruments has declined in recent years.

One characteristic of the US Treasury market that makes it a relatively more attractive destination for reserves is the large bill market. The short- term segment of the US Treasury market is much larger than its euro equivalent, mainly owing to the limited issuance of treasury bills in the euro area. The importance of this characteristic has diminished over time, however, as reserve managers have shifted into private money market instruments.

Another advantage is the homogeneity and high credit quality of the US Treasury market: there is one issuer, rated AAA. By contrast, twelve different issuers participate in the euro government securities market, and the single largest issuer – the Italian Treasury – accounts for only 30% of the outstanding stock of debt . Furthermore, several euro area governments are rated below AAA, and so the average rating of outstanding euro government securities is AA+. This is higher than the Japanese government's credit rating but one notch below the US government's.

The most important advantage the US Treasury market has over its euro or yen equivalents is its tremendous liquidity. The daily turnover of US Treasuries greatly exceeds that of any other instrument. While turnover is not synonymous with market liquidity, it can be indicative of the depth of the market, i.e. the size of the order flow that the market can accommodate without moving prices. Bid-ask spreads on US Treasuries are reportedly tighter than those on most euro area government bonds. In the euro market, bid-ask spreads are tightest for French and Italian government bonds, tighter even than for benchmark German government bonds.

That being said, some segments of euro government securities markets are as liquid as the US Treasury market. In the euro market, liquidity is concentrated in derivatives markets, in particular futures on German government bonds. Traders report that bid-ask spreads and trade sizes in the futures market for Bunds (10-year German government bonds) are similar to those in the physical market for US Treasuries. This makes Bund futures as attractive as US Treasuries for positioning and hedging purposes. However, as a medium of exchange, a physical instrument is preferred to a derivative instrument because the investment of the liquidity tranche is constrained by the need to turn assets into cash. So the depth of the US Treasury market helps to reinforce the preeminence of the US dollar as an intervention currency.

In repo markets, too, liquidity conditions favour US dollar instruments. While the introduction of the euro did much to boost the euro repo market, the dollar repo market remains the largest, most developed in the world. The growth of the dollar repo market has outpaced that of the euro market in recent years. In December 2005, the outstanding value of repo and reverse repo agreements on the books of dealers was $6.1 trillion in the dollar market, compared to $4.8 trillion in the euro market.

Moreover, the euro repo market is less deep and robust than its dollar counterpart. Since monetary union, the euro repo market has been slower to integrate than unsecured deposit markets. The cross-country dispersion relative to within-country dispersion is greater for euro repo rates than for deposit rates. The process of integration has been impeded by the absence of standardised legal documentation, among other factors. As a result, there is greater fragmentation in the euro market than in the dollar market. In the dollar repo market, almost half of all agreements had a maturity of one day and about one quarter were tri-party agreements, in which the cash and collateral legs of the transaction are settled through a common custodial bank. Furthermore, about two thirds of all transactions used US Treasuries as collateral. By contrast, in the euro repo market, one-day and tri-party agreements accounted for a relatively small proportion of the total: 10% and 16%, respectively. In addition, no one source of collateral was dominant: German government securities were used in less than 30% of all euro transactions.

The market where euro instruments compare the most favourably with US dollar instruments is that for unsecured deposits. The wholesale deposit market is larger in euros than in dollars, owing to the greater dependence of the euro area banking system on interbank funding. In the offshore (euro currency) market, the euro segment is now almost as large as the dollar segment. Whereas in 1999 euro-denominated deposits placed by non-residents in the London market were around 65% as large as dollar-denominated placements, in 2005 that proportion had risen to 83%. About 35% of all deposits held by monetary authorities are placed with banks in London, more than in any other financial centre. The decision to place reserves in the euro currency market rather than onshore was once driven by yield differences, but since 1990 other factors, such as country risk and habit, have dominated.

Moreover, the unsecured deposit market for euros is one of the most liquid markets in the world. Indeed, overnight index swaps are considered the benchmark instrument at the very short end of the euro yield curve. (An overnight index swap (OIS) is a fixed-for-floating interest rate swap with a floating rate leg tied to an index of daily Interbank rates. In the euro market, OISs are overwhelming referenced to the Euro Overnight Index Average (EONIA) rate – a weighted average of interest rates contracted on unsecured overnight loans in the euro area Interbank market). Interbank instruments are widely traded at longer maturities also. For example, the daily turnover of 3-month euro interest rate futures contracts averaged $810 billion in 2005. This was half the turnover of dollar contracts, which averaged $1.6 trillion, but far greater than the turnover of sterling or yen contracts.

The US dollar retains several advantages over the euro as a medium of exchange. The US dollar is more widely traded in foreign exchange markets, and dollar government securities and repo markets are more liquid than their euro counterparts. This supports the continued preeminence of the US dollar as a reserve currency. That being said, differences between the dollar and euro markets are small relative to differences between the dollar and other markets, and so for intervention purposes the euro is an increasingly attractive alternative to holding dollars.

Role as Unit of Account

Another key role of an international currency is as an unit of account. While in private use this role is linked to the currency of choice for invoicing, in official use it is linked to the choice of an exchange rate as a monetary anchor. Even after the collapse of the Bretton Woods system, which was effectively a gold-dollar standard, the US dollar remained the pre-eminent anchor currency. In recent years, however, the euro has played an increasingly important role in international exchange rate arrangements. Empirical evidence indicates that the euro has an increasingly important gravitational pull on other currencies.

The gravitational properties of a currency can be assessed in two different ways. First, *de jure* measures consider the weight that official exchange rate policies assign to the dollar, the euro and other currencies. It is noted that out of 150 pegged currencies listed by the IMF in 2004, 40 had the euro as an anchor currency. However, the classification of exchange rate policies is difficult, in part because some countries, such as China and Singapore, do not publish the weights of the different currencies in the baskets to which they peg. A second approach is to consider a currency's gravitational pull, based on the actual co-movement of currencies. This can be measured by the volatility of exchange rates or by the sensitivity of currencies with respect to particular exchange rates. A low volatility (or a high sensitivity) of the currency of country X with respect to the dollar could either result from the monetary framework of country X assigning weight to the dollar, or reflect synchronous business cycles and strong trade links between country X and the United States. In both cases, low exchange rate volatility (or high exchange rate sensitivity) would suggest that the dollar plays an important role as official reserve currency in country X. A greater role of the dollar in the monetary policy framework of a country typically implies a greater role of the dollar in official reserves because of foreign exchange market intervention needs and efforts to match the country's assets and liabilities. The same reasoning applies to low volatility/high sensitivity of currency X to the euro or the yen.

The gravitational role of the euro is becoming more important outside Europe. The South African rand has commoved closely with the euro in recent years, and some currencies in Latin America, most notably the Brazilian real and the Chilean peso, have tended to track the euro's movement more closely the past. By contrast, emerging market currencies in Asia still follow the dollar's movement quite closely. The US dollar, however, is still the most important currency along this dimension. Moreover, it is unclear whether the increasing gravitational pull of the euro reflects a structural change or cyclical developments. Since 2002, the US dollar has depreciated against many currencies, and so the higher co-movement of currencies with the euro may reflect temporary dollar weakness rather than a long-term increase in the euro's influence.

Role as a Store of Value

While reserve managers have in the past given greater consideration to a currency's role as a medium of exchange than to its role as a store of value, this is now changing. The accumulation of reserves over the past decade has outpaced the growth of world trade, financial flows or GDP. Total foreign currency reserves rose from 4% of GDP in 1990 to almost 10% in 2005. Consequently, reserves are now commonly perceived to be greater than needed for intervention purposes. This has led monetary authorities to focus their reserve management decisions increasingly on the maximisation of returns for a given level of risk and to place less importance on the preservation of liquidity and capital.

The diversification of reserve assets may be constrained by the composition of external liabilities. Central banks have in recent years given greater consideration to the integrated management of their assets and liabilities. To the extent that monetary authorities consider the country's international investment position when determining the allocation of their reserves, then the US dollar's share of reserves may be too low and the euro's share too high. However, the dollar's share of liabilities is significantly higher than its share of reserves, and the euro's share significantly lower. Only the yen's share is broadly in line.

Central banks might give greater weight to short-term liabilities than long-term liabilities, given the suddenness with which short-term credit can evaporate. Taking cross-border loans as a proxy for short-term external liabilities, then the currency distribution of loans is closer to that of reserves than was the currency distribution of international debt. Nevertheless, there is no consensus on the best approach to asset and liability management at central banks. Liabilities might be broadly defined, as the country's external liabilities, or narrowly defined, as the central banks' on-balance sheet liabilities. Central banks might also wish to consider potential drains on foreign currency reserves, such as foreign currency deposits placed by residents with local banks.

From the role of the financial markets in the choice of reserve currency and the macroeconomic factors that also influence this choice, it can be observed that liquidity and breadth of euro financial markets are fast approaching those of the dollar markets. This strengthen the incentive for monetary authorities to reconsider the currency composition of their reserves. Nevertheless, the introduction of the euro has not yet resulted in a significant change in the currency composition of the official reserve holdings. The US dollar has maintained its place as the dominant reserve currency, supported perhaps by the greater size of the US dollar financial markets as well as interia in the use of international currencies.

THE EURO: SUCCESSES AND CHALLENGES

The euro is the most visible symbol of European unification. It is a single currency shared by (currently) 16 of the European Union's Member States, which together make up the euro area. The introduction of the euro in 1999 was a major step in European integration. It has also been one of its major successes: around 329 million EU citizens now use it *as* their currency and enjoy its benefits, which will spread even more widely as other EU countries adopt the euro.

When the euro was launched on 1 January 1999, it became the new official currency of 11 Member States, replacing the old national currencies - such as the Deutschmark and the French franc - in two stages. First introduced as a virtual currency for cashless payments and accounting purposes, while the old currencies continued to be used for cash payments and considered as 'sub-units' of the euro, it then appeared in physical form, as bank notes and coins, on 1 January 2002.

The euro is not the currency of all EU Member States. Two countries (Denmark and the United Kingdom) agreed an 'opt-out' clause in the Treaty exempting them from participation, while the remainder (many of the newest EU members plus Sweden) have yet to meet the conditions for adopting the single currency. Once they do so, they will replace their national currency with the euro.

When the euro came into being, monetary policy became the responsibility of the independent European Central Bank (ECB), which was created for that purpose, and the national central banks of the Member States having adopted the euro. Together they compose the Eurosystem.

Fiscal policy (tax and spending) remains in the hands of individual national governments - though they undertake to adhere to commonly agreed rules on public finances known as the Stability and Growth Pact. They also retain full responsibility for their own structural policies (labour, pension and capital markets), but agree to co-ordinate them in order to achieve the common goals of stability, growth and employment.

FACTS OF THE LAST DECADE

Over ten years ago, before the euro was created, there was an academic debate turning on the theory of optimal currency areas, which questioned whether a single interest rate and, therefore, *a* single monetary policy could possibly be appropriate for such diverse countries. Ten years after the birth of the euro those who joined EMU, and many of those who did not, acknowledge the enormous advantages of being inside the monetary union. Any assessment of the first ten years of the euro should consider what the objectives were at the start of Monetary Union. Some of the objectives of the euro and the expectations it gave rise to discussed below:

The first, main objective of the euro was to create an area of monetary stability in Europe. This has been achieved. The average inflation rate between 1999 and 2008 was 2.2%, about 1 percentage point less than in the 1990s. It is also lower than the best performing countries, like Germany, before the euro. Monetary stability has been reflected also in the low level of interest rates, which is also an improvement compared with the previous decade. This suggests that monetary stability is now well entrenched in expectations.

A second objective was to ensure that this monetary stability was not attained at the expense of economic growth and stability. This too has been achieved. The GDP growth rate of the euro area over the last decade has been similar, by and large, to that of the previous decade, both in absolute and in per capita terms. Unemployment has been lower on average and employment growth stronger. All this has been achieved in spite of the more rigorous budgetary policies of the Member States, at least compared with the previous decade. It may be argued that other countries, in particular EU countries which do not have the euro, have performed even better than the euro area. The UK has had a higher average inflation rate than the euro area but also a higher growth rate; Sweden has a comparable inflation rate and higher growth. But then one has to compare like with like. In the euro area there are countries of a comparable size to the UK, like Spain, which have had even stronger growth during these years. Others though have grown less. Again, the euro area and the US are often compared, and these two monetary areas are of a size that can be compared. Over the last decade the US has recorded higher average GDP growth than the euro area only because of its higher population growth. GDP per capita has increased at exactly the same pace in the two areas. As for employment growth over the last ten years, it has been stronger in the euro area than in the US, and the rate of unemployment has decreased to a substantially greater extent. However it would be incorrect to claim that the strong employment results achieved over the last ten years are exclusively due to the euro. The improvement is more likely to stem from the structural reforms implemented in the Member States over the years.

A third objective of the euro was to move forward the integration of the financial markets. The results in this field are positive, but also uneven, depending on the market segment. Integration is more advanced in the areas close to the single monetary policy, but it also depends on the degree of integration of the underlying market infrastructure. The euro area money market, the segment closest to the single monetary policy, reached a stage of "near perfect" integration almost immediately after the introduction of the euro. The malfunctioning of recent months is common to all currencies. On the other hand, short-term debt securities (i.e. commercial paper and certificates of deposit) have remained much more fragmented. Financial integration has been fastest in the government bond market, where yields have converged and are increasingly driven by common factors, although local factors and perceived differences in credit risk continue to play a role. Likewise, the corporate bond segment is also more integrated as the various markets have merged into a single, yet diversified euro market. As a result, country- specific factors have become less important in determining corporate bond prices and spreads. Cross- border holdings of long-term debt securities of monetary financial institutions grew from about 15% in 1999 to nearly 40% in 2007. Integration in the equity markets is less advanced but shows signs of improvement. Between 1997 and 2006, euro area investors doubled their holdings of equity issued in other euro area countries to 29% of their total portfolio of euro area equity assets.

The retail banking segment has remained more fragmented. In particular, the euro area cross-country dispersion of bank interest rates, especially of interest rates on consumer loans, has remained relatively high. This reflects different conditions in national economies (e.g. credit and interest rate risk, size of firms, industrial structure and degree of capital market development), institutional factors (e.g. taxation, regulation, supervision and consumer protection) and financial structures (e.g. degree of bank/capital market financing and competitiveness). It was probably overoptimistic to expect a faster convergence in this segment.

The creation of the euro also gave rise to expectations of a broad based convergence of underlying economic developments. These expectations were quite varied, in fact. Some people expected greater divergence as a consequence of specialisation. Others expected greater convergence. The result is mixed. Some convergence has been observed, in particular in terms of business cycle and dispersion across countries, which is comparable with that among the US states. The degree of business cycle synchronisation has remained at the same levels reached in the second half of the 1990s. On the other hand, some underlying variables have diverged, in particular cost and price competitiveness, leading to an accumulation of payments imbalances within the euro area. Some countries have accumulated large current account deficits, while others have growing surpluses. It can be argued that imbalances do not matter in a monetary union, because they are automatically financed. But such imbalances might make countries more vulnerable to external shocks and their financing might become more difficult in the midst of a financial crisis, even within a monetary union.

Finally, the euro has contributed to the completion of the single European market. The advantages of the single market could be better exploited by the common currency. Trade and capital ties between euro countries have grown. In this context, few examples are listed below:

a. *The cross-border trade in goods and services in the euro area has increased by about 10 percentage points in relation to GDP since the introduction of the single currency. This can be partly attributed to the euro. Trade between individual euro countries now accounts for about half of their total exports and imports. At the same time, extra euro area trade developed very dynamically as well. Increasing trade integration within the monetary union did not come at the expense of trade with third countries. Hence, there is no "fortress Europe".*

b. The euro has promoted competition, price transparency and the convergence of prices, and has lowered transaction costs and eliminated exchange rate risk.

c. The euro has boosted direct investment within the euro area. Mergers between companies in the euro area have risen noticeably.

d. The euro has also led to a marked increase in cross-border security investments within the euro area. This is only one example of the contribution made by the single currency to the integration of the financial markets in Europe. It's not over yet. The ECB and the Eurosystem strongly support a further integration of Europe's financial markets.

These developments show that the euro is an important catalyst for the completion of the single European market. The logic of "one market, one currency" was a substantial impetus for monetary integration in Europe. It has proved to be correct.

THE ROLE OF THE EURO AMID THE CURRENT FINANCIAL MARKET TURBULENCE

The global environment has completely changed in last few years. It is marked by an intensification and broadening of the global financial market turbulence and a sharp downturn in the world economy. The tensions have increasingly spilled over from the financial sector to the real economy. Their negative effects can be felt worldwide. Since the end of 2008 virtually all economies - both of the industrialised countries and the emerging markets - have been moving in the same direction. This considerably contributes to the scale of the present downturn.

Key Systematic Problems in the Euro Area

For over two years Europe's political leaders have promised to do whatever it takes to save the euro area. Yet problems are growing and solutions still seem far off. The October 27 and December 9, 2011 agreements of European leaders failed to change the dangerous trends in Europe's economies or markets.

European Sovereign Bonds All Now Deeply Subordinated Claims on Rucssionary Economics

If one issue is to be picked that turns this crisis from a tough economic adjustment into a potentially calamitous collapse, it is the transformation of Europe's sovereign debt market. The euro area's immediate problems, in large part, reflect transition from a regime where sovereign debts were perceived to be sacrosanct ("risk-free") to one in which investors perceived that sovereign defaults were possible. Neither investors nor Europe's politicians understood the full ramifications of the no-bailout clauses in the Maastricht treaty until recently. With the new risk premium needed to compensate for default risk, some European nations will need to radically reduce their debt levels and change its maturity structure.

Crisis Spreads into Europe Core Banks and Incites Capital Flight from the Periphery

Inadequate capital levels in European banks spread crisis further by inciting flight from the periphery. If European banks are stressed for market- implied sovereign default risks, they were 200 billion to 300 billion short of capital. For the first time the IMF admitted that sovereign default risk needed to be taken into account for the largest banks in Europe. Europe's regulatory regime does not require banks to have equity capital funding for sovereign debt—there is no capital requirement, in banking jargon—so banks accumulated these debts over many years under the assumption no additional capital would be needed. They must now revisit those portfolios to take account for capital needs on risky sovereign debt.

However, the IMF analysis of the capital needs to offset this risk was odd. Markets price in a small risk of sovereign default, yet a major sovereign default would be a large, discrete event. Regulators need to decide: Sovereigns are safe, in which case banks need little capital protection against sovereign default, or they are not safe. If they are not safe, then banks need to accumulate adequate capital—raising their equity relative to total assets—to survive plausible sovereign defaults. For example, Bank for International Settlements (BIS) data show French banks in June 2011 had claims worth $109 billion (on an ultimate risk basis) on Greece, Ireland, Italy, Portugal, and Spain (GIIPS); if these nations were to default on their sovereign claims, then French banks would surely experience large losses on the entirety of this portfolio while the repercussions for France's own economy would add further domestic losses.

If sovereign default risk is not removed, then banks need nearly full equity funding to cover plausible states of nature where disorderly defaults do happen. The lesson for banks is clear: They need to reduce exposures to troubled nations and batten down the hatches.

In addition, Europe's peripheral banks are suffering large deposit losses as capital moves to safer nations. Economic capital flight is occurring through the banking sector across the euro area. According a cumulative transfer of $ 440 billion from peripheral nationals to Germany from early 2009 to October 2011. Were it not for these implicit bailouts through the payments system, the euro area would have already collapsed

Macroeconomic Programmes are Too Timid to Restore Confidence or Growth in Eurozone

While it may alreadv be too late to avoid extensive defaults, we can still consider what needs to be done to reduce the risk of default. To avoid defaults and restructuring, Europe needs to introduce policies that bring market risk premiums on sovereign (and hence bank) debts down. Investors need to feel confident that, with a 2 to 3 percent risk premium, it is worth the risk to hold onto several trillion euros worth of troubled nations' sovereign debts, as well as the much larger non-sovereign debts.

In a nation with a flexible exchange rate, adjustment is usually achieved with budget cuts and a sharp devaluation. Since euro area nations have forgone their right to devalue, they need to regain competitiveness through price and wage cuts, while even more sharply cutting budget spending. In essence, they need to increase volatility of their wages, prices, and budgets if they are prepared to forgo similar changes that could be achieved through the exchange rate.

The available evidence from the outcomes of the troika programmes in Portugal, Ireland, and Greece, as well as the recently announced budget plans in Italy and Spain, suggests current policies will fail at this task. These programmes all plan for gradual reductions in budget deficits, implying continued buildup of total government debts, while partially substituting private debt for official debt. In Portugal and Ireland the programmes rely on external financing until 2013 when it is anticipated the programme countries will reenter markets to finance ongoing budget deficits and ever higher debt stocks at modest interest rates. In Italy, optimistic growth assumptions help bring the budget to balance in 2013, but debt stocks remain far too high. Spain announced it would miss its 2011 budget deficit target of 6 percent, raising it to 8 percent. In Greece, budget revenue and GDP growth forecasts are again proving too optimistic.

Any successful programme must recognize the fact that appetite for periphery debt amongst investors will not recover to "pre-crisis" levels, because default risk is now a reality that was not seen prior to 2009 and because debt stocks are now higher in the periphery. A successful programme must take steps to quickly improve competitiveness. So far, the largely a statistical artifact driven by decline of unproductive industry in the weighting. In Portugal, the government abandoned attempts to engineer unit labour cost reductions through "internal devaluation" after meeting political opposition. In Ireland, the Croke Park accord prevents the government from further reducing public-sector wages. Despite nearly two years of troika programmes, Greek unit labour costs have hardly budged. Italian Prime Minister Mario Monti's programme includes no general wage cuts.

With sovereign risk premiums rising, and capital flowing out of the periphery from banks while deficits and competiveness improve little, it is not surprising that peripheral economies are in trouble. The current activity for Europe's major economic and troubled nations, presenting a bleak picture. It is no coincidence that a new major "downturn" started soon after German politicians made clear they were planning to let Greece default. It is also clear that the troika programmes are failing to restore growth.

The stark contrast between unemployment in Germany and the periphery reflects the dynamics of the crisis in the euro area. The strong core is becoming stronger—German unemployment is lower than it was in 2008—while Greece, Ireland, Portugal, and Spain have high unemployment that continues to rise. Italy's troubles are recent, so with a sharp recession beginning, we anticipate Italian unemployment will soon rise sharply also.

PLAYING WITH FIRE: WAYS THE EURO AREA COULD COME TO AN END

Policymakers often have trouble grasping the danger that small tail risks pose to leveraged systems. A mere 10 percent annual risk of an Italian crisis is already inconsistent with Italian long-term solvency. If Italy has a disorderly crisis, how safe are French banks? And if those banks aren't safe, how safe is France's sovereign debt? Low-probability bad events can very quickly generate a wave of collapse through leveraged systems. The concern is that, when compared with financial crises elsewhere, the potential triggers for a euro area collapse are numerous.

A Unilateral Exit, or the Credible Threat of One: An exit from the euro area can be forced in minutes. The Eurosystem only needs to cut off a national central bank from the payments system and prevent that nation from printing new cash euros. Once this is achieved, a bank deposit in Greece would no longer be the same as a deposit in Germany, because one would not be able to get cash for a Greek deposit and one would not be able to transfer it to a non-Greek bank. Of course, the moment people understand such a change could be imminent in their nation, they will run to their banks and attempt to withdraw cash or transfer funds. This is what is now happening in Greece. The country is losing 2.5 percent of GDP monthly in deposits from banks.

There would be enormous, painful ramifications for all of Europe if Greece or another nation made a disorderly exit. Since there is no legal basis for exit, all financial contracts and indebtedness between Greek and non- Greek entities would have uncertain value as the parties could dispute whether these are to be paid in drachmas or euros. Trade between the exiting nation and the rest of the euro area would dry up. The mere fact that a country did exit would have ramifications for the other troubled nations, most likely inciting further capital flight from those nations and producing sharp economic downturns. This in turn would question the viability of Europe's core banks and some of the core sovereigns. The euro itself would probably weaken sharply, and "currency risk" would be added into the euro.

The Weak Periphery Lashes Out Against Germany, While Germany Fights Back: The political dynamics of crisis invariably pit creditors against debtors, potentially leading to flare-ups that cause creditors to give up. The troubled nations already have the power to take over decision making at the ECB. They may well usurp control in order to provide much larger ECB bailouts. This would raise concerns in financial markets and could lead to rising long- term yields on all euro-denominated debts. Germany would be forced to pay more to finance itself, and German savers would ultimately be paying for the periphery bailouts through inflation and a weak euro. In Germany this would lead to rising calls to leave the euro area.

Once there is a small risk that Germany could leave, market prices for euro-denominated assets would again change sharply. New risk premiums would need to be added to national debts where nations are expected to have weak currencies, while Germany and other strong nations might see their risk premiums fall even further.

Such changes would reinforce the recent trends in which the core nations continue to strengthen relative to the periphery, but those changes would also be highly destabilizing for financial markets.

Economics of Austerity May Fail: The third risk for the euro area is that economic, political, and social realities eventually prove that the system simply cannot work. After all, the euro area is a dream of political leaders that has been imposed on disparate economies. Few nations sought popular support to create the euro. The German leadership avoided a referendum, and in France the Maastricht treaty was passed with a thin majority of 51 percent. Already the sentiments are strong in France to leave the euro area and reintroduce the franc. Even though most European leaders are highly committed to maintaining this dream, no one can be sure what the costs are in order to keep it.

A plausible negative scenario is that those costs, in the eyes of the electorate, eventually appear too high. The evidence to date suggests Europe's periphery, even in a fairly benign outcome, will be condemned to many years or even a decade of tough austerity, high unemployment, and little hope for future growth. A good comparison is the "lost decade" of the 1980s in Latin America when nations hardly grew due to the large debt overhangs from unaffordable debts. However, those nations had the benefit of flexible exchange rates, while Europe's periphery faces a more difficult period with uncompetitive economies. Latin America's problems ended only when the creditor nations accepted large write downs and debt restructuring.

Another comparison would be the heavily indebted United Kingdom during the 1920s when the government managed policies to restore currency convertibility after the war. Britain suffered with a weak economy for a decade, before ending in the Great Depression, despite a booming global economy throughout the 1920s. However, this too is not a good comparison since Britain had far more flexible wages and prices than Europe's periphery, with nominal wages falling 28 percent during the 1920–21 recession.

Markets Lose Patience: Faced with the reality of failing adjustment programmes, difficult politics, and rising risks that one or more peripheral nations may rebel, or Germany may rescind its support, investors may simply decide that the cumulative risks mean the euro area has a moderate risk of failing. The failure of the euro area will be a calamitous financial event. As Dornbusch famously remarked of the Mexican 1994–95 crisis, "It took forever and then it took a night." If one believes the euro might fail, one should avoid being invested in European financial institutions, and in euro-denominated assets, until the outcome of the new pattern of currencies is clearer. As a result, a large swathe of euro-denominated assets would quickly fall in value. The euro itself would cheapen sharply, but so would the value of European bank debt and European shares, and most sovereigns would see their bonds trade off sharply. This in turn would make it expensive for even the Germans to raise finance in euros. Despite their impeccable credit record, they would be attempting to issue bonds in what is perceived as a flawed currency.

A small risk of the euro "breaking up" would have great importance for the euro swap market. This market is used by Europe's insurance companies, banks, and pension funds to hedge their interest rate risk. A swap contract allows, for example, a pension fund to lock in a long-term interest rate for their investments, in return for promising to pay short-term interest rates to their contract counterparty. It is an important market that underlies the ability of insurance companies, pension funds, and others to make long-term commitments to provide society with annuities, pensions, and savings from insurance policies. The notional value of these swaps is many times euro area GDP.

The euro swap market could quickly collapse if markets begin to question the survival of the euro. Euro swap rates are calculated as the average interest rate paid on euro-denominated interbank loans for 44 of Europe's banks. Approximately half of these banks are in "troubled nations." So the interest rate will reflect both inflation risk and credit risk of the participating banks. If investors decided that the euro may not exist in several years' time, swap interest rates would naturally rise because people would be concerned that banks could fail and that the "euro" interest rate could turn into something else—for example, the average of a basket of new currencies with some, such as the Greek drachma, likely to be highly inflationary.

If euro swap interest rates start to reflect bank credit risk and inflation risk from a euro breakup, then the market would no longer function. A pension fund could no longer use it to lock in an interest rate on German pensions since it would not reflect the new German currency rates. The holders of these contracts would, effectively, have little idea what they would be in a few years' time. Hence, investors would try to unwind their swap contracts, while the turmoil from dislocations in this massive market would cause disruptive and rapid wealth transfers as some holders made gains while others lost. If the euro swap market ran into trouble, Europe's financial system would undoubtedly face risk of rapid systemic collapse.

This example illustrates why a small perceived risk of a euro area breakup could rapidly cause systemic financial collapse. The swap market is only one mechanism through which collapse could ensue.

On November 23, 2011 Germany was unable to sell as many bonds as it wished. The auction failure caused an immediate steepening in the German sovereign bond yield curve. Some German officials argued this failure was due to "volatile markets," but there is a more fundamental concern. Germany's ability to pay low interest rates in euro-denominated assets requires the euro area be a financially stable region. Today, German yields remain very low and are not at worrying levels. However, if these rates were to rise due to fears of currency breakup risk, then the euro area would quickly enter deep crisis as even Germany would have trouble financing itself.

DREAMS VERSUS REALITY

The overarching policy priority in Europe is to prevent further escalation of the sovereign debt and growth crisis in the euro area while working toward resolution of the underlying causes. This requires policy adjustment in a number of areas at both the country and the euro area levels. Most economies in the region need a policy mix that supports the recovery while addressing fiscal sustainability challenges and financial sector vulnerabilities.

Appropriate fiscal consolidation is an obvious priority. Euro area economies in crisis and countries with weaker fiscal positions (Italy, Slovenia) need to implement recently agreed plans to tighten the fiscal stance. Spain's new deficit target aims for a large consolidation, which is broadly appropriate, although it could have accommodated more fully the impact of the weak growth outlook. Many other euro area economies, however, should allow automatic stabilizers to operate freely to prevent still-weak activity and downside risks from dampening market confidence about growth prospects. Those with room for fiscal policy maneuvering, in terms of the strength of their fiscal accounts and their credibility with markets, should consider slowing the pace of fiscal consolidation and focusing on measures aimed at enhancing medium-term debt sustainability (Germany). In advanced economies outside the euro area, market pressure has generally remained benign and sovereign funding costs are low, so automatic stabilizers should not be constrained. In addition, some advanced economies in Europe have appropriately allowed the pace of structural fiscal adjustment to slow. Further slowing could be considered if economic conditions deteriorate. In emerging Europe, the need for fiscal consolidation varies widely; economies that have faced increased market pressure and rising yields in recent months must continue with steady consolidation (Hungary).

Given the broad need for fiscal adjustment, much of the burden of supporting growth falls on monetary policy. The policy stance should generally remain accommodative, given downside risks to growth and little danger of inflation pressure in the near term. The ECB should lower its policy rate while continuing to use unconventional policies to address banks' funding and liquidity problems. Central banks in many other advanced economies in Europe have little or no scope for easing through conventional means and must support the recovery using unconventional policies. In the United Kingdom, with inflation expected to fall below the 2 percent target amid weaker growth and commodity prices, the Bank of England can further ease its monetary policy stance. In emerging Europe, inflation pressure is set to decline rapidly in many countries, giving central banks new room for easing. Structural reforms to boost growth are also needed urgently given that the sovereign risks at the heart of the current crisis are partly related to growth prospects—or lack thereof. Product and labor market reforms can boost productivity, and they are paramount in economies with competitiveness problems and internal or external imbalances. When implemented, they can support market confidence and the sustainability of fiscal positions.

Forestalling further escalation of the crisis also requires intervention along two dimensions at the euro area level. First, crisis management facilities need to be strong. In this respect, the recent decision to combine the European Stability Mechanism (ESM) with the European Financial Stability (EFSF) is welcome and, along with other recent European efforts, will strengthen the European crisis mechanism and support the IMF's efforts to bolster the global firewall. To limit damaging deleveraging, banks need to raise capital levels, in some cases through direct government support. There is a need for a pan-euro-area facility with the capacity to take direct stakes in banks, including in countries with little fiscal room to do so themselves.

Second, over the medium term policymakers must urgently address the Economic and Monetary Union design flaws that contributed to the crisis. This is essential to the permanent restoration of market confidence. Strong mechanisms are needed to enforce responsible fiscal policies. To make the inevitable loss of national policy discretion palatable, there needs to be more fiscal risk sharing across countries, including, for example, through an expanded ESM. Other priorities are further progress in integrating financial sectors in the euro area, including through cross-border supervision, as well as resolution mechanisms and deposit insurance with a common backstop.

There is no doubt that European political leaders are highly committed to keeping the euro area together, and so far, there is widespread support from business leaders and the population to maintain it. There is also, rightly, great fear that disorderly collapse of the euro area would impose untold costs on the global economy. All these factors suggest the euro area will hold together.

However, many financial collapses started this way. A far more dramatic creation and collapse was the downfall of the ruble zone when the Soviet Union collapsed in 1991. Argentina's attempt to peg its currency to the dollar in the 1990s was initially highly successful but ended when its politicians and society could not make the adjustments needed to hold the structure together. The Baltic nations—Estonia, Latvia, and Lithuania—have managed to maintain their pegs but only after dramatic wage adjustments and recessions.

More relevant, the various exchange rate arrangements that Europe created prior to the euro all failed. With the creation of the euro, Europe's leaders raised the stakes by ensuring the costs of a new round of failures would be far greater than those of the past, but otherwise arguably little has changed to make this attempt more likely to succeed than the previous one. Small probabilities of very negative events can be destabilizing. A lot of things can go wrong at the level of individual countries within the euro area—and one country's debacle can easily spill over to affect default risk and interest rates in the other 16 countries. The euro swap market is based, in part, on interest rates charged by 44 banks in a range of countries; about half of these banks may be considered to be located in troubled or potentially troubled countries. If the euro swap market comes under pressure or ceases to function, this would have major implications for the funding of all European sovereigns— including those that are a relatively good credit risk.

At the least, we expect several more sovereign defaults and multiple further crises to plague Europe in the next several years. There is simply too much debt, and adjustment programmes are too slow to prevent it. But this prediction implies that the long-term social costs, including unemployment and recessions rather than growth, attributable to this currency union are serious. Sometimes it is easier to make these adjustments through flexible exchange rates, and we certainly would have seen more rapid recovery if peripheral nations had the leeway to use exchange rates.

When we combine multiple years of stagnation with leveraged financial institutions and nervous financial markets, a rapid shift from low-level crisis to collapse is very plausible. European leaders could take measures to reduce this risk (through further actions on sovereign debt restructuring, more aggressive economic adjustment, and increased bailout funds). However, so far, there is little political will to take these necessary measures. Europe's economy remains, therefore, in a dangerous state.

ECB AND THE INTERNATIONAL MONETARY FUND

The Articles of Agreement of the International Monetary Fund entrust it with the task of promoting, inter alia, international monetary co-operation, exchange rate stability, international trade and economic growth. The standing invitation to the ECB to attend IMF Executive Board meetings as an observer relates to the following agenda items: i) Article IV consultations on the monetary and exchange rate policies of the euro area; ii) Article IV consultations with individual euro area Member States; iii) the role of the euro in the international monetary system; and, iv) multilateral surveillance, i.e. biannual discussion of the World Economic Outlook and the International Capital Markets Report and regular discussions on world economic and market developments.

In all these discussions of the IMF Executive Board, representatives of the euro area member countries respect the allocation of competencies provided for by the Treaty. In practical terms this means, first, that insofar as the monetary policy of the euro area is concerned the ECB observer presents the policy positions of the European Community, and, second, that with regard to exchange rate matters, the Executive Director representing the Euro group Presidency and the ECB observer both present the Community position, reflecting the regular exchange of views which takes place at the euro area level, e.g. at meetings of the Euro group.

Apart from the standing invitation, the ECB observer may be invited to attend on an ad hoc basis for agenda items which both the ECB and the IMF consider to be of mutual interest for the performance of their respective mandates. It has now become common practice for the ECB observer to be invited to attend Article IV discussions concerning EU Member States which have not yet adopted the euro, given that the ECB is involved in monetary policy co-ordination procedures with the NCBs of these Member States. Another example of ad hoc participation was the last quinquennial review by the IMF Executive Board of the valuation of the Special Drawing Rights (SDRs), which resulted in a change from a country-based to a currency-based approach in order to take fully into account the introduction of the euro.

The ECB is also involved in certain IMF initiatives to strengthen the international financial architecture whenever these concern the areas of competence of the ECB. This was the case for the Code on Good Practices on Transparency in Monetary and Financial Policies. Similarly, the ECB is involved in the current process at the IMF of developing guidelines on the management of foreign exchange reserves. These guidelines will also be aimed at reducing the vulnerability of emerging market countries to financial crises.

The ECB has developed working relationships with the IMF in other areas. In particular, the ECB actively participates in the application and development of international statistical standards, such as the IMF's Balance of Payments Manual (5th edition), within the framework of the System of National Accounts 1993. Working relationships have also been developed in the framework of the Special Data Dissemination Standard (SDDS), which was established in 1996 to ensure the provision of timely, reliable, and comprehensive data by member countries to the public and to the IMF for surveillance purposes.

QUESTIONS

1. Discuss the organisation of the European System of Central Banks (ESCB) and the basic tasks carried out by the Eurosystem.
2. Critically examine the factors suggesting that the euro would become a leading international currency.
3. Compare the current role of the euro with the US dollar as a medium of exchange.
4. Discuss the functions of an international currency. Can euro assure the role of the parallel currency in countries which don't have a stable money?
5. Critically examine the factors suggesting that the euro would become a leading international currency.
6. "An important feature of the main determinants of a currency's international status is that they tend to change slowly, inducing inertia. Network externalities exacerbate this inertia and create strong path-dependence." Comment.

7. Discuss the functions of an international currency. Can euro assure the role of the parallel currency in countries which don't have a stable money?

REFERENCES

Britton, Andrew, and David Mayes. 1992. *Achieving Monetary Union in Europe.* London: National Institute of Economic and Social Research.

Committee for the Study of Economic and Monetary Union. 1989. *Report on Economic and Monetary Union in the European Community,* June.

Crockett, Andrew. 1993. "Monetary Policy Implications of Increased Capital Flows," forthcoming in Federal Reserve Bank of Kansas City, *Changing Capital Markets: Implications for Monetary Policy.*

Deutsche Bundesbank. 1992. "The Crisis Within the EMS and Its Lessons," *Deutsche Bundesbank Annual Report,* pp. 1-8.p. 69-70.

European Community, Monetary Committee. 1993. "Monetary Committee of the European Community Reports on the Lessons to Be Drawn from the Disturbances on the Foreign Exchange Markets." Europe Documents, May 26.

Feldstein, Martin. 1991. "Does One Market Require One Money?" in *Policy Implications of Trade and Currency Zones,* Federal Reserve Bank of Kansas City.

Frankel, Jefliey A., and Shang-Jin Wei. 1993. "Trade Blocs and Currency Blocs," National Bureau of Economic Re- search, working paper no. 4335, April.

Franklin, Daniel. 1993. "Better Late Than Never," in"A Rude Awakening: A Survey ofthe European Community," *The Economist,* July 3, pp. 13-15.

Friedman, Milton, and Anna Jacobson Schwartz. 1963. *A Monetary History ofthe Un ited States, 1867-1960.* Princeton, N.J.: Princeton University Press.

Friedman, Milton. 1992. "Deja Vu in Currency Markets," *The Wall Street Journal,* September 22.

Garrett, Geoffrey. 1993. "The Politics of Maastricht," *Economics and Politics,* July.

Giavazzi, Francesco, and Alberto Giovannini. 1989. *Limit- ing Exchange Rate Flexibility.* Cambridge, Mass: MIT Press.

Giovannini, Alberto. 1993. "Comment on 'Monetary Policy Implications of Increased Capital Flows," in Federal Reserve Bank of Kansas City, *Changing Capital & Markets: Implications for Monetary Policy.*

Glick, Reuven, and Michael Hutchison. 1992. "The Euro- pean Currency Crisis," Federal Reserve Bank of San Francisco, *Weekly Letter,* October 16.

Goodhart, Charles. 1990. "Economists' Perspectives on the EMS: A Review Essay," *Journal ofMonetary Economics,* December.

Hildebrandt, Paula. 1991. "The Path to European Monetary Union," Federal Reserve Bank of Kansas City, *Economic Review,* March/April.

Mundell, Robert. 1993. "EMU and the International Monetary System," Austrian National Bank, working paper no.13, July.

Soros, George. 1993. "Down with the Mark: Soros Now Targets the Bundesbank: An Open Letter from George Soros," *Times of London,* June 9.

43

INTERNATIONAL BANKING

INTRODUCTION

International banking has been an important component of a broader process of financial globalisation and integration. Historically, it has expanded in concert with international trade and has performed key functions for the business of international firms. In addition, the local operations of foreign banks have spurred the development of financial systems in emerging markets and helped to alleviate information problems via close and sustained customer relationships. The demand for financial services from multinational corporations and rapidly growing emerging markets promises to shape international banking and its contribution to economic progress in the future.

DEFINITION OF INTERNATIONAL BANKING ACTIVITIES

International banking can be defined as intermediation activity that falls into one of the following categories. The extension of credit by a bank headquartered in a particular country to residents of another country can occur via: (i) cross-border lending; (ii) local lending by affiliates established in the foreign country; or (iii) lending booked by an affiliate established in a third country (e.g. an international financial centre). In addition, the BIS international banking statistics on a residency basis include the extension of credit by a bank headquartered in a particular country to residents of the same country but in a foreign currency. The underlying financial instruments could be loans, deposits or securities as well as derivatives contracts and contingent facilities.

In order to illustrate different forms of international banking, we consider the case of a bank that is headquartered in United States and lends to a borrower located in the India. Table 1 provides a non-exhaustive list of six examples of how the lending could be extended. In examples 1 and 2, the funds are raised in United States by taking deposits from United States residents, and then lent to the an Indian borrower, either cross-border or through a local affiliate. In example 3, a depositor in India places funds in a United States bank in United States that then lends cross- border to an entity in India. Such round-tripping also qualifies as international banking.

The last three examples illustrate forms of international banking that have gained in importance over the years. Example 4 illustrates what is sometimes referred to as global banking: funds are raised in India by the Indian affiliate of a US bank and lent by the same affiliate locally to borrowers in India. Example 5 illustrates another variant of global banking, where the funds are raised in the country where the bank is headquartered but the depositor rather than the bank bears the transfer risk. Finally, example 6 illustrates the use of an international banking centre in order to raise funds and then extend a loan in two different countries, neither of which is the country in which the bank is headquartered. Most international banking transactions are variations on these examples and often also involve routing through an offshore centre in the Caribbean or Asia.

TABLE 1

How a US Bank Could Fund a Loan to an Indian Borrower

Example	*Residents of USA*				*Cross-border*	*Residents of the India*	
1.	Saver	Deposit →	Head office	Loan→		→	Borrower
2.	Saver	Deposit →	Head office	Deposit→	Bank affiliate	Loan**	Borrower
3.			Head office	←Deposit		←	Saver
				Loan→		→	Borrower
4.					Bank affiliate	←Deposit	Saver
						Loan→	Borrower
5.	Saver	→		Deposit→	Bank affiliate	Loan→	Borrower
Germany Kingdom	*Residents of border*		*Cross- the United*	*Resident of*	*Cross-border United States*	*Residents of the*	
6.	Saver →	→	Deposit	Bank affiliate→	Deposit→	→	Borrower

ORGANISATIONAL FEATURES OF INTERNATIONAL BANKING

The growth and importance of doing banking business across the border through different forms of foreign bank organisations is described below:

Correspondent Banking

An informal linkage between banks and different countries is set up when banks maintain correspondent accounts with each other. The purpose of maintaining foreign correspondents is to facilitate international payments and collections for customers. The term 'correspondent' comes from the mail or cable communications that the banks maintain when setting customer accounts.

For example, if any Indian company wishes to pay a Canadian supplier, it would ask its bank, which would then communicate with its Canadian counterpart bank by mail or cable or through SWIFT Network. The Canadian bank would credit the account of the Canadian firm, while the company's bank would debit the company's account and then settle with the Canadian bank.

Resident Representatives

In order to provide their customers help from their own personnel on the spot in foreign countries, banks open overseas business offices. These are not banking offices in the sense of accepting local deposits or providing loans. The primary purpose of these offices is to provide information about local business practices and conditions, including the credit worthiness of potential customers and the bank's clients. The resident representatives will keep in contact with local correspondent banks and provide help when needed. Representative offices are generally small; they have the appearance of an ordinary commercial office rather than a bank.

Bank Agencies

An agency is like a full-fledged bank in every respect except that it does not handle ordinary deposits. The agencies deal in the local money markets and in the foreign exchange markets, arrange loans, clear bank drafts and cheques and channel foreign funds into financial markets. Agencies also often arrange long-term loans for customers, but they deal primarily on behalf of the home office to keep it directly involved in the important foreign financial markets.

Foreign Branches

Foreign branches are operating banks like local banks, except that the directors and owners tend to reside elsewhere. Generally, foreign branches are subject to both local banking rules and the rules at home, but because they can benefit from loopholes, the extra tier of regulations is not necessarily onerous. The books of a foreign branch are incorporated with those of the parent bank, although the foreign branch will also maintain separate books for revealing separate performance, for tax purposes, and so on. The existence of foreign branches can mean very rapid cheque clearing for customers in different countries, because the debit and credit operations are internal and can be initiated by a telephone call or through SWIFT. This can offer a great advantage over the lengthy clearing that can occur via correspondents. The foreign branch also offers bank customers in small countries all the services and safety advantages of a large bank that the local market might not itself be able to support.

Foreign Subsidiaries and Affiliates

A foreign branch is a part of a parent organisation that is incorporated elsewhere. A foreign subsidiary is a locally incorporated bank that happens to be owned either completely or partially by a foreign parent. Foreign subsidiaries do all types of banking, and it may be very difficult to distinguish them from an ordinary locally owned bank except perhaps by the name.

Foreign subsidiaries are controlled by foreign owners, even if the foreign ownership is partial. Foreign affiliates are similar to subsidiaries in being locally incorporated, and so on, but they are joint ventures, and no individual foreign owner has control (even though a group of foreign owners might have control).

Consortium Banks

Consortium banks are joint ventures of the larger commercial banks. They can involve half a dozen or more partners from numerous countries. They are primarily concerned with investment, and they arrange large loans and underwrite stocks and bonds. Consortium banks are not concerned with taking deposits, and they deal only with large corporations or perhaps governments. They will take equity positions - part ownership of an investment—as well as make loans, and they are frequently busy arranging takeovers and mergers.

DEFINITION AND CLASSIFICATION IN LOANS

International bank loans are classified into two categories: foreign loans and Euroloans. Foreign loans are raised by borrowers who are foreign to the country where the loans are raised. International loans, however, mostly take the form of Euroloans or Eurocredits, which are denominated in a currency other than the currency of the country where the loans are raised. Euroloans and foreign loans are also distinguished as follows. While Euroloans are financed wholly out of Euro currency funds, irrespective of whether the borrower is a resident or a nonresident of the country in question, foreign loans are domestic currency credits extended to non-resident borrowers.

Syndicated loans (Euro or foreign) are characterised by being so large in size that it becomes necessary to form a syndicate or a group of lending banks to finance the loan. The advantage of syndication is that it enables banks to spread the risk of very large loans amongst themselves. This is important because a large multinational firm may need credit in excess of what a single bank can offer. A syndicated loan is arranged by a lead bank on behalf of a client such as a multinational firm. The lead bank seeks the participation of a group (syndicate) of banks, each providing a portion of the loan. One or more banks are designated as reference banks, which is necessary to establish the reference interest rate.

Pricing international Loans

Pricing an international loan, which amounts to the determination of the interest charged to the borrower, depends on a number of factors. It is also influenced by a combination of risk evaluation, market conditions, and shifts in the demand for and supply of loans. The following factors are important for determining the interest rate charged to the borrower.

The Spread and the Reference Rate

The interest paid on syndicated loans is usually computed by adding a spread to the London interbank offer rate (LIBOR) or another reference rate such as the US prime rate or the Singapore interbank offer rate (SIBOR). The following factors determine the spread:

1. The availability of liquidity or loanable funds relative to demand. Spreads are likely to be higher in a market that is characterised by a shortage of liquidity and excess demand for loanable funds.
2. The creditworthiness of the borrower, as high-quality borrowers are charged lower spreads than low-quality borrowers.
3. The maturity of the loan, with higher spreads charged on long-maturity loans.

In domestic bank lending, interest rates allow for the narrowest loan spread when the central government is the borrower because there is no credit risk (the government can print money or tax people to meet its debt obligations). When non-government borrowers are involved the spreads increase as a function of credit risk. In international lending, central government borrowers pay varying interest rates because of differences in perceived country risk. Other borrowers pay higher interest rates because of (i) differences in country risk, (ii) differences in credit risk, and (iii) differences in the currency of loan denomination.

The Fees Charged

In addition to interest payments, the borrower is expected to pay management fees, participation fees, commitment fees and taxes. Management fees are charged by managing banks for their services. These are one-time charges levied when the loan agreement is signed. Participation fees are divided among all banks in relation to their share of the loan. Commitment fees are charged to the borrower as a percentage of the undrawn portion of the loan. There is normally a trade-off between fees and the spread over the reference rate. Banks prefer a combination of high fees and low spreads because they can advertise a low spread (which is good for business) without losing revenue.

Currency of Denomination

The currency of denomination affects loan pricing in two ways: (i) interest rates vary from one currency to another; and (ii) the potential gain/loss on a currency must be considered when the currency of denomination is different from the base currency of the borrower.

Loan Documentation

Loan agreements specify the rights and obligations of the borrower and lender, they specify the timing, calculation and the method of paying interest, principal, and fees. Several clauses have been developed for international lending, including the following:

1. *Changes in circumstances:* If any law or regulation changes such that the loan becomes illegal, the borrower must repay the loan. A second part of the clause protects against changes in reserve requirements or changes that may lead to an increase in the bank's cost of funding the loan.
2. *Sovereign immunity:* Under most laws, a sovereign state is immune from the seizure of assets.
3. *Governing law and jurisdiction:* This clause specifies the law that governs the contract.
4. *Cross default:* A default by the borrower under any loan agreement constitutes an automatic default under the bank's agreement.
5. *Negative pledge:* This clause forbids any secured borrowing unless the bank is secured equally. It prevents a bank's position from deteriorating relative to other lenders.

Risk Sharing and Reduction

International banks use the following techniques to reduce and shift risks involved in international lending:

1. *Loan selection and structuring:* This process includes an analysis of credits to screen out inferior loans, application of loan limits, emphasis on booking higher quality credits and adherence to country, customer and currency limits.
2. *Participation in loans:* Many banks participate in large loans, each taking a small portion of the amount.
3. *Use of guarantees and insurance:* Central government agencies, central banks, and commercial banks provide loan guarantees.
4. *Floating rate loans:* These loans provide protection for the lender bank against interest rate risk (risk is shifted to the borrower).

FINANCIAL CRISIS AND REFORMS IN INTERNATIONAL BANKING

The financial crisis severely tested banking systems, and the deficiencies it revealed warranted a swift and comprehensive official response. The Basel Committee and the FSB introduced a series of strong international measures, capped by the Basel III framework issued in December 2010 (see Box-1). "Basel III" is a comprehensive set of reform measures, developed by the Basel Committee on Banking Supervision, to strengthen the regulation, supervision and risk management of the banking sector. These measures aim to:

i) improve the banking sector's ability to absorb shocks arising from financial and economic stress, whatever the source
ii) improve risk management and governance
iii) strengthen banks' transparency and disclosures.

The reforms target:

i) bank-level, or microprudential regulation, which will help raise the resilience of individual banking institutions to periods of stress.
ii) Macroprudential, system wide risks that can build up across the banking sector as well as the procyclical amplification of these risks over time. These two approaches to supervision are complementary as greater resilience at the individual bank level reduces the risk of system wide shocks.

BASEL III AND FINANCIAL STABILITY

The key elements of Base-III framework are summarized in Table-1 to provide an overview of the various measures taken by the Committee.

As the source of credit intermediation between lenders and borrowers, banks provide essential domestic and international financial services to consumers, businesses and government. A strong and resilient banking system is thus the foundation for sustainable economic growth. Throughout history, however, financial crises have occurred at one time or another in every region of the world and for a wide range of reasons. The most recent crisis, in 2007–09, revealed fundamental shortcomings in the operation and regulation of the banking system in many countries.

The crisis had its roots in the United States and spread primarily to other advanced economies, having originated in the imprudent use and inadequate regulation of complex securitisations by large banks. However, in a broader sense, the causes and evolution of the crisis reflect deficiencies that are typical of financial crises in general: investors chasing yield, too much credit, weak underwriting standards, an underpricing of risk, excessive leverage, and contagion.

TABLE-1

Key Objectives and Features of the Basel III Framework

Capital Standards

I. Raising Capital Base

Objective – Ensuring *quality, consistency* in definition across jurisdictions and *transparency* in disclosure of capital base.

Measures – I.1 Tier 1 capital predominantly held as common shares and retained earnings. I.2 Remainder of Tier 1 capital comprising of subordinate instruments with fully discretionary non-cumulative dividends and with no maturity date or incentive to redeem; I.3 Innovative hybrid instruments with an incentive to redeem would be phased out.

II. Enhancing Risk Coverage

Objective – Strengthening risk coverage of capital framework especially for on – and off – balance sheet items and derivative exposures.

Measures II.1. Introduction of stressed Value-at-Risk (VAR) capital requirement based on a continuous 12 - month period of significant financial stress; II.2. Higher capital requirements for re-securitisation in banking and trading book; I. Raising Capital Base

Objective – Ensuring *quality, consistency* in definition across jurisdictions and *transparency* in disclosure of capital base.

Measures – I.1 Tier 1 capital predominantly held as common shares and retained earnings. I.2 Remainder of Tier 1 capital comprising of subordinate instruments with fully discretionary non-cumulative dividends and with no maturity date or incentive to redeem; I.3 Innovative hybrid instruments with an incentive to redeem would be phased out.

II. Enhancing Risk Coverage

Objective – Strengthening risk coverage of capital framework especially for on – and off – balance sheet items and derivative exposures.

Measures II.1. Introduction of stressed Value-at-Risk (VAR) capital requirement based on a continuous 12 - month period of significant financial stress; II.3. Introduction of capital charge for potential mark-to-market losses related to credit valuation adjustment risks associated with deterioration in creditworthiness of counterparty; II.4. Strengthening standards for collateral management. Banks with large illiquid derivative position to a counterparty would have to apply longer margining periods for determining regulatory capital requirements.

III. Supplement Risk-based Capital Requirements with Leverage Measure

Objective – Containing leverage in the banking sector thereby mitigating risk related to deleveraging.

Measures – III.1. Introduction of a simple transparent and independent measure of leverage, comparable across jurisdictions by adjusting for differences in accounting standards.

IV. Reduce Pro-cyclicality Through Counter-cyclical Buffers

Objective – Dempening pro-cyclical movements within the banking system by making it a "shock absorber" rather than a transmitter of risk to the real economy.

Measures – IV.1. Movement to a relatively less pro-cyclical Expected Loss (EL) approach as against existing Incurred Loss (IL) and updation of supervisory guidance consistent with the EL approach; IV.2. Creation of capital conservation buffers above the minimum capital and adjust the buffer range during periods of excess credit growth.

Liquidity Standards

I. Minimum Liquidity Standards

Objective – Introducing internationally harmonized and robust liquidity standards since stronger capital requirements may be necessary but not a sufficient condition for banking sector stability.

Measures – I.1. Introduction of liquidity coverage ratio to ensure sufficient high quality liquid resources to cope with an acute stress scenario lasting one month; 1.2 introduction of net stable finding ratio, which has a longer time horizon of one year to provide sustainable maturity structure of assets and liabilities.

II. Quantitative Liquidity Metrics

Objective – Imparting consistency in quantitative metrics used by supervisors to capture liquidity risks.

Measures – II. 1. Introduction of metrics, which include among others, contractual maturity mismatch, concentration of funding, available unencumbered assets and liquidity coverage ratio by currency.

Reference:

"Basel III: A Global Regulatory Framework for More Resilient Banks and Banking System," Bank for International Settlements, June 2011.

Given the speed at which crises can arise and be transmitted around the globe, and given ever more rapid financial innovation, banks in all countries need to hold higher capital and liquidity buffers to protect the global banking system and economy from unforeseen risks. Unfortunately, memories tend to be short, and significant risks to the banking sector generally emerge after a period of complacency bred of apparent calm. Thus, the work to strengthen banking systems must be carried through now, when the crisis is still fresh in people's minds and policymakers and the wider public understand the urgency of an effective response.

With its release of the Basel III rules on 16 December 2010, the Basel Committee on Banking Supervision set out new global regulatory standards on bank capital adequacy and liquidity to correct the deficiencies revealed by the crisis. Some of the new rules represent a significant overhaul of existing global standards, others introduce rules where none previously existed. Taken together, they strengthen capital and liquidity regulation to promote more resilience in global banking. Thus fortified by Basel III, the international regulatory framework will better shield the financial sector from the next crisis, whatever its origin, and reduce the risk of spillover from the financial sector to the real economy. As risk-taking in the financial sector resumes, banks have started to accumulate capital and to adapt their funding strategies and broader business models to the new regulatory framework, which will call on them to target lower, more stable returns on equity.

HOW THE FINANCIAL CRISIS IS SHAPING REGULATORY REFORM

The severity of the crisis owed much to the fact that the banking sector in many countries had taken on too much risk without a commensurate increase in capital.

Furthermore, this inadequate *level* of capital was of insufficient *quality*, as the latter had gradually eroded. Basel III tightens capital requirements, encompasses a broader array of risks, and explicitly addresses macroprudential aspects of banking system stability.

Bank Capital

The leverage ratio will provide a backstop to the risk-based measures and help curb the build- up of excessive leverage. Basel III substantially raises the quality as well as the quantity of capital, with a much greater emphasis on common equity (Box-2). During the crisis, losses reduced banks' common equity. However, some banks maintained deceptively high ratios of Tier 1 capital to risk-weighted assets through the inclusion of other forms of financial instruments in the capital base. Moreover, non-common Tier 1 capital instruments often did not share in banks' losses through reduced coupon or principal payments and so did not contribute to maintaining the institutions as going concerns in any meaningful way. The artificially high Tier 1 risk-based ratios also meant that banks were building up high levels of leverage. Basel III therefore also introduces a simple leverage ratio that provides a backstop to the risk-based regime. The supplementary ratio, which is a measure of a bank's Tier 1 capital as a percentage of its assets plus off-balance sheet exposures and derivatives, will serve as an additional safeguard against attempts to "game" the risk-based requirements, and will mitigate model risk (Table-2). By helping contain the build-up of excessive leverage, the leverage ratio will also complement other macroprudential measures, discussed below, to reduce systemic risk.

BOX -2

Capital Instruments

The global banking system entered the crisis with an insufficient level of high-quality capital. The crisis revealed an inconsistency in how regulatory capital is defined across jurisdictions and the lack of disclosure that would have enabled the market to fully assess and compare the quality of banks' capital. In response, Basel III introduces a harmonised definition of capital that comprises the following components:

- **Common Equity Tier 1** – consists of the bank's common shares and retained earnings less regulatory adjustments (e.g. the deduction of goodwill). This component of capital fully absorbs losses while the bank remains a going concern. It is therefore the highest-quality component of a bank's capital. A key element of the new definition of capital is the greater focus on Common Equity Tier 1.
- **Additional Tier 1 capital** – consists of preferred shares and other capital instruments that comply with a set of criteria to ensure they can absorb losses while the issuing bank remains a going concern. These criteria include requirements that the instruments be subordinated, have fully discretionary non-cumulative dividends or coupons and have neither a maturity date nor an incentive to redeem.
- **Tier 2 capital** – consists of debt instruments that comply with a set of criteria to ensure they are able to absorb losses when a bank fails (i.e. when it has become a "gone concern"). These

criteria include requirements that the instruments be subordinated, have a minimum original maturity of at least five years and contain no step-ups or other incentives to redeem. Regulatory recognition of these instruments is amortised over the five years before maturity.

During the crisis, a number of distressed banks were rescued by the injection of public sector funds in the form of common equity and other forms of Tier 1 capital. While this had the effect of supporting depositors, it also meant that certain capital instruments did not absorb losses. Therefore, in addition to the characteristics noted above, instruments in Additional Tier 1 and in Tier 2 must have a feature ensuring that they can be written off or converted to common equity when the issuing bank reaches the point of non-viability (i.e. the point at which the bank is unable to support itself in the private market) as determined by the relevant authority.

The Basel III definition of capital phases out innovative hybrid capital instruments, which provided an incentive to redeem through features such as step-up clauses. It also eliminates Tier 3 capital, which was short-term subordinated debt that was previously permitted to cover market risk.

In addition to the Basel III elements of capital, certain other instruments are being considered in the context of systemically important banks:

- **Contingent capital** (also called cocos) – debt instruments that convert to Common Equity Tier 1 capital through a write-off or conversion to common shares before a bank reaches the point of non-viability.
- **Bail-in-able debt** – debt instruments that convert to Common Equity Tier 1 capital through a write- off or conversion to common shares when a bank reaches the point of non-viability.

Turning to the minimum capital requirements, the higher minimums for common equity and tier 1 capital will be phased in beginning in 2013, and will become effective at the beginning of 2015. The schedule will be as follows:

- The minimum common equity and Tier 1 requirements will increase from the current 2% and 4% levels to 3.5% and 4.5%, respectively, at the beginning of 2013.
- The minimum common equity and Tier 1 requirements will be 4% and 5.5%, respectively, starting in 2014.
- The final requirements for common equity and Tier 1 capital will be 4.5% and 6%, respectively, beginning in 2015.

The 2.5% capital conservation buffer, which will be comprised of common equity and is in addition to the 4.5% minimum requirement, will be phased in progressively starting on 1 January 2016, and will become fully effective by 1 January 2019.

Finally, the leverage ratio will also be phased in. The test (the so-called "parallel run period") will begin in 2013 and run until 2017, with a view to migrating to a Pillar 1 treatment on 1 January 2018 based on review and appropriate calibration.

TABLE 2

Strengthened Capital Framework: From Basel II to Basel III

In percentage of risk-weighted assets	*Capital requirement*							*Additional macroprudential overlay*	
	Common Equity			*Tier 1 capital*		*Total capital*		*Counter-cyclical buffer*	*Additional loss absorbing capacity for SIFI*
	Minimum	*Conservation buffer*	*Required*	*Minimum*	*Required*	*Minimum*	*Required*	*Range*	
Basel II	2			4		8			
Memo	*Equivalent to around 1% for an average international bank under the new definition*			*Equivalent to around 2% for an average international bank under the new definition*					
Basel III New definition and calibration	4.5	2.5	7.0	6	8.5	8	10.5	0-2.5	Capital surcharge for SIFLs?

*Modalities to be defined.

Risk Coverage

The Basel Committee has also improved the risk coverage of the regulatory capital framework for capital market activities – a salient feature of the recent crisis, where trading exposures accounted for much of the build-up of leverage and were an important source of losses. (Trading exposures include positions in financial instruments and commodities held either with the intent to trade them or to hedge other trading activities. For purposes of calculating regulatory capital, such positions are subject to the Basel Committee's market risk rules and are said to be held in the "trading book"). Weak capital, excessive leverage and inadequate risk coverage prevented the banking system from fully absorbing systemic trading and credit losses. Nor could it cope with the reintermediation of large off-balance sheet exposures that had built up in the shadow banking system. Under Basel III, banks will have to hold more capital against their less liquid, credit- sensitive assets whose holding periods are much longer than traditional trading positions. Trading activities will also be subject to a stressed value-at-risk requirement. In addition, securitisation exposures in the trading book will be subject to capital charges more consistent with those for the banking book. Basel III also imposes higher capital requirements for counterparty credit risk, that is, for the amount that would be lost in the event of default by a counterparty to a financial contract. Moreover, Basel III creates incentives for banks to increase the use of central counterparties (CCPs) – financial institutions that act as intermediaries between market participants while ensuring that the risk arising from banks' exposures to CCPs is adequately capitalised.

Liquidity

During the build-up to the crisis, many banks had operated with increasingly thin liquidity margins, placing undue reliance on easy access to market liquidity. At the height of the crisis, counterparties lost confidence in the liquidity of many banking institutions, severely straining their access to funding. Basel III addresses the liquidity deficiencies that the crisis laid bare. The internationally harmonised liquidity framework consists of two minimum regulatory standards: the liquidity coverage ratio (LCR) and the net stable funding ratio (NSFR). They have complementary objectives.

The LCR is designed to bolster the short-term resilience of a bank's liquidity risk profile by ensuring that it has high-quality liquid assets in sufficient quantity to survive a plausibly severe stress scenario lasting for 30 calendar days. The stress scenario, designed by the Basel Committee, incorporates many of the shocks experienced during the crisis. It includes a partial run-off of retail deposits, a partial or complete drying-up of wholesale funding sources, a need to post additional collateral due to a credit rating downgrade, and unscheduled draws on unused credit and liquidity facilities.

The NSFR is designed to promote resilience over a longer time horizon by creating additional incentives for banks to use more stable sources of funding on an ongoing basis. These standards complement the Committee's 2008 *Principles for sound liquidity risk management and supervision*, the implementation of which will be assessed in the near term.

Macroprudential Aspects

Basel III was designed to enhance both bank-specific soundness and wider banking sector stability. Thus, besides its firm-specific approaches, it incorporates macroprudential measures to explicitly address systemic risk.

During the crisis, mounting losses and the resulting strain on capital impaired banks' ability to lend – precisely at the time when economies were most in need of credit. This tendency for the financial system to amplify cyclical effects in the real economy, or procyclicality, combined with the interconnectedness of financial institutions that were considered too big to fail, exacerbated the crisis.

To help mitigate procyclicality in banking and the broader financial system, the new regulatory capital framework provides for building up capital in good times to levels above the minimum requirement. The resulting *capital conservation buffer* will help banks absorb losses during periods of financial and economic stress. As a bank's capital level moves closer to the minimum requirement, the conservation buffer imposes a progressively tightened constraint on the bank's discretionary distributions, such as dividends. Retaining a bigger proportion of earnings during a downturn will help ensure that capital remains available to support banks' ongoing business operations during the period of stress.

Basel III also introduces a *counter cyclical buffer*. It is based on the observation that private sector credit growth that is out of line with historical experience often ultimately imposes losses on the lenders. The ratio of aggregate credit to GDP will serve as the reference for the build-up of the buffer, which will be implemented through restrictions on capital distributions identical to those that apply to the conservation buffer. Within countries, the authorities will impose this buffer only when they judge that credit growth is resulting in an unacceptable build-up of system-wide risk. Conversely, the buffer will be released when, in the judgment of the authorities, the capital can help absorb banking system losses that pose a risk to financial stability. The ability to run down the buffer without penalties will help reduce the risk of constraining the availability of credit.

The macroprudential elements of Basel III contribute significantly to the development of the broader macroprudential policy framework. The BIS has advocated such a framework for some time and is encouraged to see the growth of national and international efforts to develop and implement it. However, while much has been accomplished, more needs to be done, especially on practical implementation of the broad consensus now evident around the framework's core concepts.

OUTSTANDING ISSUES AND FUTURE WORK

The reform agenda now encompasses implementation of regulations complemented by more intensive and intrusive supervision; more extensive regulation and supervision of systemically important financial institutions (SIFIs) and development of effective cross-border resolution regimes; and broader consideration of non-bank financial firms and the shadow banking system. The Basel Committee is also reviewing the distinction between the regulatory banking book and the trading book.

Implementation

The Basel III rules need to be implemented in a timely and globally consistent manner. All member countries of the Basel Committee must now translate the Basel III texts into national regulations and legislation in time to meet the 2013 deadline.

The Committee and its oversight body of Governors and Heads of Supervision have consistently stated that the new standards will be introduced in a manner that does not impede the economic recovery. Thus, they have chosen a staggered timeline for implementation . For example, the July 2009 enhancements that strengthen regulatory capital and disclosure requirements are due to take

effect no later than the end of 2011. The Basel III requirements themselves begin to take effect from the beginning of 2013 and will be phased in by 2019. This time frame includes an observation period to review the implications of the liquidity standards for individual banks, the banking sector and financial markets, with a view to addressing any unintended consequences. Similarly, the Committee will assess the impact of the leverage ratio on business models during the transition period in order to ensure that it achieves its objectives.

Like all Basel Committee standards, Basel III sets out *minimum* requirements, and the transitional arrangements are the deadlines for adopting the new standards. Countries should move faster if their banks are profitable and are able to apply the standards without having to restrict credit. Banks should not be permitted to increase their capital distributions simply because the deadline for achieving the minimum standards is still some way off, particularly if there are signs of growing macroeconomic risks and imbalances. Therefore, banks, for their part, must also begin to plan and to prepare.

Basel III is the core regulatory response to problems revealed by the financial crisis. Delay or weakening of the agreements would jeopardise financial stability and the robustness of the recovery over the long term. The full, timely and consistent implementation of *all* relevant standards by banks, along with rigorous enforcement by supervisors, is critical. Ultimately, both the official and the private sector will reap the benefits of a more stable financial system.

More Intensive and More Intrusive Supervision

Implementation efforts need to be supplemented by strong and enhanced supervision of individual banks. Strong supervision is needed to ensure that banks operate with capital levels, liquidity buffers and risk management practices that are commensurate with the risks taken. It must also address the consequences of financial innovation or risks of regulatory arbitrage that regulation cannot fully capture and, more generally, address the firm-level consequences of emerging risks and economic developments. National authorities must supervise in a more intensive and more intrusive fashion, especially for the largest and most complex banks. It will also be important to reinforce both the firm-specific and macroprudential dimensions of supervision and the way they interact.

In particular, as it carries forward its work on the implementation of the supervisory review process under Basel II (i.e. Pillar 2), the Basel Committee will foster the adoption of better supervisory practices.

Systemically Important Financial Institutions

Reducing the risks posed by financial institutions that are systemic in a global context (global systemically important financial institutions, or G-SIFIs) is a high priority for the international regulatory community. Basel III will enhance the quality and quantity of capital for all banks, but it does not fully address the externalities or spillover effects that G-SIFIs generate. Additional policy tools are necessary.

In November 2010, the FSB introduced a policy framework for these institutions. It recommends that G-SIFIs have higher loss-absorbing capacity to reflect the greater risks that they pose to the global financial system and that these institutions be subject to more intensive and coordinated resolution planning to reduce the probability and impact of their failure. This will help ensure that G-SIFIs can be closed or wound up quickly without destabilising the financial system or exposing the taxpayer to the risk of loss. In addition, the FSB calls for enhanced supervision of SIFIs that will be more intensive and effective than in the past.

The Basel Committee has developed quantitative indicators and qualitative elements to identify G-SIFIs. Work is also continuing on calibrating the additional loss absorbency that G- SIFIs should have, which could be met through some combination of common equity and contingent capital. The Committee will pursue this work in close cooperation with the FSB in the coming months.

More Effective Cross-border Bank Resolution

Higher loss-absorbing capacity for G-SIFIs and their effective resolution complement each other, but neither by itself is sufficient. The financial crisis also illustrated the importance of effective cross-border crisis management. The scope, scale and complexity of international financial transactions expanded at an unprecedented pace in the years preceding the crisis, while the tools and techniques for handling cross-border bank resolution have hardly evolved. Some of the events during the crisis revealed gaps in intervention techniques and, in many countries, a lack of appropriate resolution tools. Actions taken to resolve cross-border institutions during the crisis tended to be ad hoc, severely constrained by time, and dependent on a significant amount of official support.

In March 2010, the Basel Committee issued recommendations to strengthen national resolution powers and their cross-border implementation. The recommendations also covered firm-specific contingency planning for banks and home and host country authorities. Contagion can be reduced through risk mitigation mechanisms such as netting arrangements, collateralisation practices and the use of regulated central counterparties. These and other measures would help limit the market impact of a bank failure. The recommendations should lead to practical and credible plans to promote resilience in periods of severe financial distress and to facilitate a rapid resolution if necessary.

Building on the recommendations, the Basel Committee and the FSB are assessing progress in national and multinational efforts to enhance authorities' ability to manage and resolve distressed banking institutions in a manner that minimises disruptions to the financial system. The two bodies are evaluating legal and policy changes that would assist authorities in addressing future needs for crisis management and bank resolution.

Other Financial Sectors and Firms

Work to strengthen the regulation of SIFIs also needs to take account of differences across financial sectors. The FSB will review how the different regulatory measures fit together and whether there are inconsistencies or contradictions among the standards. For instance, deeper consideration is needed to assess the systemic importance of insurance companies and their role in financial stability. Insurance companies tend to have very different risk characteristics from those of banks, particularly regarding liquidity. Insurance company balance sheets also differ considerably across countries, for example in terms of the exposure to equity markets . Except for unusual cases such as American International Group (AIG) and the monoline insurers, these institutions proved broadly resilient during the financial crisis .

Hedge funds are another set of firms for which regulatory instruments and objectives differ sharply from those appropriate to banks. Despite major investment losses and outflows during the crisis, assets and leverage in the hedge fund sector have been broadly stable in the post-crisis period.

Shadow Banking

Shadow banking refers to credit intermediation that takes place outside the traditional banking system and involves maturity or liquidity transformation. Examples include the activities of money market funds, lending by unregulated finance companies, the issuance by specialised conduits and investment vehicles of commercial paper backed by longer-term assets, and the funding of securitisation activities through repo markets. The shadow banking system is, however, closely intertwined with the regulated system. Large banks typically draw substantial income from shadow banking activities and retain both direct and indirect credit and operational exposures to them through business lines such as loan origination, credit enhancements, backup liquidity lines, brokerage services, warehousing and credit insurance.

Shadow banking can perform valuable functions, including facilitating credit extension to certain sectors and providing banks and investors with a range of vehicles for managing credit, liquidity and maturity risks. However, the financial crisis demonstrated that shadow banking can also give rise to a number of risks in the broader financial sector. Some of these risks (such as those related to bank exposures through contingent credit lines) are being addressed through the improvements in bank regulation as well as through initiatives such as stronger regulation of credit rating agencies and money market funds. Other aspects are more difficult to deal with, especially those that call for a high degree of coordination across regulatory agencies, both within and across national boundaries. For example, judging the extent of liquidity mismatch in a bank-sponsored investment vehicle may require input from banking and market regulators in several jurisdictions.

Another lesson of the crisis was that activities in the shadow banking system need to be monitored in order to improve the ability of authorities and market participants to understand and anticipate the build-up of systemic risks. For example, in the years leading up to the crisis, US money market funds were important providers of funding to European banks. As a result, the disruption to the US money market fund sector in the aftermath of the Lehman Brothers bankruptcy in September 2008 had knock-on implications for European bank funding as well as for foreign exchange swap markets because the banks had used these instruments to swap their funding from dollars into local currencies. Existing statistical frameworks do not provide adequate information for assessing these risks .

Shadow banking's potential threats to financial stability must be reduced. First, firm-level disclosure and system-wide statistical frameworks need to be improved to ensure that the build- up of risks can be monitored properly. Improved data need to be accompanied by regular monitoring of those indicators that can be informative about the nature and locus of potential systemic risks. Second, gaps in regulation need to be identified and addressed, with the goal of reducing risky build-ups of leverage and maturity and liquidity mismatches, wherever these occur

in the financial system. Rules that mitigate these risks in a consistent way across different entities and activities would reduce the scope for regulatory arbitrage. Given the global nature of many shadow banking activities, these efforts need to be coordinated at the international level.

Other Regulatory and Supervisory Initiatives

The financial crisis exposed significant flaws in the existing regulatory capital approach to market risk and trading activities. The most immediate shortcomings were remedied in the July 2009 enhancements to the regulatory capital framework. The Basel Committee is now also carrying out a fundamental review of the trading book framework and expects to conduct a public consultation on its findings around end-2011.

There are a number of key questions: how to remove opportunities for arbitrage across the banking book and trading book, how to define trading activities, and how to capture risks in trading books (and possibly market risk more generally). Under the current regime, banking book exposures are subject to capital charges against credit risk (through the Basel II credit risk framework) and also against foreign exchange risk and commodities risk (through the market risk framework). Positions in the trading book are subject to capital charges against interest rate risk, foreign exchange risk, equity position risk and commodities risk (through the market risk framework).

INTERACTION BETWEEN BANK- AND MARKET-BASED INTERNATIONAL INTERMEDIATION

It is widely recognised that bank-based and market-based activities perform complementary functions. Both are often inseparable aspects of financial intermediation that depend heavily on the resilience of market infrastructure. The same is true in the international dimension. For instance, banks invest retail deposits in foreign securities, lengthening the intermediation chain by involving markets. Or they issue debt in international markets to fund corporate loans and other assets. International banks' reliance on market-based funding increased at the beginning of the crisis as many of them had to fund the assets of off-balance sheet vehicles that they had taken onto their balance sheets. Conversely, markets rely on banks to alleviate issues arising from limited public information about financial counterparties, especially when these issues stem from international transactions. In addition, banks provide liquidity by engaging in market-making activities, providing credit lines or custodial services.

Financial frictions help underscore the functional differences between markets and banks and hence the circumstances under which each channel for intermediation may have a comparative advantage. Bank-based intermediation may offer risk-smoothing services – by maintaining, for example, a close link between prices and fundamentals – that financial markets cannot provide. Furthermore, long-term bank-client relationships may underpin the only source of credit when asymmetric information, moral hazard or financial frictions are particularly acute .That said, bank-based intermediation could also be suboptimal if it is associated with excessive rent-seeking by banks, to the detriment of economic growth .

Market-based intermediation has a comparative advantage when diversity of opinion is important. An example in this respect is the venture capital market, often promoted as a way to finance and develop high-tech industries. Diversity of opinion also helps to distil information and embed it in prices, facilitating efficient resource allocation, particularly in high- technology R&D-type industries . In addition, markets may enhance the overall degree of corporate governance prevailing in a particular economy and facilitate risk management . At the same time, more developed financial markets may disproportionately promote the growth of industrial sectors that are relatively more in need of external finance . In addition, the market- based system is only accessible to larger companies and tends to be more volatile .

The complementarity of banks and markets goes hand in hand with a deepening and widening of the network of bank-market relations. This is likely to improve risk-sharing. At the same time, however, the strong interconnectedness of institutions and markets may also enhance the propagation of shocks across borders. This raises the question of which institutions and markets should be included in the regulatory perimeter and highlights the need for international cooperation . International cooperation should seek to restrain regulatory arbitrage by ensuring that banks and markets that perform similar functions receive similar regulatory treatment.

Long-term Developments

Functional differences between banks and markets help to illuminate how the balance between bank- and market-based intermediation evolves in individual countries (or regions). When a country is at an early stage of its economic and financial development, it typically relies heavily on international sources of intermediation. (Financial systems that are at an early stage of development are typically dominated by bank-based financial intermediation). Since it is exactly in such\ circumstances that financial frictions – associated with transactions in different currencies, across jurisdictions and time zones – are most acute, banks are virtually the only source of financing. Banks have also proven more apt at dealing with such frictions by establishing local operations in foreign countries. As the country develops, it more easily gains access to international financial markets. Typically, the initial access is effected by issuing securities in a major (foreign) currency, which helps alleviate frictions. Then, later stages are associated with foreign direct investment and with the transfer of international know-how for the development of domestic markets.

Market-based intermediation and bank-based intermediation have generally expanded in parallel, although the pace of expansion has differed across countries. How this expansion has evolved depends on historical factors, technological innovations, monetary and fiscal policies, and specific legal and accounting systems. For instance, the banking systems in Japan and Germany still account for the majority of financial system assets. Roughly 80% of euro zone non- financial credit instruments are loans, while this share is close to 50% in the United States.

In the run-up to the recent crisis, the integration of bank and market financing was taken to a new level by the development of securitisation, structured finance and the enhanced use of risk transfer instruments. These innovations reduced market incompleteness, thereby facilitating the diversification of risk by banks and the efficient allocation of capital. However, they also increased banks' vulnerability. The opaqueness and illiquidity of many securitised products have contributed to banks' credit- and funding-related stress. For instance, substantial, albeit temporary, investor demand for securitised retail exposures allowed Swedish banks to rapidly expand their lending in the Baltic region without properly evaluating the associated credit risks. Similarly, as German banks financed investments in US securities with German retail deposits, they exposed themselves to large cross-currency funding risks.

Better regulation is critical but not enough. It is just one piece of the puzzle. The promotion of financial stability requires a broad policy framework, of which prudential policy is only one element. The BIS has been a consistent and long-standing advocate of the essential role played by macroeconomic policies, both monetary and fiscal as an important element in fostering financial stability.

At the same time, the Basel Committee, its governing body and the G20 Leaders have consistently stated that the reforms will be introduced in a way that does not impede the recovery of the real economy. In addition, time is needed to translate the new internationally agreed standards into national legislation. National authorities can, and in fact should, impose higher standards if deemed appropriate in the local circumstances and prevailing economic conditions; similarly, they can impose shorter transition periods where appropriate.

The new, strengthened definition of capital will be phased in over five years: the requirements will be introduced in 2013 and fully implemented by the end of 2017. In addition, existing public sector capital injections will be grandfathered until the end of 2017. Capital instruments that no longer qualify as non-common equity Tier 1 capital or Tier 2 capital will be phased out over 10 years beginning 1 January 2013.

Basel III thus provides a combination of capital and liquidity standards that will help increase the resilience of the financial sector in the face of stress. In this context, four key points must be noted:

First, the new Basel III package affords the financial industry more clarity on the regulatory front. In today's still challenging economic and financial conditions, uncertainty is the enemy. Removing regulatory uncertainty can contribute importantly to the ongoing recovery.

Second, the new Basel III package combines enhancements at both the micro- and the macroprudential level. The new standards improve on the Basel II framework at the micro level of individual financial institutions, especially by strengthening the level and quality of capital. But Basel III also has a macroprudential overlay to promote the greater stability of the financial system as a whole. The aim is to establish appropriate capital schemes to address the procyclicality of the financial system and to deal with systemic risk. The counter cyclical capital buffer will be activated by national authorities within the general guidance provided by an international agreement, depending on circumstances in specific jurisdictions. Tools will be available to limit systemic risk, and this will surely put a premium on effective supervision within jurisdictions, as well as on international peer reviews of local arrangements to ensure their international consistency. Last but certainly not least, the foundation of a sound macroprudential framework has now been laid.

Third there will be an appropriately long transition period. The new definition of capital, higher risk weights and increased minimum requirements will entail a significant amount of additional capital. The agreed transitional arrangements will help ensure that the banking sector can meet the higher capital standards through reasonable earnings retention and capital-raising, while still supporting the flow of new lending to the economy.

Fourth, complacency must be avoided. True, the financial industry will have time to adapt so as to both maintain an adequate supply of credit for the economy and repair balance sheets. Banks and supervisors alike will have to redouble their efforts to foster behavioural changes to ensure a sustained global recovery from the deep financial crisis. From this perspective, it goes without saying that those banks that already meet the minimum standards but do not meet the conservation buffer should apply the conservation principle. In other words, they should do their best to satisfy the conservation buffer requirement as soon as reasonably possible. Supervisors, for their part, must remain vigilant and actively promote a transition to the new standards as bank- specific and broader economic conditions warrant. Market discipline also plays an important role in guarding against complacency.

QUESTIONS

1. Explain the organisational factors of international banking.
2. Describe the possible differences in risk between a purely domestic bank and an international bank.
3. Should the banking system be more closely regulated to prevent another international debt crisis or any other banking crisis?
4. Discuss the factors behind the globalisation of international banking and changing role of financial instruments.
5. Discuss the main issues of concern in international banking.
6. Identify the factors that would likely to be used by banks to assess the creditworthiness of a government and of a corporation. Why are these assessments by banks not always accurate?
7. Discuss the key elements of Basel III framework.
8. Critically examine the role of financial crisis in shaping the current regulatory reform.
9. What steps have been recently initiated to promote broader financial stability?
10. Discuss the steps taken to strengthen the capital framework from Basel II to Basel III.

REFERENCES

Beck, T, A Demirgüç-Kunt and V Maksimoviæ (2004): "Bank competition and access to finance: international evidence", *Journal of Money, Credit and Banking,* 36(3), pp 627–48.

Berger, A (2007): "Obstacles to a global banking system: old Europe versus new Europe", *Journal of Banking and Finance,* 31, pp 1955–73.

Bonin, J, I Hasan and P Wachtel (2005): "Bank performance, efficiency and ownership in transition countries", *Journal of Banking and Finance,* 29, pp 31–53.

Cerutti, E, G Dell'Ariccia, and M Martínez (2007): "How banks go abroad: branches or subsidiaries?", *Journal of Banking and Finance,* 31, pp 1669–92.

Cetorelli, N and L Goldberg (2010): "Global banks and international shock transmission: evidence from the crisis", Federal Reserve Bank of New York, manuscript.

Claessens, S, A Demirgüç-Kunt and H Huizinga (2001): "How does foreign entry affect domestic banking markets", *Journal of Banking and Finance*, 25, pp 891–911.

Clark, J and T Siems (2002): "X-efficiency in banking: looking beyond the balance sheet", *Journal of Money, Credit and Banking*, 34(4), pp 987–1013.

Goldberg, L (2009): "Understanding banking sector globalisation", *IMF Staff Papers*, 56(1).

Herrero, A and M Martinez Peria (2007): "The mix of international banks' foreign claims: determinants and implications", *Journal of Banking and Finance*, 31(6), pp 1613–31.

Jones, G (1990): "Banks as multinationals", in G Jones (ed), *Banks as multinationals*, Routledge: London.

Mathieson, D and J Roldos (2001): "The role of foreign banks in emerging markets", IMF presentation.

Papaioannou, E (2009): "What drives international bank flows? Politics, institutions and other determinants", *Journal of Development Economics*, 88(2), pp 269–81.

Stiglitz, J and B Greenwald (2003): *Towards a new paradigm in monetary economics*, Cambridge University Press.

Wang, J (2007): *Foreign banks in developing country: competition, efficiency and stability*, Beijing, RenMin Press.

World Bank (2008): "The changing role of international banking in development finance", in *Global Development Finance 2008*.

44

REVIVING THE WORLD ECONOMY

INTRODUCTION

The explanations for the global financial crisis (that reached a flash point in October 2008 with the collapse of Lehman Brothers) have been all encompassing. At macro level, they have held the loose monetary policies adopted by reserve currency-issuing advanced economies (particularly the US) in the run up to the crisis responsible on the one side and the mercantilist policies adopted by export- led economies leading to accumulation of large current account surpluses and reserves on the other. These policies were facilitated by weaknesses in the international monetary system (IMS), particularly the absence of alternative reserve assets to the dollar. Weak regulation of financial markets and intermediaries and excessive financial innovation and risk taking by finance and banking intermediaries at micro level have also figured as proximate causes of the crisis. The chapter examines the state of the global. It analyses the current global slowdown and eurozone crisis, what this means for India and the policy challenges that these international matters give rise.

FRAGILE GLOBAL RECOVERY

The global economic recovery faltered in 2011. For the year as a whole, world output grew by 3.9%, slightly slower than the average growth rate of the decade prior to the financial crisis, but down significantly from 5.3% in 2010. The pace of economic growth in advanced economies halved, to just 1.6% This reflected a significant weakening of the economy in the United States and the United Kingdom and a sharp drop in activity in Japan after the March 2011 earthquake, while growth in the euro area as a whole was broadly unchanged.

Overall, the economic momentum in advanced economies was too weak to generate a robust, self-sustaining recovery. The drag on private consumption persisted. Unemployment remained high, or even increased further. Falling property prices and high levels of debt continued to weigh on household balance sheets in the mature economies hit hardest by the financial crisis. Household sector weakness also weighed on business spending. Very weak public sector finances generally left no room for further fiscal stimulus.

Emerging market economies grew by around 6% in 2011, with the pace of growth moderating only slightly from 2010. Emerging Asia grew at 7.8%, led by China (9.2%) and India (7.2%); Latin America grew at 4.5%. Growth in central and eastern Europe was broadly unchanged at 5.3% for 2011 as a whole. However rapid growth in EMEs was in many cases associated with signs of domestic overheating, including rising inflation, strong credit growth and rising asset prices. Real credit continued to expand rapidly in emerging Asia and Latin America, and real residential property prices rose close to or above previous historical highs in major cities in China and Latin America.

Reflecting the two-speed global expansion, external imbalances remained wide. Although slightly lower than in 2010, global current account imbalances remained at about 4% of world GDP, which is high by historical standards. Major advanced economies again recorded sizeable current account deficits, with the notable exceptions of Germany and Japan. Current account surpluses in emerging Asia, though shrinking, remained sizeable. Latin America and central and eastern Europe ran current account deficits. The net private capital flow into EMEs in 2011 was still one of the strongest on record. Despite this, few emerging market currencies strengthened significantly against the major currencies, and many depreciated.

The global recovery started to falter in the second quarter of 2011. At that time, indicators of business activity weakened significantly in the United States, followed by those for EMEs; and in the second half of 2011, they deteriorated relatively sharply in Europe. The prices of many growth-sensitive financial assets declined. Major equity indices around the world fell, with the prices of cyclical stocks declining relatively sharply. Corporate bond spreads generally rose, notably for low and sub-investment grade ratings.

These developments reflected two major shocks which exposed underlying weakness in the global economy associated with domestic and external imbalances. *First*, commodity prices, which had already increased significantly, remained high against the backdrop of strong demand from EMEs. This eroded household income in the United States and other advanced economies at a time of high unemployment and ongoing balance sheet repair. In contrast, the main effect in a number of EMEs was higher inflation, which led to policy tightening. *Second*, financial market investors became increasingly wary about the credit quality of several euro area governments and the exposure of European banks to sovereign credit risk. In the second half of 2011, a sharp increase in global risk aversion, fiscal restraint and growing deleveraging pressure on banks sapped demand.

Global growth remained fragile in early 2012. Economic weakness and growing strains in global financial markets towards the end of 2011 triggered a new round of central bank support measures. The Federal Reserve committed to buy an additional $400 billion of long-dated US Treasury securities, funded by sales of shorter-term notes. It also announced that it planned to keep its short-term policy rate at exceptionally low levels until at least the end of 2014. The Bank of Japan and the Bank of England further increased the size of their asset-buying programmes. The central banks of Brazil, China, India, Indonesia, the Philippines and Turkey also loosened monetary policy. In December 2011, the ECB announced offerings of funding to euro area banks for three years, against an expanded set of collateral. Major central banks had already agreed to reduce the prices of currency swap lines between themselves, allowing them to exchange euros for dollars with banks more cheaply than previously.

These measures triggered significant improvements in bank funding markets and financial markets more broadly. The ECB's two auctions of three-year funding in December 2011 and February 2012 allowed euro area banks to prefund much of their unsecured debt redemptions due by 2014. In addition, banks used some of the cash to purchase assets, including euro area sovereign bonds. The yields on these securities declined significantly. More generally, additional policy support helped to boost a wide range of asset prices during the first few months of 2012. The completion of an orderly restructuring of Greek debt in March also removed a downside risk to asset prices.

Global economic activity seemed to recover somewhat in the first quarter of 2012. In the United States, the unemployment rate declined, hand in hand with a significant increase in consumer confidence and spending. In Japan, machinery orders and corporate investment lifted business activity, as the economy continued to rebound from the effects of the March 2011 earthquake. Following a contraction in the last quarter of 2011, GDP in the euro area stabilised. And activity in several EMEs increased at a faster pace, notably in Latin America and Southeast Asia.

That said, sustainable economic growth remained elusive, and economic activity fell in the second quarter. In April and May 2012, a number of economic indicators for the United States were weaker than expected and employment growth slowed again. Indicators of activity in China weakened significantly from the start of 2012, although this partly reflected a response to measures aimed at bringing growth down to more sustainable levels. Output growth also slowed markedly in Brazil and India, notably in the agricultural and manufacturing sectors. In the euro area, output appeared to be contracting again in the second quarter of 2012.

Financial risks in the euro area also intensified in the second quarter of 2012, driven primarily by concerns about the post-election policy orientation of Greece. Deposit and other capital outflows increased from countries perceived as vulnerable to a further deepening of the crisis. In particular, deposit withdrawals from banks in Greece reportedly accelerated in May, 2012. These banks had already lost around one third of their foreign deposits and one quarter of their domestic non-financial deposits. Foreign depositors had also withdrawn funds from banks in Ireland, Italy, Portugal and Spain, while domestic deposits had been more stable. In contrast, deposits at banks in Germany and the Netherlands increased significantly in the first quarter of 2012. Similarly, estimates of overall capital flows show net private outflows from Greece, Ireland, Italy, Portugal and Spain and inflows into Germany and the Netherlands.

ENGAGING THE WORLD ORGANISATIONS

The debates and discussions in the G 20 and other fora involving international organizations and financial institutions have been on wide-ranging issues. The question of how policies for reviving growth of individual countries impinge on the global economy and its imbalances and whether they could somehow be better coordinated has been at the centre of these discussions. These discussions are of some importance as they may, in the years to come, shape the style and substance of governance of the global economy. It is critical that the outcomes, if any, address the concerns of emerging economies (such as India) that are major drivers of global economic growth.

THE G-20

The G-20, formed in 1999 in the aftermath of the East Asian Crisis as a forum for Finance Ministers and central bank Governors, came to centre stage following the Leaders' Summit in Washington DC in November 2008. It focused on coordinated measures to address the challenges faced in the immediate aftermath of the global financial crisis. A declaration in the G-20 Summit at Pittsburgh, USA, in 2009 formally raised the forum to the level of leaders and transformed it into the premier forum for international economic cooperation.

During the global financial crisis, collective and coordinated policy action by the G-20 through macroeconomic stimulus (fiscal and monetary) and financial-sector intervention helped avoid a catastrophic meltdown. Building on this, G-20 Leaders launched the 'Framework for Strong, Sustainable, and Balanced Growth' with India and Canada as the co-chairs of the Working Group in 2009. In this signature effort of the G-20, the Mutual Assessment Process (MAP) forms a medium-term exercise to ensure that collective policy actions benefit all and policies are collectively consistent with the G-20's growth objectives.

At the 2010 summit in Seoul, the G-20 committed to working to address key imbalances that could jeopardize growth and to enhance the MAP with indicative guidelines for key imbalances. In February 2011, the G-20 agreed to include i) public debt and fiscal deficits, ii) private saving and private debt, and iii) the external position—trade balance and net investment income flows and transfers— as the key indicators for assessing external and internal imbalances. Subsequently, it was agreed that the indicative guidelines would be used to identify systemically important countries and assess each other's economic policies, suggest policy remedies, address potentially destabilizing imbalances, and set the stage for assessing the progress toward external sustainability.

In this regard, measured in terms of share in global GDP, India has been identified as systemically important economy. But it is clearly a net contributor to global demand as evidenced from its current account deficit. While India's exchange rate is largely market determined, its domestic savings are largely oriented to financing domestic investment appropriate at a stage of high growth but not at the cost of curbing consumption. Even if India is not a contributor to global imbalances, its interest clearly lies in smooth resolution of these issues and towards measures that could help revive global growth.

G-20 Agenda in 2012

Mexico has since taken over presidency of the G-20 after the Cannes Summit and released a strategic vision of the G-20 agenda spelling out the following priorities. 1) Economic stabilization and structural reforms as foundation of growth and employment. 2) Strengthening the financial system and fostering financial inclusion to promote growth. 3) Improving the international financial architecture in an interconnected world. 4) Enhancing food security and addressing commodity price volatility. 5) Promoting sustainable development and green growth in the fight against climate change.

INTERNATIONAL MONETARY SYSTEM

It has been argued that the IMS has no mechanism to prevent a build-up of imbalances on the external account and the burden of adjustment falls on deficit nations. In the run up to the crisis of 2008, it was felt that countries like the US could somehow sustain fiscal and current account deficits by virtue of the privilege of issuing a reserve currency. But this trend instead accentuated the so called external imbalances, even if it was not the primary cause of the crisis that turned global . However, the Fund is rethinking its role in the post-crisis world. But the basic question is whether the Fund is adequately equipped to be an effective guardian of global macroeconomic and financial stability. To answer this question, the IMF is looking at every aspect of its work, including how it conducts economic and financial surveillance, how it provides financing to its member countries, how it conducts its oversight of the international monetary system, and how it works with other international organizations.

The three main challenges before the fund are:

i) *Crisis prevention*. The IMF must improve its ability to assess systemic risks. National regulatory oversight after the crisis is shifting from assessing risk in individual institutions to assessing risk to the entire financial system. The IMF's surveillance covers both economic policies in individual member countries, and developments relating to the global economy as a whole. But in practice, the bulk of the Fund's efforts have been at the country level. In future, more attention should be given to the linkages and spillovers between economies. The coverage of financial sector policies is particularly important if the Fund is to be ahead of the curve in crises.

ii) *Crisis response.* In future, the IMF's crisis lending has to be of a speed, coverage, and size far beyond previous assumptions. The crisis has highlighted the risk of sudden runs on liquidity in advanced, emerging, and developing economies alike. The Fund can help by offering more flexible insurance facilities that build on recent reforms and by expanding its lending capacity. Far-reaching reforms were introduced during the crisis, but more is needed.

iii) *Stability of reserves.* The crisis has also cast a spotlight on the tension between the high demand for global liquidity by emerging market economies and the dependence on the stability of just a few suppliers of such liquidity. If the IMF's ability to prevent and respond to crises is strengthened, this could help alleviate countries' perceived need to accumulate vast reserves. It may also make sense for the Fund to back the use of a global reserve asset and other initiatives that could reduce risk in the international monetary system.

To meet this challenge, there is a need to map out exactly how the Fund should carry out its responsibility of overseeing the international monetary system, including a procedure for the Fund to analyze—and, more importantly, discuss with a wide range of policymakers—how countries' policies affect the world economy and financial system.

Clarifying the IMF's responsibilities when it comes to oversight over the financial sector is also crucial, and the Fund can do more to monitor capital movements and provide guidance on how to manage volatile flows. In this context, the buildup of international reserves as a buffer against shocks is widely expected to resume as the crisis fades. Indeed, to some extent, it already has. Such accumulation can be costly for surplus and reserve-issuing countries alike. There are three underlying problems. First, there are concerns about the availability of international liquidity in times of crisis. This prompts a precautionary reserve buildup, especially when heavy capital inflows threaten to overwhelm emerging markets. Second, there is no automatic adjustment of current account imbalances, because neither surplus countries nor reserve- issuing deficit countries face pressures to adjust. Third, the concentration of reserves in U.S. dollars reflects the absence of close substitutes that can act as a global store of value and anchor for asset and price stability.

Because it has been tasked with ensuring the stability of the international monetary system, it is required to seek solutions to these three problems. The Fund can support systemic stability by providing alternatives to reserve buildup and by helping to avoid abrupt shifts between reserve assets. A rarely discussed clause in the IMF's Articles of Agreement calls on member countries to collaborate on reserve policies. It might make sense to revive this forgotten provision as a basis for action, not least because official reserves have become large enough relative to private flows as to have significant—and potentially destabilizing—market impact, should a sudden portfolio reallocation take place.

The IMF has a chance to build on the positive role it has played in the crisis, addressing shortcomings in its mandate that have held it back when it comes to preventing and responding to crises, and helping its member countries confront pressing issues such as how to regulate banks and financial institutions.

But an updated mandate is not a silver bullet, and its capacity to resolve problems should not be oversold: a wanting mandate was not at the root of the Fund's failure to predict the crisis, and a change to the IMF's Articles of Agreement does not mean that it will be able to predict the next one. Key to the IMF's success will be the broader push for reforms now in train, especially when it comes to the institution's governance. Legitimacy in the eyes of all its member countries will ultimately decide the effectiveness of any mandate, new or old.

What underpins the IMF's role in this dynamic process is an understanding that (1) the purpose of the international financial system (of which the IMF is a key component) is to help countries develop and move up the ladder and (2) that all countries need to pursue sound macroeconomic policies in order to succeed economically. Moreover, sustaining sound macroeconomic policies is neither easy nor free of cost.

Even though the IMF does not and should not provide development finance, it does aim to contribute to the development process within its mandate, by providing temporary financing in support of countries' efforts to strengthen their policies and their balance of payments. Rather than specializing *horizontally* by providing assistance to a select section of countries, the IMF specializes *vertically* by offering to help all countries that are trying to *improve* macroeconomic policymaking. This vertical specialization is underlying rationale for the IMF as a universal financial institution.

The dynamic nature of the world economy, through which countries develop at different rates and shift—or at least know that they might shift—between providing and using the financial resources of the IMF, has, in the past, helped to ensure a measure of balance in the institution's governance. Maintaining and strengthening that balance is a key challenge in preserving the future value of the IMF as a universal financial institution. As more and more countries advance to the point where they stop viewing themselves as potential borrowers, and as others borrow continuously for long periods and lose sight of the possibility of graduating from this dependence, the dangers of polarization of the membership and marginalization of the influence of borrowers become increasingly acute.

Today, all countries that have not already achieved all of their development objectives are urged to specify quantitative and time-bound goals, set out a realistic strategy and tactics for reaching those goals, and carry out the necessary institutional and policy reforms. Developed countries have a responsibility to ensure that the global economy is conducive to development and to provide the necessary financial and other support to developing countries. An internal agencies have a responsibility to work together and with national governments to provide additional support, advice, and coordination.

The French Presidency constituted a G 20 Working group on reform of the IMS which focused, among others, on capital flows and their management (CFM), the measurement of global liquidity, holding of international reserves, and future role and composition of the special drawing rights (SDR). While the latter two issues remain areas of continuing work, drawing on the work of the IMS group, the Cannes Summit communiqué mentions that the 'Coherent Conclusions for the Management of Capital Flows' would guide the G-20 in order to reap the benefits of financial globalization, while preventing and managing risks that could undermine financial stability and sustainable growth at national and global levels.

The issue of volatility in capital flows has been of concern for several emerging markets (including India). The management of capital flows is tempered by two considerations. First, a challenge, common to most developing countries and EMEs at this juncture, arises from the uncertainties in global capital flows and monetary policies pursued in advanced countries. Emerging markets face sudden stops or reversals (witnessed in December of 2011) for reasons not necessarily linked to developments in their own economies but to serious difficulties faced by financial institutions in advanced economies. Quantitative easing pursued by monetary authorities in advanced countries (while understandable in the context of liquidity needed to repair adverse private and public balance sheets) is a relatively new phenomenon that has altered the composition of capital flows and made their management by recipients more difficult.

The second consideration arises from India's specific situation. Notwithstanding the stability of India's balance of payments after an episode in 1991, India's current account deficit has widened over the last year. The dependence on private capital inflows to finance the same has widened. It is by now known that the burden of adjustment in the current IMS falls predominantly on non-reserve-issuing current account deficit countries (like India). On that count, the Indian economy has moved towards greater openness to capital flows, albeit following a cautious and calibrated approach keeping both domestic and international factors and risks in view and through judicious use of multiple instruments.

In view of the shift in external vulnerability indicators and India's currently high dependence on imported oil, there is need to reinforce management of the capital account (which has served India well) and also encourage more stable capital flows rather than short-term flows. Countries like India may well need to rely on a matrix of choices comprising macroeconomic and macro prudential tools and other measures as policy instruments without being bound by a prescribed sequence. Under the circumstances, the fact that the 'Coherent Conclusions on Management of Capital Flows' (as endorsed by the G-20) are 'non-binding' needs to be taken note of.

An issue related to trends in global liquidity is dealing with the build-up of international reserves by some countries. It has been argued that the accumulation of reserves has negative externalities and also entails avoidable costs to the holding countries. The issue is when the holding of reserves can be deemed excessive or rather what the optimal level could be, if any, and whether some kind of 'reserve metrics' could be adopted. While the optimal size and the utility of using reserves to intervene in currency markets may be debatable, the experience, especially in the case of economies like India, has been that reserves have helped graduate to a more open economy and smoothen investment and consumption during periods of external uncertainties caused by extraneous factors. In this context, a distinction needs to be drawn between holding of reserves by countries running a current account deficit (such as India) and reserves accumulated by countries with persistent current account surpluses in addition to large sovereign wealth funds. A related set of issues on which deliberations have been going on in the G 20 concern strengthening of global financial safety nets, cooperation between the IMF and Regional Financial Agreements to help countries deal with exogenous shocks (and access emergency assistance) and the adequacy of IMF's resources to play systemic role for the benefit of its whole membership.

FINANCIAL REGULATION

The Group of 7 (G-7) countries along with a few more advanced economies with large financial sectors were the most important participants in a grouping that established the Basel Committee on Banking Supervision 1974, whose primary function was to act as a forum for coordination of supervision of the financial sector, particularly large banks, in these economies. In the wake of the major 2007-9 global financial crisis, the most severe since the 1930s, the effectiveness of financial regulation was called into question. Since then, quite significant reforms of financial regulation have taken place both within countries and internationally in terms of international regulatory standards and organizations.

In general, regulating financial markets and intermediaries and striking a balance between the need for maintaining financial stability and good market conduct without stifling innovation have always been a challenge. The global crisis brought home the inherent difficulty in doing that especially where financial institutions have had cross-border operations and exposures. This was because, with financial globalization, many banks and other financial market participants had cross-border operations but were mostly subject to national regulations.

The weaknesses in financial regulation (apart from global imbalances) were perceived as a major cause of the global crisis. The Cannes Summit communiqué 2011 reiterated the commitment that financial markets, products, and participants be regulated or subject to oversight appropriate to their circumstances in an internationally consistent and non-discriminatory way. The declaration spells out the initiatives taken that include the regulation of banks, over-the-counter (OTC) derivatives, compensation practices, and credit-rating agencies. The Cannes action plan commits to taking these initiatives further based on the work done by the Bank of International Settlements (BIS) and the Financial Stability Board (FSB) on new standards for financial regulation.

The commitment to implementing the Basel III standards for banks is of particular significance to the global economy. The implementation of Basel III capital and liquidity standards starts in 2013 with full implementation envisaged by 2019. To make sure that no financial firm is 'too big to fail' and taxpayers do not bear the costs of resolution, the FSB framework comprising new international standards for resolution, supervision, cross-border cooperation, recovery, and resolution planning from 2016 was endorsed. The FSB has also published an initial list of Globally Systemically Important Financial Institutions (G-SIFI) and a five-pronged work plan to develop guidelines on shadow banking. In order to prevent excessive risk taking and discourage excessive pay and bonuses, the FSB has developed principles and standards on compensation.

India is a member of the Basel Committee on Banking Supervision (BCBS) and FSB and is actively participating in post crisis reforms of the international regulatory and supervisory framework. The Indian financial sector is well regulated and India remains committed to adopting international standards and best practices *calibrated to its conditions*. As such, banks in India are well capitalized and it is expected that the Basel III norms are unlikely to put undue pressure on the banking system on aggregate. India had even earlier implemented some counter cyclical policies like provisioning norms and differential risk weights (for example for the real estate sector, capital markets, and personal loans) to control build-up of risks even before these were internationally proposed.

There are, however, some caveats on the implementation of the emerging regulatory standards across countries. Given that the financial sector in many countries has its specificities, and there is likely to be resistance to change from several market participants, it is yet to be seen whether all these reforms will get carried out in all the countries and not diluted. While all G-20 countries have committed to implementing Basel III, major jurisdictions have separately come out with their own regulatory standards: the Dodd Frank Act in the United States and the Vickers Commission recommendations in the

United Kingdom (see Box -1) with the EU too having its own rules. A concern that arises is that if same standards are not implemented in all jurisdictions simultaneously, there could be scope for regulatory arbitrage that could result in financial activity migrating to less-regulated jurisdictions, as well as into shadow banking. In the short run, there are also concerns that tightening of regulatory standards, even while recovery in advanced economies from the past and continuing crisis is not over, may make banks risk averse and adversely impact financial intermediation and lending to the real sector.

BOX 1

Financial Regulation: New initiatives – the US and UK

US—The Dodd-Frank Act: The financial crisis of 2007–10 led to calls for changes in the regulatory system. In June 2009, a proposal for a 'sweeping overhaul of the financial regulatory system' was introduced in the US that culminated in a legislation called The Wall Street Reform and Consumer Protection Act (also called the Dodd-Frank Act) in July 2010. This is a voluminous and overarching Act (1601 sections) with provisions for comprehensive regulation of financial markets (including the derivatives markets), consolidation of regulatory agencies, and establishing of a new oversight council called the 'Financial Stability Oversight Council' to evaluate systemic risk. The provisions also aim to address the 'too big to bail out' problem and bring in the requirement of large complex financial companies submitting plans for their orderly shutdown. The intent is that the cost arising from liquidation of large interconnected financial companies will not fall on the taxpayers. The Act incorporates what has been termed the 'Volcker rule', whereby depository banks would be prohibited from proprietary trading (similar to the prohibition of combined investment and commercial banking in the Glass–Steagall Act). The Act includes improved standards for regulation of hedge funds and credit-rating agencies, improved accounting standards, investor protection, and norms of executive compensation. As suggested in the title of the Act, it has provisions for consumer protection reforms and the establishment of a new consumer protection bureau and also a new Office of Minority and Women Inclusion as Federal banking and securities regulatory agencies.

UK—Vickers Commission report: The Independent Commission on Banking under Sir John Vickers submitted its report to the UK government in September 2011. The report starts with the argument that one of the *main reasons* for bank failure during the global crisis was that they had too little equity in relation to risk. There were few restrictions on leverage. The weights assigned in the 'risk-weighted' assets turned out unreliable. The erosion of equity led to concerns of solvency and contagion. Though risks in banking have to rest somewhere, they should not fall on the taxpayer. *Structural separation and Ring fencing:* The main recommendation is that there should be a *structural separation* between retail banking and wholesale/. investment banking. There should be a ring fence to isolate banking activities where continuous provision of service is vital to the economy and to bank customers. Domestic retail banking should be inside the ring fence. Services should not be provided from within the ring fence if they are not integral to the provision of payments services to customers in the European economic area. Banks with both retail and investment activities will need to keep these activities at arm's length but they could share information, infrastructure, etc. Structural separation would help sustain the UK's position as a pre-eminent international financial centre, while UK banking is made more resilient. *Loss absorbency:* The report is in broad agreement with the direction of Basel III but notes that it does not go far enough since the leverage cap is too lax for systemically important banks and has recommended that retail banks should have equity capital of at least 10 per cent of risk- weighted assets. The Commission has also recommended the introduction of a redirection service for personal and Small and Medium Enterprises (SME) current accounts which, among other things, would transfers accounts within seven working days.

Note: The text in the box is aimed at giving only a very brief overview of these documents and is neither exhaustive nor an interpretation.

DEVELOPMENT ISSUES

The G-20 Development Agenda comprised a Multi-Year Action Plan based on nine pillars announced at the Seoul Summit, of which the French Presidency focused on infrastructure and food security for the Cannes Summit. The other pillars are human resource development; trade; private investment and job creation; financial inclusion; growth with resilience; knowledge sharing; and domestic resource mobilization. Many of these issues have been in the subject domain of a number of developmental agencies.

While India has assigned high priority to issues relating to development appropriate to country-specific conditions, an issue deserving priority is of recycling global savings for infrastructure investment. Enhancing infrastructure investment in emerging economies and developing countries would have positive implications for rebalancing global demand as also for reviving and sustaining growth. At the same time, high savings would find productive use.

While on one side global forums like the G-20 and international regulatory bodies continued to deliberate on issues relating to financial regulation, the year 2011 was also marked by rising concern across the world that 'finance' had somehow got de-linked from serving the interests of the real economy and that various regulatory and compensation practices are out of sync with the needs of the rest of the economy.

The issue of compensation in the financial sector has been a major area of debate not just in the G-20 but also in the media in general. Similarly, the issue of financialization of commodities and speculation leading to volatility in commodity prices and the idea of implementing a tax on financial transactions have been contentious issues on which no clear consensus has emerged. Of late, an area of concern even among serious academic researchers has been whether the financial sector has become just too big in some advanced economies and whether its value addition is really genuine and correctly measured.

Regardless of whether these views and perceptions are correct or misplaced, these debates and the ongoing work need to be taken note of in policy. Fortunately, the Indian financial sector and its banks have thus far been well regulated and to ensure that it serves the real sector has been an abiding policy concern. Nevertheless, given the criticality of the role of finance in development, the Indian regulatory system would also need to maintain and strengthen its vigil to ensure that growth in the financial sector and the intermediation process go towards furthering economic development and financial inclusion.

REFORM AGENDA

Restoring confidence among private investors is paramount for the stabilization of the financial markets. The policymakers are laying foundations to support that confidence, but numerous technical, legal, and political challenges remain. The urgency of the task is also increasing, as the investors are increasingly buying protection against extreme risks, even if investing in the instruments designed to provide the protection can be costly and may prove ineffective. The realization of extreme risk in 2008 led to a material alteration in investment strategies: strong demand for insurance against tail outcomes (the risk of low-probability but high-impact events). This demand has been relatively price insensitive in the recent past, indicative of a lasting structural shift in investment strategies. New instruments have emerged to satisfy investor demand, the most notable aimed at exploiting the inverse correlation between equity prices and the expected volatility of equity markets. Global tail risks may emanate from one or more sources, such as the euro area crisis or U.S. and Japanese fiscal imbalances.

Evaluating the source of specific risks provides policymakers with a guide to areas of potential instability discussed below.

Euro Area Risks: Currency Redenomination Risk

Risks in the euro area are dominated by balance of payments imbalances across member states. Creditor countries are repatriating capital from debtor nations even when the cost of doing so is high, as demonstrated by negative nominal shorter-term interest rates in various countries. Investors are willing to accept negative interest rates as the cost of guarding against a euro breakup and the introduction of national or subregional currencies (currency redenomination risk). Creditor countries expect to see their currencies appreciate substantially, more than offsetting the negative interest rate.

Longer-Term Risks Emerging in Japan

Japan's imbalances are unique in the context of history: very high government debt yet a very large external creditor position. The resolution of these imbalances could have significant implications for both interest rates and exchange rates. The natural expectation leans to a significant increase in bond yields. Interest rate markets do indeed reflect the potential for higher yields in the medium term.

The implications for foreign exchange markets are more complex. As seen during the March 2011 natural disaster in Japan, rapid currency appreciation may occur given the potential for the repatriation of foreign assets. Alternatively, the threat of an erosion of confidence in domestic policy, or, over the longer run, of a deterioration in the current account, might cause substantial depreciation. The market has resolved these two competing forces by anticipating a very high level of medium-term volatility in the dollar-yen exchange rate, well above realized volatility and high relative to past crises.

U.S. Risks: Complacency or Confidence?

The United States has a blend of the imbalances seen in the other major countries. U.S. government debt is high, though not as high as in Japan. The United States is an international net debtor, though not to the same extent as Spain and other countries in the euro area periphery. Nevertheless, markets have a benign expectation for the resolution of U.S. imbalances. Evidence of extreme risks in interest rate and currency markets is absent at virtually all horizons.

While the capacity of the U.S. government to repay its debt is not in doubt, continued growth in macro imbalances would raise the likelihood of a misalignment of policy incentives across internal and external creditors. If the expansion of the Federal Reserve balance sheet is the last-resort policy that prevents a large rise in bond yields, the clearest transmission mechanism is currency depreciation. Medium-term expectations have been, instead, leaning toward a U.S. dollar appreciation.

In the near term, the U.S. sovereign credit default swap curve suggests that the debt ceiling, as well as the fiscal cliff, will be resolved without issue. Uncertainty about a potential technical default as a result of the debt ceiling led to credit risk in short-term default swaps rising above those over longer horizons in July 2011. No such pattern has emerged this time around. In the longer term, option markets are pricing far less fear of a rise in longer-term interest rates compared with Japan.

Financial Stability Implications

Evaluating extreme risks supports financial stability in three important ways. *First,* policymakers can disagree with the market assessment and provide targeted, logical foundations to the contrary both when there is too much and, importantly, too little concern about future imbalances. *Second,* understanding strategies that attempt to insure against extreme risks can reveal potential vulnerabilities in the financial system. Seemingly effective hedges, such as long-term euro interest rate swaps, could further concentrate counterparty exposures, exacerbating risks when extreme events occur. *Third,* changes in investment strategies lead to financial innovation. New products, particularly fast-growing ones where risk diversification is likely to lag innovation, could lead to risks simply being transferred and concentrated, and therefore should be closely monitored.

In recent times, it has been observed that even the focus of the regulatory reform agenda has shifted from the development of standards to rulemaking and implementation of Based III. Some countries are much further behind than others in the implementation process.

The liquidity requirements under Basel III—the liquidity coverage ratio (LCR) and the net stable funding ratio (NSFR)—are still some time away from implementation, with the LCR and NSFR currently within the observation period. Although the LCR rules will be clarified by early 2013, the final shape of the NFSR is less certain, as the implementation date is further out, in 2018. Further, the end-2012 deadline for trading all standardized derivatives contracts through exchanges or electronic trading platforms and clearing them where appropriate through central counterparties (CCPs) is likely to be missed because of lagging implementation at the national level.

The recovery has suffered new setbacks, and uncertainty weighs heavily on the outlook. A key reason is that policies in the major advanced economies have not rebuilt confidence in medium-term prospects. Tail risks, such as those relating to the viability of the euro area or major U.S. fiscal policy mistakes, continue to preoccupy investors. The World Economic Outlook (WEO) forecast thus sees only a gradual strengthening of activity from the relatively disappointing pace of early 2012. Projected global growth is at 3.3 and 3.6 percent in 2012 and 2013, respectively. Output is expected to remain sluggish in advanced economies but still relatively solid in many emerging market and developing economies. Unemployment is likely to stay elevated in many parts of the world. And financial conditions will remain fragile.

The WEO forecast rests on two crucial policy assumptions. The first is that European policymakers will adopt policies that gradually ease financial conditions further in periphery economies. In this regard, the European Central Bank (ECB) has recently done its part. It is now up to national policymakers to move and activate the European Stability Mechanism (ESM), while articulating a credible path and beginning to implement measures to achieve a banking union and greater fiscal integration. The second assumption is that U.S. policymakers will prevent the drastic automatic tax increases and spending cutbacks (the "fiscal cliff") implied by existing budget law, raise the U.S. federal debt ceiling in a timely manner, and make good progress toward a comprehensive plan to restore fiscal sustainability.

More generally, downside risks have increased and are considerable. The IMF staff's fan chart, which uses financial and commodity market data and analyst forecasts to gauge risks—suggests that there is now a 1 in 6 chance of global growth falling below 2 percent, which would be consistent with a recession in advanced economies and low growth in emerging market and developing economies. Ultimately, however, the WEO forecast rests on critical policy action in the euro area and the United States, and it is very difficult to estimate the probability that this action will materialize.

This juncture presents major difficulties for policymakers. In many advanced economies, injections of liquidity are having a positive impact on financial stability and output and employment, but the impact may be diminishing. Many governments have started in earnest to reduce excessive deficits, but because uncertainty is high, confidence is low, and financial sectors are weak, the significant fiscal achievements have been accompanied by disappointing growth or recessions. In emerging market and developing economies, policymakers are conscious of the need to rebuild fiscal and monetary policy space but are wondering how to calibrate policies in the face of major external downside risks.

An effective policy response in the major advanced economies is the key to improving prospects and inspiring more confidence about the future. In the short term, the main tasks are to rule out the tail risk scenarios and adopt concrete plans to bring down public debt over the medium term.

The crisis in the euro area remains the most obvious threat to the global outlook. The ECB has put in place a mechanism to improve the transmission of low policy rates to borrowing costs in the periphery, where investors' fears about the viability of the euro have pushed market rates to very high levels. The periphery economies need to continue to adjust. Governments must meet their commitment to make the euro area firewall more flexible. Specifically, the ESM must intervene in banking systems and provide support to sovereigns, while national leaders must work toward true economic and monetary union. This requires establishing a banking union with a unified financial stability framework and implementing measures toward fiscal integration, on the principle that more area-wide insurance must come with more area-wide control. Unless more action is taken soon, recent improvements in financial markets could prove fleeting.

In emerging market and developing economies, activity has been slowed by policy tightening in response to capacity constraints, weaker demand from advanced economies, and country-specific factors. Policy improvements have raised their resilience to shocks. Since the crisis erupted in 2008, expansionary policies have buffered the negative impact of the weakness in advanced economy markets: fiscal deficits have typically been above precrisis levels, whereas real interest rates have been lower. Domestic credit has grown rapidly. Over the medium term, policymakers will need to ensure that they retain the ability to respond flexibly to shocks by maintaining a sound fiscal position and by keeping inflation and credit growth at moderate rates.

Global imbalances, and the associated vulnerabilities, have diminished, but there is still a need for more decisive policy action to address them. Within the euro area, current account imbalances—the large surpluses in Germany and the Netherlands and the deficits in most periphery economies—need to adjust further. At the global level, the current account positions of the United States, the euro area as a whole, and Japan are weaker than they would be with more sustainable fiscal policies—and the real effective exchange rates of the dollar, euro, and yen are stronger. In contrast, the current account positions of many Asian economies are undesirably strong and their exchange rates undesirably weak. In part, this reflects distortions that hold back consumption. But it also reflects the effect of large-scale official accumulation of foreign exchange.

In general, the policies required to lower current account imbalances and related vulnerabilities suit the interests of the economies concerned. More adjustment in external-deficit economies and more internal demand in external-surplus economies would contribute not only to a safer global economy but also to stronger growth for all. Many external-deficit economies need further fiscal adjustment and strengthened financial sector supervision and regulation. These efforts need to be complemented with structural measures, the details of which differ widely across the external-deficit advanced and emerging market economies but include labor and product market reform, improvements to governance and the business environment, and measures to boost private saving for retirement. The structural measures needed in external-surplus economies with undervalued exchange rates also vary by country but include boosting investment in Germany, reforming the social safety net in China to encourage consumption, and reducing the accumulation of official reserves in many emerging market economies, which would also help rein in high credit and asset price growth.

Going forward, a number of forces—including the crisis itself, ongoing adjustments by market participants, crisis management responses by authorities, and an evolving regulatory reform agenda can be expected to change the structure of the financial intermediation in fundamental ways. Authorities—have made much progress on the reform agenda, but several issues still need the attention of policymakers. While being cognizant of a tendency by government to over-regulate during periods of distress (potentially stifling economic benefits), there are still some regulatory areas that remain unfinished or that may develop and require action because of unintended side effects of reform. The following is a list of those areas and a suggested agenda for further work.

I. Too Important to Fail

i) *A global-level discussion on the pros and cons of direct business activity restrictions,* because the effects of such national initiatives will not stop at the borders. This discussion should address the question of whether imposing higher costs can be expected to lower systemic risks. If not, the questions become, will restraints on activities be more effective? And what might their cross-border implications be?

ii) *Recovery and resolution planning for large institutions.* Progress so far is uneven across economies and, especially for systemically important institutions, faster progress is needed. While a so-called living will is not a panacea for reducing risk at a financial institution, the discipline of constructing such a plan for its own demise can help it sort out its internal structures and enhance its governance mechanisms to control excessive risk taking. If properly implemented, implicit guarantees would be curtailed, lowering the potential use of taxpayer funds.

II. Financial Globalization

i) *Further progress on cross-border resolution.* Globalization works best when the flows are calm and consistent and disruptions can be handled in a fair and transparent manner. Good management by financial institutions with cross-border activities, well-coordinated supervision of cross-border institutions, and transparent methods of dealing with distress are all components of healthy financial globalization. Cross-border resolution remains the most difficult component of any plan to ensure a smooth unwinding of large global institutions—burden sharing and legal commitments are areas for further clarity. The framework for coping with cross-border resolution needs to encourage operating behaviors, both by institutions themselves and by their supervisors, that reduce the likelihood of having to resort to resolution.

III. Shadow Banking

i) *Enhanced monitoring of systemic risks posed by nonbanks.* To the extent that nonbanks act like banks, a common set of prudential standards must be applied to both types of institution. Further monitoring to see where bank-like activities pose systemic concerns needs to continue and be enhanced, since some of the cost pressures on banks mean some activities will undoubtedly move into the nonbank sector.

IV. Complexity and Transparency

i) *Further thought on how to encourage the development of simpler products.* While not inhibiting innovation, we need to have ways to encourage products that can be priced more accurately to reflect risks. Both the producers of such products and their customers should be able to see clearly where risks reside. For example, the new products to securitize counterparty risks warrant close monitoring to ensure that they are transparent to investors and shareholders so they can appropriately price their exposures and to ensure that the products are not offsetting some of the goals of the new banking standards.

ii) *More information to reveal interconnections and the buildup and spillover of risk.* Lack of transparency on counterparty relationships, corporate governance structures, and other potentially risk-laden conditions blocks investors and counterparties from imposing market discipline and prevents regulators and supervisors from taking early corrective actions.

V. Over-the-counter Derivatives

i) *More consideration of risks in moving OTC derivatives contracts to central counterparties (CCPs).* Current efforts to reduce counterparty exposures through such moves come with some danger that the CCPs themselves will become too important to fail and that the "location" requirements enforced in multiple jurisdictions may create too many CCPs. These institutions could have diverse requirements and levels of oversight that would hinder the benefits of netting, increase the demands for collateral, and unnecessarily increase costs. In general, the international effort to harmonize approaches to reforms in OTC derivatives markets should be reenergized.

VI. Other Conditions

Though they are not part of the regulatory reforms effort, two conditions are essential if the reforms are to bring about a safer financial system: (1) strong supervision in implementing the reforms and (2) a private sector with the incentives to follow them. Without these elements, the reforms will wither and die.

Hence, we cannot overemphasize the importance of the role played by implementation of regulations—both in terms of the final version of rules at the national level and in terms of how those rules are interpreted and enforced within and across institutions. National and regional approaches will vary considerably, and these have the potential to alter the effectiveness of the reforms, not only for themselves but globally as well. Hence, supervision must have a global focus. But with the system remaining complex, and with the set of new (detailed and complex) regulatory initiatives being added, a political and social consensus is needed to give supervisors the will to act and to be intrusive, skeptical, proactive, comprehensive, adaptive, and conclusive.

In addition, the private sector needs to take its share of the responsibility for making financial systems safe for savers and investors—the ultimate beneficiaries. Compensation within institutions should seek to apportion rewards based on both risk and return. Governance structures should be set to support those responsible for ensuring the firm's integrity and soundness. Product development should seek to satisfy customer's bona fide needs in a manner that enables risk-adjusted pricing.

HOW HAS INDIA BEEN HIT BY THE CRISIS?

The contagion of the crisis has spread to India through all the channels – the financial channel, the real channel, and importantly, as happens in all financial crises, the confidence channel. India's financial markets – equity markets, money markets, forex markets and credit markets – had all come under pressure from a number of directions. First, as a consequence of the global liquidity squeeze, Indian banks and corporates found their overseas financing drying up, forcing corporates to shift their credit demand to the domestic banking sector. Also, in their frantic search for substitute financing, corporates withdrew their investments from domestic money market mutual funds putting redemption pressure on the mutual funds and down the line on non-banking financial companies (NBFCs) where the MFs had invested a significant portion of their funds. This substitution of overseas financing by domestic financing brought both money markets and credit markets under pressure. Second, the forex market came under pressure because of reversal of capital flows as part of the global deleveraging process. Simultaneously, corporates were converting the funds raised locally into foreign currency to meet their external obligations. Both these factors put downward pressure on the rupee. Third, the Reserve Bank's intervention in the forex market to manage the volatility in the rupee further added to liquidity tightening.

In the real sector, the transmission of the global cues to the domestic economy has been quite straight forward – through the slump in demand for exports. The United States, European Union and the Middle East, which account for three quarters of India's goods and services trade are in a synchronized down turn. Service export growth is also likely to slow in the near term as the recession deepens and financial services firms – traditionally large users of outsourcing services – are restructured. Remittances from migrant workers too are likely to slow as the Middle East adjusts to lower crude prices and advanced economies go into a recession.

Beyond the financial and real sectors of transmission the crisis also spread through the confidence channel. In sharp contrast to global financial markets, which went into a seizure on account of a crisis of confidence, Indian financial markets continued to function in an orderly manner. Nevertheless, the tightened global liquidity situation in the period immediately following the Lehman failure in mid-September 2008, coming as it did on top of a turn in the credit cycle, increased the risk aversion of the financial system and made banks cautious about lending

INDIA's RESPONSE TO THE CHALLENGE

The globalization of India has given rise to new opportunities but it has also brought with it new challenges and responsibilities. It means that the global economy can no longer be viewed from a spectator's standpoint. What happens there has large implications for India. Every time there is a major financial crisis anywhere in the world, there is need to take brace position. And, in turn, the rise and fall of India's growth rate has an impact on global growth and there is need for India to take this responsibility seriously.

The Government and the Reserve Bank of India responded to the challenge in close coordination and consultation. The main plank of the Government response was fiscal stimulus while the Reserve Bank's action comprised monetary accommodation and counter cyclical regulatory forbearance. The Reserve Bank's policy response was aimed at containing the contagion from the outside – to keep the domestic money and credit markets functioning normally and see that the liquidity stress did not trigger solvency cascades. In particular, RBI targeted three objectives: first, to maintain a comfortable rupee liquidity position; second, to augment foreign exchange liquidity; and third, to maintain a policy framework that would keep credit delivery on track so as to arrest the moderation in growth. This marked a reversal of Reserve Bank's policy stance from monetary tightening in response to heightened inflationary pressures of the previous period to monetary easing in response to easing inflationary pressures and moderation in growth in the current cycle. These measures to meet the above objectives came in several policy packages starting mid- September 2008, on occasion in response to unanticipated global developments and at other times in anticipation of the impact of potential global developments on the Indian markets.

The policy packages included, like in the case of other central banks, both conventional and unconventional measures. On the conventional side, RBI reduced the policy interest rates aggressively and rapidly, reduced the quantum of bank reserves impounded by the central bank and expanded and liberalised the refinance facilities for export credit. Measures aimed at managing forex liquidity included an upward adjustment of the interest rate ceiling on the foreign currency deposits by non-resident Indians, substantially relaxing the external commercial borrowings (ECB) regime for corporates, and allowing non-banking financial companies and housing finance companies access to foreign borrowing.

The important among the many unconventional measures taken by the Reserve Bank of India are a rupee-dollar swap facility for Indian banks to give them comfort in managing their short-term foreign funding requirements, an exclusive refinance window as also a special purpose vehicle for supporting non-banking financial companies, and expanding the lendable resources available to apex finance institutions for refinancing credit extended to small industries, housing and exports.

Recognising the depth and extraordinary impact of this crisis, the Central Government invoked the emergency provisions of the FRBM Act to seek relaxation from the fiscal targets and launched two fiscal stimulus packages in December 2008 and January 2009. These fiscal stimulus packages, together amounting to about 3 per cent of GDP, included additional public spending, particularly capital expenditure, government guaranteed funds for infrastructure spending, cuts in indirect taxes, expanded guarantee cover for credit to micro and small enterprises, and additional support to exporters. These stimulus packages came on top of an already announced expanded safety-net for rural poor, a farm loan waiver package and salary increases for government staff, all of which too should stimulate demand.

Impact of Policy Measures

Taken together, the measures put in place since mid-September 2008 have ensured that the Indian financial markets continue to function in an orderly manner. The cumulative amount of primary liquidity potentially available to the financial system through these measures is over US$ 75 bln or 7 per cent of GDP. This sizeable easing has ensured a comfortable liquidity position starting mid-November 2008 as evidenced by a number of indicators including the weighted-average call money rate, the overnight money market rate and the yield on the 10-year benchmark government security. Taking the signal from the policy rate cut, many of the big banks have reduced their benchmark prime lending rates. Bank credit has expanded too, faster than it did last year. However, Reserve Bank's rough calculations show that the overall flow of resources to the commercial sector is less than what it was last year. This is because, even though bank credit has expanded, it has not fully offset the decline in non-bank flow of resources to the commercial sector.

However, while evaluating the response to the crisis, it is important to remember that although the origins of the crisis are common around the world, the crisis has impacted different economies differently. Importantly, in advanced economies where it originated, the crisis spread from the financial sector to the real sector. In emerging economies, the transmission of external shocks to domestic vulnerabilities has typically been from the real sector to the financial sector. Countries have accordingly responded to the crisis depending on their specific country circumstances. Thus, even as policy responses across countries are broadly similar, their precise design, quantum, sequencing and timing have varied. In particular, while policy responses in advanced economies have had to contend with both the unfolding financial crisis and deepening recession, in India, the response has been predominantly driven by the need to arrest moderation in economic growth.

These initiatives can be seen within the overall context of the financial sector development in the country, particularly, in the money market, government securities market and the foreign exchange market. With the implementation of these initiatives, we can expect a continuing process of financial market development that aids the overall development process. Similar efforts are being undertaken by the Government and the securities regulator, the Securities and Exchange Board of India along with the Reserve Bank in activating the corporate debt market. As has been experienced elsewhere, among the various financial markets, the corporate debt market is indeed the most difficult to develop for a variety of reasons. A great deal of detailed work needs to be undertaken over a period of time to put in place an appropriate market micro infrastructure, trading platforms, technology and clearing and settlement systems, along with further development of both issuers and buyers. The expansion of the pension fund and insurance industries will progressively result in the presence of a larger financial investor base, which will help in the overall expansion of financial markets and in particular the corporate debt market.

India has entered a 'critical decade'. It has emerged as a large and systemically important economy on the global stage. It enjoys the unique advantage of having many economic indicators in its favour, particularly a large domestic market, robust investment-to-GDP ratio, and demographic advantage. However, all of these will need to be leveraged to get the full advantage out of them. Undoubtedly this requires India to address its internal challenges, which include the long-standing problem of poverty and the development of its social and physical infrastructure.

Given its size and its profile in the global economy, India will inevitably need to play an active role at global level, not just in debates about how to resolve the continuing crisis and prevent the recurrence of similar crises in the future, but in influencing the rules for the global economy on overarching macroeconomic issues such as trade, capital flows, financial regulation, climate change, and governance of global financial institutions.

It may be argued, and in some ways it may seem the easy option, that India should take a passive stance in the current global debate and just wait out the period of crisis. But that option is no longer realistically feasible. India is already too much a part of the global economy and polity; developments in the world will affect India deeply and what India does will affect the world. There is, therefore, a need for India to engage with the world in terms of action and ideas.

QUESTIONS

1. Discuss the cooperative efforts to strengthen the international monetary system.
2. How has India been hit by the global financial crisis? How has the government and the R B I responded to the challenge? What is the impact of policy measures?
3. Critically examine the macro prudential elements of Basel III.
4. Restoring confidence among private investors is paramount for the stabilisation of financial markets. What are the sources of specific risks which should be considered by the policymakers while setting the agenda for reform.
5. Discuss the role of IMF in post-crisis period. Is it adequately equipped to be an effective guardian of world macroeconomic and financial stability?
6. Discuss the role of international regulatory bodies in reviving the world economy.

REFERENCES

Borio, Claudio, and Philip Lowe, 2002, "Asset Prices, Financial and Monetary Stability: Exploring the Nexus," BIS Working Paper No. 114 (Basel: Bank for International Settlements).

European Central Bank (ECB), 2009, Financial Stability Review (Frankfurt, December)

International Monetary Fund (IMF), 2010b, "The State of Public Finances: Cross-Country Fiscal Monitor," IMF Staff Position Note (Washington, May).

Kang, Xiaowei, and Dimitris Melas, 2010, "A Fresh Look at the Strategic Equity Allocation of European Institutional Investors," MSCI Barra Research Insight (New York).

N'Diaye, Papa M'B. P., 2009, "Macroeconomic Implications for Hong Kong SAR of Accommodative U.S. Monetary Policy," IMF Working Paper No. 09/256 (Washington: International Monetary Fund).

Peiris, Shanaka, J., 2010, "Foreign Participation in Emerging Markets' Local Currency Bond Markets," IMF Working Paper No. 10/88 (Washington: International Monetary Fund).

Segoviano, Miguel, 2006, "Portfolio Credit Risk and Macroeconomic Shocks: Applications to Stress Testing Under Data-Restricted Environments," IMF Working Paper No. 06/283 (Washington: International Monetary Fund).

Stroebel, Johannes, and John Taylor, 2009, "Estimated Impact of the Fed's Mortgage- Backed Securities Purchase Program," NBER Working Paper 15626 (Cambridge, Massachusetts: National Bureau of Economic Research).

INDEX

C

D

F

G

R

S

T

U

V

W

Y

■■■